MW01074836

"John F. Evans's *A Guide to Biblical C*
handbook for scholars, preachers, and ،

—**C. Hassell Bullock,** Franklin S. Dyrness Professor
Emeritus of Biblical Studies, Wheaton College

"This exhaustive and practical volume is a tool that needs to be in the hands of every minister
and biblical studies teacher."

—**Gary M. Burge,** Professor of New Testament, Wheaton College

"My New Testament seminary students need this book. This will be immensely helpful for their
research on papers and for deciding which commentaries to buy for their future pastorates."

—**Robert Cara,** Hugh and Sallie Reaves Professor of New
Testament, Reformed Theological Seminary

"*A Guide to Biblical Commentaries* . . . includes many useful and insightful comments. Occasionally
I have referred to Evans's comments in these pages."

—**D. A. Carson,** Distinguished Emeritus Professor of New Testament, Trinity
Evangelical Divinity School, in *New Testament Commentary Survey*

"It is exceptionally well done and far better than anything else I have seen! The introductory
material is excellent. It seems to me to be something that will help a lot of students and pastors,
and even professors!"

—**Donald Hagner,** George Eldon Ladd Professor Emeritus
of New Testament, Fuller Theological Seminary

"In this up-to-date resource for students, pastors, and academics, Evans exceeds what is available
through other similar volumes and through the internet by virtue of his balanced and judicious
annotations. I recommend it highly!"

—**John Walton,** Professor of Old Testament, Wheaton College

"It is a boon to have this sure-footed guide available. . . . Using Evans's own system of ratings,
this book definitely gets a solid black star as an essential resource for clergy, scholars, or students
who wish to acquire a solid library of biblical commentaries."

—**Paul Foster,** Professor, University of Edinburgh, in *The Expository Times*

"This is an extraordinary work, which is clearly the fruit both of many years' work and of a deep
fascination with biblical scholarship. . . . Of course, for the advanced student or professional
scholar, the absence of works in languages other than English limits the usefulness of this book
as a research tool, but it is an excellent resource for its target audience, and I have found it helpful
for teaching."

—**Stuart Weeks,** Professor, Durham University, in *Vetus Testamentum*

# A GUIDE TO
# BIBLICAL
# COMMENTARIES
## AND REFERENCE WORKS

11*th* EDITION

# A GUIDE TO

# BIBLICAL
# COMMENTARIES

## AND REFERENCE WORKS

# JOHN F. EVANS

ZONDERVAN
ACADEMIC

ZONDERVAN ACADEMIC

*A Guide to Biblical Commentaries and Reference Works, 11th Edition*
Copyright © 2025 by John F. Evans

Published in Grand Rapids, Michigan, by Zondervan. Zondervan is a registered trademark of The Zondervan Corporation, L.L.C., a wholly owned subsidiary of HarperCollins Christian Publishing, Inc.

Requests for information should be addressed to customercare@harpercollins.com.

Zondervan titles may be purchased in bulk for educational, business, fundraising, or sales promotional use. For information, please email SpecialMarkets@Zondervan.com.

Library of Congress Cataloging-in-Publication Data

Names: Evans, John F. (John Frederick) author.
Title: A guide to Biblical commentaries and reference works / John F. Evans.
Description: 11th edition. | Grand Rapids, Michigan: Zondervan, [2024] | Includes bibliographical references and index.
Identifiers: LCCN 2024026140 (print) | LCCN 2024026141 (ebook) | ISBN 9780310150718 (paperback) | ISBN 9780310150725 (ebook)
Subjects: LCSH: Bible—Commentaries—Bibliography. | Bible—Bibliography. | BISAC: RELIGION / Biblical Studies / General | RELIGION / Biblical Commentary / General Classification: LCC Z7770 .E92 2025 BS482 (print) | LCC Z7770 BS482 (ebook) | DDC 016.2207—dc23/eng/20240717
LC record available at https://lccn.loc.gov/2024026140
LC ebook record available at https://lccn.loc.gov/2024026141

*Cover design: Tammy Johnson*
*Cover image: © Renata Sedmáková / AdobeStock*
*Interior typesetting: Sara Colley*

*Printed in the United States of America*

24 25 26 27 28 29 30 31 32 33 34 35 36 / TRM / 16 15 14 13 12 11 10 9 8 7 6 5 4 3 2 1

ותפארת בנים אבותם

PROVERBS 17:6B

TO THE MEMORY OF MY GRANDFATHER

THE REV FREDERICK WALTER EVANS

AB, BD, AM, LLD, DD

MODERATOR OF THE 1946 GENERAL ASSEMBLY, PRESBYTERIAN CHURCH USA;

FAITHFUL MINISTER OF THE GOSPEL FOR SEVENTY-TWO YEARS; 1880–1977

AND THE MEMORY OF MY FATHER

THE REV FREDERICK W. EVANS, JR

BA, BD, MA, STM, DMIN

FAITHFUL MINISTER OF THE GOSPEL FOR FORTY-FIVE YEARS; 1924–1992

~ *SEQUAR, ETSI NON PASSIBUS EQUIS* ~

I FOLLOW, THOUGH WITH UNEQUAL STEPS

# CONTENTS

# From the Author

READERS MAY WONDER WHY I undertook this project. During my senior year at Covenant Seminary, three fellow students were occasionally asking me for advice about commentaries. Eventually, they suggested that I write up a guide to OT commentaries. That guide was well-received, and, as a surprise to me, the OT Department decided to reproduce it for distribution to the students. There was a revision later that year (1989) after Professors Long and Van Groningen read the paper and made suggestions for its improvement. When NT Professors Knight and Cooper mentioned that they'd like to see a NT counterpart, I quickly demurred. After all, there were several such bibliographies, and Knight had been giving out his own fine survey for many years. When another faculty member made the same request, I decided to attempt the NT analogue and produced it while completing course work for a second degree at Covenant.

A few years later (1993) I received inquiries from friends and Covenant faculty about a revision and decided to make the effort. Revised editions were released in 1993, 1994, 1995, 1996, 2001, 2005, 2009, and 2010. I am gratified that Zondervan took on this project for a tenth Edition (2016) and now an eleventh. Receiving assistance from the late Verlyn Verbrugge, Nancy Erickson, Daniel Saxton, and the production team has been a joy.

Some may also be curious about my qualifications. I claim no great erudition in OT or NT scholarship. What I do have is a longstanding interest in theological bibliography, the blessing of a substantial personal library (in part inherited from my father and grandfather), and a sincere desire to help others make full use of the study tools available today.

After seminary I was privileged to pastor Faith Presbyterian Church (PCA) in Morganton, NC for five years. I left the pastorate in 1996 to become a missionary lecturer and first served at the Theological College of Central Africa (Zambia). Then I was on faculty at seminaries in Namibia and Kenya, eventually as Head of the Biblical Studies Department at Nairobi Evangelical Graduate School of Theology. Departing Africa after twenty years, I again served as a pastor for a time at Covenant PCA in Sun City West, AZ. God has since led me to the United Kingdom, where I lecture at Union School of Theology. The reader will detect both my pastoral and academic interests. I have often identified myself as "evangelical, catholic, and Reformed" (Nevin) in theology, as a churchman owning the heritage of all Christian history, and as being influenced by both Continental and British Calvinism.

It is a joy to acknowledge the family and friends who have supported this project over the past three decades. For this edition in particular, I wish to thank my wife Heidi for her words of encouragement and constant love. I must also mention my friends, Palmer and Joanna Robertson, who gave us a two-week stay in their Cambridge home.

Finally I am grateful yet again to the Principal and staff of Tyndale House for the opportunity to study in Cambridge. Much final revision work was done there. To one accustomed to making do with fewer library resources, Tyndale House has always been "like the garden of Eden" (Ezek 36:35).

*OMNIA IN GLORIAM DEI*

# ABBREVIATIONS

NOTE: ABBREVIATIONS FOR SERIES of commentaries are listed and annotated in the section entitled Commentary Series (see p. XX).

| | |
|---|---|
| *ABD* | *Anchor Bible Dictionary.* Edited by David Noel Freedman. 6 vols. New York: Doubleday, 1992 |
| ABRL | Anchor Bible Reference Library (now AYRL) |
| ANE | Ancient Near East(ern) |
| *ANES* | *Ancient Near Eastern Studies* |
| *AsTJ* | *Asbury Theological Journal* |
| ATD | Das Alte Testament Deutsch |
| *ATJ* | *Ashland Theological Journal* |
| *AUSS* | *Andrews University Seminary Studies* |
| AYRL | Anchor Yale Reference Library (previously ABRL) |
| B&H | Broadman & Holman (Southern Baptist publishing house) |
| *BAR* | *Biblical Archaeology Review* |
| *BASOR* | *Bulletin of the American Schools of Oriental Research* |
| *BBR* | *Bulletin for Biblical Research* |
| BETL | Bibliotheca Ephemeridum Theologicarum Lovaniensium |
| *BHQ* | *Biblia Hebraica Quinta.* Edited by A. Schenker et al. Stuttgart: Deutsche Bibelgesellschaft, 2004– |
| *BHS* | *Biblia Hebraica Stuttgartensia.* Edited by Karl Elliger and Wilhelm Rudolph. Stuttgart: Deutsche Bibelgesellschaft, 1983 |
| *Bib* | *Biblica* |
| *BibInt* | *Biblical Interpretation* |
| *BJRL* | *Bulletin of the John Rylands University Library of Manchester* |
| *BL* | *Book List*, attached to *JSOT* and *JSNT* |
| *BO* | *Bibliotheca Orientalis* |
| *BSac* | *Bibliotheca Sacra* |
| *BSB* | *Biblical Studies Bulletin* (e-journal) |
| *BTB* | *Biblical Theology Bulletin* |
| CBD | Christian Book Distributors |
| *CBQ* | *Catholic Biblical Quarterly* |
| *CBR* | *Currents in Biblical Research* (not SBL abbreviation of *CurBR*) |
| *Chm* | *Churchman* (journal), now *The Global Anglican (TGA)* |
| ch(s). | chapter(s) |
| *CJ* | *Concordia Journal* |
| CNT | Commentaire du Nouveau Testament |
| *ConcTJ* | *Concordia Theological Journal* |
| *CRBR* | *Critical Review of Books in Religion* |
| CRC | Christian Reformed Church in North America |
| CSB | Christian Standard Bible (1999–2017) |
| *CT* | *Christianity Today* |
| *CTJ* | *Calvin Theological Journal* |

| | |
|---|---|
| CUP | Cambridge University Press |
| *CurBS* | *Currents in Research: Biblical Studies* |
| *CurTM* | *Currents in Theology and Mission* |
| *DCH* | *Dictionary of Classical Hebrew*. Edited by David J. A. Clines. 9 vols. Sheffield: Sheffield Phoenix Press, 1993–2014 |
| *DenvJ* | *Denver Journal: An Online Review* |
| diss. | dissertation |
| DJD | Discoveries in the Judaean Desert. Oxford: Clarendon Press, 1955–2011 |
| *DOTPr* | *Dictionary of the Old Testament: Prophets*. Edited by Mark J. Boda and J. Gordon McConville. Downers Grove, IL: InterVarsity Press, 2012 |
| *DOTWPW* | *Dictionary of the Old Testament: Wisdom, Poetry & Writings*. Edited by Tremper Longman III and Peter Enns. Downers Grove, IL: InterVarsity Press, 2008 |
| DSS | Dead Sea Scrolls |
| DtrH | Deuteronom(ist)ic History |
| ed(s). | editor(s), edited by, edition |
| *EC* | *Early Christianity* (journal of Mohr Siebeck, 2010–) |
| ECO | A Covenant Order of Evangelical Presbyterians (formerly within PCUSA) |
| esp. | especially |
| ESV | English Standard Version (2001–) |
| ET | English Translation |
| *ETL* | *Ephemerides Theologicae Lovanienses* |
| ETS | Evangelical Theological Society |
| *EuroJTh* | *European Journal of Theology* |
| *Evangel* | *Evangel: The British Evangelical Review* |
| *EvQ* | *Evangelical Quarterly* |
| exp. | expanded |
| *ExpTim* | *Expository Times* |
| *F&M* | *Faith and Mission* |
| *Found* | *Foundations* (online journal of Affinity.org.uk) |
| FS | Festschrift |
| GNB | Good News Bible |
| *HALOT* | *Hebrew and Aramaic Lexicon of the Old Testament*. Ludwig Koehler, Walter Baumgartner, and Johann J. Stamm. Translated and edited under the supervision of Mervyn E. J. Richardson. 4 vols. Leiden: Brill, 1994–1999 |
| hb | hardback |
| *HBT* | *Horizons in Biblical Theology* |
| *HS* | *Hebrew Studies* |
| IBR | Institute for Biblical Research |
| *IBS* | *Irish Biblical Studies* |
| IBT | Interpreting Biblical Texts (Abingdon series) |
| IIS | Introducing Israel's Scriptures (Fortress series) |
| *Int* | *Interpretation* |
| *ISBE* | *International Standard Bible Encyclopedia*. Edited by Geoffrey W. Bromiley. 4 vols. rev. ed. Grand Rapids: Eerdmans, 1979–1988 |
| IVP | InterVarsity Press |
| *JAJ* | *Journal of Ancient Judaism* |
| *JAOS* | *Journal of the American Oriental Society* |
| *JBL* | *Journal of Biblical Literature* |

| | |
|---|---|
| *JBTS* | *Journal of Biblical and Theological Studies* (e-journal) |
| *JESOT* | *Journal for the Evangelical Study of the Old Testament* |
| *JETS* | *Journal of the Evangelical Theological Society* |
| *JHebS* | *Journal of Hebrew Scriptures* (e-journal) |
| *JJS* | *Journal of Jewish Studies* |
| *JNES* | *Journal of Near Eastern Studies* |
| *JR* | *Journal of Religion* |
| *JSHJ* | *Journal for the Study of the Historical Jesus* |
| *JSNT* | *Journal for the Study of the New Testament* |
| *JSOT* | *Journal for the Study of the Old Testament* |
| JSOTSup | Journal for the Study of the Old Testament Supplement Series |
| *JSS* | *Journal of Semitic Studies* |
| *JTI* | *Journal of Theological Interpretation* |
| *JTS* | *Journal of Theological Studies* |
| KAT | Kommentar zum Alten Testament |
| KEK | Kritisch-exegetischer Kommentar über das Neue Testament (Meyer-Kommentar) |
| KJV | King James Version |
| LHBOTS | The Library of Hebrew Bible/Old Testament Studies |
| LNTS | Library of New Testament Studies (monograph series) |
| LXX | Septuagint; also LXX/OG = Septuagint and Old Greek |
| *MAJT* | *Mid-America Journal of Theology* (cited by vol. number) |
| MS(S) | manuscripts |
| MT | Masoretic Text |
| n.d. | no date |
| NEB | New English Bible |
| *NIDNTT* | *New International Dictionary of New Testament Theology.* Edited by Colin Brown. 4 vols. Grand Rapids: Zondervan, 1975–1978, 1986 |
| *NIDNTTE* | *New International Dictionary of New Testament Theology & Exegesis.* Edited by Moisés Silva. 5 vols. 2nd ed. Grand Rapids: Zondervan, 2014 |
| *NIDOTTE* | *New International Dictionary of Old Testament Theology & Exegesis.* Edited by Willem A. VanGemeren. 5 vols. Grand Rapids: Zondervan, 1997 |
| NIV | New International Version |
| NJPS | *Tanakh: The Holy Scriptures: The New JPS Translation according to the Traditional Hebrew Text* |
| *NovT* | *Novum Testamentum* |
| NPP | New Perspective on Paul (see Dunn under "Pauline Studies") |
| NRSV | New Revised Standard Version |
| NSBT | New Studies in Biblical Theology |
| *NTS* | *New Testament Studies* |
| o/p | out of print |
| *Or* | *Orientalia* |
| *OTA* | *Old Testament Abstracts* |
| *OTE* | *Old Testament Essays* |
| OUP | Oxford University Press |
| P&R | Presbyterian & Reformed Publishing Co. |
| pb | paperback |
| PCA | Presbyterian Church in America |
| PCUSA | Presbyterian Church (USA) |

| | |
|---|---|
| POD | Print-on-demand (an order-fulfillment method of publication) |
| *Presb* | *Presbyterion* |
| *PRSt* | *Perspectives in Religious Studies* |
| *PSB* | *Princeton Seminary Bulletin* |
| -R | Replacement vol. in a series (e.g., TOTC-R, NICOT-R) |
| *RB* | *Revue biblique* |
| *RBL* | *Review of Biblical Literature* (online, only partially in print) |
| *RelSRev* | *Religious Studies Review* |
| repr. | reprinted |
| rev. | revised |
| *RevExp* | *Review and Expositor* |
| RSV | Revised Standard Version |
| *RTR* | *Reformed Theological Review* |
| RTS | Reformed Theological Seminary |
| *SBET* | *Scottish Bulletin of Evangelical Theology* |
| *SBJT* | *Southern Baptist Journal of Theology* |
| SBL | Society of Biblical Literature |
| *ScrB* | *Scripture Bulletin* |
| *SeTR* | *Southeastern Theological Review* |
| s/h | secondhand |
| *SJT* | *Scottish Journal of Theology* |
| SMU | Southern Methodist University |
| SNTS | Studiorum Novi Testamenti Societas |
| *SwJT* | *Southwestern Journal of Theology* |
| *TDNT* | *Theological Dictionary of the New Testament.* Edited by Gerhard Kittel and Gerhard Friedrich. Translated by Geoffrey W. Bromiley. 10 vols. Grand Rapids: Eerdmans, 1964–1976 |
| *TDOT* | *Theological Dictionary of the Old Testament.* Edited by G. Johannes Botterweck and Helmer Ringgren. Translated by John T. Willis et al. 15 vols. Grand Rapids: Eerdmans, 1974–2006 |
| TEDS | Trinity Evangelical Divinity School |
| *TGA* | *The Global Anglican*, previously *The Churchman (Chm)* |
| *Them* | *Themelios* (e-journal as of 2008) |
| *ThRef* | *Theologia Reformata* |
| *ThTo* | *Theology Today* |
| *TJ* | *Trinity Journal* |
| TPI | Trinity Press International |
| *TynBul* | *Tyndale Bulletin* |
| U. | University |
| UBS | United Bible Societies |
| vol(s). | volume(s) |
| *VT* | *Vetus Testamentum* |
| WJK | Westminster John Knox Press |
| *WTJ* | *Westminster Theological Journal* |
| WUNT | Wissenschaftliche Untersuchungen zum Neuen Testament (monograph series) |
| *ZAW* | *Zeitschrift für die alttestamentliche Wissenschaft* |

# Symbols

‡  A Work Espousing a Critical Theological Position (See Introduction for further explanation)

[𝓜]  A Work That Espouses a "Mediating" or Mildly Critical Approach to Biblical Interpretation (See Introduction)

✓  A Contribution to Scholarship and Worth Consulting, but of Debatable Value for a Pastor's Library (See Introduction)

F  A Forthcoming Volume

★  Suggested for Purchase (See Introduction)

☆  A Worthwhile Purchase, but Not a First Priority (See Introduction)

**Bold**  A Leading Commentary, Influential for Evangelical Scholarly Discussion

# INTRODUCTION

*Then Philip ran up to the chariot and heard the man reading Isaiah the prophet. "Do you understand what you are reading?" Philip asked. "How can I," he said, "unless someone explains it to me?" So he invited Philip to come up and sit with him.*

—*Acts 8:30–31*

*Meagreness, leanness, and shallowness are too often the main features of modern sermons. . . . The churches must be reminded that there can be no really powerful preaching without deep thinking, and little deep thinking without hard reading.*

—*J. C. Ryle[1]*

*[The Apostle Paul] is inspired, and yet he wants books! He has been preaching at least for thirty years, and yet he wants books! He had seen the Lord, and yet he wants books . . . He had been caught up into the third heaven, and had heard things which it was unlawful for a man to utter, yet he wants books! He had written the major part of the New Testament, and yet he wants books!*

—*C. H. Spurgeon[2]*

OVER DECADES OF MINISTRY twin convictions have grown in me. One is that the greatest longing the church has is for God himself—to know him, his glorious presence, his power, and his loving voice. The other conviction is that the church longs for her ministers to be full of God and his Word.[3] Building from this, I cannot see any pastoral ministry being effective long-term if not characterized by God's love for his people, prayerfulness, brimming confidence in the power of God's Word, and what Ryle termed "hard reading" in the study of Scripture.[4] Thank God for quality Bible commentaries which help preachers and teachers in their study! The challenge comes in recognizing quality.

Seminary students often face confusing choices in researching exegetical papers or composing sermons. They stand in the library stacks and ask themselves, "Which of these commentaries or reference works should I consult? Obviously, I can't skim even a tenth of these books on Romans; which ones are important and which ones may I safely pass by? Where should I spend my time?"

Prospective pastors or educators face a greater difficulty while searching for calls and preparing to leave for the fields of ministry to which Christ has called them. Knowing that

---

1. J. C. Ryle, "Memoir of Samuel Ward, BD," in Samuel Ward, *Sermons and Treatises* (Edinburgh: James Nichol, 1862), xvi.

2. C. H. Spurgeon, "Paul—His Cloak and His Books" (2 Tim 4:13), *Metropolitan Tabernacle Pulpit*, 9 (1863): 668.

3. See the first item in Sinclair Ferguson, "A Preacher's Decalogue," *Them* 36.2 (2011): 261–68.

4. In pressing the point I add a clarification. The expression "hard reading" does not mean general book learning, but the minister's discipline of work so as to become learned and powerful (or well versed) in the Scriptures (Acts 18:24). One could properly adapt Paul's warning in 1 Cor 4:20 to read, "the kingdom of God does not consist in [book-smarts] but in power." However, pastors are also wise to read widely outside of theology and biblical studies; see Cornelius Plantinga Jr., *Reading for Preaching: The Preacher in Conversation with Storytellers, Biographers, Poets, and Journalists* (Grand Rapids: Eerdmans, 2013).

commentaries are an important resource,[5] new graduates wonder which vols. deserve a place on the shelf. After all, they may possibly be far from a good theological library and will need an adequate personal collection to spur on their own growth in understanding the Bible. They ask, "Where should I spend my money?"

Pastors with some experience in the ministry usually keep on the lookout for new reference works, scanning booksellers' websites and catalogs a few times a year. They too wonder which commentaries would be a smart buy. This guide has been written to aid both in research and in making purchases for a personal library. It is not written for specialists—they have little need for such a guide as this—but for students and pastors, especially the evangelical and Reformed. For both students and pastors, the need for guides like this grows more acute with each passing year as the publications multiply.

To put it succinctly, we are being swamped with fine commentaries these days. The publishers have discovered that they sell well, and they are contracting for new vols. and new series all the time. None of us can keep up with the pace. But count your blessings—some top pick commentaries just five years ago are now superseded by a couple of better ones.

## TWO WARNINGS FOR ORIENTATION

It is necessary to warn the reader at the outset that commentaries should not be used as a crutch. Reading a commentary or two, or even ten, is no substitute for your own thorough initial study of the biblical text. The commentaries cannot do your work for you. They are meant to take you deeper than you have already gone and to help you check the conclusions of your own exegesis.[6] Also, commentary resources are not an excuse for neglecting the Hebrew and Greek languages, which are the best, most direct avenue to understanding and expounding the Bible in a responsible way. Charles Spurgeon said that pastors "should be able to read the Bible in the original," and he went on to explain his thinking:

---

5. Among so many excellent contributions in the Grant Osborne FS which discuss the usefulness of commentaries, see especially Robert W. Yarbrough, "The Pastoral Relevance of Commentaries" (215–34), and Walter L. Liefeld, "The Preaching Relevance of Commentaries" (235–52), in *On the Writing of New Testament Commentaries*, eds. Stanley E. Porter and Eckhard J. Schnabel (Leiden: Brill, 2013). I can highly recommend, too, the John Hartley FS: *The Genre of Biblical Commentary*, eds. Timothy D. Finlay and William Yarchin (Eugene, OR: Pickwick, 2015).

For further reflection on the art and purpose of commentary writing, see John Nolland, "The Purpose and Value of Commentaries," *JSNT* 29.3 (2007): 305–11, and the six other commentators with similar essays in that issue; Richard N. Longenecker, "On the Writing of Biblical Commentaries," in *From Biblical Criticism to Biblical Faith* (McDonald FS), eds. William Brackney and Craig Evans (Macon, GA: Mercer U. Press, 2007), 74–92; Brevard S. Childs, "The Genre of the Biblical Commentary as Problem and Challenge," in *Tehillah le-Moshe* (Greenberg FS), eds. Mordechai Cogan, Barry Eichler, and Jeffrey Tigay (Winona Lake, IN: Eisenbrauns, 1997), 185–92; Frederick W. Danker, "Commentaries and Their Uses," in *Multipurpose Tools for Bible Study*, revised and exp. ed. (Minneapolis: Fortress, 1993), 282–307; Frank H. Gorman, "Commenting on Commentary: Reflections on a Genre," in *Relating to the Text*, eds. J. Sandoval and C. Mandolfo, 100–119 (London: T&T Clark, 2003); and Walter C. Kaiser Jr., "Appendix B: The Usefulness of Biblical Commentaries for Preaching and Bible Study," in *Malachi: God's Unchanging Love* (Grand Rapids: Baker, 1984). There is excellent counsel in Brian Collins, "The Definitive Guide to Bible Commentaries: Types, Perspectives, and Use" (2023), https://www.logos.com/grow/min-bible-commentaries/.

6. Conscientious pastors often have a concern to check their faithfulness to the text by consulting trusted commentaries. All have a responsibility before God here and should be able to defend their interpretations. My brother called my attention to this withering accusation in Trollope's *Barchester Towers*: "With what complacency will a young parson deduce false conclusions from misunderstood texts, and then threaten us with all the penalties of Hades if we neglect to comply with the injunctions he has given us! Yes, my too self-confident juvenile friend, I do believe in those mysteries, which are so common in your mouth; I do believe in the unadulterated word which you hold there in your hand; but you must pardon me if, in some things, I doubt your interpretation."

Every minister should aim at a tolerable proficiency both in the Hebrew and the Greek. These two languages will give him a library at small expense, an inexhaustible thesaurus, a mine of spiritual wealth. Really the effort of acquiring a language is not so prodigious that brethren of moderate abilities should so frequently shrink from the attempt.[7]

With your seminary training, a willingness to dig, and prayer for the Spirit's illuming grace, you can competently exegete and expound the text. (Frankly, you're likely to do better than some of the commentators listed here.) Please don't cheat yourself out of that exciting learning experience. The use of commentaries apart from a careful study of the text (in the original, if possible) is a misuse of them. They are not written to relieve you of the responsibility to interpret the Scriptures, on the way to fulfilling your calling to declare the word of the Lord (Deut 5:5).

As a second warning, there is an inevitable subjectivity in compiling a selective bibliography. One Bible student is stimulated most by rigorous critical scholarship, while another perhaps views the Reformers, Puritan writings, and other classics as most valuable. It is hoped that this guide may be of some aid to both students. This list betrays my appreciation for both the older works that have stood the test of time and the more recent studies which seriously wrestle with issues of literary criticism, history, and biblical-theological interpretation. Let me elaborate.

I make no apology for emphasizing up-to-date and highly respected scholarly works in this survey. I believe that they usually best meet the needs of the pastor and student. (But see, too, my notes on old commentaries below.) Many older works—frequently the Puritans—can be faulted for not paying close enough attention to the message of the text in front of them. It is disappointing to peruse an old vol. and discover that the commentator has been distracted from the text itself by some locus of systematic theology hinted at, perhaps obliquely, in the passage.[8] Calvin's magnificent commentaries are unlike some Puritan works in this regard. The Reformer consciously rejected the Aristotelian method of establishing the meaning of a document by searching out its *loci* (i.e., its definitive concepts), and kept strictly to the task of elucidating the line of thought in the text, saving discussion of *loci* for his *Institutes of the Christian Religion*.

However, many modern commentaries have, from the pastor's point of view, worse problems. Quite a few technical works reveal little or no interest in the message and theology of the text, and the reader may feel left in Ricoeur's "desert of criticism."[9] Many commentaries have been written with "the assumption that the genetic origins of a text, often terribly hypothetical, are all one has to discover."[10] It is disappointing to spend time and money on a commentary in which the intricacies of such historical-critical debate take precedence over interpreting the text as we have it.[11] Also, some vols. hardly do more than catalog the history of scholarly opinion on each

---

7. C. H. Spurgeon, *Commenting & Commentaries* (London: Banner of Truth, 1969 reprint), 47. See also Takamitsu Muraoka, *Why Read the Bible in the Original Languages?* (Leuven: Peeters, 2020); John Piper's essay, "Brothers, Bitzer Was a Banker" (81–88), in *Brothers, We Are Not Professionals* (Nashville: B&H, 2002); Heinrich Bitzer, ed, *Light on the Path* (Grand Rapids: Baker, 1982 reprint); Jason DeRouchie, "The Profit of Employing the Biblical Languages," *Them* 37.1 (2012): 32–50; and Catherine L. McDowell and Philip H. Towner, *The Rewards of Learning Greek and Hebrew* (Peabody, MA: Hendrickson, 2021).

8. Having said that, I might add that such Puritans' digressions on systematic *loci* are usually worth reading.

9. Paul Ricoeur, *The Symbolism of Evil*, trans. Emerson Buchanan (Boston: Beacon, 1969), 349.

10. Roland E. Murphy, review of Craig G. Bartholomew, *Reading Ecclesiastes: Old Testament Exegesis and Hermeneutical Theory* (Rome: Biblical Institute Press, 1998), in *CBQ* 61.4 (1999): 735.

11. Generations of biblical scholarship fixated on historical questions, and there were indefatigable efforts both to trace the compositional history ("the text's becoming") and to "get behind the text" so as to reconstruct the religio-historical context of the writing. Often enough those reconstructions contradicted the story presented in the text. From the 1960s onward scholars have become increasingly impatient with this focus, and they have shifted from historical to literary concerns ("the text's being"). They want to study the art, the shape/structure, and the rhetoric in the final form. As one might expect, commentaries reflect this shift. Recommended reading: Craig Bartholomew, et al., eds., *"Behind" the Text: History and Biblical Interpretation* (Grand Rapids: Zondervan, 2003); David Firth and James Grant,

crux of historical criticism. Sometimes the scholar leaves you hanging and fails even to draw a conclusion. At the other end of the spectrum, the student or pastor finds many breezy homiletical commentaries that pay no serious attention to the text at all; the author's notions and observations about life in general supplant Scripture's message. How can you avoid such books?

Hopefully this survey will be some help to you, but don't depend entirely on one list. This guide is subjective and reflects my own preferences and proclivities (quirks?), which may be different from yours. You may be helped by a book I find dull and pedestrian, or, conversely, you may dislike a commentary I have suggested for purchase. It can be a matter of taste. Might the old adage apply, *de gustibus non est disputandum*—"With regard to taste, no disputing"? I urge students to use the seminary library as much as possible. Too many students fail to make best use of the library, and upon leaving school they have little idea what commentaries are out there or what kinds of books they like.

An invaluable resource for the commentary buyer is book reviews. Several evangelical journals have been especially helpful to me on account of their frequent commentary reviews: *Bulletin of Biblical Research, Calvin Theological Journal, Evangelical Quarterly, Journal of the Evangelical Theological Society, Themelios* (briefly dormant, now online free),[12] and *Westminster Theological Journal*.[13] I have cited over 12,000 reviews, both evangelical and critical, throughout this guide so that you will be able to consult them quickly without poring over the indices. These citations are intended as a check to counter subjectivity in this guide and will be found in a smaller font and in [brackets]. I also hope to save you some eye-strain, which (I laugh) may be a contribution to scholarship. Full reviews can discuss exegetical fine points and complicated interpretive issues—e.g., how to assess Elihu's discourse in Job—that my brief summaries cannot. Besides the book reviews, students are helped enormously by two publications of the Catholic Biblical Association which summarize the latest of both periodical articles and books: *Old Testament Abstracts* and *New Testament Abstracts*.

## OTHER BIBLIOGRAPHIES

The pastor or student who desires to build a fine personal library will learn much from consulting other bibliographies. Spurgeon's famous book dates from 1876 and remains quite valuable for its judicious reviews of old commentaries on both Testaments. Barber's 3-vol. survey had a wealth of bibliographical data, but often poor judgment in its recommendations. (Anything dispensational is typically given high marks, regardless of quality.) Now it is quite dated. Barber's pb vol. of 2000 is more of a supplement and does not include the huge catalog of commentaries found in the earlier set. Rosscup is the better dispensationally oriented survey. He is similar to Barber in placing a higher value on older works and in consistently recommending a narrower range of commentaries, i.e., those sharing his theology. Let me not neglect to note Robert Yost, who was inspired by Barber to produce an updated survey, *The Pastor's Library* (2017). His nearly 400-page work draws from a lifetime of ministry and teaching; his recommendations cover so much more

---

eds., *Words and the Word: Explorations in Biblical Interpretation and Literary Theory* (Nottingham: Apollos, 2008); and Thomas Olbricht, "Rhetorical Criticism in Biblical Commentaries," *CBR* 7.1 (2008): 11–36.

12. See the digital journal at http://www.thegospelcoalition.org/publications/?/themelios.

13. In addition to these, some of the best critical journals with reviews are: *Catholic Biblical Quarterly; Expository Times* (often the first review to appear); *Interpretation; Journal of Biblical Literature* (now in the auxiliary annual print publication *Review of Biblical Literature* and at http://www.bookreviews.org/); *Hebrew Studies; Biblica; Vetus Testamentum; Novum Testamentum; Journal of Hebrew Scriptures* (e-journal at http://jhsonline.org/); *Journal of Theological Studies;* and *Biblical Interpretation* (more monographs than commentaries). Other recommended evangelical periodicals are *Denver Journal* (http://www.denverseminary.edu/resources/denver-journal/); *Reformed Theological Review;* and *Trinity Journal*.

than commentaries and biblical reference resources. Yost has a familiarity with, and appreciation for, both dispensational and Reformed books. Kiehl once offered a lot of information, but few will now depend on such an old guide (current through 1986). It was evangelically oriented and, some would say, gave too much weight to Lutheran works. For a later conservative Lutheran guide to commentaries, see Brug below. Unfortunately, Stuart's 1990 guide had limited usefulness from the beginning because he made few value judgments.

Two more recent bibliographies merit special attention. The first is Bauer's large guide (2014), which covers a huge amount of ground and, therefore, is more selective. The reviews and recommendations are very intelligent, from a Wesleyan and mildly critical stance, but one wonders at points if it was selectivity or an oversight when he omitted entirely the Zondervan Exegetical Commentary on the NT and individual vols. in the NIV Application Commentary and the New American Commentary.[14] Excluding his commentary recommendations, this has been among the fullest and best bibliographic guides into the whole range of tools available for exegetical research.

Secondly, I have happily recommended the late John Glynn's work in its 10th ed. (2007) [BL 2009].[15] Glynn's perspective was unabashedly conservative, yet he covered every significant commentary series, evangelical or liberal. He was well-read and informed in his recommendations. Three drawbacks are its date, the brevity of his descriptions or reviews (often little more than a listing), and a strict focus upon works of the last 60 years or so. His wide-ranging survey of reference works and theological resources—atlases, dictionaries, hermeneutics textbooks, lexicons and grammars for the languages, introductions, systematics, and church history works—filled a real need. The commentary section is Glynn's best. Among more recent guides, only Bauer treats a similarly broad range of resources for exegesis. Note, too, that Bauer does not discuss the literature in the fields of systematic theology and church history, as does Glynn. See now the Burer-edited reworking of Glynn, discussed below.

More than just in passing, I call attention to a fine set of quick internet guides to commentaries on both Testaments. See the Grove "Biblical Studies Bulletin" edited (mostly) by Michael Thompson, Principal of Ridley Hall in Cambridge, England. He engaged leading conservative Anglican scholars—with some exceptions—to make recommendations for pastors. Would you like to know which commentaries Wenham thinks are best on Genesis? He tells you in a two-minute read. Hugh Williamson does the write-up for books on Chronicles and on Ezra–Nehemiah. In the area of NT, Peter Head among others has sage advice on the commentaries most serviceable for pastors. Occasionally I select quotes from contributors and mark them *BSB* with a date. Regrettably, it ceased publication in 2012.

Certainly one of the most useful internet guides to consulting and purchasing books is bestcommentaries.com. John Dyer has developed the site over many years, and he includes nearly exhaustive lists of the English-language Bible commentaries currently in print, links to booksellers, and purchase recommendations (Building a Commentary Library) which reflect his evangelical convictions. More precisely, Dyer "combines reviews and ratings from journals, books, and users to create an aggregate ranking for . . . commentaries."

---

14. A pastor who wants to preach on Gideon or Samson is misled if Bauer does not recommend Block's NAC work on Judges/Ruth. In Zondervan's NIVAC, the pastor is helped immensely by Enns on Exodus; Jobes on Esther; and Duguid on Ezekiel. I could list many additional jewels in other series that he misses: Milgrom on Numbers; Christopher Wright on Deuteronomy; Provan on Kings; and Murphy on Proverbs (WBC). On James he omits three top evangelical commentaries: McKnight (NICNT); Moo (Pillar); and Blomberg–Kamell (ZECNT). Once in a while, his "highly recommended" lists make no sense, as when he includes the Sanday–Headlam ICC on Romans but not Cranfield.

15. The Dallas Seminary faculty have partially continued Glynn's project. For the NT, see the 2018 Glynn–Burer update below.

Among OT annotated bibliographies, Childs's 1977 volume *Old Testament Books* is excellent but out of print (o/p). He is usually fair and worth reading cover to cover, but do note that his choices are informed by critical presuppositions. He may discount a work of quality if at odds with dominant critical theory, but the discounting is not egregious or severe. Of course Childs misses the flood of works published over the last fifty years. The aging Goldingay–Hubbard list is quite good as well (1975, 1981); I have not seen the later Goldingay revision. Tremper Longman's *Survey* was once clearly the best current bibliography here in the US, though all five editions occasionally overlooked important works.[16] The 2nd edition (1995) is not to be discarded, for it had features not included in the subsequent editions: (a) reviews of reference works like OT introductions, Hebrew grammars, etc.; (b) an appendix listing best buys; and (c) an appendix suggesting which works might be included in an ultimate reference library. Regrettably, Longman has not been updated since 2013. Moving on to an internet resource, I can heartily recommend the Denver Seminary bibliography done by Dallaire–Heim–Hess.

Among NT annotated bibliographies, Don Carson's always headed the list. In the past we used to read Carson side by side with Ralph Martin's 1984 book.[17] Both were full, wide-ranging, and well-done indeed. (Martin's guide was meant to serve as a companion to Brevard Childs's.) Carson, in contrast to Martin, was repeatedly updated; the most recent edition came out in 2013. Years ago, many regarded Carson as offering a more consistently evangelical perspective, as well as more discerning recommendations, than Martin. It would be a mistake, however, to think that Carson's conservative stance narrows the purview of his survey; he reviews the works of Bultmann alongside the Puritans. As he says, "this survey is a guide to commentaries, not orthodoxy."[18] This means he does not slight works coming out of the critical camp if they are worthy contributions (e.g., he rightly gives high marks to the Anchor Bible vols. on Luke by Fitzmyer). Carson remains an excellent guide and worth buying along with Longman; the regret is that Carson appeared over a decade ago and thousands of commentary vols. have since been published. Nijay Gupta's 2020 *Guide* is praiseworthy and more current. He does a fine job, especially in surveying and recommending more advanced and technical books. Note that he is quite selective and does not mention some major works (e.g., Boring, Edwards, Stein, Witherington on Mark). His preference is for more critical materials, open (as he is) to the New Perspective on Paul (NPP) and feminist concerns. The updating of Glynn's NT section by Burer (2018), "with contributions" by Dallas Seminary faculty, is conservative, wide-ranging, and discerning. As the reader would expect, quality dispensational books find favor and are recommended. The collaborative effort distinguishes it: Burer does Matthew to Luke, and Hebrews to 2 Peter/Jude; Johnston reviews works on Romans to Galatians, plus Thessalonians and the Pastorals; Fantin does John, the Prison Epistles, 1–3 John, and Revelation; and Bock treats Acts. The Denver Seminary NT list on the internet is updated every year and provides good guidance. These and other notable bibliographies are listed below. Bold print below indicates the more informative or instructive lists.

**Allen, David L.** *Preaching Tools: An Annotated Survey of Commentaries and Preaching Resources for Every Book of the Bible.* Fort Worth, TX: Seminary Hill Press, 2014.

Allison, Joe. *Swords and Whetstones: A Guide to Christian Bible Study Resources.* 3rd ed. Nappannee, IN: Jordan/Evangel, 1999.

---

16. In the 2003, 2007, and 2013 editions, we lacked reviews of Nelson on Deuteronomy; Hawk on Joshua; Schneider on Judges; Davidson on Psalms; the NCB volume on Hosea; Westermann on Lamentations; Macintosh's ICC on Hosea; Wolff on Micah; and all the Abingdon OT Commentaries.

17. In Google Books I've seen pages of the revision: *New Testament Books for Pastor and Teacher,* rev. ed. (Eugene, OR: Wipf & Stock, 2002).

18. D. A. Carson, *New Testament Commentary Survey,* 7th ed. (Grand Rapids: Baker Academic, 2013), viii.

Aune, David E. *Jesus and the Synoptic Gospels.* Theological Students Fellowship—Bibliographic Study Guides. Madison, WI: IVP, 1980.

Barber, Cyril J. *Best Books for Your Bible Study Library.* Neptune, NJ: Loizeaux, 2000.

Barber, Cyril J. *The Minister's Library.* 3 vols. Grand Rapids: Baker, 1974–89.

**Barber, Cyril J., and Robert M. Knauss Jr.** *An Introduction to Theological Research: A Guide for College and Seminary Students.* 2nd ed. New York: University Press of America, 2000. [*JETS* 12/01]

Barker, Kenneth L., Bruce K. Waltke, and Roy B. Zuck. *Bibliography for Old Testament Exegesis and Exposition.* Dallas: Dallas Theological Seminary, 1979.

**Bauer, David R.** *Essential Bible Study Tools for Ministry.* Nashville: Abingdon, 2014. Note the 2003 edition with Hendrickson: *An Annotated Guide to Biblical Resources for Ministry.* Even earlier was the 2nd edition of *Biblical Resources for Ministry* (Evangel, 1995).

**Bazylinski, Stanislaw.** *A Guide to Biblical Research.* 2nd enlarged ed. Rome: Gregorian & Biblical Institute Press, 2009. For the online update, see https://www.biblico.it/doc-vari /bibl_nt.html and https://www.biblico.it/doc-vari/ska_bibl.html.

***Biblical Studies Bulletin*** (*BSB*): http://grovebooks.co.uk/pages/biblical-studies-bulletin. Long edited by Michael B. Thompson of Ridley Hall, Cambridge. Ceased publication in 2012.

Brug, John F. (Wisconsin Lutheran Seminary), "Old Testament Commentaries for the Pastor's Study": www.wlsessays.net/files/BrugCommentariesOT2014.pdf. 9th ed. 2014.

**Center for Excellence in Preaching (Calvin Seminary).** "Books." https://cepreaching.org /resources/books/.

**Carson, D. A.** *New Testament Commentary Survey.* 7th ed. Grand Rapids: Baker Academic, 2013. [4th ed. 1993; 5th ed. 2001; 6th ed. 2007]

**Chester, Stephen, Max Lee, and Klyne Snodgrass.** "North Park Seminary—New Testament Bibliography, Fall 2012." https://www.northpark.edu/wp-content/uploads/New-Testament -Bibliography.pdf.

**Childs, Brevard S.** *Old Testament Books for Pastor and Teacher.* Philadelphia: Westminster, 1977.

Childs, Brevard S. *The New Testament as Canon: An Introduction.* Philadelphia: Fortress, 1985. [See "Excursus IV"]

**Clendenen, E. Ray.** "A Bibliography of Old Testament and Related Subjects: Guidance for Expositors, Updated January/2021." https://www.academia.edu/44949593/A _BIBLIOGRAPHY_OF_OLD_TESTAMENT_AND_RELATED_SUBJECTS_GUIDANCE _FOR_EXPOSITORS_Update_January_2021_.

**Conroy, Charles.** "Biblical Bibliographies" [Last updated 2023–08–30]. https://www.cjconroy .net/bibliog.htm.

**Denver Journal Bibliographies:** https://denverjournal.denverseminary.edu/the-denver-journal -article/annotated-old-testament-bibliography-2024/ (Hélène Dallaire, Knut Heim, and Richard Hess for OT); https://denverjournal.denverseminary.edu/the-denver-journal -article/new-testament-exegesis-bibliography-2024/ (Craig Blomberg, David Mathewson, and Joseph R. Dodson for NT).

**Detroit Baptist Theological Seminary.** "Basic Library Booklist: Prepared by the Faculty DBTS 2022." https://dbts.edu/basic-library-booklist/.

**Duvall, J. Scott, and J. Daniel Hays.** *Grasping God's Word.* 3rd ed. Grand Rapids: Zondervan, 2012. [See "Building a Personal Library," pp. 459–91]

**Dyer, John.** www.bestcommentaries.com.

Evans, Craig A. "New Testament Commentaries." www.craigaevans.com/teaching_materials /NT_Commentaries.doc [No longer available].

Eves, Terry, and Steven Schlei. "A Guide to Old Testament Commentaries and Reference Works." Rev. ed. 1982. Published by Westminster Seminary Bookstore, Philadelphia.

**Fee, Gordon D.** *New Testament Exegesis.* 4th ed. Louisville: WJK, 2010. [See "Aids and Resources for the Steps in Exegesis"]

Finley, Thomas J. (Talbot Seminary). www.people.biola.edu/faculty/tomf/OT_Expositional _Tools.pdf. Accessed 2005. [No longer available]

Fitzmyer, Joseph A. *An Introductory Bibliography for the Study of Scripture.* 3rd ed. Rome: Pontifical Biblical Institute, 1990.

France, R. T. *A Bibliographical Guide to New Testament Research.* Cambridge: Tyndale Fellowship for Biblical Research, 1974.

**Glynn, John.** *Commentary & Reference Survey: A Comprehensive Guide to Biblical and Theological Resources.* 10th ed. Grand Rapids: Kregel, 2007.

**Glynn, John (ed. Michael H. Burer).** *Best Bible Books: New Testament Commentaries.* Grand Rapids: Kregel Academic, 2018.

Goldingay, John. *Old Testament Commentary Survey.* Rev. ed. Leicester: Theological Students Fellowship, 1991, 1994. An earlier revision contained Robert L. Hubbard's "1981 Supplement" to the 1975 1st ed.

Goodacre, Mark. http://ntgateway.com/resource/biblio.htm.

Gorman, G. E., and Lyn Gorman. *Theological and Religious Reference Materials: General Resources and Biblical Studies.* Westport, CT; London: Greenwood Press, 1984.

**Gorman, Michael J.** *Elements of Biblical Exegesis: A Basic Guide for Students and Ministers.* 3rd ed. Grand Rapids: Baker Academic, 2020. See esp. chapter 11, "Resources for Exegesis."

**Gupta, Nijay K.** *The New Testament Commentary Guide.* Bellingham, WA: Lexham Press, 2020.

Harrington, Daniel. *The New Testament: A Bibliography.* Wilmington, DE: Michael Glazier, 1985.

**Hilbrands, Walter.** "Bibliography Old Testament Commentaries, Bibliografie Kommentare Altes Testament." April 2023. https://www.academia.edu/35181149/Bibliography_Old _Testament_Commentaries_Bibliografie_Kommentare_Altes_Testament.

**Holladay, Carl R.** *Introduction to the New Testament: Reference Edition.* Waco, TX: Baylor U. Press, 2017.

Johnston, William M. *Recent Reference Books in Religion.* Downers Grove, IL: IVP, 1996.

Kepple, Robert J., and John R. Muether. *Reference Works for Theological Research.* 3rd ed. Lanham, MD: University Press of America, 1992.

Kiehl, Erich H. *Building Your Biblical Studies Library.* St. Louis: Concordia, 1988.

**Kirby Laing Centre for Public Theology.** "Preaching the Bible for All Its Worth." *The Big Picture* 1–(2021–). https://kirbylaingcentre.co.uk/the-big-picture/online-magazine/.

**Klein, Ralph W.** http://fontes.lstc.edu/~rklein/Documents/prophets.htm (2015).

Knight, George W., III. "New Testament Commentaries for a Minister's Library." Rev. 1993. Privately produced.

**Köstenberger, Andreas J., and Richard D. Patterson.** *An Invitation to Biblical Interpretation.* Grand Rapids: Kregel, 2011. (I do not believe the 2021 2nd edition contains the commentary recommendations.)

**Longman, Tremper, III.** *Old Testament Commentary Survey.* 5th ed. Grand Rapids: Baker Academic, 2013 (1st ed. 1991; 2nd ed. 1995; 3rd ed. 2003; 4th ed. 2007).

**Martin, Ralph.** *New Testament Books for Pastor and Teacher.* Philadelphia: Westminster, 1984. On Google Books there are pages of a revised ed. (Eugene, OR: Wipf & Stock, 2002).

**Mathison, Keith.** "Top 5 Commentaries on Every Book of the Bible." (August 31, 2021). https:// www.ligonier.org/learn/articles/top-5-commentaries.

**Matthews, Christopher R., ed.** *Oxford Bibliographies in Biblical Studies.* Oxford: Oxford University Press, 2018–. https://www.oxfordbibliographies.com/obo/page/biblical-studies.

**McKnight, Scot.** "Pastor's Bookshelf" (blog posts): https://www.beliefnet.com/columnists /jesuscreed/page/2/?s=Pastor%27s+Bookshelf.

Meredith, Don (Harding School of Theology). http://hst.edu/library-resources/research-tools/. See esp. his "Commentary Recommendations" document.

Mills, Watson E. *Critical Tools for the Study of the New Testament.* Lewiston, NY: Mellen, 1995.

Moo, Douglas, ed. *An Annotated Bibliography on the Bible and the Church.* Compiled for the Alumni Association of Trinity Evangelical Divinity School, 1986.

**Moore Theological College, Sydney.** "Commentary List" (2017): https://issuu.com/moore college/docs/moore_societas_2017_online.

Oak Hill College, London (Faculty Recommendations): www.oakhill.ac.uk/resources/old _testament.html and www.oakhill.ac.uk/resources/new_testament.html. Accessed 2005. [No longer available]

**Pakala, James C.** "A Librarian's Comments on Commentaries," *Presb* 21.2–(1995–).

Pierce, Jeremy. http://parablemania.ektopos.com/archives/2006/05/forthcombook.html [No longer available].

**Porter, Stanley E., and Eckhard J. Schnabel, eds.** *On the Writing of Commentaries* (Osborne FS). Leiden; Boston: Brill, 2013. Many commentaries on NT books are surveyed.

Princeton Theological Seminary. "Recommended Old and New Testament Commentaries by the Biblical Studies Faculty of Princeton Theological Seminary" (OT list updated 2010; NT list updated 2017): http://s3.amazonaws.com/ptsem/pdfs/Recommended-Bible -Commentaries.pdf.

**Princeton Theological Seminary.** "Commentaries and Important Monographs on Books of the New Testament" (revised January 2019). https://ptsem-my.sharepoint.com/:w:/g/personal /tabitha_serrano_ptsem_edu/ETPry76g5PpDsUr1aTf2DtkB2VqdmviZq_OHCDutiC4i3w ?rtime=-8QN8gqS20g.

**Rosscup, Jim.** *Commentaries for Biblical Expositors.* Revised ed. The Woodlands, TX: Kress, 2003.

Scholer, David M. *A Basic Bibliographic Guide for New Testament Exegesis.* 2nd ed. Grand Rapids: Eerdmans, 1973.

Schreiner, Thomas R. "Select Commentaries on the Pauline Epistles." In *Interpreting the Pauline Epistles.* 2nd ed. Grand Rapids: Baker, 2011. Material shared at http://andynaselli.com /schreiners-top-three.

**Schreiner, Thomas R.** "Recommended New Testament Commentaries for Evangelical Pastors." *9Marks*, February 3, 2023. https://www.9marks.org/article/recommended-new-testament -commentaries-for-evangelical-pastors/.

Silva, Moisés. "The Silva Mind-Control Method for Buying NT Commentaries." Revised Jan. 1993. Published by Westminster Seminary Bookstore, Philadelphia.

Singleton, Steve. "Online Commentaries in Canonical Order" (links to scores of older commentaries now in public domain): http://deeperstudy.com/link/commentaries.html.

Smick, Elmer B. "A Pastor's Bibliographical Guide to the Old Testament." Rev. 1985. Privately produced at Gordon-Conwell Seminary, South Hamilton, MA.

Spurgeon, C. H. *Commenting & Commentaries.* London: Banner of Truth, 1969 repr. (1876 ed.).

Stewart, David R. *The Literature of Theology: A Guide for Students and Pastors.* Rev. ed. Louisville: WJK, 2003.

Stitzinger, James F. (The Master's Seminary, Santa Clarita, CA). "Books for Bible Expositors": http://masters.libguides.com/booksforbibleexpositors.

**Stuart, Douglas.** *A Guide to Selecting and Using Bible Commentaries.* Waco, TX: Word, 1990.

**Stuart, Douglas.** *Old Testament Exegesis.* 5th ed. Louisville: WJK, 2022. [See "Exegesis Aids & Resources"]

Sugg, Martha Aycock, and John Boone Trotti. *Building a Pastor's Library.* Richmond, VA: Union Theological Seminary, 1991.

**Tabb, Brian J.** "Comments on New Testament Commentaries." *Themelios* 48.1 (2023): https://www.thegospelcoalition.org/themelios/article/comments-on-new-testament-commentaries/.

**TGC, The Gospel Coalition.** https://www.thegospelcoalition.org/best-commentaries/ (2024).

Thomas, Derek, and John W. Tweeddale. *The Essential Commentaries for a Preacher's Library.* Revised ed. Jackson, MS: First Presbyterian Press, 2006.

Thompson, John L. "English Language Resources for Studying the History of Exegesis." http://documents.fuller.edu/sot/faculty/thompson_john/HistExeg/homepage.htm. (Extensive list of Jewish and Christian commentary resources prior to 1700.)

Thorsen, Donald A. D. *Theological Resources for Ministry: A Bibliography of Works in Theological Studies.* Nappanee, IN: Evangel Publishing House, 1996.

**Trinity Evangelical Divinity School** (Rolfing Library): http://library.tiu.edu/friendly.php?s=commentaries (OT), http://library.tiu.edu/commentaries/nt (NT).

Turner, John. "Bible Commentary Reviews": www.disciples.org/biblea.htm#Biog. [No longer available]

United Bible Societies. "Bible Commentaries" >> "List All" or "Search": http://www.ubs-translations.org/bibliographies/#c521.

Williams, Tyler F. (The King's University College, Edmonton). "Old Testament Commentary Survey": http://biblical-studies.ca/ot-commentaries.html.

Worth, Roland H., Jr. *Biblical Studies on the Internet: A Resource Guide.* 2nd ed. Jefferson, NC: McFarland, 2008.

Yost, Robert A. *The Layperson's Library: Essential Bible Study Tools for the Man and Woman in the Pew.* Eugene, OR: Wipf & Stock, 2021.

**Yost, Robert A.** *The Pastor's Library: An Annotated Bibliography of Biblical and Theological Resources for Ministry.* Eugene, OR: Wipf & Stock, 2017.

Zannoni, Arthur E. *The Old Testament: A Bibliography.* Collegeville, MN: Liturgical Press, 1992.

Here are two final notes: (1) A few commentary series (e.g., New Interpreter's Bible, Abingdon NT Commentaries, and NIV Application Commentary) include annotated bibliographies worth consulting. (2) Baker's "IBR Bibliographies" have value but most do not cover commentaries; two notable exceptions are Porter–McDonald on NT Introduction and McKnight–Williams on the Synoptic Gospels.[19]

## THE GUIDE'S FORMAT

In this guide I made no changes to the format of previous editions because that layout has been well-received and seems well suited to helping readers quickly survey the books available. I have usually starred (★) about six works for each Bible book as suggestions for purchase, allowing myself an extra selection or two for those books a preacher will often turn to (e.g., Genesis, Psalms, John, Romans). The majority of these recommended works emphasize scholarly exegesis and full theological commentary rather than devotional and sermonic helps, but I have kept in mind the need for a mix. As readers will notice, the mix I prefer includes commentaries which exegete the text in the original languages (e.g., NIGTC, BECNT, ICC); more accessible commentaries using English translations (NICOT, NICNT, NAC); and expositions which are practical in aim, relating the Bible's message to today's world (BST and NIVAC). Series such as NIGTC and BST will be helpful in different ways at different points in sermon preparation.[20] In making recommendations

---

19. Private correspondence with Rev. Doug Stelzig, a former missionary in South Africa.

20. Fred Craddock, the Bandy Distinguished Professor of Preaching and New Testament, Emeritus, at Candler School of Theology, had an interesting system of describing the books on a pastor's bookshelf. He writes of classifying

for purchases, I have mainly had pastors in mind. Preachers want reliable and accessible tools, focused more on the message of the text, which avoid being overly technical. More specifically, I have been thinking of studious pastors, who take seriously the life of the mind and the academic study of Scripture, even if academia is not their calling. (The pastorate is a higher calling in my book.) While making recommendations for purchases, I have not forgotten seminarians' interest in philology, grammar, sophisticated hermeneutical methods, cutting-edge literary analysis, bibliographies, etc. To benefit those students using this guide in their research, I have placed in bold type the authors of the weightier, more influential scholarly commentaries, i.e., those works an evangelical seminary professor would probably like to see consulted in exegetical papers.

The star-outline symbol (☆) designates a valuable commentary or reference work which would be worth buying, but would, in my judgment, be a second priority. The checkmark (British "tick") symbol (✓) designates an important scholarly work that could profitably be consulted for seminary papers, but is either difficult/expensive to obtain or of debatable value for a pastor's library. The symbol (F) indicates a forthcoming work. It must be said that some of these promised vols. will never be published.[21]

As a rule of thumb, it is unwise to purchase an entire series of commentaries, despite the lure of deep discounts. Some exceptions to this rule come to mind: Calvin's NT Commentaries, perhaps the two Tyndale series and the New International Commentary series (NICOT and NICNT). The basis for this rule is the fact that series are always uneven, some more than others, even when they are the work of only one commentator. This cuts two ways: a strong series may have weaker entries, while a mediocre series may have a couple of stellar contributions. Because of different price structures for series in electronic format (e.g., Word Biblical Commentary), this rule—that it's unwise to be buying whole series—will not be followed as regularly as it once was. *Please note: in this guide I have not included Keil & Delitzsch (OT) or Calvin's NT Commentaries among the purchase suggestions under individual books. Rather, I have assumed that many students and pastors will eventually either obtain these for their personal collections or gain free access to these classics via the internet.*

For the student just beginning to build a library, I pass along my late father's excellent advice: as you're able, buy one solid exegetical vol. and one suggestive expositional-devotional commentary for each book. I might add that it would be wise to garner the exegetical tools first and to begin with the major books of the Bible, i.e., those on which you will be preaching with some regularity. (See my appendix, An Ideal Basic Library for the Pastor.) Another, more long-term system for developing a library collection, used by probably thousands of ministers, is to purchase four to five helpful works for preaching through a book. I did this for my very first sermon series. Planning to do a full exposition of 1 Peter, I purchased Selwyn, Davids, Michaels, Grudem, and Clowney. My father encouraged me further by giving me Stuart Briscoe's book of sermons entitled *When the Going Gets Tough*. The main point is to have a smart plan in mind and keep at it.

## STANDARDS FOR EVALUATING COMMENTARIES

A few words are in order about the kinds of commentaries I have recommended.[22] What was I looking for? First, I examined a commentary for exegetical help with the text, especially at the

---

"resources for preaching according to the days of the week, Monday being farthest from the pulpit, Saturday being closest. The technically and critically heavy books . . . are called Monday books; those less so, Tuesday books. Wednesday books refer to those which are biblically and theologically substantive but which have preachers in mind. Thursday books make suggestions about how to preach their contents, Friday books contain sermon outlines, and Saturday books are collections of full sermons." *Luke*, Interpretation (Louisville: WJK, 1990), vii.

21. For an excellent, though not completely accurate, list see https://best commentaries.com/forthcoming.

22. Some of these concerns and questions were culled from the 1982 commentary guide produced by Steven Schlei and Terry Eves for Westminster Seminary students.

cruxes where help is most needed. Is the commentator learned and sensitive when it comes to language and grammar questions? Is there any analysis of structure, literary art, and rhetoric? Does the author employ traditional diachronic or recent synchronic methods (or attempt an integration of the two)? Does the commentary help me understand the flow of the story or argument (perhaps biblical discourse analysis)? Does it give evidence of the scholar's patient, hard work with the text, including a good awareness of past research? I count two strikes against scholars who have not kept up with reading in their field. Of course, some scholars give perhaps too much evidence that they read widely. From them, Andrie du Toit humorously says, "one can learn a lot about the art of compilation."[23]

My second concern was for an understanding of the historical and cultural background of the literature. Who was the author? When was it written? To whom and for what reason? What social, cultural, economic, and religious factors, in the milieu of the intended audience or readership, are key for understanding how the message was first received? What may have been the use of the text in the life of the faith community, if we know little or nothing of its author and the circumstances of composition (as with many of the psalms)? Do these facts (or guesses) throw any light on how I ought to interpret the text?

Third, does the commentator provide mature theological reflection (preferably from both the biblical theology[24] and the systematic theology angles) after making well-based exegetical decisions? The commentator ought to be alert to theological questions such as: How are themes contained in this passage anticipated earlier in Scripture? How are they developed or fulfilled later in Scripture? Does the text express truths or themes which are emphasized in the theology of the Bible book being studied: say, the new exodus theme in Ezekiel or glory in John's Gospel? How is this passage similar to others and how is it different? What is the passage's unique message? What doctrines are taught here? Does the passage shed light on doctrinal controversies? Are there tensions between the teachings in this pericope and others in Scripture that need to be appreciated, addressed, and perhaps resolved?

What a need there is for theologically astute commentary! Even with the building Theological Interpretation of Scripture (TIS) movement, we can still struggle with the problem, flatly stated by Reno, that "Theology has lost its competence in exegesis. Scripture scholars function with minimal theological training."[25]

Fourth among the concerns was to look for clarity of expression and economy of words. Books that were full in their discussion, but somewhat unfocused or prolix were sometimes excluded from the list of suggested works—many homiletical commentaries fall into this category. According to

---

23. Andrie B. du Toit, Review of Abraham J. Malherbe, *The Letters to the Thessalonians*, AB 32B (New York: Doubleday, 2000), in *RelSRev* 29.1 (2003): 46. The reviewer adds, "I once heard the late Willem van Unnik warn against writers who draw on nine other publications to produce a tenth."

24. I am among those who believe that a neglect of the biblical-theological (or redemptive-historical) approach mutes true gospel proclamation in many pulpits today. Moralizing preaching is tiresome—see "A Paper Doll King David" in *CT* 6/16/97. But it is also dangerous theologically. I implore young seminarians to get well acquainted with IVP's *New Dictionary of Biblical Theology* (2000) and to read and digest books like Sidney Greidanus's *Preaching Christ from the Old Testament* (1999); Graeme Goldsworthy's *Preaching the Whole Bible as Christian Scripture* (2000); and Edmund Clowney's *Preaching and Biblical Theology* (1961), which on p.78 boldly says,

> Preaching which ignores the *historia revelationis*, which "again and again equates Abraham and us, Moses's struggle and ours, Peter's denial and our unfaithfulness; which proceeds only illustratively, does not bring the Word of God and does not permit the church to see the glory of the work of God; it only preaches man, the sinful, the sought, the redeemed, the pious man, but not Jesus Christ." (Karl Dijk, *De Dienst der Prediking* [Kampen: Kok, 1955], 109)

25. R. R. Reno, "Series Preface," in Robert W. Jenson, *Ezekiel*, Brazos Theological Commentary on the Bible (Grand Rapids: Brazos, 2009), 13. The effects are well described by Stephen Dempster: "Theology without exegesis is speculation and exegesis without theology is antiquarian" (*Micah*, THC [Grand Rapids: Eerdmans, 2017], 37).

Calvin, *perspicua brevitas* is the chief virtue of a commentator. Along the same lines, I. Howard Marshall warned of "a real danger that pastors are going to stop reading modern commentaries simply because they haven't the time to cope with the vast mass of material in them and produce their expository sermons. Students and pastors need something more succinct!"[26] I agree with this; generally speaking, most huge books are unsuitable for a pastor's library. However, I also wish to leave room for big reference works which are more likely to take up technical questions. Hengstenberg once wrote, "There are two kinds of commentaries on Holy Scripture—those that are more adapted for perusal, and those that are more suitable for reference. Both are necessary, and it would not be desirable that either should exclude the other."[27]

Fifth, I look at the price tag. It is astonishing what some publishers ask for a book. Some superb commentaries, like the Davies–Allison ICC on Matthew, were far beyond the reach of the pastor; that 3-vol. hb set eventually came to list for over $700. Thankfully this ICC is now being released in pb at a reduced price ($273 at Amazon in 2024).

Sixth, is the work readily available for library use or purchase? It is nonsensical for me to urge readers to purchase books that are long out of print.

My seventh concern related to the genre of commentary. If the author set out to write a warm-hearted, devotional exposition with lots of anecdotes and application, I will naturally apply different standards to evaluate it than, say, a vol. in the technical series NIGTC. I asked, what kind of commentary did the person set out to write, for what kind of audience, and how well did the author accomplish his or her aim?

Eighth, the pastor asks whether the commentator can suggest ways the text may speak to contemporary issues facing the church. These days, some fine practical series, such as the NIV Application Commentary, understand the distinction between homiletical commentaries and published sermons. They seek to lay a reasonably solid exegetical foundation for understanding the meaning of the text in its ancient context before moving on to matters of contemporary application. For application, these commentaries aim to be suggestive, to present sermon seed thoughts for preachers to mull over and develop on their own. They provide guidance rather than prefabricated sermons in the guise of commentary. The better series may suggest multiple possibilities for proper application of the text's message to the people of God. Other series now in print do not seem to understand this distinction between homiletical commentaries and ready-made sermons. We all should look askance when poor quality, edited sermons which offer no serious, sustained engagement of the text are today dressed up as "commentary." What sort of book are preachers looking for? What will help them? The preface to the *New Interpreter's Bible*, in describing the aim of its practically oriented Reflections section, expresses the felt need of most ministers I know: "Preachers and teachers want some specificity about the implications of the text, but not so much specificity that the work is done for them. The ideas in the Reflections are meant to stimulate the thought of preachers and teachers, not to replace it."[28]

My comments above on homiletical commentaries may be open to misunderstanding. Books of sermons have done me a world of good; I do not denigrate them. I relish reading in vols. of sermons by the great expositors, including John Calvin, Charles Spurgeon, Campbell Morgan, Martyn Lloyd-Jones, and Kent Hughes. In this guide I recommend a few of these vols. for purchase,

---

26. I. Howard Marshall, Review of Rudolf Schnackenburg, *The Epistle to the Ephesians* (Edinburgh: T&T Clark, 1991), in *EvQ* 68.1 (1996): 70. From the OT side, Richard Coggins has spoken of commentaries having suffered "a kind of elephantiasis" (*Joel and Amos*, NCB [Sheffield: Sheffield Academic Press, 2000], vii).

27. E. W. Hengstenberg, *The Prophecies of the Prophet Ezekiel Elucidated*, trans. A. C. Murphy and J. G. Murphy (Edinburgh: T&T Clark, 1869), v.

28. "Features of the New Interpreter's Bible," *The New Interpreter's Bible*, 12 vols. (Nashville: Abingdon, 1994–2002), xviii.

not so much for their application, which often cannot easily or properly be carried over to the present day, but for their penetrating exposition which drives to the theological heart of the text.

It is appropriate to make three additional comments regarding the exegeses and expositions I recommend here. (1) I consider almost all the reader-response type works to be of diminished value for students and working pastors. (One of the rare exceptions is Clines on Job.) Too often they seem contrived and even self-indulgent, offering more insight into that particular reader's ideology than into the message of the ancient text. Don't people buy commentaries to understand the text better? In the extreme, such reader-response works betray a postmodern abandonment of the search for any communicative intent or determinate meaning in the text. (2) We are seeing a wave of interest in so-called reception history of the biblical text,[29] and more commentaries are reflecting this (e.g., BBC, S&H, HCOT, Luz on Matthew). I have often been fascinated by such materials, but I have assumed that most pastors and seminarians do not place a premium on reception history when they want to consult a commentary. (3) It is in my recommendations of expositions that my Reformed theological commitments are most obvious.

Another type of commentary, one which I rarely mention in this guide, is the single vol. Bible commentary. The pastor or student can sometimes get a wonderful overview of a Bible book using these hefty tools. I give as an example Derek Kidner's 38pp. on Isaiah in *The New Bible Commentary: Revised* (Eerdmans, 1970), later retitled *Eerdmans Bible Commentary* after the publication of the *New Bible Commentary: 21st Century Edition* (IVP, 1994). Other quality single vols. in this category are the *New International Bible Commentary* (Zondervan); *Eerdmans Commentary on the Bible* (2003) [*CBQ* 10/04]; *The HarperCollins Bible Commentary*, produced by members of SBL (1988, rev. 2000); *The New Jerome Biblical Commentary* (Prentice Hall, 1990); *The Jewish Study Bible* (OUP, 2004, 2nd ed. 2014) [*CBQ* 10/04]; *The Oxford Bible Commentary* (2001); *The New Interpreter's Study Bible* (2003); the *Africa Bible Commentary* (Zondervan, 2006); and *South Asia Bible Commentary* (Zondervan, 2015). I have not used Robert Gundry's one-vol. *Commentary on the New Testament* (Hendrickson, 2010), but I suspect it deserves the plaudits regarding its learning, wise selectivity in what it treats, and fullness (1100pp.) [*BBR* 21.4; *CBQ* 1/12; *RTR* 8/12; *Them* 8/11; *RelSRev* 6/11]. Also, I have hardly consulted those publications that proffer postmodern, ideologically oriented readings, such as the Schottroff–Wacker *Feminist Biblical Interpretation* commentary (Eerdmans, ET 2012) [*CBQ* 1/14], the Newsom–Ringe *Women's Bible Commentary* (exp. ed., 1998), and the Wisdom series.

David A. Dorsey's single vol. on the OT, *The Literary Structure of the Old Testament: A Commentary on Genesis–Malachi* (Baker, 1999), is *sui generis* and worth recommending here. Not everyone can believe that palindromes or chiasms are as common as Dorsey argues, but his 330-page book is fascinating and helpful for pastors and students [*JETS* 9/01]. At times his hermeneutical moves are brilliant (e.g., see my comment on Longman's *Job*).

## THE RANGE OF THIS GUIDE— CONSERVATIVES & CRITICS

I have included a full complement of neo-orthodox and liberal books in this guide. I might have focused more on evangelical works that are respectful of Scripture's authority. However, I have

---

29. See the vast project *Encyclopedia of the Bible and Its Reception*, eds. Dale C. Allison, Christine Helmer, Volker Leppin, Choon-Leong Seow, Hermann Spieckermann, Barry Dov Walfish, and Eric Ziolkowski (Berlin/Boston: de Gruyter, 2009–); as well as *The Journal of the Bible and Its Reception* (*JBRec*); the online journal *Relegere*, based in New Zealand; *The Oxford Handbook of the Reception History of the Bible*, eds. Michael Lieb, Emma Mason, and Jonathan Roberts (Oxford: OUP, 2011); and the inauguration of a new monograph series with Emma England and William John Lyons, eds., *Reception History and Biblical Studies: Theory and Practice* (London: Bloomsbury T&T Clark, 2015). I also recommend the multiple essays in *JSNT* 33.2 (2010).

chosen to include (and recommend on occasion) critical materials of note alongside important evangelical contributions. I have done so for several reasons. (1) The inclusion of non-conservative works will best serve the evangelical seminary student who is expected to show some familiarity with critical scholarship. I trust I am correct in assuming a certain level of theological training, sophistication, and especially spiritual discernment. (2) A few Bible books do not have a technical, recent, in-depth evangelical commentary. (3) Also, frequently many of the strongest commentaries on a given book (using the points of evaluation above) have been written by critics. Wide reading will soon convince you that "good and bad exegesis cuts across doctrinal lines and is represented at both ends of the theological spectrum."[30] (4) You will learn a great deal from the critics as you discipline yourself to read with discernment, measuring their presuppositions, methodology, and conclusions by the standard of Holy Scripture. The late F. F. Bruce once wrote, "I have sometimes learned most from scholars with whom I have agreed the least: they compel one to think and rethink."[31]

I have taken care to specify critical works listed in this guide (‡, or [*M*] if mildly critical or mediating). I hope this will enable "the fledgling student"[32] to read and make purchases with discernment. Recognizing scholars' faith commitments (in regard to the inspiration and authority of the Bible) can be helpful for knowing how to approach and digest their work. (This is especially true where those scholars [naïvely?] deny any personal faith commitment.)[33] So-called higher-critical scholarship is often anti-supernaturalist[34] and hostile to the evangelical faith. I can illustrate by quoting the liberal OT scholar, John J. Collins, who argues: "Historical criticism . . . is not compatible with a confessional theology that is committed to specific doctrines on the basis of faith." It is only "compatible with theology understood as an open-ended and critical inquiry into the meaning and function of God-language."[35] Some critical treatments are more, some less, objectionable to an evangelical pastor or student. After receiving some less-than-fair

---

30. Brevard S. Childs, *Old Testament Books for Pastor & Teacher* (Philadelphia: Westminster, 1977), 11–12.

31. F. F. Bruce, *The Epistles to the Colossians, to Philemon and to the Ephesians* (Grand Rapids: Eerdmans, 1984), xii. Beginning students can feel distress when they encounter attacks upon the Bible and contradictions of their beliefs. Here we may listen to the counsel of I. Howard Marshall: "people who disagree with you may be wrong, even if you can't immediately know how to refute them" (53). See Carl Trueman, "Interview with Professor Howard Marshall," *Them* 26.1 (2000): 48–53.

32. This is a phrase from the "Editorial Preface" of the Word Biblical Commentary series.

33. In one of his defenses against Robert Carroll's attacks on his Jeremiah scholarship, Walter Brueggemann ("Sometimes Wave, Sometimes Particle," *CBR* 8.3 [2010]: 384) protested that Carroll imagines he has no theological commitments himself. "He seems not to realize that in all our interpretation, we are, willy-nilly, exhibiting our own views of God, try as we will for critical objectivity."

34. Bultmann famously asserted, "it's impossible to use the electric light and the radio . . . and at the same time believe in the New Testament world of spirits and miracles" ("Neues Testament und Mythologie" [1941], in *Kerygma und Mythos: Ein theologisches Gespräch*, I. Band, ed. Hans Werner Bartsch, 2nd ed. [Hamburg: Herbert Reich-Evangelischer Verlag, 1951], 18).

35. "Is a Critical Biblical Theology Possible?" *The Hebrew Bible and Its Interpreters* (Winona Lake, IN: Eisenbrauns, 1990), 14. Higher criticism commonly presents two challenges to evangelical, believing scholarship. The first is a "hermeneutic of suspicion" regarding the truth claims and accuracy of the Scriptures. Michael Fox says, for example, "the willingness *not* to take a text at face value is the essence of critical scholarship" (*Character and Ideology in the Book of Esther*, 2nd ed. [Grand Rapids: Eerdmans, 2001], 148–49). The second challenge is the tendency of the more radical critics to reject the supernatural. Sheffield professor Philip R. Davies could not be clearer about his presuppositions, which amount to methodological atheism: "I don't allow divine activity or any unqualifiable or undemonstrable cause as an arguable factor in historical reconstruction, and, even if I were to accept privately the possibility of such factors, I do not see how I could integrate such explanations into anything recognizable as a historical method" ("Method and Madness: Some Remarks on Doing History with the Bible," *JBL* 114 [1995]: 703). Cf. R. Bultmann, "Is Exegesis without Presuppositions Possible?" *Existence and Faith* (New York: Meridian, 1960), 291–92. Thankfully, Davies's is still a minority view, and many moderately critical scholars would strenuously disagree. Such presuppositions make a huge difference in biblical studies, and my point here is that critical (or conservative) methodological assumptions can be noted as relevant in a guide to commentaries.

criticism, let me clarify that the symbols (‡ and 𝑀) are not marking persons so much as their scholarly work in a given instance. An individual may take a definitely critical (‡) approach in one commentary for one series (say, a technical exegesis on the Pastorals), while having a mildly critical [𝑀] orientation in a work for another series (say, a pastoral exposition on Philippians).

We must realize that everyone has to deal with the liberal–conservative divide. If some conservatives are often—more than wary—broadly dismissive of all critical scholarship, it is also true that liberals can be rudely dismissive of diligent, erudite evangelical scholars just because they belong to "the gaggle of conservatives." So much depends upon one's outlook on the church and the academy, and their relationship.[36] One caveat is for all of us: "The branding as 'liberal' or 'conservative' has too often been mistaken for engagement with the arguments put forward, and has hobbled those from across the theological spectrum who take such an exclusionary position."[37] Even as we recognize theological differences and their ramifications, we want to avoid "theological profiling" that excludes.

# BACKGROUND READING
## Dictionaries of Biblical Interpretation
Students find several reference works invaluable, beginning with the 6-vol. *Anchor Bible Dictionary* (1992). Rival works are the *New Interpreter's Dictionary of the Bible* in 5 vols. (2006–09) and de Gruyer's *Encyclopedia of the Bible and Its Reception* (2009–). Concentrating on historical and contemporary hermeneutical questions are the Coggins–Houlden *Dictionary of Biblical Interpretation* (1990); the 2-vol. *Dictionary of Biblical Interpretation* (1999), ed. John Hayes; the Stanley Porter, ed., *Dictionary of Biblical Criticism and Interpretation* (2007) [*RBL* 2011; *BTB* 11/10]; and the 2-vol. *Oxford Encyclopedia of Biblical Interpretation* (2013) [*BBR* 25.2].

## Development of Higher Criticism
Those who feel uninformed and even mystified by the complexities of scholarship and desire some orientation to the climate of critical opinion will find several books helpful. Some OT and NT Introductions include surveys of the 200-year debate over higher criticism. A book by the critic R. E. Clements, *One Hundred Years of OT Interpretation* (1976), may be useful to you. Introducing the key scholars is Mark Gignilliat, *A Brief History of OT Criticism* (2012) [*Int* 7/13; *JSOT* 37.5; *VT* 63.1; *Presb* Spr 13; *CTJ* 11/13; *DenvJ* 16; *BTB* 8/14; *JETS* 6/13]. Werner Kümmel's vol., *The New Testament: The History of the Investigation of Its Problems* (ET 1973), helps us understand theological developments in Germany. Stephen Neill's fascinating work, *The Interpretation of the NT 1861–1961*, was revised by N. T. Wright and covers the period 1861–1986. It gives an especially fine account of developments in Britain. John Riches's *A Century of NT Study* (1993) is selective in its coverage, but what it does is quite well-done [*CRBR* 1995]. No one remotely conservative rates a mention in Riches. The best book surveying the history of evangelical scholarship in the United States and its response to higher criticism is Mark Noll, *Between Faith and Criticism: Evangelicals, Scholarship, and the Bible in America* (Harper & Row, 1986; 2nd ed. Baker, 1991). None of these books, however, discusses the newer holistic literary approaches to the text.

---

36. "If you regard biblical scholarship as a critical, academic task distant to the churches but of vital importance for public discourse, you will evaluate it differently than if you see the integration of work in academic contexts with constructive theological work in church contexts as giving biblical scholarship its raison d'être." Hanna Stenström, Review of David deSilva, *Seeing Things John's Way* (Louisville: WJK, 2009), in *CBQ* 74.2 (2012): 368.

37. David W. Baker and Bill T. Arnold, eds, "Preface" in *The Face of Old Testament Studies: A Survey of Contemporary Approaches* (Grand Rapids: Baker; Leicester: Apollos, 1999), 11.

## *History of Biblical Interpretation*

To dig back further into the history of OT and NT scholarship, students turn to other works. For the whole history of biblical interpretation, pride of place now goes to the *New Cambridge History of the Bible* (4 vols., 2012–16) [*ExpTim* 3/14; *Them* 11/14]. Note that the 3-vol. *Cambridge History of the Bible* (1963–70) is still worth consulting. I believe the ambitious project edited by Hauser–Watson, *A History of Biblical Interpretation*, complements the older Cambridge set in updating the discussion. Three vols. have appeared: "Vol. 1: The Ancient Period" (Eerdmans, 2003); "Vol. 2: The Medieval through the Reformation Periods" (2009) [*JTS* 10/10; *JSOT* 35.5; *Chm* Aut 11 (Bray)]; and "Vol. 3: The Enlightenment through the Nineteenth Century" (2017) [*RTR* 4/20]. The first is strong on Jewish interpretation but weak on the canon and brief on the Fathers [2003: *Chm* Sum 08; *VT* 55.1; 2009: *EvQ* 1/13]. Reventlow's full treatment of the *History of Biblical Interpretation* is in English translation (4 vols., 2009–10) [*CBQ* 4/11; *JSS* Spr 12; *JSOT* 35.5; *ExpTim* 1/11, 3/12].

There are two stunningly comprehensive projects focused on but one Testament. Magne Saebø edits the *Hebrew Bible/Old Testament: The History of Its Interpretation*, with vols. on I/1: Antiquity (1996), I/2: The Middle Ages (2000), II: From Renaissance to the Enlightenment (2008), and III/1–2: From Modernism to Postmodernism (2013–15) [*JTS* 4/15, 10/15; *JSOT* 39.5; *VT* 63.3; *ETL* 89.4, 91.4]. The complete set boasts over 4000 pages. An enthusiastic welcome is being extended to William Baird's Fortress series, History of NT Research. Volumes slowly appeared: Vol. 1: *From Deism to Tübingen* (1992); Vol. 2: *From Jonathan Edwards to Rudolf Bultmann* (2002) [*JETS* 6/03; *CTJ* 11/04; *EuroJTh* 15.1]; and Vol. 3: *From C. H. Dodd to Hans Dieter Betz* (2013) [*JETS* 3/14; *CBQ* 7/15; *ETL* 94.1]. One telling criticism is that it focuses upon historical-critical scholarship, neglecting literary trends.

Because these reference works are daunting for beginners, I recommend three quick over-views: the basic sketch Yarchin provides in the "Introduction" (xi–xxx) to his *History of Biblical Interpretation: A Reader* (Hendrickson, 2004) [*VT* 57.2]; *A Short History of the Interpretation of the Bible* by Grant and Tracy (Fortress, 1984); and Richard Soulen's *Sacred Scripture: A Short History of Interpretation* (WJK, 2009) [*Int* 10/10; *JSOT* 35.5]. For a wise, well-balanced evangelical survey, see Gerald Bray's *Biblical Interpretation, Past & Present* (IVP, 1996), particularly for its treatment of theological currents. Because of the publisher, I had high hopes for John Court, ed., *Biblical Interpretation* (Continuum, 2004), but you can safely ignore it [*Anvil* 22.1 (Moberly)].

## *The Shape of Current Scholarship*

Those wanting a useful summary of the current *status quaestionis* in various areas of critical scholarship have in the past consulted the two vols. of essays produced by SBL: *The Hebrew Bible and Its Modern Interpreters* (1985) and *The New Testament and Its Modern Interpreters* (1989). These are now dated. More recent are the following books of note, on both Testaments: *Methods of Biblical Interpretation* (Abingdon, 2004); *To Each Its Own Meaning* (WJK, 1999); the large *Oxford Handbook of Biblical Studies* (2006) [*NovT* 49.2; *ExpTim* 11/08; *BL* 2007; *EuroJTh* 18.1]; the Barton FS, *Biblical Interpretation and Method* (2013), eds. Dell–Joyce [*JSOT* 38.5]; and Dean Deppe's *All Roads Lead to the Text* (2011). Two books devoted to postmodern approaches are Eryl Davies's *Biblical Criticism: A Guide for the Perplexed* (2013) [*JSNT* 36.5] and *New Meanings for Ancient Texts: Recent Approaches to Biblical Criticisms and Their Applications* (2013), eds. McKenzie–Kaltner [*RevExp* 8/14; *BBR* 25.2]. I expect that most biblical scholars are now relying heavily on the Oxford Handbook and Cambridge Companion series, regularly noted in this guide.

On the OT you can consult the Abingdon Press issue, *Old Testament Interpretation: Past, Present and Future* (Tucker FS, 1995); the WJK vol., *The Hebrew Bible Today: An Introduction to Critical Issues* (1998); Oxford University Press's *Text in Context* (2000); and the excellent

Petersen FS, *Method Matters* (SBL, 2009) [*JSS* Spr 12; *JSOT* 35.5; *ETL* 89.1]. Moving over to the NT, you will find helpful the collection of essays published in Porter, ed., *Handbook to Exegesis of the NT* (Brill, 1997); in Powell, ed., *The New Testament Today* (WJK, 1999); in *Approaches to NT Studies* (Sheffield, 1995), eds. Porter–Tombs; in *Method and Meaning* (Attridge FS; SBL, 2011); and in Carter–Levine, eds., *The New Testament: Methods and Meanings* (2013) [*JSNT* 37.5]. Finally, students should be reminded of the treasures in the *Anchor Bible Dictionary* (e.g., the articles on Form Criticism by Barton–Robbins) and the *New Interpreter's Dictionary of the Bible*. All the aforementioned works come out of the critical camp.

One asks, what has been produced by conservatives? Readers should note the Zondervan series Foundations of Contemporary Interpretation, now published in a one-vol. collection [*Evangel* Spr 02 (Marshall)]. For those interested in OT studies more particularly, there are two vols. to recommend: the Baker title *The Face of OT Studies* (1999) [*EvQ* 10/02; *DenvJ*]; and the collection of essays in vol.1 of the *New International Dictionary of OT Theology & Exegesis*. Both are in need of updating. Students of the NT should look up McKnight–Gupta, *The State of NT Studies* (2019), a magnificent addition to the literature. Earlier we had Dockery–Black, eds., *Interpreting the New Testament* (Broadman & Holman, 2001) [*Them* Spr 03]; *Hearing the New Testament* (Eerdmans, 1995, 2nd ed. 2010) [*JSNT* 33.5; *ExpTim* 2/11; *BTB* 11/11], ed. J. B. Green. An older McKnight–Osborne vol., *The Face of NT Studies* (2004), remains useful [*Chm* Spr 06; *BBR* 15.1; *Them* 10/06; *TJ* Fall 05; *RelSRev* 4/07; *Anvil* 22.4; *DenvJ* 11/04].

For discussion of individual interpreters, see the McKim edited *Dictionary of Major Biblical Interpreters* (IVP, 2007), which replaced the 1998 *Historical Handbook*, and the *Oxford Dictionary of the Christian Church* (3rd ed. 2005). For entries on those conservative scholars missed or ignored in other dictionaries, look up Elwell–Weaver, eds., *Bible Interpreters of the 20th Century: A Selection of Evangelical Voices* (Baker, 1999), and Larsen, ed., *Biographical Dictionary of Evangelicals* (IVP, 2003).

## *Terminology*

Some of the terminology used in biblical scholarship and in this guide to describe various herme-neutical approaches may be unfamiliar to neophyte seminarians. "What is this 'tradition-history' you mention? And what does 'diachronic' mean?" Students will find quick help in the Soulen *Handbook of Biblical Criticism* (4th ed. 2011) [*JSOT* 37.5; *ExpTim* 6/14], Randolph Tate's *Handbook for Biblical Interpretation* (2nd ed. 2012) [*JSOT* 37.5; *RevExp* 8/14], and the *Westminster Dictionary of Theological Terms* (1996). For yet more help, see the major dictionaries of biblical interpretation referenced above and the textbooks of exegesis.[38]

Philosophical sophistication is also becoming more and more necessary for high level work in theological fields. It is understandable why an information technology major or physical education major might struggle in a competitive MDiv program. A propaedeutic or quick reference is the slim dictionary *101 Key Terms in Philosophy and Their Importance for Theology* (2004), written by Kelly James Clark, Richard Lints, and James K. A. Smith. Much more in-depth are Anthony Thiselton's superlative *New Horizons in Hermeneutics* (1992) and *Thiselton on Hermeneutics* (Eerdmans, 2006) [*ExpTim* 6/07; *JTS* 4/09], which discuss the most significant

---

38. Students have long repaired to such textbooks as Barton's *Reading the OT: Method in Biblical Study* (rev. 1996); McKenzie–Haynes, eds., *To Each Its Own Meaning: An Introduction to Biblical Criticisms and Their Application* (rev. 1999); Soulen's *Handbook of Biblical Criticism* (4th ed. 2011); Hayes–Holladay, *Biblical Exegesis: A Beginner's Handbook* (4th ed. 2022); or Barton, ed., *The Cambridge Companion to Biblical Interpretation* (1998). More in depth would be the many OT and NT volumes in the Fortress Guides to Biblical Scholarship. For a good overview of the aims of, and an apology for, historical criticism, see Barton, *The Nature of Biblical Criticism* (2007) [*VT* 59.1]. More conservative overviews are available in Armerding's *The OT and Criticism* (1983) and the Klein–Blomberg–Hubbard *Introduction to Biblical Interpretation* (1993, rev. 2004) [*Them* 1/95].

philosophical currents affecting biblical studies.[39] The best counsel I can give at present, though, is to buy and digest well Thiselton's 409-page *Hermeneutics: An Introduction* (2009) [*RBL* 6/10]. He was a master teacher, a teacher of teachers, and this is about the best introduction to biblical and theological hermeneutics I've found for the bright beginner. Another vol. to consider is Porter–Robinson, *Hermeneutics: An Introduction to Interpretive Theory* (2011). For individual hot topics in hermeneutics, e.g., history, philosophy of language, and biblical-theological interpretation, see also the Paternoster/Zondervan Scripture and Hermeneutics Series (2001–) [*EuroJTh* 17.1].

## OTHER BIBLE REFERENCE WORKS

In past years, friends have asked me to expand this survey to include a full review of OT and NT reference works, such as atlases, introductions, lexicons, grammars, histories of Israel, etc. I have rejected that idea for a number of reasons I won't list here. At the end of this guide, I have provided a brief list of those works that, to my thinking, could form the nucleus of a preacher's reference library; see An Ideal Basic Library for the Pastor. For a more complete listing of OT and NT research tools, consult Longman's[40] and Carson's surveys; Danker's *Multipurpose Tools for Bible Study* (rev. 1993, 2003); the section "Exegesis Aids and Resources" in both Douglas Stuart's *Old Testament Exegesis* (5th ed. 2022) and Gordon Fee's *New Testament Exegesis* (4th ed. 2010); DeRouchie, *How to Understand and Apply the OT* (2017); Naselli, *How to Understand and Apply the NT* (2017); the *Denver Journal* bibliographies; David R. Bauer's *Essential Bible Study Tools*; and John Glynn's *Commentary and Reference Survey*, all of which are cited above.

## OLD COMMENTARIES AND FOREIGN LANGUAGE WORKS

### Old Commentaries

I have not mentioned the two famous Puritan commentaries by Matthew Henry and Matthew Poole in the section on individual books. Please don't think of them as relics. Henry, particularly, is still quite useful and, I'm glad to say, freely available online. Childs counsels:

> I would strongly recommend that pastors secure one of the great English pastors who wrote commentaries on the whole Bible. . . . These old books can work as a trap and deception if the pastor is simply looking for a retreat into the past, but if they are correctly used, innumerable riches can be tapped.[41]

Much the same thing can be said for the mountain of rich exposition in the best old sets of sermons; see, for example, the church father Chrysostom, Luther, Calvin, the Puritans, Maclaren, Spurgeon, and Campbell Morgan.

---

39. I regret that I cannot be as enthusiastic about another Thiselton issue: *A Concise Encyclopedia of the Philosophy of Religion* (2005), which is poorly edited [*SwJT* Fall 04]. A stimulating and sagacious study of the interface of hermeneutics and theology is Thiselton, *The Hermeneutics of Doctrine* (2007) [*RelSRev* 34.2; *ExpTim* 10/09].

40. Do note that Longman's 3rd and succeeding editions do not contain the thirty or so pages of reference works reviews found in the earlier editions. To read his evaluation of OT introductions, OT theologies, OT histories, Bible atlases, Hebrew lexicons, etc., look up the 2nd ed. But as you consult that 1995 edition, keep in mind the important tools published in the intervening years. Here are examples: the 2-vol. "study edition" of *The Hebrew & Aramaic Lexicon of the OT* (*HALOT*); the Provan–Long–Longman *A Biblical History of Israel*; and the 5-vol. *New International Dictionary of OT Theology & Exegesis*.

41. Childs, *Old Testament Books*, 30.

For the OT, many pastors once used the Jamieson–Fausset–Brown commentary alongside Keil & Delitzsch (KD). I would not counsel the purchase of J–F–B, which covers the NT too, because it is free online (ccel.org). Though the point can be overstressed (see below), it remains true that, for many of these older commentaries, the best insights were mined out long ago and incorporated in newer works. But if you have inherited J–F–B and have few resources, don't discard it. For comments on the KD and Lange sets, see Commentary Series below.

*Bengel's New Testament Commentary* is a great classic (1742), about 2000pp. long. John Bengel was a pioneer exegete for the modern era. I can't say I'd counsel you to buy it, however. Several other older sets on the NT should also be mentioned briefly. *Alford's Greek Testament* (6th ed. 1873) and the *Expositor's Greek Testament* (1897) both served past generations well and still have some use. I would not recommend you purchase them because they are available online. A. T. Robertson's *Word Pictures in the New Testament* (1933), though a different sort of work, would fall into the same class.

Two sets of devotional commentaries are of similar age (late 19th century) and usefulness. J. C. Ryle's *Expository Thoughts on the Gospels* is suggestive in seven pb vols. (some editions are without the more detailed notes, which include excellent quotes from the church fathers, the Reformers, and Puritans). Part of the set has been included in Crossway's Classic Commentary series. The comments are clear, edifying, and vigorously Calvinistic. H. C. G. Moule's expositions of the epistles are full of the love of Christ. Usually they have titles like *Colossians Studies*. Moule was a fine scholar as well as preacher. He produced several vols. in The Cambridge Bible for Schools & Colleges and The Cambridge Greek Testament for Schools & Colleges. Both Ryle and Moule were godly Anglican bishops. Look for their books free online.

I offer two final notes on older commentaries. First, advertisers have spent trillions to convince us that newer always means improved and older always means inferior and obsolete. One should believe them when it comes to computers. Wiser seminarians, however, should not buy into such categorizing when it comes to theological literature and the genre of commentaries in particular. Students should also be apprised that there is a growing movement within biblical studies that takes the history of interpretation more seriously—older books teach us much—and humility should incline us to join that movement.[42] My second note is a recommendation of a late Cambridge friend's work on "Pre-20th Century Commentaries on the Old Testament in Cambridge University Library." Dr. Leslie McFall spent years of work using and assessing old commentaries (17th to 19th centuries). The fruit of that labor is a list of recommended works, free at https://lmf12.files.wordpress.com/2012/11/pre-20th_century_commentaries.pdf. While you may not have access to all the Cambridge resources, you may discover some work of interest on the list which you can hunt down online.

## Foreign Language Commentaries

There isn't room in this guide to note important, individual foreign language works. Those who are doing fuller research and can handle the languages may consult those works. Strong vols. are available in French, especially in such series as *Etudes Bibliques* (e.g., Spicq on the Pastorals and Hebrews), *Commentaire de l'Ancien Testament*, *Commentaire du Nouveau Testament* (e.g., Bonnard on Matthew), *Sources Bibliques*, and *Lectio Divina* (e.g., Vesco on Psalms). For those with some proficiency in German there are the important series *Herders Theologischer*

---

42. Excellent arguments for doing so are made in Dale C. Allison, "Matthew and the History of Interpretation," *ExpTim* 120.1 (2008): 1–7. None of us wants to fall into the category of those Christian moderns chided by Mark Noll as full of "self-confidence, bordering on hubris, manifested by an extreme antitraditionalism that casually discounted the possibility of wisdom from earlier generations" (*The Scandal of the Evangelical Mind* [Grand Rapids: Eerdmans, 1994], 127). See, too, C. S. Lewis's warnings against "chronological snobbery" in his essay "On the Reading of Old Books" (*God in the Dock: Essays on Theology and Ethics*, ed. Walter Hooper [Grand Rapids: Eerdmans, 1970], 200–207).

*Kommentar* and *Regensburger Neues Testament* from Roman Catholic scholars. Catholics and Protestants collaborated to produce the *Evangelisch-katholischer Kommentar* (EKK). Largely Protestant series include *Kommentar zum Alten Testament* (KAT), *Das Alte Testament Deutsch*, *Das Neue Testament Deutsch*, *Theologischer Handkommentar*, *Zürcher Bibelkommentare*, the newer *Historisch-Theologische Auslegung Neues Testament*, and, most importantly, *Biblischer Kommentar* (BKAT) for the Old Testament and the constantly revised Meyer *Kritisch-exegetischer Kommentar* (KEK) on the New Testament. There is an abundance of good commentaries in Dutch, too (e.g., Aalders on Ezekiel, Beuken on Isaiah); see HCOT below under Commentary Series, and Commentaarreeks op het Oude Testament ("De Brug" series). And we cannot forget Modern Hebrew; e.g., see the series דעת מקרא or the more critical מקרא לישראל פירוש מדעי למקרא. For reviews of continental European works, peruse *RB*, *Ephemerides Theologicae Lovanienses*, *Biblica*, *Etudes Théologiques & Religieuses*, *ZAW* (but not *Zeitschrift für die neutestamentliche Wissenschaft*), *VT*, *NovT*, and *Theologische Literaturzeitung*. For a fairly complete list of important OT commentaries in German and Dutch, as well as English, see Hilbrands above. The current online OT and NT bibliographies from Pontifical Biblical Institute are noted under Bazylinski (above). For portions of the OT, including the Latter Prophets, Daniel, biblical theology, and history of ancient Israel, there is the magnificent Charles Conroy site (above) covering vast swathes of the commentary, monograph, and periodical literature in English, German, French, Italian, and Spanish.

# NOTES ON COMPUTER TECHNOLOGY

The world of biblical scholarship is undergoing revolutionary changes due to developments in technology. The day is dawning when serious Bible students are able to access via the internet the contents of the world's great theological libraries. (I think of Perlego and seminary reading rooms—see, e.g., Tyndale University; see also the recommendation below of Internet Archive.) One gets excited dreaming about what the future holds. But in all your dreaming about tomorrow, you can't afford to miss today's opportunities.

Up through the 8th edition of this guide, I made recommendations of Bible study software. During my two decades of missionary service in Africa, I lost my grasp of developments in the area of software. I won't take the chance of misleading you or embarrassing myself by continuing to make recommendations, except to urge more advanced students to consider Libronix Logos Bible Software (from Faithlife). The Accordance program is just as good, arguably better for technical work with the Hebrew and Greek: attractive, fast (seamless), intuitive, and easy to use. Logos users tell me they love the ability to build a large digital library, the interconnectivity, and some of the powerful search features of the program. Logos offers tons more resources for, say, sermon work; it seems they buy the rights to everything they can. (Accordance is more selective.) The downside of Logos could be that it seems slower, is more difficult to customize, and there is a longer learning curve with its more complex interface. (Sadly Hermeneutika BibleWorks ceased operations in 2018.) Those unaware of the free STEP Bible project developed at Tyndale House, Cambridge, should look at it.

One bit of advice I picked up from a blog—thank you, Dustin Battles at rootedthinking. com—is that it's wise to buy hard copies of books you plan to read cover to cover, while reference materials are best purchased for electronic use. That works for me; I have *HALOT* in hard copy and on Accordance, and the latter gets used more often. The expense can be wildly different too; the 8 vols. of *DCH* would have cost me $260 years ago through an Accordance discount, but nearly $1500 in hb.

There is a real need for up-to-date guides to both internet resources and computer-assisted theological research. Ages ago, we had Patrick Durusau, *High Places in Cyberspace: A Guide to*

*Biblical and Religious Studies, Classics, and Archaeological Resources on the Internet*, 2nd ed. (Scholars Press, 1998). Later we were helped by Roland Worth's *Biblical Studies on the Internet*, 2nd ed. (McFarland, 2008) and Montaner et al. (eds), *Computer Assisted Research on the Bible in the 21st Century* (Gorgias, 2010). Good help now is found in Michael Gorman's "Appendix D: Selected Internet Resources for Biblical Studies" to *Elements of Biblical Exegesis* (2020). At this point in time, however, we don't need print editions of such guides, only online versions. For leads to discover more that is available in the areas of databases, websites, software, linguistic tools, and stored texts, I suggest the following for a start:

Association of Christian Librarians. "Biblical & Theological Studies" acl.libguides.com/biblical studies/general.

Bible Odyssey (SBL) bibleodyssey.org.

BiblicalStudies.org.uk.

Bryan College Library. "Bible Commentaries" library.bryan.edu/bible-study-resources/bible -commentaries/. A comprehensive listing of public domain commentaries.

Digital Dead Sea Scrolls. Dss.collections.imj.org.il/

German Bible Society. "Academic Bible" academic-bible.com/en/. For reading online the latest scholarly editions (*BHS* [no *BHQ*] and NA28).

Goodacre, Mark. "New Testament Gateway" ntgateway.com.

Graduate Theological Union. "Internet Resources for Biblical Research" libguides.gtu.edu/Internet resources.

Jones, Charles E., ed. "ETANA: Electronic Tools and Ancient Near East Archives" etana.org/home. Especially useful for comparative Semitics.

Michigan State University. "Bible Resources: Internet Sites" libguides.lib.msu.edu/c.php?g=96734 &p=626911.

North Park University. "Online Resources for Biblical & Theological Studies" guides.northpark.edu /c.php?g=571810&p=3942367.

Online Critical Pseudepigrapha (SBL). http://www.purl.org/net/ocp.

Open Access Digital Theological Library. Libguides.thedtl.org/oadtl.

Oxford Biblical Studies Online (OUP). "Internet Resources" oxfordbiblicalstudies.com/resource /InternetResources.xhtml.

Patrick, Meriel. "Disentangling the Web: A Guide to Online Resources for Theology," *ExpTim* 121.5 (2010): 213–17.

Princeton Theological Seminary. "Theological Commons" commons.ptsem.edu.

Sefaria. Sefaria.org/texts/. An enormous online library of Jewish works.

Seland, Torrey. "Resource Pages for Biblical Studies" torreys.org/bible/.

Stuart, Douglas. *Old Testament Exegesis*. 5th ed. Louisville: WJK, 2022. [§ 4.12.7]

Thesaurus Linguae Graecae. "Abridged Online TLG" stephanus.tlg.uci.edu/abridged.php/.

Treat, Jay C. "Internet Resources for the Study of Judaism and Christianity" https://www.sas.upenn .edu/~jtreat/rs/resources.html.

Tufts University. "Perseus Digital Library" www.perseus.tufts.edu/hopper/. Excellent resource for the classics.

Tyndale House, Cambridge. "STEP Bible" (Scripture Tools for Every Person). Stepbible.org/. Superlatives for this free software with original texts and many translations. See also their "Tools and Links" page: https://academic.tyndalehouse.com/research/tools-and-links/.

Union Presbyterian Seminary Library. "Internet Resources for Theology Students" upsem.lib guides.com/c.php?g=648571&p=4548265.

United Theological Seminary (MN). "Biblical Studies Internet Resources" unitedseminary.edu /library/resources/religion-theology-resources/biblical-studies-internet-resources/.

University of Calgary. "Religious Studies Web Guide" libguides.ucalgary.ca/religiousstudieswebguide.
Wabash Center for Teaching and Learning in Theology and Religion. "Religion on the Web"
    wabashcenter.wabash.edu/resources/guide_headings.aspx.
Western Seminary. "Library Internet Resources" westernseminary.edu/students/portland/library
    /internet-resources.
Yale Divinity School. "EIKON: Image Database for Biblical Studies" divdl.library.yale.edu/dl/index
    .aspx?qc=Eikon.

Readers need to know about the Christian Classics Ethereal Library (www.ccel.org), now based at Calvin University. Previously Wheaton College had it. If you look up the free site, you can find an amazing assortment of materials: the writings of the church fathers, Calvin's commentaries (19th century edition), Matthew Henry, ancient Greek texts, the Hebrew OT, etc. The index is vast, and new materials are added on a regular basis. Another two free sites are Internet Archive (archive.org) and openlibrary.org, which have digitized materials from many theological libraries, including Princeton Seminary and Harvard University. Basically, if a useful old book is not in copyright, it likely has been, or soon will be, made available online.

# COMMENTARY SERIES

WHAT IS THE INTENDED readership of a specific commentary? Some of the best technical commentaries are both unsuitable for, and unusable by, the average church member, even the one who is most eager to understand the Bible. On the other hand, many well-written Bible study guides and commentaries for laypeople are considered too light to offer serious help to the studious pastor. The general reading level of the following series will be indicated by the following symbols: [L] for educated laypeople, such as the Bible study leader; [P] for theologically trained pastors and seminarians; [S] for advanced students and scholars. My rating often mixes these categories, and the first letter has the greater weight. This rating system is an adaptation of the one used by Longman's *OT Commentary Survey*.

AB ANCHOR BIBLE. ‡ (Doubleday). See AYB. [SP]

ABCS AFRICA BIBLE COMMENTARY SERIES. (Hippo Books/Zondervan). After the publication of the one-vol. *Africa Bible Commentary* (2006), it was thought wise to launch a series of pb expositions for the church. ABCS is to cover both Testaments, and the first vol. appeared in 2009. See Ngewa on the Pastorals. The tone of the series is devout evangelical Protestantism, showing concern to explain the line of thought in the text, illustrate the truths of the gospel, and make application to African life. Questions for Discussion end each unit. [PL]

AbOTC ABINGDON OLD TESTAMENT COMMENTARIES. ‡ (Abingdon). In my 2001 edition, I paid ANTC the compliment of wishing Abingdon would produce a series of similar thrust and quality on the OT. That same year saw the publication of Brueggemann's highly theological exegesis of Deuteronomy in AbOTC. Since then, this moderately critical series, with Princeton's Patrick Miller as general editor, has been something of a mixed bag. As with the NT counterpart, one expects a focus on exegesis rather than exposition. In this way it can be contrasted with the Interpretation series. The scholarship in AbOTC tends to be less original and more derivative, drawing from others' works and re-presenting the more convincing conclusions of critical scholarship. Note: I decline to use the abbreviation AOTC, departing from *The SBL Handbook of Style* (2014), because Apollos so prominently displays the same and my readers have gotten confused. [P]

ACCS ANCIENT CHRISTIAN COMMENTARY ON SCRIPTURE. (IVP). A marvelous project headed up by editor Thomas Oden, the ACCS seeks to reacquaint the church with its rich heritage of ancient commentary on Scripture. Too many biblical scholars pay little attention to anything more than a few decades old. The publisher has released a 28-vol. "series encompassing all of Scripture and offering contemporary readers the opportunity to study for themselves the key writings of the early church fathers." It is my conviction that we fail to honor the Holy Spirit, who has instructed the church from its beginning, if we neglect the insights of a Chrysostom or an Augustine. Dip into these vols. and discover for yourself the theological and devotional power of the Fathers. (See Christopher Hall's *Reading Scripture with the Church Fathers* [IVP].) The whole canon has now been covered, but keep in mind that some books receive scanty comment (341pp. on Exodus–Deuteronomy), while others get a lot (764pp. on John). An additional vol. on the Apocrypha is expected. The series is now available electronically. Cf. The Church's Bible series. [PLS]

ANTC   ABINGDON NEW TESTAMENT COMMENTARIES. ‡ (Abingdon). A series begun in 1996, now complete, which provides compact, critically informed commentaries on the NT. They are competent, non-technical, and written for students and pastors— somewhat like the Tyndale series, but liberal and perhaps more scholarly. Annotated bibliographies appear in most vols. Credit goes to the editors for keeping the commentaries so uniformly compact; some other series have less to say in twice the pages. The Gospels are appropriately allotted a good bit more space. [P]

Apollos   APOLLOS OLD TESTAMENT COMMENTARIES. (IVP–Apollos). Many eagerly awaited the first installments of this series. The choice of general editors, Gordon Wenham and David Baker, indicated to me years ago that the series would be of high quality and present evangelical, critically informed exegesis. The first two vols.—McConville on Deuteronomy and Lucas on Daniel—were well-researched, insightful, and judicious. (Regrettably, however, Lucas follows the critical line on the dating of Daniel. The lineup of contracted authors indicates that Lucas's mediating approach will be represented in some other Apollos entries.) The commentaries are intended to be both in-depth and user-friendly for pastors; McConville is less user-friendly because it's so densely packed. The editors mean for the series to be accessible to "non-experts," but the use of in-text citations may discourage some. Do continue to watch for this series, which is regularly adding vols. [PS]

Asia   ASIA BIBLE COMMENTARY. (Langham). A somewhat uneven but successful effort to provide contextualized commentary for the Asian churches. There were at least a few vols. published about 20 years ago (e.g., Trebilco–Rae, *1 Timothy*) by Asia Theological Association, but the series has been growing rapidly since 2015. Covers both OT and NT. [PL]

AYB   ANCHOR YALE BIBLE. ‡ (Yale). As originally conceived, the Anchor Bible (AB) was an interfaith project, meant to be accessible to educated laity and to provide lengthy introductions and new translations with up-to-date philological discussion. AB was not intended to be a full-orbed commentary. The series has changed markedly since the mid-1960s and now includes some of the most exhaustive commentary efforts ever attempted (Leviticus, Song of Songs, Jeremiah, Amos, 1 Peter, John's Epistles). The series is renamed to reflect the change in publisher from Doubleday to Yale. You will find AB/AYB to be rather uneven and (now) pricey. Many contributions are thin in theological interpretation, particularly the older vols., and reflect varying critical approaches. A number can be safely ignored, but others are successful efforts and can be put to good use by discerning, scholarly pastors (e.g., Proverbs, Jeremiah, Ezekiel, Jonah, Thessalonians, Timothy, James). Hebrew and Greek are transliterated. AYB is both under revision (by Yale since 2007), with replacement vols. appearing regularly, and nearing completion in the sense of covering the entire canon (about 90 vols.). The series also includes commentaries on the Apocrypha/Deuterocanonical books. I sense AYB moving in a more liberal and skeptical direction, as the previous moderate Jewish editor, David Noel Freedman, was replaced by John J. Collins. The bibliographies in recent vols. are marvelous. Volumes first appear in pricey hb and e-versions, then in less expensive pb. [SP]

BBC   BLACKWELL BIBLE COMMENTARIES. ‡ (Blackwell). A series by an Oxford-based publisher offering a reception-history approach to the Bible. As stated below in the review of the Judges vol., these can be evocative as they present centuries of much-varied cultural and artistic responses to biblical literature. I have had less opportunity to use the series and don't say much about them. [PLS]

BCBC   BELIEVERS CHURCH BIBLE COMMENTARY. [𝓜], (Herald Press). A pb set, pitched more at a general audience, and reading Scripture from the perspective of the historic Anabaptist tradition. So far it has proven to be well-written and edited. The stance on higher-critical issues varies from author to author; many are conservative and some are more critical. Generally speaking, there is a lot of "heart" and pastoral concern evident in the contributions now available. Martens on Jeremiah and Geddert on Mark are among the best of the lot. [PL]

BCOT   BAKER COMMENTARY ON THE OLD TESTAMENT. (Baker). The series began with Longman editing seven vols. on "Psalms & Wisdom" (2005–12), produced by critically aware, senior evangelical academics. Building from this are newer segments on "Pentateuch," edited by Arnold (2020–), "Historical Books" under the coeditorship of Firth–Wray Beal (2023–), and, finally, "Prophets," edited by Boda–McConville (2023–). Readers find quality exegesis that drives at the message of the text. There is a good mix of comment on the Hebrew, literary observations, sociocultural insights, and theological exposition. While diachronic concerns are not wholly absent (some mild form criticism), the focus is surely on the final form. Preachers receive good help in all the BCOT vols., while students will gain more from some entries (e.g., Psalms, Ecclesiastes, Song of Songs) than others. Probably the most critical entries thus far are *Psalms* by Goldingay and *Isaiah* by McConville, both of which can be marked [𝓜]. [PS]

BE   THE BIBLE EXPOSITION COMMENTARY. (Victor). Warren Wiersbe, once pastor of Chicago's Moody Church and regular radio preacher, was for decades publishing little popular expositions on the NT and OT. The comments are clear and simple, but not simplistic; the outlines are useful too. He has such a flair for communicating the Bible's message in a practical, warm-hearted way that a pastor might consider buying them to use alongside more in-depth exegetical books. In 1989 all the NT vols.—called the BE books—were compiled into a 2-vol. set of about 1300pp. Wiersbe finished the OT too, and all those little books filled four large hb vols. Now OT and NT fit into only two (1083 and 1533pp.). The series has a dispensational orientation. I will not be noting these commentaries below. [LP]

BECNT   BAKER EXEGETICAL COMMENTARY ON THE NEW TESTAMENT. (Baker). This series has become well-established and is among the most useful for help in exegesis of the Greek. It picked up where the Wycliffe Exegetical Commentary left off when that project had its demise in the early 1990s. See WEC, and note that there were reassignments (e.g., Schreiner rather than Moo on Romans). Pastors working with their Greek Testament may find BECNT easier to use than some other series like NIGTC and the ICC (cf. Thiselton–Garland on 1 Corinthians). The series editors are Robert Yarbrough and Joshua Jipp. Keep watching this solidly evangelical series, currently under revision (Schreiner replaces Osborne's *Revelation*), which lacks vols. on the Pastorals and Hebrews. [PS]

Belief   BELIEF: A THEOLOGICAL COMMENTARY ON THE BIBLE. ‡ (WJK). Belief is moderately critical and attempts something similar to Brazos, with leading theologians writing Bible commentaries in brief compass. See Placher's vol. on Mark (248pp.) for a model contribution. I will not make many comments on the series' vols. [PL]

BerO   BERIT OLAM. ‡ (Liturgical Press). The subtitle of this series is Studies in Hebrew Narrative and Poetry. Though the publisher is a Catholic order, it enlisted several fine Jewish contributors (e.g., Schneider on Judges, Cohn on 2 Kings, Sweeney on the Twelve) alongside Christians. These studies offer stimulating literary readings of the final form of the text and can be good complements to historically and theologically oriented commentaries. According to Cohn, "The aim of a literary commentary is not the sources, but the discourse, not the genesis of the text, but 'the text itself as a pattern of meaning and effect' (Meir Sternberg)." I believe BerO is now stalled. For the NT, Liturgical publishes Sacra Pagina, a consistently Roman Catholic series noted below. [PS]

BGI    BIG GREEK IDEA. (Kregel). Recently begun (2018–), the conservative series leads the reader through the details of the Greek text and seeks to explain the flow of thought. It seems designed first for pastors and then for seminary students. Herbert Bateman is the editor. [PS]

BGW    THE BIBLE IN GOD'S WORLD. [𝑀?], (Cascade). An OT commentary begun in 2021, with an inaugural vol. on Ecclesiastes by Goldingay. Series editors Daniel Carroll R. and Lissa Wray Beal aim for moderately sized and well-rounded treatments of "text-critical, linguistic, grammatical, contextual, and theological issues," bringing "the message of God's liberating kingdom and justice to the fore in each commentary" (ii). It is an ecumenical, international Protestant project, enlisting contributors who believe the Bible "to be the authoritative Word of God across the centuries and around the globe." For the NT the editors will be Scot McKnight and Nijay Gupta. [PS]

BHGNT    BAYLOR HANDBOOK ON THE GREEK NEW TESTAMENT. (Baylor U. Press). Edited by Martin Culy, who has contributed to several vols. (see *Acts* and *I,II,III John*), these handbooks are intended to walk the intermediate-level student through the basic lexical and syntactical issues, with little commentary or none. The scheduled authors are mainly conservative Greek grammarians at American seminaries. All the signs are that the guides (not commentaries in the traditional sense) are proving useful to students. [PS]

BHHB    BAYLOR HANDBOOK ON THE HEBREW BIBLE. (Baylor U. Press). The series complements BHGNT (see above), providing a wealth of lexical, morphological, and syntactical information for intermediate to advanced Hebrew students. So far, the vols. (e.g., Tucker on Jonah, Bandstra on Genesis, Garrett on Amos), though small in page size, are large enough with regard to number of pages to accomplish much good. BHHB does not offer commentary per se; rather, it prints the Hebrew text with a new translation and grammatical analysis. There can be a measure of discourse analysis besides. Some of the information can easily be found elsewhere, say in the morphological tagging systems of Bible study software. Overall this is a welcome series. The data presented (parsing, etc.) are not perfect but usually quite accurate. [PS]

BKAT    BIBLISCHER KOMMENTAR ALTES TESTAMENT. ‡ (Neukirchener). Many vols. in this technical OT series have been translated. BKAT is known for its thoroughness, text criticism, rigorous diachronic exegesis, and often profound theological reflection. Only the translations are noted in this guide. See Westermann's *Genesis*, Kraus on Psalms, Wildberger on Isaiah 1–39, Zimmerli's *Ezekiel*, and Wolff on several Minor Prophets, all published in the Continental Commentary (ContC) and Hermeneia (Herm) series. [S]

BMT    THE BIBLE IN MEDIEVAL TRADITION. (Eerdmans). Following on the heels of other series which present Patristic commentary (ACCS) and Reformation-era commentary (RCS), we now have a set for the Medieval period. E.g., see Levy's vol. on Galatians. [SP]

BNTC    BLACK'S NEW TESTAMENT COMMENTARY. ‡ (Hendrickson). The series was once called Harper's in America and Black's over in Britain (using the publishers' names, Harper & Row [now HarperCollins] and A. & C. Black). Though in the 1980s the American publisher Hendrickson was reprinting these vols. under the title Harper's, since around 1990 they have gone by the name Black's on both sides of the Atlantic. The series was under revision, with Henry Chadwick as general editor. Most vols. are moderately critical, models of clarity, and must be used with discernment. The best are by Barrett, Kelly, Laws, Hooker, Bockmuehl, and Boxall. I will list both the older vols. (usually o/p) and the replacement works using the same indicator, BNTC. Now appearing in pb. [PS]

Brazos   BRAZOS THEOLOGICAL COMMENTARY ON THE BIBLE. [𝑀], (Brazos). "Causing much inter-disciplinary raising of eyebrows" [*BSB* 6/06 (Briggs)], here is a brave, creative venture which enlists mainly systematic theologians to write expositions of OT and NT books. The editor writes that "commentators were chosen because of their knowledge of and expertise in using the Christian doctrinal tradition." Quite a few vols. have appeared, and some judge Brazos less than successful. The list of contributors raises questions about the goals and cohesiveness of this ecumenical project: Yale historian Pelikan (Acts), Peter Leithart of Moscow, Idaho (Kings), TEDS's Kevin Vanhoozer (Jeremiah), Princeton Seminary's Ellen Charry (Psalms), Beeson's Timothy George (James), and the Orthodox John Behr (Exodus). Editing the series is R. R. Reno of Creighton University. The series is marketed in the UK as the SCM Theological Commentary on the Bible. See Work under Deuteronomy. [PL]

BrillEC   BRILL EXEGETICAL COMMENTARY. (Brill). Reportedly, the first contribution (Pao on the Pastorals) was released late 2023 and carries a typical Brill price tag of €249. The NT series editors are Stanley Porter and Denver Seminary's David Mathewson. The announcement states, "Each volume presents detailed comments organized in four major sections: textual criticism, linguistically informed exegesis, history, and theology." [SP]

Broad   BROADMAN BIBLE COMMENTARY. [𝑀], (Broadman Press). A 12-vol. set covering both Testaments and mostly critically oriented. Rather dated at this point, BBC was never remarkable to begin with and was not used much outside Southern Baptist circles. I will not list the individual contributions to this series. Because the denominational agencies, including what is now B&H (Broadman & Holman) Publishing, are controlled by conservatives, the publishing arm has produced another, more evangelical series of commentaries. See NAC and CSC. [P]

BSC   BIBLE STUDENT'S COMMENTARY. (Zondervan). Defunct but still worth noting. Translations of the Dutch Reformed series *Korte Verklaring*, these are easy to read and have some fine biblical-theological insights. Most of the original Dutch commentaries were published in the early 1950s. BSC stalled after Ridderbos's *Matthew* (1987). Only one vol. appeared in the NT section, and there were eight for the OT, covering Genesis to Ruth as well as Isaiah. [P]

BST   BIBLE SPEAKS TODAY. (IVP). These expositions, not strictly commentaries, are of great assistance to pastors in understanding and applying God's Word. The focus is upon pericopae rather than verse-by-verse exegesis. They are reasonably priced paperbacks—only a few have been published in hardback—and are warmly recommended. They try to bridge the gap between homiletical commentaries, which often fail to pay close enough attention to the text, and scholarly works, which may seem more concerned with historical and critical issues than with the text's message. The series covers both Testaments, is under revision, and was completed by Firth, *The Message of Joshua* (Dec 2015). Buyers should be aware that the new "revised editions" (2020–2024), as far as I can tell, are little changed in substance from the originals, with some updating of language and use of the current NIV. [PL]

BTCP   BIBLICAL THEOLOGY FOR CHRISTIAN PROCLAMATION COMMENTARY. (Holman

Reference). The title was a mouthful and indicated that BTCP would concentrate on the message of the text and themes, not the technical details of exegesis. The contributions on both OT and NT were in line with the publisher's conservative Southern Baptist ethos. The hb vols. were more handbook size (21 × 13.5 cm). BTCP was dropped and restarted as EBTC (see below). [P]

Calvin   CALVIN'S COMMENTARIES. Baker once regularly reprinted the 22-vol. set, which covers both OT and NT. Specifically it was the mid-19th century production of the Calvin Translation Society. Calvin is "a superb exegete . . . [and] his insight into literary form and function is exceptional" (L. T. Johnson, *The First and Second Letters to Timothy*, p.38). The more you read him, the more you'll appreciate his nuanced, rich theological insights. Another fine point: he takes care not to allow his commentary to come between the text and the reader. His OT commentaries cover the Pentateuch, Joshua, Psalms, and Isaiah to Malachi. Banner reprinted some of these (Genesis, Jeremiah–Lamentations, Daniel, and the Minor Prophets); they did not reprint two of his best: Psalms and Isaiah. Please note that the lengthy process of retranslating his OT commentaries began under the title Rutherford House Translation, but the project stalled. Newer translations of the NT commentaries (covering all but 2–3 John and Revelation) were done under the editorial direction of D. W. and T. F. Torrance (Eerdmans). This 13-vol. set gets my highest recommendation; do add it to your library. For a detailed examination of Calvin's labors, see the two vols. by T. H. L. Parker, *Calvin's OT Commentaries* and *Calvin's NT Commentaries* (WJK, 1993), as well as the essays in D. K. McKim, ed., *Calvin and the Bible* (CUP, 2006). The 22-vol. set is cheap s/h, and free online (ccel.org). [PSL]

CBC   CAMBRIDGE BIBLE COMMENTARY ON THE NEW ENGLISH BIBLE. ‡ (CUP). This popular-level series was produced in the 1960s and 70s. The NT was completed in 1967, and the OT section was published 1971–79. These volumes were well-written examples of British moderate historical criticism during that period. I will infrequently note them. They had few sales in North America, due in part to the little-used translation upon which the series was based (NEB). See NCBC. [LP]

CBSC   CAMBRIDGE BIBLE FOR SCHOOLS & COLLEGES. [𝓜], (CUP). A late 19th and early 20th century exegetical series, once of real value to preachers and students. [PS]

CCE   CHRIST-CENTERED EXPOSITION. (Holman Reference). Meant to cover both Testaments with devotional commentaries, CCE got off to a quick start under the editorial direction of David Platt, Daniel Akin, and Tony Merida. The pb vols. have titles such as *Exalting Jesus in Ephesians*, with a length and style that is not intimidating. The editors and Baptist publisher intend for contributors to deal with larger sections of text, not move word by word or verse by verse—which makes sense from the standpoint of modern linguistics—while emphasizing the grace of God in the gospel and a Christ-centered approach. Approximately forty vols. have been released. [LP]

CCF   COMMENTARIES FOR CHRISTIAN FORMATION. [𝓜?], (Eerdmans). Begun in 2021 (see N. T. Wright on Galatians), the series seeks to "interpret Scripture in ways aimed at ordering readers' lives and worship in imitation of Christ, informing their understanding of God, and animating their participation in the church's global mission with a deepened sense of calling" (editors' Introduction). The editors are Stephen Fowl, Jennie Grillo, and Robert Wall. Top-notch scholars are being recruited: see Goldingay on Proverbs and Peeler's *Hebrews*. [PL]

CCSS   CATHOLIC COMMENTARY ON SACRED SCRIPTURE. ‡ (Baker Academic). A NT pastoral series which, the publisher says, "implements the theological principles taught by Vatican II for interpreting Scripture 'in accord with the same Spirit by which it was written'—that is, interpreting Scripture in its canonical context and in light of Catholic tradition and the analogy of faith (*Dei Verbum* 12)." It is the product of mainstream American Catholicism, with the participation of leading critics such as Harrington and Matera, and more conservative types such as Hahn. Regular references to the *Catechism of the Catholic Church* indicate that the project is as much about nurture as scholarship. Now complete as a 17-vol. set, it is written for clergy yet accessible to the laity. [PL]

CGTC   CAMBRIDGE GREEK TESTAMENT COMMENTARY. [𝓜], (CUP). Sadly, this series barely got off the ground in the late 1950s. Only two vols. were published, but both—Moule on Colossians–Philemon and Cranfield on Mark—are models of patient, careful, conservatively critical exegesis. I believe they are o/p. [PS]

ConcC   CONCORDIA COMMENTARY SERIES: A THEOLOGICAL EXPOSITION OF SACRED SCRIPTURE. (Concordia). Large-scale expositions from a conservative (Missouri Synod) Lutheran publisher, "written to enable pastors and teachers of the Word to proclaim the Gospel with greater insight, clarity, and faithfulness to the divine intent of the biblical text." Along with a commitment to inerrancy, contributors generally reject the assumptions and methods of higher criticism in favor of a grammatico-historical approach. Volumes contain valuable exegetical notes on the Hebrew and Greek, some extensive; a good grounding in the languages is necessary to use the series. The theology is soundly Lutheran, occasionally with the taking up of cudgels against Calvinism and other traditions. Critics of Concordia might call it something of a niche denominational series; there can be abundant references to Luther, the Augsburg Confession, the Formula of Concord, and the *Lutheran Service Book*. On occasion one wonders if the theological system or Bible text is driving the project forward. Readers will discover that some entries are not as rich, deep, and well-researched as their size might lead one to expect. That said, the reverent love for the Scriptures helps counterbalance any negatives. Well over 40 vols. have appeared. I am coming to appreciate the series more, the Lessing, Steinmann, and Maier vols. on the OT especially. [P]

ContC   CONTINENTAL COMMENTARIES. ‡ (Fortress, previously Augsburg). Augsburg merged with Fortress (see Hermeneia), and the two publishers, first separately and then jointly, undertook the effort of getting many scholarly German commentaries translated. The later works by Wolff for BKAT, for example, were translated for this series. ContC intended to cover both OT and NT. With Milgrom's *Leviticus* (2004), we learned that not all the vols. are European "Continental" works and that the series is possibly adopting a less technical orientation. There have been no NT publications since 1993, or OT since 2004. [SP]

CorBC   CORNERSTONE BIBLICAL COMMENTARY. (Tyndale House). After releasing the New Living Translation, the publisher commissioned a set of evangelical commentaries. The contributors are first-class, but the vols. are not in-depth. The aim of the series is to "provide pastors and laypeople with up-to-date evangelical scholarship on the Old and New Testaments. It's designed to equip pastors and Christian leaders with exegetical and theological knowledge to better understand and apply God's Word by presenting the message of each passage as well as an overview of other issues surrounding the text." Some of these vols. deserve much wider recognition: e.g., Vannoy on Samuel, Boda on Chronicles. [PL]

CritC   CRITICAL COMMENTARIES. ‡ (Sheffield Phoenix). There had been confusion about whether this OT exegetical series was cancelled. Three major commentaries appeared, all by the American Jewish scholar Lisbeth Fried: *Ezra* (2019), *Nehemiah* (2021), and *Ruth* (2023). These were joined by Lundbom on Joel (2023). [S]

CrossC   CROSSWAY CLASSIC COMMENTARIES. (Crossway). As the series title suggests, these are republications of vintage commentaries. Editors J. I. Packer and Alister McGrath chose works, from the time of the Reformation (Calvin) to the early 20th century (Griffith Thomas), which offer "practical exposition promoting godliness" (series preface). I cannot argue with any of the selections thus far; they are superb. Examples would be Calvin on John's Gospel; Luther on Galatians; Hodge on Ephesians; Spurgeon on Psalms. Some of these classics are heavily edited for a popular readership (Lightfoot on the Greek text of Philippians), or drastically scaled down in size (Owen's seven vols. on Hebrews distilled into one). The series covers mainly NT rather than OT books and is very reasonably priced in pb. [PL]

CSC CHRISTIAN STANDARD COMMENTARY. (Holman Reference). The New American Commentary (NAC) is being replaced (or refurbished?) by a new series, also from the Southern Baptist publishing arm, using their *Christian Standard Bible* (1999–2017) as a base text. The editors speak of taking an "ancient-modern approach." They mean to give attention to text criticism and analysis of the Hebrew and Greek, rhetoric, and sociohistorical and literary questions: i.e., the modern. They also intend to interpret Scripture, in accord with "the ancient commentary tradition," as "a product of complex and rich divine action." The Bible is God's word to his church and must be read as theological in nature. It "leads to spiritual and practical transformation," revealing "Christ as the center of Scripture." Already some new vols. are receiving a warm welcome; see Patrick Schreiner's *Acts* (2022) as an exemplary contribution. Most of the early releases are revisions of NAC vols.; see George on *Galatians*; Garland on *2 Corinthians*; and Smith on *Isaiah 1–39*. [PL]

DRC DIGEST OF REFORMED COMMENT. (Banner of Truth). Geoffrey Wilson, an English pastor, "has undertaken the herculean labor of distilling the best of Puritan, Reformed and modern comment on the Pauline letters in a most attractive fashion, since these quotations are interwoven with his own observations on the text of Paul's writings from a pastoral viewpoint" (Martin). I won't list these under each individual book, but you should realize they are out there. Banner rereleased the commentaries in two large vols. (2005), covering *Romans to Ephesians* and *Philippians to Hebrews and Revelation*. [PL]

DSB DAILY STUDY BIBLE. ‡ (WJK). William Barclay's well-known, popular series on the NT hardly needs an introduction. He is excellent for pithy comment and homiletical helps. Many pastors have used the series to add sparkle to their sermons. But it has something of a bad reputation among conservatives because of its decidedly liberal, critical interpretation of the Gospels. Take a look at a miracle passage to see my point. Barclay is better on the epistles, especially Hebrews. The careful student will note that in his frequent word studies he tends to over-interpret individual words and draw their significance from Classical Greek usage. The later, multiauthor OT series was designed to be a companion set to Barclay and has several evangelical contributions of note. The NT vols., though of value, will not be listed under the individual books. [PL]

Earth EARTH BIBLE COMMENTARY. ‡ (Bloomsbury T&T Clark). I will scarcely discuss this newer series, except to give my general description of its aim: the vols. are postmodern in orientation and ideologically critical, typically deconstructing the Bible in pursuit of an ecological agenda. [PL]

EB EXPOSITOR'S BIBLE. (Eerdmans–o/p). This old series (late 19th century) was long the mainstay of pastors and had an interesting Victorian flavor to it. Some of the works still have real profit to them (e.g., Genesis, Leviticus, Joshua, Samuel, Psalms, Romans, 2 Corinthians). A few have been reprinted. Some are a bit critically oriented (e.g., Farrar on Kings). Now free online (ccel.org). [PL]

EBC   EXPOSITOR'S BIBLE COMMENTARY. (Zondervan). Perhaps meant to replace the EB. There were worthy contributions to the 12-vol. set, edited by Gaebelein, but also inadequate ones. What made choices difficult was that the worthwhile and pedestrian could be bound up in the same vol. The commentators were evangelicals, writing in the 1970s and 80s. Overall, it was quite helpful considering the space allotted, but the set soon felt dated (esp. vols. 6, 10–12). Theological stance varied from book to book, but tended to be premillennial where it counts. The best were on Numbers, Samuel, Job, Psalms, Matthew, Acts, 2 Corinthians, and Revelation. Some on the NT side were published separately in pb: Matthew (2 vols.), Luke, Acts. Don't bother with the 2-vol. abridgment of EBC, *The NIV Bible Commentary*. A full-scale revision (EBCR) was released; see below. [P]

EBCR   EXPOSITOR'S BIBLE COMMENTARY, REVISED EDITION. (Zondervan). The old EBC (above) badly needed an update because of the age of the set and its unevenness in terms of both quality and quantity of comment. Psalms had an excellent 900-page exposition dating from 1990, while 1 Corinthians was published in 1976 with an allotted 120pp. The EBCR (2005–12) commissioned new book treatments in certain cases and revisions of original EBC contributions in others. This shaped up to be a very good set for pastors, and some contributions, like Psalms, are valued by students too. Because brevity of treatment is a common drawback here, I wish the series had left out the biblical text so as to provide more comment. [P]

EBTC   EVANGELICAL BIBLICAL THEOLOGY COMMENTARY. (Lexham). See BTCP above for the previous iteration. Lexham took over the series from Broadman and renamed it. While providing discussion of introductory matters and a succinct exegetical and theologically oriented commentary (with reference Hebrew and Greek), EBTC especially means to make a contribution with its section of biblical-theological essays on leading themes in each Bible book. (Hamilton on Psalms does not have such a section.) See Schreiner's *Hebrews* or Harmon's *Galatians* for examples. The series seems oriented toward conservative Baptist churches in America and evidences a concern for the church's mission. Compare THC. [P]

ECBC   EERDMANS CLASSIC BIBLICAL COMMENTARIES. ‡ (Eerdmans). Because many older Eerdmans works continue to be in demand, despite their having been replaced in such series as NICNT, the publisher is keeping them in print. An example would be F. F. Bruce on *The Epistles to the Colossians, to Philemon, and to the Ephesians*. Originally published in 1984 in NICNT, Bruce was reprinted for ECBC in 2020. See also Ladd on Revelation. [P]

ECC   EERDMANS CRITICAL COMMENTARY. ‡ (Eerdmans). Offers exhaustive and technical commentaries on both Testaments, but production has been slow. As of 2016 ECC was defunct (Lundbom, *Deuteronomy*, p.xxi), but it has restarted with Walter Wilson vols. on Matthew (2022) and Wisdom of Sirach (2023). ECC ran down much the same track as The Anchor Bible. David Noel Freedman was the general editor here—as he had been for AB—and two of the vols. which appeared were, I believe, originally intended for AB: see Quinn–Wacker on Timothy, and Barth–Blanke on Philemon. The latter vol. runs on for over 500pp. (or 20pp. per verse on average). Initially in hb, these fat vols. have been released in pb. The vol. by Shalom Paul on Isaiah 40–66 is magnificent. [SP]

EEC   EVANGELICAL EXEGETICAL COMMENTARY. (Lexham, Logos Bible Software). Planned for digital release then print. EEC was initially conceived in 2005 as a major print series under Wayne House as editor (suggesting a dispensational orientation). The project covering the OT and NT seemed derailed by financial concerns; afterwards Logos agreed to publish it digitally. One of the contracted authors, Rod Decker, reveals that the aim is to produce works "between BECNT and WBC" with regard to academic level; that's setting the bar high. It is apparent that EEC is not strictly dispensational and that print editions are slow in appearing. For examples of the series, see Tomasino on Esther, Carpenter on Exodus, Baugh on Ephesians, and Derickson on John's Epistles. Tremper Longman has become general editor, and contributors now include Goldingay on Ezekiel. [PS]

EGGNT   EXEGETICAL GUIDE TO THE GREEK NT. (B&H Academic, previously Eerdmans). Murray Harris wrote a 1991 work on Colossians as the first in a proposed 20-vol. series of guides to the Greek NT. It seemed to bode well for the series, if it ever really got off the ground. I finally concluded it wouldn't. However, in 2009 B&H took it over from Eerdmans and has successfully revived it. See Vlachos on James and Forbes on 1 Peter. By comparison with BHGNT, this series offers a measure of commentary. [PS]

EKK   EVANGELISCH–KATHOLISCHER KOMMENTAR. ‡ (Neukirchener). A prominent, large-scale German series with exacting exegesis and theological commentary on the NT. Only English translations of these vols. will be noted. See ContC and Herm in this section, Schweizer on Colossians, and Bovon's *Luke*. [S]

EPSC   EP STUDY COMMENTARY. (Evangelical Press). The UK publisher has several commentary series (see WCS below), and this one was being produced in hb. While one may be glad for the durable binding, it does make vols. more expensive as popular-level expositions for pastors. Lately vols. are being released in pb. EPSC is like the Mentor commentary (see below) with regard to reading-level and Reformed theological orientation, but EPSC sometimes has more study behind it (as shown in the citations of literature). See Duguid on Haggai–Malachi for a good example of the series. [PL]

ESVEC   ESV EXPOSITORY COMMENTARY. (Crossway). The editors of this "globally minded . . . series rich in biblical theology and broadly Reformed doctrine" are seminary profs: Iain Duguid (Westminster, Philadelphia), James Hamilton (Southern Baptist), and Jay Sklar (Covenant). Launched in 2019, the ESVEC means to provide "clear, crisp, Christ-centered explanation of the biblical text," not printed sermons, though it is "application minded" (see "Response" sections). The commentary is easy to read but studious in approach, with transliterated Hebrew and Greek, and is proving popular with pastors and laypeople. Eleven vols. were published between 2018 and 2022; only vol. 1: "Genesis–Numbers" remains to be released. [P]

FBPC   FORTRESS BIBLICAL PREACHING COMMENTARIES. ‡ (Fortress). I know of one title so far in the liberal series: Ronald Allen's *Acts of the Apostles* (2013). [PL]

FE   FOR EVERYONE SERIES. [ℳ], (WJK). These titles—a representative would be *Mark for Everyone* by N. T. Wright—share some of the same aims as DSB. (See the comparative review [*BSB* 3/12].) The series quickly developed to cover both Testaments, enlisting mainly British scholars interested in theological exposition. Wright, Goldingay, and Brueggemann are among those contributing. Though I will not be noting these under Bible books, many talk about how certain vols. (especially Wright on the Gospels) are lively and abounding with devotional insights into the text. "This enterprise is probably the most exciting thing to have happened in Christian education in Britain for many years" (*ExpTim*). I find I like Wright on the Gospels more than on the Epistles. Some OT entries have a more obvious critical/liberal orientation. [L]

Focus   FOCUS ON THE BIBLE. (Christian Focus). A thoughtful and serious, yet simple set of expositions published in the UK. The pb books were once not widely available in North America, but they are now. Almost the entire canon is covered and replacement vols. are appearing (e.g., James Hamilton's *Song of Songs* [2015] replaces Richard Brooks [1999]). American authors, as well as Brits, contribute to Focus, and the theology is warm-hearted

Calvinism. I don't always mention these publications, some of which have appeared outside the Focus series (e.g., Ralph Davis's books on Joshua, Judges). [LP]

FOTL    FORMS OF THE OLD TESTAMENT LITERATURE. ‡ (Eerdmans). A unique, specialized set offering form-critical analyses of OT books, focusing on matters of genre, setting, and structure. "[T]he entire series cannot quite decide whether it is a full-blown commentary or a form-critical survey" (Brueggemann, *JBL* 105, p.130). These studies are of interest to specialists and advanced students, but it is the rare pastor who could profit much from them. Moderately critical. Great bibliographies! For discussion of how the method has morphed, see *The Changing Face of Form Criticism for the Twenty-First Century* (2003) [*OTE* 17.3]. [S]

GAOT    GOSPEL ACCORDING TO THE OLD TESTAMENT SERIES. (P&R). Commenced by Al Groves and Tremper Longman, and now edited by Iain Duguid, GAOT is a "series of studies on the lives of Old Testament characters, written for laypeople and pastors, and designed to encourage Christ-centered reading, teaching, and preaching of the Old Testament" (publisher's description). I have purchased several of these and found both fresh theological insights and spiritual encouragement. [PL]

GNC     GOOD NEWS COMMENTARY. [𝔐], (Harper & Row). In this popularly styled series, competent scholars commented on the text of the Good News Bible/Today's English Version. Several vols. were published, but the public lost interest in the GNB after the NIV came out. See NIBC below. [P]

GS      GENEVA SERIES. (Banner of Truth). By and large, the publisher made excellent choices in republishing these old Reformed works. When used alongside a good modern exegetical commentary, these vols. on OT and NT books will aid the preacher very much. Banner is to be saluted for including Calvin's commentaries on Genesis, Jeremiah–Lamentations, Daniel, and the Minor Prophets in the series, but see Calvin above. [PLS]

HACB    HOLMAN APOLOGETICS COMMENTARY ON THE BIBLE. (B&H). The series commenced in 2013 with a vol. on *The Gospels and Acts*, and it will cover the entire Bible. Leading evangelical Bible scholars are enlisted to address the hard texts that raise questions in the minds of believers and unbelievers: alleged historical errors, ethically disturbing stories (e.g., conquest in Joshua), proof texts used by the cults, the number of temple-cleansings, etc. According to Gathercole [*Them* 11/14], "There is a consistently high quality of discussion" in the first release. I won't note these vols. under individual books. [PL]

Harper  HARPER'S NEW TESTAMENT COMMENTARY. ‡ (Harper & Row–o/p). See BNTC above.

HCOT    HISTORICAL COMMENTARY ON THE OLD TESTAMENT. ‡ (Peeters). It is good to see well esteemed works from *Commentar op het Oude Testament* coming into English translation. The Dutch series, which used to be fairly conservative under Aalders as editor, is of a high caliber and thoroughly treats philological, historical, and theological matters. The approach is mainly a restrained form of traditional historical criticism (continental European variety). It is now clear that not all the HCOT vols. will be translations of Dutch commentaries, though that is how the series began. (See Houtman on Exodus, Beuken–Koole on Isaiah, Renkema on Lamentations, Vlaardingerbroek on Zephaniah, and Spronk on Nahum.) New commentaries in English are being commissioned. Note that at the start of its history HCOT was published by Kok. [SP]

Herm    HERMENEIA. ‡ (Fortress Press). "A very high level of technical scholarship is evidenced in this . . . series" (Childs). For specialists and advanced students. Over 45 vols. of Bible commentaries have appeared. (The Apocrypha and Pseudepigrapha also have some vols.) Most are standout critical exegetical works. Generally, the older vols. are translations and offer "heavy doses of German theological discussion" (Horsley). For example, Zimmerli's and Wolff's exhaustive works come from the German series BKAT. Earlier, the OT series was more valuable than the NT, perhaps because the NT editorial board had been dominated by radical *religionsgeschichtliche* (history of religions) types who made some strange assignments (e.g., Haenchen on John and Bultmann on John's Epistles). More recent NT vols. (Achtemeier on 1 Peter, Luz on Matthew, Bovon on Luke) are more useful. Like OTL, the series has become more American with the passage of time. It continues to showcase mainly historical-critical scholarship. [S]

HGV     HEARING GOD'S VOICE. (IVP). A forthcoming series, with the first publications reportedly to appear in 2025. It aims to provide expositions of Scripture's message and to be somewhat similar to BST. [PL]

HMS     HEARING THE MESSAGE OF SCRIPTURE. (Zondervan). See ZECOT for the retitled series, which is an OT companion to ZECNT. Block is editor, and he wrote a sterling entry on Obadiah. Whereas HMS transliterated the Hebrew, the renamed series uses Hebrew typeface. Only two vols. appeared in HMS: Obadiah and Jonah. [PS]

Hodder     HODDER BIBLE COMMENTARY. (Hodder & Stoughton). At inception, with vols. soon to appear (2024). The series means to build on a solid exegetical base and provide middle-length expositions of OT and NT from an evangelical perspective, "which are doctrinally sensitive and globally aware" (series preface). There is to be close engagement with (a) the message of the text (i.e., its "own agenda"), (b) interpretation of the Scriptures over the centuries, and (c) questions of how various "cultures hear and need to hear what the Spirit is saying to the churches." Fifty vols. are planned. Some contributors are specialists in biblical studies, while others are learned pastor-theologians. [PL]

HolNT     HOLMAN NEW TESTAMENT COMMENTARY. (B&H). Begun in 1998 and completed in a mere three or four years, the series offers ready-made sermonic material. You are even provided with a closing prayer. The authors are mainly successful senior pastors of large conservative Baptist churches, though there are a few seminary faculty contributors, too. The editor and main author is Max Anders. There is little commentary on the biblical text at all, which most will view as a serious shortcoming. For pastors who have done their own in-depth study, these inexpensive hb vols. may spawn ideas for application. I will not note these under individual Bible books. OT vols. in the same mold have appeared as Holman's Old Testament Commentary (HolOT). [L]

I     INTERPRETATION. ‡ (WJK). A moderately critical series which focuses more on theological exposition than on technical, critical issues, and is designed with the pastor in mind. One of the contributors, Gaventa, says that, rather than seek to replace scholarly historical-critical works or common homiletical resources, Interpretation offers "commentary which presents the integrated result of historical and theological work with the biblical text." Some of the acclaimed entries in this series are Genesis, Exodus, Deuteronomy, Samuel, Job, Psalms, Lamentations, and 1 Corinthians—I find the OT section stronger than the NT. Now in pb. [P]

IB     INTERPRETER'S BIBLE. ‡ (Abingdon). A liberal set from the 1950s covering the entire Bible with double treatments of each book: exegesis by a scholar and homiletical comments from a pastor. The series was eventually pronounced a failure by almost everybody. The rare helpful exegetical work will be mentioned below (e.g., Wright on Deuteronomy, Bright on Joshua, Muilenburg on Second Isaiah). The homiletical sections at the bottom of the page are usually insipid and can conflict with the exegesis at the top of the page. Abingdon's full-scale revision, entitled *The New Interpreter's Bible*, was completed in 2002. See NIB. [P]

ICC       INTERNATIONAL CRITICAL COMMENTARY. ‡ (T&T Clark). Under revision. Most vols. in the series are quite dated now. Much new linguistic, textual, historical, and archaeological evidence has become available since the older publications (1895–1951), and exegetical methods have drastically changed. Some of these, however, in their full handling of the technical questions remain helpful commentaries; they are valuable for little else. Among the best of the old vintage were Genesis, Numbers, Deuteronomy, Judges, Kings, Job, Ezekiel, Daniel, Luke, Romans, 1 Corinthians, Galatians, Revelation. The series has been undergoing a thorough revision under the direction of editors G. I. Davies, G. N. Stanton (†2009), and Christopher Tuckett, with consultation of former editors J. A. Emerton (†2015) and C. E. B. Cranfield (†2015). Several works have appeared so far in the OT section (Exodus, Ecclesiastes, Isaiah, Jeremiah, Lamentations, Hosea). The NT replacement vols. on Romans, Matthew, Ephesians, 2 Corinthians, Pastoral Epistles, Acts, James, and 1 Peter are magisterial! The series is incomplete but now ambitious to publish on the Apocrypha (David Teeter, *Baruch and the Epistle of Jeremiah* [forthcoming]). Those who put off buying these vols. because of expense—e.g., the Davies–Allison set on Matthew lists for over $700 (hb)—are glad ICC is being published in pb as well, and at a huge savings. [SP]

IECOT    INTERNATIONAL EXEGETICAL COMMENTARY ON THE OT. ‡ (Kohlhammer). I have seen only a few of these vols. from Germany, but there is an impressive lineup of editors, including Adele Berlin, Bernard Levinson, and Erhard Blum. The series appears in both English and German editions and is meant to be quite broad with regard to nationality, faith, and methodology (but seeking to blend the diachronic and synchronic). As with Hermeneia and AB, the series will cover the Apocrypha. [SP]

Illum     ILLUMINATIONS. ‡ (Eerdmans). Judging by the first vol., Seow's 900pp. on *Job 1–21*, this will be an ambitious, large-scale undertaking, providing technical exegeses of the OT, NT, and Apocrypha. Its niche is an extensive treatment of reception history under the rubric History of Consequences, "meaning 'consequences' in the sense of all that comes after the Bible, as well as 'consequences' in the sense of the direct and indirect results of interpretation and reception" (series preface). Definitely a series to watch. [SP]

ITC       INTERNATIONAL THEOLOGICAL COMMENTARY ON THE HOLY SCRIPTURE. (Bloomsbury T&T Clark). Begun in 2016 (with *Joel* by Seitz), this companion of the venerable ICC "offers a verse-by-verse interpretation of the Bible that addresses its theological subject matter, gleaning the best from both the classical and modern commentary traditions and showing the doctrinal development of Scriptural truths" (preface). ITC rides the crest of the wave of theological exegesis that has been building for decades. The editors are Michael Allen and Scott Swain of RTS, thus indicating a more conservative and ecclesial orientation "marked by a creedal and confessional alertness." Some scholars involved are mildly to moderately critical. These are major works, meant to be enduring theological reference tools; examples are Bray on the Pastorals and Leithart's 900-page commentary on Revelation. Readers will encounter discussion of the original languages, literary features, history of interpretation, as well as insightful theology. With T&T Clark's cover art prominently displaying the acronym, the publisher lays claim to the ITC abbreviation, and the Eerdmans series of the same name can be designated ITC-E (see below). [SP]

ITC-E    INTERNATIONAL THEOLOGICAL COMMENTARY. ‡ (Eerdmans, now only POD). An older series of expositions (1983–98) seeking diversity of theological and cultural comment on the OT. As expected, there was unevenness: some were thin and not so helpful. Others were worth more than a second look: Brueggemann on Jeremiah;

Beeby's *Hosea*; Sakenfeld on Numbers; and Janzen's *Genesis 12–50*. Overall, I was not impressed with ITC-E. Moderately critical, with many examining the text's final form. Do not confuse with the OT and NT series now being produced by T&T Clark. [P]

IVPNT    IVP NEW TESTAMENT COMMENTARY. (IVP). Begun under editor I. Howard Marshall in 1991, IVPNT was completed in 2009. The contributors are mainly professional scholars, with a few pastors like Ray Stedman and George Stulac. While all the authors are evangelicals, some are appreciative of critical scholarship and may employ critical methods in a mild fashion. The series is practically oriented, like BST, but includes lots of good exegetical notes. I considered them a bit expensive in hb for their size and depth; they finally came out in pb. The best vols. are probably Bock on Luke; Larkin on Acts; Osborne on Romans; Belleville on 2 Corinthians; Fee on Philippians; Beale on Thessalonians; Towner on the Pastorals; Marshall on 1 Peter; and Michaels on Revelation. [P]

JPS    JPS TORAH COMMENTARY. ‡ (Jewish Publication Society). These moderately critical commentaries on the Pentateuch are useful to scholars and students. They treat the Hebrew text, provide good ANE background information, incisive exegesis from a Jewish perspective, and lots of rabbinics. The contributors may express reservations about traditional source criticism. Milgrom on Numbers is especially deep and thorough (520pp.). As an aside, it is a minor irritation learning to turn pages filled primarily with English text in the reverse direction. We have additional vols. of commentary on books outside the Pentateuch: The JPS Bible Commentary (also abbreviated JPS). See Simon on Jonah, Berlin on Esther, Fox on Ecclesiastes. [SP]

KCC    KIDNER CLASSIC COMMENTARIES. (IVP). As the much appreciated Derek Kidner works are replaced in the series for which he wrote (TOTC, BST), the publisher will keep them available in reprints. The long-lived Kidner (1913–2008) played a key role in encouraging evangelical biblical scholarship worldwide as an OT lecturer, as Warden of Tyndale House, and through his writings. [PL]

KD    KEIL & DELITZSCH. (Eerdmans or Hendrickson). For generations KD was a wise purchase for several reasons: (1) the evangelical set covers the entire OT in ten fat vols.; (2) both men were very able theologians and biblical scholars; (3) they offered a full treatment without being verbose; and (4) they were remarkably affordable (about $100 on discount). Note that the exegesis and exposition are more helpful than their dated philological comments—so you need not be put off by the Arabic you run across. These commentaries were first published 1861–75 in German. Keil did Genesis to Esther and Jeremiah to Malachi, while Franz Delitzsch covered Job to Isaiah. With all the more recent works available, I stopped recommending KD for purchase. But make no mistake, "[t]hese commentaries remain even today veritable storehouses of learning and insight" (Rogerson). In my opinion the greatest work here was Delitzsch on the Psalms. The Kindle version is under $10, and the entire set is free online (Hebrew letters sometimes corrupted by digitization). [PS]

KEL    KREGEL EXEGETICAL LIBRARY. (Kregel). This large-scale conservative series got its start in 2012 with the first of three vols. on the Psalms by Allen Ross. Though treating the original languages and offering text-critical comments, KEL is fairly accessible to those without Hebrew and Greek. Looking at Ross and at Garrett's *Commentary on Exodus*, it is clear that the exegesis does not intend to wade through all the scholarly literature and it moves directly toward drawing theological conclusions (often biblical-theological) for the church. [P]

Kerux    KERUX: AN INTEGRATIVE COMMENTARY FOR PREACHING & TEACHING. (Kregel). Quickly developing since 2019, the series has released about a dozen vols.

The conservative publisher intends Kerux to contain 44 vols. that will "accurately and authoritatively communicate the message of the divine King" (Prospectus). There seem to be some similarities with Baker's "Teach the Text Commentary" in its highly structured multiple sections and Big Idea summaries. What is more unique is the collaborative pairing of "experts in biblical exegesis" with "the best of homileticians" to produce the vols. (cf. the old IB). From what I have seen thus far, Kerux is American and Baptistic/Brethren in orientation, of middle-length, and less expensive. [PL]

Lange   LANGE'S COMMENTARY. (Scribners). A classic 19th century set (mainly 1870s) covering both Testaments that was highly valued by preachers and scholars alike. It was well-rounded, with exegetical, theological, and homiletical comment. The great historian and theologian Philip Schaff was editor of the ET. Contributors to this monumental effort were deeply learned, fairly conservative—especially by German standards—and drew from the whole history of interpretation. This series and KD introduced English readers to the best conservative continental scholarship. Originally published in 13 vols., Lange's OT series was reprinted by Zondervan in 7 huge vols. (1960). Wipf & Stock republished a portion of the OT and NT series in 2007. A couple of works were definitely worth reprinting (e.g., Bähr on Kings, Schröder on Ezekiel). The theological expositions are obviously more valuable today than the philological comments. Free online. [PS]

LCEC   LECTIO CONTINUA EXPOSITORY COMMENTARY. (Tolle Lege Press). Begun in 2012 with J. V. Fesko's *Galatians*, Lectio Continua is a conservative series "authored by an array of seasoned pastor-scholars from various Reformed denominations on both sides of the Atlantic" (Series Introduction). I will rarely note the vols. under Bible books because I have not used them. [PL]

Lenski   LENSKI'S COMMENTARY ON THE NEW TESTAMENT. (Augsburg). Depending on the printing, this Lutheran commentary is 12 or 20 vols. Lenski is similar to NTC in some ways, but not as well-done and more dated (R. C. H. Lenski, 1864–1936). A truly conservative work both in its evangelical stance and its militant defense of orthodox Lutheran distinctives (especially over against Calvinists), Lenski doesn't compete well with the other works now available to us. This series is occasionally reprinted and will not be listed below. [P]

LRC   LEXHAM RESEARCH COMMENTARY. (Lexham). I have heard of the series (specifically Widder on Jonah), but I have not used it. LRC seems to represent a sifting of others' past research, "a commentary on the commentaries," as Logos describes it. See <www.logos.com/product/189697/lexham-research-commentaries>. [P?]

Maggid   MAGGID STUDIES IN TANAKH. (Maggid). An international Jewish expositional series published in Israel, reflecting on Scripture texts. One example is Ganzel on Ezekiel. [PL]

Mentor   MENTOR COMMENTARY. (Christian Focus). Published out of Britain, these accessible commentaries by both British and American Reformed scholars aim to provide a fair measure of faithful exegesis and full theological exposition. John L. Mackay has contributed several of these hb vols.: Exodus, Jeremiah (2 vols.), Lamentations. In the USA they have been difficult and quite expensive to obtain, which is a pity since a couple of these are very good for pastors (e.g., Pratt on Chronicles). See EPSC above for a similar series. [PL]

MNT   MASTERING THE NEW TESTAMENT. (Word/Nelson). See WCC below.

MOT   MASTERING THE OLD TESTAMENT. (Word/Nelson). See WCC below.

NAC   NEW AMERICAN COMMENTARY. (B&H). A nearly complete series (1991–) on both Testaments with conservative (mostly Southern Baptist) contributors, some excellent ones too: Daniel Block, Craig Blomberg, Robert Stein, and Thomas Schreiner. They are full commentaries, some over 700pp., in a readable format. The set tends to be dispensational where it counts (i.e., Ezekiel, Daniel). Conservatives view NAC as an improvement over the old Broadman Bible Commentary, both in terms of scholarship and theological stance. That being said, Hawthorne is on the mark to say that this series usually does not break new ground or add fresh insights into the meaning of the text; rather it helpfully gleans information from recent commentaries [*JETS* 3/96]. This is probably truer for the NT than for the OT section. The stated aim of NAC is to meet the needs of ministers, not graduate students. See the Christian Standard Commentary (CSC) above for a replacement series. [P]

NBBC   NEW BEACON BIBLE COMMENTARY. (Beacon Hill). I was not acquainted with this series on both Testaments until 2010 and have only seen one vol.: Dean Fleming on Philippians. The series comes from the Wesleyan tradition and is deliberate about presenting a well-rounded work for pastors. There are sections on literary and historical background (Behind the Text), exegesis (In the Text), and application (From the Text). Any references to the original languages are transliterated. There are no footnotes or endnotes. [P]

NCB    NEW CENTURY BIBLE. ‡ (Eerdmans). Vols. treat the RSV or NRSV, ranging from mildly critical to moderately so; most are in the latter category. This exegetical series is rather undistinguished in the OT, better in the NT. Most entries were contributed by British critics, seem a bit stodgy, and offer little theological reflection. There are several excellent works in this set which can be recommended. NCB was nearly complete and under revision before it petered out. In the USA Eerdmans dropped it. Sheffield briefly picked it up in the UK, shipping what had then become expensive pb vols. to the States. The last works contracted, e.g., Joyce on Ezekiel, are published in the expensive LHBOTS. [PS]

NCBC   NEW CAMBRIDGE BIBLE COMMENTARY. ‡ (CUP). Building well upon the tradition of the accessible Cambridge Bible Commentary of the 1960s and 70s, the NCBC looks to be fuller in exegesis and more useful to students (see the recommended reading sections). The series "is pitched at a higher academic level than the old CBC" (G. I. Davies), but the intended audience is a "wide range of intellectually curious individuals," not scholars. The first releases showed that it is well-edited, well-informed, readable, and less concerned with older historical-critical (diachronic) questions than the old series. The blurb says, "Volumes utilize recent gains in rhetorical criticism, social scientific study of the Scriptures, narrative criticism, and other developing disciplines to exploit advances in biblical studies." The contributors are a diverse lot with a surprising number of Americans: liberal Protestants (Brueggemann), Catholics (Neyrey), Evangelicals (Bock, Arnold), and Jewish scholars (Halpern and Fox). The NRSV text is printed in the vols. These pb books are a bit expensive. [P]

NCCS   NEW COVENANT COMMENTARY SERIES. (Wipf & Stock, USA; Lutterworth, UK). The series began in 2009 and intends to be both internationally and theologically diverse, while remaining in the evangelical camp. "We intend the NCCS to engage in the task of biblical interpretation and theological reflection from the perspective of the global church" (preface). The first vols., by editors Keener (Romans) and Bird (Colossians, Philemon), demonstrate that the series avoids verse-by-verse exegesis and concentrates on larger units so as to help readers understand the flow of the argument or story. [P]

NIB    NEW INTERPRETER'S BIBLE. ‡ (Abingdon). Quickly brought to completion, the NIB is a major, ecumenical, 12-vol. series on both Testaments—sharing the aims but not the theological stance of the evangelical, 13-vol. EBCR. The commentaries print the NIV and NRSV, provide a basic exegesis, and have homiletical guidance for ministers. A wide (inclusive) net has been cast to enlist male and female contributors from different denominations. Even the evangelical Walter Kaiser is there. Other famous names include Dunn, Brueggemann, Wright, and Newsom. Generally, the work is very competent, moderately critical, dependable rather than bold and creative. Hermeneutical approaches vary from book to book; most seek to provide a more literary and theological reading of the final form of the text, while others employ traditional historical-critical methods. That text-centered emphasis is indicative of the sea change in biblical studies over past decades. All contributors are supposed to take the theology of the text seriously. The project is more successful than the old IB, but I'm not rushing out to buy the set. (Expense and a preference for fuller works are primary reasons.) Perhaps the NIB is most valuable for commentary on those parts of the canon which have been underserved by other scholarly series. I note each individual commentary. [P]

NIBC    NEW INTERNATIONAL BIBLICAL COMMENTARY. [*M*], (Hendrickson). This pb series was initially an attempt to refurbish the Good News Commentary by reediting those NT vols. to explain the NIV text instead of the GNB. Also, brand new commentaries were solicited. The publisher launched an OT section in 1995 with Provan's superb *1 and 2 Kings*. OT vols. have appeared regularly thereafter. Most contributors are evangelicals who are comfortable using critical methods, but a few are thoroughgoing critics (e.g., the master Catholic exegete Roland Murphy). Among the best in the series are Deuteronomy, Kings, Psalms, Isaiah, the Pastorals, Luke, Acts, Hebrews, and James. This series is one of the less expensive and is nearly complete. Now see UBC. [P]

NICNT    NEW INTERNATIONAL COMMENTARY ON THE NEW TESTAMENT. (Eerdmans). This evangelical series has been the mainstay of my own NT collection. NICNT gives readers a fairly comprehensive treatment of exegetical questions, but always with a focus on expounding the text's message. Technical discussion of the Greek text is relegated to the footnotes. "Greek clearly informs the exegesis, but the reader unfamiliar with the original language is not prevented from making good use of this commentary" (Aageson on Fee's *Thessalonians*). The quality of the set over the years owed much to its ongoing revision, also to the long-term editorial direction and several contributions of F. F. Bruce, followed by Gordon Fee. I have recommended most vols. in the collection, which covers all the NT except 2 Peter/Jude. Our long wait for vols. on Matthew and the Pastorals was rewarded with stellar works by France and Towner. With the series' revision under the capable editorship of Gordon Fee and now Joel Green (2013–), it has less and less of its old Reformed savor. Like its sister, NICOT, the series is also becoming less conservative. For another series similar to NICNT, see Pillar. [PS]

NICOT    NEW INTERNATIONAL COMMENTARY ON THE OLD TESTAMENT. (Eerdmans). Promises to continue providing pastor and teacher with a bevy of valuable exegetical tools. Thirty-eight vols. have been published (nine are replaced), and most are highly recommended. Like NICNT this evangelical series has benefitted from good editorial direction. The able Robert Hubbard headed up the project after R. K. Harrison (†1993), and Bill Arnold took over in 2020. Recent contributions to NICOT indicate a trend toward publishing more extensive commentaries which will better serve scholars' needs. The best examples are Block's two vols. on Ezekiel, totaling over 1700pp., and Boda's 850-page *Zechariah*. This trend may help explain the slowed release of new works. Eerdmans and Logos released the series electronically with NICNT. [PS]

NIGTC    NEW INTERNATIONAL GREEK TESTAMENT COMMENTARY. [*M*], (Eerdmans). A prestigious technical series, long edited by Marshall and Hagner. It is mildly critical and marked by very thorough, careful exegesis of the Greek text. Full bibliographies too. Like the ICC, NIGTC generally contains less exposition and theological reflection than preachers want. Still, the studious pastor could put these vols. to excellent use; there isn't a single poor commentary in the set. Most of the authors (Marshall, Dunn, Bruce, Thiselton, Nolland) are in the more critically oriented wing of evangelicalism; Knight and Harris are exceptions. Word is out that some older vols. (e.g., Marshall on Luke) will be revised to extend their usefulness. There have been no publications since 2016. This set is comparable to BECNT. [SP]

NIVAC  NIV APPLICATION COMMENTARY. (Zondervan). User-friendly. My enthusiasm for this evangelical series has grown. The editors did a good job enlisting both veterans and able younger scholars to contribute. The goal articulated for the series is to bridge the divide between the original context in which the biblical text spoke and the contemporary context in which the text still speaks. Better entries have a good measure of interpretation before moving on to consider practical application. That is a proper and safe pattern. But what makes NIVAC unique and even more helpful is that, in between exegesis (Original Meaning) and application (Contemporary Significance), the authors discuss the process of moving from the world of the text to our own. Often those Bridging Contexts sections offer astute counsel to preachers. Most vols. released have reached the goal. Among the more successful entries are Walton on Genesis; Enns on Exodus; Block on Deuteronomy; Jobes on Esther; Wilson on Psalms; Duguid on Ezekiel; Longman on Daniel; Moo on Romans; Hafemann on 2 Corinthians; Garland on Mark and Colossians–Philemon; Guthrie on Hebrews; and Moo on 2 Peter–Jude. Compare this series with BST. Look for the annotated bibliographies of commentaries (a few vols. don't have them). The OT and NT sections are complete. Note: I suggest buying hard copies; there have been complaints about Kindle editions. [PL]

NTC  NEW TESTAMENT COMMENTARY. (Baker). Often called "Hendriksen," after William Hendriksen (1900–82) who began the project, NTC was steadily and carefully brought to completion by Simon Kistemaker of RTS. The final issue, *Revelation*, appeared in 2001. Most students have a settled opinion about the worth of these vols. Several criticisms could be leveled (particularly at Hendriksen): they tend to be verbose, lack rigor in their grammatical and exegetical observations, jump too quickly from the text to systematic theology concerns, may pack individual words with too much theological freight, and sometimes are not so good in filling out the broader historical context. But their good points outweigh their faults. These commentaries directly serve the preacher in their full expositional style. They are distinctively Reformed, conservative, and reasonably well-grounded in their scholarship. One reviewer sums things up this way: "what it lacks in theological profundity and ethical richness it makes up for with clarity and thoroughness" (Padgett). The publisher appears to have let the 12-vol. series go o/p. [P]

NTL  NEW TESTAMENT LIBRARY. ‡ (WJK). The publisher of OTL conceived a NT counterpart which includes mid-level exegeses, reprinted classics of NT scholarship (e.g., Minear's *Images of the Church in the NT*), and other general NT reference works (theologies, hermeneutics, etc.). Some more recent commentary issues are superb: Holladay on Acts, Thompson on John. It does not appear that they provide much discussion of such technical matters as textual criticism; instead they serve preachers by focusing more on the literary features and theological message of the text. The 18 commentaries so far indicate that the series will be consistently strong. [PS]

NTM  NEW TESTAMENT MESSAGE. ‡ (Michael Glazier). These are critical expositions from Roman Catholic scholars. Usually not in-depth, they will occasionally be noted under individual books. [P]

ONTC   OSBORNE NEW TESTAMENT COMMENTARIES. (Lexham). Twelve vols. of exposition by TEDS professor emeritus Grant Osborne, completed shortly before his passing (†2018). The series is missing commentaries on Matthew, Mark, 1–2 Corinthians, the Pastorals, and the epistles of Peter, John, and Jude. The Hebrews vol. was completed in 2021 with the assistance of George Guthrie. No distractions here! Osborne sticks to the task of explaining the English text (with transliteration of all Greek references), and the vols. are remarkably clear and insightful. He rarely cites other scholars. [PL]

OOTD   AN OUTLINE OF OLD TESTAMENT DIALOGUE / *Das Alte Testament im Dialog.* (Peter Lang). I have yet to see any vols. in this newer series (but note Grossman on Ruth). It "intends to promote and stimulate the scientific dialogue between the Old Testament and its interrelated subjects." I frankly do not know what that means, but the Ruth contribution is said to be a fairly detailed literary commentary, taking up some philosophical and psychological topics. [PS?]

OTL   OLD TESTAMENT LIBRARY. ‡ (WJK). This important series used to contain mainly German works in ET and was born out of the Biblical Theology movement of the 1950s. Volumes reflect varying critical approaches and many are aging. New contributions are being added at a slow pace, and the series has become more American. A good example of this trend is Childs's *Isaiah* (2001) being added alongside the Kaiser–Westermann 3-vol. set (ET 1969–83). Some of the vols. are of real value if used with discernment. Conservatives would say they can be problematic if used as one's sole resource. This series contains other OT tools besides commentaries. The publisher is releasing both newer and older OTL vols. in pb, but they are not cheaper. E.g., Childs on Exodus in hb was earlier priced at $39.95, but the pb lists for $59.95. More positively, readers are glad the newer hb vols. have sturdy, sewn-down bindings. [PS]

OTM   OLD TESTAMENT MESSAGE. ‡ (Michael Glazier). See NTM above. [P]

Paideia   PAIDEIA COMMENTARIES ON THE NEW TESTAMENT. ‡ (Baker). Aimed at students, these exegetical commentaries are rapidly being released. The makeup of the editorial board indicates that this is a moderately critical series, similar to ANTC. (Some will not expect the "moderately critical" label on these Baker publications.) Talbert's vol., *Ephesians and Colossians* (2007), may be taken as a strong representative of Paideia, perhaps even as a model of these compact pb commentaries. Both Protestants and Catholics have been enlisted to contribute. My favorite so far is Oakes on Galatians. [P]

PCC   PAUL IN CRITICAL CONTEXTS. ‡ (Fortress). The publisher describes the series as offering "cutting-edge reexaminations of Paul through the lenses of power, gender, and ideology." [SP]

PentC   PENTECOSTAL COMMENTARY. (Deo Publishing; Brill). There are several releases, but I have only seen Fee's *Galatians* and Thomas (ed.), *The Book of the Twelve*. The series does not aim to serve the academy, and there is a modicum of interaction with scholarship. In 2023 I began to see vols. published by Brill. [P]

Pillar   PILLAR NEW TESTAMENT COMMENTARY. (Eerdmans). The vols. available are strongly evangelical, well-grounded in scholarship, insightful, and warmly recommended. The aim of Pillar is faithful exegesis moving toward biblical-theological reflection. Nearly half the series are top choices for pastors: Carson on John, Peterson on Acts, Campbell on Ephesians, Moo's *Colossians–Philemon* and *James*, and Davids on 2 Peter–Jude. The depth, format, and conservative stance of these works is similar to NICNT. That is to say, they leave the technical discussion of the original Greek text in the footnotes and concentrate on exegesis and evangelical theological reflection, rarely dealing directly with application. Carson's editorial work helps keep the standards high. [PS]

Pillar　PILLAR OLD TESTAMENT COMMENTARY. (Eerdmans). The same abbreviation (Pillar) is used for the forthcoming OT series, edited by Eric Tully. Based on reports I'm seeing, vols. may begin appearing in 2024, the contributions will emphasize exegeting the text to draw biblical-theological conclusions, and the books may not be quite as lengthy as the NT entries over the years. [PS]

Preach　THE PREACHER'S COMMENTARY. (Word/Nelson). See WCC below. The same series has also been released as Mastering the Old Testament/New Testament.

PTW　PREACHING THE WORD. (Crossway). A series of thoughtful expositions birthed by R. Kent Hughes of College Church, Wheaton, who wrote on most of the NT. Other contributors who share Hughes's warm-hearted Reformed theology are being enlisted. Philip Ryken has done Jeremiah–Lamentations and Exodus. Iain Duguid has produced a fine study of Numbers. See Hughes under Mark. Some of the vols. are exceedingly large. The series grew rapidly and is undergoing a revision to explain the ESV. Only 2 Kings, Chronicles, Ezekiel, and the Minor Prophets remain to be published. Cf. REC. [PL]

RBT　READING THE BIBLE TODAY (Aquila Press). I have not seen this series. [PL?]

RCS　REFORMATION COMMENTARY ON SCRIPTURE. (IVP Academic). Under general editor Timothy George, this set was conceived as a 28-vol. sequel to ACCS, and the first vol., *Galatians, Ephesians*, appeared in 2011. The OT section began in 2012 with *Ezekiel, Daniel*. The program is "the recovery of the robust spiritual theology and devotional treasures of the Reformation's engagement with the Bible" (General Introduction). I view RCS as valuable to preachers, Bible scholars interested in the history of interpretation, theologians, and laypeople. [PLS]

Read　READINGS: A NEW BIBLICAL COMMENTARY. ‡ (Sheffield Academic Press, now Sheffield Phoenix). Begun in 1987 and taking off in the 1990s, Readings had aims similar to Berit Olam above. (I was unsure of the series' status—still active?—but Moss on Proverbs appeared in 2015.) The editors and contributors meant to move beyond the older historical-critical methods (source, form, redaction criticism) and to study the final form of the text, using newer literary-critical and socio-rhetorical approaches. Though critical in several respects, these newer approaches sometimes read the text with more sympathy and respectfulness. See my comments on Conrad's *Zechariah* for further review of this series. Readings varies a great deal in length and depth of treatment: Miscall's Isaiah is 185pp., while the Meadowcroft *Haggai* vol. is 259pp. What confuses some is the similarity of this series to another one: OT Readings. [PS]

REC　REFORMED EXPOSITORY COMMENTARY. (P&R). Similar to PTW and a good help to preachers. REC has the following characteristics: homiletically oriented exposition, sticking close to the text; adherence to Reformed theology as outlined in the Westminster Standards; including a redemptive-historical approach; and a concern to apply the text's message to heart and daily life. The tendency here is to produce lengthy expositions, but not stodgy fare. I am enthusiastic about the series, because it is good for both mind and heart and it encourages growth in grace. (Wisdom and experience have often shown that graces are even more important than gifts in the ministry; a pastor's usefulness much depends upon character, spiritual insight, and Christlikeness.) Those working on REC include Phil Ryken, Dan Doriani, and Rick Phillips. [LP]

RNT　READING THE NEW TESTAMENT. ‡ (Crossroad, then Smyth & Helwys). Crossroad started RNT with vols. by the series editor, Baylor's conservatively critical Charles Talbert. An example is *Reading Luke* (1982). The approach is not verse-by-verse, but section-by-section (e.g., Acts 11:19–12:25). It displays interest in literary, sociohistorical, and theological questions. One of the best is Luke Timothy Johnson's *Reading Romans*. Smyth & Helwys is reissuing the vols. [P]

ROT      READING THE OLD TESTAMENT. ‡ (Smyth & Helwys). Vols. began appearing in 2011 in a series complementing RNT. The results have been mixed regarding its usefulness. See van Wijk-Bos on Samuel and Crenshaw on Job. [P]

RRA      RHETORIC OF RELIGIOUS ANTIQUITY. ‡? (Deo; now SBL). Means to provide "socio-rhetorical commentaries on the Bible and other ancient religious literature" (Deo website). One of the two main editors, V. K. Robbins, is a liberal practitioner of rhetorical criticism—see his influential book, *Exploring the Texture of Texts*—but some contracted authors are more conservative. See Jeal's *Exploring Philemon* for an example. Considering the size of Oropeza's work on 2 Corinthians, I see a major but slowly developing series ahead. [SP]

SacP     SACRA PAGINA. ‡ (Liturgical Press). A critical series on the NT produced by Catholics. Some entries in SacP are rigorous, large-scale studies, while others are less weighty. I confess I've not used these as much. They should be of greater interest to the Reformed student than the Reformed pastor. Most interesting or influential are probably Donahue–Harrington on Mark; Luke Timothy Johnson on Luke and Acts; Moloney on John; Byrne on Romans; Collins on 1 Corinthians; Matera on Galatians; and Richard on Thessalonians. This now-completed series is available in both pb and hb. [PS]

S&H      SMYTH & HELWYS BIBLE COMMENTARY. ‡ (Smyth & Helwys). An elegantly produced and moderately critical series of expositional commentaries on both Testaments. If the WJK Interpretation series is a Ford, this is a Lexus. Yes, S&H is expensive for what you get. The preacher will likely enjoy spending time with the visually stimulating vols.—they've included CDs—and appreciate their theological approach (though not always the theology, which ranges from left-wing evangelical to liberal). There is an abundance of maps, art (from the ANE to Chagall), pictures of ancient artifacts, and sidebars. Perhaps S&H aspires to redefine the commentary genre for our postmodern age (our "visual generation of believers"). A potential drawback is that readers may find the illustrations distracting and intrusive at points. Two of the first vols.—Fretheim on Jeremiah and Brueggemann on Kings—set a high standard that is generally not being met by the other contributors. Note to bibliophiles: S&H vols. have good paper and sturdy, sewn-down bindings. Because of the price tag, it's hard to recommend any but the very best in the series. [P]

SGBC     STORY OF GOD BIBLE COMMENTARY. (Zondervan). The publisher says the series "explains and illuminates each passage of Scripture in light of the Bible's grand story." Because the authors are learned scholars, and there is a focus on both the Bible's overall storyline (creation-fall-redemption-consummation) and application concerns (Living the Story), SGBC is proving popular with pastors and Bible study leaders. The intent of the publishers and general editors, Longman and McKnight, is to produce a very accessible series which, though not missing key details, keeps the big picture in view. Each passage is tackled in three sections: Listen to the Story, Explain the Story, and Live the Story. See McKnight's *Sermon on the Mount* and Cohick's *Philippians* for the initial releases in 2013. Since then the series has rapidly grown, covering about half the canon. [PL]

SRC      SOCIO-RHETORICAL COMMENTARY. (Eerdmans). I am a little uncertain about the nature of this project, for Witherington has been publishing many such commentaries, not only with Eerdmans but with IVP and others. SRC is composed of his Eerdmans releases, with a few other authors joining in; see Keener on Matthew and deSilva on Hebrews. [PS]

T@C      TEXTS @ CONTEXTS. ‡ (Fortress). Edited by two feminists, Athalya Brenner and Nicole Wilkinson Duran, these vols. each present essays by about twenty scholars on select texts in a couple of books, say, *Exodus and Deuteronomy*. It is not a comprehensive commentary. Authors are directed "to be responsibly non-objective and to represent only themselves on the biblical screen" (series preface). The faith commitments here are to "multivocality," radical reader-response interpretation, and "modifying traditional power hierarchies." I will not be noting these publications under individual Bible books. [S]

T&I    TEXT AND INTERPRETATION. ‡ (Eerdmans). A moderately critical series, practical in its aim but not all that successful. It died in the 1980s. [P]

TCB    THE CHURCH'S BIBLE. (Eerdmans). A set begun in 2004, with an intention similar to the Ancient Christian Commentary on the Scriptures (see ACCS above), but more ambitious in the amount of comment. Compared with ACCS, TCB has longer quotations and adds medieval thinkers. The first vol., *Song of Songs*, has the subtitle "Interpreted by Early Christian and Medieval Commentators" and is remarkably full at nearly 350pp. On a similar scale, how many vols. might be scheduled for Psalms? [SP]

THC    TWO HORIZONS COMMENTARY. [𝓜], (Eerdmans). Successful at blending and representing both biblical-exegetical and systematic-theological approaches to Scripture. For decades these have been viewed as divided and even in conflict. THC was introduced by a vol. of essays entitled *Between Two Horizons: Spanning NT Studies & Systematic Theology* (2000). Among excellent initial entries were Grogan on Psalms, Fowl on Philippians, and Green on 1 Peter; the series is nearing completion. The approach is more paragraph-by-paragraph than verse-by-verse. Because the series has a disciplined focus upon theological interpretation, which is where so many other series are weak, it is more valuable to preachers than its middling size might indicate. For an earlier attempt to bridge the gap between biblical scholarship and theology, see the SPCK series Biblical Foundations in Theology. [PS]

TNEBC    THROUGH NEW EYES BIBLICAL COMMENTARY. (Athanasius Press). Begun in 2007, the series "builds on the foundational Biblical-theology work of James B. Jordan and other like-minded scholars in bringing you a set of commentaries that will help you read, teach and preach through the Bible while picking up on the rich symphonic themes and the literary symbolism of the Scriptures" (publisher's description). See Leithart on Matthew for probably the best example. In my view, Jordan's work—e.g., on Judges—has serious shortcomings. [PL]

TNTC    TYNDALE NEW TESTAMENT COMMENTARIES. (Eerdmans/IVP). The set covers the NT in 20 vols. and could be a good first purchase for beginners. More advanced students will consider it useful as a quick reference. It is evangelical and is marked by attention to both text and message, broad coverage, and brief, apposite comments. Matters of critical scholarship are usually not discussed. Tyndale was long under revision; Kruse's vol. on John's Gospel (2004) completed that process for the so-called "second series" (1983–2004). More thorough revision work is being undertaken ("third series") under the editorial direction of Eckhard Schnabel. The newer editions are labeled TNTC-R. [PL]

TOTC    TYNDALE OLD TESTAMENT COMMENTARIES. (IVP). This thoroughly evangelical series is more even in quality than most, and D. J. Wiseman (†2010) deserves praise for his work as editor. "Pithy" is the best description for this set: brief, packed, often weighty exegetical comments rather than full exposition. The strongest vols. were written by Kidner, Wenham, Baldwin, and Hess. It was completed with the publication in the 1990s of long-awaited works on Joshua and Isaiah. Some are now fifty years old and need replacing (e.g., Exodus, Ezekiel). TOTC has been undergoing a thorough revision (see *Esther* by Reid, *Leviticus* by Sklar, *Psalms* by Longman), first under Martin Selman

(†2004), and then with David Firth as series editor. Buyer beware: some old vols. are being sold, say on Amazon, with inaccurate dates; for example, Taylor's 1969 *Ezekiel* is listed as 2016. [PL]

TOTE   THROUGH OLD TESTAMENT EYES. (Kregel). Treats the NT. Begun in 2017, the non-technical series puts a spotlight on the OT (and intertestamental) background of NT texts, OT quotations and allusions in the NT, literary and structural questions, theology, and life application. The intended audience is pastors and students. See Le Peau on Mark, Jobes on John, and Longman on Revelation. Given the specialized focus of the series, one might predict that it will serve more as a supplemental reference. [P]

TPI   TRINITY PRESS INTERNATIONAL NEW TESTAMENT COMMENTARY. ‡ (Trinity Press). The publisher took over the old Pelican series and commissioned new works, but not much happened. See WPC below. [PS]

TTC   TEACH THE TEXT COMMENTARY. (Baker). Sadly, the series was cancelled (2013–18). The editors, Mark Strauss and John Walton, succeeded in getting the series quickly off the ground with high standards. The structure of the commentary on the NIV had several parts: Big Idea, Key Themes, Understanding the Text, Teaching the Text (notes on how to communicate the message or themes), and Illustrating the Text (bridging the so-called two horizons). The program was to provide succinct (6-page), focused commentary on distinct pericopae, as defined by the scholar, distilling the best scholarship and helping preachers and teachers move on to explain the text's relevance. The series did not aim to break new ground with respect to scholarship but was attractive to busy pastors. Much effort was going into producing the vols. with full-color photos and maps. Perhaps the one drawback was that the series sets out to do so much in short compass—especially considering that Understanding the Text sections were divided further into four or five parts, and much space was taken up with illustrative material. The actual amount of commentary could be a bit limited. The more visually oriented one is, the more likely it is that one may regularly be distracted from reflecting on the actual commentary. See France on Luke and Bullock on Psalms for model TTC vols. [PL]

UBC   UNDERSTANDING THE BIBLE COMMENTARY SERIES. [𝔐], (Baker). The New International Biblical Commentary (see NIBC), once published by Hendrickson, was taken over by Baker and renamed. Since most of the copies in print are from NIBC, this guide continues to use the old abbreviation for older entries. Examining the latest entries, I think I detect a more critical orientation in UBC. Though the series foreword suggests an intention to pursue "vibrant biblical theology," these exegetical vols. (with some notable exceptions like *Kings* and *Deuteronomy*) tend not to have that emphasis. The editors are Robert Hubbard and Robert Johnston. [P]

UBS   UNITED BIBLE SOCIETIES: HANDBOOK SERIES. (UBS). Designed for Bible transla-tors working around the globe; the chief aim of UBS is lucidity in the receptor language. Some of these vols. can be useful to pastors who seek to understand the meaning of the original text and explain clearly the nuances of grammar and vocabulary to their congregations. Don't go looking for theology. UBS has some first-rate scholars working on this series, e.g., Ellingworth on 1 Corinthians. Normally I note these without comment. [PS]

WBC   WORD BIBLICAL COMMENTARY. [𝔐], (Word, then Nelson, now Zondervan). Valuable for its good textual work, new translations, and exegesis. At points one could wish that the contributors and editors placed greater emphasis on theological reflection. This significant series excites and frustrates at the same time. One frustration is that insightful comment on a text can be distributed across three different sections. Some have expressed surprise that many contributors to this evangelical series are, in fact, moderates. Be cautioned against buying on the basis of that label, because some, even by the most charitable estimate, do not fit into that category (e.g., note the participation of the brilliant Catholic critic, Roland Murphy, and the discussion in *ExpTim* 101, p.184). At the same time, I must say that there are numerous strong contributions to the set which can be considered top picks you would do well to add to your library. The NT series is a little more successful than the OT. For the pastor some vols. are more accessible (Leviticus, Hebrews), and some less (Ruth/Esther, Revelation). WBC is nearing completion with sixty or so available vols.—we await *1 Corinthians*—and under revision. These commentaries are a boon to students of the original languages. We are grateful that the series, under Zondervan, exchanged in-text citation for footnotes. The editors are now Nancy deClaissé-Walford (OT) and David Capes (NT). [PS]

WCC    WORD COMMUNICATOR'S COMMENTARY. (Word). This easy to read homiletical series is a mixed bag, both in regard to quality and theological stance (broadly evangelical and generally more conservative than WBC, its scholarly counterpart). WCC was completed in the early 1990s and has some good contributions (e.g., Allen on Chronicles, Stuart on Ezekiel) and some dogs (more in the NT). Usually you can ignore WCC. I note the better vols. under individual books. The series was reissued in pb by Nelson under the titles Mastering the OT and Mastering the NT. Then in the late 1990s it was again renamed as The Preacher's Commentary. Despite name and cover changes, the contents remain the same. [PL]

WEC    WYCLIFFE EXEGETICAL COMMENTARY. (Moody Press). Begun in the late 1980s, WEC looked to be a success but was killed by the publisher. The NT portion was taken over by Baker (see BECNT above). The few vols. published in WEC were solid and evangelical (e.g., Silva's *Philippians*). They provided scholarly exegesis of the Hebrew or Greek text. The OT vols. in WEC went o/p but were reprinted in pb by Biblical Studies Press (e.g., Harrison on Numbers). [PS]

Welwyn    WELWYN COMMENTARY SERIES. (Evangelical Press). Popular-level, edifying expositions for the pastor or Sunday School teacher. The comments are perceptive and simple without being obvious. This British series now covers most Bible books. P&R is the North American distributor, which tells you its Reformed orientation. I will not often comment on these. [PL]

Wesley    WESLEYAN BIBLE STUDY NEW TESTAMENT COMMENTARY. (Wesleyan Church). Though this 15-vol. set does not probe deeply, it is a useful guide for pastors seeking a reliably Wesleyan–Arminian interpretation of the Scriptures. There is also an OT set. I will not note these commentaries below. [PL]

WestBC    WESTMINSTER BIBLE COMPANION. ‡ (WJK). The Presbyterian publisher means this series to "assist laity in their study of the Bible as a guide to Christian faith and practice. Each volume explains the biblical book in its original historical context and explores its significance for faithful living today." The flavor of WestBC is somewhere between commentary and study guide, and it resembles BST in some respects. These theological expositions are based on the NRSV, and better entries serve the discerning pastor in sermon preparation. Because of the critical orientation, WestBC is not broadly recommended to Bible study groups in evangelical churches. For disparate representatives, see Peterson on Samuel and Brueggemann on Isaiah. [PL]

Wiley    WILEY BLACKWELL BIBLE COMMENTARIES. ‡ (Wiley Blackwell). The old Blackwell Bible Commentaries has been renamed, but I am continuing, for now, to use the old abbreviation, BBC. [PS]

Wisdom    WISDOM COMMENTARY. ‡ (Liturgical Press). Begun in 2015, and subtitled "A

Feminist Commentary on the Old and New Testaments." The planned 60-vol. series takes more of a "final form" literary approach, with heavy doses of ideological and feminist criticism of the text. Emancipation from androcentric and patriarchal language is only the start. [PS]

WPC   WESTMINSTER PELICAN COMMENTARY. ‡ (Westminster). This series was taken over by SCM Press in Britain and Trinity Press in North America. See TPI above. WPC included some of the old Penguin Commentaries. It was moderately to very critical, uneven, and rather undistinguished. I won't mention these under individual books, except J. P. Sweet on Revelation. [P]

ZCINT  ZONDERVAN CRITICAL INTRODUCTIONS TO THE NEW TESTAMENT. (Zondervan). Compared with ZECOT and ZECNT, more critically oriented in its subject matter and tone. The series is edited by Michael Bird and saw its first publication in 2019 with Nijay Gupta's *1 & 2 Thessalonians* (300pp.). These are not commentaries but large-scale introductions to Bible books, treating more fully the scholarly debates about the text, authorship, date, social and historical setting, etc. [SP]

ZECNT  ZONDERVAN EXEGETICAL COMMENTARY ON THE NEW TESTAMENT. (Zondervan). A conservative series, edited by Clinton Arnold, that looked promising from the start and uncommonly accessible for a commentary on the Greek. As indicated in the first vol. by Blomberg–Kamell on James (2008), ZECNT aimed to glean the best fruit from scholarly discussions, while remaining focused on close exegesis of the text. It does not try to treat all the secondary literature. Probably the feature that sets the series apart is its Translation in Graphic Layout (reflecting discourse analysis), where it "presents a translation through a diagram that helps readers visualize the flow of thought within the text" (publisher's description). Readers also find an abundance of structural outlines. There is some attention given to biblical-theological reflection and questions of contemporary relevance. ZECNT has developed quickly and is well-conceived and executed as an exegetical tool for ministers. Though some vols. are very large, it is not a heavyweight academic series such as ICC, NIGTC, WBC, and BECNT. I venture my opinion that the discourse analysis aspect is more illuminating with epistolary than narrative literature. [PS]

ZECOT  ZONDERVAN EXEGETICAL COMMENTARY ON THE OLD TESTAMENT. (Zondervan). Begun in 2013 as Hearing the Message of Scripture (see HMS), the series was retitled and reformatted to complement ZECNT. The two HMS vols. (Obadiah and Jonah) were reissued with the new cover. The subtitle of ZECOT is "A Discourse Analysis of the Hebrew Bible." It aims to uncover the theological "message intended by the author" (series preface) by close analysis of the Hebrew text and grammar issues, and especially by discourse analysis and rhetorical criticism. Like ZECNT, the series includes a graphical display of the flow of thought, or discourse structure, of each passage. It asks what the principal theological points are, and how the Bible writers make those points. Preachers will appreciate how the contributors also briefly treat questions of the Scriptures' contemporary relevance. For excellent representatives, see Sklar's *Leviticus*, Block's *Ruth*, and Boda–Conway on *Judges*. The series is growing rapidly and continues to deliver the quality I saw in early entries. It has become a favorite of mine. [PS]

ZIBBC  ZONDERVAN ILLUSTRATED BIBLE BACKGROUNDS COMMENTARY. (Zondervan). There are two sets here, the first on the NT in four vols. (2002) and the second on the OT in five vols. (2009). The series successfully uses a conservatively oriented comparative studies approach to illustrate the literary, historical, religious, cultural, and material background of the Bible. ZIBBC is beautifully produced with color photos on most pages, engaging, and instructive. Of course it is not meant to be a well-rounded commentary, but what it sets out to accomplish it does well. Gordon calls it "a major achievement." For whom is the series best suited? While it often points scholars to materials or information with which they may not be familiar, I believe pastors are the group best served. I will not be noting individual book treatments below. Note, too, that these sets are more useful than the less ambitious, older *IVP Bible Background Commentary* in two vols. A few of the contributions (Genesis, Psalms, Isaiah) have been published separately. [*BBR* 20.4; *VT* 61.3 (Gordon); *ANES* 48]. [PS]

# OLD TESTAMENT COMMENTARIES

## PENTATEUCHAL STUDIES

★ Alexander, T. Desmond. *From Paradise to the Promised Land*, 4th ed. 2022. Helpful as a theologically sensitive content survey. There is a lengthy, up-to-date evangelical assessment of the old Documentary Hypothesis and recent critiques. The main value, however, is the tracing of pentateuchal theological themes which will be developed in subsequent Scripture (OT and NT). For another, fuller content survey, see Hamilton. [3rd ed.: *BBR* 22.4; *JSOT* 37.5; *ExpTim* 10/14; *JESOT* 2.1; *TJ* Fall 14; 4th ed.: *JBTS* 8/23].

★ Alexander, T. Desmond, and David W. Baker, eds. *Dictionary of the OT: Pentateuch*, 2002. Invaluable for students. [*Them* Sum 04; *EvQ* 4/05; *CurTM* 10/05; *Anvil* 21.1].

★ Wenham, Gordon J. *Exploring the OT, Volume One: A Guide to the Pentateuch*, 2003. There is probably no better, more lucid, and accessible introduction to the Pentateuch for the beginning student (207pp.). More advanced students might skip this purchase. [*EvQ* 4/05; *JETS* 9/05; *RelSRev* 1/06; *CurTM* 6/05].

☆ Alter, Robert. ‡ *The Five Books of Moses: A Translation with Commentary*, 2004. See Genesis. [*BL* 2005].

✓ Anderson, Bradford A. ‡ *An Introduction to the Study of the Pentateuch*, 2nd ed. 2017. From T&T Clark, one of the better short treatments from a critic. [*JSOT* 42.5; *ETL* 94.1].

✓ Arnold, Bill T., ed. ‡ *The Cambridge Companion to Genesis*, 2022.

✓ Baden, Joel S. ‡ *The Composition of the Pentateuch: Renewing the Documentary Hypothesis*, 2012. In the ABRL series. [*JSOT* 39.5; *BL* 2015; *JHebS* 12].

✓ Baden, Joel S., and Jeffrey Stackert, eds. ‡ *The Oxford Handbook of the Pentateuch*, 2021.

✓ Blenkinsopp, Joseph. ‡ *The Pentateuch: An Introduction to the First Five Books of the Bible* (ABRL) 1992. Added to this is *Treasures Old and New: Essays in the Theology of the Pentateuch* (2007) [*BSac* 10/07; *JAOS* 126.4; *CJ* 10/06]. Keep in mind that the 1992 vol. was replaced by Baden (above), who surprisingly returns to something like the classic Documentary Hypothesis; also pursuing a Neo-Documentarian approach is Jeffrey Stackert, *A Prophet Like Moses* (OUP, 2014) [*BibInt* 25.1; *ETL* 91.4].

✓ Briggs, Richard S., and Joel N. Lohr, eds. [𝓜], *A Theological Introduction to the Pentateuch: Interpreting the Torah as Christian Scripture*, 2012. A FS for Moberly.

✓ Campbell, Antony, and Mark O'Brien. ‡ *Sources of the Pentateuch: Texts, Introductions, Annotations*, 1993. Following this is *Rethinking the Pentateuch: Prolegomena to the Theology of Ancient Israel* (2005). Both authors pursue and promote (with vigor) more traditional source criticism. By contrast, many evangelicals (Wenham) and critics (Whybray) believe source criticism has had poor returns for a long time.

✓ Clines, David J. A. ‡ *The Theme of the Pentateuch*, 1978, 2nd ed. 1996. A much cited study proposing partial fulfillment (and non-fulfillment) of the promises as the main theme.

✓ Crüsemann, Frank. ‡ *The Torah: Theology and Social History of OT Law*, 1996.

✓ Dozeman, Thomas B. ‡ *The Pentateuch: Introducing the Torah* (IIS) 2017. Rather more ambitious than "introducing" (over 700pp.), the author offers an astute, impressive textbook that is fully abreast of critical scholarship. [*JSOT* 42.5; *ETL* 94.1].

✓ Dozeman, Thomas, and Konrad Schmid, eds. ‡ *A Farewell to the Yahwist? The Composition of the Pentateuch in Recent European Interpretation*, 2006 [*JSS* Spr 09]. The follow-up is *The Pentateuch: International Perspectives on Current Research* (2011) [*JSS* Aut 14; *JSOT* 36.5; *ETL* 88.1].

✓ Fretheim, Terence E. ‡ (IBT) 1996. An excellent introductory guide into the Pentateuch from a moderately critical perspective. [*RelSRev* 7/98].

✓ Gertz, Jan C., Bernard M. Levinson, et al., eds. ‡ *The Formation of the Pentateuch: Bridging the Academic Cultures of Europe, Israel, and North America*, 2016. A gargantuan vol. dealing with compositional issues. [*BBR* 28.2; *JTS* 10/18; *Int* 10/19; *ETL* 94.1; *Them* 43.1].

☆ Hamilton, Victor P. *Handbook on the Pentateuch*, 1982, 2nd ed. 2005. A solid content survey, which has often seen use as a textbook.

☆ Kitchen, Kenneth A. *On the Reliability of the Old Testament*, 2003. A strong (the critics would say "strident") challenge to higher-critical skepticism about the Bible's historical worth. There is a massive amount of detail and learning here, especially ANE inscriptional and archaeological evidence. Wenham [*Anvil* 23.2] says "anyone who reads it will be bowled over by the breadth and depth of Kitchen's encyclopaedic knowledge," and he expresses hope that this "work will preserve another generation of theological students from losing faith in Scripture." [*JSOT* 27.5; *BSac* 4/05; *CTJ* 11/04; *CBQ* 7/07; *JETS* 3/05; *Them* Sum 05; *DenvJ* 5/04 (Hess); *HS* 2005; *JAOS* 124.2 (harsh); *VT* 56.2; *ExpTim* 11/04; *RTR* 4/05; *Presb* Fall 06; *RB* 4/05; *BASOR* 8/05; *CJ* 1/06]. On the dating of Deuteronomy, see also the 3–vol. Kitchen–Lawrence, *Treaty, Law and Covenant in the ANE* (2012) [*BASOR* 11/14 (Beckman)], which argues for close similarity to 2nd millennium Hittite treaties.

✓ Knight, Douglas. ‡ "The Pentateuch" (263–96) in *The Hebrew Bible and Its Modern Interpreters*, eds. Douglas Knight and Gene Tucker, 1985.

✓ Knoppers, Gary N., and Bernard M. Levinson, eds. ‡ *The Pentateuch as Torah: New Models for Understanding Its Promulgation and Acceptance*, 2007. A collection of studies by world-leading scholars, presented at an international SBL meeting, heavily revised, and reflecting the movement of scholarship toward a later dating of the pentateuchal materials and their compilation. [*BBR* 19.2; *VT* 59.2; *JHebS* 2009].

✓ Lohfink, Norbert. ‡ *Theology of the Pentateuch: Themes of the Priestly Narrative and Deuteronomy*, ET 1994.

✓ Mann, Thomas W. ‡ *The Book of the Torah: The Narrative Integrity of the Pentateuch*, 1988, 2nd ed. 2013. [*JSOT* 38.5].

✓ Moberly, R. W. L. ‡ *The Old Testament of the Old Testament*, 2001. A fascinating narratological-canonical reading and new proposal for the crux in Exodus 3 and the revelation of the divine name.

✓ Nicholson, E. W. ‡ *The Pentateuch in the Twentieth Century*, 1998. [*JBL* Sum 01].

✓ Nihan, Christophe, and Julia Rhyder, eds. ‡ *Text and Ritual in the Pentateuch*, 2021. Ritual studies are a "growth industry" today, and this vol. builds on sociological research (e.g., Catherine Bell's famous *Ritual Theory, Ritual Practice*, 2009). [*VT* 72.1; *Them* 47.2].

✓ Noth, Martin. ‡ *A History of Pentateuchal Traditions*, 1948, ET 1972.

☆ Poythress, Vern S. *The Shadow of Christ in the Law of Moses*, 1991.

✓ Rad, Gerhard von. ‡ *The Problem of the Hexateuch and Other Essays*, 1938, ET 1966.

✓ Rendtorff, Rolf. ‡ *The Problem of the Process of Transmission in the Pentateuch*, 1977, ET 1990.

✓ Rofé, A. ‡ *Introduction to the Composition of the Pentateuch*, 1999. A modification of the classic Wellhausen position.

✓ Sailhamer, John. *The Meaning of the Pentateuch: Revelation, Composition and Interpretation*, 2009. Evangelical scholarship on the canonical form, building upon *The Pentateuch as Narrative* (1992). [*BL* 2010; *BBR* 21.1; *VT* 61.4; *JETS* 12/10; *SBJT* 14.2; *Them* 11/10, 5/11; *BSac* 1/12; *BTB* 2/12].

✓ Schmid, Konrad. ‡ *The Scribes of the Torah: The Formation of the Pentateuch in Its Literary and Historical Contexts*, 2023. An enormous collection of essays from the eminent Zurich professor. Earlier he published *Genesis and the Moses Story: Israel's Dual Origins in the Hebrew Bible* (ET 2010), which was important for following continental European developments in Pentateuch scholarship [*JBL* 119.2; *JSOT* 35.5; *VT* 62.3; *RBL* 2011].

☆ Schnittjer, Gary. *The Torah Story*, 2005, 2nd ed. 2023. Wonderfully engaging textbook. Does a lot of things well: surveying Bible content, books' literary/rhetorical strategies, links to other biblical material (OT and NT). The author's fascination with biblical allusions (more diachronic version of intertextual studies) is also reflected in his huge *Old Testament Use of Old Testament* (2021) [*WTJ* Fall 22].

✓ Ska, Jean-Louis. ‡ *Introduction to Reading the Pentateuch*, ET 2006. Carr perhaps overdoes it in saying, "This book is now the best starting point for an introduction to past and present study of the formation of the Pentateuch." [*RBL*].

✓ Sparks, Kent. (IBR bibliography) 2002. [*RelSRev* 7/03; *EvQ* 1/05; *BBR* 15.1; *TJ* Spr 05].

✓ Sweeney, Marvin A. ‡ *The Pentateuch*, 2017. A brief introduction by a leading critic. [*JSOT* 47.5].

✓ Van Seters, John. ‡ *The Pentateuch: A Social-Science Commentary*, 1999, 2nd ed. 2015. [*JBL* Fall 01; *JSOT* 42.5]. Earlier vols. on the Pentateuch were: *Abraham in History and Tradition* (1975); *Prologue to History: The Yahwist as Historian in Genesis* (1992); and *The Life of Moses: The Yahwist as Historian in Exodus–Numbers* (1994). Summarizing much of his work is *The Yahwist: A Historian of Israelite Origins* (2013) [*CBQ* 1/15; *JSOT* 38.5; *JHebS* 14], where he defends a revised Documentary Hypothesis that places J in the exilic period as a "prologue" to an already existing DtrH.

☆ Vogt, Peter T. *Interpreting the Pentateuch: An Exegetical Handbook* (Kregel) 2009. Packs much useful learning and counsel into a brief guide (214pp.). [*JSOT* 37.5].

✓ Watts, J. W. ‡ *Reading Law: The Rhetorical Shaping of the Pentateuch*, 1999.

✓ Watts, James W., ed. ‡ *Persia and Torah: The Theory of Imperial Authorization of the Pentateuch* (2001). Reflects how scholarship is pushing the date of the Pentateuch later. So now we get books that never would have been written 60 years ago: Richard Wright, *Linguistic Evidence for the Pre-exilic Date of the Yahwistic Source* (2005).

☆ Wenham, Gordon J. "Pondering the Pentateuch: The Search for a New Paradigm" (116–44) in *The Face of OT Studies*, eds. Baker and Arnold, 1999.

☆ Wenham, Gordon J. *Story as Torah: Reading OT Narrative Ethically*, 2000. I have found no wiser guide to the complicated topic in the subtitle. The book, though focused mainly on Genesis, can inform one's reading of all OT narratives. [*Anvil* 19.1 (Moberly)]. For other important vols. on OT Law and ethics, see the Decalogue section below.

✓ Whybray, R. N. ‡ *Introduction to the Pentateuch*, 1995. Also important in the discussion is his earlier book, *The Making of the Pentateuch: A Methodological Study* (1987).

✓ Wolf, Herbert. *An Introduction to the Old Testament Pentateuch*, 1991.

✓ Wynn-Williams, D. J. ‡ *The State of the Pentateuch*, 1997.

# GENESIS

★ Calvin, John. (GS) 1554. I believe it is one of Calvin's three or four best commentaries. To save money, please see Calvin under Commentary Series. In an edited version, this has been included in the CrossC series (2001) [*JSOT* 27.5]. Banner has published two vols. of *Calvin's Sermons on Genesis*, up through chapter 20, in a superb ET by Rob Roy McGregor (2009–12) [*Chm* Sum 14; *RTR* 12/12].

★ **Goldingay, John.** [𝓜], (BCOT) 2020. Brief introduction and then 725pp. of lucid, mainly theological commentary. As discerning readers of his many books are aware, Goldingay has broadly evangelical sensitivities and also higher-critical commitments. Some take him to be more liberal than he is; some take him to be more conservative than he really is. His inclination here is to sidestep the question of whether the "author was seeking to write history or fiction" (5). He delineates sources (114f, 138) and supports the standard critical dating of the final form to the postexilic era, while asserting "we know virtually nothing about how Genesis came into existence" (9). But he certainly has a keen eye for theology, interpreting the text "as it stands." What I write about "double-tracking" in Goldingay's *Daniel* applies here too. His newer commentaries (e.g., *Psalms* in BCOT, *Jeremiah* in NICOT), as compared with his WBC on Daniel and ICC on Isaiah 40–66, interact with less scholarship, are less attentive to technical exegetical details, and emphasize theological exposition. (He regularly cites the church fathers [e.g., Chrysostom over 40×], the Reformers, and the rabbis [Rashi, Ibn Ezra, Qimchi, etc.].) Sometimes his translation work is unsettling and idiosyncratic—raising eyebrows among scholars—but his books are always stimulating and a good read. See Goldingay on 15:17–21 for an example of how helpful he is to expositors. More negatively, he throws in such comments as "Adam's and Eve's rebellion did not change individual human makeup, but it did fatally change the environment in which all human beings would now be born" (85). Is sin, then, merely a social contagion? [*ExpTim* 7/21; *BL* 2022; *CTJ* 4/22; *CBQ* 10/21; *JETS* 6/22; *Them* 46.1].

★ **Hamilton, Victor P.** (NICOT) 2 vols., 1989–95. Solid, dependable scholarship which can be heartily recommended. Though Wenham is more incisive, the pastor will not go wrong purchasing this as an exegetical work. Gives good attention to the exegetical details of Genesis, especially philology, semantics, and syntax. Hamilton may perhaps be faulted for giving us a better view of the trees than the forest. This is a seriously academic evangelical work, and I predict that some pastors might prefer Mathews's more accessible, less expensive commentary. [*HS* 1992, 1997; *CBQ* 1/93, 7/97; *Them* 10/93, 10/96; *ExpTim* 3/96; *EvQ* 10/98; *JETS* 6/99; *JSS* Spr 98; *RTR* 8/98; *SwJT* Spr 98]. Students should also note his well-written survey, *Handbook on the Pentateuch* (1982, 2nd ed. 2005).

★ **Mathews, Kenneth.** (NAC) 2 vols., 1996–2005; (CSC) 2nd ed. 2023–. Conservative reviewers were pleased. The 1st ed. was full (1450pp.), not quite as in-depth academically as Hamilton or Wenham, and was more accessible. Mathews gives a dependable, balanced interpretation that pastors will appreciate. This NAC might have been slightly less valuable to the student than, say, Hamilton and Wenham among evangelical works; at the same time it had a more current bibliography. Mathews was about the best in the series, and I admired his exegetical good sense. The 2nd edition (only the first vol. released as yet) is a welcome update and, in my opinion, now considerably more useful than before. Evangelical pastors would be wise to make this a top choice. [*EvQ* 10/98; *Them* 1/97; *JETS* 6/99, 3/06, 3/09; *SwJT* Fall 97, Fall 05; *HS* 1997; *CBQ* 4/06; *BSac* 7/06; 2023: *Them* 49.1].

★ Ross, Allen P. *Creation and Blessing*, 1988. A good book that has always had a spot on the purchase list. Like Aalders it is strong on theological exposition with many insights for the pastor, but is less useful to students. The work is quite lengthy at 750pp. and was released in hb and pb. Ross once taught at Dallas Seminary, then at (conservative) Trinity Episcopal School, then Beeson. See Ross's CorBC below. [*JETS* 6/90; *ATJ* 22]. Students who pass over Ross and Walton are urged to consider Collins's *Reading Genesis Well*; see below.

★ Walton, John H. (NIVAC) 2001. One of the best in the series. Richer on chs. 1–22 than 23–50.

Pastors love the guidance provided by Walton and by Ross. The author has also published vols. on ancient cosmology and the interpretation of the Creation account in our scientific age: the more technical *Genesis 1 as Ancient Cosmology* (2011) [*BBR* 22.3; *CBQ* 10/12; *JTS* 4/15; *JSS* Spr 13 (Hendel); *JSOT* 36.5; *VT* 64.2; *JETS* 6/13; *JHebS* 12]—written first, actually—and, more popularly, *The Lost World of Genesis One* (2009) [*BBR* 20.3 (Hess); *Them* 11/09; *RevExp* Spr 10; *BSac* 7/11; *SBET* Aut 11]. His conclusions seem to me to overreach; he contends that Genesis 1 concerns the functions of the created order, not the creation of matter, the substance of the universe. But why set up a kind of antithesis/dichotomy between function and the material? I find both concerns in the ANE literature, in Genesis too. He also presents the idea (depending on other OT texts) of a cosmic temple. More recent is *The Lost World of Adam and Eve* (2015) [*Them* 8/15; *CTJ* 4/16; *JSOT* 40.5], which suggests not all humanity descend from Adam and Eve.

★ **Wenham, Gordon J.** (WBC) 2 vols., 1987–94. My main exegetical reference, with about 900pp. including the introductions. This is simply one of the best evangelical biblical commentaries available on any book, treating every facet of the book's interpretation. Some conservatives would consider him a bit too conciliatory toward critical theories about multiple sources and Genesis 1–11 as "an inspired retelling of ancient oriental traditions about the origins of the world" (liii), but I'm glad he faces those issues head-on. He uses some newer literary criticism to good effect (undercutting source critical divisions) and makes helpful comments on the structure of different narratives (e.g., the flood). The theology is sound. The treatment of the Hebrew is expert. [*RTR* 5/88; *Them* 4/89; *TJ* Fall 88; *JETS* 6/97; *JSS* Spr 98; *VT* 38.2, 47.4; *BSac* 10/96; *HS* 1988; *CRBR* 1990]. See also the brief *Rethinking Genesis 1–11* (2015) [*BBR* 25.4].

☆ Aalders, G. C. (BSC) 2 vols., ET 1981. In early editions I recommended this thorough (610pp.), insightful exposition for purchase. Its strengths lie in biblical-theological comment, which is precisely where so many academic works are weak. Aalders presents a Reformed, covenantal perspective and is unquestionably orthodox. However, you will likely have difficulty obtaining this—it has been o/p for years. The Dutch original is probably the 1974 5th ed. [*HS* 1983].

F  Alexander, Desmond. (EBTC)?

✓ **Alter, Robert.** ‡ 1996. Particularly valuable for its fine, fresh translation. This Jewish scholar is known for helping spark today's strong interest in rereading Scripture from the literary angle. He rarely fails to supply fresh insights. Anyone who dips into this work will soon see how valuable and even entertaining it is. The same is true of other works of his; I get amused every time I recall his explanation of the ironies lodged in the story of Balaam and his ass (*Art of Biblical Narrative*, 1981). This vol. on Genesis is taken up into his 2004 book, *The Five Books of Moses*. See under Pentateuch above.

☆ **Arnold, Bill T.** [*M*], (NCBC) 2008. The author is in the evangelical camp—this is not a typical commentary in this mainstream critical series—yet his work is praised highly by liberal scholars like Brueggemann. Arnold is also an editor of NCBC. Here he builds on his upper-level college textbook, *Encountering the Book of Genesis* (1998), and produces an attractive, up-to-date, more exegetical work on Genesis. One of his intentions is to combine diachronic and synchronic interpretation. [*CBQ* 1/10; *BL* 2010; *BBR* 20.2; *BSac* 7/11]. By the way, the *Encountering* book is a most inviting survey, with its well-written, well-researched text, accompanied by teaching material (stated aims, study questions, etc.), many pictures and maps, and brief discussion of authorship and scholarly methods of interpretation. *Encountering* would be useful to the pastor in planning an adult Sunday School class. It was a textbook when I taught a college course on Genesis twenty years ago [*RevExp* Sum 00].

✓ Arnold, Bill T., ed. ‡ *The Cambridge Companion to Genesis*, 2022. [*CBQ* 4/23].

☆ Atkinson, David. *Genesis 1–11* (BST) 1990. Good devotional exposition; well grounded in its scholarship. Many pastors are drawn to the Atkinson and Baldwin set. [*Chm* 107.1].

F Averbeck, Richard E. (Pillar) 2024? Expected to be the inaugural vol.

F Baker, David W. (Apollos). Baker serves as coeditor of this series.

☆ **Baker, David W., with Jason Riley.** *Genesis 37–50* (BHHB) 2014. See Bandstra for the initial Genesis vol. Baker is a top-notch scholar. These 500pp. are a fine guide through the well-crafted Joseph narrative, often chosen by Hebrew teachers as a text for intermediate students. [*JSOT* 39.5].

☆ Baldwin, Joyce. *Genesis 12–50* (BST) 1986. The usual, solid work from the prolific evangelical scholar. This book is a bit better than Atkinson and is warmly recommended for preachers. [*EvQ* 1/88].

☆ **Bandstra, Barry L.** *Genesis 1–11* (BHHB) 2008. Quite full (629pp.) and helpful as a tool for students reading the Hebrew narrative. Bandstra has critical sympathies, but, because of the nature of the work, there is nothing of historical criticism to be found here. Be aware that he takes a different linguistic tack: functional grammar. One needs to read and digest the 40-page introduction that explains the approach in order to make out what he's doing. So, this book offers a lot; you can learn a new method of analyzing the grammar and syntax, as well as being guided through the Hebrew. Bandstra's Yale PhD was on Hebrew syntax. [*VT* 59.1].

Belcher, Richard P., Jr. (Focus) 2012. Have not seen it for review purposes.

✓ Bergant, Dianne. ‡ *Genesis: In the Beginning*, 2013. From a more literary-critical and moderate angle, this is very well-written. [*CBQ* 4/15; *Int* 10/15].

✓ Blenkinsopp, Joseph. ‡ *Creation, Un-Creation, Re-Creation: A Discursive Commentary on Genesis 1–11*, 2011. [*CBQ* 10/12; *JSS* Spr 14; *JSOT* 36.5; *VT* 62.2; *ExpTim* 10/12; *JHebS* 14]. His follow-up was *Abraham: The Story of a Life* (2015) [*JTS* 10/16; *JETS* 12/15; *Int* 7/17; *JSOT* 40.5; *ETL* 93.1].

☆ **Blocher, Henri.** [𝓜], *In the Beginning*, ET 1984. An important monograph on the initial three chapters by a Reformed scholar (240pp.). Covers a very broad range of issues in an incisive, capable manner. I used to include this among the recommended purchases for Genesis. [*Evangel* Sum 85; *EvQ* 7/86; *Them* 5/85]. Cf. Collins, Kelly, Walton (2009), and the arguments for an old-earth, special-creation-of-Adam position in *Seven Days that Divide the World* (2011), by John Lennox, Professor of Mathematics at Oxford [*JETS* 6/12; *Them* 11/12; *TJ* Spr 12]. Note Andrew J. Brown's twin books: *The Days of Creation: A History of Christian Interpretation of Genesis 1:1–2:3* (2014) [*JESOT* 4.1; *BBR* 26.4; *JSOT* 45.5] and *Recruiting the Ancients for the Creation Debate* (2023). See too Kyle R. Greenwood, ed., *Interpreting Genesis 1 and 2 through the Ages* (2018) [*CTJ* 4/20]. Note also Watkin (below).

Boice, James Montgomery. 3 vols., 1982–87. Boice pastored historic Tenth Presbyterian in Philadelphia (1968–2000). Many will find this exposition homiletically suggestive, but it should be checked against a scholarly commentary. I have found that Boice's expositions are better on the NT, which makes sense since his ThD from Basel was in NT. Note: I think he misinterprets ch. 23. [*JETS* 3/87].

Brichto, Herbert Chanan. ‡ *The Names of God: Poetic Readings in Biblical Beginnings*, 1998. Contains insights into the Genesis narratives.

Briscoe, D. Stuart. (WCC) 1987. Definitely one of the better vols. in the series, but not researched very deeply—check his bibliography. (Like Boice he fails to see through all the courtesies and recognize the price gouging in ch. 23 and the irony of Abraham's victimization in the light of the land promise.)

✓ **Brodie, Thomas L.** ‡ *Genesis as Dialogue: A Literary, Historical and Theological Commentary*,

2001. This Oxford work is elegantly written, over 500pp. long, and argues for unity and coherence in the book. Compare this literary reading with Alter, Waltke–Fredricks, and Cotter. [*CBQ* 10/04; *VT* 53.4; *BSac* 10/05; *JSOT* 99; *RelSRev* 10/02].

☆ **Brueggemann, Walter.** ‡ (I) 1982. His works can be serviceable for evangelicals because he treats the final form of the text (canonical approach) and has great interest in theology. Very stimulating, for the author uses clear, powerful, provocative prose to unsettle Bible readers who might settle for safe, conventional (Western, pious, upper-middle class) interpretations. He wants to draw you into what he has termed "a dangerous conversation." Read with discernment; there's an agenda which is based in part on the influence of Gottwald's sociological approach. He also shows a postmodern discomfort with absolute truth claims. In my early editions I made this a recommended purchase. [*TJ* Spr 83; *JBL* 104.1; *Int* 7/83].

F   Brueggemann, Walter. ‡ (FE) 2 vols.

Bush, George. 2 vols., 1852. Has repeatedly been reprinted. Spurgeon blasts this scholar as about the most blatant plagiarizer he's ever met up with, and he calls this work a "wholesale plunder" of Andrew Fuller and George Lawson.

Candlish, Robert S. 1869. Spurgeon's favorite—that's high praise! Strongly Reformed, theological, and lengthy. Can be quite profitable if the preacher perseveres in reading through some lengthy lectures.

✓ **Carr, David M.** ‡ *Genesis 1–11* (IECOT) 2021. An important publication, made stronger by the contributions of Erhard Blum (originally a coauthor), and classed as cutting-edge. Some will wish he had not agreed when urged to include postmodern and ideological readings (e.g., queer, postcolonial). There is an abundance of reference to ANE background materials. The notes on the Hebrew text and text criticism are excellent. Carr revives certain aspects of Wellhausen's construal of sources (P and an earlier non-P). One key interpretive move is that "Eden as a story of original sin is grounded in part on a retrospective reading of YHWH's absolute judgment on human evil at the onset of the flood (Gen 6:5–7) back into Gen 2–3." [*ETL* 3/22; *JSOT* 47.5; *CBQ* 9/23]. Carr's more technical spadework for this commentary was issued as *The Formation of Genesis 1–11* (OUP, 2020) [*JSOT* 45.5]; it focused on compositional history concerns, especially redaction. Much earlier, Carr published *Reading the Fractures of Genesis* (1996), called by many a real success in promoting a merger of "Historical and Literary Approaches" (the subtitle).

✓ **Cassuto, Umberto.** 2 vols., ET 1964. This commentary covers chs. 1–11 (with some work through 13:4 also presented) and reflects careful scholarship. Cassuto was a devout Jew who spent much of his life defending the integrity of the Pentateuch. Excellent on literary and philological details. Scholarly pastors find great profit here.

✓ Chambers, Nathan J. *Reconsidering Creation Ex Nihilo in Genesis 1*, 2021. [*SJT* 75.4; *BBR* 32.3; *Presb* Spr 22; *BL* 2022].

☆ Charles, J. Daryl, ed. *Reading Genesis 1–2: An Evangelical Conversation*, 2013. Certainly one of the best books for understanding where the lines of debate are drawn. "Star players" are here: Averbeck, Beall, Collins, Hamilton, Longman, Walton. [*BBR* 25.1; *JSOT* 39.5; *JESOT* 3.2; *RevExp* 11/14; *RTR* 8/13]. Other vols. taking up these issues are: Blocher above; Madueme–Reeves, eds., *Adam, the Fall, and Original Sin* (2014) [*Them* 8/15]; *Four Views on the Historical Adam*, eds. Barrett–Caneday (2013) [*Them* 7/14; *Anvil* 9/14]; *The Evolution of Adam* by Enns (2012) [*EQ* 10/12; *JETS* 6/12; *JESOT* 2.2; *Them* 7/12]; *The Genesis Debate: Three Views on the Days of Creation*, ed. Hagopian (2001); and Collins's books.

F   Clifford, Richard. ‡ (Herm). From a Jesuit who has a major Proverbs commentary.

✓ **Coats, George W.** ‡ (FOTL) 1983. Only of use to students interested in technical form-critical analysis. This is one of the better older vols. in the series. [*JBL* 105.1; *JETS* 9/84; *WTJ* Fall 84; *HS* 1986].

☆ **Collins, C. John.** *Genesis 1–4: A Linguistic, Literary, and Theological Commentary*, 2006. My regret is that the P&R treatment ends with ch. 4. Collins's interests, as described in the commentary subtitle, are in line with those of much of the best contemporary scholarship. The review in *ZAW* 121.1 speaks of his "discourse-oriented literary approach" and the helpful distinction he draws between the text's worldview, "intended to be normative" (Collins, p.262), and the ancient cosmology reflected in the text, i.e., "a stationary earth with an orbiting sun." He is keenly interested in, and well-qualified to address, the interface between scientific thought and Genesis. If one is particularly interested in chs. 1–4, this is an excellent commentary to pick up. [*BSac* 7/08; *JETS* 9/07]. Remaining engaged with the discussion, Collins also wrote *Did Adam and Eve Really Exist? Who They Were and Why You Should Care* (Crossway, 2011) [*EvQ* 10/12]; and a contribution to *Reading Genesis 1–2*, ed. Charles (2013). Collins is identified with the "analogical days" position.

☆ **Collins, C. John.** *Reading Genesis Well: Navigating History, Poetry, Science, and Truth in Genesis 1–11*, 2018. From a well-trained scientist and OT scholar who teaches at Covenant Seminary. His emphasis on communicative intent is helpful indeed. [*ExpTim* 6/19; *Presb* Fall 19; *BBR* 29.4; *CBQ* 1/20; *JETS* 6/19; *JSOT* 43.5; *EvQ* 91.2; *RevExp* 8/19; *Them* 44.1].

✓ **Cotter, David W.** ‡ (BerO) 2003. This Catholic priest serves as series editor. Both here and in Alter one finds literary insights. When Cotter reads Genesis, he sees "neither documents nor historical clues," but "story." [*Int* 10/04; *HS* 2003; *JSOT* 28.5; *RelSRev* 4/04; *JETS* 3/05; *JHebS* 4].

☆ Currid, John D. (EPSC) 2 vols., 2003. See Exodus for an earlier, similar 2-vol. set, which offers an accessible and creative biblical-theological exposition. Preachers, especially the Reformed, will relish this in their study.

☆ Davis, Dale Ralph. *God's Rascal: The Jacob Narrative in Genesis 25–35*, 2022. Like his other theological expositions, quite valuable to pastors. [*TGA* 12/23].

F  Day, John. ‡ *Genesis 1–11* (ICC). On the way we have been gifted with *From Creation to Babel: Studies in Genesis 1–11* (2013) [*JSOT* 38.5; *VT* 65.4] and *From Creation to Abraham* (2022) [*BBR* 33.2].

De La Torre, Miguel A. ‡ (Belief) 2011. A liberation theology approach. [*Int* 4/13; *CTJ* 11/13].

✓ Delitzsch, Franz. *A New Commentary on Genesis* (not KD) 2 vols., ET 1888. He was always brilliant and less conservative than Keil. This technical work is useful for studying the Hebrew. Later in life he began to be influenced by the Graf–Wellhausen theories of multiple sources, and this is reflected somewhat in these vols. (see vol.1, p.53). But his conclusion regarding the compositional history remained moderately conservative: "a Mosaic Thorah is the basis of the Pentateuch" (10). This 5th edition in ET has been reprinted several times.

F  Dempster, Stephen G. (ZECOT).

Dods, Marcus. [𝓜], (EB) 1893. A standard homiletical help for a bygone era.

✓ Doedens J. J. T. *The Sons of God in Genesis 6:1–4: Analysis and History of Exegesis*, 2019. A lengthy, fine PhD for Kampen. [*JTS* 4/21; *JSOT* 44.5; *CBQ* 4/20].

✓ **Driver, S. R.** ‡ (Westminster Commentaries) 1904. Perhaps the clearest, most valuable presentation of the issues from the old liberal perspective. See Skinner also for turn-of-the-century scholarship.

☆ Duguid, Iain M. *Living in the Gap between Promise and Reality: The Gospel According to Abraham* (GAOT) 1999; *Living in the Grip of Relentless Grace: The Gospel in the Lives of Isaac & Jacob* (GAOT) 2002; *Living in the Light of Inextinguishable Hope: The Gospel According to Joseph* (GAOT) 2013. Highly recommended for preachers, not only for the excellent material but also for how it models a biblical-theological approach to OT narrative. One can "go to school" on this. [2013: *Chm* Sum 15].

F  Duguid, Iain M. (ESVEC) 2024. Should prove to be a packed and wise expositional guide.

(See the author's earlier books above.) The vol. also includes Sklar on Exodus, Christine Palmer on Leviticus, and Ron Bergey on Numbers.

☆ Emadi, Samuel. *From Prisoner to Prince: The Joseph Story in Biblical Theology* (NSBT) 2022. Worth reading, and helpful in reminding us that the Joseph narratives are the longest of all the Genesis characters. Emadi, a Southern Baptist pastor, takes a canonical and typological approach. [*JETS* 3/23; *Them* 47.3].

✓ Evans, Craig A., Joel Lohr, and David Petersen, eds. ‡ *The Book of Genesis: Composition, Reception, and Interpretation*, 2012. [*BBR* 23.4; *JSOT* 37.5; *VT* 64.4].

☆ Eveson, Philip. *The Book of Origins* (Welwyn) 2001. Subtitled "Genesis Simply Explained," the pastoral exposition is the product of much pulpit experience and is often masterful at drawing out the theology of the text (580pp.). Eveson regularly makes heart-applications. Both conservative laypeople and preachers find it appealing as devotional reading. See also Leviticus, Chronicles, and Psalms; his best are the latter two (partly because they have the most study behind them).

✓ **Fokkelman, J. P.** ‡ *Narrative Art in Genesis*, 1975. This author also contributes "Genesis and Exodus" to *The Literary Guide to the Bible* (1987), eds. Alter–Kermode. See also Samuel below. The erudition here is accessible mainly to advanced students.

✓ **Fretheim, Terence.** ‡ (NIB) 1994. Rewarding as a less critical theological interpretation, but NIB vols. are so expensive that I guess many are discouraged from purchasing them. This one is more attractive than some others because it also contains Brueggemann on Exodus and Kaiser on Leviticus. Fretheim is more conservative than many critical interpreters; he refers to the early chapters as a story of the past, which, though it downplays historicity or historicality, is better than the oft-employed mythology or legend genre identification. Also, Fretheim, coming from the Lutheran tradition, has good theological perception—I would not be shy to call him one of the abler OT theologians in America. Conservatives don't follow him in his work on the suffering of God, widely used by the open theists. [*PSB* 16.3; *CBQ* 4/96; *JETS* 9/96]. Students use his theological introduction, *The Pentateuch* (1996).

Galambush, Julie. ‡ (ROT) 2018. [*Int* 1/21; *HBT* 42.1; *RevExp* 2/20].

✓ **Gertz, Jan Christian.** ‡ *Genesis 1–11* (HCOT) ET 2023. Translated from the 2nd ed. of his ATD (2021), then revised and adapted to this series. The author says it "remains a work based on the German-speaking academic tradition" (ix). One may humorously add that such a tradition also includes exceedingly long paragraphs (one on pp.153–56). A briefer Introduction (25pp.) is followed by 400pp. of exegesis, with valuable bibliographies (focused more on continental European scholarship). Gertz is a Heidelberg professor and a major player in pentateuchal studies. Along with discussion of sources and redactional activity, he offers good insights into the text. Though he sees many connections with ANE culture, conceptions, etc., and considers chs. 1–11 to be an expression of ANE myth, he asserts "the historical distinctiveness of the biblical Primeval History . . . in its aesthetics and theology" (25). [*BL* 2024].

F  Gertz, Jan Christian. ‡ (Illum).

Gibson, John C. L. ‡ (DSB) 2 vols., 1981. The series editor gives a well-done liberal exposition, but the work is now showing its age. He spends much time presenting the conclusions of 1960s and 1970s scholarship to his lay readership, who pick up this series more for devotional reasons.

Gnuse, Robert. ‡ *Misunderstood Stories: Theological Commentary on Genesis 1–11*, 2014. [*JSOT* 39.5].

Gowan, Donald E. ‡ *From Eden to Babel: A Commentary on the Book of Genesis 1–11* (ITC-E) 1988. The author is a respected OT scholar at Pittsburgh Seminary (PCUSA). This work is brief (125pp.), well-written, but not as open to the text nor as theologically perceptive as Janzen's ITC-E on chs. 12–50. [*CBQ* 51.4; *ExpTim* 8/89].

✓ Greenwood, Kyle R., ed. *Since the Beginning: Interpreting Genesis 1 and 2 through the Ages*, 2018. Baker Academic published this wide-ranging survey (over 300pp.). [*CTJ* 4/20; *JSOT* 43.5].

☆ Greidanus, Sidney. *Preaching Christ from Genesis*, 2007. The author is learned in hermeneutics, biblical theology, and homiletics. He offers superb guidance on his topic, with special attention given to handling the narrative genre and understanding the structure of the book. These 500pp. are a good antidote to moralistic preaching. The skills learned in reading such a textbook can apply to a much larger body of OT literature. For a taste, see "Detecting Plot Lines," *CTJ* 43 (2008): 64–77. [*RTR* 12/08; *CTJ* 11/08; *BL* 2008; *Chm* Sum 09; *Anvil* 26.3–4].

✓ Grossman, Jonathan. ‡ *Abram to Abraham: A Literary Analysis of the Abraham Narrative*, 2016. A large-scale work (over 500pp.), quite perceptive. [*BibInt* 27.1].

✓ **Gunkel, Hermann.** ‡ 3rd ed. 1910, ET 1997. Famous as the pioneering form-critical work on Genesis and the most influential work for scholars during the early 20th century. It was important that this finally got translated. [*ThTo* 1/98; *JSOT* 76; *CBQ* 10/98; *OTA* 2/00; *BSac* 4/98].

✓ Halton, Charles, ed. *Genesis: History, Fiction, or Neither?* 2015. Three scholars address key questions: what kind of literature is Genesis 1–3, and how do we read it? This Counterpoints vol. features Hoffmeier (historical reading), Sparks (reading as fiction), and Wenham (not a straight historical or fictional reading). The topic, as well as the related historical Adam issue, continues to receive much attention. See also Collins, Walton, and VanDoodewaard. [*JSOT* 40.5; *Them* 40.3].

☆ **Hartley, John E.** (NIBC) 2000. I have warmly commended this Methodist scholar's commentaries on Job and Leviticus. His NIBC is valuable to pastors for several reasons. The scholarship is solidly evangelical and not so dated. Also, the vol. is inexpensive and of manageable size (416pp.). You could call it among the best buys on Genesis. [*RTR* 8/01; *Them* Aut 01; *JSOT* 99 (Wenham); *Anvil* 19.1; *JHebS* 4].

✓ **Hendel, Ronald S.** ‡ *Genesis 1–11* (AYB) 2024. A 2-vol. set will replace Speiser. See Hendel's award-winning research on *The Text of Genesis 1–11: Textual Studies and Critical Edition* (OUP, 1998) [*JBL* Sum 00]. There had been a major delay, and a wide array of scholars were eagerly awaiting this AYB reference work; the first vol. by the retired Berkeley professor is approx. 450pp. See also his *Reading Genesis: Ten Methods* (CUP, 2010) [*BBR* 21.4; *JSOT* 36.5; *ExpTim* 4/12; *BibInt* 21.2].

✓ Hess, Richard S., and David T. Tsumura, eds. *"I Studied Inscriptions from Before the Flood": Ancient Near Eastern, Literary, and Linguistic Approaches to Genesis 1–11*, 1994. Some fine, older evangelical essays. Other important attempts to read the early chapters against their ANE background are: John Day, *From Creation to Babel* (2013) [*RelSRev* 9/14]; Richard Clifford, *Creation Accounts in the ANE and the Bible* (1994); and Stephanie J. Dalley, *Myths from Mesopotamia: Creation, the Flood, Gilgamesh and Others* (OUP, 1989). For a discussion of the comparative approach from a critical angle, see Christopher Hays, *Hidden Riches: A Sourcebook for the Comparative Study of the Hebrew Bible and the ANE* (2014) [*JETS* 6/15; *JESOT* 4.1; *BBR* 25.2]; a nuanced conservative reflection on the topic is found in chs. 9–11 of Collins's *Genesis 1–4*.

F   Hiebert, Theodore. ‡ (AbOTC).

☆ Hughes, R. Kent. (PTW) 2004. Expositors should consider this for purchase. The 2012 redesign for the ESV is 700pp. [*JETS* 9/05].

✓ Jacob, Benno. ‡ *The First Book of the Bible: Genesis*, ET 1974. A 358-page abridgement of an extensive Jewish commentary (1055pp.), *Das erste Buch der Tora* (1934). Wenham once said this is "of great value." See too his Exodus work.

☆ Janzen, J. Gerald. ‡ *Abraham and All the Families of the Earth: A Commentary on the Book of*

*Genesis 12–50* (ITC-E) 1993. Because the author focuses on drawing out the theology of the narratives, this book is very useful to the expositor. I consider it one of the best vols. in this series (230pp.)—"few . . . will match its depth of comment on Genesis 12–50" (W. Kaiser). For a taste, see his sparkling, cut-to-the-chase discussion of Moberly, "supersession," and the proper relation among the Abrahamic, Mosaic, and New Covenants (6–12). Janzen taught Genesis to seminary classes for decades, and it shows. I once included this on my to-buy list. He has also written on Exodus and Job. [*JETS* 3/96].

✓ Kaminski, Carol M. [*M*], *From Noah to Israel: Realization of the Primaeval Blessing after the Flood*, 2004.

✓ Keil, C. F. (KD) ET 1864. The whole set once was a recommended purchase. See under Commentary Series.

Kelly, Douglas F. *Creation and Change: Genesis 1:1–2:4 in the Light of Changing Scientific Paradigms*, 1997, rev. 2017. How do we read the biblical account of creation in our day, when evolutionary thought challenges many fundamental doctrines: God as Creator, sin and death (judgment), solidarity in our human nature, etc.? Kelly provides answers as a systematics prof at RTS Charlotte, taking a literal 24-hour days position. Cf. Blocher. [*Chm* Spr 04].

☆ Kidner, Derek. (retired TOTC) 1967. Packs an amazing amount of information and theological insight for its brief format. Excellent, but accommodates an evolutionary viewpoint, which bothered American evangelicals more than the British. Once recommended for purchase. Preachers find Kidner very suggestive for sermon prep.

Klingbeil, Gerald A., ed. *The Genesis Creation Account and Its Reverberations in the OT*, 2015. From Seventh-Day Adventist scholars. [*ExpTim* 7/16; *JSOT* 40.5].

F   Lamb, David. (EEC). A previous report was William Barrick.

Lange, Johann Peter. (Lange) ET 1868. Certainly one of the best in the series (665pp.). In his day Spurgeon judged it "in all respects beyond price" (51).

Lawson, George. *Lectures on the History of Joseph*, 1878. This theological and devotional classic has been reprinted a couple of times by Banner.

Leupold, H. C. 2 vols., 1942. A lengthy exposition by an evangelical Lutheran. Like Lenski on the NT, Leupold provides some good conservative exegesis, which often points to distinctives and concerns of Lutheran systematic theology. He has other commentaries on Psalms, Ecclesiastes, Isaiah, Daniel, and Zechariah.

✓ Longacre, Robert. *Joseph, A Story of Divine Providence: A Text Theoretical and Textlinguistic Analysis of Genesis 37 and 39–48*, 2nd ed. 2003.

☆ Longman, Tremper, III. (SGBC) 2016. Those familiar with his prodigious output will find no real surprises here in Longman's work. The commentary has much learning behind it, is clearly executed, and quite insightful (from a progressive evangelical standpoint). Unlike some of his commentaries, this is popularly written and moves quickly to application concerns. After a 25-page Intro, there are 540pp. of exposition. [*JSOT* 41.5]. See also *How to Read Genesis* (2005), which follows his like-titled handbooks on Psalms and Proverbs and is well worth reading as a popular orientation before digging deeper [*CTJ* 4/08; *JETS* 9/06; *SwJT* Fall 04; *Anvil* 23.4].

✓ Louth, Andrew, ed. *Genesis 1–11* (ACCS) 2001.

Luther, Martin. "Lectures on Genesis," *Luther's Works*, vols. 1–8, ET 1958–70.

✓ MacDonald, Nathan, Mark W. Elliott, and Grant Macaskill, eds. *Genesis and Christian Theology*, 2012. [*WTJ* Fall 12; *JSOT* 38.5; *ExpTim* 3/14; *RevExp* Sum 13; *TJ* Spr 13].

Maher, M. ‡ (OTM) 1982.

F   Mattox, Mickey L., ed. *Genesis 12–50* (RCS).

✓ **McKeown, James.** [*M*], (THC) 2008. This theological commentary was an early issue in the series (398pp.), focusing upon a triad of themes: descendants, blessing, and land. Some reviewers see the author, who teaches at Queens University, Belfast, as both evangelically rooted and conciliatory toward more liberal positions. Alongside many positive reviews, Hwang offers more criticism. [*CBQ* 4/09; *ThTo* 4/09 (Brueggemann); *JETS* 3/09 (Hwang); *BL* 2009; *JTS* 4/10; *BTB* 5/10; *ExpTim* 7/09; *Int* 4/10; *RTR* 12/09; *VT* 59.3].

✓ Mettinger, Tryggve N. D. ‡ *The Eden Narrative: A Literary and Religio-Historical Study of Genesis 2–3*, 2007.

Millard, Alan R., and Donald J. Wiseman, eds. *Essays on the Patriarchal Narratives*, 1980. An older conservative vol. on the historical character of the narratives in Genesis 12–50. More theological is Hess, Satterthwaite, and Wenham, eds.: *He Swore an Oath: Biblical Themes from Genesis 12–50* (2nd ed. 1994).

✓ Moberly, R. W. L. [*M*], *The Theology of the Book of Genesis*, 2009. From CUP's OT Theology series, and widely used. [*HBT* 32.1; *JETS* 9/10; *BBR* 21.1; *CBQ* 10/10; *JTS* 4/11; *Chm* Spr 12; *VT* 61.1; *JHebS* 11].

Morris, Henry M. *The Genesis Record*, 1976. Lengthy study, concerned with scientific issues and written for laypeople. Morris was a leader of Scientific Creationism ("Young Earth"). Not recommended. Many argue that the restricted focus upon scientific and historical issues distracts readers from the dominant theological interests of the text.

✓ **O'Connor, Kathleen M.** ‡ (S&H) 2 vols., 2018–20. A major critical commentary exploring the book from a different angle: historical criticism augmented by trauma studies. As usual with the series, the work is visually inviting and well-designed. See O'Connor's previous research on Jeremiah and Lamentations. [*BL* 2022; *CBQ* 1/20, 10/21; *Int* 1/23; *RevExp* 11/19].

Okoye, James Chukwuma. ‡ *Genesis: A Narrative-Theological Commentary*, 2 vols., 2018–20. Extensive and insightful, from a Nigerian who teaches at Duquesne. He blends older-style historical criticism and narrative criticism. Okoye's Catholic beliefs feature strongly in the theological comments. [*WTJ* Spr 21; *BBR* 29.3; *JSOT* 43.5, 45.5].

Peterson, Brian Neal. (PentC) 2022. Quite a full Pentecostal commentary (nearly 500pp.), from a prof at Lee U. [*JSOT* 47.5]. Earlier the author released a preparatory work, *Genesis as Torah: Reading Narrative as Legal Instruction* (2018), which is truly a profitable read. [*JETS* 12/18]. Cf. Wenham's *Story as Torah* under Pentateuch above.

F   Petersen, David L. ‡ (OTL-R). This is scheduled to replace von Rad.

☆ Phillips, Richard D. (REC) 2 vols., 2023. A huge set of conservative sermonic exposition (over 1300pp.) by a well-known PCA pastor.

Pink, Arthur. 1922. Cannot be recommended. Though his studies are reverent expositions, Pink is too easily distracted from the text before him and often goes overboard on typology. His earlier works (the Gleanings series published by Moody), such as this one on Genesis, tended to be dispensational and not well-grounded in scholarship. He jumped to theological concerns and present-day application before he had understood the text. An exception was his later (1956) work on Elijah, which, while not scholarly, is quite good.

✓ Plantinga, Alvin. *Science, Religion, and Naturalism: Where the Conflict Really Lies*, 2011. Not a commentary, and not an easy read, but a most useful book from OUP challenging the New Atheism. [*Chm* Sum 13 (McGrath)].

☆ Poythress, Vern S. *Interpreting Eden: A Guide to Faithfully Reading and Understanding Genesis 1–3*, 2019. Contains much wisdom for the Bible and science discussion. A good portion of this material appeared previously in *WTJ*. [*JETS* 9/19].

✓ Provan, Iain. [*M*], *Discovering Genesis*, 2016. From the Eerdmans series Discovering Biblical Texts, and briefly highlighting key interpretive issues. [*BBR* 27.2; *JETS* 9/16; *JSOT* 41.5; *Them* 43.2].

✓ **Rad, Gerhard von.** ‡ (OTL) ET 1961, rev. 1972. Building upon the form-critical work of Gunkel, von Rad was long a standard critical commentary. Examines Genesis as part of a proposed

Hexateuch (Genesis to Joshua). Even though the scholarly approach represented here has become obsolete, the commentary's highly theological discussion of the text retains value. [*ThTo* 20.1].

Reno, R. R. (Brazos) 2010. From the series editor. I have not seen this. [*CTJ* 4/11; *JETS* 12/10; *ExpTim* 11/10].

F   Römer, Thomas. ‡ *Genesis 12–50* (Herm).

Ross, Allen. (CorBC) 2008. This 550-page vol. on Genesis and Exodus (Oswalt) builds on the earlier Ross exposition, *Creation and Blessing*, but is much briefer.

☆   **Sailhamer, John H.** (EBCR) 2008. The sharp, mature, independently minded scholar taught at TEDS, Dallas Seminary, and Golden Gate Baptist Seminary. Here Sailhamer redoes Genesis after his successful effort in EBC (1990) [*Presb* Spr 91]. In the EBCR, Genesis is bound with Exodus and Leviticus. [*BL* 2010]. Do note, too, his theological-literary commentary on all five books of Moses, *The Meaning of the Pentateuch*.

✓   **Sarna, Nahum M.** ‡ (JPS) 1989. With its exegesis of the Hebrew, this is much more technical and in-depth (414pp.) than his previous work, *Understanding Genesis* (1970) [*WTJ* 30.2]. The JPS series is valuable to scholars and students, but you probably won't know quite what to do with all the rabbinics. [*ThTo* 46.3; *HS* 1992; *CRBR* 1990].

F   Schlimm, Matthew Richard. (BGW) 2024?

F   Schmid, Konrad. ‡ *Genesis 12–50* (IECOT). Partially preparing the way was *Genesis and the Moses Story* (ET 2010), with its focus on compositional history [*JHebS* 13].

✓   Schroeder, Joy A. (BMT) 2015. [*ExpTim* 5/16; *JETS* 3/16; *RTR* 12/15; *ETL* 93.4].

✓   Scullion, J. J. ‡ 1992. The literary concerns and method of interpretation here are more characteristic of critical scholarship 60 years ago. Still, it may be worth consulting for seminary papers.

✓   Sheridan, Mark, ed. *Genesis 12–50* (ACCS) 2002. See Louth above. [*Them* Spr 04; *BL* 2007].

✓   **Skinner, John.** ‡ (ICC) 1910. Back in 1977 it could be said that "[f]or a full, technical handling of the issues Skinner . . . has not been surpassed in English." Westermann's commentary was not yet translated, nor was Wenham available when Childs wrote this. Skinner is now very dated, but as an academic I still consult him on rare occasion.

✓   **Speiser, E. A.** ‡ (AB) 1964. A Jewish work of impressive scholarship for its day, with discussion of the ANE background, some source criticism, and a more literal translation. Pastors will have little use for this dated commentary. Note that exposition and theology were not among the original aims of the series. See Hendel above.

☆   **Steinmann, Andrew E.** (TOTC-R) 2019. The prolific Lutheran scholar (see Proverbs, Daniel, Ezra–Nehemiah, 1 & 2 Samuel) provides a perceptive, carefully conservative exegesis, with close attention to literary and theological features. A great replacement for Kidner's gem.

Stigers, Harold G. 1976. A strong evangelical effort in its time, exegetical in its thrust. Now it is long o/p.

F   Tatu, Silviu. ‡ (HCOT). See Gertz above.

Thomas, W. H. Griffith. 1909. This rich, somewhat dispensational, devotional commentary was first published in 3 vols. and has occasionally been reprinted.

✓   Thompson, John L., ed. *Genesis 1–11* (RCS) 2012. [*JETS* 12/13].

Towner, W. Sibley. ‡ (WestBC) 2001. I have yet to use this nearly 300-page commentary, but the reputation of the author leads me to guess it serves as a leading popular-level exposition of Genesis for liberal pastors. Compare with the fuller works by Brueggemann, Fretheim, and the Gowan–Janzen set. [*Them* Sum 05; *Anvil* 19.3].

✓   Turner, Laurence A. ‡ (Read) 2000. I've not used Turner (230pp.), who offers a narrative approach. [*JSOT* 94; *Anvil* 17.3].

VanDoodewaard, William. *The Quest for the Historical Adam*, 2015. Valuable for its survey of past discussion in church history and evangelicalism and its restatement of the most conservative young earth, literal 24-hour days interpretation (about 350pp.). I salute his zeal for defending Scripture but have concerns. The discussion of other views—even those resolutely defending a historical Adam—can seem dismissive. Alternatives to his absolute literalism deserve better: the text plainly contains a sophisticated literary style and framework, not-necessarily-endorsed features of ANE cosmology (the vault, רקיע), and an anti-polytheistic polemic. Do we dishonor our forebears if we misrepresent the diversity of views over the centuries (cf. Letham, "In the Space of Six Days," *WTJ* Fall 1999) and, more recently, within denominations (cf. PCA Creation Study Committee), as illustrating a defection from high doctrines of Scripture and Creation? Is it ironic that attacks on the Bible from scientific and historical perspectives have set the agenda for some defenders of the faith, who believe these texts must be interpreted mainly along scientific and historiographic lines? What does it mean if the likes of J. Gresham Machen (day-age) cannot pass this new test of orthodoxy? For what purpose is this vol. on the historical Adam so focused on the length of *day* in Gen 1? Because an old-earth theory does not a priori rule out macro-evolutionary origins? Is there evidence for "an inherent fluidity within nonliteral approaches" (234)? [*Them* 41.1]. On the same topic is William Lane Craig, *In Quest of the Historical Adam* (2021) [*WTJ* Spr 22; *ExpTim* 11/22; *Presb* Fall 22; *SBJT* 26.3]. See also the wide-ranging books under Charles and Collins above.

✓ **Vawter, Bruce.** ‡ 1977. This critical interpretation by a Catholic scholar was published by Doubleday and is a major work to be consulted, if one is doing exhaustive research with an interest in the results of older diachronic methods.

☆ **Waltke, Bruce, with Cathi Fredricks.** 2001. A stand-alone commentary, published by Zondervan. It is packed with much structural and rhetorical analysis, but pastors will value this most highly for its biblical-theological reflection. At points, I could wish for deeper, more current research than Waltke–Fredricks provide (e.g., following Speiser's discredited reference to Hurrian practice in explaining 12:13). For the last four editions, this was a recommended purchase. [*BSac* 1/04].

☆ **Watkin, Christopher.** *Thinking through Creation: Genesis 1 and 2 as Tools of Cultural Critique*, 2017. By a Cambridge PhD, who masterfully and even elegantly draws out the foundational truths positively taught in the creation accounts, and also how those speak to our age. Refreshing in framing a biblical life-philosophy. [*Them* 44.3]. Watkin's more ambitious undertaking is *Biblical Critical Theory: How the Bible's Unfolding Story Makes Sense of Modern Life and Culture* (2022) [*JTS* 10/23].

✓ **Westermann, Claus.** ‡ (ContC) 3 vols., ET 1984–86. Authoritative . . . 40 years ago. This mammoth work delivers to us the most thorough exegetical treatment of Genesis, with over 1500pp. of theologically charged commentary from BKAT (though I would have liked more theology in such a huge set). Westermann's approach is mainly diachronic (especially source and form-critical) while making some use of synchronic methods. This scholar was one of the Pentateuch interpreters tending toward a simpler source critical analysis, erasing "E" almost entirely. Students should note that his huge 256-page introduction to Genesis is also available in translation (1992). Those with an academic bent might be inclined to take out a bank loan to buy this. Wenham [*BSB* 3/99] speaks of how Westermann and other source critical treatments "in effect write commentaries on J's version of Genesis and P's version of Genesis rather than on the canonical Genesis" and usually "are better at describing elements within Genesis rather than the whole book." [*JBL* 6/72, 6/77; *ThTo* 43.2; *HS* 1986; *CBQ* 49.3].

Westermann, Claus. ‡ (T&I) ET 1987. This translation from a Dutch series makes his conclusions in the 3-vol. ContC available to a larger audience. Popular and more practical in its aim. [*JETS* 6/90; *EvQ* 7/89; *CBQ* 51.4].

✓ Wilson, Lindsay. *Joseph Wise and Otherwise: The Intersection of Wisdom and Covenant in Genesis 37–50*, 2004. From a fine, evangelical scholar. [*RTR* 8/10].

Young, E. J. *Studies in Genesis One*, 1964. A careful exegesis.

Young, E. J. *Genesis Three*, 1966. Subtitled "A Devotional and Expository Study."

Youngblood, Ronald. 1991. A revision of his earlier work on Genesis, and definitely one of the better popularly styled expositions. Good for a church library.

NOTES: (1) See C. S. Rodd's "Which Is the Best Commentary? II. Genesis," *ExpTim*, 3/86. (2) Despite the date, an excellent brief annotated bibliography for Genesis is R. W. L. Moberly, *Genesis 12–50* (JSOT, 1992), 102–7. (3) John Kselman, "The Book of Genesis: A Decade of Scholarly Research," *Int* 45 (1991): 380–92. (4) For a Jewish survey of scholarship, see Tammi J. Schneider, "In the Beginning and Still Today: Recent Publications on Genesis," *CBR* 18 (2020): 142–59.

# EXODUS

★ **Alexander, T. Desmond.** (Apollos) 2017. A most satisfying and full (723pp.) work, especially strong on tracing out the history of scholarship, helpful on the Hebrew text and exegetical fine points, and indicating points of biblical theology. (There is less biblical-theological reflection than I'd hoped for, however. Sometimes he merely points to another publication where he has discussed an issue of biblical theology arising in the text (e.g., see pp.131, 305; I had to remind myself that the series does not emphasize theology, though the "explanation" sections are well worth reading). He spent decades researching this Bible book. I make it my top choice for bookish pastors, but it definitely needs an exposition alongside, such as Wright or Motyer. [*JETS* 9/18; *Them* 43.2; *SeTR* 10.1 (Rooker)]. To be preferred, especially by students, to the distilled-down TTC series work (about 200pp.), released in 2016.

★ **Childs, Brevard S.** ‡ (OTL) 1974. Thorough and rewarding, this was for decades the best commentary on this portion of Scripture. "Unabashedly theological" in its purpose, Childs's work might be called "post-liberal" and a reaction against narrowly historical-critical approaches. His "Canonical Approach" is less mired in unraveling sources. He "subordinates the prehistory of the text to interpretation of its canonical form" (Danker). His concern to take into account the whole history of exegesis, ancient and modern, is laudable. Must be used with some discernment. Moderately critical. This used to be Longman's first choice. On the negative side it is half a century old; its brilliance is waning. Those wanting a more current or conservative exegesis should look up Hamilton, Currid, Garrett, or Carpenter (probably in that order). [*JBL* 95.2; *JETS* 9/75; *ThTo* 31.3].

★ **Enns, Peter.** (NIVAC) 2000. A full treatment at 600pp. The author spent much time with Exodus in his Harvard doctoral research, and was until 2008 an OT prof at Westminster, Philadelphia. Enns exhibits good sense in exegetical analysis, has an eye for theological themes, and starts the reader down the path to discovering relevant applications. Though I highly value Houtman, Cassuto, Sarna, Fretheim, and Brueggemann, my present counsel to studious pastors is buy the quartet of Alexander, Stuart, Enns, and Wright together to start. (Note: Enns has a savvy annotated bibliography on pp.37–38 which lists Houtman, Sarna, and Fretheim as "musts.")

★ Motyer, J. Alec. (BST) 2005. I love this book (327pp.) as an inexpensive, suggestive biblical-theological guide for expositors. Sterling stuff! Another help for pastors, but several times as long, would be Ryken below. [*Chm* Aut 05; *BL* 2006; *ExpTim* 2/06; *Anvil* 25.1].

★ **Stuart, Douglas.** (NAC) 2006. As with Motyer, many evangelicals were waiting for this. *Exodus* is not the academic commentary that Stuart's *Hosea–Jonah* (WBC) is, and it does not have quite the interaction with scholarship that I had hoped for. The author seems to have aimed at producing a fresh, more independent interpretation. This vol., though valuable to students, is geared more for pastors. It is a very full (826pp.), judicious exegesis to set alongside Mathews's superb *Genesis* in NAC. I note that Sklar once made this his first pick for the pastor's study [*Presb* Spr 12].

★ Wright, Christopher J. H. (SGBC) 2021. Like Motyer, a pastoral exposition. Sklar told me this is his favorite on Exodus. Surely one of the best representatives of the series, displaying what the British term exegetical nous (skill), humble attentiveness to the text (including features of the different genres) and its theology/ethics, and a remarkably clear writing style (612pp.). This is simply a joy to read, with its biblical-theological approach, seeking "a wholistic and integrated understanding of each part of Scripture in the light of the whole grand canonical narrative" (xiii). See also Wright's books on Deuteronomy, Jeremiah, Lamentations, Ezekiel, Daniel, and *The Mission of God*. All are well worth reading. Also, for understanding the ongoing relevance of biblical warnings against idolatry, see Wright's *Here Are Your Gods: Faithful Discipleship in Idolatrous Times* (2020) [*Them* 47.1]; the theological and virtue-ethics approach in Fowl, *Idolatry* (2019) [*CTJ* 4/21; *EvQ* 92.1; *SJT* 74.4]; and the biblical-theological studies by Beale, *We Become What We Worship* (2008), and Lints, *Identity and Idolatry* (2015) [*Them* 41.1].

❖ ❖ ❖ ❖ ❖ ❖

☆ Alexander, T. Desmond. (TTC) 2016. Excellent as a distillation of Apollos (see above).

F Alexander, T. Desmond, and Justin Young. (BGW).

Ashby, Godfrey. [*M*], (ITC-E) 1998. A slim, good theological interpretation with little attention given to historical and literary issues. Ashby ministered in South Africa (within the Anglican communion) and reads Exodus after seeing firsthand the injustices of apartheid. One comes away from reading Ashby with the thought that Exodus is clearly a living book for the author. [*CTJ* 11/98; *Int* 1/99; *CBQ* 7/99; *HS* 1999].

✓ Baden, Joel S. ‡ *The Book of Exodus: A Biography*, 2019. Published by Princeton, this is a probing study of the book's enduring influence. Baden thinks it is entirely fictional.

F Baden, Joel S. ‡ (AYB). Would replace Propp.

F Behr, John. (Brazos). Was at St. Vladimir's, but now professor at Aberdeen.

✓ Bimson, John J. *Redating the Exodus and Conquest*, 1978, rev. 1981. Not a commentary, but a provocative monograph, arguing for an early (15th century) date. Conservatives welcomed it as bolstering their conclusions. [*EvQ* 1/80; *JBL* 99.1; *VT* 31.1; *BAR* 13.6].

✓ Blackburn, W. Ross. *The God Who Makes Himself Known: The Missionary Heart of the Book of Exodus*, 2012. A good biblical-theological path into the book for preachers, picking up on the key use of the recognition formula—"you shall know that I am Yhwh"—though it's up for debate whether the formula's use *against* Egypt has missionary significance. [*EvQ* 4/14 (Alexander)].

✓ **Bodner, Keith.** ‡ *An Ark on the Nile: The Beginning of the Book of Exodus*, 2016. What a treat to receive this fine narrative analysis of Exod 1–2 (OUP)! [*ExpTim* 5/17; *CBQ* 7/18; *JETS* 6/17; *JSOT* 41.5].

☆ **Bruckner, James K.** [*M*], (NIBC) 2008. A readable, helpful, briefer evangelical commentary (348pp.), Bruckner is also inexpensive and could be a best buy for bargain hunters who want exegesis. The author teaches at North Park Seminary in Chicago and earlier contributed one of the better NIVAC vols. (see Jonah). He suggests a postexilic date for the final redaction of Exodus. Bruckner's theology is fairly healthy and helpful, emphasizing that the liberation was more *for* than *from*: for service (verb עבד) to God rather than narrowly from political and economic servitude/oppression. Perhaps some will argue with me, saying this deserves a spot on the recommended list, especially at the price. [*JETS* 9/09; *CBQ* 1/09; *RBL*; *BL* 2009; *JHebS* 2009].

✓ **Brueggemann, Walter.** ‡ (NIB) 1994. Here are 300pp. of stimulating theological exposition. Brueggemann is incapable of being dull. See my comments on his Genesis commentary above. [*PSB* 16.3; *CBQ* 4/96; *JETS* 9/96].

Burns, R. J. ‡ *Exodus, Leviticus, Numbers* (OTM) 1983.

Bush, George. *Notes on Exodus*, 1856. Spurgeon does not believe the American scholar plagiarized here, as on Genesis. Reprinted in pb by Kregel.

☆ **Calvin, John.** *Harmony of the Pentateuch*, 1563. Not a complete commentary on Exodus, but it does cover most of the ground. This harmony is not considered among the Reformer's best, but it should not be forgotten. See my comments under Genesis.

☆ **Carpenter, Eugene.** (EEC) 2 vols., 2016. In the 1990s we had looked for Carpenter to end the dearth of large-scale, evangelical exegetical commentaries on Exodus; this work was originally scheduled for NICOT (now see Trimm). The extensive exegesis (over 1100pp.) was completed days before the author's untimely passing (†2012). He offers a conservative introduction to the book, extensive notes on the Hebrew text, well-informed exegesis, and warm-hearted theological reflection.

✓ **Cassuto, Umberto.** ET 1967. Probably the Jewish scholar's best piece of commentary work (500pp.), hard to obtain, and "especially helpful for identifying literary patterns and allusions" (Meyers). Old Westminster's E. J. Young had high praise for Cassuto's writings. See my comments on his Genesis commentary. [*Bib* 35; *JBL* 73].

✓ Coats, George W. ‡ *Exodus 1–18* (FOTL) 1998. He also did Genesis for this series. Knierim was to complete the book of Exodus, as poor health interrupted Coats's work. This is technical, brief (178pp.), and one of the weakest entries in the series. [*JSOT* 89; *Int* 1/00; *CBQ* 1/00; *HS* 41; *RelSRev* 10/99; *JBL* Fall 01; *JSS* Spr 02].

Coggins, Richard. ‡ (Epworth) 2000. [*Anvil* 17.4].

Cole, R. Alan. (TOTC) 1973. An adequate, brief treatment from a conservative. The introduction contains a worthwhile summary of the theology of Exodus. For a long time Exodus was poorly served by evangelical commentaries, so Cole's work was more valuable than it might otherwise have been. In 1989 this was among my recommendations for purchase. [*EvQ* 4/74].

☆ **Currid, John D.** (EPSC) 2 vols., 2000–02. The author has published a book on Egypt and articles on Exodus. Here he delivers a more conservative interpretation of Exodus in about 900pp. The work is both exegetical (not too detailed) and expositional—a lot like the notes you typically find in an excellent study Bible (one which occasionally moves to consider application or to develop a devotional thought). Currid is a beloved prof at RTS, and his love for the Scriptures shines through in these pages. See his companion set on Genesis in the same series, which also is strong on redemptive-historical aspects. The pastor especially will value this.

Davies, G. Henton. ‡ (Torch) 1967. A work of 253pp., written for the general reader, though the J-E-P discussion does not interest church members. Childs called Davies "disappointing," but I think it was well-written and, though brief, serviceable for its day.

✓ **Davies, G. I.** ‡ *Exodus 1–18* (ICC) 2 vols., 2020. Truly a landmark technical exegesis, which will be consulted for many decades to come (1300pp.). ICC has never had an Exodus vol., and I was looking forward to this work after reading Davies's "The Exegesis of the Divine Name in Exodus," in Gordon, ed., *The God of Israel* (CUP, 2007). The Cambridge emeritus prof has long studied Exodus; see his *The Way of the Wilderness: A Geographical Study of* the Wilderness Itineraries in the Old Testament (1979). His discussion of textual matters (including the DSS), the plethora of proposals re. compositional history (esp. source and redaction criticism), lexical and syntactical questions, etc. is invaluable. That said, many leading Ezekiel scholars strongly dissent from his view that the Priestly author was influenced by Ezekiel (411). Somewhat surprisingly for ICC, there are theological reflections included, which he likens to the *Ziel* sections in BKAT. [*Bib* 103.2; *BL* 2022].

Davis, John D. *Moses and the Gods of Egypt*, 1971, rev. 1986. A conservative and popularly styled work by a Grace Seminary prof. He looks at Exodus "in the light of recent archaeological and historical studies" (9). Not of much help to students, and does not wrestle much with the theological message.

F   Davis, Katherine M. (née Smith). (ZECOT) 2024?

✓   **Dozeman, Thomas B.** ‡ (ECC) 2009. The large-scale (800pp.) exegesis builds upon his 1996 theological interpretation, *God at War: Power in the Exodus Tradition*, as well as *God on the Mountain: A Study of Redaction, Theology and Canon in Exodus 19–24* (1989). This well-researched vol. received a warm welcome from critical scholars, particularly those oriented toward diachronic literary criticism, but pastors of all types will probably let just the academics take account of it. Advanced students will make ready use of this, especially to understand how the work of certain pentateuchal interpreters is reshaping the discussion of genetic origins. As Davies notes, "there is little mention of the Qumran biblical scrolls" [*VT* 61.4]. [*JETS* 3/10; *BL* 2010; *CBQ* 7/10; *JTS* 10/12; *RBL* 2011; *CTJ* 11/12; *JHebS* 12]. Dozeman's follow-up was *Methods for Exodus* (CUP, 2010), evaluating various hermeneutical approaches. [*CTJ* 4/11; *JSOT* 35.5; *BibInt* 20.3; *BTB* 5/11; *RTR* 8/13].

✓   Dozeman, Thomas B., Craig A. Evans, and Joel N. Lohr, eds. ‡ *The Book of Exodus: Composition, Reception, and Interpretation*, 2014. A Brill vol. of essays. [*JSOT* 39.5; *CBQ* 7/16; *JTS* 10/16; *ETL* 92.3].

✓   **Driver, Samuel R.** ‡ (CBSC) 1911. The old standard critical work, widely used in lieu of an ICC vol. on Exodus, is jam-packed and 443pp. in length.

Dunnam, Maxie D. (WCC) 1987. The author was President of Asbury Seminary and his sermonic commentary is quite full (nearly 400pp.). This is not a throw-away, but I much prefer other expositional helps: Enns, Motyer, Ryken, J. G. Janzen, Currid.

☆   **Durham, John I.** ‡ (WBC) 1987. An extensive treatment that could have been more helpful had he followed through on his stated intent to treat the "final form" of the text. As it is, the commentary gets somewhat preoccupied with source, form, and tradition criticism—probably not what most pastors are looking for. On the plus side, Durham has more theology than some others in WBC. Advanced students will take an interest in this vol. Most evangelical pastors will prefer Stuart and Hamilton. [*HS* 1988; *RTR* 5/88; *WTJ* Spr 88; *TJ* Spr 87; *EvQ* 10/88; *Them* 1/90; *JETS* 9/89].

Ellison, H. L. (DSB) 1982. Theological, devotional exposition, but sketchy. More conservative than most other entries in DSB.

☆   Estelle, Bryan D. *Echoes of Exodus: Tracing a Biblical Motif*, 2018. A well-researched, helpful guide to how the exodus theme plays throughout Scripture (OT and NT), though he could have cited my work more carefully. [*WTJ* Spr 19; *BBR* 29.3; *CBQ* 4/19; *JETS* 12/18; *JSOT* 43.5; *RTR* 12/20; *JBTS* 4/23]. On a somewhat more popular level are the insightful *Echoes of Exodus* by Alastair Roberts and Andrew Wilson (Crossway, 2018) [*Them* 43.3] and *Exodus Old and New: A Biblical Theology of Redemption* by L. Michael Morales (IVP, 2020) [*BBR* 31.4; *JETS* 6/21; *Them* 46.2]. A bit more critically engaged are the first-rate Seth M. Ehorn, ed., *Exodus in the NT* (LNTS, 2022) [*ExpTim* 4/23; *JSOT* 47.5; *BBR* 33.2; *JETS* 9/23; *Them* 48.1] and R. Michael Fox, ed., *Reverberations of the Exodus in Scripture* (2014).

☆   **Fretheim, Terence E.** ‡ (I) 1991. Fits well with the series. An impressive theological exposition, with an emphasis on a creation theology. "Not many commentaries make a good read—as opposed to a good reference—but this is certainly one of them" [*BSB* 3/99 (Wells)]. Having used Fretheim extensively myself, I included him among my recommendations for twenty-five years, but my buy list was too long. For additional comments on Fretheim, see under Genesis above. [*CRBR* 1992; *PSB* 14.1; *ThTo* 10/91; *Int* 10/92; *CTJ* 4/95].

✓ Friedman, Richard Elliot. ‡ *The Exodus: How It Happened and Why It Matters*, 2017. Of interest for its attempt at revitalizing classic source criticism, alongside confidence that the text records an actual event.

☆ **Garrett, Duane A.** (KEL) 2014. Though less engaged with scholarly debates, this full conservative exegesis (over 700pp.) is useful to students dealing with the Hebrew. Pastors are the main beneficiaries of the commentary, which regularly makes NT connections, includes some illustrations and applications, and is similar in some ways to Currid. The theology drawn out of Exodus is, from my perspective, healthy and God-centered; e.g., see the excursus, "The Hardness of Pharaoh's Heart," pp.370–75. Another strong point is the full introduction (130pp.), tackling especially historical questions and the location of Horeb. On the weaker side, I am unconvinced that 2:23–25 is "proto-apocalyptic" or that passages such as 5:21 and 6:2–8 are best read as poetry. Garrett teaches at Southern Seminary (Baptist) and has written *Rethinking Genesis* (1991), as well as commentaries on Proverbs, Ecclesiastes, and Song of Songs. [*ExpTim* 12/15; *JTS* 4/16; *JSOT* 40.5].

☆ Gispen, W. H. (BSC) ET 1982. Helpful in much the same way as Aalders on Genesis, though the latter is richer theologically, in part because of its greater length. Pastors wanting another evangelical commentary, not a devotional-homiletical help like Ryken, could look to pick up a used copy of the o/p Gispen.

✓ **Gowan, Donald E.** ‡ *Theology in Exodus: Biblical Theology in the Form of a Commentary*, 1994. A rather different type of commentary from what pastors are used to. It is a hybrid of OT Theology and commentary. I judge the work a partial success. Gowan did make a contribution to my understanding of Exodus, e.g., with his long discussion of the divine name. [*ExpTim* 11/95; *CBQ* 7/96; *JETS* 3/97; *JSOT* 75; *Int* 7/96; *SwJT* Sum 98].

✓ **Greenberg, Moshe.** ‡ *Understanding Exodus*, 1969. Though not a lengthy study and now aging, Greenberg is still worth consulting—it is often cited (e.g., in Propp's AB). Greenberg's conservatively critical, Jewish stance is similar to Sarna's. A fine 2nd edition, edited by Tigay (2013), is subtitled "A Holistic Commentary on Exodus 1–11."

☆ **Hamilton, Victor P.** 2011. A nicely produced, middle-scale exegetical work (650pp.), published by Baker outside any series. The author is now retired from Asbury College. His introduction seems to sidestep the old questions about composition: author, date, unity of the book. The commentary is well-researched and makes a serious academic contribution (unless one wants scholarship in other languages), but it is also written in a lively style readers find engaging. Even if one is out of step with the author theologically (and theological exposition is not prominent here), this is still worth having, in large part because Hamilton is steeped in Scripture and quite perceptive in making biblical connections. (This was a recommended purchase in 2016.) The strength of the work is his patient, verse-by-verse approach; he does not offer quite as much help for understanding larger sections of text and the overall flow of the story (see Wright for this). Historical questions are not so important to Hamilton. See his profitable Baker Handbook titles. Students might note Stuart's caveats [*JESOT* 1.1]. [*BBR* 22.3; *Int* 1/13; *JSS* Aut 14; *JSOT* 36.5; *VT* 63.3; *JETS* 9/12; *ExpTim* 1/13; *RelSRev* 12/13; *TJ* Spr 14].

Harman, Allan. (Focus) 2017. Have not seen it for review purposes. The conservative Australian Presbyterian has written many valuable expositions (over 400pp.).

✓ Hawkins, Ralph K. *Discovering Exodus*, 2021. A fuller entry in Eerdmans's Discovering Biblical

Texts series of introductions, and well-done. The author has a keen interest in archaeology. [*CBQ* 7/22; *Int* 7/23].

✓ Hoffmeier, J. K. *Israel in Egypt: The Evidence for the Authenticity of the Exodus Tradition*, 1996. Solidly conservative, from OUP. See also his *Ancient Israel in Sinai* (OUP, 2005), and Hoffmeier–Millard–Rendsburg (eds), *'Did I Not Bring Israel Out of Egypt?'* (2016) [*BBR* 28.2; *JSOT* 41.5].

✓ **Houtman, Cornelis.** ‡ (HCOT) 4 vols., ET 1993–2002. Students should certainly consult Houtman, there being fewer in-depth, scholarly commentaries. It is published in pb— initially by Kok and now by Peeters—and was once difficult to obtain in the USA. Were it not so expensive ($200), I might urge that Houtman be considered for purchase by advanced students. Pastors with a scholarly bent and a sizable book allowance could profit from Houtman like they do from Westermann on Genesis or Zimmerli on Ezekiel. Among the best in its class of technical historical-critical commentary; it "provides the fullest modern treatment . . . of Exodus that is available in any language" (G. I. Davies). He says the portrayal of the plagues is to be classed as "folk tale," and "[v]iewing it as ordinary writing of history leaves one defenseless against rationalistic criticism" (vol.2, p.21). It is said that the quality of the translation is not the best. [*VT* 43, pp.115, 427–28; *VT* 48, p.572; *VT*, 51.3; *Orientalia* 48, p.885; *JSOT* 89; *BL* 1997; *CBQ* 4/01].

Humphreys, Colin. *The Miracles of Exodus*, 2003. Not recommended. [*Them* Sum 04].

Hyatt, James P. ‡ (NCB) 1971. This vol. (about 350pp.) is quite dated in approach and of little value today. Hyatt, a prof at Vanderbilt, published this just prior to his death.

F Imes, Carmen Joy. (BCOT). See under Decalogue.

✓ Jackson, Bernard S. ‡ *Wisdom-Laws: A Study of the* Mishpatim *of Exodus 21:1–22:16* (OUP) 2006. Hailed as a breakthrough study, following his many other technical publications on OT Law, such as *Studies in the Semiotics of Biblical Law* (2000). [*VT* 59.3; *BL* 2007 (Davies)]. Cf. Sprinkle below.

✓ Jacob, Benno. 1943, ET 1992. A remarkable, comprehensive (1100pp.) study of the Hebrew text by a Jewish rabbi who escaped Hitler's Germany. Many learned of this work through Childs's citations of it in the OTL. It is good to see it finally in English dress and published by Ktav. Though somewhat liberal in his general theological approach, Jacob steadfastly rejected Wellhausen's views on source criticism and the evolution of Israelite religion. [*BL* 1993; *JSOT* 79; *BSac* 10/93].

☆ Janzen, J. Gerald. ‡ (WestBC) 1997. A good theological exposition, but not as deep or thorough as Fretheim. The final six chapters are given only a glance. Could be put to excellent use in preparing a sermon. There is attention to exegetical points (and some brilliant insights along the way, e.g., at ch. 6) and to the flow of the book. This 275-page pb is well worth the money. Janzen is Harvard-trained, was ordained in the Anglican Church in Canada, and long taught OT at Christian Theological Seminary in Indianapolis (now retired). I'm glad to call him my friend. [*CBQ* 4/99; *Them* Aut 00; *Int* 1/99; *BL* 1999].

✓ Janzen, Mark D., ed. *Five Views on the Exodus: Historicity, Chronology, and Theological Implications*, 2021. From Zondervan.

☆ **Janzen, Waldemar.** (BCBC) 2000. Chooses to concentrate on the final form or canonical text, and does so even more than Childs. Though not always completely current with contemporary scholarship, Janzen is learned (Harvard PhD), devout in his Mennonite tradition, and concerned to apply Exodus in a pastoral way. I like this nearly 500-page book. [*CBQ* 1/02; *Them* Sum 03].

✓ **Johnstone, William.** ‡ (S&H) 2 vols., 2014. See his past work listed under Chronicles. Johnstone was long on faculty at Aberdeen, and his work would be classed as one of the better, full (about 925pp.) theological expositions of Exodus from a critical angle. The expense is considerable ($130 in pb), last I checked. His regular discussions of source criticism (e.g., "this reuse of D-material in P") are distracting and rather less interesting. Many pastors will chafe when Johnstone assumes a disconnect or "distance between portrayal in theological narrative and the reconstruction of actual historical events" (vol.1, p.8). [*RevExp* 2/15, 5/15; *Int* 7/16; *JSOT* 40.5].

☆ **Kaiser, Walter C.** (EBCR) 2008. The 1990 EBC was solid but only about 200pp., a portion of which was consumed printing the NIV text. Once, in a review of some commentary, Carson suggested that the book did not make up in quality what it necessarily lost by brevity; you may have the same sentiment in using Kaiser. Evangelicals once rated his exegesis highly, but there was less out there to choose from. I'm afraid the EBCR represents only a slight improvement (225pp.); there is not much updating. [*BL* 2010].

Kass, Leon R. ‡ *Founding God's Nation: Reading Exodus*, 2021. Presented as a "philosophical reading." Some term it idiosyncratic. [*ExpTim* 10/22; *BL* 2022].

✓ Keil, C. F. (KD) ET 1864. Keil was once a huge help, considering the paucity of good conservative works on Exodus. Pastors now have a good stock of commentaries.

F ~~Knierim, Rolf P.~~ ‡ *Exodus 19–40; with an Introduction to Legal Genres* (FOTL). See Coats above. I doubt there is a reassignment after his passing (2018).

✓ Langston, Scott M. ‡ (BBC) 2006. Focuses on how Exodus has been interpreted and has influenced culture. Somewhat similar, and quite stimulating, is Göran Larsson, *Bound for Freedom: The Book of Exodus in Jewish and Christian Traditions* (1999).

✓ Levy, Thomas E., Thomas Schneider, and William H. C. Propp, eds. ‡ *Israel's Exodus in Transdisciplinary Perspective*, 2015. [*JSOT* 40.5].

✓ Lienhard, Joseph T., ed. *Exodus, Leviticus, Numbers, Deuteronomy* (ACCS) 2001. [*RelSRev* 7/03; *JBL* 2007 (Davies)].

F Longman, Tremper, III. (THC). Along the way he has published *How to Read Exodus* (2009) [*JSOT* 35.5; *BSac* 4/11; *DenvJ* 14].

F MacDonald, Nathan. ‡ (ICC). His Cambridge faculty page indicates an odd division of work: *Exodus 25–31, 35–40*. See Davies above.

☆ Mackay, John L. (Mentor) 2001. This is a full (over 600pp.), conservative exposition that the pastor could put to good use. "Mackay's theological comments are a strength of this commentary" (P. Barker). There is less in the way of footnotes and bibliography to assist the student working exegetically. See his other Mentor vols. on Jeremiah, Lamentations, and Hosea; unlike *Exodus*, they discuss the Hebrew at points. [*Them* Spr 02].

F McBride, S. Dean. ‡ (Herm).

McNeile, A. H. ‡ (Westminster) 1908, 3rd ed. 1931. Best ignored now.

Merida, Tony. *Exalting Jesus in Exodus* (CCE) 2014.

Meyer, F. B. *Devotional Commentary on Exodus*, 1911, repr. 1978. Nearly 500pp. All his works are warm-hearted. For a study of the man, see Ian M. Randall, *Spirituality and Social Change: The Contribution of F. B. Meyer (1847–1929)*.

✓ **Meyers, Carol.** ‡ (NCBC) 2005. This elegantly and compactly written commentary can be recommended as a first stop for students seeking a mainstream critical interpretation of Exodus as "the commemoration of the past" and "a tribute to the imagination and creativity of those nameless people who . . . made the experiences of some the foundational stories of all" (11–12). She sees Exodus as presenting "the defining features of Israel's identity, as it took shape by the late biblical period" (xv) and as having little historical value. Known for expertise in archaeology, Meyers has a wide range of exegetical skills and provides a well-rounded commentary (except for those who want source criticism). [*CBQ* 4/07; *Int* 7/07; *HS* 2006; *BL* 2006; *JHebS*].

✓ Moberley, R. W. L. ‡ *At the Mountain of God: Story and Theology in Exodus 32–34*, 1983.

☆ Morales, L. Michael. *Exodus Old and New*, 2020. Great book! See Estelle above.

✓ Noth, Martin. ‡ (retired OTL) ET 1962. From an extraordinarily influential critical scholar, but the old Noth–von Rad schema or synthesis has badly broken down. This narrowly historical-critical work was replaced by Childs and is no longer in print. There are other Noth commentaries on Leviticus and Numbers.

F Olson, Dennis. ‡ (AbOTC).

Osborn, Noel D., and Howard A. Hatton. (UBS) 1999.

☆ Oswalt, John. (CorBC) 2008. Part of a Genesis-Exodus vol. and is excellent introductory reading. See the Ross CorBC under Genesis.

Pink, Arthur. *Gleanings in Exodus*, 1962. See Genesis. Free at PBMinistries.org.

F Polak, Frank. ‡ (BerO).

✓ **Propp, William H. C.** ‡ (AB) 2 vols., 1999–2006. As expected from the series, he delivers an exceedingly full exegesis (1500pp.). The commentary returns in some ways to a more traditional historical-critical tack (lots of E, at the expense of J), but Propp is still a very important work. While there is some theological reflection here, that is not the focus. He is more interested in the sociological factors he believes gave rise to this literature (see p.39). As Davies notes [*JSOT* 89], Propp is independent-minded and, most importantly, is the first "to be able to deal fully with manuscript evidence from Qumran." He is taken to task for his idiosyncratic translation, which is "extremely literal to the point of stiltedness." While students find Propp valuable for lexical and grammatical studies, evangelical pastors won't find as much use for this work. Denver Seminary's list makes it a top pick. [*OTA* 2/00; *ExpTim* 5/00; *Int* 1/01; *SwJT* Fall 00; *RelSRev* 10/00; *JR* 4/01; *CBQ* 1/01; *JBL* Win 01; *BL* 2008].

Ramm, Bernard. *His Way Out*, 1974. Theological interpretation of Exodus. Short and helpful for the preacher, but o/p.

F Rooker, Mark. (EBTC).

☆ Rosner, Brian S., and Paul R. Williamson, eds. *Exploring Exodus: Literary, Theological and Contemporary Approaches*, 2008. This is well described as "a survey in the use of the book of Exodus in contemporary theology, both practical and theoretical" (Fayette [*ExpTim* 5/10]).

✓ Roukema, Riemer, ed. ‡ *The Interpretation of Exodus*, 2006.

☆ Ryken, Philip G. (PTW) 2005. Rich, thoughtful, God-centered preaching in a fat vol. (cf. his *Jeremiah* in PTW). It is less attuned to OT scholarship than some other entries in the series, such as Duguid on Numbers.

F Saner, Andrea D. (ITC).

☆ **Sarna, Nahum.** ‡ (JPS) 1991. A profound, 278-page entry in this elegantly produced Jewish series; I wish it were twice as long. His learning with regard to the ANE background is most impressive. Students can learn a great deal from this exegesis, and some will find themselves getting fascinated by the ins-and-outs of rabbinic commentary. (On this point, Enns says Sarna can "direct the reader to elements of the text that Christian readers might otherwise pass over too quickly.") See his other JPS work on Genesis above. [*CBQ* 7/93]. Also note his insightful *Exploring Exodus* (1986, 1996), taking up different interpretive issues than JPS [*CRBR* 1988].

Scarlata, Mark. [𝓜], *The Abiding Presence: A Theological Commentary on Exodus*, 2018. I have not seen it, but some regard Scarlata's book as elegantly written and one of the more profitable expositions available on Exodus. [*JSOT* 43.5; *ETL* 95.1]. The American author holds a Cambridge PhD and is Senior Lecturer in OT at St. Mellitus College.

F Schmid, Konrad. ‡ (Illum).

Selvaggio, Anthony T. *From Bondage to Liberty: The Gospel according to Moses* (GAOT) 2014. Looking at Moses's life and work. [*Chm* Aut 14].

F Sklar, Jay. (ESVEC) 2024. See Duguid under Genesis. Deserves a very close look!

✓ Sprinkle, Joe M. *'The Book of the Covenant': A Literary Approach*, 1994.

F  Strawn, Brent A. (OTL-R). Would replace Childs.

F  Trimm, Charlie, and Chloe Sun. (NICOT) 2 vols. Trimm previously published *"YHWH Fights for Them!": The Divine Warrior in the Exodus Narrative* (2014), and *Fighting for the King and the Gods: A Survey of Warfare in the ANE* (2017). Dr. Sun was recently (2023) appointed to the Fuller Seminary faculty, and she has published *Conspicuous in His Absence: Studies in the Song of Songs and Esther* (2021).

✓ **Utzschneider, Helmut, and Wolfgang Oswald.** ‡ *Exodus 1–15* (IECOT) ET 2015. One of two pilot vols. for the series, this 340-page work blends synchronic and diachronic (mainly source critical) analysis. It is moderately critical and proves useful to students for its interaction with European scholarship. The source criticism—tiresome to many—is rather different from the old Wellhausen scheme and distinguishes five layers: an Older Exodus Narrative, Exodus-Mountain Narrative, DtrH, Priestly Composition, and post-Priestly insertions termed the Torah Composition. [*BBR* 24.3; *VT* 66.2; *JSOT* 45.5; *JHebS* 13].

White, John H. *Slavery to Servanthood*, 1987. These 13 lessons published by Great Commission (Adult Discipleship Series) are suggestive for either a Bible class or a sermon series. The subtitle is "Tracing the Exodus throughout Scripture." The author is a minister in the Reformed Presbyterian Church in North America ("Covenanters"). Pastors might consider this, if it remains in print.

White, Thomas Joseph. [𝓜], (Brazos) 2016. By a Dominican theologian who is an Aquinas specialist. [*JETS* 6/17].

NOTE: C. S. Rodd's "Which Is the Best Commentary? Exodus," *ExpTim*, 9/87.

# DECALOGUE & BIBLICAL LAW

★ Averbeck, Richard E. *The Old Testament Law for the Life of the Church*, 2022. More studious pastors are advised to buy Wright (below) or this fine work, where the TEDS professor emeritus is "[c]onsolidating decades of study in Old Testament Law" (Millard). Averbeck has an abiding concern for the health and maturity of the church. See his essay on "The Law and the Gospels" in Barmash (ed.) below. [*JETS* 6/23].

★ Calvin, John. *Institutes of the Christian Religion*, II.viii. Calvin's profound theological interpretation of the law has had untold influence upon political, economic, cultural, and spiritual developments in the Western world. Some may be surprised by differences between Calvin and the Puritans on the application of the moral law (e.g., the 4th commandment). By the way, the 1960 Battles translation of the *Institutes* (WJK) is the edition to buy. See Calvin's sermons and commentary below.

★ Douma, J. *The Ten Commandments: Manual for the Christian Life*, ET 1996. As the subtitle suggests, this Dutch work has a Reformed orientation. It is useful to both students and pastors; Douma has even served as a textbook in seminary ethics courses. Another rich ethics book using the Ten Words to structure much of the discussion is John Frame, *The Doctrine of the Christian Life* (2008) [*Them* 7/09].

★ Hughes, R. Kent. *The Disciplines of Grace*, 1993. An excellent modern-day exposition by the sometime pastor of the College Church in Wheaton. For the preacher, this is well worth the money. See the series PTW. Compare with Ryken.

★ Miller, Patrick D. ‡ *The Ten Commandments* (I) 2009. An extremely valuable work, especially for students of OT theology and ethics. The author long taught an ethics course at Princeton Seminary based on his research on the Decalogue. Of special note are the length of this exposition (477pp. including indices) and the exploration of "the interplay and resonance of the Commandments with many other texts" (xi) in Scripture. Academically oriented pastors will receive much stimulation reading Miller. [*BL* 2010; *JETS* 9/10; *CBQ* 10/10; *RTR* 12/10; *BTB* 2/11].

★ Ryken, Philip G. *Written in Stone: The Ten Commandments and Today's Moral Crisis*, 2008. A lively, penetrating series of sermons with both theological depth and excellent application to the church.

✓ Aaron, David H. ‡ *Etched in Stone: The Emergence of the Decalogue*, 2006. A quite critical interpretation, dating the law late (Persian era). Regrettably, there is little discussion of the text itself. The scholarship is of a high order. [*RelSRev* 9/09; *BL* 2007].

Barclay, William. ‡ *The Ten Commandments for Today*, 1973. Suggestive, and reprinted by WJK in 1998.

☆ Baker, David L. *The Decalogue: Living as the People of God*, 2017. Well-done. [*CBQ* 10/18; *Int* 1/19; *JETS* 12/17].

✓ Barmash, Pamela, ed. ‡ *The Oxford Handbook of Biblical Law*, 2019.

✓ Barton, John. ‡ *Understanding OT Ethics*, 2003. See also his *Theory and Practice in OT Ethics* (2004), and *Ethics in Ancient Israel* (OUP, 2015). Another oft-cited critical work is Waldemar Janzen, *OT Ethics* (1994). Cf. Averbeck and Wright.

☆ Bavinck, Herman. *Reformed Ethics*, Vol. 2: "The Duties of the Christian Life." ET 2021. Includes his exposition of the Ten Commandments.

☆ Braaten, Carl E., and Christopher R. Seitz, eds. ‡ *I Am the Lord Your God: Christian Reflections on the Ten Commandments*, 2005. Though somewhat critically oriented, the book benefits evangelicals. The contributors are mainly theologians instead of biblical scholars. [*RTR* 8/08; *Them* 1/06; *ExpTim* 5/06; *SJT* 63.2].

✓ Brown, William P., ed. ‡ *The Ten Commandments: The Reciprocity of Faithfulness*, 2004. This fascinating collection includes a few of the writings of church fathers and the Reformers, as well as essays from many contemporary OT scholars, theologians, and ethicists. [*CBQ* 10/05; *ExpTim* 2/06, 7/06; *CurTM* 8/06; *BL* 2007].

☆ Calvin, John. *Sermons on the Ten Commandments*, ET 1980. The Farley translation, first published by Baker, is reprinted every so often. [*WTJ* Spr 82]. Few are aware of how massive an exposition Calvin published in his *Commentaries on the Last Four Books of Moses*; see vol.1, pp.338–502; vol.2, pp.5–472; and vol.3, pp.5–201.

✓ Clines, David J. A. ‡ "The Ten Commandments, Reading from Left to Right" (26–45), in *Interested Parties: The Ideology of Writers and Readers of the Hebrew Bible* (1995). An influential denial of the Ten Words' revelatory character.

☆ Clowney, Edmund. *How Jesus Transforms the Ten Commandments*, 2007. A fresh, biblical-theological reading by the late President of Westminster Seminary in Philadelphia. Pastors and thoughtful Christians will relish this.

✓ Collins, R. F. ‡ "The Ten Commandments" in *ABD*, vol. 6.

✓ Coogan, Michael. ‡ *The Ten Commandments: A Short History of an Ancient Text*, 2014. Concerned that they not be displayed in public. [*RelSRev* 3/15; *JSOT* 41.5; *JHebS* 17].

Davidman, Joy. *Smoke on the Mountain*, 1953.

Freedman, David Noel. ‡ *The Nine Commandments*, 2000. A more popular study by a highly esteemed Jewish Bible scholar (217pp.). Conservatively critical.

Gane, Roy E. *Old Testament Law for Christians: Original Context and Enduring Application*, 2017. Includes a treatment of the Decalogue. Gane teaches at the Seventh Day Adventist Seminary. [*CTJ* 4/21; *JETS* 3/18].

Goldingay, John. [𝓜], *Old Testament Ethics: A Guided Tour*, 2019. Receiving attention as a mildly critical study from IVP Academic (though it is more a popular Bible study guide than an academic piece).

✓ Greenman, J. P., and T. Larsen, eds. *The Decalogue through the Centuries*, 2012.

✓ Harrelson, Walter. ‡ *The Ten Commandments and Human Rights*, 1980.

*Heidelberg Catechism* (1563), Questions 92–115. See also Ursinus's *Commentary on the Catechism* which has been reprinted by P&R.

Horton, Michael S. *The Law of Perfect Freedom*, 2nd ed. 2004. Another good Reformed exposition with a Lutheran tinge, some would argue.

✓ Imes, Carmen Joy. *Bearing YHWH's Name at Sinai: A Reexamination of the Name Command of the Decalogue*, 2018. An important study, arguing that the command "prohibits Israel from acting in a manner inconsistent with the responsibilities assumed upon entering into a state of belonging to ('bearing the name of') YHWH" (Hutton [*JSS* Spr 20]). See also *Bearing God's Name: Why Sinai Still Matters* (2019) [*JETS* 6/20; *Them* 45.2], dealing more generally with the Sinaitic Covenant and Ten Commandments.

✓ Kuntz, Paul G. ‡ *The Ten Commandments in History: Mosaic Paradigms for a Well-Ordered Society*, 2004. Treats the Decalogue within the history of ideas.

✓ Lalleman, Hetty. *Celebrating the Law? Rethinking OT Ethics*, 2004. A welcome evangelical treatment of the topic. Earlier we had *Toward OT Ethics* by Walter Kaiser (1983). See also Wright below.

Leithart, Peter J. *The Ten Commandments: A Guide to the Perfect Law of Liberty*, 2020. [*WTJ* Fall 20].

✓ Markl, Dominik, ed. ‡ *The Decalogue and Its Cultural Influence*, 2013. [*JSOT* 38.5; *ETL* 92.4].

Meilaender, Gilbert. *Thy Will Be Done: The Ten Commandments and the Christian Life*, 2020. A brief, more conservative, and thought-provoking Lutheran exposition. The author is a respected ethicist and theologian. [*Int* 7/21; *Them* 46.1].

Mohler, R. Albert. *Words from the Fire*, 2009. A Moody Press book, with a Reformed tone, pressing the ethical claims of the Gospel.

Morgan, G. Campbell. *The Ten Commandments*, 1901. Classic exposition.

✓ Morrow, William S. ‡ *An Introduction to Biblical Law*, 2017. [*ETL* 94.1].

✓ Nielson, E. ‡ *The Ten Commandments in New Perspective*, 1968.

☆ Packer, J. I. *Keeping the Ten Commandments*, 2008.

Patrick, Dale. ‡ *Old Testament Law*, 1985.

✓ Phillips, A. ‡ *Essays on Biblical Law*, 2002. His diss. was published as *Ancient Israel's Criminal Law: A New Approach to the Decalogue* (1970).

✓ Reventlow, Henning G., and Yair Hoffman, eds. ‡ *The Decalogue in Jewish and Christian Tradition*, 2011.

Rooker, Mark. *The Ten Commandments: Ethics for the Twenty-First Century*, 2010. I have yet to use this (B&H). See Rooker on Leviticus and Ezekiel. [*JETS* 12/10].

✓ Segal, B. Z., ed. ‡ *The Ten Commandments in History and Tradition*, ET 1990. Essays well worth looking up. The book is published by Magnes Press in Israel.

✓ Stamm, Johan Jakob, and Maurice E. Andrew. ‡ *The Ten Commandments in Recent Research*, 1967.

F   Strawn, Brent A. ‡ *Exodus 20*, 2024? For the Baker Touchstone Texts series.

✓ Strawn, Brent A., ed. ‡ *The Oxford Encyclopedia of the Bible and Law*, 2 vols., 2015.

✓ Van Harn, Roger E., ed. *The Ten Commandments for Jews, Christians, and Others*, 2007.

Wallace, R. S. *The Ten Commandments*, 1965. One could wish for a reprint.

☆ Watson, Thomas. *The Ten Commandments*, 1692. A classic Puritan exposition of the Decalogue (and the Westminster Assembly's Catechism on the Commandments, WLC Questions 100–48) which is regularly reprinted by Banner. These same 200pp. are also found in the larger work *A Body of Divinity*, also being kept in print by Banner. Watson's approximate dates were 1620–89.

✓ Westbrook, Raymond, and Bruce Wells. ‡ *Everyday Law in Biblical Israel*, 2009. "The best and most up-to-date introduction available to the theory and practice of law in biblical times" (Patrick Miller). This brief vol. (156pp.) addresses texts throughout the OT with a special focus on the *Mishpatim* of Exodus. [*JSS* Aut 13; *VT* 64.1; *JHebS* 11]. For a broader perspective, see also Bernard Levinson, ed., *Theory and Method in Biblical and Cuneiform Law* (1994), and Westbrook, ed., *A History of Ancient Near Eastern Law* (2003).

✓ Willimon, William, and Stanley Hauerwas. ‡ *The Truth about God: The Ten Commandments in Christian Life*, 1999. Engaging the debate in American religious circles, the Duke professors argue that the Decalogue does not present a set of "timeless ethical principles that are applicable to all." Rather, it guides the church community toward holiness. Cf. Kuntz's argument.

☆ Wright, Christopher J. H. *Old Testament Ethics for the People of God*, 2004. Probably the most often recommended vol. among evangelicals, but see Averbeck above. [*JSOT* 6/05].

NOTES: (1) Commentaries on the book of Deuteronomy (ch. 5) will be quite useful—e.g., in comparing the theology of the 4th commandment in Exod 20:11 with Deut 5:15. Weinfeld's *Deuteronomy 1–11* has nearly 100pp on the "Ten Words." (2) The evangelical debate over the role of the law in the Christian life can be followed in Stanley Gundry, ed., *Five Views on Law and Gospel* (1996), and Donald Alexander, ed., *Christian Spirituality: Five Views on Sanctification* (1988).

# LEVITICUS

★ Harper, G. Geoffrey. *Teaching Leviticus* (2022). Simply one of the fullest and best expositions for pastors (400pp.). A real bargain too! [*Them* 48.1]. On the way to this publication, we received *I Will Walk among You* (2018), his excellent scholarly study of Leviticus in the light of Gen 1–3. See below.

★ **Hartley, John.** (WBC) 1992. A workmanlike exegesis of the Hebrew, which has been a superb complement to Wenham for the studious. Has a full discussion of the text (nearly 500pp.) and a learned introduction (55pp.) dealing with trends in pentateuchal criticism, but is dated. More conservative than most of the other WBC on the Pentateuch. Was my first pick (but my academic bent may have been coming to the fore). The average pastor would probably want to start with Sklar's TOTC or Wenham. If you are more the advanced student type, want technical commentaries, have lots of money, and can speed read, the best choice is doubtless the combination of Milgrom's AB set and Sklar's ZECOT, supplemented by Hartley. [*SwJT* Sum 94].

★ Mathews, Kenneth. *Leviticus: Holy God, Holy People* (PTW) 2009. This vol. is near 300pp. and of good help to the expositor. From what I've seen, this manageable homiletical treatment is the equal of Ross and replaces Tidball's excellent commentary on my "buy list." See Mathews's 2-vol. NAC on Genesis. [*JETS* 12/10].

★ Ross, Allen P. *Holiness to the Lord*, 2002. Much in the same mold as his 1988 exposition of Genesis. Ross is a fine preacher's help. Cf. Tidball, Gane, and the very useful Shepherd. Expositors who love Reformed theology and old books should also consider Bonar, while I regard Balentine as the best theological interpretation from the moderately critical side. [*CBQ* 7/03; *Them* Aut 04; *JETS* 6/03; *Int* 4/03; *JSOT* 27.5].

★ **Sklar, Jay.** (ZECOT) 2023. A decade after his useful TOTC (below), the Covenant Seminary prof was given about four times the space to write this more technical study of the

Hebrew. Well-trained pastors will want to make ZECOT a first purchase, not only because it is meticulously researched over many years, judicious in its exegetical judgment, and deeply concerned with theology, but also because it is up-to-date and offers the unique feature of structural diagrams (discourse analysis). Those without Hebrew can also make excellent use of it because in the series it is one of the most accessible and most helpful vols. for application concerns. The Introduction of 65pp. is an expanded and updated version of that in TOTC, and the commentary proper surpasses 700pp. The 45-page Scripture index indicates Sklar's commitment to the principle that Scripture is its own interpreter. He interacts with the more important scholarship, such as Milgrom, Wenham, and Levine, but keeps the text as his focus. (If I had one wish, it would be for more interaction with Rendtorff and Hieke.) With the extra space, as compared with the Tyndale, he helps expositors in sections on Canonical and Theological Significance. [*BL* 2024].

★ **Wenham, Gordon J.** (NICOT) 1979. Excellent in every way for its time! Especially helpful for its theological insight. Both Stuart and Longman once called this the best. Was certainly your first choice before Hartley and Rooker came along; compare them. I really like all three. [*JBL* 100.4; *EvQ* 1/81; *JETS* 12/80]. Many will find a subsequent Wenham article instructive: "The Theology of Unclean Food," *EvQ* 53 (1981): 6–15.

Baker, David W. (CorBC) 2008. Bound with Numbers and Deuteronomy (approx. 700pp.). Dale Brueggemann (Numbers) and Eugene Merrill (Deuteronomy) are coauthors. I regret that I have not seen this.

Bailey, Lloyd R. ‡ *Leviticus–Numbers* (S&H) 2005. There is some exegetical value here, if one is seeking to consult a non-technical, moderately critical commentary. Many will turn to Bailey more for ideas on how the message of these Bible texts can relate to today's world. I do not see it as good value for the money. [*Int* 7/06].

✓ **Balentine, Samuel E.** ‡ (I) 2002. This author was chosen for his interest and expertise in scholarship on the rituals of faith and ancient Hebrew worship. See *The Torah's Vision of Worship* (1999) [*Int* 7/01; *JSS* Spr 02; *JR* 4/02]. Though not so lengthy (220pp.), the theological exposition repays study. Some evangelicals, with an aversion to anything that smacks of ritual or liturgy, are prompted here to do more careful, balanced thinking about the relation of their faith to the forms of biblical worship. Balentine taught at Union in Richmond. For a more conservative approach to OT ritual, see Gane. I pass along Jenson's recommendation that pastors consider Balentine, his favorite (as of 2010). [*ExpTim* 11/03; *JSOT* 28.5; *RelSRev* 4/04; *Int* 1/05; *JHebS* 4].

☆ Beckwith, Roger T., and Martin J. Selman, eds. *Sacrifice in the Bible*, 1995. Superb conservative essays. For background reading on the rituals and theology of Leviticus, see especially the essays of Jenson and Wenham, and note Daniel Ullucci, "Sacrifice in the Ancient Mediterranean: Recent and Current Research," *CBR* 13.3 (2015): 388–439.

Bellinger, William. [𝓜], *Leviticus, Numbers* (NIBC) 2001. The theology Bellinger draws from these Bible books is more conservative than his views on compositional history (final form in postexilic times). The commentary is well-written by a mature, conservatively critical Baptist at Baylor. [*BBR* 14.1; *JHebS* 4].

☆ Bonar, Andrew A. (GS) 1846. A lovely devotional and theological exposition by one of the godliest ministers Scotland ever knew. Heavy on typology, but not irresponsible. Exegesis should be checked against Sklar, Wenham, and Hartley. If you love Puritan-style commentaries, you will relish this.

Boyce, Richard N. ‡ *Leviticus and Numbers* (WestBC) 2008. [*JSOT* 35.5].

✓ **Budd, Philip J.** ‡ (NCB) 1996. Takes a more traditional literary-critical approach, employing source and form criticism. Students can profit from consulting Budd, but pastors find more reliable and theologically sensitive exegeses elsewhere. This replaces Snaith. For more comments on Budd, see Numbers. [*BL* 1997; *ExpTim* 10/96; *Them* 1/97; *JETS* 12/99; *JBL* Spr 98; *JSS* Aut 98; *CBQ* 1/98; *BSac* 4/97; *HS* 1998; *RelSRev* 7/97].

Bush, George. 1857. See under Exodus.

**Calvin, John.** *Harmony of the Pentateuch*, 1563. See under Exodus.

☆ Currid, John D. (EPSC) 2004. See his similar vols. on Genesis and Exodus, which are arguably more successful efforts. Still a very good book for pastors (398pp.) who want to recover for the pulpit this neglected portion of the OT. [*RTR* 8/06; *BSac* 1/07].

F Davis, Katherine M. (née Smith). (Hodder).

F Davis, Katherine M. (née Smith). (Pillar).

✓ Day, John, ed. ‡ *Temple and Worship in Biblical Israel*, 2007. Top-notch scholarship.

☆ Demarest, Gary W. (WCC) 1990. Written by an evangelical PCUSA minister, this exposition is better researched than many others in the OT series.

✓ Douglas, Mary. ‡ *Purity and Danger*, 1966. To this seminal study of the "Priestly conception of holiness" many more have been added. Douglas has also written *Implicit Meanings* (1975); *Leviticus as Literature* (1999) [*BSac* 10/03]; and *Jacob's Tears: The Priestly Work of Reconciliation* (2004). Her interdisciplinary efforts [*JR* 4/09] have encouraged many others to study these matters, especially through an anthropological approach, and there has been an explosion of work on Leviticus in the last 50 years. Note that Douglas's work has sparked a fair amount of controversy.

✓ Elliott, Mark W. *Engaging Leviticus: Reading Leviticus Theologically with Its Past Interpreters*, 2012. Includes the church fathers, medieval Christian and Jewish interpreters, the Reformers, Protestant scholastics, early Jesuits, and modern-day exegetes. Elliott, who teaches at St. Andrews, provides a vast and valuable survey in 335pp. [*JTS* 10/14; *JSOT* 38.5].

☆ Eveson, Philip H. *The Beauty of Holiness* (Welwyn) 2007. A valuable pastoral exposition by a Welsh minister who became Principal of London Theological Seminary.

☆ **Gane, Roy.** *Leviticus, Numbers* (NIVAC) 2004. I have had less opportunity to review this, but what I have read is well-researched and helpful. Gane is an able scholar, interested in religious rituals, who has published an important study of the Israelite sacrificial system, particularly the חטאת "purification offering" (*Cult and Character*, 2005) [*CBQ* 1/07; *BBR* 17.2; *JBL* Fall 06; *JAOS* 127.2; *BL* 2007; *RBL* 4/07]. All the time he spent studying the Hebrew of these two books under Professor Milgrom prepared him well to comment on them. More space in this vol. is devoted to Leviticus than Numbers; similarly the commentary on Leviticus is the stronger. Gane teaches at Andrews University (Seventh-Day Adventist), and some suspect with good reason that he has read his church's odd doctrine of the investigative judgment into the Day of Atonement; this is a problem because many pastors are most interested in ch. 16. Students and preachers both benefit from Gane.

✓ **Gerstenberger, Erhard S.** ‡ (OTL) 1993, ET 1996. A significant exegetical commentary, originally for ATD, to be consulted by students. Takes a standard critical line on most interpretive issues, dating the book in the postexilic period. The author is a prominent form critic, best known for his work on Psalms. This replaced Noth in the series. [*CBQ* 10/94; *BL* 1994; *JETS* 12/99; *JSOT* 65, 79; *Int* 10/99; *HS* 1999; *CRBR* 1995; *RelSRev* 1/98; *JR* 10/98].

F Goldingay, John. (EEC). A previous report was Richard Averbeck.

✓ **Gorman, Frank.** ‡ (ITC-E) 1997. Not as critically oriented as some others in the series, this is well-written and well-researched. He has an interest in the approach of ritual studies and the idea of enactment; see his book *The Ideology of Ritual: Space, Time and Status in the Priestly Theology* (1990). Though a slim work of about 150pp., Gorman is not so popularly styled and does not cater to the needs and interests of church people and pastors quite like some others in the series. [*CBQ* 4/99; *HS* 41; *Int* 10/99; *CTJ* 4/99; *RelSRev* 1/99; *BL* 1999].

✓ Greenberg, James A. *A New Look at Atonement in Leviticus: The Meaning and Purpose of* Kipper *Revisited*, 2019. Important reading, especially for Greenberg's survey of interpretations of כפר and his critique of Milgrom's "purge" idea (*Leviticus 1–16*, pp.1079–84). Greenberg teaches at Denver Seminary. [*Them* 2020; *JETS* 12/20; *DenvJ* 2023; *Them* 45.2 (Harper)]. See Sklar for an earlier PhD (also under Gordon Wenham) treating the topic; his most recent explanation of the "ransom and purification" view is in ZECOT, pp.28–32.

☆ Greidanus, Sidney. *Preaching Christ from Leviticus*, 2021. Apparently his last in this consistently helpful series. The introduction lays out how Greidanus combines his literary, historical, typological, theocentric, and Christocentric interpretations. His grasp of both biblical studies and homiletics is enviable. There is a bevy of suggestions for sermons (seed-thoughts) and how a minister might preach a Christ-centered series. See Duguid's review [*WTJ* Spr 23] for gentle criticism of Greidanus's dismissal of the traditional Reformed categorization of OT law as moral, civil, and ceremonial. Preachers and students both benefit from this excellent resource. [*BBR* 32.2; *Presb* Fall 21; *BL* 2022; *JETS* 9/21, 12/21].

✓ Haran, M. ‡ *Temples and Temple-Service in Ancient Israel*, 1978.

F Harper, G. Geoffrey. (BGW). See Harper above.

Harris, R. Laird. (EBC) 1990. Quite brief at only 150pp. (including NIV text). Harris was the NIV translator of Leviticus and passed away in 2008. See Hess below.

Harrison, R. K. (retired TOTC) 1980. Brief and no competition to Wenham, but was helpful and handy (252pp.). Do not discard. See Sklar. [*RTR* 9/81; *JBL* 102.1; *EvQ* 7/82].

☆ **Hess, Richard.** (EBCR) 2008. The vol. also covers Genesis (Sailhamer) and Exodus (Kaiser) and is a big improvement on the EBC. From what I see in these 265pp., and on the basis of the author's past work, I judge this to be among the best briefer evangelical exegeses of Leviticus. Theological reflection is not quite as strong. [*BL* 2010]. See also Hess on *Israelite Religions* (2007) [*WTJ* Spr 09; *BSac* 1/09; *Int* 7/09; *HBT* 30.2; *VT* 60.2; *BASOR* 2/09; *Presb* Spr 13], regarded as the standard evangelical treatment of the topic.

✓ Hieke, Thomas, and Tobias Niklas, eds. ‡ *The Day of Atonement: Its Interpretations in Early Jewish and Christian Traditions*, 2012. [*BBR* 22.4].

F Hutton, Rodney R. ‡ (FOTL).

✓ Jenson, Philip P. [𝓜], *The Priestly Vision of Holiness*, 2021. In the T&T Clark Study Guide series. Very well-done, taking standard critical positions. [*ExpTim* 4/22; *BL* 2022]. It replaced Grabbe (1993). Jenson's highly regarded, conservatively critical, revised PhD study, *Graded Holiness: A Key to the Priestly Conception of the World* (1992), can be placed alongside the Douglas work. He taught at Ridley Hall, Cambridge.

☆ **Kaiser, Walter.** (NIB) 1994. It is something of a surprise to see an evangelical writing for the *New Interpreter's Bible*, but Abingdon wanted to cast a wider net than with the old IB. Kaiser is better here than on Exodus. Because this NIB vol. also contains sterling theological commentaries on Genesis by Fretheim and on Exodus by Brueggemann, you would not go wrong buying it (if you don't mind the more liberal theology). Kaiser's contribution, perhaps by design, is briefer (a bit over 200pp.) than Fretheim (350pp.) or Brueggemann (305pp.). [*PSB* 16.3; *CBQ* 4/96; *JETS* 9/96].

Kamionkowski, S. Tamar. ‡ *Leviticus* (Wisdom) 2018. The author traces a tension between "P" material in chs. 1–16 and the later "H" (Holiness School) in chs. 17–26. As anticipated, the overtly feminist interpretation (about 400pp.) includes much discussion of gender/power dynamics. [*RBL* 4/20; *Int* 10/20; *JSOT* 43.5].

✓ Keil, C. F. (KD) ET 1864. See under Genesis.

☆ Kellogg, S. H. (EB) 1891. Reprinted by Klock & Klock and by Kregel (1988), Kellogg was a stronger entry in the old EB; pastors could put the exposition to good use if they have the funds and shelf space. The typology here is more restrained than Bonar's.

☆ **Kiuchi, Nobuyoshi.** (Apollos) 2007. The author wrote *A Study of Ḥāṭā and Ḥaṭṭā't in Leviticus 4–5* (2003), a revision of *The Purification Offering in the Priestly Literature* (1987), which received good reviews. I must mention, however, that Kiuchi's research on *ḥāṭā* (חטא) is revisionist; he argues the root term means "to hide oneself" and not "to sin" in the sense of transgressing a moral code. For a critique see Leigh M. Trevaskis, "On a Recent 'Existential' Translation of *ḥāṭā*," *VT* 59.2 (2009): 313–19. This work stimulates discussion among scholars and reflection among academically oriented pastors. Some of the exegesis is insightful, but Kiuchi should not replace Wenham and Hartley on the preacher's shelf. It seems less dependable exegetically and theologically—e.g., he speaks of Israel at Sinai as "yet unredeemed" (28)—than is required to be on the recommended list. For some rather eccentric interpretation, see his exploration of the rationale for, and symbolism behind, the clean/unclean distinction (207–10). Students must take account of Kiuchi's work. He staunchly defends Mosaic authorship. [*BL* 2008; *JETS* 3/08].

☆ **Kleinig, John W.** (ConcC) 2003. A 600-page Lutheran commentary I've had less opportunity to use. It is reputed to be a strong representative of the series, well-informed by scholarship (Cambridge PhD) and strictly adhering to a Lutheran theology. See the extensive textual notes and valuable sections on Fulfillment by Christ. [*CBQ* 4/07; *CJ* 7/05].

Knight, G. A. F. ‡ (DSB) 1981. Very rewarding in places for theology, but hampered by format and space restrictions. Moderately critical. [*EvQ* 1/84; *JETS* 6/84].

Ko, Ming Him. (Asia) 2018. I have yet to see it. [*JSOT* 45.5; *Them* 44.1].

F   Kugler, Robert. ‡ (Illum).

✓ **Levine, Baruch.** ‡ (JPS) 1989. Covers this Bible book in 284pp. Scholars often read Levine and Milgrom side by side for both Leviticus and Numbers. OT specialists have a high regard for Levine because "in philology he is nonpareil" (Milgrom, p.2438). See Numbers below. [*JR* 1/95; *CRBR* 1991; *HS* 1994 (Wenham)].

✓ Lienhard, Joseph T., ed. *Exodus, Leviticus, Numbers, Deuteronomy* (ACCS) 2001. See under Exodus.

☆ Longman, Tremper, III. *Immanuel in Our Place: Christ in Israel's Worship*, 2001. A huge help to the preacher with its redemptive-historical interpretations of OT religion and worship rituals; such a theological approach to this Bible material is not well-represented in the literature. [*Them* Aut 02; *JETS* 6/03; *F&M* Spr 03; *CJ* 7/05]. Also reflecting much work with the OT in framing a biblical theology of worship is Daniel Block's *For the Glory of God* (2014) [*ExpTim* 8/15].

Malone, Andrew S. *God's Mediators: A Biblical Theology of Priesthood*, 2017. Covers a great deal more than Leviticus. [*Them* 43.1].

Mays, James L. ‡ (Layman's Bible Commentary) 1963. Brief and popular. Once noted often in commentary surveys, but many more valuable tools are now available.

✓ **Milgrom, Jacob.** ‡ (AB) 3 vols., 1991–2001. The leading critical work. Evidently the author set out to write the most exhaustive and exhausting commentary on Leviticus ever. The three vols. total over 2700pp., with indices and bibliography included. It is a fairly technical work by one of the foremost Jewish pentateuchal scholars. Though he does engage in diachronic source and redaction criticism (P1, P2, P3, H, etc.), he is more interested in the final form of the text. This work would have been shorter had he not purposed to provide a catalog of medieval Jewish comment. He pulled some OT scholarship in a rightward direction (e.g., his arguments for P being earlier). Students will certainly look this up, but few pastors will purchase this monumental set, which was the crowning achievement of Milgrom's career. Two caveats: you may not wish to follow him in his interpretations of 17:11 (see Emile

Nicole's chapter in Hill–James, *The Glory of the Atonement,* 2004) or of the proscription of homosexual activity (see www.robgagnon.net/articles/homoMilgrom.pdf). Note also Milgrom's work on Numbers below. [*JSOT* 12/93; *JBL* Sum 93; *VT* 1/94; *Bib* 74.2; *CBQ* 1/03; *JTS* 4/02; *Int* 4/02; *BSac* 7/02; *JSOT* 99; *AsTJ,* Spr 03; *JR* 7/03; *CurTM* 12/02; *HS* 2004; *JHebS* 4; *RBL*].

Milgrom, Jacob. ‡ (ContC) 2004. I'd expected a well-done distillation of AB and a welcome addition to the literature, but it is less useful. He covers Leviticus in 344pp. [*Chm* Aut 05; *JETS* 9/05; *BL* 2005; *SwJT* Fall 04; *RelSRev* 1/06; *JHebS*; *BSac* 4/08; *ExpTim* 12/05; *Anvil* 22.4].

✓ Miller, Patrick D. ‡ *The Religion of Ancient Israel,* 2000. Not a commentary, it is highly instructive and generally dependable for students researching this key topic in Leviticus. For the evangelical student or preacher who puzzles over how to approach the latter half of Exodus and the book of Leviticus, Miller provides a store of information. See also Longman above. [*Them* Spr 02; *JTS* 4/02; *JETS* 6/03; *JBL* Spr 02; *Int* 1/02; *ThTo* 7/01; *SwJT* Sum 02; *BBR* 13.1; *DenvJ* (Hess); *Anvil* 18.4]. Cf. the major works by Hess and Zevit.

☆ Morales, L. Michael. *Who Shall Ascend the Mountain of the Lord: A Biblical Theology of the Book of Leviticus* (NSBT) 2015. One of the most profitable, thought-provoking vols. a student or pastor could read on this Bible book. [*Chm* Spr 16; *WTJ* Fall 18; *JETS* 6/17; *JSOT* 42.5; *Them* 41.2 (Harper)].

✓ Moscicke, Hans M. ‡ *Goat for Yahweh, Goat for Azazel,* 2021. Along with his diss. in the WUNT series (*The New Day of Atonement*), this is a stimulating read about the NT reception of Lev 16. [*JETS* 3/23; *JSNT* 44.5].

Moseley, Allan. *Exalting Jesus in Leviticus* (CCE) 2015.

F  Noble, John T. (BCOT).

✓ Noordtzij, A. [*M*], (BSC) 1955, ET 1982. Dated, but there is some depth of insight in Noordtzij (see Numbers as well). Though he confronts the school of Wellhausen, there are aspects of critical thought here. (Can one trace the influence of J. P. E. Pedersen?) Look this up, if you are fascinated by Leviticus.

✓ Noth, Martin. ‡ (retired OTL) ET 1965, rev. 1977. Thorough in its old-style literary-critical discussion, disassembling the text and treating it exclusively from the historical angle. Hardly any theology (o/p). See under Exodus. Replaced by Gerstenberger.

F  Palmer, Christine E. (NICOT-R). Would replace Wenham and build upon her ESVEC.

F  Palmer, Christine. (ESVEC) 2024. See Duguid under Genesis.

Porter, J. R. ‡ (CBC) 1976.

Radnor, Ephraim. (Brazos) 2008. I have not had occasion to use this. Reviews are mixed. [*JETS* 6/09; *CBQ* 4/09; *Them* 4/09; *RBL*; *BL* 2009; *CTJ* 11/11].

✓ Rendtorff, Rolf, and Robert Kugler, eds. ‡ *The Book of Leviticus: Composition and Reception,* 2003. [*JSOT* 28.5; *RelSRev* 1/06].

✓ Rhyder, Julia. ‡ *Centralizing the Cult: The Holiness Legislation in Leviticus 17–26,* 2019. [*VT* 72.2].

✓ Römer, Thomas, ed. ‡ *The Books of Leviticus and Numbers,* 2008. Essays from the Colloquium Biblicum Lovaniense. [*BL* 2009; *JTS* 4/10; *ExpTim* 5/10; *ETL* 86.1; *JHebS* 2009].

☆ **Rooker, Mark F.** *Leviticus* (NAC) 2000. A fine piece of work, nearly as useful as Wenham (who is better on ch. 16), taking account of its being more recent. Rooker did a Brandeis diss. on Ezekiel's language and is convinced we Christians need to reconsider the theological significance of the OT priestly office. Note that there is a dispensational orientation to the commentary. [*JETS* 3/02; *SwJT* Fall 01; *F&M* Fall 01].

F  Schaper, Joachim. ‡ (ICC). This is a long way off, I believe.

F  Schwartz, Baruch. ‡ (IECOT).

✓ Schwartz, Baruch J., et al., eds. *Perspectives on Purity and Purification in the Bible,* 2008. Valuable essays from SBL. [*VT* 61.3].

☆ Shepherd, Jerry E. (SGBC) 2021. A well-researched, dependable exposition from the Reformed perspective. There is a theological maturity here, and preachers will find Shepherd very instructive. (How the church needs to understand the "ritual world" presented in this literature, if she is to grasp better how it points to the atoning work of Christ!) As with Sklar's work, this SGBC may inspire a profitable sermon series or Bible study. Do note the Athas insights on p.16. One correction: Schnabel is not Edward. [*Them* 47.1].

✓ Sherwood, Stephen K. ‡ *Leviticus, Numbers, Deuteronomy* (BerO) 2002. This is one of the less successful vols. in the series. Sherwood seeks to cover a huge amount of biblical material in about 300pp., and the results are, shall we say, sketchy. There is some data here for students to work with, but little of substance for the pastor. [*JETS* 6/03; *Int* 4/03; *JSOT* 27.5; *RelSRev* 7/03].

☆ Sklar, Jay. (TOTC-R) 2013. His PhD, *Sin, Impurity, Atonement: The Priestly Conceptions* (2005) [*CBQ* 10/07; *Them* 1/07; *TJ* Spr 07; *RelSRev* 1/07; *JETS* 9/08; *BL* 2007], written under Wenham, led us to expect a fine replacement for Harrison. It is, with plenty of research behind it, clear writing, and a good eye for theological themes. The Introduction is surprisingly lengthy. More scholarly pastors should obtain his ZECOT (above). Many will be satisfied with only this TOTC on their shelf (inexpensive). If forgoing ZECOT (not desirable), buy this TOTC and Wenham together for exegetical purposes; then purchase an exposition. [*JETS* 3/16; *JSOT* 40.5; *Them* 40.3].

✓ Snaith, N. H. ‡ (retired NCB) 1967. Also covers Numbers. Critical and tends to be more academic and technical in its approach to the text than other NCB contributions. Snaith had a well-established reputation as a linguist; see his vols. of study notes on the Hebrew text published by Epworth.

Sprinkle, Joe M. *Leviticus and Numbers* (TTC) 2015. I am yet to see this approx. 450-page commentary, by a learned prof (Hebrew Union PhD) at Crossroads College, Minnesota. His doctoral work was on Exodus. [*Them* 42.2].

☆ Tidball, Derek. (BST) 2005. With a fairly full contribution to the series (327pp.), he does well in delivering a readable exposition of the message of the book. Tidball focuses on the topic of holy relationships, first of all between God and his people, and then secondly in human relationships among the Israelites. He also helps the preacher by exploring christological and other NT connections. Highly recommended by Sklar. [*Chm* Aut 08; *BL* 2006; *ExpTim* 1/07].

☆ Vasholz, Robert I. (Mentor) 2007. An exegetical and expositional work of 372pp. One reviewer [*WTJ* Fall 09] commends the fine points of exegesis but wishes for a clearer view of the big picture and a more nuanced approach to typology. Vasholz says "an allegorical approach assumes that these laws were basically to teach spiritual lessons" (143), and in rejecting allegory he appears reluctant to draw out the lessons. As his former student, I know Vasholz is useful to preachers.

✓ Vaux, Roland de. ‡ *Ancient Israel: Religious Institutions*, ET 1968. Not a commentary, but a valuable monograph on Israel's religious leadership and worship as prescribed in Leviticus.

✓ Warning, Wilfred. *Literary Artistry in Leviticus*, 1999.

✓ **Watts, James W.** ‡ *Leviticus 1–10* (HCOT) 2013; *Leviticus 11–20* (HCOT) 2023. Few are equally qualified to write a large-scale, technical commentary on Leviticus as Watts. The strong points here are skill in handling the Hebrew, decades of research and thorough knowledge of the scholarship, contributions over the years to ritual studies, rhetorical analysis, and presentation of the history of interpretation. The bibliographies are magnificent in these vols. of 550 and 575pp. He has 90pp. on ch. 16 alone. More negatively, he uses strikethroughs on "biblical texts that fail even the lowest standards of moral decency" (*Lev 11–20*, xxviii), seemingly a new step in American academic "cancel culture." Note that Watts is very expensive. [*Them* 11/14]. Some preliminary work was published as *Ritual and Rhetoric in Leviticus* (2007) [*ExpTim* 4/09; *VT* 59.2; *JSS* Spr 10; *VT* 59.2; *Bib* 91.4].

F   Wegner, Paul. (EBTC)?

✓   **Willis, Timothy M.** ‡ (AbOTC) 2009. A compact (241pp.), moderately critical exegesis with less attention to theological matters, Willis will be more useful to students than to pastors. Jenson terms it "now one of the best introductory commentaries." [*JETS* 12/09; *BL* 2010 (Jenson); *CBQ* 10/10].

F   Wright, David P. ‡ (Herm). Gary Anderson once had the contract.

Yoder, Perry. (BCBC) 2017. About 260pp of learned Mennonite commentary, plus many topical essays as appendices.

✓   Zevit, Ziony. *The Religions of Ancient Israel: A Parallactic Approach*, 2001. Hess calls this tome "the most complete inventory of the relevant data on the history of ancient Israelite religion yet available" (*Israelite Religions*, 77). [*DenvJ* 1/02; *JHebS* 4].

# NUMBERS

★ **Ashley, Timothy R.** (NICOT) 1993, 2nd ed. 2022. The large-scale work (650pp.), from a Baptist pastor and former prof at Acadia Divinity College, gives the Hebrew text almost as much attention as Harrison. The revision after thirty years represents a slight updating of the old, still-serviceable commentary; for example, he was able to make more use of Milgrom. Students find less discussion of recent scholarship (mainly in footnotes), and pastors with the original might choose not to lay out funds for the second ed. Ashley writes, "I still agree with a good deal of what I wrote." In the new book he is more open to, and appreciative of, source critical work, and he has deleted his apologetic for Mosaic authorship. He treats the final form, which "is probably postexilic, though reflecting much more ancient traditions" (Introduction). He believes "[t]he Moses we see in this text . . . is Moses as seen from centuries later and from a different perspective" (Preface). NICOT includes some excellent theological reflection. It is less conservative than the older works by Cole and Harrison. Those wanting a more in-depth exegetical work than Wenham or Sklar could make Ashley their first choice, but do compare Awabdy and Morales. [*JR* 4/95; *SwJT* Spr 98; *BSac* 10/94; *BL* 2024].

★ **Awabdy, Mark A.** [𝓜], (BCOT) 2023. A solid contribution to a high-quality series. After a shorter introduction (31pp.), readers receive a 540-page exegesis that continually focuses upon theology and how church and synagogue have reflected on Numbers. Awabdy accepts some critical conclusions about the text both shaping and being shaped by the preexilic, exilic, and postexilic Jewish communities (29, cf. Brevard Childs). He attributes material to sources plus redactors (18) and finds a "brilliant editorial design" (xii). Conservative preachers find such criticism unappealing, but the author makes so many fine biblical-theological points and NT connections—see "Implications" sections—that pastors greatly benefit from closely studying this major work. I was puzzled, however, by one "illustration" (56) and his suggestion that Christians take a Nazarite vow today (118–21); such a vow was usually temporary, and it seems better to understand Christians as eternally set apart, in union with him who consecrated himself for us (John 17:19). The author did his PhD at Asbury under Bill Arnold, contributed a vol. on Leviticus to Brill's Septuagint Commentary Series, and is adept at text criticism, structural analysis, narrative criticism, and ANE studies. Students appreciate the full bibliography (38pp.); he interacts with important Europeans (Seebass, Frevel, Schmidt, Achenbach, etc.). I wish he'd looked up Briggs. [*BL* 2024].

★ Duguid, Iain M. (PTW) 2006. I have not found any better expositional guide. There is good scholarly exegesis (in the background), stimulating biblical-theological reflection, and searching application for the people of God today. Those scouting for still more preaching helps, beyond Duguid and Sklar, should consider Philip (once on my recommended list), Reynolds, Olson, Brown, Gane, Keddie, and Sakenfeld.

★ **Milgrom, Jacob.** ‡ (JPS) 1990. An extraordinarily learned Jewish commentary which mainly treats the "final form" of the text. Students doing careful research on Numbers should consult this work (520pp.), described by Wenham [*BSB* 12/96] as "much the most stimulating historical-critical commentary." A pastor with the money and wish to build a first-class exegetical library will buy Milgrom or Levine (I prefer JPS). If you're less the scholarly type, skip this purchase or replace it with either an exegetical work (e.g., Allen) or a good exposition (e.g., Reynolds). See Milgrom under Leviticus. [*CRBR* 1992; *CBQ* 1/93; *VT* 1/94; *HS* 1995].

★ **Morales, L. Michael.** (Apollos) 2 vols., 2024. Provides a lucid, deeply spiritual and theological reading of the book, after first laying a strong, detailed exegetical foundation. The author did a PhD under Wenham, has taught for years at Greenville Presbyterian Theological Seminary, and worked ten years on this set (950pp.). Morales states, "In theological terms, Numbers is concerned profoundly with *ecclesiology*—it *is* the ecclesiology of the Torah. As such, it is no surprise that over half the occurrences of the word *'ēdâ* (congregation, community) in the HB are found within Numbers" (4). I might summarize his perspective on the message as follows. (a) The Camp of Israel, under the leadership of the tribal *neśi'im* (chiefs), enjoy YHWH's gracious presence, and guidance by his glory-cloud, in the nation's wilderness journey to the Promised Land. (b) Also, Israel's testing over a generation reveals the need for true faith, a faith that will keep covenant with her faithful God. (c) Like Israel, we Christians have been redeemed from slavery (to sin), are journeying "in the wilderness" with a God who graciously dwells among us; we drink from the spiritual Rock (1 Cor 10) and are called to respond with faith, before we gain the "land of milk and honey." I suspect many will balk at buying a two-vol. Numbers commentary, but Christ's Church will for decades be in Morales's debt for this thorough, fascinating work. It outstrips previous evangelical exegeses, and I salute him. See also his studies on the Exodus theme and Leviticus.

★ **Sklar, Jay.** (SGBC) 2023. After praiseworthy work on Leviticus, Sklar offers here a well-rounded treatment of Numbers, with both exegetical insight and sensitivity to preachers' concerns (430pp.). He builds on his notes for the *NIV Biblical Theology Study Bible* (2018). I judge that there is more research behind this vol. than most in the series. Students and pastors are helped by the lucid discussion of the book's structure, the many charts included, and the accessible treatment of theological themes. All commentaries aim to inform, but Sklar is also more reflective and attentive to how the biblical text challenges faithful readers to "live out" the story today. For example, see "What Does Ritual Impurity Have to Do with Us?" (385). If a pastor could have only one book, this would be a wise pick.

★ **Wenham, Gordon J.** (TOTC) 1981. Easy to read, very perceptive, and added luster to the series. In short compass you can't do any better (240pp.). This used to be the hands-down first choice, not only because of its excellence but also because there was pretty much nothing else. Now we have many worthy commentaries; this once neglected book is better served. Evangelical pastors can still start with Wenham, and not just because it's easier on the pocketbook. Stuart's first pick. [*TJ* Fall 82]. Also, don't miss Wenham's OT Guides vol. (1997) [*JSOT* 79; *CBQ* 7/99; *DenvJ*]. See Altmann.

F   Achenbach, Reinhard. ‡ (HCOT).

F   Albertz, Rainer, and Thomas Römer. ‡ (IECOT).

☆   **Allen, Ronald B.** (EBCR) 2012. His 1990 EBC went into greater depth (350pp.) than the other entries in that vol. (Gen–Num) and was among the most valuable in the OT set. The respected scholar began his career with a strong Dallas diss., *The Theology of the Balaam Oracles* (1973). Years ago, I nearly made Allen a recommended purchase. EBCR updates his earlier work (430pp.) and is worth consulting, alongside a couple of other strong works in Vol. 2: Numbers–Ruth. [*VT* 64.2; *JETS* 9/14; *ExpTim* 6/14; *JESOT* 2.2].

F   Altmann, Peter, and Caio Peres. (TOTC-R) 2025.

Athas, George. (Reading the Bible Today) 2016. A moderately sized (over 300pp.), accessible exegesis and exposition, published in Australia and informed by excellent study of the background. Athas has done a service to the church here. [*RTR* 12/18].

F   Averbeck, Richard. (EBTC)?

Bailey, Lloyd R. ‡ *Leviticus–Numbers* (S&H) 2005. See Leviticus.

F   Baker, David. (BCBC).

Barker, Joel, and Steven D. West. (Kerux) 2023. I have yet to see it.

☆   Bellinger, William. ‡ *Leviticus, Numbers* (NIBC) 2001. See Leviticus.

F   Bergey, Ronald. (ESVEC) 2024. See Duguid under Genesis. Bergey has long had my utmost respect for his scholarship; see under Esther.

F   Bibb, Bryan D. ‡? (WBC-R). To replace Budd. Prof. Bibb teaches at Furman and was educated at Princeton Seminary (MDiv, PhD).

Binns, L. Elliot. ‡ (Westminster) 1927.

Boyce, Richard N. ‡ *Leviticus and Numbers* (WestBC) 2008.

✓   **Briggs, Richard S.** [𝓜], *Theological Hermeneutics and the Book of Numbers as Christian Scripture*, 2018. I never fail to learn from this hermeneutically sophisticated scholar. And he has chosen a most difficult text-field to plow. Not a full commentary, the 300-page work is "part theological-hermeneutical treatise" and focuses upon six narratives in chs. 11–25. He draws from the entire history of interpretation. [*JSOT* 43.5; *ConcTJ* Win 20; *ThTo* 76.2].

☆   Brown, Raymond. (BST) 2002. Stands alongside his BST exposition of Deuteronomy and is of very good service to evangelical preachers. [*Them* Sum 03; *JSOT* 27.5; *Evangel* Spr 03].

Brueggemann, Dale A. (CorBC) 2008. See Baker under Leviticus.

✓   **Budd, Philip J.** ‡ (WBC) 1984. Well-written and of value to students with interests in diachronic criticism and the history of interpretation. Budd was the first of a spate of academic commentaries on Numbers providing an exacting exegesis of the Hebrew. Others build on his now dated work. One could wish he didn't take such a skeptical view of Numbers as history. Hardly any theology. This tome was something of a missed opportunity and is scheduled to be replaced by Bibb. [*RTR* 9/85; *EvQ* 7/87; *JBL* 106.1; *JETS* 12/85; *HS* 1987].

**Calvin, John.** *Harmony of the Pentateuch*, 1563. See under Exodus.

☆   **Cole, R. Dennis.** (NAC) 2000. The author taught at New Orleans Baptist Seminary, where he earned his doctorate. This full work (550pp.) is especially concerned with structural matters. Many have considered Numbers a catchall with a disorganized conglomeration of material. While the "generic variety that characterizes Numbers surpasses that of any other book of the Bible" (Milgrom, p.xiii), there is an inner cohesiveness found by recent commentators (Milgrom, Olson). Cole joins them in seeking to integrate the materials. He worked hard to produce this work and gives copious citations of others' research. On the negative side, he is less well versed in biblical-theological interpretation (cf. Duguid, Sakenfeld) and finely tuned narrative criticism. His literary observations sometimes lack an interpretive payoff. Also, Cole's writing style can be awkward and lack organization (e.g., p.36 has section 3 begin with subsection 8 [editor's goof?], and also has several sentences I read repeatedly without clear understanding). I prefer Ashley as a large-scale conservative commentary. Longman once gave Cole the highest rating: five stars. [*JETS* 6/02; *RelSRev* 7/02]. See also his notes for ZIBBC.

F Collins, C. John. (ZECOT).

☆ Currid, John. (EPSC) 2009. Completing the series on the Pentateuch. [*RTR* 12/12].

✓ **Davies, Eryl W.** ‡ (NCB) 1995. A sizable contribution (lxxiv + 378pp.) to the series, but its skepticism and hermeneutical approach, narrowly concerned with historical-critical issues, disappoints. That said, Davies is better than many others who run down that diachronic track. He long taught at the U. of Wales. [*ExpTim* 2/96; *Them* 10/96; *JETS* 6/98; *JSS* Aut 97; *JTS* 10/97; *JSOT* 74; *CBQ* 7/97; *RTR* 9/96; *BSac* 1/97; *HS* 1997; *RelSRev* 1/97]. More recent is an introduction, *Numbers: The Road to Freedom* (2015) [*JSOT* 40.5], republished by T&T Clark as *Numbers: An Introduction and Study Guide* (2017) [*JTS* 4/18; *JJS* 69.2].

✓ Douglas, Mary. ‡ *In the Wilderness: The Doctrine of Defilement in the Book of Numbers*, 1993. The author is best known for her decades-long anthropological research on Leviticus. [*BSac* 10/03].

✓ **Dozeman, Thomas B.** ‡ (NIB) 1998. The author is a noted exegete and theologian, who has done fine critical work on the exodus and wilderness "traditions." E.g., *God at War: Power in the Exodus Tradition* (OUP, 1996). See Dozeman under Exodus. [*ExpTim* 1/99].

Erdman, Charles R. 1952. Once a notable exposition because there were few on Numbers during his time. Erdman can be suggestive to the preacher.

F Erisman, Angela Roskop. ‡ (NCBC).

✓ Frevel, Christian. ‡ *Desert Transformations: Studies in the Book of Numbers*, 2020. An enormous body of work, with nearly 600pp of essays, some of them appearing in English for the first time. [*HBT* 44.2].

✓ Frevel, Christian, Thomas Pola, and Aaron Schart, eds. ‡ *Torah and the Book of Numbers*, 2013. Very focused on sources and redactions. [*BBR* 25.1; *CBQ* 1/15; *JSOT* 39.5].

F Fullilove, Bill. (EEC). A previous report was Dennis Cole.

☆ Gane, Roy. *Leviticus/Numbers* (NIVAC) 2004. Well worth buying, especially for pastors. See Leviticus.

✓ **Gray, George B.** ‡ (ICC) 1903. Long the standard reference work for scholars, particularly for its source critical discussion. It is still widely consulted, though none today considers it authoritative in technical matters.

F Harper, G. Geoffrey. (Pillar).

☆ **Harrison, R. K.** (was WEC) 1990. With dependable work on the Hebrew text, this was one of the more valuable evangelical works on Numbers, written by the then general editor of NICOT. Readers find it to be a well-rounded commentary treating grammatical, historical, and theological issues. One could wish that a bibliography had been appended to this worthy commentary (452pp.). It was reprinted by Baker (1992, pb 2019) and Biblical Studies Press. Because of age and strong competition, Harrison has declined in value. [*EvQ* 7/94; *JETS* 5/95; *RTR* 9/95; *CTJ* 4/95; *CBQ* 7/94].

☆ Keddie, Gordon J. *According to Promise* (Welwyn) 1992.

✓ Keil, Carl F. (KD) ET 1864. Was long an important resource. See under Genesis.

✓ **Knierim, Rolf P., and George W. Coats.** ‡ (FOTL) 2005. Mainly for advanced students interested in form criticism. [*RTR* 4/06; *CBQ* 10/05; *JTS* 10/07; *JETS* 3/06; *BSac* 7/06; *JSS* Spr 08; *BL* 2006; *VT* 57.4; *RelSRev* 4/06; *RBL*].

✓ Lee, Won W. ‡ *Punishment and Forgiveness in Israel's Migratory Campaign*, 2003. An important discussion of the structure and cohesiveness of Numbers 10:11–36:13, applying the synchronic conceptual analysis of Lee's PhD supervisor, Rolf Knierim. [*WTJ* Fall 04; *JETS* 3/05; *JTS* 10/05; *Them* Win 05; *JBL* Win 04; *JSS* Spr 06; *JNES* 4/08].

✓ **Levine, Baruch.** ‡ (AB) 2 vols., 1993–2000. A massive exegesis (about 1100pp.), like so many recent AB vols.—former editor Freedman leading the way. This work from a Jewish, critical scholar is similar to Milgrom's above, though more in-depth and diachronic in its approach and providing more discussion of the ANE context. My strong preference is for Milgrom. See Levine on Leviticus. [*PSB* 15.2; *CBQ* 1/95; *JR* 1/95; *JSS* Spr 95; *ExpTim* 5/01; *JTS* 10/01; *JETS* 6/02; *VT* 53.1; *JSOT* 94; trenchant: *CBQ* 7/01 and *Int* 10/01].

✓ Lienhard, Joseph T., ed. *Exodus, Leviticus, Numbers, Deuteronomy* (ACCS) 2001. See under Exodus.

Maarsingh, B. ‡ (T&I) 1987.

F   MacDonald, Nathan. (THC).

Mays, James L. ‡ (Layman's Bible Commentary) 1963. See Leviticus above.

✓ Moore, Michael S. *The Balaam Traditions*, 1990. Also important are J. T. Greene, *Balaam and His Interpreters: A Hermeneutical History of the Balaam Tradition* (1992), and Jonathan Miles Robker, *Balaam in Text and Tradition* (2019).

✓ **Noordtzij, A.** (BSC) 1957, ET 1983. See Leviticus above. [*JETS* 6/84].

✓ **Noth, Martin.** ‡ (OTL) ET 1968. Thorough from his particular historical-critical slant, but theologically sterile. Reprinted years ago in pb. See also his works on Exodus and Leviticus for OTL. [*JBL* 88.2 (1969)].

☆ **Olson, Dennis T.** ‡ (I) 1996. Olson, Sakenfeld, and Dozeman would be expositions recommended in mainline seminaries. Much can be learned from Olson; his work here is no breezy homiletical treatment. He presents some of the fruit of his previous research contained in *The Death of the Old and the Birth of the New: The Framework of the Book of Numbers and the Pentateuch* (1985), a significant monograph on the book's structure. His well-founded conclusion is that the book's structural movement is tied more to the shift from first to second generation than to geography. I would argue that this fine commentary is of far greater use to students than most in the series. Olson is my favorite theological interpretation from the critical side. "It is written with insight, energy and conviction . . . the most useful for the preacher today," according to Wenham [*BSB* 12/96]. [*JETS* 6/98; *BL* 1997; *CBQ* 10/97; *BSac* 10/97; *PSB* 17.3; *RelSRev* 1/97; *RBL*].

F   Paynter, Helen. (BGW).

☆ Philip, James. (WCC) 1987. A successful effort by the famous evangelical minister (†2009) at Holyrood Abbey Church in Edinburgh. Lucidly written and excellent for expositors. His better-known book is on Romans: *The Power of God*.

✓ **Pitkänen, Pekka.** [𝓜], *A Commentary on Numbers: Narrative, Ritual, and Colonialism*, 2018. Published by Routledge. See also his learned Joshua commentary below, which shows a similar penchant for moving rather quickly to ideological and political concerns. [*JSOT* 42.5].

✓ **Pressler, Carolyn.** ‡ *Numbers* (AbOTC) 2017. An engaging, concise (315pp.) exegetical treatment by a series editor, who teaches at United Seminary, Twin Cities. She suggests the Hebrews were not outside invaders but "beleaguered Canaanite peasants," who "left the coastal lowlands . . . to settle in unoccupied hill country that developed into the backbone of Israel" (4). Pastors in liberal churches gravitate toward this learned commentary, which treats social, ethical, historical, and literary issues, along with theology. [*BBR* 28.3; *Int* 1/19; *JSOT* 47.5; *JHebS* 18].

✓ Regt, Lénart J. de, and Ernst R. Wendland. (UBS) 2016. Superb, thorough (800pp.) guidance for translators ("how should the Hebrew be rendered in the target/receptor language?"), and also for any exegetes wise enough to peruse it. [*JSOT* 41.5].

☆ Reynolds, Adrian. *Teaching Numbers*, 2012. Sorry I missed this in the last edition. The exposition, by a London-based leader in the Fellowship of Independent Evangelical Churches (UK), has been praised by Duguid as providing "a wonderfully concise and helpful map to orient us to the important themes of this part of the Bible, as well as stimulating suggestions to identify how it speaks to contemporary listeners." Skillfully done!

Riggans, Walter. ‡ (DSB) 1983. Fuller than many others in the series at 252pp. and fairly well-done. [*JBL* 104.4].

F   Römer, Thomas. ‡ (Illum).

✓   **Römer, Thomas, ed.** ‡ *The Books of Leviticus and Numbers*, 2008. See Leviticus.

☆   **Sakenfeld, Katherine Doob.** ‡ (ITC-E) 1995. What I have read is superbly written and highly theological. The commentary is about 210pp. long with indices. Sakenfeld, an OT prof emerita at Princeton Seminary, is not a conservative in her views of authorship and date, but she treats the final form of the text. This book is serviceable to the evangelical pastor with discernment. [*BL* 1997; *PSB* 17.2].

✓   Sherwood, Stephen K. ‡ *Leviticus, Numbers, Deuteronomy* (BerO) 2002. See Leviticus.

✓   Snaith, N. H. ‡ (retired NCB) 1967. See under Leviticus. Now replaced by Davies.

Sprinkle, Joe M. *Leviticus and Numbers* (TTC) 2015. See Leviticus.

☆   **Stubbs, David L.** [*M*], (Brazos) 2009. An accessible theological exposition, with good literary observations, and one of the better entries in the series (272pp.). Stubbs teaches at Western Theological Seminary and is ordained in the PCUSA. [*BL* 2010; *CTJ* 4/11; *ExpTim* 6/13; *Chm* Sum 17].

Sturdy, John. ‡ (CBC) 1976.

NOTE: Mitchel Modine, "Case Studies in Recent Research on the Book of Numbers (with Attention to Non-Western Scholarship)," *CBR* 18 (2020): 246–67.

# DEUTERONOMY

★   **Arnold, Bill T.** [*M*], *The Book of Deuteronomy, Chapters 1–11* (NICOT-R) 2022. The first instalment of a monumental, thorough, highly theological work by a long-time prof at Asbury Seminary and current NICOT editor. Replaces Craigie, who was considerably more conservative. Full of insights and interaction with the best scholarship; many preachers may think the 630-page vol. too full and of greater help to Hebrew students than pastors. Arnold speaks of "the voice of Moses" in Deuteronomy but urges us to regard "the speeches . . . as that which 'later writers have reframed or thought Moses would have wanted to say in their situation' [Robson]." There was a "process by which Mosaic scribes became the voice of Moses" (17), a "long process" from the time of Hezekiah to Josiah ("perhaps the book's penultimate edition" [32]). These "early versions . . . spoke powerfully to key reading audiences in the exilic and postexilic communities" (266). Expect this to stand as a most valuable exegetical and theological reference for decades to come, though I find it less useful from the philological angle. Jenson describes it as "outstanding," and when completed "this will be the largest critical commentary published in English" [*JSOT* 47.5]. [*JETS* 9/23]. Note below the Arnold and Tucker exegetical guide to the Hebrew text of Deut 12–26, complementing Robson. [*Them* 49.1]

★   **Block, Daniel I.** (NIVAC) 2012. Breaks the series' mold somewhat in that it contains rather more scholarship (see author index) and is more valuable exegetically. Block's large vol. (880pp.) serves students' as well as preachers' interests. Those familiar with his writings— see Judges, Ruth, Ezekiel, his book on *Covenant* (2021)—need no recommendation from me to decide to buy this NIVAC. He has done brilliant and stimulating work, and the measure of his learning is that so much had to be cut that two vols. of essays were released about the same time: *The Gospel according to Moses* (2012, 394pp.) [*BBR* 23.1; *BSac* 1/14; *JESOT* 2.1], and *How I Love Your Torah, O LORD!* (2011, 270pp.) [*BBR* 22.2; *EQ* 1/13; *JETS* 9/13]. My advice to preachers is to make Block their first choice, though I don't follow him in viewing Moses's chief role as "pastor" to the nation and not seeing in 18:15, ultimately at least, an anticipation of Christ (cf. Acts 3:22). I believe the text is certainly open to Block's interpretation of "a succession of prophets" like Moses (Elijah, Jeremiah, Ezekiel) . . . *and* to a messianic figure who, in the OT faith and as a prophet, will be more approachable than the terrible Lord of Sinai (vv.16–17). Students, note the forthcoming commentary below. [*BBR* 23.3; *WTJ* Spr 13; *JSOT* 37.5; *VT* 64.4; *Them* 11/13; *JESOT* 2.1 (McConville); *TJ* Spr 14; *JETS* 6/13]. Block has one more vol. of essays: *The Triumph of Grace* (2017) [*JSOT* 47.5]. About the best discussion I've found of the authorship issue is "Recovering the Voice of Moses," *JETS* 44 (2001): 385–408 (also pp.21–67 in *The Gospel according to Moses*).

★ **Lundbom, Jack R.** ‡ 2013. Academics might wish this major reference work had been released in hb, not pb, for we had waited decades for a fine, thorough critical exegesis. Weinfeld left us hanging with his incomplete AB, and then we had the satisfaction of this large (1064pp.) commentary that includes textual criticism, ANE studies, rabbinics, rhetorical analysis of the highest quality, structural outlines, NT connections, and a fair amount of theology. Lundbom calls Deuteronomy "this homiletical treasure" (23). Rhetorical concerns are always at the forefront in this interpretation, and he finds that "inclusio and framing devices are the controlling structures" in chs. 1–28, with "a framing mode of composition" also used in 29–34 (23). He is more conservative on historical matters, believing that a first edition (chs. 1–28) possibly dates to Hezekiah's time. See also his commentary on Jeremiah, a prophecy paired with Deuteronomy from the literary and thematic/theological angles. Scholarly pastors who want to add an in-depth exegetical work alongside these suggested works will likely pick from among Weinfeld, Tigay, and Driver. Reviews fault Lundbom for not being entirely current in his scholarship and providing less lexical help [*CBQ* 10/14; *Int* 7/15; *JSOT* 38.5; *VT* 64.4; *ETL* 6/15; *ExpTim* 7/15; *JESOT* 3.2; *JSS* Spr 16; *RTR* 4/16; *JHebS* 17 (Block)]. Those without an academic bent might bypass this. More recently, he published *Deuteronomy: Law and Covenant* (2017) in the Cascade Companions series [*JSOT* 43.5].

★ **McConville, J. Gordon.** [𝓜], (Apollos) 2002. An excellent assignment! See the author's diss., *Law and Theology in Deuteronomy* (1984) [*HS* 1988]—well worth reading, by the way—for evidence of McConville's long hard work on Deuteronomy. Perhaps on the negative side, the amount of time he spent in research makes this a deep, cerebral, complicated commentary that the less studious may struggle with. For an evangelical exegetical reference, Arnold, Block, and McConville are my first picks. The commentary was discussed in a symposium; the record of the scholarly give-and-take is found in *SJT* 56.4. [*Them* Spr 04; *JETS* 6/03; *VT* 54.2; *JSOT* 27.5; *Chm* Win 04; *BSac* 4/04; *Evangel* Spr 03; *Anvil* 20.3]. See also McConville's instructive *Grace in the End: A Study in Deuteronomic Theology* (1993).

★ **Miller, Patrick D.** ‡ (I) 1990. The author is one of the most prominent American OT critics. To those sharing Miller's moderately critical views, this is probably the best theological exposition of the book, rivaled only by Brueggemann and Clements. It is quite readable and covers Deuteronomy in 245pp. [*CBQ* 10/92; *ThTo* 10/91; *BL* 1997]. Those wanting a conservative work instead could consider Craigie, Merrill, or Grisanti for exegesis, or Fernando for sermonic material.

★ Woods, Edward J. (TOTC-R) 2011. A worthy successor to Thompson, "Ted" Woods provides a solidly conservative yet fresh treatment of Deuteronomy, and there is appropriately more theology than before. (We see more clearly now than 50 years ago that Deuteronomy is a theological mountain of Himalayan size.) Personal note: Woods is a fine preacher, a sharp-eyed scholar, and was my predecessor as OT lecturer at the Theological College of Central Africa (Zambia). Go here for a concise evangelical exegesis. [*ExpTim* 8/12].

★ **Wright, Christopher J. H.** (NIBC) 1996. The author is a leading evangelical scholar; specifically, he is among the finest OT ethicists. Well-trained at Cambridge, he here delivers a popularly styled, theologically sensitive exposition. A distinctive contribution, according to McConville [*BSB* 6/99], is the commentary's "orientation to missiology, for which Deuteronomy is shown to have interesting and unexpected implications (relevant, incidentally, to the troublesome problem of the book's attitude to the non-Israelite peoples of Canaan)." You won't go wrong if you, as a pastor, make this your first purchase for reasons of cost. (Disclosure: I am biased in my assessment. A highlight of my missions experience was hosting the Wrights for dinner in our African home.) Wright also has good commentaries on Ezekiel, Jeremiah, and Lamentations. See Block above. [*JSOT* 79; *CBQ* 7/98; *Chm* 112.2; *RelSRev* 7/97].

☆ **Arnold, Bill T., and Paavo N. Tucker.** *Deuteronomy 12–26* (BHHB) 2022. See Arnold above, and Robson below. The Baylor series is splendid.

Athas, George. (RBT) 2016. I have not seen it. [*Them* 44.1].

F Ausloos, Hans. ‡ (HCOT).

Barker, Paul A. *The Triumph of Grace in Deuteronomy*, 2004. [*EuroJTh* 15.1].

Benjamin, Don C. ‡ *The Social World of Deuteronomy: A New Feminist Commentary*, 2015. A rather brief (190pp.), ideological reading.

Biddle, Mark E. ‡ (S&H) 2003. Over 500pp. of attractively presented, theological exposition from a moderately critical perspective. Not regarded as one of the best in the series.

F Block, Daniel I. (Eerdmans) 2 vols. Working so diligently on the NIVAC, Block developed more exegetical material than could be contained in that pastoral work. He told me (2015) he is producing a large work of greater use to students and fellow scholars.

✓ Block, Daniel I., and Richard L. Schultz, eds. *Sepher Torath Mosheh: Studies in the Composition and Interpretation of Deuteronomy*, 2017. Valuable, critically engaged evangelical essays, issuing from a Wheaton conference. [*BBR* 28.3; *JSOT* 43.5; *Them* 44.2].

☆ Brown, Raymond. (BST) 1993. One of the more sermonic and devotional entries in the series, this vol. is fairly full (350pp.) and works diligently to apply the message to our day. The scholarship here is not profound. Brown was formerly principal of Spurgeon's College, London and writes as a pastor; he should not be confused with Raymond E. Brown, the distinguished Catholic NT critic. This Brown wrote the BST books on Numbers, Nehemiah, and Hebrews. [*Them* 5/95; *Evangel* Spr 95; *SBET* Aut 96].

☆ **Brueggemann, Walter.** ‡ (AbOTC) 2001. See my reviews of his earlier commentaries on Genesis, Exodus, Samuel, etc. This one has a bit more exegesis and a lesser amount of high-flying, creative, theological exposition and application than in his contributions to the Interpretation series. [*CBQ* 1/03; *JETS* 12/03; *Int* 7/02; *ExpTim* 1/03; *VT* 53.2; *JSOT* 99; *ThTo* 7/02; *RelSRev* 7/03; *Anvil* 19.2; *JHebS* 4].

Cairns, Ian. ‡ (ITC-E) 1992. One of the better vols. in the series. Along with Miller, Brueggemann, and Clements, one of the best theological commentaries from the critical camp for pastors. [*HS* 1994].

**Calvin, John.** *Harmony of the Pentateuch*, 1563, ET 1852–55. Gives a great deal of space to the fifth book of Moses (available free at ccel.org). You are wise not to dole out your money for the Banner of Truth reprint, *Sermons Upon Deuteronomie*. I agree with Childs that this 1584 edition is "virtually inaccessible" and really cannot be used as a tool because of its antiquated script and translation. Leave it for the bibliophile with lots of money to spend on an impressive looking library.

✓ **Christensen, Duane L.** (WBC) 2 vols., 2001–02. The initial release, *Deuteronomy 1–11* (1993), was not well-received; Christensen went back to work to expand and defend his approach. The actual amount of commentary in the older vol. was less than expected from WBC. The newer set is much fuller (900pp.). Christensen calls this Bible book a "didactic poem" (*Deut. 1–11*, p.lx) and is mainly occupied with structural and rhythmical analysis. Academic types will compare this set to other technical commentaries and find he pursues a different agenda. Pastors will find it slow going as they plow through arcane stuff, irrelevant for preaching. Students might be intrigued, however. Reviewers call the new set an improvement but still question the interpretive approach. See also his Nahum work [*JETS* 12/03, 5/05; *CBQ* 1/04; *Them* Spr 04; *Int* 1/04; *JSOT* 27.5; *BBR* 14.2; *BSac* 10/03].

✓ Christensen, Duane L., ed. [*M*], *A Song of Power and the Power of Song: Essays on the Book of Deuteronomy*, 1993. A collection students should not miss. [*Them* 1/95].

✓ **Clements, Ronald E.** ‡ (NIB) 1998. The author builds upon his 1969 study of the theological issues: *God's Chosen People*. The NIB work is seeing much use in mainline circles. [*ExpTim* 1/99]. Close on its heels was a Preacher's Commentary published in 2001 by Epworth [*JSOT* 99; *Anvil* 19.2].

Cook, Stephen L. ‡ *Reading Deuteronomy* (ROT) 2015. I have not seen it.

☆ **Craigie, Peter C.** (retired NICOT) 1976. For its time, a substantial, accurate exegesis from an exceptional Hebraist (see his translation). Craigie used to be evangelical pastors' first pick for careful work with the English text and understanding the covenant treaty background. But we long lacked a full-length evangelical treatment of the Hebrew, which McConville has partially supplied. Craigie was thought a bit dry, so pastors wanted an expositional work like C. Wright alongside. It is still worth buying but shows its age, and I dropped it as a recommendation. See Arnold's NICOT above. [*EvQ* 10/77; *JBL* 6/78].

☆ Currid, John D. (EPSC) 2006. This follows his solid, readable commentaries on Genesis, Exodus, and Leviticus. Pastors will find Professor Currid a dependable guide in both exegesis and (Reformed) theological exposition. [*RTR* 4/09].

F   DeRouchie, Jason. (Pillar). He wrote his PhD under Block on chs. 5–11, *A Call to Covenant Love* (2007). With Gile and Turner, he edited the large Block FS on Deuteronomy, *For Our Good Always* (2013).

✓ **Driver, Samuel R.** ‡ (ICC) 1895. Still very helpful for minutiae, especially the Hebrew, but there is little interest in theology. Driver's liberal classic was acclaimed as one of the best vols. in the old series and is consulted often by scholars—"still an indispensable tool," says McConville [*BSB* 6/99]. Some refer to Lundbom as Driver's successor, but "Driver . . . is where everyone has to begin" (Lundbom, xix).

☆ Fernando, Ajith. (PTW) 2012. It is fitting that a world Christian leader with so much "heart" writes this sermonic material on Deuteronomy with its emphasis on a religion of the heart. I regret that I have only dipped into the work (765pp.), but it comes highly recommended by Robson [*Them* 11/12]. Much study went into this, and he is ready with illustrations and applications of the message.

☆ Firth, David G., and Philip S. Johnston, eds. *Interpreting Deuteronomy: Issues and Approaches*, 2012. A product of Tyndale Fellowship and a superb book for students, with essays by leading evangelical scholars. [*JSOT* 38.5; *Them* 4/14; *JESOT* 2.2; *TJ* Fall 14].

Gerbrandt, Gerald E. [*M*], (BCBC) 2015. One of the largest vols. in the Mennonite series (over 550pp.). Gerbrandt speaks of the book as containing "clues for gracious living." There is much valuable commentary here, with substantial research behind it, though I found "The Text in the Life of the Church" segments sometimes disappointing.

Grisanti, Michael A. (EBCR) 2012. Replacing Kalland, this is a competent, strongly conservative commentary for pastors (355pp.), though the 7-page introduction disappoints. Grisanti teaches at The Master's Seminary (MacArthur's school). It seems that his work dates to around 2005, and there was a publication delay. See Allen under Numbers.

☆ **Harstad, Adolph L.** (ConcC) 2022. Another enormous conservative Lutheran reference work (approx. 1000pp.), fitting well into the series. It has a treasure of exegetical and theological comment, with pastoral reflection and suggestions for applying the gospel. You will find another large-scale Harstad vol. treating Joshua.

F   Hernández, Dominick S. (BCOT).

Kalland, Earle S. (EBC) 1992. Had a practical, devotional tone—of use to pastors, but not to students (230pp.). In Vol. 3: Deuteronomy–Samuel. See Grisanti above.

F   Josberger, Rebekah. (EEC). A previous report was Abner Chou.

✓   Keil, C. F. (KD) ET 1864. See under Genesis.

✓   Kitchen, Kenneth A., and Paul J. N. Lawrence. *Treaty, Law and Covenant in the Ancient Near East*, 3 vols., 2012. This marks the culmination of Kitchen's decades of form-critical research into all the extant ANE treaties, placing the biblical texts (esp. Deuteronomy, late 2nd millennium) in their chronological context. [*BBR* 24.4 (Hess)].

Kline, Meredith G. *Treaty of the Great King*, 1963. A favorite of many conservatives, decades ago (o/p). As the title indicates, Kline argues for an early (2nd-millennium) covenant treaty structure. He gave us one of the better brief commentaries in the old one-vol. *Wycliffe Bible Commentary*, including the substance of *Treaty*. [*WTJ* 26.2].

☆   Konkel, August H. (ESVEC) 2021. Nearly 300pp in the fat vol. covering Deut to Ruth. All the expositions here are edifying and of value to pastors. The commentators take different positions on dating, with Konkel reading Deut as essentially Mosaic but having a final form date during the divided monarchy. Reimer dates the book of Joshua to the exile, while Van Pelt suggests that Samuel authored Judges. [*JETS* 6/22].

✓   Levinson, Bernard M. ‡ *Deuteronomy and the Hermeneutics of Legal Innovation*, 1997. An OUP issue, quite influential in scholarly discussion. Now added is *Legal Revision and Religious Renewal* (CUP, 2008) [*BibInt* 18.4].

F   Levinson, Bernard M. ‡ (Herm). The earlier announcement was Blaulik and Lohfink.

✓   Lienhard, Joseph T., ed. *Exodus, Leviticus, Numbers, Deuteronomy* (ACCS) 2001. See under Exodus.

Luther, Martin. "Lectures on Deuteronomy," *Luther's Works*, Vol. 9, ET 1960.

Mann, Thomas W. ‡ (WestBC) 1996. The author once taught at Princeton Seminary. See my comments above on the series as a whole. [*Int* 7/96; *BL* 1997; *CBQ* 7/97; *RelSRev* 1/97].

F   Markl, Dominik. ‡ (Illum).

Maxwell, J. C. (WCC) 1987. Fuller than some others in the series at 350pp. Helpful overall.

✓   **Mayes, A. D. H.** ‡ (NCB) 1979. More substantial than NCB usually is (416pp.), and a fairly good representative of this moderately critical British series. Students can consult this work, long praised in critical circles. [*JBL* 102.3; *TJ* Fall 80].

☆   **Merrill, Eugene H.** (NAC) 1994. Though not considered an incisive work that advances scholarly discussion, it is a very good and full commentary (477pp.)—I could well include it above. Most pastors would gain from adding this dependably conservative work to their personal libraries, but note Millar's CSC below. In a number of ways, Merrill provides an updating of Craigie and Thompson, the evangelical standbys from the 1970s. Furthermore, he develops the intriguing suggestion made by Yehezkel Kaufmann that Deuteronomy's legislation is organized according to the Decalogue. [*EvQ* 10/96; *JETS* 9/96; *HS* 1995]. See also "Deuteronomy and de Wette," *JESOT* 1.1 (2012): 25–42.

Merrill, Eugene H. (CorBC) 2008. See Baker under Leviticus.

✓   Millar, J. Gary. *Now Choose Life: Theology and Ethics in Deuteronomy*, 1998. The reworked Oxford DPhil by Millar is conservative, fairly accessible, and well worth reading by evangelical preachers. [*JNES* 10/07]. See Millar below.

F   Millar, J. Gary. (EBTC)?

F   Millar, J. Gary. (CSC).

✓   **Nelson, Richard D.** ‡ (OTL-R) 2002. A 400-page commentary to replace von Rad and sit alongside Nelson's *Joshua* in the same series. If McConville was an esteemed conservative exegesis published in 2002, Nelson was an authoritative liberal counterpart from the same year. Ralph Klein said it "ranks first." For further comment on this scholar, see under Joshua. Students should certainly consult such a mature critical work. [*JTS* 10/04; *CBQ* 1/04; *ExpTim* 11/03; *JSOT* 28.5; *RelSRev* 1/04; *BBR* 15.1; *JETS* 12/04; *CurTM* 4/05 (Klein); *JHebS* 4; *RBL*].

✓ Nicholson, E. W. ‡ *Deuteronomy and Tradition*, 1967. The Oxford don changed his mind a bit; see *Deuteronomy and the Judaean Diaspora* (2014) [*JJS* 66.1; *BBR* 25.2].

Payne, D. F. [*M*], (DSB) 1985. A more conservative and useful vol. in the series.

✓ Polzin, Robert. ‡ *Moses and the Deuteronomist: A Literary Study of the Deuteronomic History: Part One. Deuteronomy, Joshua, Judges*, 1980. Of greater value for Joshua and Judges than for Deuteronomy.

✓ **Rad, Gerhard von.** ‡ (retired OTL) ET 1966. Still a noted critical commentary, but it is quite brief and has become obsolete as an exegetical tool. He gives a lot of attention to the prehistory of the text (tradition history). The author's forte was biblical theology, and the theological discussion here had more lasting value than the exegesis. "His recognition that Deuteronomy has the characteristics of preaching has endured," says McConville [*BSB* 6/99]. Replaced by Nelson. [*ThTo* 24.3]. See also von Rad's theological essays: *Studies in Deuteronomy* (ET 1953).

F   Richter, Sandra L. (CCF).

F   Richter, Sandy. (THC).

☆ **Ridderbos, Jan.** (BSC) 1950–51, ET 1984. Much good theology, but the author did better on Isaiah (BSC). Years ago I used to recommend this for purchase; it is now o/p.

☆ **Robson, James E.** *Deuteronomy 1–11* (BHHB) 2016. Block puts it well: "an invaluable reference work for commentators and translators, and an extremely helpful textbook in exegesis courses" (370pp.). See Arnold–Tucker above for the complement. [*BBR* 27.4; *JSOT* 41.5]. On the way we received Robson's *Honey from the Rock: Deuteronomy for the People of God* (2013), applying the message in very thoughtful ways [*Chm* Win 13].

✓ Schmid, Konrad, and Raymond F. Person Jr., eds. ‡ *Deuteronomy in the Pentateuch, Hexateuch, and the Deuteronomistic History*, 2012.

✓ Sherwood, Stephen K. ‡ *Leviticus, Numbers, Deuteronomy* (BerO) 2002. See under Leviticus.

Smith, George Adam. ‡ (CBSC) 1918. Still referenced in the literature. For a study of the enigmatic man—who was deeply affected by Moody's preaching and pushed German higher criticism in Britain—see Iain Campbell, *Fixing the Indemnity: The Life and Work of Sir George Adam Smith (1856–1942)*.

✓ Stackert, Jeffrey. ‡ *Deuteronomy and the Pentateuch*, 2022. From a highly regarded source critic, this is published in AYRL. [*JSOT* 47.5].

F   Stackert, Jeffrey, and Joel S. Baden. ‡ (IECOT).

F   Strawn, Brent. ‡? (NCBC).

F   Theocharous, Myrto. (SGBC)?

Thompson, Deanna A. ‡ (Belief) 2014. [*RevExp* 11/14; *Int* 4/16].

Thompson, J. A. (retired TOTC) 1974. Has been helpful, in my view, and worth the money. Like Craigie, he finds a covenant treaty structure in the book. The drawback is the age of the vol. See Woods. [*EvQ* 1/76; *JETS* 6/77; *JBL* 95.2].

F   Tiffany, Frederick G. ‡ (FOTL).

✓ **Tigay, Jeffrey H.** ‡ (JPS) 1996. See my comments above on the series. Students should not miss this as they work with the Hebrew (548pp.), for it is a top scholarly commentary on Deuteronomy. The Jewish scholar takes more interest in source criticism than evangelicals will. Moshe Greenberg can be considered to have had a hand in this publication, since he made available to Tigay his own notes on the whole book. [*JBL* Win 97].

✓ Vogt, Peter T. *Deuteronomic Theology and the Significance of Torah: A Reappraisal*, 2006. A valuable PhD. "Certainly, widespread assumptions about how the book reflects a secularization and demythologization of earlier modes of thinking, acting, and seeing will require reevaluation in the light of Vogt's careful reading of the text of Deuteronomy" (Miller). [*EuroJTh* 18.2].

F   Vogt, Peter T. (ZECOT).

☆ **Weinfeld, Moshe.** ‡ *Deuteronomy 1–11* (AB) 1991. One of the world's most respected Jewish exegetes, Weinfeld was especially known for his *Deuteronomy and the Deuteronomic School* (Clarendon, 1972). This work is very full and scholarly (458pp.) and has over 90pp. on the Ten Words. Specialists were excited about it, and more academically minded pastors benefit if they make the purchase. "Indispensable for the serious student" (Clements). [*JBL* Sum 93; *JSS* Spr 93, Spr 94; *HS* 1996]. There were to be two more vols., but Prof. Weinfeld's death (2009) left the set incomplete. I saw news that David Seely is working on *Deuteronomy 12–34*.

Work, Telford. [*M*], (Brazos) 2009. The author earned a PhD at Duke and teaches theology at Westmont. I have had less opportunity to use this theological commentary. For exegetical guidance, Work appears to draw mainly on Tigay, Brueggemann, Nelson, and Alter. He walks through the text using the topics of faith, hope, and love (circumscribed allegory) to illumine the plain meaning in stimulating ways. I have not used it enough to make up my mind about this and some other Brazos titles that seem to range into a kind of Christian midrash at points. Generally, I'm not impressed, but this is a better vol. in the series. [*JTI* Spr 10; *JETS* 6/10; *Int* 4/10 (Nelson); *BL* 2010; *CTJ* 11/11].

Wright, G. E. ‡ (IB) 1953. To be valued more than most commentaries in the old series because of the author's academic rigor and theological interests.

NOTE: Under the auspices of the U. of Vienna, Braulik and Lohfink developed a free interactive Analytical Bibliography for Deuteronomy (*AnaBiDeut*). The reach and size of the database are stunning: in 2010 nearly 12,000 titles and 22,000 ch./v. references to Bible passages. Besides the main German version (anabideut.univie.ac.at), there is an English one dated 2015 [*VT* 61.3], now hosted by the U. of Minnesota.

# READING NARRATIVE & THE FORMER PROPHETS

NOTE: The terms Former Prophets and Deuteronom(ist)ic History both designate the sequence of four books in the Hebrew Bible: Joshua, Judges, Samuel, and Kings.

★ Alter, Robert. ‡ *The Art of Biblical Narrative*, 1981. This classic ought to be read in the library, if you don't purchase it. (Alter is cheap as a used book.) It represents the exciting "Bible as Literature" movement, which took hold in the 1970s. To see what he himself does in translating (superbly) and commenting literarily on these books, see *Ancient Israel: The Former Prophets* (2013), incorporating *The David Story* (1999).

★ Arnold, Bill T., and H. G. M. Williamson, eds. [*M*], *Dictionary of the Old Testament: Historical Books*, 2005. More valuable for academic than pastoral work. Indispensable for serious study of this portion of the Bible. Articles are by conservatives and moderate critics. Does not treat Ruth or Esther. [*CTJ* 11/07; *CBQ* 1/07; *SBET* Spr 08; *BSac* 1/07].

★ Fokkelman, J. P. ‡ *Reading Biblical Narrative: An Introductory Guide*, ET 1999. Among the very best introductions available to students. See the ten guiding questions on pp.208–9. Compare with Walsh below. [*Them* Aut 00; *RelSRev* 1/01; *CBQ* 4/01; *BSac* 10/03; *VT* 54.1, see Moberly's cautions in *VT* 53.2].

★ Howard, David M. *An Introduction to the Old Testament Historical Books*, 1993. This fine conservative textbook can be compared with the briefer, more current Satterthwaite–McConville below. [*CTJ* 11/96].

★ Long, V. Phillips. *The Art of Biblical History*, 1994. A thought-provoking and trustworthy guide into the basic questions arising from this literature: What kind of literature is this? What were the narrators seeking to accomplish? How did they intend their books to be read? For more probing discussion of OT historiography and the challenge of skeptical "minimalists," see Day and Long–Wenham–Baker below, and then the Provan–Long–Longman vol., *A Biblical History of Israel* (2003, 2nd ed. 2015).

★ Pratt, Richard L. *He Gave Us Stories: The Bible Student's Guide to Interpreting OT Narratives*, 1990. Ryken (below) and Pratt are valuable and accessible evangelical introductions to the topic, and they both help students read OT narrative theologically. Pratt has the more redemptive-historical perspective.

★ Satterthwaite, Philip E., and J. Gordon McConville. *Exploring the OT, Vol. 2: A Guide to the Historical Books*, 2007. Start here for an introduction to Joshua through Esther, combined with some content survey (e.g., Hamilton). [*ExpTim* 11/08; *JETS* 9/08; *Anvil* 26.1].

✓ Amit, Yairah. ‡ *Reading Biblical Narrative: Literary Criticism and the Hebrew Bible*, 2001. [*Int* 4/02; *JSS* Aut 03; *BSac* 10/03]. See also *Hidden Polemics in Biblical Narrative* (2000).

☆ Arnold, Bill T., and Richard S. Hess, eds. *Ancient Israel's History: An Introduction to Issues and Sources*, 2014. A leading evangelical work, useful for research on the Pentateuch and Prophets as well. [*JSOT* 39.5; *Them* 8/15].

✓ Bar-Efrat, Shimon. ‡ *Narrative Art in the Bible*, 1989. Superb work by an Israeli scholar.

✓ Barstad, Hans. ‡ *History and the Hebrew Bible*, 2008. Includes what Williamson terms the "extremely influential monograph *The Myth of the Empty Land* (1996)." [*ExpTim* 11/09].

✓ Berlin, Adele. ‡ *Poetics and Interpretation of Biblical Narrative*, 1983.

✓ Briggs, Richard S. [𝓜], *The Virtuous Reader: OT Narrative and Interpretive Virtue*, 2010. A fine, rewarding, integrative piece. [*Them* 11/10 (Provan); *BSB* 3/12].

✓ Campbell, Antony F., and Mark A. O'Brien. ‡ *Unfolding the Deuteronomistic History: Origins, Upgrades, Present Text*, 2000. [*BSac* 4/02].

✓ Campbell, Antony F. ‡ *Joshua to Chronicles: An Introduction*, 2004. [*CBQ* 10/05; *BBR* 17.2; *JETS* 3/06; *RelSRev* 7/05].

Cate, Robert L. *An Introduction to the Historical Books of the Old Testament*, 1994. Does not compare favorably with Howard or Satterthwaite–McConville.

✓ Childs, Brevard S. ‡ "Introduction to the Former Prophets," in *Introduction to the OT as Scripture*, 1979. Having taught courses on these books over the years, I assure you there is, in fact, a huge difference between regarding this literature as prophetic or as composing a Deuteronomistic History. Wrestle with Childs's thoughts on the topic (229–38). See also Kaufmann under Joshua.

☆ Chisholm, Robert B. *Interpreting the Historical Books: An Exegetical Handbook*, 2006. [*JETS* 12/07; *JSS* Spr 08; *BL* 2008].

✓ Day, John, ed. ‡ *In Search of Pre-Exilic Israel*, 2004. Essays, some from Oxford dons, critiquing the revisionist minimalist school.

✓ De Pury, A., T. Römer, and J.-D. Macchi, eds. ‡ *Israel Constructs Its History: Deuteronomistic Historiography in Recent Research*, 2000. [*Them* Aut 01; *BSac* 7/02].

✓ Dearman, J. Andrew. [𝓜], *Reading Hebrew Bible Narratives*, 2019. From OUP. [*BBR* 29.3].

✓ Dever, William G. ‡ *Beyond the Texts: An Archaeological Portrait of Ancient Israel and Judah*, 2017. A full accounting of the conclusions of a leading voice in the field. Do consult it and also Hess's review essay [*BBR* 30.2]. [*CBQ* 10/18]. Earlier Dever published the provocative *What*

*Did the Biblical Writers Know and When Did They Know It?* (2001) [*JAOS* 122.3 (Rainey); *Anvil* 19.4 (G. I. Davies)].

✓ Earl, Douglas S. ‡ *Reading OT Narrative as Christian Scripture*, 2017. Stimulating, from a moderately critical position.

✓ Fewell, Danna Nolan, ed. ‡ *The Oxford Handbook of Biblical Narrative*, 2016. Covers both OT and NT. [*RBL* 2018; *CBQ* 1/18; *JTS* 4/18; *ETL* 93.3].

✓ Frei, Hans W. ‡ *The Eclipse of Biblical Narrative*, 1974.

✓ Fretheim, Terence E. ‡ *Deuteronomic History*, 1983. From the IBT series.

✓ Grabbe, Lester L. ‡ *What Do We Know and How Do We Know It?* 2007. The author is associated with the so-called revisionists/minimalists, and this book is useful to students for getting to know the lines of the debate over the history of Israel. Cf. Dever, and also Kitchen, who argues we know a lot more than Grabbe thinks. [*BASOR* 2/10 (Halpern, Dever); *Int* 7/09; *TJ* Fall 09; *VT* 60.1 (Moberly); *JTS* 4/09 (Williamson)].

✓ Gunn, David M., and Danna Nolan Fewell. ‡ *Narrative in the Hebrew Bible*, 1993. For more advanced readers.

☆ Hamilton, Victor. *Handbook on the Historical Books*, 2001. A good content survey, just as valuable (but in different ways) as Howard. Note that Hamilton seems more interested in the Former Prophets than Chronicles to Esther. Earlier he did a *Handbook on the Pentateuch*. [*RTR* 8/02; *Them* Sum 03; *TJ* Spr 03; *JSOT* 99; *BSac* 10/03].

✓ Halpern, Baruch. ‡ *The First Historians: The Hebrew Bible and History*, 1988. An exploration of the redactional approach to the so-called Deuteronomistic History.

✓ Heller, Roy L. ‡ *Narrative Structure and Discourse Constellations: An Analysis of Clause Function in Biblical Hebrew Prose*, 2004. So much can be learned here from the SMU prof! If memory serves, this was originally a Yale PhD.

☆ Howard, David M., and Michael A. Grisanti, eds. *Giving the Sense: Understanding and Using OT Historical Texts*, 2003. A large collection of essays by leading conservative scholars on the main questions and problems faced by interpreters and preachers. [*Them* Sum 05; *Chm* Win 05; *Anvil* 22.1].

✓ Jacobs, Mignon R., and Raymond F. Person Jr., eds. ‡ *Israelite Prophecy and the Deuteronomistic History*, 2013. Collected essays from SBL. [*CBQ* 10/14; *ETL* 90.3; *Them* 8/15].

✓ Kelle, Brad E., and Brent A. Strawn, eds. ‡ *The Oxford Handbook of the Historical Books of the Hebrew Bible*, 2020. As Firth writes [*ExpTim* 7/22], it is a very useful reference, once one gets past the slight oddity of the vol. not treating Ruth and Esther—the Arnold–Williamson *Dictionary* doesn't either. See Morgan below. [*BBR* 32.4; *BL* 2022].

☆ Kermode, Frank, and Robert Alter, eds. ‡ *The Literary Guide to the Bible*, 1987. This and Ryken below are good places to start understanding a literary approach. Kermode–Alter offers essays which introduce the Bible books. Available in pb.

☆ Kitchen, Kenneth A. *On the Reliability of the OT*, 2003. See under Pentateuch.

✓ Knoppers, Gary N., and J. Gordon McConville, eds. *Reconsidering Israel and Judah: Recent Studies on the Deuteronomistic History*, 2000. [*JSS* Aut 02; *RelSRev* 1/02; *CurTM* 2/02].

✓ Kort, W. ‡ *Story, Text and Scripture: Literary Interests in Biblical Narrative*, 1988.

✓ Leuchter, Mark A., and David T. Lamb. ‡ *The Historical Writings: Introducing Israel's Historical Literature* (IIS) 2016. An extensive (530 pp.) Fortress collaboration between a prominent Jewish HB scholar and a well-trained (Oxford DPhil) Christian seminary prof. The evangelical, Lamb, does Joshua, Judges, and Kings—see his SGBC on Kings—and his contributions are a bit (almost imperceptibly) more conservatively critical [𝓜]. Leuchter, Director of Jewish Studies at Temple U., covers Samuel, Chronicles, and Ezra–Nehemiah. [*JETS* 9/17].

✓ Long, V. P., G. J. Wenham, and D. W. Baker, eds. *Windows into OT History: Evidence, Argument, and the Crisis of "Biblical Israel,"* 2002. [*RTR* 12/02; *Them* Aut 03; *BSac* 10/03; *RelSRev* 10/03;

*EvQ* 10/04]. For another, more archaeologically based challenge to minimalist scholarship (Davies, Thompson, Lemche), see Dever above.

✓ Long, Burke O. 1984. ‡ *1 Kings with an Introduction to Historical Literature* (FOTL) 1984.

Mann, Thomas W. ‡ *The Book of the Former Prophets*, 2011. [*Int* 7/12; *JSOT* 36.5].

☆ Mathewson, Steven D. *The Art of Preaching OT Narrative*, 2nd ed. 2021. Fine book! [*Them* 47.1; *JBTS* 6/22].

✓ Mayes, A. D. H. ‡ *The Story of Israel between Settlement and Exile*, 1983.

☆ McConville, J. Gordon. *Grace in the End: A Study in Deuteronomic Theology*, 1993. A good help to preachers as well as students. [*SBET* Aut 94].

✓ McKenzie, Steven L. ‡ *Introduction to the Historical Books: Strategies for Reading*, 2010. See his "Deuteronomistic History" in *ABD* (1992). [*BBR* 21.4; *Int* 10/12; *JSOT* 35.5; *RBL* 2011; *JETS* 9/10; *ETL* 89.1].

✓ Millard, A. R., James K. Hoffmeier, and David W. Baker, eds. *Faith, Tradition, and History: Old Testament Historiography in Its Near Eastern Context*, 1994. Conservative discussion of the topic.

✓ Mills, Mary E. ‡ *Joshua to Kings: History, Story, Theology*, 3rd ed. 2016. Provides an overview for students (190pp.), from the T&T Clark Approaches series.

✓ Miscall, Peter D. ‡ "Introduction to Narrative Literature," *New Interpreter's Bible*, Vol. II, 1998.

✓ Moore, Megan Bishop, and Brad E. Kelle. [𝓜], *Biblical History and Israel's Past*, 2011. Traces "the Changing Study of the Bible and History," including the minimalist-maximalist debate. [*CBQ* 1/13; *JTS* 4/14; *VT* 62.3; *BSac* 7/13; *BASOR* 5/13; *BTB* 11/12; *JETS* 3/12].

✓ Morgan, Donn F., ed. ‡ *Oxford Handbook of the Writings of the Hebrew Bible*, 2019. For those unfamiliar with the Hebrew canon and the "Writings" designation, this vol. treats Psalms, Job, Proverbs, Ruth, Song of Songs, Qohelet (Ecclesiastes), Lamentations, Esther, Daniel, Ezra–Nehemiah, Chronicles. [*BBR* 29.4; *Int* 1/20; *JSOT* 43.5].

✓ Nelson, Richard D. ‡ *The Historical Books*, 1998. See also his oft-cited book, *The Double Redaction of the Deuteronomistic History* (1981), and his more recent critical history of OT times: *Historical Roots of the OT (1200–63 BCE)* (2014) [*CBQ* 7/15].

✓ Noth, Martin. ‡ *The Deuteronomistic History*, ET 1981. The first half of *Über-lieferungsgeschichtliche Studien* (1943, 3rd ed. 1967). The classic text on the topic, later nuanced by Cross in *Canaanite Myth and Hebrew Epic* (1973).

✓ Person, Raymond F. ‡ *The Deuteronomic School: History, Social Setting, and Literature*, 2002. [*Int* 7/03; *ExpTim* 7/03; *JBL* Spr 03; *VT* 54.4; *BiblInt* 12.4].

✓ Peterson, Brian Neil. *The Authors of the Deuteronomistic History*, 2014. Dates the availability and influence of Deuteronomic ideas quite early, and McConville welcomes the work as "a stimulating new analysis of the origins and composition of the DtrH." [*JSOT* 39.5; *JETS* 6/15; *VT* 66.3; *JTS* 4/16; *JHebS* 17].

✓ Polzin, Robert. ‡ *Moses and the Deuteronomist*, 1980.

✓ Powell, M. A. ‡ *What Is Narrative Criticism?* 1990. Good for reading alongside is Satterthwaite, "Narrative Criticism: The Theological Implications of Narrative Techniques," *NIDOTTE*, Vol. 1:125–33.

✓ Provan, Iain W. *1 and 2 Kings* (NIBC) 1995. See the introduction. Another good initial read is Provan, "The Historical Books of the Old Testament" in *The Cambridge Companion to Biblical Interpretation* (1998). His challenge to today's trend toward reading this material as historicized fiction is most clearly stated in the *Congress Volume Oslo 1998* ("In the Stable with the Dwarves," pp.281–319).

✓ Rad, Gerhard von. ‡ "The Deuteronomistic Theology of History in the Books of Kings," in *Studies in Deuteronomy*, ET 1953.

✓ Römer, Thomas. ‡ *The So-Called Deuteronomistic History: A Sociological, Historical and*

*Literary Introduction*, 2007. Influential work, arguing for a later dating of the whole DtrH. [*HS* 2008; *VT* 58.4; *RelSRev* 9/09; *BL* 2007; *CTJ* 11/10].

☆ Ryken, Leland. *Words of Delight: A Literary Introduction to the Bible*, 1987, 2nd ed. 1992. An evangelical standard.

✓ Simon, Uriel. ‡ *Reading Prophetic Narratives*, ET 1997. A brilliant narratological study of selected texts: 1 Sam 1–3; 28; 2 Sam 10–12; 1 Kgs 13; 17–19; and 2 Kgs 4. This Jewish scholar offers an exciting blend of literary and theological insights.

✓ Sternberg, Meir. ‡ *The Poetics of Biblical Narrative: Ideological Literature and the Drama of Reading*, 1985. Somewhat controversial as an introduction, but one of the three or four most important works on the topic.

✓ Walsh, Jerome T. ‡ *Style and Structure in Biblical Hebrew Narrative*, 2001. For students this is a fine introduction to OT narrators' conventions and stylistic devices. [*CBQ* 10/03; *ExpTim* 2/02; *HS* 2003; *JHebS* 4]. Further, we have Walsh's *Old Testament Narrative: A Guide to Interpretation* (2009) [*JSOT* 35.5; *VT* 62.3; *JETS* 12/11; *ExpTim* 9/12; *DenvJ* 14].

✓ Watson, Duane F., and Alan J. Hauser. ‡ *Rhetorical Criticism of the Bible, A Comprehensive Bibliography with Notes on History and Method*, 1994. For advanced readers.

✓ Weinfeld, Moshe. ‡ *Deuteronomy and the Deuteronomic School*, 1972.

# JOSHUA

★ **Butler, Trent C.** (WBC) 2 vols., 2nd ed. 2014. Erudite. The 1983 edition (310pp.) gave greater attention to archaeological findings than did Woudstra and was seen as a major, mildly critical work. Many conservatives said that the exegesis was misdirected, being framed by his arguments for "a protracted period of tradition formation and preservation" (xl) and an exilic date (DtrH). The late date can tend to destroy any historical value given to the book—the distant past is ordinarily dim as well. Nevertheless, Butler's work had strengths in other areas and was regularly consulted by students. Scholarly pastors who read Hebrew bought it too. [*RTR* 5/84; *EvQ* 10/85; *HS* 1985]. In the impressive update of 2014 (over 900pp.), the Introduction alone is 160pp. It is more conservative in approach and tone—see his acknowledgement of past criticisms in the Author's Preface. Cf. his 2009 WBC on Judges. Butler "places the Joshua materials in the Solomonic period" (11) and continues to see centuries-long redactional work. (By the way, arguments for an earlier dating of the book of Joshua are well presented by Waltke in *ISBE, Revised* and in Howard.) Pastors probably ignore the longer Source, Redaction and Form sections (e.g., pp.278–92). The handling of the Hebrew is extensive, the exegesis is thorough, and Butler's constant concern is to explain the theological message. The bibliographies are magnificent. [*JSOT* 39.5].

★ **Firth, David.** (EBTC) 2021. Building on his briefer BST (below), Firth offers a faithful, very satisfying exegesis and theological exposition (400pp.). The first 65pp. have an Introduction and eight essays on theological themes. Because he is so adept at narrative analysis and has a good theological mind, this is a sterling purchase for pastors. Evangelical students interested in the historical and archaeological backdrop, exegetical fine points, and the message of the book of Joshua will also gravitate to this. There is some Hebrew script in the commentary, but it remains accessible to those without the language. I have no reservation or hesitation in recommending Firth, and for getting at the message of Joshua many preachers would happily make this a top choice. See the pastorally sensitive "Bridge" sections. [*BL* 2022; *CBQ* 1/23; *JETS* 3/22; *Them* 46.3].

★ **Goldingay, John.** [𝑀], (BCOT) 2023. After a 48-page Introduction, the prodigious author has 385pp. of exegesis and theological exposition. Goldingay emphasizes covenant and explains well how the book "relates to the Torah on one side and to Judges through Kings on the other. . . . Joshua faces both ways narratively and theologically; it occupies a pivotal place in the sequence of works from Genesis through Kings" (7–8). He sees those behind the Joshua scroll as setting down "the deposit of the corporate memory of the people who won [in the conflict with the Canaanites] and who knew that it was Yahweh who had enabled that victory." He suggests the memory was "more selective than inventive" (11), but on the worrying side, accounts could be "fictionalized" (141) and "the scriptwriters" reworked the story "over more or less a millennium" (12). On the topic of violence, Goldingay sagely argues that "settlement and conquest is a universal phenomenon," and he critiques some postmodern and postcolonial interpreters of "othering" the book and the Israelites (25). The exegesis is narratively sensitive, stimulating, and consistently insightful; the theology is also stimulating, in part because you may disagree with him; e.g., "the devoting was Joshua's idea" (31) and not a commissioning from God. There are not a few moments of brilliance. In his interpretation of the spies and Rahab (103), he remarks that "the second Joshua or second Jesus . . . is happy to be entertained in Jericho by a 'sinner' (Luke 19:1–9)." Finally, there is good interaction with the rabbis (Qimchi, Rashi) and church fathers (esp. Origen's *Homilies*). See Goldingay under Genesis, Psalms, and Hosea (all BCOT), as well as Isaiah and Jeremiah. [*JETS* 3/24].

★ **Hawk, L. Daniel.** [𝓜], (BerO) 2000. A 344-page work giving diligent attention to the narrator's art and purposes. Hawk teaches at Ashland Seminary, and this is a more conservative vol. in the series. He builds upon his fine earlier study of different plots, their twists and turns, in *Every Promise Fulfilled* (WJK, 1991) [*CRBR* 1993; *CBQ* 1/94; *HS* 1994]. The commentary will be of greater interest to students and scholarly pastors. [*CBQ* 4/02; *Them* Aut 01; *Int* 7/02; *HS* 2002; *JSOT* 99; *F&M* Fall 01; *RelSRev* 1/02]. He added another study, *Joshua in 3-D: A Commentary on Biblical Conquest and Manifest Destiny* (2010), that wrestles "with the question of how Joshua can contribute meaningfully to Christian theology and mission in the twenty-first century" (Preface). He suggests readers may at points wish to identify with the indigene rather than the invader and engages in ideological criticism. [*BBR* 21.3; *EvQ* 1/13; *JSOT* 38.5; *JHebS* 3].

★ **Hess, Richard S.** (TOTC) 1996. A very fine addition to the Tyndale series. As one would expect of Hess, this is a well-researched work that takes a thoroughly conservative approach. I was glad to see it because of its thoughtful discussion of archaeological, historical, and literary issues. Thankfully, this commentator takes an interest in the theology of the book; many in the past have not. Preachers and students appreciate this balanced commentary. [*Chm* 111.3; *Them* 2/99; *JETS* 6/99; *BL* 1997; *RelSRev* 1/98].

★ **Howard, David M.** (NAC) 1998. The author did a creditable job in his *Introduction to the OT Historical Books* (1993), and here he builds upon that work. Evangelical pastors have been delighted with the help they get from Hess and Howard: both are most trustworthy guides. I long wished Howard had given us more, for we lacked major, up-to-date, evangelical commentaries to replace Woudstra. Holds to an early date, 15th century. [*HS* 01; *DenvJ*].

★ **Hubbard, Robert.** (NIVAC) 2009. I expected it to be among the best in NIVAC (as a preacher's series), at least from the exegesis standpoint, judging from the quality of his past work. It is, and presents a surprisingly full treatment (652pp.), alongside Block's NIVAC on Deuteronomy. Note that his approach is not as conservative as the NAC and TOTC. Those scouting for more pastoral/devotional helps should consider Ralph Davis, Firth (BST), Jackman, Martin, Reimer, and Wray Beal below. [*JETS* 12/10].

✓ Amos, N. Scott, ed. *Joshua, Judges, Ruth* (RCS) 2020. [*JTS* 4/23].

Auld, A. Graeme. ‡ *Joshua, Judges, and Ruth* (DSB) 1984. Quite suggestive in its exposition

(290pp.). Auld discounts these books historically and dates them late, but his is still one of the better vols. in DSB and is profitable reading for one interested in the theology of the text. [*Them* 1/86; *EvQ* 10/86]. Students note Auld's *Joshua Retold: Synoptic Perspectives* (1998) [*JBL* Win 01; *DenvJ*], which prepares the way for the ICC below.

F   Auld, A. Graeme. ‡ (ICC).

✓   Bekkum, Koert van. ‡ *From Conquest to Coexistence: Ideology and Antiquarian Intent in the Historiography of Israel's Settlement in Canaan*, 2011.

F   Beynon, Graham. (Hodder) 2024?

✓   Bimson, John. *Redating the Exodus and Conquest*, 1978, rev. 1981. See under Exodus.

    Blaikie, W. G. (EB) 1893. Reprinted by Klock & Klock (1978) and Solid Ground Christian Books (2005), and now free online. This is a superb exposition by a Free Church of Scotland luminary with suggestive ideas for pastors. In 1989 when few resources were available on Joshua, I recommended its purchase.

☆   Boice, James M. *Joshua: We Will Serve the Lord*, 1989. About 200pp. of sermons.

✓   **Boling, Robert G., and G. Ernest Wright.** ‡ (retired AB) 1982. Dated. It had the strengths and weaknesses of the old AB, with much information on archaeology and historical backdrop. Wright contributed only the introduction, which is a pity since he had greater sensitivity to matters theological. See Boling on Judges. [*JBL* 103.3].

✓   Bright, John. ‡ (IB) 1953. Formerly it was valued highly because of the dearth of commentaries on Joshua. Bright was a leading OT historian, more conservative in his critical outlook (Albright school); he also had theological insight. See Coote below.

    **Calvin, John.** 1563, ET 1854. According to his friend Beza, this was Calvin's last commentary. The reader will notice that the work, due to physical weakness, is comparatively brief. Still, there is much excellent material here.

    Coleson, Joseph. (CorBC) 2012. Bound with Judges (Stone) and Ruth (Driesbach). Much ground is covered quickly in this 560-page book. I have used it very little, but some have shared their high opinion of the three sections. Without a doubt, Stone's contribution on Judges should be looked up; he crystalizes the issues and has excellent insights.

    Cooke, G. A. ‡ (CBSC) 1918.

✓   Coote, Robert B. ‡ (NIB) 1998. The old IB had a valuable commentary on Joshua by Bright, but NIB offers little help to either the student (on account of brevity) or the pastor (on account of a negative, dismissive interpretation of Scripture). [*ExpTim* 1/99].

    Creach, Jerome. ‡ (I) 2003. A surprisingly brief vol. (130pp.) for a 24-chapter Bible book which preachers find a challenge. Not as successful an entry in the series. He gives us hardly more than a glance at chs. 13–22. [*CBQ* 10/04; *Int* 10/04; *EuroJTh* 18.2].

☆   **Dallaire, Hélène M.** (EBCR) 2012. The author teaches at Denver Seminary, is an able Hebraist, and writes well. Pastors find her commentary a well-rounded, helpful guide, though it is brief (225pp.). There are insights; e.g., Joshua had learned by personal experience (Num 13) that just two spies could do the job. See Allen under Numbers.

F   Dallaire, Hélène. (ZECOT).

    Davis, John J. *Conquest and Crisis*, 1969, 3rd ed. 2008. A popular-level, brief, conservative commentary, covering Joshua to Ruth. Useful to lay readers.

☆   Davis, D. Ralph. *No Falling Words*, 1988. Sermonic material, published by Baker, from a former OT prof at RTS. See under Judges for further comments applicable here. Preachers find this very suggestive. I bought it myself. If you are less bookish, I'd suggest dropping the Butler, Goldingay, and Hawk recommendations and purchasing this. [*Chm* Sum 02].

✓   **Dozeman, Thomas B.** ‡ (AYB) 2 vols., 2015–23. A replacement for Boling–Wright, Dozeman is impressively detailed and thorough (approx. 1000pp.) as a historical-critical exegesis of the Hebrew (giving constant attention to the LXX too). Certainly in the top rank of academic reference tools on this literature, despite a few idiosyncratic views. He is critical of the DtrH thesis and chooses to interpret "Joshua as an independent book written during the postexilic period from a northern point of view" (5). Joshua uses pentateuchal materials and "represents a Samarian myth of origin in which the promised land is heavily populated with kings and royal city-states requiring holy war to empty the land of its urban culture.... The message of the book ... is one of opposition to foreign rule in the promised land, represented by city-states; over against this the author idealizes a more primitive and rural life" (31). The skepticism regarding any historical value of the book of Joshua will be off-putting to most pastors. [*BBR* 26.2; *JSOT* 41.5; *ExpTim* 8/16].

✓ Earl, Douglas S. ‡ *Reading Joshua as Christian Scripture*, 2010. A Durham PhD that dispenses with historical categories and provides a close literary reading. The original function of the myth-narrative, he says, was to reshape the community identity (along Deuteronomic lines) by creating a cultural memory. There is heavy use of Ricoeur, with attention paid to the church's interpretation of Joshua from the early Fathers to Calvin. [*BBR* 21.2; *JTS* 4/11; *JSOT* 35.5; *VT* 61.4; *RBL* 2/11; *JETS* 3/11; *Them* 11/10; *DenvJ* 15; *JHebS* 11]. He summarizes his views in *The Joshua Delusion?* (2010), which includes a critique from Chris Wright [*Int* 10/12; *JSOT* 37.5; *ExpTim* 10/12].

☆ Firth, David G. (BST) 2015. The exposition (256pp.) completed the OT series, offering a very good narrative reading, as well as wise theological guidance on *The Message of Joshua*. Pastors especially should consider this for purchase, but compare with Firth's EBTC above. He has other commentaries on Esther (BST) and Samuel (Apollos). [*Chm* Aut 16; *JETS* 6/16; *Them* 41.2 (Howard)].

✓ Franke, John R., ed. *Joshua, Judges, Ruth, 1–2 Samuel* (ACCS) 2005. [*BL* 2008].

Garstang, John. *The Foundations of Biblical History, Joshua, Judges*, 1931. Pastors long looked to this work for answers to questions about archaeology and geography relating to Joshua and Judges. Garstang is terribly out of date. Findings from excavating Jericho (1930–36), written up in *The Story of Jericho* (rev. ed. 1948), were challenged by a subsequent dig (1952–58). See Hess and Butler instead.

☆ **Goslinga, C. J.** (BSC) 1955, ET 1986. Also treats Judges and Ruth (558pp.). Theologically sensitive, Goslinga would be a worthy addition to a pastor's library, but is long o/p.

✓ **Gray, John.** ‡ (NCB) 1967, rev. 1986. Covers Judges and Ruth as well. Though not one of the stronger vols. in NCB, this vol. is regularly cited in the literature. Critical and skeptical for its time, Gray now sounds less critical as so much historical scholarship has become radicalized.

F   Greenspoon, Leonard. ‡ (JPS). The scholar wrote a Harvard diss. on Joshua.

✓ Hall, Sarah Lebhar. *Conquering Character: The Characterization of Joshua in Joshua 1–11*, 2010. A fine Cambridge diss. on a fascinating topic. [*JTS* 4/11; *JSOT* 35.5; *JHebS* 13].

Hamlin, E. John. ‡ (ITC-E) 1984. A theological interpretation which received some favorable reviews. I find it to be of indifferent value. [*WTJ* Spr 88; *JETS* 9/84; *ExpTim* 8/84].

☆ **Harris, J. G.**, C. Brown, and M. Moore. *Joshua, Judges, Ruth* (NIBC) 2000. The treatments of Judges (160pp.) and Ruth (80pp.) are considerably fuller than the Joshua section (130pp.). The publisher might well have devoted, instead, a whole vol. to Joshua with its 24 chapters, especially since Harris does an admirable job on Joshua, given space constraints. The commentary has received generally favorable reviews, with a warmer reception given to Judges than to Ruth. [*RTR* 8/01; *Them* Spr 02; *Int* 1/02; *HS* 2002; *JSOT* 99; *SwJT* Fall 01; *Anvil* 19.3; *JHebS* 4].

☆ **Harstad, Adolph L.** (ConcC) 2004. A huge (906pp.) undertaking, typical of the conservative Lutheran series. Harstad provides both exegetical guidance for seminarians and pastors studying the Hebrew and theological (christological) reflection. It is a reverent reading of Scripture but, on the negative side, is regarded by some as insufficiently rigorous for the academy. In light of the paucity of thorough evangelical expositions, it is very welcome. [*EvQ* 10/07; *CBQ* 7/06; *JETS* 12/06; *BL* 2006; *BSac* 4/08].

F    Hawkins, Ralph. (EEC).

✓    Hess, Richard S., Gerald A. Klingbeil, and Paul J. Ray, Jr., eds. *Critical Issues in Early Israelite History*, 2008. No doubt many dismiss this vol. as out of step with today's increasingly skeptical historiography, but the scholarship here is of a high caliber, with eight essays relating to the Joshua narrative.

✓    Hess, Richard S., and Elmer Martens, eds. *War in the Bible and Terrorism in the Twenty-First Century*, 2008. Older books include John Wood, *Perspectives on War in the Bible* (1998); Susan Niditch, *War in the Hebrew Bible* (1993); and Peter C. Craigie, *The Problem of War in the OT* (1978). For more on the topic of warfare in OT times, see T. R. Hobbs's *A Time for War* (1989); M. G. Hasel's *Military Practice and Polemic: Israel's Laws of Warfare in Near Eastern Context* (2005); *War and Ethics in the ANE* (2009) by C. L. Crouch [*BBR* 22.1]; Boyd Seevers's *Warfare in the OT* (2013) [*CBQ* 1/15; *ExpTim* 7/15; *Them* 4/14; *JESOT* 3.2; *BTB* 45.3]; and literature cited in Charles Trimm, "Recent Research on Warfare in the OT," *CBR* 10.2 (2012): 171–216. Trimm's large-scale work is *Fighting for the King and the Gods: A Survey of Warfare in the ANE* (2017).

Hinlicky, Paul R. ‡ (Brazos) 2021. By a Lutheran theologian, retired from Roanoke College. He offers some fine theological discussion, well described as a "literary-spiritual" reading (7) and conservatively critical, though it is (quietly) anchored in a higher-critical understanding of the literature. Hinlicky regularly explores connections with the New Joshua of the NT. [*JETS* 6/23].

Hoppe, L. ‡ *Joshua, Judges* (OTM) 1982.

Huffman, John A. (WCC) 1986. Huffman makes one of the better contributions to the series. Will prompt the preacher to think theologically and practically about Joshua. The author is an evangelical PCUSA pastor.

☆    Jackman, David. (PTW) 2014. Briefer than many in the series (224pp.), but by a master preacher and trainer of preachers (former President of Proclamation Trust, UK). Anyone looking for a vol. of sermons could pick this. Most pastors will find more help here than in Hawk. As an added plus, Jackman has a beautiful British essay style.

✓    Kaufmann, Yehezkel. *The Biblical Account of the Conquest of Canaan*, ET 1953, 2nd ed. 1985. Kaufmann presents a conservative Jewish interpretation of the narrative and issues a bracing challenge to proponents of the DtrH theory.

✓    Keil, Carl F. (KD) ET 1865. Able, old exegesis and theological exposition.

F    Knight, Douglas A. ‡ (NCBC). The author is an expert on tradition history.

F    Knight, Michelle E. (BGW).

Laughlin, John C. H. ‡ *Reading Joshua: A Historical-Critical/Archaeological Commentary*, 2015. From the Baptist publisher Smyth & Helwys.

Madvig, Donald H. (EBC) 1992. Pedestrian. It was brief at 130pp. and had fewer exegetical notes than others in the series. See Dallaire above.

☆    Martin, Oren R. *Bound for the Promised Land: The Land Promise in God's Redemptive Plan* (NSBT) 2015. Well covers a key theological theme in the OT and NT, especially prominent in the Pentateuch and Joshua. [*WTJ* Fall 16; *JETS* 12/15; *Them* 42.2]. See also Koorevaar–Paul, eds., *The Earth and the Land: Studies about the Value of the Land of Israel in the OT and Afterwards* (2018).

☆    Mathews, Kenneth A. (TTC) 2016. Does very well as a simple, straightforward, brief study tool for pastors and Sunday School teachers. The author is a fine scholar (see his NAC on Genesis), but he wears his considerable learning lightly here. This has potential to become a favorite among pastors.

✓ Matties, Gordon. [𝓜], (BCBC) 2012. Readers sense Matties is superbly trained, diligently studious, and ethically conscientious in "a difficult conversation . . . even an argument with" Joshua. He has long taught at Canadian Mennonite University, and his Peace Church tradition motivates him to engage, not avoid, "biblical texts that have been used to justify colonialism, conquest, occupation, and ethnic cleansing" (Preface). Predictably, the issue of continuity vs. discontinuity between the Testaments is at the fore. He decides that Joshua is not a conquest narrative per se, and it needs to be interpreted via an intrabiblical conversation. At points Matties finds himself in disagreement with the text (530pp.).

F  McCarter, P. Kyle. ‡ (Herm). A leading critical commentary for years to come?

✓ **McConville, J. Gordon, and Stephen Williams.** [𝓜], (THC) 2010. McConville provides able, though not detailed, exegesis (80pp.), and Williams, a systematics professor, joins him in offering mature and helpful theological reflection (both systematics and biblical theology). As Firth notes, Williams's work takes up about 60 percent of the book, "and it is not always clear that the commentary itself has had a significant effect on the theological developments that are offered." The two share a Northern Ireland Presbyterian heritage. [*JSOT* 35.5; *VT* 61.4 (Firth), 62.3; *JETS* 6/11; *ExpTim* 3/11; *BTB* 2/12; *BSB* 6/11]. See McConville's Phoenix Guide, *Joshua: Crossing Divides* (2013) [*JSOT* 38.5; *JJS* 69.2], republished by T&T Clark in 2017 [*BBR* 27.3; *JTS* 4/18; *JSOT* 38.5, 41.5].

F  Meer, Michaël van der, and Cor de Vos. ‡ (IECOT).

✓ Miller, J. M., and Gene M. Tucker. ‡ (CBC) 1974. Both scholars had well-established reputations in critical scholarship. Miller made OT history his specialty. They are quite skeptical about the historical value of the book of Joshua.

✓ Mitchell, Gordon. ‡ *Together in the Land: A Reading of the Book of Joshua*, 1993. Works such as Mitchell, Hawk encourage others to apply narrative criticism. See Hall.

✓ **Nelson, Richard D.** ‡ (OTL-R) 1997. Nelson made the Deuteronomistic History (DtrH) his specialty and here provides us with a 310-page commentary in a prestigious series. The author is solidly in the liberal camp and, in paying close attention to historical questions, discounts Joshua's historical value. This is another vol. for the scholarly pastor who is building a first-rate personal library, but note that Nelson does not help much with the Hebrew text. See Soggin. [*Them* 11/99; *JETS* 9/99; *JBL* Spr 99; *Int* 10/98; *CBQ* 4/99; *HS* 1999; *ThTo* 1/99; *RelSRev* 7/98; *RBL*].

✓ Noort, Ed, ed. ‡ *The Book of Joshua*, 2012. A 650-page vol. of essays in BETL, showcasing mainly continental European scholarship. [*ETL* 92.4; *JHebS* 14].

Pink, Arthur. *Gleanings in Joshua*, 1964. See under Genesis. This was one of his last series and is better than Genesis and Exodus.

☆ **Pitkänen, Pekka M. A.** [𝓜], (Apollos) 2010. The series can focus more on theology and the message of the text than is the case here. Pitkänen's keen interest is reading Joshua in a postcolonial world (74–99), but he also pays attention to literary form and structure (much interaction with Nelson), narratological features, archaeological research, history, and placing the story in the wider ANE context. The Introduction is full (80pp.), and the commentary runs for 300pp., including 12 excursuses. There is a conservative take on the history question: "actual historical events, even though one cannot prove the matter" (40). Partly because of scant biblical theology and its being less engagingly written, I recommend Pitkänen more as a supplement to the likes of Hess and Hubbard, not as a pastor's sole resource. Some might allege he has an ax to grind as he discusses the Israeli-Palestinian conflict and other situations of "indigenous peoples" suffering violence and "ethnic cleansing"; e.g., he takes swipes at the Puritans in America ("genocidal thinking"). His research is tinged with ideological criticism; see his "Pentateuch–Joshua: A Settler-Colonial Document of a Supplanting Society," *Settler Colonial Studies* 4.3 (2014): 227–44. [*JSOT* 35.5; *ExpTim* 5/12].

✓ **Polzin, Robert.** ‡ *Moses and the Deuteronomist: A Literary Study of the Deuteronomic History: Part One. Deuteronomy, Joshua, Judges*, 1980.

Pressler, Carolyn. ‡ *Joshua, Judges, and Ruth* (WestBC) 2002. [*ExpTim* 8/03; *JSOT* 27.5].

☆ Reimer, David. (ESVEC) 2021. A noteworthy theological exposition from a veteran scholar once Dean at Faith Mission Bible College in Edinburgh and Honorary Lecturer at St. Andrews. See Konkel under Deuteronomy.

✓ **Rösel, Hartmut N.** ‡ (HCOT) 2011. Steps away from discussions of a Hexateuch or DtrH to treat the book more on its own. Because Rösel has expertise in archaeology and historical geography, the vol. is strong in those areas—the only index is Site Identifications. He is interested in a supposedly complex compositional history (five stages) and skeptical about the book's historical value. "The book of Joshua does not reflect the actual historical process that led to the existence of Israel in their land" (15). He sees little sense in writing up a theology of the book himself, and, surprisingly, chooses instead to summarize Calvin's theological insights on Joshua (10–14). The work is mid-sized (380pp.), treats the Hebrew text, and contains full bibliographies. [*JSOT* 37.5; *JHebS* 12].

Schaeffer, Francis. *Joshua and the Flow of Biblical History*, 1975.

F   Schneider, Tammi. ‡ (Illum).

✓ **Sharp, Carolyn J.** ‡ (S&H) 2019. A fairly thorough, liberal commentary (400pp.), with strong interests in narrative criticism (literary structure, characterization), and postmodern, postcolonial interpretation. Sharp writes in a very engaging manner, deconstructing an "appalling" book with its ANE "ideology that a deity chooses sides and renders military aid in military conflicts" (1). She reads very much "against the grain." [*CBQ* 10/21; *Int* 7/22].

Smith, Robert. *Exalting Jesus in Joshua* (CCE) 2023.

✓ **Soggin, J. Alberto.** ‡ (retired OTL) ET 1972. Mainly concerned with archaeological, geographical, and historical problems of the text. Soggin is rather dated and comes to standard critical conclusions (DtrH, etc.). Pastors should not expect to find theological help in this o/p work, which is replaced by Nelson. See also Judges.

✓ Stern, Philip D. ‡ *The Biblical Ḥerem: A Window on Israel's Religious Experience*, 1991. See also Lilley, "Understanding the Ḥerem," *TynBul* 44 (1993): 169–77. Difficulties in explaining the term are explored in Younger, "Some Recent Discussion of Ḥērem," in *Far from Minimal* (Davies FS), eds. Burns–Rogerson (2012), pp.505–22. A reception historical account is Hofreiter, *Making Sense of Old Testament Genocide* (OUP, 2018). See also Note #3 below.

☆ Tidball, Derek. *Lead Like Joshua: Lessons for Today*, 2017. The former Principal of London Bible College has a passion for inspiring and training church leaders, and this IVP issue uses Joshua as a model of biblical leadership to follow. (I believe he's well aware that Joshua wasn't written for that main purpose.) Contains fine insights.

✓ Wijk-Bos, Johanna W. H. van. ‡ *The End of the Beginning: Joshua & Judges*, 2019. From a veteran feminist scholar, this is part of a multi-vol. series also covering Samuel and Kings. The author is astute narratologically and writes very well. [*JSOT* 44.5; *BBR* 30.4; *CBQ* 10/21; *JETS* 6/20; *Int* 7/21].

✓ Winther-Nielsen, Nicolai. *A Functional Discourse Grammar of Joshua*, 1995. Of course there is a lot of technical linguistics here, but for those who understand it, Winther-Nielsen is useful indeed (353pp.).

☆ **Woudstra, Marten.** (NICOT) 1981. Long a recommended purchase. Though we could have used more help with the Hebrew, this work served us well for decades. There is excellent discussion of theology and ethics in the introduction, but not as much as might be hoped for in the commentary proper. No evangelical work prior to Hess and Howard came close to Woudstra. Now dated. [*TJ* Spr 83; *JETS* 9/82; *JBL* 102.2; *WTJ* Spr 82].

☆ Wray Beal, Lissa M. (SGBC) 2019. Over 400pp., quickly moving from a reading of the text in its background ("Listen to the Story" in ANE context) to concise, basic exposition ("Explain the Story") and application ("Live the Story") sections. Wray Beal's book is solid, frequently insightful, and fits well into the series format; it is becoming a favorite of mine. She "works with the premise that real events underlie the account in Joshua," while being alert to "artful telling" that "utilizes techniques such as hyperbole and narrative characterization to shape events for theological purposes" (34–35). In a few spots the applications are an odd fit; e.g., after the story of Ai's capture she writes at some length about historic injustices in Canada's Residential School system for "First Nations" children (190–92). [*JETS* 3/20; *Them* 45.1 (Hawk); *WTJ* Spr 24].

✓ Younger, K. Lawson. *Ancient Conquest Accounts: A Study in Ancient Near Eastern and Biblical History Writing*, 1990.

NOTES: (1) Be sure to consult atlases and OT histories. Among the latter, many evangelical OT scholars now recommend *A Biblical History of Israel* by Provan–Long–Longman (WJK, 2nd ed. 2015) and Merrill's *Kingdom of Priests* (Baker, 2nd ed. 2008). (2) See "Joshua: An Annotated Bibliography," *SwJT* 41.1 (1998): 102–10. (3) Understandably, many struggle with the slaughter in the book of Joshua. How do we read those narratives and make sense of them ethically, and what do they teach about the God of the Bible? The best quick help I can offer is to recommend Christopher J. H. Wright, "Appendix: What about the Canaanites?" in *Old Testament Ethics for the People of God* (IVP, 2004), 472–80, and the literature he cites there. A book edited by Stanley Gundry debates the better explanations: *Show Them No Mercy: Four Views of God and Canaanite Genocide* (Zondervan, 2003). See also Trimm, *The Destruction of the Canaanites: God, Genocide, and Biblical Interpretation* (2022) [*JETS* 9/22; *DenvJ* (Hess); *Presb* Spr 22; *CBQ* 7/23]; Mariottini, *Divine Violence and the Character of God* (2022) [*JETS* 3/23]; Versluis, *The Command to Exterminate the Canaanites: Deuteronomy 7* (2017) [*BBR* 27.3]; the Walton–Walton revisionist study, *The Lost World of the Israelite Conquest* (2017) [*JETS* 3/18; *SJT* 72.4; *Them* 43.1]; Thomas–Evans–Copan, eds., *Holy War in the Bible: Christian Morality and an OT Problem* (IVP, 2013) [*BBR* 24.2]; and Copan–Flannagan, *Did God Really Command Genocide?* (2014) [*Them* 8/15; *JETS* 12/15]. From other angles come Berthelot–David–Hirschman, eds., *The Gift of the Land and the Fate of the Canaanites in Jewish Thought* (OUP, 2014) [*BBR* 24.3], and Seibert, *The Violence of Scripture: Overcoming the OT's Troubling Legacy* (Fortress, 2012). Pursuing the theology are von Rad, *Holy War in Ancient Israel* (ET 1991); Longman–Reid, *God Is a Warrior* (1995); the Anabaptist Lind, *Yahweh Is a Warrior* (1980); and Hawk, *The Violence of the Biblical God* (2019) [*CBQ* 7/20; *Int* 4/21; *SJT* 73.2]. See also Hess–Martens above.

# JUDGES

★ **Beldman, David J. H.** (THC) 2020. Follows a diss. on *The Completion of Judges: Strategies of Ending in Judges 17–21* (2017) [*VT* 69.4; *BBR* 28.2; *CBQ* 4/19; *JSOT* 42.5], and a fine brief introduction to the book: *Deserting the King* (2017). After an Introduction (55pp.) there is chapter-by-chapter theologically oriented exegesis (174pp.) and a section of theological essays (over 70pp.). Someone suggests that, though in an overtly theological series, this commentary is more astute in its literary insights and exegesis than in theology [*BBR* 31.1], but I count it a successful contribution to the series. Beldman teaches at Redeemer U., Ontario, and has Reformed convictions. [*RB* 4/22; *ZAW* 134.1; *ExpTim* 6/20; *BL* 2022; *JTS* 4/22; *JETS* 9/20; *Int* 7/22].

★ **Block, Daniel.** *Judges–Ruth* (NAC) 1999. Once the obvious first choice for the pastor's library, this extensive work (767pp.) filled a huge hole as it provides a careful treatment of introductory matters, adequate and balanced exegesis, and good theological interpretation. After Block's appearance we still awaited a technical exegesis of the Hebrew by a conservative, and Butler began to meet our need. Now also see Boda–Conway. Looking over these recommendations, the student and more scholarly pastor might especially consider Boda–Conway, Butler, and Webb for purchase. Another pastor might prefer starting with NAC or NICOT and then adding the superb BST and WCC expositions, and Davis. My counsel: mix and match these works as you please. Note that a CSC revision has been announced. Worth mentioning is that Block wrote the comprehensive NICOT on Ezekiel, NIVAC on Deuteronomy, and ZECOT on Ruth. [*JETS* 9/01; *BSac* 10/01].

★ **Boda, Mark J., and Mary L. Conway.** (ZECOT) 2022. Was so eager to see this! An enormous (880pp of commentary plus appendices), detailed reference work with fine sensitivity to philology and syntax, literary structure, narratology (including discourse analysis), and the theology in the Hebrew text. Honestly, I find the discourse analysis here to be more sophisticated than in most of the other ZECOT vols. One could spend many months digesting all the learning in this well-rounded tome, a landmark commentary for decades to come. Pastors will certainly want Block and Webb in their libraries, but this is now my first choice. Preparatory for the collaboration here was Boda's publication in EBCR (see below) and Conway's *Judging the Judges: A Narrative Appraisal Analysis* (2019) [*JSOT* 45.5]. The two are McMaster colleagues, with Conway now emerita.

★ **Butler, Trent.** (WBC) 2009. He did *Joshua*, one of the first vols. in the series. This fat book (xcii + 538pp.) came a quarter century later and was more conservative in approach to such matters as dating (composed in "the opening years of the divided monarchy" [lxxiv]). Butler does not attribute the Judges material to a Deuteronomist. He offers a thorough commentary with textual criticism, philology and grammar, form and narrative/rhetorical criticism, historical study, and theological reflection (a bit, anyway). Once again WBC provides us with nearly exhaustive bibliographies. There is less biblical theology, which made me more eager for Webb. A criticism could be that he so catalogs others' arguments that some pages are composed of nearly 3/4 quotation (e.g., pp.282, 325, 443); occasionally I am left without a clear idea of Butler's own conclusion. Students will relish the extensive research. The average pastor might pass this by and prefer a homiletical exposition. [*Int* 7/10; *CBQ* 4/11; *JETS* 12/10; *RevExp* Spr 11].

★ **Webb, Barry G.** (NICOT) 2012. Evangelicals have made impressive strides in Judges research. As anticipated, Webb here built on his diss.—see below—and is top-notch with regard to exegesis, narratological discussion, and theological interpretation. How to pick between Block and Webb? Students will quickly surmise that Webb is not so engaged with historical questions; he does not try "to achieve the kind of exhaustive thoroughness that insists on putting back into the text all the data that the author has left out" (xvi). On a hard topic, see "The Wars of Judges as Christian Scripture," *RTR* 67.1 (2008): 18–28. Also, see below his entry in PTW, which some will prefer to the exegetical NICOT. [*BBR* 23.3; *JTS* 10/14; *JSOT* 37.5; *RTR* 4/13; *ExpTim* 1/14; *BSac* 4/13; *RevExp* Fall 13; *RelSRev* 9/14; *RTR* 4/13; *VT* 66.2].

★ Webb, Barry. *Judges and Ruth: God in Chaos* (PTW) 2015. Offers a model for preaching the books which is guided by fine biblical scholarship (never in the forefront), literary sensitivity, and a biblical-theological approach (300pp.). Block has a glowing endorsement: "Webb is not only the finest interpreter of Judges, he is also the book's finest expositor." The vol. "is a great gift first to preachers, but ultimately to God's people who will hear from them the living and life-giving Word of the Lord from these books." [*JETS* 9/16].

★ **Younger, K. Lawson.** *Judges/Ruth* (NIVAC) 2002, rev. 2021. More exegetical than the OT series as a whole and is, therefore, useful to students as well as pastors. Conversely, it is less helpful as a guide to applying the message of Judges to the present day. It starts expositors down the path of applying the Scriptures but does not accompany them as long a distance. The author is a much respected scholar at TEDS, who has expertise in the ancient Near Eastern background of the Bible and has coedited the standard reference set, *The Context of Scripture*. He agrees with Block, who said the theme of Judges is "the Canaanization of Israelite society during the period of the settlement."

Ackerman, Susan. ‡ *Warrior, Dancer, Seductress, Queen: Women in Judges and Biblical Israel*, 1998. In the ABRL series.

✓ Amit, Yairah. ‡ *The Book of Judges: The Art of Editing*, 1998. A literary reading and redactional study published by Brill.

✓ Amos, N. Scott, ed. *Joshua, Judges, Ruth* (RCS) 2020.

✓ **Assis, Elie.** [𝓜], *Before There Were Kings: A Literary Analysis of the Book of Judges*, 2024. By a conservatively critical Israeli academic. See also his work on Joel.

Auld, A. Graeme. ‡ (DSB) 1984. See under Joshua. Auld has thought deeply about the book of Judges and its relevance today. He taught at Edinburgh, is liberal in theology, and does well (within the confines of the series) in literary analysis.

✓ Bal, Mieke. ‡ *Murder and Difference*, 1988; *Death and Dissymmetry*, 1988. These two works are similar in their literary approach to texts in Judges and their postmodern and feminist concerns. They are learned and provocative, "focusing on characters rather than storyline, practices rather than events" (Groom [*BSB* 9/98]).

Barber, Cyril J. *Judges: A Narrative of God's Power*, 1990.

Biddle, Mark E. ‡ *Reading Judges* (ROT) 2012. I have not used this yet. [*Int* 7/14].

☆ **Boda, Mark J.** (EBCR) 2012. Among the strongest in the series. Boda is well-trained (Cambridge PhD), adept at biblical theology, and a veteran commentator. Here he offers a 245-page exegesis, which does well with historical questions, narrative, lexical and grammatical issues, scholarly interaction, biblical connections, themes, and (briefly) message. There is no better concise treatment of Judges from an evangelical; one senses that Boda is held back by word count from doing far, far more. See Allen under Numbers. Students now immediately turn to ZECOT (above).

✓ Bodner, Keith, and Benjamin J. M. Johnson, eds. ‡? *Characters and Characterization in the Book of Judges*, 2024. Expected to be rich, from LHBOTS. I have yet to see it. See the companion vols. on Samuel and Kings.

☆ **Boling, Robert G.** ‡ (AB) 1975. Lots of information and, like the AB on Joshua, reflects the more conservative historical approach of the Albright school. The student or scholarly pastor doing a thorough study of the book of Judges (esp. the Hebrew) can use this work; the average pastor will not benefit so much. Boling had prominence as the leading critical work mainly because there were so few quality, in-depth works on Judges, and I used to recommend this for purchase. Now dated and outstripped by newer works, including Sasson (Boling's replacement). [*JBL* 95.1].

Branson, Robert D. 2009. A Wesleyan commentary I have not seen.

☆ **Brensinger, Terry L.** [𝓜], (BCBC) 1999. Conservatively critical assumptions do not intrude on his work of commenting theologically and practically on Judges. Though there is not a great deal of interaction with scholarship, the author does make good use of some literary treatments (e.g., Webb). This vol. could be put to excellent use by pastors because he has a fine grasp of the flow of the book. There is a bit over 200pp. of actual commentary. At points I wonder if he moralizes the text in ways probably not intended by the narrator, e.g., interpreting Samson's character as a bad example not to follow. While that's true, of course, is the Samson story in the Bible mainly to warn us all against hedonism and immoral sex? Brensinger does less to place the text in the course of redemptive history; Davis and Webb do a better job in that respect. [*CBQ* 4/01; *CTJ* 11/01].

✓ Brettler, Marc Zvi. ‡ *The Book of Judges*, 2002. A well-written introduction to reading the book in order to discover its historical and literary concerns. [*Int* 1/03; *RelSRev* 1/03].

F Brettler, Marc Zvi. ‡ (IECOT).

✓ **Burney, C. F.** ‡ 2nd ed. 1920. Continues to be of philological value for those reading the Hebrew. Burney had many of the same aims as Moore and continues to be consulted widely. For example, Lindars (below) cites him 55 times. [*JBL* 90.2].

Cassel, P. (Lange) ET 1872. Years ago some thought it quite good, in light of the scarcity of theological works on Judges. Moore asserted that it offered "ingeniously perverse exegesis" (l). Covers both Judges and Ruth. Spurgeon found the Joshua work by Fay in the same vol. inferior. See Cassel on Esther.

☆ **Chisholm, Robert B., Jr.** *A Commentary on Judges and Ruth* (KEL) 2013. There is much to like about this book: the author has taught the material in the original for decades, the introduction is quite full (nearly 90pp.), the "literary-theological method" (14) serves pastors' needs well, and it is fairly easy to read. The exegesis of Judges is thorough, perceptive, and slightly over 400pp. Note to preachers: the 15-page Modern Proclamation of Judges section (86–101), mapping out a ten-part sermon series, duplicates material found in the commentary proper. Compare with Block, Butler, and Webb. [*JETS* 12/14; *Them* 7/14; *BBR* 26.1; *JSOT* 40.5].

Cundall, A. E., and Leon Morris. *Judges and Ruth* (retired TOTC) 1968. Cundall's work (about 200pp.) was once a first choice only because there was little else to choose from. He gives Judges a high credit rating historically. Morris's commentary on Ruth is quite full (100pp.), considering the series. See Evans below.

☆ Davis, D. Ralph. *Judges: Such a Great Salvation*, 1990. A homiletical commentary of excellent value. Maybe a bit too racy and clever to my liking at points, but I don't want to be dismissive. Davis is a good student of the Scriptures, and this book helps those it aims to: pastors and Sunday School teachers with the boldness to enter this forbidding territory. He also has expositions of Joshua, Samuel, Kings, and Daniel, and all of them helpfully emphasize a redemptive-historical approach. Preachers should consider buying these books. I myself purchased all of them.

F Duguid, Iain. *Judges, Ruth* (EBTC)?

☆ Evans, Mary J. *Judges and Ruth* (TOTC-R) 2017. Replacing the old Cundall–Morris was necessary, and Evans delivered a concise, solid exegesis. She has about 215pp on Judges and 70pp on Ruth; for both books she somewhat downplays the theme of monarchy (or an apology for the Davidic kingship). [*BBR* 29.2; *JETS* 9/18; *JSOT* 43.5].

✓ Exum, J. Cheryl. ‡ *Samson and Delilah: Selected Essays*, 2020. [*CBQ* 7/21].

Fausset, Andrew R. (GS) [1885] 1999. About the most valuable old evangelical commentary, reprinted in 1977 by James & Klock. Banner added this to their Geneva Series, and the inclusion indicates its conservative, expository character (340pp.). Be aware of heavy typology (e.g., the dew representing Israel, pp.120–26). [*Evangel* Aut 01].

✓ Franke, John R., ed. *Joshua, Judges, Ruth, 1–2 Samuel* (ACCS) 2005.

✓ **Frolov, Serge.** ‡ (FOTL) 2013. The author teaches at SMU and offers a "full-fledged form critical investigation" (374pp.). It is a sign of the times that he launches the book with a succinct apology for form criticism (1–2) and an explanation of his conviction that "exegesis should proceed, in the first instance, in the mode suggested by the interpreted text. Specifically, since the entire Enneateuch (Genesis–Kings) . . . presents itself as an integral composition, it will be mostly read as such, i.e., from the synchronic perspective" (3). There is little of a diachronic approach here, so we are presented with what some call "the new face of form-criticism" (an Eerdmans book-title). Frolov is a shrewd exegete—Butler speaks of "his mastery of syntax." [*CBQ* 7/14 (Butler); *JETS* 12/13; *RelSRev* 3/14; *JHebS* 14].

García Bachmann, Mercedes L. ‡ (Wisdom) 2018. [*Int* 10/21; *JSOT* 43.5].

Garstang, John. 1931. See under Joshua.

F  Gorospe, Athena E. (SGBC).

☆  Goslinga, C. J. (BSC) 1966, ET 1986. See under Joshua. Now o/p. I used to recommend this for purchase for its theological worth, but that was back when we had little from evangelicals besides Cundall's TOTC.

✓  **Gray, John.** ‡ (NCB) 1967, rev. 1986. See under Joshua.

✓  Grossman, David. [𝓜], *Lion's Honey: The Myth*, 2005. A more conservative Jewish reading of the Samson cycle, using narratological and psychological approaches.

Groves, Alan. *New Geneva Study Bible*, 1995. My friend was also slated to write the Judges vol. for THC, but he lost a brave fight with cancer. See Beldman above.

Gunn, David M. ‡ (BBC) 2005. Evocative as it presents centuries of much-varied cultural and artistic responses (artwork, music) to the stories of Judges. [*EvQ* 10/07; *RBL* 10/05].

✓  Hamley, Isabelle. ‡ *God of Justice and Mercy: A Theological Commentary on Judges*, 2020. Praised by Firth as providing "a rich combination of literary awareness and close attention to the text" [*BL* 2022].

✓  Hamlin, E. J. ‡ (ITC-E) 1990. Strange in places, but ITC-E was meant to be a little exotic. Hamlin is worth looking at. Webb has a judicious critique [*RTR* 5/91].

☆  Harris, J. G., **Cheryl Brown**, and M. Moore. *Joshua, Judges, Ruth* (NIBC) 2000. See Joshua above.

F  Hugenberger, Gordon. (Apollos). The author teaches at Gordon-Conwell Seminary.

☆  Jackman, David. *Judges, Ruth* (WCC) 1991. The well-known evangelical Anglican does very fine work here. Judged as valuable as Wilcock or Davis in the category of theological exposition (300pp. on Judges). Was a purchase recommendation in past editions, and pastors are still wise to purchase this (and consider the other two).

Jeter, Joseph R. ‡ *Preaching Judges*, 2003. Should we attempt to preach on this dark, difficult material? Practically speaking, many preachers believe we should not. Jeter makes a good case for opening up Judges in the pulpit. He is an engaging read, with a liberal slant. The homiletics prof at Brite is fairly open to the text. He appears to eschew christological interpretation in his homiletical strategy. [*Int* 7/05; *CTJ* 4/10].

Jordan, James B. *Judges—God's War against Humanism*, 1985. While appreciating his concern to make this Bible book applicable to our context, I can't call this effort a success. Jordan can be insightful at times, but, more often than not, he seems to lack balance and good judgment in his exegesis, theological points, and application. He needs some stricter controls in his hermeneutical method. The symbolism and allegorizing can be wild! He sometimes needs more guidance than he provides.

☆  Keddie, Gordon J. *Even in Darkness* (WCS on Judges and Ruth) 1985.

✓  Keil, Carl F. (KD) ET 1865.

☆  Keller, Timothy. *Judges for You*, 2013. I know little about the series, but it offers material for congregational Bible studies. Keller (200pp.) makes wise homiletical moves (invaluable for Judges), is gospel-centered, and well worth looking up. I bought it.

✓  Klein, Lillian R. ‡ *The Triumph of Irony in the Book of Judges*, 1988. This literary study may prove more useful to students than most of the commentaries available.

☆  Kuruvilla, Abraham. *Judges: A Theological Commentary for Preachers*, 2017. Fascinating story here of an Indian dermatologist who later took degrees in theology (Aberdeen PhD) and now teaches preaching at Dallas Seminary. The book is highly praised by Block as providing a "sensitive literary and theological reading." [*JSOT* 43.5].

Lewis, Arthur. *Judges and Ruth*, 1979. Evangelical exposition published by Moody.

✓ **Lindars, Barnabas.** ‡ *Judges 1–5* (intended for ICC) 1995. The Catholic scholar long taught at Manchester and was an accomplished OT and NT exegete. Sadly, he died before he could complete this work, and the publisher released it outside the ICC series. (A 19th century interpreter, Bachmann, also only got to ch. 5.) Here you'll find approximately 300pp. of exceedingly careful and comprehensive textual analysis which will be valued by serious researchers for decades to come. [*ExpTim* 12/95; *Them* 1/97; *JETS* 6/97; *CBQ* 7/97; *SJT* 52.2; *SwJT* Spr 98; *BSac* 4/96; *HS* 1997].

✓ Martin, Lee Roy. *The Unheard Voice of God: A Pentecostal Hearing of the Book of Judges*, 2008. He terms it a "literary-theological reading . . . that examines the role of God." It is said to be quite well-done [*VT* 61.1]. I have not seen it.

✓ **Matthews, Victor H.** [𝓜], *Judges & Ruth* (NCBC) 2004. The successful first vol. of the CUP series. Matthews is known for his interest in social scientific research, and is helpful for the study of the background. Among scholars enlisted for NCBC, he is one of the less critical. It is surprising that Matthews cites a number of Block's articles but misses his commentary. He offers bibliographical guidance on pp.18–36. [*CBQ* 1/05; *JETS* 6/05; *Int* 1/06; *BSac* 10/06; *BL* 2005].

F Maybie, Fred. (EEC).

F Mayes, A. D. H. ‡ (ICC-R). Mayes is to pick up the project after Lindars, but I do not expect him to incorporate Lindars's treatment of chs. 1–5. Note his *Judges* (1985) in OT Guides, one of the best in the series.

☆ **McCann, J. Clinton.** ‡ (I) 2002. A thoughtful, though brief (139pp.), exposition from the mildly critical camp, focusing upon the theology in the text and preaching concerns. The author is best known as a leading Psalms scholar. [*CBQ* 7/03; *ExpTim* 10/03; *JSOT* 28.5; *SwJT* Fall 03; *RelSRev* 10/03; *BSac* 10/05; *CurTM* 10/05; *JHebS* 4].

F Mobley, Gregory. ‡ (Illum). The Harvard grad earlier published his PhD as *Samson and the Liminal Hero in the Ancient Near East* (2006).

✓ **Moore, George F.** ‡ (ICC) 1908. Long the classic to consult for detailed textual work. While students must take account of Moore's brilliant research, pastors have little use for it and may be put off by the negatively critical spirit the author projects (often harsh with other scholars). See Burney.

✓ **Nelson, Richard D.** ‡ 2017. From a veteran scholar on the DtrH, this exegesis (350pp.) complements his previous works on Deuteronomy, Joshua, and Kings. Despite the thin Introduction (and a lack of interaction with secondary literature), the expensive vol. is important and will be cited by scholars for decades to come for its form-critical interpretation of the biblical material, including Nelson's own translation. Each portion of text is discussed in sections on "Structure and Rhetoric" (synchronic) and "Genre and Composition" (diachronic). [*JSS* Spr 19; *JSOT* 42.5; *JJS* 70.2; *Them* 43.3].

✓ **Niditch, Susan.** ‡ (OTL-R) 2008. Replaces Soggin and is fairly brief for the series, with the commentary portion running to 211pp., including the biblical text. The appendix, "A Literal Translation of Judges" (213–81), is a waste of space since it often has a stilted character and sometimes differs little from the translation already offered in the commentary (cf. 14:1–4 in both). Niditch is well-known for a feminist and folklorist perspective in reading Bible tales. See her influential work, *Oral World and Written Word* (1996). This well-written OTL vol. will be of interest to academics but few pastors. [*CBQ* 4/09; *ExpTim* 4/09; *RBL*; *JETS* 9/08; *CurTM* 2/09; *BL* 2009; *BSac* 4/10 (Chisholm); *Int* 4/09 (Meyers); *WTJ* Spr 11].

✓ **O'Connell, Robert H.** ‡ *The Rhetoric of the Book of Judges*, 1996. This Cambridge diss. "represents the most thorough literary analysis of the book of Judges available in English" (Block). Compare with Webb below. [*JETS* 3/99; *JTS* 4/98; *Bib* 80.2; *CBQ* 7/98].

✓ Ogden, Graham S., and Lynell Zogbo. *A Handbook of Judges* (UBS) 2019. A huge work (1000pp.) for translators, valuable for exegetes as well. [*JSOT* 44.5].

✓ **Olson, Dennis T.** ‡ (NIB) 1998. One of the best available critical treatments of exegetical and expositional matters. The author previously did first-rate work on Numbers. [*ExpTim* 1/99].

✓ **Polzin, Robert.** ‡ *Moses and the Deuteronomist: A Literary Study of the Deuteronomic History: Part One. Deuteronomy, Joshua, Judges*, 1980. Presents a redactional approach that assumes various unrelated tales were woven together and interpreted by an editor, who created a coherent whole.

Pressler, Carolyn. ‡ *Joshua, Judges, and Ruth* (WestBC) 2002.

Redmond, Eric C. *Exalting Jesus in Judges and Ruth* (CCE) 2023.

Rogers, Richard. 1615 Original. The massive work, containing over 100 sermons by an English Puritan, has been reprinted by Banner of Truth in a "Facsimile Edition."

F  Ross, Jillian L. (Pillar).

✓ Ryan, Roger. ‡ (Read) 2007. Said to pursue competently a narrative-critical approach and read the text with a good measure of sympathy (221pp.). [*BL* 2008; *VT* 60.2].

F  Sanderson, Judith E. ‡ (S&H).

✓ **Sasson, Jack M.** ‡ *Judges 1–12* (AYB) 2014. The Sasson set replaces Boling, and the first vol. has 536pp. of commentary (in smaller font than in AB). This profoundly learned Jewish scholar teaches at Vanderbilt and pursues a rather more skeptical reading of Judges than Boling's. Many evangelicals will likely count his *Jonah* vol. more successful and useful to them. Advanced students and scholars are grateful for the 60-page bibliography, Sasson's extraordinary knowledge of ANE literature and cultures, comparative Semitics, close reading of the Hebrew and its literary artistry, citation of variant readings (without emending the text), and the treatment of the whole history of interpretation. [*BBR* 24.4; *ETL* 6/15; *ExpTim* 2/16; *JSOT* 41.5; *JHebS* 15].

☆ **Schneider, Tammi.** ‡ (BerO) 2000. A well-researched, moderately detailed, and provocative literary reading of Judges that well complements historical and theological commentaries. This is *not* to say Schneider takes no interest in the theology of the book. She does (from a Jewish perspective), and she makes astute comments on such issues as leadership and covenant faithfulness. I value her literary sensitivity, revealed particularly in her discussion of the women of Judges (commonly "foils" for male characters or male society). She has a contagious enthusiasm for the text in her 290pp. I bought this and learned much. More for students or pastors with academic proclivities. [*Int* 1/01; *RelSRev* 1/01; *OTA* 10/00; *CBQ* 10/02; *HS* 01; *JSOT* 94; *RelSRev* 1/01; *RBL*; *JHebS* 3].

☆ Schwab, George M. *Right in Their Own Eyes: The Gospel According to Judges* (GAOT) 2011. Compare with Keller. A bit too much alliteration in the chapter titles, but quite useful to preachers. [*JESOT* 1.2].

☆ Smit, Laura A., and Stephen E. Fowl. *Judges & Ruth* (Brazos) 2018. Smit's contribution on Judges has helpful literary analysis (following Gooding's chiastic structure), is highly theological (from a Reformed angle), and worth reading. (She was originally ordained in the PCUSA and has been on faculty at Calvin College since 1999. She is a theologian, having done doctoral work on Bonaventure.) Fowl offers wise guidance on theological interpretation of Ruth, though it is less attentive to exegetical questions and surprisingly brief (35pp.). [*CTJ* 11/19; *ExpTim* 1/20; *BBR* 31.1; *JETS* 9/19; *JSOT* 43.5].

✓ **Smith, Mark S., and Elizabeth Bloch-Smith.** ‡ *Judges 1* (Herm) 2021. The couple at Princeton Seminary cover 1:1–10:5 in extraordinary detail (700pp. plus huge indexes). They follow the series pattern—Zimmerli's *Ezekiel* being an exception—of doing "relatively little theological reflection or 'biblical theology,'" while still attempting "to convey the religious worldview of the texts (what might be regarded as their own 'theologies')" (49). The thoroughness and technical detail are impressive: text criticism, lexical matters, comparative Semitics, syntax, sociohistorical study, ANE religion, geography, archaeology, fine narrative criticism, and diachronic literary research. Little reception history, however (cf. Gunn, Spronk). Most of the recent major Judges commentaries focus on the final form, with the diachronic eschewed or downplayed; this vol. takes diachronic questions seriously. In their redaction criticism they conclude that "the book retains yet submerges literary dissonance" (18). The authors see multiple strata, with materials collected/edited from the Omride era to the postexilic period, and conclude, "it seems that all too often historical truth in Judges lies beyond reach" (21). With all this learning and technical detail for an erudite readership, why are the Greek and Hebrew transliterated? [*JETS* 3/22; *BL* 2024].

✓ **Soggin, J. Alberto.** ‡ (retired OTL) ET 1981, 2nd ed. 1987. Remains an important older work from the standpoint of historical-critical scholarship. Theological reflection is beyond his ken. I consider *Judges* better than Soggin's earlier *Joshua* in OTL. See Niditch above for Soggin's replacement. [*HS* 1983; *JTS* 33].

✓ **Spronk, Klaas.** ‡ (HCOT) 2019. A full (500pp.), technical critical work that reads the book as from a single "talented author living in the early Hellenistic period" (ix). Spronk takes "Historical" in the series title as an opportunity to pay close attention to the history of interpretation and reception history; the bibliographies, then, are rich and long. He spent 20 years researching and writing, and this work is a more valuable scholarly resource as a result. In some spots (e.g., the translation of 18:7) the English editing needed greater care. Note, Spronk also did Nahum in the series. [*BL* 2022].

☆ **Stone, Lawson.** (CorBC) 2012. See Coleson under Joshua. Regrettably, the last edition of this guide did not offer a review of Stone's contribution. It is exceptionally insightful and longer (310pp.) than most in the series. Students as well as preachers ought certainly to use this.

☆ Van Pelt, Miles V. (ESVEC) 2021. From a well-known Hebrew prof at RTS. See Konkel under Deut.

☆ Way, Kenneth C. *Judges and Ruth* (TTC) 2016. He earned a Hebrew Union PhD and teaches at Talbot. The brief vol. (about 230pp.) is praised by Block and Younger.

✓ **Webb, Barry G.** *The Book of Judges: An Integrated Reading*, 1987, 2008. Pastors and scholars have long been frustrated by the atomistic approach of verse-by-verse commentaries: too often the thread of the theological argument is lost and larger literary structures of the book are obscured. Some feel the need for a more integrated, synthetic approach that goes beyond the older diachronic studies. The value of such an approach is demonstrated here. This readable Sheffield PhD contains a sensitive literary analysis of the book as a complex whole and complements other works that focus on the historical and theological. Webb's study is of immense help to any scholarly pastor preaching or teaching through Judges (even if you disagree with him over the centrality of the Jephthah narrative). Compare with O'Connell. Note Webb's NICOT above. [*EvQ* 1/89; *RTR* 5/88; *Them* 10/88; more critical are *HS* 1989, *CRBR* 1990].

Wijk-Bos, Johanna W. H. van. ‡ *The End of the Beginning: Joshua & Judges*, 2019. See under Joshua.

☆ Wilcock, Michael. (BST) 1993. A suggestive exposition for the preacher, rivaled by Jackman. Wilcock also did Chronicles and Revelation for this series. Some of the interpretations offered in this BST entry are a bit surprising and out of the ordinary; I am tempted to say off-beat. [*Them* 10/94; *Evangel* Spr 95; *SBET* Sum 93 (Hess)].

Wolf, Herbert. (EBC) 1992. Rather brief (130pp.) and mainly concerned with filling out the historical picture; he capably does that. There is not much theology or literary interest; he didn't use Webb. See Boda.

Wood, Leon. *Distressing Days of the Judges*, 1975. Fact-filled, but no biblical-theological reflection. Some find the dispensational Wood helpful, but I came away disappointed the few times I consulted him. Influential in conservative circles decades ago, when there was nothing else but Cundall. Wood has been reprinted.

✓ Yee, Gale A., ed. ‡ *Judges and Method: New Approaches in Biblical Studies*, 1995, 2nd ed. 2007. [*JTS* 10/08; *BibInt* 17 (Schneider); *ExpTim* 10/09; *HBT* 30.2 (Butler)].

NOTES: (1) An essay especially helpful for the preacher to look up is Daniel Block's "The Period of the Judges: Religious Disintegration under Tribal Rule," in the Harrison FS, *Israel's Apostasy and Restoration* (Baker, 1988), pp.39–58. (2) See Raymond Bayley's "Which Is the Best Commentary? 14. Judges," *ExpTim* 2/92. (3) See, too, K. M. Craig, "Judges in Recent Research," *CBR* 1.2 (2003): 159–85; and Kelly J. Murphy, "Judges in Recent Research," *CBR* 15 (2017): 179–213.

# RUTH

★ **Block, Daniel I.** (ZECOT) 2015. With this first entry in the retitled series (cf. HMS), Block provides a more extensive and scholarly treatment of Ruth than in NAC (see below). I call it the studious pastor's first pick because of the thoroughness and quality of the research (approx. 270pp.), including interaction with more recent scholarship, Block's expert discussion of the Hebrew, good sense exegetically, and his full comments on the text's "Canonical and Practical Significance" (many sermon seed thoughts are offered). Other strong points are narratological sensitivity, discourse analysis, clarity of writing, and a focus on David ("royal reading"). Block is highly recommended as a solidly evangelical work, though I don't entirely buy his reading the book as a drama. He puzzlingly renders תחלה in 1:22 as "end" (100). Note: he names the other kinsman "Peloni Almoni," in the sense of "Mr. So-and-So." [*Chm* Win 18; *ExpTim* 2/17; *BBR* 26.4; *CBQ* 4/17; *JETS* 12/16; *JSOT* 41.5].

★ **Bush, Frederic.** [𝓜], *Ruth, Esther* (WBC) 1996. Treats technical issues, such as text criticism and philology, at greater depth than Hubbard. The literary-critical approach yields many insights on the narrative art. A superb scholarly work, though most evangelicals date the book much earlier than the early postexilic period. Among the contributions is a thorough discussion and a new proposal for understanding *gōʾēl* (גאל); cf. Hubbard. This is for students and scholarly pastors. As noted above in the Commentary Series section, Bush is a more technical, less accessible vol. in WBC. If you don't want this, you have another fine Ruth commentary by buying Younger on Judges. [*JETS* 3/99; *RTR* 9–12/97; *SwJT* Spr 00; *BSac* 10/98].

★ Duguid, Iain M. *Esther and Ruth* (REC) 2005. The vol. on two challenging books for preachers builds on careful exegesis, clearly expounds the theology of the text, and makes wise moves toward application. See his other books for preachers on Ezekiel and Haggai–Malachi. I confess I feel a bit lost in recommending theological expositions of Ruth since we are spoiled for choice. Just as rich as Duguid is Ferguson. Webb, Atkinson, and Ulrich are preachers' favorites too. [*JSOT* 41.5].

★ **Lau, Peter H. W.** (NICOT-R) 2023. Replaces Hubbard, which I so enjoyed over the decades. Lau receives a warm welcome, however, as a lengthy (307-page), fresh, and even fascinating reading. He builds upon a Sydney PhD, published as *Identity and Ethics in the Book of Ruth* (2011); cf. with Hawk's use of social-identity theory. Born in Hong Kong but reared in Sydney, and also having had cross-cultural ministry experience elsewhere in Asia, Lau is well-positioned to write this commentary on the story of Ruth the alien. Both the well-rounded exegesis (including text criticism, extensive notes on the Hebrew, narratology) and the theological reflection are highly intelligent, full of insight, and lucid. He is open to what I might term "chastened postmodern approaches"; see his 2015 essay "Another Postcolonial Reading." I highly recommend the NICOT to students and well-trained pastors. Interestingly, Lau also trained as a physician and has an ongoing, limited medical practice, besides his teaching career. See also Lau and Goswell below. [*JETS* 12/23; *BL* 2024; *BBR* 33.4].

★ **McKeown, James.** (THC) 2015. The author taught at Union Theological College, Belfast and is an astute interpreter of the OT. Earlier he contributed *Genesis* to THC. McKeown (146pp.) reads Ruth in conjunction with other texts, most helpfully Genesis (cf. themes of blessing, famine, land, marriage, seed, etc). He focuses on Ruth within the canon and its theological intention, not spending much time on such things as legal transactions, "since it was not the narrator's purpose to teach us the complex details of Israelite customs and law" (1). In addition to sections of commentary and Canonical Context, he also offers character studies and discussion of theological themes, feminist approaches, and the book's missiological significance. [*JETS* 6/15; *BBR* 26.2; *JTS* 4/16; *JSOT* 40.5].

☆ **Alter, Robert.** ‡ *Strong as Death Is Love: The Song of Songs, Ruth, Esther, Jonah, and Daniel*, 2015. The author has long been engaged in translating and writing brief literary commentaries on the biblical corpora (see Pentateuch, Former Prophets, Psalms, Wisdom Lit.). They are stimulating and masterful.

✓ Amos, N. Scott, ed. *Joshua, Judges, Ruth* (RCS) 2020.

☆ Ash, Christopher. *Teaching Ruth & Esther*, 2018. Great for expositional preachers.

☆ Atkinson, David. (BST) 1983. An excellent contribution to the series, unfolding the many theological themes in this jewel of a book (128pp.). The author is a retired Anglican bishop, formerly a college chaplain in Oxford. [*WTJ* Spr 84].

Auld, A. Graeme. ‡ (DSB) 1984. See under Joshua.

☆ **Block, Daniel.** *Judges–Ruth* (NAC) 1999. Recommended above for Judges. Block's NAC on Ruth does not disappoint (though not quite as strong as the Judges portion) and has been useful to students for its interaction with Hubbard, Sasson, Bush, etc. Block's ZECOT outstrips this NAC, especially for Hebrew students.

✓ **Campbell, Edward F.** ‡ (retired AB) 1975. A good, thorough commentary, one of the better older contributions to AB in the OT section. Campbell reflects the more conservative (among critical scholars) historical approach of Albright. This did not compare with Hubbard, though. Replaced by Schipper. [*JBL* 9/77].

Campbell, Iain D. *The Gospel according to Ruth*, 2003. By a godly and learned Scottish pastor and subtitled "Devotional Studies." A blessing to pastors and lay readers.

☆ **Chisholm, Robert B., Jr.** *A Commentary on Judges and Ruth* (KEL) 2013. See under Judges. The Ruth segment contains 33pp. of introduction and 115pp. of commentary. Because, unlike with Judges, we had lacked a fully up-to-date evangelical commentary on Ruth, Chisholm (along with Hawk and Block) was, when published, all the more valuable for interacting with recent scholarly literature. Many pastors and students will want this.

✓ Clark, Gordon R. *The Word Ḥesed in the Hebrew Bible*, 1993. A leading semantic study, especially relevant for researching the book of Ruth. [*Them* 20.2]. Cf. Sakenfeld.

Davis, Ellen F. *Who Are You, My Daughter? Reading Ruth through Image and Text*, 2003. Accompanying Davis's insightful translation and exegetical notes are woodcuts by Margaret Adams Parker. An enjoyable read.

✓ De Waard, Jan, and Eugene A. Nida. *A Handbook on the Book of Ruth* (UBS) 1992.

Dharamraj, Havilah, and Philip Ewan Yalla. (Asia) 2019. Subtitled "A Pastoral and Contextual Commentary." Note her earlier work on the Song of Songs. [*BL* 2022].

Driesbach, Jason. (CorBC) 2012. See Coleson under Joshua.

F   Duguid, Iain. *Judges, Ruth* (EBTC)?

✓   **Eskenazi, Tamara Cohn, and Tikva Frymer-Kensky.** ‡ (JPS) 2011. Following a well-researched 60-page introduction, Eskenazi uses her late colleague's extensive notes on chs. 1–2 to supplement her own exegetical work in a 100-page commentary. The result is a robust narrative reading with close attention paid to rabbinics and centuries of Jewish interpretation. The authors propose a late date, in the Persian period, for the composition of Ruth. They join the growing number who believe the union of Ruth and Boaz was not levirate marriage. [*JHebS* 12].

☆   Evans, Mary J. *Judges and Ruth* (TOTC-R) 2017. See under Judges.

✓   **Farmer, Kathleen A. Robertson.** ‡ (NIB) 1998. Well-done. I am inclined to call it one of the best in the entire OT section of the series. [*ExpTim* 1/99].

✓   **Fentress-Williams, Judy.** ‡ (AbOTC) 2012. The author teaches at Virginia Theological Seminary (Episcopal). She offers a careful, well-written literary reading of Ruth, the strength of which "is surely in its attention to the . . . internal and external dialogues" (Bechtel [*Int* 1/14]). [*JSOT* 37.5; *JHebS* 15].

☆   Ferguson, Sinclair B. *Faithful God: An Exposition of the Book of Ruth*, 2005. A small book (160pp.) born out of a Bible conference series, but there is a great deal of study and theological reflection behind these edited sermons. I consider this model preaching: powerful yet tender, thoughtful yet simple, attentive to the OT message and to how the NT gospel connects, and edifying. See his commentaries on Daniel, Jonah, and the Sermon on the Mount.

✓   Fewell, Danna N., and David Gunn. ‡ *Compromising Redemption: Relating Characters in the Book of Ruth*, 1990. Another leading study which examines literary structure, characterization, and thematic development. I recommend skipping the dramatic retelling of the story (23–66) to get to the "close reading" (69–105). I note in passing an insightful, brief reading that is similar in approach: Phyllis Trible's chapter on Ruth in *God and the Rhetoric of Sexuality* (1992).

✓   Franke, John R., ed. *Joshua, Judges, Ruth, 1–2 Samuel* (ACCS) 2005.

✓   **Fried, Lisbeth S.** ‡ (CritC) 2023. Reads the book as fiction. Marks a thoroughgoing application of Propp's folklorist approach (cf. Sasson). The exegesis is provocative and reasonably full (197pp. with bibliography). She emphasizes the "otherness" of the main character. "The purpose of making Ruth a Moabite can then only be to shock the reader. It increases her otherness since she is from one of the forbidden peoples" (11). Fried dates the final form to the Maccabean age and has a revisionist interpretation: "the book is a reaction against the new condition in the Hellenistic period of the malleability of identity. . . . [T]he author is claiming that the stranger, especially the *female* stranger, is deceitful and should not be trusted" (11–12). [*BL* 2024].

F   Gesundheit, Shimon. ‡ (IECOT).

Goslinga, C. J. (BSC) 1966, ET 1986. See Joshua above.

✓   **Gow, Murray D.** *The Book of Ruth: Its Structure, Theme and Purpose*, 1992. A stimulating literary reading of the book from a conservative scholar. Gow suggests that the book of Ruth is quite early—authored by the Prophet Nathan—and that it offers an apology for King David and his Moabite ancestry. [*SBET* Aut 93; *RTR* 5/97; *Them* 4/96; *BSac* 7/95].

✓   **Gray, John.** ‡ (NCB) 1967, rev. 1986. See Joshua above.

F   Greenstein, Edward L. ‡ (Herm).

✓   **Grossman, Jonathan.** ‡ *Ruth: Bridges and Boundaries* (OOTD) 2015. I have yet to see this Jewish work in a new (expensive) commentary series, but it is said to be extremely detailed as a literary study (350pp.), also employing psychological theories. The author lectures at Bar-Ilan and has an impressive monograph on Esther. [*JSOT* 43.5].

✓ Hals, Ronald M. ‡ *The Theology of the Book of Ruth*, 1969. [*JBL* 89.1].

F Hamley, Isabelle. (EEC). A previous report was Ronald Youngblood.

✓ Hamlin, E. John. ‡ *There Is a Future: Ruth* (ITC-E) 1996. Of some help with exposition, but it has declined in value. [*VT* 47.2; *RTR* 9/96; *HS* 1997; *RelSRev* 1/97].

☆ Hannah, Mary Willson. (ESVEC) 2021. An engaging, insightful expositional treatment from the director of Women in Ministry at Second Presbyterian Church, Memphis. See Konkel under Deuteronomy.

☆ Harris, J. G., C. Brown, and **M. Moore.** *Joshua, Judges, Ruth* (NIBC) 2000. See Joshua above.

☆ **Hawk, L. Daniel.** [𝓜], (Apollos) 2015. A slim vol. (140pp.) which accomplishes much with its fresh translation, selective notes on the Hebrew, structural analysis, remarkably perceptive narrative criticism, and exegetical digging. Certain features of the work make it more interesting to students than pastors. Hawk seems to understand Ruth reflecting the past as a cultural projection, by which the community shapes its own identity and values. He regards the book "as a narrative of dissent probably written in response to the reforms of Nehemiah and Ezra" (36)—Hubbard critiqued this notion in the 1980s. It's hard for me to see how, in Hawk's reading, Ruth is the revealed word of God. See his BerO work on Joshua, also very well-written. [*JTS* 4/17; *JETS* 3/16; *Them* 41.1 (Lau)].

☆ **Holmstedt, Robert D.** (BHHB) 2010. Much more here than one might expect (220pp.). Very well-done for Hebrew students. [*JSOT* 35.5; *VT* 61.1; *ExpTim* 12/10; *JHebS* 11].

  Howell, Adam J. 2022. Subtitled "A Guide to Reading Biblical Hebrew." I have not seen it, but it is said to supply ample help to students (300pp.). [*JETS* 12/22].

☆ **Hubbard, Robert L.** (retired NICOT) 1988. A very substantial, satisfying commentary (316pp.) on this short book. Hubbard treats everything, and frankly, if pastors have this, they are well-supplied on Ruth. Even now, after its replacement! When it appeared, it was the best in the series by a long shot, and Stuart's and Longman's first choice. The only drawback is the age of the book. Hubbard, as editor for NICOT, enlisted Lau to replace him. Compare with Block's ZECOT. [*WTJ* Spr 91; *Them* 10/91; *HS* 1990; *Chm* 104.2; *ExpTim* 8/89].

  Huey, F. B. (EBC) 1992. A readable, informed work (40pp.), displaying an interest in historical, literary, and theological issues, but not all that penetrating. See Schwab.

☆ Jackman, David. *Judges, Ruth* (WCC) 1991. See under Judges. Well-done, but only half the size of Atkinson.

✓ Jones, Edward Allen, III. ‡ *Reading Ruth in the Restoration Period: A Call for Inclusion*, 2016. Receiving good attention by scholars. [*JETS* 3/17].

✓ **Joüon, Paul.** ‡ *Ruth: A Philological and Exegetical Commentary*, ET 2013. Homer Heater Jr., retired Capital Seminary professor, thought this older work (1953, rev. 1986) worthy of translation. If they can find a copy, students benefit from consulting Joüon.

☆ Keddie, Gordon J. *Even in Darkness* (WCS) 1985. Covers Judges and Ruth.

✓ Keil, Carl F. (KD) ET 1865.

✓ Knight, G. A. F. ‡ (Torch Bible Commentaries) 2nd ed. 1966.

F Korpel, Marjo C. A. ‡ (HCOT). This scholar has already produced a groundbreaking study of *The Structure of the Book of Ruth* (2001) [*RelSRev* 1/03; *JHebS* 4].

✓ **LaCocque, André.** ‡ (ContC) ET 2004. This is a major exegetical and theological commentary, as befits the series, but one that also has several demerits. The author does not interact much with other scholars' views. There is a deep skepticism (the setting is "quite fictitious," p.18) and a controlling opinion that "the 'attitudes and actions' of Ruth's main characters 'make no sense' in any period prior to the postexilic" (Moore). LaCocque sees subversive elements everywhere, it seems. Pastors will pass this by, but students doing advanced work on Ruth should not ignore this independent-minded exegesis. See also his work on Daniel. [*CBQ* 1/06; *JETS* 3/06; *Int* 4/06; *BL* 2005; *RelSRev* 7/05; *JHebS*; *RBL*; *CurTM* 8/06].

☆ Lau, Peter H. W., and Gregory Goswell. *Unceasing Kindness: A Biblical Theology of Ruth* (NSBT) 2016. Readers come away with a much, much deeper appreciation for the Bible story and the profound theological themes in the book. See Lau's NICOT above. [*Chm Win* 17; *ExpTim* 7/17; *JETS* 6/17; *JSOT* 41.5; *Them* 42.3 (Webb)].

Lawson, George. *Expositions of Ruth and Esther*, 1805. A classic, occasionally reprinted.

✓ Laffey, Alice, and Mahri Leonard-Fleckman. ‡ (Wisdom) 2017. A highly competent, lengthy (225pp.), strongly feminist interpretation. [*Int* 10/20; *JSOT* 42.5].

✓ **Linafelt, Tod**, and Timothy K. Beal. ‡ *Ruth, Esther* (BerO) 1999. Fairly full, for the series, on the two books (approx. 100 + 135pp.). Beal's work on Esther is cleverer and better, in my judgment, than Linafelt's, but both engage in what might be termed ideological manipulations of the text. Some of the newer literary criticism is tamer, more responsible text-oriented interpretation, but the reader-oriented, ideological approaches—predominant here—are often not seeking determinate meaning in the text at all. This vol. is stimulating for students, but you won't learn as much about Ruth and Esther as you hope. [*JSOT* 89; *OTA* 6/00; *Int* 4/01; *CBQ* 1/01; *RelSRev* 10/02; *JHebS* 4].

☆ Luter, A. Boyd, and Barry C. Davis. *God Behind the Seen*, 1996. A large vol. on Ruth and Esther (350pp.) published in Baker's Expositor's Guide to the Historical Books. This book provides good homiletical direction for the pastor, but perhaps is not as helpful as its size might indicate. [*JETS* 3/99; *BSac* 1/97].

✓ Matthews, Victor H. [𝓜], *Judges & Ruth* (NCBC) 2004. See Judges above. The commentary section on Ruth is short (27pp.), and the valuable portion of his treatment is perhaps the bibliographical guidance (213–16).

Morris, Leon. (retired TOTC) 1968. Bound with Cundall on Judges. Morris is edifying and, as a NT specialist, makes good NT connections. Pastors used to have little else.

✓ Murphy, Roland E. ‡ *Job, Proverbs, Ruth, Canticles, Ecclesiastes, Esther* (FOTL) 1981. He was, in my opinion, the foremost American scholar in the field of wisdom literature. This form-critical research of Ruth is for students and OT specialists, and it has a dated feel. [*WTJ* Spr 84; *JETS* 9/82; *JBL* 103.3; *ThTo* 39.4].

✓ **Nielsen, Kirsten.** ‡ (OTL) 1997. The reviews all note her interest in intertextuality, and this book does succeed in prompting the thoughtful reader to explore possible interplay between the text/story of Ruth and other biblical texts. See especially her exploration of links to Genesis 38, though most scholars now want to distinguish more strictly the gō'ēl tradition from the levirate (e.g., Hubbard, 57). I bought Nielsen and found her reading of the nighttime encounter scandalous. Of greater interest to students than to preachers. [*JBL* Sum 99; *JSOT* 79; *Bib* 79.3; *Int* 1/99; *CBQ* 4/98; *HS* 1998; *RBL*].

Piper, John. *A Sweet and Bitter Providence*, 2010. An exposition I have not seen, now republished as *Sex, Race, and the Sovereignty of God* (2022).

Pressler, Carolyn. ‡ *Joshua, Judges, and Ruth* (WestBC) 2002.

✓ **Queen-Sutherland, Kandy.** ‡ *Ruth & Esther* (S&H) 2016. An exceedingly full, feminist interpretation (over 500pp.) by a Baptist religion prof at Stetson U. As a surprise, she explores connections between the two books (Megilloth bookends); they are not separate commentaries. Readers are entertained by the included art and reception history. No evangelical scholarship is used, not even Hubbard. [*Int* 1/19]. The author also is scheduled to contribute a vol. on Song of Songs and Lamentations.

Redmond, Eric C. *Exalting Jesus in Judges and Ruth* (CCE) 2023.

☆ Roop, Eugene F. [𝓜], *Ruth, Jonah, Esther* (BCBC) 2002. One of the best in the Anabaptist series (280pp.). The author did his PhD at Claremont and was President of Bethany Seminary, Indiana. The three Bible books are treated from the literary and theological angles, though Roop sometimes fails to draw conclusions on difficult points.

☆ **Sakenfeld, Katharine Doob.** ‡ (I) 1999. An attractive 90-page work, which fails even to mention Hubbard. Sakenfeld was an excellent choice for this exposition—see *The Meaning of Ḥesed in the Hebrew Bible* (1978)—and voices feminist concerns at junctures. The theological discussion is quite well-done and helps the preacher. Chisholm puts it on his highly recommended list. However, the list price ($40 hb, $30 pb) may discourage some from buying. [*JSOT* 89; *OTA* 6/00; *Int* 4/01; *VT* 51.3; *JSOT* 94].

✓ **Sasson, Jack M.** ‡ *Ruth: A New Translation with a Philological Commentary and a Formalist–Folklorist Interpretation*, 1989. This Sheffield work interests academics because it applies some of the newer literary-critical methods (Vladimir Propp-influenced) to uncover the narrative artistry. Almost 300pp. Hubbard questions Sasson's philology at numerous points and finds him lacking in theological interest. An earlier form of this commentary was published under the same title by Johns Hopkins in 1979. His work on Jonah is better. [*JBL* 100.4; *JETS* 12/80].

✓ **Schipper, Jeremy.** ‡ (AYB-R) 2016. Replaces Campbell, and of similar length (190pp.). The author is a Princeton Seminary grad (PhD), teaching at Temple. As expected from the series, there is good technical help for those reading the Hebrew. For example, he has one of the most satisfying commentary discussions of the anomaly of masculine suffixes having feminine antecedents (1:8, 9, 11, 13, 19, 22 [pronoun]; 4:11). Schipper offers a fine literary reading, which will sensitize students to the narrative art in the Hebrew. I noted an openness to queer interpretation (34–38) and a couple off-beat comments that might annoy conservative pastors (the Ruth character is a seductress, disrobing at the threshing floor). You can call this a postmodern commentary. [*BBR* 26.3; *JETS* 12/18; *JSOT* 42.5; *Them* 43.3 (Lau)].

☆ **Schwab, George.** (EBCR) 2012. A rather brief entry (58pp.), with an Introduction pastors may find less approachable (focused on history of composition, from early origins to "some creative development . . . in the postexilic period"). Preachers may also be uncomfortable with Schwab's interpretation that Ruth "clearly makes herself sexually available to Boaz" on her night visit, though he stops short of saying there was immorality. "Ruth and Boaz trust each other's character in this risky encounter; they both 'maintain their righteousness'" (1335). There is value in the narrative reading here and the theological Reflection sections. See Allen under Numbers.

Smit, Laura A., and Stephen E. Fowl. *Judges & Ruth* (Brazos) 2018. See under Judges.

Strain, David. *Ruth & Esther* (Focus) 2018. See under Esther.

☆ Taylor, Marion Ann. *Ruth, Esther* (SGBC) 2020. See under Esther.

✓ Tooman, William A., with Marian Kelsey. ‡ *(Re)reading Ruth*, 2022. Tooman has distinguished himself as a much-cited Ezekiel scholar, and he is slated to write the ICC on Ruth. [*JSOT* 47.5; *CBQ* 7/23].

☆ Ulrich, Dean R. *From Famine to Fullness: The Gospel according to Ruth* (GAOT) 2007. A good purchase for the preacher, Ulrich's work is readable, well-informed by OT scholarship (Westminster PhD), theologically insightful, and keen to apply the text to daily life. In line with the subtitle, the exposition brings out gospel themes and provides guidance for a redemptive-historical approach—no barren moralism here.

✓ Van Wolde, Ellen J. ‡ *Ruth and Naomi*, 1997. The scholar is known for her semiotic/structuralist approach to OT narrative and her feminist interpretation. [*Int* 7/99].

✓ **Vance, D. R.** *A Hebrew Reader for Ruth*, 2003. Useful and well-produced. Cf. Holmstedt. [*VT* 54.4; *JAOS* 123.4].

☆ Way, Kenneth C. *Judges and Ruth* (TTC) 2016. See under Judges.

☆ Webb, Barry. *Judges and Ruth* (PTW) 2015. See under Judges.

☆ Webb, Barry G. *Five Festal Garments: Christian Reflections on the Song of Songs, Ruth,*

*Lamentations, Ecclesiastes and Esther*, 2000. This 150-page book offers a biblical-theological interpretation of the message of each of the five *Megilloth* (scrolls). I found it stimulating for both teaching and preaching purposes. It is recognized as all the more valuable by the fact that these Bible books are among the most difficult for preachers to handle. [*EvQ* 7/03; *VT* 51.4; *Chm* Aut 01].

☆ **Wilch, John R.** (ConcC) 2006. I have hardly used this large (405pp.) Lutheran work, but found extensive notes on the Hebrew preceding the homiletically styled exposition. Wilch regularly draws on other commentaries, including the major German ones (Gressmann, Gerlemann, Rudolph, Hertzberg). He served the Lord as a pastor and seminary prof. Highly praised by Chisholm. [*JETS* 9/07; *BSac* 10/09; *BL* 2007].

F   Wray Beal, Lissa M. (BGW).

F   Yoder, Christine. ‡ (Illum).

☆ Younger, K. Lawson. *Judges/Ruth* (NIVAC) 2002, rev. 2021. A recommended purchase under Judges.

NOTES: (1) Amy Erickson and Andrew Davis review, "Recent Research on the Megilloth," *CBR* 14 (2016) 298–318. (2) Jennifer M. Matheny, "Ruth in Recent Research," *CBR* 19 (2020): 8–35.

# SAMUEL

★ Arnold, Bill T. (NIVAC) 2003. Preachers value Arnold's large exposition (681pp.), built upon good exegesis, especially for sermon preparation. Cf. Brueggemann, Davis, and Woodhouse. Students of the Hebrew might replace this selection with McCarter or the Klein–Anderson set.

★ Evans, Paul S. (SGBC) 2018. A fresh, lucid, nearly 500-page exposition from a younger prof at McMaster. Evans knows the scholarship and also has a practiced hand at theological reflection and application in the church. (Growing up in a pastor's home has its advantages!) He is an exegete, but that is not his main brief here. Evans has also published a couple of books on 2 Kings, and all this research prepares him for his daunting assignment to write two NICOT vols. on Chronicles. Evans writes that, though the speeches in the book of Samuel should be thought of as "largely the creative work of the historian" (23) and as "structuring devices" (24), "we have every reason to trust [the book's] story" (28). I'm not comfortable with his view that this "[h]istoriography is written in a literary form similar to fiction" (25), but this is a brilliantly executed book. [*ExpTim* 3/19; *Presb* Fall 19; *BBR* 29.1; *JETS* 3/19; *JSOT* 43.5; *EvQ* 93.2].

★ **Firth, David G.** (Apollos) 2009. Many features impress here (614pp.). Firth knows the scholarship, is courageous to challenge the critical consensus at points (e.g., the DtrH), patient in exegetical analysis, readable (less technical), sensitive to literary devices, and has a sharp eye for biblical-theological themes. There is less textual analysis. A special feature is his gathering many of Fokkelman's literary insights from that 4-vol. set which few have time or competence to work through. The bibliography includes several 2007 works (but not Tsumura). Only rarely will British parlance confuse Americans (e.g., "kit-bearer"). One difference I have with Firth is his interpretation of the sex in 2 Sam. 11 as less about lust and more about "an assault on Uriah that ultimately requires his murder" (415). He says David "is not trying to cover his tracks but rather trying to create a legal pretence for Uriah's execution" (418). I aver that David *does* rather than "does not send for a woman because he sees her beauty" (417), and I think he subsequently attempts a cover-up. Believing that both students and pastors will benefit greatly from buying this book, I reckon it to be my first choice as an exegetical reference. [*JSOT* 35.5; *Chm* Win 11]. Do not confuse this with his 2013 Phoenix Guide [*JSOT* 38.5], rereleased in 2017 as a T&T Clark Study Guide [*BBR* 27.4; *JTS* 4/18; *JJS* 69.2]. See also his books on Esther and Joshua.

★ **Gordon, Robert P.** [𝓜], *1 & 2 Samuel: A Commentary*, 1986. Students and pastors both appreciate this superb Zondervan work, which employs literary methods to shed new light on the text. Gordon had become more difficult to obtain, and for that reason I moved it off the recommended purchase list (and Bergen on). It is widely available again and back on the list. Gordon retired as Regius Professor of Hebrew in Cambridge. [*Them* 1/88; *RTR* 1/88]. Not to be confused with *I and II Samuel* (JSOT, 1984), a book of essays helping students grasp the issues addressed by scholars. [*EvQ* 10/86].

★ **Long, V. Philips.** (TOTC-R) 2020. My former prof did a difficult job well, handling in small compass a huge Bible book and replacing a sterling Baldwin TOTC. By comparison, Long treats more issues in the MT and interacts with more scholarship. He also follows in the footsteps of his Cambridge supervisor, Gordon, who wrote an admirable literary commentary on Samuel with fine theological insight. Earlier, Long had done the *New Geneva Study Bible* notes (reworked in the *Reformation Study Bible*), and the Samuel entry in ZIBBC. [*BBR* 32.1; *RTR* 12/20]. Students can look up his PhD on the story of Saul's reign (published 1989 [*CRBR* 1991]) and his *The Art of Biblical History (1994)* [*TJ* Fall 95; *VT* 47.1].

★ **Vannoy, J. Robert.** (CorBC) 2009. The author was long Professor of OT at Biblical Seminary in Hatfield, PA and did a superb job on Samuel and Kings in the notes of the *NIV Study Bible* (1985), especially considering the prescribed length. He was a fine biblical theologian and a safe pair of hands in dealing with this literature exegetically and expositionally. More effort and care went into this vol. than most others in CorBC, and I'm glad to see interaction with a fair number of Dutch works missed by other scholars (e.g., M. R. van den Berg, H. de Jong). Simply put, this insightful, mid-sized commentary (450pp.) deserves to be better known than it is. The scholarly pastor will indeed learn from this, and the average pastor would be well-served having only this on the shelf (more well-rounded than Firth). [*Presb* Spr 12].

★ Woodhouse, John. (PTW) 2 vols., 2008–15. The expositions (672 and 688pp.), by a former Principal of Moore College in Sydney, build upon solid OT scholarship (Manchester PhD), are easy to read, and prompt the preacher to read 1–2 Samuel christologically. The anointed leaders point to Christ in both their successes and failures, the latter giving the people of God a heightened sense of need for a perfectly righteous king. Pastors will want these books on their shelf, not only for their exposition of Samuel but also as a model for doing biblical-theological interpretation of OT narrative (cf. Van't Veer on Kings) and for their devotional value.

★ **Youngblood, Ronald F.** (EBCR) 2009. An updating of the well-rounded 1992 EBC was welcome; I wished for more thorough revision, however (590pp.). Perhaps most useful for its literary reading (building on the works of Fokkelman, Eslinger, Gunn, Gordon, Miscall), textual criticism, and mature exegesis, Youngblood reminds me of VanGemeren on Psalms and Carson on Matthew in that this work is fuller and more academic than its companion in the EBCR vol. (Vol. 3: 1 Sam–2 Kgs). My counsel once was to make EBC your first choice, but I have reassessed the options. Pastors can buy Firth or Vannoy for exegesis. Students gravitate toward AB, NICOT, OTL, WBC, and Steinmann, and they can consult Fokkelman in the library.

Ackroyd, Peter R. ‡ (CBC) 2 vols., 1977. Once a leading British critical scholar, Ackroyd did a capable job of explaining the books to a popular audience. Discounts the historical value of these Scriptures.

✓ **Alter, Robert.** ‡ *The David Story: A Translation with Commentary of 1 and 2 Samuel*, 1999. Pick this up to get a fresh literary reading of Samuel from a Jewish perspective. Alter has been a leading expert on ancient Hebrew narrative. He notes some of the insights found in modern Hebrew commentaries (e.g., Bar-Efrat and Garsiel). The translation is occasionally too literal but frequently brilliant; the commentary he offers is selective. Such selective engagement with the text is not such a bad thing. (One of the problems with the modern commentary genre is that scholars are required to say something about everything, whether or not they have anything to say.) See further comment on Alter's work under Genesis. Note also: this David book has been included in Alter's *Ancient Israel* (see under Reading Narrative).

☆ **Anderson, A. A.** ‡ *2 Samuel* (WBC) 1989. A fine complement to Klein's work, though marred by many typos. Anderson is no conservative, but he is a very capable British exegete who uses a more restrained critical approach. Note to students: on text-critical questions you will find Driver, Tsumura, McCarter, and the WBC set most helpful. [*WTJ* Fall 92; *JTS* 4/91; *EvQ* 7/91; *CBQ* 4/91; *RTR* 9/90; *Them* 10/92; *Chm* 104.3; *CRBR* 1991].

✓ **Auld, A. Graeme.** ‡ (OTL-R) 2011. The author, at the forefront of "the Edinburgh School," contests the priority of Samuel–Kings over Chronicles. Both drew with adaptation from a common source, he says. That thesis has sparked debate. See his *Kings Without Privilege* (1994) and *Samuel at the Threshold* (2004) [*BSac* 4/08; *ExpTim* 10/05 (Williamson)]. Auld has a disciplined focus on David: "all the other personalities are there so that we may see and know David better" (2). His work is valuable for its select use of the DSS evidence, general text criticism (copious notes on the codices of LXX), and close literary reading. I like his turns of phrase: e.g., "He finds at first trial what the Philistine champion discovers fatally late, that heavy armor constitutes an impediment, not a protection" (211). Pastors can make good use of Auld, even as they balk at his proposals about the development of Samuel as literature. [*BBR* 22.4; *CBQ* 7/13; *Int* 4/13 (Klein); *JSOT* 36.5 (Firth); *JESOT* 2.1; *RevExp* Fall 12; *BTB* 2/14; *SJT* 67.2].

✓ Auld, A. Graeme, and Erik Eynikel, eds. ‡ *For and Against David: Story and History in the Books of Samuel*, 2010.

☆ **Baldwin, Joyce G.** (retired TOTC) 1988. We went so long without a good, conservative commentary on the books of Samuel. Then we quickly got several: Gordon, Baldwin, Youngblood, and Bergen. Baldwin's 300-page work is compact, very readable, and satisfying as more of a quick reference. Careful scholarship underlies her conclusions. The vol. is helpful for theology too. Now see Long. [*EvQ* 1/91; *Them* 1/92; *Chm* 104.4].

Barron, Robert. *2 Samuel* (Brazos) 2017. From a scholarly Roman Catholic bishop, academic administrator, and popular Catholic apologist. [*JETS* 12/15].

☆ **Bergen, Robert D.** (NAC) 1996. Long recommended for purchase by Denver Seminary faculty, and upon taking a closer look at Bergen, I made it a pick too. The commentary (470pp.) is well-balanced and readable, with good attention given to historical, literary, and theological issues. Distinguishing the work is Bergen's use of discourse analysis; he edited a book on *Biblical Hebrew and Discourse Linguistics* (1994). Still a smart buy, but not a top choice.

✓ **Birch, Bruce C.** ‡ (NIB) 1998. Quite full at nearly 350 large pages. Birch knows this literature well, having written his diss. on *The Rise of the Israelite Monarchy: The Growth and Development of I Samuel 7–15* (1976). He ignores almost all evangelical works on Samuel. [*ExpTim* 1/99].

Blaikie, W. G. (EB) 1888. Reprinted by Klock & Klock (1978) and Nabu Press (2010). This 2-vol. work is esteemed by all to be one of the best in the Expositor's Bible. Blaikie still aids the preacher, but not the student. See Joshua also.

F   Block, Daniel. (BCBC).

☆ Boda, Mark J. *After God's Own Heart: The Gospel according to David* (GAOT) 2007. Penetrating theological exposition. I only wish it were longer.

✓ **Bodner, Keith.** ‡ *1 Samuel: A Narrative Commentary*, 2008. Originally planned for the Readings series, this 340-page commentary has both a perceptive literary approach and respect for the text. Don't look for theology here. [*BL* 2009; *BSac* 4/11].

✓ Bodner, Keith, and Benjamin J. M. Johnson, eds. ‡ *Characters and Characterization in the Book of Samuel*, 2019. Leading scholars contribute 17 essays. [*VT* 71.3; *BL* 2022; *BBR* 30.4; *CBQ* 1/21; [*Them* 2020; *JETS* 12/20; *DenvJ* 2023; *Them* 45.2 (Harper)].].

✓ Borgman, Paul. *David, Saul, and God: Rediscovering an Ancient Story*, 2008. A keen narrative analysis from a Gordon College English prof (OUP). [*RBL* 2011].

☆ **Brueggemann, Walter.** ‡ (I) 1990. About the best exposition one can find from the critical side (360pp.). This is yet another work by the prolific scholar which really gets you thinking (see Genesis). Use with discernment; there's a good bit with which evangelicals will disagree. Compare with Davis below, which many pastors will prefer. If one likes books of sermons, Woodhouse provides more in the way of pastoral exposition than anyone else. [*CRBR* 1991; *CBQ* 1/92; *ThTo* 4/91; *Int* 7/92; *HS* 1993]. See Brueggemann's essays in *David and His Theologian* (2011) [*CBQ* 1/13].

☆ Calvin, John. *Sermons on 2 Samuel 1–13*, ET 1992. For the preacher, this large work repays study. Douglas Kelly, systematics prof at RTS Charlotte, is responsible for the Banner translation. This is the first time in English for the sermons, delivered in French. [*RTR* 9/95; *SBET* Spr 95].

✓ **Campbell, Antony F.** ‡ (FOTL) 2 vols., 2003–05. Campbell, a brilliant Jesuit, is known for being revisionist on issues of form-critical methodology. He is just as interested in the final form of the book of Samuel (the synchronic) as he is in the compositional history (the diachronic). This is only for advanced students and specialists. [*RTR* 4/04, 12/05; *BSac* 7/06; *JETS* 9/04; *Int* 10/04, 4/08; *JSOT* 28.5; *VT* 54.4; *CBQ* 1/05, 1/06; *JTS* 4/06; *JSS* Spr 06; *JNES* 7/08, 1/09; *RBL*; *Presb* Spr 06; *JAOS* 124.1, 126.4; *ExpTim* 5/06].

☆ **Cartledge, Tony W.** ‡ (S&H) 2001. A full (over 700pp.), competent exposition. Very little of the OT scholarship upon which he builds is cited, and this makes the vol. less useful to the student. Cartledge seems to take a more conservative approach; though he may not himself have full confidence in the historicity of the narrative, he interprets the theological story as we have it. [*Int* 10/04; *JSOT* 99; *CurTM* 4/04].

Chafin, Kenneth L. (WCC) 1989. Not a poor entry, but not rich either. [*Chm* 104.4].

✓ Chapman, Stephen B. ‡ *1 Samuel as Christian Scripture: A Theological Commentary*, 2016. An Eerdmans release with incisive reflections on the text and contemporary applications. [*ExpTim* 3/17; *CBQ* 7/17; *JTS* 4/17; *JETS* 6/17; *Int* 7/18; *JSOT* 41.5; *JHebS* 17].

☆ Chisholm, Robert B., Jr. (TTC) 2013. The author is a solid scholar at Dallas Seminary with long experience teaching the Former Prophets (see Judges). My sense is that, in order to accomplish all the TTC goals, a much fuller commentary was needed than this 320-page vol. for all the material in 1–2 Samuel (twice the verses of Judges–Ruth). One three-chapter pericope is treated in six pages. That said, pastors will gain much from using Chisholm in sermon prep. [*JETS* 12/13; *BSac* 4/15].

F Chisholm, Robert B., Jr. (ZECOT).

Conroy, C. ‡ *1–2 Samuel, 1–2 Kings* (OTM) 1983.

✓ Cooper, Derek, and Martin J. Lohrmann, eds. *1–2 Samuel, 1–2 Kings, 1–2 Chronicles* (RCS) 2016.

☆ Davis, Dale Ralph. *1 Samuel—Looking on the Heart*, 1988; *2 Samuel—Out of Every Adversity*, 1999. Published in the UK by Christian Focus (over 550pp.). Many prefer this set to Brueggemann; both authors offer quite lively and perceptive theological readings (one evangelical, the other not). [*TJ* Fall 96; *RTR* 9/96; *Anvil* 18.4 (Evans)]. See my comments on his Joshua and Judges books.

✓ **Driver, Samuel R.** ‡ *Notes on the Hebrew Text and the Topography of the Books of Samuel*, 2nd ed. 1913. One of the great works of textual criticism—on a book that really needed it! This is not a commentary, but must be included on our list. Reprinted in 1984 (Alpha). To review what we have learned since Driver, including the 4QSam discoveries, see Philippe Hugo, "Text History of the Books of Samuel: An Assessment of the Recent Research," in Hugo–Schenker, eds, *Archaeology of the Books of Samuel* (Brill, 2010)—especially his fine bibliography.

✓ Edenburg, Cynthia, and Juha Pakkala, eds. ‡ *Is Samuel among the Deuteronomists? Current Views on the Place of Samuel in a DtrH*, 2013. [*CBQ* 10/14; *ETL* 90.3].

Erdmann, Chr. Fr. David. (Lange) ET 1877. Well over 600pp.

✓ **Evans, Mary J.** (NIBC) 2000. Covers the vast material of 1–2 Samuel in 288pp., which seems slight in the larger-print NIBC format. Power and political power-plays are major motifs or themes in her commentary; while interesting, her focus does not seem as beneficial to the preacher. Worth consulting for its attention to narrative, though not a technical work for students. See also the expositional BST below. Evans has written an introduction to OT prophecy entitled *Prophets of the Lord* (1992). [*ExpTim* 2/01; *Int* 7/01; *SwJT* Sum 01; *CBQ* 1/01; *RTR* 12/01; *JSOT* 94; *Chm* Spr 01; *Anvil* 19.3; *JHebS* 4].

☆ Evans, Mary J. (BST) 2004, rev. 2022. Perhaps one of the less helpful theological expositions in this series, yet there are many insights here. As with the NIBC above, Evans's literary interests are up front. [*Chm* Spr 06; *Anvil* 21.4]. I've yet to see the revision.

F  Flanders, Denise C. (BGW).

✓ **Fokkelman, Jan P.** ‡ *Narrative Art and Poetry in the Books of Samuel: A Full Interpretation Based on Stylistic and Structural Analyses*, 1981–93. Four vols. containing over 2000pp. of painstaking literary research. Though not a full-orbed commentary, this set is valued very highly by advanced students and OT specialists with an interest in the art of OT narrative. Do not expect theological reflection. See also the poetry studies of this Leiden professor which focus on Job and Psalms. [*JSS* Spr 99; *JSOT* 65; *CBQ* 1/94].

✓ Franke, John R., ed. *Joshua, Judges, Ruth, 1–2 Samuel* (ACCS) 2005.

Gehrke, R. D. (ConcC) 1968. Evangelical and Lutheran, in the old series.

Goldingay, John. *The Theology of the Books of Samuel*, 2024. From CUP.

✓ Gunn, David M. ‡ *The Fate of King Saul*, 1980; *The Story of King David*, 1978.

F  Gunn, David M. ‡ (BBC).

✓ Halpern, Baruch. *David's Secret Demons: Messiah, Murderer, Traitor, King*, 2001. More of a historical-archaeological study by a conservatively critical Jewish scholar.

F  Halpern, Baruch. ‡ (Herm).

✓ **Hertzberg, H. W.** ‡ (retired OTL) ET 1964. One of the better older entries in the series, Hertzberg gave attention to historical and literary details and was occasionally alert to theological motifs too. This classic of German scholarship is rather dated. See Auld.

✓ **Hoffner, Harry.** (EEC) 2015. The author was a world-leading Hittite scholar (†2015) on faculty at the U. of Chicago. The work is reportedly quite lengthy, released digitally (logos.com), but not yet in print. I've not seen it but expect it to be of higher caliber in terms of historical and lexical (Hebrew) scholarship.

F  Hunziker-Rodewald, Regine. ‡ *1 Samuel 1–15* (IECOT).

F  Hutton, Jeremy, and Sara Kipfer. ‡ (Illum). A fine preparation is the collection of essays they edited: *The Book of Samuel and Its Response to Monarchy* (2021) [*JBTS* 12/22].

Jenson, David H. ‡ (Belief) 2015. The author is a theology prof at Austin Presbyterian Seminary. [*ExpTim* 6/16; *JETS* 6/16; *JSOT* 40.5; *RTR* 12/15].

✓ **Jobling, David.** ‡ *1 Samuel* (BerO) 1998. If anything, Jobling is a provocateur. Here you find structuralism, Marxist analysis, and a variety of reading strategies. After using Jobling's postmodern work, you know better what you yourself think about the text. As you disagree with his interpretations, you are forced to come up with reasons for disagreeing. Sometimes he has excellent insights, e.g., on the timing of Hannah's song: the dedication of the child. [*CBQ* 7/99; *RelSRev* 7/99; *BL* 1999; *Int* 4/01; *JBL* Sum 01; *RBL*].

☆ Keddie, Gordon J. *Dawn of a Kingdom* (WCS on 1 Samuel) 1988; *Triumph of the King* (WCS on 2 Samuel) 1990. These two are well-done and will help the expositor.

✓ Keil, C. F. (KD) ET 1872.

F Kim, Jichan. ‡ *2 Samuel* (HCOT).

Kim, Koowon. *1 Samuel* (Asia) 2018. [*BL* 2022; *Them* 44.2].

✓ Kirkpatrick, A. F. [𝓜], (CBSC) 1881–88, rev. 1930. Still surprisingly useful, the "revised and reset" ed. is 469pp. The author has a fine Psalms vol.

F Klein, Johannes. ‡ *1 Samuel 16—2 Samuel 5* (IECOT).

☆ **Klein, Ralph.** ‡ *1 Samuel* (WBC) 1983, 2nd ed. 2009. Quite useful—Klein is one of the most accomplished OT text critics—and fairly thorough. It serves well as a corrective to McCarter. Intended for scholars, and pastors who have kept up with the Hebrew. There is not much theology here to speak of, though Klein, a Lutheran scholar, has interests in that area. The rev. ed. of 2009 runs to 350pp. The difference is merely an additional chapter: "My Commentary on 1 Samuel after Twenty-five Years." [*RTR* 1/85; *WTJ* Fall 84; *EvQ* 4/87; *JBL* 104.4; *BL* 2010].

Leithart, Peter J. *A Son to Me: An Exposition of 1 & 2 Samuel*, 2003. See Leithart under Kings. [*JETS* 3/05].

☆ Mackay, John L. "1–2 Samuel" in *1 Samuel–2 Chronicles* (ESVEC) 2019. All three portions of this enormous exposition (over 1300pp.) are solid and of real help to preachers. Gary Millar does "Kings," while John Olley covers "Chronicles." [*JETS* 3/20, 9/20].

F Marsman, Hennie J., Eveline van Staalduine-Sulman. ‡ *1 Samuel* (HCOT).

Mauchline, J. ‡ (NCB) 1971. One of the weakest entries in the series.

✓ **McCarter, P. Kyle.** ‡ (AB) 2 vols., 1980–84. About the fullest commentary to date on Samuel (over 1000pp.) and a leading scholarly work, in part because McCarter had access to the DSS. (See also Ulrich, *The Qumran Text of Samuel and Josephus*, 1978). McCarter's approach to textual criticism could, in my opinion, use more restraint and respect for the MT. He engages in traditio-historical analysis but has little interest in theology. The academically oriented pastor could put this set to good use, especially its detailed textual notes. Among OT scholars McCarter is considered to be more conservatively critical on questions of historicity. Also, he is an expert in textual criticism. The Denver Seminary faculty continue to make this their top pick (alongside Firth and Tsumura). [*JBL* 101.3; *Bib* 67.1].

McKane, William. ‡ (Torch Bible Commentaries) 1963. Quite critical.

✓ Miscall, P. D. ‡ *1 Samuel: A Literary Reading*, 1986. For students interested in the diverse approaches of the new literary criticism used with OT narrative. [*HS* 1988; *CRBR* 1988].

✓ **Morrison, Craig E.** ‡ *2 Samuel* (BerO) 2013. The author of this literary study teaches at Pontifical Biblical Institute in Rome. I have used it sparingly but find Morrison very perceptive in his discussion of structure, characterization, plot development, themes, Hebrew phrasing (leitmotifs), etc. There is a measure of reception history presented as well. The intentions of the series do not include diachronic analysis and research of historical backdrop. [*CBQ* 10/14; *JSOT* 39.5; *ETL* 6/15; *JTS* 10/15].

Murphy, Francesca Aran. *1 Samuel* (Brazos) 2010. [*JETS* 6/11; *ExpTim* 11/11].

F Naumann, Thomas. ‡ *2 Samuel 6–24* (IECOT).

✓ Omanson, Roger, and John Ellington. (UBS) 2 vols., 2001. Useful for exegetes (1280pp.).

Payne, David F. [𝓜], (DSB) 1982. Conservative for the series, and insightful on more the devotional level.

☆ Peterson, Eugene H. (WestBC) 1999. Unlike others in the series, this is not critically oriented and is entirely composed of devotional reflection and application—with little historical background information and few literary insights. In short, negatively, this is not valuable as a guide into the text. However, it is so pastoral and spiritually minded that readers will relish it for quiet times. I sense that Peterson has responsibly researched the text, but in his writing he chooses to concentrate on devotional pearls. Often I'd be critical of this approach, but I enjoyed reading in the book after sweating it through an exegesis of the Hebrew. I predict that any preacher, by reading this, could learn about feeding the sheep and preaching Christ from the OT. Consider this devotional material, not a commentary. [*ThTo* 7/00; *Int* 1/01; *JSOT* 94].

☆ Phillips, Richard D. (REC) 2 vols., 2012–18. Full exposition at over 1000pp. and of similar quality as his other REC vols. Pastors should consider it. As an OT lecturer, I opine that more interaction with the best up-to-date commentaries would have improved and deepened Phillips's work. Cf. Woodhouse above. [*JETS* 6/19; *JSOT* 41.5].

Pink, Arthur. *The Life of David*, 1958. Exceedingly lengthy exposition.

✓ Pisano, Stephen. ‡ *Additions or Omissions in the Books of Samuel: The Significant Pluses and Minuses in the Massoretic, LXX and Qumran Texts*, 1984.

✓ **Polzin, Robert.** ‡ *Samuel and the Deuteronomist: A Literary Study of the Deuteronomic History, I Samuel*, 1989; *David and the Deuteronomist: A Literary Study of the Deuteronomic History, II Samuel*, 1993. Polzin has been a challenging, provocative voice among those calling for literary readings of Scripture. Often it seems to me he reads against the grain of the text rather than with it. Still, this is important material in the scholarly discussion. Compare with Fokkelman. [*HS* 1993; *CRBR* 1990].

Robinson, Gnana. *Let Us Be Like the Nations: 1 & 2 Samuel* (ITC-E) 1993. This exposition, written by the principal of a seminary in India, interacts little with the scholarly literature and does not bother to discuss critical issues. The focus is on the storyline and the contemporary relevance of the message. Of more interest to the preacher than to the student.

✓ Rost, Leonhard. ‡ *The Succession to the Throne of David*, 1926, ET 1982. Constantly cited. For recent scholarship on the topic, see Andrew Knapp, "The Succession Narrative in Twenty-first-century Research," *CBR* 19 (2021): 211–34.

Smith, Henry Preserved. ‡ (ICC) 1899. Still cited, but lackluster.

☆ **Steinmann, Andrew E.** (ConcC) 2 vols., 2016–17. Strong, consistently insightful, full (600pp. + 500pp.) commentaries on the Hebrew from a confessional Lutheran stance. It aims to be a one-stop shop, from meticulous research on the background (history, archaeology) and detailed textual notes, all the way to guidance on sermon prep. Steinmann helps both the student and the pastor seeking to preach Christ from these narratives. These vols. really should be better known outside the Missouri Synod. The author amazes with his productivity; see under Ezra–Nehemiah. [*BSac* 1/18; *BBR* 27.3; *JETS* 9/17].

Sweeney, Marvin A. ‡ (NCBC) 2023. Announced but I've had little opportunity to use it. The 25pp. of Introduction and Suggested Readings are followed by a concise, learned, critical exegesis of nearly 300pp. from a Jewish perspective. [*BL* 2024].

Swindoll, Charles. *David: A Man of Passion and Destiny*, 1996. The review in *CT* (6/16/97) is instructive and might save you disappointment and a few shekels.

Thomas, Heath, and J. D. Greear. *Exalting Jesus in 1 & 2 Samuel* (CCE) 2016. Thomas I recognize as a capable OT scholar.

☆ **Tsumura, David Toshio.** (NICOT) 2 vols., 2007–19. Proves more useful to students working closely with the Hebrew text—he usually defends the MT (xi)—than to pastors interested in theological exposition, though there is some theology certainly. Tsumura is esteemed as learned on text-critical, philological, and grammatical/syntactical matters; he also does well with discourse analysis. He often focuses on the historical backdrop and reliability of Samuel. The stance taken on introductory matters is solidly conservative. I tend to agree with Williamson who says this commentary "will probably be consulted more for its particular strengths than for general purposes." The second vol. is less in-depth and, perhaps more so than the first, best used as a student's exegetical reference. If you are more academically minded, move this up onto the recommended list. [*BBR* 19.1; *CBQ* 1/08; *Int* 10/08; *HS* 2008; *BL* 2008; *ExpTim* 5/08; *VT* 58.3 (Williamson); *JETS* 3/08, 9/20; *RBL*; *RelSRev* 9/09; *Anvil* 25.4; *Bib* 92.1].

F   Vaillancourt, Ian J. (Pillar) 2 vols.

✓   Van Seters, John. ‡ *The Biblical Saga of King David*, 2009. A major work pushing the date of composition to the late Persian, even early Hellenistic era. See his many works on the Pentateuch and the DtrH. [*BL* 2010; *CBQ* 1/11; *VT* 61.3; *Bib* 92.4; *RevExp* Fall 11; *JJS* 62.1].

✓   Wijk-Bos, Johanna W. H. van. ‡ *The Road to Kingship: 1–2 Samuel*, 2020. From her multi-volume series, *A People and a Land*, covering all four Former Prophets. Strongly feminist, insightful, and taking a narrative-critical approach. [*BL* 2022; *BBR* 31.1; *CBQ* 10/21; *JETS* 9/20]. In her earlier *Reading Samuel* (ROT, 2011), she provides a compact (250pp.) narrative-critical and theological interpretation [*Int* 4/14].

F   Wu, Daniel. (EBTC)?

NOTES: (1) OT Histories are invaluable here. Likewise for Kings, Chronicles, and Ezra–Nehemiah. See the Note under Joshua. (2) David Firth, "Some Reflections on Current Narrative Research on the Book of Samuel," *SeTR* 10.1 (2019): 3–31.

# KINGS

★   Dillard, Raymond B. *Faith in the Face of Apostasy: The Gospel According to Elijah and Elisha* (GAOT) 1999. A 170-page P&R pb, presenting the thoughtful biblical-theological approach Dillard did so well in the seminary classroom. He leads you first to hear "the authentic voice of the OT" (my terms) and then teaches how to preach Christ out of the OT. I bought the book. Students working with the Hebrew might bypass this and Olley to purchase the 2-vol. AB and/or Sweeney. [*RTR* 12/00].

★   **Hobbs, T. R.** [*M*], *2 Kings* (WBC) 1985. Until the mid-1990s it was difficult to suggest commentaries; so little had been written covering this fascinating portion of Scripture. Hobbs had begun to meet the need. The work is thorough, reads narrative well, and provides help with the Hebrew. Would be a worthy addition to your library, though it does not have all the elements I look for in an exegesis. Hobbs's approach is less critical than DeVries's. I find little objectionable here. [*RTR* 5/87; *TJ* Fall 86; *CRBR* 1988]. See his *1, 2 Kings* (1989) in Word Biblical Themes.

★   **House, Paul.** (NAC) 1995. A solid, well-rounded effort, House's vol. filled a void in the conservative pastor's library. (Expositors had inadequate resources on Kings prior to NAC and NIBC.) It is valuable exegetically and theologically. After teaching at a variety of schools, including Taylor, Southern Baptist, and Wheaton, he joined Beeson. See Lamentations and Isaiah. [*VT* 7/96; *JETS* 12/97; *BL* 1997; *BSac* 1/96].

★   Olley, John W. (BST) 2011. The author, long at Baptist Theological College of Western Australia, is a superb Septuagint scholar (linguistic/philological ability does shine through at points). Here he demonstrates sagacity as a theological expositor for the church and a pastor's heart to apply the truths of Scripture. This is ripe fruit. Olley's strengths are depth of learning, mature theological reflection, a sensitivity to narrative features, experience in intercultural ministry, readability, and application. The low price makes the book even more attractive to pastors. Students also profit from consulting it (e.g., chiastic outline of 1 Kgs 1–11 on p.61). [*Chm* Aut 13; *JESOT* 1.2].

★ **Provan, Iain. W.** (NIBC) 1995. Launched the series' OT section, and its theological exposition is profitable for pastors. The author's previous work—see *Hezekiah and the Book of Kings* (1988)—was somewhat critical and diachronic, but the superb NIBC takes a more synchronic, evangelical approach, with good attention paid to literary features. And this believing scholar at Regent in Vancouver took the heat for his courageous stance; see *JBL* Win 95, pp.585–606, 683–705, and his essay in *Congress Volume Oslo 1998*. [*BL* 1997; *CBQ* 4/98; *RTR* 4/01]. Students enjoy his witty contribution of *1 & 2 Kings* (1997) to Sheffield's OT Guides series [*EvQ* 10/99; *JSOT* 79; *DenvJ*].

★ **Wray Beal, Lissa.** (Apollos) 2014. The author, previously at Providence Seminary, teaches at Wycliffe College, Toronto, and presents us with an engagingly written, thorough commentary of 550pp. It is solidly evangelical in approach, but critically informed in its discussion of historiography, chronology, literary readings, etc. Basically, her approach to historiographical issues (36–41) mirrors that of Provan–Long–Longman in their *Biblical History*. Wray Beal has confidence in Thiele's work on regnal chronologies. She has shown herself to be an accomplished narrative critic in her PhD, *The Deuteronomist's Prophet* (2007), on the story of Jehu in 2 Kgs 9–10; it is in this area that she makes her strongest contribution. Pastors can ignore the discussions of compositional history (a pre-Dtr story, a post-Dtr composition, the DtrH). Because the Elijah narratives are a favorite, I had hoped for fuller commentary there, preferably one enriched by interaction with Uriel Simon's *Reading Prophetic Narratives* (1997). Her theological Explanation sections are thoughtful and include connections to themes in NT proclamation. [*JSOT* 40.5].

F   Aucker, W. Brian. (Pillar) 2 vols.

Auld, A. Graeme. ‡ (DSB) 1986. In much the same mold as his *Joshua, Judges, and Ruth* for DSB. More helpful to expositors than to students. Well-done from the critical angle. His scholarly work on Kings is well-represented by *Life in Kings: Reshaping the Royal Story in the Hebrew Bible* (2017) [*BBR* 28.3; *ETL* 94.2], which analyzes the textual history of Kings while arguing that Samuel–Kings was not used by the Chronicler as a source.

✓ Bähr, Karl Chr. W. F. (Lange) ET 1872. One of the best in that old series. Includes not only exegesis but also a most suggestive homiletical section. The 570-page vol. (minuscule print) is praised to high heaven by Spurgeon, and, in looking over the copy passed down to me from my grandfather, I concluded it deserved the praise. Zondervan reprinted this in 1960. I used to say, "Would that somebody would again reprint Bähr!" Now available free online.

☆ Barnes, William H. *1–2 Kings* (CorBC) 2012. Certainly helpful and highly competent, though brief (400pp., including the biblical text). The author did a ThD at Harvard, published as *Studies in the Chronology of the Divided Monarchy of Israel* (1991).

Belz, Mark. *A Journey to Wholeness: The Gospel according to Naaman's Slave Girl* (GAOT) 2015. Not much Bible material to work with, but what a story!

F   Bergen, Robert D. (EBTC)?

✓ Bodner, Keith. ‡ *Jeroboam's Royal Drama*, 2012 [*VT* 65.2; *JHebS* 13]; *Elisha's Profile in the Book of Kings*, 2013 [*JSOT* 38.5; *VT* 65.3; *Int* 1/16; *SJT* 70.3]. Consistently brilliant in his literary insights, Bodner followed up these character studies with *The Theology of the Book of Kings* (2019) from CUP [*JSOT* 44.5; *VT* 70.2; *BBR* 31.4; *CBQ* 4/21; *JTS* 4/20; *JSOT* 44.5]. See also Bodner-Johnson.

✓ Bodner, Keith, and Benjamin J. M. Johnson, eds. ‡ *Characters and Characterization in the Book of Kings*, 2019. See Bodner–Johnson on Samuel. [*VT* 71.3; *BL* 2022; *BBR* 30.4].

F Brubacher, Gordon. (BCBC).

☆ **Brueggemann, Walter.** ‡ (S&H) 2000. This author of many commentaries loves OT theology, is creative and imaginative—communicating well with postmoderns. Brueggemann's S&H vol. is weighty (over 600pp.) and expensive. See his other works under Genesis, Exodus, Samuel, Isaiah, and Jeremiah. This is well worth purchasing, but only if used a good bit (approx. $70 in pb). [*Int* 1/02; *JSOT* 99; *RelSRev* 10/01; *CurTM* 2/02]. He built well off his 2-vol. Knox Preaching Guides set (1982).

✓ Burney, Charles F. ‡ *Notes on the Hebrew Text of the Books of Kings*, 1903. Good text-critical work, now superseded by the ICC and others. Reprinted by CUP (1983). The same scholar gave us the massive 2-vol. study on the Hebrew text of Judges.

✓ **Cogan, Mordechai, and Hayim Tadmor.** ‡ *II Kings* (AB) 1988; *I Kings* (AB) 2001. The technical, critical set by two Israeli scholars espouses the now-standard double Deuteronomistic redaction; the authors would be considered conservatively critical within the OT guild. The vol. on 1 Kings, done by Cogan alone, contains the introduction. The AB set is valuable for specialists and should be considered for purchase by scholarly pastors—the Denver Seminary bibliography recommends Cogan–Tadmor as a top pick. The authors' expertise lies in Mesopotamian history in the 1st millennium BC, and they provide extensive documentation for their historical conclusions. There is a lack of theology. [*JBL* 108.4; *HS* 1990; *BSac* 1/04; *JHebS* 4].

✓ **Cohn, Robert L.** ‡ *2 Kings* (BerO) 2000. At 175pp. it is not a full-scale commentary on 2 Kings, but what it sets out to do—see BerO in the Commentary Series section—it does well. Note Walsh's much fuller BerO work below. What theological reflection there is comes from a Jewish perspective. [*OTA* 10/00; *Int* 7/01; *CBQ* 7/01; *HS* 2002; *JSOT* 94; *RelSRev* 1/01; *JHebS* 3].

Conroy, C. ‡ *1–2 Samuel, 1–2 Kings* (OTM) 1983.

✓ Conti, Marco, ed. *1–2 Kings, 1–2 Chronicles, Ezra, Nehemiah, Esther* (ACCS) 2008.

✓ Cooper, Derek, and Martin J. Lohrmann, eds. *1–2 Samuel, 1–2 Kings, 1–2 Chronicles* (RCS) 2016.

Davies, John A. (EPSC) 2012. I have not seen it. [*RTR* 12/12].

☆ Davis, Dale Ralph. *The Wisdom and the Folly*, 2002; *The Power and the Fury*, 2005. The first vol., an engaging 350-page exposition of 1 Kings, was published and warmly received in the UK. I never did see it in an American bookstore. (Believe it or not, I found a copy in central Africa!) Now both vols. are available on Amazon. The set of nearly 700pp. would be a wise purchase for expositors. See his other lively theological commentaries on Joshua, Judges, and Samuel. Preachers might want to move this set up to the starred category. [*Chm* Aut 02, Win 06].

✓ **DeVries, Simon.** ‡ *1 Kings* (WBC) 1985, 2nd ed. 2003. Not so thorough or responsible as Hobbs, and takes a dimmer view of the book's historical worth. DeVries's other works show more interest in theological issues than he manifests here; this vol. is a dry well for expositors. Still, it should be consulted for academic work. I regret that the 2nd edition offers no revision of the original commentary; it only adds 16pp. of "Supplemental Bibliography" and a five-page excursus attacking the "minimalists" in OT scholarship, who denigrate the Scriptures as a source for history. If you own 1985, don't bother with 2003. [*Bib* 68.1; *RTR* 5/86; *JETS* 12/86; *HS* 1986].

F Dharamraj, Havilah. (TOTC-R) 2025. To build upon *A Prophet Like Moses? A Narrative-Theological Reading of the Elijah Stories* (2011) [*JSOT* 37.5]. Though without the historical prowess of Wiseman, whom she replaces in the series, Dharamraj will give closer attention to the literary and theological aspects of the text. Exciting prospect!

Dilday, Russell H. (WCC) 1987. Some reviewers called this homiletical commentary strong, while others found it mediocre. I vote more with the former group. Though Dilday misses the riches that can be mined out with a redemptive-historical approach, he does well at giving relevant background information (e.g., 1 Kgs 16:29–34). Quite full at over 500pp.

F   Dubovsky, Peter. ‡ (Illum).

Ellul, Jacques. [𝓜], *The Politics of God and the Politics of Man*, ET 1972. He is always brilliant and interesting. A bold exposition of extensive parts of 2 Kings (esp. the Elisha cycle). Theologically sensitive (essentially a Barthian viewpoint), christological, and conservatively critical. Well worth buying if you find the book s/h. [*JBL* 92.3].

☆   Ellsworth, Roger. (Welwyn) 2 vols., 2000, 2002. Well-done, accessible pastoral expositions (approx. 500pp.) from a Reformed viewpoint. Cf. Ryken and Woodhouse.

Farrar, Frederic W. [𝓜], (EB) 1892–93. Was reprinted, but difficult to obtain apart from the whole EB set. Now free online. "A rich and vigorous exposition," says Childs. There are some critical, rationalistic conclusions (e.g., comments on 1 Kgs 17:6).

☆   Fretheim, Terence. [𝓜], (WestBC) 1999. Fulfills the aims of the series. Though some may consider this vol. a bit too short at 228pp. to cover such a vast amount of material, Fretheim's theological and practical insights make this reasonably priced pb a wise purchase for the preacher. Treats the final form of the text and is accurately assessed as mildly critical—certainly less critical and more in sympathy with the text than Nelson (see both on 2 Kgs 4). [*JSOT* 89; *Int* 4/00; *CBQ* 1/00; *RelSRev* 4/00].

✓   **Fritz, Volkmar.** ‡ (ContC) 1996–98, ET 2003. The historically oriented commentary did not have the best reception (450pp.). The main complaints are a narrow interest in discerning compositional layers and a lack of interest in theology. The strength of the author is archaeology. Though less technical than others in ContC, Fritz is not for pastors. Students look in vain for discussion of text-critical matters, philology, grammar, narrative features, and theology. [*CBQ* 10/04; *JSOT* 28.5; *JHebS* 4; *RBL*; *ExpTim* 6/06; *CTJ* 4/10].

F   Fyall, Robert. (Mentor).

✓   Garsiel, Moshe. *From Earth to Heaven: A Literary Study of the Elijah Stories in the Book of Kings*, 2014. Brilliant work from the Israeli, who specializes in archaeology, history, and literary readings. [*JHebS* 14].

Grabbe, Lester. ‡ *1 & 2 Kings: An Introduction and Study Guide*, 2017. [*JJS* 69.2].

✓   **Gray, John.** ‡ (retired OTL) 1963, rev. 1970. Provan remarked that few commentaries on the historical books helped preachers: "Too often historical issues have dominated, leaving little room for narrative and theological concerns" [*BSB* 3/97]. Gray is a case in point. Though he presents a lot of information (802pp.), he is dry as dust. Pastors glean very little to help them in sermon prep; Gray seems to have no interest in theology. It had been considered a more important academic commentary, but is rather dated at this point (and o/p). Students can still consult it for research, but not before Sweeney's replacement in OTL. [*JBL* 93.3].

✓   Heller, Roy L. ‡ *The Characters of Elijah and Elisha and the Deuteronomic Evaluation of Prophecy*, 2018. Close narratological reading. [*JSS* Spr 21; *ExpTim* 10/20].

✓   **Hens-Piazza, Gina.** ‡ (AbOTC) 2006. The author is a proponent of both *The New Historicism* (2002), a postmodern approach, and socio-rhetorical interpretation. Her interests are mainly literary and theological, rather than historical. The Hebrew is hardly mentioned. Reviews are mixed, with Miscall regarding her work as uneven and somewhat lacking in critical rigor, and Nelson praising it as a competent, accessible exegesis. She engages the text with a hermeneutic of suspicion and at points will deconstruct the narrative and the heroes of the story. [*CBQ* 7/07; *Int* 7/07; *BL* 2008; *JETS* 3/09; *JHebS* 2009 (Wray Beal)].

F   Hess, Richard. (NICOT). Previously David Howard was said to have the contract. We have always lacked a heavyweight evangelical commentary on Kings.

F   Hoyt, JoAnna M. (ZECOT).

✓   Israel, Alex. *I Kings: Torn in Two* (MST) 2013; *II Kings: A Whirlwind* (MST) 2019. An Israeli rabbi gives a stimulating reading.

Jeyaraj, Jesudason Baskar. (Asia) 2022. [*JSOT* 47.5].

✓   **Jones, Gwilym H.** ‡ (NCB) 2 vols., 1984. Critical, lengthy (650pp.), and sometimes of help. Jones is definitely preferable to Gray, but still is too skeptical and narrowly concerned with historical-critical issues. When it appeared, it was among the best critical works, and advanced students considered it for purchase. Now Jones seems rather dated. [*JETS* 12/85; *ExpTim* 12/85].

Jost, Lynn. [*M*], *1 & 2 Kings* (BCBC) 2021. His 500-page exposition provides good service, especially for his Anabaptist tradition. Jost has been a missionary in Spain, a pastor, and a seminary prof.

F   Kalimi, Isaac. ‡ *2 Kings* (HCOT). Preparing the way is *Writing and Rewriting the Story of Solomon in Ancient Israel* (CUP, 2019), a more conservatively critical work on characterization, also useful for Chronicles study [*VT* 69.3; *JSOT* 43.5; *ETL* 97.1].

✓   Keil, C. F. (KD) ET 1857. My habit was to look up Keil first, before Provan and House came along. He is at his best in the historical material, and "often surprises the reader with a profound theological insight" (Childs). In a sense we still await Keil's replacement. NAC and NIBC are great to have, and Wray Beal is an excellent, fuller addition, but the task remains for an evangelical to give us an extensive exegetical study on the Hebrew text of Kings—especially 1 Kings, since we have Hobbs on 2 Kings.

✓   **Knoppers, Gary N.** [*M*], *Two Nations under God: The Deuteronomistic History of Solomon and the Dual Monarchies*, 1993–94. This 2-vol. PhD for Harvard contains some valuable commentary on the text of Kings. Knoppers's work has been appreciated by evangelicals because it shows more respect for the text as providing valuable historical evidence (unlike some radically skeptical scholarship by the likes of P. R. Davies and T. L. Thompson). He was conservatively critical and often wrote good reviews in *CTJ*. [*JETS* 9/96; *JBL* Win 96; *JTS* 10/96; *Int* 7/96; *CBQ* 1/96].

☆   Konkel, August H. (NIVAC) 2006. Appropriately, a larger vol. (704pp.) in the series. I have had less opportunity to review this, but I agree with my friend, John Glynn, who proofread the book for Zondervan and called it "a very solid effort, multifaceted in Hebrew, ANE, archeological, and theological coverage."

☆   Lamb, David T. (SGBC) 2021. Clear, readable, and theologically sensitive, with approx. 500pp. of commentary. The author did an Oxford DPhil on Kings, teaches at Missio Seminary, and has some excellent insights, especially on the Elijah–Elisha narratives. The work is conservative, but some of Lamb's scholarship elsewhere is critical in a reserved way (see his coauthored intro to the historical literature).

☆   Leithart, Peter J. (Brazos) 2006. The author has a brilliant mind and moves text-by-text, sometimes in a more cursory manner, offering theological exposition and redemptive-historical insights. There is heavy typology in service of christological interpretation. (He writes more as a systematic theologian than as an OT scholar.) Though Leithart's connections to the Federal Vision theology will be off-putting to some, he has done good work here. At points, the book is more stimulating than it is a dependable guide through the text. Longman praises this. See also his books on Samuel, Chronicles, and Revelation [*JETS* 12/07; *Int* 1/08; *BL* 2007; *ThTo* 4/09; *ExpTim* 9/07; *RelSRev* 3/08].

✓   Lemaire, André, and Baruch Halpern, eds. ‡ *The Book of Kings: Sources, Composition, Historiography and Reception*, 2010. An enormous (710-page) treasure of Brill essays, nearly a dictionary, on the topics taken up in an introduction to this Bible book. [*JTS* 4/15; *JSOT* 35.5; *VT* 64.1].

✓ Leuchter, Mark, and Klaus-Peter Adam, eds. ‡ *Soundings in Kings: Perspectives and Methods in Contemporary Scholarship*, 2010. [*BibInt* 21.1].

✓ **Long, Burke O.** ‡ (FOTL) 2 vols., 1984–91. For advanced students interested in a form-critical approach to Kings. However, as a welcome development, Long departs somewhat from the standard format of the series and offers more extensive commentary on the structure and literary art of the text. A good bit can be learned from this nearly 600-page set. [*JBL* 9/86, Sum 93; *RTR* 5/93; *JETS* 3/96; *JR* 7/93].

✓ Lovell, Nathan. *The Book of Kings and Exilic Identity: 1 and 2 Kings as a Work of Political Historiography*, 2021. A keen mind! [*Them* 46.2].

☆ **Maier, Walter A., III.** *1 Kings* (ConcC), 2 vols., 2018–19. This set is a testament to learning and diligence (and *Sitzfleisch*?), offering an enormous store of material for Bible teachers and preachers, especially in the conservative Lutheran tradition. After over 200pp of introductory material, Maier (Harvard PhD) spends 1400pp exegeting and expounding the Hebrew text, with many excursuses on historical and theological questions and many homiletical hints. Praiseworthy! Here there is more exegetical help on 1 Kings for evangelical pastors than anywhere else. [*BBR* 29.4, 31.2; *JETS* 12/20].

✓ **McKenzie, Steven L.** ‡ *1 Kings 16–2 Kings 16* (IECOT) 2019. One of the more valuable vols. in the series so far for scholars (approx. 530pp.). It is rigorously historical-critical, with a proposal of seven layers of tradition (3 strata brought together in the original text and 4 phases of later editing). Synchronic Analysis sections precede the Diachronic Analysis; the former are much more interesting, I think. The major surprise is text-critical, where McKenzie does not offer a straight translation of the MT, as one would expect, but makes choices as he goes along about what seems original. In almost every chapter he departs from the MT somewhere to translate the Old Greek. Occasionally, his suggestions grate: e.g., Elisha fathered the Shunammite's son. This is a "landmark" scholarly treatment, but its influence may be lessened somewhat by 1–2 Kings being divided among three commentators. [*Bib* 101.4; *BL* 2022; *CBQ* 10/20; *ETL* 97.2].

Merida, Tony. *Exalting Jesus in 1 & 2 Kings* (CCE) 2015. One Amazon reviewer thought it "more or less a copy" of Dale Ralph Davis's commentary.

☆ Millar, J. Gary. "1–2 Kings" in *1 Samuel–2 Chronicles* (ESVEC) 2019. See Mackay under Samuel.

✓ **Montgomery, James A., and H. S. Gehman.** ‡ (ICC) 1951. A classic. "A superb example of text critical scholarship" (Childs). Adequate historical treatment as well (for its time), but Montgomery had no real theological interest. This was the last of the old ICC to see publication, and it is still frequently consulted.

✓ **Mulder, Martin J.** ‡ *1 Kings*. Vol. 1, 1 Kings 1–11 (HCOT) ET 1998. Over 600pp. of minute exegesis. This set promises to be the most thorough, technical historical-critical investigation yet of 1 Kings, and as such it will be invaluable to students. All we had on the Hebrew text of 1 Kings previously was WBC and ICC, with help from the AB. Mulder of Leiden is deceased (†1994); Jurie le Roux of Pretoria (below) will carry on the project. [*Bib* 81.3; *RelSRev* 7/00].

✓ **Nelson, Richard.** ‡ (I) 1987. The author is well-known for his work on the supposed double Deuteronomistic redaction of these books. Despite the attention he pays to the message and theology of the text (in line with the series' aims), he retains a strong interest in narrower literary and historical issues. Noteworthy for preachers, especially because expositions of Kings are fewer. Compare with Brueggemann and Fretheim, who have more to say theologically.

F O'Kane, Martin. ‡ *1 and 2 Kings through the Centuries* (BBC).

✓ Omanson, Roger, and John Ellington. *A Handbook on 1–2 Kings* (UBS) 2 vols., 2008. [*BL* 2009].

F Oswalt, John N. (EEC) 2025? Next in the OT series? Given the author's reputation, this may be a fine, extensive exegesis and a first choice for many. See Oswalt on Isaiah.

Park, Song-Mi Suzie. ‡ *2 Kings* (Wisdom) 2019. [*JSOT* 44.5; *Int* 4/22].

Patterson, Richard D., and Hermann J. Austel. (EBCR) 2009. Their 1988 EBC was useful for the average pastor, but many found it not very penetrating as it tended merely to retell the biblical story with some accompanying historical sidelights and literary observations. The revised commentary is more of an update than 1–2 Samuel in the same vol. but suffers on account of its brevity (340pp., including the Bible text) and lack of biblical-theological reflection.

☆ Pink, Arthur. *Elijah*, 1956. Pink's most profitable exposition: warmly commended. Banner has been keeping it in print, but be sure to check his exegesis. Pink's other exposition of Kings, *Gleanings from Elisha*, is not so good.

☆ Rice, Gene. [*M*], *1 Kings: Nations under God* (ITC-E) 1990. A stronger vol. in the series for the preacher, packed with relevant exegetical points and theological reflection. Little here could prove objectionable to evangelicals. Once praised by Longman.

Robinson, J. ‡ (CBC) 2 vols., 1972–1976.

F  Roux, Jurie le. ‡ *1 Kings*. Vol. 2, 1 Kings 12–22 (HCOT). See Mulder above.

☆ Ryken, Philip G. (REC) 2 vols., 2011–19. One of the best in this sermonic series. Ryken is learned (Oxford DPhil), exegetically perceptive, theologically astute, skillful in exposition, creative, and even entertaining (587pp.). He has the "ability to blend exegetical detail with canonical and doctrinal development into an accessible and coherent form that is . . . spiritually invigorating" (Oeste [*JETS* 3/12]). Note his redemptive-historical approach. Ryken once pastored historic Tenth Presbyterian (PCA), Philadelphia and is the current President of Wheaton. [*Chm* Aut 13; *JSOT* 41.5; *JETS* 12/19]. Cf. Woodhouse.

Schreiner, David B., and Lee Compson. (Kerux) 2022. I have not seen it. [*JETS* 3/23].

✓ **Seow, Choon-Leong.** ‡ (NIB) 1999. Well-researched, yet surprisingly brief. The brevity is especially noticeable when one considers that both the NIV and NRSV texts are printed out, leaving less room for interpretation. Some other NIB commentaries are much fuller; for example, while Kings (118pp. in *BHS*) has only 295pp. of discussion, Ezekiel (95pp. in *BHS*) was allocated 533pp. This scholar has standout commentaries on Ecclesiastes and Job. His theology is liberal. [*ExpTim* 2/00; *CTJ* 11/01].

Skinner, John. ‡ (Century Bible) 1904. By the author of *Genesis* in the ICC.

F  Spina, Frank Anthony. (THC).

✓ **Sweeney, Marvin A.** ‡ (OTL-R) 2007. The erudite Jewish scholar should be consulted by students for a recent historical-critical commentary. An introduction of 44pp. is followed by 424pp. of compact, rigorous exegesis. Sweeney is especially interested in King Josiah's place in the DtrH (a Josianic redaction, among four other strata); see *King Josiah of Judah* (OUP, 2001) [*JAOS* 122.1]. His work replaces Gray's much fatter vol. and, like its predecessor, really does not venture much into theological interpretation. With regard to historical approach, Sweeney views himself as charting a middle way between those who read the Bible as fiction and those accepting the Bible's historical claims more at face value. Alongside the diachronic interests he has displayed over many years, he also takes seriously the final form of the text (the synchronic). [*WTJ* Fall 08; *CBQ* 4/08; *BL* 2008; *ExpTim* 4/09; *Them* 4/09; *VT* 58.4 (Williamson); *RBL*; *BBR* 20.1; *Int* 10/09].

✓ Thiele, Edwin R. *The Mysterious Numbers of the Hebrew Kings*, 1951, rev. 1965 and 1983. The thesis is rather complex, but I think Thiele did a brilliant job of dealing with the difficult problem of chronology from a conservative angle, though scholars like to point out that problems still exist [*JBL* 3/79]. Many believe that a few adjustments with co-regencies—see McFall, "A Translation Guide to the Chronological Data in Kings and Chronicles," *BSac* 148.1 (1991): 3–45 [available free on the internet]—cause the problems to disappear. Cf. J. Finegan, *Handbook of Biblical Chronology* (1998), who accepts the Thiele–McFall synthesis. Another strong work on chronology, this one from the critical camp, is Hayes–Hooker, *A New Chronology for the Kings of Israel and Judah and Its Implications for Biblical History and Literature* (1988). Also touted is Galil, *The Chronology of the Kings of Israel and Judah* (Brill, 1996) [*JTS* 4/98; *VT* 49.4]. Tetley has a more radical try at untangling the knots in *The Reconstructed Chronology of the Divided Kingdom* (2005) [*VT* 57.4; *JNES* 7/08 (Klein); *AUSS* 45.2]. However, I am most impressed with Bieke Mahieu, "A Revised Chronology for the Kings of Israel and Judah," *RB* 129 (2022): 505–44, whose proposal includes a chart comparing the leading interpretations. Finally, I applaud the meticulous work of Steinmann, *From Abraham to Paul: A Biblical Chronology* (2011).

✓ Vannoy, J. Robert. *NIV Study Bible* notes, 1985. See under Samuel. Superb biblical theology! You will be surprised, if you look closely at the notes, how packed it is.

☆ Van't Veer, M. B. *My God Is Yahweh*, ET 1980. What a delight to come across this outstanding 400-page exposition of Elijah's early ministry (1 Kgs 16:34–19:21)! To say that this man was theologically perceptive is an understatement. I can scarcely find any finer biblical theology drawn from the historical literature of the OT. Go to school on this. Van't Veer was published by Paideia/Premier, is long o/p, and can be purchased used; I once had it as a recommended purchase. Cf. the Jewish work of Simon mentioned above under Reading Narrative.

☆ Wallace R. S. *Readings in 1 Kings*, 1995; *Readings in 2 Kings*, 1997. These two vols. build upon his older rich exposition, *Elijah and Elisha*. [*SBET* Spr 98].

☆ **Walsh, Jerome T.** ‡ *1 Kings* (BerO) 1996. The first in the series, and set a high standard. Walsh has fresh and fascinating literary insights. (Not long ago it was the case that few commentaries on 1 Kings showed interest in the narrative art of the book.) Students and scholarly pastors will enjoy this 400-page work which focuses on the final form, but that is not to say the commentary is less accessible or difficult reading. Those not theologically trained can use it. Little here would be objectionable to evangelical interpreters. [*JSOT* 79; *JETS* 6/99; *CBQ* 4/97; *JBL* Spr 98; *RBL*].

Wijk-Bos, Johanna W. H. van. ‡ *The Land and Its Kings: 1–2 Kings*, 2020. Strongly feminist. See the companion vols. on Joshua–Judges and Samuel. [*BL* 2022; *BBR* 31.3; *CBQ* 10/21; *JETS* 3/21; *Int* 1/22].

F  Wilson, Robert R. ‡ (Herm). The scholar is brilliant from the sociological angle.

☆ **Wiseman, D. J.** (TOTC) 1993. The author (†2010) was universally held in high esteem; he was chosen as editor of this series, which tells you something. Wiseman is especially noted for historical studies of the ANE, Assyriology in particular. See, e.g., his groundbreaking *Chronicles of the Chaldean Kings* (1956). The commentary's strength is in providing information on the historical background—Provan and House are much better on the message of Kings. Up until the 2001 edition of this guide, I recommended this TOTC for purchase. See Keil above. [*CTJ* 11/94; *EvQ* 4/95; *Evangel* Spr 95; *JSOT* 61; *SwJT* Sum 94; *SBET* Aut 96]. See Dharamraj for a replacement.

☆ Woodhouse, John. *1 Kings* (PTW) 2018. The author was Principal of Moore College, Sydney (2002–13). His large and thorough exposition (nearly 800pp.) is superb in building a solid exegetical foundation and then for offering preaching hints from a conservative Reformed perspective. [*JETS* 9/19]. He is said to be working on *2 Kings*. See Woodhouse under 1–2 Samuel, and compare with Ryken on Kings.

NOTE: Michael Avioz, "The Book of Kings in Recent Research (Part I)," *CBR* 4.1 (2005): 11–55; and "The Book of Kings in Recent Research (Part II), *CBR* 5.1 (2006): 11–57.

# CHRONICLES

NOTE: American missionaries joke about the paralysis of indecision they experience when, previously deprived, they come home and face a million choices in a supermarket. Evans is having that kind of experience here with Chronicles commentaries. Please mix and match according to your needs and interests. All these recommended works are worth having.

★ **Boda, Mark.** (CorBC) 2010. Without question one of the best, clearest evangelical books on Chronicles available to pastors (456pp.). Some see a drawback in the series' being based on the NLT, but that should not dissuade you from using Boda. He knows the scholarship and guides readers to make sense of the text theologically, even the most difficult portions (e.g., genealogies). See Boda on Judges, Haggai–Zechariah.

★ **Dillard, Raymond.** *2 Chronicles* (WBC) 1987. So many fine commentaries on Chronicles! Dillard is excellent all-round, with creative biblical theology enriching a pastor's study of this long-neglected book—no lack of scholarly interest now. Though committed to inerrancy, he did not skirt the hard exegetical issues and drew some conclusions that raised questions among fellow conservatives. (He resigned from ETS about the time this vol. came out.) His death in 1993 was a terrible loss to Westminster Seminary, OT scholarship, and the church. Longman's first pick. [*JBL* 108.3; *HS* 1989; *JTS* 4/89].

★ Eveson, Philip H. (Focus) 2 vols., 2024. The Welsh pastor-scholar receives plaudits for his theological expositions, and this 700-page set should gain him still more praise. (See his similar works on Genesis, Leviticus, and Psalms—this and *Psalms* are the best.) Formerly the Principal of London Theological Seminary, Eveson draws on respected scholarship, including Japhet, Knoppers, and Germans such as Rudolph, Willi, and Plöger. There is occasional reference to the Hebrew in transliteration, but the commentary is accessible to a lay readership. It is one of the best for pastors. Every portion of text has an "Application" section, and the set contains 90 "Group Discussion Questions."

★ **Hill, Andrew E.** (NIVAC) 2003. Provides a fine mix of exegesis and guidance for application. The research is solid, and the vol. is quite full for the series (700pp.). Though it is a book for preachers, students can also benefit as they ask their questions: What does a learned evangelical approach to Chronicles look like? What are its challenges and advantages? The theological exposition rightly picks up on the God-centeredness of the Chronicler's main themes (covenant, worship, etc.) and message, and Hill makes a compelling argument for this literature being well-suited for preaching to a postmodern, self-absorbed culture (39–41). [*JETS* 6/05; *CTJ* 4/10].

★ **Japhet, Sara.** [*M*], (OTL) 1993. Magnificent and very valuable, particularly to specialists and scholarly pastors. Japhet is "the doyenne of Chronicles studies" (Williamson), and her conservatively critical work is rivaled only by Klein as the largest commentary yet on 1–2 Chronicles (1104pp.). A keen Jewish scholar, she worked on the exegesis and theology of Chronicles for decades. It seems a pity not to have any indices. The average pastor might well leave this off the to-buy list. For a fine, more accessible substitute, consider McKenzie or Williamson. See Blenkinsopp under Ezra–Nehemiah. [*WTJ* Spr 95; *Int* 4/96; *CBQ* 10/95; *JR* 4/95; *JSS* Spr 95; *JSOT* 65; *BSac* 1/95; *HS* 1995]. Students note her republished study focusing on the Chronicler's distinctives: *The Ideology of the Book of Chronicles and Its Place in Biblical Thought* (1989, 2009) [*RBL*; *BL* 2010], which is tremendously influential. Useful for both Chronicles and Ezra–Nehemiah studies is *From the Rivers of Babylon to the Highlands of Judah: Collected Studies on the Restoration Period* (2006).

★ Kaminski, Carol M. (SGBC) 2023. More for pastors than students, though the author is learned (Cambridge PhD) and the work has depth (570pp.). I was eager to see this after it was praised by Sklar as containing "wonderfully rich biblical theology along with helpful exposition in general," even of the genealogies and why they are important (private correspondence). In keeping with the series aims, Kaminski devotes attention to pastoral application. The "Live the Story" segments are not "preachy" but quite thought-provoking. E.g., "Perhaps the loss [of a sense] of God's holiness in the church is the direct result of our neglect of the OT in preaching and teaching. Stories of God's unapproachable holiness are intended to draw us into a deeper understanding of God's character, resulting in praise and worship, but also fear and reverence for his holy name" (148). A great theological commentary! Cf. Hahn. The only drawback is a neglect of Knoppers's AB; she has but one citation of it (178). Kaminski works well as a pastor's first choice.

★ **Knoppers, Gary.** [𝑀], *I Chronicles* (AB-R) 2 vols., 2004. The author last taught at Notre Dame and was mourned by the entire OT guild (†2018). This was to have been a replacement set on all of Chronicles (see Myers); we received the fullest, most probing commentary ever published on 1 Chronicles (1000pp.). The textual criticism is exceedingly thorough and careful. Also see Knoppers under Kings. Few pastors have the money or the interest for this, but it is a marvel, worthy of inclusion among the recommended picks. As a technical exegesis, not an exposition, this is nearly definitive—Klein is the only close competitor. Though Knoppers was theologically astute, the AB provides less theology. [*JTS* 4/06; *Int* 7/06; *JSS* Aut 07; *BL* 2005; *Bib* 87.4; *RelSRev* 4/07; *RBL*].

★ Pratt, Richard. (Mentor) 1998. This 512-page, mainly theological commentary is somewhat like Currid's on Exodus. I think Pratt may have gotten started on this by contributing the Chronicles notes to the *New Geneva Study Bible* (*Reformation Study Bible*). I haven't used this commentary extensively, but commend it to pastors for their consideration. More expositional than exegetical. The author has done good work with OT narrative—*He Gave Us Stories* (1990)—and taught at RTS in Orlando. Compare with Hill. Other fine expositional helps are Allen (WCC), McConville, and Wilcock. [*Them* 6/00].

✓ Ackroyd, P. R. ‡ (Torch) 1973. Of note because of the author's "important role in the general rehabilitation of the Chronicler" [*BSB* 12/00]. But, Williamson adds, "the commentary itself is very brief, and seems to have been hurriedly written." Ackroyd's expertise lay in the exilic and postexilic literature. See also his OTL vol., *Exile and Restoration* (1968), and book of collected essays, *The Chronicler in His Age* (1991), which contains a lifetime of learning (397pp.).

☆ Allen, Leslie C. [𝑀], (WCC) 1987. So good I wanted to include it above, years ago. A tremendous amount of research lies behind it: his 2-vol. PhD concerned the LXX of Chronicles. Allen's is one of the best researched vols. in the series, alongside Hubbard on Proverbs; Ecclesiastes–Song of Songs. For another, more exegetical work from Allen, see immediately below.

✓ **Allen, Leslie C.** [𝑀], (NIB) 1999. See Allen above; here he has reworked some of his earlier material. Those building a first-class library will buy this mature commentary (360pp.). [*ExpTim* 2/00; *CTJ* 11/01]. For introductory matters, Allen's T&T Clark "Study Guide" (2021) is perfect for students [*ExpTim* 4/22; *BL* 2022].

F  Bautch, Richard J. ‡ *II Chronicles* (AYB). See Knoppers above.

✓ Beentjes, Pancratius C. ‡ *Tradition and Transformation in the Book of Chronicles*, 2008. [*BibInt* 19.4].

✓ Ben Zvi, Ehud. ‡ *History, Literature and Theology in the Book of Chronicles*, 2006. [*BibInt* 19.3].

F  Ben Zvi, Ehud. ‡ (IECOT). There is a report of *1 Chronicles* appearing in 2024.

✓ Ben Zvi, Ehud, and Diana V. Edelman, eds. *What Was Authoritative for Chronicles?* 2011. A dozen important essays; the most intriguing topic for me was the Chronicler and the prophets (Jonker and Warhurst). [*BBR* 22.3; *CBQ* 4/13; *JTS* 4/13; *JSOT* 36.5; *VT* 63.1].

☆ **Braun, Roddy.** [𝓜], *1 Chronicles* (WBC) 1986. Quite helpful, especially on the genealogies. Braun is more technical but not as interesting as NCB. He knows Chronicles well and brings out some fine theological points. The Lutheran scholar employs some newer-style literary criticism but doesn't handle the text with the same respect as Dillard. (I wish he did not regard chs. 23–27 as secondary.) Advanced students may want to buy this, but note the critical review in *HS* 1987. Both Knoppers and Klein have far eclipsed Braun, but those works are more expensive too. [*EvQ* 10/88; *RTR* 9/87; *CRBR* 1988].

Coggins, R. J. ‡ (CBC) 1976. One of the best in the series. [*EvQ* 10/77].

✓ Conti, Marco, ed. *1–2 Kings, 1–2 Chronicles, Ezra, Nehemiah, Esther* (ACCS) 2008.

✓ Cooper, Derek, and Martin J. Lohrmann, eds. *1–2 Samuel, 1–2 Kings, 1–2 Chronicles* (RCS) 2016.

✓ Curtis, E. L., and A. A. Madsen. ‡ (ICC) 1910. A reference tool from a time when Chronicles was widely ignored. Has been consulted on technical questions by those interested in history of interpretation. Quite liberal and skeptical.

✓ **DeVries, Simon J.** ‡ (FOTL) 1989. A full-scale work (439pp.) to be consulted by students with form-critical interests. Once in the evangelical camp, DeVries became more critical. See under Kings. [*WTJ* Fall 91; *JETS* 6/92; *Them* 4/91; *BSac* 1/92; *HS* 1990; *CRBR* 1991].

✓ **Dirksen, Peter B.** ‡ *1 Chronicles* (HCOT) 2003, ET 2005. A technical exegesis of the Hebrew, of manageable size (356pp.) and of value to students. It does not compete favorably, however, with the newer scholarly commentaries by Knoppers and Klein, nor with the older Japhet. As with some other continental European series, the treatment of a passage is divided into too many sections: Introduction; Translation; Essentials and Perspectives; Scholarly Exposition (I); Scholarly Exposition (II); e.g., see pp.93–98. I regret there are no indices. Kalimi is scheduled to complete the set. [*BBR* 19.1; *VT* 57.3].

F   Duke, Rodney K. (Apollos). In 1990 he published his Emory diss., *The Persuasive Appeal of the Chronicler: A Rhetorical Analysis.*

F   Evans, Paul S. (NICOT) 2 vols.

✓ Evans, Paul, and Tyler Williams, eds. ‡ *Chronicling the Chronicler*, 2013. [*CBQ* 7/15; *VT* 66.1].

✓ French, Blaire A. ‡ *Chronicles through the Centuries* (BBC) 2016. [*JTS* 4/18; *JSOT* 43.5].

Goldsworthy, Graeme. (RBT) 2021. I have not seen it. [*Them* 47.3].

✓ Graham, Patrick, Kenneth Hoglund, and Steven McKenzie, eds. ‡ *The Chronicler as Historian*, 1997. Here the leading critical scholars on Chronicles contribute influential articles to a Sheffield collection. [*EvQ* 7/02; *BibInt* 9.2]. Added to this vol. are *The Chronicler as Author: Studies in Text and Texture* (1999) [*CurTM* 12/02], and a 2003 FS for Ralph Klein, *The Chronicler as Theologian*, edited by Graham–McKenzie–Knoppers [*HS* 2005; *VT* 57.1].

☆ **Hahn, Scott.** *The Kingdom of God as Liturgical Empire*, 2012. From an able OT scholar, once a conservative Presbyterian but now a Catholic apologist. In using this brief (204pp.) exposition, I've found very rich, stimulating biblical theology. Hahn gives extra attention to 1 Chr 17: "God's covenant with David is the theological summit of the salvation story the Chronicler has come to tell" (68). The book is given strong commendation on the *DenvJ* list, and it deserves the praise. Readers should be aware that Hahn assumes they have a good theological education (e.g., references to haggadah) and can follow his typological interpretations. His main thesis? "The Chronicler indeed presents us with a utopia. It is not an ideal political economy or kingdom, but a liturgical empire, a multinational kingdom ordered to offer sacrifice and praise to the living God" (23). Also, "the kingdom of God is sacramental" (101). [*BBR* 23.1; *Int* 7/13; *ExpTim* 3/13; *Them* 7/14; *BTB* 8/14].

Hicks, John Mark. (College Press NIV Commentary) 2001. A rather large (540-page) exposition which tends to concentrate on theological matters. [*RelSRev* 4/02].

Hooker, Paul K. ‡ (WestBC) 2001. Compare with Tuell's exposition of similar length (see *Them*, which finds Hooker more exegetical and more liberal). It is well-done and highly theological from the critical camp. Preachers can learn from this reasonably priced pb (about 300pp.), but it is not as much homiletical help as some expect from this series. [*Them* Spr 04; *CTJ* 11/03; *Int* 4/04; *ExpTim* 2/03; *RelSRev* 4/02; see Williamson in *JSOT* 27.5].

F   House, Paul, and Todd Borger. (EBTC)?

F   Janzen, David. ‡ (Illum).

✓   **Jarick, John.** ‡ (Read) 2 vols., 2002–07. An important literary-critical reading, one which is pursued without constant comparisons to Samuel–Kings. Jarick is on faculty at Oxford. [*BL* 2005, 2009; *RBL*; *JTS* 10/09; *ExpTim* 11/09 (Klein)].

F   Johnson, Benjamin. (EEC). A previous report was Eugene Mayhew.

✓   **Johnstone, William.** ‡ 2 vols., 1997. This Sheffield commentary of over 700pp. tends to spurn historical questions and take up theological ones. It is a fresh, sympathetic reading of the text without a lot of wrangles with others' views. On the downside, Williamson says the work is "sometimes idiosyncratic" [*BSB* 12/00]. Johnstone contends that Chronicles is "a highly integrated theological statement . . . concerned with the universal relationship between God and humanity, and the vocation of Israel within that relationship" (I: p.10). See also his 1998 work, *Chronicles and Exodus*. [*JBL* Spr 00; *JSOT* 79; *ExpTim* 10/98; *CBQ* 4/99; *RelSRev* 10/98; *EvQ* 4/03].

✓   **Jonker, Louis C.** ‡ (UBC) 2013. From a sharp Stellenbosch prof who participated for some time in the tightly knit guild of Chronicles scholars. He treats the book in four sections: From the Beginning (1 Chr 1–9), David (1 Chr 10–29), Solomon (2 Chr 1–9), and Rehoboam to Cyrus (2 Chr 10–36). He dates it to the mid-fourth century and agrees with the growing consensus of "a separate literary composition from Ezra-Nehemiah" (11). He designates the book "'reforming history' . . . to describe the intention or purpose of this work and to characterize its hermeneutical dynamics" (15), as it retells the story using earlier sources (DtrH) and traditions. The commentary is exegetical, well-informed, and similar in some respects to McKenzie (325pp.). [*JESOT* 3.2].

F   Kalimi, Isaac. ‡ *2 Chronicles* (HCOT). Note Peeters's decision to divide Chronicles between two scholars. Kalimi proved his mettle in such works as *The Reshaping of Ancient Israelite History in Chronicles* (2005) [*JETS* 6/06; *TJ* Fall 08; *JBL* Win 05; *JSS* Aut 07; *BL* 2006], which is a high-level, detailed discussion of the Chronicler's redaction-work; *An Ancient Israelite Historian* (2005) [*BL* 2006], a collection of essays; and *Writing and Rewriting the Story of Solomon in Ancient Israel* (CUP, 2019) [*CBQ* 1/20].

✓   Keil, Carl F. (KD) ET 1872. Years ago, Keil was "invaluable as a very learned and carefully argued commentary which defends a traditional orthodox Protestant position" (Childs).

✓   Kelly, Brian E. *Retribution and Eschatology in Chronicles*, 1996.

✓   **Klein, Ralph.** ‡ (Herm) 2 vols., 2006–12. Magisterial! Klein has been well-connected with, and productive among, the leading Chronicles scholars. This comprehensive, technical exegesis may be the capstone of his honored career—which began, by the way, with a Harvard diss. on Chronicles. He has strong historical interests and is an accomplished text critic. There is more theology in these vols. (562 and 592pp.) than in many others in Hermeneia, and Klein pays special attention to the theme of divine retribution. He joins most leading scholars in distinguishing the Chronicler and his perspective from Ezra–Nehemiah. See this Lutheran scholar's past work on Samuel, which makes him an astute commentator on the Chronicler's redactional activity. [*JETS* 9/07; *SwJT* Fall 05; *Int* 7/08; *VT* 59.1; *CurTM* 6/07; *ExpTim* 9/07; *JHebS* 13; *RBL*; *CBQ* 7/09; *BL* 2007; *JSOT* 41.5].

☆   Konkel, August H. (BCBC) 2016. Have not used it much, but I recognize the author produces good, faithful scholarship. He has been a Canadian pastor, professor, and seminary President. The Anabaptist series is of less interest to those outside that camp. (Konkel did his PhD at Westminster.) See under Kings.

☆ Leithart, Peter J. (Brazos) 2019. After doing a good job on 1–2 Kings for the series, Leithart offers an engaging, insightful theological exposition of the Chronicler's work (about 260pp.). Of particular interest is his idea that music and a theology of music/worship lie at the heart of the Bible book. Those familiar with his past work (and expecting some focus on matters ecclesiological?) are not disappointed. [*ExpTim* 6/20; *JETS* 3/20; *JSOT* 45.5 (Goldingay); *Them* 47.1].

✓ **Levin, Yigal.** ‡ *The Chronicles of the Kings of Judah: 2 Chronicles 10–36*, 2017. Originally intended for ECC; see the publication story in *Bib* 99.1. Levin offers a fine translation of the MT, with copious textual notes and much discussion of archaeology and historical questions. Literary features and the theology of the Chronicler receive somewhat less attention. Three vols. are to appear in reverse order: the next one scheduled will cover 1 Chr 10 to 2 Chr 9. This excellent research can be put to good use alongside Japhet, Klein, and Dillard. [*JSS* Spr 19; *BBR* 27.4; *JSOT* 42.5].

☆ Mabie, Frederick J. (EBCR) 2010. Drawing on much of the best scholarship (Japhet, WBC, Schniedewind, Johnstone), he offers a strongly conservative interpretation (315pp.). Perhaps the advance on earlier writers like Payne is that Mabie approaches Chronicles on its own terms; he is less interested in a "synoptic approach" that regularly reads Chronicles as compared with Samuel–Kings (38, n.60). I find this well-done, but I believe a book like Hill or Boda is preferable for theological exposition.

✓ Mason, Rex. ‡ *Preaching the Tradition*, 1990.

☆ McConville, J. Gordon. (DSB) 1984. Most stimulating for pastors despite severe space limitations. This is a great little commentary by an able British evangelical scholar. In early editions I included this among my purchase recommendations. [*EvQ* 7/86].

☆ **McKenzie, Steven L.** ‡ (AbOTC) 2004. An excellent exegetical work in pb by one of the leaders in recent Chronicles scholarship. I consider it something like a new Williamson, though slightly more critically oriented. All of Chronicles is covered in about 380pp. Recommended for both students and pastors who desire a careful exegesis in line with the generally accepted conclusions of current critical scholarship. [*CBQ* 1/07; *JETS* 3/06; *Int* 4/05; *BL* 2005].

☆ **Merrill, Eugene H.** (KEL) 2015. Over 600pp., representing years of diligent study by a senior evangelical OT scholar who retired from Dallas Seminary in 2013. I class this as a leading conservative commentary with strengths in traditional grammatico-historical exegesis and theological reflection. As expected from one with such a widely used OT history textbook, *Kingdom of Priests* (2nd ed. 2008), Merrill has an enviable and wide knowledge of the details of Israelite and ANE history. Many pastors will count this a top choice, though it says less to assist preachers with their concern for contemporary relevance. Note "The Theology of the 'Chronicler': What Difference Does It Make?" *JETS* 59 (2016): 691–700. See also his publications on Deuteronomy and Haggai–Malachi. [*BBR* 27.1; *JETS* 12/16; *JSOT* 40.5 (Williamson); *Them* 42.1].

✓ Myers, J. M. ‡ (AB) 2 vols., 1965. Has a stress on archaeological finds. Myers was good on background, not so strong on interpretation and theology—in other words, he was more in line with AB's original aims. Today it is considered a dated, weaker entry in the series and is scheduled for full retirement. See Knoppers above.

☆ Olley, John W. "1–2 Chronicles" in *1 Samuel–2 Chronicles* (ESVEC) 2019. See Mackay under Samuel. I have not used this vol., but I know Olley to be an astute exegete and theologian. See his BST on Kings.

✓ Omanson, Roger L., and John E. Ellington. (UBS) 2 vols., 2015. A huge project (over 1400pp.) by the same authors of the *Handbooks* on Samuel and Kings. Quite useful to exegetes!

F  Palmer, Christine. (ZECOT).

Payne, J. Barton. (EBC) 1988. Takes a more conservative approach than Williamson. Though Payne was a remarkable scholar (making many contributions to OT scholarship prior to his mountain-climbing death in 1979), other, more recent works would be better guides. Obviously completed a decade prior to publication. See Maybie above.

✓ Person, Raymond F. ‡ *The Deuteronomic History and the Book of Chronicles: Scribal Works in an Oral World*, 2010. Drafting a proposal that seems in line with the Edinburgh School (see Auld under Samuel), Person dates the DtrH as well as Chronicles to the Persian period. He considers them competing historiographies, descended from a common source. [*JSS* Aut 12; *JSOT* 35.5; *RBL* 2011; *JETS* 3/11; *ETL* 89.4; *BibInt* 21.3; *RelSRev* 6/13].

✓ **Redditt, Paul L.** ‡ (S&H) 2020. Haven't used it much (460pp.), but the author consistently takes a stricter historical-critical approach in his commentaries. Here Redditt seems less interested in 1 Chronicles; the treatment of 2 Chronicles is nearly twice as long. Look up his other books, including the S&H on Ezra–Nehemiah. [*CBQ* 10/21; *Int* 1/22].

✓ Riley, William. ‡ *King and Cultus in Chronicles*, 1993.

F   Ristau, Kenneth A. (WBC-R) 2 vols. Scheduled to replace Braun and Dillard.

F   Schniedewind, William M. ‡ (NCBC). I expect this to be a fine work.

☆ **Selman, Martin J.** (TOTC) 2 vols., 1994. Well over 500pp. of informed, conservative comment. He was able to build upon the excellent WBC set. I would not quarrel with anyone recommending this as a first purchase for a pastor's library; the price is right. Selman is particularly interested in theology and a good partner to Williamson's or Japhet's exegesis. [*Them* 10/95; *JETS* 6/97; *JSOT* 71; *BSac* 7/95; *Chm* 110.2].

✓ Sparks, James T. *The Chronicler's Genealogies*, 2008. A Murdoch University diss. by an Australian evangelical, published by SBL. The subtitle is "Towards an Understanding of 1 Chronicles 1–9." [*CBQ* 4/11; *Bib* 92.3].

☆ **Thompson, J. A.** (NAC) 1994. From the pen of a respected, productive Australian, this is solid and fairly full (400pp.). The exegesis is in line with the publisher's commitment to inerrancy; it would not be inaccurate to term it a newer, more thorough Barton Payne. As usual with NAC, not as penetrating as some other commentaries. Thompson has also written works on Jeremiah and Deuteronomy. [*SwJT* Fall 96; *VT* 46.4; *JSOT* 76; *HS* 1997].

☆ **Tuell, Steven S.** ‡ (I) 2001. The 250-page exposition shows the author's concern to see Chronicles, as a less popular portion of the Bible, preached more often. It is well-written (see his treatment of 1 Chr 17) and theologically oriented. He reads Chronicles as being of one piece with Ezra–Nehemiah. Tuell wrote a PhD and commentary on Ezekiel. [*CBQ* 10/03; *Them* Spr 04; *Int* 1/03; *ExpTim* 10/04; *HBT* 12/02; *JSOT* 99; *SwJT* Fall 04; *Anvil* 19.4].

☆ Wilcock, Michael. (BST) 1987. Years ago I said, if you can afford a third homiletical commentary (after Pratt and Hill), this one might barely nose out McConville and Allen (WCC). Yet they, not Wilcock, are the OT scholars. All three are worth the money. [*EvQ* 10/88; *RTR* 1/88; *Evangel* Win 88; *Chm* 107.1].

Wilkinson, Bruce. *The Prayer of Jabez*, 2000. Yes, I'm jocular here. But for a perceptive review from an OT scholar, see Schultz, "Praying Jabez's Prayer" in *TJ* Spr 03.

F   Williams, Joshua E., and Calvin F. Pearson. (Kerux) 2024.

☆ **Williamson, H. G. M.** [𝓜], (NCB) 1982. A treasure trove. According to Dillard decades ago, this was the best commentary on all of Chronicles. Well-reasoned and conservatively critical in his conclusions, Williamson seems to disdain (as unscholarly) attempts at harmonization (Chronicles with Samuel–Kings). Sadly, this has gone o/p, and I removed it from the to-buy list. Compare with McKenzie. For a companion vol. to the NCB, see Williamson under Ezra–Nehemiah. [*Them* 9/85; *ExpTim* 6/83].

F   Wright, John W. ‡ (BerO).

NOTES: (1) William Johnstone's "Which Is the Best Commentary? 11. The Chronicler's Work," *ExpTim* 10/90. (2) Rodney K. Duke, "Recent Research in Chronicles," *CBR* 8.1 (2009): 10–50. (3) Students wanting to compare Samuel–Kings with Chronicles should consult one of the harmonies authored by Crockett (1959); Newsome (Baker, 1986); or Endres–Millar–Burns (Liturgical, 1998). The last two are much to be preferred. I chose to buy Endres. Students of the Hebrew can avail themselves of Jürgen Kegler and Matthias Augustin, *Synopse zum chronistischen Geschichtswerk* (Frankfurt: Peter Lang, 1984), or Abba Bendavid, *Parallels in the Bible* [מקבילות במקרא] (Jerusalem: Carta, 1972).

# EZRA–NEHEMIAH

★ Fyall, Robert. *Ezra and Haggai* (BST) 2010. A worthy series addition, Fyall's work expounds this odd pairing of Bible books with exegetical skill, mature theological sense, and spiritual insight. (Then again, perhaps not so odd; both books concern the rebuilding of the temple.) The author has also published a fine book on Job in NSBT. [*Chm* Spr 11; *JETS* 12/11; *ExpTim* 3/12].

★ **Harrington, Hannah K.** (NICOT-R) 2022. A welcome replacement for Fensham, with greater thoroughness (500pp.) and balance of hermeneutical approaches, far more interaction with scholarship (Steinmann too, happily), and a wealth of 23 excursuses. This is a very good book! Harrington has long worked in the field of Second Temple Judaism and on purity issues in the DSS (ritual-physical as well as moral). She explains how Ezra–Nehemiah is "an early repository of valuable information regarding key concepts in Second Temple Judaism." Though preferring Smith in certain respects, I esteem Harrington as an excellent, learned guide through this literature. Here is a taste (7): "The central focus of the Nehemiah Memoir . . . is not the wall but the rebuilding of the community by means of the Torah and covenant renewal. After Nehemiah secures the city with the wall (Neh 1–6), Israel can then focus on the more significant matter of rededication to keeping God's law (Neh 8–10). It is only after the reading of the Torah (Neh 8) and the people's promise to keep it (Neh 9–10) that the people are fit to move in and repopulate the holy city of Jerusalem (Neh 11:1)." [*RelSRev* 12/22; *JETS* 3/23; *JSOT* 47.5].

★ **Kidner, Derek.** (retired TOTC) 1979. An excellent, brief commentary that "deserves high praise," according to Williamson [*BSB* 9/00]: "his verse-by-verse comments never fail to provide fruit for searching reflection." Kidner does not attribute these books to the Chronicler and takes a more conservative approach than Williamson. Perhaps no one could write a short OT commentary as well as Kidner. The replacement is by Lorein. [*WTJ* Fall 80; *JBL* 100.4; *JETS* 3/82].

★ **Lorein, Geert W.** (TOTC-R) 2024. From a mature, respected professor at Leuven (Evangelical Theological Faculty). Earlier, Lorein published a Dutch commentary on these books (2010), but this is a fresh work, replacing Kidner. He has a 30-page bibliography, a longer Introduction (58pp.), and 200pp. of learned, fairly clear exegesis. The work is well-rounded, treating "all levels of the text: linguistic, historical, literary (not only for aesthetical reasons, but also because literary devices tell us something about the author's intentions), and theological." He is on guard against liberalism (179) and has high confidence in the reliability of the story: "in Ezra-Neh. we have to do with historiography without an elevated literary style (but with a tight structure)" (3). Lorein is less approachable and provides more technical detail than the Tyndale readership is accustomed to, especially in the Intro (e.g., his discussion of the language, text, versions, and canon [34–51]; his translations of Akkadian and Old Persian texts; and a paragraph on Nehemiah's animal [165]).

★ **Petter, Donna, and Thomas Petter.** (NIVAC) 2021. This able husband and wife teach at Gordon-Conwell, and their 500-page book completes the series. She commented on Ezra, and he did Nehemiah, after which they worked as a team to edit. Both exhibit their learning in Hebrew/Aramaic exegesis, archaeology, history, and solid biblical theology, but in keeping with the series' aim the commentary is accessible. Useful for students and pastors; the latter would be helped by digesting the section on "Nehemiah as a Leadership Manual?" (479–81) before embarking on a sermon series.

★ **Smith, Gary V.** (ZECOT) 2022. What a need this entry and Harrington fill, as we once had a paucity of first-rate scholarly commentaries from evangelicals! In fact, until very recently Ezra–Nehemiah was more underserved by both evangelicals and the critics than any other portion of Scripture. With his 35-page Introduction and 425pp. of well-rounded commentary, Smith builds upon his 2010 CorBC, which also covered Esther. He is a careful, faithful, mature, judicious scholar; some pastors might term the retired professor "a safe pair of hands." Preachers appreciate the God-centered theology drawn out of the text, and students find the discourse analysis to be a unique contribution. Block made a good choice in asking his former colleague to write this vol. There is coverage of most of the more important secondary literature, though by comparison less than Harrington. On the downside, he avoids text-critical questions, sticks almost exclusively to English-language scholarship, and cites an earlier Harrington essay as "Harrison." [*BL* 2024].

★ **Williamson, H. G. M.** [𝓜], (WBC) 1985. Long *the* benchmark study and the evangelical pastor's first choice in an exegetical work, though the vol. made concessions to critical positions. Following on his superb Chronicles commentary, this work furnished further proof that Williamson was one of the world's foremost scholars in the area of postexilic history and literature. Now one has to say the Emeritus Regius Professor of Hebrew in Oxford is among the world's foremost OT scholars, period (see Isaiah). This rigorous WBC is not for the slothful. Williamson subsequently wrote [*BSB* 9/00], "I have been gratified to learn that preachers too have found it useful, perhaps especially in the 'explanation' sections, where I in fact wrote up my own sermon notes." [*CRBR* 1988; *RTR* 9/86; *TJ* Spr 86; *Them* 10/87; *JETS* 3/87; *HS* 1986]. For a more accessible overview of Ezra–Nehemiah and key interpretive issues, see his slim 1987 OT Guides vol. For further historical research, see his *Studies in Persian Period History and Historiography* (2004).

✓ Ackroyd, P. R. ‡ (Torch) 1973. Bound with his Chronicles commentary. This is one of the more valuable critical works suitable for beginners.

Adeney, Walter F. (EB) 1893. Leaving off the Esther portion of this classic, Klock & Klock reprinted *Ezra and Nehemiah* in 1980.

☆ **Allen, Leslie, and Timothy Laniak.** [𝓜], *Ezra, Nehemiah, Esther* (NIBC) 2003. Allen, an expert on Chronicles, contributes the commentary on Ezra and Nehemiah. It is well-researched and well-written. And the price is right for those who are on a tight budget. Conservative evangelicals will find Allen somewhat critical and will prefer Laniak's approach in this joint effort. See Esther. [*CBQ* 10/04; *RTR* 12/04; *JETS* 12/04; *Int* 4/05; *BSac* 10/05].

☆ Aucker, W. Brian. "Ezra-Nehemiah" in *Ezra–Job* (ESVEC) 2020.

Batten, L. W. ‡ (ICC) 1913. Has retained value, more so than some others in the old series.

✓ **Becking, Bob.** ‡ *Ezra–Nehemiah* (HCOT) 2018. A translation of his 2017 book in "de Prediking van het Oude Testament," a series he coedited for 30 years. Becking is now Emeritus after decades at Utrecht, and this substantive, mature work (330pp., no indexes) will be a standard historical-critical commentary for many years to come. Strangely, though, such a work in HCOT offers less discussion of the historical setting. He is attuned to English-language as well as continental European scholarship. He does not read the two books as a unity, and they seem to be dated to the later Persian era (early fourth century). Ezra, he says, is pseudepigraphic and presents "a bogus history" (6). [*BBR* 30.1 (Smith); *RB* 127.4; *JSOT* 47.5; *Them* 44.2].

☆ Benn, Wallace P. *Ezra, Nehemiah, and Esther* (PTW) 2021. From an admirably gifted preacher in the Church of England. Those desiring a profitable homiletical exposition will enjoy this; perhaps they will also wish it were a bit longer than 175pp. There are nine sermonic segments for Ezra, twelve for Nehemiah, and five for Esther. [*JETS* 3/23].

✓ **Blenkinsopp, Joseph.** ‡ (OTL) 1988. The full-length commentary was an important addition to the literature at the time, though perhaps not as seasoned as some others listed here. Blenkinsopp took issue with the growing consensus (Batten, Japhet, Williamson, Klein, Braun, Dillard, Schunck) distinguishing the author(s) of Ezra–Nehemiah from the Chronicler. This question of whether or not Chronicles and Ezra–Nehemiah come from the same hand has continued to generate work, but the consensus strengthens by the year (see Boda–Redditt). [*Bib* 71.1; *JSS* Spr 90; *HS* 1990]. Blenkinsopp kept thinking and wrote *Judaism, the First Phase: The Place of Ezra and Nehemiah in the Origins of Judaism* (2009) [*CBQ* 4/10; *RBL* 8/10; *JTS* 10/10; *JSS* Spr 12; *VT* 61.3; *BTB* 2/12]; his program continued to be predominantly historical-critical. The Catholic scholar also produced the 3-vol. AB set on Isaiah.

✓ Boda, Mark J., and Paul L. Redditt, eds. ‡ *Unity and Disunity in Ezra-Nehemiah: Redaction, Rhetoric, and Reader,* 2008. Quite a large body of then cutting-edge scholarship (384pp.), divided over Ezra–Nehemiah being a single, coherent book or two, but generally holding that Chronicles and Ezra–Nehemiah are not two parts of an overall chronistic history. [*JSOT* 35.5].

☆ Boice, James M. *Nehemiah,* 1990. Another exposition from the late pastor of Tenth Presbyterian, Philadelphia (PCA). More useful than Swindoll for the expositor because he sticks more with the text. Well, to be honest, I like his theology better as well.

☆ **Breneman, Mervin.** *Ezra, Nehemiah, Esther* (NAC) 1993. Ably covers the books in 383pp. and would be a good purchase for pastors to make. It is less valuable to students. Recommended for purchase in previous editions of this guide, but I was less enthusiastic about this vol. Compare Breneman with Fensham, and see the reviews [*JETS* 9/96 (Baldwin); *VT* 46.2 (Williamson)].

✓ Briant, Pierre. *From Cyrus to Alexander: A History of the Persian Empire,* ET 2002. Indispensable for background research (1200pp.), especially the sifting of historical realities from ancient Greek propaganda. [*JNES* 65.2; *BASOR* 332].

Brockington, Leonard H. ‡ (retired NCB) 1969. A weak entry replaced by Clines.

Brown, A. Philip, II. *Hope Amidst Ruin: A Literary and Theological Analysis of Ezra,* 2009. Lengthy, from Bob Jones U. Press. Praised by Hamilton. I haven't seen it.

☆ Brown, Raymond. *The Message of Nehemiah* (BST) 1998. Will serve the pastor much like Packer does. This author has contributed several other commentaries to BST: Numbers, Deuteronomy, Hebrews. [*BL* 1999; *Them* 11/99; *Chm* 113.2].

F  Buster, Aubrey E. (BGW). By a younger Wheaton faculty member.

☆ **Clines, David J. A.** [*M*], (NCB) 1984. Covers Ezra, Nehemiah, and Esther. His work here is erudite and careful; also he uses the newer literary criticism to good effect. This commentary is still one of the best available and serviceable for evangelicals. Clines became increasingly critical over the decades, and his newer work cannot possibly be classed as "mediating." See Clines under Esther and Job. [*ExpTim* 12/85; *JETS* 12/85; *Them* 9/85].

Coggins, R. J. ‡ (CBC) 1976. Not as good as on Chronicles, but still a strong effort. [*EvQ* 10/77].

✓ Conti, Marco, ed. *1–2 Kings, 1–2 Chronicles, Ezra, Nehemiah, Esther* (ACCS) 2008.

☆ **Cook, John A.** *Aramaic Ezra and Daniel* (BHHB) 2019. Extremely useful for students who are learning to read and interpret biblical Aramaic passages. You may wish to note discussion of the jussive in one review [*ExpTim* 1/20; *CBQ* 10/19; *JSOT* 47.5].

✓ **Davies, Gordon F.** ‡ (BerO) 1999. Uses discourse analysis and speech-act theory to produce some good insights for students. Excluding the printing of Bible passages, Davies offers about 100pp. of commentary and reflects on sections of narrative (not verse-by-verse). On the negative side, the discussion can be rather selective and some texts are neglected. [*JSOT* 89; *RelSRev* 10/99; *CBQ* 10/00; *Int* 4/01; *JETS* 9/01].

F   Ehrlich, Carl. ‡ (Illum).

✓ Escott, Timothy R. [𝓜], *Faithfulness and Restoration: Towards Reading Ezra-Nehemiah as Christian Scripture*, 2023. A fine Durham PhD. [*BL* 2024].

✓ **Eskenazi, Tamara Cohn.** ‡ *Ezra* (AYB) 2023. Replaces Myers. Eskenazi has published very well-received work on these books, beginning with *In an Age of Prose: A Literary Approach to Ezra-Nehemiah* (1988) [*HS* 1990 (Dillard); *CRBR* 1990]. Specialists all expected this AYB to be a jewel. Who better than Williamson can summarize the vol.'s significance? "The culmination of a lifetime of research on the book of Ezra by a most distinguished scholar." She has long taught at Hebrew Union College, Los Angeles. The work is more useful to students than pastors (450pp.).

✓ Eskenazi, Tamara C., and Kent H. Richards, eds. ‡ *Second Temple Studies 2: Temple and Community in the Persian Period*, 1994. There are several other titles named *Second Temple Studies*, edited by P. R. Davies and John Halligan.

Evers, Stan K. *Doing a Great Work: Ezra and Nehemiah Simply Explained* (Welwyn) 1996. This devotional and expositional commentary runs to about 225pp. and emphasizes God-centered faith, service, and worship.

✓ **Fensham, F. Charles.** (retired NICOT) 1982. Good work by a strong Semitics scholar, which is not quite so demanding on the reader as Williamson, who incidentally found this vol. "uniformly disappointing" [*BSB* 9/00]. Fensham is less critical and easier for fledgling students and busy pastors. Like Blenkinsopp, Fensham attributes these books to the Chronicler. He provides a healthy amount of detail, particularly in the areas of historical-cultural backdrop and Hebrew/Aramaic, but I judge it to be less valuable as a well-rounded commentary in literary and theological analysis. Early editions of this guide recommended Fensham for purchase, but now see Harrington above. [*JBL* 104.1; *JTS* 4/85; *HS* 1983].

✓ Frevel, Christian, ed. ‡ *Mixed Marriages: Intermarriage and Group Identity in the Second Temple Period*, 2011. [*VT* 64.2].

✓ **Fried, Lisbeth S.** ‡ *Ezra: A Commentary* (CritC) 2015, rev. 2017. Eventually published by Sheffield Phoenix, after the ECC series stalled, this is an erudite, more technical exegetical work (450pp.). See also her *Nehemiah* below. What made her project noteworthy is that we hadn't seen any in-depth commentaries on the Hebrew/Aramaic text since the 1980s, though Steinmann's conservative Lutheran work is certainly valuable. See now Becking, Eskenazi, and Smith also. In Fried's historical criticism, Ezra was a Persian official, reporting on the province of Yehud. "From the point of view of the local Judean hierarchy . . . Ezra and Nehemiah represent the occupying powers—the enemy" (17). She dates the composition to the Hellenistic era. [*JSS* Aut 19; *JSOT* 41.5; *ETL* 93.1; *JHebS* 17]. Prior to this, she published *Ezra and the Law in History and Tradition* (2014) [*CBQ* 4/15; *JSOT* 39.5; *JHebS* 15].

✓ **Fried, Lisbeth S.** ‡ *Nehemiah: A Commentary* (CritC) 2021. Though she holds to the one-book theory, Fried published her commentary in separate vols. (See *Ezra* above.) Call this "a continuation" (xix), with strengths in archaeology, history, Hebrew, and ancient literary context. The work is slightly inconsistent in using both transliteration and Hebrew typeface. I felt disappointment when Fried terms the thrilling night ride of ch. 2 "a Hellenistic insertion" (70). Be aware that she distinguishes two main "I-reports" in her historical criticism: one pertains to the wall-building Nehemiah mentioned by Ben Sira, and another is from a governor of Judah (Neh 5, 13) she takes to be Yeho'ezer. "[A] late editor may have interleaved two separate genuine first-person accounts" (9). Fried oddly claims an editor was influenced by Aristotle. [*CBQ* 4/24].

F   Fulton, Deirdre N. (WBC-R). Scheduled to replace the magnificent Williamson. By a Baylor prof with strong archaeological interests.

Goswell, Gregory. (EPSC) 2014. I have not seen this exposition, said to be 450pp. Goswell is an able, theologically astute Australian; currently he is Academic Dean at Christ College, The Presbyterian Theological Centre, Sydney.

✓   Grabbe, Lester L. ‡ (OT Readings) 1998. A very critical, close reading of the text. Williamson [*BSB* 9/00] once suggested going here "for a radical shake-up." [*OTA* 2/00; *JSS* Spr 02; *Anvil* 17.3].

F   Green, Douglas J. (SGBC).

Hamilton, James M., Jr. *Exalting Jesus in Ezra-Nehemiah* (CCE) 2014. A conservative exposition that keeps its eye trained on biblical-theological themes and to which many pastors will gravitate. The author teaches at Southern Seminary (Baptist).

F   Hill, Andrew. *Ezra, Nehemiah, Esther* (EBTC)?

F   Hogg, David, ed. *Ezra, Nehemiah, Esther, Job* (RCS).

✓   Hoglund, Kenneth E. ‡ *Achaemenid Imperial Administration in Syria-Palestine and the Missions of Ezra and Nehemiah*, 1992.

☆   Holmgren, F. C. ‡ (ITC-E) 1987. Better than some others in the series, of which the author was a general editor, and his theological exposition can complement the more exegetical works of Kidner, Williamson, etc. [*HS* 1988].

✓   Kalimi, Isaac, ed. ‡ *New Perspectives on Ezra-Nehemiah*, 2012. A collection of essays by leading scholars who are conservatively or moderately critical. [*CBQ* 1/13; *JTS* 4/13; *JSOT* 38.5; *VT* 63.1; *ExpTim* 4/13; *JHebS* 12].

✓   Keil, Carl F. (KD) ET 1873.

✓   **Klein, Ralph W.** ‡ (NIB) 1999. A little less than 200pp. and well-done. For pastors, many call this the best critical work since WBC in combining exegesis and theological exposition. Student exegetes will be attracted to the good material here as well. This contribution can be considered among the most useful in the OT section of the NIB. Klein delivered a monumental Chronicles commentary and wrote the WBC on *1 Samuel*. [*ExpTim* 2/00; *CTJ* 11/01].

F   Klingbeil, Gerald. (Apollos).

F   Klouda Sharp, Sheri L. (CSC).

F   Knoppers, Gary, and Oded Lipschits. ‡ (Herm). Reassignment after Knoppers's passing?

Laird, Donna. ‡ *Negotiating Power in Ezra-Nehemiah*, 2016.

Laney, J. Carl. 1982. Popularly styled and published by Moody Press.

Levering, Matthew. (Brazos) 2007. I have not used this. [*CBQ* 7/08; *JETS* 12/08; *BL* 2008 (Williamson); *JTI* Spr 10; *HBT* 31 (Dearman); *CTJ* 11/11; *RelSRev* 6/11].

Loken, Israel. (EEC) 2011. Has been released digitally but not in print.

☆   McConville, J. Gordon. *Ezra, Nehemiah, Esther* (DSB) 1985. Long recommended for purchase. Though hindered by brevity and format, McConville gave us another fine devotional exposition (see Chronicles). Excellent scholarship undergirds his commentary. [*Them* 9/85]. There has been a paucity of expositional helps. Cf. Brown, Fyall, Throntveit, and the very full Steinmann.

✓   **Myers, J. M.** ‡ (AB) 1965. Has the same strengths and weaknesses as his Chronicles vols. and had been considered a standard historical-critical commentary. It has sharply declined in value since the publication of Clines and Williamson. See Eskenazi.

F   Nam, Roger S. (OTL-R). Would replace Blenkinsopp.

✓   **Noss, Philip A., and Kenneth Thomas.** *A Handbook on Ezra and Nehemiah* (UBS) 2005. This large translation help (577pp.) was classed as more valuable than some other UBS Handbooks, considering its date and the lack of resources then available on Ezra–Nehemiah. [*BL* 2006].

☆   Nykolaishen, Douglas J. E., and Andrew J. Schmutzer. *Ezra, Nehemiah, and Esther* (TTC) 2018. Clear and of value, though brief. Schmutzer does the Esther section. [*Them* 45.2].

☆   Packer, J. I. *A Passion for Faithfulness: Wisdom from the Book of Nehemiah*, 1995. Much here to spur on pastors to think theologically and devotionally. [*Them* 1/96].

Rata, Tiberius. (Mentor) 2010. An informative, very conservative commentary of 185pp. (large font), plus a 28-page introduction. Concluding the work is an appendix proposing that Ezra and Nehemiah authored their respective books (225–39).

✓   **Redditt, Paul L.** ‡ (S&H) 2014. From an experienced commentator on postexilic literature (see Chronicles, Daniel, and Haggai–Malachi), and employing mainly a historical-critical approach. Because of the size of the work (341pp.) and its interaction with scholarship (though little besides English), students will learn from Redditt. Pastors won't be so impressed with discussions of redactional layers, a compositional history stretching as late as the 160s BC, and "Connections" sections that seem weak on the message and theology of the text. Note that Ezra receives much more commentary than Nehemiah (125pp.), and Redditt disapproves of Nehemiah's "ethnic discrimination."

Roberts, Mark D. (WCC) 1993. One of the fuller expositional commentaries. Covers Ezra through Esther.

✓   Ryle, H. E. (CBSC) 1897. According to Williamson, this packed little vol. (328pp.) was the best of the older English-language commentaries for pointing out key interpretive issues. It may still be useful to consult, if a student is doing fuller research.

Shao, Joseph Too, and Rosa Ching Shao. (Asia) 2019. [*BL* 2022].

☆   **Shepherd, David J., and Christopher J. H. Wright.** (THC) 2018. The Introduction (10pp.) and Commentaries (100pp.) are fairly short and perhaps less useful as a result; Shepherd is the commentator. Three theological essays follow (100pp.)—the two by Wright are the highlight for me—and are very worthwhile for students and pastors. A fine book! [*ExpTim* 7/19; *BBR* 28.3; *CBQ* 10/19; *Int* 10/19; *JSOT* 43.5; *RTR* 4/19].

Smith, Gary V. (CorBC) 2010. Bound with Esther. See his other commentaries on Isaiah and Amos. Of course, now one has recourse to Smith's large-scale ZECOT above.

☆   **Steinmann, Andrew E.** (ConcC) 2010. It is remarkable that he has churned out such a quick succession of huge commentaries: the 628-page *Daniel* (2008) was followed by the 719-page *Proverbs* (2009). Now comes this *Ezra and Nehemiah* which is 675pp. Clearly he is making a sacrificial effort to serve the church. I have only sparingly used Steinmann, and find him to be quite thorough (he had room to be). There are a few editing problems (e.g., sizing the Hebrew font on p.608). He can perhaps be faulted for inattention to narrative studies and jumping too quickly to NT reflections. I needed more interpretation of the message to its ancient Jewish audience, instead of lifting Bible teachings straight from the OT textual world into today's (Lutheran) church context with a law-gospel dichotomy. But let me be clear: Steinmann's is an impressive, judicious, very well-executed work—one of the best for evangelicals. [*BBR* 22.4; *JETS* 9/11].

Swindoll, Charles R. *Hand Me Another Brick*, 1978. Aims to help the preacher with Nehemiah. Weak in biblical theology, it can still be suggestive for sermon preparation. Compare with Boice, Evers, Packer, Roberts, and Thomas.

☆   Thomas, Derek W. H. *Ezra & Nehemiah* (REC) 2016. A strong entry in the series and thorough as an exposition (over 400pp.). [*JETS* 9/17].

☆ **Throntveit, Mark A.** ‡ (I) 1992. Seems thin compared, say, to Roberts's expositional help, but is better informed. This work is more probing and learned than might first appear. Gives good direction to the expositor who wants to understand the message of the text. Throntveit, van Wijk-Bos, Holmgren, and Klein would be the first recourse for those seeking a thoughtful critical and theological exposition. [*Int* 1/94; *BSac* 7/93; *HS* 1993; *CRBR* 1993].

✓ Tiemeyer, Lena-Sofia. [𝔐], *Ezra-Nehemiah: Israel's Quest for Identity*, 2017. Quite useful, brief guide to the two books, as well as to scholarship (T&T Clark Study Guides to the OT). [*JSS* Spr 20; *ExpTim* 8/18; *CBQ* 10/19; *JSOT* 42.5; *JJS* 69.2; *ETL* 94.2].

☆ Ulrich, Dean R. *Now and Not Yet: Theology and Mission in Ezra-Nehemiah* (NSBT) 2021. From a PCA pastor and sometime seminary prof who wrote a biblical-theological study on Ruth, *From Famine to Fullness.* Here the "not yet" elements, mentioned in the title, look ahead to the coming of Christ. Stimulating for preachers. [*JSOT* 47.5 (Williamson); *JETS* 12/22].

White, John. *Excellence in Leadership*, 1986. An IVP issue which sold well.

Wijk-Bos, Johanna W. H. van. ‡ *Ezra, Nehemiah, and Esther* (WestBC) 1998. I find Throntveit to be a much better researched work, but van Wijk-Bos is regarded as offering good help to the more liberally oriented expositor. Evangelicals will struggle at points with her labeling as "prejudice," "sexism," and "intolerance" some of the key concerns of the text. [*JSOT* 84; *Int* 10/99].

F   Wright, Jacob. ‡ (IECOT).

☆ **Yamauchi, Edwin.** (EBCR) 2010. The 1988 EBC was a strong work by an able historian. He chaired the Biblical Studies department at Miami U., Ohio, and pastors knew that Yamauchi was a trustworthy guide into the Persian era and these books. (They were glad, too, that Smick's fine contribution on Job was bound in the same vol.) After writing the EBC he further showed his expertise in Persian-era history with his acclaimed *Persia and the Bible* (1990). EBCR is a full, improved work for pastors (230pp.), superb on background. Weaknesses? The author is less adept at theological reflection.

Zakheim, Dov S. *Nehemiah: Statesman and Sage* (MST) 2016. Something of a political biography by a Jewish, former senior US government official.

# ESTHER

★ **Allen, Leslie, and Timothy Laniak.** *Ezra, Nehemiah, Esther* (NIBC) 2003. Laniak comments on Esther (100pp.), building on *Shame and Honor in the Book of Esther* (1998). He taught at Gordon-Conwell, Charlotte. This pb is among the best buys on Esther (cf. Baldwin, Reid, Firth). Laniak is also an excellent guide into the theology of the book. I commend his overall conclusion, "It is not so much the *presence* of God but the *hiddenness* of God in human events that the story articulates. To be hidden is to be present yet unseen" (185). I still ponder his suggestion that "being a Jew means being the presence of YHWH in the world. We look in vain to find his name in Esther because his identity is joined to that of his people" (187). See Ezra–Nehemiah.

★ **Bush, Frederic W.** [𝔐], *Ruth, Esther* (WBC) 1996. Primarily interested in the form, function, and theology of the stories, not their historicity. For brief discussion of the scroll and history, see the LaSor–Hubbard–Bush *OT Survey* (2nd ed. 1996). Pastors with a scholarly bent use Bush in their study of the original text (noting the strength of his lexical work), and they also definitely want access to Fox's technical exegesis and Berlin's sensitive literary reading for JPS. This is excellent, but not one of the more readable or accessible commentaries in WBC. [*JETS* 3/99; *RTR* 9–12/97; *SwJT* Spr 00; *BSac* 10/98].

★ **Duguid, Iain M.** *Esther and Ruth* (REC) 2005. A well-thought-out, suggestive homiletical approach. In the same series, he has also done a superb job on Daniel. Pastors find Duguid and Firth brimming with ideas they can develop in expository sermons.

★ **Firth, David.** (BST) 2010. A mature, perceptive exposition for pastors. Firth has preached through this book and taught it numerous times in academic settings, and readers quickly realize he understands how the parts of the book come together in presenting *The Message of Esther*. The low price helps make this a preacher's best buy. It is worth adding that students will find some shrewd academic points made in Firth's introduction. Firth did ministry in his native Australia, missionary work in Africa (two colleges), and now lectures at Trinity, Bristol. See also his major commentaries on Joshua and Samuel. [*JSOT* 35.5; *Chm* Aut 11; *JETS* 3/11].

★ **Jobes, Karen H.** (NIVAC) 1999. The pastor or teacher will find much help here. The author did her Westminster Seminary diss. on the LXX of Esther and wants this oft-neglected Bible book to receive its due. Though the main thrust of this work is theology and application, there is a lot of exegetical worth here too. She refuses to pit literary achievement against historicity (31) but also believes "some expressions in the story may have been intended for literary effect, not for historical accuracy as we define it today" (36). In the past I suggested Jobes or Baldwin as a pastor's first choice. [*DenvJ*]. For a slight update on introductory matters, see Jobes's sections on "Esther" in *DOTWPW* (2008).

★ **Tomasino, Anthony.** [*M*], (EEC) 2013 digital, 2016 print. Because in-depth evangelical exegeses are thin on the ground—only Bush from the mid-1990s—I was delighted to find this lengthy work (365pp.). Tomasino, a Methodist minister and capable scholar (Chicago PhD), has published award-winning work (on ancient Jewish interpretation of Daniel) and teaches at Bethel College (IN). After a thorough, judicious introduction (130pp.), he provides an analysis of the Hebrew which is alert to textual issues (MT, LXX, Alpha-Text, Syriac), historical questions, narrative features, biblical theology, and history of interpretation, as well as the proclamation and application interests of preachers. He asserts, "there was no such thing as an 'accidentally secular' story in the ancient world," and at some stage in the book's transmission history references to God were "deliberately banished." Examining the hiddenness of God and "the complementary nature of 'divine action and human initiative' [Clines]," he argues that "certainly, divine Providence is primary, since it is Providence that creates the situation where human action can make a difference" (119). He faces historical problems head-on and is honest about the lack of solutions at several points. He concludes that, while much in the book squares with what we know about 5th century Persia (see his 40-page "Esther" in ZIBBC), "the book has taken some literary license in telling its story" (58). "The book of Esther is, above all, a work of literature" (59). Because of the quality, extensiveness, and accessibility of the work, Tomasino can serve as a studious pastor's first pick; others might prefer Baldwin to Bush and Tomasino. See also Steinmann below.

❖ ❖ ❖ ❖ ❖

Adam, Peter. *Esther: For Such a Time as This* (Reading the Bible Today) 2018. An exposition from Australia, said to be very stimulating for pastors. [*JETS* 9/19; *RTR* 8/19].

☆ **Alter, Robert.** ‡ *Strong as Death Is Love: The Song of Songs, Ruth, Esther, Jonah, and Daniel*, 2015. See under Ruth.

Anderson, Bernhard W. ‡ (IB) 1954.

☆ Ash, Christopher. *Teaching Ruth & Esther*, 2018. Great for expositional preachers.

☆ **Baldwin, Joyce G.** (retired TOTC) 1984. Typical of her always helpful, well-researched work. For obvious reasons you will appreciate her womanly perspective on this particular book. Baldwin used to be the pastor's first choice for an accessible exegesis, though McConville is better at showing Esther's relevance for today, and Jobes is more up-to-date and well rounded (exegesis and exposition). In 1990 Baldwin was Stuart's favorite. See Reid for the replacement Tyndale. I was a bit sorry to move this off the recommended list in my 9th edition. [*JETS* 12/85].

Barkhuizen, Wayne K. *God Behind the Scenes*, 2016. A simple but perceptive exposition from a South African pastor, with prompts for contemporary application. I pass along the recommendations of both Firth and Tomasino.

✓ **Bechtel, Carol.** ‡ (I) 2002. A well-written, more liberal exposition that follows several of the leads offered in Berlin's commentary. The literary reading, with its focus upon such things as characterization, could help preachers and teachers who take up Esther. Theologically, Bechtel is less help than some other books on Esther and even other vols. in the Interpretation series. [*CBQ* 1/04; *Int* 10/03; *JSOT* 27.5; *SwJT* Fall 03; *CJ* 7/05; *BSac* 7/04; *RBL*].

Beckett, Michael. *Gospel in Esther*, 2002. This more allegorical reading, while interesting, is not recommended. [*Chm* Aut 03].

☆ Benn, Wallace P. *Ezra, Nehemiah, and Esther* (PTW) 2021. See under Ezra–Nehemiah.

✓ **Berg, Sandra B.** ‡ *The Book of Esther: Motifs, Themes, and Structure*, 1979. A significant, oft-cited work, pointing to the striking parallels with the Joseph narrative. Students should take account of this Vanderbilt PhD. [*JBL* 100.2].

✓ Bergey, Ronald L. ‡ "The Book of Esther—Its Place in the Linguistic Milieu of Post-Exilic Biblical Hebrew Prose." PhD diss., Dropsie College, 1983. The only unpublished diss. I will mention.

☆ **Berlin, Adele.** ‡ (JPS) 2001. The author here makes a major contribution to Esther scholarship; she maintains the high standards set in her Zephaniah AB. But this work for JPS has a different focus, as she writes for an audience keenly interested in the history of Jewish interpretation. Her literary approach to Esther is laid out in a *JBL* article (Spr 2001). Berlin is mainly for students, and those doing advanced studies should definitely buy this. She identifies the genre of the book as burlesque or farce (xix); she probably does more than any scholar in exploring comedic elements. While she helpfully highlights the many humorous and ironic twists in the story, she downplays any historical value of the text. [*JETS* 12/02; *Int* 1/02; *VT* 53.4; *JSOT* 99; *RBL*; *JHebS* 3].

☆ **Breneman, Mervin.** *Ezra, Nehemiah, Esther* (NAC) 1993. See under Ezra–Nehemiah.

Brockington, L. H. ‡ (NCB) 1969. See Ezra–Nehemiah above.

✓ **Brown, Erica.** ‡ *Esther: Power, Fate and Fragility in Exile* (MST) 2020. A large-scale scholarly Jewish commentary (500pp.), drawing heavily on Jewish interpretation over the centuries, and displaying a knack for narratological, psychological, sociological, and feminist interpretation.

✓ Candido, Dionisio. *Synopsis of the Book of Esther*, 2023. Technical reference, showing correspondences among the MT, Old Greek, Alpha Text, Old Latin, Vulgate, etc.

✓ Carruthers, Jo. ‡ (BBC) 2008. A full and fascinating reception history. [*CBQ* 7/09; *RelSRev* 9/09; *Anvil* 26.2; *JTS* 4/11; *Int* 1/11].

Cassel, Paulus. *An Explanatory Commentary on Esther*, ET 1888. Few know of this large-scale exposition (400pp.) for it appeared too late to be noted in Spurgeon's catalog. Cassel was a famous, conservative prof at Berlin—a Jewish Christian actually—and there is a historical orientation to this commentary.

☆ **Clines, David J. A.** [*M*], (NCB) 1984. See under Ezra–Nehemiah. Advanced students note his Sheffield monograph, *The Esther Scroll* (1984), which includes some brilliant comments on the author's/redactor's literary skill [*HS* 1988 (Fox)]. This same scholar produced the massive WBC set on Job. Sadly, Clines now repudiates his fairly conservative approach in this more traditionally styled NCB work; see "Esther and the Future of Commentary" in Greenspoon–Crawford below.

Coggins, R. J. and S. P. Re'emi. ‡ *Nahum, Obadiah, Esther* (ITC-E) 1985. Notable mainly because commentaries on these Bible books are fewer. This commentary employs the usual critical methods and examines the relationship between the people of God and several surrounding nations: Assyria, Edom, and the Medo-Persian Empire.

✓ Conti, Marco, ed. *1–2 Kings, 1–2 Chronicles, Ezra, Nehemiah, Esther* (ACCS) 2008.

✓ Craig, Kenneth. ‡ *Reading Esther: A Case for the Literary Carnivalesque*, 1995. Representing a similar approach is Andre LaCocque, *Esther Regina: A Bakhtinian Reading* (2008) [*BibInt* 18.3].

✓ Crawford, Sidnie White. ‡ (NIB) 1999. About 120pp. [*ExpTim* 2/00; *CTJ* 11/01].

✓ Crawford, Sidnie White, and Leonard J. Greenspoon, eds. ‡ *The Book of Esther in Modern Research*, 2003. [*Them* 5/08; *ExpTim* 6/05].

F   Dallaire, Hélène. (Apollos). An earlier report was Gerald Klingbeil.

✓ Davidovich, Tal. ‡ *Esther, Queen of the Jews: The Status and Position of Esther in the OT*, 2013. [*CBQ* 4/14; *JSOT* 41.5].

✓ **Day, Linda M.** ‡ (AbOTC) 2005. As expected in the series, Day provides a compact exegesis, well-informed by critical scholarship. She writes well and with insight. Her strength is a close literary reading (especially characterization), while some reviews find Day weaker in research of the historical-cultural backdrop and textual issues. She offers a largely atheological, feminist approach to the message of the book: "Esther, the hiding Jew, is analogous to the closeted gay" (3), while Mordecai the childless bachelor "represents an ambiguous sexual identity" (61). This makes Day unsuitable for evangelical pastors, who might be tempted to query whether she has bought an import license. [*CBQ* 7/08; *JETS* 12/06; *Int* 10/06; *BL* 2006; *VT* 57.3; *JHebS*; *HBT* 29.2; *RBL*; *RelSRev* 9/09 (Sweeney)]. See also her diss., *Three Faces of a Queen: Characterization in the Books of Esther* (1995).

F   De Troyer, Kristin. ‡ (Herm).

Dowden, Landon. *Exalting Jesus in Esther* (CCE) 2019.

✓ Firth, David G., and Brittany N. Melton, eds. *Reading Esther Intertextually*, 2022. A collection of sixteen essays, deserving close attention by advanced students. [*JSOT* 47.5].

✓ Fountain, A. Kay. ‡ *Literary and Empirical Readings of the Books of Esther*, 2002. [*RBL* 11/03].

☆ **Fox, Michael V.** ‡ *Character and Ideology in the Book of Esther*, 1991, 2nd ed. 2001. This highly touted work must be consulted by students; it does contain a commentary (13–130, 274–87). Though Fox thinks the book has historical intentions, and the author "almost certainly meant us to read the book as a precise report of actual historical events" (138), Fox takes a quite skeptical position on the book's historical value: "certainly a fictional creation" (131). Students appreciate the 2nd edition's postscript, "A Decade of Esther Scholarship," though it's now dated. [*JSOT* 55; *Bib* 75.1; *JR* 1/94; *RTR* 12/02; *JTS* 4/03; *VT* 53.1; *JSOT* 99; *JSS* Spr 04; *JETS* 12/02 (Jobes)]. On compositional history Fox wrote *The Redaction of the Books of Esther* (1991). See Fox's works on Proverbs, Qoheleth, and Song of Songs below. [*JSOT* 55; *Bib* 75.1; *JR* 1/94; *RTR* 12/02; *JTS* 4/03; *VT* 53.1; *JSOT* 99; *JSS* Spr 04; *JETS* 12/02 (Jobes)].

✓ **Gordis, Robert.** ‡ *Megillat Esther: The Masoretic Hebrew Text with Introduction, New Translation and Commentary*, 1974. Judicious, conservatively critical Jewish scholarship. A large portion of this slim vol. is taken up with the printing of a Purim Service. For a distillation of Gordis's insights, see his later articles: "Studies in the Esther Narrative," *JBL* 95 (1976): 43–58; "Religion, Wisdom and History in the Book of Esther—A New Solution to an Old Crux," *JBL* 100 (1981): 359–88. It is good to read him saying in *JBL* 95, "the author of Esther has an excellent familiarity with Persian law, custom, and languages in the Achaemenid period" (44).

✓ Greenspoon, Leonard, and Sidnie White Crawford, eds. ‡ *Esther*, 2003. These are collected essays of value to students and scholars.

☆ Gregory, Bryan R. *Inconspicuous Providence: The Gospel according to Esther* (GAOT) 2014.

First-rate for pastors, particularly in its suggestions for preaching Christ. Students can learn here too, as Gregory has numerous insights, some delightful, in his close reading of the text. [*Chm* Win 15; *WTJ* Fall 15].

✓ **Grossman, Jonathan.** [*M*], *Esther: The Outer Narrative and Its Hidden Reading*, 2011. A fascinating study, one of the better in recent years, suggesting the interplay of two phenomena: "dynamic analogies" with characters in other Bible narratives and "veiled messages" in the use of literary devices. The author is a more conservative Jewish critic, teaching at Bar-Ilan, and he uses Bakhtin's idea of literary carnivalesque (235). [*BBR* 22.3; *VT* 66.1; *JSOT* 43.5].

✓ **Hazony, Yoram.** ‡ *God and Politics in Esther*, 2016. A brilliant Jewish exploration of the whole book (moves chapter by chapter), focusing on the topic of politics, and published by CUP. Called a *tour de force* by Tamara Eskenazi. (Note: an earlier Shalem edition was titled *The Dawn.*) [*JSS* Spr 19; *JTS* 10/17].

F   Hill, Andrew. *Ezra, Nehemiah, Esther* (EBTC)?

F   Hogg, David, ed. *Ezra, Nehemiah, Esther, Job* (RCS).

☆ **Holmstedt, Robert D., and John Screnock.** (BHHB) 2015. The broad consensus is that Baylor has done Hebrew students a magnificent service in producing this series. The quality of scholarship is very high. One complaint has been about obscure linguistic jargon in discussions of syntax, semantics of the Hebrew verbal system, word order, etc.; this vol. might be classed as one of the less approachable. But the payoff, if you're able to grasp their analysis (with the help of their introduction and glossary), is huge. Holmstedt–Screnock is a jewel, providing help with the Hebrew that is difficult to find elsewhere. [*BBR* 26.2; *JSOT* 40.5; *ExpTim* 1/17; *CBQ* 10/16; *Them* 41.3].

F   Hubbard, Robert. (NICOT). In his work on Ruth, Hubbard set an extraordinarily high standard of scholarship for the series, of which he became general editor.

Huey, F. B. (EBC) 1988. Only 65pp. on ten chapters. See Phillips.

✓ Kahana, Hanna. *Esther: Juxtaposition of the Septuagint Translation with the Hebrew Text*, 2005. Though focused mainly on the LXX, Kahana pays close attention to the Hebrew text (moving word by word) to evaluate the ancient translator's methods and translational preferences (474pp.). An enormous amount of time and work went into this, but note the caveats in Jobes's review [*JTS* 10/07].

✓ Keil, Carl F. (KD) ET 1873.

Knight, G. A. F. ‡ (Torch) 1955. Also covers Song of Songs and Lamentations.

✓ Koller, Aaron. ‡ *Esther in Ancient Jewish Thought*, 2014. [*JJS* 66.1; *JSOT* 41.5].

F   Korpel, Marjo C. A. ‡ (HCOT).

✓ Larkin, Katrina J. A. ‡ *Ruth and Esther*, 1995. A slim vol. in the OT Guides series, helpfully reviewing the history of interpretation.

Lau, Peter H. W. (Asia) 2018. Said to be very well-done. [*JSOT* 45.5; *Them* 45.2].

☆ **Levenson, Jon D.** ‡ (OTL) 1997. Alongside Bush, Berlin, and Fox, this vol. by a Jewish commentator is one of the finest scholarly commentaries to be published in English in decades. Levenson does not believe there is much, if any, history in the book; instead there is an "enormous amount of exaggeration and inaccuracy" (26). Those less interested in technical translation issues and more interested in a literary reading or theology might want OTL instead of WBC. As a plus, Levenson treats the Additions to Esther, which have been receiving much appreciative attention in scholarship. [*JBL* Spr 99; *JSOT* 79; *Bib* 79.3; *CBQ* 7/98; *HS* 1998; *RelSRev* 10/97, 10/98; *RBL*].

✓ **Linafelt, Tod, and Timothy K. Beal.** ‡ *Ruth, Esther* (BerO) 1999. See Linafelt's Ruth above, and note Beal's earlier ideologically charged reading in *The Book of Hiding: Gender, Ethnicity, Annihilation, and Esther* (1997), the title of which uses the wordplay on Esther (אסתר) and "to hide" (סתר).

✓ Lubetski, Edith, and Meir Lubetski, eds. *The Book of Esther: A Classified Bibliography*, 2008. [*RBL* 8/10].

☆ Luter, A. Boyd, and Barry C. Davis. *God behind the Seen*, 1996. See Ruth above.

✓ **Macchi, Jean-Daniel.** ‡ (IECOT) ET 2019. A major scholarly exegesis by a Geneva professor; the work is lengthy (310pp.) and an adaptation of Macchi's 2016 *Commentaire de l'Ancien Testament* (535pp.). The book was helped along by editor Adele Berlin. Macchi dates "proto-Esther" to the late third century BC and believes the material was reworked in the Maccabean era, eventuating in a text-form that developed into the MT. Thus there is a redaction-critical orientation to the commentary, and I judge the diachronic interests here more prevalent than the synchronic. [*JSOT* 45.5; *ETL* 97.1].

☆ McConville, J. Gordon. (DSB) 1985. See under Ezra–Nehemiah. This was Longman's first choice many years ago.

F  Melton, Brittany N. (BGW). By a fine younger scholar (Cambridge PhD), now at Regent, who has worked on the Megilloth and coedited *Reading Esther Intertextually* (2022).

✓ **Moore, Carey A.** ‡ (AB) 1971. Offered some philological aid, but, like most of the old AB contributions, was "theologically anemic" (Kiehl). Moore is regarded as dated. The approach is somewhat conservative within the critical ranks, arguing for an earlier date of composition. [*JBL* 6/77]. Subsequently, Moore did scholarship a favor by republishing many of the most influential German, French, and English journal articles (1895–1977) in *Studies in the Book of Esther* (1982).

✓ Murphy, Roland E. ‡ (FOTL) 1981. See under Ruth.

✓ Omanson, Roger L., and Philip A. Noss. *A Handbook on the Book of Esther: The Hebrew and Greek Texts* (UBS) 1997. As the subtitle makes clear, this also covers the deuterocanonical additions (263–356).

☆ Ortlund, Eric. "Esther" in *Ezra–Job* (ESVEC) 2020.

✓ **Paton, L. B.** ‡ (ICC) 1908. Some solid work with the MT, which has held up reasonably well over the years. Hardly valuable for much besides philology and textual criticism. Highly skeptical: "it is doubtful whether even a historical kernel underlies its narrative" (75). Paton's reading of the story is astonishingly negative. He asserts, "There is not one noble character in the book. . . . Morally Est. falls far below the general level of the OT, and even of the Apocrypha. The verdict of Luther is not too severe: 'I am so hostile to this book that I wish it did not exist.'" (96).

☆ **Phillips, Elaine.** (EBCR) 2010. A huge improvement over Huey's 65pp. in EBC, both in terms of thoroughness and scholarship (105pp.). The author taught at Gordon College and is adept at Hebrew exegesis, literary analysis (esp. tracing themes), and history of research. She is very well-informed about Jewish interpretation (e.g., rabbinic tradition). While acknowledging the difficulties, Phillips has confidence in the reliability of the book historically. Vol. 4 in EBCR covers Chronicles to Job.

Prime, Derek. *Esther Simply Explained*, 2001. A well-done, edifying exposition from an English pastor in the Reformed Baptist circle. [*Evangel* Spr 04].

✓ **Queen-Sutherland, Kandy.** ‡ *Ruth & Esther* (S&H) 2016. See under Ruth.

☆ **Reid, Debra.** (TOTC-R) 2008. Though having a higher page count (168pp.), Reid is approximately the same length as the Baldwin work it replaces. (This is the first of the TOTC replacement vols.) I agree with those who find in Reid an inclination to read the story as fictitious. She offers less comment on historical questions and chooses to emphasize literary features. Her narratological discussion is very good, by the way. At the same time she generally avoids the genre question: "it is advisable not to put the text into a genre straitjacket, but to be alert to the plethora of possibilities" (34). I find Jobes and Firth more satisfying and clear about genre. [*JETS* 9/09; *BL* 2009; *EQ* 4/10].

Roberts, Mark D. (WCC) 1993. Covers Ezra through Esther.

Rodriguez, A. M. *Esther: A Theological Approach*, 1995.

F Rogland, Max. (ZECOT).

✓ Roop, Eugene F. [𝓜], *Ruth, Jonah, Esther* (BCBC) 2002. See under Ruth.

F Ross, Jillian L. (BCOT).

✓ Ruiz-Ortiz, Francisco Javier. ‡ *The Dynamics of Violence and Revenge in the Hebrew Book of Esther*, 2017. [*Bib* 99.3].

F Schifferdecker, Kathryn. ‡ (Illum).

☆ Schmutzer, Andrew J. (TTC) 2018. See Nykolaishen under Ezra–Nehemiah.

☆ Smith, Gary V. (CorBC) 2010. See Ezra and Nehemiah. Worthwhile.

F **Steinmann, Andrew E.** (CSC) 2024. Expect a solidly conservative, well-rounded exegesis, possibly to be considered a first choice by many pastors. Interestingly, the stalwart, industrious Lutheran author is writing in a Southern Baptist series. Steinmann has published several vols. in ConcC, including *Ezra-Nehemiah*, as well as *Genesis* in TOTC.

Strain, David. *Ruth & Esther* (Focus) 2018. Said to be a fine pastoral commentary (approx. 175pp.) by a PCA minister, published by Christian Focus in the UK.

Sun, Chloe T. *Conspicuous in His Absence: Studies in the Song of Songs and Esther*, 2021. A theological exploration of divine absence, from IVP. [*BBR* 32.4; *BL* 2022].

☆ Taylor, Marion Ann. *Ruth, Esther* (SGBC) 2020. Well-researched exegesis and exposition by an Anglican at Wycliffe College, U. of Toronto. Her main area of expertise is nineteenth century OT interpretation.

Thomas, W. Ian. *If I Perish, I Perish: The Christian Life as Seen in Esther*, 1967. Pastors of an earlier generation had Major Thomas on their shelf, but I recommend Firth, Jobes, Duguid, and Webb for guidance in reading Esther as Christian Scripture. There is heavy, pious allegorizing: wicked Haman going to the gallows typifies how "my old sinful nature was nailed to the cross with the Lord Jesus Christ—executed and buried" (109).

☆ Webb, Barry G. *Five Festal Garments: Christian Reflections on the Song of Songs, Ruth, Lamentations, Ecclesiastes and Esther*, 2000. Offers good help to the preacher (on books where help is very much needed), especially with its wise guidance into theological interpretation. See under Ruth.

Wells, Samuel, and George Sumner. [𝓜], *Esther & Daniel* (Brazos) 2013. Wells has served as dean of the chapel at Duke and an Anglican vicar in London. The vol. is a good representative of the series. [*BBR* 24.2; *JETS* 3/14; *TJ* Spr 15].

Wijk-Bos, Johanna W. H. van. ‡ *Ezra, Nehemiah, and Esther* (WestBC) 1998. See Ezra–Nehemiah above.

✓ Wills, Lawrence M. ‡ *The Jew in the Court of the Foreign King: Ancient Jewish Court Legends*, 1990. A much-cited Harvard study, with wide application to biblical materials.

✓ Yamauchi, Edwin M. *Persia and the Bible*, 1990. See under Ezra–Nehemiah, where the monumental study of Briant, *From Cyrus to Alexander*, is also referenced.

NOTES: (1) For a brief discussion of Esther and scholarly skepticism about the story's relation to history, see Provan–Long–Longman, *A Biblical History of Israel* (2015), pp.400–402. On the same topic one can also consult *DOTWPW*. (2) Amy Erickson and Andrew Davis review "Recent Research on the Megilloth," *CBR* 14 (2016) 298–318.

# POETRY & WISDOM LITERATURE

★ Bartholomew, Craig G., and Ryan P. O'Dowd. *Old Testament Wisdom Literature: A Theological Introduction*, 2011. Does very well at situating this corpus within the frame of an overall

Christian theology and exploring its cultural implications. "The eclipse of creation and the marginalization of the biblical Wisdom literature has left us bereft of sheer wonder at God's ways with his world" (14–15) and hindered us from understanding God's purpose of re-creation in the redemption accomplished by Christ. I like their definition of wisdom. Besides offering an astute theological overview of the literature, the authors have a larger aim: "to open a dialogue about what it means to embrace and embody a theology of OT wisdom" (16). There is much here for both student and pastor. [*EvQ* 1/13; *Chm* Sum 12; *ExpTim* 1/12 (Dell); *JESOT* 1.2; *JETS* 3/12].

★ Fokkelman, J. P. ‡ *Reading Biblical Poetry*, 2001. An understanding of Hebrew poetry is crucial for interpreting every OT book in our English canon after Esther, except Daniel. There is scarcely a better introductory guide than this one for the pastor. Adele Berlin says, "Few books for the uninitiated reader capture as much sophisticated information in such an intelligible way." For his application of the approach, see Job and Psalms. [*CBQ* 10/03; *ThTo* 1/03; *BBR* 15.2; *RelSRev* 10/06; *DenvJ* 1/02]. Compare with Alter's stimulating *Art of Biblical Poetry*, and the much slimmer Petersen–Richards. On parallelism, Berlin (2008) should be read, and Watson can serve as a more advanced textbook. Do note Dobbs–Allsopp too.

★ Longman, Tremper, III. [*M*], *The Fear of the Lord Is Wisdom: A Theological Introduction to Wisdom in Israel*, 2017. Certainly one of the best of its kind, with the bonus of discussing the influence of wisdom on intertestamental and NT literature (300pp.). Longman is especially valued for discussing the latest scholarship on the (now disputed) genre of wisdom literature, as well as for his four decades of research on OT wisdom (see his commentaries on Job, Proverbs, and Ecclesiastes). He seems to have moved in two questionable directions. Earlier he argued that "Woman Wisdom is a personification of Yahweh's wisdom" (*Proverbs*, 212) but now contends she "actually represents Yahweh himself" (24). Also, in his discussion of gender (199–213), Longman is more open to an ideological criticism of Scripture; he appears to label both ancient Israelite society and OT wisdom teachings as misogynistic and patriarchal. [*JETS* 3/18; *JSOT* 42.5; *DenvJ* 9/17].

★ Longman, Tremper, III, and Peter Enns, eds. *Dictionary of the OT: Wisdom, Poetry & Writings*, 2008. As with the companion IVP dictionaries on the Pentateuch, Historical Books, and Prophets, this gem is especially for students. It covers Psalms, the Wisdom literature, and the *Megilloth*: Ruth, Song of Songs, Ecclesiastes, Lamentations, and Esther. [*EvQ* 4/09; *BBR* 20.1; *CBQ* 10/09].

★ Robertson, O. Palmer. *The Christ of Wisdom: A Redemptive-Historical Exploration of the Wisdom Books of the OT*, 2017. Remarkably, both a fresh, creative take and a seasoned, mature theological investigation of this literature. Robertson is extremely useful, and also more useful when alongside, say, a Bartholomew–O'Dowd. [*WTJ* Spr 18; *JETS* 3/18; *Found* Aut 17].

✧ ✧ ✧ ✧ ✧ ✧

✓ Adams, Samuel L., and Matthew Goff, eds. ‡ *The Wiley Blackwell Companion to Wisdom Literature*, 2020. [*Int* 7/21; *JSOT* 45.5; *JTS* 4/24].

☆ Alter, Robert. ‡ *The Art of Biblical Poetry*, 1985. One of the most influential books on Hebrew poetry, offering his own approach to interpreting ancient poetic technique and critiquing the work of Kugel and others. [*VT* 1/93].

☆ Alter, Robert. ‡ *The Wisdom Books: Job, Proverbs, and Ecclesiastes*, 2010. Another in Alter's fine series of translations and brief literary commentaries. They are all very well-done and stimulating.

✓ Balentine, Samuel E. ‡ *Wisdom Literature*, 2018. Can be regarded as one of the best brief, critical introductions. [*Int* 4/2; *JSOT* 47.5].

☆ Belcher, Richard P., Jr. *Finding Favour in the Sight of God: A Theology of Wisdom Literature* (NSBT) 2018. A solid, approachable theological introduction to this literature, with a conservative review of scholarly perspectives. The interpretation of Qohelet is decidedly negative. [*JBTS*].

☆ Berlin, Adele. ‡ *The Dynamics of Biblical Parallelism*, 1985, 2nd ed. 2008. Still the best, most manageable introduction to the subject. Note that the basic text is unchanged in the 2nd edition, which is regrettable. [*ExpTim* 4/09; *JTS* 4/09 (Watson); *JHebS* 2009]. Beginners will enjoy Berlin's "Introduction to Hebrew Poetry" in Vol. 4 of the NIB (1996) [*DenvJ*], while advanced students researching parallelism supplement Berlin's *Dynamics* with Watson (see below); Lunn (below); Dobbs-Allsopp (below); and (if German-readers) Andreas Wagner, ed., *Parallelismus Membrorum* (2007).

Berry, D. K. *An Introduction to Wisdom and Poetry of the OT*, 1995. Received mixed reviews. [*JETS* 12/99; *VT* 46.4; *CBQ* 10/96].

✓ Blenkinsopp, Joseph. ‡ *Wisdom and Law in the Old Testament*, 1983, rev. 1995.

✓ Boda, Mark J., Russell L. Meek, and William R. Osborne, eds. *Riddles and Revelations: Explorations in the Relationship between Wisdom and Prophecy in the Hebrew Bible*, 2018. Much needed, well-handled, and fascinating! [*BBR* 29.2; *CBQ* 10/19; *JSOT* 43.5].

☆ Brown, William P. ‡ *Wisdom's Wonder: Character, Creation, and Crisis in the Bible's Wisdom Literature*, 2014. A superb book. [*BBR* 25.1; *JSOT* 39.5; *JETS* 12/14; *RevExp* 11/14; *JTS* 10/15; *Int* 10/15; *JHebS* 15]. The previous edition was *Character in Crisis* (1996) [*JETS* 12/99; *Int* 10/97; *CBQ* 1/97; *RTR* 5/97; *HS* 1997; *PSB* 18.3].

☆ Bullock, C. Hassell. *An Introduction to the Poetic Books of the OT*, 1979, rev. 1988, 2007. A valuable evangelical treatment, strangely missed by Enns. Cf. Estes below.

✓ Clements, R. E. ‡ *Wisdom in Theology*, 1989. [*VT* 46.2; *JSOT* 62; *CBQ* 10/94; *CRBR* 1994].

✓ Clifford, Richard J. ‡ *The Wisdom Literature*, 1998. From the IBT series.

✓ Clifford, Richard J., ed. ‡ *Wisdom Literature in Mesopotamia and Israel*, 2007. [*DenvJ*].

✓ Clines, David J. A., ed. *The Poetical Books: A Sheffield Reader*, 1997. Essays selected from *JSOT*. Similar is David E. Orton, ed., *Poetry in the Hebrew Bible* (2000), which collects key *VT* articles.

✓ Couey, J. Blake, and Elaine T. James, eds. ‡ *Biblical Poetry and the Art of Close Reading*, 2018. Fine essays published by CUP.

☆ Crenshaw, James. ‡ *Old Testament Wisdom: An Introduction*, 1981, 1998, 3rd ed. 2010. All consider this a most valuable, even invaluable work from the critical camp. Students will wrestle with it and appreciate the 2010 added chapter on seeking the knowledge of God. [*JBL* 102.2; *Them* 2/00; *HS* 41; *SJT* 55.1; *JSOT* 35.5; *ExpTim* 12/11; *BSB* 6/11; *JHebS* 11].

✓ Cross, Frank Moore, & David Noel Freedman. ‡ *Studies in Ancient Yahwistic Poetry*, 1975.

Curtis, Edward M. *Interpreting the Wisdom Books*, 2017. Definitely a solid vol. in the Kregel series. Curtis has the wisdom and experience of a long, fruitful career (at Talbot) to inform this "Exegetical Handbook" on the Wisdom literature (165pp.). However, it is a bit dated—see the appendix on "Computer and Internet Resources for OT Exegesis"—and provides less guidance regarding theological interpretation. [*JETS* 9/18; *JSOT* 42.5].

✓ Day, J., R. P. Gordon, and H. G. M. Williamson, eds. ‡ *Wisdom in Ancient Israel: Essays in Honour of J. A. Emerton*, 1995. A superb collection.

✓ Dell, Katharine J. ‡ *The Solomonic Corpus of 'Wisdom' and Its Influence*, 2020. Issued by OUP, from a leading contributor to discussions of wisdom. [*WTJ* Fall 22; *JTS* 4/24].

✓ Dell, Katharine J., Suzanna R. Millar, and Arthur Jan Keefer, eds. ‡ *The Cambridge Companion to Biblical Wisdom Literature*, 2022. [*JSOT* 47.5; *JTS* 4/24].

✓ Dobbs-Allsopp, F. W. *On Biblical Poetry*, 2015. An enormous and enormously learned OUP issue (560pp.), guaranteed to shake up scholarship. He seeks "to conceive biblical poetry again beyond the idea of a defining parallelism" (4). Newsom predicts, "His challenging analysis of biblical poetry as part of the free verse tradition will set scholarship on a new and more productive path." Why, however, does Oxford torment scholars by giving them endnotes? [*CBQ* 4/18; *JETS* 9/16; *Int* 10/17; *BibInt* 25.1].

✓ Enns, Peter. *Poetry & Wisdom* (IBR Bibliographies) 1997. Gave trusty help in researching wisdom literature generally and the books of Job–Song of Songs, plus Lamentations. Now dated. [*RelSRev* 10/98].

☆ Estes, Daniel J. *Handbook on the Wisdom Books and Psalms*, 2005. A fine, fuller, dependable introduction and content survey from a veteran evangelical scholar. He also has commentaries on Job, Psalms, and Song of Songs. [*CBQ* 7/07; *JETS* 6/07; *VT* 57.4; *RelSRev* 10/06 (Crenshaw); *BSac* 1/07; *BL* 2007 (Dell)].

✓ Fiddes, Paul S. *Seeing the World and Knowing God: Hebrew Wisdom and Christian Doctrine in a Late-Modern Context*, 2013. An OUP issue. [*CBQ* 7/14; *VT* 64.4].

✓ Firth, David G., and Lindsay Wilson, eds. *Interpreting Old Testament Wisdom Literature*, 2017. As a collection of essays, this is outstanding in coverage and quality. Some of the scholarship would be marked [𝓜]. [*JSOT* 42.5].

✓ Follis, Elaine, ed. ‡ *Directions in Biblical Hebrew Poetry*, 1987.

✓ Ford, David, and Graham Stanton, eds. ‡ *Reading Texts, Seeking Wisdom: Scripture and Theology*, 2004. Deals with NT and Theology too.

✓ Gammie, John G., and Leo G. Perdue, eds. ‡ *The Sage in Israel and the Ancient Near East*, 1990. For its time, I can hardly think of a more judicious selection of articles (on the critical side) for the student of OT wisdom. [*VT* 46.3; *JSOT* 58]. Another, earlier collection was *Israelite Wisdom: Theological and Literary Essays* (1978). The latest collection is Perdue, ed., *Scribes, Sages, and Seers* (2008) [*JSOT* 35.5].

✓ Geller, S. A. ‡ *Parallelism in Early Biblical Poetry*, 1979.

Goh, Samuel T. S. *The Basics of Hebrew Poetry*, 2017. Well accomplishes its aims.

☆ Goldsworthy, Graeme. *Gospel and Wisdom: Israel Wisdom Literature in the Christian Life*, 1987. Excellent as a quick theological introduction.

Golka, F. W. ‡ *The Leopard's Spots: Biblical and African Wisdom in Proverbs*, 1993. Pursues a fascinating track—comparing biblical and African proverbs—in his argument that the proverb "is chiefly indigenous, popular wisdom," not necessarily tied to wisdom schools or the royal court context. Others recently have drawn the same conclusion while arguing different points. [*VT* 45.4; *JSOT* 64].

✓ Gordis, Robert. ‡ *The Word and the Book*, 1976. See also *Poets, Prophets, and Sages* (1971). Both are still of value, despite their age.

✓ Hallo, William W., and K. Lawson Younger, eds. *Context of Scripture*, 3 vols., 1997–2002. A replacement for the old standard collection of ANE literature edited by Pritchard, useful for comparative work on the ancient international wisdom movement. This topic generates a lot of work and is controversial. Cf. G. E. Bryce, *A Legacy of Wisdom: The Egyptian Contribution to the Wisdom of Israel* (1979), and K. A. Kitchen, "Proverbs and Wisdom Books of the Ancient Near East," *TynBul* 28 (1977): 69–114; these discuss Amenemope.

Hildebrandt, Samuel. *Vast as the Sea: Hebrew Poetry and the Human Condition*, 2023.

✓ James, Elaine T. ‡ *An Invitation to Biblical Poetry*, 2022. Handles the subject succinctly (about 200pp.), clearly (where others may use much unexplained jargon), and very well. By a Princeton Seminary prof, and from OUP. Her tendency is to stress indeterminate meaning. [*CBQ* 7/23].

✓ Jarick, John, ed. ‡ *Perspectives on Israelite Wisdom: Proceedings of the Oxford OT Seminar*, 2016. [*VT* 67.2; *JTS* 10/16; *JSOT* 40.5; *JJS* 67.2].

☆ Kidner, Derek. *The Wisdom of Proverbs, Job and Ecclesiastes*, 1985. It remains a wise guide, engagingly written. Long on the to-buy list. [*Presb* Spr 87].

☆ Kugel, J. L. ‡ *The Idea of Biblical Poetry*, 1981. Challenges the emphasis on parallelism. One of the most discussed books on the topic over the last four decades. [*JBL* 102.4].

✓ Kynes, Will. *An Obituary for 'Wisdom Literature': The Birth, Death, and Intertextual Reintegration of a Biblical Corpus*, 2019. From OUP, "a methodologically sophisticated appeal not to let taxonomy restrict our view of the conversations a text may be involved in" (Stephen Long [*CBQ* 1/20]). Kynes addresses a hot topic: Do we not need a more flexible approach to genres (plural), with intertextual sensitivity? [*JTS* 4/20; *JETS* 12/20; *BBR* 30.2].

✓ Kynes, Will, ed. ‡ *The Oxford Handbook of Wisdom and the Bible*, 2021. The leading essay by Kynes (not ‡) on the "Past, Present, and Future" is sterling stuff, summarizing his *Obituary* vol. [*Them* 48.1; *JBTS* 12/21].

Lowth, Robert. *Lectures on the Sacred Poetry of the Hebrews*, ET 1815 (*De sacra poesi Hebraeorum praelectiones*, 1753). This was the groundbreaking work on the subject by an English bishop.

☆ Lucas, Ernest C. [*M*], *Exploring the OT: A Guide to the Psalms & Wisdom Literature*, 2003. There are few better, more accessible guides into this diverse literature for the beginning student (200pp.). [*RelSRev* 4/06; *Anvil* 21.2].

✓ Lunn, Nicholas P. *Word-Order Variation in Biblical Hebrew Poetry*, 2006. [*JTS* 4/08].

✓ McLaughlin, John L. ‡ *An Introduction to Israel's Wisdom Tradition*, 2018. One of the stronger, more concise, and approachable intros available, from a moderately critical perspective. This is ripe fruit from a mature Toronto prof. [*BBR* 29.1; *CBQ* 1/20; *JTS* 10/20; *JETS* 3/19; *Int* 4/20; *JSOT* 43.5].

Morgan, Donn F. ‡ *Wisdom in the OT Traditions*, 1981.

✓ Morgan, Donn F., ed. ‡ *Oxford Handbook of the Writings of the Hebrew Bible*, 2019. See under Reading Narrative & the Former Prophets above.

☆ Murphy, Roland E. ‡ *The Tree of Life: An Exploration of Biblical Wisdom Literature* (ABRL) 1990, 1996, 3rd ed. 2002. In previous editions of this guide I recommended this as a purchase, since Murphy was a world authority on this literature. [*JSS* Aut 98; *HS* 41; *CRBR* 1992; *RelSRev* 10/97; *VT* 54.4]. See also his *Wisdom Literature and Psalms* (1983) from the IBT series, and his FOTL vol. listed under Ruth.

✓ O'Connor, M. *Hebrew Verse Structure*, 1980. The 1997 reissue contains a significant "Afterword." Advanced Hebrew readers can also consult Holladay's *JBL* articles (vol.118), interacting with O'Connor.

☆ Perdue, Leo G. ‡ *Wisdom and Creation: The Theology of Wisdom Literature*, 1994. Though his treatment of "Lady Wisdom" is unsatisfactory (84–94) and he maintains a strange distinction between the creation of the cosmos and the creation of humanity—never found in ANE cosmogonies, by the way—Perdue's work is superb to start you thinking about this topic, which is sometimes neglected in seminaries. In several ways he develops Zimmerli's dictum, "Wisdom thinks resolutely within the framework of a theology of creation" (*SJT* 6/64). Perdue and von Rad have probably been the two most suggestive vols. on the theology of these Bible books. [*Int* 1/96; *ThTo* 1/96; *JETS* 12/96; *JBL* Spr 96; *CBQ* 4/96; *JR* 10/96].

✓ Perdue, Leo G. ‡ *Wisdom Literature: A Theological History*, 2007. The fruit of a lifetime of study on biblical wisdom, this is an in-depth survey textbook which includes Ben Sira and The Wisdom of Solomon and which further develops the ideas in *Wisdom and Creation* (above). [*CBQ* 10/08; *Int* 4/08; *JETS* 3/09; *BBR* 19.3; *ExpTim* 8/09; *HBT* 30.2; *VT* 59.3 (McConville); *Them* 11/09]. Perdue goes over similar ground in *The Sword and the Stylus: An Introduction to Wisdom in the Age of Empires* (2008), but with more of a focus on the historical-social context and the international wisdom movement [*CBQ* 4/09; *JETS* 3/10; *BL* 2009; *ExpTim* 10/09;

*Int* 4/10]. I come away from reading this author mightily impressed by his scholarship but wishing he were more impressed by differences between Israel's Scripture and the nations' wisdom.

☆ Petersen, David L., and Kent Harold Richards. ‡ *Interpreting Biblical Poetry* (Guides to Biblical Scholarship) 1992. [*CRBR* 1994].

☆ Rad, Gerhard von. ‡ *Wisdom in Israel*, 1972. A classic indeed! Advanced students will look to purchase this.

✓ Scott, R. B. Y. ‡ *The Way of Wisdom in the Old Testament*, 1971, rev. 1988. [*JBL* 92.3].

✓ Sneed, Mark R. ‡ *The Social World of the Sages: An Introduction to the Israelite and Jewish Wisdom Literature*, 2015. A large textbook mainly focused on background. [*CBQ* 4/16; *JTS* 10/16; *JSOT* 40.5; *JHebS* 17]. Sneed also edited a masterful collection of essays provocatively titled, *Was There a Wisdom Tradition?* (2015) [*CBQ* 4/17; *RB* 124.2; *BibInt* 26.2; *ETL* 93.1; *VT* 67.1; *JSS* Spr 18; *JHebS* 17].

✓ Sparks, Kenton L. *Ancient Texts for the Study of the Hebrew Bible: A Guide to the Background Literature*, 2005. See pp.56–83 for a good selection of introductory readings in wisdom texts; then move on to Hallo.

☆ Watson, W. G. E. *Classical Hebrew Poetry: A Guide to Its Techniques*, 1984. An excellent textbook, probably the best single vol. for one who's already done some serious study. The strength of the work lies in its "catalogs (of literary-poetic techniques) for reference rather than treatments outlining any particular way of reading poetry" (Howard). Watson followed up with *Traditional Techniques in Classical Hebrew Verse* (1994), which was partially an updating of his previous efforts.

✓ Weeks, Stuart. ‡ *Early Israelite Wisdom*, 1994. Revisionist scholarship, said to be one of the best introductions to the wisdom literature (Waltke). Check the caveats in the reviews. [*JETS* 6/97; *JBL* Spr 96; *JSS* Aut 95; *JSOT* 71]. See also *An Introduction to the Study of Wisdom Literature* (2010) [*JTS* 4/12; *Int* 10/12; *JHebS* 11] and his impressive *Ecclesiastes* in the ICC.

✓ Westermann, Claus. ‡ *Roots of Wisdom: The Oldest Proverbs of Israel and Other Peoples*, 1995. [*Int* 1/97; *HS* 1996].

NOTES: (1) See the 2-part review-essay by J. Kenneth Kuntz on "Biblical Hebrew Poetry in Recent Research," *CurBS* 6 (1998) and 7 (1999). (2) Also see articles on Hebrew Poetry in *ABD*; *New Interpreter's Dictionary of the Bible*; and *International Standard Bible Encyclopedia, Revised*. (3) There is a superb bibliography on Hebrew poetry at John Hobbins's site: www .ancienthebrewpoetry.typepad.com. (4) Quite helpful is Katharine Dell, "Reviewing Recent Research on the Wisdom Literature," *ExpTim* 119.6 (2008): 261–69.

# JOB

★ Ash, Christopher. (PTW) 2014. Preachers worldwide sing Ash's praises for this nearly 500-page work, which is fuller and more mature than his earlier homiletical study, *Out of the Storm: Grappling with God in the Book of Job* (IVP, 2004) [*BL* 2005]. It is rich and powerful as a theological exposition and is recommended for pastors. I suggest that, along with Ash and Walton, preachers should also look at Calvin (and Derek Thomas's guide), Ortlund, Webb, O'Donnell, Atkinson, Balentine, Janzen, Jones, and Campbell Morgan. [*JETS* 9/15].

★ **Clines, David J. A.** ‡ (WBC) 3 vols., 1989–2011. A set overwhelming in its erudition and painstaking work with the Hebrew (over 1500pp.). Clines has had tremendous influence in OT scholarship as a proponent of the new literary criticism at Sheffield, as editor of the periodical *JSOT*, and as a philologist, editing the huge *DCH*. I'll be frank here: Clines's more recent work worried me and made me suspect that vols. 2 and 3 would be more ideologically left-wing—i.e., his reader-response deconstruction—and less useful. Specifically, I was troubled by his chapter in *The Book of Job* (1994), edited by Beuken; and by "Job's Fifth Friend: An Ethical Critique of the Book of Job," *BibInt* 12.3 (2004): 233–50. For scholarly types these vols. are magisterial, though sometimes pushing quirky interpretations (e.g., vegetarian reading) and doubtful reconstructions of the canonical text (especially chs. 26–27). The average pastor will never be able to put the wealth of material here to full use. Those wanting more accessible commentaries instead have the other superb works listed here. Clines is Longman's favorite on Job. [*Bib* 72.3; *JETS* 3/94 (Smick); *JTS* 4/91; *EvQ* 7/92; *CBQ* 4/92; *Int* 4/91; *ExpTim* 6/90; *RTR* 9/90; *VT* 10/95; *CTJ* 4/92; *ExpTim* 5/09 (Hartley); *BL* 2007, 2014]. See also his collected *Joban Papers* (2023) for an academic audience.

★ **Hartley, John.** (NICOT) 1988. This substantial commentary (550pp.) ably treats the literary features and theology of Job (see the so-called christological texts). It is well-informed on the whole range of scholarly opinion and provides a good bit of discussion on the many text-critical issues (conservative attitude toward the MT). Argues that the affinity between the book of Job and Isaiah 40–55 is best explained as Isaianic dependence on Job (and dates both early). The vol. is workmanlike and, prior to the release of Longman, was regarded as the best evangelical work. Note that a huge amount of work has been done in Job scholarship, especially by Clines, since Hartley appeared. [*HS* 1991].

★ **Longman, Tremper, III.** (BCOT) 2012. A companion to his *Proverbs* in the same series. Again, I might wish for more interaction with other scholars, but the vol. is pitched just right for studious pastors, who should think of Longman as a good first choice. It provides a fine translation and a measure of help with the difficult Hebrew, is sensitive to poetic conventions and imagery, concentrates on the theological message, and includes mature reflection on the book's place in the Christian canon. He regards wisdom as the primary theme and believes "Job's suffering is the foil that allows a discussion of wisdom" (66). The Redeemer text in 19:25–26 is "an example of [Job's] most optimistic thinking" (261), and "it seems likely that God is the redeemer" (260). The *śāṭān* figure in chs. 1–2 is taken to be "one of God's angelic associates . . . but not Satan himself" (82). Has Longman overemphasized the irritation, anger, and sarcasm in God's rebuke (chs. 38–41), to the neglect of a latent positive message? Perhaps. In his *Literary Structure of the OT* (1999), David Dorsey has shown the multiplied verbal links between Job's anguished speeches, especially the lament in ch. 3, and God's response at the close of the book; this proves that God has indeed heard his servant and kept a record (see 19:23). [*CBQ* 7/13; *JSOT* 37.5; *JETS* 12/13; *Them* 11/13; *JESOT* 2.1; *RevExp* Win 13; *RelSRev* 6/13; *SJT* 67.4; *BBR* 25.3].

★ **Walton, John H.** (NIVAC) 2012. Besides taking up old interpretive questions with a fresh perspective, this 469-page exposition also livens up the discussion by including a chapter-by-chapter dialogue ("Kelly's Story" sections) with one of Walton's insightful Wheaton students. Kelly Lemon Vizcaino suffered painfully since a debilitating car accident. Walton argues that the book of Job is not meant "to give an answer to suffering or to provide a theodicy," and it does not intend "to present Job as a role model" (20). Also, Job's righteousness is not on trial. "Though Job and his friends may believe he is on trial, . . . it is God's policies that have been called into question, and he therefore takes the role of defendant. Job . . . is not on trial" (21). Walton's approach is stimulating, as he treats retribution and the idea of disinterested righteousness. I suggest, though, that both God and Job are on trial. The Bible often teaches that the honor/integrity/righteousness of those who bear God's name is bound up with God and his honor/integrity/righteousness. Cannot both God's and Job's righteousness be under assault? Also, many disagree with Walton in de-linking the "accuser" (שָׂטָן), whom he terms an "amoral" Challenger (67), with the NT's "Satan" (σατανᾶς). I predict pastors may be disappointed, too, on p.218 where he "denies that Job's confidence in 19:25 . . . anticipates Christ" (Lewis [*WTJ* Spr 13]). He sees historical questions as largely irrelevant to interpretation. The book is well-done. [*BBR* 23.3; *JSOT* 37.5; *Them* 11/13; *JESOT* 2.2; *TJ* Fall 13; *JETS* 6/13]. See also Walton and Longman, *How to Read Job* (2015) [*JETS* 12/16; *JSOT* 40.5].

★ **Webb, Barry G.** (EBTC) 2023. About 470pp. of accessible, thoughtful, wise exegetical comment, plus biblical-theological discussion. Webb over and over has proven himself a superb guide for interpreting and preaching the OT; see Judges, Zechariah, and his *Five Festal Garments*. He blends together, as well as anyone really, sensitive literary readings and a biblical-theological approach. The Biblical and Theological Themes section is 50pp. It must be noted that his work here was marked by personal suffering as he battled two forms of unrelated cancer; thank God, he has been in remission several years. This EBTC partners well with Clines's monumental WBC because (a) Webb's PhD was supervised by Clines and Gunn, (b) he uses the WBC as his main dialogue partner, and (c) Webb has "often differed with him on larger matters of interpretation" (xvi). [*BL* 2024].

★ **Wilson, Lindsay.** (THC) 2015. A masterful theological exposition, displaying strong interest in canonical interpretation. As is customary with THC, the vol. has two halves: a solid, concise exegetical treatment (1–210) and a wide-ranging section of thematic and theological essays (211–382). Wilson has given us a wise, mature work—one of the best in the series. In the accuser he sees "the role of one who was later to become Satan as we know him" (32). He is resistant to the idea that Job, in some direct sense, is the word of God about Christ. It's more complicated. So, "identifying Christ with the mediator figure of the book does not do justice to the book of Job in its canonical form. Instead, such an identification proposes too easy a solution that actually domesticates . . . what is meant to be an unsettling book" (318). The author teaches OT at Ridley Melbourne College and has a Reformed perspective. [*BBR* 26.2; *CBQ* 7/16; *JTS* 10/16; *JETS* 3/16 (Bullock); *Int* 4/18; *JSOT* 40.5].

☆ **Alden, Robert L.** (NAC) 1993. Though not written at the same level of scholarship as NICOT or especially WBC, this is a fine commentary (432pp.). Alden's work is helpful and clear, but the reviews are mixed. [*WTJ* Spr 95; *CBQ* 10/95; *SwJT* Spr 95; *JSOT* 63].

Allen, David L. *Exalting Jesus in Job* (CCE) 2022.

☆ **Andersen, Francis I.** (TOTC) 1976. Wrestles very well with Job's difficult message. The few textual notes are quite valuable too; Andersen is a renowned grammarian. This 300-page work has retained its value over the years and been a purchase recommendation in previous editions of this guide. Andersen has multiple commentaries in the AB (Hosea, Amos, Micah, Habakkuk) that are not so theological. [*JBL* 3/78; *EvQ* 4/78].

☆ Atkinson, David. (BST) 1992. Another successful effort by the author of the vols. on Genesis 1–11 and Ruth in this series. I only wish he had written at greater length. Atkinson was recommended in early editions of this guide. [*EvQ* 7/93; *Them* 1/94; *SBET* Aut 96].

☆ **Balentine, Samuel E.** ‡ (S&H) 2006. One of the strongest, most substantive (750pp.) entries in the series, written by the OT editor, this Job vol. makes a contribution to scholarship. Reviewers have piled up superlatives, overdoing it perhaps. The value of the work is not in any treatment of historical-critical questions (which are generally avoided), but in its profound, sustained, and wide-ranging theological reflection (suffering, evil, creation, God's rule). "Yet for all the intellectual breadth and seriousness of these discussions, they are eminently accessible and deeply evocative for the pastoral tasks of preaching, teaching, and pastoral care" (Newsom). This is a purchase recommendation ($72 in pb) for those with a big book allowance who intend to spend a lot of time with Job. I like the less expensive Janzen just as much, among critical writers. [*CBQ* 4/08; *JETS* 6/08; *Int* 1/08; *RBL*].

Students should note his reception-history study, *Have You Considered My Servant Job? Understanding the Biblical Archetype of Patience* (2015) [*Int* 1/17; *JSOT* 40.5], and *"Look at Me and Be Appalled": Essays on Job, Theology, and Ethics* (2021)

Ball, C. J. ‡ 1922. A detailed philological commentary (OUP), showcasing the author's learning in comparative Semitics. From the beginning, however, it was in the shadow of the great ICC.

☆ Belcher, Richard P., Jr. (Focus) 2017. As with his expositional works on Ecclesiastes, the RTS prof shows himself here to be studious, with an evident love for the Lord, the Bible, and the church. The tone of the Focus commentary is somewhat traditional and devotional (approx. 350pp.). His inspiring biographical "About Pierce" sections reminded me of Walton's "Kelly's Story" vignettes. [*JETS* 9/18].

Bergant, D. ‡ *Job, Ecclesiastes* (OTM) 1982.

✓ Beuken, W. A. M., ed. ‡ *The Book of Job*, 1994. Important gathered essays for BETL.

Brown, Michael L. 2019. Writing as an evangelical Christian with a Jewish heritage and good training (PhD, NYU), the author reportedly provides a fresh translation, learned commentary, and then a good measure of theological reflection (about 400pp.). Boda has praised the work: "exemplifies the best in confessional interpretation." I regret I have not seen it. [*BL* 2022].

F   Burrell, David. (Brazos).

☆ Calvin, John. *Sermons on Job*, 3 vols., ET 2022. What a marvelous Banner of Truth project (2100pp.), with Rob Roy McGregor as translator! The 159 sermons (1554–55) are justly famous as representing some of the Reformer's most searching and profound preaching. Previously we had only a selection in the 1952 Nixon translation, reissued by Baker (1979) and Solid Ground (2011). Note that there was an earlier Banner reprint of the 1584 Golding translation of all the sermons in a Facsimile Edition, but the 16th century translations were not very accessible on account of language, Elizabethan spelling, and print quality. See also Schreiner and Thomas below. [*EvQ* 7/53; *CTJ* 11/95; *SBET* Spr 94].

Chase, Steven. ‡ (Belief) 2013. [*BBR* 24.4].

Cotton, Bill. (Focus) 2001. Brief exposition (176pp.), giving close attention to the narrative framework and biography: "we shall treat Job as a real man" (7). Cotton taught at Moorlands.

✓ Crenshaw, James. ‡ *Reading Job* (ROT) 2011. [*Int* 10/13].

✓ Davidson, Andrew B. ‡ (CBSC) 1884, 1918. An old standby, still referenced and quoted in the scholarship.

Davy, Tim J. *The Book of Job and the Mission of God, 2020.* [*Found* Spr 22].

✓ Delitzsch, Franz. (KD) ET 1866. While Keil was a stand-out commentator on the historical books, Delitzsch was unsurpassed in his day as a scholar on the poetical books.

✓ Dell, Katharine J. ‡ *Job: An Introduction and Study Guide*, 2017. On the conservatively critical side, this intro for students by the well-known Cambridge scholar is hard to beat (about 110pp.). [*JTS* 4/19; *JSOT* 41.5; *JJS* 69.2].

✓ Dell, Katharine J., and Will Kynes, eds. ‡ *Reading Job Intertextually*, 2013. [*JTS* 4/15; *JSOT* 38.5; *JHebS* 17; *Them* 40.3]. See also Dell's Phoenix Guide, *Job: Where Shall Wisdom Be Found?* (2013) [*JSOT* 38.5].

✓ **Dhorme, Edouard.** ‡ 1926, ET 1967. A massive work, of interest to academic types, with "exhaustive handling of the textual problems" (Childs). Though it has the reputation of a classic, its value declined with all the developments in the study of philology and Hebrew poetry. As a reviewer noted, Dhorme himself made huge contributions to those developments by helping to decipher Ugaritic, the comparative study of which has shone much light on Job's language and grammar. Thereby he ironically contributed to the obsolescence of his previous work. Still, this brilliant study continues to be consulted for its discussion of grammar and syntax. Reprinted by Nelson in 1984. [*JBL* 87.1].

✓ **Driver, Samuel R., and George B. Gray.** ‡ (ICC) 1921. A great classic, which has retained value for philological and syntactical work.

☆ Estes, Daniel J. (TTC) 2013. The author is well-qualified as a veteran scholar to write on Job; he published Baker's *Handbook on the Wisdom Books and Psalms* (2005), as well as the Apollos vol. on Song of Songs. He writes clearly and has the knack for distilling the best scholarship (265pp.). As expected, the series does not break new ground here with respect to scholarship, but busy pastors will like this. Each of the 42 chapters is allocated a teaching/preaching unit of 6pp. However, along with one reviewer, I can't recommend that many sermons on the speeches of Eliphaz, Bildad, Zophar, and Elihu, alongside only four on God's speeches [*JETS* 3/14]. Those who don't buy the TTC can still benefit substantially from reading his "Communicating the Book of Job in the Twenty-First Century," *Them* 40.2 (2015): 243–52.

✓ **Fokkelman, J. P.** *Major Poems of the Hebrew Bible*, vols. 1–4, 1998–2004. Following his enormous project covering Hebrew narrative (see Samuel), Fokkelman took up the structural analysis of poetry. He examines more the surface structures revealed in *analyse structurelle* than the deeper structures of *analyse structurale* (semiotics). Vol. 1: Exodus 15, Deuteronomy 32, Job 3 [*CBQ* 4/99; *Bib* 81.2]. Vol. 2: 85 Psalms and Job 4–14 [*CBQ* 7/01; *Bib* 83.1]. Vol. 3: The Remaining 65 Psalms [*CBQ* 7/04; *Bib* 86.4; *VT* 56.4]. Vol. 4: Job 15–42 [*CBQ* 1/06; *JSS* Spr 07; *Bib* 88.2; *VT* 56.4; *RelSRev* 10/06]. This set is only for advanced students who have patience with detail-work. There is no theological interest here. His more recent investigation, again emphasizing poetics, is *The Book of Job in Form: A Literary Translation with Commentary* (2012) [*JSOT* 37.5; *JHebS* 13]. Readers should discount all the syllable-counting in numerical analyses.

F   Fox, Michael V. ‡ (OTL-R). Reports are that Scott Jones will be coauthor.

✓ **Fyall, Robert S.** *Now My Eyes Have Seen You: Images of Creation and Evil in the Book of Job*, 2002. An evangelical minister and university lecturer here revises his very perceptive and theological Edinburgh PhD thesis: quite a profitable monograph and surprisingly accessible to non-specialists. An early popular-level exposition was *How Does God Treat His Friends?* (1995).

F   Garrett, Duane A. (EEC) 2024. To be released soon. Worth a very close look.

    Gibson, E. C. S. [*M*], (Westminster Commentaries) 1919. Still of some value.

    Gibson, J. C. L. ‡ (DSB) 1985.

✓ **Good, Edwin M.** ‡ *In Turns of Tempest: A Reading of Job, with a Translation*, 1990. A literary study with an abundance of fresh insights (Stanford). I regard this as a valuable and erudite treatment of Job (496pp.). But be warned: Good is a proponent of deconstructive indeterminacy—there is no one right meaning to be determined, rather there are infinite meanings. [*HS* 1992; *CRBR* 1992].

✓ Gordis, Robert. ‡ *The Book of God and Man*, 1965. A study preliminary to the work below. Gordis was once the leading Jewish authority on Job. Extremely learned.

✓ **Gordis, Robert.** ‡ 1978. A detailed textual and philological commentary on the Hebrew, published by Ktav, with good attention to the history of exegesis. An enormous amount of work went into this tome and specialists fell in love with it. There has been high demand for this Jewish work on the s/h market. [*JBL* 12/79].

F   Gorospe, Athena E. (ZECOT).

✓ **Gray, John.** ‡ 2010. Quite a story behind this work: when Prof. Gray of Aberdeen died in 2000, a full Job commentary in typescript was discovered among his belongings. Clines edited the work and saw to its publication (over 500pp.), commending it with the remark,

"The chief interest of the work lies in its philological observations" (viii). Students of the Hebrew should take note. [*BBR* 23.2].

F  Greenstein, Edward L. ‡ (Herm). Previously he was listed for BerO, and Harvard's Michael David Coogan had the Herm contract. The foretaste of Greenstein's work is *Job: A New Translation* (Yale, 2019), which includes copious notes. Brilliant work with the oh-so-difficult Hebrew! In the opinion of some, however, Greenstein's rearrangement of material (e.g., 4:12–21 is considered Job's speech [joined to ch. 3], and the poetic masterpiece of ch. 28 is relocated to the end of Elihu's speeches) introduces new problems after he has worked well to solve other difficulties. [*JSOT* 44.5; *CBQ* 4/20; *JTS* 10/21].

☆  **Habel, Norman C.** [*M*], (OTL) 1985. Formerly at Concordia in St. Louis, Habel is "mildly critical" here (Kiehl). He emphasizes theology in this astute, thorough study, arguing for the unity of Job and treating the final form of the text (except at chs. 25–27). Like Gordis, this is highly regarded by scholars, and a pastor wishing to build a first-class reference library will purchase it. Crenshaw once called Habel "the best commentary in English." The conservative Anglican scholar Motyer said, "it is hard to conceive that the book of Job can ever receive a richer or more satisfying treatment than Habel provides." Do not confuse this work, published in hb and pb, with Habel's CBC (1975) or *Job* (1982) in the Knox Preaching Guides. [*ExpTim* 12/85; *JETS* 3/87; *HS* 1987; *Chm* 102.1]. In the last couple decades, he took a pronounced ideological turn; see *Finding Wisdom in Nature: An Eco-Wisdom Reading of the Book of Job* (2014) [*BibInt* 25.1].

✓  **Ḥakham, Amos.** *The Bible: Job with the Jerusalem Commentary*, 1970, ET 2009. A large-scale work (456pp.), similar in quality to his Psalms commentary. What I have seen impresses me as a fresh, skillful, conservative handling of the MT; what Ḥakham does not do is lay out all the exegetical options for difficult texts like 19:25–26. In line with some old Jewish traditions (*Baba Bathra* 15a), he takes the book of Job to be a fable (xv). This is translated out of the Hebrew series *Da'at Miqra* and beautifully printed on large (8¹/₂ × 10) pages. The author also has commentaries on Exodus, Isaiah, and the Five Scrolls (Ruth, Song of Songs, Qoheleth, Lamentations, and Esther). Those familiar with the rich medieval tradition of Jewish philological exegesis (פשט) will recognize Ḥakham as one of its heirs.

F  Hogg, David, ed. *Ezra, Nehemiah, Esther, Job* (RCS).

Holbert, John C. ‡ *Preaching Job*, 1999. A thoughtful, liberal Methodist approach, written by a professor of homiletics at SMU.

Jackson, David R. *Crying Out for Vindication: The Gospel according to Job* (GAOT) 2007. I have not seen it, but the series seems uniformly helpful.

✓  **Janzen, J. Gerald.** ‡ (I) 1990. A great entry in the series and an intelligent, reflective companion while reading Job. Never dull, Janzen is to be considered about the best, most thought-provoking exposition written for the expositor and coming from the (moderately) critical camp; cf. Balentine. You are guaranteed to find frequent fresh insights. For further comment on this theologically oriented exegete, see Genesis and Exodus. [*ThTo* 43.4]. Another Janzen book is *At the Scent of Water: The Ground of Hope in the Book of Job* (2009). It is meant to be accessible to pastors but includes some technical discussion for students' benefit (152pp.) [*RBL* 6/10; *BL* 2010; *RevExp* Spr 10; *CBQ* 4/11; *RelSRev* 3/11].

✓  Jarick, John. ‡ (Read) 1998. [*ExpTim* 1/00].

Jones, Hywel R. (EPSC) 2007. A spiritually edifying exposition by a professor of practical theology at Westminster Seminary, California. Previously he had pastored in the UK and served as Editorial Director at Banner of Truth. The publisher describes Jones's focus as "reading the Old Testament book through the eyes of New Testament revelation." Preachers will enjoy this (304pp.).

✓ Jones, Scott C. *Rumors of Wisdom: Job 28 as Poetry*, 2009. Painstaking analysis of the great poem, with some revisionist ideas (e.g., it isn't about mining). [*JHebS* 11].

Kissane, Edward J. 1939. A learned and conservative Catholic scholar, Kissane produced this as an accessible summary of his more extensive work on the Hebrew text (which he could not afford to get published). Clines regularly cites him—then again, Clines regularly cites about everyone.

F   Köhlmoos, Melanie. ‡ (IECOT).

☆ Konkel, August H., and Tremper Longman III. *Job, Ecclesiastes, Song of Songs* (CorBC) 2006. Job is well-handled by Konkel in 250pp. The vol. is a solid representative of the series.

Kravitz, Leonard S., and Kerry M. Olitzky. *The Book of Job: A Modern Translation and Commentary*, 2017. A Jewish work I have not seen. [*JSOT* 43.5].

☆ Kynes, Bill, and Will Kynes. *Defiant Faith in the Face of Suffering*, 2022. A dialogical approach to a biblical book of dialogue. Pastor Bill develops wise sermonic material, and his scholar son Will speaks to more academic questions. [*JTS* 4/23; *JETS* 6/23].

F   Legaspi, Michael C. (CCF).

✓ Lewis, Andrew Zack. *Approaching Job*, 2017. In the Cascade Companions series. [*CBQ* 4/18; *JSOT* 43.5].

✓ Lugt, Pieter van der. ‡ *Rhetorical Criticism & the Poetry of the Book of Job*, 1995. For those with the learning to delve into it, he provides an astonishing amount of detail on the Hebrew text, verbal repetitions, perceived chiasms, strophic analysis, etc.

✓ Manley, Johanna, ed. *Wisdom, Let Us Attend: Job, the Fathers, and the Old Testament*, 1997. A huge patristic anthology, of which only "Book 1" is relevant. Commended by Webb.

Mason, Mike. *The Gospel according to Job: An Honest Look at Pain and Doubt from the Life of One Who Lost Everything*, 1994. Extensive (448pp.), soul-searching, and brief (two-page) meditations based on the story and poetry of Job. Mason's devotional work has some profound insights and is published by Crossway. Not for students. [*BSac* 7/95].

McKenna, David L. (WCC) 1986. Meant to be suggestive for the preacher. [*RTR* 9/87].

Morgan, G. Campbell. *The Answers of Jesus to Job*, 1950. Suggests a fascinating homiletical approach, focused on Job's agonizing questions, which pulls both Testaments together. Job is often neglected in the pulpit, and this little study could prompt many pastors to attempt their very first series of expository messages on the book.

✓ **Murphy, Roland E.** ‡ (FOTL) 1981. See under Ruth. Also see next entry.

✓ Murphy, Roland E. ‡ *The Book of Job: A Short Reading*, 1999. "The primary merit of the book lies in its succinctness and consistency" (G. Y. Kwak). About 140pp. [*JSOT* 89; *RelSRev* 7/00; *ScrB* 1/01; *CBQ* 10/00; *Int* 7/01; *JETS* 9/01; *HS* 2001; *VT* 51.3].

F   Neff, Robert. (BCBC).

✓ **Newsom, Carol A.** ‡ (NIB) 1996. One of the best literary commentaries on Job, Newsom is in vol.4 of the series. The author is Emerita at Candler (Emory) and regarded as a leading American OT scholar. She uses literary theory (especially Bakhtin's dialogism) adroitly and finds much irony in Job. Because this commentary is bound up with Berlin's fine, succinct Introduction to Hebrew Poetry and McCann's (at the time) cutting-edge commentary on Psalms, some pastors wanting to build a first-rate exegetical library will consider purchasing this. [*CurTM* 6/97]. There's more from Newsom in *The Book of Job: A Contest of Moral Imagination* (OUP, 2003) [*CBQ* 10/04; *JTS* 4/04; *Int* 4/04; *JSOT* 28.5; *ThTo* 4/04; *VT* 57.2; *JR* 4/04 (Levenson); *DenvJ*].

F   Nõmmik, Urmas. (HCOT).

☆ O'Donnell, Douglas Sean. (ESVEC) 2020. The author is truly gifted in exposition.

✓ Oeming, Manfred, and Konrad Schmid. ‡ *Job's Journey: Stations of Suffering*, ET 2015. Brief, perceptive scholarly monograph. [*BBR* 27.1; *CBQ* 10/17; *JSOT* 41.5; *JHebS* 17].

☆ Ortlund, Eric. *Suffering Wisely and Well: The Grief of Job and the Grace of God*, 2022. A brief (approx. 170pp.), most thoughtful pastoral reflection on Job and its message. Quite honestly, one of the best books available on the popular side. The author teaches Hebrew and OT at Oak Hill College in the UK. [*JETS* 12/22].

✓ Perdue, Leo G., and W. Clark Gilpin, eds. *The Voice from the Whirlwind: Interpreting the Book of Job*, 1992. A collection of more influential essays.

✓ **Pope, Marvin H.** ‡ (AB) 1965, 3rd ed. 1973. Helpful translation with minute attention to philological details. This has had a strong appeal to specialists especially because of Pope's great learning in the area of comparative ANE literature. Pastors won't find much help here; it will seem a dry well. For another Pope work, see Song of Songs.

✓ Reardon, Patrick Henry. *The Trial of Job: Orthodox Christian Reflections on the Book of Job*, 2005.

✓ **Reyburn, W. D.** (UBS) 1992. A *Handbook* with 840pp. of lexical and exegetical guidance for translators. There is not the theological reflection one would expect from traditional commentaries, but this is quite valuable for helping the expositor explain the meaning of Job's difficult Hebrew text. [*CBQ* 10/94].

Rodd, C. S. ‡ (Epworth) 1990.

✓ **Rowley, H. H.** ‡ (NCB) 1970. Good exegesis in brief compass from a moderately critical perspective. Rowley was a most learned, judicious OT scholar of mid-20th century Britain. His turns of phrase are sometimes remarkable; e.g., he speaks of how, in ch. 4, Eliphaz's "theology has dried the springs of true sympathy" (50). [*EvQ* 4/72].

✓ **Scheindlin, Raymond P.** ‡ *The Book of Job: Translation, Introduction, and Notes*, 1998. "A fresh and bold translation" by a scholar "concerned to break through the confines of conventional interpretation" (Dell). [*JSOT* 84; *RelSRev* 7/00].

✓ Schreiner, Susan E. ‡ *Where Shall Wisdom Be Found? Calvin's Exegesis of Job from Medieval and Modern Perspectives*, 1994. Brilliant, and commended by Webb.

Selms, A. van. ‡ (T&I) ET 1985. Eerdmans would better have translated the South African scholar's much fuller "Prediking van het Oude Testament" 2-vol. set than the "Tekst en Toelichting" work, which I found too cursory (160pp.). [*Bib* 66.4; *HS* 1986].

✓ **Seow, Choon-Leong.** ‡ *Job 1–21* (Illum) 2013. Like Clines, this large-scale exegesis is exceedingly erudite and of greatest interest to advanced students and the best-trained pastors. If you don't have an academic bent, pass it by. Seow serves as general editor for the series and made the first contribution here. Long at Princeton Seminary and now on faculty at Vanderbilt, he is well-known for authoring a Hebrew grammar and the stellar AB vol. on Ecclesiastes. One can say, all Job scholarship must now begin with Clines and Seow. The strengths of this vol. are mature scholarship; detailed, thorough analysis of the Hebrew text; its handling of poetry; depth of learning in OT and ANE wisdom; and its interest in reception history ("Consequences"). Evangelicals are likely to conclude that Seow's theology leaves a lot to be desired; e.g., he views the rude Adversary as "a hypostasis, an extension of divine personality . . . a projection of divine doubt about human integrity" (256). (Cf. Clines whose theological reading suggests the *Satan* reflects more the "dark" side of the divine personality, or is a pointer to "a God who doubts himself" [*Job 1–20*, p.22].) Because of its price and incomplete status, Seow is left off the recommended purchase list. [*CBQ* 7/14; *Int* 1/15; *JSOT* 38.5; *JETS* 12/14; *ETL* 91.1; *JESOT* 3.2; *RelSRev* 9/14; *Bib* 96.3; *BBR* 25.3; *JHebS* 14].

F Shields, Martin A. (SGBC). In the meantime, look up "Was Elihu Right?" *JESOT* 3.2 (2014): 155–70, quite useful for surveying the much-varied interpretations of chs. 32–37.

✓ Simonetti, Manlio, and Marco Conti, eds. (ACCS) 2006. [*BL* 2007].

Simundson, Daniel J. ‡ 1986. This Lutheran OT scholar with experience in hospital chaplaincy has produced a theological commentary arguing that Job is about the meaning of suffering rather than theology (the freedom and justice of God). It may be better to believe that Job 1:22 suggests the justice of God as the central issue, though we fall into the trap of Job's comforters if we treat the issue theoretically as if "conducting a seminar on theodicy at the local university" (20). [*CRBR* 1988; *WTJ* Fall 87].

☆ **Smick, Elmer B., and Tremper Longman III.** (EBCR) 2010. In the 1988 EBC, Smick gave us the product of long years of study; though brief (220pp.) it was one of the best evangelical commentaries for pastors. He was respected as a fine Hebraist (Dropsie PhD) with valuable experience defending the faith. With Smick gone from the scene (†1994), Longman updated the work for EBCR (245pp.); he says in his *Survey*, "I did not conform it to my own approach to the book."

Terrien, S. L. ‡ (IB—Introduction & Exegesis) 1954. Has some contribution to make and is still consulted, though scholars pay greater attention to his later commentary for *Commentaire de l'Ancien Testament* (1963, 2nd ed. 2005). This same scholar has published a huge one-vol. commentary on Psalms.

Thomas, David. 1878. This lengthy exposition, first titled *Problemata Mundi*, might help on theological themes. Thomas was reprinted by Kregel in 1982 and Kessinger in 2010.

☆ Thomas, Derek. *When the Storm Breaks* (Welwyn) 1995. Pastors receive wise theological guidance in this exposition, which is strongly recommended by Fyall [*BSB* 3/98]. Thomas is a Welsh preacher-professor with deep appreciation for Calvin's exposition; see his academic work, *Calvin's Teaching on Job* (Mentor, 2004) [*BSac* 7/06], which can be read alongside the research of Schreiner (above) and Paolo de Petris, *Calvin's* Theodicy *and the Hiddenness of God: Calvin's* Sermons on the Book of Job (2012).

F   Thomas, Heath A. (CSC). To replace Alden.

F   Tucker, W. Dennis, Jr. (TOTC-R). Would replace Andersen.

✓   **Tur-Sinai, N. H. (H. Torczyner).** *The Book of Job: A New Commentary*, rev. 1967. The fruit of a long career teaching the Hebrew Bible and a 50-year fascination with Job, this is a full, learned commentary for advanced students (nearly 600pp.).

✓   Vesely, Patricia. ‡ *Friendship and Virtue Ethics in the Book of Job*, 2019. Represents "an innovative approach within the field of biblical studies" (Dell [*JTS* 4/20]). [*CBQ* 4/20].

Vicchio, Stephen J. *The Book of Job: A History of Interpretation and a Commentary*, 2020. I have yet to see this substantial research (about 390pp.), but it has been termed "an anthology of citations" (Cioată [*JSOT* 45.5]). What I have come across is the 3-vol. history of interpretation: *The Image of the Biblical Job: A History* (2006), treating the ancient, medieval, and modern world.

✓   Westermann, Claus. ‡ *The Structure of the Book of Job: A Form-Critical Analysis*, ET 1981. Not a commentary.

Wharton, James A. ‡ (WestBC) 1999. This 200-page exposition may be compared with Gibson and Atkinson. It would not be an unwise purchase for pastors, though his critical perspective intrudes at points and impoverishes the theological discussion. See the review in *JSOT* 89. [*Int* 1/01; *Them* 6/00; *PSB* 21.1; *PRSt* Sum 00; *CBQ* 10/00; *HBT* 6/01].

✓   **Whybray, Norman.** ‡ (Read) 1998. A prolific scholar on Israel's poetic literature, Whybray here presents a fine personal literary reading. [*JSOT* 84; *Bib* 80.4; *CBQ* 4/00; *RelSRev* 4/00].

☆ **Wilson, Gerald H.** (NIBC) 2007. Published after Wilson died suddenly (2005); how appropriate, then, are his closing words in this commentary! One of the largest vols. in the series (494pp.), well-grounded in scholarship, and useful to both pastors and students. He made his mark as a cutting-edge Psalms scholar and was adept at handling poetry. The theology drawn out emphasizes the sovereignty of God; he sees Job as realizing that his affliction "must fall within the divine purposes" (466). Wilson reads the Redeemer text (19:25) as expressing hope "that God at his core is essentially just, and that he will, if Job's case could only come before him, *necessarily* assume the role of advocate for the innocent and defenseless" (208). He takes the traditional view of ch. 28 as belonging to Job. Regrettably, the adjective "bombastic" is used for the divine speeches in chs. 38–41. Because NIBC is priced cheaply, call this *the* bargain purchase on Job. [*JETS* 12/07; *BSac* 1/08; *BTB* 2/08; *RBL*; *BL* 2009 (Clines); *BBR* 19.3].

Wolfers, David. *Deep Things Out of Darkness*, 1995. A sizable Eerdmans vol. that includes a new translation, essays, and a commentary. The author was a physician who gave up his practice to devote the last 20 years of his life to researching the book of Job. [*JSOT* 72; *BL* 1996; *CBQ* 1/97; *HS* 1997].

Zöckler, Otto. (Lange) ET 1872. About 400pp. of exegetical, theological, and practical comment.

✓ Zuck, Roy B., ed. *Sitting with Job. Selected Studies on the Book of Job*, 1992. Zuck has done similar projects with Proverbs and Ecclesiastes, though with arguably indifferent results. There is unevenness in his choice of material, and the reader may wonder what criteria were used in the selection process. Still, he does provide the student and pastor with ready access to materials that may prove difficult to find. Most of the articles he has selected are well worth reading. [*VT* 47.4; *JSOT* 64; *BSac* 1/93].

✓ Zuckerman, Bruce. ‡ *Job the Silent: A Study in Historical Counterpoint*, 1998. [*JSOT* 84; *HS* 1992].

NOTES: (1) C. S. Rodd's "Which Is the Best Commentary? IV. Job," *ExpTim* 9/86. (2) Carol A. Newsom, "Re-considering Job," *CBR* 5.2 (2007): 155–82.

# PSALMS

NOTE: The recommendations amply serve preachers' interests. There is less, however, to assist students who pore over the Hebrew and wrestle with technical aspects of the text. In fact, we are somewhat lacking in current, thorough scholarly exegeses of the Hebrew. See Hossfeld–Zenger and Böhler; the WBC vols. by Craigie–Tate–Allen; Kraus; Goldingay (BCOT); NICOT; and Ḥakham.

★ **Bullock, C. Hassell.** (TTC) 2 vols., 2015–17. The mature product of four decades of teaching and preaching, this well-rounded commentary is valuable for many reasons. Bullock loves the Psalms, treats each poem in its canonical context (making connections with other psalms and Scriptures), is a careful exegete of the Hebrew, is theologically penetrating, and provides a fresh, spiritual reading of the poetry. I don't know that I have ever simply enjoyed using a commentary more (about 1200pp.). Two quibbles are a lack of diacritical marks in transliterating the Hebrew (e.g., no distinguishing *he* and *ḥet*) and how the Illustrating the Text sections are sometimes less apropos and connected to the exegetical/theological interpretation. If I were pastoring, I think I might make this my first pick. Bullock earned his PhD at Hebrew Union College and is emeritus at Wheaton. Because Baker was in the process of cancelling the series, Vol. 2: *Psalms 73–150* was released with lower production values (pb) and no illustrations. Disappointingly, then, the set does not match, but it is still one to buy. [*JETS* 12/18; *Them* 43.2]. The latest is a 180-page, delightful *Theology from the Psalms* (2023). [*BL* 2024].

★ **Calvin, John.** 1557, ET 1845–49. Free online! Childs judged the Reformer's work here "one of his most magnificent achievements" (2500pp.). Calvin is particularly useful because many of today's scholarly commentaries fail to deliver a satisfying theological exposition. His lectures were born out of his sermons, and it shows in his christological interpretations. (He was criticized, however, by the Lutheran Hunnius in the 16th century for not doing more; see G. Sujin Pak, *The Judaizing Calvin* [OUP, 2009] [*SJT* 67.1], which defends Calvin.)

Calvin scholarship is enriched with Herman Selderhuis, *Calvin's Theology of the Psalms* (2007) [*Presb* Fall 08; *ThTo* 7/09].

★ **Mays, James L.** ‡ (I) 1994. Covers the Psalter in one vol., packing into 450pp. a great deal of insight. You'll find it is rather sketchy on some less attractive psalms. Mays is a veteran at writing commentaries, so this is a mature product. But it is also fresh, riding the crest of the wave of works which focus a bit less on categorizing individual psalms (à la Gunkel) and attempt more of what Howard calls a "holistic analysis of the entire Psalter." "Today . . . the prevailing interest in Psalms studies has to do with questions about the composition, editorial unity, and overall message of the Psalter as a *book* (i.e., as a literary and canonical entity that coheres with respect to structure and message) and with how individual psalms and collections fit together." (Not all have jumped on this wagon, however; cf. Whybray's *Reading the Psalms as a Book* [1996].) Mays's commentary reflects "the abundant energy of contemporary Psalms scholarship" (J. K. Kuntz). Along with Miller's and Brueggemann's vols., the best in the OT series. [*Them* 1/96; *ExpTim* 12/94; *Int* 4/96; *ThTo* 4/95; *PSB* 16.1; *JETS* 3/99; *CBQ* 1/96; *RelSRev* 1/98]. Also worth consulting are Mays's *The Lord Reigns: A Theological Handbook to the Psalms* (1994) [*JBL* Fall 96; *Int* 4/96], and *Preaching and Teaching the Psalms* (2006) [*ExpTim* 3/07]. Pastors, especially those with less academic proclivities, may want to choose Hamilton, Collins, or Eveson instead.

★ **Ross, Allen P.** (KEL), 3 vols., 2011–15. From a well-trained (Cambridge PhD), veteran expositor (see Genesis, Leviticus, and Proverbs), who taught at Dallas Seminary, Trinity Episcopal, and Beeson. Ross presents a full exegesis of the text, making regular reference to the Hebrew, that moves toward his main goal of theological exposition and even homiletical hints (over 2700pp.). Pastors will find it clear and accessible, well-organized, stimulating, and spiritually edifying. The KEL series is not finely, expensively produced—I think of the typesetting—but this Ross set has excellent content, useful even for more academic purposes. See, for example, the text criticism. (With a smaller font and an editing down of "his sometimes prolix homiletic style" [*JTS* 4/15], this could have been two fat vols.) Students should not expect discussion of canonical shaping; he treats each psalm on its own. While the Introduction is pleasingly full (155pp.), there are two disappointments for students: much of the scholarship cited there is dated, and the brief overview of parallelism is weak. [*JSOT* 38.5, 41.5; *JETS* 9/14, 3/17; *BBR* 25.2, 28.1; *ExpTim* 1/17; *WTJ* Spr 17; *JTS* 10/17].

★ **Tucker, W. Dennis, Jr., and Jamie A. Grant.** *Psalms, Volume 2* (NIVAC) 2018. A huge vol. (1072pp.) on Psalms 73–150, completing what Wilson so ably began. Initially, after Wilson's death, I had doubts the series would ever have a balanced set on Psalms. Doubts entirely removed now! Tucker and Grant have produced a splendid complement to Wilson, allying themselves closely with his approach. The exegetical work represented is well-informed by the best scholarship, insightful, and as thorough as Wilson's. Students discover analysis of the finer grammatical details, strophes, themes, and connections between psalms. Think of this vol. as standing alongside Wilson, Block on Deuteronomy, Hubbard on Joshua, Duguid on Ezekiel, and Boda on Haggai/Zechariah as one of the most learned and exegetically fruitful books in the series. Of course, the vol. is also in an "Application" series. The concern that the psalms be understood in their use and application to worship and everyday life brings the authors more in tune with the poetry's original purpose. Moreover, it prepares them to give excellent guidance to pastors, liturgists, musicians, and all readers who seek to draw near to God. (Grant is responsible for Books III and IV, while Tucker does Book V.) [*BBR* 30.2; *CBQ* 7/21; *JETS* 3/19; *JSOT* 43.5; *Them* 44.1]. See also Tucker's *Constructing and Deconstructing Power in Psalms 107–150* (2014) [*JSS* Aut 16].

★ **VanGemeren, Willem A.** (EBCR) 2008. The 1991 EBC edition—still useful, by the way—had almost 900 closely packed pages of commentary from a Reformed viewpoint. The revision is a slight update (see pp.34–37) but not an expansion; the larger font size accounts for the increased page count (1000pp.). Some bibliographies are reduced (cf. pp.39–47, 573, and 880 in the old edition with the new bibliographies). Longman used to say that, if a pastor could have only one work on Psalms, this is it. Compare with Bullock. Pastors will learn much from VanGemeren's biblical-theological approach here. Unlike the old edition, VanGemeren makes up the whole EBCR Vol. 5. [*BL* 2010].

★ **Wilson, Gerald H.** *Psalms, Volume 1* (NIVAC) 2002. Covers Psalms 1–72, and published prior to Wilson's unexpected death (†2005). Even though this is not meant to be a high-powered scholarly work, there is superb, well-informed exegesis here. And when you look at the size of the vol. (1024pp.) together with the scholar's reputation, you know it is a good value. The expositor will relish this. Wilson's Yale diss. on *The Editing of the Hebrew Psalter* (1985) has had extraordinary influence over the years—that is partly what I refer to in my comments on Mays above (the interest in, and emphasis on, canonical placement). For a review and critique of Wilson's overall work, see David C. Mitchell, "Lord, Remember David," *VT* 56.4 (2006): 526–48. [*EuroJTh* 16.2].

✧ ✧ ✧ ✧ ✧ ✧

F   Abernethy, Andrew, and Elizabeth Backfish. (EEC). Another report lists Andrew Abernethy and Michael McKelvey.

Akin, Daniel L. *Exalting Jesus in Psalm 119* (CCE) 2021.

Akin, Daniel L., and Tony Merida. *Exalting Jesus in Psalms 101–150* (CCE) 2021.

Alden, Robert. *Psalms: Songs of Discipleship*, 3 vols., 1975. A seminarian once told me this was his favorite. Alden was a fine scholar but writes popularly here.

Alexander, Joseph A. 1850. Reprinted as a classic commentary from a prof at Old Princeton. Much of the material here is admittedly from the great German scholar, Hengstenberg. As an exposition it retains value. [*WTJ* 18.1].

☆ **Allen, Leslie C.** [*M*], *Psalms 101–150* (WBC) 1983, rev. 2002. A good commentary that, nevertheless, left me somewhat dissatisfied—particularly in the area of theological exposition. But Allen is "very helpful in the area of structure of the Psalms he covers" (Longman). The student will find more to appreciate than the pastor. In the last few editions of the guide, despite some misgivings, I recommended this for purchase because it works with the Hebrew. I am glad to say the revision does more to highlight the NT use and interpretation of these psalms. Note that in recent decades we have all become more sensitized to the problem of ignoring the canonical division into five books, and Allen includes introductions to Book IV (90–106) and Book V (107–50). Students note serious problems with the final forms of certain Hebrew letters in the revision; e.g., μ replaces כ. [*JTS* 4/04; *WTJ* Fall 84; *JTS* 10/90; *JBL* 104.4; *JETS* 9/84; *CBQ* 1/04; *Int* 1/05]. My judgment now of the Allen–Craigie–Tate set is that more diligent students of the Hebrew should buy it, but pastors can bypass it.

☆ **Alter, Robert.** 2007. The fresh translation well conveys the power and compactness of the Hebrew poetry. Alter is a forceful intellect who taught for decades at Berkeley. The 500-page vol. includes a brief, unusually insightful exegetical commentary from a Jewish perspective. Most helpful for its rendering of the Hebrew (few emendations of the MT), for prompting readers to reflect on the nuances of the original, and for its discussion of literary features such as parallelism. [*WTJ* Fall 08; *JETS* 9/08; *BL* 2010].

✓ **Anderson, A. A.** ‡ (NCB) 2 vols., 1972. A sober-minded survey of previous scholarship and careful form-critical exegesis from a middle-of-the-road critical perspective. This was a suggested purchase in early editions of this guide, but now we have Bullock, Goldingay, WBC, EBC/EBCR, ContC, and NICOT.

✓ Anderson, Bernhard W. ‡ *Out of the Depths: The Psalms Speak to Us Today*, 1974, 3rd ed. 2000. Long a standard handbook for reading the Psalms form-critically. [*OTA* 10/00; *JSOT* 94].

☆ Ash, Christopher. *Teaching Psalms*, 2 vols., 2017–18. The veteran preacher and one-time head of Proclamation Trust UK is writer-in-residence at Tyndale House, Cambridge. His first vol. here is described as a handbook on how to pray and teach the Psalms; the difficulties we face in the Psalms; and integrating the Psalms into the biblical story. Vol. 2 is a quick but careful overview of the whole Psalter. Ash told me he has a four-vol. exposition (Crossway) in the works, expected in mid-2024. He is a godly and most perceptive reader of Scripture, who has always impressed me with his ability to apply the Scriptures to the heart. He passed along his recommendations of the two-vol. sets by Hamilton and by Eveson.

☆ Bailey, Kenneth E. *The Good Shepherd: A Thousand Year Journey from Psalm 23 to the NT*, 2014. Surprisingly lengthy (approx. 260pp.) and rather like the psalm's rich feast that the Lord prepares for his own. Warmly recommended, and complements his books on the Gospels. [*WTJ* Fall 15; *CBQ* 7/17; *Int* 1/17; *Them* 40.2]. See also Briggs below.

✓ Barbiero, Gianni, Marco Pavan, and Johannes Schnocks, eds. ‡ *The Formation of the Hebrew Psalter*, 2021. Essays for 2019 SBL International Meeting in Rome.

Belcher, Richard. *The Messiah and the Psalms: Preaching Christ from all the Psalms*, 2014. Seems to take the approach that every psalm is messianic.

F Bellinger, William H. ‡ (S&H). His much-used introduction is *Psalms: A Guide to Studying the Psalter* (1990, 2nd ed. 2012) [*BBR* 23.2; *JSOT* 38.5].

Bergant, Dianne. ‡ (NColBC) 2 vols., 2013.

✓ **Berlin, Adele.** ‡ *Psalms 120–150* (JPS) 2023. Though not a work of great length (about 230pp.), the exegesis of the Hebrew and exposition are astute and have real depth. Draws heavily on the long Jewish interpretive tradition and millennia of liturgical usage. Berlin is selective in her interaction with contemporary scholarship but treats the best [*BL* 2024]. Note her other commentaries on Esther, Lamentations, and Zephaniah, and *The Dynamics of Biblical Parallelism* (rev. 2008).

F Berlin, Adele, and Andrea Weiss. ‡ (IECOT).

✓ Blaising, Craig A., and Carmen S. Hardin, eds. *Psalm 1–50* (ACCS) 2008.

F Boda, Mark. *Psalms 1–41* (ICC-R). Worth noting in passing is Boda–Chau–Tanner, eds., *Inner Biblical Allusion in the Poetry of Wisdom and Psalms* (2018).

F Böhler, Dieter. ‡. Will it become *Psalms 1* (Herm)? After the passing of Hossfeld (†2015) and Zenger (†2010), leaving both the Herders and Hermeneia series incomplete, Böhler wrote a massive German commentary on Pss. 1–50 (40-page Introduction + 860pp. of commentary), published in 2021, which, I heard, is being translated. (I'm inclined to trust reports of *Psalms 1* being written instead by Schnocks and Liess [see Schnocks below].) It is impressive! The vol. does not match up completely with Hossfeld–Zenger, for they were more interested in reception history and the diachronic, esp. redaction criticism. By contrast, Böhler focuses more upon the synchronic. All three scholars are Catholics. [*JSOT* 47.5].

☆ Boice, James Montgomery. 3 vols., 1994–98. A set of sermonic expositions, best used alongside strong, up-to-date exegeses. It proves quite useful to preachers.

F Botha, Phil J., and Gert T. M. Prinsloo. ‡ (HCOT).

✓ **Bratcher, R. G., and W. D. Reyburn.** *A Handbook on Psalms* (UBS) 1991. Over 1200pp. and well worth consulting. Years ago McCann praised it: "An indispensable resource not only for translators but also for every student, commentator, and teacher of the Book of Psalms." [*CRBR* 1993].

Bridges, Charles. *Psalm 119* (Banner reprint) 1857. An exposition some friends use in their quiet times. Could be added to one's library, not as a necessary commentary, but as devotional literature. Has something of a Puritan flavor. See Proverbs.

Briggs, C. A., and E. G. Briggs. ‡ (ICC) 2 vols., 1907–09. Of little account today.

☆ Briggs, Richard S. *The Lord Is My Shepherd: Psalm 23 in the Life of the Church* (Touchstone) 2021. By an expert in OT hermeneutics. [*JETS* 9/22; *ExpTim* 9/22; *TGA* Dec 22; *BL* 2022]. Perhaps the best devotional is David Gibson, *The Lord of Psalm 23* (2023). Cf. Willard's excellent *Life without Lack* (2018) [*DenvJ* 7/18].

✓ Broderson, Alma. ‡ *The End of the Psalter*, 2017. An Oxford DPhil, completed under Barton's direction, focusing upon the last five psalms and challenging the recent canonical "shape and shaping" approaches. [*Bib* 99.3].

☆ Brown, William P. ‡ *Seeing the Psalms: A Theology of Metaphor*, 2003. Can be strongly recommended to students exploring either the psalmists' use of metaphors or the theology of the Psalter. More academically oriented pastors find plenty of grist for the mill here. [*Them* Sum 04; *Int* 7/03; *ExpTim* 11/03; *HBT* 12/03; *JSOT* 28.5; *BBR* 14.2; *VT* 54.4; *BibInt* 14.3; *SJT* 60.3; *Anvil* 20.4]. Subsequently he wrote the 2010 Psalms vol. in IBT [*Int* 4/12; *JSOT* 36.5; *JETS* 9/11], which differs somewhat from a standard introductory textbook. See also *Deep Calls to Deep: The Psalms in Dialogue amid Disruption* (2021), a theological and pastoral engagement with the Psalms as "a little Bible" (Luther), so as to address the "profound disruption and rancorous division" in American society. [*Int* 4/23].

F Brown, William P. ‡ (OTL-R). This should be superb.

✓ Brown, William P., ed. ‡ *Oxford Handbook of the Psalms*, 2014. An immense amount of diverse scholarship is distilled here, treating ANE backgrounds, language, ancient translations, compositional history, reception history, interpretive approaches, theology, and "Practicing the Psalms." [*JSOT* 39.5; *ExpTim* 6/15; *BBR* 25.3; *Int* 1/16; *ETL* 91.4].

☆ **Broyles, Craig C.** (NIBC) 1999. His diss., *The Conflict of Faith and Experience in the Psalms* (1989), was a fine piece with good discussion of form-critical categories; Broyles distinguishes psalms of plea and psalms of complaint. The NIBC is well-done for a one-vol. commentary (525pp.). He is more interested in "the psalms' original use as liturgies" (8) and in treating them singly; he is less interested in connections between psalms and the structure of the whole Psalter (cf. Wilson, Mays). Reviews were laudatory, and since NIBC is priced reasonably, it would be a wise purchase, even a best bargain pb on Psalms. Cf. Longman. [*Int* 10/00; *Crux* 6/00; *RTR* 8/00; *Them* Spr 01; *VT* 51.2; *JTS* 4/01; *CBQ* 10/01; *JETS* 9/01; *HS* 2001; *JSOT* 94; *RelSRev* 7/02; *Chm* Aut 01].

✓ **Brueggemann, Walter.** ‡ *Praying the Psalms*, 1982, 2nd ed. 2007 [*VT* 58.4]; and *The Message of the Psalms: A Theological Commentary*, 1984. His most important articles relating to the Psalms were gathered into one vol. by Patrick Miller: *The Psalms and the Life of Faith* (1995). He is a shrewd and veteran interpreter, and made a major contribution to critical scholarship on the Psalms with his "life of faith" approach. He famously recategorized the laments/complaints, thanksgiving psalms, and hymns as psalms of disorientation, reorientation, and orientation. See Brueggemann's other commentaries on Genesis, Exodus, Samuel, Kings, and Isaiah. As usual, his works are packed theologically.

☆ **Brueggemann, Walter, and William Bellinger.** ‡ (NCBC) 2014. For a concise, more liberal, highly theological interpretation of the Psalms, one can hardly do better than this 620-page commentary. The approach is mainly form-critical, but they are mindful of questions about how the Psalter all fits together. [*JTS* 4/16; *Int* 1/17; *JSOT* 41.5].

☆ Bullock, C. Hassell. *Encountering the Book of Psalms*, 2001, 2nd ed. 2018. An excellent piece of work that a long-ago seminary grad could use as a refresher. One of the best in the series, and I chose it as a primary textbook in a 2010 course. [*Them* Spr 04; *RTR* 8/02; *JETS* 6/03; *ExpTim* 12/02; *JSOT* 99; *SBET* Aut 02; *BSac* 4/03; *CJ* 1/05; 2018: *BBR* 30.1]. See Bullock's commentary above.

Byassee, Jason. [*M*], *Psalms 101–150* (Brazos) 2018. "Drawing on 'christologically maximalist' readings of Augustine and others" (Boersma), with something of a focus on allegory, and written by a Methodist prof of homiletics at Vancouver School of Theology. "Preachers will perhaps be his most appreciative audience" (McCann). Byassee has suggestions for creative application of the psalms. [*ExpTim* 3/22; *BSac* 7/20; *CBQ* 7/21; *JETS* 3/19; *JSOT* 43.5].

Charry, Ellen T. ‡ *Psalms 1–50* (Brazos) 2015. By a prominent systematic theologian at Princeton Seminary. I have not used it. [*ExpTim* 9/16; *CBQ* 10/18; *JETS* 12/16; *Int* 4/18].

✓ **Clifford, Richard J.** ‡ (AbOTC) 2 vols., 2002–03. Turn to this for a concise critical exegesis of the Psalter. Clifford attempts one of the first rhetorical-critical readings of the entire Psalter (cf. Schaefer below). What he aims to do, he does well. Students discover that Clifford does not cite much Psalms scholarship. See Clifford under Proverbs. [*CBQ* 4/04; *JSOT* 28.5; *CBQ* 4/05; *JETS* 3/05, 6/05; *Int* 1/05; *VT* 56.4; *RBL*; *JHebS* 4].

✓ Cohen, A. ‡ *Psalms. Hebrew Text, English Translation and Commentary*, 1992.

✓ Cole, Robert. *The Shape and Message of Book III: Psalms 73–89*, 2000; *Psalms 1–2: Gateway to the Psalter*, 2013 [*JSOT* 38.5; *JESOT* 3.1; *JHebS* 17]. He pursues what he terms "interpsalmic exegesis."

☆ **Collins, C. John.** (ESVEC) 2022. A lengthy treatment (approx. 700pp.) in Vol. V: Psalms–Song of Solomon. The blending of serious exegesis and theological "Comment" with reflective "Response" sections, often focused on Christ in the Psalms, is a boon to preachers preparing to teach and preach. Not sermonic, but there is an abundance of seed-thoughts for sermons. Collins says his distinctive contribution is in developing more fully and consistently the insight that these are "poems intended to be sung: not doctrinal treatises, nor even sermons" (C. S. Lewis).

F   Cooper, Alan. ‡ *Psalms II (42–72)* (Illum).

☆ **Craigie, Peter C.** *Psalms 1–50* (WBC) 1983, 2nd ed. 2004. Once regarded as among the best OT commentaries from an evangelical, Craigie is valuable not only for its superb introduction, learning in ANE background, and solid exegesis, but also for lexical work and its evaluation of Dahood's bold translation (see below). He ably sifts out the more appropriate suggestions. Like Allen, this WBC doesn't often relate the Psalms to the NT. There have been such major developments in Psalms studies since the 1980s that Craigie is not valued so highly now; it's behind the curve. Nelson tried to remedy this, with a measure of success, by providing a 2004 supplement (115pp.) that reviews recent scholarship and updates the bibliographies. Pastors with the 1st edition need not replace it, as the commentary section remains unchanged. Students want the 2nd edition. [*WTJ* Fall 84; *RTR* 9/83; *TJ* Fall 91; *JBL* 104.2; *EvQ* 4/87; *HS* 1984; *ExpTim* 2/09].

✓ Creach, Jerome F. D. ‡ *Discovering Psalms: Content, Interpretation, Reception*, 2020. [*BBR* 31.4; *JETS* 9/21; *Int* 4/22; *JSOT* 45.5].

✓ Crenshaw, James. *The Psalms: An Introduction*, 2001. [*RTR* 12/01; *Them* Sum 02; *JETS* 6/03; *Int* 4/02; *HS* 01; *TJ* Spr 04; *JSOT* 99; *SwJT* Fall 01; *RelSRev* 1/02].

✓ Crow, Loren D. ‡ *The Songs of Ascents (Psalms 120–134): Their Place in Israelite History and Religion*, 1996. A worthy Vanderbilt PhD.

Dahood, Mitchell. ‡ (AB) 3 vols., 1965–70. A wholesale reinterpretation of the Psalter on the basis of Ugaritic studies. Idiosyncratic! You might be curious enough to consult Dahood in writing an exegetical paper, but it would be best to leave it to the scholars to debate his novel suggestions. The fact that Longman, a specialist in the area of ANE cognate languages, dismisses this work outright should make you extremely cautious. See Strawn below, due to replace Dahood. [*JBL* 88.2, 93.2].

☆ Davidson, Robert. [𝓜], *The Vitality of Worship* (meant for ITC-E) 1998. Called a superb theological work by McCann. I'd say that, for the pastor, it is perhaps the most valuable expositional-devotional work on the Psalms from a mainline church position (Church of Scotland, which Davidson served as General Assembly Moderator). Published in pb by Eerdmans, this delightful book often mines the richest veins of Reformed comment, including Calvin. Because of a relative lack of interaction with more recent Psalms scholarship, students will not value this conservatively critical vol. as highly. [*Int* 4/99; *CBQ* 10/99; *RTR* 8/00; *HS* 1999; *ExpTim* 5/01; *JTS* 4/02; *VT* 51.3].

✓ deClaissé-Walford, Nancy. ‡ *Psalms: Books 4–5* (Wisdom) 2020. In addition to covering Book IV (Pss 90–106), the author revisits many of the psalms she interpreted in NICOT (Pss 107–150), but with a strongly feminist reading strategy. [*BL* 2022; *CBQ* 7/21].

F deClaissé-Walford, Nancy. ‡ *Psalms 1–72* (WBC-R). Replacing Craigie and Tate. Among these seventy-two, she did Pss 42–51 for the earlier NICOT vol.

✓ deClaissé-Walford, Nancy, ed. ‡ *The Shape and Shaping of the Book of Psalms: The Current State of Scholarship*, 2014. [*JSOT* 39.5; *ExpTim* 9/15; *VT* 67.1; *JSS* Aut 16; *JTS* 10/15; *ETL* 91.4; *JHebS* 17]. For important earlier work on the "shaping" question, see Wilson–McCann–deClaissé-Walford, *Reading from the Beginning* (1997).

☆ **deClaissé-Walford, Nancy, Rolf A. Jacobson, and Beth LaNeel Tanner.** [*M*], (NICOT) 2014. Two selling points are: it is one vol. (1010pp.) and represents cutting-edge Psalms scholarship (think SBL seminar group). The authors are the most critically oriented ever to write for NICOT; as a result students and scholars are more attracted to the work than evangelical pastors. The trio is adept in handling the Hebrew and extremely well-informed in contemporary research, but there is less attention given to the great commentators prior to the 20th century. The comments for each psalm are signed by one of the three; consequently there is less cross-referencing between psalms. Jacobson's work seems the strongest here. (How can Tanner [540] believe that the world Lennon wishes for ["Imagine"] "is the very same world reflected in this prayer-wish" of Ps 67?) Because the whole biblical corpus takes the figure of King David as the wellspring of the Psalter, it is odd to have the psalmist regularly presented as "she." Another questionable feature is their decision not to translate *ḥesed*, rendered "steadfast love" in ESV. The vol. better serves those desiring a reference tool than those preparing to preach the message of a psalm. See deClaissé-Walford's essay in Gillingham (2013) for an explanation of the trio's approach: "On Translating the Poetry of the Psalms"—Johnston's response is worth reading too. Also noteworthy is "Both Sides Now: A Feminist Reading of the Enthronement Psalms," *RevExp* 112 (2015): 226–38. [*JSOT* 39.5; *VT* 66.3 (Gillingham is astute); *ExpTim* 9/16; *BBR* 26.1; *CBQ* 4/16 (Longman); *JETS* 3/16; *RevExp* 2/19; *Them* 41.3].

✓ **Delitzsch, Franz.** (KD) 1859–60, 2nd ed. 1867, ET 1871. His 3-vol. work is masterful but not easy to wade through. I would argue that it is this commentary in the KD set (and subsequent German editions up to the 5th in 1894) which has had the greatest, longest-lasting impact on scholarship. Delitzsch continues to be cited constantly, and the German work was reissued in 2005 [*BL* 2007]. Students should make use of this, assured that they will be surprised at numerous turns by the freshness of the treatment. Such learning! The latest English edition I found is the Eaton translation (Hodder & Stoughton, 1894) of the 4th edition (1883). The common KD reprints have the translation of the 2nd edition of 1867. See also Kirkpatrick below.

☆ Dickson, David. (GS) 1653–55. The Puritans wrote few substantial commentaries on OT books. The few they did write are mostly on Psalms. Dickson's lovely commentary is representative of their best work. "The exegesis is warm, vigorous, bold and devotional and is highly recommended" (Childs). Pastors who appreciate Dickson might also want to look up the commentaries of Owen, Sibbes, and Spurgeon.

Eaton, J. H. ‡ (Torch) 1967. More valuable than one might think, looking at its size (317pp.). A representative interpretation from the cultic and ritual camp; he buys Mowinckel lock, stock, and barrel. See also Eaton below.

✓ **Eaton, John H.** [*M*], *The Psalms: A Historical and Spiritual Commentary, with an Introduction* *and New Translation*, 2003. Students now take account of this fatter (536-page) commentary produced near the close of the author's career as a Psalms expert, rather than the Torch vol. He continues to read a great many of the Psalms as representing the voice of the king, in line with his thesis in *Kingship and the Psalms* (1986). What has changed over the years is that Eaton pursues a more literary approach, which is in line with the dominant trend in Psalm studies. Grant says, "Readers . . . should be careful to make their way to the appendix at the back of the book as they study each psalm. It is there that we find some very helpful discussion of translation questions and the historical interpretation of the text. . . . This is a truly sympathetic commentary with a great grasp of the tone and spiritual purpose" of each psalm. [*CBQ* 4/05; *JTS* 4/05; *VT* 56.4; *ExpTim* 12/04; *Anvil* 21.4; *EuroJTh* 16.2 (Grant)]. A more devotional and popular reading is *Psalms for Life: Hearing and Praying the Book of Psalms* (2006) [*RTR* 4/08; *BL* 2008].

F   Elliott, Mark W. *Psalms 42–72* (ITC) 2024.

☆   **Estes, Daniel J.** *Psalms 73–150* (NAC) 2019. The first installment of a two-vol. set, which distills much learning and takes an approach Estes terms "ecclesial biblical theology" (after Leithart). Without ignoring canonical ordering and connections among psalms, he chooses to focus on "the primary task of appreciating what each individual psalm is communicating in its own right" and each text's poetic and rhetorical devices. What makes the poem distinctive? How did these songs as "performed texts . . . affect those who sing them"? There is a maturity here, with regard to decades of university teaching and long experience in church work, but I also find evidence of his fresh research. Due to "a good deal of textual fluidity in the superscriptions" (MT, LXX, DSS), he makes only light use of them. For pastors, an excellent commentary, inexpensive for its size (650pp.).

☆   Eveson, Philip. (Welwyn) 2 vols. 2015. Refreshing, wonderfully mature Christian interpretation. Any Bible-believing pastor would relish this exposition (over 950pp.), written by a Welsh former pastor (Presbyterian) and Principal of London Theological Seminary. Eveson is an astute reader, with much to teach, and, even more importantly, he has a heart attuned to the God of the Psalter. He has many of what I term sermon seed-thoughts. See Ash above. [*Chm* Aut 16].

F   Firth, David G. (Apollos). Wenham was originally slated to produce this.

☆   Firth, David G., and Philip S. Johnston, eds. *Interpreting the Psalms*, 2005. These collected essays are just right for introducing seminarians to developments in the field of Psalms scholarship. The British edition orders the editors as Johnston and Firth. [*Chm* Spr 07; *CBQ* 4/07; *BL* 2006; *VT* 57.4; *BSac* 1/07; *CJ* 4/07; *ExpTim* 7/06; *Evangel* Aut 07; *Anvil* 23.3].

✓   Flint, Peter, and Patrick Miller, eds. ‡ *The Book of Psalms: Composition and Reception*, 2005. Contains cutting-edge scholarship. [*JTS* 4/06; *VT* 57.3; *CurTM* 8/06].

✓   **Fokkelman, J. P.** ‡ *Major Poems of the Hebrew Bible: At the Interface of Prosody and Structural Analysis*, Vol. 2, 2000; Vol. 3, 2003. Extremely detailed structural analysis (see under Job) with scarcely any theological points. [*CBQ* 7/01, 7/04; *JSOT* 28.5]. He also published a large (A4 size) printing of the Hebrew text, divided into cola, verses, and strophes: *The Psalms in Form: The Hebrew Psalter in its Poetic Shape* (2002).

✓   Foster, Robert L., and David M. Howard, eds. *"My Words Are Lovely": Studies in the Rhetoric of the Psalms*, 2008. [*BL* 2009; *JHebS* 2009].

☆   Futato, Mark D. (CorBC) 2009. Paired with Schwab on Proverbs in a 669-page vol. The two commentaries are sound guides, accessible to educated lay readers. Futato has published both a popular introduction to the Psalter, *Transformed by Praise* (2002), and a more technical exegetical handbook, *Interpreting the Psalms* (2007). The latter is a dependable tool for seminarians beginning to use Hebrew in exegesis and for pastors wanting something like a refresher course [*BTB* 2/08; *JETS* 9/08; *BL* 2009; *HBT* 31.2].

F    Geller, Stephen. ‡ (Herm). This Jewish scholar used to teach at Dropsie and earlier did some of the very best work on parallelism in Hebrew poetry. This then would be a companion to Hossfeld–Zenger.

✓    **Gerstenberger, E. S.** ‡ *Psalms, Part 1: With an Introduction to Cultic Poetry* (FOTL) 1989; *Psalms, Part 2, and Lamentations* (FOTL) 2001. A big name in Psalms study—"perhaps the most disciplined and intentional form critic of the present generation of scholars of the Hebrew Bible" (Brueggemann)! Gerstenberger is only for advanced students. Along with Westermann and Kraus, he has urged some important revisions of Gunkel's form-critical categories. Of greater value for Psalms than Lamentations. [*Bib* 71.3; *JETS* 6/92; *Int* 1/91; *Them* 10/91; *HS* 1990; *Them* Spr 04; *BSac* 10/03; *JTS* 10/02; *JSS* Spr 03; *VT* 53.1; *JSOT* 99].

✓    Gillingham, Susan. *Psalms through the Centuries* (BBC) 2008, 2018, 2022. Three vols. of reception history, generating excitement among many, especially in Britain. I predict this set will have long-enduring value. Cf. Holladay below. [*ExpTim* 7/09; *Int* 4/10 (McCann); *Anvil* 26.3–4 (Firth); *JTS* 10/13; *JSOT* 47.5; *CBQ* 4/24]. See also *A Journey of Two Psalms: The Reception of Psalms 1 and 2 in Jewish and Christian Tradition* (OUP, 2014) [*CBQ* 4/15; *JJS* 66.1]. Further, Gillingham has a widely used introduction: *The Poems and Psalms of the Hebrew Bible* (OUP, 1994).

✓    Gillingham, Susan, ed. ‡ *Jewish and Christian Approaches to the Psalms*, 2013. Most stimulating, from a 2010 Oxford conference. Hossfeld and Steiner contribute "Problems and Prospects in Psalter Studies" (240–58). [*CBQ* 4/14; *JTS* 4/14; *Int* 7/14; *JSOT* 39.5; *JSS* Spr 15; *ExpTim* 7/14; *JESOT* 3.1; *VT* 65.4].

F    Gillmayr-Bucher, Susanne. ‡ *Psalms III (90–106)* (Illum).

     Goldingay, John. *Songs in a Strange Land: Psalms 42–51* (was BST) 1977. See BCOT.

☆    **Goldingay, John.** [𝓜], (BCOT) 3 vols., 2006–08. The fullest exegesis and theological exposition of the Psalms (near 2200pp.) to be published in a long time, but there is a caveat for pastors. Goldingay treats the Psalms mostly within their OT context, and so the commentary may be considered deficient by those wanting a more forthrightly Christian or NT-related interpretation. In this respect his work is different from others in the BCOT series. The best Christian reflection in these vols., what there is, comes from quotes of church fathers and Reformers. Goldingay is less interested in the older diachronic methods and prefers to treat the final form of the Hebrew. He's also not enamored of the newer questions about the shape and shaping of the Psalter as a whole book; his focus is the individual psalm. (But as my friend Steffen Jenkins says, this does not stop him from making some brilliant connections with surrounding psalms.) His basic interpretive questions are form-critical: what categories of psalms do we perceive, and what was their use in the community of faith? The author is a British evangelical who has published widely in the fields of exegesis (see Genesis, Joshua, Isaiah, Jeremiah, and Daniel), hermeneutics, and biblical theology; for an assessment of his critical views in this commentary, see VanGemeren [*Them* 11/09]. These nicely bound vols. are accessible to pastors, many of whom will make this purchase. [*CBQ* 10/08; *Int* 10/07, 7/11; *BL* 2007, 2008, 2010; *VT* 59.1, 59.4; *ExpTim* 2/09; *JETS* 3/08, 12/09, 3/10; *RBL; JHebS* 2009 (McCann); *BSac* 7/08; *BBR* 19.2, 19.4].

✓    **Goulder, Michael D.** ‡ *Studies in the Psalter I–IV* (JSOTSup) 4 Vols, 1982–1998. A huge project spanning many years. Goulder is a trenchant critic who is unafraid to challenge consensus (with wit) where he believes it necessary. There is both much detailed exegesis of individual psalms and a general interpretive scheme which places great weight on the psalms' order. This is a set for students to consult; it is of little account to pastors. [*EvQ* 1/01; *JSS* Spr 01].

☆    Greidanus, Sidney. *Preaching Christ from the Psalms*, 2016. One of the last in an eminently useful series—see Genesis, Leviticus, Ecclesiastes, Daniel. [*BBR* 28.2; *JSOT* 41.5].

☆    **Grogan, Geoffrey W.** (THC) 2008. A delightful, brief theological exposition with select exegetical notes on the Hebrew. Gillingham is correct to say it suffers somewhat on account of its brevity. I can think of few better introductory guides into the Psalter's theology than the 200-page concluding section: "Theological Horizons of Psalms." [*RTR* 12/08; *VT* 59.1; *JETS* 12/09; *BL* 2009; *BTB* 2/10; *CBQ* 10/09; *ExpTim* 7/09 (Gillingham); *RTR* 12/10]. Earlier he wrote *Prayer, Praise & Prophecy: A Theology of the Psalms* (2001).

✓ Gunkel, Hermann. ‡ *Introduction to the Psalms: The Genres of the Religious Lyric of Israel*, 1933, ET 1998. The classic of early form-critical scholarship on Psalms. Still influential. [*JETS* 12/99; *Int* 7/99].

✓ Ḥakham, Amos. *The Bible: Psalms with the Jerusalem Commentary*, 3 vols., 1979–81, ET 2003. This large-scale work (1400pp.) is a translation from the Hebrew series *Da'at Miqra* and deserves to be better known. Barry Eichler sums up its strengths: "articulate exposition of the Psalms, often reflecting the discerning insights of classical Jewish exegesis . . . lucid translation . . . with a serious philological commentary containing grammatical and textual notes." I would add that Ḥakham highlights many psalm parallels (a kind of *intra*textuality). The tone of the commentary is devout, conservative (Judaism), and theological—scarcely anything here might be termed higher-critical. If you sample this, you will use it again and again. See also Ḥakham under Job.

☆ **Hamilton, James M., Jr.** (EBTC) 2 vols., 2021. About 1200pp., including both the CSB and author's own translation. I was pleased to see a measure of discussion of the editing of the Psalms (canonical context) and connections among the poems. Puts forward the idea that an overarching "narrative message of the Psalter was David's own idea," and later psalmists "added to the project" (50). That seems quite a stretch. Much learning here, yet its theological exposition is accessible, breathing out a love for Scripture. Valuable for preachers, some of whom now speak of this set as their favorite Psalms commentary. Any drawbacks? Hamilton states his working "hypothesis," that "a psalm's superscription comes from the hand of the psalm's author" (50). All well and good, but he seems to dismiss summarily the careful scholarship of those who wrestle with the real and extensive problem of textual pluriformity: variation between the Hebrew and LXX in the titles. [*JETS* 6/22; *JSOT* 47.5 (Gillingham); *Them* 47.3].

Harman, Allan M. (Mentor) 1998. A briefer (450pp.) theological exposition from a conservative Presbyterian scholar in Australia. What is confusing perhaps is that the author has rewritten and expanded the whole commentary in two vols. (2011). The new set is both exegetical and devotional, thoughtful, and the product of one who seems to live in the Psalms. [*Chm* Aut 13].

✓ Holladay, William L. ‡ *The Psalms through Three Thousand Years: Prayerbook of a Cloud of Witnesses*, 1993. There is nothing like this and Gillingham's BBC for appreciating the history of Jewish and Christian use of the Psalms. Another resource is Attridge and Fassler, eds., *Psalms in Community: Jewish and Christian Textual, Liturgical, and Artistic Traditions* (SBL, 2003) [*JNES* 4/10].

Holtvlüwer, Peter H., ed. *Christ's Psalms, Our Psalms*, 4 vols., 2020. An enormous exposition I have not seen, coming out of the Canadian Reformed Church. [*JETS* 6/21].

Hopkins, Denise Dombkowski. ‡ *Psalms: Books 2–3* (Wisdom) 2016. [*Int* 10/18; *JSOT* 42.5].

✓ **Hossfeld, Frank-Lothar, and Erich Zenger.** ‡ *Psalms 2* (Herm) 2000, ET 2005; *Psalms 3* (Herm) 2008, ET 2011. Most stimulating. For specialists there is an astonishing amount of learning in these vols., each covering 50 psalms. "Two themes run through their commentary like a crimson thread: poetics and the interplay of anthropology and theology" (Crenshaw [*CBQ* 10/12]). As one would expect from Hermeneia, Hossfeld and Zenger present a technical exegesis and take up questions related to the psalms' compositional/redactional history. They tend to attribute rather late dates to individual psalms. They are also interested in the overall message of the Psalter and the relation between the part (the individual psalm) and the whole. The set pays close attention to what might be termed an intertextuality of text production and reception. (In passing let me note that Vesco's French commentary is brilliant for a canonical reading too.) Advanced students will interact with their conclusions, but few pastors will pay the price for this expensive work. After the death of Zenger (†2010), we wondered if *Psalms 1* (Psalms 1–50) would ever appear; it was to include their Introduction. German-readers can consult their 310-page *Die Psalmen I: Psalm 1–50* in *Die Neue Echter Bibel* (1993). See Böhler (above) for a possible *Psalms 1* in the series; more likely is a 2022 report I have from Beat Weber of a vol. by Schnocks and Liess (see below). [*CTJ* 4/06; *Int* 4/07, 4/13; *BL* 2006, 2014; *RelSRev* 1/07, 9/13; *BSac* 4/08; *RBL*; *ExpTim* 7/06; *EuroJTh* 16.2, 18.2; *BBR* 23.1; *VT* 63.3].

✓ Howard, David M., and Andrew J. Schmutzer, eds. *Reading the Psalms Theologically*, 2023. Among the essays is Howard–Snearly, "Reading the Psalter as a Unified Book: Recent Trends." See also the Psalms essays in *JETS* 9/23. [*Them* 48.2; *BL* 2024].

✓ Human, D. J., and G. J. Steyn, eds. ‡ *Psalms and Hebrews: Studies in Reception*, 2010. "Project Psalms" out of Pretoria has sponsored conferences since 2002. This is one of many LHBOTS publications from those annual meetings. [*VT* 64.2; *Them* 5/11]. See also *Psalmody and Liturgy* (2004), *Psalms and Mythology* (2007); *Psalmody and Poetry in OT Ethics* (2012).

✓ Hunter, Alastair G. ‡ (Read) 1999. Not a full commentary, but a stimulating attempt to coordinate older methods with newer literary (often postmodern) approaches. [*ExpTim* 4/00; *Int* 7/01]. See also *An Introduction to the Psalms* (2008) [*BL* 2009; *BBR* 21.1].

✓ Jacobson, Rolf A., ed. ‡ *Soundings in the Theology of the Psalms: Perspectives and Methods in Contemporary Scholarship*, 2011. [*JSOT* 35.5; *VT* 61.4, 62.2; *BibInt* 20.4; *JESOT* 1.2].

✓ Janowski, Bernd. ‡ *Arguing with God: A Theological Anthropology of the Psalms*, 2013. [*CBQ* 1/15; *RevExp* 11/14].

☆ Jenkins, Steffen G. *Imprecations in the Psalms: Love for Enemies in Hard Places*, 2022. My colleague's diss., completed under Gordon Wenham, breaks new ground as a sensitive rereading of this poetry, within the overall shape of the Psalter, as not ultimately and bitterly retributive in nature. He insists that imprecations be interpreted firstly in their immediate literary contexts: surrounding psalms, and the book of Psalms. (His particular focus is Pss 1–3, 7, 18, and Book V.) "Even imprecatory psalms show concern for the welfare of the enemy, including not only leniency in punishment but also forgiveness and a desire for their repentance and blessing" (272). Hunter says this "is one of those rare works which should make a real change in the way scholars . . . can make sense of what at first sight appear to be alienating ancient materials" [*JSOT* 47.5]. [*ExpTim* 7/23; *SBJT* 26.3; *TGA* 9/23; *JETS* 12/22].

Johnston, James. *The Psalms: Vol. 1, Psalms 1 to 41* (PTW) 2015. The author has a TEDS PhD, pastors Tulsa Bible Church, and is a visiting lecturer at Jordan Evangelical Seminary. Regrettably, I have not seen it. [*JETS* 9/15].

F Jones, Scott. *Psalms I (1–41)* (Illum).

F Katanacho, Yohanna. (SGBC). Previously Elizabeth Hayes was listed.

☆ **Kidner, Derek.** (KCC, retired TOTC) 2 vols., 1973–75. Over the years I've often started with Kidner, especially for quick reference. He never fails me when I am looking for theological insights. Kidner offered a discerning corrective for the cultic interpretations in the older, more critical commentaries (e.g., Weiser and sometimes Anderson). This was a favorite of Stuart and Longman. In most previous editions of my guide, Kidner was a recommended purchase. See Longman below. [*JETS* 3/75, 12/76].

✓ **Kirkpatrick, A. F.** (CBSC) 1892–1902. Reprinted long ago in Baker's Thornapple series and by Scripture Truth Book Co. Definitely one of the best in the OT section of the old Cambridge series. I have found great profit in this solidly packed vol. (100pp. of introduction, 850pp. of commentary), which follows the old conservative grammatico-historical approach we also see in Delitzsch. Though dated, it retains value. Kirkpatrick's prose is elegant.

Kissane, Edward J. [𝓜], 2 vols., 1953–54. A famous pre-Vatican II Catholic work.

Knight, George A. F. [𝓜], (DSB) 2 vols., 1982. Over 700pp. of fine theological exposition and devotional reflection. The author (†2002) was both a missionary and a conservatively critical OT scholar in Britain. Worth looking up.

F   Knowles, Melody. ‡ *Psalms III (97–155)* (Illum). That title contains no typo; in the LXX there is Psalm 151, and in the Syriac and a Qumran scroll there are extra psalms.

✓   **Kraus, Hans-Joachim.** ‡ (ContC) 2 vols., ET 1987–89. Translated out of BKAT (1961–66; rev. 1978), together with the author's *Theology of the Psalms* (ET 1986) [*JBL* 101.2]. The set has been quite important and totals about 1100pp. Scholars are presently wrestling with the "problem of how to evaluate justly the relative proportions of individual creativity and social convention in the process of poetic composition" (Gerstenberger). Kraus argues that they should be viewed more as private compositions, which is the more traditional view. He also refines the form-critical categories which have customarily been used in cataloging the Psalms. Indispensable for scholars, this has been one of my favorite technical commentaries. The more historical approach here, however, has become dated. [*TJ* Fall 91; *CBQ* 7/91; *Int* 4/91; *ExpTim* 1/92; *ThTo* 46.2].

✓   Laurence, Trevor. *Cursing with God: The Imprecatory Psalms and the Ethics of Christian Prayer,* 2022. Based on an Exeter PhD and published by Baylor. Laurence combines redemptive-historical (biblical-theological), narrative ethics, and liturgical performance approaches, arguing "that prayerful enactment of the imprecatory psalms is an obligatory exercise of the church's God-given calling as a royal priesthood in God's story" (blurb) [*BL* 2024]. Cf. Jenkins above, Kit Barker's *Imprecation as Divine Discourse: Speech Act Theory, Dual Authorship, and Theological Interpretation* (2016) [*BBR* 28.2], and the works cited in Note #1 below.

Lennox, Stephen J. *Psalms: A Bible Commentary in the Wesleyan Tradition,* 1999.

Leupold, H. C. 1959. Once listed as "the best commentary on this book" (TEDS annotated bibliography), Leupold is not as penetrating as other works and appeared before the later 20th century explosion of research into Hebrew poetry. Helpful for gaining insight into conservative Lutheran theological interpretation.

✓   Lewis, C. S. *Reflections on the Psalms,* 1958. A delightful, insightful, very quotable little book, but I can't recommend following him on imprecations. See Collins above.

Limburg, James. ‡ (WestBC) 2000. The largest vol. in the series thus far at 500pp. (one of the best too), Limburg is useful to consult for a moderately critical exposition. The reviews have been warm. For preachers. [*ExpTim* 5/01; *CBQ* 10/01; *JETS* 3/02; *Int* 1/02; *VT* 53.1; *JSOT* 94; *BBR* 12.1; *Them* Sum 05; *Anvil* 18.4 (Johnston)].

✓   Linville, James R. "Psalm 22:17B: A New Guess," *JBL* 124 (2005): 733–44. How do we read 22:16 (English text), which contains "one of the most vexed lexical problems in biblical interpretation"? Linville surveys the many suggestions and offers his own (which I do not follow). Many commentaries are frankly disappointing on this crux, and I wish more reckoned fully with the evidence from the DSS (4QPs^f) and especially the Naḥal Ḥever scrap from the 1st century AD (5/6ḤevPs, Col. XI, frag. 9; see *DJD*, vol.38, pp.159–60, and Plate XXVII), which seems to corroborate the minority of Hebrew MSS (כארו) and the readings in the ancient versions, including the LXX (ὤρυξαν, "they dug"). The NIV and ESV are translating a well-attested textual tradition with "they pierced." See also Gregory Vall, "Psalm 22:17B: 'The Old Guess'," *JBL* 116 (1997): 45–56, and Delitzsch, *Die Psalmen* (5th ed. 1894), pp.214–15.

Lloyd-Jones, D. Martyn. *Faith on Trial*, 1965. A moving exposition of Psalm 73 by the great expositor. This work is spiritually refreshing and challenging. Now published with his fine exposition of Habakkuk in *Faith Tried and Triumphant* (1987).

☆ Longman, Tremper, III. *How to Read the Psalms*, 1988. A useful handbook for the student wanting to get acquainted with the Hebrew Hymnal and to learn to interpret it. Not a commentary, though it includes some insightful studies of a few psalms as models. Accomplishing similar goals but critically oriented is James Crenshaw's *The Psalms: An Introduction* (2001).

☆ **Longman, Tremper, III.** (TOTC-R) 2014. What Kidner did so well, Longman does for the 21st century, even if not as tightly written. Look no further if you need a quick, concise reference for evangelical exegesis (about 450pp.). Each psalm is discussed in Context (genre mainly) and Comment sections, prior to a couple of paragraphs on Meaning that include christological reflection. The one drawback is that, like Ross, Longman treats each psalm pretty much on its own; there is hardly any canonical reading taking place. Note: Longman is now consulting editor for the series. Preachers and counselors find much wisdom in *Cry of the Soul* (1994), cowritten with Dan Allender, "which looks at our emotional lives through the prism of the Psalms" (10). [*Them* 8/15; *JTS* 10/16; *JETS* 9/15; *JSOT* 40.5].

✓ Lugt, Pieter van der. *Cantos and Strophes in Biblical Hebrew Poetry*, 3 vols., 2006–13. An enormous project focused on the Psalms. [*JSOT* 39.5].

Luther, Martin. "First Lectures on the Psalms," vols. 10–11 in *Luther's Works*, 1513–15, ET 1974–76; "Selected Psalms, I–III," vols. 12–14 in *Luther's Works*, 1521–46, ET 1955–58. Both as a monk and afterwards, Luther's daily life was suffused with meditation on the Psalms.

Maclaren, Alexander. (EB) 1893. Representing some of the best of 19th century exposition, this was reprinted by Klock & Klock. Now free online.

Marlowe, W. Creighton, and Charles H. Savelle, Jr. *Psalms, Volume 1: The Wisdom Psalms* (Kerux) 2021. I have yet to see this. [*JETS* 6/22].

✓ **McCann, J. Clinton.** ‡ (NIB) 1996. Found in vol.4 of the series. The author taught at Eden Seminary, St. Louis, chaired the SBL Psalms group, and is a proponent of the new approach to the Psalms (cf. *The Shape and Shaping of the Psalter*, ed. McCann [1993]). Students make ready use of this commentary, one of the best in the NIB. [*DenvJ*]. See also McCann's *Theological Introduction to the Book of Psalms: The Psalms as Torah* (1993), used as a textbook in some evangelical seminaries [*CRBR* 1995; *RelSRev* 1/98].

✓ Miller, Patrick. ‡ *Interpreting the Psalms*, 1986. Has long been, and still remains, one of the best written and widely used introductions to the Psalms. More recent and on related topics are *They Cried to the Lord: The Form and Theology of Biblical Prayer* (1994), and *The Lord of the Psalms* (2013) [*RevExp* 8/14].

✓ Mowinckel, Sigmund. ‡ *The Psalms in Israel's Worship*, 2 Vols., ET 1962. A seminal introduction—not a commentary—which sought to understand the Psalms as the compositions of temple singers and musicians and as destined for cultic use. Placed great stress upon an annual festival, which celebrated the enthronement of Yahweh. In the mid-20th century Mowinckel was the don of the many Scandinavians studying the poetical books. Eerdmans republished Mowinckel as one pb vol. (2004). See also Eaton and Weiser. [*VT* 57.3; *ExpTim* 10/05]. Mowinckel's accompanying *Psalm Studies* are now translated in 2 vols. (SBL, 2014) [*JSOT* 39.5; *ETL* 91.4].

Murphy, Roland E. ‡ *The Gift of the Psalms*, 2000. [*Int* 4/02; *JSOT* 99].

F  Nasuti, Harry. ‡ *Psalms II (73–89)* (Illum).

Oesterley, W. O. E. ‡ 1939. Still occasionally cited in the literature (600pp.).

☆ **Perowne, J. J. S.** 2 vols., 5th ed. 1883. A masterful classic. Childs says, "Its strength lies in its close attention to the Hebrew text." He adds, "the writer has a good knowledge of the history of exegesis and a profound sense of the unity of the two Testaments," and "provides an excellent balance to the modern commentaries which seldom deal with the New Testament's use of the Psalter." Perowne was reprinted, is free online, and is still worth consulting as a compendium of the best old commentary on the Psalms.

Phillips, Richard D. *Psalms 42–72* (REC) 2019; *Psalms 73–106* (REC) 2020. Theologically strong sermons, from a conservative Presbyterian pastor. There is much here to feed the soul. [2020: *JETS* 12/21].

Platt, David, Jim Shaddix, and Matt Mason. *Exalting Jesus in Psalms 51–100* (CCE) 2020.

Plumer, W. S. (GS) 1867. A massive work (1211pp.) that I've never had the opportunity to use. Spurgeon records that he did not find Plumer all that helpful.

☆ Robertson, O. Palmer. *The Flow of the Psalms: Discovering Their Structure and Theology*, 2015. Offers a creative canonical, biblical-theological reading to show a narrative progression in the Psalter's arrangement. Robertson finds a redemptive-historical framework which moves from a thematically programmatic Pss. 1–2, to confrontation of David's enemies (Book I), to communication with the nations (Book II), to devastation for disobedient Israel (Book III), to maturation of renewed Israel under *Yahweh Malak* (Book IV), to consummation (Book V). [*Chm* Win 16; *WTJ* Fall 16; *JETS* 12/15; *JSOT* 41.5; *Found* Aut 16]. His earlier *Psalms in Congregational Celebration* (1995) represents model preaching on 25 psalms by this pastor, seminary principal, and missionary.

✓ Sabourin, Leopold. ‡ 2 vols, 1969. A moderate Catholic work which emphasizes the private origin of this poetry (contra Mowinckel, Weiser, et al.). At one time it was valued by specialists for its bibliographies. [*JBL* 89.2].

☆ **Saleska, Timothy E.** *Psalms 1–50* (ConcC) 2020. The author has an OT doctorate (Hebrew Union), pastoral experience, and strong preaching interests. The vol. of about 450pp. is helpful on a number of levels, and confessional Lutherans prize it.

✓ Sarna, Nahum. *Songs of the Heart: An Introduction to the Book of Psalms*, 1993. I bought this book of sensitive Jewish readings of select psalms and found it stimulating.

☆ **Schaefer, Konrad.** ‡ (BerO) 2001. A literary reading with 45pp. of introduction plus 358pp. of commentary; it is one of the best in the series. Schaefer's approach has been strongly influenced by the pioneering literary critic Luis Alonso Schökel (known for *A Manual of Hebrew Poetics*, 1988). It can be very profitably used alongside form-critical and exposi-tional commentaries. [*Int* 4/02; *ExpTim* 9/02; *HS* 2003; *JSOT* 99; *CBQ* 7/05].

✓ Schmutzer, Andrew J., and David M. Howard, eds. *The Psalms: Language for All Seasons of the Soul*, 2013. A conservative (Moody Press), somewhat uneven collection from ETS, including essays from Howard, Longman, Waltke, and VanGemeren. [*JESOT* 4.1].

F   Schnocks, Johannes, and Kathrin Liess. ‡ *Psalms 1* (Herm). See Hossfeld–Zenger.

✓ Selderhuis, Herman J., ed. (RCS) 2 vols., 2015–18. Judicious selections of the best expositions of the Psalms in the Reformation era. [*JETS* 6/19].

✓ Seybold, Klaus. *Introducing the Psalms*, ET 1990. An important work, complemented by his finely compressed exegesis in *Handbuch zum Alten Testament* (1996).

Shead, Andrew G., ed. *Stirred by a Noble Theme: The Book of Psalms in the Life of the Church*, 2013. From a conference at Moore College, Sydney. [*Chm* Sum 14].

Smith, J. Josh, and Daniel L. Akin. *Exalting Jesus in Psalms 1–50* (CCE) 2022.

F   Sommer, Benjamin D., Mark Zvi Brettler, Alan Cooper, and Yair Zakovich. ‡ (JPS). See Berlin above. A recent announcement listed Sommer, *Psalms I: 1–30*; Cooper, *Psalms II: 31–60*; Zakovitch, *Psalms III: 61–90*; and Brettler, *Psalms IV: 91–119*.

Spurgeon, Charles H. *The Treasury of David*, 1870–85. Many reprints available, free online. Spurgeon is rich theologically and serves as a compendium of scores of old classics, including the Puritans. Unhappily, the exposition is sometimes unrelated to the text, and verbose. This is for the preacher rather than the scholar and should only be used with ready reference to a couple of good exegetical works. This exposition was edited down to two pb vols. for CrossC.

F   Strawn, Brent A. ‡ (AYB). To be a replacement for Dahood.

☆  **Tate, Marvin E.** [𝓜], *Psalms 51–100* (WBC) 1990. More extensive (578pp.) than the other WBC vols. (Allen, Craigie), more in tune with scholarly developments since the mid-1980s, but perhaps not always as incisive in its exegesis. Has many of the strengths and weaknesses of the series as a whole. The strong points are that Tate shares some of Mays's interests and provides ample notes on the Hebrew. He was among my recommended purchases through the 9th edition. [*JTS* 4/94; *JSOT* 62; *HS* 1993].

✓  **Terrien, Samuel L.** ‡ (ECC) 2003. Completed shortly before the professor's death at age 91: "a monumental tribute to a great scholar of the past, but will hardly be monumental for the future" (Johnston). This nearly 1000-page tome is faulted for being dated in scholarship, and yet "erudition and elevated language grace the commentary throughout" (Ryan). The theology here has sparkle and imagination, focusing a good bit on the theme of divine presence/absence—this was expected and in line with his 1978 OT Theology, *The Elusive Presence*. Eerdmans released a pb reprint in two vols. [*CBQ* 7/04; *RTR* 8/03; *JTS* 10/03; *ExpTim* 1/04; *JSOT* 28.5; *ThTo* 4/04; *Int* 10/05; *BSac* 4/06; *HS* 2005; *VT* 55.2 (Johnston); *JNES* 7/07; *TJ* Fall 04 (VanGemeren); *Anvil* 21.4; *EuroJTh* 16.1].

F   Tucker, W. Dennis, Jr. *Psalms 73–150* (WBC-R). See his well-conceived study, *Constructing and Deconstructing Power in Psalms 107–150* (2014) [*JSOT* 40.5], and his coauthored NIVAC above.

✓  Van Hecke, Pierre, and Antje Labahn, eds. ‡ *Metaphors in the Psalms*, 2010. Helpful indeed, from BETL. [*ETL* 6/15; *BBR* 21.4; *JHebS* 14]. See also Van Hecke, ed., *Metaphor in the Hebrew Bible* (2005).

Villanueva, Federico G. (Asia) 2 vols., 2016, 2022. Regrettably, I have yet to see this. The Filipino author reportedly interprets the second half of the Psalter from the perspectives of trauma and exile. [*BL* 2022, 2023].

✓  Wallace, Howard N. ‡ (Read) 2009.

☆  **Waltke, Bruce K., James M. Houston, with Erika Moore.** *The Psalms as Christian Lament: A Historical Commentary*, 2014. Given that the church often struggles to understand and employ the complaint psalms in private and public worship, this commentary on Pss 5–7, 32, 38–39, 44, 102, 130, and 143 accomplishes a lot of good (nearly 300pp.). It draws from the history of interpretation (from the church fathers to Calvin), works through the text exegetically, and makes searching spiritual application. [*CBQ* 4/15; *JSOT* 39.5; *Chm* Aut 14; *RTR* 12/14; *JETS* 3/15; *JESOT* 4.1; *ExpTim* 8/15; *Int* 10/16; *Them* 40.3]. Earlier, the authors gave us a meaty vol. (572pp.), *The Psalms as Christian Worship* (2010), treating those Psalms (1–4, 8, 15–16, 19, 22–23, 51, 110, and 139) deemed to hold special significance for the church [*BBR* 21.4; *EvQ* 1/12 (Allen); *JTS* 10/11; *JSOT* 35.5; *Chm* Aut 13; *VT* 62.3; *RTR* 12/12; *JETS* 6/11; *RevExp* Spr 12; *TJ* Spr 12]. More recently, *The Psalms as Christian Praise* (2019) treats Pss 90–93, 95–100, 103–104 [*ExpTim* 11/20; *TGA* Sum 22; *BBR* 30.4; *CBQ* 10/20]. It has been an enormous interdisciplinary commentary project. Note to students: the work focuses primarily on the theological message, and there is little said on such matters as philology and poetry—an exception is the discussion of 22:16 (see 2010, p.393). Waltke's exegesis is well-done. Finally comes an enormous introduction: *How to Read & Understand the Psalms* (2023) [*Them* 48.3], written with Fred G. Zaspel.

☆  **Waltner, James.** [𝓜], (BCBC) 2006. This fat pb (831pp.) by a studious old Anabaptist pastor has devotional value, though there is also some critical orientation. He has obviously spent thousands of hours exegeting and meditating upon the psalms. Pastors will appreciate how Waltner draws attention to related Bible passages (intertexts). To get the flavor of the work, see Ps. 67, the great missionary psalm. [*JETS* 12/08].

F   Webster, Brian L. (ZECOT) 4 vols.

Webster, Douglas D. *The Psalms: Jesus's Prayer Book*, 4 vols., 2023. Extensive devotional readings (1200pp.) from a Beeson professor of pastoral theology and preaching. I have not seen it. [*JETS* 3/24; *BL* 2024].

✓ **Weiser, Artur.** ‡ (OTL) ET 1962. Was a leading critical commentary but has seriously aged. Develops many of Mowinckel's cultic themes relating to the hypothetical annual festival; this is Weiser's prime demerit. (Note to students: Weiser redefines the festival as centered on covenant rather than Yahweh's enthronement.) The work has its weaknesses, but on the plus side is concerned with theology, the idea of the covenant, and its place in the people's worship. Not to be discarded.

✓ Wendland, Ernst R. *Studies in the Psalms: Literary-Structural Analysis with Application to Translation*, 2017. Ever since we had a dinner together in Johannesburg in 1998, I have been impressed with Ernie's brilliant mind. And he is such a skilled reader of texts. These 550pp. of essays are very instructive. [*Them* 43.3].

☆ Wenham, Gordon. *Psalms as Torah: Reading Biblical Song Ethically*, 2012; *The Psalter Reclaimed: Praying and Praising with the Psalms*, 2013. I cannot think of a better, more thought-provoking, more edifying introduction to using the Psalms than these two books, especially the *Torah* pb. For my study purposes and walk with God, they accomplish more good than most of the commentaries I have. [2012: *BBR* 23.1; *WTJ* Spr 15; *EvQ* 4/14; *JTS* 4/13; *Int* 4/13 (McCann); *Them* 7/12; *BSac* 7/14; *JESOT* 1.1; 2013: *Them* 11/13].

✓ Wesselschmidt, Quentin F., ed. *Psalms 51–150* (ACCS) 2007. [*BL* 2009].

✓ **Westermann, Claus.** ‡ *The Living Psalms*, ET 1989. A famous form critic here explains the book theologically [*JR* 4/91]. See also *The Psalms: Structure, Content and Message* (ET 1980) [*JBL* 101.2]; and *Praise and Lament in the Psalms* (ET 1981), which includes Westermann's widely influential *The Praise of God in the Psalms* (ET 1965). Along with Brueggemann who builds upon him, Westermann transformed the older form-critical approach to the Psalms and reinvigorated scholarship.

☆ Wilcock, Michael. (BST) 2 vols., 2001. This set, by the author of several BST vols. (Judges, Chronicles, Luke, Revelation), can be recommended to pastors. [*JSOT* 99; *Chm* Spr 05; *Them* Sum 05; *Evangel* Sum 03; *Anvil* 19.3].

✓ Willgren, David. ‡ *The Formation of the 'Book' of Psalms*, 2016. A well-researched Lund diss. that challenges the prevalence of wholistic analysis, i.e., Psalter interpretation [*ExpTim* 3/21; *BBR* 27.2; *JSOT* 41.5]. See also Brodersen above. Confusingly, Willgren has another version of the doctoral work: *Like a Garden of Flowers: A Study of the Formation of the 'Book' of Psalms* (2016) [*WTJ* Spr 17].

Williams, Donald M. (WCC) 2 vols., 1986–89. One of the largest in the series (1034pp.). The running exposition unfortunately seems to lack the insight and synthesis of material one finds in the best WCC vols.—too little time spent with the text? The impression is of a very well-trained, but time-pressed expositor. On the plus side, Williams's comments are theologically sound and don't lead the reader astray. The vols. have the usual anecdotal, practical thrust one expects from the series, usually found more in the introduction and conclusion sections. Longman's assessment is more positive in *Survey* (3rd ed.). [*CBQ* 4/92; *Chm* 104.4].

✓ Witherington, Ben, III. *Psalms Old and New: Exegesis, Intertextuality, and Hermeneutics*, 2017. See his similar vol. on Isaiah, also published by Fortress. Again, Witherington focuses special attention on the NT use of OT material, the psalms here. [*JETS* 6/18; *JSOT* 42.5].

☆ Witvliet, John D. *The Biblical Psalms in Christian Worship: A Brief Introduction & Guide to Resources*, 2007. Fits a niche with its synthesis of biblical scholarship, history of worship, musicology, and liturgics (suggestions for using Psalms corporately). The best way to learn the Psalms is by using them! The author heads the Calvin Institute of Christian Worship, but this 169-page handbook treats nearly all Christian traditions.

✓ Zenger, Erich, ed. ‡ *The Composition of the Book of Psalms*, 2010. Another huge vol. of essays from BETL, about 60 percent in English. [*BBR* 22.4; *JSOT* 37.5; *ETL* 87.4].

NOTES: (1) The imprecatory Psalms have long baffled Christians. An old influential study of this troubling literature is Chalmers Martin, "Imprecations in the Psalms," *Princeton Theological Review* (1903): 537–53; it is reprinted in Kaiser, ed., *Classical Evangelical Essays in OT Interpretation*. Five newer conservative contributions to the discussion are: James Adams's *War Psalms of the Prince of Peace* (P&R, 1991, rev. 2016) [*Chm* Spr 18]; John Day's *Crying for Justice* (IVP, 2005) [*BL* 2007; *EvQ* 4/07]; David Firth's *Surrendering Retribution in the Psalms* (Paternoster, 2005) [*CBQ* 1/07; *Them* 10/06; *ExpTim* 10/06; *EvQ* 4/07]; Jenkins (above); and Laurence (above). On the critical side, consult Erich Zenger's *A God of Vengeance? Understanding the Psalms of Divine Wrath* (1996) [*JSOT* 79]; William Morrow's *Protest Against God* (2007) [*Bib* 91.4]; and Elisabet Nord, *Vindicating Vengeance and Violence?* (2023). (2) Some scholars are now more trusting of the superscriptions. See Bruce Waltke, "Superscripts, Postscripts, or Both," *JBL* 110 (1991): 583–96; Dale Brueggemann, "Psalms 4: Titles," in *DOTWPW* (2008), 613–21; and Ian Vaillancourt, "Reading Psalm Superscriptions through the Centuries," *Them* 48.2 (2023). (3) For reviews of developments in Psalms scholarship, see Susan Gillingham, "Studies of the Psalms: Retrospect and Prospect," *ExpTim* 119.5 (2008): 209–16; David Howard's chapter in Firth–Johnston above; J. Kenneth Kuntz, "Continuing the Engagement: Psalms Research Since the Early 1990s," *CBR* 10.3 (2012): 321–78; Gert T. M. Prinsloo, "Reading the Masoretic Psalter as a Book: Editorial Trends and Redactional Trajectories," *CBR* 19 (2021): 145–77; Howard and Schmutzer (above); and J. Clinton McCann, "Psalm Studies Today," *JETS* 66.3 (2023): 473–80.

# PROVERBS

★ **Ansberry, Christopher B.** [𝓜], (ZECOT) 2024. Follows his introduction, *Reading Wisdom and Psalms as Christian Scripture* (2024). The author teaches at Grove City College, after some years at Oak Hill, London. I regard him as a very capable younger scholar (Wheaton PhD) and worth reading, despite an earlier unfair attack on the historical scholarship of a previous generation of conservatives: see *Evangelical Faith and the Challenge of Historical Criticism* (2013) [*Them* 39.1], edited by Hays and Ansberry. The sizable ZECOT vol. (650pp.) builds upon his doctoral work, *Be Wise, My Son, and Make My Heart Glad: An Exploration of the Courtly Nature of the Book of Proverbs* (2011), and demonstrates how he is a sophisticated reader of biblical texts and writes in an accessible manner. He is influenced by William Brown's brilliant work on both moral/character formation and a "didactic movement" in Proverbs (61). What Ansberry terms the "progressive pedagogical scheme" (60) moves from elementary (10:1–15:33) to intermediate (16:1–22:16) to vocational (22:17–24:34) to advanced wisdom (25:1–29:27). This commentary holds real value for learned ministers and Hebrew students, especially those interested in discourse analysis and rhetorical criticism. Some may class the theology (more in the OT context) to be healthier than the stance on hermeneutics and critical issues.

★ **Fox, Michael.** ‡ (AB) 2 vols., 2000–09. The brilliant set replaces Scott. Fox previously did first-rate work on Esther, Ecclesiastes, and Song of Songs. He then devoted many years to

Proverbs, publishing excellent essays while writing his AB set; e.g., "The Social Location of the Book of Proverbs" in *Texts, Temples, and Traditions* (Haran FS, 1996), 227–39. The Jewish prof takes honors as the leading, most comprehensive, critical commentary available (cf. Loader, Schipper). Note that AB is not for the faint of heart: it is packed with technical philological and textual research, and it extends to 1200pp. With Dell, I do not recommend following Fox in his developmental view of Israelite wisdom: "from pragmatic, to moral to the more theological figure of Wisdom." For advanced students and scholarly pastors. [*ExpTim* 5/01, 9/10 (Dell); *CBQ* 10/01; *JTS* 10/01; *JETS* 3/02; *Int* 10/02, 4/11 (Brown); *BSac* 10/02; *VT* 53.2; *HBT* 6/02; *JSOT* 94; *CurTM* 10/04; *JSOT* 36.5; *BBR* 13.2; 20.3; *JHebS* 12].

★ Koptak, Paul E. (NIVAC) 2003. The fullest preacher's commentary now available at over 700pp. Koptak is a prof at North Park Seminary in Chicago and an insightful guide through Proverbs. It would be an excellent addition to the pastor's library, for moving toward application. [*WTJ* Spr 06]. See also O'Dowd, Bridges, Kitchen, Ortlund.

★ **Longman, Tremper, III.** (BCOT) 2006. A very good interpretation, but I had expected something more in-depth and useful to students (in line with Hess on Song of Songs); I was slightly disappointed. Since then I have come to recognize that Longman chose to wear his learning lightly. He knows Proverbs and Proverbs scholarship well. His focus on the text's theological message and ethical instruction is just what pastors want. They will think this commentary is pitched at just the right level and is written for them. The 30 essays in the appendix, synthesizing Proverbs' teaching on various topics, are worth the price of the book. [*JETS* 3/08; *BL* 2007 (Firth)]. If you buy this, you do not need to bother with Longman's *How to Read Proverbs* (2002) [*RelSRev* 7/03; *CTJ* 11/04], which is a well-written introduction and hermeneutical guide that can be compared with the earlier *How to Read the Psalms* (1988).

★ O'Dowd, Ryan P. (SGBC) 2017. By comparison with the later ESVEC (below), this treats the NIV, has more focus on biblical-theological reflection, more analysis of contemporary culture, and illustrative material (430pp.). He writes well, mainly for a lay audience, and draws from the best scholarship: Fox, Van Leeuwen, Heim, and especially Waltke. The author has a Liverpool doctorate, pastors an Anglican church in New York, and engages in university ministry. I call it a delightful book, though, as a practical commentary on wisdom, it has less discussion of "The Story of God." Students might pass this by. [*ExpTim* 6/18; *JETS* 3/18; *JSOT* 42.5; *DenvJ* 1/18].

★ **Overland, Paul.** (Apollos) 2022. The ripe fruit of long-term research on the wisdom literature. Overland teaches at Ashland Seminary and offers careful and comprehensive exegetical analysis (approx. 650pp.), evidencing a concern to explain "clusters of sayings" in context and how the book coheres. (This concern can be a corrective for those who instinctively plan to preach thematically on scattered proverbs [cf. McKane's approach and the Ross topical index].) Somewhat like ZECOT, his commentary helpfully sets the translation and structural outline side by side. This is undoubtedly a help to preachers in developing messages on sections of Proverbs, though Overland offers less in the way of exposition (see instead O'Dowd, Koptak, Kitchen, Ortlund). Students note that he does not deal much with recent scholarship; he interacts mainly with Fox and Waltke. I find Overland well-balanced: he can deal meticulously with details but is also great at showing connections and interpreting the book more holistically ("a bookwide instructional scheme"). For study purposes, now my favorite single vol. on Proverbs.

★ **Waltke, Bruce.** (NICOT) 2 vols., 2004–05. This was a publishing event for which some of us waited nearly 20 years. His past articles on Proverbs suggested that his commentary would be full, conservative (à la Kidner), and highly theological. We had to content ourselves with Waltke's "Theology of Proverbs" in *NIDOTTE*, and "Wisdom Literature" in *The Face* *of OT Studies* (1999). This commentary outdistances all previous evangelical exegeses of Proverbs and is my first choice for pastors and students. Students learn much from the introduction and bibliography here, which run to 170pp. As one would expect from an expert grammarian, the discussion of the Hebrew text is superb (and difficult reading for non-specialists). When it appeared, it was the fullest, most well-rounded English-language commentary ever published on Proverbs; it should not be regarded, however, as more scholarly than Fox. For a stimulating example of how Waltke sees the wisdom of Proverbs applying in our cultural context, see "Righteousness in Proverbs" in *WTJ* 70.2 (2008). [*RTR* 12/06; *WTJ* Spr 06; *CBQ* 4/08; *JTS* 4/06; *JETS* 9/05, 6/06; *Int* 4/06; *BSac* 10/06; *BL* 2005, 2006; *JAOS* 126.1 (harsh); *VT* 57.3; *RBL*; *JHebS*; *CurTM* 6/07]. Those daunted by such a thorough and erudite work (1175pp.) should consider Waltke–De Silva (below).

★ **Wilson, Lindsay.** (TOTC-R) 2018. A superb replacement for Kidner's little classic and to be regarded as one of the outstanding newer entries in the series. Treats the background/context and exegetical matters in a careful yet concise manner. The theological reflection and limited discussion of "Ministry Issues" are mature and wise. I agree with one reviewer [*JETS* 12/18] who especially commends one of Wilson's hermeneutical principles: "Always approach the individual proverbs through the gateway of chapters 1–9" (45). Wilson has taught for three decades at Ridley, Melbourne. [*BBR* 29.4; *JTS* 10/18; *JSOT* 43.5]. See also his Job commentary in THC.

Aitken, K. T. ‡ (DSB) 1986.

Akin, Daniel L., and Jonathan Akin. *Exalting Jesus in Proverbs* (CCE) 2017. Earlier, J. Akin published *Preaching Christ from Proverbs* (2015).

☆ Alden, Robert. 1983. The average reader will find Alden's commentary helpful for its practical suggestions. Most pastors, I think, are looking for something more thorough. Still, it is recommended for your consideration. [*WTJ* Spr 86; *JETS* 12/84].

Arnot, William. 1882. This well-known exposition was reprinted by Kregel.

☆ Atkinson, David. (BST) 1996. Well-done, though sketchy in places. [*Them* 11/99; *VT* 47.3].

Bellis, Alice Ogden. ‡ (Wisdom) 2018. Offers a "gender-sensitive reading" and can be classed as a stronger entry in the series. [*JSOT* 44.5; *CBQ* 1/20; *Int* 7/22; *HBT* 42.2].

✓ Böstrom, L. ‡ *The God of the Sages: The Portrayal of God in the Book of Proverbs*, 1990.

Brady, Gary. *Heavenly Wisdom: Proverbs Simply Explained* (Welwyn) 2003. Good exposition with application of the biblical material by a London pastor, and surprisingly full (812pp.).

☆ Bridges, Charles. (GS) 1846. Good for the soul, this wise old classic helps the pastor (650pp.). Childs's gentle critique of moralisms is probably deserved. I used to include it among my recommendations, but the more modern expositions displace it. Note that it is now free online. Bridges was edited down for CrossC (2001). [*JSOT* 27.5].

✓ **Clifford, Richard J.** ‡ (OTL-R) 1999. Replaces McKane's erudite but flawed work. Clifford builds upon his 1995 monograph, *The Book of Proverbs and Our Search for Wisdom.* (By the way, I regard it as a better piece than the commentary.) As an academic who regularly taught a course on Psalms and Wisdom, I bought this OTL, but I don't recommend it to pastors. The upshot of one negative but fair review is that the Jesuit critic "offers few new solutions to the many problems in Proverbs" and, in interpretation, too often moves outside the context of Hebrew society and Scripture—he repeatedly reads Proverbs "in terms of Mesopotamian mythology" [*BL* 2000]. On the plus side, he pays attention to rhetoric, asking "how did the instructions and maxims engage its audience?" (vii). [*JR* 4/00; *ExpTim* 5/00; *CBQ* 7/00; *Int* 10/00; *PSB* 21.2; *OTA* 2/00; *JTS* 4/04 (more positive)].

✓ Davis, Ellen F. ‡ *Proverbs, Ecclesiastes, and the Song of Songs* (WestBC) 2000. The author wrote a superb Yale diss. on Ezekiel and teaches at Duke. This treatment is competent, theologically oriented, and quite full for the WestBC series at 272pp. Worth consulting as a fresh exposition. More conservatively critical. [*ExpTim* 5/01; *VT* 53.2; *JSOT* 94; *RelSRev* 10/01].

✓ **Delitzsch, Franz.** (KD) ET 1875. He is truly at his best in this material: a giant still worth consulting, alongside the heavyweights: Waltke, Fox, Loader, and Schipper.

✓ Dell, Katharine J. ‡ *The Book of Proverbs in Social and Theological Context*, 2006. From CUP. [*JR* 7/08; *ExpTim* 4/07; *Them* 5/08; *CJ* 7/08; *Bib* 90.3; *BL* 2007]. A follow-up is *The Theology of the Book of Proverbs* (2023) [*BL* 2024].

✓ Dell, Katharine J., and Will Kynes, eds. ‡ *Reading Proverbs Intertextually*, 2019. [*JSOT* 43.5].

✓ Errington, Andrew. *Every Good Path: Wisdom and Practical Reason in Christian Ethics and the Book of Proverbs*, 2020. Dell calls it "a fascinating synthesis" [*ExpTim* 7/20]. [*JTS* 4/21].

F  Estelle, Bryan. (EEC).

✓ Estes, Daniel. *Hear, My Son*, 1997. Brief, probing evangelical exposition of chs. 1–9, focusing upon themes related to "personal formation" and moral education.

✓ Farmer, K. A. [*M*], *Proverbs and Ecclesiastes* (ITC-E) 1991. Argues the two books were companions, meant to be read together. Applies feminist concerns. [*CRBR* 1993].

✓ Fink, David, ed. *Proverbs, Ecclesiastes, Song of Songs* (RCS) 2023.

☆ **Fox, Michael.** ‡ (AB) 2 vols., 2000–09. The brilliant set replaces Scott. Fox previously did first-rate work on Esther, Ecclesiastes, and Song of Songs. He then devoted many years to Proverbs, publishing excellent essays while writing his AB set; e.g., "The Social Location of the Book of Proverbs" in *Texts, Temples, and Traditions* (Haran FS, 1996), 227–39. The Jewish prof takes honors as the leading, most comprehensive, critical commentary available (cf. Loader, Schipper). Note that AB is not for the faint of heart: it is packed with technical philological and textual research, and it extends to 1200pp. With Dell I do not recommend following Fox in his developmental view of Israelite wisdom: "from pragmatic, to moral to the more theological figure of Wisdom." Invaluable for advanced students. [*ExpTim* 5/01, 9/10 (Dell); *CBQ* 10/01; *JTS* 10/01; *JETS* 3/02; *Int* 10/02, 4/11 (Brown); *BSac* 10/02; *VT* 53.2; *HBT* 6/02; *JSOT* 94; *CurTM* 10/04; *JSOT* 36.5; *BBR* 13.2; 20.3; *JHebS* 12].

✓ Fox, Michael V. משלי *Proverbs: An Eclectic Edition with Introduction and Textual Commentary*, 2015. From an SBL project, "HBCE: The Hebrew Bible: A Critical Edition" (500pp.). Indispensable for scholars. [*JSS* Aut 18; *CBQ* 1/16; *JSOT* 40.5; *ETL* 92.3].

☆ **Garrett, Duane A.** *Proverbs, Ecclesiastes, Song of Songs* (NAC) 1993. A thoughtful, clear 448-page work from a scholar at Southern Seminary. Mainly an exposition for pastors, but Garrett knew the direction scholarship was headed and used some of the best of it: he interprets individual proverbs within larger literary units. The vol. was valued more around the turn of millennium because, relative to some other Bible books, there were fewer good commentaries on Proverbs. We have much more to choose from now. The Denver Seminary faculty used to recommend purchasing Garrett; the quality of the work and also the coverage of three Bible books likely played a part in their value judgment. [*VT* 7/96; *CBQ* 7/94; *BSac* 10/94; *HS* 1995].

F  Gianto, Agustinus. ‡ (Illum).

☆ **Goldingay, John.** (CCF) 2023. With regard to genre and material, Proverbs lends itself to the reflective, "Christian formation" approach taken in this series. With fewer hard questions of higher criticism in play, Goldingay focuses on what he does best: theological exposition with appreciation of the treasures from past interpreters (rabbis, church fathers, the Reformers). Happily, he had good space made available to him to provide a fuller discussion (over 450pp.). Pastors who are less academically oriented may prefer this to Waltke. Cf. with O'Dowd's SGBC.

✓ **Heim, Knut.** *Poetic Imagination in Proverbs: Variant Repetitions and the Nature of Poetry,*

2013. An expansion of his work *Like Grapes of Gold Set in Silver: An Interpretation of Proverbial Clusters in Proverbs 10:1–22:16* (2001) [*DenvJ*]. Heim is noteworthy for proposing the meaningful arrangement of individual proverbs in clusters; this book deserves the plaudits it received. [*BBR* 24.1; *WTJ* Spr 15; *CBQ* 10/14; *JSOT* 38.5].

Horne, Milton P. ‡ *Proverbs–Ecclesiastes* (S&H) 2003. The exposition draws from the fine exegeses published in major commentary series. Horne does not interact much with conservative scholarship. Like all S&H vols. which are meant to be visually engaging, it is nicely presented (578pp.). He teaches at William Jewell College. [*CJ* 1/06].

☆ **Hubbard, David A.** (WCC) 1989. A lengthy study (487pp.) by the late President of Fuller Seminary. The commentary handles a large portion of Proverbs in topical format. There is more scholarship behind this book than just about any other in the series. "This volume (like the volume on Daniel) makes the whole series worthwhile!" says Motyer. More for pastors than students. In the first ten editions, this was a recommended purchase; it remains a smart buy. [*JETS* 3/94; *BSac* 4/92; *Chm* 104.4].

F   Johnston, Gordon. (Kregel).

✓   Jones, Edgar. ‡ (Torch) 1961.

F   Joosten, Jan. [*M*], (ICC). Will this ever appear?

✓   Keefer, Arthur Jan. *Proverbs 1–9 as an Introduction to the Book of Proverbs*, 2020. Most welcome as "an original and valuable contribution" [*Bib* 102.4]. [*Presb* Fall 21; *BL* 2022; *BBR* 33.2; *JBTS* 2/21]. See also *The Book of Proverbs and Virtue Ethics: Integrating the Biblical and Philosophical Traditions* (2020). [*JTS* 4/22; *CBQ* 1/24].

☆ **Kidner, Derek.** (retired TOTC) 1964. Excellent introduction. Solid exegesis, though too brief in some places. It includes fine summary treatments of various words and topics covered in Proverbs and was once Longman's and Stuart's first choice. See Hubbard and Ross for other conservative works on a par with Kidner. See Wilson above.

Kitchen, John. (Mentor) 2006. Quite a large pastoral and devotional work (789pp.). [*JETS* 12/08].

F   Krispenz, Jutta. ‡ (IECOT).

Lawson, George. 1821. A reverent exposition, reprinted by Kregel.

Lennox, Stephen J. *Proverbs: A Bible Commentary in the Wesleyan Tradition*, 1998.

✓ **Loader, James A.** ‡ *Proverbs 1–9* (HCOT) 2014; *Proverbs 10–15* (HCOT) 2022. An impressive senior scholar, Loader travels the historical-critical avenue in researching the text (in line with the series title), but there are abundant philological, grammatical, structural, poetical, and reception history insights here too. This is a full, technical work (400 + 700pp.) that has the advantage of interacting with the Fox set. I value the excursus on "The Reception of Proverbs 8." A friend has suggested that Loader could well have dealt more with the ANE context and, at points, been less cautious in stating his own conclusions regarding exegetical options. Clearly, the trajectory is to produce the most comprehensive critical Proverbs commentary ever. [*OTE* 28.2].

☆ **Lucas, Ernest.** (THC) 2015. He was a good choice for this substantial work (380pp.), blending exegetical commentary and more sustained theological reflection. A publisher's blurb says Lucas "takes a unique 'cluster' approach to the book of Proverbs, studying it thematically and showing how it speaks to such issues as character formation, gender relations, wealth and poverty, interpersonal communication, science and religion, and care for the environment." (Note, however, that it is not so "unique"; see Heim.) Ten "theological horizons" essays, which I judge to be more valuable than the exegesis, round out the vol. This is a solid and clearly executed work. [*BBR* 26.3; *JTS* 4/17; *JETS* 9/17; *JSOT* 40.5; *Them* 43.2].

F   McCreesh, Thomas. ‡ (BerO).

✓ **McKane, William.** ‡ (retired OTL) 1970. Learned and dated. Helpful introduction, but "the exegesis is dominated by a larger theory respecting the development of Israel's wisdom," according to Childs. "McKane envisions a growth from an early non-theological stage of simple empirical observation to a subsequent growth of 'God language'. The effect of these rigid categories is to rob the proverbs of much of their theological vitality." Also, he regularly jumps about, organizing his discussion of verses according to topic. Simply put, a scholar's commentary. Other works are of greater value to pastors, and more current in their scholarship as well. Replaced by Clifford. [*JBL* 90.2].

Miller, John W. (BCBC) 2004. Well accomplishes the aims of the series. This 351-page commentary treats much of the material in a topical rather than verse-by-verse manner. [*JETS* 3/06].

✓ Moss, Alan. ‡ (Read) 2015. A fair representative of the series (175pp.), that, because of its more literary approach, complements the strongly grammatical-historical commentaries by Fox and Waltke. Imagery is key here. "Most attention is given . . . to the context of the passages within the book sections, and within the whole unfolding educational text" (2). There is some focus, too, on a wider canonical context, but little interest in the ANE background. See the lengthy appendix on the figure of "Solomon as the Author of Proverbs." Moss wrote a Queensland PhD on Proverbs' Personified Wisdom texts. [*JSOT* 40.5].

☆ **Murphy, Roland E.** ‡ (WBC) 1998. I like this work, for a variety of reasons. See my comments on Murphy's WBC on Ecclesiastes. Note that he previously wrote a more compact, popularly styled commentary on Proverbs for NIBC (see below). This WBC has more to offer as the in-depth treatment. I used to regard it as the best exegetical work for the well-trained pastor, but Waltke and Fox clearly supersede it. Though the 375-page book remains quite useful to students and to pastors working with the Hebrew, those with a healthy book budget will want Fox. [*CBQ* 7/00; *Int* 10/00; *JBL* Fall 01; *RelSRev* 10/01; *Chm* Spr 01].

Murphy, Roland E. ‡ (FOTL) 1981. Preceded WBC above. See under Ruth.

Murphy, Roland E., and Elizabeth Huwiler. [*M*], *Proverbs, Ecclesiastes & Song of Songs* (NIBC) 1996. Murphy contributes Proverbs here, while Huwiler takes the shorter books. Both do a good job within the confines of the series, though I judge the treatments of Proverbs and the Song to be better than Ecclesiastes. The Proverbs section is rather brief. Murphy's WBC is recommended, not NIBC, especially for pastors using the Hebrew. [*JSOT* 89, 94; *CBQ* 10/00; *Chm* Win 00; *RTR* 4/01; *Them* Spr 01; *EvQ* 10/01; *VT* 53.2].

☆ O'Dowd, Ryan Patrick. (ESVEC) 2022. A different format and base translation, but SGBC (above) and this are similarly useful and praiseworthy. Weighing in favor of the ESVEC work is its pairing with other strong works (see O'Donnell under Song of Songs).

✓ Oesterley, William O. E. ‡ (Westminster) 1929. Though dated, Oesterley retains some of its original value. Crenshaw, I discovered, agrees with this assessment: "Valuable insights give this commentary staying power." Fairly complete in its treatment.

☆ Ortlund, Raymond C. *Proverbs: Wisdom that Works* (PTW) 2012. Sidney Greidanus states that this vol. "models powerful, profound, relevant expository preaching" and is "[a] superb source for preachers preparing a series of . . . sermons on the book of Proverbs and for Bible study groups interested in . . . biblical wisdom." I agree. Ortlund is a pastor-scholar, and he has done the church a service here.

Pauw, Amy Plantinga. ‡ *Proverbs and Ecclesiastes* (Belief) 2015.

☆ **Perdue, Leo G.** ‡ (I) 2000. Well-done, indeed, but perhaps not what pastors expect from the series. There is less verse-by-verse commentary and more discussion of the book's development of topics/themes in their theological and social context (late date). Much attention is paid to larger literary units. At times he seems to be attempting, in a fine essay style, to synthesize the diverse materials. This is a critical work, dating both the materials and their redaction to the Persian period. The origin and early dating of this wisdom within the book itself (Solomon, Hezekiah, etc.) is "the fiction of tradition" (64).

In brief, this is a more scholarly, and less accessible, vol. in the series. It is one of the least successful in the series at helping preachers move toward application. [*ExpTim* 5/01; *Them* Sum 02; *Int* 1/02; *VT* 51.4; *HBT* 6/02; *JSOT* 94; *RelSRev* 10/01; *Anvil* 18.4].

✓ Reyburn, William D., and Euan McG. Fry. (UBS) 2000. This 700-page book can aid students as well as translators. [*RelSRev* 10/01].

☆ **Ross, Allen P.** (EBCR) 2008. His 1991 EBC was among the best in the set, and EBCR extends the commentary's usefulness. At approximately 250pp., Ross is nearly as valuable as some of the suggested purchases above. The scholarship is careful, and the preacher's needs and interests are kept in mind. The topical index appended to the introduction is among the better ones available to the student in English (38–45). Proverbs is bound with commentaries on Ecclesiastes by Shepherd, Song of Songs by Schwab, and Isaiah by Grogan. See the author's other works under Genesis, Leviticus, and Psalms. [*BL* 2010].

F Ross, Allen P. (EBTC)? See his EBCR above.

✓ Sandoval, Timothy J. [𝓜], *The Moral Vision of Proverbs: A Virtue-Oriented Approach to Wisdom*, 2024. Quite engaging and stimulating.

✓ **Schipper, Bernd U.** ‡ *Proverbs 1–15* (Herm) ET 2019. Another BKAT contribution (2018) to the series. Schipper dates the collection to the late Persian or early Hellenistic period. His huge work is important for relating together Torah/law (esp. Deuteronomy) and wisdom, once classed as unbridgeably divided. (On this see also *The Hermeneutics of Torah: Proverbs 2, Deuteronomy, and the Composition of Proverbs 1–9* [ET 2021] [*BBR* 33.2].) Schipper is distinguished by his focus on the book of Proverbs' placement in the international wisdom movement; he pays especially close attention to Egyptian wisdom as a major influence. (Evangelicals will, instead, want to emphasize more the uniqueness of wisdom in Proverbs as divinely revealed and highly theological, with references to "the fear of Yahweh.") It boggles the mind to have such a wealth of thorough, technical scholarship available in Waltke, Fox, Loader, Schipper, etc. [*BBR* 31.1; *Int* 10/21 (Brown)].

☆ Schwab, George. (CorBC) 2009. Bound with Futato's Psalms commentary. Together the entries compose a larger-sized vol. in the series (over 650pp.). Both scholars are Reformed, competent, and helpful. Since CorBC is aimed at pastors and lay readers of the NLT, I should note that Futato is an easier read than Schwab.

☆ Schwáb, Zoltán. [𝓜], *Proverbs: Wisdom Calls*, 2023. An excellent, more conservative entry in the T&T Clark Study Guides series. [*BL* 2024].

Scott, Robert B. Y. ‡ *Proverbs, Ecclesiastes* (retired AB) 1965. Years ago, Scott was somewhat valuable for its translation and introduction. It contains little exposition and is too brief. See Fox above.

✓ **Steinmann, Andrew E.** (ConcC) 2009. I have made less use of this 719-page exegesis *cum* theological exposition. What I have read is lucid and judicious, but Waltke has much fuller research. The author has served long years as a seminary professor and has large-scale Concordia works on Samuel, Ezra–Nehemiah, and Daniel. Valuable to students for his marshalling evidence that chs. 1–9 and 10–24 reveal a consistent vocabulary and viewpoint. [*JETS* 3/11; *BSac* 1/11].

✓ Stewart, Anne W. [𝓜], *Poetic Ethics in Proverbs: Wisdom Literature and the Shaping of the Moral Self*, 2016. Brilliant, well-written research, focusing on "how a person's capacity for mature forms of moral reasoning is rooted in the concept of *mûsār* ('discipline'), which is heuristically explored in four modes: rebuke, motivation, desire, and imagination.... This is one of the best books on Proverbs that I have ever read" (Moberly [*JSOT* 42.5]).

Toy, Crawford H. ‡ (ICC) 1904. Long used as a reference in dealing with the Hebrew text and the history of interpretation, but only advanced students doing the most in-depth research should bother with it now. See Joosten.

☆ Trier, Daniel. *Proverbs and Ecclesiastes* (Brazos) 2011. The author is a prof at Wheaton and has a fine theological mind. [*CBQ* 4/15; *BBR* 26.1].

☆ **Van Leeuwen, Raymond.** [𝓜], (NIB) 1997. The editors gave him about 250pp., and he did remarkably well within those constraints. Van Leeuwen is particularly valuable for his efforts to interpret individual proverbs within larger literary units. Students should not miss this commentary, probably the best briefer one on Proverbs. If the vol. were not so expensive, and if I valued some of Van Leeuwen's companions, it would be easier to consider this for purchase. (Ecclesiastes, Song of Songs, Wisdom of Solomon, and Sirach are less useful.)

☆ **Waltke, Bruce K., and Ivan D. V. De Silva.** *Proverbs: A Shorter Commentary*, 2021. The monumental and comprehensive NICOT is here distilled so as to make its learning more accessible (approx. 450pp.). My friend Art Keefer [*VT* 72.3] judges the summaries to be "punchier" and skillfully done, compared with the earlier work, "which detailed literary relationships of almost every scale." Many pastors would agree that it is "concise, convenient, and welcomely reliable" as an abridgement. Another selling point: "On the whole, commentaries on . . . Proverbs remain over-simplified or over-specialized to aid most non-specialists. This commentary strikes a rather lonely middle ground." Time-starved pastors may prefer this to NICOT. Note that there is here some updating of the older set. [*ExpTim* 11/21; *Presb* Fall 22; *BL* 2022; *WTJ* Fall 21; *JETS* 12/21; *CBQ* 7/22].

✓ Weeks, Stuart. ‡ *Instruction and Imagery in Proverbs 1–9* (OUP) 2007. Brilliant work which unsettles some longstanding critical scholarship; specifically, he posits that the first nine chapters are "a single composition, with a more-or-less coherent viewpoint." [*JR* 10/08; *VT* 58.2; *Them* 9/08].

✓ **Whybray, R. N.** ‡ (NCB) 1994. A substantial vol. of nearly 480pp. (xxxiii + 446) that builds on his earlier CBC (1972). Crenshaw once spoke of this NCB as "judicious, perhaps the most useful commentary in English." Whybray is a moderate British critic, and his work here is strong. Also note his monographs: *The Book of Proverbs: A Survey of Modern Study* (1995), which is masterful [*JSS* Spr 00; *RelSRev* 1/98]; *The Composition of the Book of Proverbs* (1994); *Wealth and Poverty in the Book of Proverbs* (1990); and *Wisdom in Proverbs* (1965), which treats the concept of wisdom in Proverbs 1:1–9:45. Note: In the mid-1990s I recommended Whybray for purchase. [*JETS* 12/97; *CBQ* 10/96; *RTR* 1/97; *JSS* Spr 99; *HS* 1997].

F   Wilson, Lindsay. (BGW). See also Wilson's TOTC above.

✓ Wright, J. Robert, ed. *Proverbs, Ecclesiastes, Song of Solomon* (ACCS) 2004. [*CTJ* 4/07; *JETS* 3/06; *BL* 2007].

✓ Yoder, Christine Roy. ‡ (AbOTC) 2009. A good example of the series, with middle-of-the-road, concise scholarship on exegetical questions and little exposition. Yoder sees a lack of purposeful editorial arrangement in Proverbs and displays good interpretive skill. Call this a useful quick reference tool. [*ExpTim* 8/10; *BL* 2010 (Weeks)].

Zöckler, Otto. (Lange) ET 1870. The vol. covers Proverbs through Song of Solomon.

NOTES: (1) See Alice Ogden Bellis, "Proverbs in Recent Research," *CBR* 20 (2022): 133–64.

# ECCLESIASTES

★ **Bartholomew, Craig G.** (BOTC) 2009. His PhD, *Reading Ecclesiastes* (1998) [*Chm* Aut 01; *Int* 4/00], demonstrated his excellent grasp of scholarly developments and hermeneutics. It probed the philosophical underpinnings or presuppositions of contemporary OT scholarship, with particular reference to Ecclesiastes. This commentary (448pp.) then revealed Bartholomew's exegetical skill and keen interest in biblical theology. He chooses to translate *hebel* (הבל) as "enigmatic," arguing against Seow's rendering of "vanity" and his idea that the word reflects Qoheleth's anthropology. Bartholomew says, "Rather than his anthropology, what is at stake in Qohelet's quest is his epistemology, how we come to know that we can trust the results of our explorations. Qohelet embarks on a quest for knowledge, and it is this exploration of the meaning of life that continually runs down into the conclusion: utterly *hebel*" (106). Though not convinced the quest is quite so philosophical—Qoheleth seeks satisfaction (1:8) and "to see what is good to do" (2:3)—I make this my first pick as a scholarly exegesis. Pastors are glad that "[h]is applications . . . to postmodernism, psychology, spiritual formation, and preaching are replete with insight" (Estes). Students note that critical scholars complain Bartholomew tends to make Qoheleth too "orthodox." Compare with Seow, Murphy, Krüger, Gordis, and Fox. [*JETS* 6/10; *BSac* 7/10; *HBT* 32.1; *BL* 2010; *CBQ* 7/10; *RelSRev* 12/09 (Crenshaw); *BBR* 21.2 (Estes); *CTJ* 4/11 (Greidanus); *RevExp* Fall 10; *BTB* 2/12].

★ **Enns, Peter.** [𝓜], (THC) 2011. Controversial in some circles, Enns is unquestionably an able commentator on Scripture, with rigorous training (Harvard PhD). See his work on Exodus. There are many fine points: careful work with the text, a constant focus on the message, a theological exposition (according to his "Christotelic" model), his discussion of *hebel* (esp. pp.126–28), and an explanation of "the ambiguous nature of wisdom for Qohelet. . . . Wisdom is both a trusted ally and an undependable business partner, as much a victim of death as anything or anyone else." Enns is absolutely right that how one understands the relation of the frame-narrator and the Qohelet figure (speaking in the first person in the book's main body) determines how one reads the overall message. He does not follow Longman's line of interpretation. [*BBR* 22.3, 31.1; *CBQ* 10/12; *JSOT* 36.5; *JETS* 6/12; *TJ* Fall 13].

★ **Fredericks, Daniel C.**, and Daniel J. Estes. *Ecclesiastes & Song of Songs* (Apollos) 2010. Judging from the strength of Fredericks's diss. on *Qoheleth's Language* (1988), which argued the case for an earlier dating of the book, I expected this to be a competent, strongly conservative work. It is indeed excellent, and more approachable than Bartholomew as a briefer work (250pp.). Fredericks steers away from interpretations of *hebel* as "vanity, futile, meaningless, absurd, foul, false" because these "are inconsistent with the explicit content of Ecclesiastes, or are foreign to the OT's meanings" of the word. Instead, "by considering *hebel* to mean 'temporary', the reader will discover a book that speaks clearly to the effects of the Fall" (70). "The book's message is clearly about *transience*, not minimal purposefulness" (43). He helpfully cites James 4:14 as a NT parallel. I propose that pastors will find this to be one of the three or four most serviceable commentaries on Qoheleth, even though I balk at his view that "the book consoles rather than disturbs the realist" (45). There are reviews of his PhD work [*JTS* 4/90; *CBQ* 4/91; *JBL* Win 89; *HS* 1990]. His partner, Estes, does a capable job on Song of Songs; they are a well-matched pair. [*JSOT* 35.5; *Chm* Spr 14; *JETS* 9/11; *BSac* 1/12].

★ Gibson, David. *Living Life Backward: How Ecclesiastes Teaches Us to Live in Light of the End*, 2017. For pastors, a fascinating avenue into the baffling book. The author has a brilliant mind with fine training (Aberdeen PhD), and he has applied himself well to the task of interpreting the Bible book. Gibson pastors Trinity Church, Aberdeen, and I can tell he has preached the material. I picked up this Crossway title because a fellow scholar working on Ecclesiastes said it is the best exposition he has ever read. I believe Gibson's earlier *Destiny: Learning to Live by Preparing to Die* (IVP, 2016) may be the same book. Note that it is not a full exposition; he leaves out chs. 6, 8, and 10. [*Found* Aut 17].

★ **Kidner, Derek.** *A Time to Mourn and a Time to Dance* (BST) 1976. I am not satisfied with his thesis that the "Preacher" merely assumes the posture of the secularist—his dark mood and worldly perspective—for the sake of apologetics. Surely, instead, we are reading the record of Qoheleth's inner turmoil and debate. But this is still a great book for the preacher. Compare with Hubbard, Enns, Provan, Brown, Greidanus, Ryken, O'Donnell, Gibson, and Chris Wright; these expositional helps are tops for the pastor's study. [*EvQ* 1/77; *JETS* 3/78].

★ **Longman, Tremper, III.** (NICOT) 1998. Influential in conservative circles on the issue of authorship and genre, Longman speaks of Qoheleth as "framed wisdom autobiography" (17). I wrestle with some interpretive maneuvers in this fine NICOT. Though there is obviously an editorial voice (frame-narrator) in chs. 1 and 12, does setting pious editor over against skeptical Qoheleth serve to answer the problems and resolve the tensions? Does not the epilogist affirm the wisdom of the Teacher (12:9)? One comes away from Longman wondering if anything positive, from the NT standpoint, can be said for the Teacher's message. Instead, the message must be challenged and wholly redirected at the conclusion of the book. "Here is the conclusion of the matter": there is nothing like Longman to sensitize the reader to the tension between much of Qoheleth's seemingly secular advice and other biblical exhortations (self-denial, etc.). The pastor who uses this will be helped in preaching Christ, but this is not a definitive evangelical commentary like, say, Boda on Zechariah. Perhaps, owing to the diversity of opinions, a definitive evangelical commentary can never be written on Ecclesiastes. For understanding the message of Ecclesiastes, I prefer Hubbard's and Enns's lines of interpretation and am intrigued by Fredericks (who finds a bit too positive a message). [*JBL* Win 99; *JSOT* 79; *Int* 1/99; *CBQ* 1/99; *SwJT* Fall 99; *BSac* 4/98; *HS* 1999; *RelSRev* 7/98; *VT* 54.2]. Longman's views are distilled in CorBC; see Konkel–Longman below.

★ **Provan, Iain.** *Ecclesiastes, Song of Songs* (NIVAC) 2001. The interpretation of Ecclesiastes is, in my opinion, more convincing and helpful than that of the Song. In the latter he revives the so-called dramatic interpretation (cf. Delitzsch); specifically he opts for the three-character version, proposed long ago by Ibn Ezra, then by Ewald, and developed by S. R. Driver. This reading of the Song reminds me of *The Princess Bride*, in which a lovely, simple girl is taken by royalty, but she pines for her one true love, a country boy. Provan also has excellent commentaries on Kings and Lamentations.

Akin, Daniel L., and Jonathan Akin. *Exalting Jesus in Ecclesiastes* (CCE) 2016.

✓ **Athas, George.** [𝓜], *Ecclesiastes, Song of Songs* (SGBC) 2020. A full commentary (400pp.) and more valuable entry in the series, scholarship-wise. Athas, an able Hebraist who teaches at Moore in Sydney, demonstrates his learning in wider ANE studies. For Ecclesiastes, he takes the narrator to be a later member of the Davidic royal family (now displaced, 220s BC [58]). The Qohelet figure's material (1:2–12:8) is read in a strongly negative fashion: "descends into the disorderly, before expiring with one last discernible sigh at the end. . . . The whole movement gives a sense of uncontrolled, heavy descent into darkness and oblivion, capturing perfectly Qohelet's sense of the fate of humanity and, more particularly, the Jewish nation" (41) under the Ptolemies. As regards the Song, Athas dates the book extremely late (mid-160s BC) and adopts the three-character interpretation (a love triangle). Before the maiden is taken by the "villainous playboy king" (358), she sleeps with her shepherd-boyfriend in a "do or die" move. (Though widespread in liberal studies—e.g., see J. L. Andruska, "Unmarried Lovers in the Song of Songs," *JTS* 72 (2021): 1–18—this idea of celebrated unmarried sex in the Bible is surprising for a more conservative series.) Behind all this, Athas thinks, the book's poetry is alluding to the Seleucid tyranny, massacre of the Jews in 167 BC, and the Maccabean revolt. I am not convinced by the interpretations or the strictly constructed historical contexts. [*BBR* 31.3; *JETS* 9/20].

✓ Barbour, Jennifer. ‡ *The Story of Israel in the Book of Qohelet: Ecclesiastes as Cultural Memory*, 2012. Published by OUP. [*JHebS* 13].

✓ **Barton, George A.** ‡ (ICC) 1908. Treats the book as quite late. He may still be of some use to students researching philology, textual issues, and history of interpretation. Barton's own contribution to interpretation is unsatisfactory, as he opts to explain the tensions in the book by source criticism.

Belcher, Richard P., Jr. (EPSC) 2014. An extensive exposition (500pp.), followed by a more exegetically focused "Mentor" vol. of 430pp. (2017). The author is capable, studious, and has an evident love for God and the church. I have questions, however, about Belcher's understanding of the book and the Hebrew wisdom tradition.

Bennett, Stephen J. *Ecclesiastes/Lamentations: A Commentary in the Wesleyan Tradition* (NBBC) 2010. [*JETS* 3/12].

Bergant, Dianne. ‡ *Job, Ecclesiastes* (OTM) 1982.

✓ Berlejung, A., and P. van Hecke, eds. *The Language of Qohelet in Its Context* (Schoors FS), 2007. An enormous vol. (742pp.).

✓ Boda, Mark J., Tremper Longman III, and Christian G. Rata, eds. *The Words of the Wise Are Like Goads: Engaging Qohelet in the 21st Century*, 2013. An enormous wealth of essays here (about 500pp.) in this Eisenbrauns book. [*CBQ* 10/13; *JSOT* 38.5].

Bollhagen, James G. (ConcC) 2011. I have scarcely used this full (440pp.), confessional Lutheran exegesis and exposition. [*JETS* 9/12; *RBL* 4/14; *SeTR* 3.2 (Estes)].

F Breed, Brennan, and Davis Hankins. ‡ (Illum).

Bridges, Charles. (GS) 1860. Not his best effort, but still helpful to some all the same for theology and pastoral reflection. See his more famous work on Proverbs.

✓ Brown, Erica. (Maggid) 2023. Offers an engaging, very full (over 500pp.), conservative Jewish exposition of the book as "the search for meaning" (mentioned in the title). The author has also contributed the Esther and Jonah vols. to the series. The Preface reads, "this book emerges primarily from the study of classical Jewish scholarship, from talmudic and midrashic interpretations to medieval and pre-modern commentators."

☆ **Brown, William P.** ‡ (I) 2000. Though brief, this is a very good, informed, and balanced book to guide the expositor. I bought Brown for his theological interpretation. Brown dates the book earlier (ca. 300 BC) than some critics. He interacts less with scholarship than students would prefer. The author now teaches at Columbia Seminary and has published several well-received books on Psalms and the wisdom literature. [*OTA* 10/00; *Them* Spr 01; *Int* 7/01; *VT* 53.2; *JSOT* 94; *SwJT* Sum 02; *RelSRev* 1/01 (Crenshaw)]. Do note that Brown's positive reading of Ecclesiastes here has developed into something far more mature and nuanced in *Wisdom's Wonder* (2014).

✓ Christianson, Eric S. *Ecclesiastes through the Centuries* (BBC) 2007. [*BL* 2007].

✓ **Crenshaw, James L.** ‡ (OTL) 1987. The leading critical authority on sapiential literature offers a 32-page intro and 138pp. of commentary (no indices). He compels you to think hard about the perplexing tensions in the message of the book, which he dates between 250 BC and 225 BC, and champions the view that Qoheleth is best read as a bitter skeptic. Frankly, numbers had hoped for a more substantial, thorough commentary, especially in documented interaction with other scholarly views, and were disappointed. I admit I don't care for this commentary. Longman likes it a lot, however, which may explain why his NICOT follows OTL in its deeply pessimistic reading of Qoheleth's worldview. [*TJ* Spr 88; *HS* 1989]. Crenshaw's views are slightly updated in his fine textbook *Old Testament Wisdom* (rev. 2010). There are additional studies in *Qoheleth: The Ironic Wink* (2013) [*CBQ* 7/14; *JSOT* 38.5; *JTS* 4/16].

Currid, John D. (Welwyn) 2015. I regret I have not seen it.

Curtis, Edward M. *Ecclesiastes and Song of Songs* (TTC) 2013. I have not seen it (178pp.), but one review says that, although it "does not offer new insights," the vol. is "a good starting point" for pastors and teachers [*JESOT* 3.2].

Davidson, Robert. [*M*], *Ecclesiastes and Song of Solomon* (DSB) 1986. A well-researched devotional commentary, marred slightly by its critical approach.

✓ Davis, Ellen F. ‡ *Proverbs, Ecclesiastes, and the Song of Songs* (WestBC) 2000. See Proverbs above.

✓ Delitzsch, Franz. (KD) ET 1891. Full of insight.

F Dell, Katharine. ‡ (ECC). She is also scheduled for an installment in IECOT. Along the way she wrote a quality monograph on *Interpreting Ecclesiastes: Readers Old and New* (2013) [*CBQ* 10/14; *JSOT* 38.5; *RevExp* 5/15; *BBR* 26.1; *JHebS* 14], and coedited (with Kynes) *Reading Ecclesiastes Intertextually* (2014) [*JTS* 10/15; *JSOT* 40.5].

✓ **Duncan, Julie Ann.** ‡ (AbOTC) 2017. Well-written, thorough, and to be regarded as one of the strongest vols. in the series. Alongside the exegesis, Duncan offers an existential and liberal theological interpretation that interacts with literature and philosophy, ancient and modern. She teaches at Garrett-Evangelical. Much to appreciate here. There is wisdom in her rendering *hebel* as "vapor" to keep the metaphor before the reader: "to translate all occurrences of *hebel* with any single abstract term will invariably prove a misfit" (9). [*CBQ* 7/18; *Int* 4/19; *JSOT* 47.5].

✓ **Eaton, Michael A.** (retired TOTC) 1983. Not one of the strongest in the series. Still, students should consult it. Eaton's is a voice to be counted in the debates on this book. Some conservative scholars have a higher opinion of this book. For example, Hill and Walton call Eaton "the most helpful of the evangelical commentaries" (*Survey of the OT* [2000], 372). Eaton reads the message of the book more positively: "It is an essay in apologetics. It defends the life of faith in a generous God by pointing to the grimness of the alternative" (44). See Heim. [*EvQ* 7/86; *WTJ* Fall 84].

✓ Ellul, Jacques. [*M*], *Reason for Being: A Meditation on Ecclesiastes*, ET 1990. Focuses less on exegesis and more on the meaning and theology of the book. As with all Ellul's books, this examines the Scriptures' relevance today in a most incisive fashion. His essay style is a joy to read, but the message may afflict the comfortable/contented. See another of his works under Kings. [*RTR* 5/92].

Eswine, Zack. *Recovering Eden: The Gospel according to Ecclesiastes* (GAOT) 2014. I regret I have not seen it, but it is said to be quite useful for pastors, and well-written. [*WTJ* Spr 15].

✓ Farmer, K. A. [*M*], *Proverbs and Ecclesiastes* (ITC-E) 1991. See Proverbs above.

☆ Ferguson, Sinclair. *The Pundit's Folly: Chronicles of an Empty Life*, 1995. More an evangelistic tool, treating major ideas in Ecclesiastes, less an exposition. Brilliantly done. Somewhat similar is another slim Banner issue, hard to put down: Peter Barnes, *Both Sides Now: Ecclesiastes and the Human Condition* (2004). Cf. Gibson above.

✓ Fink, David, ed. *Proverbs, Ecclesiastes, Song of Songs* (RCS) 2023.

☆ **Fox, Michael V.** ‡ *A Time to Tear Down and a Time to Build Up: A Rereading of Ecclesiastes*, 1999. "Fox's rereading of Qoheleth is priceless" (Murphy) and influential in critical debate. I accept his theory that the book is a narrative unity in which the voice of an anonymous frame-narrator quotes the words of the persona Qoheleth (though form criticism is of less value for this Bible book). I am not convinced that "absurd" is the best rendering of *hebel*, or that we should read the book as if it were existentialist literature. Fox says he is impressed with the similarities between Qoheleth and Camus (see pp.8–15), and I think that mostly explains his approach. He here updates and expands his earlier *Qohelet and His Contradictions* (1989), which was an erudite, lengthy (almost 400pp.) study. It also included a brief commentary [*JTS* 10/90; *CBQ* 4/91]. *A Time to Tear Down* is definitely worth consulting!

Fox is a Jewish scholar and his work is a favorite of Longman. This and Seow are "must buys" for the scholarly pastor with money and keen interest in OT wisdom literature. [*JSOT* 89; *PSB* 21.3; *ExpTim* 12/00; *Int* 7/00; *CBQ* 4/00; *Them* Aut 00; *JR* 7/00; *Bib* 82.1; *RTR* 4/01; *EvQ* 10/01; *VT* 53.2].

✓ **Fox, Michael V.** ‡ (JPS) 2004. JPS offers a more concise, slightly more accessible commentary, and more discussion of traditional Jewish reflection on Qoheleth than the previous Fox entry. [*JETS* 6/05; *Int* 4/05; *BL* 2006; *BSac* 7/07; *RBL*].

Fuerst, W. J. ‡ *The Books of Ruth, Esther, Ecclesiastes, The Song of Songs, Lamentations* (CBC) 1975.

F Garfinkel, Stephen. ‡ (BerO).

☆ **Garrett, Duane A.** *Proverbs, Ecclesiastes, Song of Songs* (NAC) 1993. See Proverbs.

✓ Ginsburg, Christian David. *The Song of Songs and Coheleth*, 1857–61. The work of a somewhat critical, converted Jewish scholar which is well-known for its treatment of the history of exegesis (27–243 in the 1861 *Coheleth*). It is worth consulting the 1970 Ktav reprint. This scholar should be distinguished from the liberal H. L. Ginsberg, who authored *Supplementary Studies in Koheleth* (1952).

☆ **Goldingay, John.** [𝓜], (BGW) 2021. A major new interpretation (300pp.) in a major new series. The Fuller professor emeritus puts on full display his independent streak, exegetical skill, and theological depth. Consistently taking critical positions on introductory issues, Goldingay dates the book quite late. There are oddities here, with *qōhelet* rendered "Congregationalist," *hokmāh* rendered "smartness" instead of "wisdom" (though many humans are exceedingly intelligent but morally foolish). On the other hand, there is commendable restraint and reluctance to overinterpret the key word *hebel*, translated more literally as "mere breath." This vol. is a real success, and it includes some touching personal notes (e.g., p.55). Note: Goldingay uses "Qohelet" to refer to the book and its author; by "Congregationalist" he means the figure created by the author, or a pen name for the voice speaking throughout the book (34). [*BBR* 32.3; *BL* 2022; *JETS* 9/22].

✓ **Gordis, Robert.** [𝓜], *Koheleth: The Man and His World*, 1951, 3rd ed. 1968. Magnificent! One of the best exegetical commentaries on the book, rivaling Seow, Fox, and Murphy except that it is more dated. Gordis was a leading Jewish scholar of a previous generation, known for careful and thorough textual work and profound learning in the Jewish exegetical tradition. Fairly conservative.

☆ Greidanus, Sidney. *Preaching Christ from Ecclesiastes: Foundations for Expository Sermons*, 2010. A difficult task requires a rather full book on the topic (376pp.). See his earlier helpful works on *Preaching Christ from the OT* and *Preaching Christ from Genesis*. The author is professor emeritus of preaching at Calvin Seminary. [*JSOT* 35.5; *RTR* 4/11; *ExpTim* 7/12 (Bartholomew); *TJ* Spr 11].

✓ **Heim, Knut M.** (TOTC-R) 2019. Replaces Eaton. An intriguing, less conventional reading of Ecclesiastes, suggesting the use of "calculated hyper-ambiguity" and "underdetermined language." Heim says "the book as we now have it is the written record of a speech sequence similar to the routines of modern stand-up comedians, who use the medium of comedy to critique problematic issues" (x). To what degree is irony, subversion, and political satire present? He dates the book to the third century and Ptolemaic rule: "Ecclesiastes is resistance literature" (6). In my view Heim offers a thought experiment that makes Ecclesiastes an outlier in the OT canon. See also Heim on Proverbs. [*CTJ* 4/21; *BBR* 31.3].

F Heim, Knut M. (ZECOT).

✓ **Hengstenberg, Ernst W.** 1860. Childs calls it his best—a full, vigorous commentary. Reprinted by Sovereign Grace (1960). Now free online. Still worth consulting, if one is pursuing fuller research. Critical scholars sometimes accused Hengstenberg of confusing apologetics and exegesis, but here that is not an issue.

F   Hernández, Dominick S. (EEC). From a well-trained Talbot prof. A previous report listed Bob McCabe and Kyle Dunham.

☆   **Holmstedt, Robert D., John A. Cook, and Phillip S. Marshall.** *Qoheleth* (BHHB) 2017. Among the most detailed (310pp.), technical, and valuable series entries, especially on account of (a) these three authors' expertise in Hebrew grammar/syntax and linguistics, and (b) the baffling linguistic profile of Qoheleth. To make proper use of this handbook, one needs to digest the linguistic terminology and approach (see pp.3–33). Their dating is early- to mid-Hellenistic era. They leave הבל untranslated. [*BBR* 29.3; *CBQ* 10/18; *JSOT* 43.5].

Horne, Milton P. ‡ *Proverbs–Ecclesiastes* (S&H) 2003. See under Proverbs.

☆   **Hubbard, David A.** *Ecclesiastes–Song of Solomon* (WCC) 1993. Building on his insightful little book entitled *Beyond Futility* (1976), Hubbard is stronger on "Koheleth" (238pp.) than the Song (93pp.). Excellent for the pastor! Both Hubbard and Kidner are also worth reading by the student for their discussion of the message of the book. Only the dating of Qoheleth (4th or early 3rd century BC) might suggest the commentary is mildly critical [𝓜]. Past editions of this guide recommended Hubbard for purchase.

✓   Jones, Edgar. ‡ (Torch) 1961.

Kaiser, Walter C. *Ecclesiastes: Total Life*, 1979. Well-researched, practical exposition, but I prefer Kidner. The approach here raises questions. Bible students struggle with the severe tensions in Ecclesiastes between dark despair and hope, skepticism and faith. How can both attitudes or outlooks be contained, even integrated, in one book? What do we do with the contradictions? I believe these true-to-life tensions need to be retained in our interpretation, rather than resolved in some facile way. Liberals have tended to overemphasize the forlorn, skeptical tone of the book, while some believers have overstressed the notes of hope and the positive exhortations. I am less than pleased with any commentary which attempts to ease these tensions. I find that Kaiser tends to relativize the pessimistic/skeptical portions and misses the pathos of the book. See Perry below.

Keddie, Gordon. *Looking for the Good Life*, 1991. A popular-level P&R exposition from a devout Reformed Presbyterian minister.

✓   Keefer, Arthur Jan. *Ecclesiastes and the Meaning of Life in the Ancient World*, 2022. From CUP. The study does not deal with "how Ecclesiastes informs the meaning of one's life today" (x), but implications are there. He draws from psychological research and probes how meaning in life connects with suffering, when the latter tends to strip away coherence, significance, and purpose. [*Or* 91.3; *TGA* 12/23; *CBQ* 4/24].

Konkel, August H., and Tremper Longman III. *Job, Ecclesiastes, Song of Songs* (CorBC) 2006. Longman offers the commentary on the latter two Bible books, distilling his scholarship published earlier in NICOT.

✓   **Krüger, Thomas.** ‡ (Herm) ET 2004. Specialists and advanced students take note of this technical exegesis, which includes 38pp. of introduction, 180pp. of commentary on the Hebrew, and one of the fullest bibliographies for Qoheleth studies (55pp.). There is heavy interaction with German scholarship. Krüger says that reconstructing the history of the text's origin is his special focus. He also devotes attention to structural issues and textual criticism. While he finds rhetorically cohesive units in the book, Qoheleth as a whole is contradictory ("conveys no clear teaching") and reveals an internal debate. Within the book, he says, "the form of wisdom teaching . . . is adopted critically and ironically," and so we can draw "no direct conclusions regarding the social and institutional context in which and for which it was written" (12). Krüger attempts to teach us how much we don't know. Not for pastors. He varies his interpretation of *hebel* as meaning "futility" or "fleeting" in different places. Ralph Klein calls this "the best of the current commentaries on Ecclesiastes/Qoheleth." [*ExpTim* 2/06; *BSac* 4/08; *CurTM* 6/07 (Klein)].

Leupold, H. C. 1952. A thorough, old Lutheran exegesis. See Leupold under Genesis.

Limburg, James. ‡ *Encountering Ecclesiastes*, 2006. A thoughtful, brief, personal exposition, more along thematic lines, from a retired Lutheran OT scholar. It is meant for preachers interested in Qoheleth's message. [*ExpTim* 10/07; *Chm* Aut 09].

✓ **Loader, J. A.** ‡ (T&I) ET 1986. His more important (and provocative) work was *Polar Structures in the Book of Qoheleth* (1979). The commentary is supposedly written for pastors and laypeople, but few such folk find it accessible. [*HS* 1987; *Chm* 101.1 (Kidner)].

✓ **Lohfink, Norbert.** ‡ (ContC) ET 2003. The effort expended both to translate the 1980 German work and to expand it subsequently shows its importance. As compared with other recent commentaries, Lohfink tends to put more emphasis upon the positive message of the book—and this was before Whybray's interpretation. There is also more Christian reflection than we might have anticipated. Another contribution is said to be the structural analysis, which differs from the famous A. D. G. Wright structure I like (see below). This vol. is more accessible than some others in the same series; Lohfink states upfront that he did not set out to write an academic commentary (vii). [*JTS* 4/04; *JSOT* 28.5; *Int* 1/05; *CJ* 7/05; *JBL* Fall 04 (Van Leeuwen); *RBL*; *JHebS*].

F  Lucas, Ernest. *Ecclesiastes, Song of Songs* (EBTC)?

Luther, Martin. ET 1972. His exposition is found in Vol. 15 of *Luther's Works*.

✓ Meek, Russell L., and David J. H. Beldman. *A Classified Bibliography on Ecclesiastes*, 2019. [*JSOT* 44.5; *BBR* 30.4; *Int* 1/21].

Miersma, Thomas. 2022. Subtitled "A Reflective Exposition." [*JETS* 6/23].

✓ **Miller, Douglas B.** (BCBC) 2010. Quite useful. Earlier he published *Symbol and Rhetoric in Ecclesiastes: The Place of Hebel in Qohelet's Work* (2002), which is very instructive, even if his conclusion (bad/foul air) doesn't hold up. [*JR* 1/05; *JNES* 7/07]. He still recognizes that "not everything is *hebel* in the same way" (154). "Apparent inconsistencies in the way *hebel* is used are actually due to the multivalency of this tensive symbol" (161). The foci are transience, insubstantiality, and foulness (e.g., it is bad for wealth to be passed on to a fool [2:18–19]).

Moore, T. M. *Ecclesiastes: Ancient Wisdom When All Else Fails*, 2001. Translates the text into a poetic form more familiar to Westerners: iambic pentameter. From IVP.

Murphy, Roland E. ‡ (FOTL) 1981. See under Ruth. Superseded by WBC below.

☆ **Murphy, Roland E.** ‡ (WBC) 1992. Among the strongest studies of the Hebrew available, from a world authority on the wisdom literature. There is a lengthy introduction and 155pp. of commentary. Murphy works hard to do justice to the tension between joyful preacher (3:11–13; 8:15) and the frustrated skeptic (2:10ff; 4:1ff). Not as in-depth as his Hermeneia vol. on Song of Songs, but this WBC was a recommended purchase for many editions of my guide. Bartholomew took its place. (By the way, I regard Seow as equally valuable.) [*RTR* 9/93; *Int* 7/95; *BSac* 4/94].

Murphy, Roland E., and Elizabeth Huwiler. [𝓜], *Proverbs, Ecclesiastes & Song of Songs* (NIBC) 1996. See Proverbs above.

☆ O'Donnell, Douglas Sean. (REC) 2014. I have only briefly looked at these sermons, but the book receives strong commendations (220pp.). The gentleman has a flair for preaching, it must be said, and communicates a heart full of the gospel. I find O'Donnell to be an able, wise expositor, though some of his interpretive moves are a bit more folksy (e.g., referring to "Pastor Solomon") or sentimental (6) than I'd recommend. His is a more positive reading of the book's message (cf. Eaton). O'Donnell pastored in the PCA before moving to an academic post in Australia. See also his work on Song of Songs. [*JSOT* 43.5].

✓ **Ogden, Graham S.** ‡ (Read) 1987, 2nd ed. 2007. An influential Sheffield study, not to be missed by students. He was among those, early on, who urged a more positive reading. Ogden is a favorite of Bartholomew. See also the handbook below. A couple of fellow scholars once told me this was their favorite book on Qoheleth. [*Bib* 71.3; *CRBR* 1989; *RBL*].

✓ **Ogden, Graham S., and Lynell Zogbo.** (UBS) 1998. The *Handbook* runs to 471pp.

Olyott, Stuart J. *A Life Worth Living and a Lord Worth Loving* (Welwyn) 1983. Covers Ecclesiastes and the Song.

Pauw, Amy Plantinga. ‡ *Proverbs and Ecclesiastes* (Belief) 2015. [*BBR* 31.1].

✓ Perry, T. A. *The Book of Ecclesiastes (Qohelet) and the Path to Joyous Living*, 2015. From CUP, and reminding me a bit of Walter Kaiser's astonishing claim that "the mood of Ecclesiastes is one of delight" (42). [*JSOT* 42.5].

✓ Peterson, Brian Neil. *Qoheleth's Hope: The Message of Ecclesiastes in a Broken World*, 2020. Pursues mainly a rhetorical approach, emphasizing life's transience. Despite the Fortress imprint, this is a more conservative study. Peterson disagrees with scholars who offer more pessimistic interpretations of *hebel* and the book; he finds instead a more positive, even pious, message. [*JSOT* 44.5; *CBQ* 7/20].

✓ Plumptre, Edward H. ‡ (CBSC) 1881. Childs's favorite (back in the 1970s) among commentaries in English. The author is notable in the history of interpretation for pressing arguments that Qoheleth betrays the influence of Greek thought.

Reynolds, Edward. 1669, repr. 1998. A massive Puritan exposition found in Reynolds's collected works, reprinted by Soli Deo Gloria. Now free online.

☆ Rogland, Max. (ESVEC) 2022. Astute training in Hebrew Bible (Leiden PhD) is here married to a shepherd's heart. The author pastors a PCA congregation in Columbia, SC, has taught OT at Erskine Seminary, has preached through the book, and previously did the notes for Ecclesiastes in the *ESV Study Bible*.

☆ Ryken, Philip G. *Ecclesiastes: Why Everything Matters* (PTW) 2010. The author is always brimming with ideas for exposition and application. See his big books on Exodus, Jeremiah, Luke, etc. [*Them* 41.3].

✓ **Schoors, Antoon.** ‡ (HCOT) 2013. The capstone of a career (†2023), the last thirty-five years of which centered on Ecclesiastes, this massive commentary (nearly 50pp. of bibliography, 854pp. of commentary) by Schoors will keep fellow scholars busy for an equally long period. He builds upon his extensive research of the language of the book published in two vols., *The Preacher Sought to Find Pleasing Words* (1992, 2004). In a tome of this size, readers regret a lack of indices. Schoors's conclusions? He says "it is not possible to detect a clear literary structure in the book" (19), that Qoheleth is a realist and skeptic, "but remains a searching believer" (20), that the dating is the Hellenistic period (3rd–2nd cent. BC), and that Qoheleth's "image of God leaves a fatalistic impression" (22). [*RB* 123.1].

✓ Schoors, A., ed. ‡ *Qohelet in the Context of Wisdom*, 1998. From the 1997 Colloquium Biblicum Lovaniense, this contained cutting-edge scholarship for its time (526pp.).

Scott, Robert B. Y. ‡ (retired AB) 1965. See Proverbs above. Seow replaced Scott.

✓ Segal, Benjamin J. ‡ *Kohelet's Pursuit of Truth*, 2016. Offers a fresh translation of the Hebrew (with notes), quotes from the rabbis (Rashi, Ibn Ezra, etc.), and "a new reading" of the book. [*BBR* 27.4; *CBQ* 1/20].

☆ **Seow, Choon-Leong.** ‡ (AB) 1997. Reviewers have given this vol. high praise. "[I]f readers and pastors can afford only one book on Ecclesiastes, I would suggest Seow" (Van Leeuwen). It might be instructive to learn that the Denver Seminary OT faculty pick Seow and Bartholomew as their favorites. Seow dates the book to the Persian period—earlier than many other critical scholars—and seems disposed to take the view that the book is a substantial unity. There is a wealth of textual study, linguistic analysis, and theological interpretation in this commentary, aimed at scholars, yet accessible and readable. He urges that we see Qoheleth as a wise realist. Most pastors will skip this, but advanced students should buy it (s/h?). See my remarks on Fox above. [*JBL* Fall 99; *PSB* 20.2; *JSOT* 79; *Int* 1/99; *JR* 10/98].

Shaw, Benjamin. 2008. Mainly an exposition, issued by Banner of Truth and arguing for Solomonic authorship. [*RTR* 4/23].

☆ Shepherd, Jerry. (EBCR) 2008. I have not had much opportunity to use this 110-page commentary, but what I have seen is well-studied and well-written. What a change from EBC! Shepherd's approach to the message of the book owes much to Longman: "Qohelet serves as a foil for the frame-narrator to get across his message of the danger of pessimistic, skeptical wisdom" (269). He admits that this stance raises serious questions as to whether we should even preach and teach out of Qoheleth's words. See J. Stafford Wright for the weaker EBC predecessor. [*BL* 2010].

✓ Shields, Martin A. *The End of Wisdom: A Reappraisal of the Historical and Canonical Function of Ecclesiastes*, 2006. Runs as far as possible with the negative reading of Qoheleth (see Crenshaw and Longman). [*BL* 2007; *RBL* 6/09]. As he wrote in *TynBul* 50 (1999): 139, "it is clear that the wisdom of Qohelet has gone astray . . . and is ultimately incompatible with the message of the remainder of the canon."

✓ **Towner, W. Sibley.** ‡ (NIB) 1997. This commentary is a little short of 100pp. and does not compete seriously with heavyweight works like Longman, Murphy, Fox, and Seow. This is a fallback for students. Qoheleth is dated around 250 BC. Towner is best known for his commentary on Daniel.

Trier, Daniel. *Proverbs and Ecclesiastes* (Brazos) 2011. [*CBQ* 4/15; *BBR* 31.1].

Turner, Marie. ‡ (Earth) 2017. [*JETS* 6/18].

☆ Webb, Barry G. *Five Festal Garments: Christian Reflections on the Song of Songs, Ruth, Lamentations, Ecclesiastes and Esther*, 2000. See under Ruth.

✓ **Weeks, Stuart.** ‡ (ICC-R) 2 vols., 2020–22. Eagerly awaited, but Weeks outstripped my expectations! Replaces Barton. After about 225pp. of Introduction, we are treated to an astonishingly thorough (over 1100pp.) and fresh exegesis with magnificent textual notes. He dates the book to the Hellenistic period, not earlier than 300 BC. In his interpretation, the use of *hebel* does not point so much to the absurdity of life, or epistemological skepticism, or the world as incomprehensible. Rather, the problem is more human finitude ("limits of our own perception" [27]) and fallibility where we misapprehend reality. "The idea of an illusion . . . and of corresponding human delusion or confusion, comes close to catching the sense of *hebel* both in Ecclesiastes and in many of the other texts where it is used" (28). Weeks does not distinguish between the author of the narrative frame and of the monologue; they are one and the same. This is a landmark technical reference and now my first choice in that category. Students especially will appreciate the bibliography. [*BL* 2022; *JTS* 4/22, 10/22; *JETS* 3/22, 12/22]. See Weeks under Wisdom Literature and Proverbs above and note his preliminary *Ecclesiastes and Scepticism* (2012) [*JSOT* 37.5; *VT* 63.3; *JHebS* 13], which distances Qoheleth from a skeptical tradition, and *The Making of Many Books: Printed Works on Ecclesiastes 1523–1875* (2014) [*BBR* 25.2; *VT* 66.3; *JJS* 66.2].

✓ Whitley, C. F. ‡ *Koheleth: His Language and Thought*, 1979. A detailed, technical treatment of the book.

✓ **Whybray, R. N.** ‡ (NCB) 1989. One of the more important critical commentaries, this parts company from the usual critical interpretations in that it emphasizes the positive, even joyful aspects in Ecclesiastes. He builds on his earlier article, "Qohelet: Preacher of Joy," *JSOT* 23 (1982): 87–92. (On the same topic, see Eunny P. Lee's *The Vitality of Enjoyment in Qohelet's Theological Rhetoric* [2005].) Whybray's vol. is quite useful, though I think he dulls the sharp pessimistic edge of the Bible book. [*CBQ* 7/91; *RTR* 9/90; *HS* 1990]. See also Whybray's entry in Sheffield's OT Guides (1989).

Williams, A. L. ‡ (CBSC) 1922.

Wolfe, Lisa Michele. ‡ (Wisdom) 2020. [*Int* 1/22; *JSOT* 45.5].

Wright, A. D. G. ‡ "Ecclesiastes," *New Jerome Bible Commentary*, 1990. A stand-out treatment in a one-vol. commentary. The author made a significant contribution to scholarship with articles on the structure of the book. See "The Riddle of the Sphinx: The Structure of the Book of Qoheleth," *CBQ* 30 (1968): 313–34; and "The Riddle of the Sphinx Revisited," *CBQ* 42 (1980): 38–51.

Wright, C. H. H. 1883. Still consulted by scholars.

☆ Wright, Christopher J. H. *Hearing the Message of Ecclesiastes*, 2023. As Bartholomew puts it well, "Wright is not only a brilliant scholar, but also a great communicator." See the similar exposition on Daniel. Well worth the money.

✓ Wright, J. Robert, ed. *Proverbs, Ecclesiastes, Song of Solomon* (ACCS) 2004. [*CTJ* 4/07].

Wright, J. Stafford. (EBC) 1991. Found a prominent note of joy in Ecclesiastes. These 60pp. were thoughtful at points and included application, but Wright did not probe deeply. It helped that, in the editing process, John Walton strengthened the introduction. This EBC was weak. See Shepherd.

✓ Zuck, Roy B., ed. *Reflecting with Solomon: Selected Studies on the Book of Ecclesiastes*, 1994. A sizable (432pp.) collection of book chapters and journal articles—some significant from an academic standpoint, some not at all—treating the text and message of Ecclesiastes. Contributors range all the way from critical scholars like Crenshaw, Fox, and Murphy to evangelical pastors like Wiersbe. [*Them* 1/96].

NOTES: (1) Amy Erickson and Andrew Davis review "Recent Research on the Megilloth," *CBR* 14 (2016) 298–318. (2) Russell L. Meek, "Twentieth and Twenty-first-century Readings of *Hebel* (הבל) in Ecclesiastes," *CBR* 14.3 (2016): 279–97; (3) Elizabeth Mehlman and Russell L. Meek, "Sputtering at the Start Line? Trends in Theological Interpretation of Scripture through Three Theological Commentaries on Ecclesiastes," *BBR* 31.1 (2021): 16–38.

# SONG OF SONGS

★ **Duguid, Iain M.** (TOTC-R) 2015. The author combines the best qualities of a Bible commentator: faith, learning, a literary sensibility, exegetical good sense, solid theology, and a lucid writing style. I've read everything from his Cambridge PhD to his sermonic work and never been disappointed. This is an excellent replacement vol. in Tyndale, doing justice to the called-for natural interpretation while retaining elements of a spiritual approach (28). I am in hearty agreement with Duguid on the key question: "whether the central relationship of the Song is intended by God as a typological picture of . . . Christ and his church . . . , or if the background . . . is more properly to be found in the world of wisdom literature" (34). The Song "is best understood as a wisdom piece" (36). The three-character view receives a shrewd critique. See Carr for the retired work. Note Duguid's sermons in REC. [*Them* 8/15; *JTS* 10/16; *JETS* 9/15; *JSOT* 40.5].

★ Fredericks, Daniel C., and **Daniel J. Estes.** *Ecclesiastes & Song of Songs* (Apollos) 2010. Prior to writing his commentary, Estes taught classes on the Song in his church and college for 25 years. This is a wise, mature work and a dependable tool for pastors and teachers. There are no new, revolutionary interpretive schemes. He avoids reading the Song as an allegory of divine love. "Neither is it a drama or narrative tracing the actual experience of a specific couple. The extravagant descriptions, rather, seem to point in the direction of an idealization of love" (300), prompting "reflection on the nature of love itself" (Webb). Estes believes this biblical poetry, focused on erotic love, is a corrective to debased sexuality in the world of the ANE and today. He says "the numerous links to the wisdom literature suggests [*sic*] an additional didactic purpose as the Song endeavors to teach about the nature of intimacy" (300). Note that Estes permits himself the minor literary license of referring to the Beloved as by name: Shulammith. This is a more conservative vol. in the series; for additional comment see Ecclesiastes. Note also Estes's *Handbook on the Wisdom Books and Psalms* (2005).

★ **Gledhill, Tom.** (BST) 1994. A very full exposition (254pp.), including a study guide. He says he plows his own furrow (13) without a lot of interaction with other interpreters. I like his approach. Longman once gave this book his highest recommendation (5 stars). Compare with Provan. [*JETS* 12/96; *CTJ* 4/96].

★ **Hess, Richard S.** (BCOT) 2005. An excellent, substantial commentary that interacts a good bit with Longman (series editor), as well as with other important scholarship, and which contains insights related to the ANE background (archaeology, Semitics, comparative literature, cultural studies, etc.). This is judicious evangelical scholarship, and well-written. Some will prefer Hess, who argues "the book represents a poetic unity" (34), to (the similarly learned) Longman, who sees an anthology in the book. Hess is now the reference vol. I reach for first, if I have background-related questions. [*EvQ* 7/08; *CBQ* 7/07; *BBR* 18.2; *JETS* 12/05; *BSac* 7/06; *BL* 2006; *VT* 58.4; *RBL*; *JHebS*]. Advanced students will perceive among these recommended purchases the lack of a top-rank technical work on the Hebrew; they should consider Murphy, Keel, Fox, and Fishbane. Exum contains some important scholarship too.

★ **Longman, Tremper, III.** (NICOT) 2001. A well-rounded, satisfying reference work which treats questions regarding the original text; the structure, imagery and conventions of the Hebrew poetry; the possible social and cultural background; verse-by-verse exegesis; and theology, while making suggestions for contemporary application (see pp.58–70). The introduction is pleasingly full, especially on the history of interpretation (20–47). This or Hess should be an evangelical pastor's first purchase for the Song. Realistically, most pastors would be content with either Hess or Longman on their shelf—or even just Duguid. There is some truth in Gledhill's assertion [*Them* Sum 03] that Longman gives us a better view of the trees than the forest; I believe reading the Song as "an anthology of love poems" (58) "on a common and generally erotic theme" (56) leads him to pay less attention to the whole. One heartily concurs that "the pressing concern for exegesis of the Song is unpacking the metaphors and explaining the effect it has on us as readers" (43). [*RTR* 4/02; *JTS* 4/03; *Int* 10/02; *VT* 53.1; *JSOT* 99; *CBQ* 4/04 (peevish); *SwJT* Spr 03; *F&M*, Fall 02; *ExpTim* 11/04]. The NICOT work is distilled in CorBC; see Konkel–Longman.

★ O'Donnell, Douglas Sean. (PTW) 2012. If you're a preacher drawn to attempt an exposition of the Song, then this vol. offers a hundred or more good ideas for how to go about it. Duguid writes, "Doug O'Donnell has given us a masterful exposition that unfolds the book's very real wisdom for human relationships in a way that constantly and without allegory points us to the gospel. Highly recommended!" See Duguid above.

Akin, Daniel L. *Exalting Jesus in Song of Songs* (CCE) 2015.

☆ **Alter, Robert.** ‡ *Strong as Death Is Love: The Song of Songs, Ruth, Esther, Jonah, and Daniel,* 2015. See under Ruth.

✓ Andruska, Jennifer. *Wise and Foolish Love in the Song of Songs,* 2018. A revised Cambridge PhD. [*JTS* 10/21].

✓ **Assis, Elie.** [*M*], *Flashes of Fire: A Literary Analysis of the Song of Songs,* 2009. An Israeli scholar at Bar-Ilan, Assis has written an excellent but cost-prohibitive commentary in LHBOTS. Not to be missed by students is the analysis of the characters' dialogue. Another benefit of consulting him, and Fishbane too, is the access gained to modern Hebrew works, including the impressive Zakovitch. I appreciate Assis's reading of the Song more as a unity. [*RBL* 2011; *JHebS* 12].

✓ **Athas, George.** *Ecclesiastes, Song of Songs* (SGBC) 2020. See Ecclesiastes.

✓ **Barbiero, Gianni.** ‡ *Song of Songs: A Close Reading*, ET 2011. A Brill issue, combining literary sensitivity with theological interest, and interpreting the Song as a "unitary poem," not an anthology. He finds no narrative, "no coherent love story here" (505). [*WTJ* Fall 13 (Duguid); *JSOT* 36.5 (Exum)].

✓ **Bergant, Dianne.** ‡ (BerO) 2001. One of the better liberal commentaries, which emphasizes a literary approach (in keeping with the series aims). Compare with Exum's fuller work, which has strengths in the same area. Beautifully written, and suggestive in the best sense of the word. Since the most prominent voice in the Song is the maiden's, I believe it helps to read a woman's interpretation. Bergant teaches at Catholic Theological Union, Chicago. [*Int* 10/02; *JSOT* 28.5; *RBL*; *JHebS* 4 (negative)].

F  Berlin, Adele. ‡ (Herm). Scheduled to replace Murphy.

Bernard of Clairvaux. 1135–53. A medieval allegorical approach. There are various translated editions of the 86 sermons.

✓ **Bloch, Ariel, and Chana Bloch.** ‡ 1995. A Random House hb (republished in 1998 by U. of California), noted by many especially for its translation and poetic sensitivity. This fine study includes about 90pp. of commentary on the Hebrew text and should be taken into account by students. [*JSOT* 72; *JSS*, Spr 98; *BL* 1999; *HS* 1996; *VT* 51.2; *RelSRev* 10/01].

✓ **Brenner, Athalya.** ‡ *The Song of Songs* (OT Guides) 1989. Later complemented by her edited vol., *A Feminist Companion to the Song of Songs* (1993).

F  Bucher, Christina. (BCBC).

Burrowes, George. (GS) 1853. Allegorical approach. Compare with Durham in the same Reformed series.

☆ **Carr, G. Lloyd.** (retired TOTC) 1983. A full (for Tyndale—175pp.), informative commentary on this short book. Years ago Carr was the favorite evangelical work of Longman and Stuart. I once said the average pastor probably doesn't feel the need for anything more than this. [*EvQ* 4/86]. See Duguid.

F  Clark, Ros. (Hodder).

Cox, Harvey, and Stephanie Paulsell. ‡ *Lamentations and the Song of Songs* (Belief) 2012. The author of the commentary on the Song is Paulsell.

Curtis, Edward M. *Ecclesiastes and Song of Songs* (TTC) 2013. See Ecclesiastes.

Davidson, Robert. [*M*], (DSB) 1986. See Ecclesiastes.

✓ Davis, Ellen F. ‡ *Proverbs, Ecclesiastes, and the Song of Songs* (WestBC) 2000. See Proverbs above.

✓ Delitzsch, Franz. (KD) ET 1891. An important commentary in the history of interpretation, even if not convincing. Delitzsch put forward the idea that the song was a drama.

☆ **Dharamraj, Havilah.** *Altogether Lovely: A Thematic and Intertextual Reading of the Song of Songs*, 2018. Extraordinarily insightful. Published by Fortress. Without hesitation I call her interpretation one of my favorites on the Song. [*Int* 7/20].

Dillow, S. J. *Solomon on Sex*, 1977. I would ignore this one. See Glickman below.

F  Dobbs-Allsopp, Frederick W. ‡ (ECC).

☆ Duguid, Iain M. (REC) 2016. Just as helpful as his exegetical work in TOTC, but running in a homiletical direction. Splendid for pastors and laypeople (170pp.). See his expositions of Ezekiel, Genesis, Ruth & Esther, Daniel, and several Minor Prophets. [*JSOT* 41.5].

Durham, James. (GS) 1668. Takes an allegorical approach; highly valued by Spurgeon. See Burrowes above. This is available free online.

✓ Elliott, M. Timothea. ‡ *The Literary Unity of the Canticle*, 1989. Often cited.

✓ **Exum, J. Cheryl.** ‡ (OTL) 2005. Completes the OTL coverage of the OT canon, and is a brilliant reading by a leading literary critic. Though not extreme, Exum's approach is more reader-centered. She has long had an interest in the Song; note her article, "A Literary and Structural Analysis of the Song of Songs," *ZAW* 85 (1973): 47–79. Academics with an interest in OT poetry (and gender studies) definitely want this, but pastors prefer working with Hess, Estes, and Longman. [*CBQ* 10/06; *JTS* 10/07; *JETS* 6/07; *Int* 1/07; *Bib* 89.3; *BibInt* 16.1; *BSac* 4/07; *JAOS* 126.4; *RBL*; *JNES* 4/10; *RevExp* Spr 08; *BL* 2007].

✓ **Falk, Marcia.** ‡ *Love Lyrics from the Bible: A Translation and Literary Study of the Song of Songs*, 1982. An exceedingly fine poetic translation and some cogent arguments that we cannot discover a dramatic structure or plot as such. This work, originally a diss. for Stanford, was updated in 1990 as *The Song of Songs: A New Translation and Interpretation*. The translation was published alone in pb in 1993. "It's always a thrill when (as rarely happens) the scholar's mind and the poet's soul come together" (A. Rich). Like the Song itself, Falk's is "a delightful book" (Moshe Greenberg).

✓ Fink, David, ed. *Proverbs, Ecclesiastes, Song of Songs* (RCS) 2023.

✓ Fischer, Stefan, and Gavin Fernandes, eds. ‡ *The Song of Songs Afresh: Perspectives on a Biblical Love Poem*, 2019. Mainly conference papers. [*JSOT* 44.5; *VT* 70.4; *ETL* 97.4].

✓ **Fishbane, Michael.** ‡ (JPS) 2015. Brilliant, and the fullest entry in the series so far (about 380pp.), considering the size of the Song. The author made his reputation mainly with *Biblical Interpretation in Ancient Israel* (1985), and the strong points here are exegesis, the history of Jewish interpretation, and his inner-biblical connections. If your interests are more scholarly, then this is a splendid work to consult (especially the *Peshat* or plain-sense sections). The other levels of commentary are *Derash* (midrashic reflections, often of an allegorical sort), *Remez* (allegorical reading "in terms of individual spirituality"), and *Sod* (mystical level—think Kabbalah, which is best avoided entirely). Fishbane views the Song as "a collection of love lyrics that emerged . . . over a period of centuries. Only then—as a literary whole—did this work become Scripture" (xxi). He believes that because it "offered the opportunity to present the entire history of Israel in terms of love dialogues between God and Israel" (xx), "the Song entered the canon . . . as *the* religious lyric par excellence." He makes a good case for a simpler reading of the book as involving only a maiden and her beloved, with "the figure of a king as a trope for a male lover" (18). [*JSOT* 40.5; *BibInt* 26.3].

✓ Fox, Michael V. ‡ *The Song of Songs and Ancient Egyptian Love Songs*, 1985. Murphy calls it "a superb accomplishment." The in-depth study includes a fresh translation and commentary. One drawback is that Fox insists, "as a matter of doctrine" (Hess, 139), that the lovers must be unmarried. Cf. Estes, 293–99. Fox establishes by his research into comparative ANE literature that love songs are a distinguishable genre, and that Song of Songs should be interpreted for what it is: a celebration of human sexual love. Scholars debate his conclusion that "the Song is a single poem composed, originally at least, by a single poet. The poet may have used earlier materials" (220). [*Bib* 68.1; *HS* 1985].

Garrett, Duane A. *Proverbs, Ecclesiastes, Song of Songs* (NAC) 1993. See Proverbs. For the student, this competent commentary is outstripped by the WBC.

☆ **Garrett, Duane,** and Paul House. *Song of Songs, Lamentations* (WBC) 2004. These authors picked up the project after Hubbard died. The result is a solid exegesis, more conservative than most WBC vols. on the OT. Garrett does Song of Songs, building upon his mid-level NAC. The work is appreciated by students and pastors working with the Hebrew. However, I regard a number of Garrett's conclusions, especially those along the psychological line, as being too speculative. Hess, Longman, and Duguid are more trustworthy, in my opinion.

I am more enthusiastic about House's work in this vol. Once a recommended purchase, Garrett dropped off the list. [*JETS* 9/05; *Int* 7/05; *ExpTim* 9/09; *BL* 2007].

✓ Ginsburg, C. D. 1857–61. See under Ecclesiastes. He develops the drama interpretation of the Song.

☆ Glickman, S. Craig. *A Song for Lovers*, 1976; *Solomon's Song of Love*, 2004. A much better, practically minded commentary than Dillow. (Dillow is too practically minded, if you know what I mean.)

✓ **Gordis, Robert.** ‡ *The Song of Songs and Lamentations*, 1954, rev. 1974. A very fine discussion of the technical data, but scholarship on the Song has come a long way in recent decades. Gordis was an astute, conservatively critical scholar, specializing in the poetical and wisdom literature. See his other works on Job and Ecclesiastes.

Griffiths, Paul. (Brazos) 2011. I have not used it, but I've heard he uses the Vulgate as his source text. [*BBR* 22.3; *CTJ* 4/12; *ExpTim* 8/13; *JETS* 3/12; *JHebS* 14].

✓ Hagedorn, Anselm C., ed. ‡ *Perspectives on the Song of Songs: Comparative Approaches to a Biblical Text*, 2005. [*BL* 2006; *JTS* 4/09].

F  Halvorson-Taylor, Martien. ‡ (IECOT).

Hamilton, James M. (Focus on the Bible) 2015. Sermonic material. A bit of a stretch, to my way of thinking: "Solomon *intended* his audience to see . . . a typified Messiah" (32), but there is excellent material here. [*Them* 8/15; *Chm* Spr 16]. His maximalist approach is explained further in the textbook *Typology* (2022) [*WTJ* Fall 23].

✓ Hauge, Martin Ravndal. ‡ *Solomon the Lover and the Shape of the Song of Songs*, 2015. [*JSOT* 40.5].

F  Hernández, Dominick S. (NICOT-R). Would replace Longman.

☆ Hubbard, David A. *Ecclesiastes–Song of Solomon* (WCC) 1993. I long recommended this vol. for Ecclesiastes. Hubbard did a fine job on the Song too. There was to have been another more scholarly work on the Song (WBC), but Hubbard died suddenly, soon after retiring (†1996). See Garrett and House above.

✓ Japhet, Sara, and Barry Dov Walfish, eds. *The Way of Lovers: The Oxford Anonymous Commentary on the Song of Songs (Bodleian Library, MS Opp.625): An Edition of the Hebrew Text, with English Translation and Introduction*, 2017. Remarkable medieval Jewish work, published by Brill. [*JSOT* 42.5 (Watson)].

✓ **Jenson, Robert W.** [𝓜], (I) 2005. By a systematic theologian who chooses to "read the Song as a solicitation of theological allegory" and argues that "the Song's canonical plain sense *rightly* takes human sexual love as an analogue of the love between the Lord and Israel" (13). For more on this scholar, see his work on Ezekiel. Cf. Knight below. [*JETS* 9/06; *Int* 1/07; *HBT* 29.1; *BL* 2007].

F  Johnston, Gordon. (Kregel).

✓ **Keel, Othmar.** ‡ (ContC) ET 1994. Downplays the erotic a bit and is praised by some prominent scholars as about the best technical interpretation available. At 272 packed pages, it rivals Murphy and Pope in scholarship and detail. My preference for Murphy is slight. "For all its appeal to ANE carvings and imagery as parallels, this commentary is typically postmodern" (M. Elliott). [*ExpTim* 3/95; *JETS* 12/96; *JSOT* 68; *Them* 4/96].

Kinlaw, Dennis F. (EBC) 1991. A 44-page exposition, regarded as a "weak link" in the series. See now Schwab's replacement.

✓ **Knight, G. A. F.,** and F. W. Golka. ‡ *The Song of Songs and Jonah* (ITC-E) 1988. As a surprise to some in the 1980s, Knight revived the interpretation of the Song as referring to the love relationship between God and humanity. See also his 1955 Torch commentary which covers this book. By the way, pursuing basically the same line of interpretation are Jenson; the well-written OUP diss. by Edmeé Kingsmill, *The Song of Songs and Eros of God* (2009) [*BL*

2010]; and Larry Lyke's *"I Will Espouse You Forever": The Song of Songs and the Theology of Love in the Hebrew Bible* (2007) [*VT* 59.2]. I believe I have seen enough to call this a trend.

☆ Konkel, August H., and Tremper Longman III. *Job, Ecclesiastes, Song of Songs* (CorBC) 2006. See under Ecclesiastes. Longman is valuable as a succinct exposition.

✓ LaCocque, André. ‡ *Romance She Wrote: A Hermeneutical Essay on Song of Songs*, 1998. Argues for female authorship and a subversive intent.

✓ Landy, Francis. ‡ *Paradoxes of Paradise: Identity and Difference in the Song of Songs*, 1983; 2nd ed. 2011. A valuable, early literary study. [*JSOT* 37.5].

F Lucas, Ernest. *Ecclesiastes, Song of Songs* (EBTC)?

Luter, Boyd. (EEC) 2013–digital. I have not seen this work.

Luther, Martin. ET 1972. Found in the 15th vol. of *Luther's Works*.

✓ **Mitchell, Christopher W.** (ConcC) 2003. Had to see this work to believe it. Yes, it is 1300pp. (without the bibliography)—could anyone fail to get lost in the detail of a book this fat? The Song is only 117 verses of poetry! The introduction alone is 543pp. According to reviewers, the quality of scholarship in this tome is higher than usual for the series. The textual notes, christological interpretations, and recommendations for using the Song in Lutheran worship are extensive. [*EvQ* 7/08; *CBQ* 7/06; *BSac* 1/07; *CJ* 10/06].

☆ **Murphy, Roland.** ‡ (Herm) 1990. Magisterial! Few will spring for this vol. at the bookstore, but it is arguably the best technical exegesis of the love poem. Keel, Fox, Fishbane, and Pope are rivals, with rather different interests. Murphy is especially useful because he treats the "final form" of the text. It tickles me to think of a Catholic priest writing the best-rated modern commentary on Song of Songs. See also his 1981 FOTL work under Ruth. In early editions of this guide, Murphy was a recommended purchase, but it is less suitable for pastors. For more on this scholar, see the memorial in *CBQ* 10/02. See Berlin for an expected replacement. [*JBL* Fall 93; *JTS* 4/93; *CBQ* 10/92; *VT* 1/96; *Them* 10/94].

Murphy, Roland E., and Elizabeth Huwiler. [*M*], *Proverbs, Ecclesiastes & Song of Songs* (NIBC) 1996. See Proverbs above.

✓ Noegel, Scott B., and Gary A. Rendsburg. *Solomon's Vineyard: Literary and Linguistic Studies in the Song of Songs*, 2009. [*CBQ* 1/11; *JSS* Spr 12; *JSOT* 35.5; *RBL* 2011].

✓ Norris, Richard A., Jr., ed. (TCB) 2004. The inaugural vol. (347pp.) in the series. [*CTJ* 4/07; *VT* 55.3; *BibInt* 13.4; *Pro Ecclesia* Win 09].

☆ O'Donnell, Douglas Sean. (ESVEC) 2022. Good coverage, though briefer (50pp.). In the same Vol. V, which is arguably about the best in the whole OT series, we have Collins on Psalms, O'Dowd on Proverbs, and Rogland on Ecclesiastes. Please note the O'Donnell PTW above.

Ogden, Graham S., and Lynell Zogbo. (UBS) 1998.

Olyott, Stuart J. *A Life Worth Living and a Lord Worth Loving* (Welwyn) 1983.

✓ Pardes, Ilana. ‡ *The Song of Songs: A Biography*, 2019. In actuality, more a reception history study. [*Int* 4/21].

✓ **Pope, Marvin H.** ‡ (AB) 1977. Excels in presenting philological detail and the history of interpretation. Longman once celebrated this tome as "one of the best commentaries written on any book of the Bible." But then he added, "His overall approach to the book as connected with the love and death cults of the ancient world leaves much to be desired." In brief, an eccentric commentary only an OT specialist could love. Few ministers have money for an older work of this size (750pp.) and type on a book they rarely preach from. See Pope on Job. [*JBL* 3/79; *ExpTim* 12/78].

☆ Provan, Iain. *Ecclesiastes, Song of Songs* (NIVAC) 2001. See under Ecclesiastes.

F Queen-Sutherland, Kandy. (S&H)? See under Ruth.

✓ Roberts, D. Phillip. *Let Me See Your Form: Seeking Poetic Structure in the Song of Songs*, 2007.

A lengthy, lightly revised 2001 PhD for Westminster Seminary with meticulous exegesis of the Hebrew. Sadly, it is a posthumous publication (†2005).

F   Schellenberg, Annette. ‡ (Illum).

☆ Schwab, George. (EBCR) 2008. A great improvement on Kinlaw's EBC. Schwab earned a PhD at Westminster Seminary and is also a trained counselor. He teaches at Erskine Seminary. He earlier published *The Song of Songs' Cautionary Message Concerning Human Love* (2002), offering good guidance on a variety of questions including the marital status of the lovers in the early chapters. His work in EBCR is a little over 60pp. and is well worth looking up. [*BL* 2010].

Seerveld, C. *The Greatest Song*, 1967. Clearly presents the three-player drama view.

✓ **Snaith, John G.** ‡ (NCB) 1993. The phrase-by-phrase exegesis by a Cambridge lecturer (140pp.) is quite useful to the student, but less so to the preacher. Snaith does not interact as much as he could with other scholars' views; he does not cite Keel. [*JTS* 4/94; *VT* 47.1; *JSOT* 64; *CRBR* 1995; *Criswell Th. Rev.* Spr 94].

Spencer, F. Scott. ‡ (Wisdom) 2017. [*CBQ* 7/18; *Int* 4/19; *JSOT* 42.5].

✓ **Stoop-van Paridon, P. W. T.** ‡ *The Song of Songs: A Philological Analysis of the Hebrew Book* שיר השירים (Peeters) ET 2005. A massive Leiden diss. (539pp.), only for the most patient specialists. Reads the Song as a drama. [*Bib* 89.4; *BL* 2007 (Watson)].

F   Sun, Chloe T. (BGW). For an initial foray, see Sun under Esther.

✓ Van Hecke, Pierre, ed. ‡ *The Song of Songs in Its Context: Words for Love, Love for Words*, 2020. Another huge work in BETL, with anticipated cutting-edge scholarship (630pp.). A veritable feast for the scholar!

F   Van Pelt, Miles V. (ZECOT).

F   Watson, Wilfred G. E. ‡ (HCOT).

☆ Webb, Barry G. *Five Festal Garments: Christian Reflections on the Song of Songs, Ruth, Lamentations, Ecclesiastes and Esther*, 2000. Excellent reading for expositors and teachers, especially as a theological guide. See under Ruth.

✓ Weems, Renita J. ‡ (NIB) 1997. By a learned Vanderbilt prof (70pp.). She obviously has an affinity for the "black-skinned" maiden with her poetic longings. (Perhaps we need a reminder here, however, that the "blackness . . . has nothing to do with race" [Fox, 101].) Weems causes the reader to reflect upon the possible literary purposes of the poet. She takes a feminist approach, as expected from the author of *Battered Love: Marriage, Sex, and Violence in the Hebrew Prophets* (1995). I found myself frequently disagreeing with her conclusions and perspective, especially where feminist resentments seem to rise to the surface (e.g., p.381).

Wesley, John. *Explanatory Notes on the Old Testament*, Volume 3, 1765. Allegory.

✓ Wright, J. Robert, ed. *Proverbs, Ecclesiastes, Song of Solomon* (ACCS) 2004. [*CTJ* 4/07].

NOTES: (1) Students interested in the history of various interpretations would also do well to consult H. H. Rowley's "The Interpretation of the Song of Songs," *JTS* 38 (1937). This article is revised and expanded in *The Servant of the Lord and Other Essays on the Old Testament* (Blackwell, 1965). See also the discussions of the history of interpretation in Pope (140pp.), Murphy, Longman, Garrett's WBC, and Fishbane. (2) Amy Erickson and Andrew Davis review "Recent Research on the Megilloth," *CBR* 14 (2016) 298–318. (3) An attractive introduction is Eric Ortlund, "The Wisdom of the Song of Songs," *Them* 45.3 (2020).

# PROPHETS & PROPHETIC LITERATURE

★ Boda, Mark J., and J. Gordon McConville, eds. *Dictionary of the OT: Prophets*, 2012. A magnificent addition to the IVP series and indispensable resource for serious students of this literature. Articles come from conservative and critically oriented evangelicals, and some are "mediating." [*JETS* 12/13; *Them* 4/14; *JESOT* 1.1; *Anvil* 3/14].

★ Chisholm, Robert B. *Handbook on the Prophets*, 2002. This is more content-survey than introduction; readers will find it to be mildly dispensational, learned, and well-written. [*Them* Sum 04; *CJ* 10/05; *RelSRev* 4/06; *DenvJ* 1/03; *JHebS* 4].

★ Cook, Stephen L., John T. Strong, and Steven S. Tuell. ‡ *The Prophets: Introducing Israel's Prophetic Writings* (IIS) 2022. In so many ways, attractive and well-done from the critical angle (about 550pp.). Students should take notice of this work, as it is both current and impressively researched. One puzzles, however, over three fine Ezekiel scholars failing to mention, let alone discuss, the recognition formula. I expect evangelical pastors would prefer Hoffmeier below.

★ McConville, J. Gordon. [𝓜], *Exploring the OT, Volume 4: The Prophets*, 2002. As is true of Wenham's vol. on the Pentateuch in this series, I cannot think of a better initial guide into this portion of the Scriptures, especially for introducing scholarly questions. It is a work of British evangelical scholarship and has a less conservative feel than many American evangelical books on the prophets—my own conclusions are more in line with Tully's. [*Them* Spr 04; *JETS* 9/04; *ExpTim* 7/03; *Anvil* 20.3].

★ Robertson, O. Palmer. *The Christ of the Prophets*, 2004. Superb as a conservative Reformed theological survey (517pp.). [*TJ* Spr 06].

★ Tully, Eric J. *Reading the Prophets as Christian Scripture: A Literary, Canonical, and Theological Introduction*, 2022. A 400-page textbook from a prof at TEDS, published in an attractive format by Baker Academic. Tully emphasizes the gripping theological messages within a covenant context. Though handling basic introductory issues (rarely any Hebrew/Aramaic), he probes deeply enough to be useful as a longer-term reference. About the best recent conservative book of its type. (Cf. Hoffmeier.) Reading it could be a refresher course for pastors, years out of seminary. [*RelSRev* 9/22; *ExpTim* 7/23, 8/23; *TGA* 3/23; *CBQ* 9/23; *BBR* 33.2; *Them* 47.3; *JETS* 12/22 (Bullock)].

★ VanGemeren, Willem A. *Interpreting the Prophetic Word*, 1990. Pays good attention to theology in the prophets and is a reliable guide for pastors and students. [*Chm* 111.4].

❖ ❖ ❖ ❖ ❖ ❖

✓ Achtemeier, Paul J., and James Luther Mays, eds. ‡ *Interpreting the Prophets*, 1987.

✓ Ackroyd, Peter R. ‡ *Exile and Restoration*, 1968.

✓ Alter, Robert. ‡ *The Hebrew Bible*, Vol. 2: *The Prophets*, 2019. Translation seeking fidelity to the Hebrew in fine literary English. The brief commentary holds value as well.

☆ Baker, David W. "Israelite Prophets and Prophecy" (266–94) in Baker–Arnold, eds., *The Face of OT Studies* (1999). More up-to-date are Robert R. Wilson, "Current Issues in the Study of OT Prophecy" (38–47), in Kaltner–Stulman, eds, *Inspired Speech* (2004); Lena-Sofia Tiemeyer, "Recent Currents in Research on the Prophetic Literature," *ExpTim* 119.4 (2008): 161–69; and Brad Kelle, "The Phenomenon of Israelite Prophecy in Contemporary Scholarship," *CBR* 12.3 (2014): 275–320. All four are exceptionally helpful for understanding currents in scholarship.

✓ Barton, John. ‡ *Oracles of God: Perceptions of Prophecy in Israel after the Exile*, 1986, 2007. See also Ehud ben Zvi, ed., "Rereading Oracles of God: Twenty Years after John Barton, *Oracles of God: Perceptions of Prophecy in Israel after the Exile* (London: Darton, Longman and Todd, 1986)," *JHebS* 7, Article 14 (online).

✓ Blenkinsopp, Joseph. ‡ *A History of Prophecy in Israel*, 1983, rev. 1996. Advanced students and academically oriented pastors learn much from this more traditional historical-critical introduction. However, scholars today often choose to approach prophecy differently, researching the use of metaphor, inner-biblical interpretation, poetry in prophetic language, rhetoric, etc., in a more holistic, final-form approach (cf. Seitz). As good as Blenkinsopp, but briefer, are Sweeney and Petersen below. See also his *Prophecy and Canon* (1977).

✓ Boda, Mark J., and Lissa M. Wray Beal, eds. *Prophets, Prophecy, and Ancient Israelite Historiography*, 2013. Just as useful for the study of the Former Prophets as the Latter. [*CBQ* 1/14; *JSOT* 38.5; *VT* 64.4].

✓ Brueggemann, Walter. ‡ *The Prophetic Imagination*, 1978, 2nd ed. 2001.

☆ Bullock, C. Hassell. *An Introduction to the OT Prophetic Books*, 1986. Compares with G. Smith below as a fine conservative intro. It now has a dated feel and has lost value as a textbook. The 2007 edition was more a reformatting rather than a true revision—e.g., the Ezekiel section has but one reference to a work published after 1982.

✓ Carroll, Robert P. ‡ *When Prophecy Failed*, 1979. This very critical, influential study argues that so-called "prophecy" is ever failing, and the community's leaders, dealing with the "cognitive dissonance" thus produced, reshape the materials to interpret new contingencies and revitalize the people's hope.

✓ Carroll R., M. Daniel. *The Lord Roars: Recovering the Prophetic Voice for Today*, 2022. Concerned to understand the ancient prophets' messages and their contemporary application through a vital/active faith. The focus is on Amos, Isaiah, and Micah (especially their social critique). [*Int* 10/23; *CBQ* 4/24].

✓ Chalmers, Aaron. [𝔐], *Interpreting the Prophets: Reading, Understanding and Preaching from the Worlds of the Prophets*, 2015. Accomplishes quite a lot in 170pp., focused on the historical, theological, and rhetorical worlds. Very well-done, by a critically aware evangelical Australian. [*Them* 41.2].

✓ Childs, Brevard S. ‡ *Introduction to the Old Testament as Scripture*, 1979. The Prophets section is still shrewd and instructive.

✓ Clements, R. E. ‡ *Old Testament Prophecy: From Oracles to Canon*, 1996. Preachers will be glad to find an emphasis on theology here. [*JETS* 6/98; *JBL* Spr 98; *JSS* Spr 99; *CBQ* 4/97; *HS* 1997]. Earlier Clements wrote *Prophecy and Tradition* (1975).

✓ Conrad, Edgar. ‡ *Reading the Latter Prophets: Towards a New Canonical Criticism*, 2003.

✓ Crenshaw, James. ‡ *Prophets, Sages & Poets*, 2006.

Davidson, A. B. [𝔐], *Old Testament Prophecy*, 1904. A classic in the history of British scholarship, introducing some of the ideas of German criticism to the English-speaking world.

✓ Davies, Philip R., and David J. A. Clines, eds. ‡ *Among the Prophets*, 1993. Add to this Davies, ed., *The Prophets: A Sheffield Reader* (1996), which includes influential articles such as Hans Barstad's "No Prophets? Recent Developments in Biblical Prophetic Research."

✓ Davis, Ellen F. ‡ *Biblical Prophecy: Perspectives for Christian Theology, Discipleship, and Ministry* (I) 2014. Offers something of a corrective to critical scholarship. Fascinatingly, as she argues for a new approach, I recognize an "old path": emphasizing the prophets' writing ministry as interpreters of earlier revelation/Scripture.

✓ Day, John, ed. ‡ *Prophecy and the Prophets in Ancient Israel: Proceedings of the Oxford OT Seminar*, 2010. [*BBR* 21.4; *RelSRev* 6/12; *JHebS* 11].

Emmerson, Grace, ed. ‡ *Prophets and Poets: A Companion to the Prophetic Books of the OT*, 1997.

✓ Fishbane, Michael. ‡ *Biblical Interpretation in Ancient Israel*, 1985. Hugely important, arguing that the Hebrew Bible is an exegetical work in its own right, often interpreting earlier Scriptures. The prophets receive close attention.

☆ Gordon, Robert P., ed. ‡ *The Place Is Too Small for Us: The Israelite Prophets in Recent Scholarship*, 1995. A superb collection for students to consult. [*Them* 1/97; *JETS* 3/99].

✓ Gowan, Donald E. ‡ *Theology of the Prophetic Books: The Death and Resurrection of Israel*, 1998. [*ThTo* 10/99; *CBQ* 10/99; *RelSRev* 7/99].

Habel, Norman. ‡ "The Form and Significance of the Call Narratives," *ZAW* 77 (1965): 297–323.

Hayes, John H. ‡ "The History of Form-Critical Study of Prophecy," in *SBL 1973 Seminar Papers*.

☆ Hays, J. Daniel. *The Message of the Prophets: A Survey of the Prophetic and Apocalyptic Books of the OT*, 2010. More of an evangelical introduction to the prophets than to scholarship on the prophets. So attractively produced! [*JSOT* 41.5].

Hengstenberg, Ernst. *Christology of the Old Testament and a Commentary on the Messianic Predictions*, ET 1836–39. See also Van Groningen.

✓ Heschel, Abraham. ‡ *The Prophets*, 2 vols., 1962. A classic of Jewish interpretation.

✓ Hillers, Delbert. ‡ *Treaty Curses and the Old Testament Prophets*, 1964.

☆ Hoffmeier, James K. *The Prophets of Israel*, 2021. The emeritus professor from TEDS is deeply learned in OT studies, ANE history, Egyptology, and archaeology, but this book represents accessible scholarship. He does well in treating the message of the prophets, even in a warm-hearted way, but the strength of his work is in explaining background issues (including geography). Fascinating for those with historical interests. Wonderful photos! From Kregel. [*CBQ* 4/23; *JETS* 6/22].

✓ Holt, Else K., Hyun Chul Paul Kim, and Andrew Mein, eds. ‡ *Concerning the Nations: Essays on the Oracles against the Nations in Isaiah, Jeremiah and Ezekiel*, 2015. [*JTS* 4/17; *Them* 42.2]. On the same topic, see Bezzel–Becker–de Jong, eds., *Prophecy and Foreign Nations* (2022) [*JSOT* 47.5].

Hutton, Rodney. ‡ *Fortress Introduction to the Prophets*, 2004. Very brief.

✓ Koch, Klaus. ‡ *The Prophets*, 2 vols., ET 1983–84. [*JBL* 105.3].

✓ Kratz, Reinhard G. ‡ *The Prophets of Israel*, ET 2015. Quite critical, as a brief introduction with strong diachronic interests. [*JSOT* 42.5].

✓ Lindblom, J. ‡ *Prophecy in Ancient Israel*, ET 1962.

✓ Matthews, Victor H. ‡ *The Hebrew Prophets and Their Social World*, 2001, 2nd ed. 2012. [*Int* 7/03; *ExpTim* 3/03; *VT* 54.2; 2012: *JTS* 4/15; *JESOT* 2.2].

✓ Mays, James Luther, and Paul J. Achtemeier, eds. ‡ *Interpreting the Prophets*, 1987.

✓ McEntire, Mark. ‡ *A Chorus of Prophetic Voices*, 2015. One of the better moderately critical introductions for a beginning student. [*BibInt* 26.3].

Mowinckel, Sigmund. ‡ *Prophecy and Tradition*, ET 1946.

Muilenburg, J. ‡ "The 'Office' of the Prophet in Ancient Israel," (74–97) in Hyatt, ed., *The Bible in Modern Scholarship* (1967).

Newsome, James D. ‡ *The Hebrew Prophets*, 1984.

✓ Nissinen, Martti. ‡ *Ancient Prophecy: Near Eastern, Biblical, and Greek Perspectives*, 2017. Almost all one could hope for as a deeply learned introduction to prophecy in the ANE context, bearing in mind that he is extremely skeptical about the OT books accurately preserving the activity and oracles of Israel's prophets. From OUP. [*BBR* 29.2]. Cf. Jonathan Stökl, *Prophecy in the Ancient Near East: A Philological and Sociological Comparison* (2012).

✓ Nissinen, Martti, C. L. Seow, and Robert K. Ritner. ‡ *Prophets and Prophecy in the Ancient Near East*, 2003, 2nd ed. 2019. [*DenvJ* 10/04; *RBL*; 2019: *BBR* 30.3]. See also the earlier Nissinen, ed., *Prophecy in Its Ancient Near Eastern Context* (2000).

✓ Nielsen, K. ‡ *Yahweh as Prosecutor and Judge: An Investigation of the Prophetic Lawsuit*, 1978.

✓ Nogalski, James D. ‡ *Introduction to the Hebrew Prophets*, 2018. Has a special interest in The Twelve and redaction-critical approaches. [*BBR* 29.2; *Int* 7/19; *ETL* 94.3; *RevExp* 5/19]. Earlier he wrote *Interpreting Prophetic Literature: Historical and Exegetical Tools for Reading the Prophets* (2015) [*JETS* 6/16; *Int* 7/18; *JSOT* 40.5; *BibInt* 26.3].

✓ Peckham, Brian. ‡ *History & Prophecy* (ABRL) 1993.

☆ Petersen, D. L. ‡ *The Prophetic Literature*, 2002. [*Int* 4/03; *ExpTim* 3/03; *BSac* 10/04; *HBT* 12/03; *CJ* 1/07]. He has done much work in the area; see his *Late Israelite Prophecy* (1977), *The Roles of Israel's Prophets* (1981), and OTL vols. on Haggai–Malachi.

✓ Rad, Gerhard von. ‡ *Old Testament Theology*, Vol. II, ET 1965; *The Message of the Prophets*, ET 1967.

✓ Redditt, Paul. ‡ *Introduction to the Prophets*, 2008. A historical-critical introduction. [*VT* 59.4 (Williamson); *ETL* 86.1; *RelSRev* 12/09; *Them* 4/10; *Int* 7/11; *JSS* Aut 12].

Robinson, T. H. ‡ *Prophecy and the Prophets in Ancient Israel*, 2nd ed. 1953.

Rofé, Alexander. ‡ *Introduction to the Prophetic Literature*, 1997.

Rowley, H. H. ‡ *Studies in Old Testament Prophecy*, 1950.

☆ Sandy, D. Brent. *Plowshares & Pruning Hooks: Rethinking the Language of Biblical Prophecy and Apocalyptic*, 2002. Fine conservative treatment of prophecy, which served well as a textbook (IVP). There is but one 25-page chapter on apocalyptic.

✓ Sandy, D. Brent, and Daniel M. O'Hare. *Prophecy and Apocalyptic: An Annotated Bibliography* (IBR) 2007. Includes a selective bibliography for each of the Major and Minor Prophets. There was once an online supplement at ibr-bbr.org. [*RelSRev* 9/08].

Sawyer, John F. A. ‡ *Prophecy and the Biblical Prophets*, rev. ed. 1993.

☆ Seitz, Christopher R. ‡ *Prophecy and Hermeneutics: Toward a New Introduction to the Prophets*, 2007. Mainly focused upon Isaiah and "The Twelve," Seitz explores the newer canonical, holistic approaches, as opposed to the older historical-critical scholarship that tended to fragment the text. [*EvQ* 7/08; *JETS* 6/08; *JTS* 10/08; *Int* 7/08; *RelSRev* 12/08; *HBT* 31.2; *Them* 7/09; *BBR* 21.2]. Added later is *The Goodly Fellowship of the Prophets* (2009) [*JHebS* 12].

✓ Sharp, Carolyn J., ed. ‡ *The Oxford Handbook of the Prophets*, 2016. [*JSOT* 41.5; *ETL* 93.3]. A major reference work. For Sharp's own conclusions, see *The Prophetic Literature* (2019) [*BBR* 30.4; *Int* 7/20; *JSOT* 45.5].

☆ Smith, Gary V. *An Introduction to the Hebrew Prophets: The Prophets as Preachers*, 1994. [*VT* 47.1]. Building on this is *Interpreting the Prophetic Books: An Exegetical Handbook* (2014) [*WTJ* Fall 16; *JETS* 9/15, 12/16; *ExpTim* 3/17; *JSOT* 40.5].

Smith, W. Robertson. ‡ *The Prophets of Israel*, 1895.

✓ Stulman, Louis, and Hyun Chul Paul Kim. ‡ *You Are My People: An Introduction to Prophetic Literature*, 2010. [*TJ* Spr 12].

☆ Sweeney, Marvin A. ‡ *The Prophetic Literature*, 2006. From the widely used IBT series, this is among the best brief critical introductions to the subject [*CBQ* 7/06; *Int* 4/07; *VT* 57.4; *ExpTim* 4/07; *CJ* 4/07; *BL* 2007; *Anvil* 23.4]. Also notable are *Form and Intertextuality in Prophetic and Apocalyptic Literature* (2005) [*JTS* 10/07], and *Reading Prophetic Books* (2014) [*JTS* 4/16; *ETL* 93.3].

☆ Van Groningen, Gerard. *Messianic Revelation in the Old Testament*, 1990.

✓ Wendland, Ernst. *Prophetic Rhetoric: Case Studies in Text Analysis and Translation*, 2nd ed. 2014. There is a mountain of discourse analysis research in these collected essays (700pp.), by a missionary scholar at Stellenbosch.

✓ Westermann, Claus. ‡ *The Basic Forms of Prophetic Speech*, ET 1967; *Prophetic Oracles of Salvation in the OT*, ET 1991. Seminal form-critical work.

✓ Wilson, Robert R. ‡ *Prophecy and Society in Ancient Israel*, 1980. A classic that encouraged many to take up sociological research. For more on this, see Thomas W. Overholt, *Channels of Prophecy: The Social Dynamics of Prophetic Activity*, 1989.

Wood, Leon. *The Prophets of Israel*, 1979. Classic, learned dispensational textbook.

☆ Young, Edward J. *My Servants the Prophets*, 1952. Retains value because Young points to the wide cleavage between the critic and the believing scholar on the matter of prophecy. Young would agree with Calvin, who directed his readers "to trace the Prophets [back] to the Law, from which they derived their doctrine, like streams from a fountain; for they placed it before them as a rule, so that they may be justly held and declared to be its interpreters, who utter nothing but what is connected with the Law" (Preface to Isaiah). The believing scholar teaches that the prophets were interpreters of the Law who were calling the people back to the covenant relationship Yahweh established first in choosing Abraham and then in redeeming his descendants out of Egypt (all recorded in Scripture). The written Law begat the prophets, not the other way around, as the critics have often taught. [*EvQ* 4/53].

✓ Zimmerli, Walther. ‡ *The Law and the Prophets*, ET 1965. Also, some of his key articles are collected in *The Fiery Throne: The Prophets and OT Theology* (ET 2003).

NOTE: The literature on the prophets is copious, and this must be a very selective list of excellent and influential works.

# ISAIAH

★ Calvin, John. 1551. "One of the Reformer's best" (Childs). Previously, this 2000-page commentary was available only in the Baker set, but Crossway issued a much condensed CrossC pb edition (2000) [*JSOT* 94]. Free online!

★ **McConville, J. Gordon.** [*M*], (BCOT) 2023. From the series coeditor, who has published excellent vols. on Deuteronomy and the prophets. After a surprisingly short Introduction (17pp.), the commentary becomes pleasingly full at over 700pp. McConville finds much historical ambiguity; "the composition evinces a historical layering in which the horizons subtly shift." He argues there are numerous examples in Isaiah of "the subordination of historical reference to theological and thematic ordering" (4). The work is impressive on a number of levels: knowledge of scholarship, exegetical care, thoroughness (without obsessing over being an exhaustive treatment), handling of the Hebrew (in transliteration), theological interest, and literary sensitivity with an appreciation for the structuring both of oracles and the book. He sees fine connections among texts, in a kind of *intra*-textuality. I like the commentary a lot, though the historical-critical stance disappoints. According to McConville, "the book presumably grew incrementally over a long period" (11), from the day of Isaiah ben Amoz down to the Persian era. He is not clear on how one should explain the unity of the prophecy. As he proceeds to comment on the chapters, he concludes sections with "a short theological reflection." I expect, the more academic you are, the more you'll appreciate what he seeks to achieve. I'm already learning more from him than almost anyone else. For a more conservative and less demanding exegesis, see House or Mackay. [*BL* 2024].

★ **Motyer, J. Alec.** 1993. An excellent exegetical and expositional commentary in the mold of TOTC except more lengthy (544pp.). This should be reckoned the best one-vol. evangelical work on Isaiah—a good first choice—though the critics pan it for maintaining the authorial integrity of all 66 chs. Motyer researched Isaiah for decades, has a valuable structural analysis, includes astute theological comment, and views the messianic hope as central to the prophecy. The work mainly puts forward the author's mature research and is not a repository of others' scholarship. That is not to say, however, it is an isolated piece of work. Students, note the misspelling "Wilderberger" (*passim*). See also his TOTC below. Motyer wrote the BST vols. on Amos, Philippians, and James. By the way, the pronunciation of the surname is "Mōh-teer." [*BSac* 1/96; *VT* 10/94; *CBQ* 7/95; *EvQ* 4/95; *Them* 1/95; *SwJT* Spr 95; *JETS* 12/96; *SBET* Spr 96].

★ **Oswalt, John.** (NICOT-R) 2 vols., 1986–98. With capable scholarship (especially in the areas of text criticism and grammatical analysis), Oswalt takes a decidedly and dependably conservative approach. The commentary is not yet dated, though some might wish for an appendix discussing the vast amount of recent research into "Isaianic coherence." In the rich theology of the prophecy, Oswalt highlights the contrast between the greatness of a holy God and the corruption of humanity, on the one hand, and, on the other, the "amazing paradox that if humanity will lay aside its pretensions to deity, the true God will raise us to fellowship with himself" (vol.1, p.32). The matter of true service and servanthood repeatedly comes to the fore. See also his NIVAC below, which distills the scholarship in NICOT and may be more useful to the busy expositor. [*Bib* 69.2; *TJ* Spr 87; *WTJ* Fall 87; *JETS* 9/88, 12/99; *JSOT* 84; *Int* 4/00; *SwJT* Spr 99; *RelSRev* 1/99; *CBQ* 1/02; *DenvJ*]. Oswalt's essays are collected in *The Holy One of Israel* (2014).

★ **Smith, Gary V.** (NAC) 2 vols., 2007–09; (CSC) 2nd ed. 2021–. This rivals Oswalt as a full (over 1400pp.), highly competent, conservative exegesis; it beats Oswalt in the sense that Smith interacts with two decades of more recent scholarship. He has already published a good bit on the prophets and has a first-rate commentary on Amos. Is this set the studious evangelical pastor's first choice? After evaluating, I agree with the Denver Seminary faculty who once made this a top pick. Take note that Smith pays especially close attention to chs. 40–66. For a précis of his conservative arguments, see "Isaiah 40–55," *JETS* 54 (2011): 701–13. Happily, this excellent set is being updated, not only to remain useful but to become all the more useful. [*BBR* 22.2].

★ Webb, Barry. (BST) 1996. A high compliment paid to a book is that one wishes to have written it—or to have been able to have crafted such a fine book. Webb's is exactly the kind of approach that makes the OT come alive. It is (1) conservative and evangelical, viewing the text as God's authoritative revelation; (2) rich in theology (a biblical-theological approach); (3) sensitive to the literary features of the Bible; and (4) engagingly written. Pastors can start off with Motyer, Oswalt, Smith, and Webb, then perhaps buy McConville, if they have a scholarly bent. Desiring more sermon help? See House, Lessing, Mackay, Ortlund, and Oswalt's NIVAC. [*Them* 10/97; *BL* 1997; *RelSRev* 7/98].

☆ Abernethy, Andrew T. *Discovering Isaiah*, 2021. Excellent, full introduction to the background, interpretation, and theology of the prophecy, with some added reception history. The Wheaton prof wrote for a more critical audience (SPCK, Eerdmans) and hid somewhat his conservative views. [*CBQ* 7/22; *Int* 4/23; *JSOT* 47.5; *Them* 48.3]. Abernethy is influenced by the biblical-theological, canonical approach. He also wrote *The Book of Isaiah and God's Kingdom* (2016) [*JETS* 9/17; *JSOT* 41.5; *Them* 42.3], a superb entry in NSBT.

☆ Alexander, J. A. 1847. A standard resource for generations, by an old Princeton Seminary professor. Mature theological reflection abounds. Free online. [*EvQ* 4/54].

✓ Allis, O. T. *The Unity of Isaiah*, 1950. A valuable old defense of the orthodox position, explaining why the issue has been a watershed for biblical studies and theology. See Young below.

✓ Aster, Shawn Zelig. *Reflections of Empire in Isaiah 1–39: Responses to Assyrian Ideology*, 2017. Most stimulating work from a conservatively critical Israeli.

✓ **Baltzer, Klaus.** ‡ *Deutero-Isaiah* (Herm) ET 2001. A translation of the 680-page commentary on Isaiah 40–55 in KAT (1999). Baltzer worked on it for decades, and his proposal proved controversial in critical circles. He supposes the prophecies are set in the form of a liturgical drama (in six scenes), are to be dated to the mid-5th century BC, and are drawing from the Pentateuch (among several intertexts). There is less text criticism than we have come to expect in Hermeneia, and less theological reflection, too, than in some other works, e.g., Zimmerli's *Ezekiel*. Of interest only to specialists and advanced students. See Roberts below. [*CBQ* 1/04; *JTS* 4/02; *JBL* Spr 04; *JETS* 6/03; *Int* 7/03; *ExpTim* 8/01; *SJT* 56.1; *CurTM* 2/03; *RBL*; *JHebS*; *DenvJ* 1/03; *JHebS* 4].

☆ **Bartelt, Andrew H.** *Isaiah 1–12* (ConcC) 2024. Builds upon a monograph, *The Book around Immanuel: Style and Structure in Isaiah 2–12* (1996). Bartelt had the benefit of consulting the vast scholarship on these chapters, e.g., Williamson's ICC vols., and his work is all the stronger for that. I believe it is the most exhaustive conservative exegesis ever produced on these twelve chapters (800pp.). The notes on the Hebrew are extensive, but readers without the language expertise can still profitably consult it, bypassing the "Textual Notes" sections. See also Lessing and Raabe.

✓ Bautch, Richard J., Joachim Eck, and Burkard M. Zapff, eds. ‡ *Isaiah and the Twelve: Parallels, Similarities, and Differences*, 2020. [*JSOT* 47.5].

✓ **Beuken, Willem A. M.** ‡ *Isaiah II, Chapters 28–39* (HCOT) ET 2000. The vol. contains hardly any introduction, but 420pp. of detailed exegesis. It is valued highly for its intertextual interests. Childs speaks of how his "illuminating articles and magisterial 4-vol. commentary in Dutch on chs. 40–66 have opened the way to a new era in interpreting the book of Isaiah." Would that some publisher would undertake to put Beuken's vols. on chs. 1–12 (2003), chs. 13–27 (2007), and chs. 40–66 (1979–89) into English! See *Bib* 72.2 (1991). [*CBQ* 4/01; *JETS* 6/03; *VT* 51.4; *JSOT* 94]. The series companions are Groenewald for chs. 1–27 and Koole for chs. 40–66.

Beyer, Bryan E. *Encountering the Book of Isaiah*, 2007. A useful college-level handbook. [*CBQ* 7/08; *TJ* Fall 08; *ExpTim* 10/08 (Goldingay); *RelSRev* 3/08; *JETS* 9/08].

✓ **Blenkinsopp, Joseph.** ‡ (AB) 3 vols., 2000–2003. By a leading Catholic scholar, long at Notre Dame (†2022). In the first vol., he takes a conventional historical-critical approach, offering a good translation (68pp.), 39-page introduction, 53-page bibliography, and 319pp. of exegesis. The commentary is not as full as some other AB entries, such as Lundbom on Jeremiah. Blenkinsopp believes "that the book has undergone successive restructurings and rearrangements in the course of a long editorial history" (83), and these diachronic matters are of greater interest to him than a reading of Isaiah as a rhetorical and structural unity. I grow weary of all the confident talk about "editorial addenda," their dating, and even the frame of mind or intention of the "scribes" responsible (e.g., *ad locum* 19:16–25). Vols. 2–3 carry forward Blenkinsopp's program. The set is for students, not pastors. [*JTS* 10/04; *CBQ* 7/01, 10/03, 7/04; *JETS* 12/02; *JBL* Spr, Fall 04; *CurTM* 12/02; *Int* 7/02; *HS* 2003; *SwJT* Fall 01; *VT* 54.1, 54.4; *JSOT* 94, 27.5 and 28.5; *JSS* Aut 05, Spr 06; *BSac* 10/04, 1/06; *JSS* Aut 02; *HS* 2004 (Williamson); *Bib* 83.2, 84.3, and 85.3 (Beuken); *SJT* 60.4 (Seitz); *RelSRev* 10/04 (Sweeney); *RBL*; *CurTM* 8/06].

Block, Daniel I., and Richard L. Schultz, eds. *Bind Up the Testimony: Explorations in the Genesis of the Book of Isaiah*, 2015. From a Wheaton colloquium.

✓ Bock, Darrell L., and Mitch Glaser, eds. *The Gospel according to Isaiah 53: Encountering the Suffering Servant in Jewish and Christian Theology*, 2012. Evangelical essays.

F Boda, Mark J. (SGBC).

☆ Brueggemann, Walter. ‡ (WestBC) 2 vols., 1998. About 575pp. of theological commentary aimed at educated laity, but of real assistance to pastors as well. Read with discernment, e.g., at ch. 53. See also his works on Genesis, Exodus, Samuel, and Jeremiah. Those stimulated by interaction with the critics may like the more liberal, provocative Brueggemann. [*Them* 11/99; *JSOT* 89; *Int* 10/99; *HBT* 12/03].

☆ Chester, Tim. *Isaiah for You*, 2021. Thought-provoking exposition by an English pastor with a PhD. In this case and Webb's, the brevity means it fills a need.

☆ **Childs, Brevard S.** ‡ (OTL) 2001. A major interpretation, picking up where he left off in his *Introduction to the OT as Scripture*. Childs believes that "the crucial questions turn . . . on how one understands the process of the book's editorial shaping" (371). If only there were more focus on the final shape. Frankly, he spends more time discussing diachronic issues and pursuing his redactional approach than expected. There is also less theology than I'd hoped. I judge it to be less useful to evangelical pastors than Childs's *Exodus*. Consider it valuable to students for its review of the history of interpretation, exegetical findings, and for passing on the insights of some key European interpreters (Beuken, Steck, Elliger). Motyer [*Anvil* 19.3] expresses disappointment with this work. See the older Isaiah vols. in OTL by Kaiser and Westermann. [*CBQ* 1/02; *Them* Spr 02; *JETS* 12/02; *JBL* Sum 02; *Int* 10/02; *ExpTim* 11/01; *BSac* 10/02; *Bib* 83.4; *BibInt* 12.3; *JSOT* 99; *SwJT* Sum 02; *Chm* Win 01; *BBR* 14.2; *ThTo* 4/02 (Williamson); *CurTM* 2/02 (Klein); *RBL*; *Evangel* Sum 02]. More discussion of the history of interpretation is offered in *The Struggle to Understand Isaiah as Christian Scripture* (2004) [*RTR* 4/05; *CBQ* 1/06; *JETS* 12/05; *Int* 1/06; *BL* 2005; *ExpTim* 1/07; *Anvil* 23.1 (Motyer); *EuroJTh* 18.1 (Firth)].

✓ **Clements, Ronald E.** ‡ *Isaiah 1–39* (NCB) 1980. Has value as a reference tool for students. Prior to Childs, I judged the 2-vol. NCB set and 3-vol. OTL commentary to be close rivals for pride of place as the best completed critical exegesis of this prophecy. Both sets employ a form-critical approach, with NCB being more restrained. [*WTJ* Fall 83; *ExpTim* 9/81; *EvQ* 4/82; *JBL* 102.1].

F  Collins, C. John (EBTC)?

✓ Conrad, Edward W. ‡ *Reading Isaiah*, 1991. Literary analysis which lends support (unintentionally) to other, even evangelical, readings of the prophecy as a coherent whole. [*BSac* 4/92; *HS* 1992].

F  Couey, J. Blake. ‡ *Isaiah 1–39*. I don't know which series. Couey's published PhD, *Reading the Poetry of First Isaiah* (Oxford, 2015), does not cover a great deal of text, but he provides one of the more fruitful explorations of Hebrew poetry generally (including currents in research) and the features of Isaiah's poetry specifically. [*JETS* 6/16; *JSOT* 40.5; *BibInt* 25.3; *JHebS* 17].

F  Couey, J. Blake, and Christopher Frechette. ‡ (Illum).

Davis, Andrew M. *Exalting Jesus in Isaiah* (CCE) 2017.

☆ Davis, Dale Ralph. *Stump Kingdom: Isaiah 6–12*, 2017. A welcome theological exposition (8 sermons). See Davis's other works on Joshua to Kings, Daniel, etc. [*WTJ* Fall 18].

✓ Delitzsch, Franz. (KD has the 2nd ed., 1869). "A monument of immense learning" (Childs). This work is justly famous. Conservatives regret that Delitzsch came to moderate his position on the unity of Isaiah in his 4th edition of this commentary (1889). All four editions were translated into English.

F  Dempsey, Carol. ‡ *Isaiah 1–39* (BerO). See Franke and Niskanen.

✓ Elliott, Mark W., ed. *Isaiah 40–66* (ACCS) 2007. [*BL* 2008].

F  Fantuzzo, Chris. (THC).

☆ Firth, David G., and H. G. M. Williamson, eds. *Interpreting Isaiah: Issues and Approaches*, 2009. These 287pp. are from Tyndale Fellowship. See the similar Firth-edited vol. on Psalms. [*ExpTim* 7/10; *BBR* 21.4; *JSOT* 35.5; *Chm* Win 12; *BSac* 7/11; *DenvJ* 13].

Fisher, Jeff, ed. *Isaiah 1–39* (RCS) 2024. I have not seen it yet.

F  Franke, Chris. ‡ *Isaiah 40–55* (BerO). Her diss. was *Isaiah 46, 47, and 48: A New Literary-Critical Reading* (1994). See Dempsey and Niskanen.

Friesen, Ivan D. ‡ (BCBC) 2009. Well-informed in his critical scholarship (Toronto PhD), the author writes for pastors, especially those sharing his Mennonite faith. Friesen sees the prophecy as cohesive because it is a "composite unity," and he then pursues a theological reading and issues of application.

☆ Fyall, Bob. "Isaiah" (ESVEC) 2022. The massive Volume VI in the set (over 1200pp.) covers

Isaiah (19–417), then "Jeremiah" by Hwang (421–783), "Lamentations" by Gibson (787–905), and "Ezekiel" by Duguid (909–1208). Among these, Gibson's is by far the fullest. Fyall is retired Senior Tutor, Cornhill Training Course, Scotland, and a veteran commentator. Call his section thoughtful, with sound theology and a wide knowledge of Scripture.

F   Gentry, Peter J. (ZECOT). Preliminary to this is Rico and Gentry, *The Mother of the Infant King, Isaiah 7:14: ʿalmâ and parthenos in the World of the Bible* (2020) [*CBQ* 1/22].

F   Gignilliat, Mark S. (CCF).

☆   **Goldingay, John.** ‡ (NIBC) 2001. While I like the often-brilliant theological reading here, I am concerned how his higher-critical approach pulls evangelical scholarship to the left. He argues for four voices (or pens), for the theological unity of the prophecy (through redaction and inner-biblical interpretation), and for a postexilic date of the final form. Goldingay taught at Fuller Seminary. Helpful to pastors—students mainly use Goldingay's more scholarly works for ICC (see below). [*CBQ* 10/04; *Int* 1/04; *HS* 2006; *JHebS* 4]. Perhaps his final books on Isaiah are *The Theology of the Book of Isaiah* (2014) [*Int* 7/16; *JSOT* 40.5] and *Isaiah for Everyone* (2015).

✓   **Goldingay, John.** ‡ *Isaiah 56–66* (ICC–new series) 2014. A separate work (about 550pp.) from the ICC set on chs. 40–55 below, but builds off of it. Goldingay follows the same program with much the same depth and thoroughness, except that the commentary is structured a bit differently. ("Translation and Notes" and "Introduction" now head each larger literary section, in addition to the verse-by-verse "Comment" subsections.) This work also has more on the message. He emphasizes the interrelation of the different parts of the prophecy and calls chs. 56–66 "an exercise in scriptural interpretation" (46). Of enduring value to scholars, except those who believe that the most complex redaction-critical theories are still *de rigueur*. (He writes, "the assumption that we can establish how the chapters came into being is fallacious" [9].) One annoyance: why transliterate the Hebrew in the main text of the commentary, considering the ICC audience? [*CBQ* 4/15; *JTS* 4/15; *JSOT* 38.5; *Them* 7/14 (Oswalt)].

✓   **Goldingay, John.** ‡ *The Message of Isaiah 40–55: A Literary-Theological Commentary,* 2005. This more accessible vol. builds upon his ICC (below) and presents Goldingay's theological conclusions, but without such a mass of technical scholarship on the exegetical fine points like textual criticism. However, it is still a very full treatment (600pp.) of these 16 chapters. Regrettably, *The Message* is rather expensive. See also the author's (happily inexpensive) NIBC work above on the whole prophecy. [*CBQ* 7/07; *RelSRev* 1/07; *CJ* Win 09; *ExpTim* 5/07; *RBL*; *BSac* 7/08; *Int* 1/09; *BL* 2007].

✓   **Goldingay, John, and David Payne.** ‡ *Isaiah 40–55* (ICC) 2 vols., 2006. Supposedly completed six years before publication. Pastors with financial means prefer the 2005 one-vol. commentary above. This ICC is expensive and, with its severe focus on minutiae, is meant for scholars and reference libraries. With regard to critical orientation, the ICC works on Isaiah by Goldingay–Payne and Williamson must be classed as more conservative. The difference, in my opinion, between *Isaiah 40–55* and Williamson is that the latter is more interested in redaction and twice as thorough in textual analysis. Though "more conservative," Goldingay–Payne do uphold the critical conclusion that Second Isaiah addresses the Israel of the Babylonian exile (ca. 540 BC). The exegesis is more focused on the final form (9) than expected from ICC. Because much of the theological reflection was jettisoned—see the Literary-Theological Commentary above—this ICC seems dry and even truncated in one respect. Isn't the point of meticulous exegesis to drive at the message of this highly theological literature? Yes, but ICC always tends to leave that theological work to readers. [*CBQ* 4/08; *Int* 1/09; *BL* 2008; *RelSRev* 10/07 (Sweeney); *RBL*; *BSac* 10/08; *JETS* 12/09; *HS* 2009].

✓ **Gray, George B.** ‡ *Isaiah 1–27* (ICC) 1912. Years ago it offered students much help with philology, grammar, etc. In the history of scholarship, it is a pity that Gray's completed commentary on chs. 28–39 in this same series was never published. See Williamson below for a developing replacement set.

F   Groenewald, Alphonso. ‡ *Isaiah 1–27* (HCOT).

☆ **Grogan, Geoffrey W.** (EBCR) 2008. The author has updated and improved his 1986 EBC for a new generation of seminarians and ministers. It is a better updating than some of the other EBC works received. This thoughtful exegesis with exposition runs to about 430pp. and is a very good, sound guide to Isaiah. [*BL* 2010].

✓ **Hanson, Paul D.** ‡ *Isaiah 40–66* (I) 1995. A 272-page work, by an expert on apocalyptic, completing the Isaiah set which Seitz began. Hanson emphasizes "God's compassionate justice" as the central theme. The approach is broadly liberal and highly theological. [*JETS* 3/99; *CBQ* 1/97; *BSac* 4/97; *HS* 1997; *RelSRev* 1/97].

✓ Hayes, John H., and Stuart A. Irvine. ‡ *Isaiah: His Times and His Preaching*, 1987. A commentary on so-called First Isaiah (chs. 1–39) with a critical orientation. But the authors go their own more conservative way in attributing almost all the material in these chapters to Isaiah ben Amoz. "The major contribution of this work . . . is their focus on the historical backdrop of the latter half of the eighth century without which . . . Isaiah remains incomprehensible" (Vasholz). Because historical concerns dominate, this work feels dated in approach. [*Presb* Spr 90; *JTS* 10/90; *CRBR* 1991; *ExpTim* 8/89].

F   Hays, Christopher B. ‡? (OTL-R). Would replace Childs.

Heffelfinger, Katie. ‡ *Isaiah 40–66* (NCBC) 2024. See also Stromberg.

Horton, Stanley M. 2000. A full exegesis by a Pentecostal, focused on historical and theological points.

☆ **House, Paul R.** (Mentor) 2 vols., 2019. Will delight many pastors and laypeople as a lucid, conservative, theologically oriented exegesis (approx. 1500pp.). House is a fine, solid scholar; see 1–2 Kings, Lamentations, and Daniel. There are similarities between this set and Mackay's, but House is more widely read and attuned to Isaianic scholarship. He seeks to read the prophecies with sensitivity to the 8th century historical context, relating specific oracles to the successive reigns of Uzziah, Jotham, Ahaz, and Hezekiah. Tracing evidence of "Assyrian-era settings in Isaiah" and reading the relevant ANE background literature, he finds "a consecutive historical framework" (24–25) in the prophecy. The vols. abound in theological insights. A downside would be no interaction with Williamson's ICC. The average Bible-believing pastor would find Mentor considerably more approachable, straightforward, and useful than McConville's BCOT.

✓ Janowski, Bernd, and Peter Stuhlmacher, eds. *The Suffering Servant: Isaiah 53 in Jewish and Christian Sources*, 2004. Also see Bock–Glaser above; MacLeod below; and Antti Laato, *Who Is the Servant of the Lord? Jewish and Christian Interpretations on Isaiah 53 from Antiquity to the Middle Ages* (2012) [*CBQ* 1/15 (Williamson)].

✓ **Kaiser, Otto.** ‡ *Isaiah 1–12* (OTL) ET 1972, rev. 1983; *Isaiah 13–39* (OTL) ET 1974. A prominent historical-critical exegesis. Note that this German became more radical since he began commenting on Isaiah and seems supremely confident about his redaction theories. Westermann completes this series. Compare with Clements and the much more thorough Wildberger. [*ExpTim* 6/83; *JBL* 94.3].

Kim, Hyun Chul Paul. ‡ (ROT) 2016. Interested in intertextual research. [*Int* 4/19].

✓ Kissane, Edward J. 2 vols., 1941–44. This Irish Catholic took a more conservative approach. Oswalt often quotes Kissane, whose work is "very impressive" (Childs).

✓ **Knight, G. A. F.** ‡ (ITC-E) 2 vols., 1984–85. About 330pp. of exposition of chs. 40–66. Knight is better than many other critics' interpretations. The theology he draws out is also more conservative. Back in 1965 Knight published *Deutero-Isaiah*, a well-received commentary in which he tried to reconstruct a 6th century BC milieu of chs. 40–55.

✓ **Koole, Jan L.** ‡ *Isaiah III* (HCOT) 3 vols., ET 1997–2001. Among the three vols., which cover chs. 40–48, 49–55, and 56–66, there are about 1700pp. of detailed commentary: a rich harvest of sober, meticulous, Dutch critical scholarship. Koole's more traditional historical-critical approach can be contrasted with Beuken's. Students, don't be confused by the title, *Isaiah III*. Koole covers so-called Second and Third Isaiah. [*CBQ* 1/99, 7/99; *JBL* Spr 01; *RelSRev* 10/99, 7/00; *BL* 1998, 1999; *JSOT* 27.5].

☆ **Lessing, R. Reed.** *Isaiah 40–55* (ConcC) 2011; *Isaiah 56–66* (ConcC) 2014. The division of chapters in these vols. does not indicate acceptance of higher-critical conclusions regarding compositional history. As expected from this series, there is valuable guidance offered to ministers in working through the Hebrew text, confessional Lutheran theological interpretation, and ample preaching suggestions. The set is full enough (1210pp.) to accomplish a great deal. [chs. 40–55: *BBR* 23.4 (Smith); *JETS* 12/13; *JESOT* 1.2; chs. 56–66: *JESOT* 4.1; *BBR* 25.4; *JETS* 9/15].

Leupold, H. C. 2 vols., 1968–71. There is some solid exposition here from a conservative Lutheran angle, but the ConcC vols. are much to be preferred.

☆ Lloyd-Jones, D. Martyn. *The All-Sufficient God*, 2005. Fine sermons on ch. 40, from Banner.

Lozano, Gilberto. [𝓜], *Isaiah 40–66* (NBBC) 2020. A briefer Wesleyan exposition; he does not interact with much conservative scholarship.

✓ Lynch, Matthew J. ‡ *First Isaiah and the Disappearance of the Gods*, 2021. Useful for critiquing a commonly held idea. "Biblical scholars routinely portray Isa 1–39 as a way station toward the 'fully fledged' or 'uncompromising' monotheism in Isa 40–55" (1). [*Bib* 104.1].

☆ **Mackay, John L.** *Isaiah* (EPSC) 2 vols., 2008–2009. A conservative Presbyterian exegesis and exposition published in the UK, totaling over 1400pp. The author has many commentaries on OT books (e.g., see Jeremiah), and all are characterized by a disciplined focus on the text, not scholarly opinions, and by a devotion to Scripture as "divinely-given." He views redaction-critical concerns as more of a distraction, possibly even as distorting our understanding. Mackay attends to detail but always aims to explicate the theological message. [*SBET* Spr 09].

☆ MacLeod, David J. *The Suffering Servant of the Lord*, 2019. Waltke terms it "a splendid exposition" of ch. 53.

MacRae, Allan A. *The Gospel of Isaiah*, 1977. An exposition of 40:1–56:8 by a scholar who left the Northern Presbyterians (old PCUSA) over liberalism and the reorganization of Princeton Seminary. It focuses on Christ, the true Servant of Yahweh, and is perhaps worth a one-time read through. MacRae had the best of scholarly training, but this Moody pb is on a popular level.

✓ Margalioth, Rachel. *The Indivisible Isaiah*, ET 1964. Conservatives were enthusiastic about this apology for the traditional position, translated from modern Hebrew. Not a commentary. Her work anticipated much of the scholarly interest today in the coherence and (redactional) unity of Isaiah.

☆ McConville, J. Gordon. [𝓜], *The Suffering Servant: Isaiah 53*, 2023. For the Baker Touchstone Texts series. See also his major commentary above. [*BL* 2024].

McKenna, David. (WCC) 2 vols., 1994.

McKenzie, J. L. ‡ *Second Isaiah* (retired AB) 1968. Not so valuable. Covers all of chs. 40–66, not merely 40–55, despite the reader's expectations. McKenzie was replaced in the series by Blenkinsopp. [*JBL* 88.1].

✓ McKinion, Steven A., ed. *Isaiah 1–39* (ACCS) 2004. [*BL* 2008].

✓ **Miscall, Peter D.** ‡ (Read) 1993, 2nd ed. 2006. Interprets the prophecy as a whole, while ignoring the "seams" between the different Isaiahs that critical scholars allege. It had a friendly reception. [*CBQ* 7/94; *CRBR* 1995; *BL* 2008]. Added to it is Quinn-Miscall, *Reading Isaiah: Poetry and Vision* (2002) [*Int* 7/03; *VT* 54.3; *BibInt* 12.1; *Evangel* Spr 05].

☆ Motyer, J. Alec. (retired TOTC) 1999. Presents the author's conclusions from his 1993 commentary above (not much of the intervening Isaiah scholarship was discussed). Having both vols. is a waste of shelf space. No commentary I have seen rivals this Tyndale vol. in terms of compression. [*Chm* Spr 00; *Them* Spr 01; *EvQ* 7/04; *JETS* 9/01; *JSOT* 94].

✓ Muilenburg, James. ‡ (IB–exegesis section) 1956. For his time, he offered a brilliant treatment of chs. 40–66. See Scott below.

✓ **Niskanen, Paul V.** ‡ *Isaiah 56–66* (BerO) 2014. After about 15pp. of introductory material, the author commences a close literary examination of the poetry. The commentary is not extensive (100pp.) but still has plenty of insights for students of the Hebrew. Niskanen explores intratextual connections among the chapters and with Isaiah 1–55, discovering evidence that "Third Isaiah" preserves and extends the themes/concerns of the "eighth century prophet." [*JTS* 4/16; *JSOT* 40.5].

✓ North, C. R. ‡ *Isaiah 40–55* (Torch) 1952. Longman found North valuable, especially on the Servant Songs. Note also the more technical work, *The Second Isaiah* (1964).

✓ Ogden, Graham S., and Jan Sterk. (UBS) 2 vols., 2011. About 1900pp.

☆ Ortlund, Raymond C. (PTW) 2005. The exposition of over 450pp. reads like printed sermons; that might not sound exciting, but Ortlund is both an OT scholar and an engaging preacher (founded Immanuel Church, Nashville). He provides good guidance to today's expositors (48 sermons on the 66 chs.). What he does not provide is a lot of his undergirding exegesis. [*JETS* 3/07; *BSac* 1/07; *CJ* 4/07].

☆ Oswalt, John. (NIVAC) 2003. A single-vol. exposition (700pp.), building upon his twenty years of research for NICOT above. Pastors will take an interest in it, perhaps buying this NIVAC or Ortlund's PTW, but students will make use of Oswalt's older, more academic work.

✓ Parry, Donald W. *Exploring the Isaiah Scrolls and Their Textual Variants*, 2020. Extremely detailed evaluation of DSS evidence. [*RelSRev* 9/22; *JTS* 10/20; *JETS* 12/21; *JJS* 71.2].

✓ **Paul, Shalom.** ‡ *Isaiah 40–66* (ECC) 2012. From a very learned, perceptive, conservatively critical Jewish scholar, whose 2-vol. Magnes Press commentary in Hebrew appeared in 2008 [*BL* 2009; *VT* 59.2; *RBL* 2011]. That was translated and then reworked for this 650-page technical work. It contains much textual criticism, lexical and grammatical analysis, comparative Semitics, historical study, inner-biblical interpretation, review of the history of interpretation, and a close literary reading. There is less of a theological intention here and little interaction with leading interpreters (Goldingay, Williamson, Beuken). Paul sees the supposed "watershed" between chs. 55 and 56 as "artificial" and reads 40–66 as "one coherent opus composed by a single prophet" (11–12). Scholars are marvelously equipped by Paul and Goldingay (ICC) to dig deeper into this literature. [*JSOT* 37.5; *VT* 59.2, 63.1; *JETS* 12/13; *JSS* Aut 15; *ExpTim* 8/13; *JESOT* 2.1 (Oswalt); *JJS* 66.1 (Williamson); *RelSRev* 9/13; *JSS* Aut 15; *JHebS* 15].

Pawson, David. *Come with Me through Isaiah*, 2010. A homiletical and devotional treatment by a well-known English pastor.

✓ Pieper, August. *Isaiah II: An Exposition of Isaiah 40–66*, ET 1979. A conservative Lutheran, Pieper provides a careful exegesis based on thorough work with the MT, and theological exposition. Cf. Lessing.

☆ **Raabe, Paul R.** *Isaiah 13–27* (ConcC) 2023. Valuable to students and ministers as an exegesis and theological interpretation from a conservative Lutheran perspective (500pp.). Previously he wrote a major commentary on Obadiah. See also Bartelt and Lessing.

F   Raabe, Paul R., and Ryan Tietz. *Isaiah 28–39* (ConcC). Will complete a five-vol. set.

☆ Ridderbos, Jan. (BSC) ET 1984. Though shorter than many other commentaries on Isaiah, Ridderbos offers valuable theological exposition in a readable translation. Now o/p. Before Motyer was published and Oswalt was completed, Longman counseled you to purchase this first. [*WTJ* Spr 88; *JETS* 3/87].

✓ **Roberts, J. J. M.** ‡ *First Isaiah* (Herm) 2015. Considering the author's scholarly reputation as a Princeton Seminary prof and author of the acclaimed OTL vol. on *Nahum, Habakkuk, and Zephaniah*, as well as the prestige of the Hermeneia series, the appearance of this commentary was a major publishing event. I had not expected so brief an Introduction. As anticipated, it has a highly technical, moderate historical-critical orientation, and it is rich in ANE comparative studies. Other key strengths here are discussion of text-critical issues, a wise restraint about any redaction questions, full bibliographies, and mature scholarship (after four decades of Isaiah research). Do note, however, that not much 21st century scholarship is cited. Roberts includes more theological reflection than some other recent contributors to the series. See Baltzer above, and cf. Williamson. [*BBR* 27.1; *JTS* 4/18; *Int* 1/18; *JSOT* 41.5].

F Roberts, Megan, and Kevin Foth. (EEC). A previous report was Todd S. Beall.

Ross, Barry L. *Isaiah 1–39* (NBBC) 2016. A mature work by a scholar long at Anderson University (Indiana) and strong on the ANE background. See Lozano above.

Sawyer, John F. A. ‡ (DSB) 2 vols., 1984–86. Critical exposition. [*EvQ* 10/86].

✓ Sawyer, John F. A. ‡ *Isaiah through the Centuries* (BBC) 2017. By a pioneer in reception history research; see Sawyer's much-cited *The Fifth Gospel: Isaiah in the History of Christianity* (CUP, 1996) [*EvQ* 1/03]. [*Bib* 99.4; *ExpTim* 12/18; *JSOT* 43.5].

F Schuele, Andreas. ‡ *Third Isaiah* (Herm). See also Roberts and Baltzer.

F Schultz, Richard. (Apollos). Will this be a one-vol. conservative exegesis to rival Motyer and McConville? Schultz is an able evangelical who did his Yale PhD on Isaiah.

Scott, R. B. Y. ‡ (IB–exegesis section) 1956. Covers the first 39 chs. Among older commentaries, this was prized by Childs. Scott was combined with Muilenburg's exegesis of the Book of Comfort, chs. 40–66. Decades ago this 2-part work in IB was an important reference, but most ignore it today.

✓ **Seitz, Christopher R.** ‡ *Isaiah 1–39* (I) 1993. He has done important work on Isaiah, both before and after this more conservatively critical commentary. For unfolding the message of these oracles, the Interpretation series is more interesting than the old OTL or NCB, and preachers have gravitated toward Seitz and Hanson (above). See the next entry. [*Int* 7/95; *JR* 4/95; *JETS* 3/99; *JBL* Fall 95; *BSac* 4/96; *HS* 1995; *AsTJ* Fall 97].

✓ **Seitz, Christopher R.** ‡ *Isaiah 40–66* (NIB) 2001. Completes his treatment of the prophecy, though in different series. The approaches and depth of treatment are similar. Seitz has an eagle eye for theological themes. "First Isaiah" in the NIB is covered by Tucker. [*CurTM* 2/03].

✓ Skinner, John. ‡ (CBSC) 2 vols., 1910–15.

Smith, G. A. ‡ (EB) 1888.

F Stromberg, Jacob. ‡ *Isaiah 1–39* (NCBC). An earlier report was David Baer.

F Stromberg, Jacob. ‡ *Isaiah 28–39* (ICC).

✓ **Sweeney, Marvin A.** ‡ (FOTL) 2 vols., 1996–2016. Sweeney teaches at Claremont and is a trenchant Jewish scholar. This set will be cited in the literature for a long time to come. Students consult it for bibliography, form-critical, redactional, and structural analysis. In the initial vol., the author did better than most others in the series at examining texts within the prophecy's structure as a whole—i.e., more attention is paid to the final form. [*BSac* 1/97; *JETS* 6/98; *JSS* Spr 98; *Bib* 78.2; *BL* 1997; *CBQ* 4/98; *HS* 1999; *BibInt* 9.1]. Sweeney's *Isaiah 40–66* maintains the same high standards, though he scarcely interacts with Goldingay. [*Bib* 98.4 (Williamson); *BBR* 27.2; *JETS* 3/17; *JSOT* 41.5; *JHebS* 17].

☆ Thomas, Derek. *God Delivers: Isaiah Simply Explained* (Welwyn) 1991. A solid, spiritually helpful, Reformed exposition pitched at a level suitable for both laity and ministers. See also his books on Job. [*SBET* Aut 96].

✓ Tiemeyer, Lena-Sofia. [𝓜], *For the Comfort of Zion: The Geographical and Theological Location of Isaiah 40–55*, 2011. Argues for Judahite provenance. [*ExpTim* 5/13].

✓ Tiemeyer, Lena-Sofia, ed. ‡ *The Oxford Handbook of Isaiah*, 2020. [*BL* 2022; *DenvJ* 2023; *ETL* 9/23].

✓ Tucker, Gene M. ‡ *Isaiah 1–39* (NIB) 2001. Was a leading form critic, and his 300-page interpretation is less valuable for theological reflection than Seitz on chs. 40–66.

✓ **Tull, Patricia K.** ‡ *Isaiah 1–39* (S&H) 2010. Her Emory PhD topic (under the name Willey) was well-chosen: *Remember the Former Things: The Recollection of Previous Texts in Second Isaiah* (1997). Tull is an able scholar, emerita at Louisville Presbyterian Seminary, and there is much here (568pp.) for students and academically oriented pastors, especially on inner-biblical interpretation (or intertextuality) and the history of interpretation. The theological exposition is fresh and well-done from the liberal angle. [*CBQ* 1/13 (Williamson); *Int* 4/12].

✓ Van Ruiten, J., and M. Vervenne, eds. ‡ *Studies in the Book of Isaiah* (Beuken FS), 1997.

✓ Vermeylen, J., ed. ‡ *The Book of Isaiah*, 1989.

Vine, William E. 1953. Once commended by F. F. Bruce: "The author has concentrated on the moral and spiritual lessons of Isaiah, and presented them in a way which will prove very helpful for the general reader." Vine wrote expositions of both OT and NT books, and they have been reprinted.

Walker, Larry L., and Elmer A. Martens. *Isaiah, Jeremiah, Lamentations* (CorBC) 2005. I've not had opportunity to use this vol. Walker's work was originally scheduled for NAC.

✓ **Watts, John D. W.** ‡ (WBC) 2 vols., 1985–87, rev. 2005. I'm not enthusiastic about the set. Watts presents Isaiah as a drama, and, while there is much learning to appreciate, I find the scheme too farfetched and idiosyncratic to be of much help. Watts concludes that the Isaianic materials were gathered and reshaped quite late, about 435 BC (xli). As noted by one reviewer [*BL* 2007 (Day)], among his oddest conclusions is "that the 'messianic' oracles in Isaiah 9 and 11 are to be regarded as the words of Isaiah's opponents." Thirty years ago it had some prominence as one of the few recent, complete technical exegeses. Happily, the revision is substantive. [*HS* 1987, 1993; *RTR* 1/87; *ExpTim* 3/88, 1/91; *JETS* 9/88, 3/94; *Them* 10/89; *EvQ* 10/88; *Chm* 102.2; *CRBR* 1988, 1992].

☆ Wegner, Paul D. (TOTC-R) 2021. It is sad to say goodbye to the predecessor Motyer, which was excellent, though very dense. Wegner, who has long taught at Phoenix and now Gateway seminaries, has written a solid exegesis which is easier reading. Like Motyer, he is a stalwart defender of the unity of the prophecy as authored by Isaiah ben Amoz. Useful as a less expensive and concise commentary, though those committed to historical criticism see Wegner as less serviceable [*JSOT* 47.5 (Williamson)].

✓ **Westermann, Claus.** ‡ *Isaiah 40–66* (OTL) 1969. Some theology buried in form-critical analysis of the oracles. This is a rigorous, important critical work, sitting alongside Kaiser's less useful Isaiah vols. in the old OTL. Scholars still make constant reference to Westermann. More academically oriented pastors and students consult it. See Childs above. [*JBL* 88.3].

✓ **Whybray, R. Norman.** ‡ *Isaiah 40–66* (NCB) 1975. [*EvQ* 10/76].

✓ **Wildberger, Hans.** ‡ (ContC) 3 vols., ET 1991–2002. A BKAT treasure trove for specialists, with a measure of theology. The vols. cover chs. 1–12, 13–27, and 28–39. Typical of older German scholarship, Wildberger views it as his task to delineate the earliest individual prophetic utterances by form-critical means and then trace the development of the book through its redactional layers. Wildberger treats the text with more respect than Kaiser and is more confident we can reconstruct the historical proclamation of Isaiah ben Amoz. It is instructive to note that the *JBL* reviewer, Blank, finds little to which an adherent of Judaism would object. Note also that vol.3 contains the introduction. [*JBL* 91.1, 94.2; *SwJT* Fall 93; *JSOT* 89, 27.5; *JETS* 12/99; *BSac* 1/93; *RelSRev* 7/98; *JSS* Spr 02; *RelSRev* 1/04; *Int* 10/05; *RBL*].

Wilken, Robert Louis, ed. (TCB) 2007. Nearly 600pp. of patristic and medieval commentary. Compare this with ACCS. [*Chm* Win 08; *RTR* 8/08; *JTS* 10/08; *ExpTim* 4/08; *VT* 58.3 (Williamson); *Pro Ecclesia* Win 09; *RelSRev* 3/11].

Williams, Jenni. ‡ *The Kingdom of Our God*, 2019. A succinct theological commentary by a British academic and vicar in Oxford. [*CTJ* 11/21; *CBQ* 1/21].

✓ **Williamson, H. G. M.** ‡ *Isaiah 1–5* (ICC) 2006; *Isaiah 6–12* (ICC) 2018. I pile up superlatives for the fullest technical OT commentary I have ever seen. Specialists expected these vols. on chs. 1–27 to be a conservatively critical, invaluable reference work (particularly for diachronic and textual issues), and they are not disappointed. In his historical criticism Williamson posits the usual threefold division of Isaiah and argues for a definite redactional unity. But it's complicated: the authors of chs. 40–66 consciously used First Isaiah as a model, yet much of chs. 1–12 bears the marks of a late-exilic redaction by Deutero-Isaiah. For example, as he reads the Immanuel saying, Williamson speaks of "the probably exilic date for its incorporation in the book" (160). He told me (March 2023) that he has in manuscript his commentary on chs. 13–20, and there will be two more vols. on 21–27. He is Emeritus Regius Professor of Hebrew in Oxford, with a background in evangelical circles in the UK. [*JTS* 4/08; *VT* 60.1 (Millard), 69.2; *Bib* 91.2; *BL* 2007; 2018: *Bib* 100.1; *JSS* Aut 20; *BBR* 29.1; *CBQ* 10/20; *JTS* 4/20; *JSOT* 43.5 (Moberly); *JJS* 70.1]. See also his monographs, *The Book Called Isaiah* (1994) [*JETS* 3/98; *JSS* Spr 96; *JTS* 10/96], and *Variations on a Theme: King, Messiah, and the Servant in the Book of Isaiah* (1998) [*SJT* 53.4].

✓ Witherington, Ben, III. [𝓜], *Isaiah Old and New: Exegesis, Intertextuality, and Hermeneutics*, 2017. Having written commentaries on the whole NT, Witherington here writes a lengthy (500pp.), mildly critical study on Isaiah with special attention given to the NT use of Isaianic materials (400 quotes and allusions in the NT). See his discussions of differences between the MT and the LXX. He writes, "one can make a strong case for the hermeneutical centrality of Isaiah for the majority of NT books" (2). He posits a much later Second and Third Isaiah. Published by Fortress. [*CBQ* 1/18; *JETS* 3/18; *JSOT* 42.5].

Wolf, Herbert. *Interpreting Isaiah: The Suffering and Glory of the Messiah*, 1985. A conservative, popularly styled commentary, focused upon Messianic revelation. Written more for an educated lay readership. Wolf contributed Judges in EBC.

✓ **Young, E. J.** (retired NICOT) 3 vols., 1965–72. A solid, learned commentary for its time. There was much to appreciate in the vols., but the set now feels older than it is, and readers may feel they are plodding through the text. There is not as much theology as could be hoped for in such a massive work (1640pp.). Young died soon after completing the manuscript (†1968). See Oswalt. [*EvQ* 7/73]. Students can consult Young's strong apologetic for the unity of the prophecy: *Who Wrote Isaiah?* (1958). For an older review of the history of Isaianic interpretation, see his *Studies in Isaiah* (1954).

Youngblood, Ronald. 2nd ed. 1993. A thoughtful, popularly styled exposition (174pp.).

NOTES: (1) Richard J. Coggins's "Which Is the Best Commentary? 12. Isaiah," *ExpTim* 1/91. (2) See the four review-essays gathered in Alan J. Hauser, *Recent Research on the Major Prophets* (2008); two of them are drawn from *CRBS*. (3) The most valuable quick review of current scholarship is Williamson's leading chapter in Firth–Williamson above.

# JEREMIAH

NOTE: Choices among evangelical exegetical works aren't so clear for Jeremiah. Over the decades, what we thought to be the best are now older (Thompson and Martens), and some of the newer are not the most suitable. For this reason I include a greater number of recommendations below, and readers may sort through them. Do mix and match according to your needs and interests. All are worth having.

★ **Allen, Leslie C.** ‡ (OTL-R) 2008. An excellent addition to OTL (550pp.), replacing Carroll, who was both influential and rather out of sympathy with the text (finding little coherence, little reliable historical information about Jeremiah, and regarding large portions of text as later redactions). Allen taught at Fuller but is more critical than some might guess; he sometimes finds less material belonging to the prophet than, say, Holladay (Allen, 509–10). That said, he is also more conservative theologically than the usual OTL contributor. Though majoring on the final form, he is also more interested in literary development (diachrony) than many younger OT scholars. Were there more theology (and discussion of NT connections), it might more easily be recommended to students for purchase; this deficiency also makes the book less useful for the pastor's study. As expected from Allen, he deals a good bit with textual issues (MT vs. LXX). Strong points include his attention to the rhetorical structure and style of the prophecy, and a learned handling of the main historical, linguistic, and form-critical questions. One also appreciates the discussion of "the purposeful trajectory of overriding grace that stretches over the book like a rainbow" (17). Allen is a veteran commentator; see Chronicles, Psalms, Ezekiel, and Joel. [*JETS* 6/10; *Int* 1/10; *BL* 2010; *VT* 60.2; *Anvil* 26.3–4; *RelSRev* 6/13; *JHebS* 11].

★ Calvin, John. (GS) 5 vols., 1563, ET 1850–55. Astonishingly, 2,400 pages! Its theological treatment more than made up for Thompson's inadequacy; they are good companions. An edited version (320pp.) of both Jeremiah and Lamentations is published in CrossC (2000) [*JSOT* 94]. Free online (ccel.org)! By contrast his *Sermons on Jeremiah* (ET 1990) from Edwin Mellen Press was prohibitively costly.

★ Dearman, J. Andrew. [𝓜], *Jeremiah, Lamentations* (NIVAC) 2002. Offers a nearly 500-page exposition which will aid pastors, but students will have less use for it. His past work has been mildly critical. See also Lamentations, and his Hosea work. [*RTR* 1/96].

★ **Fretheim, Terence E.** [𝓜], (S&H) 2002. An expensive work ($75) of nearly 700pp., focused on theological exposition. I find this to be an unusually astute reading. Fretheim is a veteran writer of commentaries, having done Genesis, Exodus, and Kings in other series. Wright has said, alongside Lundbom, he finds "Fretheim and Stulman to be the most stimulating and insightful" (10). If you balk at the price, look for a s/h copy or for another (critical) theological treatment: Stulman, Bracke, Clements, or Brueggemann. For a conservative substitute, try Martens or Longman. [*Int* 4/04; *CBQ* 1/05; *CJ* 4/06].

★ **Goldingay, John.** [𝓜], (NICOT-R) 2021. Massively learned, lucid, and lauded by conservatives and critics alike (970pp.). Replaces Thompson; by comparison he concentrates more on flow of thought, rhetoric, and theological nuance than on historical matters and exegetical fine points. Having both vols. isn't a bad thing. All the interaction with the likes of Allen, Brueggemann, Calvin, Carroll, Fretheim, Holladay, Lundbom, McKane, older German commentators, and contemporary trauma studies enriches the discussion. Goldingay's register can be informal ("have it in their backpack") and he includes good illustrations. He has less interest in "textual genetics" (12), but dates final editing to the Babylonian period. In my opinion, *Jeremiah* is among Goldingay's two or three most useful works to date. [*JETS* 9/22; *JSOT* 47.5; *JTS* 10/23]. From the same year we have *The Theology of Jeremiah* (IVP, 2021) [*ExpTim* 11/21; *RTR* 8/21; *JETS* 9/21; *Int* 10/22; *JSOT* 47.5].

★ **Lalleman, Hetty.** *Jeremiah and Lamentations* (TOTC-R) 2013. An OT tutor at Spurgeon's College, London, the author did her PhD on Jeremiah and published a 2004 Dutch commentary on the prophecy. Especially appreciated are her full, well-informed introductions. She is an excellent guide, too, in the exegesis sections, with literary sensitivity and good theological sense. Let me note that historical-literary exegesis rather than a christological reading is at the fore in this larger Tyndale vol. (360pp.). As expected from the series, Lalleman has a disciplined focus upon the text, not scholarly debates. See Harrison. [*JESOT* 2.2 (Dearman)].

★ **Lundbom, Jack R.** [𝓜], (AB) 3 vols., 1999–2004. Replaces Bright and follows the recent AB pattern of exhaustively detailed exegesis. This is a magnificent achievement, with attention given not only to modern exegesis, but also to the history of interpretation (Calvin cited more than Carroll). Lundbom must be consulted by students, but pastors may find less use for it. Though well-written and accessible, the sheer detail (2207pp.) can overwhelm. More scholarly pastors, however, will be delighted to own the set. The key contributions are its attention to textual criticism (usually supporting the MT) and rhetorical study (vol.23A, pp.68–85)—the latter a lively topic in current scholarly discussion of the prophets. His approach to Jeremiah is not nearly as skeptical as some others' (e.g., Carroll), and he finds trustworthy biographical information. He emphasizes the unity, coherence, and literary artistry in the final form of the text, rejecting attempts to get "behind the text" and discover many layers or voices. Along with Hill on Malachi, this is a more conservative contribution to AB, but don't call it evangelical. See Holladay below. It is much to be regretted that Yale hiked the price (list over $300). If you can't handle this heavyweight—academically or financially—and you don't mind a mildly to moderately critical work, try Allen or Stulman (the more synchronic of the two). [*Int* 7/01, 10/05; *CBQ* 4/01, 7/05, 7/06; *CurTM* 10/04; *JTS* 10/07; *JBL* Sum 05; *BL* 2005; *VT* 56.2; *RelSRev* 1/05, 7/05; *RBL*; *ExpTim* 8/06]. Lundbom's latest are *Jeremiah among the Prophets* (2012), a 150-page summary treatment [*Int* 4/14; *Them* 7/14; *JESOT* 3.2 (Tiemeyer); *ExpTim* 7/16; *JSOT* 41.5]; *Writing Up Jeremiah: The Prophet and the Book* (2013) [*JSOT* 39.5; *JESOT* 3.2; *RelSRev* 9/14]; and the "Cascade Companion," *Jeremiah: Prophet Like Moses* (2015), which is a simpler introduction to the prophecy and its themes (with study questions).

★ Mackay, John L. (Mentor) 2 vols., 2004. The theological approach is strongly conservative and Reformed. He provides a full (over 1100pp.), accessible exposition for pastors; all the exegesis is aimed at illumining the message. The purpose is not to provide a sophisticated academic commentary, though Mackay is clearly a diligent, practiced student of God's word. He writes lucidly, treats lexical and syntactical matters, interacts with some of the better commentaries (mainly the historically oriented Keil, Holladay, Carroll, WBC, and Thompson), and even includes a few well-chosen illustrations (e.g., p.117). He is remarkably useful to the preacher.

★ Wright, Christopher J. H. (BST) 2014. Following on his Ezekiel vol. in BST, this *Message of Jeremiah* (448pp.) is exactly the thoughtful study companion pastors want handy. Much research lies behind the writing, and the exposition is both engaging and deeply satisfying. His earlier work on Deuteronomy (NIBC) prepared the way for this, since Jeremiah's theological outlook is consistently Deuteronomic. Shead says "Wright is first and last a missionary writer, and though at times he may be more focused on mission than Jeremiah was, his comments are salient, and constitute his most original contribution to Jeremiah studies" [*Chm* Aut 14]. [*JSOT* 40.5].

F  Arnold, William. (Apollos).

✓  Barstad, Hans M., and Reinhard G. Kratz, eds. ‡ *Prophecy in the Book of Jeremiah*, 2009. Essays from a 2007 Edinburgh conference. [*BBR* 21.2].

Boadt, Lawrence. ‡ (OTM) 2 vols., 1982. Also treats Nahum, Habakkuk, and Zephaniah. This Catholic (†2010) was highly respected for his work in the prophets and was a gracious, conservatively critical scholar.

✓ Bodner, Keith. ‡ *After the Invasion: A Reading of Jeremiah 40–44*, 2015. A well-received narrative-critical study (Oxford). [*CBQ* 1/17; *JTS* 10/16; *JETS* 3/16; *JSOT* 40.5; *JHebS* 17].

☆ Bracke, John M. ‡ (WestBC) 2 vols., 2000. Treats Lamentations too, and I value the set especially for that section (60 out of 470pp.). Bracke follows Brueggemann in three respects: (1) he taught at Eden Seminary, where Brueggemann formerly was on faculty, (2) he has written a fine theological exposition of Jeremiah, and (3) he takes more of a canonical approach. See Lamentations below. [*OTA* 10/00; *JSOT* 94].

✓ **Bright, John.** ‡ (retired AB) 1965. Years ago, classed as an especially good treatment of the historical background, offering some theology and a few homiletical hints. Bright was a more conservative AB vol. and more in line with the series' original aims. A frustration for readers is that the author rearranged the text according to chronological sequence. This aged commentary was replaced by Lundbom.

☆ **Brown, Michael.** (EBCR) 2010. Volume 7 contains Jeremiah to Ezekiel. Brown's work is quite full (550pp.) and entirely new, not a revision of Feinberg below. Firth well describes it as "a fairly traditional reading of Jeremiah . . . made distinctive by his use of rabbinic material in elucidating the text" [*JSOT* 37.5]. The work is solid and mostly exegetical, as compared to expositional.

☆ **Brueggemann, Walter.** ‡ (ITC-E) 2 vols., 1988–91, rev. 1998. One of the most valuable theological works from a critical standpoint. He focuses less on historical criticism and more on the message of the final form of the text (about 540pp.). [*CRBR* 1993; *BL* 1990, 1993; *CBQ* 7/91; *RTR* 1/90, 9/94; *BSac* 7/92; *HS* 1990, 1993]. This was republished (with a slight update) in a more convenient one-vol. format: *A Commentary on Jeremiah: Exile and Homecoming* (1998). [*JETS* 12/99; *ExpTim* 10/98; *CBQ* 4/00; *SwJT* Fall 98; *HS* 1999; *RBL*]. Another two works are his collected essays, *Like Fire in the Bones: Listening for the Prophetic Word in Jeremiah* (2006) [*CBQ* 7/07; *JR* 7/08; *EuroJTh* 18.2; *RelSRev* 3/11], and his Cambridge vol. on *The Theology of the Book of Jeremiah* (2007) [*Int* 7/08; *JR* 4/08; *CBQ* 7/08; *EuroJTh* 18.1]. See Brueggemann's other commentaries on Genesis, Exodus, Samuel, Kings, and Isaiah.

✓ Callaway, Mary Chilton. ‡ *Jeremiah Through the Centuries* (BBC) 2020. An inviting book, prompting broad reflection. [*BBR* 32.4; *JSOT* 47.5; *JTS* 10/23].

✓ **Carroll, Robert P.** ‡ (retired OTL) 1986. A huge tome (870pp.), building upon his monograph, *From Chaos to Covenant* (1981). After such a long stretch of time when no scholarly commentaries appeared except NICOT, we rapidly received Carroll, Holladay, Jones, WBC, McKane, and three vols. of Lundbom! Carroll is quite critical, denigrating any approach that tries to make sense out of the book's historical aspects and to form a portrait of the man Jeremiah and his life. (In his view, that portrait is irretrievable because redactors have completely reworked the traditions for a subsequent generation.) He also applies some heavy ideological criticism. Advanced students have to take account of Carroll as "the most influential [Jeremiah] interpreter of our generation" (Brueggemann [*CBR* 6/10]), but this is not for pastors. See Carroll under Prophets & Prophetic Literature above. This work had a better reception in the UK than in the USA, and Sheffield Phoenix reissued a 2-vol. edition in 2006. For Carroll's later, changed views regarding Jeremiah, see his essays in Diamond–O'Connor–Stulman. See Allen above. [*CBQ* 7/91; *TJ* Fall 87; *JETS* 9/88; *Int* 7/88 (Brueggemann); *JSOT* 45; *BibInt* 17 (2009)].

✓ Carvalho, Corrine. ‡ (ROT) 2017. A quickly moving, brief literary study by a learned (Yale PhD) and incisive scholar, who has also worked on Ezekiel. [*BBR* 28.3; *Int* 1/10].

✓ **Clements, R. E.** ‡ (I) 1988. Rather brief (276pp.) on such a big, complex book (the Bible's longest). Pursues the aims of the series well enough. Still considered a leading exposition from the critical camp. Clements was a respected, moderately critical scholar (†2024) who taught at Cambridge and London. [*JETS* 6/92; *CBQ* 4/91; *CRBR* 1990].

✓ **Craigie, Peter C., Page H. Kelley, and Joel F. Drinkard, Jr.** [𝑀], *Jeremiah 1–25* (WBC) 1991. The work begun by Craigie had to be completed by the others when he died in a car accident (†1985). They are mainly responsible for the commentary, not Craigie. It covers the first 25 chapters in 375pp. Their approach includes careful textual criticism (using the DSS and expressing confidence in the MT), conservative form criticism, and ample research in the vast literature. Those seeking another careful exegetical work will find this less rigorous than Lundbom or Holladay, but also less liberal (than Holladay) and less expensive. [*CBQ* 7/93; *VT* 46.2; *BSac* 7/93]. See Keown below.

✓ Crouch, C. L. ‡ *An Introduction to the Study of Jeremiah*, 2017. From T&T Clark. Well-done, in describing the turn to literary and postmodern approaches (evangelical scholarship is not mentioned). It fills a real gap, because Jeremiah studies have been chaotic and in ferment for decades. [*BBR* 27.3; *CBQ* 7/18; *JTS* 4/18; *JSOT* 42.5; *JJS* 69.2; *ETL* 94.3; *JHebS* 17].

Davidson, Robert. ‡ (DSB) 2 vols., 1983–85. Covers Lamentations as well (in 45pp.). Writing a popularly styled devotional commentary, Davidson does not go much into issues of criticism. More useful than many other liberal works on this book. From the critical angle you may prefer the fuller ITC-E or WestBC.

F Dempster, Stephen. *Jeremiah, Lamentations* (EBTC)?

✓ Diamond, A. R. P., K. M. O'Connor, and L. Stulman, eds. ‡ *Troubling Jeremiah*, 1999. Cutting-edge scholarship at the time. As Lim has suggested [*BibInt* 22.2], one can trace a multi-decade revolution in Jeremiah studies by examining various collections of essays: *A Prophet to the Nations* (1984), ed. Perdue; then *Troubling Jeremiah* (1999); then *Jeremiah (Dis)placed: New Directions in Writing/Reading Jeremiah* (2011), eds. Diamond–Stulman [*JTS* 4/13; *JSOT* 36.5; *VT* 67.1]. Now we have *Jeremiah Invented* (2015), eds. Holt–Sharp [*BibInt* 26.2].

Feinberg, Charles L. (EBC) 1986. A dispensational work from an able Hebraist, once published separately in pb. [*JBL* 103.4]. See Brown above.

F Firth, Jill. (BGW).

✓ Fischer, Georg. ‡ *Jeremiah Studies: From Text and Contexts to Theology*, ET 2020. From a Jesuit, one of the world's most respected interpreters of Jeremiah, who produced the 1500-page Herders Kommentar (2005). His labors in researching intertextuality (or inner-biblical interpretation)—"the most distinctive literary feature of Jer" (35)—have been so fruitful. He also contends that the prophecy "depends" on "all the books of the Torah" (129). There are 24 essays here. [*WTJ* Fall 22; *RelSRev* 3/22].

Garrett, Duane, and Calvin F. Pearson. *Jeremiah and Lamentations* (Kerux) 2022. Regrettably, I have not seen this, but it has been said that the exegesis and exposition sections are considerably stronger than the preaching and application segments. [*JETS* 3/23; *JSOT* 47.5].

F Graves, Michael. *Jeremiah and Lamentations* (ITC). I also salute Graves of Wheaton for his translation of the Jerome vol. below; earlier he had published *Jerome's Hebrew Philology* (Brill, 2007).

Guest, John. (WCC) 1988. Covers Lamentations too. Specialists will not regard this as stellar Bible interpretation, but it is thoughtful and better than some in the series.

F Halpern, Baruch. ‡ (NCBC).

Harrison, R. K. (retired TOTC) 1973. A good older treatment which was even more valuable because it covered Lamentations as well. Pastors added this to their library for its coverage, evangelical stance, and dependable scholarship in brief compass (240pp.). Now replaced by Lalleman. [*EvQ* 7/74].

☆ Hays, J. Daniel. *Jeremiah and Lamentations* (TTC) 2016. Has a gift for communicating clearly and in an engaging manner. Readers find attractively presented material (in keeping with the series' design), offering brief (or "focused") exegetical comments, exposition of the message, and illustrations. I regard Hays as a strong entry in Teach the Text (approx. 365pp.), released shortly before the series was cancelled. He is good for keeping "the big picture" in view.

☆ **Holladay, William.** ‡ (Herm) 2 vols., 1986–89. Before Lundbom was complete, I regarded this as the best technical historical-critical exegesis available. Holladay was perhaps America's foremost Jeremianic scholar. He used a lot of form criticism and took a more conservative approach than Carroll or McKane. "In a magisterial effort, he sought to push to its furthest reach the direct and concrete connection between text and specific historical location" (Brueggemann). The scholarly pastor who desires to build a first-class exegetical library can save up to buy this expensive set. Among reviews note especially Williamson's [*VT* 7/93] and Brueggemann's critiques [*Int* 42]. [*Bib* 69.3; *SJT* 89.1, 93.1; *JETS* 9/88, 9/92; *JSOT* 45; *JBL* 107.4; *CBQ* 10/91; *ExpTim* 6/90; *HS* 1991]. A brief, more accessible interpretation from Holladay is *Jeremiah: A Fresh Reading* (1990).

☆ **Huey, F. B.** *Jeremiah, Lamentations* (NAC) 1993. This was the first OT vol. in the NAC and runs to 512pp. It received fairly generous reviews [*CBQ* 7/95; *Them* 5/95]. Lawson Younger notes that "Huey's commentary on Jeremiah is stronger than his commentary on Lamentations." When in past editions I recommended this, I did so with less enthusiasm (especially for students) because of depth of treatment and my sense that this work, though competent, was already becoming dated. [*VT* 46.3; *HS* 1995].

☆ Hwang, Jerry. "Jeremiah" (ESVEC) 2022. See Fyall under Isaiah. Good learning lies behind Hwang's exposition, and he shows aptitude for narrative and poetic analysis. Also, it is instructive to follow this Dean at Singapore Bible College in his exploration of "The *Missio Dei* as an Integrative Motif in Jeremiah" (title of a 2013 *BBR* essay). There is a freshness here.

✓ St. Jerome, *Commentary on Jeremiah* (Ancient Christian Texts) ET 2012. Covers up to ch. 32.

✓ **Jones, Douglas Rawlinson.** ‡ (NCB) 1992. Fairly typical of the series: solid but unexciting phrase-by-phrase exegesis (560pp.). Jones did not interact much with other major works at the time. On the plus side, he is less focused on diachronic issues and treats the text with more respect than some other commentators. [*JBL* 113.2; *VT* 7/96].

☆ **Kaiser, Walter C., Jr., and Tiberius Rata.** *Walking the Ancient Paths*, 2019. A large-scale conservative exegesis and exposition (over 600pp.), including some devotional thoughts and application. Mainly for pastors, with some fn. discussion of the MT and LXX. This is fairly easy to read, however, and useful to educated laypeople. I see it as less valuable to students, in terms of academic rigor. [*JSOT* 44.5; *JETS* 12/19; *BTB* 52.2; *RTR* 4/23].

Katho, Robert Bungishabaku. *Jeremiah and Lamentations* (ABCS) 2011. Insights from a Congolese scholar whose land is war-torn.

✓ Keil, Carl F. (KD) ET 1874.

✓ **Keown, Gerald L., Pamela J. Scalise, and Thomas G. Smothers.** [𝓜], *Jeremiah 26–52* (WBC) 1995. Completes the WBC set (see Craigie above). I note the publisher's strange decision to use six scholars on this prophecy, with not one of them contributing to both vols. Deadlines! A bit uneven in quality and thoroughness, it is still useful to students. [*SwJT* Fall 98; *RelSRev* 10/98].

☆ Kidner, Derek. *The Message of Jeremiah* (KCC, retired BST) 1987. A good, lively help to preachers. One only wishes the exposition were more in-depth—176pp. on the Bible's longest book is short indeed. See Wright. [*Evangel* Sum 88].

✓ **King, Philip J.** *Jeremiah: An Archaeological Companion*, 1993. This is an excellent book on its particular topic. [*Them* 1/95; *HS* 1995; *CRBR* 1990, 1995].

Laetsch, Theodore. 1952. A reverent Lutheran exposition directly serving the preacher. In the late 1980s I recommended its purchase. Laetsch well communicates the painful message of this book; theology is his main thrust. Covers Lamentations too (30 of 412pp.). [*Int* 7/53].

F  Lindo, Ron. (EEC).

☆ **Longman, Tremper, III.** *Jeremiah, Lamentations* (NIBC) 2008. Here the author moves away from his area of specialization (wisdom literature). It is a handy (400pp.), inexpensive, accessible evangelical commentary with a mix of both exegesis and exposition. I find his theology healthy and helpful. [*CBQ* 4/09 (Lundbom); *RelSRev* 3/08; *JETS* 3/09; *BL* 2009; *RTR* 4/09; *RevExp* Sum 09; *BBR* 21.2; *BSac* 1/11].

✓  Lundbom, Jack, Craig A. Evans, and Bradford Anderson, eds. ‡ *The Book of Jeremiah: Composition, Reception, and Interpretation*, 2018. Approximately 500pp., from a large-scale, quickly developing Brill series. [*JTS* 4/20; *JSOT* 43.5].

F  Maier, Christl M. ‡ *Jeremiah 1–25* (IECOT). See Sharp.

☆ **Martens, Elmer A.** (BCBC) 1986. Valuable for its exposition. Written on the popular level (327pp.), and deserves to be better known among preachers. The same could be said for Martens's fine OT Theology, *God's Design* (3rd ed. 1998). He is well-read in the field and astute theologically. See also Walker below. [*WTJ* Spr 89; *JETS* 3/91].

✓  McConville, J. Gordon. *Judgment and Promise*, 1993. An excellent work which points to the important theological relationship between Deuteronomy and Jeremiah and discusses it from the conservative angle. Students, look this up! [*JSS* Aut 96; *CBQ* 10/94; *Them* 1/95; *SBET* Spr 94, Spr 97].

✓  **McKane, William P.** ‡ (ICC) 2 vols., 1986–96. Meticulous textual and philological work and very critical. As one would expect, he has modeled his commentary after earlier ICC vols. If anything, McKane limited himself to philological and syntactical concerns even more than the old series. Personally, I often find it nigh impenetrable. McKane continues to believe the old theory that prophecies of deliverance and restoration must be dated to the postexilic period. Redaction-critical concerns dominate the discussion (note his idea of a "rolling corpus"), and there is little theological reflection. This is only for specialists, but students should try to consult it for in-depth exegetical work. [*Them* 4/88; *JETS* 9/88; *JBL* 107.1; *Int* 7/88 (Brueggemann); *JSOT* 45; *EvQ* 7/99; *JSS* Aut 98; *JTS* 4/99 (Carroll); *BL* 1987, 1997; *HS* 1998; *RelSRev* 1/98].

McKeating, Henry. ‡ (Epworth) 1999. For preachers. [*Anvil* 18.4 (McConville)].

✓  **Miller, Patrick D.** ‡ (NIB) 2001. Of special interest because Miller well knows Deuteronomy, the theological mate to Jeremiah. The commentary here is strong, but I wish that the longest book of the Bible had been allocated more than 370pp. in the series—Ezekiel by comparison gets over 500pp. So much space is taken up by printing the full NRSV and NIV text. Miller probes questions of contemporary application from the liberal angle.

✓  Mills, Mary E. ‡ *Jeremiah: An Introduction and Study Guide*, 2017. [*JTS* 4/18; *JSOT* 40.5; *JJS* 69.2].

Morgan, G. Campbell. *Studies in the Prophecy of Jeremiah*, 1931. A well-known exposition from one of the 20th century's greatest preachers, reprinted in 1963 and 1982.

Nägelsbach, C. W. (Lange) ET 1871. Covers both Jeremiah and Lamentations.

✓  Najman, Hindy, and Konrad Schmid, eds. ‡ *Jeremiah's Scriptures: Production, Reception, Interaction, and Transformation*, 2016. An exceeding rich resource for scholars (612pp.), issuing from a large 2014 conference. [*ETL* 94.3].

✓  Newman, Barclay M., and Philip C. Stine. (UBS) 2004. This "Handbook" is 1052pp.

Nicholson, E. W. ‡ (CBC) 2 vols., 1973–75. More important for scholars is his *Preaching to the Exiles: A Study of the Prose Tradition in the Book of Jeremiah* (1970), which sees the prophecy as being produced by Deuteronomic preachers who reworked Jeremianic traditions (the prose sections in particular) to address the postexilic situation. A similar diachronic theory stands behind a couple of other well-known commentaries: McKane and Clements.

✓   O'Connor, Kathleen M. ‡ *The Confessions of Jeremiah: Their Interpretation and Role in Chapters 1–25*, 1988. Published a year prior was the similarly strong diss. by A. R. Diamond, *The Confessions of Jeremiah in Context* (1987). O'Connor also wrote *Jeremiah: Pain and Promise* (2011), a brief, "very thoughtful exploration of the disaster/trauma themes in Jeremiah" (Fretheim [*Int* 4/13]). [*VT* 65.2; *ExpTim* 8/13; *BibInt* 22.2; *RelSRev* 6/13].

Orelli, H. C. von. ET 1889. This exposition, once reprinted by Klock & Klock, is now digitized and freely available online.

F   Patton, Matthew H. (ZECOT).

Peake, A. S. ‡ (Century Bible) 1910–12. Perhaps still worth consulting.

F   Peels, Eric. *Jeremiah 30–52* (HCOT).

☆   Ryken, Philip. *Jeremiah and Lamentations* (PTW) 2000. The first OT vol. complementing Kent Hughes's expositions on the NT, this is an excellent book to get one thinking homiletically. It is also a tome of 790pp. Ryken has a DPhil from Oxford, is a gifted preacher, pastored Tenth Presbyterian in Philadelphia, and is President of Wheaton. An ESV version came out in 2016. See also his *Exodus* in the same series.

✓   Schroeder, Joy A., ed. (BMT) 2017. [*ExpTim* 11/18; *JSOT* 42.5; *ETL* 96.4].

✓   **Sharp, Carolyn J.** ‡ *Jeremiah 26–52* (IECOT) 2021. A major exegetical work. I was expecting strong ideological criticism from her. [*RelSRev* 6/23]. With Maier she edited *Prophecy and Power: Jeremiah in Feminist and Postcolonial Perspective* (LHBOTS, 2013).

F   Shead, Andrew G. *Jeremiah, Lamentations* (SGBC). Along the way we received *A Mouth Full of Fire* (2012), a 300-page biblical theology of Jeremiah, which gives special attention to the doctrine of the word of God, argues well for the theological coherence of the prophecy, and has been well-received. [*BBR* 24.4 (Allen); *WTJ* Fall 13; *JSOT* 38.5; *RTR* 4/13; *JETS* 9/13; *Them* 11/13; *RTR* 4/13; *VT* 66.2].

✓   Skinner, John. ‡ *Prophecy and Religion*, 1922. A seminal work, long consulted by scholars. One could say with Davies [*BSB* 6/03] that Skinner "treats the book as the spiritual biography of Jeremiah." [*ExpTim* 9/78].

✓   Smith, G. A. ‡ 1929.

Smith, Steven. *Exalting Jesus in Jeremiah and Lamentations* (CCE) 2019.

Stedman, Ray C. *Expository Studies in Jeremiah*, 1976. About 250pp. of basic sermon material broken down into 14 studies.

☆   **Stulman, Louis.** ‡ (AbOTC) 2005. The author did doctoral work on the prose sermons in Jeremiah and here provides an accessible exegesis which is interested in finding literary structure and theological meaning (in what seems a disorganized book). It is well-grounded in scholarship, though it wears its learning lightly, and explains the text instead of scholars' disagreements about Jeremiah. Stulman's focus is certainly upon the final form of the text. Students should note his discussion of "macro-units" of text and their contribution to overall coherence in the book. Stulman is a little more conservative a critic on composition history (cf. Allen). [*CBQ* 1/06; *JETS* 3/06; *Int* 1/06; *BL* 2006; *BibInt* 15.1; *ExpTim* 2/06; *RBL*; *CJ* 1/07; *JHebS*; *HBT* 29.1 (Dearman)].

✓   Stulman, Louis, and Edward Silver, eds. ‡ *The Oxford Handbook of Jeremiah*, 2021. Not to be missed by students. [*ExpTim* 12/22; *JSOT* 47.5; *ETL* 9/23].

F   Sweeney, Marvin. ‡ (Illum).

☆   **Thompson, J. A.** (retired NICOT) 1980. Most experienced conservative pastors have used this as their first resource. Something of an evangelical standard, but unexciting and too thin in its theological discussion. There are many NT allusions to (even citations of) Jeremiah that Thompson misses. He has an excellent 130-page introduction, now dated, and a fine treatment of historical data. In the past, Longman and Stuart said Thompson was the best conservative work. Still very much worth considering for a pastor's library, if s/h prices drop. See Goldingay above. More current evangelical exegeses are Brown and Longman. [*TJ* Fall 81; *JBL* 101.4; *JETS* 9/81].

✓  Tyler, J. Jeffrey, ed. *Jeremiah, Lamentations* (RCS) 2018.

F  Vanhoozer, Kevin. (Brazos). To be one of the more conservative books in the series.

F  Viviano, Pauline A. ‡ *Jeremiah and Lamentations* (BerO).

Waard, Jan de. *A Handbook on Jeremiah*, 2003. Treats text-critical issues, for translators.

☆  Walker, Larry L., and Elmer A. Martens. *Isaiah, Jeremiah, Lamentations* (CorBC) 2005. I have not yet had opportunity to use this vol. Martens contributes the commentary on Jeremiah–Lamentations. Knowing his excellent, somewhat fuller BCBC from 20 years prior (see Martens above), I expect the second half of this CorBC is very strong and worth buying.

F  Wearne, Gareth. ‡ *Jeremiah 1–29* (HCOT).

F  Weis, Richard D. ‡ (FOTL).

✓  Wenthe, Dean O., ed. *Jeremiah, Lamentations* (ACCS) 2009. [*JSOT* 35.5].

Wilcock, Michael. *Jeremiah & Lamentations* (Focus) rev. 2013. Though rather brief (270pp.), the work by an evangelical Anglican contains plenty of insight and clear exposition. See Wilcock's other commentaries on Judges, Chronicles, Psalms, Luke, and Revelation.

F  Wray Beal, Lissa. (BCOT).

NOTES: (1) C. S. Rodd's "Which Is the Best Commentary? VI. Jeremiah," *ExpTim* 3/87. (2) Claire E. Carroll, "Another Dodecade: A Dialectic Model of the Decentred Universe of Jeremiah Studies 1996–2008," *CBR* 8.2 (2010): 162–82. (3) Robert Carroll has two reviews of Jeremiah studies in *CurBS* (vol.4, pp.115–59, and vol.8, pp.18–58), which are helpfully collected in Alan J. Hauser, ed., *Recent Research on the Major Prophets* (2008); Carroll's are supplemented by a sagacious review-essay by A. R. P. Diamond.

# LAMENTATIONS

★  Calvin, John. (GS) 1563. A deeply moving set of lectures, as the Reformer reflects on both the pathos of the literature and its witness to the sufferings of God's people and ultimately to Christ who suffered for them. Quite lengthy (250pp.). Free online! See Calvin under Commentary Series.

★  Dearman, J. Andrew. [𝑀], *Jeremiah/Lamentations* (NIVAC) 2002. Has been one of the best resources available to the pastor preaching on Lamentations. While students may be instructed by Dearman's engagement with other scholarly views and interpretations, the main help of this commentary is its guidance for proclamation. Dearman, a more conservative PCUSA minister, teaches at Fuller. See his Hosea work. [*CTJ* 4/04].

★  Garrett, Duane, and **Paul House.** *Song of Songs, Lamentations* (WBC) 2004. See Song of Songs. House contributes the commentary on Lamentations in this vol., and I class it as better than Garrett's work. (House seems more dependable as a guide toward exposition.) This has been, without question, the most thorough evangelical commentary on this portion of Scripture (205pp.); now cf. Goldingay. Those working in the Hebrew are glad to have it. Because of the veritable explosion of scholarship on Lamentations in recent decades, WBC's bibliographical help alone was worth the price of the book when it appeared. Other key commentaries for students are: Berlin (from whom House draws much), Salters, Hillers, Renkema, Westermann, Gordis, and now Goldingay. [*JETS* 9/05; *Int* 7/05; *ExpTim* 9/09].

★  **Goldingay, John.** [𝑀], (NICOT) 2022. Lamentations research is something of a "growth industry" these days, and Goldingay's fine, erudite vol. both benefits from this upsurge and contributes to it. He excels, as always, in illuminating the background matters, working through exegetical issues in a most engaging way, and then delivering fresh theological insights. Sometimes, with his independent streak, his interpretative work can be unsettling (e.g., his translation). Why "Ms Zion" for בת־ציון? He writes so well, even powerfully, that he was an excellent choice to comment on this emotionally charged poetry, especially after just completing his huge NICOT on Jeremiah—the work is stronger for the paired research, but *Jeremiah* is better. There is literary sensitivity here, an able handling of ANE comparative literature and the Hebrew text, an openness to learn from grief and trauma studies, knowledge of the history of interpretation, and pastorally helpful sections of "A Reader's Response" by an ancient worshiper. We needed this commentary! [*Presb* Fall 22; *CBQ* 4/23; *JSOT* 47.5 (Reimer); *ZAW* 135.2].

★ **Parry, Robin A.** (THC) 2010. Not just a theological commentary with a christological empha- sis, Parry is saluted by Wright as offering "the most sure-footed guide, with exceptionally clear exegesis of the most disputed sections" (Preface). [*BBR* 22.2; *JSOT* 35.5; *Chm* Sum 12]. This very good book (280pp.) is complemented by Parry–Thomas, eds., *Great Is Thy Faithfulness? Reading Lamentations as Sacred Scripture* (2011), the essays of which seek to draw upon the book's reception history to answer the question of "how . . . Lamentations could serve as sacred Scripture for the church" (xiii–xiv) and how this poetry is the word of God. [*BBR* 22.2; *JSOT* 37.5; *VT* 65.2; *JETS* 3/11; *BTB* 5/12; *SJT* 66.4; *TJ* Spr 11]. Some readers might want it noted that Parry came out in favor of a form of universalism (see *EvQ* 1/12).

★ Wright, Christopher J. H. (BST) 2015. After writing eminently useful, clear expositions of Ezekiel and Jeremiah for BST, Wright here adds the vol. between them. For preachers to have both Parry and Wright (145pp.) available is a blessing and joy (though the poetry in Lamentations is "tear-soaked"); I would not want to be without either of them. The 45-page Introduction is better than you find in some more in-depth exegetical com- mentaries. Cook offers a critique, however, on the application side. [*Chm* Spr 17; *JETS* 3/16 (Cook); *JSOT* 40.5].

✓ **Albrektson, B.** ‡ *Studies in the Text and Theology of the Book of Lamentations*, 1963. Moved the scholarly discussion farther along, especially with his critique of Gottwald and his counter-proposals regarding the theology of the book. Albrektson construes Lamentations as presenting an acute tension between two teachings: breaking covenant with God brings retribution (Deuteronomic theology) and belief in God's promises of protection for Jerusalem (the Zion theology of the psalmists).

☆ **Allen, Leslie C.** [𝓜], *A Liturgy of Grief: A Pastoral Commentary on Lamentations*, 2011. The author explains, "This book, which endeavors to integrate biblical scholarship and pastoral care, is what happens when an Old Testament professor looks at Lamentations through a chaplain's eyes" (ix). Allen put in 1800 hours of volunteer chaplaincy work at a hospital and is eager to see the Scriptures bring help to both the grief-stricken and those who minister to the grieving. See his past work on Chronicles, Psalms, Jeremiah, and Ezekiel. He offers his own translation with notes, clear and accessible exposition, and often eloquent application (190pp.)—a very good book. [*BBR* 22.3; *EQ* 1/13; *CBQ* 4/13; *Int* 4/13; *JSOT* 36.5; *ExpTim* 12/12; *RevExp* Spr 12; *RelSRev* 6/13; *TJ* Fall 12].

✓ **Assis, Elie.** [𝓜], *Lamentations: From Despair to Prayer*, ET 2022. Certainly a most worth- while, verse-by-verse literary analysis (288pp.). Those without Hebrew will not be able to make full use of the study. From a professor at Bar-Ilan, who has extensive knowledge of contemporary scholarship and the history of Jewish interpretation. [*BL* 2024].

Bailey, Wilma Ann, and Christina Bucher. [𝓜], *Lamentations, Song of Songs* (BCBC) 2015. A fuller, strong representative of the series.

Bennett, Stephen J. *Ecclesiastes/Lamentations* (NBBC) 2010. See Ecclesiastes.

✓ **Bergant, Dianne.** ‡ (AbOTC) 2003. This scholar, Emerita at Catholic Theological Union, Chicago, has written much on OT poetry (e.g., Song of Songs). Her writing is clear, her exegesis is laudably careful, and she cares about the theology of the book. [*CBQ* 4/04; *JETS* 9/04; *Int* 10/04; *JSOT* 28.5].

☆ **Berlin, Adele.** ‡ (OTL) 2002. A superb study of the Hebrew, paying attention to rhetorical and poetic features—more on metaphor and imagery than on parallelism, the building and declining acrostic patterns, and structure. Berlin aims to keep the forest, not just the trees, in view. Students must take account of her findings, but most pastors won't be able to make full use of the scholarship here (e.g., discussion of the genre "Jerusalem lament" here and in Psalms 74, 79, 102, 137, etc). Theologically, this Jewish author is keenly interested in the faith community's response to an evil catastrophe. Her focus is more on the human side, not on the divine and how this book's heart-cry is also divine revelation. In other words, she is less helpful in addressing preachers' concern as to what God is saying in Lamentations. There is some feminist critique and less interest in historical criticism (e.g., form criticism), textual criticism, and philology. Berlin offers her own translation. The 135-page vol. is now less expensive in pb. [*CTJ* 4/04; *CBQ* 10/03; *Int* 10/03; *ExpTim* 8/03; *HBT* 12/02; *JSOT* 28.5; *BBR* 14.2; *BSac* 1/05; *CurTM* 10/05; *RBL*].

✓ **Berman, Joshua A.** ‡ (NCBC) 2023. By a Bar-Ilan faculty member. Cf. the work of Assis at the same university. Berman claims the book demonstrates "how biblical writers offered support to their communities"; in this case we find "a pastoral mentor who engages in a series of dialogues with a second constructed character, daughter Zion, who embodies the traumatized community of survivors." A substantial and thoughtful commentary (175pp.), dedicated to family members who died in the Holocaust. [*BL* 2024; *JTS* 4/24].

✓ Berrigan, Daniel. ‡ *Lamentations: From New York to Kabul and Beyond*, 2002. A most thoughtful reflection piece from a Jesuit, relating the book to modern tragedy.

✓ Bier, Miriam J. [𝓜], *'Perhaps There Is Hope': Reading Lamentations as a Polyphony of Pain, Penitence, and Protest*, 2015. Has valuable exegetical insights and could be termed a multiperspectival study, considering different voices in tension (LHBOTS). [*VT* 67.1; *JSS* Spr 18; *JTS* 4/18; *JSOT* 40.5]. A much more negative study along these lines is Carleen Mandolfo, *Daughter Zion Talks Back to the Prophets* (2007).

F  Boda, Mark. (BCOT).

☆ Bracke, John M. ‡ *Jeremiah 30–52 and Lamentations* (WestBC) 2000. Gives serious attention to the book (60pp.). This is to be considered, from a critical standpoint, one of the better theological expositions for pastors.

☆ Brooks, Richard. *Great Is Your Faithfulness* (Welwyn) 1989. A Reformed exposition which is quite full (160pp.) for its series and has a lot of heart.

Chou, Abner. (EEC) 2014–digital. I have not seen this work.

Cox, Harvey, and Stephanie Paulsell. ‡ *Lamentations and the Song of Songs* (Belief) 2012. Cox writes on Lamentations. [*Int* 4/13; *RevExp* Spr 13].

Davidson, Robert. ‡ *Jeremiah, Volume 2, and Lamentations* (DSB) 1985. See Jeremiah.

F  Dempster, Stephen. *Jeremiah, Lamentations* (EBTC)?

Dickson, David. *Sermons on Jeremiah's Lamentations*, 2020. Never-before-published material from a prominent Scottish Presbyterian (1583–1663), who wrote a praiseworthy Psalms commentary.

☆ **Dobbs-Allsopp, F. W.** ‡ (I) 2002. Alongside Allen, one of the best theological expositions from the critical camp for preachers. But students are mistaken to think this slim vol. useful only for theological reflection. Dobbs-Allsopp has published much on Lamentations, and, from early in his career, been regarded as an authority on this literature and the city-lament genre. He would be classed as moderately critical. One caveat for evangelicals: his liberal theology, seemingly opposed to the doctrines of God's wrath and judgment, leads him to some offensive conclusions about the portrait of God in the book. See his work *On Biblical Poetry* (2015). [*CTJ* 4/04; *CBQ* 4/03; *Int* 1/03; *HBT* 12/02; *JSOT* 27.5; *BBR* 14.2; *BSac* 4/05; *SwJT* Fall 04; *RelSRev* 10/06; *JHebS* 4].

Ellison, H. L. (EBC) 1986. A highly respected Jewish Christian scholar who for many years taught at London Bible College, Cambridge University, and Moorlands Bible College. Ellison was a "moderating" influence on evangelical OT scholarship years ago. His work here deserves praise and aids the pastor.

☆ **Ferris, Paul.** (EBCR) 2010. I expected this to be quite good, and it is. The emphasis is upon exegesis, and Ferris displays admirable literary and theological sensitivity (65pp.). Some pastors would be happy to have only this on their shelves to cover this Bible book. Note that, contrary to the series' intention, occasionally Hebrew script creeps into the commentary sections (e.g., pp.616, 639). See his diss. on *The Genre of Communal Lament in the Bible and the Ancient Near East* (1992).

Garrett, Duane, and Calvin F. Pearson. *Jeremiah and Lamentations* (Kerux) 2022. See under Jeremiah.

✓ **Gerstenberger, E. S.** ‡ *Psalms, Part 2, and Lamentations* (FOTL) 2001. Advanced students may consult this form-critical treatment.

☆ Gibson, Jonathan. "Lamentations" (ESVEC) 2022. See Fyall under Isaiah. While the entire vol. is worthwhile, this segment is fuller, more in-depth (120pp.), and represents one of the best conservative expositions I've found on this book. Gibson is well-trained (Cambridge PhD) and is the junior OT prof at Westminster, Philadelphia. He was also a fine choice for this work as a man with "heart."

✓ **Gordis, Robert.** ‡ 1954, rev. 1974. See under Song of Songs. An earlier commentary on Lamentations in *Jewish Quarterly Review* (1967–68) was published as a monograph (1968). Then that work was thoroughly revised and expanded for the 1974 edition. This is one of the most valuable older studies of the Hebrew text.

✓ Gottwald, N. K. ‡ *Studies in the Book of Lamentations*, 1959, rev. 1962.

F   Graves, Michael. *Jeremiah and Lamentations* (ITC).

F   Greenstein, Edward. ‡ (JPS).

F   Gruber, Mayer. ‡ (Illum).

Guest, John. (WCC) 1988. See under Jeremiah.

Habel, Norman C. [𝓜], (Concordia, old series) 1968. Safe to ignore.

Harrison, R. K. (retired TOTC) 1973. See under Jeremiah, and note Lalleman below.

Hays, J. Daniel. *Jeremiah and Lamentations* (TTC) 2016. See under Jeremiah.

✓ Hens-Piazza, Gina. ‡ (Wisdom) 2017. Feminist, urging readers to "reject the patriarchal theology of a violent God" [*Int* 4/19]. [*CBQ* 1/19; *JSOT* 42.5].

☆ **Hillers, Delbert R.** ‡ (AB) 1972, rev. 1992. Excellent, with careful exegesis (fairly mild in its criticism), offering help with the Hebrew, and some theological insights. This AB (165pp.) almost doubled in size from the first edition. Hillers was long the best scholarly work in English—for German readers there has been incredible wealth: Kraus, Plöger, Rudolph, Weiser, Wiesmann, and Westermann. Years ago, Longman and Stuart agreed that Hillers's commentary had no serious rivals, but now we have a good number of excellent books. Students and more academically oriented pastors will best appreciate this work; the average pastor would have plenty even with Parry and Wright.

☆ **Huey, F. B.** (NAC) 1993. See under Jeremiah. This vol. is not as recommended for interpreting Lamentations.

✓ Joyce, Paul M., and Diana Lipton. ‡ *Lamentations through the Centuries* (BBC) 2013. As the collaborators put it, "reception exegesis," and I call it marvelously done. [*JSOT* 38.5; *VT* 65.2; *ExpTim* 5/14; *JTS* 10/16; *SJT* 69.3].

Kaiser, Walter. *A Biblical Approach to Suffering: A Study of Lamentations*, 1982. Written with the pastor's needs in mind. Republished as *Grief & Pain in the Plan of God* (2010).

✓ Keil, Carl F. (KD) ET 1874.

✓ Knight, G. A. F. ‡ (Torch) 1955.

✓ Kotzé, Gideon R. *The Qumran Manuscripts of Lamentations*, 2013. [*VT* 67.3].

Laetsch, Theodore. 1952. Bound together with the Jeremiah commentary. Written for pastors.

☆ **Lalleman, Hetty.** *Jeremiah and Lamentations* (TOTC-R) 2013. See under Jeremiah.

✓ Lee, Nancy C., and Carleen Mandolfo, eds. ‡ *Lamentations in Ancient and Contemporary Cultural Contexts*, 2008. This book of essays, not commentary, reveals the shape of recent scholarship, and is especially welcome because Lamentations has been a growth industry since 1990. But there is more, as the vol. includes lengthy discussions of the lament genre and its use in various contexts. [*RBL*; *BL* 2009; *VT* 59.4; *ExpTim* 9/10; *JSS* Spr 11; *RelSRev* 3/11].

✓ Linafelt, Tod. ‡ *Surviving Lamentations: Catastrophe, Lament and Protest in the Afterlife of a Biblical Book*, 2000. [*ThTo* 1/01; *Int* 7/01; *CBQ* 1/01; *JBL* Win 01].

☆ **Longman, Tremper, III.** *Jeremiah, Lamentations* (NIBC) 2008. See under Jeremiah.

☆ **Mackay, John L.** (Mentor) 2008. A solid 220-page exposition with a strongly conservative, Reformed orientation. It was preceded by a 2-vol. set on Jeremiah. See also Mackay's well-done "Mentor" vol. on Hosea. All his works are best appreciated by expositors. Students learn from them too (exegesis is carefully done), but they may desire more rigor and discussion of technical questions.

✓ Martin-Achard, R., and S. Paul Re'emi. ‡ *Amos and Lamentations* (ITC-E) 1984. Not particularly remarkable, but was once worth consulting because of a paucity of works.

F   Michel, Andreas. ‡ (IECOT).

✓ Middlemas, Jill. ‡ *The Troubles of Templeless Judah*, 2005. This Oxford imprint has nearly 60pp. (171–228) treating Lamentations and is worth consulting. [*VT* 57.1]. See also her *Lamentations: An Introduction and Study Guide*, 2021. [*ExpTim* 2/22; *BL* 2022].

Nägelsbach, C. W. (Lange) ET 1871.

✓ **O'Connor, Kathleen M.** ‡ (NIB) 2001. Added to this is an eloquent applicatory exposition published by Orbis: *Lamentations and the Tears of the World* (2002) [*BibInt* 13.2]. O'Connor is an able, learned scholar and an excellent writer, exploring the staggering grief expressed in the text. Hers is a more negative interpretation of the book, more as a cry against God's injustice than a lament over terrible judgment. Berlin is similar on this point.

Peake, A. S. ‡ 1912. Bound with Jeremiah.

☆ **Provan, Iain W.** [*M*], (NCB) 1991. This 160-page work received good reviews. Provan became more conservative after his doctoral days and taught at Regent College, Vancouver. Though trained thoroughly in a more diachronic approach, he is interested in synchronic literary readings. He is also surprisingly agnostic about the historical backdrop. Many pastors will find the less expensive Provan more than adequate for their library. Became difficult to obtain after Eerdmans dropped the series, but Regent College did a reprint (2016). [*VT* 4/95; *JETS* 6/95; *BSac* 10/92].

F   Queen-Sutherland, Kandy. ‡ (S&H). See under Ruth.

✓ **Renkema, Johan.** ‡ (HCOT) ET 1998. Translated from the Dutch and a stunningly comprehensive work of 641pp. Makes compelling arguments for the unity of the book. Despite the series title, this is more a literary than a historical commentary. Renkema certainly makes "a strong contribution to the burgeoning scholarship on the Book of Lamentations" (*CBQ*). [*JSOT* 84; *Bib* 81.2; *CBQ* 4/00; *OTA* 2/00; *JBL* Spr 01; *VT* 51.3].

✓ **Reyburn, William D.** (UBS) 1992. Well-deserves to be consulted, though some of the lengthy discussion meant to help translators sift through appropriate terms in various target languages won't be relevant.

F   Roberts, J. J. M. ‡ (Herm). But this was not on a recent Fortress list.

☆ Ryken, Philip. *Jeremiah and Lamentations* (PTW) 2000. See Jeremiah above. Ryken was a recommended purchase in 2010, and still should be for preachers.

✓ **Salters, R. B.** ‡ (ICC) 2010. Preparing the way was an OT Guides vol. on *Jonah and Lamentations* (1994). After a more compact introduction of 30pp., Salters offers a quite lengthy commentary (nearly 350pp.) that aims "to wrestle with the complexities of the Masoretic text" (ix), do thorough text criticism, understand the text against its ANE background, survey the history of interpretation (including Calvin and plenty of rabbinics), and draw exegetical conclusions. The vol. has on display all the usual ICC rigor and denseness, though some readers might appreciate closer attention to literary/poetic features. Also, the ICC hardly touches on theology. The one major lack is indices. Note that since 1994 Salters has changed his mind on the unity of the book and single-authorship. [*BBR* 21.3 (Thomas); *CBQ* 4/12; *JSS* Spr 15; *JSOT* 35.5; *JESOT* 1.1; *JTS* 10/16].

F   Shead, Andrew G. *Jeremiah, Lamentations* (SGBC).

Smith, Steven. *Exalting Jesus in Jeremiah and Lamentations* (CCE) 2019.

F   Sun, Chloe T. (BGW).

✓ **Thomas, Heath A.** *Poetry and Theology in the Book of Lamentations: The Aesthetics of an Open Text*, 2013. A revision of his Gloucester PhD.

✓ Thomas, Heath A., and Brittany N. Melton, eds. *Reading Lamentations Intertextually*, 2023. Essayists "read between texts" in Scripture, as well as ancient and modern literature. The contributors are a mix of evangelicals and critics. [*BL* 2022; *CBQ* 1/24].

✓ Tyler, J. Jeffrey, ed. *Jeremiah, Lamentations* (RCS) 2018.

F   Viviano, Pauline A. ‡ *Jeremiah and Lamentations* (BerO). Publication had been expected in 2009. The author is a Catholic teaching at Loyola University.

☆ Walker, Larry L., and Elmer A. Martens. *Isaiah, Jeremiah, Lamentations* (CorBC) 2005. See under Jeremiah.

☆ Webb, Barry G. *Five Festal Garments: Christian Reflections on the Song of Songs, Ruth, Lamentations, Ecclesiastes and Esther*, 2000. See under Ruth.

✓ Wenthe, Dean O., ed. *Jeremiah, Lamentations* (ACCS) 2009. [*JSOT* 35.5].

✓ **Westermann, Claus.** ‡ *Lamentations: Issues and Interpretation*, 1990, ET 1994. Includes over 100pp. of commentary. The author suffered during WWII, and this prepared him to reflect profoundly on the place, meaning, and expression of suffering in the life of God's people. Perhaps the most outstanding and valuable section of Westermann is on the history of interpretation. This vol. is called by one reviewer "a *sine qua non* of Lamentations study." It will long be useful to serious researchers. [*ExpTim* 3/95; *Them* 1/96; *JSS* Spr 96].

Wilcock, Michael. *Jeremiah & Lamentations* (Focus) rev. 2013. See under Jeremiah.

✓ Yansen, James W. S., Jr. *Daughter Zion's Trauma: A Trauma-Informed Reading of the Book of Lamentations*, 2019. From a Seventh-Day Adventist pastor who earned his PhD at Boston University. [*JSOT* 47.5].

F   Young, May. (Pillar).

F   Youngblood, Kevin J. (ZECOT).

✓ **Ziegler, Yael.** [𝔐], (Maggid) 2021. Critically engaged, but the product of conservative Judaism. Because the work is lengthy (over 500pp.), deeply thought through, interested in intertextual connections with the rest of the Hebrew Bible, and "informed by deep psychological and spiritual understanding" (Kass), it is well worth noting. Ziegler also wrote a stimulating Maggid vol. on Ruth.

NOTES: (1) C. W. Miller, "The Book of Lamentations in Recent Research," *CBR* 1.1 (2002): 9–29. (2) Heath A. Thomas, "A Survey of Research on Lamentations (2002–2012)," *CBR* 12.1 (2013): 8–38. (3) Amy Erickson and Andrew Davis review, "Recent Research on the Megilloth," *CBR* 14 (2016) 298–318.

# EZEKIEL

★ **Block, Daniel.** (NICOT) 2 vols., 1997–98. Like Oswalt's *Isaiah* in the series, a massive 2-vol. work (over 1700pp.). Block's set is painstakingly exegetical, includes some mild form criticism and rhetorical criticism, and is mainly concerned with the final form of the text (à la Greenberg). An outstanding work: comprehensive in scope, lucid, quick to discuss both biblical and extrabiblical parallels, structural patterns, grammar, and translation issues. The organization of the vols. is similar to BKAT or WBC, which some believe makes them easier to consult. After his 60-page introduction, Block deals with each section of text in (a) translation; (b) nature and design; (c) verse-by-verse exegesis; and (d) theological implications. Though I would never want to be without Zimmerli and Greenberg–Cook, this is the best pick for the studious evangelical pastor. The manuscript was submitted in early 1994. *Full disclosure: Block was the external examiner for my dissertation.* [CBQ 4/99, 10/99; Bib 80.1; Int 7/99; JETS 12/99; WTJ Spr 99; SwJT Fall 00, Sum 01; BSac 10/98, 7/99; BL 1998, 1999; JSOT 78; RelSRev 10/99]. Students are glad to see a collection of Block's many Ezekiel articles in two 2013 vols: *By the River Chebar* and *Beyond the River Chebar* [BBR 24.3; JSOT 38.5; ExpTim 2/15; RelSRev 6/14; VT 65.4; Int 4/16].

★ **Duguid, Iain M.** (NIVAC) 1999. His 550-page exposition builds upon doctoral research in Cambridge: *Ezekiel and the Leaders of Israel* (1994). Duguid has taught at Westminster California, Grove City College, and now Westminster Philadelphia. I like his biblical-theological approach which is sensitive to redemptive history themes. Though he was a young scholar when he wrote this vol., there is mature reflection, as seen in the lengthy Authors Cited index which includes church fathers and Puritans alongside OT scholars. This book easily beats Stuart for a place on the pastor's shelf; Duguid knows the literature better and digs deeper. I warmly commend Duguid's work—buy it prior to Stuart and Wright—which is aimed at meeting the inadequacy he perceives in Block and Greenberg (see his review of Block [WTJ Spr 99]). Students will find savvy exegesis here. By the way, people ask me how to pronounce his name; it is "Do-good." More recently he contributed "Ezekiel" to the sixth vol. of ESVEC (2022); see Fyall under Isaiah. Duguid's brief section on "Preaching from Ezekiel" (915) has excellent advice! For a succinct, pastoral exposition, one must look far and wide for anything better.

★ **Hilber, John W.** 2019. Was to have been TTC, but the series was cancelled. Hilber is well-trained (Cambridge PhD), hermeneutically shrewd, has a pastor's heart, and writes with admirable clarity. He has taught at Dallas Seminary, Grand Rapids Theological Seminary, and McMaster. The subtitle, "A Focused Commentary for Preaching and Teaching," indicates his focus on the oracles' message, themes, interpretive highlights, and constructing a bridge to application. Note that the last nine chapters are covered in 24 pages (241–64). There is limited interaction with scholarship; mainly the NICOT and AYB sets are cited, with some regular references also to Wright's BST and Bodi's research in ZIBBC. This recommendation is for the sake of busy pastors. [JSOT 44.5; JETS 6/20].

★ **Joyce, Paul.** [𝓜], 2007. Ezekiel scholars expected a strong entry, considering the promise shown in his DPhil, *Divine Initiative and Human Response in Ezekiel* (1989) [CRBR 1990], and the leadership he has given to the SBL Ezekiel study group. Originally this commentary was scheduled for release in NCB, but that series is defunct. Joyce has taught at Oxford and now London, and has given us a stellar, compact (somewhat selective), theologically oriented exegesis in about 300pp. One no longer has to pay $140 for the hb; a pb edition has been released. I am glad for this because Joyce deserves wide usage. [*BL* 2008; *ExpTim* 7/08; *JHebS* 2008 (Sweeney); *RBL* 11/08 (Tuell); *JTS* 4/10; *BibInt* 18.2; *CBQ* 7/09; *HS* 2009; *JSS* Aut 09 (Allen); *JSOT* 35.5; *BibInt* 18.2; *RelSRev* 6/11; *SJT* 64.2]. I am glad to pass on Joyce's commendation of Duguid and Wright as well suited for "preachers seeking encouragement and help in relating Ezekiel to the present day" [*BSB* 12/06].

★ Stuart, Douglas. (WCC) 1989. A more substantial vol. than one normally finds in WCC and a good theological guide. Stuart is one of the few full-time biblical scholars who has written for the WCC; he has pastored a church besides being Professor of OT at Gordon-Conwell. This is a solid commentary for pastors, though now dated and less informed by scholarship. I only wish he (and other commentators) had wrestled more with the constant refrain, "you/they shall know that I am Yahweh." (See Evans and Zimmerli below.) Stuart is widely and cheaply available s/h.

★ Wright, Christopher J. H. (BST) 2001. A fine pb for preachers, which could spark many sermons. Wright has long loved the book and Ezekiel's theology (see his editor's column in *Them* 5/94), and it shows in his exposition here (368pp.). Note that he does not treat chs. 12–13, 15, 17, 19, and 21–22. As a BST work it contains a pleasing amount of exegesis; some others in the series do not. One quibble: I question his proposal that Ezekiel teaches the salvation of the nations, even while I love his passion for missions reflected in his best-known book, *The Mission of God* (2006), a most impressive piece of work. [*JSOT* 99 (2002); *Chm* Win 02; *Them* Sum 05; *Anvil* 19.4, 20.4 (Renz)]. Other commentaries from Wright's pen are on Deuteronomy, Jeremiah, Lamentations, Daniel, and Habakkuk.

✓ Alexander, Ralph H. (EBCR) 2010. The author's 1986 EBC saw a fair amount of use as a conservative work, in part because there was little out there at the time (Keil, Taylor, Feinberg). Today, even with the 2010 update, Alexander seems to lack depth compared to other publications; we're grateful to have it though. He is premillennial in his interpretation of the latter chapters (280pp.). See Brown on Jeremiah.

☆ **Allen, Leslie C.** [𝔐], *Ezekiel 20–48* (WBC) 1990; *Ezekiel 1–19* (WBC) 1994. The initial vol. picked up where Brownlee left off and did a competent job. Quite valuable as a reference tool because of its strong scholarship and close working with the Hebrew. He states on pp.xix–xx that he carves out a niche for himself between practitioners of traditional historical-critical methods, especially form criticism (Zimmerli), and those using a synchronic approach on the final form of the text (Greenberg). Allen does not often relate Ezekiel's message to the NT. Conservatives especially disagree with his treatment of the prophecy's (alleged) multiple layers of redaction material. Also, I have greater confidence in the MT over against the LXX than Allen. The 1994 vol. replaces Brownlee and completes a useful reference set. Prior to NICOT, when I recommended Zimmerli, I wrote, "the frugal may prefer Allen to Zimmerli (Allen's two vols. together cost about the same as one Hermeneia vol.)." [*CRBR* 1996; *WTJ* Fall 91; *VT* 1/93; *CBQ* 10/92; *SwJT* Spr 96; *JTS* 4/96; *JSOT* 74; *OTA* 2/96; *BSac* 1/96; *HS* 1993].

✓ Beckwith, Carl L., ed. *Ezekiel, Daniel* (RCS) 2012. The first OT entry in the series, Beckwith makes for fascinating reading, though many will prefer to read the full comments of, say, Calvin, rather than mere excerpts. The vol. is richer on Daniel, chiefly because more Reformers wrote on it. [*JSOT* 37.5; *RelSRev* 6/13].

Blackwood, Andrew W. *Ezekiel: Prophecy of Hope*, 1965; *The Other Son of Man: Ezekiel/Jesus*,

1966. The sermonic material in these books gives good direction to the preacher. Blackwood was the longtime conservative homiletics prof at Princeton Seminary (my father's in fact).

✓ **Blenkinsopp, Joseph.** ‡ (I) 1990. A good exposition which fulfills the aims of the series. Blenkinsopp was an expert on OT prophecy—see his AB set on Isaiah. This vol. is not as good as Stuart, though, in explaining the message of the book. One minus, relative to Stuart, is his historical-critical approach (closer to Zimmerli than Greenberg). Another main drawback would be Blenkinsopp's general failure to discuss views which differ from his own. [*CBQ* 1/93; *Int* 1/92; *JETS* 6/95; *CTJ* 4/91; *HS* 1991; *CRBR* 1992].

✓ **Bodi, Daniel.** "Ezekiel" in *ZIBBC*, 2009. About 120pp. of astute, very profitable research on the prophecy's ANE backdrop, with regard to history, archaeology, culture, literature, religion, and politics. Cited by many!

✓ Bowen, Nancy. ‡ (AbOTC) 2010. Sharply critical in its interpretation, especially where the oracles or theology seem offensive to feminist sensibilities. Other vols. in the series include more straightforward exegesis, and Bowen is an atypical contribution (328pp.). Smith-Christopher's endorsement explains that she "is particularly interesting as she weaves contemporary culture, trauma studies, and even insights of traditional 'Spirituals' where Ezekiel was a favored subject." [*BSB* 6/11].

Briscoe, D. Stuart. *All Things Weird and Wonderful*, 1977. A somewhat dispensational, popular exposition by an English pastor in America.

✓ Brownlee, William H. ‡ *Ezekiel 1–19* (WBC) 1986. Called a memorial vol. The Claremont prof died before the commentary could be completed. Some good scholarship at points, but in the main a disappointment. Brownlee fell into the more critically oriented wing of evangelicalism, and I mark his work as critical (‡) because he argues against a Babylonian locale for the prophecies and because of all the supposed redaction. Actually, one could argue that he was more eccentric than liberal. This WBC is basically a museum piece; see Allen. [*RTR* 9/87; *WTJ* Fall 88; *Them* 4/90; *EvQ* 1/89; *HS* 1987].

☆ Calvin, John. 1564. Covers only the first 20 chs. and is less valuable for that reason. The lectures were halted by serious illness, and the preface for its first publication was written by Beza after Calvin's death. Much fine theology here. There are two editions available: the Calvin Translation Society (1849–50)—free online—and the Rutherford House translation covering Ezekiel 1–12 (ET 1994). Strange but true: Ezekiel has been termed "the Calvin of the OT" (Peake, 1904).

✓ Carvalho, Corrine, ed. ‡ *The Oxford Handbook of Ezekiel*, 2023.

☆ Clements, Ronald E. ‡ (WestBC) 1996. A moderately critical treatment of the message. Clements attends to expositional and theological concerns rather than textual issues. He seeks to understand Ezekiel with traditio-historical research. Less helpful to preachers, for he concentrated almost wholly on what Ezekiel *meant* and not on what it *means* today. Clements knows the prophecy well. He undertook the translation of Zimmerli's first vol. [*Them* 2/99; *Int* 1/98; *CBQ* 10/97; *SwJT* Sum 98; *BSac* 4/98; *HBT* 6/97].

☆ **Cook, Stephen L.** ‡ *Ezekiel 38–48* (AYB) 2018. Greenberg's two vols. on chs. 1–37 were monumental for Ezekiel studies, with incalculable influence. There were repeated attempts to complete the AB set—see Milgrom below—and I'm delighted with how expertly Cook finished the task. He was an excellent choice because of his fine scholarship; a felt "kinship with [Greenberg] in several of his emphases"; his presentation of "insights from traditional premodern Jewish commentators" (xi); and his previous research on apocalyptic (see Apocalyptic Literature below). It was from Greenberg that Cook first learned "the great exegetical and theological payoff of *visualizing* the text's architectural details" (xi–xii), and the figures in the book do prove to be a highlight (but see Duguid's caution [*Them* 45.1]). I also value him highly for cataloguing and sorting through the various approaches to interpreting chs. 40–48, where scholarship has made huge strides over the last three decades. I have always regarded these eleven chs. as the most difficult portion of the HB, after Job (and possibly Hosea), with all their hapaxes, details, and peculiarities. All the more reason, then, to salute Cook for his translation, textual notes, and detailed commentary (300pp.). Three minor quibbles are with his greater reliance on the LXX, and with the renderings "mortal one" (for בֶּן־אָדָם) and "the word . . . *happened* to me" (for the prophetic word formula). [*BBR* 29.4; *RBL* 1/20 (Ganzel); *JETS* 6/20].

✓   Cook, Stephen L., and Corrine L. Patton, eds. ‡ *Ezekiel's Hierarchical World*, 2004. Collected essays from SBL symposia. [*JSS* Spr 08; *VT* 57.3].

✓   **Cooke, G. A.** ‡ (ICC) 1937. Fairly conservative as a commentator on Ezekiel in the 1930s; in some respects Cooke's approach anticipated developments in Ezekiel studies 20 years later. "Cooke stands out for his particularly careful work on the text" (Zimmerli). The student will find this ICC easier to use than many others in the series.

✓   **Cooper, Lamar E.** (NAC) 1994. Well-written from a dispensational perspective, but not a profound work (NAC usually does not aim to be). Useful for understanding the dispensational approach to this book. The Reformed pastor will find Duguid to be more helpful and a sounder theological guide. There are both scathing reviews [*JSOT* 12/95; *VT* 46.2] and fairer, kinder ones [*HS* 1995 (Boadt)].

☆   Craigie, Peter C. (DSB) 1983. Lots here for pastors. Good scholarship underlies this devotional exposition. Provides more background information than most in DSB. Longman once suggested you start here, and I recommended buying it. [*JBL* 104.4].

✓   **Darr, Katheryn Pfisterer.** ‡ (NIB) 2001. A pleasingly full interpretation (over 530pp.) that students should consult. Darr is more conservative (like Greenberg and Block) in the way she treats the text and questions of compositional history. I have few quarrels with her approach—only where a reader-oriented emphasis seems overdone. Count this as one of the top five or six commentaries on the book at present.

✓   Davidson, Andrew B. [*M*], (CBSC) 1916. In my opinion, Davidson's vols. were among the best in this old series. They are always lucid and reflect thorough scholarship. This particular book is still consulted. Davidson was partly responsible for the infusion of continental higher criticism into British scholarship.

✓   Davis, Ellen F. ‡ *Swallowing the Scroll*, 1989. Not a commentary, but a revised Yale PhD. Along with Childs's *Introduction to the OT as Scripture*, Davis pointed Ezekiel scholarship in a new direction by critiquing Zimmerli's approach of form criticism. She argues that "the very thing for which we lack evidence is the fundamental stratum of orally conceived preaching" (17), and that students of the prophecy should recognize that Ezekiel was composed as a literary work and must be interpreted as such.

F   Dharamraj, Havilah. (SGBC). See Song of Songs.

✓   Dowden, Landon. *Exalting Jesus in Ezekiel* (CCE) 2015.

☆   **Eichrodt, Walther.** ‡ (OTL) ET 1970. Has been a highly respected critical work. The vol. focuses on his forte, biblical theology, and is valuable for that theological discussion. The commentary is marred somewhat by textual emendations in deference to the shorter LXX (see his introduction, p.12). [*JBL* 86.3]. See Lyons below.

✓   Evans, John F. *You Shall Know That I Am Yahweh: An Inner-Biblical Interpretation of Ezekiel's Recognition Formula*, 2019. A technical study on what has been termed "the keynote of Ezek.'s prophecies" (S. R. Driver) and "the most decisive characteristic of Ezekiel's theology" (Boadt). [*RBL* 5/20, 8/20; *JSOT* 44.5; *ThRef* 64.3; *BL* 2020; *BO* 78.1–2].

F   Evans, John F. (Hodder). Will give close attention to the recognition formula (over 70×).

☆   Fairbairn, Patrick. 2nd ed. 1855. Reprinted by Klock & Klock (1989) and Wakeman (2000), this warm exposition was long a useful tool for pastors. The approach is strongly theological with stresses on covenant and amillennial eschatology. Fairbairn was a pastor and professor in the (Presbyterian) Free Church of Scotland. Today, pastors will view recent commentaries as more valuable, but if you are the type who loves Banner's Geneva Series, do consider this. Free online.

Feinberg, Charles L. 1969. From the dispensational camp. An exposition rather than exegesis, written with the lay reader in mind. Better, from that same theological perspective are Cooper and Rooker.

✓ **Ganzel, Tova.** [*M*], (Maggid) ET 2020. The Israeli author is a fine Ezekiel scholar, informed by the history of Jewish exegesis but also drawing from Christian interpreters. The commentary, from a conservative Jewish series, is thoughtful and accessible (328pp.). "In general, I have tried to avoid explaining the meaning of individual words and verses, focusing instead on the themes arising from them" (Preface). So much to appreciate here, though I demur where she speaks of "the *absence* of love, compassion, and sorrow in this book" (312); see the intense grief in 9:8; 11:13. [*Them* 46.3]. Her more technical and recent work is *Ezekiel's Visionary Temple in Babylonian Context* (2021) [*CBQ* 4/23].

F  Goldingay, John. (EEC). A previous report was Mark Rooker. I saw a 2023 draft of a major, lengthy exegetical commentary (330,000 words) and eagerly await it.

☆ **Greenberg, Moshe.** [*M*], *Ezekiel 1–20* (AB) 1983; *Ezekiel 21–37* (AB) 1997. This scintillating commentary far extends our scholarly understanding. An excellent resource for its philological work and its sensitive, patient literary reading of Ezekiel. (See his explanation of his "holistic interpretation" in *Ezekiel 1–20*, pp.18–27.) Greenberg teases out interesting links with other biblical texts. He has high respect for the Hebrew text and takes a conservative approach toward text criticism. This exegesis and Zimmerli's are the most influential right now in academic circles—two of the very best critical commentaries written on any OT book. (Block writes, "No scholar has had a greater influence on my understanding of and approach to the book than Professor Greenberg.") This work does not provide any Christian interpretation of this prophecy for Greenberg's faith was Judaism; that is not to say there is no theology here. See Cook above for *Ezekiel 38–48* (but also note Milgrom below). That makes three AB 3-vol. sets on the Major Prophets. [*JBL* 105.1; *Int* 38, pp. 210–17; *JETS* 12/99; *WTJ* Spr 99; *JSOT* 79; *JR* 7/99].

☆ Greenhill, William. (GS) 1645–67, 1995 reprint. As is typical of Puritan works, Greenhill is very large (859pp.) and provides good food for thought, if one is willing to plow through a lot of pages. I was pleasantly surprised by Greenhill because I expected him to expound points of systematic theology suggested by the text (the typical Puritan approach) and provide less exegesis and interpretive comment than he does. He generally sticks with the text. [*CTJ* 11/95; *RTR* 9/95].

✓ **Gross, Carl, and Philip C. Stine.** (UBS) 2016. I'd wondered when such a translator's *Handbook on Ezekiel* might see the light of day—a huge undertaking (1225pp.). Though not a commentary per se, it is quite valuable for students. Sadly, my copy's binding broke the first time I opened it. [*JSOT* 42.5 (Joyce)].

✓ **Hals, R. M.** ‡ (FOTL) 1989. One of the best vols. in this form-critical series and especially useful to specialists, but few others. [*CRBR* 1991; *HS* 1991; *JETS* 9/92; *VT* 7/93; *Them* 10/91].

✓ Hengstenberg, E. W. ET 1869. Pastors in past generations found this helpful and it remains valuable, but today it is hard to find a copy (o/p). Now free online. Hengstenberg and Keil were stalwart conservatives in German OT scholarship, fighting the incoming tide of what was termed "destructive criticism" during the mid-19th century.

✓ **Hummel, Horace D.** (ConcC) 2 Vols., 2005–07. A massive conservative Lutheran treatment of Ezekiel by a longtime seminary professor. There is exegesis of the Hebrew, but the theological (quite christological) exposition of the prophet's message is accessible to laypeople.

The first vol. runs over 600pp., and the second is nearly 900. One of the better works in the series (see under Commentary Series). [*EvQ* 10/07; *BSac* 7/06; *JETS* 3/09].

☆ Jenson, Robert W. [*M*], (Brazos) 2009. About 350pp. of theological reflections by a systematic theologian (Lutheran). Jenson became a more conservative voice in mainline circles, eventually at the Center for Theological Inquiry, Princeton. He issued appeals for the church to return to a sturdy Nicene faith. Pannenberg spoke of him as "one of the most original and knowledgeable theologians of our time." Thankfully, this commentary on Ezekiel is more closely tied to the text than some other entries in Brazos. It is stimulating, wide-ranging, brainy stuff, but students find minimal interaction with OT scholarship. [*JTI* Spr 10; *BL* 2010; *CTJ* 11/11; *JETS* 12/10].

✓ Joyce, Paul M., and Dalit Rom-Shiloni, eds. ‡ *The God Ezekiel Creates*, 2014. Stimulating essays from SBL. [*JSOT* 39.5; *JSS* Aut 17; *CBQ* 7/16; *JHebS* 18].

F Keating, Daniel A. (CCSS) 2024.

✓ Kemp, Joel B. [*M*], *Ezekiel, Law, and Judahite Identity*, 2020. A Boston PhD examining the "juridical diction and legal imagery" so as to recover the "legal framework" that is "one of the bases the book uses to articulate a vision for Judahite identity" (32). Kemp's background piqued my interest: he previously earned a Harvard JD.

✓ Keil, Carl F. (KD) ET 1882. I found this commentary rich and full (860pp.). Excellent treatment of theological issues and careful (now very dated) work with the language.

✓ **Kelle, Brad E.** [*M*], (NBBC) 2013. Interesting mix of solid research, Wesleyan-oriented theological reflection, insights from trauma studies, and application. Kelle is well-respected for his scholarship on the prophets, writes well, and his book is accessible to non-specialists. [*RelSRev* 6/13].

F Konkel, Michael. ‡ (IECOT).

F Launderville, Dale. ‡ (Illum).

✓ Lee, Lydia. *Mapping Judah's Fate in Ezekiel's Oracles against the Nations*, 2016. [*BibInt* 26.4; *ETL* 93.1].

✓ Levenson, Jon D. ‡ *Theology of the Restoration of Ezekiel 40–48*, 1976. A brilliant scholarly monograph, one with origins as a Harvard dissertation, with much to teach the student. Conservatively critical.

Lind, Millard. [*M*], (BCBC) 1996. The author and series come out of the Anabaptist tradition, and the peace-movement affiliation is reflected in the exegesis and application. Lind dethe-ologizes Gog and understands it as a reference, not to ungodly powers who fiercely oppose the people and purposes of God, but as a "metaphor for greedy, militaristic politics" (317). A proper reading of Ezekiel 38–39 then leads us to fight the Strategic Defense Initiative of the Republicans (321). All very interesting, but I count it one example among several where Lind seems to father his own convictions onto the prophet and mutes "the authentic voice of the OT." [*OTA* 10/97; *RelSRev* 1/98].

✓ Lust, J., ed. ‡ *Ezekiel and His Book*, 1986. A much-cited collection of essays.

☆ Lyons, Michael A. [*M*], *An Introduction to the Study of Ezekiel*, 2015. Superb! [*VT* 67.1; *CBQ* 10/16; *JETS* 6/16; *JSOT* 40.5; *ETL* 92.2; *JHebS* 17].

F Lyons, Michael A. [*M*?] (OTL-R). Previously he wrote one of the best PhD dissertations I've seen: *From Law to Prophecy: Ezekiel's Use of the Holiness Code* (2009). Conservatively critical, Lyons argues that the prophet was an interpreter of the law. [*BBR* 21.1]. Along a similar track is Jason Gile, *Ezekiel and the World of Deuteronomy* (2021) [*ExpTim* 12/22].

☆ **Mackay, John L.** (Mentor) 2 vols., 2018. See his other commentaries, esp. *Jeremiah*. The author (†2018) long taught at the Free Church College, now Edinburgh Theological Seminary. These vols. total about 1300pp. (large print), having strengths in Hebrew lexicology, exegesis, and theological exposition (conservative and winsomely Reformed). There is less interaction with OT scholarship. Pastors will find in Mackay a devout, wise guide through one of the most challenging, baffling Bible books. [*MAJT* 33].

F   Mein, Andrew. ‡ (BBC). From a recognized Ezekiel scholar (Oxford DPhil), who long coedited LHBOTS. See also Joyce–Mein, eds., *After Ezekiel: Essays on the Reception of a Difficult Prophet* (2011) [*JSOT* 38.5; *BibInt* 20.4; *JHebS* 12].

☆   **Milgrom, Jacob, and Daniel I. Block.** [*M*], *Ezekiel's Hope: A Commentary on Ezekiel 38–48*, 2012. Complicated story here. Greenberg had a long illness and passed away in 2010 without completing his AB. The respected Jewish critic, Milgrom, agreed to author the final vol., but he died a month after Greenberg. Shortly before his death, he enlisted Block to help him prepare his manuscript. The result is this conversation between the two, and we are grateful it has appeared (outside any series). There are a few oddities—e.g., Milgrom thinks the temple of chs. 40–48 was patterned on Delphi. Block and Joel Duman (Milgrom's assistant) have completed a successful rescue operation. Still, this is Milgrom's book in the main, and he sometimes "was delighted to do battle with Block" (xvii). [*BBR* 23.4 (Martens); *CBQ* 10/13; *JSOT* 38.5; *VT* 64.2; *Them* 11/14].

Naylor, Peter. (EPSC) 2011. Regrettably the English pastor (†2007) did not live to see his exposition published (800pp.). Naylor was a Reformed Baptist who trained at London, Hebrew University, and Potchefstroom. He offers a phrase-by-phrase interpretation of his own translation, with Application sections at the close of each chapter. He believes Ezek 34–39 "refer to the spiritual renewal of Israel, Abraham's natural children, at some time prior to the Second Coming of Christ," and "chapters 40–48 have to do with the heavenly scene" (11). [*RTR* 8/13].

✓   **Odell, Margaret S.** ‡ (S&H) 2005. The author has engaged in Ezekiel studies since the 1990s, including (often leading) participation in SBL's Ezekiel Seminar. She knows the scholarship, has thought deeply about Ezekiel and its relevance, and writes well. A major commentary! My trouble is that Odell believes we must look outside the prophet's Jewish heritage (see p.4) to find the main ideas or models influencing Ezekiel as a cohesive, primarily literary prophecy. For example, she goes to 7th century Assyrian building inscriptions, when I go to Exodus, Leviticus. Darr's more mainstream exposition, though without Odell's visually engaging illustrations, is more theological and valuable among critical interpretations. [*Int* 4/07; *ThTo* 1/07; *RBL*; *CJ* 7/07].

✓   Odell, Margaret S., and John T. Strong, eds. ‡ *The Book of Ezekiel: Theological and Anthropological Perspectives*, 2000. This book of essays from SBL was followed by Cook–Patton above. [*VT* 55.2; *JAOS* 123.4].

F   Patton, Corrine. ‡ *Ezekiel 25–48* (HCOT). See Herrie van Rooy below.

✓   Peterson, Brian Neil. *Ezekiel in Context: Ezekiel's Message Understood in Its Historical Setting of Covenant Curses, and ANE Mythological Motifs*, 2012. [*JHebS* 14].

F   Petter, Donna. (Pillar) 2 vols. Will build on her published Toronto PhD, *The Book of Ezekiel and Mesopotamian City Laments* (2011).

✓   Renz, Thomas. *The Rhetorical Function of the Book of Ezekiel*, 1999. An excellent PhD.

Rooker, Mark F. (HolOT) 2005. An exposition building upon a Brandeis dissertation (under Fishbane). I regard Rooker as the best contribution to a rather weak series. Somewhat dispensational.

F   Rooy, Herrie F. van. ‡ *Ezekiel 1–24* (HCOT). See Corrine Patton above.

F   Ruiz, Jean-Pierre. ‡ (BerO).

Schröder, F. W. J. (Lange) ET 1873. This remarkable but forgotten work examines all aspects of the prophecy. It is conservative in approach with full exegesis and many homiletical hints. In the 1960s Feinberg said that this was still "among the finest on Ezekiel." Wipf & Stock reprinted Schröder in 2007. It is now free online.

Skinner, John. ‡ (EB) 1895.

✓ Stevenson, Kenneth, and Michael Glerup, eds. *Ezekiel, Daniel* (ACCS) 2008. Some of us find it regrettable that Ezekiel has far fewer pages in this vol. than Daniel.

F  Stovell, Beth M. (BCOT).

Sweeney, Marvin A. ‡ *Reading Ezekiel* (ROT) 2013. [*RelSRev* 3/14].

Taylor, John. (TOTC) 1969. A competent exegesis by an Anglican bishop. Helpful for the beginner, but Ezekiel studies have come a long way since 1969. Quite readable; I read it all the way through.

☆ Thomas, Derek. *God Strengthens: Ezekiel Simply Explained* (Welwyn) 1991.

Thompson, David L., and Eugene Carpenter. *Ezekiel, Daniel* (CorBC) 2010. Thompson, a writer and minister in the Wesleyan Church, contributed the Ezekiel commentary.

F  Toffelmire, Colin. (ZECOT). Previously he has researched Joel.

✓ Tooman, William A., and Michael A. Lyons, eds. ‡ *Transforming Visions: Transformations of Text, Tradition, and Theology in Ezekiel*, 2010. [*CBQ* 1/13; *JSOT* 35.5; *VT* 61.4; *ExpTim* 5/13; *RelSRev* 3/11; *JHebS* 11].

✓ Tooman, William A., and Penelope Barter, eds. ‡ *Ezekiel: Current Debates and Future Directions*, 2017. An extensive set of essays (over 500pp.), describing the "state of the question" in research. [*BBR* 28.2; *JSOT* 42.5].

☆ **Tuell, Steven S.** ‡ (NIBC) 2009. A vol. of 368pp., written by a recognized Ezekiel scholar at Pittsburgh Seminary (PCUSA). I would class this inexpensive and well-written exegesis as moderately critical. Many pastors may find the discussion of compositional history a distraction, especially when he argues for a tension between redactional layers (i.e., between chs. 1–39 and 40–48). [*JETS* 9/09; *Them* 4/10; *BTB* 8/10; *BBR* 21.2; *Int* 7/12 (Allen); *RTR* 8/12; *HS* 2010; *JHebS* 13].

✓ Vawter, Bruce, and Leslie J. Hoppe. ‡ (ITC-E) 1991. As a brief critical treatment with theological concerns, this has value. [*HS* 1993].

✓ Vries, Pieter de. *The Kābôd of Yhwh in the Old Testament, with Particular Reference to the Book of Ezekiel*, 2016. [*JHebS* 17].

✓ Wevers, John W. ‡ (NCB) 1969. Gives a concise, useful treatment of the historical-critical issues confronting the interpreter 50 years ago, but the commentary is not very interesting and is hard of hearing when it comes to theology. See Joyce.

F  Williamson, Paul. (EBTC)?

✓ Wu, Daniel Y. *Honor, Shame, and Guilt: Social-Scientific Approaches to the Book of Ezekiel*, 2016. [*CBQ* 10/17; *JETS* 6/17; *JSOT* 41.5; *JHebS* 17; *Them* 42.2 (Duguid)].

☆ **Zimmerli, Walther.** ‡ (Herm) 2 vols., ET 1979–82. "It is hard to believe that this exhaustive commentary will be superseded within the next few generations" (Childs). Relatively critical, the magisterial work reflects a lifetime of assiduous textual, form-critical, and tradition-history research. This commentary is not for everyone, but if you have a keen mind and are very serious about studying the Hebrew text and understanding Ezekiel in-depth, you ought to purchase these vols. The cost is substantial, so I counsel you not to invest your money if you're not planning on investing hard hours of study. But if you buy it, this exegesis will more than repay study. Prior to Block, I recommended purchasing Zimmerli, not only for the technical detail but also for the profound theological engagement with the text. [*JBL* 105.2; *ThTo* 37.1; *CBQ* 10/81; *Int* 4/84; *HS* 1984]. Note: students may want to consult Zimmerli's little book of essays entitled *I Am Yahweh* (ET 1982), which includes an important study of the "recognition formula" (see also Evans above).

NOTES: (1) See the three review-essays now gathered in Alan J. Hauser, ed., *Recent Research on the Major Prophets* (Sheffield Phoenix, 2008). They are: K. Pfisterer Darr, "Ezekiel among the Critics," *CurBS* 2 (1994): 9–24; Risa Levitt Kohn, "Ezekiel at the Turn of the Century," *CBR* 2.1 (2003): 9–31; and *idem*, "Ezekiel Update." (2) John Olley, "Trajectories of Ezekiel," *CBR* 9.2 (2011): 137–70, and *CBR* 10.1 (2011): 53–80.

# DANIEL

★ **Baldwin, Joyce G.** (retired TOTC) 1978. First-rate when it appeared, but showing its age in areas (e.g., the handling of apocalyptic). Fine introduction, responsible exegesis, and solid theological comment. She packs a great deal of content into 210pp. The 75-page introduction alone is probably worth the price of the book. Years ago, this was Stuart's first pick among the conservative works. The critical commentator Redditt, even in 2008, called this excellent. Was reset in a more readable typeface and reissued in 2009. Now replaced by House. [*WTJ* Fall 79; *EvQ* 4/79; *JBL* 99.3; *JETS* 12/80].

★ Calvin, John. (GS) 1561, ET 1852–53. About 800pp. of commentary from the Reformer, free online. Calvin was being retranslated, and the first Eerdmans vol. (chs. 1–6) appeared in 1993 ("Rutherford House Translation"). The project died.

★ Duguid, Iain M. (REC) 2008. Exemplary expositions by a fine OT scholar, one who spends time in the pulpit. They prompt preachers to interpret Daniel along redemptive-historical lines and develop the connections between the Testaments. Despite the series being termed "commentary," this is a book of sermonic material. [*JETS* 3/09; *JSOT* 41.5]. See Duguid on Genesis, Numbers, Ruth/Esther, Song of Songs, and Ezekiel.

★ Ferguson, Sinclair B. (WCC) 1988. Anyone who has read his books will be interested in obtaining this. He was pastor at St. George's Tron in Glasgow and First Presbyterian (ARP) in Columbia, SC, but much of his career was spent teaching systematics at Westminster Philadelphia. Along with Stuart on Ezekiel, perhaps the best in the WCC series in providing theological guidance. Ferguson tries to be suggestive rather than exhaustive. There are helpful anecdotes, pastoral insight, great theology, and *sane* exposition on a book that needs it. Compare with Longman, Davis, Greidanus, Wallace, and Wright; all six are superb.

★ **Goldingay, John.** ‡ (WBC) 1989, rev. 2019. Though standing painfully loose on introductory matters (assumes a late date and doubts the inspiring stories are grounded in historical events), Goldingay gives us a valuable commentary for close work with the Hebrew and Aramaic. He engages in what may be termed "double tracking," often masterfully drawing out the theological message (even from an evangelical perspective), while talking about folk-tales and legendary materials. He debases the coinage with which he trades. It all makes some conservatives nervous about the future of Anglo-American evangelical scholarship. He reads the visions "as a pesher or actualization of earlier Aramaic material now appearing in chs. 2–7" (578), yet, in his view, "points of difference—indeed, of tension— between the stories and the visions are a key to recognizing the theological significance of Daniel as a whole" (580). Though WBC makes few concessions to preachers' concerns and determinedly sticks to exegesis, this vol. includes some very thoughtful application. Advanced students and scholarly pastors definitely want this; cf. Collins, also considered indispensable. The commentary revision is major (500pp.) and the bibliography superlative (70pp.)! [*Them* 1/92; *CRBR* 1990; *Them* 46.1 (Meadowcroft)].

★ **House, Paul R.** (TOTC-R) 2018. Regarding Baldwin, he writes, "Readers will note that I build on her work; I do not presume to replace it." This Tyndale is remarkably clear in style, insightful, and dependable exegetically. Unlike Baldwin who defended an early date, House is tentative: "the author . . . most likely lived in Babylon," and the composition "could be as early as the late sixth century BC" (27). He identifies the book's main theological theme to be "God's kingdom rising" (1). As a quick reference, this well-informed, judicious, sometimes cautious book is easy to recommend. [*ExpTim* 1/20; *Presb* Spr 19; *BBR* 30.1; *JSOT* 43.5].

★ **Longman, Tremper, III.** (NIVAC) 1999. Like Ferguson, his former Westminster colleague, Longman is a great expositional and theological help. Of course, they also share a Reformed orientation. Where they differ is their areas of expertise: Longman is an OT scholar and Ferguson a systematic theologian who is nonetheless alert to redemptive-historical themes. I would not want to pick between them. Be assured they both will inspire you to do a sermon series on Daniel. (Aside: Longman does not express strong confidence in his conservative views on the dating issue.) Also from Longman is *How to Read Daniel* (2020), providing a fine introduction and a measure of concise, popularly written commentary (90pp.). I came away, however, thinking that the 35-page section addressing American cultural and political issues (from a progressive evangelical viewpoint) was the main thrust. [*BL* 2022; *BBR* 31.2; *JETS* 12/20; *DenvJ* 23].

★ **Widder, Wendy.** (ZECOT) 2023. Pursues different aims from her SGBC (below) and is on a whole other level, in discussing the Hebrew, textual criticism, and Runge-style discourse analysis. As the fuller, more in-depth work (550pp.), ZECOT is to be preferred by students and the best-trained pastors. All preachers can benefit from the 100pp. devoted to the Canonical and Theological Significance sections. Widder is learned, has done careful and thorough research, and writes very well. She is quite open to higher criticism, in theory at least: "There are evangelical scholars with high views of Scripture's inspiration and authority" who date the book to the second century, and "the date of Daniel should not be a litmus test of orthodoxy." Her own position is fairly conservative, believing that "the book of Daniel reflects real events that happened to a real Daniel in Babylonian exile, and that the prophecies recorded in the visions are accurate" (30–31).

Akin, Daniel L. *Exalting Jesus in Daniel* (CCE) 2017.

☆ **Alter, Robert.** ‡ *Strong as Death Is Love: The Song of Songs, Ruth, Esther, Jonah, and Daniel*, 2015. See under Ruth.

✓ Anderson, Robert. *Daniel in the Critics' Den*, 1902. An old apology for the traditional view of Daniel as 6th century prophecy. Don't confuse this work with Josh McDowell's popular book of the same title.

Anderson, Robert A. ‡ *Signs and Wonders* (ITC-E) 1984.

✓ Archer, Gleason L. (EBC) 1985. Premillennial, but not dispensational. He was a stalwart opponent of higher criticism and offered more of a historical exegesis, defending a 6th century date. (Find those arguments also in his OT introduction.) Theological interpretation was not his strong point—he was brilliant in other ways. See Hill below. [*JBL* 3/87].

✓ Beckwith, Carl L., ed. *Ezekiel, Daniel* (RCS) 2012. See under Ezekiel.

F Beyerle, Stefan. ‡ (HCOT).

☆ Boice, James M. *An Expositional Commentary*, 1989.

F Breed, Brennan. ‡ (I). This would replace Towner.

✓ Buchanan, George Wesley. ‡ (Mellen Biblical Commentaries) 1999. I have yet to see this large (500pp.) and expensive vol., reprinted by Wipf & Stock in 2005. It reportedly is especially concerned with intertextuality. [*OTA* 10/00; *JSOT* 94].

Carpenter, Eugene. (CorBC) 2010. Carpenter did the work on Daniel in vol. #9: *Ezekiel, Daniel*. David L. Thompson is responsible for Ezekiel. I have not seen this (448pp.).

F Chan, Michael. (BCOT).

☆ Chapell, Bryan. *Standing Your Ground*, 1990. Like Boice, this series of sermons served preachers well as a model for preaching Christ from this OT book and was attractive because of its reasonable price. In 2014, *The Gospel according to Daniel* was released, also by Baker. I've not seen the newer issue, but the author told me "the opening chapters are an expansion, but the second half of the book is all new material."

✓ Charles, R. H. ‡ 1929. Charles is best known for editing the massive *Apocrypha and Pseudepigrapha of the OT* and his two vols. on Revelation in the ICC. Here he takes up an OT apocalyptic book. This work on Daniel was published by Oxford's Clarendon Press and is very technical.

☆ Chase, Mitchell L. "Daniel" in *Daniel–Malachi* (ESVEC) 2018. Worth obtaining by pastors due to its coverage of thirteen books (750pp.), as well as quality. Some of the expositions have the strongest of research foundations (e.g., Timmer on Nahum, Petterson on Zechariah).

✓ **Collins, John J.** ‡ *Daniel. With an Introduction to Apocalyptic Literature* (FOTL) 1984. A slim, useful handbook which fulfills the aims of the series. The author built on his earlier monograph *The Apocalyptic Vision of the Book of Daniel* (1977). FOTL is superseded by Hermeneia below. [*EvQ* 4/87; *JBL* 106.2; *JETS* 12/85; *Evangel* Spr 86; *Them* 1/86].

✓ **Collins, John J.** ‡ (Herm) 1993. A comprehensive historical-critical exegesis (528pp.), following on the heels of the FOTL above, and the leader in its category. Though Montgomery will still be consulted for decades to come, Collins is considered the most important reference for specialists (philology, text criticism, the Old Greek additions, etc.). Note, however, that he largely confines himself to the older historical and literary-critical methods, which is in keeping with the overall aims of the series (excluding Shalom Paul on Amos). Collins is also a world-leading expert on apocalyptic. Compare with Goldingay, who has much more to say theologically. Pastors will much prefer WBC. [*Bib* 77.4; *JSOT* 6/95; *CBQ* 10/95; *JTS* 4/95; *Int* 1/96; *Them* 10/95; *JETS* 3/98; *JSS* Spr 99; *VT* 46.4; *SJT* 49.3; *JR* 7/96].

✓ Collins, John J., and Peter W. Flint, eds. ‡ *The Book of Daniel, Composition and Reception*, 2 vols., 2001. A huge project (over 700pp.) in a Brill series. [*JTS* 4/03; *JBL* Fall 02; *JSOT* 99; *RelSRev* 10/02; *BBR* 14.2].

☆ **Cook, John A.** *Aramaic Ezra and Daniel* (BHHB) 2019. See under Ezra.

F Cook, Stephen L. ‡ (BCOT). See his astute books on Ezekiel and Apocalyptic. One can expect standard critical positions on introductory issues.

Culver, R. D. *Daniel and the Latter Days*, 1954. Similar to Walvoord in being strongly dispensational. See Miller and Tanner for the best current presentations of that more literalistic, prophetic approach to Daniel.

✓ Davies, Philip R. ‡ (OT Guides) 1985. Quick survey of critical scholarship and its conclusions done by a brilliant and radically critical Sheffield professor.

☆ Davis, Dale Ralph. (BST-R) 2013. A veteran commentator (see Joshua, Judges, Samuel, Kings), Davis offers a strong, concise biblical-theological exposition from a Reformed viewpoint (170pp.). Can be recommended without hesitation to preachers or a Bible study group. I predict many pastors would prefer Davis to a couple recommendations above. As with his other books, I bought it. [*Chm* Sum 14; *Them* 11/14; *Anvil* 3/14; *JSOT* 40.5].

F Dimant, Devorah. ‡ (IECOT).

✓ DiTommaso, Lorenzo. ‡ *The Book of Daniel and the Apocryphal Daniel Literature*, 2005. A huge Brill study mainly focused on the Apocryphal literature.

✓ Driver, Samuel R. ‡ (CBSC) 1900. This is a classic statement of the liberal position. The old Robert Anderson published his response two years later (1902).

Edlin, Jim. [*M*], (NBBC) 2009. [*RelSRev* 3/11].

✓ **Fewell, Danna Nolan.** ‡ *Circle of Sovereignty*, 1988, 2nd ed. 1991. Provides a "close reading" of chs. 1–6, using the new literary criticism. This work is often cited in the literature and deserves attention as one of the first examples of narrative criticism in Daniel studies. The conclusion drawn, that the stories develop the theme of conflict between human and divine sovereignty (the kingdom of God), is convincing and also helps readers integrate the stories with the visions. Conservatives will probably ignore the reader-response elements here. [*CRBR* 1991].

F   Finley, Thomas J. (Kerux?).

☆   Fyall, Robert. (Focus) 1998. A warm, devout exposition from a conservative, very capable Reformed OT scholar in Scotland. Much wisdom here!

✓   Gaston, Thomas E. *Historical Issues in the Book of Daniel*, 2016. A defense of the historical value of the book, written by a learned man (Oxford DPhil) and published by Paternoster. There was a 2009 edition by TaanathShiloh [*JSOT* 36.5; *VT* 61.4 (Millard)].

✓   **Gowan, Donald E.** ‡ (AbOTC) 2001. Another accessible, mainline critical exegesis. Those intimidated by Goldingay and Collins might turn here. Gowan's theological interpretation emphasizes the sovereign rule of God as the hope of the faithful in trying situations. Lucas knows Daniel scholarship better than Gowan and is a better, more conservative guide for exegesis and theology. [*CBQ* 7/03; *JETS* 6/03; *ExpTim* 3/03; *JSOT* 99; *ThTo* 7/02; *JHebS* 4].

☆   Greidanus, Sidney. *Preaching Christ from Daniel*, 2012. Following up his books on Genesis and Ecclesiastes, the retired Calvin Seminary professor of homiletics gives superb guidance on this subject (both interpreting the message of Daniel and approaching the preaching task). He is solidly conservative in approach and will be a help to any evangelical expositor (450pp.). Three model sermons are in an appendix. For a taste see "Applying Daniel's Messages to the Church Today," *CTJ* 47 (2012): 257–74, which includes a clever Berkouwer illustration of a Christian perspective on the Last Days: "We are now traveling along the edge of time, like walking a trail winding along the edge of a cliff." [*CTJ* 11/14; *JSOT* 38.5; *JETS* 9/13; *SBET* Aut 14; *RTR* 8/13; *Chm* Spr 18].

☆   Hamilton, James M., Jr. *With the Clouds of Heaven: The Book of Daniel in Biblical Theology* (NSBT) 2014. Offers a canonical reading with real insight (about 230pp.). The NT use of Daniel materials is covered, but Hamilton gives somewhat less attention to the deadly serious stories in chs. 3–6. Pastors planning a sermon series on Daniel would be enriched by this study of all the connections with other Bible books. [*JETS* 12/14; *Chm* Sum 16].

☆   Harman, Allan. (EPSC) 2007. A full (333pp.), fresh, conservative interpretation which will aid preachers especially. Harman can teach the student too, but this does not contain the detailed and deep scholarship one finds in technical works. He places emphasis, rightly in my view, on the kingdom theology in the book. [*RTR* 4/08].

✓   **Hartman, L. F., and A. A. DiLella.** ‡ (AB) 1978. Though not one of the stronger AB vols., in places it contributes to the scholarly discussion. The authors are Catholic critics who well present the scholarly arguments that the stories and visions address the situation of the Maccabean revolt and its aftermath. [*JBL* 12/79].

Heaton, E. ‡ (Torch) 1956.

Hebbard, Aaron B. ‡ *Reading Daniel as a Text in Theological Hermeneutics*, 2009. [*JETS* 6/10].

Helm, David. *Daniel for You*, 2015. Sermonic material. I have not seen it, but I know Helm to be a most thoughtful preacher. See Keller on Judges, and Helm on 1–2 Peter, Jude.

☆   **Hill, Andrew.** (EBCR) 2008. The fine piece of work (190pp.) is an improvement upon Archer in terms of usefulness to the expository preacher (more literary and theological insight). While solidly conservative, the tone of Hill's commentary is less polemical than Archer on historical-critical matters. As with the old EBC, a vol. on Daniel to Malachi completes the OT section. Worth buying. [*BL* 2010].

✓   Holm, Tawny L. ‡ *Of Courtiers and Kings: The Biblical Daniel Narratives and Ancient Story-Collections*, 2013. A Johns Hopkins dissertation. [*Bib* 96.3].

St. Jerome. *Jerome's Commentary on Daniel*, ET 1977. Translation was done by Archer. Those with French have Régis Courtray, *Jérôme: Commentaire sur Daniel* (2019) and *Prophète des temps derniers: Jérôme commente Daniel* (2009).

Jordan, James B. *The Handwriting on the Wall*, 2007. A theological exposition (over 700pp.) that is best avoided. The defects of his Judges work are present here (e.g., p.115).

✓ Keil, Carl F. (KD) ET 1872.

✓ **Lacocque, André.** ‡ ET 1979. John Knox Press thought this French work important enough to put into translation. Accessible to non-specialists, but includes notes on the Hebrew. Davies opines that the work can be "erratic, but often brilliant, especially on the literary qualities of Daniel" (9). Note: the author, long at Chicago Theological Seminary, prefers the spelling LaCocque. He followed up his quite critical commentary with *Daniel in His Time* (1988). [*EvQ* 4/79; *JBL* 100.2; *RTR* 1/80].

Lang, George H. *The Histories and Prophecies of Daniel*. 1950. This work expounds the book within a historic premillennial framework.

Lederach, Paul. [*M*], (BCBC) 1994. Wants to take a mediating position, that the stories are early but the book is 2nd century BC. Lederach is an educator rather than OT specialist. This is not designed for students.

Leupold, H. C. 1969. Another fairly thorough exposition from this old evangelical Lutheran scholar. Steinmann is much to be preferred. [*WTJ* 13.1].

☆ **Lucas, Ernest C.** [*M*], (Apollos) 2002. With regard to critical dating and main lines of interpretation, this well-researched vol. can be likened to Goldingay. (Lucas believes "it is possible to make a reasoned, and reasonable, defence of a late sixth-century or early fifth-century date for the book," but doesn't.) Perhaps one might say it is like an updated, less technical Goldingay (1989). Some conservatives hoped the series would offer an updated, more technical Baldwin instead. Most pastors would be content with the exegetical guidance offered in the trio of Baldwin, House, and Longman; they would not feel a lack without Goldingay, Lucas, and Collins on their shelf. Students learn more from Goldingay than Lucas. [*Them* Sum 04; *JETS* 6/03; *Int* 4/04; *JSOT* 27.5; *Chm* Sum 04; *EvQ* 1/05; *Evangel* Sum 04; *Anvil* 20.3].

F Mastin, Brian. ‡ (ICC-R).

✓ Meadowcroft, Tim. *Like the Stars Forever: Narrative and Theology in the Book of Daniel*, 2020. Worthwhile essays. [*JSOT* 45.5; *Them* 46.2].

✓ **Miller, Stephen R.** (NAC) 1994. Though I've made less use of this sizeable exegesis (352pp.), I know Miller and Tanner are the best dispensational interpretations. It is well described as more moderate dispensationalism—more cognizant of, and in tune with, developments in broader evangelicalism than that school used to be. The conclusions are "vintage dispensationalism" (Schibler), except for his interpretation of chs. 10–11. Compare with Wood and Walvoord. I regard Miller as much more valuable, both in terms of OT studies and theology. [*Them* 10/95; *CBQ* 1/97].

✓ **Montgomery, James A.** ‡ (ICC) 1927. Definitely a classic with its full treatment of textual and philological matters, but little theology. Prior to Goldingay and Collins's Hermeneia—to consider only works in English—Montgomery's technical commentary was *the* starting point in scholarly discussion. It still is *a* key starting point. Young constantly interacts with the ICC.

✓ **Nelson, William.** [*M*], (UBC) 2012. Well-informed exegesis by an evangelical at Westmont. Nelson has a Harvard PhD and adopts a critical stance on many issues. E.g., traditions about Daniel originally circulated independently of traditions about the three heroes, Hananiah, Azariah, and Mishael; we know this, he says, because we find no Daniel in ch. 3 and no three friends in ch. 6 (53–54). He concludes that here and there we find "a somewhat fictionalized account told for theological purposes" (146). He says, "there are good reasons for questioning whether the prayer [ch. 9] belongs to the earliest stratum of the book" (222) and believes it is a later interpolation. Students find Nelson a useful reference, but pastors may be disappointed by how the critical and historical cast of the commentary leaves less space for theological engagement with the text (320pp.).

✓ **Newsom, Carol A.** ‡ (OTL-R) 2014. Nothing routine here. Scholars were glad to see a more up-to-date critical commentary appear (400pp.); that had been a need. Regrettably, the only evangelicals mentioned by Newsom are old dispensationalists, Scofield and Larkin (charts included). The strengths here are discussion of current scholarship (e.g., postcolonial interpretation of chs. 1–6), a close narrative reading, harvesting the insights of research on apocalyptic (that field has grown immensely since Porteous's day), careful exegesis, and a fresh theological approach. Here is a taste: "While one can certainly read these narratives in light of the challenges posed to the Jewish characters . . . a good case can be made that the true focus is on the figure of the Gentile king. The drama of the stories can be grasped in terms of whether or how the Gentile king will recognize the true nature of eternal divine sovereignty and the actual source of his own, delegated sovereignty" (33). Note that the focus is not on linguistic details. Brennan W. Breed assisted with supplementary sections on reception history (art images included). [*JETS* 6/15; *BBR* 25.2; *CBQ* 1/16].

Olyott, Stuart. *Dare to Stand Alone* (Welwyn) 1982. Provides expositional help.

Pace, Sharon. ‡ (S&H) 2008. The veteran Marquette scholar offers a theological exposition (350pp.), building on historical-critical conclusions. I judge it is of less use to students than many others in the series. Perhaps Pace is of limited use for (evangelical) pastors too, since the reflections on contemporary relevance ("Connections") tend not to focus on the text as God's word or as containing any gospel. E.g., see pp.183–92, where the story of Belshazzar's feast is a springboard to talk about inter-religious respect and dialogue. Is that what ch. 5 is about? [*JETS* 3/10; *Int* 7/09 (Towner)].

✓ Péter-Contesse, René, and John Ellington. (UBS) 1994. One of the later issues in the series, full (352pp.), and reasonably priced. [*CBQ* 7/95; *JSOT* 90].

☆ Pierce, Ronald W. (TTC) 2015. A succinct (200pp.), attractive, and well-balanced evangelical interpretation for pastors, by a prof at Talbot (dispensational). He states that he pursues a "canonical theology approach" (9) and, wisely in my view, sees the central theme of the book as "God's sovereign control [as King] over humanity, from exiles to kings to kingdoms."

✓ **Porteous, Norman W.** ‡ (retired OTL) 1965, rev. 1979. Once it could be said that Porteous "often penetrates to the heart of the theological issue and sets the critical questions in a fresh light" (Childs). He interpreted Daniel as 2nd century history rather than revelatory prophecy, constantly pointing to the clash between Hellenism and Judaism. Porteous was more expositional than exegetical, and built on Montgomery. This work became less important with the passage of time; it has been replaced by Newsom.

Pusey, E. B. 1869. Reprinted years ago by Klock & Klock. Larsen (*JTS* 60.2 [2009]: 490) termed it "an extremely thorough and formidable piece of scholarship" in defense of the integrity and historicity of the book. Now free online.

✓ **Redditt, Paul L.** ‡ (NCB) 1999. The last OT vol. in the defunct series; Redditt's work on Haggai to Malachi in 1995 was next to last. The commentary is based on the NRSV and of reasonable size for NCB's format: xxvi + 211pp. The historical-critical exegesis seems pedestrian. [*JSOT* 89; *ExpTim* 4/00; *RelSRev* 1/01; *CBQ* 10/00; *Them* Spr 01; *JTS* 4/01].

✓ Russell, D. S. ‡ (DSB) 1981. Russell published important books and journal articles on apocalyptic literature, so this more lengthy work for the devotional DSB (244pp.) interested me. Takes the standard critical line on date. There is further work in his *Daniel, An Active Volcano: Reflections on the Book of Daniel* (1989).

F   Segal, Michael. ‡ (AYB). Along the way, the Hebrew University professor has given us *Dreams, Riddles, and Visions: Textual, Contextual, and Intertextual Approaches to the Book of Daniel* (2016) [*JTS* 4/19; *JSOT* 43.5].

Seow, Choon-Leong. ‡ (WestBC) 2003. This same author produced the well-received *Ecclesiastes* in AB. Here Seow provides a liberal exposition, accessible even to a lay readership. [*CBQ* 7/04; *Int* 10/03; *JSOT* 28.5; *HS* 2004; *JAOS* 124.4; *JHebS* 4].

F   Seow, Choon-Leong. ‡ (Illum). I assume this would follow the completion of his *Job* set.

✓   **Smith-Christopher, Daniel L.** ‡ (NIB) 1996. Found in Vol. 7 (17–152), covering Daniel and the Minor Prophets. [*CurTM* 6/97]. Also to be noted is his vol., *A Biblical Theology of Exile* (2002) [*VT* 54.4; *BibInt* 13.3], which is eminently worthwhile for students of Jeremiah, Lamentations, and Ezekiel.

☆   **Sprinkle, Joe M.** (EBTC) 2021. A quality exegesis and theological exposition, defending an early date (in the same vein as his old teacher, Gleason Archer). The commentary is over 300pp and is followed by 90pp of essays on theological themes of the book. The latter will, I predict, provide much grist for preachers' mills; they focus on theology proper, messianic revelation, and a theology of history. Though he deals with the Hebrew and Aramaic, Sprinkle's writing is accessible, and pastors are praising his work as tailored to their needs. [*JETS* 9/22 (Steinmann); *BL* 2022; *CBQ* 4/22].

☆   **Steinmann, Andrew E.** (ConcC) 2008. The Lutheran series continues to build a tradition of issuing large-scale theological commentaries. The mold is an older-style grammatico-historical exegesis with much attention to philology, grammar, etc. Steinmann is over 650pp. and emphasizes both the historicity of the stories and a christological approach to the book. The author is learned and clear, in writing for both students and pastors. Specialists will not judge this to be a new (and conservative) Montgomery, but pastors of conservative congregations will find Steinmann quite useful. He has many sermon suggestions. Well worth buying! [*RBL* 6/10; *CBQ* 10/10].

✓   Stevenson, Kenneth, and Michael Glerup, eds. *Ezekiel, Daniel* (ACCS) 2008. See Ezekiel.

Stortz, Rodney. (PTW) 2004. Born out of the sermons of an able Presbyterian pastor in St. Louis (PCA), this exposition had to be published posthumously.

Sumner, George. [𝓜], (Brazos) 2013. In *Esther & Daniel*, coauthored by Wells.

☆   **Tanner, J. Paul.** (EEC) 2020. An enormous conservative work (850pp.) on the Hebrew and Aramaic text, displaying a keen interest in dispensational eschatology and love for Scripture. The fulsome introduction includes a fine discussion of the book's structure. Tanner's exegetical and expositional commentary bears fruit in his "Application and Devotional Implications" sections. There is much to learn here, even by those who disagree with his theological approach. Clearly, he worked on this EEC a very long time, and it can be classed as an impressive reference that evangelicals will use for decades to come. I'm glad to have it on my shelf. It is fair to say, however, that, apart from an "interesting proposal for an overlapping structure of the book," the commentary "breaks little new ground" (Atkins [*JSOT* 45.5]). [*BBR* 32.2; *JETS* 9/21; *CBQ* 4/22].

✓   **Towner, W. S.** ‡ (I) 1984. Proportional to length of the text, this entry is more in-depth than others in the series, but not one of the best. Theological, practical, with a liberal viewpoint. The author is explicit about his anti-supernaturalist assumptions: there is no such thing as predictive prophecy. The "inspired writers" were "limited in the same way all other human beings are, namely, by an inability to foresee the future" (178). Consider this Porteous's replacement for the shelves of liberal pastors, but Towner has less exegesis and is expositional. Widely used and quoted. [*JBL* 105.2].

Veldkamp, Herman. *Dreams and Dictators*, ET 1978. A very perceptive theological commentary written in sermonic style by a conservative, Reformed minister in the Netherlands. The pastor with this on hand will be helped in preaching Christ from Daniel's prophecy, but Veldkamp is difficult to obtain.

☆ Wallace, R. S. (retired BST) 1979. Originally published as *The Lord Is King*. Evangelicals have found it worthwhile for its excellent theological exposition, and because Wallace maintained the early date on Daniel—which probably irked his colleagues at Columbia Seminary, where he taught Biblical Theology. I agree with him that the kingdom of God may be the main theme. Well worth the price. See Davis. [*EvQ* 4/80].

F   Walton, John H., and Aubrey E. Buster. (NICOT). The two are Wheaton colleagues, and Buster published *Remembering the Story of Israel: Historical Summaries and Memory Formation in Second Temple Judaism* (2022) with CUP.

Walvoord, John F. *Daniel, The Key to Prophetic Revelation*, 1971. By the sometime President of Dallas Seminary. Strongly dispensational and more oriented toward dogmatics than OT interpretation—not recommended, though there are insights (e.g., the king's political designs in 3:1–7). See Miller above.

☆ Widder, Wendy L. (SGBC) 2016. Certainly worthwhile for pastors and Bible teachers (244pp.). The author worked at Logos Software and was a teaching fellow at the University of the Free State. While being critically engaged, Widder takes traditional, conservative positions on critical issues. She says that "current arguments about *ex eventu* pseudonymous prophecy being an inappropriate genre for God to have used are less than persuasive" to her, but she prefers an earlier date and believes that "the accounts . . . reflect events that happened to a real Daniel and his Judean peers in sixth-century BC Babylonian exile" (5). Unlike many evangelicals, she argues the fourth human kingdom is Greece. [*DenvJ* 1/19; *JETS* 6/17, 9/18; *JSOT* 41.5]. She contributes a more technical Daniel commentary to ZECOT (above); students turn there instead. Application concerns ("Live the Story") and illustrative material are more prominent in SGBC.

✓ Wilson, Robert Dick. *Studies in the Book of Daniel*, 1917; *Studies in the Book of Daniel: Second Series*, 1938. These present a thorough, dated apology for the traditional position. From the pen of one of old Princeton's greatest OT scholars. Young followed in his train. More recent conservative work is well-represented in Gaston (above).

✓ Wiseman, D. J., ed. *Notes on Some Problems in the Book of Daniel*, 1965. Not a commentary but provides well-informed answers to some issues raised by the critics; the issues haven't changed as much as some think.

Wood, Leon J. 1973. A comprehensive commentary from the dispensational camp, and prior to Miller the best presentation of that position by a long shot.

✓ Woude, A. S. van der, ed. ‡ *The Book of Daniel, in the Light of New Findings*, 1993. At the time, cutting-edge essays from many of the world's leading scholars on Daniel.

☆ Wright, Christopher J. H. *Hearing the Message of Daniel*, 2017. So very good, clear, and insightful. This is somewhat like his BST vols. on Jeremiah, Lamentations, and Ezekiel, except that it is less a commentary (12) and Wright has less exegesis and avoids most introductory issues. Contains an abundance of sermon illustrations (more from his British context) and works best as a devotional and preacher's exposition (250pp.). He was a missionary in India, and his cultural critique of the West may strike some as strident. [*Chm* Spr 18; *BBR* 27.3; *JSOT* 42.5; *JETS* 12/17; *DenvJ* 3/18].

☆ **Young, E. J.** (GS) 1949. Though quite old, it remains a valuable exegetical work from an evangelical amillennial perspective. Young and Baldwin have been viewed as a conservative corrective to critical works like Montgomery, Porteous, and Goldingay. One drawback is that Young, like the ICC work he builds upon, did not have access to the Qumran literature or to the important Babylonian Chronicles, published in 1956. [*EvQ* 10/49]. Over the years both Eerdmans and Banner have kept this commentary in print. See also Young's *Messianic Prophecies of Daniel* (1954).

NOTE: David Valeta, "The Book of Daniel in Recent Research (Part 1)," *CBR* 6.3 (2008): 330–54, and Amy C. Merrill Willis, "A Reversal of Fortunes: Daniel among the Scholars, *CBR* 16 (2018): 107–30.

## APOCALYPTIC LITERATURE

NOTE: Back in 1989 I recommended Hanson, *The Dawn of Apocalyptic* (1979), which dealt primarily with the OT, and Morris's *Apocalyptic* (1972), which was both a conservative counterbalance and more focused on the NT. Both works are dated. My purchase suggestions are now Murphy and Taylor. The old Collins definition of apocalyptic in *Semeia* (1979) still holds up well: "a genre of revelatory literature with a narrative framework, in which a revelation is mediated by an otherworldly being to a human recipient, disclosing a transcendent reality which is both temporal, insofar as it envisages eschatological salvation, and spatial, insofar as it involves another, supernatural world." To get a quick initial grasp of both the OT genre and recent scholarly work, I recommend a perusal of (1) Longman–Dillard, *An Introduction to the OT*, pp.384–89; (2) Hanson's "Appendix: An Overview of Early Jewish and Christian Apocalypticism," pp.427–44 in *The Dawn of Apocalyptic* (1979); (3) Oswalt's essay below; and (4) T. J. Johnson's "Apocalypticism, Apocalyptic Literature," pp.36–43 in *DOTPr*. For discussions of apocalyptic in the NT more up-to-date than Morris, see especially Pate and the articles below by Aune–Geddert–Evans, Helyer, and Kreitzer, and *What Are They Saying about New Testament Apocalyptic?* by Lewis—see Lewis's annotated bibliography (108–15). The fullest, most current bibliographic list I have found is Conroy's: <https://www.cjconroy.net/bib/apoc-gen.htm>.

★ Murphy, Frederick J. ‡ *Apocalypticism in the Bible and Its World: A Comprehensive Introduction*, 2012. Despite the Baker imprint, this is a critical treatment (429pp.). The book won awards and contains much instructive material, though reviewers rightly complain about Murphy conflating apocalypticism and eschatology. The author had a Harvard PhD and was a former Jesuit, who taught at Holy Cross (†2011). Though a NT scholar, Murphy knew OT scholarship well, as shown in his earlier "Introduction to Apocalyptic Literature" in NIB, Vol. 7 (1996), and the review essay, "Apocalypses and Apocalypticism: The State of the Question," *CurBS* 2 (1994): 147–79. A specialist in OT might prefer to purchase Collins's *The Apocalyptic Imagination* (1998). Other good general introductions covering OT and NT are Cook's *The Apocalyptic Literature* (2003) and the more popularly written Carey (2005). [*BBR* 24.1; *Int* 1/14; *TJ* Spr 15].

★ Taylor, Richard A. *Interpreting Apocalyptic Literature: An Exegetical Handbook*, 2016. Regrettably, evangelicals have not written a major scholarly introduction I can recommend; this veteran Dallas Seminary prof did not set out to write one. But Taylor offers a basic, discerning summary of the existing scholarship and provides intelligent guidelines for interpretation. He treats "the main features, themes, origins, development, and purpose of Jewish apocalyptic literature," discusses "the broader context of ancient apocalyptic thought," and provides hermeneutical guidelines and two sample interpretations of OT texts. [*ExpTim* 5/17; *JETS* 6/17; *JSOT* 42.5; *Them* 42.1].

✧ ✧ ✧ ✧ ✧

✓ Aune, D. E., T. J. Geddert, and C. A. Evans. "Apocalypticism" (45–58), in *Dictionary of NT Background*, 2000. One does well to start here for an introduction to the topic as it concerns the NT.

✓ Aune, David E. *Apocalypticism, Prophecy, and Magic in Early Christianity: Collected Essays*, 2006 (Baker, 2008). Of "unquestionable utility for scholars of Revelation" (DiTommaso), but also helpful well beyond that.

Barr, James. ‡ "Jewish Apocalyptic in Recent Scholarly Study," *BJRL* 58 (1975): 9–35.

✓ Bauckham, Richard. *The Fate of the Dead: Studies on the Jewish and Christian Apocalypses*, 1998.

Block, Daniel I. "Preaching OT Apocalyptic to a NT Church," *CTJ* 41.1 (2006): 17–52. Normally I don't list articles, but this is a gem on the book of Daniel, with wise guidance for handling other texts. There are other fine essays in *CTJ* 41.1 on the theme of "Preaching Apocalyptic Texts." Monographs addressing the theme include Leah D. Schade and Jerry L. Sumney, *Apocalypse When?* (2020); Larry Paul Jones and Jerry L. Sumney, *Preaching Apocalyptic Texts* (1999); and Dorothy Jonaitis, *Unmasking Apocalyptic Texts: A Guide to Preaching and Teaching* (2005).

☆ Carey, Greg. ‡ *Apocalyptic Literature in the NT*, 2016. [*CBQ* 7/17].

☆ Carey, Greg. ‡ *Ultimate Things: An Introduction to Jewish and Christian Apocalyptic Literature*, 2005.

✓ Charlesworth, James H., ed. *The OT Pseudepigrapha. Vol. 1: Apocalyptic Literature and Testaments*, 1983. The standard reference for Jewish apocalyptic texts, superseding the 1913 R. H. Charles set. See also the St. Andrews project *OT Pseudepigrapha: More Noncanonical Scriptures*, vol.1 (2013) [*ExpTim* 11/14], and the Online Critical Pseudepigrapha (http://www .purl.org/net/ocp).

✓ Cohn, Norman. ‡ *Cosmos, Chaos, and the World to Come: The Ancient Roots of Apocalyptic Faith*, 2nd ed. 2001. A Yale issue. Readers can dampen the Zoroastrian stress.

☆ Collins, John J. ‡ *The Apocalyptic Imagination: An Introduction to Jewish Apocalyptic Literature*, 3rd ed. 2016. This is the premier scholarly introduction to apocalyptic as "the Jewish Matrix of Christianity" (the 1984 subtitle). The slight drawback for readers wanting a general introduction to the genre/literature is that Collins only deals with the NT in a concluding chapter. Collins's own views feature strongly here, as one would expect. [*BBR* 26.3; *JSNT* 39.5]. Note the responses in Crawford–Wassén, eds., *Apocalyptic Thinking in Early Judaism: Engaging with John Collins'* The Apocalyptic Imagination (2018) [*ETL* 94.3]. See, too, Collins's 1984 FOTL vol. on Daniel and his collected essays since 2000: *Apocalypse, Prophecy, and Pseudepigraphy* (2015) [*JJS* Spr 21; *BBR* 26.3; *JTS* 4/18; *ETL* 93.4].

✓ Collins, John J., ed. ‡ *The Oxford Handbook of Apocalyptic Literature*, 2014. "A thematic and phenomenological exploration of apocalypticism in the Judaic and Christian traditions" (OUP blurb), that also includes chapters on "the appropriation of apocalypticism in the modern world." [*ExpTim* 11/14; *ETL* 91.4].

✓ Collins, John J., Bernard McGinn, and Stephen J. Stein, eds. ‡ *The Encyclopedia of Apocalypticism*, 3 vols., 1998. The broadest available treatment of the genre, thought forms, and historical development (both ancient and modern) of the tradition. This massive work (1520pp.) on ANE, Jewish, and Christian apocalypticism contains careful distinctions among, and definitions of, apocalypse (genre), apocalypticism (ideology), and apocalyptic eschatology. Authoritative as a survey of the whole history. Do note that the set is composed of long essays and is not in a typical encyclopedia format. Only Volume 1 deals directly with biblical materials. [*RelSRev* 7/00; *JR* 10/00; *WTJ* Fall 02].

✓ Collins, J. J., and J. H. Charlesworth, eds. ‡ *Mysteries and Revelations: Apocalyptic Studies since the Uppsala Convention*, 1991.

☆ Cook, Stephen L. ‡ *The Apocalyptic Literature*, 2003. A fine vol. in the IBT series, well worth purchasing. Do note that his specialty is OT. [*JETS* 3/05]. Earlier Cook gave us *Prophecy and Apocalypticism: The Postexilic Social Setting* (1995). There, using a social-scientific method and focusing on Ezek 38–39, Zech 1–8, and Joel, he challenges the usual interpretation of apocalyptic as always originating among the alienated, powerless, and deprived.

✓ Davis, Joshua B., and Douglas Harink, eds. ‡ *Apocalyptic and the Future of Theology: With and Beyond J. Louis Martyn*, 2012. For NT and Theology. [*RelSRev* 12/13].

✓ DiTommaso, Lorenzo. "Apocalypses and Apocalypticism in Antiquity (Part I)," *CBR* 5.2 (2007): 235–86. The second review-essay appeared in *CBR* 5.3 (2007): 367–432.

✓ DiTommaso, Lorenzo, and Matthew Goff, eds. ‡ *Reimagining Apocalypticism: Apocalyptic Literature in the Dead Sea Scrolls and Related Writings*, 2023.

✓ Elliott, John K., ed. *The Apocryphal NT: A Collection of Apocryphal Christian Literature in an English Translation*, 1993. Standard Oxford resource.

  Frost, S. B. ‡ *Old Testament Apocalyptic*, 1952.

✓ Grabbe, L. L., and R. D. Haak, eds. ‡ *Knowing the End from the Beginning: The Prophetic, the Apocalyptic, and Their Relationship*, 2003.

☆ Hanson, Paul D. ‡ *The Dawn of Apocalyptic: The Historical and Sociological Roots of Jewish Apocalyptic Eschatology*, 1975, rev. 1979; and *Old Testament Apocalyptic*, 1987. The former is his major work (still in print), and the latter is a shorter, popular work in IBT. Hanson and Collins have been leading American OT critics dealing with the genre. Hanson in particular is noted for stressing the relationship between apocalyptic and prophecy, whereas others like von Rad urge that apocalyptic has little to do with prophecy and should be linked instead with wisdom traditions. See also his summary of past work on the topic in SBL's *The Hebrew Bible and Its Modern Interpreters* (1985), and in *ABD*. For a more accessible and up-to-date introduction, see Carey. [*JSOT* 14 (Carroll)].

✓ Hanson, Paul D., ed. ‡ *Visionaries and Their Apocalypses*, 1983. A collection of key early essays in the field. Also a standard from the same era is J. J. Collins, ed., *Apocalypse: The Morphology of a Genre* (*Semeia* 14 [1979]), which built well upon Hanson's *Dawn* and is constantly cited.

✓ Hellholm, David, ed. ‡ *Apocalypticism in the Mediterranean World and the Near East*, 1983. A giant leap forward in the study of the genre for its time, this product of the 1979 International Colloquium on Apocalypticism (Uppsala) remains important today. See Collins–Charlesworth for a follow-up.

✓ Helyer, Larry R. *Exploring Jewish Literature of the Second Temple Period: A Guide for NT Students*, 2002. A leading textbook (nearly 500pp.), that covers apocalyptic and so much more. More recent from Helyer is "Apocalypticism" (252–63) in Green–McDonald, eds, *The World of the NT* (2013).

✓ Horsley, Richard A. ‡ *Revolt of the Scribes: Resistance and Apocalyptic Origins*, 2010. [*JJS* 64.1].

✓ Koch, Klaus. ‡ *The Rediscovery of Apocalyptic*, ET 1972.

✓ Kreitzer, Larry J. "Apocalyptic, Apocalypticism" (55–68), in *Dictionary of the Later NT and Its Developments*, edited by Martin and Davids (1997).

  Ladd, George E. "Why Not Prophetic-Apocalyptic?" *JBL* 76 (1957): 192–200. For study of the book of Revelation. The author's article on "Apocalyptic Literature" in *ISBE, Revised* (I:151–61) is a more conservative take on the topic, well worth reading alongside Collins, Hanson, Murphy, etc.

☆ Lewis, Scott M. ‡ *What Are They Saying about NT Apocalyptic?* 2004. A basic, concise discussion. [*CBQ* 10/04].

✓ Marcus, Joel, and Marion L. Soards, eds. ‡ *Apocalyptic and the New Testament*, 1989.

✓ McAllister, Colin, ed. ‡ *The Cambridge Companion to Apocalyptic Literature*, 2020. By comparison with the *Oxford Handbook*, this vol. is more concerned with how the litera-ture has been interpreted and used down through history. Also focusing less on biblical literature is Daly, ed., *Apocalyptic Thought in Early Christianity* (2009).

✓ Minear, Paul S. ‡ *New Testament Apocalyptic* (IBT) 1981. Important early book.

☆ Morris, Leon. *Apocalyptic*, 1972. For pastors at least, this is still a useful brief introduction to the topic from the conservative standpoint (Morris's expertise was in NT). Because the book is quite old, students would be wise to start elsewhere. [*EvQ* 1/75].

✓ Nickelsburg, George W. E. ‡ *Jewish Literature Between the Bible and the Mishnah: An Historical and Literary Introduction*, 2nd ed. 2005. From an authority on Second Temple Judaism, critical of attempts to link the rise of apocalyptic with the OT wisdom literature.

✓ Oswalt, John N. "Recent Studies in Old Testament Apocalyptic" (369–90), in *The Face of OT Studies*, eds. Baker and Arnold (1999).

☆ Pate, C. Marvin. *Interpreting Revelation and Other Apocalyptic Literature: An Exegetical Handbook*, 2016. Taylor is the OT companion in the Kregel series. Pate is adept at pointing out similarities and parallels among apocalyptic texts, but he has less of a focus on the book of Revelation than his title would indicate.

✓ Portier-Young, Anathea E. ‡ *Apocalypse against Empire: Theologies of Resistance in Early Judaism*, 2011. A superb in-depth discussion of the social setting of early Jewish apocalypses, using trauma studies and other social scientific approaches. [*Them* 7/12; *HS* 2012; *TJ* Fall 13].

✓ Reddish, Mitchell G., ed. ‡ *Apocalyptic Literature: A Reader*, 1990. Those who want to move beyond this, see Charlesworth, ed., *The OT Pseudepigrapha, Vol 1: Apocalyptic Literature and Testaments*, 1983. Another route is to use Online Critical Pseudepigrapha (see Charlesworth above). For NT-era materials, see Elliott.

✓ Reynolds, Benjamin E., and Loren T. Stuckenbruck, eds. ‡ *The Jewish Apocalyptic Tradition and the Shaping of NT Thought*, 2017. Touches on all the NT literature.

✓ Rowland, Christopher. ‡ *The Open Heaven*, 1982. More useful for NT students. The same is true for his tome of collected essays: *"By an Immediate Revelation": Studies in Apocalypticism, Its Origins and Effects* (2022).

✓ Rowley, H. H. ‡ *The Relevance of Apocalyptic*, 3rd ed. 1963.

✓ Russell, D. S. ‡ *Divine Disclosure: An Introduction to Jewish Apocalyptic* (1992). It is best now not to rely on his earlier scholarly output: *The Method and Message of Jewish Apocalyptic: 200 B.C.–A.D. 100* (OTL) 1964. On a more basic level are *Apocalyptic: Ancient and Modern* (1978), and *Prophecy and the Apocalyptic Dream* (1994).

✓ Sacchi, Paolo. ‡ *Jewish Apocalyptic and Its History*, ET 1996.

☆ Sandy, D. Brent, and Daniel M. O'Hare. *Prophecy and Apocalyptic: An Annotated Bibliography*, 2007. See under Prophets. Students doing more extensive work in these areas have made the purchase. Note also that Sandy's *Plowshares & Pruning Hooks* (2002) contains a sensible brief conservative discussion of apocalyptic (203–27).

✓ Schmithals, W. ‡ *The Apocalyptic Movement: Introduction and Interpretation*, ET 1975.

✓ Stone, Michael E. ‡ "Apocalyptic Literature" (383–441), in Stone, ed., *Jewish Writings of the Second Temple Period*, 1984.

✓ Tomasino, Anthony J. *Judaism before Jesus: The Events & Ideas That Shaped the New Testament World*, 2003. Only touches on apocalyptic in this "introduction for the uninitiated," but noted here for explaining the wider context in simpler terms.

✓ VanderKam, James C. ‡ *An Introduction to Early Judaism*, 2001. From a world authority on the DSS. His article on "Apocalyptic Literature" (305–22) in the *Cambridge Companion to Biblical Interpretation* (1998) holds value.

✓ VanderKam, James C., and William Adler, eds. ‡ *The Jewish Apocalyptic Heritage in Early Christianity*, 1996.

✓ Watson, Duane F., ed. ‡ *The Intertexture of Apocalyptic Discourse in the NT*, 2002.
✓ Wright, Benjamin G., III, and Lawrence M. Wills, eds. ‡ *Conflicted Boundaries in Wisdom and Apocalypticism* (SBL) 2005.

# THE TWELVE MINOR PROPHETS

★ Calvin, John. *Commentaries on the Twelve Minor Prophets* (GS) 5 vols., 1559. A most helpful and full guide to theological exposition, which can be put to good use alongside the modern exegeses. Extends to 500pp. on Hosea, which gives one a sense for the fullness of the treatment. Both GS and Baker have reprinted the mid-19th century translation—now free online. See Calvin under Commentary Series.

★ **McComiskey, Thomas E., ed.** *The Minor Prophets: An Exegetical and Expository Commentary*, 1992–98. A Baker set, originally published in three vols. and available in a single vol. (nearly 1500pp.) at a cheaper price. It is beautifully presented, a delight to use, and "should be a first resource to look at when asking what the Hebrew text of the Minor Prophets says" (Oswalt). Perhaps the most valuable book treatments are Hosea, Zechariah (McComiskey), Joel (Dillard), Micah (Waltke), and Nahum (Longman). The series includes the RSV and the scholar's own translation; then it treats the Hebrew in an exegesis section and concludes each pericope with a theological exposition. Contributors are listed below. My recommendation is to buy the single vol., but years have passed, and it is not the first-stop resource it was. [*BL* 1993, 1995, 1999; *EvQ* 1/94; *Them* 10/93; *VT* 47.1; *BSac* 10/94; *HS* 1994, 1997, 2000; *RelSRev* 7/99].

Achtemeier, Elizabeth. ‡ *Preaching from the Minor Prophets*, 1998. Highly regarded.
✓ Albertz, Rainer, James Nogalski, Jakob Wöhrle, eds. ‡ *Perspectives on the Formation of the Book of the Twelve*, 2012. [*BBR* 25.1; *CBQ* 7/14; *JSOT* 38.5].
✓ Athas, George, Beth M. Stovell, Daniel Timmer, and Colin M. Toffelmire, eds. *Theodicy and Hope in the Book of the Twelve*, 2021. [*ExpTim* 8/22; *Them* 48.3].
☆ Bartholomew, Craig G., and Heath A. Thomas. *The Minor Prophets: A Theological Introduction*, 2023. [*BL* 2024].
✓ Boda, Mark J., Michael H. Floyd, and Colin M. Toffelmire, eds. ‡ *The Book of the Twelve and the New Form Criticism*, 2015. [*ExpTim* 11/18; *CBQ* 1/17; *JSOT* 42.5].
☆ Boice, James Montgomery. 2 vols., 1986. An exposition of great help to pastors. I used Boice on Jonah and found him suggestive. The scholarship could be updated at points; use only with a thorough exegetical commentary. Premillennial. [*JETS* 9/91].
☆ Craigie, Peter C. (DSB) 2 vols., 1985. In the main, an inspiring devotional commentary. Some may be disappointed with his reading of Jonah as a parable. For preachers one of the very best sets covering the Twelve. The Craigie and McConville commentaries are the best in the DSB OT section. [*EvQ* 7/86].
✓ Di Pede, Elena, and Donatella Scaiola, eds. ‡ *The Book of the Twelve—One Book or Many?* 2016. Papers from the 2015 Metz Conference.
Driver, S. R. ‡ (Century Bible) 2 vols., 1906. He is still consulted by some.
✓ Fabry, Heinz-Josef, ed. ‡ *The Books of the Twelve Prophets: Minor Prophets–Major Theologies*, 2018. A major European project of collected essays (580pp.), issuing from the Colloquium Biblicum Lovaniense 2016. [*JSOT* 47.5].
Feinberg, Charles L. 1947–52. A capable work for the evangelical church long ago, still in print. Formerly published as *Major Messages of the Minor Prophets*.
F Ferguson, Sinclair. (PTW). I don't know if this is still planned.

✓ Ferreiro, Alberto, ed. *The Twelve Prophets* (ACCS) 2003. [*BSac* 7/05; *BL* 2007].

✓ Firth, David G., and Brittany N. Melton, eds. *Reading the Book of the Twelve Minor Prophets*, 2022. From the Tyndale Fellowship. [*JSOT* 47.5; *Them* 48.3; *BBR* 33.4; *Them* 48.3].

☆ Fuhr, Richard Alan, Jr., and Gary Yates. *The Message of the Twelve: Hearing the Voice of the Minor Prophets*, 2016. Conservative intro. [*JETS* 3/17; *JSOT* 41.5; *RB* 126.1; *Them* 42.1].

✓ Gelston, Anthony, ed. *BHQ: The Twelve Minor Prophets*, 2010. Replacing *BHS*.

Hailey, Homer. 1972. Includes a paraphrase and brief exposition.

✓ House, Paul R. *The Unity of the Twelve*, 1990. Helped to spur research with its thesis that the Minor Prophets are organized along the lines of thematic/theological progression, from sin to judgment to restoration. See also Barry Alan Jones, *The Formation of the Book of the Twelve: A Study in Text and Canon* (1995).

Hutcheson, G. 1657. A reprinted Puritan work I've never seen.

✓ Keil, Carl F. (KD) ET 1871. The careful, conservative exegesis here—this vol. is among Keil's best—has long been appreciated. Conservatives do not use it as much now, with the multiplicity of newer works. Now free online.

Laetsch, Theodore. 1956. Shares the same qualities as his devotional exposition of Jeremiah–Lamentations, and was valued more when resources were scarcer.

Lange's Commentary. ET 1874. The commentaries by Paul Kleinert on Obadiah through Zephaniah are especially deserving of mention. Free online.

✓ LeCureux, Jason T. *The Thematic Unity of the Book of the Twelve*, 2012. [*JHebS* 13].

☆ Longman, Tremper, III, and David E. Garland, eds. *Daniel–Malachi* (EBCR) 2008. As with the corresponding 1985 EBC vol., this is worth owning, especially for those just beginning to build a library, since it offers quick, wide coverage of these Bible books. There is also similarity in that most of the authors have premillennial convictions. The EBCR is more even in quality and much improved over the old EBC [*JETS* 3/87], which felt dated even in the 1990s.

Morgan, G. Campbell. *Voices of Twelve Hebrew Prophets*, n.d.; *The Minor Prophets*, 1960. The former is a series of expositions, and the latter prints the KJV, with outlines and brief analyses of the Twelve, their messages, and their relevance today.

✓ Nogalski, James D., and Marvin A. Sweeney, eds. ‡ *Reading and Hearing the Book of the Twelve*, 2000. Presents discussions within SBL, and is important reading for advanced students. As with Psalms, scholarship is wanting to interpret the collection more as a cohesive and coherent whole, rather than as strictly independent and individual writings. [*CBQ* 1/03; *HS* 2002; *VT* 53.1; *JSS* Spr 04]. See Paul Redditt, "The Formation of the Book of the Twelve: A Review of Research," in *SBL 2001 Seminar Papers* (58–80). For a protest against this shift, read Ehud Ben Zvi, "Twelve Prophetic Books or 'The Twelve': A Few Preliminary Considerations," in *Forming Prophetic Literature: Essays on Isaiah and the Twelve in Honor of John D. W. Watts* (1996), 125–56. The debate continues in Ben Zvi–Nogalski, eds., *Two Sides of a Coin* (2009) [*VT* 61.1; *RBL* 2011].

✓ **Nogalski, James D.** ‡ *The Book of the Twelve* (S&H) 2 vols., 2011. By a leading American scholar on this literature, preferring mainly a historical-critical approach (form criticism, redactional processes, etc). Because of his close familiarity with scholarship—including reading the Twelve as a "single collection" and some rhetorical criticism—his set should be more serviceable to students than most other S&H vols. The theologically oriented "Connections" sections are rather less useful than the exegesis. [*Int* 7/13; *RelSRev* 9/13]. For Nogalski's collected essays, see *The Book of the Twelve and Beyond* (2017) [*ETL* 94.3]. Also, note his more recent NICOT vols. on Joel and Micah.

✓ O'Brien, Julia M., ed. ‡ *The Oxford Handbook of the Minor Prophets*, 2021. [*TGA* Sum 22; *BL* 2022; *ETL* 9/23].

Orelli, Conrad von. 1893. By a moderately conservative Swiss-German. Free online.

F Pak, Sujin, ed. (RCS).

Pusey, Edward B. 2 vols., 1860. The same commentary as in the classic set, "Barnes' Notes." A mature exposition with attention given to interpreters down through the centuries. Not as strong as some of Pusey's other studies.

✓ Redditt, Paul L., and Aaron Schart, eds. ‡ *Thematic Threads in the Book of the Twelve*, 2003. These collected SBL essays are a follow-up to Nogalski–Sweeney above. [*JBL* Fall 04; *RelSRev* 4/07; *CJ* 4/05; *BL* 2007]. Sadly, the link to the Nogalski–Schart bibliography (www.uni-due .de/Ev-Theologie/twelve/12b_bib.htm) is broken.

✓ Shepherd, Michael. *A Commentary on the Book of the Twelve* (KEL) 2018. The Cedarville prof follows recent scholarship emphasizing the unity, coherence, and progression within the Twelve (traditionally a single corpus). Cf. House, Nogalski–Sweeney, Redditt–Schart, Tiemeyer–Wöhrle, etc. Instead of reading these prophets as separate and disconnected, Shepherd "follows the compositional strategy of a single author" (12). That means Shepherd does not provide introductions to individual books, with discussion of each prophet's setting, etc. (Will KEL's typical readership understand what is being done?) The commentary is learned and stimulating (500pp.), addressing Odil Steck's concern for "how a prophetic book should be read according to the desire of those who shaped it during its formative period" (18). [*TGA* Sum 22; *JETS* 6/19].

Smith, George A. ‡ (EB) 1901. The liberal standard of a former generation of preachers. Today's evangelical pastor won't get much of anything out of it.

F Stovell, Beth M. (SGBC) 2 vols.

☆ Stovell, Beth M., and Daniel J. Fuller. *The Book of the Twelve*, 2022. From the Cascade Companions series and one of the best of the more accessible introductions available.

✓ **Sweeney, Marvin A.** ‡ *The Twelve Prophets* (BerO) 2 vols., 2000. About 750pp. of careful, fresh literary analysis. Though Sweeney is one of the leading American scholars on OT prophecy, this set does not have the same research behind it that, say, McComiskey above has. It will be of special interest to students because Sweeney, more than most, explores the literary and theological links among the Twelve. Note that Sweeney has more in the way of diachronic interests than some others in the series, and his faith is Judaism. [*ScrB* 1/01; *CBQ* 10/01; *ExpTim* 7/01; *HS* 2002; *VT* 53.1; *JSOT* 99; *RelSRev* 7/03].

☆ Thomas, John Christopher, ed. *The Book of the Twelve* (PentC) 2020. Ample commentary with nine contributors, including Idestrom, Wessels, and Harrington (735pp.). Well-done!

✓ Tiemeyer, Lena-Sofia, and Jakob Wöhrle, eds. ‡ *The Book of the Twelve: Composition, Reception, and Interpretation*, 2021. An enormous, magnificent Brill collection of essays (600pp.), exploring "an overall message and intention" in the Book and summarizing research over the last several decades. [*CBQ* 7/22; *ETL* 3/22; *VT* 71.3; *JTS* 4/22; *CBQ* 7/22; *JSOT* 45.5].

NOTES: (1) Added to the discussion of Nogalski–Sweeney above are Paul Redditt, "Recent Research on the Book of the Twelve as One Book," *CurBS* 9 (2001): 47–80; and the essays in "Twelve, Book of the," *DOTPr*, 788–817. (2) The journal *Interpretation* devoted the Spring 2007 issue to the Twelve, and the discussion is quite stimulating.

# HOSEA

★ **Dearman, J. Andrew.** [*M*], (NICOT) 2010. Provides the church with probably the best evangelical exegesis; cf. Hwang. Dearman is full (400pp.), conversant with important scholarship, sensitive to literary features, extremely well-informed on sociohistorical and archaeological background issues, and provides good (mildly critical) theological exposition. I am delighted with the astute discussion of the Hebrew and the treatment of "Hosea's Theology" (29–59). Other high-points are the discussion of Baalism in the 8th century, early covenant theology in the writing prophets, and the controversial topics of sexual infidelity and metaphor in this prophetic book. My only unfulfilled wish was for exegetical sections to draw more theological conclusions. Dearman is a PCUSA minister at Fuller, Houston, who wrote the NIVAC on *Jeremiah–Lamentations*. This is the studious pastor's first pick. [*BBR* 21.4; *Int* 4/12; *JSOT* 36.5; *VT* 61.4; *RTR* 4/11; *JETS* 12/11 (Smith); *ExpTim* 6/11; *Them* 11/11; *RelSRev* 6/12; *TJ* Spr 14; *BSB* 9/11; *JHebS* 12].

★ **Hwang, Jerry.** *Hosea* (ZECOT) 2021. After the 66-page Translation and Introduction sections, Hwang provides an extensive (265-page) conservative exegesis of the Hebrew text, employing discourse analysis and other hermeneutical methods, with theological reflection. I found myself trusting this younger scholar's exegetical ability and judgment. He earned his PhD at Wheaton (studying under Block) and is a sensitive, astute reader of texts. There is a good measure of interaction with other scholars (a wise selection too of interlocutors), but he refrains from discussing at length the various views. Hwang might have offered more help on text-critical questions—Hosea's text is not in good shape—and connections with other Bible books, esp. Jeremiah and Ezekiel, but I don't want to quibble. [*JETS* 9/21; *Them* 47.1 (Routledge)].

★ **Kidner, Derek.** *Love to the Loveless* (BST) 1981. A boon for the preacher. Full of pastoral and theological insight into the message of the prophecy and backed up with competent scholarship. [*EvQ* 1/84].

★ **McComiskey, Thomas E.** 1992. See McComiskey under The Twelve Minor Prophets. This is already a suggested purchase.

★ **Moon, Joshua N.** (Apollos) 2018. The author states that his work "hopes, from start to finish, to be a theological commentary" (28). He uses, in a perspicacious way I might add, an honor-shame cultural lens to interpret chs. 1–3. Unlike most scholars, he finds in 6:7 a reference to the first man; this accords with his more conservative Reformed emphasis on covenant. (Moon is a graduate of Covenant Seminary.) The commentary is judicious, well-focused, and fairly succinct in its treatment of the text; it is not a commentary on Hosea scholarship. In my view, pastors will find it both an accessible, learned guide for exegesis and sensitive to their preaching concerns. Thousands of preachers will want Moon. [*Presb* Spr 21; *BBR* 29.3; *JETS* 6/19; *JSOT* 43.5].

★ Smith, Gary V. *Hosea/Amos/Micah* (NIVAC) 2001. Pastors will appreciate the guidance of this OT professor in learning how to apply the message of these three lengthier Minor Prophets. About 180pp. are devoted to Hosea. Amos is treated to 215pp. of commentary, and Micah to nearly 170pp. Do note that, while this is more of a homiletical commentary, Smith has a good measure of dependable exegesis as well.

★ **Stuart, Douglas.** *Hosea–Jonah* (WBC) 1987. First-rate, original work by a Gordon-Conwell prof and one of the best in the OT series. Some evangelicals find Stuart readier to emend the MT tradition than they are. Also, he does not always set forth opposing viewpoints (e.g., at Hosea 6:7). Yet there is so much good to say about it. Stuart is especially valuable because he views the prophetic office much as Calvin did: the prophets' foremost calling was to be interpreters of the Torah, demanding a loving loyalty and trust in the God of the covenant. Longman says this should be a priority; I agree. There are reports of a forthcoming revision by Stuart. [*JETS* 9/92].

☆ **Andersen, Francis I., and David Noel Freedman.** [*M*], (AB) 1980. The most thorough work on this prophet (699pp.) with nearly exhaustive textual analysis. There is an excellent conservative commentary by Andersen (he contributed *Job* in TOTC). Freedman's syllable counting can be discounted. I fear, though, that pastors don't have the time to work through a tome like this or Macintosh's. Hubbard, McComiskey, etc. are excellent in shorter compass. [*JBL* 101.2; *ThTo* 38.1; *JSS* Aut 88].

✓ Achtemeier, Elizabeth. [*M*], *Minor Prophets I* (NIBC) 1995. Covers Hosea through Micah. The author is conservatively critical and a respected scholar. Ten years previously, she published *Nahum–Malachi* in the Interpretation series, so this NIBC work marks her completion of the Twelve. [*Them* 10/97; *WTJ* Spr 99; *JSOT* 79; *Int* 7/98; *Chm* 113.1; *RelSRev* 10/97; *RTR* 4/01].

Barrett, Michael V. P. *Love Divine and Unfailing: The Gospel according to Hosea* (GAOT) 2008. I regret I have not seen it.

F Bass, Derek. *Hosea, Joel, Obadiah* (EEC). An earlier report had Gary Yates.

✓ **Beeby, H. D.** [*M*], (ITC-E) 1989. I like this conservatively critical interpretation better than any other in this series, excepting those on Genesis 12–50 and Jeremiah. Some good theological reflection (189pp.). Beeby was a missionary prof in Taiwan and had a role, with others like Newbigin, in the "Gospel and our Culture" movement. [*CBQ* 10/91; *HS* 1991].

✓ **Ben Zvi, Ehud.** ‡ *Hosea* (FOTL) 2005. A rigorous contribution to the series, giving evidence that the whole form-critical enterprise is reforming and has moved with the rest of scholarship toward synchronic readings (e.g., Ben Zvi speaks of *Sitz im Buch*, not *Sitz im Leben*). This "is a significant work not only on the book of Hosea, but also on the theory of literary study of the Bible" (Hutton). [*RTR* 8/07; *CBQ* 10/06; *JETS* 6/07; *Int* 4/07; *JSS* Aut 08; *BL* 2006; *VT* 57.4; *ExpTim* 11/06; *JAOS* 126.4 (Hutton); *RBL*; *CJ* 7/07].

Bentley, David. *Hosea & Obadiah: Turning Back to God* (Welwyn) 2000. Praiseworthy as a pastoral exposition from the United Kingdom.

☆ Birch, Bruce C. [*M*], *Hosea, Joel, Amos* (WestBC) 1997. For the series, this is a more evangelically oriented interpretation. Birch's commentary especially focuses upon the social critique offered by these prophets. It is well-written and speaks to the heart of the human problem: the problem of the human heart. E.g., see his poignant comments on p.91. [*Them* 2/00; *JSOT* 79; *CBQ* 7/98; *RelSRev* 7/98].

✓ Blois, Kees de, Louis Dorn, Gerrit van Steenbergen, and John A. Thompson. *A Handbook on Hosea and Joel* (UBS) 2020. [*BL* 2022].

F Bons, Eberhard. ‡ (IECOT).

Brown, Sydney L. ‡ (Westminster) 1932.

✓ **Brueggemann, Walter.** ‡ *Tradition for Crisis*, 1968. Pays good attention to the book's so-called complexes of tradition (Patriarchs, Exodus, Sinai covenant, etc.) and to theological issues. This has been a seminal work over the years. [*JBL* 91.1].

Burroughs, Jeremiah. *An Exposition of the Prophecy of Hosea*, 1643. One of the greatest Puritan OT commentaries (699pp.), completed posthumously.

☆ **Carroll R., M. Daniel.** (EBCR) 2008. The former Denver Seminary prof is incisive and does consistently high-quality, carefully researched work. I am very pleased with this contribution. One wishes for more than 90pp. See Amos. [*BL* 2010].

☆ Chester, Tim. (Focus) 2014. A most thoughtful exposition (over 200pp.) from the UK.

F Collett, Don. (ITC).

✓ **Davies, G. I.** ‡ (NCB) 1992. A very thorough work (315pp.) by a leading OT scholar (Cambridge), to be consulted by students. Many years of research went into this. Yes, chs. 1 and 3 can be difficult to bring together, but Davies strangely argues that Gomer the prostitute bore Hosea's children but was never his wife (108). Only this late in the decline of Western morals could the notion of Hosea as "john" be countenanced! [*SwJT* Spr 94; *VT* 46.3; *RTR* 1/97; *CRBR* 1994]. Davies also has a vol. in the OT Guides series (1993).

F Dewrell, Heath, and Brian Rainey. ‡ (Illum).

Doorly, William. ‡ *Prophet of Love: Understanding the Book of Hosea*, 1991.

✓ Emmerson, G. I. ‡ *Hosea: A Northern Prophet in Southern Perspective*, 1984. A valuable JSOT monograph, notable for its cautious approach to the redaction issue. [*Them* 9/85].

☆ Fretheim, Terence E. [𝓜], *Reading Hosea–Micah* (ROT) 2013. The author is always a stimulating theological read, and he writes enough here (225pp.) to benefit pastors who are looking for help in preaching on the Twelve. [*Them* 4/14; *Int* 10/15].

☆ **Garrett, Duane.** *Hosea, Joel* (NAC) 1997. Surely one of the better entries in the OT series, and previously a recommended purchase. It can't compete with AB, WBC, and ICC in detail of scholarship, but it presents the fruits of much commentary work over the preceding 30 years. This solidly conservative treatment is a good choice for most pastors. Garrett also did the NAC on *Proverbs, Ecclesiastes, and Song of Songs*; this is a better piece of work.

☆ **Goldingay, John.** [𝓜], *Hosea–Micah* (BCOT) 2021. Builds on long experience as a commentator on the Prophets; see the author's vols. on Isaiah and Jeremiah, as well as Genesis, Joshua, and Psalms in BCOT. Here with the Minor Prophets, we are happy for the fresh, often-novel translation, though there are oddities causing readers to stumble (e.g., Hos 11 with *Miṣrayim* for Egypt, *Masters* for Baals, *'Eprayim* for Ephraim). Goldingay has abundant exegetical and theological insights (many from Calvin), along with a somewhat critical orientation in this mid-sized work (nearly 500pp.). His 40-page treatment of Jonah exemplifies this, reading the story as an "inspired and authoritative" parable. He writes in a consistently engaging style and shows interest in application to life (e.g., cultural critique of the affluent West). [*ExpTim* 9/21; *BBR* 32.2; *BL* 2022; *JETS* 3/22].

✓ **Gruber, Mayer I.** ‡ *Hosea: A Textual Commentary* (LHBOTS) 2017. A mammoth technical work (600pp.) by a retired prof at Ben-Gurion, who uses multiple hermeneutical approaches and is a leading critic of both the usual interpretation of chs. 1–2 (Hosea betrayed by Gomer) and "the scholarly myth of cultic prostitution" (4). This is a repository of much of the best Jewish learning, alongside important research on historical questions, Hebrew poetics, and rhetoric. [*ExpTim* 10/18; *BBR* 29.1; *CBQ* 1/21; *JSOT* 42.5; *JJS* 70.2; *JHebS* 18].

☆ Guenther, Allen R. *Hosea, Amos* (BCBC) 1998. A fine, devout treatment of these two more significant Minor Prophets. The commentary is geared for the pastor or studious lay reader, employs both diachronic and synchronic approaches, and has many insights. Quite full at over 400pp. [*CBQ* 4/00].

✓ **Hamborg, Graham R.** ‡ *Hosea, Joel, Amos* (NCBC) 2023. For the series, a fairly lengthy exegesis by an academic ordained in the Church of England. He has a brief Introduction (15pp.), then treats the three prophets as individual books in a more diachronic manner (esp. redaction criticism). He is "seeking to find interpretive meaning in all the significant stages of composition which can plausibly be identified" (5). Predictably, texts mentioning covenant are said to be quite late (see 112). What about reading the three as part of The Book of the Twelve? While terming it "a valid interpretive approach" and discussing "intertextual links, catchwords, and themes" shared by the three (11), Hamborg is less interested in reading them as part of one book. The three commentaries total 360pp. Some find the work slightly more difficult to use because of less specific page headings—"Commentary on Hosea" runs from p.35 to p.188. [*BL* 2024].

Harper, W. R. ‡ (retired ICC) 1905. Some technical information can be gleaned from the three older ICC vols. on the Minor Prophets, but it is usually buried deep in a lot of outdated scholarship. Other vols. (AB, Herm, OTL, WBC, new ICC, NICOT) will be more helpful in this regard. Macintosh replaces Harper.

☆ **Hubbard, David A.** [𝓜], (retired TOTC) 1989. Perhaps the most scholarly entry in the old series, and allocated more space than others. It is a careful exegesis which pays close attention to theology. Hubbard was in the critically oriented wing of evangelical scholarship and exerted a strong influence on evangelicalism as editor for WBC and President of Fuller Seminary. A favorite of Longman. Replaced by Routledge.

F **King, Andrew M.** (Pillar).

✓ **King, Philip.** ‡ *Amos, Hosea and Micah: An Archaeological Commentary*, 1988. Excellent. See Jeremiah also.

Knight, G. A. F. ‡ (Torch) 1960. Mildly critical and filled with insightful comments.

✓ **Landy, Francis.** ‡ (Read) 1995. He is an acute reader of texts, especially from a rhetorical angle. Goldingay cites this exegesis repeatedly.

✓ **Lim, Bo H., and Daniel Castelo.** [𝔐], (THC) 2015. A well-studied exegesis of Hosea and inter-disciplinary theological discussion from two faculty colleagues at Seattle Pacific. Lim, the OT prof, provides a valuable commentary of 143pp.; he seeks to read individual oracles "dialogically, in light of the literary context of the whole book" (134). Castelo teaches systematics, and he contributes 100pp. of essays on theological interpretation, covenant and "God-knowledge," "marriage, sexuality, and covenant faithfulness," and "Readers of Terror." There is quite a mix here: historical-critical research, rhetorical study, rabbinics, biblical theology, metaphor theory, discussion of gender issues, counseling insights from EFT (emotionally focused couple therapy). Hermeneutically, the authors are inclined to pursue a postmodern reader-centered approach (see p.10). The vol. is of greater use to academics than pastors. [*ExpTim* 8/16; *BBR* 26.2; *CBQ* 7/17; *JTS* 4/19; *JETS* 6/16; *JSOT* 40.5; *HBT* 38.1; *Them* 41.3].

✓ Limburg, James. ‡ *Hosea–Micah* (I) 1988. A solid entry in the series, though somewhat brief in covering these six prophets (201pp.). [*CRBR* 1990].

☆ Mackay, John L. (Mentor) 2012. A learned theological exposition from a prof at Free Church College, Edinburgh (375pp.). It possesses the same qualities as his large Jeremiah and Lamentations expositions, though perhaps with less interaction with other scholars. Mackay does spell out the exegetical options (e.g., at 6:7), but sometimes without citations of those advancing those opinions. He is judicious and writes lucidly for pastors.

✓ **Macintosh, A. A.** ‡ (ICC) 1997. Replaces Harper. "An important landmark in the study of Hosea" (Davies), with the philological strengths we normally associate with ICC. There is more focus upon the text and less on the text's alleged pre-history (esp. redaction) than we find in McKane's Jeremiah set for ICC. Also distinctive for the series is the author's effort "to mediate the insights of the medieval Jewish writers" (R. P. Gordon). Evangelicals will find his approach more conservative than most in the ICC—I'm almost inclined to mark it [𝔐]. [*Chm* 113.4; *JETS* 9/99; *JSOT* 79; *CBQ* 7/98; *OTA* 10/97; *RelSRev* 7/98; *EvQ* 4/01; *VT* 51.1; *DenvJ*].

McKeating, H. ‡ *Amos, Hosea, Micah* (CBC) 1971. Longman once gave this four stars; why I don't know. McKeating covers these larger Minor Prophets in about 200pp., and is a good, interesting work from the critical perspective.

✓ **Mays, James L.** ‡ (OTL) 1969. One of the strongest vols. in OTL, and I valued it highly. Seems to have been written with studious pastors in mind. He concentrates on Hosea's message. Stuart once said this is the best liberal work on Hosea. Students must reckon with a flood of scholarship on this prophet since Mays was published. [*WTJ* 34.1].

Morgan, G. Campbell. *Hosea: The Heart and Holiness of God*, 1934. A very helpful exposition by Lloyd-Jones's famous predecessor at Westminster Chapel, London. Penetrates to the core of Hosea's message. This has been repeatedly reprinted and sits on many a veteran pastor's shelf.

Ogilvie, Lloyd J. *Hosea, Joel, Amos, Obadiah, Jonah* (WCC) 1992.

☆ Ortlund, Raymond C., Jr. *Whoredom: God's Unfaithful Wife in Biblical Theology* (NSBT) 1996. Shocking title, but a very good book, treating Hosea and much of the OT alongside NT texts. The book was reissued as *God's Unfaithful Wife: A Biblical Theology of Spiritual Adultery* (2002).

☆ Patterson, Richard. (CorBC) 2008. This 672-page book is the joint effort of Patterson and Andrew Hill, covering all the Minor Prophets in the New Living Translation. It is competent and handy. Not for students.

F Petterson, Anthony. (EBTC)? Would cover Hosea to Micah.

Phillips, Richard D. (REC) 2021. Well-crafted sermonic material from a conservative Presbyterian angle (about 250pp.), but one might look up Sprinkle's critique [*JETS* 9/22].

F Roberts, J. J. M. ‡ (NCBC).

☆ **Routledge, Robin.** (TOTC-R) 2020. An admirable, succinct yet thorough, exegetical treatment of Hosea, with much excellent theological reflection. The commentary is well-researched, sifting through the important scholarship, and a wise guide for students and pastors. Some might prefer to buy Routledge, as handier than the larger-scale works recommended above. A worthy replacement for Hubbard.

F Ruiten, Jacques van. ‡ (HCOT).

☆ Schwab, George M. "Hosea" in *Daniel–Malachi* (ESVEC) 2018. See Chase under Daniel.

✓ Simundson, Daniel. ‡ *Hosea, Joel, Amos, Obadiah, Jonah, Micah* (AbOTC) 2005. An exegetical work not as dense as many others in the series and thought by some reviewers to be a weaker AbOTC. Others like Ralph Klein praise it (but they share critical and Lutheran commitments). I was not impressed. It is clearly written and accessible. [*CBQ* 4/06; *JETS* 9/06; *Int* 1/06; *BL* 2006; *CurTM* 6/05; *RBL*; *ExpTim* 4/06; *HBT* 29.2].

F Stovell, Beth M. (BGW).

☆ **Tully, Eric J.** (BHHB) 2018. Hebrew readers need more help with Hosea than with most other Bible books, and this vol. by a TEDS prof is exceptionally useful. See also Gruber. [*JSS* Spr 20; *ExpTim* 4/19; *BBR* 29.4; *CBQ* 7/19; *JSOT* 43.5].

Vawter, Bruce. ‡ *Amos, Hosea, Micah* (OTM) 1981. The author is a respected critic, but other works, from both liberal and conservative camps, are much more thorough.

Ward, James M. ‡ *Hosea: A Theological Commentary*, 1966. Critically oriented and widely used decades ago.

✓ **Wolff, Hans Walter.** ‡ (Herm) ET 1974. Was the old standard critical exegesis, along with AB. Liberal and technical. Advanced students find a mine of information here, especially with regard to textual criticism, form-critical analysis, tradition-history research, and theological commentary. Wolff was assigned the monumental task of treating all 12 Minor Prophets for BKAT. Each of his works is a standout commentary: Hosea; Joel–Amos; Obadiah–Jonah; Micah; and Haggai. The fledgling student would do well to steer clear of Wolff until capable of handling these with some discernment and understanding of Wolff's methodology. Now o/p.

Wood, Leon J. (EBC) 1985. Quite brief. See Carroll R. for Wood's replacement.

✓ Yee, Gale A. ‡ (NIB) 1996. Students may find reason to consult this commentary, which builds upon her earlier *Composition and Tradition in the Book of Hosea* (1987).

NOTES: (1) Harry Mowvley's "Which Is the Best Commentary? XVI. Amos and Hosea," *Exp-Tim*, 9/92. (2) Brad Kelle, "Hosea 1–3 in Twentieth-Century Scholarship," *CBR* 7.2 (2009): 179–216; and "Hosea 4–14 in Twentieth-Century Scholarship," *CBR* 8.3 (2010): 314–75. (3) Consult the above section, The Twelve Minor Prophets

# JOEL

★ Baker, David W. *Joel, Obadiah, Malachi* (NIVAC) 2006. Considering the brevity of the three Bible books, this 352-page homiletical commentary seems pleasingly full. In relation to other vols. in the series as a whole, generally speaking, I find Baker provides better exegetical guidance but fewer wise thoughts on application. [*Anvil* 24.4].

★ **Barker, Joel.** (ZECOT) 2020. A consistently helpful, conservative exegesis, offering a fresh translation and notes on the Hebrew, and majoring on rhetorical and discourse analysis (155pp.). Barker draws excellent theological conclusions too—see his good discussion of the day of Yahweh theme—and many students and well-trained pastors will make this a first choice. He dates the prophecy a bit later (early postexilic). While he considers reading Joel as part of the Book of the Twelve, and examines connections among the Twelve, he is more guarded than, say, Nogalski. Barker is interested in "preserving the unique contribution of each book" (34) and exploring links to other prophecies as well (esp. Isaiah and Jeremiah). [*RelSRev* 3/22]. He was building on an excellent McMaster diss.; see *From the Depths of Despair to the Promise of Presence: A Rhetorical Reading of the Book of Joel* (2014) [*BBR* 24.4; *JSOT* 39.5; *JESOT* 4.1].

★ **Dillard, Raymond.** 1992. See McComiskey under "Twelve Minor Prophets." Long my favorite on Joel, Dillard of Westminster Philadelphia was able to build on Stuart's and Allen's excellent work. It is an interesting study to compare Dillard and Stuart on the question of whether to take the locust invasion of ch. 1 as literal or metaphorical. Great theology here for the preacher! Students will also make ready use of Allen, Assis, Barker, Barton, Coggins, Crenshaw, Finley, Nogalski, Seitz, and Wolff.

★ **Nogalski, James D.** ‡ *The Books of Joel, Obadiah, and Jonah* (NICOT-R) 2023. Replaces Allen, but here the Micah commentary is separate. The Baylor prof, who has devoted decades to studying the Twelve, published the 2-vol. S&H set (see "Twelve Minor Prophets" above). He is justly famous for "exploring the literary, canonical, theological, historical, and sociological implications of an ancient Jewish and Christian tradition concerning the Twelve Prophets" as a single scroll. For all three prophecies here, Nogalski emphasizes their connections as parts of that collection, and I often find the linkage fascinating—not that I find his brand of redaction criticism appealing. He is a rigorous scholar, and also one of the most critical ever to contribute to this series. (In fact he is not known for making much use of evangelical scholarship.) He distinguishes between an eighth century (fictional) literary setting for the three and a final form in the postexilic period. Happily, Nogalski had much more space in this vol. (400pp.) than in S&H (145pp. on the three). Students are glad for the erudition and current bibliography. Pastors will sense that they are not the intended audience, given the vol.'s historical criticism and less theological orientation (cf. S&H). Surprisingly, he seems unaware of Barker's books on Joel. [*JETS* 3/24; *BL* 2024; *JTS* 4/24].

★ Robertson, O. Palmer. *Prophet of the Coming Day of the Lord* (Welwyn) 1995. Normally I do not recommend these popularly styled paperbacks, but the theological exposition here is rich. Students will look elsewhere. Pastors may supplement this with Robertson's theological introduction, *The Christ of the Prophets* (2004).

★ **Stuart, Douglas.** (WBC) 1987. See Hosea above.

✓ Achtemeier, Elizabeth. [𝓜], *Minor Prophets I* (NIBC) 1995. See Hosea above. This same scholar also contributed the Joel commentary for NIB (1996).

☆ **Allen, Leslie C.** [𝓜], *The Books of Joel, Obadiah, Jonah and Micah* (retired NICOT) 1976. A good commentary, but I'm bothered by some of his critical conclusions. Despite the volume's age, it is still one of the top evangelical works on Joel and "[o]ffers a very valuable survey of earlier scholarship" (Mason, 10). [*JBL* 3/78].

✓ **Assis, Elie.** ‡ *The Book of Joel: A Prophet between Calamity and Hope*, 2013. A LHBOTS issue of good length (275pp.), Assis's commentary treats the Hebrew text but is fairly accessible to those without the language (if not confused by Hebrew versification). He is interested in rhetoric and structure, has respect for the Scriptures, and seeks to draw out the book's theological message. Though he is an Israeli, most of his dialogue partners here are European and North American Christian scholars. Assis dates the prophecy to the exilic period, which is earlier than many, including Allen. It is of interest that Calvin thought the dating issue of little importance. [*EvQ* 4/14; *CBQ* 10/14; *JTS* 10/13; *JSOT* 39.5; *JJS* 66.1; *VT* 65.4; *JHebS* 13].

✓  **Barton, John.** ‡ *Joel and Obadiah* (OTL) 2001. One expects a highly competent commentary from this well-read Oxford scholar, and Barton delivers. The list price ($50) for this slim vol. (170pp.) causes pastors to look elsewhere for reference works on these short prophets. Students can make ready use of it in the library. The exegesis is mainly pursued with older historical-critical methods, and there is a good measure of theological reflection. [*CBQ* 10/02; *Them* Aut 02; *JTS* 4/03; *Int* 10/02; *ExpTim* 1/03; *Bib* 84.3; *VT* 54.2; *JSOT* 27.5; *RelSRev* 7/02; *Chm* Sum 05; *BSac* 4/03; *RBL*; *Anvil* 19.4].

F   Bass, Derek. *Hosea, Joel, Obadiah* (EEC). An earlier report had Gary Yates.

✓  Bewer, J. A. ‡ (ICC) 1911.

☆  Birch, Bruce C. ‡ *Hosea, Joel, Amos* (WestBC) 1997. See Hosea.

Busenitz, Irvin Albert. *Joel and Obadiah* (Mentor) 2003. I've not used the book, but it is said to be a clear, fairly full theological exposition at 288pp. The conservative author taught for many years at Talbot and at The Master's Seminary. [*Chm* Spr 05; *RTR* 4/05].

✓  **Coggins, Richard J.** ‡ *Joel and Amos* (NCB) 2000. Marked the brief continuation of the series with a British publisher (Sheffield); I've not seen the work in North America. I found Coggins to be succinct (170pp.), well-reasoned, and helpful in discussing inner-biblical allusions and interpretation. Preachers are helped less in discerning the prophetic message. [*ExpTim* 5/01; *CBQ* 10/01; *JSOT* 94; *RelSRev* 1/03; *Anvil* 18.3 (Renz)].

✓  **Crenshaw, James.** ‡ (AB) 1995. About 240pp. and adds luster to the series. Crenshaw is known as a trenchant critic, long at Vanderbilt, then at Duke. In my opinion this and Wolff have been the most important liberal works. He reads the prophecy purely in its OT situation, with scarcely a reference to the NT. The scholarly pastor who intends to do some preaching on Joel should consider buying this. See Wolff below. [*JETS* 3/99; *BSac* 4/97].

✓  Driver, Samuel R. ‡ *Joel and Amos* (CBSC) 1897. Classic liberal work by one of the greatest British scholars around the turn of the century. There was a later revision (1915) with additions by H. C. O. Lanchester.

☆  **Finley, Thomas J.** *Joel, Amos, Obadiah* (WEC) 1990. A careful, balanced work, similar to Stuart's in that both are thoroughly evangelical, exegetical, and treat the Hebrew. Finley is worth buying, if you desire to build a first-class reference library. Moody allowed it to go o/p, but Biblical Studies Press reissued it (2003), with some revisions related to the use of the NET Bible. Longman has high regard for the work. [*JETS* 9/93].

☆  Fretheim, Terence E. [*M*], *Reading Hosea–Micah* (ROT) 2013. See Hosea.

☆  **Garrett, Duane.** *Hosea, Joel* (NAC) 1997. See Hosea. One of the fullest (over 400pp., 120pp. on Joel) and best in the OT series. We had lacked a major, fully up-to-date evangelical commentary on Joel, but now we have admirable studies by Barker, Nogalski, and Hadjiev. This remains a very good, serviceable guide for pastors; those wanting a substitute for the critically oriented Nogalski can choose Garrett.

☆  **Goldingay, John.** [*M*], *Hosea–Micah* (BCOT) 2021. See under Hosea.

☆  **Hadjiev, Tchavdar S.** *Joel and Amos* (TOTC-R) 2020. Replaces Hubbard. The author is a shrewd exegete and forceful writer, originally from Bulgaria, who did an Oxford DPhil (*The Composition and Redaction of the Book of Amos*, 2009 [*JHebS* 11]) and teaches in Belfast.

Note also his T&T Clark Study Guide for *Joel, Obadiah, Habakkuk and Zephaniah* (2020) [*VT* 72.1; *BL* 2022]. He reads the Minor Prophets more separately than as the Book of the Twelve. [*BL* 2022].

F   Hagedorn, Anselm. ‡ *Joel, Obadiah* (IECOT).

✓   **Hamborg, Graham R.** ‡ *Hosea, Joel, Amos* (NCBC) 2023. See under Hosea.

☆   Harman, Allan. "Joel" in *Daniel–Malachi* (ESVEC) 2018. See Chase under Daniel.

F   Hiebert, Ted. ‡ (Herm). To be added alongside Wolff (below), and Paul on Amos.

☆   **Hubbard, David A.** [𝓜], *Joel and Amos* (retired TOTC) 1989. Very useful and full treatment for the series (245pp.). An excellent companion to the suggested works above. See also under Hosea. [*EvQ* 7/92; *Evangel* Win 89; *BSac* 10/92]. Replaced by Hadjiev.

F   Hwang, Jerry. *Joel and Obadiah* (BGW).

F   Kwakkel, Gert. ‡ (HCOT).

✓   Limburg, James. ‡ *Hosea–Micah* (I) 1988. See under Hosea.

✓   **Lundbom, Jack R.** [𝓜], (CritC) 2023. Though not of much length (90pp.), a careful, quite useful work of scholarship. Readers may be fascinated by the inclusion of a photo album of the 1915 locust plague in Jerusalem.

✓   Mason, Rex. ‡ *Zephaniah, Habakkuk, Joel* (OT Guides) 1994.

Ogden, G. S., and R. R. Deutsch. ‡ *Joel and Malachi* (ITC-E) 1987.

Ogilvie, Lloyd J. *Hosea, Joel, Amos, Obadiah, Jonah* (WCC) 1992.

☆   **Patterson, Richard D.** (EBCR) 2008. The earlier EBC (1985) was a solid work from this well-respected scholar, now retired from Liberty. It was updated in these 38pp., and remains worthwhile for pastors. Students look for more, however. [*BL* 2010].

F   Petterson, Anthony. (EBTC)? Would cover Hosea to Micah.

Prinsloo, Willem S. ‡ *The Theology of the Book of Joel*, 1985.

☆   Prior, David. *Joel, Micah, Habakkuk* (BST) 1998. Fairly full at over 250pp. I am not sure why these three prophets were grouped together for this exposition. Well-done in the main, with many insights into the texts and their applicability in the world today. This can be recommended to all preachers. [*Chm* 113.4; *CTJ* 4/01].

☆   Rhys Jones, Iwan. *Joel and Obadiah* (Focus) 2015. Quite useful and accessible, though there is careful study of the Hebrew behind it. When the vol. appeared, it was especially valuable because of the relative neglect of Obadiah in scholarship. The author is a good friend of mine. [*Chm* Win 18; *ExpTim* 10/16].

F   Roberts, J. J. M. ‡ (NCBC).

F   Ruiz, Jean-Pierre. ‡ *Joel & Obadiah* (Illum).

✓   **Seitz, Christopher R.** [𝓜], (ITC) 2016. The first issue of T&T Clark's already impressive series, but this can be distinguished from some other early ITC entries by its laying more of a historical-critical foundation. As always, Seitz has canonical interpretation as a focal point—see his discussion of biblical intertexts—and is a good, insightful read (235pp.). As with much current scholarship, he explores connections among The Twelve. Note that he includes German texts. He has taught at both St. Andrews and Wycliffe College, Toronto, and is highly esteemed for his expertise in the prophets and biblical theology. See his books on *Prophecy and Hermeneutics*, Isaiah, and Colossians. [*JSS* Spr 18; *Presb* Spr 20; *BBR* 27.1; *JTS* 10/17; *JETS* 9/17; *JSOT* 41.5].

Shao, Joseph Too, and Rosa Ching Shao. *Joel, Nahum, and Malachi* (Asia) 2021. [*BL* 2022].

✓   Simundson, Daniel. ‡ *Hosea, Joel, Amos, Obadiah, Jonah, Micah* (AbOTC) 2005. See under Hosea.

✓   **Strazicich, John.** *Joel's Use of Scripture and the Scripture's Use of Joel*, 2007. A Brill issue, very valuable not only on its topic but also for bibliographical purposes. It provides enough commentary to be placed in bold.

✓ Thompson, John A. "The Book of Joel, Exegesis" (IB) 1956. Said by Mason to be an "excellent commentary by one who studied the book in great depth over a long period" (10).

✓ **Toffelmire, Colin.** *A Discourse and Register Analysis of the Prophetic Book of Joel*, 2016. His revised McMaster PhD, done under Boda, which applies Systemic Functional Linguistics and a nuanced form criticism. Much of the study constitutes a commentary on the prophecy. [*JSOT* 42.5; *JHebS* 17].

✓ Troxel, Ronald L. [𝓜], *Joel: Scope, Genre(s), and Meaning*, 2015. Capably undertaken and praiseworthy. [*JHebS* 17].

✓ **Wolff, Hans Walter.** ‡ *Joel and Amos* (Herm) ET 1977. Another exhaustive, rigorous critical resource from BKAT. See comments under Hosea. Wolff's treatment of Joel is not quite as thorough as that of Amos, but, then again, a little less thoroughness in excavating redactional layers in Amos (six!) might actually have improved the commentary. For purposes of grasping up-to-date scholarship (especially in the North American context), students need to depend upon Hadjiev, Barker, and Nogalski. Wolff's theological interests are always close to the surface, and he argues for the unity of Joel.

NOTES: (1) Consult the above section, The Twelve Minor Prophets. (2) See the review of research in Richard Coggins, "Joel," *CBR* 2.1 (2003): 85–103, and Ronald Troxel, "The Fate of Joel in the Redaction of the Twelve," *CBR* 13.2 (2015): 152–74.

# AMOS

★ **Carroll R., M. Daniel.** (NICOT) 2020. Like Boda on Zechariah, this is so thorough, probing, and insightful that it's an obvious first choice for a scholarly Amos commentary within broader evangelicalism. Has a remarkable amount of interaction with the most important literature. Though appreciative of historical-critical research, he "pursues a primarily synchronic reading" (45). As one who saw firsthand the suffering and carnage of war in Central America, and who struggled to understand a biblical response to social injustice, Carroll wants to "stimulate others to appreciate the incomparable value of . . . Amos for a world needing a moral compass and an authentic prophetic word" (xiv). He displays remarkable literary sensitivity and has for many years used social-science approaches to Bible interpretation. Call this a *magnum opus* (520pp, including a 112-page intro). [*RelSRev* 12/22; *VT* 71.2; *ExpTim* 4/21; *ZAW* 134.2; *BL* 2022; *BBR* 31.4; *JTS* 10/22; *JETS* 9/21; *Int* 4/23; *Them* 46.2]. See also his *Contexts for Amos* (1992); and *Amos, The Prophet and His Oracles* (2002) [*CBQ* 7/03; *SwJT* Fall 04; *Int* 4/04; *JSOT* 28.5; *JAOS* 123.3; *CBQ* 10/21].

★ Motyer, J. A. *The Day of the Lion* (BST) 1975. Typical of the series in general. An OT specialist, Motyer also contributed the Philippians and James vols. to BST; he always proved to be perceptive and edifying in his theological expositions. See his books on Isaiah and Exodus. [*EvQ* 10/75; *JETS* 12/75].

★ **Niehaus, Jeffery.** 1992. See McComiskey under Twelve Minor Prophets. This is already a suggested purchase. The author's strengths in the area of ANE studies well complement the other recommended works on this prophecy.

★ **Smith, Gary V.** (Mentor) rev. 1998. A thorough exegesis, initially issued by Zondervan (1989), and the best conservative work on Amos prior to Carroll R. (fuller than Stuart, Niehaus). "A magisterial treatment" (Longman), and could still be a first choice. The 400-page Mentor is a slight revision. Though these five purchase selections are probably the most useful for pastors, students give prominence to the critical works by Paul, Andersen–Freedman, Wolff, Eidevall, Jeremias, and Mays (probably in that order). For pastoral reflection and application, Smith's NIVAC on *Hosea/Amos/Micah* is quite good but not stellar. His commentaries put me in a quandary: which to recommend? The earlier exegesis has much more to teach, and the later NIVAC has more practical help for preachers moving from ancient text to application. The author taught at Midwestern Baptist Seminary, Union U., and Bethel Seminary. [*CRBR* 1990; *Them* 2/00].

★ **Stuart, Douglas.** (WBC) 1987. See Hosea above.

✓ Achtemeier, Elizabeth. [*M*], *Minor Prophets I* (NIBC) 1995. See Hosea above.

✓ **Andersen, Francis I., and David Noel Freedman.** [*M*], (AB) 1989. Their superlative *Hosea* was 650pp. This exhaustive work on a shorter prophecy is 1050pp! We would have been better served by a rigorous pruning of material. I guess it is tough to edit your own work— Freedman was general editor for the series. Among the best, most complete commentaries on Amos, but I won't recommend its purchase unless you are an advanced student or scholarly pastor. (I am trying to be a realist; unless you are an OT specialist, you will be lost in the detail.) This vol. and those on Hosea and Micah are generally mild in their criticism, compared with most others in the AB. I do not recommend their speculative proposal for a multiphase development of the prophet's career. [*SJT* 93.2; *JBL* Fall 91; *Int* 4/91; *CBQ* 7/91; *JNES* 4/95; *HS* 1991].

✓ Auld, A. Graeme. ‡ (OT Guides) 1986.

✓ Barton, John. ‡ *The Theology of the Book of Amos*, 2012. [*JTS* 4/14; *Int* 4/13; *JESOT* 3.2; *DenvJ* 16; *RelSRev* 9/13].

Beeley, Ray. 1970. This is a fine 120-page commentary by a godly English schoolmaster, published by Banner. He draws from Calvin, the Puritans, and other old classics, and includes searching questions for applying the message.

☆ Birch, Bruce C. ‡ *Hosea, Joel, Amos* (WestBC) 1997. See Hosea.

F Cardiff, Peter. (Apollos). Naylor was once listed as under contract.

✓ **Coggins, Richard J.** ‡ *Joel and Amos* (NCB) 2000. See Joel above.

Cripps, Richard S. ‡ 1955. An old work by a Cambridge don (first ed., 1929).

F Crouch, Carly L. ‡ (OTL-R). Would replace Jeremias.

✓ Davis, Andrew R. ‡ *The Book of Amos and Its Audiences*, 2023. From CUP. A substantial (over 300pp.) and sustained argument for a lengthy, complex compositional history. Utilizing John Stuart Mill's concept of "overhearing," Davis proposes that numerous scribes developed the oracles to speak to multiple audiences, later than the putative audience. "The overhearing audience is . . . entrapped and implicated in oracular speech condemning others" (Hibbard [*CBQ* 9/23]). [*BL* 2024].

F Dijkstra, Meindert. ‡ (HCOT).

✓ Driver, Samuel R. ‡ *Joel and Amos* (CBSC) 1897. More valuable than Cripps and Harper, says Childs. See under Joel.

✓ **Eidevall, Göran.** ‡ (AYB) 2017. A work of technical scholarship, replacing Andersen and Freedman. By comparison, this AYB is more negatively critical. Eidevall is on faculty at Uppsala and, with Clines, urges us "to distance ourselves from the prophetic voice" and not "simply buy the ideology of the text" (32). He applies redaction criticism to discern editing work (three stages) and theological diversity in the book; at the same time he describes Amos "as a carefully structured literary composition" (10). Interpreters, he says, should shift attention from biographical speculation, i.e., from the elusive *prophet* active in Israel, to the contents of the *book*, which was edited in Judah. The review of the history of interpretation, text criticism, and handling of the Hebrew are astute. [*BBR* 28.3 (Carroll R.)].

☆ **Finley, Thomas J.** *Joel, Amos, Obadiah* (WEC) 1990. See under Joel.

Fretheim, Terence E. [*M*], *Reading Hosea–Micah* (ROT) 2013. See Hosea.

☆ **Garrett, Duane.** *Amos: A Handbook on the Hebrew Text* (BHHB) 2008. See under Commentary Series. The author here is a much-published, conservative Southern Baptist, and his work is full (304pp.) and helpful to students, as well as to pastors wanting to stay in the Hebrew. [*RelSRev* 9/09; *JHebS* 2010; *CBQ* 4/10; *VT* 60.3; *ExpTim* 7/11].

☆ **Goldingay, John.** [*M*], *Hosea–Micah* (BCOT) 2021. See under Hosea.

F Gordon, Robert P. [*M*], (ICC-R). Will be a treat. Gordon retired as Regius Professor of Hebrew in Cambridge and has more conservative sensibilities. A long way off?

✓ **Gowan, Donald E.** ‡ (NIB) 1996.

☆ Guenther, Allen R. (BCBC) 1998. See under Hosea.

☆ **Hadjiev, Tchavdar S.** *Joel and Amos* (TOTC-R) 2020. See under Joel. The doctoral work behind this Tyndale was heavily redaction-critical. Still, *The Composition and Redaction of the Book of Amos* (2009) provides a most helpful summary of previous critical work on Amos. Some would challenge the monograph as speculative, and he admits his reconstruction is "highly hypothetical" (208).

✓ Hagedorn, Anselm C., and Andrew Mein, eds. ‡ *Aspects of Amos: Exegesis and Interpretation*, 2011. [*CBQ* 1/13; *JTS* 4/12; *JSOT* 35.5; *VT* 62.4; *BibInt* 22.1; *JHebS* 12].

✓ **Hamborg, Graham R.** ‡ *Hosea, Joel, Amos* (NCBC) 2023. See under Hosea.

✓ **Hammershaimb, Erling.** ‡ ET 1970. Deals with technical matters, but is still fairly accessible. It has been one of the standard commentaries but has steadily lost value over recent decades with all the new publications. [*JBL* 91.2].

☆ Harman, Allan. *Amos: The Shepherd Prophet*, 2021. A solidly conservative exposition, containing exegetical insights and a pastoral concern for application. From Banner of Truth. [*RTR* 12/21].

✓ Harper, W. R. ‡ (ICC) 1905.

✓ **Hasel, Gerhard F.** *Understanding the Book of Amos*, 1991. Excellent analysis of the book, especially for its time, treating all the basic introductory questions and issues of interpretation. [*BSac* 4/93; *CRBR* 1992]. Books of this kind are multiplying: see Auld and Carroll R. above, Houston and Watts below. I call Carroll R. the best of the lot.

✓ **Hayes, John H.** ‡ *Amos: The Eighth Century Prophet*, 1988. [*CRBR* 1990].

☆ Hill, Andrew. (CorBC) 2008. See under Hosea.

✓ Houston, Walter J. ‡ *Amos: An Introduction and Study Guide*, 2017. One of the best in the T&T Clark series, from a British academic. [*BBR* 27.3; *JSOT* 40.5; *JJS* 69.2]. He also wrote *Justice for the Poor?* (2020).

☆ **Hoyt, JoAnna M.** *Amos, Jonah, & Micah* (EEC) 2019. A large-scale (850pp.) conservative work that displays strengths in Hebrew, linguistics, and discourse analysis. I was glad to see her rather full textual notes—as a teacher of Hebrew I have this on my shelf and refer to it. Hoyt did her PhD at Dallas Seminary. She does not seem interested in reading The Twelve as a book. Also, she does not rehash traditional interpretations but wrestles with the text and occasionally proposes fresh, debatable readings (e.g., Jonah 4:11). [*JSOT* 44.5; *BBR* 31.1; *JETS* 6/20].

☆ **Hubbard, David A.** [*M*], *Joel and Amos* (retired TOTC) 1989. See under Joel.

✓ **Jeremias, Jörg.** ‡ (OTL) 1995, ET 1998. As is typical of much German OT scholarship, "Jeremias's leading concern is the history of the growth and composition of the book" (Tucker). That critical approach wearies many of us today. Still, this is an important commentary for students to consult. [*JBL* Fall 97; *JTS* 10/96; *BL* 1996; *Int* 7/00; *CBQ* 7/97; *PSB* 21.1; *RelSRev* 10/98; *RBL*; *DenvJ*].

F Joyce, Paul. ‡ (Illum).

✓ Kapelrud, A. S. ‡ *Central Ideas in Amos*, 1961.

Keddie, Gordon. *The Lord Is His Name* (Welwyn) 1986. Warm-hearted exposition.

F   Kessler, Rainer. ‡ (IECOT). The preliminary German publication was released in 2021 [*JSOT* 47.5]. As is typical of German higher criticism, the author confidently discerns multiple layers of redaction over a long period (200 years, in this case).

✓   **King, Philip.** ‡ *Amos, Hosea and Micah: An Archaeological Commentary*, 1988.

F   Lee, Won. ‡ *Amos* (FOTL).

☆   **Lessing, R. Reed.** (ConcC) 2009. An enormous work (691pp.) that nearly rivals in size the Andersen–Freedman AB. Smith calls it "an excellent work" [*BBR* 22.2], but one that depends heavily on three commentaries (Paul, Niehaus, and Andersen–Freedman). Its strengths are thoroughness (no surprise) and a patient exegetical treatment of the Hebrew. Those from the Lutheran tradition, and many outside it, will value its theological exposition and christological approach.

✓   Limburg, James. ‡ *Hosea–Micah* (I) 1988. See under Hosea.

☆   **McComiskey, Thomas E., and Tremper Longman III.** (EBCR) 2008. The 1985 EBC by McComiskey was a solid work (possibly the leading evangelical commentary when it appeared), and Longman has made it better. (But a bibliography of six items?) These 70pp. are valuable for both exegesis and theological exposition. [*BL* 2010].

    McKeating, H. ‡ (CBC) 1971. See under Hosea.

☆   McKelvey, Michael. "Amos" in *Daniel–Malachi* (ESVEC) 2018. See Chase under Daniel.

✓   Martin-Achard, R. ‡ (ITC-E) 1984. See under Lamentations. Hubbard uses Martin-Achard a good bit.

☆   **Mays, James L.** ‡ (retired OTL) 1969. Decades ago, pastors looking for a supplement to Stuart and Smith were wise to pick up this commentary, but now it is dated. Newer works have greater appeal to the pastor. Mays is moderately critical in approach and one of the most thoughtful liberal commentators on the OT. See Jeremias for a replacement. The publisher is keeping Mays in print. [*WTJ* 34.1].

F   Möller, Karl. (THC). Preparing the way is his dissertation, *A Prophet in Debate: The Rhetoric of Persuasion in the Book of Amos* (2003) [*BibInt* 12.4].

    Ogden, Graham S. ‡ *Amos and Micah* (Read) 2024. I have not seen it yet.

    Ogilvie, Lloyd J. *Hosea, Joel, Amos, Obadiah, Jonah* (WCC) 1992.

☆   **Paul, Shalom.** ‡ (Herm) 1991. A most impressive work (409pp.) by a Jewish exegete, hailed by many as pointing in a more productive scholarly direction. Not a replacement for Wolff, but a complementary study which takes a holistic, more conservative approach to the text. Along with Andersen–Freedman and Wolff, a leading technical commentary. Pastors with the money and desire to build a first-class reference library will consider buying Paul. I bought it and found the vol. to be the most stimulating and satisfying exegesis available on Amos for examining literary features, but I realize most pastors do not share my academic interests. There is little theology here. [*CBQ* 1/93; *JBL* Sum 93; *Int* 4/93; *VT* 4/95; *Them* 10/94; *JSOT* 57; *BSac* 10/92].

F   Petterson, Anthony. (EBTC)? Would cover Hosea to Micah.

F   Roberts, J. J. M. ‡ (NCBC).

✓   Simundson, Daniel. ‡ *Hosea, Joel, Amos, Obadiah, Jonah, Micah* (AbOTC) 2005. See under Hosea.

☆   **Smith, Billy K.**, and Frank S. Page. *Amos, Obadiah, Jonah* (NAC) 1995. Fulfills the aims of the series. The section on Amos is the best here in this 300-page vol.; Obadiah and Jonah are thought to be among the poorer contributions to NAC. [*JETS* 3/98; *VT* 47.1; *JSOT* 76; *SwJT* Spr 98; *HS* 1997].

☆   Smith, Gary V. *Hosea/Amos/Micah* (NIVAC) 2001. Has been recommended for purchase under Hosea. Many pastors will want NIVAC for Amos. See Smith's earlier *Amos* listed above.

✓   **Soggin, J. Alberto.** ‡ ET 1987. This critical exegesis was published by Fortress and, for students at least, is worth consulting. Regrettably, the approach is strictly historical-critical. See Soggin under Joshua and Judges. [*Them* 1/89; *JBL* Sum 89].

Thorogood, Bernard. ‡ *A Guide to the Book of Amos*, 1971.

Vawter, Bruce. ‡ *Amos, Hosea, Micah* (OTM) 1981. See under Hosea.

Veldkamp, Herman. *The Farmer from Tekoa*, ET 1977. Rich sermonic material from a master preacher in the Dutch Reformed Church.

Waard, Jan de, and William Allen Smalley. (UBS) 1994.

✓ **Watts, John D. W.** [𝓜], *Vision and Prophecy in Amos*, 1958, 2nd ed. 1997. [*DenvJ*].

✓ **Wolff, H. W.** ‡ (Herm) ET 1977. See Joel above. [*JBL* 90.4].

F   Wu, Daniel. (ZECOT).

NOTES: (1) Consult the above section, The Twelve Minor Prophets. (2) See M. Daniel Carroll R., "Twenty Years of Amos Research," *CBR* 18 (2019): 32–58.

# OBADIAH

★ Baker, David W. *Joel, Obadiah, Malachi* (NIVAC) 2006. See under Joel. This meets a real need, since we have lacked a good selection of strong expositions that offer guidance in applying Obadiah today.

★ **Block, Daniel I.** (ZECOT) 2013, 2nd ed. 2017. Every publication from Block is a happy event. Subtitled "The Kingship Belongs to YHWH," this full (110pp.) theological commentary employs discourse analysis and rhetorical criticism and has real value for students and bookish pastors. It's my first pick. The author, who also serves as series editor, offers a fine translation and an insightful treatment of the Hebrew text. (The 1st edition used transliteration instead of a Hebrew font.) See Ezekiel, Judges, Ruth, and Deuteronomy for other works by the enormously productive, now retired Wheaton scholar. For reference purposes I now reach for Block and Raabe together, then Nogalski (most up-to-date). [*JSOT* 39.5; *JETS* 9/14, 9/18; *JESOT* 3.2; *DenvJ* 18; *ExpTim* 3/20; *JSOT* 42.5].

★ **Niehaus, Jeffrey.** *The Minor Prophets: An Exegetical and Expository Commentary*, Vol. 2, ed. Thomas E. McComiskey, 1993. Already recommended for purchase; see the section above on the Twelve Minor Prophets. This second vol. in the set is every bit as strong as the first. On Obadiah specifically, Niehaus and Stuart were the best works prior to Raabe. The number of good exegetical commentaries on this long-neglected prophet is nothing short of astonishing. Finding expositional help, however, has long been more difficult with Obadiah; see Baker, Bridger, Brown, Busenitz, Calvin, Marbury, and Ogilvie.

★ **Nogalski, James D.** *The Books of Joel, Obadiah, and Jonah* (NICOT) 2023. See under Joel. Listed as a purchase here primarily for students' benefit—many pastors would prefer Phillips below.

★ **Raabe, Paul R.** (AB) 1996. A very substantial single vol. on Obadiah (273pp.). Few have the money to buy a book like this on such a short prophecy, but it has been the best (partly because fullest) scholarly exegesis—it is rivaled in size only by Ben Zvi and Renkema. Raabe is emeritus at conservative Concordia Seminary, St. Louis and shows great ability in ANE background studies, philology, close textual work, and weighing other scholars' work. [*JBL* Fall 00; *JSOT* 79; *CBQ* 1/99; *RelSRev* 7/97; *RBL*].

★ **Stuart, Douglas.** (WBC) 1987. See Hosea above.

✓ **Achtemeier, Elizabeth.** [𝓜], *Minor Prophets I* (NIBC) 1995. See Hosea above.

☆ **Allen, Leslie C.** [𝓜], (retired NICOT) 1976. See Joel above.

☆ **Armerding, Carl E.** (EBCR) 2008. The old EBC (1985) contained dependable, brief scholarship, and here Armerding updates his work. A lot of pastors would probably be content to have only these 27pp. on this prophecy, which is so often ignored or regarded as unattractive. [*BL* 2010].

☆ **Baker, David, T. D. Alexander, and Bruce Waltke.** *Obadiah, Jonah, and Micah* (retired TOTC) 1988. A 207-page gem, mainly because of Waltke's work on Micah and Alexander's 45-page, thoughtful introduction to Jonah (which defends the traditional position). Baker's commentary on Obadiah is well-reasoned, balanced, and valuable—no throw-away. Even if this is all you have on Obadiah, you may think you're still in good shape. [*JETS* 6/92]. Note Baker's later homiletical commentary above.

✓ **Barton, John.** ‡ *Joel and Obadiah* (OTL) 2001. See Joel above.

F  Bass, Derek. *Hosea, Joel, Obadiah* (EEC). An earlier report had Gary Yates.

✓ Becking, Bob, ed. ‡ (Read) 2016. Unusual in its multi-author, essay approach to the book. The appearance of Ogden more recently might suggest the publisher desired a commentary format instead. [*JSOT* 41.5].

✓ **Ben Zvi, Ehud.** ‡ *A Historical-Critical Study of the Book of Obadiah*, 1996. See also his form-critical work on Hosea and Micah in FOTL. Students consult this commentary for the rare exegetical paper on this Minor Prophet. Much attention is paid here to the putative readers. Ben Zvi is notable for his rigor, depth, and thoroughness (286pp.). [*CBQ* 7/98; *HS* 1999; *RelSRev* 7/97].

✓ Bentley, David. *Hosea & Obadiah: Turning Back to God* (Welwyn) 2000. See Hosea.

✓ Bewer, J. A. ‡ (ICC) 1911.

☆ Bridger, Gordon. *The Message of Obadiah, Nahum & Zephaniah* (BST) 2010. The author is an evangelical Anglican parish priest and former Principal of Oak Hill College, now retired. Preachers will find his exposition of these neglected prophets satisfyingly full (307pp.), thought-provoking, and readable. There is a basis, though, for criticism that Bridger is less engaged with the text than other BST entries. [*JSOT* 35.5; *JETS* 9/11; *RelSRev* 6/13].

☆ Brown, William P. ‡ *Obadiah through Malachi* (WestBC) 1996. One of the few and most helpful pastoral expositions of Obadiah. Brown has also written a well-received exposition of Ecclesiastes. There are few remarks here to suggest higher criticism. [*JSOT* 79; *CBQ* 10/98; *RelSRev* 1/98; *Int* 7/98].

Busenitz, Irvin Albert. *Joel and Obadiah* (Mentor) 2003. See under Joel.

Clark, David J., Norm Mundhenk et al. *A Handbook on the Books of Obadiah, Jonah, and Micah* (UBS) 1993.

✓ **Coggins, R. J., and S. P. Re'emi.** ‡ *Nahum, Obadiah, Esther* (ITC-E) 1985. See under Esther. Mason once called Coggins's work on Nahum here "[t]he best of recent commentaries, emphasizing the function and cultic setting of such prophecy" (56). Obadiah is similarly well-done from the historical-critical angle (38pp.).

✓ Crowell, Bradley L. ‡ *Edom at the Edge of Empire: A Social and Political History*, 2022. A most impressive piece of scholarship from SBL Press (500pp.), and helpful for understanding the background of Obadiah's oracles. See also D. V. Edelman, ed., *You Shall Not Abhor an Edomite for He Is Your Brother: Edom and Seir in History and Tradition* (1995); and John R. Bartlett, *Edom and the Edomites* (1989).

✓ Dicou, Bert. ‡ *Edom, Israel's Brother and Antagonist: The Role of Edom in Biblical Prophecy and Story*, 1994, repr. 2009. From JSOTSup, treating the major oracles against Edom/Mt. Seir (Is 34; Jer 49; Ezek 35; and Obadiah) as well as the Genesis story of Esau. I believe it was originally a U. of Amsterdam doctoral study.

Eaton, J. H. ‡ *Obadiah, Nahum, Habakkuk, and Zephaniah* (Torch) 1961. At one time it was considered very useful because there were few commentators.

✓ Field, David. 2008. Subtitled "A Practical Commentary."

☆ **Finley, Thomas J.** *Joel, Amos, Obadiah* (WEC) 1990. See under Joel.

Fretheim, Terence E. [𝓜], *Reading Hosea–Micah* (ROT) 2013. See Hosea.

☆ **Goldingay, John.** [𝓜], *Hosea–Micah* (BCOT) 2021. See under Hosea.

✓ Hadjiev, Tchavdar S. *Joel, Obadiah, Habakkuk and Zephaniah*, 2020. See under Joel.

F Hagedorn, Anselm. ‡ *Joel, Obadiah* (IECOT).

F Hwang, Jerry. *Joel and Obadiah* (BGW).

✓ **Jenson, Philip Peter.** [𝓜], *Obadiah, Jonah, Micah: A Theological Commentary*, 2008. Like Joyce's choice vol. on Ezekiel, this was to have been published in NCB, now defunct. The compact exegesis of 227pp. with indices aims at explaining the theological message in its original context, with a few Christian reflections. The book divides as follows: Obadiah, pp.3–27; Jonah, 29–93; Micah, 95–189. Jenson is reluctant to say much about compositional history since it is speculative; he prefers to take a canonical, synchronic approach. With regard to Jonah, he sees serious problems with reading it as a historical account and with discerning a fitting genre categorization. "Most recent commentators wisely leave the genre as general as possible" (34) and speak of "story." In coming to the exegetical treatment of the text, one finds Jenson astute, careful, and responsible. He taught at the evangelical Trinity College, Bristol, and Ridley Hall, Cambridge. For reasons of price ($220), this regrettably has to be consulted in the library. I have yet to see a pb. [*CBQ* 10/09; *BL* 2010; *VT* 60.2 (Williamson); *JHebS* 2009; *JSS* Spr 12; *RBL* 2011; *RelSRev* 3/11].

Kleinert, Paul. (Lange) ET 1874.

✓ Limburg, James. ‡ *Hosea–Micah* (I) 1988. See under Hosea.

Marbury, Edward. *Obadiah and Habakkuk*, 1649 (1865 ed. repr.). This Puritan work offers a lengthy, profound Reformed exposition of these books. I've not used it much but know it was warmly commended by Spurgeon. Available free online.

✓ Mason, Rex. ‡ *Micah, Nahum, Obadiah* (OT Guides) 1991.

✓ **Ogden, Graham S.** ‡ *Obadiah and Haggai* (Read) 2022. A fuller, more in-depth commentary (about 30pp. on Obadiah and 95pp. on Haggai) than one might expect from the series, but the tone is rather negatively critical. The author seems fixated on a theory: "so much happens in an oral culture between an original pronouncement by a prophet or storyteller, its repetition, transmission within the community, and its eventual recording." Haggai "would almost certainly have been illiterate" (53). Similarly, Obadiah has a difficult-to-trace compositional history, and the book is "a collection of oral responses to Edom and the nations over an extended period" (7). The bibliographies are surprisingly weak and dated. [*JSOT* 47.5].

Ogilvie, Lloyd J. *Hosea, Joel, Amos, Obadiah, Jonah* (WCC) 1992.

✓ **Pagan, Samuel.** ‡ (NIB) 1996.

Perowne, T. T. *Obadiah and Jonah* (CBSC) 1889.

F Petterson, Anthony. (EBTC)? Would cover Hosea to Micah.

☆ **Phillips, Elaine.** *Obadiah, Jonah & Micah* (Apollos) 2022. Approx. 400pp. from a beloved prof, now retired, at Gordon College. Previously she wrote "Esther" for EBCR. She is a learned Hebraist, a masterful teacher, and a devout Christian with a love for Scripture. Her work here is one of the more conservative and approachable vols. in the series for students and pastors. She does explore thematic and lexical connections within the three books, also considering their placement among the Twelve. She finds it may be elusive, however, "determining intentional shaping of the entire [Book of the Twelve] corpus." As Renz notes [*JSOT* 47.5], there is less theological interpretation than some readers might desire, but this tends to be true of the series as a whole.

✓ **Renkema, John.** ‡ (HCOT) ET 2003. A well-done, large-scale (224pp.), technical study, more focused upon the old historical-critical concerns. Hebrew students will certainly consult it as a leading reference work. Compare with Raabe and Block, who are more conservative. [*JSOT* 28.5; *VT* 57.2; *RelSRev* 10/04 (Sweeney)].

☆ Rhys Jones, Iwan. *Joel and Obadiah* (Focus) 2015. See under Joel.

☆ Rogland, Max. "Obadiah" in *Daniel–Malachi* (ESVEC) 2018. See Chase under Daniel.

F Ruiz, Jean-Pierre. ‡ *Joel & Obadiah* (Illum).

✓ Simundson, Daniel. ‡ *Hosea, Joel, Amos, Obadiah, Jonah, Micah* (AbOTC) 2005. See under Hosea.

Smith, Billy K., and Frank S. Page. *Amos, Obadiah, Jonah* (NAC) 1995. See under Amos.

✓ **Thompson, John A.** "The Book of Obadiah, Exegesis" (IB) 1956. Few works in vol.6 are worthwhile, but this and Thomas's "Haggai" and "Zechariah 1–8" have been.

F Tietz, Ryan. (ConcC).

☆ **Timmer, Daniel C.** *Obadiah, Jonah and Micah* (TOTC-R) 2021. A fine exegetical handbook for these prophets, following Timmer's doctoral work on *The Non-Israelite Nations in the Book of the Twelve* (2015) [*JHebS* 17], his recent Nahum commentary, and his theological study of Jonah, *A Gracious and Compassionate God* (2011). This replaces Baker–Alexander–Waltke.

✓ **Watts, John D. W.** ‡ *Obadiah: A Critical, Exegetical Commentary*, 1969. Important since it was long the most in-depth commentary on the tiny book. Watts was occasionally reprinted. "His cultic interpretation can be safely ignored" (Childs). If you plan to do a lot of study in Obadiah, you want to look this up. Watts was usually spoken of as the authority to consult, at least prior to the publication of Raabe. [*JBL* 90.2]. He also has a later commentary on this book in CBC (1975).

✓ **Wolff, H. W.** ‡ *Obadiah and Jonah* (ContC) ET 1986. Another translation from the BKAT series, but this time the publisher for Wolff's work was Augsburg rather than Fortress. (Those two publishing houses eventually merged.) The vol. meets the same standards established in the earlier Hermeneia commentaries. The student must consult Wolff on technical issues. Wolff's strengths were form criticism, tradition-history, and theological interpretation. See Hosea. [*JBL* 99.2; *CRBR* 1988].

NOTE: Consult the list of works in the above section The Twelve Minor Prophets.

# JONAH

★ Bruckner, James K. *Jonah, Nahum, Habakkuk, Zephaniah* (NIVAC) 2004. Preachers especially esteem this as an excellent addition to the series. Together with my friend, Dale Brueggemann [*CTJ* 4/08], I find his treatment of Jonah inferior to the fine exposition of Nahum through Zephaniah. The particular weakness is a straining to rehabilitate Jonah as a good prophet. As I wrote earlier, one needs to remember that prophets, priests, and kings (2 Sam 11 and 24) point to Christ—the need for a perfect prophet, priest, and king—in their failures as well as their successes. I note, however, that Longman disagrees and finds the Jonah section "the most stimulating." Alongside this book and Ferguson, preachers should also consider Brown, Keddie, Martin, Nixon, Estelle, Phillips, and Robertson.

★ Ferguson, Sinclair. *Man Overboard*, 1982. Reprinted by Banner (2008), this wise, theologically insightful study in sermonic form was originally from Tyndale House Publishers. I consider the vol. to be model preaching. See also under Daniel.

★ **Nogalski, James D.** ‡ *The Books of Joel, Obadiah, and Jonah* (NICOT) 2023. See under Joel and Obadiah, where the vol. has already been recommended to advanced students. For Jonah I expect most pastors might prefer Nixon, Hoyt, or Elaine Phillips.

★ **Sasson, Jack M.** ‡ (retired AB) 1990. Masterful. Along with Wolff, one of the leading scholarly exegeses. Sasson's approach is essentially synchronic, using the new literary criticism and focusing on the text's *being* rather than its *becoming*. Much fuller in its discussion than ContC or OTL, it is often consulted, and scholarly pastors will want to purchase it. See Graybill below. [*JBL* Spr 92; *CBQ* 1/93; *Int* 7/92; *JNES* 4/95; *AsTJ* Fall 92].

★ **Stuart, Douglas.** (WBC) 1987. See Hosea above. Evangelicals value this reverent defense of the miraculous in Jonah's prophecy, but there is far more substance to the work than just that. The exegesis is well-reasoned and insightful. Stuart's literary observations and theological guidance meet the needs of preachers.

★ **Timmer, Daniel C.** *Obadiah, Jonah and Micah* (TOTC-R) 2021. See under Obadiah. Previously we were blessed with *A Gracious and Compassionate God: Mission, Salvation, and Spirituality in the Book of Jonah* (2011), from NSBT [*Them* 11/12].

★ **Youngblood, Kevin J.** (ZECOT) 2nd ed. 2019. Deft rhetorical analysis is paired with discourse analysis (text linguistics) in the service of providing solid theological exposition. Those who can handle the Hebrew will be able to make fullest use of this, but it is accessible to those without that competence. He nuances his position on the genre question, saying that, "while [it] . . . relates historical events, the book of Jonah was not written as strict historiography" (31). Youngblood believes "the author's interests were more theological and didactic than historical and chronological," and this accounts for the story having "less historical detail." A very fine book for both preachers and teachers, written with remarkable clarity. It may prove helpful, too, to those who desire to learn by example how to apply discourse analysis to OT texts. My first pick. [*JSOT* 39.5; *JESOT* 3.2; *BTB* 5/15].

✓ Aalders, G. Charles. *The Problem of the Book of Jonah*, ET 1948. A short defense of the book as fitting the genre of history and as credible.

✓ Achtemeier, Elizabeth. [𝓜], *Minor Prophets I* (NIBC) 1995. See Hosea above.

☆ **Alexander, T. D.** (retired TOTC) 1988. See Baker (TOTC) under Obadiah. Alexander has excellent theological insights. He ably defends his conservative approach to the prophecy in this commentary. You might also consult "Jonah and Genre," *TynBul* 36 (1985): 35–59, a significant, wisely cautious article for conservatives to read. [*JETS* 6/92].

☆ **Allen, Leslie C.** [𝓜], (retired NICOT) 1976. See Joel above and Micah below. The major deficiency here is the brevity of the commentary, a little over 30pp; by contrast Stuart spends 67pp. Allen reads Jonah as a non-historical parable, though it is certainly not an impossible "sea yarn"—see note #4 below. This was long a leading evangelical commentary. Replaced by Nogalski.

☆ **Alter, Robert.** ‡ *Strong as Death Is Love: The Song of Songs, Ruth, Esther, Jonah, and Daniel*, 2015. See under Ruth.

☆ **Baldwin-Caine, Joyce.** *The Minor Prophets: An Exegetical and Expository Commentary*, Vol. 2, ed. Thomas E. McComiskey, 1993. A solid work which rivals the other evangelical commentaries now available, but this was perhaps not her finest hour—see her numerous vols. in the Tyndale series. It is not among my top picks for Jonah, but the whole set has been recommended for purchase.

✓ Bewer, J. A. ‡ (ICC) 1912.

☆ Brown, William P. ‡ *Obadiah–Malachi* (WestBC) 1996. Well-done and conservatively critical. See Obadiah.

Cary, Phillip. ‡ (Brazos) 2008. I have not yet had a chance to explore this exposition by an Augustine scholar, said by reviewers to read Jonah as a humorous allegory. [*JETS* 6/09; *HBT* 31.2; *BL* 2010; *RelSRev* 9/09; *CBQ* 4/10; *BBR* 21.3; *Int* 1/11].

F   Claassens, L. Juliana M. ‡ (OTL) 2024. By a feminist prof at Stellenbosch. Her past work displays an interest in trauma studies, queer interpretation, gender, and sexuality.

Clark, David J., Norm Mundhenk, et al. *A Handbook on the Books of Obadiah, Jonah, and Micah* (UBS) 1993.

Ellison, H. L. (EBC) 1985. Honorably retired and replaced by Walton.

✓   Ellul, Jacques. [𝓜], *The Judgment of Jonah*, ET 1971. A stimulating and successful study, interpreting the book christologically; it is more of a reflection on Jonah than an exegesis or textual exposition. Though difficult to pinpoint on the theological spectrum, Ellul was essentially Barthian. See his books on Kings and Ecclesiastes.

✓   **Erickson, Amy.** ‡ (Illum) 2021. Few Bible narratives have had so many representations in literature, visual arts, etc. As Limburg said, "Jonah is everywhere!" Erickson, an able Hebraist who teaches at Iliff, can be congratulated for dealing more fully with this reception history ("History of Consequences"). She also offers a major detailed commentary, interesting throughout, that challenges the common interpretations: text-as-satire or obstinate, xenophobic, runaway prophet (not to be emulated). The latter of these she sees as "anti-Judaic," following Sherwood. Erickson's view is that the story has elements of parody and the figure of Jonah represents Jewish elite in Persian Yehud, the literati, critiqued as religious authoritarians who misused Scripture and misrepresented God. [*ExpTim* 9/22; *BBR* 32.4; *BL* 2022; *CBQ* 4/22].

☆   Estelle, Bryan D. *Salvation through Judgment and Mercy: The Gospel according to Jonah* (GAOT) 2005. An attractive, well-studied, biblical-theological reading (157pp.) by a prof at Westminster, California. Suitable for pastors and Bible study groups.

Fairbairn, Patrick. 1849. Another classic 19th century exposition, besides Martin, which would provide preachers with grist for the mill. Free online.

F   Fischer, Irmtraud. ‡ (IECOT).

Fretheim, T. E. [𝓜], *The Message of Jonah*, 1977. Warmly received in mainline circles as a theological exposition and literary analysis. It remains useful, if you make allowances for his critical stance. [*JBL* 9/79].

Fretheim, Terence E. [𝓜], *Reading Hosea–Micah* (ROT) 2013. See Hosea.

☆   **Goldingay, John.** [𝓜], *Hosea–Micah* (BCOT) 2021. See under Hosea.

✓   **Graybill, Rhiannon, John Kaltner, and Steven L. McKenzie.** ‡ (AYB-R) 2023. Replaces Sasson, and quite lengthy (well over 300pp.). Graybill is known for her feminist publications, especially in the field of gender and sexuality studies on the Hebrew Bible; see her *Texts after Terror* (OUP, 2021). Kaltner and McKenzie bring expertise in historical criticism, exegetical method, and Islamic studies. With the exception of bibliographical help, I prefer Sasson.

✓   **Hasel, Gerhard F.** [𝓜], *Jonah: Messenger of the Eleventh Hour*, 1976. A fine treatment of Jonah by an able biblical theologian.

☆   **Hoyt, JoAnna M.** *Amos, Jonah, & Micah* (EEC) 2019. See under Amos.

✓   **Hunter, Alistair G.** ‡ *The Judgement of Jonah*, 2022. The LHBOTS issue is a serious work of scholarship, includes a commentary, and makes for some unsettling reading. "Nineveh" is supposed to be recognized as a cipher for Jerusalem? [*JSOT* 47.5].

✓   **Jenson, Philip Peter.** [𝓜], *Obadiah, Jonah, Micah: A Theological Commentary*, 2008. See under Obadiah.

✓   **Kamp, Albert H.** ‡ *Inner Worlds: A Cognitive Linguistic Approach to the Book of Jonah*, ET 2004.

☆   Keddie, Gordon J. *Preacher on the Run* (Welwyn) 1986.

Kleinert, Paul. (Lange) ET 1874. Defends reading the account as historical.

Knight, G. A. F., and F. W. Golka. ‡ *The Song of Songs and Jonah* (ITC-E) 1988.

☆ **Lessing, R. Reed.** (ConcC) 2007. A large (451pp.), reverent exegetical and theological treatment from an OT scholar at Concordia Seminary. It is panned by critics for taking the fish story literally. He aims to help preachers and students in christological interpretation and with proclamation. The usual Lutheran move from Law to Grace is common here. The complaint of some is that, as he labors to explain elements of NT theology in Jonah, he seems to mute the "authentic voice of the OT." Students can expect to find penetrating exegesis of the Hebrew, especially in the area of literary parallels (biblical intertexts). [*JETS* 12/08; *BSac* 10/09; *VT* 60.1; *CBQ* 7/10].

Limburg, James. ‡ *Hosea–Micah* (I) 1988. See under Hosea. For expositors.

✓ **Limburg, James.** ‡ (OTL) 1993. More thorough and scholarly than his treatment of Jonah in the Interpretation series. Still, at 123pp. it appears brief compared to, say, Sasson's work, which I also find more interesting. P. R. Davies writes with characteristic bite, "Rarely do I think a commentary might have been longer; here is an exception." Certainly classed as one of the most important commentaries from the critical camp. Some (e.g., Jenson [*BSB* 9/96]) have recommended Limburg highly. [*ThTo* 4/94; *Int* 4/95; *JTS* 4/95; *VT* 10/95; *JSOT* 3/95; *Them* 10/95; *JETS* 3/96; *JSOT* 65; *HS* 1995, 1996].

Mackay, John L. *Jonah, Micah, Nahum, Habakkuk, Zephaniah* (Focus) 2008. Lengthy exposition (420pp.) from a Reformed perspective.

Magonet, Jonathan. *Form and Meaning: Studies in Literary Techniques in the Book of Jonah*, 1983.

☆ Martin, Hugh. (GS) 1870, 3rd ed. 1889. A classic theological exposition from the 19th century. Spurgeon rather overstated his case, even for his own day, when he wrote, "No one who has it will need any other." Still, it is very good, edifying, and was worth buying for its thoughtfulness, "unexcelled warmth and fervour" (Murray). In 1990 I made this a purchase recommendation (359pp.), but it is free online. Frankly, it is one of my favorite older commentaries on either Testament.

✓ **Niditch, Susan.** ‡ (Herm) 2023. The author trained at Harvard and has taught at Amherst since 1978. She is known for her research on folklore, orality in the production of Hebrew literature, and personal religion in the ANE. In something of a departure from the series, Niditch provides a large helping of reception history, alongside the expected historical criticism, textual criticism, technical notes, and exegetical treatment (123pp., plus a pleasingly full 22-page bibliography). As with Trible, she offers a stimulating narrative-critical reading. The interaction with scholarship, including conservatives such as Stuart, is impressive: for example, over 90% of pp.22–24 is footnotes. There certainly are longer exegeses in the world's libraries, but this is among the more detailed and learned. She offers little exposition here. Niditch is not enamored with approaches to reading The Twelve as an integrated whole, but she gives attention to such research (11). In my opinion, Sasson and Niditch are the best, most useful critical commentaries on Jonah (in English); I have yet to use Graybill et al. much. [*JETS* 9/23; *CBQ* 4/24; *BL* 2024].

☆ **Nixon, Rosemary A.** (BST) 2003. Though open to interpreting Jonah as allegory, Nixon is not insistent on that reading scheme. She is sharp in picking up literary features and offers a surprisingly full theological exposition (about 220pp. on four short chapters). There is real learning here, and students can profitably consult Nixon. Evangelical pastors will find this BST homiletically rich and stimulating. [*JETS* 9/04; *JSOT* 28.5].

Ogilvie, Lloyd J. *Hosea, Joel, Amos, Obadiah, Jonah* (WCC) 1992.

☆ Patterson, Richard. (CorBC) 2008. See under Hosea.

Perowne, T. T. *Obadiah and Jonah* (CBSC) 1889.

F   Petterson, Anthony. (EBTC)? Would cover Hosea to Micah.

☆ **Phillips, Elaine.** *Obadiah, Jonah & Micah* (Apollos) 2022. See under Obadiah.

☆ Phillips, Richard D. *Jonah & Micah* (REC) 2010. I have only used this briefly (355pp.). He is a veteran expositor (see Zechariah, Hebrews), and this is quite useful as an example of rich, well-studied gospel preaching. Because there is so much competition among devotional-sermonic books on Jonah, I suspect that his treatment of Micah (20 sermons, 220pp.) meets more of a need. [*JSOT* 41.5].

F Potgieter, Johannes H. ‡ (HCOT).

Redmond, Eric, Bill Curtis, and Ken Fentress. *Exalting Jesus in Jonah, Micah, Nahum, Habakkuk* (CCE) 2016.

☆ Robertson, O. Palmer. *Jonah: A Study in Compassion*, 1990. An exposition from one of today's more insightful OT theologians in the Reformed camp. Published by Banner.

Roop, Eugene F. [*M*], *Ruth, Jonah, Esther* (BCBC) 2002. See under Ruth.

Shao, Rosa Ching. (Asia) 2021. [*BL* 2022].

✓ **Simon, Uriel.** [*M*], (JPS) ET 1999. The first JPS outside the Pentateuch. "The author tries to combine the insights of the traditional Jewish commentators and modern biblical exegesis" [*JSOT* 89]. Though not of much length (xliii + 52pp.), this will set you back $50. Whew! A helpful commentary with much to offer in theological reflection (especially on the theme of God's compassion versus the prophet's demand for justice), grammatical analysis, and literary sensitivity. I find little here which could be termed higher-critical, except the notion that the story is fictionalized. [*Int* 10/00; *CBQ* 4/00; *RelSRev* 1/01; *DenvJ*; *JHebS* 3].

✓ Simundson, Daniel. ‡ *Hosea, Joel, Amos, Obadiah, Jonah, Micah* (AbOTC) 2005. See under Hosea.

☆ Sklar, Jay. "Jonah" in *Daniel–Malachi* (ESVEC) 2018. See Chase under Daniel.

Smith, Billy K., and Frank S. Page. *Amos, Obadiah, Jonah* (NAC) 1995. See under Amos.

✓ Tiemeyer, L. S. [*M*], *Jonah through the Centuries* (BBC) 2021. Extensive reception history, exceptionally well-done. [*JSOT* 47.5; *JTS* 10/23]. Other similar efforts are Erickson (above) and Yvonne Sherwood, *A Biblical Text and Its Afterlives: The Survival of Jonah in Western Culture* (2000).

✓ **Trible, Phyllis.** ‡ *Rhetorical Criticism: Context, Method, and the Book of Jonah*, 1995. From the Fortress series, Guides to Biblical Scholarship. She discusses the new rhetorical approaches and then applies the methods in interpreting Jonah. All in all, an excellent introduction to the newer synchronic approaches and a very rich reading of Jonah—she wrote her 1963 diss. on Jonah. [*CBQ* 7/96; *JBL* Win 95; *Int* 1/97; *JR* 1/97]. Mention should also be made of her Jonah contribution to *NIB*, 1996.

☆ **Tucker, W. Dennis.** *Jonah: A Handbook on the Hebrew Text* (BHHB) 2006, rev. 2018. The first vol. in the Baylor series (see under Commentary Series). Not a commentary in the traditional sense, this work helps students and pastors to make good progress in reading the Hebrew. The revised edition shifts away from an older model of discourse analysis (Longacre's) to use "generative grammar" (1). That is Holmstedt's more sophisticated linguistic approach, represented in the 2010 BHHB vol. on Ruth. There is certainly a long learning curve with the technical linguistic terminology, but students wrestling with it can gain so much. More for advanced Hebrew students? Regrettably, as Jarick notes [*JSOT* 43.5], the fledgling Hebrew reader—Jonah is often a first set text for such a student—may find the linguistics baffling. [*VT* 58.1; *ExpTim* 9/08; *JETS* 3/08; 2018: *CBQ* 7/19; *ExpTim* 5/19].

☆ **Walton, John H.** (EBCR) 2008. A very fine replacement for Ellison—one of the two or three best entries in the vol. The quality makes one wish for more than 38pp. The stance is conservative, believing "the Israelite audience would have considered the narrative a reflection of reality" (463), and he follows their lead. But this is not a "journalistic history." There is more straight exegesis here and less theological reflection. [*BL* 2010].

Widder, Wendy. (LRC) 2017. I have not seen it.

✓ **Wolff, H. W.** ‡ (ContC) ET 1986. See Obadiah above.

NOTES: (1) Consult the above section The Twelve Minor Prophets. (2) In this modern age with its short attention span, few OT books are as inviting as Jonah to the minister inclined to systematic book expositions. One article well worth reading prior to preaching on Jonah is John H. Stek's "The Message of the Book of Jonah," *CTJ* 4 (1969): 23–50. (3) See Kenneth Craig, "Jonah in Recent Research," *CurBS* 7 (1999): 97–118, and Aron Tillema, "The Book of Jonah in Recent Research," *CBR* 21 (2023): 145–77. (4) Critical scholars often speak of Jonah as a fictionalized story, perhaps in the genre of parable or allegory. Many church folk, too, consider it a fish tale, and the expositor certainly must deal with the genre question before commencing a sermon series. With my own congregation I made the following points (in simpler language). First, it is a mistake to make the story's historicity and matters of piscine/cetacean anatomy our major concern. See the sage remarks of Ferguson (p.45) on this point. Second, while mere stories can teach truth (e.g., Jesus's parables), there are still reasons in the Jonah text for reading the account in a more straightforward fashion, not as a parable. "The incident is reported very matter-of-factly" (Brown, p.23). On the all-important genre question, see Alexander above. Third, there have been similar stupendous stories told of "fish swallows person." Some are obviously fiction while others seem quite within the realm of history (cf. Sasson, pp.150–51; *Princeton Theological Review* 25 [1927] 630–42; but note also *ExpTim* 17 [1905/6]: 521 and *ExpTim* 18 [1906/7]: 239). Finally, our approach to Scripture ought to be "faith seeking understanding" (*fides quaerens intellectum*—Anselm). We begin our search with faith, not rationalism and positivism, which a priori reject all supernatural claims. Instead of the world's "seeing is believing" skepticism, we stand on Jesus's principle that only by believing will we see—see the glory of God (John 11:40).

# MICAH

★ **Andersen, Francis I., and David Noel Freedman.** [𝓜], (retired AB) 2000. Essentially completed in 1993, and specialists were kept waiting. Along with Waltke, one of the most comprehensive exegeses available, though lacking in the area of theological reflection. (Its strength is philology.) The brilliant coauthors have a history of collaboration—see Hosea and Amos above. Freedman was editor of AB and *ABD*. This 600-page work is definitely for the academically inclined; the average pastor has difficulty digesting the material here without surrendering the time necessary for personal reflection and meditation. Students appreciate the 67-page bibliography. The approach is cautiously critical, patiently exegetical, detail-oriented, and inclined to treat the text's final form. Do note that Hillers and Wolff (ContC) below are both valuable in their own way—perhaps just as valuable for scholarship as Andersen–Freedman. Pastors not interested in buying this more expensive and technical vol. should rely on Waltke and McComiskey–Longman for exegetical help. [CBQ 7/01; JTS 10/01; JETS 12/02; JBL Sum 02; JSS Spr 03; BSac 4/02; VT 53.2; JSOT 94; RelSRev 4/02; BBR 13.2; TJ Fall 04; Int 1/05; RBL; DenvJ 1/02 (Carroll R)].

★ Davis, Dale Ralph. (EPSC) 2010. A very fine Reformed exposition for pastors, including some discussion of the Hebrew. The whole book is aimed at the theological message and can be used devotionally (180pp.). There is less available currently to assist preachers with Micah, so I'm glad to see the appearance of Davis—he is more learned in the OT than some other expositors: Prior, Rick Phillips, Boice. [RTR 12/11]. Others offering good homiletical suggestions on Micah are Calvin and Craigie (see Twelve Minor Prophets above). Attractive critical expositions for pastors would be Brown and Limburg.

★ **Dempster, Stephen G.** (THC) 2017. If every vol. in the series were this fine and consistently useful, I'd buy the entire set. Building upon a solid exegetical base, Dempster moves on to display what Block terms "a whole-Bible theological acumen." The commentary is well laid-out, easy to use (even easier if you have Hebrew), clearly written, full of astute research, and passionate about the prophetic message (262pp.). He covers well the original historical contexts of the oracles, later literary contexts (including the Twelve), the structure of the book, connections among texts, and the need to read Micah as an integral whole (see 31–33). He is also shrewd about the history of scholarship. [*Chm* Spr 19; *BBR* 28.3; *JETS* 6/18; *Int* 10/19; *JSOT* 42.5; *CBQ* 4/20]. See also Dempster's ESVEC below.

★ Smith, Gary V. *Hosea/Amos/Micah* (NIVAC) 2001. See Hosea above.

★ Timmer, Daniel C. *Obadiah, Jonah and Micah* (TOTC-R) 2021. See Obadiah. For a quick exegetical reference on Micah, the old Tyndale by Waltke (see Baker under Obadiah), or the new Tyndale by Timmer is hard to beat.

★ **Waltke, Bruce K.** *A Commentary on Micah*, 2007. Don't get confused. Waltke has three different works on Micah. First came the Tyndale (1988), superb but brief [*JETS* 6/92]. In 1993 he gave us a fuller exegesis with much more discussion of the Hebrew; see the McComiskey-edited work below. Finally came the 2007 commentary, which is twice the length of the 1993 work and is the best evangelical exegesis (nearly definitive from the grammatico-historical angle). Students and scholarly pastors should all start here, after first doing their own exegesis. Waltke is such a good Hebraist! [*CTJ* 4/08; *RTR* 12/07; *CBQ* 1/08; *BBR* 19.1; *JTS* 4/08; *Int* 7/08; *BL* 2008; *VT* 58.3; *RelSRev* 12/08; *JETS* 3/08].

F Abernethy, Andrew. (Pillar).

✓ Achtemeier, Elizabeth. [𝓜], *Minor Prophets I* (NIBC) 1995. See Hosea above.

Alfaro, Juan I. ‡ (ITC-E) 1989. Interesting majority-world perspective on Micah's issues of wealth and poverty (only 85pp.). Many Westerners do need their eyes opened to the fact that economic justice is a theological and spiritual concern. [*CBQ* 1/91; *HS* 1991].

☆ **Allen, Leslie C.** [𝓜], (retired NICOT) 1976. See Joel above. Allen gives proportionally more space and careful attention to Micah than to the other three books covered: Jonah's four chapters get about 30pp., and Micah's seven chapters get 140pp. of exegesis. Unfortunately, Allen treats portions of chs. 4 and 7 as non-Mican, which I consider unnecessary. So often a more fragmentary reading causes the interpreter to miss points in the book's unfolding theology. For one attempt to redress this limitation (though he denies single authorship), see David Hagstrom, *The Coherence of the Book of Micah: A Literary Analysis* (1988). Also note Cuffey below. Allen is a good work to have, but I do not rave about it. See Nogalski below.

☆ **Barker, Kenneth L.,** and Waylon Bailey. *Micah, Nahum, Habakkuk, Zephaniah* (NAC) 1999. A very competent dispensational treatment by Barker that many pastors would prefer to the huge technical AB above. Bailey covers the three shorter books here. [*JETS* 9/00].

✓ **Becking, Bob.** ‡ (AYB-R) 2023. Replaces Andersen–Freedman and is 40% the length at 255pp. As expected, the author concentrates attention on compositional history and redaction criticism, though he does have his reservations about the method (14). Because the earlier AB vol. took a final-form approach, it was considerably more useful to pastors in trying to get at the message of the text. Honestly, I value this new vol. especially for the review of scholarship, Rabbinics, impressive bibliography, and textual notes. (Micah's Hebrew is quite the challenge, as my students discover each year.) Becking long taught at Utrecht. [*BL* 2024].

✓ **Ben Zvi, Ehud.** ‡ (FOTL) 2000. Here the erudite Jewish scholar, long at Alberta, has written a dense form-critical treatment (200pp.). It is a more critical interpretation than some other first-rate scholars have offered (e.g., Andersen–Freedman). As with all of FOTL, this is solely of interest to academics. Ben Zvi is well-known for advocating that form-critical researchers consider "prophetic book" as a form. What is revisionist here is that, while older typical forms are discarded as useful categories, his form-critical approach treats every unit in Micah as a "prophetic reading." [OTA 10/00; JTS 4/01; CBQ 1/01; JETS 3/02; JBL Win 01; HS 2002; VT 51.4; JSOT 94; RelSRev 4/03].

☆ Bentley, Michael. *Balancing the Books* (WCS on Micah and Nahum) 1994.

☆ Brown, William P. ‡ *Obadiah–Malachi* (WestBC) 1996. See Obadiah.

☆ Calvin, John. *Sermons on Micah*, ET 1990. An initial translation in hb was terribly expensive; Blair Reynolds was the translator (Mellen, 1990). Later, P&R released an inexpensive 424-page pb rendering by Ben Farley: *Sermons on the Book of Micah* (2003). This is different from the commentary and makes for fascinating reading.

Clark, David J., Norm Mundhenk, et al. *A Handbook on the Books of Obadiah, Jonah, and Micah* (UBS) 1993.

✓ Cuffey, Kenneth H. ‡ *The Literary Coherence of the Book of Micah*, 2015. [JSS Spr 18; JTS 10/16; JSOT 40.5; Them 41.3].

☆ Dempster, Stephen. "Micah" in *Daniel–Malachi* (ESVEC) 2018. See Chase under Daniel.

Ferreira, Johan., with Ruth House. (Asia) 2017. [BL 2022].

Fretheim, Terence E. [*M*], *Reading Hosea–Micah* (ROT) 2013. See Hosea.

✓ **Gignilliat, Mark S.** (ITC) 2019. An early vol. in the series and certainly a major theological (canonical) reading of about 250pp. The Beeson prof closely engages with the history of OT interpretation (a forte of his) in a redemptive-historical and trinitarian approach. He engages with "the Old Testament as an abiding theological witness whose authorial voice and governed deployment remain under the providential care of our Triune God" (13). Gignilliat is learned (St. Andrews PhD), an able Hebraist and exegete, and attentive to the best scholarship. Note: he includes untranslated German. An excellent book at a silly price ($130). [JSOT 44.5; VT 70.2; BBR 30.3; ETL 96.4].

☆ **Goldingay, John.** [*M*], *Hosea–Micah* (BCOT) 2021. See under Hosea.

☆ Hill, Andrew. (CorBC) 2008. See under Hosea.

✓ **Hillers, D. R.** ‡ (Herm) 1984. With 21pp. of introduction and 70pp. of packed exegesis, Hillers is more concise than Wolff and much more cautious in its critical approach (avoids redaction-critical analysis). A good, solid technical piece of work. Scholarly students and pastors (with money) wanting to do close work with the Hebrew text of Micah might be interested in obtaining this. Hillers was Stuart's first choice in 1990, but it has become dated. [TJ Fall 84; HS 1985].

☆ **Hoyt, JoAnna M.** *Amos, Jonah, & Micah* (EEC) 2019. See under Amos.

✓ Jacobs, Mignon R. [*M*], *The Conceptual Coherence of the Book of Micah*, 2001. A reworked Claremont dissertation, completed under Knierim and employing his concept-critical method. The prophecy is coherent, she argues, mainly as the result of redactors' work, contemporizing even the oldest material.

✓ **Jenson, Philip Peter.** [*M*], *Obadiah, Jonah, Micah: A Theological Commentary*, 2008. See under Obadiah.

☆ Kaiser, Walter. *Micah, Nahum, Habakkuk, Zephaniah, Haggai, Zechariah, Malachi* (WCC) 1993. If looking for homiletical help on these books, this vol. provides broad coverage (nearly 500pp.). It has pastoral insight and, as one of few WCC written by a professional OT scholar, is better researched than most. The average preacher will prefer, and be more than satisfied with, having Waltke, Davis, and Gary Smith on the shelf. Kaiser could be an inexpensive add-on (cheap s/h).

✓ **King, Philip.** ‡ *Amos, Hosea and Micah: An Archaeological Commentary*, 1988.

✓ Kleinert, Paul. (Lange) ET 1874.

✓ Limburg, James. ‡ *Hosea–Micah* (I) 1988. See under Hosea.

Mackay, John L. *Jonah, Micah, Nahum, Habakkuk, Zephaniah* (Focus) 2008. See Jonah.

✓ Mason, Rex. ‡ *Micah, Nahum, Obadiah* (OT Guides) 1991.

☆ **Mays, James L.** ‡ (retired OTL) 1976. Still one of the more suggestive critical commentaries available. It is thorough, readable, and asks many of the right theological questions. His position is a bit more critical than Allen's, for he denies most of the book to Micah. Not as worthy as his OTL vols. on Hosea and Amos. By the way, Mays later did exceptionally fine work on Psalms. See Smith-Christopher below. [*JBL* 6/78].

☆ **McComiskey, Thomas E., and Tremper Longman III.** (EBCR) 2008. The 1985 EBC, authored by McComiskey, is superseded by EBCR. McComiskey–Longman is to be considered among the finest brief (60pp.) evangelical treatments of this prophecy.

✓ **McKane, William.** ‡ 1998. From T&T Clark, the detailed critical exegesis runs to 256pp. Micah suffers division into three parts at the hands of this scholar, who did Jeremiah for ICC. Only chs. 1–3 are supposed to have come from the 8th century prophet. Few younger scholars today—outside Germany, I should say—have McKane's confidence that they can decide what the prophet could and could not have said (and therefore what must be ascribed to later redaction). For advanced students and scholars. [*BL* 1999; *EvQ* 7/00; *JTS* 10/99; *CBQ* 10/99; *OTA* 6/99; *RelSRev* 7/99; *JSS* Spr 01; *VT* 51.3].

McKeating, H. ‡ (CBC) 1971. See under Hosea.

✓ **Moor, Johannes C. de.** ‡ (HCOT) 2020. A major technical vol. (35-page intro and 340pp of exegesis) from a pioneer in structural analysis of Hebrew poetry. As a critic de Moor has a more respectful attitude toward the text. He regards a limited amount of the prophecy to come from a redactor and is tentative about his conclusions (14). He states that he was working on Micah for 60 years! Quite expensive ($95). This is a favorite of mine and will be a trusted reference work for decades to come. [*JSOT* 47.5].

☆ **Nogalski, James D.** ‡ (NICOT-R) 2024. Replaces Allen but is a stand-alone Micah vol. See Nogalski under Joel. Advanced students will be those most attracted to this, especially with its up-to-date bibliography, extensive textual notes, and discussion of cutting-edge scholarship (e.g., "Reading Micah in the Twelve," 26–37). He posits an eighth century "early core," with further "development of the book" (chs. 6–7) after Jerusalem's destruction, and a "later anthology" (chs. 4–5) of hopeful messages added in the postexilic era (1–2). Nogalski thinks we have prophecy after the fact: oracles are put in the mouth of the eighth century prophet, and the postexilic community is encouraged by hearing "prophecies" of the fall of Assyria and Babylon and the salvation of Zion. (These events have "already occurred and that knowledge provides comfort and confidence in Yahweh's fidelity" [12].) The exegesis (45–235) is clearly written, critical, and of greatest value to those reading the poetry in Hebrew. I missed seeing much interaction with Hillers, Waltke, and de Moor. Preachers find some reflection on contemporary application, more to the USA (see pp.134–35).

✓ **O'Brien, Julia.** ‡ (Wisdom) 2015. Though not a fan of this overtly feminist series, I recognize O'Brien's skill and insight as a critical commentator. [*CBQ* 4/17; *Int* 4/18; *JSOT* 40.5; *BibInt* 26.1].

Ogden, Graham S. ‡ *Amos and Micah* (Read) 2024. I have not seen it yet.

F Ollenburger, Ben. (BCBC).

F Petterson, Anthony. (EBTC)? Would cover Hosea to Micah.

☆ **Phillips, Elaine.** *Obadiah, Jonah & Micah* (Apollos) 2022. See under Obadiah.

☆ Phillips, Richard D. *Jonah & Micah* (REC) 2010. See under Jonah. This would be an excellent purchase for the preacher.

☆ Prior, David. *Joel, Micah, Habakkuk* (BST) 1998. See Joel above.

Redmond, Eric, Bill Curtis, and Ken Fentress. *Exalting Jesus in Jonah, Micah, Nahum, Habakkuk* (CCE) 2016.

F  Sharp, Carolyn. ‡ (Illum).

F  Sharp, Sheri L. Klouda. (ZECOT).

✓  **Shaw, Charles S.** ‡ *The Speeches of Micah: A Rhetorical-Historical Analysis*, 1993.

✓  **Simundson, Daniel J.** ‡ (NIB) 1996. See also the next entry.

✓  Simundson, Daniel. ‡ *Hosea, Joel, Amos, Obadiah, Jonah, Micah* (AbOTC) 2005. See under Hosea.

✓  Smith, J. M. P. ‡ (ICC) 1911.

✓  **Smith, Ralph L.** ‡ *Micah–Malachi* (WBC) 1984. Workmanlike, but not very stimulating. Not up to the standard of Stuart's *Hosea–Jonah*, and more critical. I had hoped for more theological discussion. Overall, it is a disappointment, though offering some help with the Hebrew. While students will consult Smith for papers, pastors will probably steer clear of this older WBC. In past editions I expressed my hope for a replacement. See Stuart below. [*RTR* 1/86; *ExpTim* 6/85; *JBL* 105.3; *JETS* 6/85; *HS* 1984].

✓  **Smith-Christopher, Daniel L.** ‡ (OTL-R) 2015. Replaces Mays (see above) and represents first-rate critical scholarship (227pp.), but with a political/ideological edge. The author has been productively engaged in sociohistorical and trauma studies of OT texts for decades, and has an excellent mind (Oxford DPhil). This will be a leading liberal interpretation for many years to come. Smith-Christopher moves (too?) quickly from exegesis to theological and cultural application (ancient world and today), much of it being a protest against Western affluence, abuse of the poor, colonial seizure of ancestral land (128), etc. With his Quaker background, he supports radical labor movements' opposition to war (99). He suggests "antimilitary populism as the ideological context for reading Micah" (20); I suggest that is reading "against the grain" in spots (e.g., 4:13; 5:6, 8–9). For another commentary of his, see the NIB on Daniel. [*JETS* 3/17; *Int* 7/17; *JSOT* 40.5; *JHebS* 17].

☆  **Soenksen, Jason R.** (ConcC) 2020. Approx. 625pp. with extensive textual notes on the Hebrew and versions, interaction with leading commentators (quotes in German, French, and Latin), discussion of NT use of Micah's oracles, and literary and rhetorical insights. Something of a repository of scholarship with much sifting through exegetical options, theological discussion, and many preaching helps. An admirable reference work for students and learned ministers.

F  Stuart, Douglas. *Micah–Malachi* (WBC-R). To replace Ralph Smith.

Vawter, Bruce. ‡ *Amos, Hosea, Micah* (OTM) 1981. See under Hosea.

☆  **Waltke, Bruce K.** *The Minor Prophets: An Exegetical and Expository Commentary*, Vol. 2, ed. Thomas E. McComiskey, 1993. Prior to the fuller 2007 work above, I urged people to start here. Still a very satisfying exegesis for pastors, who might even prefer this more condensed commentary (which is still quite full with 175 large pages).

✓  **Wolff, H. W.** ‡ (ContC) ET 1990. See under Hosea. Once again, as with the earlier BKAT vols. in translation, Wolff provides very valuable textual and exegetical notes, prior to probing theological reflection (240pp.). No question, this continues to be a standard reference commentary. The demerits of the earlier Wolff vols. (Hosea, Joel–Amos, Obadiah–Jonah) are present here too. [*SJT* 93.4; *Int* 7/91].

✓  Wolff, H. W. ‡ *Micah the Prophet*, ET 1981. A different work than his entry in ContC, as is clear from the German title, best translated *Conversing with Micah*. This contains exposition and essays with some rich homiletical thoughts. Seems less critical in its approach than his other commentaries because he addresses a different audience: the church rather than the academy. [*ExpTim* 1/82].

✓  **Zapff, Burkard M.** ‡ (IECOT) ET 2022. The orientation of this major scholarly work is historical-critical, with some attention given to other textual traditions besides the MT (LXX, and to a lesser degree the Peshitta). Zapff is on faculty at Katholischen Universität Eichstätt-Ingolstadt, and he earlier published a heavily redaction-critical monograph (*Habilitationsschrift*) on Micah (1997). [*JSOT* 47.5; *RelSRev* 6/23].

NOTES: (1) Consult the above section The Twelve Minor Prophets. (2) See Sheri L. Klouda, "Micah: An Annotated Bibliography," *SwJT* 46.1 (2003): 48–56. (3) Mignon Jacobs, "Bridging the Times: Trends in Micah Studies since 1985," *CBR* 4.3 (2006): 293–329.

# NAHUM

★ Bruckner, James K. *Jonah, Nahum, Habakkuk, Zephaniah* (NIVAC) 2004. See under Jonah. Other worthwhile pastoral commentaries are Boice, Calvin, Bridger, Craigie, and Kaiser; more critical are Achtemeier and Brown.

★ **Cook, Gregory D.** *Severe Compassion: The Gospel according to Nahum* (GAOT) 2016. Surprisingly full exposition (230pp.) from a Reformed angle, with plenty of exegetical expertise behind it (2014 Westminster Seminary PhD on Nahum). Valuable indeed for students as well as preachers, who may find it too full for their liking. [*JETS* 12/16; *Them* 42.1 (Timmer)].

★ **Longman, Tremper, III.** *The Minor Prophets: An Exegetical and Expository Commentary*, Vol. 2, ed. Thomas E. McComiskey, 1993. I prefer Longman's exegesis to Patterson's lengthier treatment (below). This was his first scholarly commentary, and it is well-informed and presented. He did much research and reflection on the divine warrior theme (*God Is a Warrior*, 1995) and expertly covers this prophecy about Yahweh's vengeance on Assyria. Longman and Robertson have been a well-matched pair.

★ **Renz, Thomas.** *The Books of Nahum, Habakkuk, and Zephaniah* (NICOT-R) 2021. It is a treat to have such a thorough (approx. 650pp.), well-rounded, and rich exegetical replacement for Robertson. Preachers and students alike appreciate Renz's literary and theological sensitivity, as well as the notes on the Hebrew. (Text-critical remarks are conservative toward the MT.) He treats the final form and has less confidence in redaction-critical approaches; he has a strong interest in prophetic rhetoric. Renz also prefers to read these prophets individually, unconvinced The Twelve ought to be read as a coherent whole. This is usually the first reference I now pull off the shelf for the three books, though he is somewhat independent-minded. [*JTS* 9/22 (Hadjiev); *VT* 72.3; *BBR* 32.1; *BL* 2022; *JTS* 10/22; *JETS* 6/22].

★ **Robertson, O. Palmer.** *Nahum, Habakkuk and Zephaniah* (retired NICOT) 1990. Quickly established itself as the standard conservative commentary on these books, i.e., for the pastor's study. Robertson excels at theological exposition, but has less for students in the way of scholarly helps (philology, grammar, textual criticism, etc). The relative neglect suffered by these books makes a detailed exegesis of the Hebrew text the more valuable. Even as an aging vol., Robertson retains much value for the preacher who wants to get at the message of the text. See Renz above. [*WTJ* Spr 92; *Them* 1/93; *Int* 1/92; *CBQ* 7/92; *JETS* 6/95; *HS* 1994; *CRBR* 1992].

★ **Timmer, Daniel C.** (ZECOT) 2020. Alongside Renz, my favorite scholarly commentary on this prophecy. Timmer teaches at Puritan Reformed Seminary in Grand Rapids and on the Faculté de Théologie Évangélique, Montreal. His interests and expertise are wide-ranging: ANE studies, history, literary and rhetorical research, and biblical theology. Though he has deep understanding of theories about the unity of the Twelve (see under Obadiah), Timmer "bypasses questions related to the Twelve as a collection in favor of biblical-theological reflection that reckons with the fundamental unity of the Bible as a whole" (58). There is so much here for the pastor who has Hebrew. Those without the language might choose to use Timmer's ESVEC below. [*Them* 46.1]. Students should note his Cambridge issue: *The Theology of Nahum, Habakkuk, and Zephaniah* (2024).

☆ Achtemeier, Elizabeth. [*M*], *Nahum–Malachi* (I) 1986. Good from a more conservatively critical perspective, even distinguished. You may think it suffers a bit, however, on account of its brevity (200pp.). As expected from this series, she focuses on the theological message and writes mainly for pastors. [*CRBR* 1988].

☆ **Armerding, Carl E.** (EBCR) 2008. A good, solid commentary made better with the revision. The 1985 EBC was easy to recommend, for we had hardly any exegetical commentaries on Nahum. Now we have several excellent ones, and the competition makes Armerding's EBCR seem less substantial, at least for students (47pp.).

☆ **Baker, David.** *Nahum, Habakkuk and Zephaniah* (retired TOTC) 1988. A thoughtful, well-researched vol. of 120pp., the first pick in my 1989 guide. All three Bible books are well-covered. See Snyman. [*EvQ* 1/91; *JETS* 9/92].

☆ Barker, Kenneth L., and **Waylon Bailey.** *Micah, Nahum, Habakkuk, Zephaniah* (NAC) 1999. Bailey covers the three shorter books here, and some judge his work to be a better guide than Barker's Micah commentary in this same vol. This is very well-done and of value to students as well as pastors. Years ago, it nearly deserved a place on the recommended purchase list. Praised by Longman.

☆ Bentley, Michael. *Balancing the Books* (WCS on Micah and Nahum) 1994.

Boadt, Lawrence. ‡ *Jeremiah 26–52, Habakkuk, Zephaniah, Nahum* (OTM) 1982.

✓ **Bosman, Jan Petrus.** ‡ *Social Identity in Nahum: A Theological-Ethical Enquiry*, 2008. Hard to follow at points, but the Stellenbosch diss. includes valuable commentary.

☆ Bridger, Gordon. *The Message of Obadiah, Nahum & Zephaniah* (BST) 2010. See Obadiah.

☆ Brown, William P. ‡ *Obadiah–Malachi* (WestBC) 1996. See Obadiah.

F Callender, Dexter. ‡ *Nahum, Habakkuk, and Zephaniah* (Illum).

F Cathcart, Kevin J. ‡ (ICC). Scholars anticipate good things, as the research on this Minor Prophet goes back to his much-cited *Nahum in the Light of Northwest Semitic* (1973).

✓ **Christensen, Duane.** (AYB) 2009. Not for the faint-hearted! He delivered an extremely detailed, conservatively critical exegesis (464pp.). Pastors won't invest in it (previously $85 list), but doctoral students will, if focusing on Nahum. The obvious strengths are exhaustiveness, poetic analysis (both larger structures and the fine points), interaction with previous interpreters, and bibliography (82pp.). Very simply, nothing compares with this in scope. The problem is digging through all the idiosyncratic "logoprosodic analysis" of "the numerical and musical composition of the biblical text." Here are examples: "the balance in terms of mora count becomes (24 + 16) ‖ (16 + 25) = 40 ‖ 41 morae" (389). "The invariant five tones on the central axis (C G D A E) provide five pentatonic modal permutations" (37). Got that? Some bright students might be able to learn German and digest Rudolph's great commentary or Heinz-Josef Fabry's vol. in Herders (2006) sooner than they could pick up on what the author is doing here. Christensen is obviously a genius, and you will discover he also has a large WBC on Deuteronomy. [*JETS* 9/10; *CBQ* 10/10 (Renz); *Int* 1/12; *JSOT* 36.5; *ExpTim* 11/11; *RelSRev* 6/11].

✓ Clark, David J., and Howard A. Hatton. (UBS) 1989. Covers Nahum to Zephaniah in 357pp. [*CRBR* 1992].

F Clendenen, Ray. (EBTC)? Would cover Nahum to Malachi.

✓ **Coggins, R. J.,** and S. P. Re'emi. ‡ *Nahum, Obadiah, Esther* (ITC-E) 1985. One of the best commentaries oriented more toward historical criticism (63pp.). See under Esther and Obadiah. The problem that pastors may find in Coggins's work, both here and elsewhere, is that he tends to emphasize the great distance between the ancient text and modern day and what terribly hard work it is to find the text's relevance.

✓ Coggins, Richard, and Jin H. Han. ‡ *Six Minor Prophets through the Centuries* (BBC) 2011. See Nahum. Reception history of Nahum to Malachi. [*JTS* 4/17].

F Crow, Timothy. *Nahum, Habakkuk and Zephaniah* (Apollos). By a Baptist pastor and adjunct prof at Ashland Seminary, who studied under Millard at Liverpool. Crow has strong historical and archaeological interests.

✓ Davidson, A. B. [*M*], (CBSC) 1896. Also covers Habakkuk and Zephaniah. One of the old mildly critical scholars from Britain.

✓ **Dietrich, Walter.** ‡ *Nahum, Habakkuk, Zephaniah* (IECOT) 2014, ET 2016. About 250pp, from a retired Bern professor. Certainly to be classed as an erudite, clearly written, and leading critical commentary. Dietrich seeks to blend older diachronic and newer synchronic approaches. The translation is less than felicitous. [*JSOT* 41.5; *JHebS* 17].

Eaton, J. H. ‡ (Torch) 1961. See under Obadiah.

F Firth, David. *Nahum, Habakkuk, Zephaniah* (EEC). An earlier report was Kevin Warstler.

✓ **Floyd, Michael H.** ‡ *Minor Prophets, Part 2* (FOTL) 1999. Over 650pp. of extremely detailed form-critical and structural analysis of the last six Minor Prophets. In keeping with developments in form-critical research, Floyd shows interest in synchronic concerns, as well as diachronic. Has become a standard reference work on these books. [*JTS* 4/01; *Int* 7/01; *CBQ* 4/02; *JSS* Spr 03; *HS* 2003; *VT* 51.4; *JSOT* 94; *RelSRev* 4/03; *JAOS* 122.1].

Gafney, Wilda C. M. ‡ *Nahum, Habakkuk, Zephaniah* (Wisdom) 2017. [*Int* 4/19; *JSOT* 42.5].

✓ Garcia-Treto, Francisco O. ‡ (NIB) 1996.

☆ Goldingay, John, and Pamela Scalise. [*M*], *Minor Prophets II* (NIBC) 2009. Goldingay covers Nahum to Haggai, and his colleague at Fuller Seminary treats Zechariah and Malachi. I've not had opportunity to do more than scan this vol., but these authors are recognized, productive scholars. Expect clarity and critical acumen in a briefer exegesis. [*RTR* 4/11; *BTB* 5/11; *RelSRev* 3/11; *JHebS* 12].

F Hernández, Dominick S. *Nahum, Habakkuk, and Zephaniah* (BGW).

☆ Kaiser, Walter. *Micah, Nahum, Habakkuk, Zephaniah, Haggai, Zechariah, Malachi* (WCC) 1993. See under Micah.

Kleinert, Paul. (Lange) ET 1874.

F Machinist, Peter. ‡ (Herm).

✓ Mack, Russell. *Neo-Assyrian Prophecy and the Hebrew Bible: Nahum, Habakkuk, and Zephaniah*, 2011. A Hebrew Union College PhD. [*JESOT* 2.2].

Mackay, John L. *Jonah, Micah, Nahum, Habakkuk, Zephaniah* (Focus) 2008. See Jonah.

☆ **Maier, Walter A.** 1959 (posthumous). A conservative Lutheran, technical exegesis, once the longest on Nahum in any language (370pp.). Christensen now wins that prize. Maier is an aging (essentially late 1940s) work—still a good purchase for in-depth study. But it should be used with a more up-to-date commentary, especially on issues like textual criticism. Was Stuart's favorite back in 1990; it wouldn't be now.

✓ Mason, Rex. ‡ *Micah, Nahum, Obadiah* (OT Guides) 1991.

✓ O'Brien, Julia. ‡ *Nahum, Habakkuk, Zephaniah, Haggai, Zechariah, Malachi* (AbOTC) 2004. A brief (326-page) and competent exegesis, sometimes regrettably out of sympathy with the theology of these prophets (e.g., pp.288–89). See her earlier commentary below. [*CBQ* 7/05; *Int* 1/06; *BL* 2005; *RBL*; *ExpTim* 10/05]. O'Brien's program for interpreting the prophets' theology is set out in *Challenging Prophetic Metaphor: Theology and Ideology in the Prophets* (2008) [*CBQ* 4/10].

✓ **O'Brien, Julia.** ‡ (Read) 2002. This is much more in-depth on Nahum (162pp.) than the AbOTC. She employs more postmodern synchronic analysis (intertextuality, etc.) in this work, which is of greater interest to students (especially those seeking a feminist reading) than to evangelical pastors. [*Them* Spr 04; *RelSRev* 1/04; *BBR* 16.1; *BL* 2006, 2010; *JHebS* 4].

☆ Patterson, Richard D. (CorBC) 2008. See under Hosea. He builds on WEC (below).

☆ **Patterson, Richard D.** *Nahum, Habakkuk, and Zephaniah* (WEC) 1991. Provides the Hebrew exegetical helps for the student which aren't so plentiful in Robertson. Patterson is admired as a leading evangelical OT scholar, and he was one of the OT editors for this series (with Ronald Youngblood). A full treatment (416pp.), this vol. went o/p with Moody but was reprinted by Biblical Studies Press.

Redmond, Eric, Bill Curtis, and Ken Fentress. *Exalting Jesus in Jonah, Micah, Nahum, Habakkuk* (CCE) 2016.

☆ **Roberts, J. J. M.** ‡ *Nahum, Habakkuk, Zephaniah* (OTL) 1991. Has been the leading critical interpretation of these three books (223pp.). The author is retired from Princeton Seminary and is a proficient text critic, exegete, and theologian. "Roberts' commentary . . . is a jewel" (Hillers), and would not be an unwise purchase for the pastor who enjoys digging deep. I bought it and found it rich. See also Roberts on Isaiah. [*CBQ* 7/93; *JBL* Spr 93; *ThTo* 4/92; *JR* 10/94; *JETS* 6/95; *BSac* 1/93].

Shao, Joseph Too, and Rosa Ching Shao. *Joel, Nahum, and Malachi* (Asia) 2021.

✓ Smith, J. M. P. ‡ (ICC) 1911.

✓ **Smith, Ralph L.** ‡ (WBC) 1984. See Micah above.

☆ **Snyman, S. D.** *Nahum, Habakkuk and Zephaniah* (TOTC-R) 2020. Replaces Baker. With his past research on the Twelve (see Malachi), this prof at U. of the Free State is a fine choice for this contribution. I think that many pastors would be satisfied with only this on their shelf for the three briefer prophecies.

✓ **Spronk, Klaas.** ‡ (HCOT) ET 1997. A very full, originally Dutch commentary for specialists and students: 144pp. of introduction and exegesis. Spronk is keen to detail as far as possible the historical setting of the prophecy, which he dates earlier (660 BC) than many scholars. [*JSOT* 79; *RelSRev* 7/98; *JBL* Spr 01].

F  Stuart, Douglas. *Micah–Malachi* (WBC-R). See under Micah.

F  Thomas, Heath A. *Nahum–Malachi* (BCOT). Goldingay was previously listed.

☆ Timmer, Daniel. "Nahum" in *Daniel–Malachi* (ESVEC) 2018. See Chase under Daniel.

✓ Tuell, Steven. ‡ *Reading Nahum–Malachi* (Read) 2016. [*Int* 1/18].

NOTES: (1) Consult the above section The Twelve Minor Prophets. (2) Michael Weigl, "Current Research on the Book of Nahum: Exegetical Methodologies in Turmoil?" *CurBS* 9 (2001): 81–130; and Barry A. Jones, "The Seventh-Century Prophets in Twenty-first Century Research," *CBR* 14 (2016): 129–75.

# HABAKKUK

★ Bruckner, James K. *Jonah, Nahum, Habakkuk, Zephaniah* (NIVAC) 2004. See under Jonah.

★ Lloyd-Jones, D. Martyn. *From Fear to Faith*, 1953. Rich exposition from a Reformed perspective. Those looking to make the purchase find it is republished with a 1965 exposition of Psalm 73 under the title *Faith Tried and Triumphant* (IVP, 1987). [*EvQ* 7/54]. Cf. Wright below.

★ **Renz, Thomas.** *The Books of Nahum, Habakkuk, and Zephaniah* (NICOT-R) 2021. See under Nahum.

★ **Robertson, O. Palmer.** (retired NICOT) 1990. See under Nahum. The more scholarly pastor would probably also want to consider purchasing Roberts below, in addition to these recommended works. See Renz above.

★ **Thomas, Heath A.** (THC) 2018. The author was given a great deal of space (224pp.) on such a brief prophecy; this vol. is longer than the THC on *Ecclesiastes* and nearly as long as those on *Joshua* and *Hosea*. If there is one regret, it is the relative brevity of the commentary on ch. 3 (143–53, including a two-page excursus). The theological essays at the back (157–211) set this book apart and add considerably to its value. Thomas draws from a number of the church fathers (Cyril, Irenaeus, Jerome, Theodoret) and Luther and Calvin. Pastors will appreciate how Thomas expounds the prophet's "robust vision of God and faithfulness, especially amid human prayer and pain" (9). Daniel Block's blurb says this "represents theological interpretation at its best." [*JETS* 3/19; *Int* 7/22; *JSOT* 43.5; *CBQ* 4/20].

★ **Turner, Kenneth J.** (ZECOT) 2023. Surprisingly lengthy, by a Toccoa Falls prof who trained at Southern Seminary (260pp.). Though I missed interaction with some major commentators (Calvin, Floyd, Hiebert, Nogalski, Renz, Sweeney, Thomas) and I would hesitate to call it brilliant, Turner's work is solidly researched and quite useful. There is a careful treatment of the Hebrew poetry, workmanlike application of discourse analysis (cf. Fuller, with whom he conversed "over a couple of years" [19]), and healthy theological reflection on the OT message and NT "appropriations." He is critical of a more forensic reading of 2:4b and likes to think of אמונה in terms of "fidelity" or "allegiance," with a relational focus (122–27).

❖ ❖ ❖ ❖ ❖ ❖

Achtemeier, Elizabeth. [𝓜], (I) 1986. See Nahum above.

☆ **Andersen, Francis I.** [𝓜], (AB) 2001. Advanced students and specialists have a treat here, but most pastors find this 400-page book daunting. Helpful in the areas of philology, poetic analysis, structure, textual criticism, and translation, but draws relatively few theological conclusions. See the other Andersen–Freedman AB vols. on Hosea, Amos, and Micah. If you are more academically oriented and plan to spend good time mining this prophecy to its depths, buy this. Because of a major price rise, Andersen is no longer a purchase recommendation; it was one for fifteen years. [*JTS* 10/02; *Int* 7/02; *ExpTim* 6/02; *BSac* 10/02; *Bib* 83.3; *JSOT* 99; *JHebS* 4].

☆ **Armerding, Carl E.** (EBCR) 2008. Happily, the fine 1985 EBC (a leading commentary of its time) has extended life in the EBCR (44pp.). On the negative side, there is less revision and update here. On the positive side, for students at least, there is fuller research and discussion of the Hebrew than in a lot of other EBCR contributions. See also his Obadiah and Nahum.

☆ Baker, D. (retired TOTC) 1988. See Nahum above.

☆ Barker, Kenneth L., and **Waylon Bailey.** *Micah, Nahum, Habakkuk, Zephaniah* (NAC) 1999. See Nahum above.

✓ Boadt, Lawrence. ‡ *Jeremiah 26–52, Habakkuk, Zephaniah, Nahum* (OTM) 1982. This is well-done, by a highly esteemed, conservatively critical Catholic scholar.

**Booth, Susan Maxwell.** (CSC) 2024. The author is Professor of Evangelism and Missions at Canadian (Southern) Baptist Theological Seminary in Cochrane, Alberta. She also has a background of studying literature and takes a strong interest in rhetoric and the literary structure of the prophecy. I have only seen a few pages of this vol. (dated 2023), said to be over 300pp.—the preview was not full enough to make a recommendation. Booth writes well and seems to have both a fine theological mind and a heart devoted to Christ.

☆ Brown, William P. ‡ *Obadiah–Malachi* (WestBC) 1996. See Obadiah.

☆ **Bruce, F. F.** *The Minor Prophets: An Exegetical and Expository Commentary*, Vol. 2, ed. Thomas E. McComiskey, 1993. Many students do not realize that Bruce, long the editor of the

NICNT series, also commented on OT books in an able, sober way—see "The Legacy of F. F. Bruce" in *CT*, Nov. 5, 1999. This is not one of my first picks on Habakkuk, but I have recommended the whole set above.

F   Callender, Dexter. ‡ *Nahum, Habakkuk, and Zephaniah* (Illum).

F   Cathcart, Kevin J. ‡ (ICC–new series). See under Nahum.

✓   Clark, David J., and Howard A. Hatton. (UBS) 1989. See Nahum above.

F   Clendenen, Ray. (EBTC)? Would cover Nahum to Malachi.

✓   Coggins, Richard, and Jin H. Han. ‡ (BBC) 2011. See Nahum.

F   Crow, Timothy. *Nahum, Habakkuk and Zephaniah* (Apollos). See Nahum.

Currid, John D. (Welwyn) 2009. I imagine this is excellent for expositors, but I have not seen it. Currid has published much on the Pentateuch and been an OT professor at RTS for decades.

Davidson, A. B. [𝓜], (CBSC) 1896. See Nahum above.

✓   **Dietrich, Walter.** ‡ *Nahum, Habakkuk, Zephaniah* (IECOT) 2014, ET 2016. See Nahum.

Eaton, J. H. ‡ (Torch) 1961. See under Obadiah.

☆   Firth, David. "Habakkuk" in *Daniel–Malachi* (ESVEC) 2018. See Chase under Daniel.

F   Firth, David. *Nahum, Habakkuk, Zephaniah* (EEC). An earlier report had Kevin Warstler.

✓   **Floyd, Michael H.** ‡ *Minor Prophets, Part 2* (FOTL) 1999. See Nahum above.

✓   **Fuller, David J.** *A Discourse Analysis of Habakkuk*, 2020. An enormous Brill release (approx. 380pp.) of his McMaster PhD (under Boda), applying Systemic-Functional Linguistics. Anyone doing detailed, scholarly work on this brief prophecy should consult Fuller. Fine bibliography! [*JSOT* 44.5; *JSS* Aut 21; *RelSRev* 9/22; *JETS* 12/20].

Gafney, Wilda C. M. ‡ *Nahum, Habakkuk, Zephaniah* (Wisdom) 2017. See Nahum.

☆   Goldingay, John, and Pamela Scalise. *Minor Prophets II* (NIBC) 2009. See under Nahum.

✓   Gowan, Donald E. ‡ *The Triumph of Faith in Habakkuk*, 1976. This useful theological study was published by John Knox Press. Suitable even for a lay readership.

✓   **Haak, Robert D.** ‡ *Habakkuk*, 1992. A revised Chicago PhD, which treats the political context, contains extensive textual and translation notes—essentially a technical commentary—and received much attention in scholarship. [*CBQ* 7/93; *JBL* Fall 93; *JTS* 4/93; *JSS* Aut 98; *VT* 46.3; *JSOT* 59; *BSac* 1/95; *HS* 1993].

✓   Hadjiev, Tchavdar S. *Joel, Obadiah, Habakkuk and Zephaniah*, 2020. See under Joel.

✓   Harper, Joshua L. *Habakkuk, Zephaniah, and Haggai: A Handbook on the Greek Text*, 2023. Not a reference work normally noted in this guide, but my former colleague's study is valuable for LXX/Greek and text-critical research. He builds on his Cambridge PhD on Habakkuk.

F   Hernández, Dominick S. *Nahum, Habakkuk, and Zephaniah* (BGW).

✓   **Hiebert, Theodore.** ‡ (NIB) 1996. Rather brief. His research goes back to a 1984 Harvard PhD, published as *God of My Victory: The Ancient Hymn of Habakkuk 3* (1986).

Idestrom, Rebecca G. S. (PentC) 2020. Well-done in brief compass.

☆   Kaiser, Walter. *Micah, Nahum, Habakkuk, Zephaniah, Haggai, Zechariah, Malachi* (WCC) 1993. See under Micah.

Kleinert, Paul. (Lange) ET 1874.

Ko, Grace. *Theodicy in Habakkuk*, 2014. [*JHebS* 16].

✓   Mack, Russell. *Neo-Assyrian Prophecy and the Hebrew Bible*, 2011. See Nahum.

Mackay, John L. *Jonah, Micah, Nahum, Habakkuk, Zephaniah* (Focus) 2008. See Jonah.

Marbury, E. *Obadiah and Habakkuk*, 1650. See under Obadiah.

✓   Mason, Rex. ‡ *Zephaniah, Habakkuk, Joel* (OT Guides) 1994.

✓   O'Brien, Julia. ‡ *Nahum, Habakkuk, Zephaniah, Haggai, Zechariah, Malachi* (AbOTC) 2004. See under Nahum.

☆   **Patterson, Richard.** (WEC) 1993. See under Nahum. Here he builds on his article, "The

Psalm of Habakkuk," in *Grace Theological Journal* 8 (1987): 163–94. This commentary on Habakkuk may be the best researched in the vol. and should be more widely available than it is.

☆ Patterson, Richard. (CorBC) 2008. See under Hosea.

F Prinsloo, Gert T. M. ‡ (HCOT).

☆ Prior, David. *Joel, Micah, Habakkuk* (BST) 1998. See Joel above.

   Redmond, Eric, Bill Curtis, and Ken Fentress. *Exalting Jesus in Jonah, Micah, Nahum, Habakkuk* (CCE) 2016.

☆ **Roberts, J. J. M.** ‡ *Nahum, Habakkuk, Zephaniah* (OTL) 1991. See under Nahum.

✓ **Smith, Ralph L.** ‡ (WBC) 1984. See Micah above.

☆ **Snyman, S. D.** *Nahum, Habakkuk and Zephaniah* (TOTC-R) 2020. See Nahum.

F Stuart, Douglas. *Micah–Malachi* (WBC-R). See under Micah.

✓ Szeles, Maria E. ‡ *Habakkuk, Zephaniah* (ITC-E) 1987. [*JETS* 3/91; *Evangel* Spr 90; *HS* 1989].

F Thomas, Heath A. *Nahum–Malachi* (BCOT). Goldingay was previously listed. The forthcoming work, of necessity, will be briefer on Habakkuk than the THC above.

✓ Timmer, Daniel C. *The Theology of Nahum, Habakkuk, and Zephaniah*, 2024. From CUP.

✓ Tuell, Steven. ‡ *Reading Nahum–Malachi* (Read) 2016. See Nahum.

F Vanderhooft, David. ‡ (Herm).

✓ Ward, W. H. ‡ (ICC) 1911.

☆ Wiersbe, Warren W. *From Worry to Worship*, 1983. This popular exposition rivals Lloyd-Jones. Wiersbe is easier reading, but Lloyd-Jones is more penetrating and forceful.

   Wright, Christopher J. H. *Hearing the Message of Habakkuk*, 2024. Probably in the same, fine mold as his pastoral expositions of Daniel and Ecclesiastes. I've not seen it but strongly urge preachers to consider it.

NOTES: (1) Consult the above section The Twelve Minor Prophets. (2) Oskar Dangl, "Habakkuk in Recent Research," *CurBS* 9 (2001): 131–68; and Barry A. Jones, "The Seventh-Century Prophets in Twenty-first Century Research," *CBR* 14 (2016): 129–75. (3) E. Ray Clendenen, "Salvation by Faith or Faithfulness in the Book of Habakkuk?" *BBR* 24.4 (2014): 505–13.

# ZEPHANIAH

★ **Berlin, Adele.** ‡ (AB) 1994. One of the three most complete scholarly commentaries available on this Bible book (too much of an expense to recommend to pastors for purchase?). The Jewish author is a shrewd exegete, shows good respect for the text, and treats the final form. She has gained quite a reputation for her analysis of rhetorical devices, particularly parallelism, in the Hebrew Bible. The AB's literary sensitivity and "close reading" is the perfect complement to Robertson's theological exposition. Students will also gravitate toward Sweeney, Vlaardingerbroek, and Roberts. Pastors who would prefer an evangelical commentary can replace this recommendation with Bailey. [*SwJT* Spr 96; *JETS* 9/98; *Int* 10/96; *CBQ* 1/97].

★ Bruckner, James K. *Jonah, Nahum, Habakkuk, Zephaniah* (NIVAC) 2004. See under Jonah. Other expository helps for the pastor's study, of which there are fewer on this prophecy, would be Calvin, Craigie, Boice, and Mackay. More critical but well-done are Achtemeier and Brown.

★ Duguid, Iain M., and Matthew P. Harmon. *Zephaniah, Haggai, Malachi* (REC) 2018. The first two sermonic expositions are Duguid's work, while that of Malachi is a cooperative effort—Harmon previously was Duguid's ministerial associate. Valuable indeed for all preachers (approx. 190pp.). See Duguid's many books on Ezekiel, Numbers, Ruth, Esther, Song of Songs, etc.

★ **Motyer, J. Alec.** *The Minor Prophets: An Exegetical and Expository Commentary*, Vol. 3, ed.

Thomas E. McComiskey, 1998. I have already recommended the set for purchase above. Motyer was a veteran at writing commentaries, and I argue he did his best work on the prophetic literature. This is excellent. [*BSac* 1/99].

★ **Renz, Thomas.** *The Books of Nahum, Habakkuk, and Zephaniah* (NICOT-R) 2021. See Nahum. His 225-page commentary on this prophet is wonderfully thorough, perceptive, and pastoral; it is becoming my favorite.

★ **Robertson, O. Palmer.** (retired NICOT) 1990. See under Nahum. His 95-page treatment of Zephaniah is especially fine.

Achtemeier, Elizabeth. [𝓜], (I) 1986. See Nahum above.

✓ **Ball, Ivan J., Jr.** *Zephaniah: A Rhetorical Study*, 1988. A large PhD from the 1970s (308pp.), published much later, and one of the best early applications of Muilenburg's approach. Praised by Francis Andersen and often cited by Berlin.

☆ **Baker, D.** (retired TOTC) 1988. See Nahum above. Was Stuart's favorite in 1990.

☆ Barker, Kenneth L., and **Waylon Bailey.** *Micah, Nahum, Habakkuk, Zephaniah* (NAC) 1999. See Nahum above. With over 120 quality pages on this brief prophecy, the well-read Bailey deserves wide use by both students and pastors.

✓ **Bennett, Robert A.** ‡ (NIB) 1996. An approachable, liberal interpretation (45pp.).

✓ **Ben Zvi, E.** ‡ *A Historical-Critical Study of the Book of Zephaniah*, 1991. Contains a lengthy commentary, which reveals the author's overriding form-critical concerns, and a vast section of exegetical and thematic notes. Regarded as one of the three or four most important technical exegeses, published by de Gruyter. [*JSOT* 58].

Boadt, Lawrence. ‡ *Jeremiah 26–52, Habakkuk, Zephaniah, Nahum* (OTM) 1982.

☆ Bridger, Gordon. *The Message of Obadiah, Nahum & Zephaniah* (BST) 2010. See Obadiah.

☆ Brown, William P. ‡ *Obadiah–Malachi* (WestBC) 1996. See Obadiah.

F Callender, Dexter. ‡ *Nahum, Habakkuk, and Zephaniah* (Illum).

F Cathcart, Kevin J. ‡ (ICC–new series). See under Nahum.

✓ Clark, David J., and Howard A. Hatton. (UBS) 1989. See Nahum above.

F Clendenen, Ray. (EBTC)? Would cover Nahum to Malachi.

✓ Coggins, Richard, and Jin H. Han. ‡ (BBC) 2011. See Nahum.

F Crow, Timothy. *Nahum, Habakkuk and Zephaniah* (Apollos). See Nahum.

✓ Davidson, A. B. [𝓜], (CBSC) 1896. See Nahum above.

F DeRouchie, Jason S. (ZECOT). In the meantime see ESVEC.

☆ DeRouchie, Jason S. "Zephaniah" in *Daniel–Malachi* (ESVEC) 2018. See Chase under Daniel.

✓ **Dietrich, Walter.** ‡ *Nahum, Habakkuk, Zephaniah* (IECOT) 2014, ET 2016. See Nahum.

Eaton, J. H. ‡ (Torch) 1961. See under Obadiah.

F Firth, David. *Nahum, Habakkuk, Zephaniah* (EEC). An earlier report had Kevin Warstler.

✓ **Floyd, Michael H.** ‡ *Minor Prophets, Part 2* (FOTL) 1999. See Nahum above.

Fries, Micah. *Exalting Jesus in Zephaniah, Haggai, Zechariah, Malachi* (CCE) 2015.

Gafney, Wilda C. M. ‡ *Nahum, Habakkuk, Zephaniah* (Wisdom) 2017. See Nahum.

☆ Goldingay, John, and Pamela Scalise. *Minor Prophets II* (NIBC) 2009. See under Nahum.

✓ Hadjiev, Tchavdar S. *Joel, Obadiah, Habakkuk and Zephaniah*, 2020. See under Joel.

F Hernández, Dominick S. *Nahum, Habakkuk, and Zephaniah* (BGW).

✓ **House, Paul R.** *Zephaniah: A Prophetic Drama*, 1988. This dissertation for Southern Baptist Seminary has a unique approach and includes a brief commentary. The evangelical author also has capable works on 1 & 2 Kings, Lamentations, Daniel, and a full-length OT Theology. [*JBL* Fall 00; *CBQ* 7/90; *Int* 10/90; *Chm* 103.4].

Idestrom, Rebecca G. S. (PentC) 2020. Again, well-done.

☆ Kaiser, Walter. (WCC) 1993. See under Micah.

✓ **Kapelrud, Arvid S.** ‡ *The Message of the Prophet Zephaniah: Morphology and Ideas*, 1975. A major scholarly work out of Oslo, now available online (Internet Archive).

✓ Kleinert, Paul. (Lange) ET 1874.

✓ Mack, Russell. *Neo-Assyrian Prophecy and the Hebrew Bible*, 2011. See Nahum.

Mackay, John L. *Jonah, Micah, Nahum, Habakkuk, Zephaniah* (Focus) 2008. See Jonah.

✓ Mason, Rex. ‡ *Zephaniah, Habakkuk, Joel* (OT Guides) 1994.

✓ O'Brien, Julia. ‡ *Nahum, Habakkuk, Zephaniah, Haggai, Zechariah, Malachi* (AbOTC) 2004. See under Nahum.

☆ **Patterson, Richard D.** (WEC) 1993. See under Nahum.

☆ Patterson, Richard D. (CorBC) 2008. See under Hosea.

☆ **Roberts, J. J. M.** ‡ *Nahum, Habakkuk, Zephaniah* (OTL) 1991. See under Nahum.

✓ Ryou, Daniel Hojoon. ‡ *Zephaniah's Oracles against the Nations: A Synchronic and Diachronic Study of Zephaniah 2:1–3:8*, 1995. A research for the Free University of Amsterdam.

Smith, Gary V., and Timothy D. Sprankle. *Zephaniah–Malachi* (Kerux) 2020. I have not seen this, but it is said to be a model commentary in the series. [*JETS* 3/21].

✓ Smith, J. M. P. ‡ (ICC) 1911.

✓ **Smith, Ralph L.** ‡ (WBC) 1984. See Micah above.

☆ **Snyman, S. D.** *Nahum, Habakkuk and Zephaniah* (TOTC-R) 2020. See Nahum.

F   Stuart, Douglas. *Micah–Malachi* (WBC-R). See under Micah.

✓ **Sweeney, Marvin A.** ‡ (Herm) 2003. The author teaches at Claremont. This is an exceedingly thorough and rigorous text-critical and (newer style) form-critical analysis, the conclusions of which can be compared with Floyd and Ben Zvi. Conservative readers like Sweeney's arguments for an earlier, preexilic dating (with little secondary material). For a more diachronic approach, it is the authoritative commentary to consult (but cf. Vlaardingerbroek). Berlin's more literary reading complements it nicely. [*JTS* 10/04; *CBQ* 10/04; *JSOT* 28.5; *JETS* 12/04; *Int* 10/05; *VT* 57.1; *JNES* 7/08; *CurTM* 6/05; *RBL*; *JHebS* (Watts)].

✓ Szeles, Maria E. ‡ *Habakkuk, Zephaniah* (ITC-E) 1987. [*JETS* 3/91; *HS* 1989].

✓ Tuell, Steven. ‡ *Reading Nahum–Malachi* (Read) 2016. See Nahum.

F   Thomas, Heath A. *Nahum–Malachi* (BCOT). Goldingay was previously listed.

✓ Timmer, Daniel C. *The Theology of Nahum, Habakkuk, and Zephaniah*, 2024. From CUP.

✓ Tuell, Steven. ‡ *Reading Nahum–Malachi* (Read) 2016. See Nahum.

✓ **Vlaardingerbroek, Johannes.** ‡ (HCOT) ET 1999. A 222-page translation from the Dutch, called "a splendid tool" by Mason [*JSOT* 89]. The thorough exegesis provided here will be consulted by students of the prophets for decades. Vlaardingerbroek rivals Berlin in quality and depth, though the exegetical method has a different focus (more historical-critical), and he is not as practiced a literary critic as she. [*RelSRev* 4/00].

☆ **Walker, Larry.** (EBCR) 2008. I have not used this 45-page commentary much but am glad there is a revised and updated work. Walker's work was not considered one of the best in the 1985 EBC, but he is a capable scholar and has done a thorough rewrite here, with many notes on the Hebrew. Worth having.

☆ Webber, Daniel. *Zephaniah: The Coming of the Warrior King* (Welwyn) 2004. Somehow missed in previous editions. It is surprisingly full (190pp.) as an exposition. The author served as a pastor and then as Director of European Missionary Fellowship.

NOTES: (1) Consult the above section The Twelve Minor Prophets. (2) For a review-essay on scholarship, appearing prior to his commentary, see Marvin A. Sweeney, "Zephaniah: A Paradigm for the Study of the Prophetic Books," *CurBS* 7 (1999): 119–45. (3) Note Barry A. Jones, "The Seventh-Century Prophets in Twenty-first Century Research," *CBR* 14 (2016): 129–75.

# HAGGAI

★ **Boda, Mark J.** *Haggai, Zechariah* (NIVAC) 2004. A well-researched exposition by a Westminster Seminary grad who did a Cambridge PhD on Zechariah. Boda teaches at McMaster and is considered a leading scholar on this literature. After an 84-page Introduction, he devotes 90pp. to Haggai and 370pp. to Zechariah. He is not as courageous as I wish he were on the higher-critical issue of a divided Zechariah. Both exegetically and theologically, the work is deeply satisfying; a little less satisfying is his guidance in application. For additional help in discerning the contemporary relevance of these books, one could look up the BST vols. or, from the more critical side, Achtemeier and Brown. [*CTJ* 4/08]. Students gladly use another Boda work too: *Haggai and Zechariah Research: A Bibliographic Survey* (2003) [*BL* 2005; *RelSRev* 1/05; *VT* 55.3; *ExpTim* 11/04].

★ Fyall, Robert. *The Message of Ezra and Haggai* (BST) 2010. See Ezra. This is an excellent help to expositors, written by a man with a good theological head and an ability to probe the relevance of the Bible's message today (46pp.). He has repeatedly preached on Haggai, and that makes all the difference. If one wants sermons specifically, see Duguid's REC, which some would argue is equally useful.

★ **Jacobs, Mignon R.** [𝓜], *The Books of Haggai and Malachi* (NICOT-R) 2018. Replaces Verhoef. An able Hebrew exegete, trained at Claremont (under Knierim), Jacobs does well in discussing the historical backdrop, the Hebrew (in transliteration), the literary structure, and flow of the oracles. She has produced a full, major commentary (336pp.), informed by scholarship, with plenty of detailed textual notes. Her preference often is not to provide "a single, decisive interpretation," but to allow interpretive options to "coexist" even where they are "potentially competing" (xiii). Much can be learned from Jacobs, but there are downsides. She doesn't use *BHQ*. At points, I find her writing less than clear, and her use of the term "intertextual" is confusing (though I have for over 30 years closely read the scholarship on intertextuality). Her interpretation of the difficult divorce text, Mal 2:16, is less plausible (251)—see Hugenberger under Malachi. In her feminism Jacobs will go to some lengths to avoid a masculine pronoun for God (xiv). Finally, there is less discussion of theology and NT connections than I am accustomed to in the series. To sum up: more geared for students than pastors. [*Presb* Fall 18; *BBR* 28.3; *CBQ* 4/19 (Hill); *JETS* 9/18; *Int* 1/20; *JSOT* 42.5; *Them* 44.2].

★ **Motyer, J. Alec.** *The Minor Prophets: An Exegetical and Expository Commentary*, Vol. 3, ed. Thomas E. McComiskey, 1998. I have already recommended the set for purchase above. This is as valuable as Verhoef and is a little briefer. Motyer instinctively drives to the heart of a passage and its theological message. He has a strongly conservative stance on critical issues. See Zephaniah.

★ **Petterson, Anthony R.** *Haggai, Zechariah & Malachi* (Apollos) 2015. The author lectures at Morling College in Australia, having previously pastored Baptist churches in Sydney and Dublin. His doctoral research was on Zechariah (see under Zechariah). His commentary is of good length (over 400pp.) and shows him to be an adept exegete. After 20pp. of General Introduction, situating the prophets in their historical, canonical, and biblical-theological contexts, Haggai receives a 45-page treatment, with a fresh translation, notes on the text (text-critical, lexical, and syntactical), discussion of the form and structure, exegetical comment, and theological explanation. Each prophecy is treated more on its own, with less attention paid to interpretation of canonical placement within The Book of the Twelve. This Apollos vol. benefits both students and pastors, who will appreciate the references to the NT. [*JETS* 3/16 (Duguid); *JSOT* 40.5; *Them* 40.3]. Two notes for students: first, the older Verhoef is far more extensive (150pp.) than Petterson on Haggai and should not be missed; second, the major scholarly works are Koopmans, Meyers–Meyers, Petersen, Meadowcroft, and Wolff.

★ **Taylor, Richard A., and E. Ray Clendenen.** *Haggai, Malachi* (NAC) 2004. A vol. so thoroughly researched and well-done that one may call it a replacement for Verhoef's conservative exegesis. Both Taylor's "Haggai" and Clendenen's slightly less technical "Malachi" are competent and full (496pp. total). There are differences in hermeneutical approach between these two. While Taylor pursues a traditional grammatico-historical exegesis, long taught at his own Dallas Seminary, Clendenen practices discourse analysis. Boda and Motyer provide more biblical-theological reflection than Taylor. Yes, there is a dispensational orientation here, but it is not so noticeable. [*CBQ* 7/05; *JETS* 9/05; *BSac* 7/06; *SwJT* Fall 04].

✓ Achtemeier, Elizabeth. [*M*], (I) 1986. See Nahum above.

Alden, Robert L. (EBC) 1985. Fine work from a well-known evangelical who taught at Denver Seminary, now with the Lord. See Merrill's EBCR below.

☆ **Baldwin, Joyce G.** *Haggai, Zechariah, Malachi* (retired TOTC) 1972. This excellent work used to be the first choice for pastors, and it remains a smart purchase. In 2010 I wrote of the need for an updated TOTC after Meyers, Petersen, Verhoef, and Wolff. Now see the Hill replacement.

✓ **Barker, John Robert.** ‡ *Disputed Temple: A Rhetorical Analysis of the Book of Haggai*, 2017. A major study (about 290pp. with bibliography), treating text-critical, redaction-critical, and sociohistorical matters as well as rhetoric. Barker includes a commentary of 110pp. He teaches at Catholic Theological Union, Chicago. [*CBQ* 1/20].

Barnes, W. E. ‡ *Haggai, Zechariah, Malachi* (CBSC) 1917.

☆ Bentley, Michael. *Building for God's Glory* (WCS on Haggai and Zechariah) 1989.

✓ Boda, Mark, and Michael Floyd, eds. *Tradition in Transition: Haggai and Zechariah 1–8 in the Trajectory of Hebrew Theology*, 2008. [*CBQ* 1/10; *BL* 2010; *RelSRev* 3/11].

☆ Brown, William P. ‡ *Obadiah–Malachi* (WestBC) 1996. See Obadiah.

✓ **Clark, David J., and Howard A. Hatton.** *A Handbook on Haggai, Zechariah, and Malachi* (UBS) 2002. [*CBQ* 10/04].

F Clendenen, Ray. (EBTC)? Would cover Nahum to Malachi.

✓ Coggins, Richard, and Jin H. Han. ‡ (BBC) 2011. See Nahum. Note too Coggins's brief *Haggai, Zechariah, Malachi* (1987) in OT Guides.

F Cook, Stephen. ‡ *Haggai & Zechariah* (Illum).

F Coover-Cox, Dorian, and Daniel Lowery. *Haggai, Zechariah, Malachi* (EEC)?

Davis, Stacy. ‡ *Haggai, Malachi* (Wisdom) 2015. [*CBQ* 4/17; *Int* 4/18; *JSOT* 42.5].

✓ Driver, Samuel R. ‡ (Century Bible) 1906. See Nahum above.

☆ Duguid, Iain M. *Haggai, Zechariah, Malachi* (EPSC) 2010. I was in a quandary because I wanted to recommend that pastors purchase this rich, succinct theological exposition (255pp.). It is built on exegetical decisions (as far as I have checked) with which I agree all the way down the line. The problem was that, with a larger font and being written on a popular level, the book didn't have enough substance for its high price in hb. It is now out in pb but still costs about $30. Unless they look closely, students may miss the fact that Duguid offers his own (fine) translation. See the author's other works on Genesis, Ezekiel, Ruth & Esther, and Daniel.

☆ Duguid, Iain, and Matthew P. Harmon. *Zephaniah, Haggai, Malachi* (REC) 2018. See Zephaniah above. The sermons here (4) are about the best I've found on Haggai.

✓ **Floyd, Michael H.** ‡ *Minor Prophets, Part 2* (FOTL) 1999. See Nahum above.

✓ Foster, Robert L. ‡ *The Theology of the Books of Haggai and Zechariah*, 2021. Fairly full treatment (over 250pp.) both of blocks of text and of the books' overall theological concerns. From CUP. [*HBT* 44.1; *ExpTim* 6/21; *BL* 2022; *Int* 4/23].

Fries, Micah. *Exalting Jesus in Zephaniah, Haggai, Zechariah, Malachi* (CCE) 2015.

☆ Goldingay, John, and Pamela Scalise. *Minor Prophets II* (NIBC) 2009. See under Nahum.

F   Hanson, Paul D. ‡ (Herm). I doubt this will appear; Hanson passed away in 2023.

☆ Hill, Andrew. (CorBC) 2008. See under Hosea.

☆ **Hill, Andrew.** *Haggai, Zechariah and Malachi* (TOTC-R) 2012. The Wheaton prof builds upon his earlier work in both CorBC (on all three prophets) and AB (on Malachi). He gives special attention to intertextual relationships (12), and this compact commentary (about 350pp.) contains much fine exegesis and some theological interpretation. Like Baldwin, it includes more detail (e.g., discussion of Hebrew) than some other TOTC, and lay readers may struggle to follow it at points. Baldwin is still of great value, but Hill has the benefit of drawing on four decades of more recent research. (E.g., Hill points to the excellent scholarship on Zechariah's prologue that "seeks to tie both halves of Zechariah together lexically, thematically, and theologically, by relating the message . . . to the generalized call to repentance voiced in the earlier prophets in Zechariah 1:4" [112].) Having both Tyndale vols. is not a bad idea. [*Chm* Win 13].

✓ Jones, D. R. ‡ *Haggai, Zechariah, Malachi* (Torch) 1962. A brief, critical work of value years ago.

☆ Kaiser, Walter. (WCC) 1993. See under Micah.

✓ **Kessler, John.** *The Book of Haggai: Prophecy and Society in Early Persian Yehud*, 2002. A very large, expert, and more conservative study of Haggai's prophecy, taken as a reproclamation of past traditions or Scriptures. This vol. contains much of the material one would expect in a commentary. [*JSOT* 27.5; *VT* 54.4].

✓ **Koopmans, William T.** [𝓜], (HCOT) 2017. Admirably thorough as a technical reference (365pp.), Koopmans covers text-critical, lexical, grammatical, historical, and theological matters, with ample discussion of ANE background materials and an additional "Structural Analysis of Haggai as Poetic Prose" (299–365). He is a learned pastor (Kampen ThD) in the CRC and worked 24 years on this project. Despite the lack of indexes, the inconsistency of blending transliteration and Hebrew typeface, and the less-than-expected theological reflection, this is my favorite scholarly work on Haggai. We are all indebted to Koopmans for his labors, and all hereafter will build on him. This would certainly be a recommended purchase, were it affordable; it is so cost-prohibitive ($93 in pb) that few will access it outside of institutional libraries. [*Downside Review* 137.2].

☆ Mackay, John L. *Haggai, Zechariah, Malachi: God's Restored People*, 1994. Published by Christian Focus, this was until recently (see Duguid) about the best popular-level exposition from the Reformed side. I find it especially useful for Zechariah.

✓ **March, W. Eugene.** ‡ (NIB) 1996.

F   Marshall, Phillip S. (ZECOT).

✓ Mason, R. A. ‡ (CBC) 1977. Covers through Malachi. Mason has been a leading scholar on Zechariah since his groundbreaking dissertation, "The Use of Earlier Biblical Material in Zechariah 9–14: A Study in Inner Biblical Exegesis" (London, 1973), which has more recently seen publication (see Boda–Floyd under Zechariah).

✓ **Meadowcroft, Tim.** *Haggai* (Read) 2006. This exceedingly full exegesis (259pp.) has much to offer: historical-critical investigation (form, redaction, and reception history), a literary reading, discourse analysis, and theology. There are also forays into speech-act theory and contemporary application. Needless to say, there is a good mix of hermeneutics to try to meld. Discourse analysis features most prominently. He treats the prophecy as a unity. Meadowcroft teaches at Bible College of New Zealand. Along with Koopmans, a very intelligent, masterful work of scholarship. [*CBQ* 4/09; *BL* 2008; *RelSRev* 12/09].

☆ **Merrill, Eugene H.** *Haggai, Zechariah, Malachi* (intended for WEC?) 1994. Careful, dependable, and can certainly be appreciated by all evangelicals. Dispensationalists interpreting Zechariah will find it to be especially serviceable. Because it is thorough and includes Hebrew exegesis, and because there are fewer conservative scholarly works on these books, preachers and students do well to consult Merrill, even buy it. It went o/p with Moody but was reprinted by Biblical Studies Press. [*BSac* 7/96].

☆ Merrill, Eugene H. (EBCR) 2008. This replaces Alden's contribution to the old EBC and is a fine summary of his earlier dependable work (22pp.).

☆ **Meyers, Carol L., and Eric M. Meyers.** ‡ *Haggai, Zechariah 1–8* (AB) 1988. Very well-received by the scholarly world, moderately critical, helpful for philological details, and especially valuable for historical background. The Meyers couple, on faculty at Duke, provide an excellent commentary on Haggai (Introduction + 84pp.). The Zechariah treatment is even fuller and more detailed—perhaps more critical too. Compare this vol. with Petersen. The serious drawback, from a pastor's perspective at least, is that Meyers–Meyers and Petersen both have little to say theologically. [*JBL* 107.3, 114.3].

Mitchell, H. G. ‡ (ICC) 1912.

Moore, Thomas V. *Haggai, Zechariah, Malachi* (GS) 1856. A warm Reformed exposition from the 19th century, but not one of the best in the series. Still in print, but also available online. For pastors, not students.

✓ O'Brien, Julia. ‡ *Nahum, Habakkuk, Zephaniah, Haggai, Zechariah, Malachi* (AbOTC) 2004. See under Nahum.

Perowne, T. T. *Haggai and Zechariah* (CBSC) 1888, 2nd ed. 1901. Fairly conservative work by a leading scholar of that day that was replaced by Barnes.

☆ **Petersen, David L.** ‡ *Haggai, Zechariah 1–8* (OTL) 1984. Moderately critical, this commentary has many fine points. It repays close study, but read with discernment. Not dissimilar in its approach and conclusions to the Meyerses' work. OTL, AB, and ContC are leading critical exegeses available in English. See Zechariah. [*JBL* 105.4].

✓ **Redditt, Paul L.** ‡ *Haggai, Zechariah, Malachi* (NCB) 1995. Covers the Bible texts phrase-by-phrase (about 220pp.). He is professor emeritus at Georgetown College (KY), and strongly prefers a diachronic approach (positing multiple redactions) to newer literary-critical methods. Worth consulting for exegesis, but I doubt you will find it stimulating. [*CBQ* 7/96; *JETS* 6/97; *JSS* Spr 97; *VT* 47.1; *RTR* 1/97; *HS* 1997; *CRBR* 1996; *RBL*].

☆ **Rogland, Max.** *Haggai and Zechariah 1–8* (BHHB) 2016. One of the clearest and most helpful vols. in an excellent series for Hebrew students. [*JSS* Aut 18; *BBR* 27.3; *JSOT* 41.5].

F Shelley, Patricia. (BCBC).

Smith, Gary V., and Timothy D. Sprankle. *Zephaniah–Malachi* (Kerux) 2020. See Zephaniah.

✓ **Smith, Ralph L.** ‡ (WBC) 1984. See Micah above.

✓ Stead, Michael R. *Haggai, Zechariah, and Malachi: An Introduction and Study Guide*, 2022. [*JTS* 10/22; *ExpTim* 7/23, 8/23].

☆ Stead, Michael. "Haggai" in *Daniel–Malachi* (ESVEC) 2018. See Chase under Daniel.

F Stuart, Douglas. *Micah–Malachi* (WBC-R). See under Micah.

✓ **Stuhlmueller, C.** ‡ *Haggai and Zechariah* (ITC-E) 1988. One of the series' best, along with Brueggemann's *Jeremiah*, even though somewhat brief (165pp.). [*Evangel* Win 89].

F Thomas, Heath A. *Nahum–Malachi* (BCOT). Goldingay was previously listed.

✓ Thomas, D. Winton. "The Book of Haggai—Exegesis" (IB) 1956. Because the author was an excellent philologist, this is still worthwhile.

✓ **Tollington, Janet.** ‡ *Tradition and Innovation in Haggai and Zechariah 1–8* (JSOTSup) 1993. An Oxford dissertation.

✓ Tuell, Steven. ‡ *Reading Nahum–Malachi* (Read) 2016. See Nahum.

☆ **Verhoef, Pieter A.** *Haggai, Malachi* (retired NICOT) 1987. Was on the recommended list years ago, but replaced in the series by Jacobs. It is still classed as a major reference work because of its depth: 150pp. on Haggai, and 200pp. on Malachi. One only wished the Stellenbosch professor emeritus had had opportunity to interact with Petersen's 1984 work. Written at a higher scholarly level than most of the older NICOT vols., Verhoef's work (Motyer's too) complemented Baldwin well. [*WTJ* Spr 89; *JETS* 12/88; *Them* 4/88; *ExpTim* 3/88; *HS* 1987].

F    Wöhrle, Jakob. ‡ *Haggai, Zechariah 1–8* (IECOT).

✓    **Wolff, H. W.** ‡ (ContC) ET 1988. Certainly a leading critical exegesis for students to consult. As one might expect from this scholar, Wolff pays close attention to what he perceives as a complicated compositional history with three "growth-rings" (18). He pursues a form-critical and tradition history approach with theological goals. See his other vols. under Hosea, Joel–Amos, Obadiah–Jonah, and Micah.

NOTES: (1) Consult the above section The Twelve Minor Prophets. (2) Mark Boda, "Majoring on the Minors: Recent Research on Haggai and Zechariah," *CBR* 2.1 (2003): 33–68.

# ZECHARIAH

★    Baldwin, Joyce G. (retired TOTC) 1972. See Haggai above. Back in 1999 Wolters said, "For the preacher, the best current scholarly commentary in English is probably the little jewel by . . . Baldwin," despite her "rather debatable overall literary structure" for the whole book of Zechariah [*BSB* 9/99]. While we long had Verhoef's erudite work on Haggai and Malachi to complement Baldwin, we sadly lacked an in-depth, evangelical work on Zechariah. Merrill and McComiskey came along and were a good help, then accompanied by Klein, but students looked for something more thorough. We certainly have it in Boda's NICOT! Students needing technical help should also go find Wolters, Meyers–Meyers, and Petersen in the library.

★    **Boda, Mark J.** (NICOT) 2015. What a magnificent, comprehensive commentary (782pp.)! Most pastors are happy enough with Boda's extensive NIVAC on Zechariah (370 of 540pp.), but NICOT is easily the studious pastor's first choice for an exegesis. With the combination of Boda and Wolters—they will dominate the field for decades—Zechariah is so well served by scholarly evangelical commentaries. Boda had studied and preached upon the prophet for 25 years, and it shows. (A page and half of the bibliography are his own publications.) There is painstaking textual work, lexical research, discussion of historical and religious background, compositional history, literary and structural analysis, restrained form criticism, brilliant intertextual study, thorough exegesis, and biblical-theological exposition. He finds evidence of editorial shaping of autobiographical accounts, original vision reports, and oracle collections extending over decades. At the same time as he recognizes distinctions between the styles of chs. 1–8 and 9–14, he adduces strong reasons for his reading Zechariah as a single book. He shows interest in canonical shaping (literary links to Haggai and Malachi) and suggests that chs. 9–14 were joined to an already integrated Haggai 1–Zech 8 work (the final form in mid- to late-fifth century). Boda is a remarkably clear writer, even when treating technical matters. [*Bib* 98.3; *WTJ* Fall 17; *CBQ* 4/18; *JTS* 10/16; *JETS* 12/16; *JSOT* 41.5 (Mason); *RevExp* 11/19; *Them* 41.3]. Students relish his collected essays in the 2-vol. *Exploring Zechariah* (2017) [*ExpTim* 8/18, 6/19; *CBQ* 7/19; *JSOT* 42.5; *ETL* 94.3].

★    **Klein, George L.** (NAC) 2008. This exegesis is more extensive (450pp.) and contains more substantive research than most other vols. in the series. The treatment of the Hebrew is careful and workmanlike. The theological approach is that of moderate or progressive dispensationalism. Citing some of Blaising's work, Klein argues that "it remains preferable to view biblical references to 'Israel' as applying to national Israel, not the Church" (67). Reformed students of biblical prophecy prefer Boda, Wolters, Webb, and McComiskey at such points of interpretation where Klein marks a hard distinction between the OT and the NT people of God. Leaving aside eschatology, this is a useful companion in walking through the text. [*RelSRev* 9/09].

★ **McComiskey, Thomas E.** *The Minor Prophets: An Exegetical and Expository Commentary*, Vol. 3, ed. McComiskey, 1998. Up to the same excellent standard found in "Hosea." It is a dependable exegesis with solid theology (240pp.), now outstripped in scholarship by Wolters and Boda. The whole set has been recommended above.

★ **Petterson, Anthony R.** (Apollos) 2015. See Haggai. The 210pp. on Zechariah are the best segment of the work. Petterson's doctoral research, *Behold Your King* (2009) [*CBQ* 1/11; *JTS* 10/10; *JSOT* 37.5; *VT* 61.4; *RelSRev* 9/13; *JHebS* 11], focused upon the Davidic hope in Zechariah, and he argued for thematic unity (chs. 1–8 with 9–14) in that oft-divided book. See his summary article in *JSOT* 35.2. A very well-informed exegesis of Zechariah for pastors, who might shy away from the marvelously detailed vols. by Wolters and Boda (NICOT). [*Chm* Aut 16]. Also note Petterson below.

★ Webb, Barry G. (BST) 2003. The exposition includes careful, insightful exegesis and especially rich biblical-theological reflection—excellent for evangelical pastors (170pp.). Webb also produced the fine vol. on Isaiah in the series. [*JSOT* 28.5; *Chm* Win 10].

Achtemeier, Elizabeth. [𝓜], (I) 1986. See Nahum above.

☆ **Barker, Kenneth L.** (EBCR) 2008. This revision of EBC (1985) is dispensationally oriented, but still valuable to others who do not take that stance. Barker is well-trained in Semitics (Dropsie PhD) and highly respected in evangelical circles, notably for his work as general editor of the *NIV Study Bible*. He produced the helpful notes on this book for the *NIV Study Bible* (1985, rev. 2002). His work here in EBCR is about 90pp.

✓ Barnes, W. E. ‡ *Haggai, Zechariah, Malachi* (CBSC) 1917.

Baron, David. 3rd ed. 1919. A substantial exposition, repeatedly reprinted by various publishers. Baron was a converted Jew and strongly premillennial.

☆ Bentley, Michael. *Building for God's Glory* (WCS on Haggai & Zechariah) 1989. For the expositor.

☆ **Boda, Mark J.** *Haggai, Zechariah* (NIVAC) 2004. See Haggai above, for which this vol. is already a recommended purchase. Note Boda's NICOT above.

✓ Boda, Mark J., and Michael H. Floyd, eds. [𝓜], *Bringing Out the Treasure: Inner Biblical Allusion in Zechariah 9–14* (JSOTSup) 2003. Includes the publication of Mason's groundbreaking PhD, noted above under Haggai. [*RelSRev* 10/04].

✓ Boda, Mark, and Michael Floyd, eds. [𝓜], *Tradition in Transition: Haggai and Zechariah 1–8 in the Trajectory of Hebrew Theology*, 2008. Invaluable essays, especially on Zechariah. [*CBQ* 1/10; *BL* 2010; *RelSRev* 3/11].

☆ Brown, William P. ‡ *Obadiah–Malachi* (WestBC) 1996. See Obadiah.

✓ **Clark, David J., and Howard A. Hatton.** (UBS) 2002. See under Haggai.

F Clendenen, Ray. (EBTC)? Would cover Nahum to Malachi.

✓ Coggins, Richard, and Jin H. Han. ‡ (BBC) 2011. See Nahum. Note too Coggins's brief *Haggai, Zechariah, Malachi* (1987) in OT Guides.

✓ **Conrad, Edgar W.** ‡ *Zechariah* (Read) 1999. At points Conrad is for me like a breath of fresh air. Reading Zechariah as a whole, instead of as a divided book, makes fresh insights possible. I am not saying he thinks the book is totally cohesive, however. Conrad uses literary methods like intertextuality in mainly unobjectionable ways. Some evangelical scholars will applaud Conrad's methods and conclusions; all can learn from them. About 220pp. [*JSOT* 89; *CBQ* 7/00; *Int* 1/00; *OTA* 2/00; *RelSRev* 1/00].

F   Cook, Stephen. ‡ *Haggai & Zechariah* (Illum).

F   Coover-Cox, Dorian, and Daniel Lowery. *Haggai, Zechariah, Malachi* (EEC)?

✓   Curtis, Byron G. *Up the Steep and Stony Road: The Book of Zechariah in Social Location Trajectory Analysis*, 2006. A Westminster Seminary dissertation defending both the unity of the prophecy and authorship by the historical Zechariah. I confess I am not clear on his hermeneutical method. [*CBQ* 1/08].

☆   Duguid, Iain M. *Haggai, Zechariah, Malachi* (EPSC) 2010. See under Haggai.

Feinberg, Charles L. *God Remembers*, 4th ed. 1979. Dispensationalists gravitate to the apocalyptic literature (Daniel, Zechariah, and Revelation). This commentary is valuable to those sharing their perspective, but Reformed interpreters will not be able to agree with this scholar's approach. Eschatology is the thrust here: Feinberg is militantly dispensational, strictly separating God's program for Jews and Gentiles. He does, however, helpfully include many rabbinic quotes from Kimḥi and others. Barker, Merrill, and Klein are more moderate from a similar theological stance.

✓   **Floyd, Michael H.** ‡ *Minor Prophets, Part 2* (FOTL) 1999. See Nahum above.

✓   Foster, Robert L. ‡ *The Theology of the Books of Haggai and Zechariah*, 2021. See Haggai.

Fries, Micah. *Exalting Jesus in Zephaniah, Haggai, Zechariah, Malachi* (CCE) 2015.

Goldingay, John, and Pamela Scalise. *Minor Prophets II* (NIBC) 2009. See under Nahum. Scalise treats the last two prophets, Zechariah and Malachi, in this vol.

Gregory, Bryan R. *Looking for God in an Age of Discouragement: The Gospel according to Zechariah* (GAOT) 2010. Praised by Boda. I've not seen it.

F   Hanson, Paul D. ‡ (Herm). I doubt this will appear; Hanson passed away in 2023.

☆   Hill, Andrew. (CorBC) 2008. See under Hosea.

☆   **Hill, Andrew.** *Haggai, Zechariah and Malachi* (TOTC-R) 2012. See Haggai. Excellent as a quick reference. Hill seemed to me a bit unclear on 6:9–15: is the builder "the one who sprouts out of Joshua" (177) or Joshua (180)?

✓   Jones, D. R. ‡ *Haggai, Zechariah, Malachi* (Torch) 1962.

F   Jones, Jennifer Brown. (ZECOT).

☆   Kaiser, Walter. *Micah, Nahum, Habakkuk, Zephaniah, Haggai, Zechariah, Malachi* (WCC) 1993. See under Micah. This is a suggestive, full (135-page) exposition of this prophet; the approach is premillennial.

Kersten, G. H. *The Night Visions of Zechariah*, ET 1995. Subtitled "A Practical Exposition" (about 500pp.) and issued by the Netherlands Reformed Book and Publishing Committee, out of Grand Rapids. The Dutch original was published posthumously in 1953.

☆   Kline, Meredith G. *Glory in Our Midst: A Biblical-Theological Reading of Zechariah's Night Visions*, 2001. A full, vigorous theological exposition (300pp.) issued by Wipf & Stock. I regret I've had less opportunity to use this. He is so creative that readers may find him both stimulating and mystifying (how did he come up with that?).

☆   **Lessing, R. Reed.** (ConcC) 2021. Has done Jonah, Amos, and Isaiah 40–66 for the series. There is said to be adept handling of the Hebrew and exegetical cruxes (approx. 540pp.), but I have yet to see this vol. The hollow star is based on his past work.

Leupold, H. C. 1956. A dated, fairly thorough commentary, offering a traditional, conservative Lutheran interpretation (amillennial perspective).

☆   Mackay, John L. *Haggai, Zechariah, Malachi: God's Restored People*, 1994. See under Haggai.

✓   Mason, R. A. ‡ (CBC) 1977. See under Haggai.

☆   **Merrill, Eugene H.** *Haggai, Zechariah, Malachi*, 1994. See under Haggai. Has a dispensational orientation; Merrill is among the best, most judicious OT scholars in that camp. His work treats the Hebrew and is of greater value than Barker or Feinberg from that perspective. Many pastors would want to purchase this; I did.

☆ **Meyers, Carol L., and Eric M. Meyers.** ‡ (AB) 2 vols., 1987–93. See Haggai above. The second vol. is astonishingly full; *Zechariah 9–14* runs to 552pp.! They do not hold to the unity of Zechariah, but do take a more conservative approach to the text than many critics. There is an immense amount of learning in the set. Among critical commentaries on Zechariah, this is the first I reach for, if I'm not time-pressed. One caveat, though: pastors interested in theology find that both the AB and OTL sets read the book more as political document—answering scholars' questions about the sociopolitical context—and may disappoint in their theological discussion. This deficiency seemed glaring with the arrival of Boda's NICOT. [*JBL* 114.3].

Mitchell, H. G. ‡ (ICC) 1912.

☆ Moore, Thomas V. (GS) 1856. See Haggai above.

✓ O'Brien, Julia. ‡ *Nahum, Habakkuk, Zephaniah, Haggai, Zechariah, Malachi* (AbOTC) 2004. See under Nahum.

✓ **Ollenburger, Ben C.** [𝓜], (NIB) 1996.

Perowne, T. T. *Haggai and Zechariah* (CBSC) 1888, 2nd ed. 1901. Fairly conservative work by a leading scholar of that day; it was replaced by Barnes.

☆ **Petersen, David L.** ‡ *Haggai, Zechariah 1–8* (OTL) 1984; *Zechariah 9–14 and Malachi* (OTL) 1995. See Haggai above. He does not hold to the unity of Zechariah. The pastor wanting to build a first-rate exegetical library might purchase the OTL set for its careful form-critical treatment and as a handier guide than AB. The Meyerses' AB set is much fuller and marginally more useful for certain kinds of work with the text. [*Int* 1/97; *CBQ* 7/96; *JTS* 10/96; *JETS* 6/97; *JSS* Spr 97; *JTS* 10/96; *JSOT* 76; *SwJT*, Sum 98; *BSac* 4/96].

☆ Petterson, Anthony R. "Zechariah" in *Daniel–Malachi* (ESVEC) 2018. See Chase under Daniel.

☆ Phillips, Richard D. (REC) 2007. Faithful, Christ-centered expository preaching, and well-done. Much material here (351pp.). See REC under Commentary Series, and note Phillips's other REC vols., e.g., Hebrews. [*JETS* 9/08; *JSOT* 41.5 (Tiemeyer, negative)].

✓ **Redditt, Paul L.** ‡ *Haggai, Zechariah, Malachi* (NCB) 1995. See Haggai above.

✓ **Redditt, Paul L.** ‡ *Zechariah 9–14* (IECOT) 2012. The author, now retired from Georgetown College (KY), updates and deepens his earlier NCB research. He remains convinced that discerning redactional layers is key to understanding the text; the chapters grew up around "four collections of traditional eschatological hope (9:1–17; 10:3b–12; 12:1–4a, 5, 8–9; and 14:1–13, 14b–21)." He also briefly discusses the material synchronically, as it relates to the whole of The Twelve. Curiously, I found that an "Al Wolters" (see below) on Amazon panned the work as a "rehash" with "many misprints and philological mistakes." [*BBR* 24.2; *CBQ* 7/13; *VT* 63.4; *RevExp* 2/14; *RelSRev* 9/13].

☆ **Rogland, Max.** *Haggai and Zechariah 1–8* (BHHB) 2016. See under Haggai.

F Shelley, Patricia. (BCBC).

Smith, Gary V., and Timothy D. Sprankle. *Zephaniah–Malachi* (Kerux) 2020. See Zephaniah.

✓ **Smith, Ralph L.** ‡ (WBC) 1984. See Micah above. He believes Zechariah 9–14 to be a later gloss.

✓ Stead, Michael R. *Haggai, Zechariah, and Malachi*, 2022. See Haggai for this very useful "Introduction and Study Guide" by the now Bishop of South Sydney. Previously, he did important work on *The Intertextuality of Zechariah 1–8* (2009) [*JSS* Aut 11; *VT* 61.3; *RelSRev* 6/11; *JHebS* 12].

F Stuart, Douglas. *Micah–Malachi* (WBC-R). See under Micah. Stuart had been slated to do the NICOT vol. on Zechariah, but that research will go into WBC.

✓ **Stuhlmueller, C.** ‡ *Haggai and Zechariah* (ITC-E) 1988.

✓ Thomas, D. Winton. "The Book of Zechariah 1–8, Exegesis" (IB) 1956. Because the author was an excellent philologist, this is still worthwhile.

F   Thomas, Heath A. *Nahum–Malachi* (BCOT). Goldingay was previously listed.

✓   Tiemeyer, Lena-Sofia. ‡ *Zechariah and His Visions*, 2015. Recognized as first-rate scholarship, using form criticism to analyze the vision reports in chs. 1–6 and to argue that they present actual visionary experience. [*JSOT* 39.5; *Bib* 97.1; *JSS* Spr 19; *CBQ* 7/16; *JTS* 10/17; *JHebS* 17]. Tiemeyer's strong interest in redaction criticism is reflected in her subsequent vol., *Zechariah's Vision Report and Its Earliest Interpreters* (2016) [*JSOT* 41.5; *JHebS* 17].

F   Timmer, Daniel C. (Pillar).

✓   Tuell, Steven. ‡ *Reading Nahum–Malachi* (Read) 2016. See Nahum.

Unger, Merrill. 1963. A dispensational exposition, based on the Hebrew.

✓   Wenzel, Heiko. *Reading Zechariah with Zechariah 1:1–6 as the Introduction to the Entire Book*, 2011. Quite stimulating, a Wheaton PhD.

F   Wöhrle, Jakob. ‡ *Haggai, Zechariah 1–8* (IECOT).

✓   **Wolters, Al.** (HCOT) 2014. Simply put, this is excellent through and through. Wolters worked on the prophecy for well over two decades, and he covers pretty much everything. As the jacket blurb says, the work makes several notable contributions: "close attention to philological detail, with a special focus on textual criticism, lexical semantics, and literary wordplay"; treatment of the entire history of interpretation, including rabbinics; intertextual studies; Christian theological interpretation; and a new proposal regarding composition. He dispenses with the usual two-part division and argues that the prophecy "consists instead of three independent and quite different parts, each of which is attributable to the prophet after whom the book is named." Warning: this is a dense work (473pp.). The list price has dropped from $130 to $93 in pb. [*JTS* 10/15]. See also "Confessional Criticism and the Night Visions of Zechariah" in *Renewing Biblical Interpretation, Scripture and Hermeneutics*, Bartholomew et al., eds. (2000).

✓   Wright, C. H. H. *Zechariah and His Prophecies*, 1879. Fascinating for the student of Zechariah. These were the Bampton Lectures of 1878 and go into great depth (about 600pp.). This is a true classic in the history of interpretation and for generations was a favorite among conservatives. Reprinted by Klock & Klock in 1980.

NOTES: (1) Consult the above section The Twelve Minor Prophets. (2) See Michael Floyd's "Zechariah and Changing Views of Second Temple Judaism in Recent Commentaries," *RelSRev* 25.3 (1999): 257–63. (3) Mark Boda, "Majoring on the Minors: Recent Research on Haggai and Zechariah," *CBR* 2.1 (2003): 33–68.

# MALACHI

★   Adam, Peter. (BST) 2013. The Australian knows Malachi well, having preached and taught it for decades. His biblical-theological approach helps make the exposition Christ-centered and edifying. Pastors are instructed by his emphasis on corporate, as opposed to individual, application of the message. Adam's BST represents healthy, robust preaching. Compared with some others in the series, however, there is less exegesis and interaction with current scholarship. As Clendenen notes [*Them* 11/14], this presents a problem at 2:16 where he follows the 1984 NIV (cf. ESV and 2011 NIV). [*JSOT* 40.5].

★   **Hill, Andrew.** (AB) 1998. A full-length, satisfying work from an evangelical—not really expected in AB, which is more ecumenical than anticipated. (Hill came to the attention of AB's editor, David Noel Freedman, through doctoral studies at Michigan.) Competes with Tucker as the best commentary on the book for exegetical help (because fullest, 425pp.), though compare with Snyman and Stuart. There is more theological reflection here than in most AB vols. Advanced students interested in the finer points of philology and grammar may be disappointed by Hill's discussion in places; see Jack Collins's review in *TJ* Fall 00. [*BL* 1999; *EvQ* 4/00; *JBL* Win 99; *JTS* 10/99; *Bib* 81.1; *Int* 4/99; *AsTJ* Fall 99; *JR* 10/99; *RBL*; *DenvJ*]. For a distillation, see Hill's TOTC and CorBC below.

★ **Petterson, Anthony R.** *Haggai, Zechariah & Malachi* (Apollos) 2015. See under Haggai. Though not as strong as his Zechariah section, Malachi is well-done in 85pp.

★ **Ross, Allen P.** *Malachi Then and Now: An Expository Commentary Based on Detailed Exegetical Analysis*, 2nd ed. 2018. A number of aims are adroitly pursued: providing a textbook on exegetical method and sermon preparation; modeling "detailed exegetical analysis" of the Hebrew text and theological exposition; offering theological reflection on the NT use of Malachi's oracles; and guidance for homiletics and application. Ross is truly an "old hand" at this, and his books are a blessing; see Genesis, Leviticus, Psalms, Proverbs. [*JETS* 3/17].

★ **Stuart, Douglas.** *The Minor Prophets: An Exegetical and Expository Commentary*, Vol. 3, ed. Thomas E. McComiskey, 1998. This set is already recommended for purchase above. Stuart's handling of the Hebrew is lucid, accurate, and reliable.

★ Taylor, Richard A., and **E. Ray Clendenen.** *Haggai, Malachi* (NAC) 2004. See Haggai.

★ **Tucker, W. Dennis, Jr.** (ZECOT) 2024. The Baylor prof previously distinguished himself with a Hebrew handbook on Jonah, a Psalms monograph, and *Psalms, Volume 2* in NIVAC (coauthored with Grant). Tucker is now my first pick for a reference commentary because it is fully up-to-date, exceptionally careful, detailed, and insightful in treating the Hebrew; attuned to rhetoric and discourse structures; linguistically sophisticated; conversant with all the major scholarship; and shrewd in sorting through the exegetical options. There is certainly fine theological interpretation as well—see the eight Canonical and Theological Significance sections—and a zeroing in on Malachi's deeper concerns, for example, in 2:14–16. "Divorcing the 'wife of their youth' is not the issue; it is the symptom. With this act, the husbands practiced a form of infidelity to their community and, worse yet, infidelity to the God who served as a witness to that marriage. . . . [W]hat YHWH longs for is a community absent of such faithless action (בגד), fully committed to one another, and unflinching in their devotedness to their God" (107). However, the prime strength of the vol. is close, technical exegesis. Hebrew students and the best-trained pastors will most appreciate Tucker (191pp.). Those without much language learning will be grateful that glosses (translations) are given for all Hebrew words and phrases.

✓ Achtemeier, Elizabeth. [*M*], (I) 1986. See Nahum above.

Alden, Robert L. (EBC) 1985. See under Haggai.

☆ Baker, David W. *Joel, Obadiah, Malachi* (NIVAC) 2006. Meets a real need, since we lack a good selection of strong expositions which offer guidance in applying Malachi today (105pp. on Malachi). I missed not having any discussion of tithing, which inevitably comes up for discussion in the churches. See under Joel.

☆ **Baldwin, Joyce G.** (retired TOTC) 1972. See Haggai above.

Barnes, W. E. ‡ *Haggai, Zechariah, Malachi* (CBSC) 1917.

☆ Benton, John. *Losing Touch with the Living God* (Welwyn) 1985. Reformed exposition with close application to the heart.

☆ Brown, William P. ‡ *Obadiah–Malachi* (WestBC) 1996. See Obadiah.

✓ **Clark, David J., and Howard A. Hatton.** (UBS) 2002. See under Haggai.

F Clendenen, Ray. (EBTC)? Would cover Nahum to Malachi.

✓ Coggins, Richard, and Jin H. Han. ‡ (BBC) 2011. See Nahum. Note too Coggins's brief *Haggai, Zechariah, Malachi* (1987) in OT Guides.

F   Coover-Cox, Dorian, and Daniel Lowery. *Haggai, Zechariah, Malachi* (EEC)?

Davis, Stacy. ‡ *Haggai, Malachi* (Wisdom) 2015. See under Haggai.

☆ Duguid, Iain M. *Haggai, Zechariah, Malachi* (EPSC) 2010. See under Haggai. It is worth noting that Duguid handles the difficult divorce text very well and succinctly.

☆ Duguid, Iain, and Matthew P. Harmon. *Zephaniah, Haggai, Malachi* (REC) 2018. See Zephaniah above. The sermons on Malachi (7) are shared between them. Well-done!

☆ **Eddinger, Terry W.** *Malachi: A Handbook on the Hebrew Text* (BHHB) 2012. A good aid in translating the text and sorting out lexical forms and the grammar. It would have been advantageous for him to use the 2010 *BHQ* instead of *BHS*; did it come too late? The crux at 2:16 could have been better researched and handled. [*JSOT* 39.5; *RelSRev* 6/13].

✓ **Floyd, Michael H.** ‡ *Minor Prophets, Part 2* (FOTL) 1999. See Nahum above.

✓ Fox, R. Michael. *A Message from the Great King: Reading Malachi in Light of Ancient Persian Royal Messenger Texts from the Time of Xerxes*, 2015. [*JSOT* 41.5].

Fries, Micah. *Exalting Jesus in Zephaniah, Haggai, Zechariah, Malachi* (CCE) 2015.

✓ Gibson, Jonathan. *Covenant Continuity and Fidelity: A Study of Inner-Biblical Allusion and Exegesis in Malachi*, 2016. A Cambridge PhD, published in LHBOTS. Gibson now teaches at Westminster Philadelphia. With Williamson, one can suggest that Gibson is "becoming a benchmark study of an important element of Malachi's composition and theology" [*JJS* 70.2]. [*JSS* Aut 18; *ExpTim* 6/17; *JSOT* 41.5; *JHebS* 17].

✓ **Glazier-McDonald, Beth.** ‡ *Malachi: The Divine Messenger*, 1987. Esteemed as a very important technical commentary (275pp.), originally a U. of Chicago PhD, and published by Scholars Press. Students should certainly consult the work. Its judiciousness in exegesis and maturity in sifting the scholarship are unlike most doctoral projects. [*JBL* Spr 89].

Goldingay, John, and Pamela Scalise. *Minor Prophets II* (NIBC) 2009. See under Nahum. Scalise treats the last two prophets, Zechariah and Malachi, in this vol.

F   Hardy, H. H., II. (BGW). The author teaches at Southeastern Baptist.

☆ Hill, Andrew. (CorBC) 2008. Slightly updates and popularizes the in-depth commentary in his AB work. See under Hosea.

☆ Hill, Andrew. *Haggai, Zechariah and Malachi* (TOTC-R) 2012. See Haggai, as well as his CorBC and AB entries above.

✓ Hugenberger, Gordon P. *Marriage as a Covenant*, 1994. Not a commentary. This is a sterling dissertation, published by Brill and then Baker. Hugenberger focuses on the Malachi 2 text but treats other Scriptures as well. This work is of interest to ethicists as well as OT exegetes. [*JBL* Sum 95; *VT* 46.3]. I am convinced by such scholars as Glazier-McDonald, Hugenberger, and Stuart that the Hebrew of 2:16 (backed by a correct interpretation of the LXX) is best read as a conditional sentence: "if one, hating [his wife], divorces . . . he covers his clothes with violence/crime" (cf. NIV 2011, ESV, and Ps 73:6).

☆ **Jacobs, Mignon R.** *The Books of Haggai and Malachi* (NICOT) 2018. See Haggai. Students will certainly gravitate to this full exegesis (over 200pp.).

☆ **Kaiser, Walter C.** *Malachi: God's Unchanging Love*, 1984. With an analysis of the MT, the exposition is full, readable, and well-researched. Kaiser is concerned to discuss the theological issues and their contemporary relevance. He has a surprising bonus; Appendix B is entitled "The Usefulness of Biblical Commentaries for Preaching and Bible Study." I consider this pb more useful than Kaiser's WCC on Malachi below. The student prefers to work with this commentary because of the Hebrew. Preachers pressed for time will be tempted to opt for the Communicator's Commentary. [*JETS* 6/85].

☆ Kaiser, Walter. *Micah, Nahum, Habakkuk, Zephaniah, Haggai, Zechariah, Malachi* (WCC) 1993. See Micah.

F   Kalimi, Isaac. ‡ (Herm).

F Körting, Corinna. ‡ (Illum).

✓ Jones, D. R. ‡ *Haggai, Zechariah, Malachi* (Torch) 1962.

☆ Mackay, John L. *Haggai, Zechariah, Malachi: God's Restored People*, 1994. See Haggai.

✓ Mason, R. A. ‡ (CBC) 1977.

☆ **Merrill, Eugene H.** *Haggai, Zechariah, Malachi*, 1994. See Haggai and Zechariah above.

☆ **Merrill, Eugene H.** (EBCR) 2008. There are few good evangelical works to compete with this for brevity (27pp.). Students should mainly use the fuller work of 1994.

Moore, Thomas V. (GS) 1856. See Haggai above.

☆ Morgan, G. Campbell. *Malachi's Message for Today*, 1972 reprint. A series by one of the 20th century's greatest Bible expositors, formerly titled *Wherein Have We Robbed God?* (1898). The book of six messages remains very suggestive and well worth buying, if you can find it s/h. See Hosea above.

✓ O'Brien, Julia. ‡ *Nahum, Habakkuk, Zephaniah, Haggai, Zechariah, Malachi* (AbOTC) 2004. See under Nahum.

Ogden, G. S., and R. R. Deutsch. ‡ *Joel and Malachi* (ITC-E) 1987.

☆ Ortlund, Eric. "Malachi" in *Daniel–Malachi* (ESVEC) 2018. See Chase under Daniel.

☆ **Petersen, David L.** ‡ (OTL) 1995. See Zechariah above.

✓ **Redditt, Paul L.** ‡ *Haggai, Zechariah, Malachi* (NCB) 1995. See Haggai above.

✓ **Schart, Aaron.** ‡ (IECOT) ET 2021. A major scholarly work, though not of great length. The 19-page Introduction is followed by nearly 120pp. of exegesis. In accord with the series aims, there is synchronic and diachronic (esp. form and redaction criticism) analysis, followed by a Synthesis which may include discussion of NT "reception" of the text. The textual notes are limited and astute; for some technical questions, he refers readers to the recent German commentaries by Meinhold and Kessler. [*JSOT* 47.5; *ETL* 9/23].

✓ Schuller, Eileen M. ‡ (NIB) 1996.

Shao, Joseph Too, and Rosa Ching Shao. *Joel, Nahum, and Malachi* (Asia) 2021.

F Shelley, Patricia. (BCBC).

Smith, Gary V., and Timothy D. Sprankle. *Zephaniah–Malachi* (Kerux) 2020. See Zephaniah.

✓ Smith, J. M. P. ‡ (ICC) 1912.

✓ **Smith, Ralph L.** ‡ (WBC) 1984. See Micah above.

✓ **Snyman, S. D. (Fanie).** [𝔐], (HCOT) 2015. A well-rounded, major, mildly critical work on the Hebrew (192pp.), building on a more popular 1995 Afrikaans commentary. One of the best reference works available, really. The author has worked on Malachi for nearly 30 years, finds "a mixture of genres . . . in each of the six units" (10), discusses antitheses in the prophecy, and has a healthy interest in the theology of the text. As usual with HCOT, the bibliographies are valuable. I find Snyman to be an astute, responsible exegete who has read widely (e.g., see his discussion of 2:16).

Stead, Michael R. *Haggai, Zechariah, and Malachi*, 2022. See under Haggai.

F Stuart, Douglas. *Micah–Malachi* (WBC-R). See under Micah.

F Thomas, Heath A. *Nahum–Malachi* (BCOT). Goldingay was previously listed.

✓ Tuell, Steven. ‡ *Reading Nahum–Malachi* (Read) 2016. See Nahum.

☆ **Verhoef, Pieter A.** (NICOT) 1987. See Haggai above. Though this vol. began to have a somewhat dated feel, the rigorous exegesis and theological reflection long kept it on the recommended list. In my opinion, he does not get the crux at 2:16 right. Quite full on Malachi at 200pp.

NOTES: (1) Consult the above section The Twelve Minor Prophets. (2) I recommend looking up David Jones's article, "Malachi on Divorce," *Presb* 15.1 (1989): 16–22. His defense of the superior Septuagintal reading—once properly understood—is on target, and one needs to note it. He takes issue with a number of scholars over their exegesis of 2:16. Jones's further research on the LXX is reflected in an article published in *JBL* (Win 1990). Another fine article is Markus Zehnder, "A Fresh Look at Malachi II 13–16," *VT* 53.2 (2003): 224–59. Among the commentaries, Clendenen has an especially full (14pp.) and carefully thought-through exegesis of 2:15b–16.

# NEW TESTAMENT COMMENTARIES

★ Beale, G. K., and D. A. Carson, eds. *Commentary on the NT Use of the OT*, 2007. Since the church has always held to the principle that Scripture interprets Scripture and the relationship between the Testaments is key for understanding each, works such as this prove spiritually and academically useful to a high degree. [*CBQ* 1/09; *RelSRev* 9/08; *JETS* 6/09; *BBR* 19.2; *BL* 2009; *NovT* 52.2; *EuroJTh* 18.2]. To follow current evangelical debates about interpreting the OT in the NT, see Berding and Lunde, eds., *Three Views on the NT Use of the OT* (2008), and Dan McCartney and Peter Enns, "Matthew and Hosea: A Response to John Sailhamer," *WTJ* 63 (2001): 97–105. For a critical orientation to the *status quaestionis*, see Susan Docherty, "NT Scriptural Interpretation in Its Early Jewish Context," *NovT* 57.1 (2015): 1–19; David Allen and Steve Smith, eds., *Methodology in the Use of the OT in the New* (2019); and the large-scale Henze–Lincicum, eds., *Israel's Scriptures in Early Christian Writings* (2023). Quite wide-ranging is Blowers–Martens, eds., *The Oxford Handbook of Early Christian Biblical Interpretation* (2019).
★ Beale, G. K., D. A. Carson, Benjamin L. Gladd, and Andrew David Naselli, eds. *Dictionary of the NT Use of the OT*, 2023.
★ *Calvin's NT Commentaries*. D. W. Torrance and T. F. Torrance, eds., ET 1958–72. In 12 vols. and published by Eerdmans. Calvin's theological comments have carried great weight for centuries, and these translations are adept. He covers all the NT except three books (2–3 John, Revelation). This set of Calvin is to be preferred to (still serviceable) reprints of the 19th century edition by the Calvin Translation Society (free online). [*EvQ* 7/98].
★ Metzger, Bruce. *A Textual Commentary on the Greek NT*, 2nd ed. 1994. [*JBL* 92.4]. Another, less in-depth UBS option is Roger L. Omanson, *A Textual Guide to the Greek NT* (2006) [*NovT* 50.3; *ExpTim* 11/07].

## JESUS & GOSPELS RESEARCH

★ Bauckham, Richard. *Jesus and the Eyewitnesses: The Gospels as Eyewitness Testimony*, 2006, 2nd ed. 2017. The thesis of this conservative work has had a major impact in broader scholarship and is attacked by skeptics. Gathercole of Cambridge terms it "the most significant recent book in my discipline" (2017: xi). [*Bib* 90.1; *JSNT* 31.2 (discussion); *NovT* 52.1; *JSHJ* 6.2 (discussion); *EuroJTh* 16.2; *Chm* Win 18; *ExpTim* 2/18; *JTS* 4/19; *ETL* 95.2; *JSNT* 40.5]. On memory studies particularly, I urge students to read Bauckham's essay in *JSHJ* 16.2/3 (2018). See also Bauckham below and under John's Gospel, and also his profound essays on Christology in *Jesus and the God of Israel* (2008).
★ Blomberg, Craig L. *Jesus and the Gospels: An Introduction and Survey*, 1997, 2nd ed. 2009. I have not found a better accessible evangelical content-survey. The companion is *From Pentecost to Patmos* (2006, 2nd ed. 2021).
★ Green, Joel B., Jeannine K. Brown, and Nicholas Perrin, eds. [𝓜], *Dictionary of Jesus and the Gospels*, 2nd ed. 2013. The first of IVP's famous "black dictionaries," Green–McKnight–Marshall (1992) was a standard evangelical reference work, though some of the contributors

were leading critics (e.g., Allison, Danker, and Painter). Now it is revised and, I argue, a bit more critically oriented. [*Them* 4/15].

★ Pennington, Jonathan T. *Reading the Gospels Wisely*, 2012. A wise and even entertaining "Narrative and Theological Introduction," engaging the key issues and questions.

★ Wenham, David. *Jesus in Context: Making Sense of the Historical Figure*, 2021. Valuable defense of the Gospels' historical value. From CUP. [*JETS* 9/22; *JSNT* 44.5].

★ Wenham, David, and Steve Walton. *Exploring the NT: A Guide to the Gospels & Acts*, 3rd ed. 2021. All six vols. in this IVP/SPCK series are worth purchasing. [*Anvil* 19.3].

✓ Aland, Kurt, ed. *Synopsis Quattuor Evangeliorum*, 15th ed. 1996; *Synopsis of the Four Gospels: Greek-English Edition*, 10th ed. 1993. Some cannot recommend Zeba Crook's all-English *Parallel Gospels* (2012) because the translation hardly is one [*JTS* 10/13].

✓ Allen, Garrick V., et al., eds. *Son of God: Divine Sonship in Jewish and Christian Antiquity*, 2019. [*JTS* 4/20; *JSNT* 42.5].

✓ Allison, Dale C. ‡ *Jesus of Nazareth: Millenarian Prophet*, 1998. See also the cleverly titled *The Historical Christ and the Theological Jesus* (2009) [*Them* 11/09; *JTS* 4/10; *JETS* 6/10; *CBQ* 7/10; *DenvJ* 3/09 (Blomberg); *BL* 2010; *Int* 10/10; *BTB* 5/11]; *Constructing Jesus: Memory, Imagination, and History* (2010) [*EvQ* 1/12 (Wenham); *CBQ* 4/12; *JSNT* 33.5; *Them* 11/11; *BSac* 7/13; *RelSRev* 6/11]; and *The Resurrection of Jesus: Apologetics, Polemics, History* (2021) [*CBQ* 4/23; *BBR* 33.4].

✓ Andrejevs, Olegs, Simon J. Joseph, Edmondo Lupieri, and Joseph Verheyden, eds. ‡ *The Synoptic Problem 2022: Proceedings of the Loyola U. Conference*, 2023.

✓ Bailey, Kenneth E. *Jesus through Middle Eastern Eyes: Cultural Studies in the Gospels*, 2008. See also his research listed under Parables below. [*EQ* 7/09; *CBQ* 7/11].

✓ Barnett, Paul. *Finding the Historical Christ*, 2009. [*BL* 2010; *CBQ* 1/11; *JTS* 4/13].

✓ Barton, Stephen C., and Todd Brewer, eds. ‡ *The Cambridge Companion to the Gospels*, 2nd ed. 2021. [*ExpTim* 12/22; *JSNT* 45.5].

✓ Bauckham, Richard. *"Son of Man," Volume One: Early Jewish Literature*, 2023. God willing, the first of an extensive, magisterial 2-vol. treatment of the Son of Man designation. Volume Two "will parse the meaning of 'Son of Man' in the Gospels." The project meets a need! [*Them* 48.3; *JETS* 3/24; *WTJ* Spr 24].

✓ Bauckham, Richard, ed. *The Gospels for All Christians: Rethinking the Gospel Audiences*, 1998. A corrective for the widespread notion that the Gospels were produced out of, and for, specific communities (see Stendahl on Matthew, Martyn on John); but Bauckham faces resistance [*JSNT* 84].

✓ Beilby, James K., and Paul Rhodes Eddy, eds. *The Historical Jesus: Five Views*, 2009. Getting Crossan, L. T. Johnson, Dunn, and Bock together in one book was a good idea and quite a feat. [*RevExp* Spr 10; *BBR* 21.2; *CTJ* 11/11; *JSNT* 33.5; *JETS* 3/11; *SBET* Aut 11; *TJ* Fall 10].

✓ Beitzel, Barry J., ed. *Lexham Geographic Commentary on the Gospels*, 2016. Unique, welcome resource. Note Sleeman's critique [*JETS* 6/19]. [*ETL* 95.2; *JSNT* 41.5; *Them* 43.3].

✓ Bernier, Jonathan. ‡ *The Quest for the Historical Jesus after the Demise of Authenticity*, 2016. [*BibInt* 26.3 (Keener)].

✓ Bird, Michael F. *The Gospel of the Lord: How the Early Church Wrote the Story of Jesus*, 2014. A major study commended "most warmly" by Dunn [*JTS* 4/15]. [*WTJ* Fall 16; *BBR* 26.3; *JETS* 9/15; *Int* 10/16; *EvQ* 10/15 (Wenham); *Them* 40.3]. More recent is *Jesus the Eternal Son: Answering Adoptionist Christology* (2017) [*JETS* 3/18].

✓ Black, C. Clifton. ‡ *The Rhetoric of the Gospel: Theological Artistry in the Gospels and Acts*, 2nd ed. 2013. Note also his invitation to read the Synoptics in a fresh fashion: *A Three-Dimensional Jesus* (2023).

✓ Black, David Alan, and David R. Beck, eds. *Rethinking the Synoptic Problem*, 2001.

☆ Blomberg, Craig L. *The Historical Reliability of the Gospels*, 1987, rev. 2007. [*BL* 2009; *RBL* 2011]. See his companion vols. on the reliability of John's Gospel (2001) and, more broadly, *The Historical Reliability of the NT* (2016) [*BBR* 27.3; *JETS* 6/18].

☆ Bock, Darrell L. *Jesus according to Scripture*, 2002, 2nd ed. with Benjamin Simpson 2017. A massive study (750pp.) of the witness of the four Gospels to Jesus [*JSHJ* 1.2; *Them* 43.2]. This is complemented by their *Jesus the God-Man* (2016). Earlier Bock published *Studying the Historical Jesus* (2002), a "Guide to Sources and Methods."

✓ Bock, Darrell L., and G. J. Herrick. *Jesus in Context: Background Readings for Gospel Study*, 2005.

✓ Bock, Darrell L., and J. Ed Komoszewski, eds. *Jesus, Skepticism, and the Problem of History: Criteria and Context in the Study of Christian Origins*, 2019. [*JETS* 12/20].

✓ Bock, Darrell L., and Robert L. Webb, eds. *Key Events in the Life of the Historical Jesus*, 2009. Nearly 950pp. of conservative essays from IBR: "a monumental achievement" (Barnett [*Them* 7/12]). [*BBR* 21.4; *JTS* 10/11; *JSNT* 33.5; *JETS* 3/11; *BTB* 11/12; *TJ* Spr 11].

✓ Bockmuehl, Markus. [𝓜], *This Jesus: Martyr, Lord, Messiah*, 1994. Later he would edit *The Cambridge Companion to Jesus* (2001) [*Anvil* 20.2].

✓ Bockmuehl, Markus, and Donald Hagner, eds. [𝓜], *The Written Gospel*, 2005. A fine FS for Graham Stanton. [*Anvil* 24.1 (France); *Evangel* Spr 07 (Wenham)].

✓ Bockmuehl, Marcus, and James Carleton Paget, eds. ‡ *Redemption and Resistance: The Messianic Hopes of Jews and Christians in Antiquity*, 2007. Valuable for so much more than just the study of the four Gospels.

✓ Brown, Colin., with Craig A. Evans. *A History of the Quests for the Historical Jesus*, 2 vols., 2022. An enormous, comprehensive, evaluative survey, published by Zondervan, lauded by liberals and conservatives alike. [*JETS* 9/23].

☆ **Brown, Raymond E.** ‡ *The Birth of the Messiah*, 1977, rev. 1993. A notable, exceedingly full, and moderately critical commentary on the birth and infancy narratives in Matthew and Luke. Brown was a Catholic priest who taught at Union Seminary, New York. Best appreciated by the scholarly pastor who reads quickly. [*JBL* 9/79; *EvQ* 4/80].

✓ **Brown, Raymond E.** ‡ *The Death of the Messiah*, 2 vols., 1994. This astonishingly learned historical and theological commentary on the passion narratives is over 1500pp. long—much too long to recommend to the pastor, despite its value. [*Int* 4/96; *PSB* 16.3; *JBL* Sum 96; *Chm* 108.4; *HBT* 12/96].

✓ Bryan, Christopher. [𝓜], *The Resurrection of the Messiah*, 2011. A lengthy OUP issue defending the bodily resurrection. [*CBQ* 4/13 (Wright); *JTS* 4/12; *RelSRev* 9/12].

✓ Bultmann, Rudolph. ‡ *The History of the Synoptic Tradition*, rev. 1963.

✓ Burkett, Delbert, ed. ‡ *The Blackwell Companion to Jesus*, 2011. [*JTS* 10/11; *JSNT* 34.5; *EvQ* 4/16].

☆ Burridge, Richard A. [𝓜], *Four Gospels, One Jesus? A Symbolic Reading*, 1994, 2005, 3rd ed. 2014. [*RevExp* 2/15; *CBQ* 10/15]. Note too the brilliant, widely cited dissertation, *What Are the Gospels? A Comparison with Graeco-Roman Biography* (1992, 2004, 3rd ed. 2018) [*CBQ* 4/20; *JSNT* 42.5]. On the influence of the latter, see Steve Walton, "What Are the Gospels?" *CBR* 14 (2015): 81–93.

✓ Carroll, John T. ‡ *Jesus and the Gospels: An Introduction*, 2016. Well-received and widely used textbook in mainline liberal circles. [*Int* 7/18; *JSNT* 39.5].

✓ Carter, Warren. ‡ *Jesus and the Empire of God*, 2021. Partly a summarizing of his important past work (see under Matthew). [*JSNT* 44.5].

✓ Chapman, David W., and Eckhard J. Schnabel. *The Trial and Crucifixion of Jesus*, 2015. A huge, brilliant research in WUNT. [*BSac* 10/17; *BBR* 25.3 (Gathercole); *JTS* 4/17 (Cook); *JETS* 9/16; *JSNT* 38.5; *Them* 40.3]. Note too Chapman's Cambridge PhD, *Ancient Jewish and*

*Christian Perceptions of Crucifixion* (2010) [*BTB* 5/12]; the controversial Gunnar Samuelsson, *Crucifixion in Antiquity* (2nd ed. 2013); and Cook below.

✓ Charlesworth, James H., ed. ‡ *Jesus and Archaeology*, 2006. [*JSHJ* 8.2 (2010)].

✓ Charlesworth, James H., with Brian Rhea and Petr Pokorný, eds. ‡ *Jesus Research: New Methodologies and Perceptions*, 2014. [*BBR* 24.4 (Blomberg); *JTS* 4/11; *JSNT* 37.5; *ExpTim* 2/15]. There was an earlier vol., *Jesus Research: An International Perspective* (2009) [*TJ* Fall 10].

✓ Chilton, Bruce, and Craig A. Evans, eds. [*M*], *Studying the Historical Jesus*, 1994; *Jesus in Context: Temple, Purity, and Restoration*, 1997; and *Authenticating the Words of Jesus*, 1999. All three vols. are from Brill.

✓ Collins, John J., and Daniel C. Harlow, eds. ‡ *The Eerdmans Dictionary of Early Judaism*, 2010. Quite useful. [*NovT* 54.2; *Them* 5/11; *BTB* 5/12; *JJS* 63.2; *RelSRev* 3/12; *TJ* Spr 12].

✓ Cook, John Granger. *Crucifixion in the Mediterranean World*, 2014. A substantial updating and expansion of Hengel's classic *Crucifixion* (ET 1977). [*JSNT* 37.5; *BSac* 10/17; *BBR* 26.4; *Int* 7/17; *RB* 123.2]. See Chapman above. At the prompting of his pastor father, Cook has also produced the scholarly study *Empty Tomb, Resurrection, Apotheosis* (2018) [*BBR* 30.2; *NovT* 63.1; *JTS* 10/21].

✓ Crossan, John Dominic. ‡ *The Historical Jesus*, 1991. Highly critical and tendentious piece [*Int* 7/93; *CBQ* 7/93], followed by *Jesus: A Revolutionary Biography* (1994).

✓ Crowe, Brandon D. *The Last Adam: A Theology of the Obedient Life of Jesus in the Gospels*, 2017. On a neglected topic. [*JETS* 12/17]. Along the same track is *Why Did Jesus Live a Perfect Life?* (2021) [*JSNT* 44.5].

✓ Dawes, Gregory W., ed. ‡ *The Historical Jesus Quest: Landmarks in the Search for the Jesus of History*, 1999. Useful for surveying past work. [*JSHJ* 1.2].

✓ Dawson, Nancy S. *All the Genealogies of the Bible*, 2023. Nothing quite like this large resource, completed with the assistance of Eugene Merrill and Andreas Köstenberger.

✓ DelHousaye, John. *The Fourfold Gospel*, 2020–. I have thus far seen two vols. in this unusual project, which is part synopsis/harmony (treating parallel texts together), part commentary (including citations of the church fathers and Greco-Roman literature), part application of the medieval *quadriga* (four senses of Scripture), part learned and thoughtful devotional application. An enormous amount of study has gone into this, and I can see how some would find it engrossing and of spiritual benefit. [*JSNT* 45.5].

✓ Denton, Donald L., Jr. *Historiography and Hermeneutics in Jesus Studies: An Examination of the Work of John Dominic Crossan and Ben F. Meyer*, 2004.

✓ Dungan, David Laird. ‡ *The Synoptic Problem: The Canon, the Text, the Composition, and the Interpretation of the Gospels*, 1999.

✓ Dunn, James D. G. [*M*], *Jesus according to the NT*, 2019. Besides a synthesis, Dunn also briefly covers "Jesus according to Acts," "Jesus according to Paul," "Jesus according to Hebrews," etc. [*JETS* 12/19; *JSNT* 42.5].

✓ Dunn, James D. G. [*M*], *Jesus Remembered*, 2003. Yet again, Dunn has offered an enormous, lucid study for students. Blomberg writes, "While not replacing Wright in boldness of hypothesis and scope of coverage nor Meier in painstaking analysis of minute detail, Dunn's work deserves to take its place with that of Wright and Meier as one of the three most significant, comprehensive historical Jesus studies of our generation." [*JSHJ* 3.1; *Anvil* 22.3; *DenvJ* 1/03 (Blomberg)]. See also *Jesus, Paul, and the Gospels* (2011) [*CBQ* 4/13; *Int* 7/12; *BTB* 8/12; *BSB* 12/11; *JETS* 3/12], and his essays in *The Oral Gospel Tradition* (2013) [*Them* 43.1].

✓ Dunn, James D. G., and Scot McKnight, eds. *The Historical Jesus in Recent Research*, 2005. Influential essays in the field over a 150-year period, in Eisenbrauns's Sources for Biblical and Theological Study series. [*JSHJ* 5.1].

✓ Eddy, P. R., and Gregory A. Boyd. *The Jesus Legend: A Case for the Historical Reliability of the Synoptic Jesus Tradition*, 2007.

✓ Edwards, James R. *The Hebrew Gospel and the Development of the Synoptic Tradition*, 2009. His claims have drawn controversy. [*ExpTim* 6/10; *JSNT* 33.5; *JETS* 3/11; *Them* 8/11; *BSac* 4/11; *RevExp* Sum 10; *RelSRev* 9/10]. See Edwards under Luke.

✓ Evans, Craig A., ed. *Encyclopedia of the Historical Jesus*, 2008. Also titled *The Routledge Encyclopedia of the Historical Jesus* (2010) [*JJS* 66.2]. Earlier he edited a 4-vol. set, *The Historical Jesus* (2004). Evans has been productive, authoring the cleverly titled Clarendon issue, *The Historical Christ and the Jesus of Faith* (1996); a book against the skeptics: *Fabricating Jesus* (IVP, 2006) [*BL* 2009]; the IBR Bibliography, *Jesus* (1992); and *Jesus and His World: The Archaeological Evidence* (2012) [*JETS* 12/12; *ExpTim* 4/13].

✓ Evans, Craig A., and David Mishkin, eds. *A Handbook on the Jewish Roots of the Gospels*, 2021. Taking up many key topics, this is a great resource—could serve brilliantly as a secondary textbook in a Gospels course (approx. 350pp.).

✓ Evans, Craig A., and James A. Sanders, eds. *The Gospels and the Scriptures of Israel*, 1994. On the same fascinating topic, see Willard Swartley, *Israel's Scripture Traditions and the Synoptic Traditions* (1994), Christopher M. Tuckett, ed., *The Scriptures in the Gospels* (1997), and Richard B. Hays's *Reading Backwards: Figural Christology and the Fourfold Gospel Witness* (2014).

✓ Eve, Eric. ‡ *The Jewish Context of Jesus' Miracles*, 2002. A shorter, more popular version is *The Healer from Nazareth* (2009).

✓ Foster, Paul, et al., eds. ‡ *New Studies in the Synoptic Problem: Oxford Conference, April 2008* (Tuckett FS), 2011. From BETL. [*NovT* 54.2; *ExpTim* 4/12; *BBR* 26.1]. See now Andrejevs, et al. (2023) above.

✓ Gathercole, Simon. *The Gospel and the Gospels*, 2022. A weighty and "splendid book" (Koester) by a Cambridge professor, arguing that the Four Gospels can be distinguished from the non-canonical gospels by their theology, especially their salvation message focused upon the teachings, death, and resurrection of Jesus. Gathercole laid a deep foundation for this study with some of the very best research on the non-canonical gospels (e.g., Gospel of Thomas). [*JETS* 6/23; *WTJ* Spr 24].

✓ Gathercole, Simon. *The Pre-Existent Son: Recovering the Christologies of Matthew, Mark, and Luke*, 2006. [*RTR* 12/12].

✓ Gaventa, Beverly Roberts, and Richard B. Hays, eds. ‡ *Seeking the Identity of Jesus: A Pilgrimage*, 2008. First-rate essays illustrating the resistance of mildly and moderately critical scholars to today's hypercritical reconstructions of the historical Jesus. [*JSNT* 32.3 (review discussion); *BL* 2009; *Them* 7/09; *JSNT* 3/10].

✓ Gladd, Benjamin L. *Handbook on the Gospels*, 2021. One of the better textbooks, taking a canonical approach. From Baker (446pp.). [*JSNT* 44.5].

✓ Goldsworthy, Adrian. ‡ *Pax Romana: War, Peace, and Conquest in the Roman World*, 2016. Noted because of its brilliance and references to NT Scriptures. Craig Evans calls Goldsworthy "essential reading for NT students and scholars" [*BBR* 27.3].

✓ Harding, Mark, and Alanna Nobbs, eds. *The Content and Setting of the Gospel Tradition*, 2010. A product of Australian scholars, highly recommended. [*Them* 5/11].

✓ Hays, Richard B. [*M*], *Reading Backwards: Figural Christology and the Fourfold Gospel*, 2014. Argues that the figure of Jesus and the Gospels are best understood when grappling with the OT texts used to present the Christ. [*CBQ* 1/16; *JETS* 9/15; *Int* 10/16; *RB* 123.4; *BibInt* 24.3; *JSNT* 38.5; *Them* 41.3]. An even fuller discussion is *Echoes of Scripture in the Gospels* (2016) [*ExpTim* 9/16; *CTJ* 11/17; *BBR* 27.1; *CBQ* 1/18; *JTS* 4/17; *JETS* 3/17; *Int* 1/18 (Watson); *NovT* 60.1; *SJT* 71.2; *JSNT* 39.5; *Them* 41.3].

✓ Hengel, Martin. [*M*], *The Four Gospels and the One Gospel of Jesus Christ*, 2000. Reflects a lifetime of study by a leading German NT professor. [*Anvil* 19.1]. Worth noting is that Hengel is fully on board with the idea that the Gospels were not produced for single communities but were general ("catholic") tracts; cf. Bauckham, ed., *The Gospels for All Christians*.

✓ Hengel, Martin, and Anna Maria Schwemer. [*M*], *Jesus and Judaism*, ET 2019. Skeptical German scholars wanted to ignore this when it first appeared (2007). A hefty work of prodigious scholarship (750pp.). [*JSNT* 43.5; *Them* 45.3].

✓ Hezser, Catherine, ed. ‡ *The Oxford Handbook of Jewish Daily Life in Roman Palestine*, 2010. [*BBR* 23.2].

✓ Holmén, Tom, and Stanley E. Porter, eds. ‡ *Handbook for the Study of the Historical Jesus*, 4 vols., 2011. This fine set is over 3600pp! Handbook? Costing $1300? [*BBR* 21.3; *JSNT* 34.5; *JETS* 9/12; *ETL* 89.4; *Them* 8/11 (Blomberg); *BTB* 11/13; *RelSRev* 6/13].

✓ Horsley, Richard A. ‡ *Jesus and the Politics of Roman Palestine*, 2014. [*CBQ* 7/15].

☆ Hurtado, Larry W. *Lord Jesus Christ: Devotion to Jesus in Earliest Christianity*, 2003. Lucid, impressive, and influential scholarship, drawing together NT research, early Christian history, and theology (Christology). [*JSHJ* 3.1]. Added to this is *How on Earth Did Jesus Become God?* (2005) [*JSHJ* 5.2].

✓ Hurtado, Larry W., and Paul L. Owen, eds. *'Who Is This Son of Man?' The Latest Scholarship on a Puzzling Expression of the Historical Jesus*, 2011. [*CBQ* 7/13; *JSNT* 34.5; *JETS* 6/12; *BibInt* 22.3; *BTB* 11/13; *JJS* 66.2; *RelSRev* 9/12]. This book is somewhat in critique of Maurice Casey, *The Solution to the 'Son of Man' Problem* (2007) [*JJS* 64.1], who drives a wedge between Jesus's Aramaic expression and the Greek of the Evangelists. See also Bauckham above and Mogens Müller, *The Expression 'Son of Man' and the Development of Christology: A History of Interpretation* (2008) [*JJS* 63.1; *JTS* 10/13].

✓ Johnson, Luke Timothy. ‡ *The Real Jesus*, 1996. One of the best critiques of the so-called Third Quest, by a conservatively critical Catholic.

✓ Joseph, Simon J. *Jesus and the Temple: The Crucifixion in Its Jewish Context*, 2016. [*JSNT* 39.5].

☆ Keener, Craig S. *The Historical Jesus of the Gospels*, 2009. A large (831pp.) and learned treatment of the biblical material and scholarship today. [*Them* 4/10; *BBR* 21.4; *CBQ* 4/11; *JSNT* 33.5; *RBL* 2011; *JETS* 3/11; *BTB* 2/11; *SBET* Aut 11; *RelSRev* 9/11; *TJ* Fall 12]. Added to this is the 2-vol., stunningly comprehensive *Miracles: The Credibility of the NT Accounts* (2011) [*JSNT* 35.5; *JETS* 12/12; *Them* 4/12; *DenvJ* 15; *TJ* Fall 13].

☆ Keener, Craig S. *Christobiography: Memory, History, and the Reliability of the Gospels*, 2019. Another enormous work from Keener (700pp.), this one seeking to "contribute to the epistemology of historical-Jesus research" (20). [*RevExp* 5/21; *Presb* Spr 20; *WTJ* Fall 20; *CTJ* 4/21; *BBR* 30.2 (Blomberg); *CBQ* 1/21; *JETS* 9/20; *Int* 4/21; *BSac* 4/21; *JSNT* 42.5; *Them* 48.3].

✓ Keith, Chris. [*M*], *Jesus against the Scribal Elite: The Origins of the Conflict*, 2014. Though the thesis is arguably overblown, Keith is on to something. [*JSHJ* 14.3; *JSNT* 43.5].

✓ Kelber, Werner. ‡ *The Oral and the Written Gospel*, 1983. The challenges to, and refinement of, the thesis continue in Thatcher, ed., *Jesus, the Voice, and the Text: Beyond The Oral and the Written Gospel* (2008) [*BL* 2010].

✓ Kelber, Werner, and Samuel Byrskog, eds. ‡ *Jesus in Memory*, 2009.

✓ Kingsbury, Jack D., ed. ‡ *Gospel Interpretation: Narrative-Critical and Social-Scientific Approaches*, 1997.

✓ Kirk, J. R. Daniel. ‡ *A Man Attested by God*, 2016. Along with his controversial position on sexual ethics, this book by Kirk, attacking the idea of a "high Christology" in the Synoptics, led to his leaving Fuller. He thinks Jesus was presented as an idealized human figure. [*JETS* 9/17; *Int* 10/18; *RB* 125.2; *SJT* 71.1 (Gathercole); *JSNT* 39.5].

✓ Knoppers, Gary N. [*M*], *Jews and Samaritans: The Origins and History of Their Early Relations*,

2013. A brilliant OT scholar offers a fresh research of the relationship, published by OUP. Called a "landmark" study [*CBQ* 1/15], and proves useful for studies in the OT, the Gospels, and Acts. [*Int* 7/14; *JHebS* 14]. See also Pummer, *The Samaritans: A Profile* (2015).

✓ Koester, Helmut. ‡ *Ancient Christian Gospels: Their History and Development*, 1990.

✓ Levering, Matthew. *Did Jesus Rise from the Dead? Historical and Theological Reflections*, 2019. An intelligent, conservative Catholic work, from OUP. [*CBQ* 4/20].

✓ Licona, Michael R. *The Resurrection of Jesus*, 2010. A huge IVP issue. [*JETS* 12/11].

✓ Licona, Michael R. *Why Are There Differences in the Gospels? What Can We Learn from Ancient Biography?* 2017. From OUP. [*WTJ* Fall 17; *BBR* 28.1; *JETS* 3/18; *JSNT* 40.5; *Them* 42.1 (Strauss)].

✓ Loader, William. ‡ *Jesus' Attitude Towards the Law*, 2002.

✓ Marcus, Joel. ‡ *John the Baptist in History and Theology*, 2018. See also the issue of *JSHJ* 19.1 (2021), dedicated to reviewing his revisionist study. [*JETS* 6/20; *CBQ* 4/20].

✓ McDonald, Lee Martin. *The Story of Jesus in History and Faith: An Introduction*, 2013. One of the better books for getting started. [*JETS* 9/14].

✓ McKnight, Scot. *Jesus and His Death: Historiography, the Historical Jesus, and Atonement Theory*, 2005. [*JSHJ* 5.1].

✓ McKnight, Scot, and Matthew C. Williams. *The Synoptic Gospels: An Annotated Bibliography*, 2000. From the IBR Bibliographies project, published by Baker. Needing an update is McKnight's useful *Interpreting the Synoptic Gospels* (1987).

✓ McKnight, Scot, and Joseph B. Modica, eds. *Who Do My Opponents Say that I Am? An Investigation of the Accusations against the Historical Jesus*, 2008. Evangelical essays approaching the issue of Jesus's identity from a different angle. [*JETS* 6/09; *BL* 2009 (Head); *EuroJTh* 18.2].

✓ Meier, John P. ‡ *A Marginal Jew: Rethinking the Historical Jesus* (ABRL) 5 vols., 1991–2016. Probably the fullest, most detailed study ever produced in the field (3500pp.). I venture my opinion that little here will help the evangelical preacher. [*CBQ* 7/10; *BTB* 8/10; *JETS* 9/10; *JTS* 10/13; *Int* 10/10; *ExpTim* 11/10; *Them* 11/10]. His Vol. V, subtitled "Probing the Authority of the Parables" [*ExpTim* 9/16; *BBR* 27.1; *CBQ* 7/20; *Int* 1/18], has been called somewhat "disappointing" [*JETS* 12/17 (Blomberg)].

Meyer, Ben F. ‡ *The Aims of Jesus*, 1979. Though dated now, many still count it as seminal (certainly influencing N. T. Wright) as it applies Lonergan's "critical realism."

✓ Moyise, Steve. ‡ *Jesus and Scripture: Studying the NT Use of the OT*, 2010. [*CBQ* 1/13; *JSNT* 33.5; *Them* 4/12; *JETS* 3/12].

✓ Murphy, Francesca Aran, ed. ‡ *The Oxford Handbook of Christology*, 2015. Treats both Bible and theology. [*JSNT* 38.5].

✓ Murphy, Frederick J. ‡ *An Introduction to Jesus and the Gospels*, 2005. By an authority on Jewish and Christian apocalypticism.

✓ Novenson, Matthew V. ‡ *The Grammar of Messianism: An Ancient Jewish Political Idiom and Its Users*, 2017. An OUP historical survey of the idea and various Jewish movements; this is a widely discussed book [*ExpTim* 4/18]. Earlier he wrote *Christ among the Messiahs* (OUP, 2012), which is important for Pauline studies.

✓ Perkins, Pheme. ‡ *Introduction to the Synoptic Gospels*, 2007. [*BL* 2009; *Anvil* 26.3–4]. Also notable is her *Resurrection: NT Witness and Contemporary Reflection* (1984).

✓ Perrin, Nicholas. *Jesus the Priest*, 2018. Drawing on the Synoptics. [*JSNT* 41.5].

✓ Pitre, Brant. [𝓜], *Jesus and the Last Supper*, 2015. Enormous, wide-ranging work on the topic, by a conservatively critical Catholic. [*BBR* 26.3; *JTS* 4/17; *JETS* 3/17 (Perrin); *ETL* 94.2; *JSHJ* 15.1; *SJT* 70.2; *JSNT* 38.5].

☆ Porter, Stanley E., and Bryan R. Dyer, eds. *The Synoptic Problem: Four Views*, 2016. Clear presentations of the two-source proposal (Evans: Markan priority + Q), Farrer hypothesis

(Goodacre: Markan priority, no Q), Griesbach hypothesis (Peabody: Matthean priority, followed by Luke and Mark), and "Orality and Memory hypothesis" (Riesner). [*Presb* Spr 18; *BBR* 27.2; *JETS* 9/17; *JSNT* 39.5].

✓ Powell, Mark Allan. ‡ *Jesus as a Figure in History: How Modern Historians View the Man from Galilee*, 1998, 2nd ed. 2013. One of the most widely used textbooks. [*JSNT* 36.5; *RevExp* 2/15; *BTB* 5/15].

✓ Poythress, Vern. *Inerrancy and the Gospels: A God-Centered Approach to the Challenges of Harmonization*, 2012. Few write at such length on this, in part because scholars tend to play up the distinctiveness of each instead of harmonizing. [*JETS* 12/13; *Them* 7/13; *BSac* 4/13; *DenvJ* 16].

✓ Reid, Duncan G. *Miracle Tradition, Rhetoric, and the Synoptic Tradition*, 2016. Called a "seminal study" of solutions to the synoptic problem [*ExpTim* 10/18].

✓ Reynolds, Benjamin E., ed. ‡ *The Son of Man Problem: Critical Readings*, 2018. [*JETS* 9/19].

✓ Riches, John. ‡ *The World of Jesus: First-Century Judaism in Crisis*, 1990. A Cambridge issue. For a well-written evangelical treatment, consult James Jeffers, *The Graeco-Roman World of the NT Era* (IVP, 1999).

✓ Riches, J., W. R. Telford, and C. M. Tuckett, with an Introduction by S. McKnight. ‡ *The Synoptic Gospels*, 2001. Collected vols. from Sheffield's New Testament Guides.

☆ Robertson, O. Palmer. *Christ of the Consummation: A NT Biblical Theology*, Vol. 1: "The Testimony of the Four Gospels," 2022. An inspiring redemptive-historical approach to the Gospels that would help any student or preacher (330pp.). My friend self-consciously carries forward Geerhardus Vos's study of "the historic progressiveness of the revelation process" as no one else has. What is the revelation connected with various phases: Jesus's nativity, John the Baptist, the temptation of Jesus, etc.? With his excellent theological mind, Robertson does justice to the distinctiveness of each evangelist's portrait of Jesus but aims at something higher: how they together testify to the Savior, how they together are revealing the unfolding story of redemption in Christ. There is an admirable maturity here. See his other books on *The Christ of the Covenants* (1980), *The Christ of the Prophets* (2004), *The Christ of Wisdom* (2017), etc.

✓ Robinson, James M., et al., eds. ‡ *The Critical Edition of Q* (Herm) 2000.

✓ Sanders, E. P. ‡ *Jesus and Judaism*, 1985. Followed by *The Historical Figure of Jesus* (1993).

☆ Schnabel, Eckhard J. *Jesus in Jerusalem: The Last Days*, 2018. A mammoth vol. (over 600pp.) that might be compared to Raymond Brown's *The Death of the Messiah* (1994), but more conservative, up-to-date, and with different foci. Students and pastors can learn so much! [*ExpTim* 2/19; *BBR* 29.1; *JTS* 10/19; *JETS* 9/19 (Blomberg); *JSNT* 41.5; *RevExp* 11/19]. His collected essays are a treasure: *Jesus, Paul, and the Early Church* (2018) [*Them* 45.2].

✓ Schröter, Jens, and Christine Jacobi, eds. ‡ *The Jesus Handbook*, 2017, ET 2022. Large vol. of essays more focused on historical questions and the debates over the life of Jesus. [*JSNT* 41.5; *ExpTim* 8/23; *CBQ* 1/24; *JTS* 4/24].

✓ Schweitzer, Albert. ‡ *The Quest of the Historical Jesus*, ET 2000. The famous 1906 demolition of the liberal 19th century Life of Jesus research. Bowden's translation (2000) is altogether a better, clearer work than the abbreviated 1911 2nd edition by Montgomery.

✓ Sievers, Joseph, and Amy-Jill Levine, eds. ‡ *The Pharisees*, 2021. A significant collection of 25 conference papers, "as close to an exhaustive account of the Pharisees in history and culture as has ever been done" (Novenson [*JSNT* 45.5]). [*Int* 10/23]. Cf. Yinger, *The Pharisees* (2022) [*Them* 48.1].

✓ Spencer, F. Scott. *The Passions of the Christ: The Emotional Life of Jesus in the Gospels*, 2021. [*JETS* 9/22; *CBQ* 7/22; *JSNT* 44.5].

✓ Stanton, Graham N. ‡ *The Gospels and Jesus*, 1989, 2nd ed. 2002. An Oxford publication and certainly among the best moderately critical introductions to the subject. See also his essays in *Jesus and Gospel* (2004).

✓ Stegemann, W., B. J. Malina, and G. Theissen, eds. ‡ *The Social Setting of Jesus and the Gospels*, 2002. [*JSHJ* 2.1].

☆ Stein, Robert H. *Studying the Synoptic Gospels: Origin and Interpretation*, 2001. This mature evangelical book focuses on the Synoptic Problem and older diachronic methods. It is an expanded 2nd ed. of *The Synoptic Problem: An Introduction* (1987). Also valuable is his *Jesus the Messiah: A Survey of the Life of Christ* (1996), widely used in Bible colleges and seminaries.

☆ Strauss, M. L. *Four Portraits, One Jesus: An Introduction to Jesus and the Gospels*, 2007, 2nd ed. 2020. One of the best, most inviting evangelical introductions. Works well in the classroom. [*BL* 2009; *Presb* Spr 21; *DenvJ* 23].

✓ Theissen, Gerd, and Dagmar Winter. ‡ *The Quest for the Plausible Jesus: The Question of Criteria*, ET 2002. Theissen is a leading European scholar in historical-Jesus study. [*JBL* Aut 99; *JTS* 49.2; *JSHJ* 1.2]. On the same specific topic is Porter, *The Criteria for Authenticity in Historical-Jesus Research* (2000).

✓ Tuckett, Christopher. ‡ *From the Sayings to the Gospels*, 2014. A convenient collection of the vast output of articles by a prominent critic, mainly touching on the Synoptic tradition and Q. [*NovT* 57.1].

☆ Turner, David L. *Interpreting the Gospels and Acts: An Exegetical Handbook*, 2019. Certainly deserves praise. [*JETS* 9/20; *Them* 45.2].

✓ Twelftree, Graham H. *Jesus the Miracle Worker: A Historical & Theological Study*, 1999. Cf. the Keener set on the topic. See also Twelftree's series of books on exorcism in the NT (1985–2007) [*CBQ* 10/10]. From the more liberal side, read Horsley, *Empowering the People: Jesus, Healing and Exorcism* (2022) [*JSNT* 45.5].

✓ Vermes, Geza. ‡ *Jesus the Jew: A Historian's Reading of the Gospels*, 1973.

✓ Wassén, Cecilia, and Tobias Hägerland. ‡ *Jesus the Apocalyptic Prophet*, ET 2021.

☆ Watson, Francis. ‡ *Gospel Writing: A Canonical Perspective*, 2013. The author, who has contributed so helpfully to Pauline studies, here "engages the historical, hermeneutical, and theological aspects of Gospel transmission and later canonization" (Milinovich [*CBQ* 1/15]). A major work, termed paradigm-shifting. [*JTS* 4/14; *JSNT* 36.5 and 12/14; *JETS* 3/14; *Them* 11/14 (Blomberg); *RelSRev* 9/14; *ETL* 92.4]. See Hamilton–Willitts, eds., *Writing the Gospels: A Dialogue with Francis Watson* (2019) [*Presb* Fall 19; *JSNT* 42.5]. More recent from Watson are *The Fourfold Gospel: A Theological Reading of the NT Portraits* (2016) [*WTJ* Spr 17; *BBR* 27.4; *CBQ* 7/18; *JTS* 4/17; *Int* 7/17; *HBT* 42.1; *Them* 41.3; *DenvJ* 5/18], which is probably the best introduction to his Gospels work; and *What Is a Gospel?* (2022) [*ExpTim* 6/23; *JSNT* 45.5].

☆ Williams, Peter J. *Can We Trust the Gospels?* 2018. Has appeal as a brief, popularly written (but learned) book to put in the hands of those with questions. My friend is Principal of Tyndale House and a superb scholar. [*JETS* 12/19; *EvQ* 93.1; *Them* 44.2]. See also his gem on the parables, especially Luke 15: *The Surprising Genius of Jesus* (2023).

Witherington, Ben, III. *The Jesus Quest: The Third Search for the Jew of Nazareth*, 1995, 2nd ed. 1997.

✓ Wright, N. T. [*M*], *Jesus and the Victory of God*, 1996; *The Resurrection of the Son of God*, 2003. Two vols. (#2 and #3) from the author's series, Christian Origins and the Question of God. A tour de force which seeks to understand, through research mainly on the Synoptics, "how Jesus' whole life, not just his death on the cross in isolation, was somehow 'gospel'" (*JVG*, xiv). Wright reads the Gospels against the backdrop of Jewish apocalyptic thinking, but is more moderate than critics like Allison and Ehrman. The series is an apology for rigorous historical study of what he believes to be the most important religious question of all. Everywhere in evidence is his ability to write "with such power and fluency" (Dunn). For *The Resurrection of the Son of God* [*Evangel* Sum 04 (Turner); *DenvJ* 1/03 (Blomberg)], the review discussion in *JSHJ* 3.2 (2005) is well worth looking up, including as it does Wright, Allison, Habermas, Goulder, Hurtado, and Evans.

NOTES: (1) Judith A. Diehl, "What is a 'Gospel'? Recent Studies in the Gospel Genre," *CBR* 9.2 (2011): 171–99. (2) In order to use many of the Gospels commentaries you must learn something about redaction criticism. A quick way is to study Don Carson's 24-page pamphlet, "Redaction Criticism: The Nature of an Interpretive Tool" (Christianity Today Institute, 1985), or the relevant section in *An Introduction to the NT* (2005) by Carson and Moo.

# MATTHEW

★ **Carson, Donald.** (EBCR) 2010. Updates the 1984 EBC. Even after the appearance of France, this may still be the most generally useful commentary on Matthew for the pastor (650pp.). The adjective that comes to mind is "sure-footed." Carson was allowed a great deal more space than other contributors to the series and used it well. There is mild redaction criticism. It was said of the EBC, "He has done his homework with great care, and regularly launches into very thorough explanations of particular exegetical, historical or theological points" [*BSB* 9/04]. I am delighted that Carson's revision (EBCR) gives extended life to this commentary. [*JETS* 6/85; *TJ* Spr 85]. Pastors will also note Carson's homiletical expositions of the Sermon on the Mount (see below) and Matthew 8–10 entitled *When Jesus Confronts the World* (1987). These expositions are essentially sermonic, but of a much higher caliber intellectually than the typical sermon. He also has one of the best study guides: *God with Us: Themes from Matthew* (1995, 2009).

★ **France, Richard T.** (NICNT) 2007. Those who anticipate forthcoming commentaries had a long wait for NICNT on Matthew. Several scholars in succession had contracts. France delivered, building upon his TNTC gem (see below). This could be considered the top pick for the evangelical pastor—but be aware of some of the exegetically and theologically controversial positions noted by Agan [*Presb* Spr 09]. France (†2012) was one of the most respected evangelical NT scholars in the world, "a Matthean scholar par excellence" (Hagner), and he set out to "locate the individual parts of the gospel within the overall narrative flow of the whole" (xviii). One caution: many would challenge his argument that the "coming of the Son of Man" in 24:29–31 is not the parousia. [*JTS* 10/08; *CJ* Win 09; *BL* 2008; *ExpTim* 2/08; *RelSRev* 12/08; *JETS* 12/08 (Turner); *BSac* 10/08; *Anvil* 25.3].

★ **Keener, Craig S.** 1999, (SRC) 2009. The first edition was a massive one-vol. work (721 + 300pp. of bibliography and indices), of real usefulness to both pastor and student. Keener chose to focus especially upon "the social-historical contexts of Matthew and his traditions on the one hand, and pericope-by-pericope suggestions concerning the nature of Matthew's exhortations to his Christian audience on the other" (1). The new edition is a revision and slight expansion; it complements Carson very well. Do not confuse this large pb with Keener's much briefer IVPNT, which preachers will find more accessible. [*ThTo* 1/00; *Int* 10/00; *Them* Aut 00; *Presb* Spr 00; *ScrB* 7/00; *Bib* 82.1; *SwJT* Spr 01; *EvQ* 1/04; *JETS* 9/01; *TJ* Spr 02; *RelSRev* 4/01; *DenvJ*]. See Jesus & Gospels Research (above), John, Acts, Galatians, and 1 Peter.

★ **Nolland, John.** [*M*], (NIGTC) 2005. As expected, Nolland has largely followed the research methods used in his 3-vol. WBC on Luke and produced a redaction-critical exegesis which is exceedingly thorough (nearly 1300pp. + 200pp. of bibliography). One difference is the more contemporary feel of *Matthew*, as Nolland gives greater attention to narrative criticism. I regard this as a better work for pastors than the earlier *Luke* because it is a little more focused on the text as we have it and spends much less time on the ins-and-outs of scholarly discussion. Contrariwise, some students might want more interaction with other exegetes. This is clearly one of the best commentaries on the Greek text, more accessible than Davies–Allison. The bibliographies are nearly exhaustive. Nolland wants to date Matthew prior to AD 70, yet thinks it "most unlikely" that the Apostle Matthew authored the Gospel. [*JTS* 10/07; *JETS* 9/06; *BL* 2007; *RB* 1/08; *NovT* 48.4; *RelSRev* 10/06; *BSac* 7/07; *ExpTim* 7/06].

★ **Quarles, Charles.** (EBTC) 2022. The author is well-known for his years of focused research on Matthew—see his EGGNT below—and here offers a sizeable exegetical and biblical-theological work (approx. 780pp.). I imagine this is rapidly becoming a favorite among Southern Baptists and also those outside that body. Students might choose his stellar EGGNT instead. [*JSNT* 45.5].

★ Wilkins, Michael J. (NIVAC) 2004. The largest vol. in the series (over 1000pp.) and built on a strong exegetical foundation. Wilkins develops the theme of discipleship, upon which he has written a monograph. The author completed his PhD at Fuller Seminary, has done pastoral ministry at a Presbyterian church, and now teaches at Talbot Seminary. As a preacher's companion alongside the more exegetical works, Wilkins has a much fuller discussion (e.g., see the Beatitudes) than most preacher's commentaries, but Green's BST may be just as good a value for the money. Also in the category of pastoral expositions well worth buying are: Reeves, O'Donnell, and Doriani. [*JETS* 6/05].

Alexander, J. A. 1861. Once reprinted from time to time, this is a classic by an amazing Princeton Seminary polymath, who served alternately as Professor of OT, Church History, and NT. The commentary was interrupted at ch. 16 by Alexander's last illness; the remainder of the Gospel (chs. 17–28) was covered by his previously prepared chapter summaries.

Allen, O. Wesley, Jr. ‡ (FBPC) 2013. [*JSNT* 36.5].

Allen, W. C. ‡ (retired ICC) 3rd ed. 1922. Scholars are divided over the value of this ICC. Carson rates it low, while Danker rates it more highly. Considering Carson's past work with Matthew, I place more weight on his judgment.

✓ Allison, Dale C. ‡ *Studies in Matthew: Interpretation Past and Present*, 2005. Collected essays from the main author of the Davies–Allison ICC set. [*JETS* 12/06; *JBL* Win 06; *BL* 2007]. Another, most stimulating read for students is *The New Moses: A Matthean Typology* (1993).

✓ Anderson, Craig Evan, and Matthew Ryan Hauge, eds. ‡ *Character Studies in the Gospel of Matthew*, 2024.

Argyle, A. W. ‡ (CBC) 1963.

✓ Aune, David E., ed. [*M*], *The Gospel of Matthew in Current Study*, 2001. [*WTJ* Fall 03; *RTR* 12/02; *SwJT* Sum 02; *RelSRev* 1/02; *BBR* 13.1; *Anvil* 21.2]. More dated on the same topic is Bauer–Powell, eds., *Treasures Old and New: Recent Contributions to Matthean Studies* (1996).

✓ Balch, David L., ed. ‡ *Social History of the Matthean Community*, 1991. Approaching the same topic is Saldarini, *Matthew's Christian-Jewish Community* (1994).

☆ Bauer, David R. *The Gospel of the Son of God: An Introduction to Matthew*, 2019. Has received plaudits. Boxall says the work "includes one of the finest discussions I have read of fulfillment and the kingdom in Matthew" [*Int* 10/21]. [*BBR* 31.3; *CBQ* 10/20; *JETS* 6/21]. Also from Bauer is *The Structure of Matthew's Gospel* (2015).

✓ Beare, Francis. ‡ 1981. Though a technical, lengthy commentary and widely consulted at one time, Beare is not regarded as of great value at this point. The scholarly approach seemed rather dated even when it appeared in print. [*JBL* 103.1].

F Beaton, Rick. ‡ (BNTC).

✓  Becker, Eve-Marie, and Anders Runesson, eds. ‡ *Mark and Matthew I-II*, 2 vols., 2011–13. See David Sim's essay, "Matthew: The Current State of Research." [*BBR* 24.2; *JSNT* 34.5].

☆  **Blomberg, Craig.** (NAC) 1992. A work containing great insight, just as one would expect in light of his previous research on the Gospels (e.g., *The Historical Reliability of the Gospels*) and parables (see that section below). This commentary is 460pp. long and does not directly treat the Greek text, though one senses that all the research is there to back up his conclusions. Along with Stein's *Luke*, Pohill's *Acts*, Garland's *2 Corinthians*, and Schreiner on *1, 2 Peter, Jude*, this is the best in the NT series. Nearly as valuable to the pastor as any of the above recommended commentaries on Matthew. The more I've used this, the more I have come to appreciate it. Comparing Keener with Blomberg, the former has more primary source material and an impressive bibliography, while the latter is a wiser, more mature guide in exposition, with a minimum of distractions. Blomberg is also half the price. I am eager to see a forthcoming CSC revised edition. [*Them* 10/94; *CTJ* 11/94; *CBQ* 1/94; *CRBR* 1994].

☆  Boice, James Montgomery. 2 vols., 2001. Of value to preachers. See John's Gospel.

✓  **Boring, Eugene.** ‡ (NIB) 1995. The author also has major commentaries published on Mark's Gospel, Thessalonians, and Revelation. [*JETS* 3/99].

Bornkamm, Günther, Gerhard Barth, and Heinz Held. ‡ *Tradition and Interpretation in Matthew*, ET 1963. Significant for launching redaction criticism on this Gospel.

✓  Boxall, Ian. [𝓜], *Discovering Matthew: Content, Interpretation, Reception*, 2015. [*WTJ* Fall 17; *Int* 1/18; *JSNT* 38.5].

✓  Boxall, Ian. [𝓜], *Matthew through the Centuries*, 2019. [*JSNT* 45.5].

Broadus, J. A. 1886. An old standby of preachers which can still be consulted with profit. Its strengths lie more in the area of exposition and homiletical hints than exegesis.

☆  Brown, Jeannine K. (TTC) 2015. The author is a capable scholar who writes well, and there is a wise selectivity about aspects of Matthew's Gospel which she engages in this succinct commentary for pastors (approx. 330pp.). She seeks to uncover the narrative theology in the text, understand the sociocultural backdrop of the stories and teaching, and trace how the theology (with its ethics) in Matthew's account of Jesus should shape the Christian community.

✓  **Brown, Jeannine K., and Kyle A. Roberts.** [𝓜], (THC) 2018. A blend of mainly narrative-critical commentary (270pp.) and theological essays (250pp.), which some say "proves to be a masterful example of the marriage between biblical studies and theology" [*CTJ* 4/20]. To my taste, the initial Brown section is more respectful of scriptural authority and most valuable. The collaborative essay section explores many topics from global, feminist, liberation, and political perspectives. [*RevExp* 11/21; *BBR* 29.3; *JETS* 3/20 (Turner); *Int* 4/21; *JSNT* 41.5; *DenvJ* 23]. Note that Roberts is known for *A Complicated Pregnancy* (2017), his book denying the Virgin Birth.

☆  **Bruner, Frederick D.** [𝓜], *The Christbook (Matthew 1–12)*, 1987; *The Churchbook (Matthew 13–28)*, 1990. These books are subtitled, "A Historical/Theological Commentary." The set was revised (2004), interacting with the massive amount of NT scholarship published the previous 20 years (Davies–Allison, Luz, etc.) and with influential theologians. These massive vols. (1400pp. total) are stimulating, mildly critical, and underline many preaching themes in Matthew's Gospel. Bruner is a mainline Presbyterian, known earlier for his valuable doctoral work in systematics, *A Theology of the Holy Spirit* (1970); this background helps explain why he is so theologically attentive. [*EvQ* 10/88; *RTR* 1/88, 5/92; *JETS* 3/91; *Anvil* 22.3; *EvQ* 4/05; *Them* 4/06; *BL* 2005; *SwJT* Fall 04; *ExpTim* 5/05; *CurTM* 12/07; *BSB* 9/04]. See also under John.

✓  Buchanan, George Wesley. ‡ (Mellen Biblical Commentary) 2 vols., 1996. The set costs only $239.90. I never saw this, but it was among the first works in a unique series of intertextual studies (now defunct). See Revelation. [*RelSRev* 1/98].

F   Capes, David B. (BGW).

F   Carter, Warren. ‡ (Illum). Previously he has written the well-regarded *Matthew: Storyteller, Interpreter, Evangelist* (rev. 2004) and a sociopolitical reading, *Matthew and the Margins* (2001). See Parables of Jesus (below).

Case-Winters, Anna. ‡ (Belief) 2015.

☆ **Chamblin, Knox.** (Mentor) 2 vols., 2010. A much beloved prof at RTS, Chamblin retired in 2001. This large work (1500pp.) is steadfastly, carefully exegetical, not so expositional—important to make clear because Mentor often is equally expositional and exegetical. There is a dated feel to the work; I found consistent use of BAGD, not BDAG, and no citations of literature appearing after Keener (1999), except one 2001 *WTJ* essay. Preachers will find a reverent tone and a number of insights.

✓ **Culpepper, R. Alan.** ‡ (NTL) 2021. Eagerly awaited by many, and a quite full (600pp.) interpretation. There is a measure of narrative criticism (though nowhere to the same degree as in his John research), but no bracketing of historical-critical interests. (See his past work on the Fourth Gospel, on Luke for NIB, and Mark for S&H.) Culpepper selects key textual issues and has notes on his own translation. Ten excursuses situate the Gospel in the first-century world and Second Temple Judaism. The question driving the research is Louis Martyn's (2): "Where does the document we are reading belong in the strains and stresses characteristic of early Christian history?" Culpepper's answer: the Matthean church was composed of law-observant Jews, elevated Peter, presumably had contact with Pauline Christians, and made "a concerted effort to construct an alternate path" for their community. "In the NT, Matthew is most closely related to James, in opposition to Paul's law-free mission to gentiles" (26). Many will critique such a construal and argue that the Gospels are not sectarian documents but written for a broad audience (see Bauckham under Jesus & Gospels Research). This is a well-written piece of mature scholarship and, in mainline Protestant circles especially, will be recommended as a first pick commentary on Matthew. [*Int* 4/23; *RevExp* 11/22; *JSNT* 45.5].

✓ **Davies, W. D., and Dale Allison.** ‡ (ICC-R) 3 vols., 1988–97. With painstaking work on the Greek text, the authors come to mainstream critical conclusions. Specialists value this magisterial and encyclopedic work as the finest exegetical tool available (2400pp.). Compare with Luz, which along with the ICC is an authoritative reference set. Replaces Allen in the series. These fat vols. must be consulted, but have become way too expensive, even in the pb editions released in 2004 (now totaling $270 on Amazon). I can no longer recommend the set's purchase. Advanced students will use it in the library, and the most diligent, scholarly, and well-heeled of pastors can buy it. [*JTS* 4/92; *JBL* Sum 91; *CBQ* 10/91; *Int* 7/91; *ExpTim* 2/93; *ThTo* 47.1; *EvQ* 10/98; *NovT* 41.2; *CTJ* 11/91, 4/94; *Bib* 78.4; *SJT* 54.1; *DenvJ*]. There is also a 2004 abridgment by Allison [*JTS* 10/07; *BL* 2006; *RelSRev* 10/06].

Dickson, David. (GS) 1647. Banner thankfully reset this Puritan classic in modern typeface. Retains value as a theological exposition but is not as worthwhile as his Psalms work. [*EvQ* 4/84].

☆ Doriani, Daniel. (REC) 2 vols., 2008. Exemplary sermons that are the fruit of long academic study—he taught a course on this Gospel for many years at Covenant Seminary—and that nurture the church with the life-giving word. Doriani models how to expound the Scriptures from the redemptive-historical angle.

☆ Doriani, Daniel. "Matthew" in *Matthew–Luke* (ESVEC) 2021. The author's exposition is full yet more concise than his REC above. All three Synoptics are very well-covered: Bayer does Mark, and Tom Schreiner treats Luke.

☆ **Evans, Craig A.** (NCBC) 2012. Beautifully produced, evangelical, and insightful, which is what was expected, given Evans's reputation as a top Gospels specialist. (He has written commentaries on the other Synoptics, including an especially thorough one on Mark. Since Matthew uses almost 90 percent of Mark's content, we can say Evans was well-prepared for this assignment.) His focus is on the text and, though citing much of the most important scholarship, "kept the engagement with scholarly literature to a minimum" (xv). Evans's handling of sociocultural and religious background is outstanding. Quite useful to students as a recent issue and for its learning in extrabiblical literature. [*VT* 64.1; *JETS* 3/13]. See also Carlston–Evans, *From Synagogue to Ecclesia* (2014), surveying theological motifs: "a major contribution to Matthean studies" (Foster [*ExpTim* 9/15]).

Fenton, J. ‡ (WPC) 1977. Critically oriented and uneven.

Filson, Floyd V. ‡ (BNTC) 1971. Disappointing, considering Filson's gifts.

☆ France, Richard T. (TNTC) 1985. Replaced Tasker's contribution. This is an excellent work, supplemented by his monograph, *Matthew: Evangelist and Teacher* (1989) [*JETS* 9/92]. Years ago, France's TNTC edged out Morris (but not Blomberg) as a pick for Greekless readers, especially if conserving funds. I was delighted with this fuller Tyndale entry (416pp.), and was even happier with the NICNT above, though the interpretation of ch. 24 is still off the mark.

✓ Gardner, Richard B. (BCBC) 1991. Received a laudatory review in *CRBR* 1992.

☆ Garland, David E. *Reading Matthew: A Literary and Theological Commentary*, 1993. Well-done indeed, and providing remarkable help per page read (270pp.). This same evangelical scholar has written vols. on Mark, Luke, both 1 and 2 Corinthians, and Colossians–Philemon. [*JETS* 9/97; *CBQ* 10/94; *CRBR* 1994; *RelSRev* 4/97].

☆ **Gibbs, Jeffrey A.** (ConcC) 3 vols., 2006–18. In keeping with the series' pattern, a massive and conservative Lutheran exposition. The vols. run to 1660pp. I have had less opportunity to use them, but find Gibbs to be an able exegete who writes with mind and heart. He studied under Kingsbury and follows him in his narrative approach, finding a tripart structure: 1:1–4:16; 4:17–16:20; 16:21–28:20. He consults much of the important literature in his exegesis, but scholarly interaction isn't the main aim in this pastor's commentary. [*BL* 2008; *JETS* 3/08; *BSac* 4/09; *CBQ* 4/12].

Green, H. Benedict. ‡ 1975. An OUP issue, packing a lot of background information into small compass. At one time this was worth consulting, if one were doing more thorough research, but can now be safely ignored.

☆ Green, Michael. (BST) 2001. An excellent companion (350pp.) to the more exegetical works I recommend. Should it be added to your own list? Students may hold off, but many pastors will buy Green as a homiletical aid. He taught a course on Matthew at Regent College and builds upon his earlier exposition, *Matthew for Today* (1988). Preachers on the lookout for additional expository helps might consider the sermonic vols. by Doriani, Boice, and O'Donnell, the commentaries by Bruner and Reeves, and the vintage Ryle.

✓ **Gundry, Robert.** [*M*], *Matthew: A Commentary on His Literary and Theological Art*, 1982, rev. 1994. A brilliant, erratic commentary coming out of the evangelical ranks—originally written for EBC, believe it or not. One of the most heavily redaction-critical works on Matthew, interpreting many elements of the story as midrash. It's hard to assess the author's true critical stance, for he states his full belief in the inspiration and authority of Scripture. [*WTJ* Fall 83; *JBL* 103.3; *EvQ* 7/83; *JETS* 3/83, 3/84; *TJ* Spr 82 (Carson)]. The 744-page revision is renamed, *Matthew: A Commentary on His Handbook for a Mixed Church under Persecution*, and attempts to answer the criticisms leveled at Gundry's method (e.g., "Where are the methodological controls?"). As a plus, Gundry prompts us to consider Matthew's distinctiveness as a gospel: a matter of vital interest to every preacher.

F  Gurtner, Daniel M. (WBC-R). Would replace Hagner.

✓ Gurtner, Daniel M., and John Nolland, eds. *Built upon the Rock: Studies in the Gospel of*

*Matthew*, 2008. From the Tyndale Fellowship NT Study Group, this represents some of the best evangelical scholarship. [*BL* 2009].

☆ **Hagner, Donald.** [*M*], (WBC) 2 vols., 1993–95. A fine redaction-critical work, called "certainly one of the best available" [*BSB* 9/04]. Just a quick look at the first vol.'s 75pp. of introduction and 400pp. of comment on chs. 1–13 shows this historically oriented exegesis to be quite thorough, and the second vol. is even better. Unlike some other massive works, Hagner is interesting throughout and does not get lost plowing through technical issues; he gives a great deal of attention to Matthew's distinctive message. The pastor working in the Greek should find this WBC very helpful. Hagner, now retired from Fuller Seminary, asks many of the right theological questions. There is less narrative criticism. Many probably bought this set in lieu of the expensive ICC vols.—Hagner's two vols. together cost half the price of a single ICC hb. [*Them* 10/96; *JETS* 3/99; *JBL* Sum 96; *JTS* 4/96 & 4/01; *TJ* Spr 98; *CTJ* 11/00; *RTR* 1/97; *RelSRev* 10/97].

Hare, Douglas R. A. ‡ (I) 1993. I have not used this work (320pp.), but it was called splendid by one reviewer. His Mark commentary in WestBC is highly theological and well-done too. [*CBQ* 7/94; *CRBR* 1994; *HBT* 6/94].

✓ **Harrington, Daniel J.** ‡ (SacP) 1991. The Jesuit author is also editor for this Catholic NT series, which is of greater interest to the student than the preacher. Evaluating the series as a whole, I judge the SacP vols. on the Gospels most valuable. That being said, *Matthew* is the weakest of the four. [*CBQ* 7/93; *Int* 10/93; *EvQ* 1/95; *Bib* 75.1; *CRBR* 1993].

✓ Hatina, Thomas R., ed. *Biblical Interpretation in Early Christian Gospels. II. The Gospel of Matthew*, 2008. For two companion vols., see Hatina under Mark and Luke. [*BL* 2010].

Hauerwas, Stanley. ‡ (Brazos) 2006. An exposition by a famous American theologian, prompting preachers to think hard about Matthew's message today. Reviewers are less sanguine about the quality of exegesis underlying the sometimes insightful exposition; see p.18 for a hint of his struggle to launch into the rough waters of commentary-writing and for his scheme to retell Matthew's story. Here is a provocative quote, reflecting on ch. 4: "Give the devil his due. He understands, as is seldom acknowledged particularly in our day, that politics is about worship and sacrifice." [*CBQ* 7/08; *JETS* 6/08; *BL* 2008].

Hendriksen, William. (NTC) 1976. Has been valuable for preachers, especially those in the Reformed camp. He probes a number of Matthew's theological emphases such as the kingdom of God. Very long (over 1000pp.) and sometimes prolix, this is one of his better commentaries.

✓ **Hill, David.** ‡ (NCB) 1972. A moderately critical commentary which in the past was quite useful for students, less so for pastors. Years ago Hill was Ralph Martin's first pick. With the passage of time, this commentary has much declined in value and is nowhere near the top of anyone's list. [*EvQ* 1/73].

✓ Kampen, John. ‡ *Matthew within Sectarian Judaism*, 2019. From AYBRL and treating a major topic of discussion in Matthean scholarship. [*JETS* 12/20; *JSNT* 42.5].

☆ Keener, Craig S. (IVPNT) 1997. Well-done. See Keener above.

✓ Kingsbury, Jack D. ‡ *Matthew: Structure, Christology, Kingdom*, 1975; *Matthew as Story*, 2nd ed. 1988. These redaction and narrative-critical works have had great influence in the discussion of Matthew's theology. Some of his conclusions are distilled in his brief Proclamation Commentary (1981). [*RTR* 1/77; *JBL* 6/77; *EvQ* 4/77].

✓ Kirk, Alan. ‡ *Q in Matthew: Ancient Media, Memory, and Early Scribal Transmission of the Jesus Tradition*, 2016. From a pioneer in "social memory" studies, and receiving much attention [*JSHJ* 15.1].

✓ **Konradt, Matthias.** ‡ 2015, ET 2020. A stand-alone commentary of moderate length (approx. 450pp.), translated by Eugene Boring and published by Baylor. Scholarly and theological, but not so technical. The author has for some time been a productive Matthean scholar, and he has much to say. [*ExpTim* 3/23; *BBR* 31.4; *CBQ* 4/22]. See his earlier *Israel, Church, and the Gentiles in the Gospel of Matthew* (2014) [*Them* 41.1].

✓ Lee, Jason K., and William M. Marsh, eds. (RCS) 2021. [*RelSRev* 9/22].

☆ Leithart, Peter J. *The Gospel of Matthew Through New Eyes* (TNEBC) 2 vols., 2017–18. A stimulating, fresh, even provocative survey of the Gospel (600pp.), intending "to show that Matthew organized his account of the life of Jesus as an Irenaean recapitulation of Israel's history, in which Jesus replays both major individual roles in that history (Moses, David, Solomon, Elisha, Jeremiah) as well as the role of the nation herself" (7). Strongly from a biblical-theological angle and quite accessible to a lay readership. Honestly, there are insights on every page, though some of his connections are debatable. See my comments on his *Revelation* and *1 and 2 Kings*.

Long, Thomas G. ‡ (WestBC) 1997. [*Int* 10/98; *PSB* 19.2; *RelSRev* 10/98].

F   Lowery, David, and John Lowery. (EEC)?

**Luz, Ulrich.** ‡ *Matthew 1–7* (ContC) ET 1989. Should be passed over in preference for the reformatted, retranslated Hermeneia vol. below [*ExpTim* 10/07]. This ContC vol. is translated by Linss from the 1985 edition, while the 2007 translation by Crouch comes from a revised German edition. [*JBL* Fall 92; *Int* 7/91; *ExpTim* 2/93; *CTJ* 4/94].

✓ **Luz, Ulrich.** ‡ *Matthew 8–20* (Herm) 1997, ET 2001; *Matthew 21–28* (Herm) 1997–2002, ET 2005; *Matthew 1–7* (Herm) 2002, ET 2007. If you have means and are an academic, buy this. A brilliant technical work translated out of the German EKK, this commentary is more accessible than ICC—for example, there is not a lot of textual criticism—and more concerned with interpreting Matthew's theology. Luz, a prof at Bern, is certainly worth consulting, particularly for the attention he pays to what German-speakers call *Wirkungsgeschichte* (more "reception history" than "history of interpretation"); there is much artwork included. The four vols. in German (1997–2002) become three in English. Note that this is a distinctive contribution to this Fortress series, one that is more useful to preachers than the vols. on Mark and John. See Luz above. [*CBQ* 1/02, 1/07; *JBL* Win 02; *Int* 1/03, 4/09; *HBT* 6/02; *SwJT* Spr 02; *JR* 7/02; *RelSRev* 1/02; *CurTM* 12/03; *JETS* 6/08; *BL* 2007, 2008; *ThTo* 4/08; *RelSRev* 10/06; *BSac* 4/07; *NovT* 52.3]. Students can also look up his *Studies in Matthew*, ET 2005 [*EvQ* 10/07; *RTR* 12/07; *JTS* 10/06; *JETS* 6/06; *Them* 5/07; *JBL* Win 06; *BL* 2006; *RelSRev* 4/07, 9/08; *BTB* Win 07], and the 1995 Cambridge work, *The Theology of the Gospel of Matthew* [*Int* 7/97; *JR* 4/97; *HBT* 12/96].

Mac Arthur, John. 4 vols., 1985–89. These Matthew vols. were among the first published in this ambitious project to cover the whole NT. About 27 vols. are out. I have to say I'm not real impressed with these expositions. There is some fine sermonic material in them, and I'm glad they're out there for lay preachers and Sunday School teachers, but I would not consider them the most dependable tools for seminary-trained pastors. Only to be used after one's own exegesis. Of a similar genre (practical exposition) but a bit more like commentaries are the vols. in PTW, mostly by Kent Hughes. On Matthew's Gospel compare O'Donnell. [*JETS* 3/87].

✓ Machen, J. Gresham. *The Virgin Birth of Christ*, 1930. The classic defense of Bible teaching, still being challenged. See *Born of a Virgin?* (2013) by Lincoln [*ExpTim* 11/14; *DenvJ* 17].

✓ Malina, Bruce J., and Richard L. Rohrbaugh. ‡ *Social-Science Commentary on the Synoptic Gospels*, 1992.

Mann, C. S., and William Albright. ‡ (AB) 1971. Has a huge introduction, but spotty and disappointing exegesis. They defend the Griesbach Hypothesis (i.e., reject Markan priority and Matthew's dependence on the Second Gospel). This hypothesis, which goes back to the early church and held sway until it went into eclipse in the early 1800s, was revived by

W. R. Farmer's *The Synoptic Problem* (1964) [*EvQ* 10/77]. See also Farmer's vol., *The Gospel of Jesus*. For a thoroughgoing critique of that thesis, consult C. M. Tuckett's *The Revival of the Griesbach Hypothesis* (CUP, 1983). Attacking both the Griesbach Hypothesis and Q is Mark Goodacre, *The Case against Q* (2002) [*NovT* 46.4; *ExpTim* 12/05]. A lively evangelical roundtable discussion of the various synoptic theories is Black–Beck, eds., *Rethinking the Synoptic Problem* (2001) [*NovT* 49.2]. See also Porter–Dyer under "Jesus & Gospels Research."

✓ McNeile, A. H. ‡ 1915. On the Greek text, and still useful for that reason—more so than Allen's old ICC.

Meier, John P. ‡ (NTM) 1979. A critical Catholic commentary by one who took a lead role in Gospels scholarship. His influence continues, and the controversial 5-vol. set, *A Marginal Jew: Rethinking the Historical Jesus*, displeases evangelicals. Meier contributed to the spate of recent critical books, which amounts to a Third Quest to reconstruct the Jesus of history. This movement, while not as radical as the "New Quest" Renewed (exemplified in the works of Mack and Crossan), alleges there is less continuity between the historical Jesus and the Christ of faith. [*JBL* 101.2].

F   Meier, John P. ‡ (~~AYB~~). Expect a reassignment after his passing (2022).

Mitch, Curtis, and Edward Sri. ‡ (CCSS) 2010.

☆ **Morris, Leon.** (Pillar) 1992. Joins his earlier commentaries on John and Romans; all are useful works for the expositor. This book on Matthew is not scintillating and doesn't break new ground, but it is solid, basic, dependable, and reverent. Like Hendriksen, its size and thoroughness are strengths. Compare with Blomberg's more incisive and up-to-date work. [*Int* 1/94; *EvQ* 1/95; *RTR* 1/94; *CRBR* 1994].

Mounce, Robert A. (NIBC) 1985. Highly regarded by some as a basic work for introducing this Gospel to beginning students. Mounce has written other fine commentaries, especially the NICNT on Revelation.

Mullins, Michael. *The Gospel of Matthew*, 2007. A large work (661pp.) I have never seen, published in Dublin. [*ExpTim* 7/09].

✓ Newman, B. M., and P. C. Stine. (UBS) 1988. A translator's handbook which is over 900pp.

✓ Neyrey, J. H. ‡ *Honor and Shame in the Gospel of Matthew*, 1998.

☆ O'Donnell, Douglas Sean. (PTW) 2013. Highly praised as a homiletical work by Yarbrough of Covenant Seminary (1088pp.). O'Donnell's studies in Matthew continued with an Aberdeen PhD, *"O Woman, Great Is Your Faith!": Faith in the Gospel of Matthew* (2021) [*JSNT* 45.5].

☆ **Olmstead, Wesley.** (BHGNT) 2 vols., 2019. I have not used it extensively, but it seems superbly done and interesting throughout—quite a compliment for a lengthy work (700pp.) on lexical, grammatical, and syntactical matters! Additionally, Olmstead can indicate the exegetical and theological payoff of his observations. [*ExpTim* 9/19; *CBQ* 4/20].

☆ **Osborne, Grant R.** (ZECNT) 2010. Doing what he does best, Osborne approaches this Gospel using a chastened redaction criticism to offer a careful, thorough exegesis of the Greek (over 1100pp.). He also employs a style of discourse analysis with text diagrams, in keeping with the series aims. Osborne (†2018) was a respected senior scholar, with major commentaries under his belt (e.g., *Revelation* in BECNT), and he taught Matthew to seminarians for over 30 years. He also did much pastoral work and knew what preachers need. Anyone desiring help with preparing expositional sermons will find it in abundance here. Blomberg [*DenvJ* 14] terms it "my preferred commentary on Matthew," except when he wants exhaustive technical discussion. Could easily go on the to-buy list. [*Them* 36.2; *BBR* 21.4; *JSNT* 34.5; *RBL* 2011 (Keener); *JETS* 12/11; *ExpTim* 8/12; *Them* 8/11; *BSac* 10/11].

✓ **Overman, J. Andrew.** ‡ *Church and Community in Crisis: The Gospel According to Matthew*, 1996. A fine 400-page work from the New Testament in Context series. The author is particularly interested in "the social world of the Matthean Community" (the subtitle of his 1990 Fortress vol.). This work in pb is more important than its size might first indicate, though the community idea has come in for deserved criticism.

F    Pao, David W. (TNTC-R). Would replace France.

Patte, Daniel. ‡ 1987. Subtitled "A Structural Commentary on Matthew's Faith." Patte does not attempt to answer all the questions taken up in a full-orbed critical commentary. Those curious about the hermeneutical approach—part of the New Literary Criticism—can consult his *What Is Structural Exegesis?* Truth be told, structuralism's star was fading even when this was published. [*JBL* 107.4; *CRBR* 1990].

✓    Pennington, Jonathan T. *Heaven and Earth in the Gospel of Matthew*, 2007. Originally published by Brill, the work argues that "kingdom of heaven" is not an insignificant variant on "kingdom of God." The reviews have been laudatory. [*BBR* 19.4].

F    Pennington, Jonathan T. (Pillar-R). Would replace Morris.

✓    Piotrowski, Nicholas G. *Matthew's New David at the End of Exile*, 2016. [*JETS* 12/17].

Platt, David. *Exalting Jesus in Matthew* (CCE) 2013.

✓    Plummer, Alfred. 1915. Reprinted many times but, like Allen and McNeile, is dated.

✓    Powell, Mark Allan. ‡ *Chasing the Eastern Star: Adventures in Biblical Reader-Response Criticism*, 2001. After explaining his take on this controversial method, Powell applies it to the story of the Magi. As several reviews have stated, the author is engaging and witty. [*Evangel* Sum 03; *Anvil* 19.3].

✓    Powell, Mark Allan, ed. ‡ *Methods for Matthew*, 2009. The publisher (CUP) describes this as "a primer on six exegetical approaches that have proved to be especially useful and popular." Leading scholars contribute. [*BBR* 20.2; *Int* 10/11; *JETS* 3/11; *ExpTim* 4/11].

✓    Quarles, Charles L. *A Theology of Matthew*, 2013. From the P&R series Explorations in Biblical Theology. [*WTJ* Fall 14; *Chm* Win 14; *JETS* 3/15; *Them* 4/14].

☆    **Quarles, Charles.** (EGGNT) 2017. Very well-done as a guide for students into lexical, grammatical, and syntactical matters. What distinguishes the work is the measure of high-quality discourse analysis he adds to the mix. Note that Quarles also includes homiletical thoughts. Compare with Olmstead. [*ExpTim* 5/18; *JSNT* 41.5].

☆    Reeves, Rodney. (SGBC) 2017. Writing in a most engaging style, the Baptist author provides a well-studied and organized interpretation of the text before moving to contemporary application. His strong interests in discipleship and spirituality shine through. I find Reeves to be a careful and sensitive interpreter; he delves deeply into the text so as to explain details of Matthew's narrative and theology. Perhaps stronger on exposition and spiritual application than exegesis, but Reeves has done much homework in the best technical commentaries. An enjoyable read, and one of the best recent expositions of this Gospel! Reeves is a prof who loves the church and has served as interim preacher at more than thirty congregations (219). *DenvJ* makes this one of their top picks for pastors (550pp.). [*JSNT* 41.5].

✓    Riches, J., and D. C. Sim, eds. ‡ *The Gospel of Matthew in Its Roman Imperial Context*, 2005.

☆    Ridderbos, Herman. (BSC) 1952–54, ET 1987. Quite helpful theologically and in a readable format [*JETS* 3/91 (Carson)]. My former prof, Karl Cooper, told me that Ridderbos's *The Coming of the Kingdom* (1962) is even more helpful and stimulating for work in Matthew's Gospel. He was right.

Runesson, Anders. ‡ *Divine Wrath and Salvation in Matthew*, 2016. A major, impressively detailed study (465pp.). [*JSNT* 40.5; *RevExp* 2/19]. In my opinion, Matthew comes across as covenantal nomism on steroids (salvation through Torah-observance): "the Mosaic covenant is what Matthew's Jesus is restoring in order to save his people" (203). But Runesson's work is indicative of a major trend in Gospels research: interpretation *within* the Jewish context, not against the background of Judaism. See also Runesson–Gurtner (eds.), *Matthew within Judaism: Israel and the Nations in the First Gospel* (2020).

☆ Ryle, J. C. (CrossC) 1993.

✓ **Schnackenburg, Rudolf.** ‡ 1985–87, ET 2002. From a leading German NT scholar. This commentary can be consulted by students who want a more historically oriented and theological work from a Catholic and critical perspective. It is heavy on redaction criticism. I'd say this Eerdmans pb (329pp.) was not one of his stronger efforts. Schnackenburg is better known for brilliant works on John's Gospel, Ephesians, and John's Epistles. [*EvQ* 7/04; *RTR* 12/03; *JETS* 12/03; *Int* 7/03; *ExpTim* 10/04; *CurTM* 12/03].

✓ Schreiner, Patrick. *Matthew, Disciple and Scribe*, 2019. A Baker issue that illumines how the scribe-teacher Matthew writes about the sage-teacher Jesus. [*WTJ* Spr 20; *JETS* 12/20; *Int* 4/22 (Brown); *EvQ* 93.2; *JSNT* 42.5; *Them* 45.1; *DenvJ* 24]. His PhD was *The Body of Jesus: A Spatial Analysis of the Kingdom in Matthew* (2016) [*JSNT* 39.5].

✓ Schweizer, Eduard. ‡ ET 1975. His three vols. on the Synoptics make ready use of redaction criticism and are designed for pastors, often with good insights. Much better on Mark and Luke than on Matthew. Carson notes that "in this volume Schweizer devotes almost all his space to non-Markan material in Matthew, making the work almost useless to those who do not have the other commentary." [*RTR* 1/77; *EvQ* 7/76].

✓ **Senior, Donald.** ‡ (ANTC) 1998. Though not often interacting with other scholarly positions—see the skimpy bibliography—Senior's work is among the best compact exegetical commentaries on this Gospel from the critical side. Cf. the Allison abridgement. The author, a recognized expert on Matthew, teaches at Catholic Theological Union, Chicago, has written *What Are They Saying about Matthew?* (2nd ed. 1996), and also contributed *Matthew* to IBT (1997). [*CBQ* 1/00; *ThTo* 7/98; *RelSRev* 7/99].

✓ Senior, Donald, ed. ‡ *The Gospel of Matthew at the Crossroads of Early Christianity*, 2011. Another huge vol. from BETL. [*BBR* 23.4; *JSNT* 35.5; *ExpTim* 12/12].

F Sider-Hamilton, Catherine. (NCCS).

✓ Sim, David C. ‡ *The Gospel of Matthew and Christian Judaism*, 1998.

✓ Simonetti, Manlio, ed. (ACCS) 2 vols., 2001–02. [*JETS* 9/03; *RelSRev* 10/02; *BBR* 13.1].

Smith, Robert. ‡ (Augsburg Commentary on the NT) 1988.

Spurgeon, Charles. *The Gospel of the Kingdom*, 1893. Reprinted from time to time.

✓ Stanton, Graham. ‡ *A Gospel for a New People*, 1992. A very stimulating read for the student and one of my favorite books on Matthew. See also his collected essays: *The Interpretation of Matthew* (1983, 2nd ed. 1995), and *Studies in Matthew and Early Christianity* (2013).

✓ Stendahl, Krister. ‡ *The School of St. Matthew and Its Use of the OT*, 1954, 2nd ed. 1968. One of the first studies attempting to trace the alleged influence of the believing communities surrounding the Apostles on the shaping of the Gospels. [*JBL* 89.2]. Compare with Martyn's *History and Theology in the Fourth Gospel* (1968) and R. E. Brown's work on the Johannine literature, *The Community of the Beloved Disciple* (1979).

✓ Stonehouse, Ned B. *The Witness of Matthew and Mark to Christ*, 1944. To appreciate the significance of this work and its companion, *The Witness of Luke to Christ*, see Silva's two articles on "Ned B. Stonehouse and Redaction Criticism" in *WTJ* 40. Both of Stonehouse's works were combined in one vol.: *The Witness of the Synoptic Gospels to Christ* (1979). You'll find the author to be both a superb exegete and a pioneer.

✓ **Talbert, Charles H.** ‡ (Paideia) 2010. "What is offered here is an attempt at a fresh reading of the First Gospel" (Preface), with a first-century reader-centered approach ("reading with the authorial audience"). Talbert is a respected Baylor academic, learned in his field; I think his essays are more valuable than some of his commentary work (over 320pp.). He usually brackets historical issues, but dates the Gospel a bit later (80–100). As Davids notes, there is nary a Greek letter or a transliterated word in the book [*BBR* 21.4]. [*CBQ* 1/12; *Int* 4/12; *ExpTim* 6/11].

Tasker, R. V. G. (retired TNTC) 1961. Has had some value as a quick reference.

☆ **Turner, David L.** (BECNT) 2008. A competent conservative exegesis by a prof at Grand Rapids Theological Seminary who has been publishing on Matthew for a long time. Turner associates himself with the progressive dispensational camp along with such people as Bock. He reads the Gospel as coming from a "Christian-Jewish" perspective, "as the voice of 'Jews for Jesus' as it were" (3). Interestingly, he did doctoral studies at Hebrew Union College as well as Grace Seminary. A strength of the commentary is his focus upon the narrative, its features and flow. He eschews a redactional approach which might read "Matthew as an adaptation of Mark" (3). [*ExpTim* 5/09; *RelSRev* 12/08; *Them* 9/08; *JETS* 9/09; *BL* 2009; *CBQ* 10/11]. I count this vol. among the weaker entries in the very strong BECNT.

Turner, David L., *The Gospel of Matthew*, and Darrell L. Bock, *The Gospel of Mark* (CorBC) 2005. Solid conservative scholarship, more from a moderate dispensational perspective. Both concisely cover the basic issues and then move toward application. [*JETS* 12/07].

✓ Vine, Cedric E. W. ‡ *The Audience of Matthew: An Appraisal of the Local Audience Thesis*, 2014. In the LNTS series, and criticizing the local audience theory.

✓ Waetjen, Herman C. ‡ *Matthew's Theology of Fulfillment, Its Universality and Its Ethnicity: God's New Israel as the Pioneer of God's New Humanity*, 2019. Actually a commentary. [*BBR* 30.3; *BibInt* 27.2; *JSNT* 40.5].

— Williams, D. H. (TCB) 2018. [*JSNT* 41.5].

Willitts, Joel. *Matthew's Messianic Shepherd-King*, 2007. [*JETS* 3/09; *EuroJTh* 18.1].

✓ **Wilson, Walter T.** [𝓜], (ECC) 2 vols., 2022. A major, large-scale work by a Candler prof, who earlier published *Healing in the Gospel of Matthew* (2014) [*JSNT* 38.5]. The commentary is well-informed by Matthean scholarship and reads the Gospel as "a catechetical work that expresses the ideological and institutional concerns of a faction of disaffected Jewish followers of Jesus in the late first century" (blurb). [*ExpTim* 5/23; *RelSRev* 9/23; *JETS* 3/24].

✓ **Witherington, Ben, III.** (S&H) 2006. This exposition, by perhaps the most prolific NT scholar today, would be cause for more preachers' celebration, were it not so poorly edited and proofread, if proofread at all [*DenJ* 11/06]. Though not a work of profound scholarship, it is the product of careful study and is a help to those preparing sermons (550pp.). His writing and some of the accompanying artwork (e.g., p.518) provoke reflection. As with his work on John's Gospel, he attempts a "sapiential reading," wanting to interpret Matthew as owing much to ancient Israel's wisdom tradition. The thesis is less than convincing, in my opinion. [*Int* 1/08; *RelSRev* 12/08].

NOTES: (1) Please remember the recommendation of Calvin's Commentaries. (2) See Richard France, "Matthew's Gospel in Recent Study," *Them*, 1/89; John Ziesler's "Which Is the Best Commentary? I. Matthew," *ExpTim*, 12/85; David C. Sim, "The Synoptic Gospels," *ExpTim*, 4/08. (3) Darrell L. Bock, "Commentaries on the Synoptic Gospels" (339–63), in *On the Writing of NT Commentaries*, eds. Porter and Schnabel, cited in the Introduction.

## SERMON ON THE MOUNT

★ Ferguson, Sinclair B. *Kingdom Living in a Fallen World*, 1986. Excellent, edifying study now being published by Banner of Truth under the title *The Sermon on the Mount*. Ferguson's is one of the very best devotional works on the Sermon, and has served well, I know, as a guide for Bible studies. [*RTR* 9/88; *SBET* Spr 90].

★ Lloyd-Jones, D. Martyn. 1959–60. A lengthy, reverent, penetrating exposition, which deserves a place on every pastor's shelf! Lloyd-Jones's collection of sermons will never lose its value to the preacher. Has been reprinted many times.

★ **Pennington, Jonathan T.** *The Sermon on the Mount and Human Flourishing*, 2017. A remarkable, fresh interpretation which will spawn many a sermon (from more academic ministers) and possibly provoke NT profs to revise their lecture notes. A Baker Academic release. [*JETS* 6/18; *Them* 44.3].

★ Stott, John R. W. (BST) 1978. Formerly titled *Christian Counter-Culture* (210pp.), this is "a very crisp, clear and brief analysis" of the Sermon on the Mount, "standing alongside Lloyd-Jones" (George Knight). [*ExpTim* 5/78; *EvQ* 7/78; *JETS* 6/80].

✧ ✧ ✧ ✧ ✧ ✧

Akin, Daniel L. *Exalting Jesus in the Sermon on the Mount* (CCE) 2019.

✓ **Allison, Dale C., Jr.** ‡ 1999. Building upon the 3-vol. ICC on Matthew, "this book is to be commended to students and general readers alike" (Ruth Edwards). [*ExpTim* 1/00; *RelSRev* 1/01].

Augsburger, Myron. *The Expanded Life*, 1972. A popularly styled exposition.

✓ **Baasland, Ernst.** ‡ *Parables and Rhetoric in the Sermon on the Mount*, 2015. A valuable, large-scale (650pp.), technical treatment of Matthew 5–7, written by a retired Norwegian scholar and former Lutheran bishop. He argues that both the parabolic language (a third of the material) and the rhetorical argumentation in the Sermon have been neglected in scholarship. [*ExpTim* 2/16; *RB* 128.4; *JSNT* 38.5; *Them* 41.1]. His collected essays on the Sermon are in *Radical Philosophy of Life* (2020).

Barclay, William. ‡ *And Jesus Said*, 1970.

✓ Bauman, Clarence. ‡ 1985. Large-scale, from Mercer U. Press. Originally Bauman's Edinburgh PhD, it focuses on cataloging the modern history of interpretation.

✓ **Betz, Hans Dieter.** ‡ (Herm) 1995. A huge (768-page) commentary on both Matthew 5–7 and Luke 6, which should be consulted. No previous exegetical work on the Sermon on the Mount has ever run to this length. This detailed, technical commentary emphasizes parallel texts and issues of rhetorical criticism; Betz writes for specialists. It is the rare expositor who could put this tome to good use. Rather critical in its orientation. See also his *Essays on the Sermon on the Mount* (1985). [*ThTo* 10/96; *JETS* 6/99; *JBL* Spr 98; *Int* 7/97; *CBQ* 4/97; *SwJT* Sum 96; *PSB* 17.3; *JR* 1/98].

✓ Black, C. Clifton. ‡ *The Lord's Prayer*, 2018. In the Interpretation series. [*Int* 1/20; *SJT* 73.3; *JSNT* 42.5].

Boice, James M. 1972. A sermonic exposition of value, from early in his pastoral ministry.

☆ Bonhoeffer, Dietrich. [𝓜], *The Cost of Discipleship*, ET 1959. Includes some arresting exposition of sections of the Sermon on the Mount. He argues that "only those who believe obey, . . . only those who obey believe" (68). Bonhoeffer's personal history is well-known. Connected with the Neo-Orthodox Confessing Church during the Third Reich, he was imprisoned at Buchenwald for opposing Hitler and finally martyred by the S.S. at Flossenbürg concentration camp. For a scholarly edition see *Discipleship*, vol.4 in his collected works (Fortress, 1996).

✓ Bradshaw, Timothy. ‡ *Praying as Believing: The Lord's Prayer and the Christian Doctrine of God*, 1998.

☆ Calvin, John. *Sermons on the Beatitudes*, 1560, ET 2006. A brief (114pp.) but precious book. [*Presb* Fall 07; *RTR* 8/09; *Chm* Aut 12; *RTR* 8/10].

☆ Carson, Donald. 1978. A superb exposition with exegetical depth to it. This was reprinted in 1999 by Global Christian Publishers, combined in an inexpensive pb with Carson's exposition of Matthew 8–10, *When Jesus Confronts the World*. I expect this will retain value over the years. A wise purchase for pastors.

✓ Carter, Warren. *What Are They Saying about Matthew's Sermon on the Mount?* 1994. Students can make excellent use of Carter.

Chambers, Oswald. *Studies in the Sermon on the Mount*, 1960 reprint.

✓ **Davies, W. D.** ‡ *The Setting of the Sermon on the Mount*, 1964. A scholarly study of great importance, though Guelich and Betz became the premier studies.

✓ Eklund, Rebekah. *The Beatitudes through the Ages*, 2021. Includes some fine interpretive work on the texts of Matthew and Luke before presenting a thorough reception-history research. [*WTJ* Spr 22; *JETS* 3/22; *Int* 4/23].

☆ Doriani, Daniel M. 2006. Well-done, full, Reformed exposition.

Fleer, David, and Dave Bland, eds. ‡ *Preaching the Sermon on the Mount*, 2007.

✓ Greenman, Jeffrey, Timothy Larsen, and Stephen Spencer, eds. *The Sermon on the Mount through the Centuries*, 2007. Not to be missed! Cf. Eklund. [*RelSRev* 3/08].

☆ **Guelich, Robert A.** [𝓜], 1982. This immensely learned, mildly critical book has a wealth of information and, though aging, is still regarded as a standard historical-critical commentary on this portion of Scripture. Compare to the other heavyweight academic studies by Allison, Betz, and Davies. Was reprinted by W Publishing Group in pb, but now seems o/p. Recommended for purchase in all previous editions of the guide. [*JBL* 103.3; *TJ* Fall 83 (Wenham)].

☆ Gupta, Nijay K. *The Lord's Prayer* (S&H) 2017. Nothing quite like this surprisingly full work (pushing 200pp.) for setting the context (OT prayers, Jewish prayers, Jesus's own prayer life, etc.), and Gupta's exegesis and exposition are impressive in content and presentation (many visual aids). [*JETS* 9/19; *Int* 7/19].

Hart, Addison Hodges. *Taking Jesus at His Word*, 2012. [*ExpTim* 10/14; *RevExp* Sum 13].

Hauerwas, Stanley, and William H. Willimon. [𝓜], *Lord, Teach Us to Pray: The Lord's Prayer and the Christian Life*, 1996. Well-received, widely used pastoral treatment from two famous mainline Protestants.

Hendriksen, William. 1934.

☆ Hughes, R. Kent. (PTW) 2001. Another really thoughtful evangelical exposition to compete with Stott, Lloyd-Jones, Ferguson, etc. [*BSac* 1/03].

Hunter, A. M. [𝓜], *A Pattern for Life*, 1965. Any who have used Hunter's works are grateful for his clear style and insights. He was a very careful, mildly critical NT prof at Aberdeen.

✓ Jeremias, Joachim. ‡ ET 1961.

Kendall, R. T. 2011. About 400pp. of sermonic/devotional material by a successor of Martyn Lloyd-Jones at Westminster Chapel. [*BSac* 1/13].

✓ Kissinger, W. S. ‡ *The Sermon on the Mount: A History of Interpretation and Bibliography*, 1975.

✓ Klein, William W. *Become What You Are: Spiritual Formation according to the Sermon on the Mount*, 2006. Helpful in its move from analysis of the text to practice.

✓ Lapide, Pinchas. ‡ ET 1986. Influential interpretation, from an Orthodox Jewish perspective, indicting the church. Published by Orbis, but o/p.

✓ Levine, Amy-Jill. ‡ 2020. Termed "a beginner's guide," from a brilliant, liberal Jewish scholar at Vanderbilt. [*JETS* 6/21].

✓ Lundbom, Jack R. [𝓜], *Jesus' Sermon on the Mount: Mandating a Better Righteousness*, 2015. Something of a rarity for a major OT scholar to write such a full expositional commentary on the Sermon. [*CBQ* 1/19; *JETS* 12/16; *Int* 7/17].

Luther, Martin. "The Sermon on the Mount (Sermons)," *Luther's Works*, vol. 21, ET 1956.

✓ Mattison, William C., III. *The Sermon on the Mount and Moral Theology: A Virtue Perspective*, 2017. Readers will take away "a greater appreciation of both the Sermon and Thomas Aquinas" (Ridlehoover [*CBQ* 4/20]). [*SJT* 72.2].

☆ **McKnight, Scot.** (SGBC) 2013. Though not in an academic series, McKnight distills an abundance of good scholarship and is useful to students. The main users of this SGBC (300pp.), however, will be pastors and Bible study leaders. He terms himself Anabaptist (254) and, at the outset, protests against interpreters who have "softened, reduced, recontextualized, and in some cases abandoned what Jesus taught" (1). [*JETS* 9/14].

✓ Patte, Daniel. ‡ *The Challenge of Discipleship: A Critical Study of the Sermon on the Mount as Scripture*, 1999. [*Int* 4/01].

Pelikan, Jaroslav. ‡ *Divine Rhetoric: The Sermon on the Mount as Message and as Model in Augustine, Chrysostom, and Luther*, 2001.

☆ Quarles, Charles. *Sermon on the Mount: Restoring Christ's Message to the Modern Church*, 2011. A large (over 350pp.), conservative Baptist work. [*JETS* 9/12].

✓ Ridlehoover, Charles Nathan. *The Lord's Prayer and the Sermon on the Mount in Matthew's Gospel*, 2020. A valuable PhD arguing that the Prayer is not an intrusion. [*CBQ* 4/21; *JETS* 3/21; *JSNT* 43.5].

Rohr, Richard. *Jesus' Alternative Plan*, 2023. From the best-selling contemplative Catholic. Earlier there was *Jesus' Plan for a New World* (1996).

✓ Roitto, Rikard, Colleen Shantz, and Petri Luomanen, eds. ‡ *Social and Cognitive Perspectives on the Sermon on the Mount*, 2021. More abstruse. [*JSNT* 45.5].

Schnackenburg, Rudolf. ‡ *All Things Are Possible to Believers: Reflections on the Lord's Prayer and the Sermon on the Mount*, ET 1995.

✓ **Strecker, Georg.** ‡ ET 1988. An exegetical commentary published by Abingdon, which is "heavily Germanic and theological" [*ExpTim* 3/90]; it should be consulted by students who want to get a historical-critical reading.

✓ Talbert, Charles H. ‡ *Reading the Sermon on the Mount*, 2004 (Baker, 2006). [*BL* 2005, 2007; *BSac* 1/08].

✓ Vaught, Carl G. [𝓜], 1987, rev. 2001. Subtitled *A Theological Interpretation*, and now published by Baylor. [*CRBR* 1989].

✓ Welch, John W. ‡ *The Sermon on the Mount in Light of the Temple*, 2009.

F Wenham, David.

Wright, William M., IV. *The Lord's Prayer*, 2023. [*ExpTim* 10/23].

NOTE: Five fine books specifically on the Lord's Prayer are: Thomas Watson's Puritan exposition; Helmut Thielicke's sermons, *Our Heavenly Father*; the 1992 supplementary issue of the *PSB* on the Lord's Prayer ("1991 Frederick Neumann Symposium"); Kenneth Stevenson's historical study, *The Lord's Prayer: A Text in Tradition* (2004); and Jeffrey B. Gibson, *The Disciples' Prayers: The Prayer Jesus Taught in Its Historical Setting* (Fortress, 2015).

# MARK

★ **Edwards, James.** (Pillar) 2002. Clearly written, good and solid, offering a satisfying exegesis and theological discussion. Reviewers were very pleased with this 552-page vol., which pays attention both to matters of historical background and narrative analysis (for more of the latter, see SacP, BCBC, Witherington III, and Moloney). The greatest strength here may be his attention to extrabiblical Jewish literature. Stein, France, and Strauss take pride of place as leading evangelical exegeses, but they deal directly with the Greek, and some preachers may find Edwards less threatening (cf. Lane). See also his *Luke*. [*CTJ* 4/04; *Them* Aut 03; *Int* 1/03; *JETS* 6/03 (Stein); *SwJT* Spr 03; *RelSRev* 7/03; *EvQ* 10/04; *BBR* 13.2; *RTR* 8/08; *Anvil* 20.1].

★ **France, Richard T.** (NIGTC) 2002. I find I now turn first to France and Stein (in that order) as reference tools on technical questions. This is a mature and excellent piece of work on the Greek text. Many, however, will refuse to follow him in his interpretation of the coming of the Son of Man texts. (See under Matthew.) For the student and academically oriented pastor, the (slightly more) critically oriented Guelich and Evans set is nearly as valuable as NIGTC. [*CTJ* 4/04; *Them* Sum 03; *JTS* 10/03; *JETS* 6/03; *Int* 1/03; *TJ* Fall 03; *RelSRev* 7/02; *BBR* 13.2; *RTR* 8/06; *CurTM* 12/05; *Anvil* 22.2].

★ Garland, David. (NIVAC) 1996. The author also contributed the Colossians–Philemon commentary in this series. Though English is good, this is fuller (630pp.) and of greater help to the expositor. Less informed by NT scholarship but also very useful are Hughes and English below. Garland knows the Gospels; see his earlier work on Matthew as well. One of the best in the series. He has added *A Theology of Mark's Gospel* (2015) [*ExpTim* 4/16; *WTJ* Spr 18; *BBR* 26.4; *JETS* 9/16; *Int* 4/16; *JSNT* 38.5], which is extensive (650pp.), brilliant, and serves both academics and expositors.

★ Gombis, Timothy G. (SGBC) 2021. Full (575pp.) and engagingly written, with an interest in narratology and many insights. Gombis is less interested in synoptic comparisons. He presents Mark as "a highly subversive and utterly unique gospel" that "moves along at breakneck speed, with everything happening 'immediately'" (5). Like Gundry, he sees the cross as absolutely central to the book's message, for it "shapes and orients Jesus's identity as ruler of God's kingdom, and it defines and determines the mode of life in that kingdom. . . . The cross is a totalizing and relativizing reality that has cosmic, communal, social, political, economic, relational, and personal implications" (9). Certainly, an enjoyable read that will inspire many a sermon series.

★ **Schnabel, Eckhard J.** (TNTC-R) 2017. By the series editor, and replacing Cole. Unless one is looking for sparkling narratological insights, this is just about perfect as a basic conservative exegesis (440pp.). The interpretive decisions are consistently trustworthy. It may be the best TNTC I have ever used, to be compared, in an earlier generation of the series, with the excellent Stott on John's Letters, Marshall on Acts, and France on Matthew. One can be grateful that the new generation of TNTC includes more discussion of the text's theology. But like the older entries, Schnabel is packed—a model of concision. The only drawback is, as my wife says, there is no running header to help you find passages, and time is wasted hunting. [*JETS* 3/19]. See Schnabel's other books on *Jesus in Jerusalem*, Acts, and Paul.

★ **Stein, Robert H.** (BECNT) 2008. Cause for rejoicing! Like France, Stein offers solid technical exegesis which is also quite readable. For decades Stein has been a leading American evangelical scholar on the Synoptics, and I opine that he has given us some of his best work, near the close of his career, in this full commentary (864pp.). He gives considerable space to a discussion of the original ending or lack of one. See also his NAC work on Luke; both tend to pursue redaction-critical questions instead of literary/narratological ones. Having a literary reading (e.g., Moloney or Witherington III) and an incisive critical interpretation (e.g., Hooker or Marcus) alongside Stein makes for a well-rounded discussion. [*JETS* 12/09; *ExpTim* 10/09; *CBQ* 7/10; *BBR* 20.2; *BL* 2010]. Also from Stein is *Jesus, the Temple, and the Coming of the Son of Man: A Commentary on Mark 13* (2014) [*JETS* 12/15].

★ **Strauss, Mark L.** (ZECNT) 2014. The author had opportunity to dig deeper into Mark's Gospel after having reworked Wessel's contribution for EBCR. He knows the Gospels well—see his *Four Portraits, One Jesus* (2007) [*RelSRev* 9/12]—and has produced a large (730pp.), well-rounded commentary that treats matters of translation, literary structure, the flow of argument/story, exegesis, theological exposition, and application. The reader comes to appreciate, as Strauss himself does, the Gospel "author's literary design and theological skill," which yields "a well-structured, powerful theological drama that catches the reader up and carries them to a new destination" (Preface). Strauss is learned (Aberdeen PhD), articulate, and serves on the faculty of Bethel Seminary. A stronger vol. in the series. [*JSNT* 37.5; *BBR* 25.2; *Chm* Win 18; *JETS* 12/15; *DenvJ* 5/16].

❖ ❖ ❖ ❖ ❖

Akin, Daniel L. *Exalting Jesus in Mark* (CCE) 2014.

Alexander, J. A. (GS) 1858. Though dated, it is still useful as a theological exposition. Alexander has other commentaries on Psalms, Isaiah, Matthew, and Acts.

✓ **Anderson, Hugh.** ‡ (NCB) 1976. Frustrating in its skeptical approach, but a noted work. Ralph Martin used to recommend this NCB, with its full introduction, and decades ago I consulted it for a scholarly, critical perspective. Like Hill on Matthew, this no longer has prominence among commentaries.

✓ Anderson, Janice Capel, and Stephen D. Moore, eds. ‡ *Mark & Method: New Approaches in Biblical Studies*, 1992, 2nd ed. 2008. This touted book should not be missed by students working on Mark or even the Synoptics generally, if they seek an understanding of the shape of Gospels study today. [*BibInt* 18.3; *RelSRev* 9/09; *BL* 2010].

Barbieri, Louis. (Moody Gospel Commentary) 1995. A full, popular-level work in pb.

☆ Bayer, Hans. "Mark" in *Matthew–Luke* (ESVEC) 2021. See Doriani under Matthew.

✓ **Beasley-Murray, George R.** [𝓜], *Jesus and the Last Days: A Commentary on Mark 13*, 1957, rev. 1993. The revision published by Hendrickson is 600pp. long and gives a thorough, rich treatment of Jesus's eschatological teaching.

✓ Beavis, Mary Ann. ‡ (Paideia) 2011. The author did her PhD on Mark at Cambridge in the mid-1980s, and she has contributed a lucid exegetical treatment of the Gospel, particularly a sensitive narrative reading. She spells out her commitments on p.29: "academic, Anglican, liberal, feminist, social-justice oriented." [*BBR* 22.4; *Int* 4/13; *JSNT* 35.5; *ExpTim* 11/12; *TJ* Spr 14].

✓ Becker, Eve-Marie, and Anders Runesson, eds. ‡ *Mark and Matthew I-II*, 2 vols., 2011–13. See Cilliars Breytenbach, "Current Research on the Gospel according to Mark." [*BBR* 24.2].

✓ **Black, C. Clifton.** ‡ (ANTC) 2011. I have had less opportunity to use this commentary, but the author is a well-respected critic. [*CBQ* 1/14; *Int* 7/15; *JSNT* 35.5; *ExpTim* 3/13]. His dissertation was a blockbuster in critiquing the redaction-critical approach: *The Disciples according to Mark* (1989, 2nd ed. 2012) [*BTB* 5/15]. Capping Black's career in Markan research is *Mark's Gospel: History, Theology, Interpretation* (2023).

☆ Blackwell, Ben C., John K. Goodrich, and Jason Maston, eds. *Reading Mark in Context: Jesus and Second Temple Judaism*, 2018. Published by Zondervan. [*JETS* 9/19 (Stein); *JSNT* 41.5; *RevExp* 5/20].

☆ Bock, Darrell. "The Gospel of Mark" (CorBC) 2005. See Turner under Matthew.

☆ **Bock, Darrell.** (NCBC) 2015. Exactly the solid work one would expect of this Gospels expert (390pp.). Because of the recent date and Bock's goal "to reflect the discussion [the major commentaries] raise about the book" (xi), this CUP issue will be useful to both students and pastors. He comes to traditional conclusions on matters of authorship, date, provenance, and genre (ancient *bios* "that presents Jesus as a hero whose life is worthy of reflection and emulation," 37). He is an unusually gifted and productive exegete, as seen here and in his works on Jesus, Luke, and Acts. Another remarkable thing about this NCBC is that Bock devotes 65pp. to bibliography. [*Chm* Win 18; *JTS* 10/18; *JETS* 12/16].

F Bolt, Peter. (EBTC)? Building upon *The Cross from a Distance: Atonement in Mark's Gospel* (2004) in NSBT.

✓ Bond, Helen K. ‡ *The First Biography of Jesus: Genre and Meaning in Mark's Gospel*, 2020. Monograph by a professor at Edinburgh, which Black terms "scholarship of the highest order" [*Int* 7/21]. [*ExpTim* 10/21; *WTJ* Fall 20; *CBQ* 10/21; *JETS* 6/21; *NovT* 62.4; *EvQ* 93.2; *JSNT* 43.5; *Them* 45.3 (Walton)].

✓ **Boring, M. Eugene.** ‡ (NTL) 2006. Considered in the top rank of mid-level critical commentaries, Boring "emphasizes Mark's theological creativity as an evangelist" (Bock). Not only is this work quite full (482pp.), it is also a model of compressed historical scholarship, and the reader gets a great deal of information for the time invested. I have to class it as one of the better contributions to the NTL series. Boring pays attention to literary or narrative features but asserts that "the substantive content of Mark's narrative is theological" (24). There is properly a focus on Christ, since "[t]he Gospel of Mark is narrative Christology" (8). The translation offered is forceful and fresh. Boring holds that the evangelist drew from oral traditions, not being an eyewitness. Here "the approach is still heavily indebted to form-critical insights" (Foster). At points I find myself in strong disagreement with him, as when he contends that "for Mark, 'Son of David' is a misunderstanding of Jesus' true identity" (305). [*Int* 10/08; *BL* 2008; *RelSRev* 4/07; *ExpTim* 12/07; *CurTM* 12/08].

F   Botha, P. J. J. (RRA).

✓   Botner, Max. *Jesus Christ as the Son of David in the Gospel of Mark*, 2019. [*JSNT* 42.5].

Bratcher, R. G., and E. A. Nida. (UBS) 1961. One of the oldest in the series.

☆   Brooks, James A. (NAC) 1991. Some reviewers find it not as full, insightful, or well-informed as the other NAC vols. on the Gospels. Clifton Black sees Brooks as surprisingly open to higher criticism. I have not made enough use of it to justify a strong personal opinion. Carson ranks this highly. [*EvQ* 1/94; *ThTo* 10/93; *CRBR* 1994].

F   Campos, Mateus F. de. (BGW). Building upon his strong Cambridge PhD, *Resisting Jesus: A Narrative and Intertextual Analysis of Mark's Portrayal of the Disciples of Jesus* (2021) [*JSNT* 45.5; *JTS* 10/23].

Carter, Warren. ‡ (Wisdom) 2019. A large feminist commentary. [*Int* 1/21; *JSNT* 43.5].

✓   Chilton, Bruce, Darrell Bock et al., eds. *A Comparative Handbook to the Gospel of Mark: Comparisons with Pseudepigrapha, the Qumran Scrolls, and Rabbinic Literature*, 2010. From the Brill project, NT Gospels in Their Judaic Context, which aims to be a new "Strack und Billerbeck"—nothing to worry about, if you don't know what this means. [*BBR* 21.3 (Evans); *JETS* 3/11; *BTB* 8/12; *RelSRev* 6/12].

☆   Cole, R. Alan. (retired TNTC) rev. 1989. Though not one of the best entries in the series, it is serviceable and thoughtful. The newer edition was more of a revision than many others in the series. See Schnabel. [*RTR* 5/91].

☆   **Cranfield, C. E. B.** [𝓜], (CGTC) 1959. A clear, balanced, sensible commentary which you will consult often once you've sampled it. Mildly critical with incisive exegesis. Cranfield's method does not seem to have been influenced much by Marxsen's redaction-critical approach (see p.478). For work on the Greek text, scholarly pastors keep this handy. I am not sure it remains in print. Through six editions of this guide I recommended Cranfield for purchase, but its place was given to France.

✓   **Culpepper, R. Alan.** ‡ (S&H) 2007. One of the best in the NT section of this series. The author is especially known for his expertise in narrative criticism, and in particular his research on the narratives in John. I have found this commentary (622pp.) to be uncommonly insightful, with points a preacher can bring into sermons. E.g., 30 years ago I found it stunning that after cleansing the leper, who previously had been ostracized from the community, Jesus is put in the position of having to "stay outside in lonely places" due to the healed man's disobedience (1:45). Culpepper picks up on such narrative features and reflects on them theologically. [*RelSRev* 3/08; *Int* 4/09].

☆   **Decker, Rodney J.** (BHGNT) 2 vols., 2014. Over 600pp. of learned analysis of the Greek by a late veteran Baptist scholar (†2014). The set is not inexpensive, but I can think of few better tools for one to learn verse-by-verse exegesis of Greek narrative.

✓   **Donahue, John, and Daniel Harrington.** ‡ (SacP) 2002. This large-scale (488pp.) Catholic work interprets Mark through research into intertextuality, besides other more tried methods like redaction criticism and narrative criticism. There is great learning here as two veteran scholars have teamed up (Donahue is primarily responsible for 1–8 and 14; Harrington does the rest). [*CBQ* 1/03; *JETS* 6/03; *Int* 1/03; *RelSRev* 10/02].

Dowd, Sharyn. ‡ *Reading Mark* (RNT) 2000.

F   Dunn, James D. G. [𝓜], (ICC-R). Expect a reassignment after his passing (†2020).

☆   English, Donald. (BST) 1992. A boon for the expositor. Very well-written, with many theological and pastoral insights. [*Chm* 109.2].

☆   **Evans, Craig.** [𝓜], *Mark 8:27–16:20* (WBC) 2001. Completes the work Guelich so ably began. It is very full (nearly 100pp. of introduction and 500pp. of commentary), and the theological approach seems to be similar to Gundry's. As we have come to expect of WBC, the bibliographies are very well prepared. Unfortunately, there are more than a few editorial problems—e.g., on p.131 the Hebrew for Jericho is misspelled in one place and in another Jerusalem is mistakenly written for Jericho. I value Evans more highly than Guelich, and not only because of more current bibliographies. He is set to revise his vol. and replace Guelich's. Students and scholarly pastors won't want to be without Evans in working with the Greek. [*CTJ* 11/02; *NovT* 44.4]. Note that this world-class scholar did *Luke* for NIBC.

☆   Ferguson, Sinclair. *Let's Study Mark*, 1999. Outstandingly clear and theological.

✓   **Focant, Camille.** ‡ 2004, ET 2012. A work 30 years in the making, building upon his many essays (collected in *Marc, un évangile étonnant*, BETL, 2006). Though treating historical-critical concerns (e.g., through redaction criticism), Focant delivers mainly a narrative-critical interpretation in this important major commentary (approx. 750pp.), published by Pickwick. [*NovT* 56.2; *CBQ* 4/14; *ETL* 84.1, 89.4; *JETS* 6/13 (Stein)].

☆   **Geddert, Timothy.** (BCBC) 2001. An excellent, more literary commentary, which is one of the very best in the NT section of the series. The Anabaptist author did previous work (Aberdeen PhD) on the Olivet Discourse in Mark. There is much to be enthusiastic about here. [*JETS* 9/02; *RelSRev* 10/01].

Gould, E. P. ‡ (ICC) 1896. Can be safely ignored.

☆   **Guelich, Robert A.** [𝓜], *Mark 1–8:26* (WBC) 1989. A standard scholarly commentary to be consulted. Draws heavily from German scholarship on this Gospel (Gnilka, Pesch, etc.) and is interested in tradition history. Sadly, Guelich died (†1991) in the prime of his career before finishing Mark for the series. Evans completed the 2-vol. set, and these both are highly recommended for advanced students. Guelich is the same scholar who produced the exceptional study of the Sermon on the Mount. This WBC is to be replaced; see Craig Evans above. [*CRBR* 1992; *EvQ* 4/92; *CBQ* 10/91; *Them* 10/91].

☆   **Gundry, Robert.** *Mark: A Commentary on His Apology for the Cross*, 1993. An exhaustive and penetrating study of this Gospel (1069pp. in small print!). The subtitle gives his perspective on Mark's purpose. Many are intimidated by the price tag and the sheer size and detail of this work. It is more of a purchase priority if you are an advanced student or scholarly pastor. Gundry's friend, Moisés Silva, calls it "an enormous treasure of information." Douglas Moo says the provocative commentary "enhances this scholar's reputation as an original and independent thinker." Released in a 2-vol. pb in 2004. [*JBL* 113.4; *CBQ* 4/95; *Them* 10/94; *CTJ* 4/95; *ExpTim* 1/95; *EvQ* 1/97; *SJT* 50.1; *Chm* 111.4].

☆   **Hare, Douglas R. A.** ‡ (WestBC) 1996. Fairly good. Has received complimentary reviews as a "thoroughly theological commentary" (Allison). The author, Emeritus Professor of NT at Pittsburgh Seminary (PCUSA), also wrote the Matthew vol. for the Interpretation series. [*Int* 1/98; *HBT* 12/98].

✓   Hatina, Thomas R., ed. *Biblical Interpretation in Early Christian Gospels. I. The Gospel of Mark*, 2006. For two companion vols., see Hatina under Matthew and Luke.

Healy, Mary. ‡ (CCSS) 2008. The initial vol. in the series. [*CBQ* 7/10].

F   Henderson, Susanne Watts. ‡ (Illum).

☆ Hendriksen, William. (NTC) 1975. Not as prolix nor as good as *Matthew* in the series. The pastor could put his theological exposition to good use, though the student will be looking for a more rigorous work. [*RTR* 1/76].

✓ Hengel, Martin. [𝓜], *Studies in the Gospel of Mark*, ET 1985. The measure of Hengel's significance is other commentators' heavy use of him.

   Hiebert, D. E. rev. 1979. An evangelical commentary of some size organized around the servant theme.

☆ **Hooker, Morna.** ‡ (BNTC) 1992. This replacement work for Johnson is a big improvement. Hooker has 411pp. of phrase-by-phrase exposition and is easily accessible to non-specialists. This is also a significant exegesis for students to consult. Hooker's stature among NT scholars and the low price of this vol. make it among the "best buys" for students. An excellent commentary which is moderately critical. [*EvQ* 7/93; *ExpTim* 2/93; *RTR* 9/92, 1/94; *JBL* Spr 94; *JTS* 4/94; *Them* 10/94].

✓ Huebenthal, Sandra. ‡ *Reading Mark's Gospel as a Text from Collective Memory*, 2020. [*BBR* 31.2; *Int* 10/21].

☆ Hughes, R. Kent. (PTW) 2015. Carson has spoken of PTW as one of the best in the genre of sermonic commentary. The series, which includes good theology, much illustrative material, and application, covers the entire NT; the OT section is nearly done. Hughes was pastor of the College Church in Wheaton, IL. The original commentary on Mark was 480pp. in 2-vols. (1989), while the ESV edition is a single vol. See Garland above. [*JETS* 12/92].

   Hunter, A. M. [𝓜], (Torch Bible Commentary) 1967. Good, but sketchy compared with the recent exegetical commentaries on Mark.

☆ **Hurtado, Larry W.** [𝓜], (NIBC) 1989. A 320-page work certainly worth consulting. Hurtado was a much respected professor (†2019) at Edinburgh.

✓ **Iersel, Bas M. F. van.** ‡ *Mark: A Reader-Response Commentary*, ET 1998. [*CBQ* 7/00; *Bib* 81.2; *JBL* Win 00; *JTS* 4/01; *RelSRev* 10/01]. Previously there was the more accessible *Reading Mark* (ET 1986) [*Bib* 70.4].

   Jeffrey, David Lyle. (Brazos) 2012. [*CBQ* 1/14].

   Johnson, Sherman E. ‡ (retired BNTC) 1960. Never particularly helpful. See Hooker.

F  Joynes, Christine. ‡ (BBC).

✓ Juel, Donald H. ‡ (IBT) 1999. A serviceable introduction to Markan studies by a Princeton Seminary professor.

✓ Kealy, Sean P. *A History of the Interpretation of the Gospel of Mark*, vols. I and II/1–2, 2007. [*CBQ* 4/11].

F  Keener, Craig. *Mark* (ICC-R). Will be fascinating to see how this turns out, given Keener's faith in the Scriptures. I saw this reported in a Gupta interview of Keener.

   Kernaghan, Ron. (IVPNT) 2007. The author is a PCUSA minister connected to Fuller Seminary. I have not had opportunity to use this. [*BL* 2008].

✓ Kuruvilla, Abraham. 2012. Subtitled "A Theological Commentary for Preachers." [*ExpTim* 6/13].

☆ **Lane, William.** (NICNT) 1974. Long considered the most valuable work for evangelical pastors. Edwards's Pillar challenged its place, to say nothing of the fuller, more recent works like France, Gundry, WBC, Stein. Lane employs a mild form of redaction criticism (see p.7) in a responsible way. He has a standout commentary on Hebrews. For students' sake I have removed this from the purchase list, but pastors should still seriously consider it. [*WTJ* Spr 77; *RTR* 9/74; *JBL* 94.3; *EvQ* 1/75].

   Le Peau, Andrew T. (TOTE) 2017. [*JETS* 6/18].

F  Lyons-Pardue, Kara. (CCF).

MacArthur, John. 2 vols., 2015. Many preachers will gravitate toward this sermonic material from the famous "Grace to You" expositor. Compare with Hughes.

✓ Malbon, Elizabeth S. ‡ *Mark's Jesus: Characterization as Narrative Christology*, 2014.

✓ Malina, Bruce J., and Richard L. Rohrbaugh. ‡ *Social-Science Commentary on the Synoptic Gospels*, 1992.

✓ **Mann, C. S.** ‡ (retired AB) 1986. A critical commentary arguing the Griesbach Hypothesis. See Albright under Matthew, but note that this vol. is better and worth consulting by students. Those who use it will find that the introduction is massive and the exegesis a bit disappointing. Mann has been replaced; see Marcus below. [*ThTo* 44.2].

✓ **Marcus, Joel.** ‡ (AYB) 2 vols., 2000–09. Replaces Mann. The set has a 65-page introduction, 49pp. of bibliography, and over 1000pp. of mainly historical-critical exegesis. The work can be compared to Guelich's, though more liberal, skeptical, and stressing apocalyptic. What I have read of Marcus is pleasingly full, but I have not always trusted his exegetical judgment (e.g., at 1:43). He notes some of the surprising ironies in Mark and the development of Isaianic themes (e.g., God's way of holy war to liberate his people). As mentioned below, Marcus and Yarbro Collins are the leading critical technical commentaries on this Gospel. [*JTS* 4/02; *Int* 1/02, 4/11; *ExpTim* 8/01; *NovT* 44.3; *BBR* 13.2, 20.2; *RBL* 6/10; *HBT* 32.1; *CBQ* 4/10 (Moloney); *JETS* 9/10 (Stein)]. Marcus has made a special study of *The Mystery of the Kingdom of God* (1986) and christological exegesis of the OT in Mark: *The Way of the Lord* (1992) [*TJ* Spr 94; *CTJ* 4/95]).

Martin, Ralph P. [*M*], *Mark: Evangelist and Theologian*, 1973. Not a commentary, but one of the helpful introductions to the four evangelists published by Zondervan. Not as good as Marshall on Luke or France on Matthew. [*JBL* 94.1].

✓ Marxsen, Willi. ‡ *Mark the Evangelist*, 1956, ET 1969. The groundbreaking redactional study on Mark and quite critical. To investigate more recent redaction criticism on this Gospel, see *The Disciples according to Mark* (1989) by C. C. Black.

✓ Miller, Susan E. ‡ *Women in Mark's Gospel*, 2004. In LNTS. See under John too.

☆ **Moloney, Francis J.** ‡ 2002. A lucid, mid-level commentary from Hendrickson (outside any series), with a moderately critical Catholic perspective. It blends literary, historical, and theological concerns and can be compared to Donahue–Harrington above. He seeks and finds narrative coherence. Quite a number of leading scholars have highly praised this: "the finest one-volume commentary in English on Mark that I know" (Black). Moloney was reissued by Baker in 2012. The author is better known for his extensive work on John. [*JTS* 10/04; *CBQ* 1/04; *RTR* 12/03; *JETS* 9/04; *ExpTim* 1/04, 4/14; *RelSRev* 1/03; *Bib* 85.4; *Int* 10/05; *BL* 2005; *CurTM* 10/05]. See the added introductory study of Mark (2004): *Mark: Storyteller, Interpreter, Evangelist* [*NovT* 48.4; *ExpTim* 3/07]. Further reflection on the ending of Mark and a "narrative commentary on the resurrection accounts in the four Gospels" is found in *The Resurrection of the Messiah* (2013) [*CBQ* 7/15; *JETS* 6/15].

F  Moritz, Thorsten. (THC).

Moule, C. F. D. ‡ (CBC) 1965. Insightful, as Moule always was, but brief.

Myers, Ched. ‡ *Binding the Strong Man: A Political Reading of Mark's Story of Jesus*, 1988. This lengthy (500pp.) Orbis publication applies both literary criticism and a (leftist) political hermeneutic. I note it because it won a book award and was praised outlandishly—"most important commentary . . . since Barth's Romans."

Nineham, Dennis E. ‡ (Pelican) 1963. Destructively critical, as expected from a contributor to *The Myth of God Incarnate*. Though cited by some, it can be ignored, unless you are especially interested in form criticism.

✓ Oden, Thomas C., and Christopher Hall, eds. (ACCS) 1998. [*RelSRev* 7/99; *EvQ* 7/02; *NovT* 42.4].

O'Donnell, Douglas Sean. *Expository Reflections on the Gospels: Mark*, 2024. Said to be an excellent, large vol. (over 550pp.) of sermonic material, but I've not seen it.

☆ Osborne, Grant R. (TTC) 2014. The veteran Gospels scholar at TEDS (†2018) had the exegetical expertise and teaching experience to write a fine, concise commentary for pastors (335pp.). There are many insights and seed-thoughts for sermons. [*BSac* 4/16].

✓ **Perkins, Pheme.** ‡ (NIB) 1995. The author is a prof at Boston College and has written many books in the NT field. See, for example, Ephesians. Perkins's work on Mark fits well into this much-used series for pastors. [*JETS* 3/99]. Her further research on the Gospels is published as *Introduction to the Synoptic Gospels* (2007) [*ExpTim* 11/08].

F Gladd, Benjamin. (EEC). A reassignment after Rodney Decker's death.

Placher, William C. ‡ (Belief) 2010. By the late series editor. [*Int* 7/11; *JSNT* 34.5; *JETS* 6/11; *ExpTim* 12/11; *RelSRev* 3/12; *SJT* 66.4].

✓ Plummer, Alfred. [𝓜], 1914. A dated, learned commentary on the Greek text.

F Powery, Emerson Byron. (PC).

Rawlison, A. E. J. ‡ (Westminster) 1949. Can be ignored, despite Childs's comment.

✓ **Rhodes, David, and Donald Michie.** ‡ *Mark As Story*, 1982, 2nd ed. 1999, 3rd ed. 2012. Riches says (with some disapproval) this interpretation "has been influential among a growing circle . . . in the States who wish to see the abandonment in biblical study of historical in favour of literary modes of investigation" (*A Century of NT Study*, 165) [*JSNT* 35.5]. The measure of its impact is the 2011 celebratory Brill monograph, *Mark as Story: Retrospect and Prospect*, eds. Kelly Iverson and Christopher Skinner [*EvQ* 10/13; *CBQ* 7/13; *JSNT* 34.5; *JETS* 12/12; *RelSRev* 3/13].

✓ **Robbins, Vernon.** ‡ *Jesus the Teacher: A Socio-Rhetorical Interpretation of Mark*, 1992. Robbins teaches at Emory and has for some time been encouraging an integrated model of biblical interpretation, emphasizing synchronic methodologies. His book *Exploring the Texture of Texts* (1996) has been seminal for many. Quite critical. Compare with the evangelical Witherington below.

☆ Ryle, J. C. (CrossC) 1993.

✓ **Schweizer, Eduard.** ‡ ET 1970. Much better on Mark than on Matthew. If you do some sifting, Schweizer is well worth reading. This vol. was written essentially for pastors, and readers with a sharp eye will find many theological insights and homiletical hints.

F Shively, Elizabeth Evans. (NIGTC-R). Would replace France.

✓ Skinner, Christopher W., and Matthew Ryan Hauge, eds. ‡ *Character Studies and the Gospel of Mark*, 2014. [*JETS* 12/15].

Smuts, P. W. *Mark by the Book: A New Multidirectional Method for Understanding the Synoptic Gospels*, 2013. [*Them* 11/13]. I have yet to see it.

✓ Struthers-Malbon, Elizabeth. ‡ *Mark's Jesus: Characterization as Narrative Christology*, 2009. Published by Baylor.

✓ Swete, H. B. [𝓜], 1895, 3rd ed. 1927. Something of a classic, at least for its full treatment of the Greek text, but Swete is eclipsed by more recent commentaries.

Tan, Kim Huat. (NCCS) 2016. "All in all, this is a first-rate, up-to-date commentary" (Wenham [*JSNT* 39.5]). The author teaches at Trinity Theological College, Singapore.

F Tait, Edwin Woodruff, ed. (RCS).

✓ **Taylor, Vincent.** ‡ 1952, 2nd ed. 1966. Admirable as a full-scale, painstaking work on the Greek, this was the first thoroughgoing form-critical analysis of Mark. Taylor's vol. is less valuable for its theology. This has long been used alongside Cranfield and now feels dated.

✓ Telford, W. R. ‡ *The Theology of the Gospel of Mark*, 1999. Prior to this work for CUP [*EvQ* 7/01], he edited *The Interpretation of Mark* (1985). For a massive history of research, see *Writing on the Gospel of Mark* (2009) [*NovT* 52.4; *JSNT* 33.5; *Them* 11/10; *RelSRev* 12/11].

Thurston, Bonnie. ‡ *Preaching Mark*, 2002. [*Int* 1/03; *SwJT* Spr 03].

☆ **Voelz, James W.** (ConcC) 2 vols., 2013–19. The level and quality of engagement with the

Greek text is very high, and I regard Voelz as one of the best, most rigorous contributions to this large-scale, confessional Lutheran series. Taking a step further, I call it one of the best reference tools on Mark's Gospel for students and learned pastors. J. K. Elliot says it is "stimulating, engagingly written, and erudite" [*NovT* 56.4]. Now complete with 1270pp., it is also about the fullest commentary on Mark's Gospel ever written. The bonus for preachers is how the set moves to Lutheran Christocentric reflection and homiletics. [*BBR* 25.1; *CBQ* 7/18; *JETS* 9/15; *Int* 4/16; *NovT* 63.2 (in French); *JSNT* 43.5].

F   Watts, Rikk E. (NICNT-R). The author teaches at Regent College, Vancouver. Expect this to give prominence to the theme of *Isaiah's New Exodus and Mark* (1997).

☆ **Wessel, Walter W., and Mark L. Strauss.** (EBCR) 2010. While Wessel's 1984 EBC was competent [*TJ* Spr 85], some preferred fuller works and ignored it. The new work is a major improvement, as Strauss has done a creditable job bringing Wessel (†2002) up to date. Again a briefer "Mark" (671–989) is paired with a more helpful, twice-as-long "Matthew." Many young preachers, who buy this vol. 9 for the highly rated Carson, will be content with Wessel–Strauss on Mark, at least for a while.

☆ **Williams, Joel F.** (EGGNT) 2020. Excellent and "fit for purpose," as the Brits say, within this series on the Greek. The wise homiletical suggestions are a bonus. [*Presb* Fall 20; *ExpTim* 10/23].

Williamson, Lamar. ‡ (I) 1983. I have never used it enough to form an opinion. Others assess it as a useful preacher's commentary.

☆ **Witherington, Ben, III.** *The Gospel of Mark: A Socio-Rhetorical Commentary* (SRC) 2001. Mark is the subject of an increasing number of literary studies, chiefly concerned with the nature of the text, its rhetoric, settings, plot, and characterization. This 450-page work is a good representative of a conservative literary approach; cf. the liberal Robbins above. For further review see SRC under Commentary Series and the comments under 1 Corinthians. Previously a recommended purchase. [*CTJ* 4/04; *CBQ* 4/02; *Them* Spr 03; *JETS* 9/02; *Int* 7/02; *ExpTim* 8/01; *TJ* Spr 02; *SwJT* Fall 02; *RelSRev* 10/01; *BBR* 13.2; *Anvil* 19.4].

✓ **Yarbro Collins, Adela.** ‡ (Herm) 2007. A publishing event! NT specialists were eagerly anticipating this technical, historical-critical exegesis for many years. It is quite critical in orientation (Bultmann is a favorite citation) and builds on earlier research in *The Beginning of the Gospel: Probings of Mark in Context* (1992), as well as an abundance of journal articles. Yarbro Collins believes Mark has a long, complicated compositional history and can be termed "an eschatological counterpart of an older biblical genre, the foundational sacred history." In many places she shows she shares her husband's (OT scholar John J. Collins) keen interest in apocalyptic. Portions of Mark receive extremely detailed exegesis, while others do not (e.g., four pages on 1:35–45). Students must take account of this 800-page reference work, especially the massive number of literary parallels from the ancient world she adduces to help interpret this Gospel. This and Marcus would be the leading liberal technical commentaries now. [*NovT* 51.2; *RelSRev* 3/08; *JETS* 3/09; *BL* 2009; *Int* 1/09 (Boring); *CBQ* 1/13].

NOTES: (1) See Hurtado's article on "The Gospel of Mark in Recent Study" in *Them* 1/89; and (2) John Ziesler's "Which Is the Best Commentary? VII. Mark," *ExpTim* 6/87. (3) Darrell L. Bock, "Commentaries on the Synoptic Gospels" (339–63), in *On the Writing of NT Commentaries*, eds. Porter–Schnabel, cited in the Introduction.

# LUKE

NOTE: I do not see a standout exposition for pastors, though Garland provides a measure of help in applying the text to heart and life. Compare the following: Bock's NIVAC (previously recommended), Ryken, Calvin, France, Hughes, Just (Lutheran), Gooding, and Wilcock. Luke's Gospel is well served by exegetical works.

★ **Bock, Darrell.** (BECNT) 2 vols., 1994–96. The first vol. (nearly 1000pp.) was once described as "the most extensive, up-to-date, and consistently evangelical commentary on the first portion of Luke." Bock is not up-to-date now, but still of great value. None matches his thoroughness. Compared with other major exegetical works on the Greek text (i.e., Fitzmyer, Marshall, Nolland, and Bovon), this set is more accessible (less technical), conservative, and theological. (Bock is a senior prof at Dallas and a leader in progressive dispensationalism.) It is valuable for text criticism too. Stein's expertise in redaction criticism and Green's more refined literary investigations have complemented Bock's grammatico-historical approach. For three decades I have loved this set ($110 on sale), but I'm tempted to recommend Garland as a first choice for pastors because of date, price ($40 on sale), and his application. See the other two Bock works below. [*Presb* Fall 95; *RTR* 1/96; *JETS* 9/98 (Blomberg); *JBL* Spr 98; *WTJ* Spr 96; *TJ* Fall 96; *SwJT* Fall 97; *AsTJ* Fall 98; *RelSRev* 1/98]. Warmly welcomed is his full (over 400pp.) summary theological treatment: *A Theology of Luke and Acts*, 2012 [*EvQ* 4/14; *CBQ* 1/14; *JSNT* 35.5; *JETS* 3/13; *Them* 11/12; *BSac* 4/13; *TJ* Fall 13]—it's good to be reminded that Luke–Acts is 25 percent of the NT. See Eklund below.

★ **Edwards, James R.** (Pillar) 2015. Perhaps it was through unusual circumstances that Edwards was enlisted by the series editor to contribute this Luke commentary after he had already done the Pillar entry on Mark (xiii), but the church is glad he took on the assignment. There are 750pp. of introductory material and commentary, and readers will find him to be thorough, lucid, and reliable as an exegete. Not surprisingly, the work has similar emphases and strengths as Edwards's *Mark*. One difference comes as the result of his research on *The Hebrew Gospel* (2009)—see under Jesus & Gospels Research. He now believes that Luke made use of both Mark and a supposed "Hebrew Gospel" as sources, along with a so-called "Double Tradition" containing material common to Matthew and Luke (see pp.14–18). There is much interaction with the scholarly literature (esp. Bovon, Fitzmyer, Plummer, Wolter, and German scholars generally), but to keep this an approachable pastor's reference the discussion is limited mostly to footnotes. [*WTJ* Fall 15; *BBR* 26.4; *Int* 4/19; *RTR* 12/15; *JSNT* 38.5].

★ **Garland, David E.** (ZECNT) 2011. Some have the gift of writing consistently insightful, crystal-clear commentaries for pastors, while inspiring a love for Scripture; Garland has it. This is a very long book (950pp. of introduction and commentary), but it reads well and will be extremely useful to busy pastors in preparing expository sermons. Because Garland has previously published well-received works on Matthew and Mark, he is sensitive to the distinctiveness of Luke among the Synoptics. Note that the series not only probes the background and structure of the text on the way to treating exegetical fine points (Greek text), but it also stimulates the preacher to think about appropriate application. This works well as a first choice for pastors, though they may be slightly disappointed with the brevity of the Introduction (20pp.). See my comments above on Bock. [*JETS* 12/12; *DenvJ* 15].

★ **Green, Joel B.** [*M*], (NICNT-R) 1997. A fine, recommendable work, but perhaps best not used by itself. Though so much work had lately been done on Luke, Green brought a fresh, more literary approach, which can be compared with L. T. Johnson's and Carroll's. (I use them just as much.) He is less interested in historical questions. Evangelical pastors found that this vol. had a less conservative feel than others in NICNT. It replaced Geldenhuys. [*EvQ* 7/99; *Them* 5/99; *JTS* 10/99; *Bib* 79.4; *CBQ* 1/99; *Chm* 113.2; *RelSRev* 10/98; *Presb* Spr 00]. See also Green's well-written vol. on Luke in the Cambridge NT Theology series (1995) [*Them* 10/97; *Int* 7/97; *JR* 1/97; *CRBR* 1996; *CBQ* 1/97]; *Conversion in Luke–Acts* (2015) [*ExpTim* 8/16; *CBQ* 1/18;

*JETS* 12/16; *Int* 10/18; *BibInt* 26.1; *Them* 43.2]; collected essays in *Luke as Narrative Theologian* (2020) [*RelSRev* 3/22; *RevExp* 5/22]; and an up-to-date introduction, *Discovering Luke: Content, Interpretation, Reception* (2021) [*RelSRev* 9/22; *JETS* 3/23]. He also edited *Methods for Luke* (CUP, 2010) [*RBL* 8/10; *ExpTim* 3/11; *BTB* 11/11].

★ **Perrin, Nicholas.** (TNTC-R) 2022. Just as Morris, replaced by Perrin, was long the best concise exegesis on Luke, this is a jewel and a first choice as a quick reference. Perrin's work is fairly full, though, at over 500pp., and he is able to probe more deeply and come up with insights.

❖ ❖ ❖ ❖ ❖ ❖

Anyabwile, Thabiti. *Exalting Jesus in Luke* (CCE) 2018.

Arndt, W. F. 1956. A conservative Lutheran work designed for the pastor.

Arterbury, Andrew E. ‡ (RNT) 2019. Subtitled "A Literary and Theological Commentary." [*CBQ* 4/21].

F  Aune, David. ‡ *Luke–Acts* (Illum).

✓  Bartholomew, Craig G., Joel B. Green, Anthony Thiselton, eds. *Reading Luke: Interpretation, Reflection, Formation*, 2005. Essays published in Zondervan's Scripture and Hermeneutics Series. [*JETS* 9/06; *Evangel* Aut 07].

F  Bauckham, Richard. [𝓜], (ICC–new series). This may be a long way off, since Bauckham is mainly focused on the Son of Man title.

Bentley, Michael. *Saving a Fallen World* (Welwyn) 1992.

☆ Bock, Darrell. (IVPNT) 1994. A fine, well-informed commentary of about 400pp. that the pastor can put to good use, being more manageable than the huge BECNT set. He aims to make the conclusions of his exegetical work in BECNT above available to a broader audience, but I do not think he gave us his best work here. [*Presb* Fall 95].

☆ Bock, Darrell. (NIVAC) 1996. "Bock has turned Lukan commentary into a growth industry" (C. R. Matthews). Yes, three different commentaries in a three-year span! BECNT offers full exegesis, theological reflection, and hints for application. IVPNT makes Bock's exegetical conclusions more accessible to a general audience and begins the move from text to sermon. NIVAC moves more quickly from original message to significance today (homiletical musings). Busy pastors might be tempted to bypass the massive BECNT in favor of NIVAC, but I can't recommend that, unless money is a key factor.

Borgman, Paul. *The Way according to Luke: Hearing the Whole Story of Luke-Acts*, 2006. A narrative reading (400pp.) by a Gordon College English prof.

✓ **Bovon, François.** ‡ (Herm) 3 vols., ET 2002–2013. A truly great commentary! The vol. covering 1:1–9:50, translated from the German (EKK, 1989), introduces 3-vols. of technical exegesis and probing theological interpretation (approx. 1400pp.). Vols. 2–3 are from the French (CNT, 1996/2001, 2009). This huge work's availability in the three languages indicates its influence in European scholarship and its value; only for advanced students. Note that Bovon has not divided the Lukan material in Hermeneia as he has in the 4-vol. German and French commentaries. *Luke 2* covers 9:51–19:27, and *Luke 3* provides an exegesis of 19:28–24:53. [*Int* 7/03; *ExpTim* 1/03; *CurTM* 4/05; *CBQ* 10/11]. Likely the most valuable critical introduction to Luke and Lukan scholarship is Bovon's 681-page *Luke the Theologian: Fifty-Five Years of Research* (1950–2005) in its 2nd edition (2006) [*ExpTim* 2/07], while the fullest survey is Seán P. Kealy's 1250-page *The Interpretation of the Gospel of Luke*, 2 vols. (2005).

Brawley, Robert. ‡ 2020. Subtitled "A Social Identity Commentary." [*JTS* 4/22; *JSNT* 43.5].

☆ **Brown, R. E.** ‡ *The Birth of the Messiah*, 1977, rev. 1993. See Jesus & Gospels Research.

Browning, W. R. F. ‡ (Torch) 1982. Somewhat similar to Caird below: too brief to compete with the major works, but insightful nonetheless.

✓ Bryan, David K., and David W. Pao, eds. *Ascent into Heaven in Luke-Acts: New Explorations of Luke's Narrative Hinge*, 2016. Fine lineup of essayists (Walton, Pao, Porter, Sleeman, Farrow) on a neglected topic. See Sleeman under Acts.

✓ Caird, G. B. ‡ (Pelican) 1963. One of the best in the series. Caird was always incisive.

☆ Calvin, John. *Songs of the Nativity: Selected Sermons on Luke 1 & 2*, 2008. [*RTR* 8/10].

☆ **Carroll, John T.** ‡ (NTL) 2012. After a rather brief 15-page introduction, this Union Seminary, Virginia prof devotes 480pp. to a clear exegesis of the text. Carroll provides a "synchronic narrative analysis that attends closely to literary shaping of the canonical form of the Gospel of Luke" (9), with a bit of redaction criticism thrown in. Because of its focus on the literary qualities and message of the text, I predict that many pastors will gravitate toward this vol., which stands among the best and most interesting in NTL (see also de Boer on Galatians and Johnson on Hebrews). There is less engagement with various scholarly debates; perhaps it is slightly less useful to students on that account. It's worth remarking, too, that Carroll is an enjoyable read, since most commentaries aren't. He shows a reluctance to take any firm positions on authorship or date (75–125 CE, p.4). [*CBQ* 7/14; *Int* 10/13; *JSNT* 36.5; *RevExp* 5/15].

Chen, Diane G. (NCCS) 2017. Well-written and about 320pp. Chen earned her PhD at Fuller and is an ordained elder in the ECO.

Craddock, Fred B. ‡ (I) 1990. Mainly for the communicator and very well-done from a moderately critical angle. [*Int* 1/92; *ThTo* 48.2; *CRBR* 1992; *AsTJ* Fall 92].

Creed, J. M. ‡ 1930. Highly critical and dated. Though still cited in the literature, Creed can be safely ignored.

✓ **Culpepper, R. Alan.** ‡ (NIB) 1995. This Baylor professor is well-known for his literary-critical work on John's Gospel (see below). His commentary on Luke will be of more use to the student than the pastor, though he seeks to assist preachers. [*JETS* 3/99].

☆ **Culy, Martin M., Mikeal C. Parsons, and Joshua J. Stiggall.** (BHGNT) 2010. Praised by a number of scholars as a well-done, thorough lexical and grammatical analysis of the Greek text (over 800pp.). [*JSNT* 34.5; *ExpTim* 12/11].

☆ **Danker, Frederick.** ‡ *Jesus and the New Age*, 1972, rev. 1988. A most stimulating commentary (430pp.)—a favorite of Marshall. Danker's immense learning in the classics is put to good use, and there are many insights a preacher would find suggestive for sermon preparation. This is Danker of the BDAG lexicon. [*CRBR* 1990].

Davis, Dale Ralph. (Focus) 2 vols., 2021. I have yet to see it.

F   DeLong, Kindalee Pfremmer. (SGBC).

✓ Dicken, Frank, and Julia Snyder, eds. ‡ *Characters and Characterization in Luke-Acts*, 2016. [*JSNT* 39.5].

F   Dinkler, Michal Beth. (NIGTC-R). Would replace Marshall.

F   Eklund, Rebekah. (BECNT). Replacing Bock, which is a surprise.

✓ **Ellis, E. E.** [𝓜], (NCB) 2nd ed. 1974. Still valuable, especially for understanding passages as a whole and their historical backdrop. An appealing evangelical work which is mildly critical and astute. Advanced students also note his monograph, *Eschatology in Luke* (1972). Marshall really liked Ellis's lengthy introduction.

☆ **Evans, Craig A.** [𝓜], (NIBC) 1990. Over 400pp. Worthwhile to consult and perhaps purchase. Don't confuse with C. F. Evans, the very liberal scholar who has published a substantial work on Luke for TPI. A pastor friend, John Turner, once said in his commentary review that "Evans has stimulated a number of sermon ideas for me." Note also his work on Mark for WBC.

✓ Evans, C. F. ‡ (TPI) 1990. The work to consult to get the radical, Jesus Seminar type of interpretation of this Gospel. This is a large (933pp.), significant work from the far left. The SCM 2nd edition (2008) is really just a reprint. [*JTS* 4/91; *CBQ* 7/92; *BL* 2010].

☆ **Fitzmyer, Joseph A.** ‡ (AB) 2 vols., 1981–85. Even Marshall humbly called this work the best on Luke. Over the years I have encouraged advanced students especially to consider buying this moderately critical Catholic commentary. The long-lived Fitzmyer (1920–2016) was a leading authority on Aramaic and the Semitic background of the NT. Many pastors find the historically oriented set too skeptical as a commentary on the Greek text and are glad to have Bock's BECNT instead. Compare with Marshall and Nolland below. [*Int* 7/83; *SJT* 42.2; *JBL* 9/87; *EvQ* 10/83, 1/88; *ExpTim* 6/83]. See also Fitzmyer's follow-up study, *Luke the Theologian* (1989) [*JTS* 10/90; *JBL* Win 91; *EvQ* 4/91; *CBQ* 10/91]. Finally, note that Fitzmyer published much in AB: Acts, Romans, 1 Corinthians, Philemon.

☆ France, R. T. (TTC) 2013. Regrettably, the British scholar did not live to see this vol. (†2012), which rounds out his studies on the Synoptics. The other two commentaries were exceptional academic works, while this one is a more accessible, to the point (400pp.) pastor's commentary, including much illustrative material. Recommended to all expository preachers. [*JSNT* 36.5].

Gadenz, Pablo T. ‡ (CCSS) 2018. A successful entry in the Catholic series, with a more devotional flavor. [*BBR* 32.1; *CBQ* 1/20; *JSNT* 41.5].

Geldenhuys, J. Norval. (retired NICNT) 1951. The first NICNT, Geldenhuys once served preachers well with its spiritually edifying exposition. E.g., his theological comments (479–87) on the Triumphal Entry are among the more fruitful I have found for the pastor. Also, at 670pp. it was a full work that covered many of the questions raised by the average Bible student. Similar to NTC in Reformed orientation.

Godet, Frederic. ET 1893. Pastors for generations relied on Godet's insightful theological commentaries, which were reprinted by Kregel 1977–81. A great pastor-scholar with Arminian theology, Godet withdrew from the Swiss state church in protest against liberalism. He helped found a seminary where he served as a professor in exegesis. He is not as good here as on John's Gospel. His gifts as a commentator are reviewed in Warfield's *Selected Shorter Writings* (I: 432–36).

González, Justo L. ‡ (Belief) 2010. From the author of one of the most widely used church histories, *The Story of Christianity* (2 vols., rev. 2010), and the 3-vol. *A History of Christian Thought*. Quite insightful and one of the best in the series. [*CBQ* 4/12; *Int* 7/11; *JSNT* 34.5; *RevExp* Sum 11].

☆ Gooding, David. 1987. A very useful study guide, though not so detailed, with application for our time (350pp.). Gooding's work is expositional (not verse-by-verse), focused on "Luke's flow of thought" (7), with many narrative insights and some mild redaction criticism. [*Evangel* Win 88; *EvQ* 7/89].

✓ **Goulder, Michael D.** ‡ *Luke: A New Paradigm*, 2 vols., 1989. A painstaking study (824pp.), interpreting Luke as dependent upon Mark *and* Matthew. The alleged sayings-source Q is dispensed with. Gives close attention to material unique to Luke and challenges traditional source criticism and redaction criticism. Includes a technical commentary of 600pp. which applies his "new paradigm." [*WTJ* Fall 91; *JTS* 4/92; *JBL* Spr 91]. The Goulder thesis is now being pushed by his student, Mark Goodacre, in such vols. as *The Case against Q* (2002) and Goodacre-Perrin, eds., *Questioning Q* (2004) [*BTB* Spr 06].

F Gray, Timothy. ‡ (CCSS).

✓ Gustafsson, Daniel. *Aspects of Coherency in Luke's Composite Christology*, 2022. [*JETS* 6/23].

✓ Hatina, Thomas R., ed. *Biblical Interpretation in Early Christian Gospels. III. The Gospel of Luke*, 2010. For two companion vols., see Hatina under Matthew and Mark.

Hendriksen, William. (NTC) 1978. This was his lengthiest commentary at 1122pp., and probably his most homiletically styled work too. [*RTR* 5/80].

☆ Hughes, R. Kent. (PTW) 2014. See Mark's Gospel. Nearly 1000pp., the original version of the homiletical work was 2 vols. (1998). It has been reedited to explain the ESV.

☆ **Jeffrey, David Lyle.** (Brazos) 2012. If all the vols. in the series were of this quality, Brazos would have a much higher profile. Jeffrey has little to satisfy those with historical questions, but offers a solid literary and theological reading. Like Gooding, a real help to preachers. [*ExpTim* 8/13 (Marshall); *TJ* Fall 14].

☆ **Johnson, Luke Timothy.** ‡ (SacP) 1991. Delivers an interesting, sensitive, literary reading of this Gospel (466pp.). Advanced students can learn a lot here, especially because Johnson has respect for the text. There is less of a hermeneutic of suspicion. To be more accurate, there is suspicion of any attempt, either hyper-critical (Jesus Seminar) or supposedly uncritical (evangelicals), to discover the historical Jesus. See his controversial book, *The Real Jesus: The Misguided Quest for the Historical Jesus and the Truth of the Traditional Gospels* (1996), and the high-level discussion of it in *BBR* 7 (1997). This SacP was among Carson's top picks in 2007. [*JBL* 113.2; *Int* 10/93; *Bib* 74.2; *CBQ* 1/93]. It was wise for the series' editors to allow Johnson to contribute *Acts* as well; Johnson wrote his dissertation on Luke–Acts. In another series (AB), Johnson wrote on James and Timothy.

✓ **Just, Arthur A.** (ConcC) 2 vols., 1996–97. A large-scale (1066-pp.) work with real exegetical value and theological exposition in a confessional Lutheran mold. The author is well-educated (Yale and Durham, beyond Concordia Seminary), and his aim is to assist the studious preacher who is reading through the Greek to compose a sermon.

✓ Just, Arthur A., ed. (ACCS) 2003. [*RelSRev* 4/04].

✓ Kreitzer, Beth, ed. (RCS) 2015.

F Lanier, Gregory. (CSC). To replace Stein.

Leaney, A. R. C. ‡ (BNTC) 1958.

✓ **Levine, Amy-Jill, and Ben Witherington III.** (NCBC) 2018. An extraordinary collaboration between a Jewish feminist from Vanderbilt and an evangelical Methodist from Asbury. There is much learning here, accessibly presented (approx. 700pp.). [*CBQ* 10/19; *JSNT* 41.5].

☆ **Liefeld, Walter L., and David W. Pao.** (EBCR) 2007. The original Liefeld EBC (1984) was regarded as a very good entry, despite its brevity. [*TJ* Spr 85]. The older work has been improved in this collaborative effort of 320pp. It is competent, insightful, and well-written throughout. Found in vol. 10, covering Luke to Acts.

Lieu, Judith. ‡ (Epworth Commentaries) 1997. Written for pastors.

✓ Malina, Bruce J., and Richard L. Rohrbaugh. ‡ *Social-Science Commentary on the Synoptic Gospels*, 1992.

☆ **Marshall, I. Howard.** [𝓜], (NIGTC) 1978. Still one of the five most important scholarly commentaries on Luke. It is more conservative than Fitzmyer—cf. their approaches to redaction and historical questions—and was Silva's first pick years ago. Many pastors prefer Marshall's evangelical approach to Fitzmyer's assiduous criticism. Unfortunately, the format of this work (about 900pp.) is somewhat self-defeating. It is laborious to use Marshall because, in Carson's words, it is so "densely-packed," with notes incorporated into the text of the commentary. But diligence on the part of the student does pay off. The advanced student working on Luke will want Marshall and Fitzmyer, in addition to Bock and Bovon. Rather than write a new introduction for this vol., Marshall refers readers to his excellent *Luke: Historian and Theologian* (1970, rev. 1979, enlarged ed. 1989), discussed at length in a 2022 memorial journal issue [*EvQ* 93.2]. Though I haven't included this monograph among the above recommendations, it has long been a smart buy for studies in Luke and Acts. [*WTJ* Spr 80; *RTR* 1/79; *EvQ* 10/79].

✓ Moessner, David Paul. ‡ *Luke the Historian of Israel's Legacy, Theologian of Israel's 'Christ'*, 2016. An influential attempt to read Luke and Acts as a unit. [*ETL* 94.4; *JSNT* 39.5].

Morgan, G. Campbell. 1931. I do not intend to list all of Campbell Morgan's thoughtful expositions, but pastors should be reminded that they are available and useful. He was Lloyd-Jones's famous predecessor at Westminster Chapel, London.

☆ Morris, Leon. (retired TNTC) 1974, rev. 1988. Helpful and handy, Morris was definitely one of the more insightful works in the series. The financially strapped preacher could start here. The revision is minor. [*EvQ* 1/75].

✓ **Nolland, John.** [*M*], (WBC) 3 vols., 1989–93. One would have thought there was little to say after Marshall and Fitzmyer got done, but Nolland wrote a fine, heavily redaction-critical commentary that goes on and on for 1300pp. After sampling it, one comes to the conclusion that this is more of an academic commentary; Nolland seems to spend proportionally more time interacting with the literature on Luke than bringing out the meaning of the evangelist himself. In other words, those working on the graduate level will find these three vols. more useful than the expositor preparing for Sunday. I find Nolland quite useful for his discussion of Synoptic parallels. This set received mixed reviews. One of the best is *CRBR* 1995. [*WTJ* Fall 91; *JTS* 4/91, 10/95; *EvQ* 1/93, 4/96; *CBQ* 4/92; *RTR* 1/91; *Them* 1/92, 5/95; *BSac* 7/93]. Reports are that Kindalee DeLong will join Nolland in revising the set.

F   Orr, Peter. (EEC). A previous report was Stanley Porter.

Osborne, Grant R. (ONTC) 2018. See under Commentary Series.

✓ **Parsons, Mikeal C.** ‡ (Paideia) 2015. The author has published a lot on Luke–Acts. E.g., see his *Luke: Storyteller, Interpreter, Evangelist* (2007) [*BBR* 19.1; *RelSRev* 12/08], and BHGNT above (see Culy). This is a good representative of the series (about 360pp.), with strengths in literary and socio-rhetorical analysis. [*WTJ* Spr 17; *CBQ* 1/16; *Int* 10/16; *RB* 125.2; *JSNT* 38.5].

Pate, C. Marvin. (Moody Gospel Commentary) 1995. A fuller, popular-level pb.

✓ Pitts, Andrew W. *History, Biography, and the Genre of Luke-Acts: An Exploration of Literary Divergence in Greek Narrative Discourse*, 2019. An important, revised doctoral study (under Porter) challenging the "biography" designation. See the probing review by Burridge [*JETS* 3/21]. [*Them* 45.1 (Walton)].

✓ **Plummer, Alfred.** (ICC) 5th ed. 1922. The standard of its day and still useful for work in the Greek. Silva called it first-rate. This commentary was about the most conservative work ever published in ICC. Should now be used in conjunction with AB, NIGTC, BECNT, WBC, and Herm.

✓ Porter, Stanley E., and Ron C. Fay, eds. *Luke-Acts in Modern Scholarship*, 2021. Essays on leading scholars of last 150 years. [*JETS* 9/22].

Powery, Emerson B. [*M*], *The Good Samaritan: Luke 10 for the Life of the Church*, 2022. Stimulating, from a progressive evangelical angle. [*Int* 10/23].

Reicke, Bo. ‡ *The Gospel of Luke*, 1964.

Reid, Barbara E., and Shelly Matthews. ‡ (Wisdom) 2 vols., 2021. [*CBQ* 7/22, 4/23; *Int* 1/23; *JSNT* 45.5].

Reilling, R., and J. L. Swellengrebel. (UBS) 1971. A translator's handbook of nearly 800pp.

Ringe, Sharon H. ‡ (WestBC) 1996. A feminist treatment by one of the editors of *The Women's Bible Commentary*. [*Int* 1/98; *CBQ* 4/97].

F   Robbins, Vernon K. ‡ (RRA).

✓ Rowe, C. Kavin. *Early Narrative Christology: The Lord in the Gospel of Luke*, 2009.

☆ Ryken, Philip. (REC) 2 vols., 2009. Excellent sermonic material indeed! Were it not, then 1300pp. would seem awfully excessive. Ryken has followed the grand tradition of Boice, his predecessor at famous Tenth Presbyterian. See his other large-scale expositions of Exodus, 1 Kings, Jeremiah, Galatians, and 1 Timothy.

☆ Ryle, J. C. (CrossC) 1997.

Schertz, Mary H. (BCBC) 2023. I have yet to see this Anabaptist commentary (440pp.).

☆ Schreiner, Thomas. "Luke" in *Matthew–Luke* (ESVEC) 2021. See Doriani under Matthew.

✓ Schweizer, Eduard. ‡ ET 1984. See under Mark.

✓ Spencer, F. Scott. ‡ *The Gospel of Luke and Acts of the Apostles*, 2008. This entry in Abingdon's IBT series gives less attention to Acts. [*BL* 2009; *Int* 7/10].

☆ **Spencer, F. Scott.** ‡ (THC) 2019. Never expected a THC vol. this size, with 635pp. of commentary and about 90pp. of theological essays. Spencer has previously done praiseworthy work on both Luke and Acts, and in this hefty book he demonstrates his narratological expertise. I predict this book will have "staying power" as a multidisciplinary, creative, and most stimulating engagement with the text, regularly keeping theological questions and concerns at the fore. Spencer avoids the atomization problem, often found in verse-by-verse (even word-by-word) exegeses, and deals with Luke section-by-section (5). Theologically, he draws from a broad spectrum: the church fathers, to the Reformers, to Joel Green and Moltmann (favorites). The work thankfully is not a commentary on the commentators. Literary insights abound, and this work is not simply going over the same ground as other commentators. The register can be chatty, and humorously you get a citation of Sapolski, *Why Zebras Don't Get Ulcers*, but this is a probing, most thoughtful work. [*BBR* 30.2; *Int* 1/22; *JSNT* 42.5; *RevExp* 11/20].

☆ **Stein, Robert H.** (NAC) 1992. The heftiest (642pp.), and one of the most thoughtful, in the series. "Written with a pastor's heart," says Steve Walton [*BSB* 12/97]. Stein is an experienced, very sharp exegete (see his BECNT on Mark). Among the many features here to appreciate is "a regular summing up of Luke's distinctive redactional emphases in each passage" (Blomberg). Note that Stein uses the terminology "composition criticism" instead of "redaction." This work proves to be a good counterbalance to Green. [*ThTo* 10/93; *EvQ* 7/94; *JETS* 6/96; *CRBR* 1994].

✓ Stonehouse, Ned B. *The Witness of the Synoptic Gospels to Christ*, 1979 reprint. See under Matthew.

✓ **Talbert, Charles H.** ‡ *Reading Luke: A Literary and Theological Commentary on the Third Gospel* (RNT) 1982. Provocative and packed commentary by a leading American Lukan scholar. The evangelical pastor found this useful years ago, but it is less valuable today. See also Talbert's books on John, Acts, and Corinthians. [*JBL* 104.2].

✓ **Tannehill, Robert C.** ‡ *The Narrative Unity of Luke-Acts, A Literary Interpretation*, 2 vols., 1990–91. An exciting study that provided a synchronic, literary reading of the final form of the Lukan corpus. There are many insights in this Fortress set. See the next entry. [*Bib* 69.1; *CRBR* 1988 (more critical)].

✓ **Tannehill, Robert C.** ‡ (ANTC) 1996. This 378-page entry updates his past work and makes his conclusions available in a less expensive pb format. [*Int* 7/98; *RelSRev* 1/98].

☆ **Thompson, Alan J.** (EGGNT) 2017. I agree with Carson: "Thompson's fine volume on Luke succinctly provides judicious explanation of the Greek syntax, structure, grammatical options, the flow of the argument, and more." The provision of some homiletical hints indicates that this is no mere morphological and syntactical tagging exercise; Thompson has a commentary element. [*WTJ* Spr 19; *Them* 42.3].

✓ Tiede, David L. ‡ (Augsburg NT Commentary) 1988. This full Lutheran work (457pp.) is praised by Danker, who knows this Gospel well. [*CRBR* 1991].

Trites, Allison. (CorBC) 2006. Also covers Acts (Larkin). I have not seen this.

✓ Verheyden, J., ed. *The Unity of Luke-Acts*, 1999. Huge BETL vol.

Vinson, Richard B. ‡ (S&H) 2008. Substantial research underlies this, one of the largest vols. in the series (760pp.). Vinson is open to "suspicious readings" of Luke and makes it a goal of his interpretation "to offer readings that support the full participation of women in ministry" (19). Application parts of this exposition sometimes have an oddly loaded, unpracticed feel to them (e.g., commending the example of elaborate, expensive preparations for death after an ominous palm-reading, p.473). Vinson teaches at Salem College in North Carolina. [*Int* 4/10].

☆ Wilcock, Michael. (BST) 1979. Formerly titled *The Saviour of the World*. Directly serves the expositor as it explains pericopae (not a verse-by-verse commentary).

F  Wilkins, Michael. (EBTC)? See Wilkins under Matthew.

✓ Wilson, Benjamin R. *The Saving Cross of the Suffering Christ: The Death of Jesus in Lukan Soteriology*, 2016. Notable as a fine Cambridge PhD. [*JETS* 9/17].

✓ **Wolter, Michael.** ‡ 2 vol., ET 2016–17. A massive, detailed commentary from *Handbuch zum Neuen Testament*, in Baylor's well-executed translation. Students welcome this, as it represents some of the best German scholarship and includes the fullest kind of interaction with recent continental research. [*BBR* 28.1, 30.2; *Int* 7/18; *JSNT* 41.5].

NOTES: (1) See Marshall's article, "The Present State of Lucan Studies," in *Them*, 1/89; and (2) C. S. Rodd, "Two Commentaries on Luke," *ExpTim* 9/90. (3) Darrell L. Bock, "Commentaries on the Synoptic Gospels" (339–63), in *On the Writing of NT Commentaries*, eds. Porter and Schnabel, cited in the Introduction.

# JOHN

★ **Barrett, C. K.** ‡ 2nd ed. 1978. Moloney terms this "precise but rich." The Germans translated it for their prestigious NT series, MeyerK (1990). I call Barrett indispensable for the student and scholarly pastor doing exegesis of the Greek text. Yes, you must have a handle on Greek to make good use of this. Amazingly thorough, compressed and well-reasoned from the critical angle (638pp.), with some fine theological points: "the Father is God sending and commanding, the Son is God sent and obedient" (468). The commentary really has not changed much since it was first published in 1955. Some would say that Barrett's argument has been partially vitiated because of a shift in scholarly opinion toward identifying a Palestinian milieu for the Fourth Gospel (see Martyn below). The work is complemented by *Essays on John* (1982). Barrett is one of Carson's and Silva's favorite critical works. Compare with Brown's more expensive set, which some say has more for the pastor. Evangelicals may want the *caveat emptor* that Barrett believes the Fourth Gospel is theologically creative in presenting Jesus traditions with little historical value. Any who wish to stick with conservative exegeses are urged to buy Kruse or Blomberg instead. [*EvQ* 4/79; *JBL* 99.4].

★ Burge, Gary. (NIVAC) 2000. A sizable (600-page) homiletical commentary building upon a solid foundation of NT scholarship (see Burge below). Burge did a PhD at Aberdeen and teaches at Wheaton. This vol. ventures some bold, thought-provoking application and well complements these other exegeses. Other wise purchases for preachers would be Hughes, Boice, Milne, and Morris's *Reflections*. [*CTJ* 11/01]. Note his subsequent *Interpreting the Gospel of John* (2nd ed. 2013) [*CTJ* 4/18].

★ **Carson, Donald.** (Pillar) 1991. Still the evangelical pastor's first choice. The vol. was originally intended as Tasker's replacement in TNTC, and I'm glad it proved much too lengthy. Boice—who, incidentally, did his dissertation on John's Gospel and took six years preaching through John—called this 700-page work "the most exciting, helpful, and sound commentary on the Gospel of John in decades." I used it extensively during a 15-month series and found Boice's comments on target. The strengths of his earlier Matthew commentary are mirrored here. [*WTJ* Fall 92 (Silva); *CBQ* 7/92; *RTR* 5/92; *EvQ* 1/95; *JETS* 6/95; *CRBR* 1992]. Pastors might also note Carson's exposition of chs. 14–17, *The Farewell Discourse and Final Prayer of Jesus* (1981). My counsel to the average pastor would be to buy Carson, then Michaels and/or Klink, and finally an expositional work. The more scholarly can then add some combination of Keener, Barrett, Thompson, Ridderbos, WBC, Lincoln, Morris, Blomberg, Moloney, and perhaps Brown or Schnackenburg—but do start with Keener and Barrett.

★ **Keener, Craig.** 2 vols., 2003. An exceedingly full evangelical interpretation, which displaced Morris on my list of suggestions. But perhaps Keener is too full for the pastor (1600pp.). As with his huge commentaries on Matthew and Acts, this is long on historical, cultural, and ancient literary background. (He adduces too many supposed parallels, in my opinion, but I don't complain.) Those who want a more manageable evangelical commentary in one vol. can repair to Blomberg, or the TNTC by Kruse. Students willing to work through the astonishing amount of detail find the set a masterful guide into John's Gospel, where, Augustine famously said, a child may safely wade and an elephant can swim. The size and weight here suggest more the elephant. [*CBQ* 10/04; *ExpTim* 8/04; *SwJT* Fall 05; *RTR* 12/08; *JTS* 10/05; *Int* 7/06; *BSac* 1/09; *EuroJTh* 15.2].

★ **Klink, Edward W., III.** (ZECNT) 2016. By a former Talbot prof, who now pastors an Evangelical Free Church. Klink builds on his doctoral research at St. Andrews (under Bauckham), published as *The Sheep of the Fold: The Audience and Origin of the Gospel of John* (2007), which Kysar termed "splendid" [*Bib* 90.1]. It presents a trenchant critique of the scholarship about John being written for a single Christian community. [*BBR* 19.2 (Carson)]. Klink's focus in ZECNT is resolutely and creatively theological; preachers will appreciate this, though some may question whether all his points are truly text-based. Also, Klink's concern "is not to conjecture about the shared (or lack of shared) material [with the Synoptics] or to reconstruct an event in light of the four accounts so as to align them into one, but to interpret [the events of Jesus's life] . . . through the . . . lens of the Fourth Gospel" (732). Strengths of the work include thoroughness (920pp.), a surprisingly full explanation of his theological commitments and "confessional approach" (21–41), constant interaction with the major English-language commentaries, reading John in the light of the whole canon (a huge Scripture Index), and the usual ZECNT graphical layout of the Greek. [*BBR* 27.3; *CBQ* 4/18; *JETS* 3/18; *JSNT* 40.5].

★ **Michaels, J. Ramsey.** (NICNT-R) 2010. The fat, trusty Morris vol. was retired to give place to this even larger tome (about 1100pp.), the size and detail of which may discourage busy pastors from using it. Michaels builds upon his earlier NIBC (below) and has obviously thought long and hard about the Gospel. He has always seemed to me a more independently minded gentleman, and, though very well-informed, he is not concerned to interact with all the available scholarship. (Reviewers are critical at this point.) In other words, this is a fresh take on John, specified as "synchronic" (xii), though with less interest in newer literary studies. There is less, too, on background, which is Keener's strength, and he leaves aside some historical and chronological issues (e.g., the temple cleansing). Where does it rank? I continue to regard Carson as the pastor's first choice, even though it dates to 1991. This NICNT (which is perhaps not as reliable a guide) is a complement to it. Michaels's handling of the Greek and the basic exegetical questions is admirable. He is now retired; he taught for a couple of decades at Gordon-Conwell and then was long at Missouri State. See also 1 Peter, Revelation, and Hebrews. [*CBQ* 4/12; *JTS* 10/11; *JSNT* 33.5; *Chm* Sum 12; *JETS* 12/11; *ExpTim* 3/11; *Them* 5/11 (Harris); *BSac* 4/12; *DenvJ* 14; *RelSRev* 9/11; *TJ* Fall 12].

★ **Ridderbos, Herman.** *The Gospel of John: A Theological Commentary*, ET 1997. You ought to consider this for purchase, as extensive as it is, and as masterful a theologian as Ridderbos is. Though rich and profound, this work is not always lucid in ET and is not easy for beginners. Some pastors might prefer another book, but Ridderbos has a different, fresh approach; he is not going over the same ground, as with many other commentators. [*Them* 5/99; *JETS* 9/99; *WTJ* Fall 97; *TJ* Spr 98; *Int* 7/98; *CBQ* 1/99; *RTR* 8/98].

❖ ❖ ❖ ❖ ❖ ❖

F   Anderson, Paul. ‡ (S&H). The author is known for *The Christology of the Fourth Gospel* (1996, enlarged ed. 2010) [*JSNT* 34.5]. On the way to S&H he offers *The Riddles of the Fourth Gospel: An Introduction to John* (2011) [*Int* 7/12; *JSNT* 34.5; *JETS* 12/12; *BibInt* 21.1; *RelSRev* 9/14].

✓   Anderson, Paul N., Felix Just, and Tom Thatcher, eds. ‡ *John, Jesus, and History*. Vol. I: *Critical Appraisals of Critical Views*, 2007. [*BL* 2009; *JSHJ* 7.1]. Volume II is *Aspects of Historicity in the Fourth Gospel* (2009) [*JSNT* 33.5; *ExpTim* 10/10]. Volume III is *Glimpses of Jesus through the Johannine Lens* (2016) [*JSNT* 39.5].

✓   Ashton, John. ‡ *Understanding the Fourth Gospel*, 1993, 2nd ed. 2007. Published by OUP (624pp. in 1993) and seeks to interpret John with reference to apocalyptic. [*JBL* Spr 93; *JTS* 10/92; *ExpTim* 10/91, 11/07]. Added to this is *The Gospel of John and Christian Origins* (2014) [*JSNT* 37.5] and the Ashton-edited collection of various scholars' essays in *The Interpretation of John* (2nd ed. 1997) [*RelSRev* 7/00].

F   Attridge, Harold. ‡ (Herm). Some initial work is *Essays on John and Hebrews* (2010).

Bartholomä, Philipp. *The Johannine Discourses and the Teaching of Jesus in the Synoptics*, 2012. A fine Leuven PhD on a topic of perennial interest. [*JETS* 6/13].

F   Bauckham, Richard. [𝓜], (NIGTC). Could make a major contribution to scholarship here, especially as he argues further the thesis proposed in Bauckham, ed., *The Gospels for All Christians: Rethinking the Gospel Audiences* (1998), which takes aim at the widely held idea of a conflicted Johannine Community. His thesis, that the Gospels are general tracts for all Christians, is applied to all four. He builds brilliantly on it in *The Testimony of the Beloved Disciple* (2007) [*JETS* 9/08; *CTJ* 11/09; *EvQ* 7/09; *DenvJ* 12/07; *JSHJ* 8.2; *RelSRev* 3/12], though I disagree with him identifying the author as John the Elder, not John, son of Zebedee. Cf. Martyn (below) and Klink (above). For Bauckham's rejection of a source and form-critical approach, see *Jesus and the Eyewitnesses: The Gospels as Eyewitness Testimony* (2006) [*BBR* 19.1; *JTS* 4/08; *TJ* Spr 08; *JSNT* 12/08; *Them* 5/08 (Wenham)]. Then we received *Gospel of Glory: Major Themes in Johannine Theology* (2015), each essay of which is self-contained. [*WTJ* Fall 16; *CBQ* 4/16; *JETS* 6/16; *Int* 7/17; *JSNT* 38.5; *Them* 41.1].

F   Bauckham, Richard. [𝓜], (THC).

✓   Bauckham, Richard, and Carl Mosser, eds. *The Gospel of John and Christian Theology*, 2008. [*CBQ* 4/09; *ExpTim* 4/09; *TJ* Spr 09; *Chm* Sum 09; *Them* 4/10; *BL* 2009; *RelSRev* 12/09].

✓   **Beasley-Murray, George R.** [𝓜], (WBC) 1987, 2nd ed. 1999. Highly respected as an erudite, closely packed commentary. I was somewhat disappointed by its critical stance on a number of issues. Barrett and Brown are better coming from the critical perspective, and Carson is more dependable and insightful from a consistently evangelical viewpoint. This vol., says Silva, is exceeding rich on the last half of the Gospel. The 2nd edition contains the same commentary and a much-lengthened introduction and bibliography. Students should note that the addendum gives an especially fine account of major developments in studies on John from the late 1970s to late 90s. [*JTS* 40.1; *JBL* Win 89; *WTJ* Fall 88; *JBL* 108.4; *RTR* 1/88; *Chm* 104.1]. Students may consult his follow-up work, *Gospel of Life: Theology in the Fourth Gospel* (1991).

✓   Behr, John. [𝓜], *John the Theologian and His Pascal Gospel*, 2019. A multidisciplinary work from OUP by a famous patristics scholar—his recent study of Origen's *On First Principles* is magisterial. (And there is a good measure of retrieval work here, as Behr digs into patristic *theological* interpretation of John's Gospel, as contrasted to contemporary *historical* research within biblical studies.) [*JETS* 6/20; *Them* 44.3].

✓   Bennema, Cornelis. *Encountering Jesus: Character Studies in the Gospel of John*, 2nd ed. 2014. [*CBQ* 4/16]. Cf. the popular-level Watson and Culy, *The Making of a Disciple: Character Studies in the Gospel of John* (2021) [*JSNT* 45.5].

Bernard, J. H. ‡ (ICC) 2 vols., 1928. Can be ignored at this stage. See both de Boer and McHugh below.

✓ **Beutler, Johannes.** ‡ ET 2017. A large-scale (550-page), technical, Catholic commentary, from Eerdmans, containing heavy doses of interaction with fellow Catholics and German scholars. Moloney says it takes English-only readers "into the exciting world of the best of European Johannine scholarship" (xii). Close attention is paid to literary structure and narrative development (around the theme of journeys). John 21 is regarded as *relecture*, a "rereading" of earlier passages in the tradition—an important idea for Beutler (and others, such as Zumstein). In truth, this book represents the man's life work, 50 years of research. [*Chm* Spr 20; *JETS* 9/18; *BSac* 7/21; *JSNT* 40.5].

☆ **Blomberg, Craig.** *The Historical Reliability of John's Gospel*, 2002. Not only does the Denver prof address the scholarly wrangle mentioned in the book title, he also has a commentary in these pages. This is a good piece of work by a leading evangelical that can be recommended to both students and pastors. [*Them* Aut 02; *JETS* 6/03]. See also his *Jesus the Purifier: John's Gospel and the Fourth Quest for the Historical Jesus* (2023). As Keener puts it, "Readers essentially get two good books here: a fair and extremely helpful survey of the history of Jesus research, suitable for a historical Jesus course, that does not leave out voices often marginalized by Bultmannians, and a case for why John's Gospel belongs in historical Jesus research." [*Int* 10/23; *JETS* 3/24].

F   Boer, Martinus C. de. ‡ *John 1–6* (ICC-R) 2025. See Bernard (above) and McHugh (below).

☆ Boice, James Montgomery. 1975–79. A huge vol. of exposition—really printed sermons (his series began in 1971). Boice here builds on his doctoral work at Basel. This would be useful to the preacher looking for a guide in preaching through John (hopefully more quickly). For further review of Boice's work, see Genesis. The later multivol. sets which he wrote (e.g., Psalms, Matthew) are better, more mature preaching.

☆ **Borchert, Gerald L.** (NAC) 2 vols., 1996–2002. The set has received generally favorable reviews and has good research behind it, but I do not place Borchert in the top rank of evangelical commentators. Of special interest to some is the author's proposal regarding an alternative structuring of the Fourth Gospel. He sees ch. 1 as introductory. What follows are three sections he terms cycles: the Cana Cycle (2:1–4:54); the Festival Cycle (5:1–11:57); and the Farewell Cycle (13:1–17:26). The pivot in the middle is ch. 12, while the passion and resurrection narratives form the Gospel's conclusion. Students could make use of Borchert. [*Them* Sum 04; *JETS* 9/04].

☆ Bowsher, Clive. *Life in the Son: Exploring Participation and Union with Christ in John's Gospel and Letters*, 2023. From the NSBT series. A welcome research, given that union with Christ has more often been explored from the Pauline studies angle (173pp.). On the related topic of "Abiding in Christ in the Johannine Writings" (the subtitle), see Rodney Reeves, *Spirituality according to John* (IVP, 2021) [*JSNT* 45.5].

✓ **Brant, Jo-Ann A.** ‡ (Paideia) 2011. A 290-page exegesis from a Goshen College prof, which takes a fresh literary-rhetorical approach and moves along at a good pace. It has a contemporary feel, as she makes diverse connections to popular culture. The theological reading is odd in places; e.g., she believes Jesus's prayer language in 17:9–10 "is perhaps best described as boasting." [*CBQ* 7/13; *JSNT* 35.5; *ExpTim* 9/12; *TJ* Fall 12].

✓ **Brodie, Thomas L.** ‡ 1993. This OUP work is subtitled "A Literary and Theological Commentary" (625pp.), and urges readers to consider the evidence for literary unity and coherence. Compare this with another Catholic literary interpretation: Moloney. [*JTS* 4/95; *JETS* 3/96; *JBL* Sum 95].

✓ Brown, Christopher B., ed. *John 13–21* (RCS) 2021. See also Farmer below.

☆ **Brown, R. E.** ‡ (AB) 2 vols., 1966–70. Rich and incisive exegesis with a treasure trove of notes.

This commentary, by one of the most prominent Catholic NT scholars of the 20th century, is quite a work to set one thinking, especially since there's a good bit for an evangelical to disagree with (e.g., sacramental emphases). Brown's work is also significant because he was one of the first to recognize the importance of the Qumran discoveries for Johannine studies and to emphasize a Palestinian setting. Among critical works I have sometimes found Brown marginally more useful than Barrett. The scholarly student or pastor with means might try to obtain both. Brown's work on a revision of the commentary was cut short by his death in 1998. [*JBL* 90.3]. The new introduction with updated notes was edited by Moloney, filling almost 400pp., and published in 2003 [*JTS* 4/05; *ThTo* 7/04 (Moody Smith)]. Additionally, see Brown's AB on John's Epistles.

✓ Brown, Sherri, and Francis J. Moloney. ‡ *Interpreting the Gospel and Letters of John*, 2017. A rather full Catholic introduction, moderately critical, from Eerdmans. [*JSNT* 40.5].

✓ Brown, Sherri, and Christopher W. Skinner, eds. ‡ *Johannine Ethics: The Moral World of the Gospel and Epistles of John*, 2017. [*JSNT* 40.5]. Cf. the different approach in Bennema, *Mimesis in the Johannine Literature* (2017) [*JSNT* 40.5].

☆ Bruce, F. F. 1983. Once it was hard to beat this 400-page commentary in terms of value for your money ($10 in pb). Bruce offers a solid, sober, careful grammatico-historical interpretation of John. Eerdmans also published a one-vol. 600-page hb which included Bruce's work on John's Epistles. [*Them* 1/85; *EvQ* 4/86; *ThTo* 41.4].

☆ **Bruner, Frederick Dale.** [*M*], 2012. Bruner was known for his large-scale, 2-vol. Matthew commentary, and then Eerdmans published his follow-up work of 1300pp. on John. The strengths of the author are theological rather than exegetical, in the minds of some NT scholars. Preachers definitely find Bruner stimulating, but more as "a companion volume than a stand-alone text" (Koester [*Int* 10/13]). [*JSNT* 35.5; *RTR* 12/14; *JETS* 12/13; *RelSRev* 12/12; *TJ* Spr 13].

F Bryan, Steve. (BECNT). Long a missionary in Ethiopia, Bryan has taught at TEDS since 2016. This replaces Köstenberger.

✓ **Bultmann, Rudolf.** ‡ ET 1971. Called by many Bultmann's greatest work, this commentary is radically critical, proposes a complex source theory, and is stimulating (because it compels the reader to interact). It once had towering stature, but John studies moved sharply away from his thesis that the Fourth Gospel addresses a gnostic viewpoint and should be interpreted against a Hellenistic, non-Christian background of Mandaeism (see comments on Barrett above). Ironically, Bultmann the demythologizer did a lot of mischief in pushing the pre-Christian gnostic redeemer myth (shown to be baseless). This is only for advanced students.

✓ Burge, Gary. *The Anointed Community: The Holy Spirit in the Johannine Tradition*, 1987. Not a commentary, but a PhD on the doctrine of the Holy Spirit in this literature. Such a work was needed "since pneumatology plays a fundamental role in the very fabric of the Fourth Gospel" (Silva). [*WTJ* Spr 88; *JBL* 108.1]. Also helpful is Burge's *Interpreting the Gospel of John* (2nd ed. 2013) [*JSNT* 37.5], with a commentary guide as an appendix. See his NIVAC on John's Gospel (above) and John's Epistles.

✓ Byers, Andrew J. *Ecclesiology and Theosis in the Gospel of John*, 2017. In SNTSMS from CUP. [*JSNT* 40.5]. More recent is a hard-hitting critique of widely accepted theses that John is a sectarian and anti-Jewish tract: *John and Others: Jewish Relations, Christian Origins, and the Sectarian Hermeneutic* (2021) [*Int* 10/23].

✓ Byrne, Brendon. ‡ *Life Abounding: A Reading of John's Gospel*, 2014. An approachable, insightful Jesuit exposition. [*CBQ* 10/15].

Calvin, John. (CrossC) 1994. The full commentary is free online.

F Caneday, Ardel. (EBTC)?

Carter, Matt, and Josh Wredeberg. *Exalting Jesus in John* (CCE) 2017.

✓ Carter, Warren. ‡ *John: Storyteller, Interpreter, Evangelist*, 2006. One of the better introductions to John and Johannine scholarship. [*BL* 2008; *ExpTim* 2/08; *BTB* Spr 08]. More important from the scholarly side is *John and Empire* (2008) [*Pacifica* 22.1; *BibInt* 18.3].

✓ Charlesworth, James H. ‡ *Jesus as Mirrored in John*, 2019. [*JSNT* 42.5].

Coloe, Mary L. ‡ (Wisdom) 2 vols., 2021. Ties the Gospel to biblical and extrabiblical wisdom literature, arguing that "Jesus's words and deeds embody Sophia throughout the narrative." With her strongly feminist approach, Coloe thinks "the incarnation destroys dualistic views of spirit/matter, male/female" (13). [*CBQ* 1/23, 7/23; *JSNT* 45.5; *Int* 10/23].

✓ Coloe, Mary L., and Tom Thatcher, eds. ‡ *John, Qumran, and the DSS: Sixty Years of Discovery and Debate* (SBL) 2011. [*CBQ* 1/14; *JSNT* 34.5].

✓ **Culpepper, R. Alan.** ‡ *Anatomy of the Fourth Gospel: A Study in Literary Design*, 1983. A signal book, not only for Johannine studies but also for the whole NT discipline. Culpepper applies the new literary criticism to John. Though his conclusions are not compatible with a high view of Scripture, students should acquaint themselves with the work. For an update and survey of scholarship, consult *The Gospel and Letters of John* (IBT) 1998; he gives the Letters little attention (mainly pp.251–83). See Moloney's works and Thatcher–Moore for further research into John as narrative. [*TJ* Fall 83].

✓ Dodd, C. H. ‡ *The Interpretation of the Fourth Gospel*, 1953. Once a seminal study of the ideas behind and in this Gospel. Stresses a Hellenistic background, which is less plausible. He later published *Historical Tradition in the Fourth Gospel* (1963). See Thatcher–Williams, eds., *Engaging with C. H. Dodd on the Gospel of John* (CUP, 2013) [*CBQ* 4/15; *JTS* 10/14].

Dods, Marcus. [*M*], (EB, and Expositor's Greek Testament) 1886 and 1897. These are still somewhat useful. Dods imbibed some old-style liberalism.

Edwards, Mark. ‡ (BBC) 2004. [*EuroJTh* 15.2].

Edwards, Ruth. ‡ *Discovering John: Content, Interpretation, Reception*, 2nd ed. 2015. [*JSNT* 38.5].

Ellis, Peter F. ‡ *The Genius of John: A Composition-Critical Commentary on the Fourth Gospel*, 1984. This Catholic scholar pursues a narrative-critical approach, coming to some surprisingly conservative conclusions about the composition of John and its literary unity. The last two paragraphs are worth reading over and over.

✓ Elowsky, Joel C., ed. (ACCS) 2 vols., 2006–07.

✓ Farmer, Craig S., ed. *John 1–12* (RCS) 2014. See also C. B. Brown above.

✓ **Ford, David F.** ‡ 2021. Originally intended for the Belief series. Subtitled "A Theological Commentary," from a celebrated Irish Anglican who is Regius Professor of Divinity Emeritus in Cambridge. Ford is known for pursuing interfaith dialogue (what he terms "Scriptural Reasoning"). The work is highly intelligent and spends good time discussing themes of belief, light, life, truth, and love, as well as how John might be read alongside other Scriptures. Ford's intertextual approach is key, as John is "marinated" in the LXX; John "often quotes it and, even more frequently, echoes it" (2). Ford is a marvelous guide into such biblical connections, even if you disagree with his theology. He discerns three main emphases: (1) who Jesus is; (2) the Spirit given without measure for the ongoing drama of loving; and (3) God and all people, all creation (4–11). The author has few references to other interpreters, but his 443-page exposition is the product of twenty years of reflection on John. It is more conservatively critical and has been received with alacrity by mainline Protestants. [*Theology* 5/22; *BBR* 32.4; *JSNT* 44.5; *Int* 10/23; *JETS* 12/22].

✓ Frey, Jörg. ‡ *The Glory of the Crucified One: Christology and Theology in the Gospel of John*, ET 2018. Important essays from a Jesuit scholar. [*ExpTim* 6/19; *BBR* 30.1; *Them* 44.1]. See also Frey's critique of the Johannine Community thesis: *Theology and History in the Fourth Gospel* (2018) [*JTS* 10/20; *JETS* 12/19; *SJT* 73.3; *JSNT* 41.5], and cf. the title of Martyn's study.

Godet, Frederic. ET 1886. A classic for pastors, containing 1100pp. of masterful exposition and theological exegesis. You can ignore the discourses on the religious issues of his day. "The thoughtful reader will always discern practical applications if he or she ponders Godet's remarks" (Carson). See his commentaries on Luke, Romans, and 1 Corinthians, which have been reprinted. All are free online.

✓ Gorman, Michael J. [𝓜], *Abide and Go: Missional Theosis in the Gospel of John*, 2018. [*Int* 1/21; *JSNT* 41.5].

✓ **Haenchen, Ernst.** ‡ (Herm) 2 vols., ET 1984. This expensive, very critical work was called a major disappointment by almost everyone except the neo-Bultmannians. Completed posthumously by a student of Haenchen. Dated and sketchy at points. You'd best ignore it, unless you are doing full research at an advanced level.

☆ Hamilton, James M., Jr. "John" in *John–Acts* (ESVEC) 2021. A strong theological exposition by a Southern Baptist prof and preacher (who contributed the highly praised *Psalms* to EBTC). In this same, slightly less hefty ESVEC vol. (570pp.), Vickers treats Acts.

☆ **Harris, Murray J.** (EGGNT) 2015. Has the quality of his *Colossians–Philemon*, and arguably provides a better view of the trees than the woods. After a 12-page Introduction, Harris offers about 340pp. of expert exegetical guidance to Greek readers, adding bibliographical and homiletical suggestions. The reviews have been favorable. [*ExpTim* 4/16; *JETS* 3/17; *RTR* 8/16].

F Heever, G. van den. (RRA).

Heil, John Paul. ‡ *The Gospel of John: Worship for Divine Life Eternal*, 2016. [*CBQ* 7/18].

Hendriksen, William. (NTC) 1953. This commentary is not so prolix as some later ones, but it is also more dated. Sturdy, Reformed, and needs to be checked against more recent works. Of little use to students.

✓ **Hoskyns, Edwyn, and F. N. Davey.** ‡ 1940, 2nd ed. 1957. A very rich theological commentary with a Barthian slant. In fact, Hoskyns interrupted his work on John's Gospel to translate Barth's *Römerbrief* after he had experienced a conversion from a liberal religion of experience to a religion of revelation. Unlike much English biblical scholarship from the 1920s and 30s, this work retains value down to today. For an account of the author's life work, see John M. Court, "Edwyn Clement Hoskyns (9th August 1884–28th June 1937)," *ExpTim* 118 (2007): 331–36. [*WTJ* Fall 40].

☆ Hughes, R. Kent. (PTW) 1999. An outstanding choice for the preacher, if used in conjunction with a solid exegetical work. Approximately 500pp. See Mark above.

✓ Hunt, Steven A., D. Francois Tolmie, and Ruben Zimmerman, eds. ‡ *Character Studies in the Fourth Gospel*, 2013. [*JSNT* 36.5; *JETS* 12/14; *CBQ* 10/15]. For a more conservative study, see Cornelis Bennema, *Encountering Jesus: Character Studies in the Gospel of John* (2009, 2nd ed. 2014) [*JSNT* 37.5; *Them* 5/11; *BTB* 5/11; *RelSRev* 6/11], now complemented by a broader study, *A Theory of Character in NT Narrative* (2014) [*JETS* 6/15; *JSNT* 37.5].

Hunter, A. M. [𝓜], (CBC) 1965. Insightful in brief compass.

Hutcheson, George. (GS) 1657. A great Puritan exposition. Spurgeon wrote that it was "excellent; beyond all praise . . . a full-stored treasury of sound theology, holy thought, and marrowy doctrine." Recommended for lovers of the Puritans.

☆ **Jobes, Karen H.** (TOTE) 2021. Quite useful in two respects: Jobes closely, though not exhaustively, examines the Fourth Gospel verse-by-verse with an eye to the OT/Jewish background, and her application to the church is rich and searching. A great book! [*JETS* 9/22; *RTR* 12/22; *CBQ* 1/23; *JSNT* 45.5].

Kanagaraj, Jey. (NCCS) 2013. The author teaches at Hindustan Bible Institute and College in India. [*JSNT* 36.5; *ExpTim* 3/16].

Keddie, Gordon J. (EPSC) 2 vols., 2001. [*Evangel* Spr 05].

✓ Keith, Chris. ‡ *The Pericope Adulterae, the Gospel of John, and the Literacy of Jesus*, 2009. [*JTS* 10/14; *BibInt* 20.2; *RelSRev* 3/11]. See also the essays in Black–Cerone (eds), *The Pericope of the Adulteress in Contemporary Research* (2016) [*NovT* 58.4; *JSNT* 39.5], and the large text-critical and reception-history study by Jennifer Knust and Tommy Wasserman, *To Cast the First Stone* (2019) [*JETS* 3/21; *NovT* 61.4; *BSac* 1/21].

Kellum, L. Scott. *Preaching the Farewell Discourse: An Expository Walk-Through of John 13:31–17:26*, 2014. [*Chm* Spr 15; *Them* 11/14].

F Klink, Edward W., III. (CCF). See also his ZECNT work above.

✓ Koester, Craig R. ‡ *Symbolism in the Fourth Gospel: Meaning, Mystery, Community*, 2nd ed. 2003; *The Word of Life: A Theology of John's Gospel*, 2008 [*JETS* 3/10; *Int* 10/09; *BL* 2010; *EvQ* 7/11; *ExpTim* 6/12].

✓ Koester, Craig R., ed. *Portraits of Jesus in the Gospel of John*, 2019. [*JSNT* 42.5].

**Köstenberger, Andreas J.** (BECNT) 2004. Withdrawn 2017, due to "a series of inadvertently unattributed references" to Carson's work. See Bryan for a replacement. [*CBQ* 1/06; *BBR* 16.2; *JETS* 9/05; *BSac* 4/06; *SwJT* Fall 05; *Them* 10/05; *BL* 2006; *SBET* Aut 06; *RelSRev* 1/06; *ExpTim* 5/06; *EuroJTh* 15.2]. Köstenberger's college-level textbook is *Encountering John* (2nd ed. 2013) [*JSNT* 37.5; 1999: *JSNT* 12/00; *CTJ* 11/00; *JETS* 9/01], and, below, *A Theology of John's Gospel and Letters*.

F Köstenberger, Andreas. (EEC). An older report had Hall Harris.

✓ Köstenberger, Andreas J. *A Theology of John's Gospel and Letters*, 2009. The first installment in an 8-vol. series, Biblical Theology of the NT (BTNT), edited by Köstenberger. [*Them* 7/10 (Kruse); *SBET* Aut 10; *BBR* 20.4; *CBQ* 1/11; *JSNT* 33.5; *JETS* 12/10; *DenvJ* 14]. See above; he published a great deal over the decade (1999–2009), including (with Scott R. Swain) the coauthored *Father, Son and Spirit: The Trinity and John's Gospel* (2008).

☆ **Kruse, Colin G.** (TNTC) 2004, rev. 2017. The initial handy 395-page exegesis replaced Tasker and completed the initial revision of the Tyndale NT ("second series"). Then its revision (467pp.) was among the first of the "third series." Kruse knows the Johannine literature well—he produced the Pillar commentary on the Epistles—and does a fine job here. He chooses not to follow the scholars reading the Gospel as addressed to a particular Johannine community. This is what I would give to the thoughtful lay leader who is studying John's Gospel and who has questions that require well-founded and succinct answers. This can also serve the pastor well as a quick reference. Worth buying. [*DenvJ* 8/04; *CBQ* 4/07; *ExpTim* 11/04; *Anvil* 21.4 (Smalley); *JSNT* 40.5].

✓ Kysar, Robert. ‡ *The Fourth Evangelist and His Gospel*, 1975. Surveys issues in the interpretation of John. See also his Augsburg Commentary (1986). Students doing literature review will certainly consult *Voyages with John* (2005) and weigh his critique of Martyn's work.

Laney, J. Carl. (Moody Gospel Commentary) 1992. A popular-level pb (407pp.).

✓ Lierman, John, ed. *Challenging Perspectives on the Gospel of John*, 2006. These essays from the Tyndale Fellowship explore new and different paths, often challenging dominant theories in higher criticism. [*BBR* 19.1; *JETS* 9/08; *EuroJTh* 17.1].

✓ Lieu, Judith M., and Martinus C. de Boer, eds. ‡ *The Oxford Handbook of Johannine Studies*, 2019. Does not cover Revelation. [*BBR* 29.2; *RB* 127.3; *BSac* 1/21].

Lightfoot, J. B. 2015. Subtitled "A Newly Discovered Commentary" and published by IVP (over 350pp.). [*CBQ* 1/17; *JSNT* 38.5]. See Lightfoot under Acts.

Lightfoot, R. H. ‡ 1969. A scholarly commentary published by Oxford.

✓ **Lincoln, Andrew T.** ‡ (BNTC) 2005. In the longest contribution to the series so far (584pp.), Lincoln provides a fresh, lucid, mainly narrative and theological commentary. I found insights on nearly every page. When interpreting the passion narratives, he runs down the track set out in *Truth on Trial: The Lawsuit Motif in John's Gospel* (2000) [*BBR* 16.2; *JTS*

4/07]. This is an important, moderately critical work for students to consult. He knows the scholarship and can summarize it well, but there is less interaction with differing views. As with many other critics, Lincoln does not read John as providing a historically grounded, reliable portrait of Jesus; there is a measure of "embellishment and invention" (49) and "more legendary elements" (39). [*CTJ* 4/07; *BBR* 17.2; *JTS* 10/07; *JETS* 12/06; *JSNT* 3/07; *BL* 2007; *DenvJ* 1/06 (Blomberg); *ExpTim* 3/06; *RelSRev* 3/11].

✓ **Lindars, Barnabas.** ‡ (NCB) 1972. A highly praised commentary from a late, prominent Roman Catholic scholar who long taught at Manchester. Students benefit from consulting this, even though there have been many developments in Johannine research since. Moderately critical. [*EvQ* 4/73; *JBL* 95.4].

✓ Loader, William. ‡ *Jesus in St. John's Gospel: Structure and Issues in Johannine Christology*, 2017. The 3rd ed. of this major study. [*CBQ* 4/20; *SJT* 72.1; *JSNT* 40.5].

Lüthi, Walter. ‡ 1942, ET 1960. Expositions by a once famous German Catholic preacher.

✓ **Malina, Bruce J., and Richard L. Rohrbaugh.** ‡ *A Social-Science Commentary on the Gospel of John*, 1998. [*JBL* Sum 00; *CBQ* 4/00; *RelSRev* 4/99].

F Marshall, Bruce. (Brazos).

Martin, Francis, and William M. Wright IV. ‡ (CCSS) 2015. Highly readable Catholic commentary, praised by Peter Davids [*BBR* 26.3].

✓ Martyn, J. Louis. ‡ *History and Theology in the Fourth Gospel*, 1968; 3rd ed. (NTL) 2003. This study revolutionized John studies years ago and was further developed by others like Raymond Brown. But the notion that John's Gospel throughout reflects the history and conflicts of a mainly Jewish, Johannine Community—and is therefore more narrowly focused than a general Christian tract—has been challenged by Bauckham, Carson, and others. [*ThTo* 10/03]. See Wally Cirafesi, "The Johannine Community Hypothesis (1968–Present)," *CBR* 12.2 (2014): 173–93.

✓ **McHugh, John.** ‡ *John 1–4* (ICC-R) 2008. Might have joined the ranks of Brown, Schnackenburg, Lindars, and Moloney as an immensely learned Catholic commentary on John's Gospel. McHugh was to replace Bernard. (Now see de Boer.) Sadly, the author died after making just a start, and Stanton (in the closing months of his own life) put it into publishable form. Foster calls it "a fragmentary work with no great coherence. Readers are only left with a sense of what might have been." Students doing full research on the early chapters may make use of it. [*ExpTim* 7/09; *NovT* 52.3; *BL* 2010; *RelSRev* 12/12].

Michaels, J. Ramsey. (NIBC) 1989. Updated the 1984 entry in GNC to explain the NIV. At 400pp. it is a probing exegesis, but see his NICNT above.

✓ Miller, Susan E. ‡ *Women in John's Gospel*, 2023. See Miller under Mark too.

☆ Milne, Bruce. (BST) 1993. Has 320pp. of exposition of John's message. The theology drawn from John is well-founded. Includes as an appendix a study guide which could be put to good use in a Bible study format.

✓ **Moloney, Francis J.** ‡ (SacP) 1998. Highly theological from a Catholic perspective, but also attentive to literary and rhetorical features of the text. Moloney attempts to aid preachers in calling their congregations to the response of faith. I call it a real success. The SacP vol. of nearly 600pp. follows on the heels of a 3-vol. set which focused more on reader and narrator (that term is preferred over evangelist). Those titles are *Belief in the Word: Reading John 1–4* (1993); *Signs and Shadows: Reading John 5–12* (1996); and *Glory Not Dishonor: Reading John 13–21* (1998). Those three vols. total about 700pp. [*Bib* 80.4; *Int* 1/99; *CBQ* 7/99; *RelSRev* 7/00]. See also the follow-up essays, *The Gospel of John: Text and Context* (2005) [*JTS* 10/07; *BL* 2006], and a fine monograph on *Love in the Gospel of John* (2013) [*CBQ* 7/15; *ExpTim* 7/15; *RevExp* 5/15; *BSac* 7/15; *JTS* 4/16].

☆ **Morris, Leon.** (retired NICNT) 1971, rev. 1995. Morris was long the standard among evangelical works, and prior to my 7th edition I always recommended its purchase. However, I prefer Carson's approach to Morris's "strictly earthly-historical view of Jesus' ministry" (Carson's phrase). Still, the evangelical pastor is very much helped by Morris. [*EvQ* 1/73; *JBL* 91.3; *RelSRev* 4/99]. Honestly, the Sunday School teacher and expositor find nearly as much help—of a different kind—in *Reflections on the Gospel of John*, 4 vols. (1986–89), later published by Hendrickson in one hb (760pp.). Students should note his suggestive work on the theology of the Gospel: *Jesus Is the Christ* (1989). Michaels replaced Morris.

☆ Mounce, Robert. (EBCR) 2007. The author writes expressly for pastors in these 300pp. Students will see, even in the 3-page introduction, that this is not written for them. Mounce is well-informed, insightful, and clear.

✓ Myers, Alicia D. ‡ *Reading John and 1, 2, 3 John: A Literary and Theological Commentary*, 2019. [*CBQ* 4/21]. Previously, she helped edit *Abiding Words: The Use of Scripture in the Gospel of John* (SBL, 2015) [*JSNT* 38.5].

✓ Newman, B. H., and E. A. Nida. (UBS) 1980.

✓ **Neyrey, Jerome H.** ‡ (NCBC) 2007. This work by a Notre Dame scholar is one place to go for a critically oriented, up-to-date, social science perspective. Students appreciate his bibliographical guidance (28–36). [2007: *CBQ* 7/08; *BL* 2008; *ExpTim* 3/08 (Keener); *RBL* 7/10; *HBT* 29.2; *Anvil* 25.3; *JSNT* 33.5; *BSac* 1/12; *BTB* 5/11]. See too his complementing essays in *The Gospel of John in Cultural and Historical Perspective* (2009) [*Int* 1/12; *ExpTim* 9/10].

Ngewa, Samuel. 2003. A good-sized, helpful commentary, published by Evangelical Publishing House, Nairobi, and written by a former colleague at Nairobi Evangelical Graduate School of Theology. It is a reflective, warm-hearted work for pastors.

☆ **Novakovic, Lidija.** (BHGNT) 2 vols., 2020. Thorough and careful work, focused on the technicalities of the Greek text, done by the Baylor prof and series coeditor (725pp.). Cf. with the briefer Harris EGGNT, aiming to provide greater assistance to expositors.

✓ **O'Day, Gail.** ‡ (NIB) 1995. The author teaches at Emory, and her commentary is bound up with Culpepper's work on Luke. I have not examined her work closely (370pp.). [*JETS* 3/99]. Note that she has also coauthored a more accessible exposition with Susan E. Hylen in WestBC (2006) [*Int* 1/08].

Osborne, Grant R. (ONTC) 2018. See under Commentary Series.

F   Painter, John. ‡ (SRC). Earlier he wrote *The Quest for Messiah: The History, Literature, and Theology of the Johannine Community* (2nd ed. 1993). Compare Brown.

F   Parsenios, George. ‡ (Illum).

F   Paul, Ian. (BGW).

F   Perrin, Nicholas. (SGBC).

Peterson, Robert. *Getting to Know John's Gospel*, 1989. Not a commentary, but a study guide which takes "a fresh look at its main ideas." With its 13 chs., this works well as a quarter-long Sunday School study. It fits a niche few other publications do.

Phillips, Richard D. (REC) 2 vols., 2014. Regrettably, I have yet to see this set, but it is reportedly over 1400pp. I've heard the gentleman preach, and I expect many find these sermons a blessing to their heart and life.

Pink, Arthur. 1945. If you are looking for a fat vol. of exposition, buy Boice.

Plummer. Alfred. 1882. Reprinted in 1981, but among the older English commentaries, Westcott's two are more useful.

✓ Porter, Stanley E., and Andrew K. Gabriel. *Johannine Writings and Apocalyptic: An Annotated Bibliography*, 2013. [*JETS* 12/14; *JSNT* 37.5]. Also from Porter is *John, His Gospel, and Jesus: In Pursuit of the Johannine Voice* (2015). [*WTJ* Fall 16; *JSNT* 38.5].

✓ Porter, Stanley E., and Ron C. Fay, eds. *The Gospel of John in Modern Interpretation*, 2018. Of value to students for its vignettes of eight major Johannine scholars. [*JETS* 6/20].

✓ Porter, Stanley E., and Andrew W. Pitts, eds. *Johannine Christology*, 2020. [*JSNT* 44.5].

✓ Rainbow, Paul A. *Johannine Theology: The Gospel, the Epistles, and the Apocalypse*, 2014. Given a warm review by Blomberg. [*BBR* 26.1; *JETS* 12/15]. I've yet to use it. Cf. Marvin Pate's *The Writings of John* (2011) [*JETS* 6/12; *JSNT* 37.5].

✓ Reinhartz, Adele. ‡ *Cast Out of the Covenant: Jews and Anti-Judaism in the Gospel of John*, 2018. A much-discussed scholarly work on Johannine theology [*RBL* 2019 (Byers); *CBQ* 1/20 (Lieu); *Int* 10/20; *JSNT* 41.5], following the earlier *Befriending the Beloved Disciple: A Jewish Reading of the Gospel of John* (2001). A valuable doctoral work on the topic is Jonathan Numada, *John and Anti-Judaism: Reading the Gospel in Light of Greco-Roman Culture* (2021) [*JETS* 9/22; *JSNT* 45.5].

✓ Reynolds, Benjamin, and Gabriele Boccaccini, eds. ‡ *Reading the Gospel of John's Christology as Jewish Messianism*, 2018. "Over against previous assumptions that John's high Christology marks a decisive break with Judaism, this provocative collection suggests that John's Gospel should be located firmly within its wider Jewish milieu" (Coutts [*JTS* 4/20]). [*JSNT* 42.5].

F  Richards, E. Randolph. (WBC-R). Replacing Beasley-Murray.

  Sanders, J. N., and B. A. Mastin. ‡ (BNTC) 1968. Never very good to begin with and now replaced by Lincoln.

✓ **Schnackenburg, R.** ‡ 3 vols., ET 1968–82. This is surely one of the most valuable scholarly commentaries available and one of the best examples of the moderately critical scholarship coming out of the Catholic Church—a monument to it, really. Moody Smith says, "Schnackenburg is for the European scene what Raymond Brown has been for the American." Note: Schnackenburg became, like Brown (compare his commentaries on the Gospel and the Epistles), more critical with the passage of time. The third vol. does not compare favorably with the first. There is also a fourth vol. with essays to consult, but only if you read German (*IV: Ergänzende Auslegungen und Exkurse*, 1984). The author has other standout commentaries in ET on Ephesians and John's Epistles.

✓ Segovia, Fernando, ed. ‡ *"What Is John?" Readers and Readings of the Fourth Gospel*, 1996. A collection of essays that deal primarily with the newer hermeneutical approaches and with important theological issues in John under discussion today. Also worthwhile, especially in researching some of the older historical scholarly questions, is *The Johannine Writings*, eds. Porter–Evans (1995). [*RelSRev* 1/99, 4/99].

✓ Skinner, Christopher W., ed. ‡ *Characters and Characterization in the Gospel of John*, 2013. [*CBQ* 4/15; *JETS* 9/14].

  Sloyan, Gerard. ‡ (I) 1988. Not of much account, I'm afraid.

✓ Smalley, S. S. *John: Evangelist and Interpreter*, 1978, 2nd ed. 1998. [*EvQ* 10/78; *JETS* 6/80]. Smalley also did the WBC on John's Epistles and is right at home in the literature. He takes a more critical view on issues such as authorship.

✓ **Smith, D. Moody, Jr.** ‡ (ANTC) 1999. This 400-page commentary, by a man Barrett calls "one of the highest authorities on St. John's Gospel," is not to be missed. Though not extensively footnoted and not evidencing much interaction with other scholars' work (especially in the area of narrative criticism), there is mature scholarship undergirding his clearly argued conclusions. [*CBQ* 1/04; *Them* Aut 01; *Int* 4/04; *RelSRev* 10/02; *JTS* 10/01 (more critical)]. For a critical theological introduction to John's Gospel, see Smith's 1995 vol. in the CUP NT Theology series [*Int* 1/97; *CRBR* 1996 (Carson)]. Two more works are *John among the Gospels: The Relationship in Twentieth-Century Scholarship* (2nd ed. 2001) [*JTS* 10/03; *JBL* Sum 04; *RelSRev* 7/03] and *The Fourth Gospel in Four Dimensions: Judaism and Jesus, the Gospels and Scripture* (2008) [*CBQ* 7/10].

✓ Stewart, Bryan A., and Michael A. Thomas. (TCB) 2018. [*JSNT* 41.5].

✓ Stibbe, Mark W. G. ‡ (Read) 1993. [*CBQ* 10/94].

Stevick, Daniel B. ‡ *A Commentary on John 13–17,* 2011. A lively exposition, meant to assist preachers. [*JTS* 4/13; *Int* 10/12; *JSNT* 34.5; *ExpTim* 11/12; *RelSRev* 3/13].

F   Swartley, Willard. (BCBC).

✓   Talbert, Charles H. ‡ *Reading John: A Literary and Theological Commentary on the Fourth Gospel and the Johannine Epistles* (RNT) 1992, rev. 2005. This study complements his work on Luke and Corinthians. [*CRBR* 1994; *RevExp* 2/15].

Tasker, R. V. G. (retired TNTC) 1960. Retains more value than some think (230pp.), and is still good to lend to a Sunday School teacher. See Kruse's newer TNTC.

Tenney, Merrill C. *John: The Gospel of Belief,* 1948. A popularly styled exposition, later joined by Tenney's weak EBC (1981). Can be honorably retired.

✓   Thatcher, Tom, and Stephen D. Moore, eds. ‡ *Anatomies of Narrative Criticism: The Past, Present, and Futures of the Fourth Gospel as Literature,* 2008. Compare these essays with the Culpepper work they celebrate. [*JETS* 12/09; *BL* 2010; *ExpTim* 1/12; *BibInt* 18.4]. Also for students is Thatcher, ed., *What We Have Heard from the Beginning: The Past, Present, and Future of Johannine Studies* (2007) [*BBR* 19.3].

☆   **Thompson, Marianne Meye.** [𝓜], (NTL) 2015. Well-done, accessible, and conservative relative to the series. Earlier she wrote *The Humanity of Jesus in the Fourth Gospel* (1988) and *The God of the Gospel of John* (2001) [*Anvil* 19.4 (Smalley)]. This 450-page work, written by a veteran Fuller Seminary prof and PCUSA minister, can certainly be classed as one of the best in the series. Thompson was working on John's Gospel for seventeen years. Students will appreciate her insights on narrative, rhetoric, and theology, as well as the (smaller) measure of interaction with current scholarship. [*BSac* 10/17; *CBQ* 1/17; *JETS* 12/16 (Klink); *Int* 7/17; *JSNT* 38.5; *Them* 41.2].

✓   Van Belle, Gilbert, Jan Gabriël van der Watt, and P. J. Maritz, eds. *Theology and Christology in the Fourth Gospel,* 2005. A BETL vol. from SNTS.

✓   **Wahlde, Urban C. von.** ‡ *The Gospel and Letters of John* (ECC) 3 vols., 2010. A huge project (over 2000pp.) to be "greeted with enthusiasm by those who look to source analysis as a key to understanding these writings" (Swetnam [*CBQ* 7/12]). There is no question of the learning here, of which scholars will take account. Note that von Wahlde's assumptions regarding a Johannine Community make this extensive commentary set of less use to those critical of that long influential theory (see Bauckham). [*CBQ* 7/12; *JSNT* 34.5; *ExpTim* 7/11; *Them* 8/11; *RevExp* Spr 12; *RelSRev* 9/13; *JETS* 3/12].

Wallace, Ronald S. *The Gospel of John, Chapters 1–21: Pastoral and Theological Studies,* 2003. A lovely, brief exposition (327pp.). See also under Daniel and Kings.

✓   Watt, Jan van der. ‡ *An Introduction to the Johannine Gospel and Letters,* 2007. [*BL* 2009].

Watt, Jan van der, and Ruben Zimmerman, eds. ‡ *Rethinking the Ethics of John,* 2012. Treats the epistles as well. [*JSNT* 36.1 (Koester); *ExpTim* 9/14].

✓   **Weinrich, William.** *John 1:1–7:1* (ConcC) 2015; *John 7:2–12:50* (ConcC) 2022. What adds interest here is the author's long career as Professor of Early Church and Patristic Studies. I am yet to see this work, but it attempts a nearly exhaustive exegetical and theological commentary within his conservative Lutheran tradition. The second vol. on just six chapters runs to 800pp. [*BSac* 1/18].

✓   Westcott, B. F. 1889, 1908. There are two different commentaries being reprinted: the earlier work treats the English text, and the later one exegetes the Greek. Both are classics, remarkably penetrating, and still on the shelves of many pastors.

✓   Williams, Catrin H., and Christopher Rowland, eds. ‡ *John's Gospel and Intimations of Apocalyptic,* 2013. Building off of Ashton's work. [*JSNT* 36.5].

Whitacre, Rodney. (IVPNT) 1999. I have not used it, but both Carson and Smalley commend it. [*CTJ* 11/00; *Anvil* 17.3 (Smalley)].

✓ **Witherington, Ben, III.** *John's Wisdom: A Commentary on the Fourth Gospel*, 1995. This amazingly prolific scholar has published a couple of dozen other NT commentaries and full-scale works on NT Theology and *Paul's Narrative Thought World* (1994). All the books are worth consulting, but they needed better editing and proofreading. In this distinctive commentary, close attention is paid to narrative and various themes, especially wisdom. I must say the author has not convinced me that wisdom is a strong motif in the Fourth Gospel (note that σοφία and σοφός are not even found there). This vol. has numerous insights, though it is not one of Witherington's more successful efforts. See 1 Corinthians. [*EvQ* 1/98; *JETS* 3/99; *Int* 7/97; *CBQ* 10/97].

Yarbrough, Robert. (Everyman's Bible Commentary) 1991. A popularly styled, well-researched book, with more substance to it than the other vols. in the series. Offers an annotated bibliography too (216pp.).

NOTE: See Don Carson's articles, "Selected Recent Studies of the Fourth Gospel," in *Them* 14.2., and "Recent Literature on the Fourth Gospel: Some Reflections," in *Them* 9.1. Other articles to help students understand where Johannine scholarship has come from are: S. S. Smalley, "Keeping Up with Recent Studies; XII. St. John's Gospel," *ExpTim* 1/86; D. Moody Smith, "The Contribution of J. Louis Martyn to the Understanding of the Gospel of John," in *The Conversation Continues* (Nashville: Abingdon, 1990); Klaus Scholtissek, "Johannine Studies: A Survey of Recent Research with Special Regard to German Contributions," (part I) *CurBS* 6 (1998): 227–59, and (part II) *CurBS* 9 (2001): 277–305; Paul N. Anderson, "Beyond the Shade of the Oak Tree: The Recent Growth of Johannine Studies," *ExpTim* 119.8 (2008): 365–73; and Francis Moloney, "Recent Johannine Studies," *ExpTim* 4/12 and 6/12.

# THE PARABLES OF JESUS

★ Blomberg, Craig. *Interpreting the Parables*, 1990, 2nd ed. 2012. A superb contribution, which I've long argued should be required reading in a Gospels course. Prior to Wenham and Blomberg we'd lacked solid, scholarly introductions from an evangelical standpoint. The newer edition (430pp.) is a major updating and expansion. See Boucher below. [*Bib* 72.4; *JETS* 6/92; *EvQ* 7/92; *Chm* 104.4]. Also excellent is Blomberg's *Preaching the Parables* (2004) [*CTJ* 4/05; *Them* Win 05; *TJ* Spr 05; *Int* 7/06].

★ Snodgrass, Klyne R. [*M*], *Stories with Intent: A Comprehensive Guide to the Parables of Jesus*, 2008, 2nd ed. 2018. Snodgrass intended this tome (900pp.) to be a resource book for the parables, i.e., what the professor with expertise in parables wanted to put in students' hands. With the 2nd edition's chapter on "Recent Contributions to Parable Interpretation," it remains an up-to-date treatment from an evangelical fully abreast of scholarship—his earlier surveys of the field were "Modern Approaches to the Parables," in *The Face of NT Studies* (2004) and "From Allegorizing to Allegorizing" in Longenecker, ed., *The Challenge of Jesus' Parables* (2000). Especially appreciated by this student of the OT is the author's effort to place Jesus's parabolic teaching in the context of the Jewish prophetic tradition. Though seminarians prefer Wenham and Blomberg as introductory reading, this vol. is now the main reference text. Already in 2010 I termed this a "landmark study." [*ThTo* 1/09; *ExpTim* 5/08; *TJ* Spr 09; *RelSRev* 9/08; *Them* 9/08 (Wenham); *JETS* 6/09; *JTS* 4/09; *BL* 2009; *BBR* 19.4 (Blomberg); *EvQ* 7/09; *Int* 4/09 (Hultgren); *RTR* 4/09; *RevExp* Fall 09; *RTR* 8/22; *ExpTim* 5/18; *JSNT* 41.5; *RevExp* 5/19].

★ Wenham, David. 1989. As part of IVP's The Jesus Library, this has been the best, most inviting popular introduction to the parables on the market—by one of the editors of the *Gospel Perspectives* vols. [*EvQ* 4/91].

☆ Bailey, Kenneth E. *Poet & Peasant and Through Peasant Eyes*, 1976, 1980, Combined ed. 1983. Argues capably that the parables can only be fully understood when studied in their cultural context. Our occidental canons of interpretation can be misleading. [*WTJ* Fall 78, Spr 81; *JETS* 3/82; *JBL* 96.4, 102.2].

✓ Boucher, Madeleine. ‡ *The Mysterious Parable: A Literary Study*, 1977. A much needed critique of the customary distinction—argued by Jülicher (1899), Jeremias, and Dodd—between parable (one point) and allegory (many points). Blomberg also presses this critique in a measured way. [*JBL* 12/78].

Bruce, A. B. *The Parabolic Teaching of Christ*, 1908. Still of some value, especially for those interested in the history of interpretation. Pastors should only use Bruce in conjunction with more recent works.

✓ Buttrick, David. ‡ *Speaking Parables: A Homiletic Guide*, 2000. No froth! Buttrick is a most thoughtful and skilled homiletician, and his guide will stimulate readers to approach the parables in fresh ways that capture the frequent surprises found in Jesus's stories.

Capon, Robert. ‡ *Kingdom, Grace, Judgment*, 2001. Bold exposition.

✓ Carter, Warren, and John Paul Heil. ‡ *Matthew's Parables: Audience-Oriented Perspectives*, 1998. [*JTS* 51.1].

✓ Culpepper, R. Alan. ‡ *The People of the Parables: Galilee in the Time of Jesus*, 2024. Certainly a remarkable and fresh approach, dealing with the sociocultural, political, and religious background of Jesus's teaching. Insights abound (approx. 335pp.).

✓ Dodd, C. H. ‡ *The Parables of the Kingdom*, 1935. A classic in the field.

✓ Donahue, John R. ‡ *The Gospel in Parable*, 1988.

✓ Drury, John. ‡ *The Parables in the Gospels*, 1985. Like Donahue, often cited.

✓ Forbes, Greg W. *The God of Old: The Role of Lukan Parables in the Purpose of Luke's Gospel*, 2000. Quite helpful.

✓ Gowler, David B. ‡ *What Are They Saying about the Parables?* 2000. A good introduction to where parable research had been and where it might be headed. [*Int* 7/01]. Happily, we also have *The Parables after Jesus: Their Imaginative Receptions across Two Millennia* (2017) [*CBQ* 7/20].

✓ Hedrick, Charles W. ‡ *Many Things in Parables: Jesus and His Modern Critics*, 2004. An important scholar who previously wrote *Parables as Poetic Fictions* (1994).

✓ Herzog, William R. ‡ *Parables as Subversive Speech: Jesus as Pedagogue of the Oppressed*, 1994.

☆ Hultgren, Arland J. ‡ 2000. Considered by many a tour de force (500pp.), which introduces and comments upon the parables. There is good balance and judgment in Hultgren's discussions. While he warns against a return to an allegorical method of interpretation, he also notes that parable and allegory were not sharply differentiated in Jesus's world. In the NT parables there are allegorical elements to which the reader should be alert. Hultgren provides a digest of much of the best work on parables and should be classed as moderately critical. I once recommended Hultgren for purchase, but have given his place to Snodgrass. [*ExpTim* 5/01; *SwJT* Sum 01; *CBQ* 4/01; *EvQ* 7/03; *CTJ* 11/01; *JETS* 12/01; *TJ* Fall 02; *HBT* 6/02; *RelSRev* 1/02; *WTJ* Fall 01 (Poythress, more critical)].

✓ Hunter, A. M. [𝓜], *Interpreting the Parables*, 1960. A lucid, helpful introduction, but rather brief. See also his later work, *The Parables Then and Now* (1971).

☆ Jeremias, Joachim. ‡ *The Parables of Jesus*, ET 1963. The classic treatment of the genre. All modern discussion has had to begin with Dodd and Jeremias. Here you find both strong criticism of allegorizing and a strong interest in possible reconstructions of the original parables (after being corrupted or reworked by the early church).

✓ Johnston, Robert M., and Harvey K. McArthur. *They Also Taught in Parables*, 1990.

✓ Jones, Ivor Harold. ‡ *The Matthean Parables: A Literary and Historical Commentary*, 1995. An enormous work. [*JTS* 48.1 (Nolland)].

☆ Jones, Peter R. *Studying the Parables of Jesus*, 1999. Another good evangelical introduction.

Keach, Benjamin. *Exposition of the Parables*, 1701, repr. 1974. An enormous work (900pp.) by a much-persecuted Baptist preacher in England. Can be passed over.

✓ Kissinger, Warren S. ‡ *The Parables of Jesus: A History of Interpretation and Bibliography*, 1979. Those who are interested in an updated bibliography should see Blomberg (2012) and Snodgrass above. The masterful old review was Blomberg, "The Parables of Jesus: Current Trends and Needs in Research," in *Studying the Historical Jesus* (Brill, 1994). [*JBL* 101.1].

☆ Kistemaker, Simon J. 1980, rev. 2002. A worthwhile reference book for pastors that explains each parable in the Synoptics. A good expositional tool, revised to become even better. The theology is solidly Reformed. [*WTJ* Spr 81; *RTR* 1/82; *JETS* 3/82].

✓ Lambrecht, Jan. ‡ *Out of the Treasure: The Parables in the Gospel of Matthew*, 1991. His more general introduction was *Once More Astonished* (1981).

Linnemann, Eta. ‡ ET 1966. A bright German scholar's treatment of the parables. It is of interest to note that the former student of Bultmann renounced her critical works, including this one, and converted to evangelicalism.

Lischer, Richard. ‡ *Reading the Parables*, 2014. For preachers. [*RevExp* 2/15; *Int* 4/16].

✓ Lohfink, Gerhard. ‡ *The Forty Parables of Jesus*, ET 2021. A study and pastoral exposition from the Catholic Tübingen professor.

☆ Long, Thomas G. ‡ *Proclaiming the Parables: Preaching and Teaching the Kingdom of God*, 2024. From a Presbyterian professor, retired from Candler and one of the foremost homileticians in America. From the liberal side this is likely the best, most interesting book on the topic.

✓ Longenecker, Richard, ed. *The Challenge of Jesus' Parables*, 2000. [*EvQ* 4/02; *RTR* 8/02; *Them* Aut 02; *DenvJ*; *Anvil* 19.3].

Marshall, I. Howard. *Eschatology and the Parables*, 1963.

MacArthur, John. *Parables*, 2015. Sermonic material by a famous American pastor.

✓ Meier, John P. ‡ *A Marginal Jew*. Vol. V, 2016. See under "Jesus & Gospels Research."

✓ Michaels, J. Ramsey. *Servant and Son: Jesus in Parable and Gospel*, 1981.

✓ Perrin, Norman. ‡ *Jesus and the Language of the Kingdom*, 1976. Includes a survey of parable research since Jeremias together with his own critical views. Can be updated by checking the articles and vols. referenced with Kissinger above. You could also see *The NT and Its Modern Interpreters* and Scott.

Schottroff, Luise. ‡ ET 2006. [*JSHJ* 5.2].

✓ Scott, Bernard Brandon. ‡ *Hear Then the Parable: A Commentary on the Parables of Jesus*, 1989. A 427-page work published by Fortress. Prior to Hultgren's appearance this was the fullest critical commentary on the parables. Scott's work exemplifies the highly skeptical work done, for example, in the Jesus Seminar. E.g., he pays a lot of attention to the Gospel of Thomas. [*SJT* 93.2; *JBL* Win 91; *CBQ* 4/92; *Int* 7/91].

✓ Shillington, V. George, ed. ‡ *Jesus and His Parables*, 1997.

✓ Sider, John W. *Interpreting the Parables*, 1995. [*JETS* 6/98].

✓ Sirico, Robert. *The Economics of the Parables*, 2022. A well-written study by a Catholic priest who is President of Acton Institute, promoting free-market economics.

✓ Stein, Robert H. *An Introduction to the Parables of Jesus*, 1981. An excellent conservative work. [*EvQ* 1/84; *WTJ* Spr 82; *JETS* 9/82].

✓ Strong, Justin David. ‡ *The Fables of Jesus in the Gospel of Luke*, 2021. [*JSNT* 45.5].

✓ Via, Dan O. ‡ *The Parables: Their Literary and Existential Dimensions*, 1967.

✓ Westermann, Claus. ‡ *The Parables of Jesus in the Light of the OT*, ET 1990.

✓ Young, Brad H. ‡ *Jesus and His Jewish Parables: Rediscovering the Roots of Jesus' Teaching*, 1989 [*EvQ* 4/91]; *The Parables: Jewish Tradition and Christian Interpretation*, 1998. He studied under Flusser in Jerusalem.

✓ Zimmermann, Ruben. ‡ *Puzzling the Parables of Jesus*, 2015. A well-informed research by a Mainz professor. [*CBQ* 7/18; *JTS* 10/17].

# ACTS

★ **Bock, Darrell.** (BECNT) 2007. Follows the 2-vol. set on Luke in the same series. Perhaps Bock fills the role that Bruce's two works once did for evangelical pastors and students, in that he also has strong historical interests and takes a more conventional grammatico-historical approach to exegesis. I'm not convinced that Bock quite lives up to the standards set in his *Luke*, which was over twice as lengthy, but *Acts* is still a very valuable tool. I find Bock and Peterson to be a well-matched pair, with the latter providing more theology. One small complaint: more text criticism in a commentary on the Greek text would have been helpful. Ready yourself for evangelical exegesis of the Greek to become even richer with Walton. [*BL* 2008; *ExpTim* 1/09; *JETS* 12/08; *CBQ* 10/09 (Pervo, severe); *ExpTim* 11/09; *Int* 7/09; *Anvil* 26.2; *EuroJTh* 18.1].

★ **Holladay, Carl R.** ‡ (NTL) 2016. Among accessible, mid-level, critical exegeses, this masterful work (513pp of actual commentary) ranks at the top of my list. Holladay long taught at Emory, and Acts has been a favorite PhD seminar for him. I find him astute in his literary and narratological comments, responsible in his historical and archaeological research, open to the theology of the text, and more conservatively critical. Sleeman is right: "Holladay's refreshingly limited engagement with other commentators will make me turn to him over and over again. In an age when too many . . . engage with too many commentators, Holladay prioritises the text and its world, and we are the beneficiaries of his labours" [*ExpTim* 11/17]. If you don't want a critical work, you might consider Bruce's NICNT, D. Johnson, Larkin, Longenecker, Marshall, or Schreiner. [*BBR* 27.4; *JSNT* 39.5].

★ **Keener, Craig.** (NCBC) 2020. At 635pp., a condensation of the stunning 4-vol. research (see below). It calls to mind the Oliver Wendell Holmes quip: "For the simplicity on this side of complexity, I wouldn't give you a fig. But for the simplicity on the other side of complexity, for that I would give you anything I have." Students note his collected essays: *Between History and Spirit* (2020) [*Presb* Spr 20].

★ **Peterson, David G.** (Pillar) 2009. Certainly to be ranked as one of the best for the pastor seeking a robustly theological exposition, well-grounded in careful exegesis. The whole book is solid and balanced and, prior to Schnabel, I made it my first pick. No aspect of interpretation is given short shrift: textual criticism, philology and grammar, literary analysis, history, theology. The author teaches at Moore College, the vibrant seminary of the Anglican diocese of Sydney with a conservative and Reformed orientation. Previously he was Principal of Oak Hill College, London. At 790pp. this was the fullest vol. in the series (until 1 Corinthians); extensive interaction with many leading works on Luke–Acts dictated its large size (see the author index). But there were important works missed, such as Fitzmyer; for a critical review on this point, see Foster. Like Dennis Johnson, Peterson approaches Acts along redemptive-historical lines, but is also strong on narrative. See Marshall–Peterson below. [*Them* 11/09; *BBR* 20.1; *ExpTim* 6/10; *CBQ* 7/10; *DenvJ* 1/10; *BL* 2010 (Foster); *Chm* Sum 14; *JETS* 3/11 (Polhill); *DenvJ* 13].

★ **Schnabel, Eckhard J.** (ZECNT) 2012. What adds interest here is the author's fine research, already published in two immense books (2004): *Early Christian Mission*, Vol. 1: Jesus and the Twelve, Vol. 2: Paul and the Early Church. See also *Paul the Missionary: Realities,*

*Strategies, and Methods* (2008), which offers a different avenue into the material. The ZECNT is a massive work (over 1100pp.), and the e-version is even longer, including material cut from the book. Still, it is lucid and accessible for a work on the Greek; Schnabel serves well as a first pick. Pastors will find him to be well-rounded, providing expert exegesis and thoughtful Theology in Application sections. Any weaknesses? The textual criticism (important for Acts) does not appear to be as thoroughly and carefully done, which is more of a concern for students than busy pastors. Questions can be raised about his translating βαπτίζω with "immerse" (which lacks the semi-technical meaning of "baptize" in Christian parlance). Schnabel long taught at TEDS but is now at Gordon-Conwell. [*NovT* 55.4; *BBR* 24.3 (Blomberg); *Chm* Spr 14; *JETS* 3/14 (Polhill)].

★ Stott, John R. W. *The Spirit, the Church and the World* (BST) 1990. Certainly what you would expect from Stott: an excellent, clear, theological, and pastoral exposition. This 400-page work is as valuable as any book can be to the preacher. Released in hb initially, then in pb as *The Message of Acts*. [*CTJ* 4/91, 11/94; *Chm* 104.3]. Also excellent for approaching homiletical questions are Larkin, Fernando, Dennis Johnson, Hughes, Green, and Pinter.

★ **Walton, Steve.** (WBC) 3 vols., 2024 –. The author told me the first vol. would appear by Nov 2024. Having seen a 600-page draft of *Acts 1:1–9:42*, I believe this sets a new standard for balanced evangelical exegesis of Acts. (For thoroughness and Greco-Roman literary context, the standard is set by Keener, though Walton's sifting of the ancient literature sometimes gives me clearer understanding.) I looked forward to a sensitive literary (narrative-critical) reading and the exegesis of the Greek, with his Reformed theological interpretation; I was not disappointed. It is fresh, not derivative scholarship. His decades of research on Acts have produced superb essays and books, including *Reading Acts Theologically* (2022) [*Them* 47.3; *BBR* 33.4]. Students of the Greek will find abundant help (e.g., 21 notes on the eleven verses in 9:32–42). Preachers will appreciate how Walton keeps his focus on the text, not all the ins-and-outs of scholarly discussion, and has such a lucid, accessible, and God-centered exposition. All readers benefit from the wisdom and maturity in his interpretive work; see, for example, his weighing the two sides of the "conversion or call" of Saul debate. When complete, this commentary may well be my favorite on Acts.

❖ ❖ ❖ ❖ ❖

Alexander, J. A. (GS) Third ed. 1875. A lengthy, reverent exposition from one of old Princeton's greatest scholars; it needs to be supplemented by more recent scholarly commentaries. Free online.

F   Alexander, Loveday. ‡ *Acts* (BNTC). The author is a classicist who became an authority on Acts, and British academics tell me to expect a "cracker" (excellent/exciting piece of work). See her collected essays, *Acts in its Ancient Literary Context* (2005) [*JETS* 6/07; *Int* 1/09; *JR* 1/07; *RelSRev* 3/08; *BBR* 20.2; *EuroJTh* 18.1; *BibInt* 19.3]. She is particularly interested in genre and makes a substantial contribution to scholarship in that area, arguing that Acts does not fit neatly the category of historiography, yet seems a factual account.

Allen, Ronald J. ‡ (FBPC) 2013. Quite liberal, process theology. [*Int* 7/15; *JSNT* 36.5].

Arrington, French L. 1988. This is subtitled "A Pentecostal Commentary."

F   Aune, David. ‡ *Luke–Acts* (Illum).

✓ **Barrett, C. K.** ‡ (ICC) 2 vols., 1994–98. What excitement this generated! Scholars expected it to be the crowning achievement of a long career, and it is. Barrett takes a different view of Luke's historical accuracy than evangelical scholarship, but it is less objectionable than the corrosive skepticism in Haenchen and Conzelmann, whom he continually quotes in German. (And you have Latin citations from Bengel, St. Jerome, etc.) This 2-vol. set is one of the most valuable, most detailed exegeses of the Greek text of Acts ever published in any language (1272pp.) . . . and the most expensive. I used to say that scholarly pastors, and only scholarly ones, will want to take out a bank loan to buy this. (Even in pb the set costs $190—years ago CBD had it for $50.) Unfortunately, as Kern writes, "because of its impenetrability to many, it may join that body of literature which is more often cited than read." As Walton notes, the weaknesses of the set are in the areas of narrative and theology: probably a big letdown for pastors. If you are a student ambitious to do a PhD in NT, you'll want this as a reference work. Be assured that Barrett will serve as a standard reference for decades. [*JETS* 3/98, 6/01; *NovT* 42.2; *RTR* 12/99; *RelSRev* 7/99; *Anvil* 18.3 (Walton)]. An abridgment in pb came out in 2002 [*Them* Aut 03; *RelSRev* 10/03].

☆ **Bauer, David R.** *The Book of Acts as Story: A Narrative-Critical Study*, 2021. A most welcome publication, examining plot development, literary structure, and theology. [*WTJ* Spr 22; *JETS* 6/22; *CBQ* 7/22; *Int* 4/23; *JSNT* 44.5; *ExpTim* 7/22 (Walton)]. Cf. Tannehill, L. T. Johnson, Parsons, Spencer, Talbert, and Witherington.

☆ Boice, James Montgomery. *Acts: An Expositional Commentary*, 1997. About 450pp. of fine, mature preaching.

☆ **Bruce, F. F.** *The Acts of the Apostles*, 1951/1952, 3rd ed. 1990. Vintage Bruce: judicious exegesis. Treats the Greek text and assists the student—it is less help with exposition. Most preachers prefer the NICNT (below). I used to select this vol. on the Greek for purchase instead, because the introduction is fuller and better, and because the other suggested works were so strong on exposition, but did not help as much with the original—textual criticism is important on Acts. (Note: Metzger's *Textual Commentary on the Greek NT* is also a big help.) The availability of Barrett's magisterial set, the arrival of Bock, and the promise of Walton mean that Bruce on the Greek is less valuable now. Reprinted by Wipf & Stock in 2000. [*Evangel* Sum 92; *EvQ* 7/94].

☆ **Bruce, F. F.** (NICNT) 1954, rev. 1988. One could have wished in the revision for more attention to theology and the missionary aspect of the book, and Bruce admits this weakness (xvii). It is not enough to encourage readers to make up what is lacking by reading Marshall's *Luke: Historian and Theologian*. As a historical commentary, however, Bruce's NICNT is still among the best for the pastor. Having both commentaries—the vol. on the Greek text (see above) and the more expositional NICNT—is not a bad idea. Years ago the pastor looking for a single vol. to cover Acts might have preferred Longenecker or Marshall (as the more balanced works) to Bruce's NICNT. Note that this work is to be replaced by Green's more literary commentary. Peterson displaced this among my purchase recommendations. [*EvQ* 7/90; *JTS* 4/90].

✓ Bryan, David K., and David W. Pao, eds. *Ascent into Heaven in Luke-Acts: New Explorations of Luke's Narrative Hinge*, 2016. [*JSNT* 40.5].

✓ Burke, Trevor J., and Brian S. Rosner, eds. *Paul as Missionary*, 2011.

☆ Calvin, John. (CrossC) 1995. The commentary has been carefully distilled down.

☆ Calvin, John. *Sermons on the Acts of the Apostles: Chapters 1–7*, ET 2008. Banner of Truth has fat vols. of Calvin's sermons on several Bible books: Genesis, Samuel, Job, Galatians, Ephesians, and the Pastorals. These 700pp. contain 44 sermons plus a fine introduction to Calvin the preacher. [*RTR* 8/09].

Chance, J. Bradley. ‡ (S&H) 2007. I've used this book less. The author, a prof at William Jewell, reads Acts reflectively and with a liberal theology. E.g., he uses Sallie McFague's writings and the film *Chocolat* to draw connections between Paul's speech to his would-be killers in ch. 22 and our need today for the virtues of inclusion and acceptance (420). Pinnock's open theism is attractive to him. [*Int* 4/09].

Cho, Youngmo, and Hyung Dae Park (NCCS) 2 vols., 2019. [*JSNT* 44.5].

✓ Chung-Kim, Esther, ed. (RCS) 2014.

✓ **Conzelmann, Hans.** ‡ (Herm) 1963, ET 1987. Along with Haenchen this has been a standard critical commentary. Takes a very skeptical view of the historical worth of Acts. German and English scholarship tend to go their separate ways on this point, though I once hoped works like Hengel's *Acts and the History of Earliest Christianity* (ET 1979) might dampen German radicalism. Conzelmann is no longer as important a reference as when first published. [*Them* 10/88]. See Pervo below.

✓ Crowe, Brandon D. *The Hope of Israel: The Resurrection of Christ in the Acts of the Apostles*, 2020. Well-done, from a conservative Reformed angle. [*RevExp* 8/21 (Walton); *ExpTim* 11/22; *CBQ* 4/21; *JETS* 3/21; *JSNT* 43.5; *Them* 45.2]. A somewhat broader study is Kevin Anderson, *"But God Raised Him from the Dead": The Theology of Jesus' Resurrection in Luke-Acts* (2007).

☆ **Culy, Martin M., Mikeal C. Parsons, and Josiah D. Hall.** (BHGNT) Rev. ed. 2022. As the beginning of the series (2003), Culy–Parsons was recommended as a careful, thorough (579pp.) guide to lexical, grammatical, and textual analysis of Acts. The two-vol. revision involved Hall and is much expanded (approx. 900pp.). See below Parsons's commentary on the English text. [*EvQ* 10/07; *JSNT* 12/05; *RelSRev* 1/05; *ExpTim* 9/06; Revised: *ExpTim* 9/23; *Them* 49.1].

✓ **Dunn, James D. G.** [𝓜], (Narrative Commentaries) 1996. Originally published by Epworth (UK) and TPI (USA), this well-written commentary (354pp.) was reissued by Eerdmans in 2016 [*ExpTim* 2/18; *JSNT* 39.5]. Gaventa noted that, despite the series title, Dunn has less interest in matters literary and narratological. As one might expect from him, there is a good measure of theology. If you keep in mind his own approach to Paul, this is a serviceable commentary for the pastor [*RelSRev* 10/98], but Dunn has not given us his best work here. For students the more important vol. to take account of, regarding Dunn's study of Acts and understanding of the early history of the church (Easter to AD 70), is the enormous and engaging *Beginning from Jerusalem* (2009) [*JETS* 3/10; *RTR* 4/10; *TJ* Spr 10; *Them* 4/10 (Barnett); *DenvJ* 1/10; *Int* 7/10; *BL* 2010; *CBQ* 10/11; *JTS* 4/12; *DenvJ* 13]. His series, Christianity in the Making, concludes with vol. 3: *Neither Jew Nor Greek* (2015), moving from AD 70 to the mid-2nd century.

Faw, Chalmer E. (BCBC) 1993.

☆ Fernando, Ajith. (NIVAC) 1998. Well-done exposition, comparable to Stott, from a Sri Lankan church leader. A number of preachers have spoken to me about the help Fernando gives them. There is a lot of heart and conviction here, but less in the way of careful, nuanced scholarship.

☆ **Fitzmyer, Joseph A.** ‡ (AB) 1998. A fitting companion to his work on Luke, though not as thorough. This big (824pp.), moderately critical Catholic commentary is not quite as technical or full as Barrett, but is nearly as valuable. In reviewing AB and Barrett's ICC, one may also say, "Their discussion of issues of theological importance . . . is not as extensive as one might hope for" (*NT Abstracts*). That is a serious demerit from the pastor's perspective. Students can consult this more classically styled commentary for historical investigation, textual issues, and form criticism. But for up-to-date literary/rhetorical analysis, see L. T. Johnson, Spencer, and Witherington. Fitzmyer has fairly traditional critical views on authorship and tentatively assigns an intermediate date of 80–85. I am glad to have Barrett's and Fitzmyer's high-quality, technical commentaries on the Greek text of this, the largest book in the NT, which unfortunately has more than its share of text-critical problems. See Munck. [*Int* 7/99; *CBQ* 7/00; *JBL* Spr 00; *NovT* 42.2; *Bib* 76.3; *ThTo* 7/99; *SJT* 57.1 (Walton)].

✓ Foakes-Jackson, F. J., and Kirsopp Lake, eds. ‡ *The Beginnings of Christianity*, Part I: The Acts of the Apostles, 1920–33. Vols. 4 and 5 of "the monumental classic" (Carson) still see use today, the former being a commentary on Acts and the latter a vol. of additional notes and essays.

✓ Gasque, W. Ward. *History of the Criticism of the Acts of the Apostles*, 1975. This excellent book is still valuable for advanced students working on a *Forschungsbericht* (history of research). Gasque was once under contract to write the NIGTC, in collaboration with the late Colin Hemer, who had considerable historical expertise.

✓ **Gaventa, Beverly.** ‡ (ANTC) 2003. Nothing better than this and Barrett's abridgment for getting a concise critical exegesis. In more liberal Reformed circles, say at Princeton Seminary, this would be a recommended first stop for pastors, before they move on to expositional commentaries. She aimed to produce a dependable tool for ministry. One criticism might be that Gaventa gives less attention to the historical-cultural context. She concentrates on Acts as the unfolding story of God's plan and actions in and through the church. [*CBQ* 7/04; *ExpTim* 8/04; *RelSRev* 4/04; *EvQ* 1/07; *JETS* 3/05; *Int* 7/05; *BL* 2005].

Gloag, Paton J. 2 vols., 1870. Reprinted classic exegesis by a worthy Presbyterian Scot.

F   Green, Joel. (NICNT-R). Will follow his work on Luke (same series). See Bruce.

☆ Green, Michael. *Thirty Years That Changed the World: The Book of Acts for Today*, 2004. Excellent for pastors!

Hackett, Horatio B. 1851. This old 325-page commentary from a moderately Calvinistic perspective was reprinted by Kregel in 1992. Alexander is better.

✓ **Haenchen, Ernst.** ‡ ET 1971. A translation from the MeyerK series, Haenchen has long been one of the most influential commentaries in Acts scholarship. It is very demanding on the reader, highly theological, and radically critical in the neo-Bultmannian sense. This vol. disparages Luke as historian in order to focus upon the theological import of the story. Advanced students should wrestle with it, while pastors choose to leave it alone. Rather dated at this point. [*EvQ* 1/72, 4/78].

Hanson, R. P. C. ‡ (New Clarendon) 1967.

Harrison, E. F. *The Expanding Church*, 1976. A simply written but insightful exposition.

Harvey, John D., and David Gentino. (Kerux) 2023. I've not seen it (approx. 450pp.).

✓ Hemer, Colin. *The Book of Acts in the Setting of Hellenistic History*, 1989. Excellent piece of scholarship, challenging German skepticism regarding the reliability of Acts. How tragic that in 1987 this man with such promise died so suddenly (in his friend D. A. Carson's arms)!

✓ Holmes, Christopher R. J. *Hearing and Doing: The Speeches in Acts and the Essence of Christianity*, 2022. A theological exegesis that plunges deep.

✓ Hornik, Heidi J., and Mikeal C. Parsons. ‡ (BBC) 2016. History of interpretation.

☆ Hughes, R. Kent. (PTW) 1996. About 350 pages. See under Mark.

Jennings, Willie James. ‡ (Belief) 2017. Explores theological implications of the text with a strong interest in postcolonial criticism, race theory, and social justice. See his work *The Christian Imagination: Theology and the Origin of Race* (Yale, 2011). Jennings now teaches at Yale Divinity, and he attempts here to deconstruct the text as betraying a churchly "segregationist trajectory" (146) from the very beginning. [*Int* 1/10; *SJT* 72.1].

✓ Jervell, J. ‡ *The Theology of the Acts of the Apostles* (Cambridge) 1996. The influential German scholar stirred up much discussion with his proposal that Acts should be read as having a strongly Jewish character. (Note: He wrote a 1998 commentary replacing Haenchen in MeyerK.)

☆ Jipp, Joshua W. *Reading Acts*, 2018. A very fine, brief introduction from a TEDS prof in the Cascade Companions series. [*JETS* 3/20; *NovT* 61.4; *JSNT* 41.5].

☆ **Johnson, Dennis.** *The Message of Acts in the History of Redemption*, 1997. Valuable because, though we have redemptive-historical treatments of the Gospels and Paul's letters (e.g., Ridderbos), there's nothing quite like this on Acts. Johnson taught at Westminster California and also wrote on Revelation. Accessible and suggestive for pastors, but students will learn much, too. The exposition is a corrective for those tempted to believe the early church's experience is the norm for today: apostles, resurrections, prophetic revelations on a par with Scripture, etc. A smart purchase!

☆ **Johnson, Luke Timothy.** ‡ (SacP) 1992. Continues his previous efforts in explaining Lukan material. See Johnson under Luke. Both *Luke* and *Acts* were well-received and more oriented toward contemporary literary theory than others in the series. Scholarly pastors will be interested in this. I consider Johnson among the best, most interesting critical commentaries on Acts over the last 30 years. Johnson can be innovative and independent-minded. On the negative side, he does not interact with much evangelical scholarship besides Bruce—no citations of Marshall or Longenecker. From a more conservative angle, Walton's WBC will offer an exacting literary reading. [*CBQ* 7/94; *CRBR* 1994]. Very helpful background reading for Acts is Johnson's *Among the Gentiles: Greco-Roman Religion & Christianity* (2009) [*Chm* Aut 11].

Keddie, Gordon J. *You Are My Witnesses* (Welwyn) 1993.

✓ **Kee, Howard Clark.** ‡ *To Every Nation under Heaven* (NT in Context) 1997. Superb on background, well-written, and accessible. By a leading scholar. [*Int* 1/99; *CBQ* 4/99].

☆ **Keener, Craig S.** 4 vols., 2012–15. Gives "comprehensive" a new significance—"an entire library on Acts in commentary form" (Bockmuehl). The first vol. released by Baker warned us of a colossal work: *Acts: An Exegetical Commentary, Introduction and 1:1–2:47* (1036pp.). Succeeding vols. cover chs. 3–14 (2013); chs. 15–23 (2014); and chs. 24–28 (2015). Aune has referred to it as "an incredibly detailed megacommentary . . . unlikely to be surpassed in the foreseeable future." The strengths are in the areas of socio-cultural background, citations of an astonishing amount of ancient literature and Acts scholarship, and excursuses treating topics relevant to Acts (e.g., dreams, patron–client relationships, Tyrian purple, ancient anti-Judaism). It does less in treating text-critical, lexical, and Greek grammar questions. What I've seen of his exegesis is first-rate, but the trouble is that it seems buried under the encyclopedic details; with difficulty will the reader gather what is the theological message of a pericope. He writes well, though. What is the set's significance? First, it is an imposing argument to assign full historical value to Acts (cf. Pervo). Second, as George Guthrie once said to me about a Keener book, it is "worth its weight in gold in terms of primary source material." Pastors don't have the money or time for a 4500-page academic reference. The advanced student and NT professor, if well-heeled, probably won't hesitate to buy the set. I am clueless as to how Keener amasses such detailed information and finds energy to write so many pages. [*WTJ* Fall 13, Spr 17; *BBR* 23.4, 26.2; *CBQ* 4/14; *Int* 10/14; *JETS* 6/14; *JSNT* 37.5, 38.5; *ExpTim* 8/13, 6/15; *Bib* 95.1; *BSac* 10/13, 7/16; *TJ* Spr 15; *Them* 8/15; *JTS* 10/16].

☆ Kellum, L. Scott. (EGGNT) 2020. Fine work of approx. 300pp. Cf. Culy, Parsons, and Hall in BHGNT. [*Presb* Fall 21].

F Kellum, L. Scott. (EEC). An earlier report was Daniel Huffman.

☆ Kistemaker, Simon J. (NTC) 1990. No disappointment here; it is one of the most valuable vols. in the series (1010pp.). Many preachers will gravitate toward this solidly Reformed work, but you might note Longenecker's caveats. [*WTJ* Fall 93; *CTJ* 11/92].

Krodel, G. A. ‡ (Augsburg Commentary) 1986. Though learned, full, and accessible, it takes a skeptical approach, making it less useful to evangelicals. [*JETS* 9/89; *CRBR* 1988].

✓ Kucicki, Janusz. *The Function of the Speeches in the Acts of the Apostles*, 2018. [*JSNT* 41.5; *RevExp* 8/20 (Walton)].

Kurz, William S. ‡ (CCSS) 2013. [*Int* 4/16].

☆ **Larkin, William.** (IVPNT) 1995. Having heard Larkin lecture, I know it is helpful to preachers for understanding the missionary outreach of the early church and the message of Acts.

Appropriately this is one of the largest vols. in the series (400pp.). The balance of exegesis (winsomely Reformed), theological exposition, and application makes it a good first purchase for pastors. Great insight. [*RelSRev* 4/97].

Larkin, William J. (CorBC) 2006. Bound with Luke (Trites). I've not seen it.

✓ **Lightfoot, J. B.** *The Acts of the Apostles: A Newly Discovered Commentary*, 2014. Through the efforts of Witherington and others, we have a previously unpublished work from "perhaps the greatest New Testament exegete in the nineteenth-century English-speaking world" (Keener). Best known for commentaries on Galatians, Philippians, and Colossians–Philemon, Lightfoot (1828–89) had *Acts* in progress when he died. Of greater interest to students than pastors (400pp.). [*JSNT* 37.5; *JETS* 9/15; *Them* 40.3].

☆ Lloyd-Jones, D. Martyn. *Authentic Christianity: Studies in the Book of Acts*, 6 vols., 1999–2006. The Doctor's last series at Westminster Chapel, on Acts 1–8. [*RTR* 4/07].

☆ **Longenecker, Richard.** (EBCR) 2007. Along with Carson's *Matthew*, the best NT entry in the old EBC (1981). Longenecker was full (370pp.) and nicely balanced as a sagacious exegesis and exposition—an excellent buy for pastors. [*EvQ* 7/83; *JETS* 6/81]. The EBCR is a welcome revision of 437pp., though I wish the update were more thorough, with more citations of the recent literature (e.g., in the Introduction). Some of the revisions are excisions of his discussion of contemporary relevance; cf. p.339 (1981) and p.816 (2007).

Lüdemann, G. ‡ *Early Christianity according to the Traditions in Acts*, ET 1989. The research is in line with much German scholarship and mainly treats older literary questions about the alleged growth of apostolic traditions. Highly skeptical.

MacArthur, John. 2 vols., 1994–96. See Matthew for a review of the series.

✓ Malina, Bruce J., and John J. Pilch. ‡ 2008. I admit to being baffled by this "Social Science Commentary." Malina–Pilch strangely view the early Christian mission as producing a *Heidenrein* (heathen-free) community where all have become "Judean" (Jewish). [*CBQ* 1/09; *BL* 2010].

Maloney, Linda M., and Ivoni Richter Reimer. ‡ (Wisdom) 2022.

☆ **Marshall, I. Howard.** (TNTC) 1980. Given a warm welcome, Marshall is excellent in almost every way—a little less conservative, though, than some would prefer. This is Marshall's expert sequel to his detailed commentary on Luke's Gospel. There is good balance between treating the history and theology of the text (see Bruce's NICNT above) [*RTR* 5/81]. For an updated introduction to Acts and Acts scholarship, see his superb 1992 contribution to the New Testament Guides series [*CRBR* 1993].

✓ Marshall, I. Howard, and David Peterson, eds. *Witness to the Gospel: The Theology of Acts*, 1993. Not a commentary, but collected essays meant to complement the Eerdmans multivol. series The Book of Acts in Its First-Century Setting. A very important and useful book! [*Int* 4/00; *RTR* 8/99; *RelSRev* 4/99; *ScrB* 1/99].

✓ Martin, Francis, ed. (ACCS) 2006. [*BL* 2007; *EuroJTh* 18.1].

Merida, Tony. *Exalting Jesus in Acts* (CCE) 2017.

Milne, Bruce. *Acts: Witnesses to Him*, 2010. [*RTR* 8/13].

✓ Moyise, Steve. ‡ *The Later NT Writers and Scripture: The OT in Acts, Hebrews, the Catholic Epistles and Revelation*, 2012. Joins his earlier works on *Jesus and Scripture* and *Paul and Scripture* to complete a set on the subject. [*CBQ* 10/13; *JSNT* 35.5; *JETS* 3/13].

Munck, Johannes. ‡ (retired AB) 1967. Brief and disappointing in light of his past works. Munck was a more conservative voice among continental critics. See Fitzmyer.

Neil, William. [𝓜], (NCB) 1973, rev. 1981. Good but undistinguished.

Newman, B. M., and E. A. Nida. (UBS) 1972. An older handbook for Bible translators.

Osborne, Grant R. (ONTC) 2019. See under Commentary Series.

☆ Padilla, Osvaldo. *The Acts of the Apostles: Interpretation, History and Theology*, 2016. Endeavors to give this generation an introduction similar to the 1970 I. Howard Marshall title, *Luke: Historian & Theologian.* [*WTJ* Fall 18; *JTS* 4/17; *JETS* 3/17; *DenvJ* 6/16].

✓ **Parsons, Mikeal C.** ‡ (Paideia) 2008. The approach is mainly narrative criticism, with rhetorical and compositional strategies in focus. His few historical judgments tend to be in line with Pervo (with whom he wrote *Rethinking the Unity of Luke and Acts*, 1993). E.g., Parsons dates Acts to ca. AD 110, perhaps some 20 years after the Gospel. [*CBQ* 7/09; *ExpTim* 11/09; *RelSRev* 9/09; *BL* 2010; *Int* 7/11]. For more on the unity challenge, see Gregory–Rowe, eds., *Rethinking the Unity and Reception of Luke and Acts* (2010) [*JTS* 4/11].

Pelikan, Jaroslav. ‡ (Brazos) 2006. This is the inaugural vol. in Brazos, and I was not sure what it meant for the future of the series. On the one hand, Pelikan, a preeminent church historian, is an amazingly learned guide for readers interested to "place Acts in theological conversation with centuries of Christian creeds and other rules of faith" (Weaver). On the other, the commentary is "as much topic-driven as text-driven" and is deficient as an exegetical help. Some may wish to turn to this after all the exegesis is done. [*CTJ* 11/06; *CBQ* 4/08; *JETS* 12/06; *BL* 2007; *ExpTim* 12/07].

F   Penner, T. (RRA).

✓ **Pervo, Richard I.** ‡ (Herm) 2009. A rigorous 800-page technical exegesis (100pp. of bibliography and indices), added to the series alongside Conzelmann. Pervo proposed that Acts fits the genre of historical novel (*Profit with Delight: The Literary Genre of the Acts of the Apostles*, 1987) and dates to ca. 110–120 (*Dating Acts*, 2006 [*CBQ* 10/07]). While students make use of this expensive reference work in libraries, few pastors will invest their time and money here. The author presents "a wealth of insights into the literary context of Acts. Techniques of rhetoric, narration and characterization are emphasized" (Elliott). What quickly comes across to readers is that "Pervo is extremely sceptical about the historical worth of Acts" (Edwards) and dismissive of conservatives. [*JETS* 6/09 (Keener); *ExpTim* 9/09; *NovT* 52.3 (Elliott); *BBR* 20.2 (Schnabel); *BL* 2010 (Edwards); *CBQ* 1/12]. For a summary of his interpretation, see *The Mystery of Acts: Unravelling Its Story* (2008) [*CBQ* 10/09].

✓ Phillips, Thomas E., ed. ‡ *Contemporary Studies in Acts*, 2009. From SBL. [*BL* 2010].

☆ Pinter, Dean. (SGBC) 2019. The product of a well-read parish priest in the Anglican Church of Canada. Pinter studied at Regent College and Durham (PhD); he provokes good reflection on the text, and especially how it speaks to us and applies today. His strong theological influences seem to be Fee, Dunn, Wright, and McKnight. The full contribution (590pp.) fits very well into the series and is easy to recommend.

☆ **Polhill, John B.** (NAC) 1992. A full and informed exposition (550pp.), written on a level easily understood by educated laypeople. Competes with Blomberg on Matthew and Stein on Luke as the best in the NT series. Well worth buying. This is also a commentary for students; Fitzmyer surprisingly quotes it more than Pesch, Roloff, or Bruce. [*EvQ* 1/94; *ThTo* 10/93; *CRBR* 1994; *Bib* 75.4].

F   Porter, Stanley E. (NIGTC). By a world-recognized grammarian, who helped develop verbal aspect theory. In preparation for the commentary, he wrote *The Paul of Acts: Essays in Literary Criticism, Rhetoric and Theology* (1999) [*JSNT* 76].

✓ Rackham, R. B. (Westminster) 1901, 5th ed. 1910. "Written from a 'high' Episcopalian viewpoint" (Martin), has verve, and discusses the message of the text from a number of angles. Because Rackham shows an interest in matters ecclesial, I count this a useful work for evangelical preachers today—too many of whom lack interest in ecclesiology. Look for it s/h. [*JETS* 6/79].

✓ Rowe, C. Kavin. *World Upside Down: Reading Acts in the Graeco-Roman Age*, 2009. The measure of this book's importance is the high-level reviews on the pages of *JSNT* 33.3 (2011). [*JETS* 12/10; *SBET* Aut 11; *SJT* 64.3].

☆ **Schreiner, Patrick.** (CSC) 2022. The author, Tom Schreiner's son, seeks to "distill and highlight especially the *narratival* and *theological* content of Acts with an eye toward the *ecclesial*." He is a gifted Bible interpreter and writes in a lucid and engaging way. Pastors will be his main audience. What distinguishes the work is "a more symbolic/figural approach to Acts than many commentaries." Also, he writes that he does "*not shy away from jumping to other canonical and biblical-theological connections. I won't only look for themes in Luke-Acts but the entire Christian canon to enlighten the reading*" (Preface).

Skinner, Matthew L. ‡ *Intrusive God, Disruptive Gospel*, 2015. Thoughtful, more popular-level, mainline Protestant study, alert to narratological and theological themes (185pp.). [*Them* 40.3].

✓ Sleeman, Matthew. *Geography and the Ascension Narrative in Acts*, 2009. From CUP.

Smith, Daniel Lynwood, and Zachary Lundin Kostopoulos. ‡ "Biography, History, and the Genre of Luke-Acts," *NTS* 63 (2017): 390–410. A survey of proposals, including Gregory Sterling's *Historiography and Self-Definition* (1992) that emphasizes apologetic interests.

✓ Soards, Marion L. [𝓜], *The Speeches in Acts*, 1994.

✓ **Spencer, F. Scott.** ‡ (Read) 1997, 2nd ed. 2004. The fresh, literary interpretation is a more significant contribution than its size might indicate. For students. Spencer previously did excellent work on the character of Philip in the Acts narrative. In the 2nd ed. (Hendrickson), the body of the commentary is left unchanged. [*Int* 4/99, 7/05; *CBQ* 4/99; *CTJ* 11/07; *EvQ* 10/07; *Chm* Aut 06; *RTR* 12/05; *RelSRev* 1/06]. See under Luke.

✓ Strutwolf, Holger, et al., eds. *Novum Testamentum Editio Critica Maior: III Acts of the Apostles*, 4 vols., 2017. A full accounting for manuscript evidence for the (troublesome) text of Acts. What a meticulous and "stunning research tool" for scholars [*ExpTim* 4/18]! [*BBR* 28.2; *JTS* 4/18].

✓ **Talbert, Charles.** ‡ *Reading Acts* (RNT) 1997, rev. 2005. Like Spencer from the same year, Talbert focuses upon literary features as pointers to theology.

✓ Tannehill, Robert. ‡ *The Narrative Unity of Luke-Acts, A Literary Interpretation*, 2 vols., 1990–91. See under Luke. [*CBQ* 4/92].

Thomas, Derek W. H. (REC) 2011. I have not seen it (750pp.). [*Chm* Aut 13].

☆ Thompson, Alan J. *The Acts of the Risen Lord Jesus*, 2011. A very fine biblical-theological overview from NSBT (230pp.)—great for expositional preachers—building upon his well-received *One Lord, One People: The Unity of the Church in Acts in Its Literary Setting* (2008). [*EvQ* 4/14 (Walton); *JETS* 3/13; *ExpTim* 2/13; *Them* 11/11; *RelSRev* 12/12; *TJ* Spr 14].

F Thompson, Alan J. (EBTC)?

✓ Troftgruben, Troy. ‡ *A Conclusion Unhindered: A Study of the Ending of Acts within Its Literary Environment*, 2010. [*JETS* 12/11 (Walton); *BBR* 22.2].

✓ Verheyden, J., ed. ‡ *The Unity of Luke-Acts*, 1999. Huge BETL vol.

☆ Vickers, Brian J. "Acts" in *John–Acts* (ESVEC) 2021. See Hamilton under John.

Walaskay, Paul W. ‡ (WestBC) 1998. [*RelSRev* 7/99; *Int* 7/02].

☆ **Wall, Robert W.** (NIB) 2002. One of the more conservative contributions to the NIB project in the NT section. Wall is an able scholar, known for his interest in final-form exegetical methods, such as canonical criticism. He was able to build upon the mountain of research in AB, ICC, SacP, etc. See Wall's other commentaries on Colossians, James, and Revelation.

✓ Walton, Steve, Thomas E. Phillips, Lloyd Keith Pietersen, and F. Scott Spencer, eds. *Reading Acts Today*, 2011. A FS for Loveday Alexander brimming with the best scholarship and focusing on varied approaches to the book. [*Them* 4/12].

Waters, Guy Prentiss. (EPSC) 2014. An extensive exposition (600pp.) by a thoughtful PCA theologian. I regret I have not seen it.

F Weatherley, J. (THC). There is a conflicting report that Bauckham has the contract.

**Williams, C. S. C.** ‡ (BNTC) 1957, rev. 1969. A once useful but now dated work, with the more moderate historical perspective of the British critics. The pastor with Bruce, Longenecker, or Marshall wouldn't have much use for it.

☆ **Williams, David John.** (NIBC) 1990. Quite full at 493pp., worth consulting, and reasonably priced. The work (in GNC) was given a warm review by Colin Hemer [*JETS* 3/87].

Willimon, William. [*M*], (I) 1988. Skimpy compared with other works on Acts. Good for communicators, from a mildly critical angle, but not a major interpretive work.

✓ Winter, Bruce W., et al. *The Book of Acts in Its First Century Setting*, 1993–. A series of the highest scholarly caliber, mildly critical in approach, and indispensable to the serious student. Five vols. came out, and the sixth was issued as Marshall–Peterson (see above). [*EvQ* 7/97; *JETS* 12/96, 9/97, 6/99; *CTJ* 11/96; *CBQ* 4/97, 10/97, 4/99; *Presb* Spr 96; *JSNT* 71].

☆ **Witherington, Ben, III.** 1997. Another of this prolific evangelical's "socio-rhetorical" commentaries. Carson thinks the author did some of his best work here. See my comments under 1 Corinthians. I used to include Witherington among the purchases because his approach is different from my other suggestions and yields key insights (a goodly number of which are picked up by Peterson). By the way, Johnson and Spencer also provide fine works with literary/rhetorical savvy. Cf. the forthcoming Green and Walton, with their similar narrative interests. Note: The 900-page commentary is very comprehensive, exploring more side roads than you'll probably care to. If you love to read and have found Witherington's works stimulating, then do move this up to the top pick category. [*JBL* Sum 99; *Bib* 81.1; *Int* 4/99; *CBQ* 4/99; *AsTJ* Fall 98 (Marshall)].

☆ Wright, Tom (N. T.). *Acts for Everyone*, 2 vols., 2008. A sparkling exposition of 480pp. [*ExpTim* 4/09; *BL* 2009].

NOTES: (1) See I. H. Marshall's "The Present State of Lucan Studies," in *Them* 1/89 and "Recent Commentaries on the Acts of the Apostles" by Ward Gasque in *Them* 10/88. (2) John Ziesler's "Which Is the Best Commentary? V. Acts of the Apostles," *ExpTim*, 12/86. (3) Students are helped by two review-essays. One by Patrick Spencer considers a specific scholarly controversy, "The Unity of Luke-Acts," *CBR* 5.3 (2007): 341–66. The other is a more comprehensive review: Todd Penner, "Madness in the Method? The Acts of the Apostles in Current Study," *CBR* 2.2 (2004): 223–93. (4) Saving the briefest for last, I urge students to read I. Howard Marshall, "Acts in Current Study," *ExpTim* 115 (2003): 49–52.

# PAULINE STUDIES

★ Bruce, F. F. *Paul: Apostle of the Heart Set Free*, 1977. Has a well-deserved reputation as a rich, trustworthy overview of Paul as a man, his travels, and his theology. Bruce wrote commentaries on just about every epistle of Paul, so this book is well-informed, to put it mildly. Note: some Reformed interpreters (e.g., George Knight) disagree with a certain antinomianism they detect in Bruce's review of Paul's theology. For a more recent book accomplishing many of Bruce's same aims, see Polhill below. We are still waiting, really, for Bruce's replacement. [*RTR* 5/78; *EvQ* 10/78; *ThTo* 35.3].

★ Campbell, Constantine R. *Paul and Union with Christ: An Exegetical and Theological Study*, 2012. The teaching of our being "in Christ" is seen more and more as "of utmost importance" to Paul's theology of salvation and vital for the Christian life. Campbell demonstrates these twin points in his thorough (480pp.) work, which took the 2014 *Christianity Today* book award for biblical studies. Union "does not occupy the 'center' of [Paul's] theological framework. It is, rather, the essential ingredient that binds all other elements together" (39). Cf. Macaskill below, who says Campbell "is highly sensitive to the range of associations that the phrase has and does not press these into a particular scheme" (38–39). See Johnson's [*JETS* 6/13] appreciation and critique. [*Int* 10/14; *JSNT* 35.5; *Them* 7/13; *TJ* Spr 15; *RTR* 12/15]. More from the historical and theological angles, one can consult Robert Letham's *Union with Christ* (2011) [*Chm* Aut 14]; Marcus Peter Johnson's *One with Christ* (2013); and the published dissertations of Mark A. Garcia (*Life in Christ*, 2008) and William B. Evans (*Imputation and Impartation*, 2008). See also J. T. Billings's *Union with Christ: Reframing Theology and Ministry for the Church* (2011) [*Int* 4/13; *Chm* Aut 14]. Note both Thate–Vanhoozer–Campbell and Hewitt below.

★ Gaffin, Richard B. *Resurrection and Redemption: A Study in Paul's Soteriology*, 2nd ed. 1987. Formerly titled *The Centrality of the Resurrection* (1978). I cannot think of any more valuable 125pp. of text on Paul's theology. The student or pastor who digests this will gain an exciting perspective on Paul's theology and an appreciation for the truth that, in union with Christ, his resurrection life is ours. Can radically change the way preachers approach Paul's letters. [*JETS* 12/80]. Similarly useful is Gaffin's *By Faith, Not by Sight: Paul and the Order of Salvation* (Paternoster, 2006), which discusses theology's *ordo salutis* and the doctrine of union with Christ, seen as the dominant, organizing truth in Paul's soteriology. See also Con Campbell above.

★ McKnight, Scot, Lynn H. Cohick, and Nijay K. Gupta, eds. [*M*], *Dictionary of Paul and His Letters*, 2023. The old edition (1993), edited by Hawthorne–Martin–Reid, need not be discarded [*JETS* 12/96; *Them* 1/95; *ExpTim* 9/23; *CBQ* 1/24].

★ Moo, Douglas J. *A Theology of Paul and His Letters*, 2021. Ripe fruit from a lifetime of scholarly engagement with Paul. Such a treat, this thorough (700pp.) survey, serving as an up-to-date seminary textbook and marvelously wise refresher course for pastors! Moo says "that participation in Christ, or union with Christ, might serve as the web that holds Paul's theology together" (37), emphasizing that believers are brought into "the new realm" headed by Christ (locative sense) and "the idea of incorporation into Christ and the benefits he has won for us in his redemptive work" (39). Moo's theology is baptistic and a "tweaking of Reformed theology" (30); as an OT lecturer I disagree "that the biblical use of 'covenant' language focuses more on discontinuity than continuity" (29). Note that it is a book of two halves: the first treats individual letters and the second gives a synthesis of Paul's overall theology. [*JETS* 9/22; *WTJ* Spr 22; *TGA* 9/23].

★ Ridderbos, Herman. *Paul: An Outline of His Theology*, ET 1975. Though the translation makes for tough going in places, this work has a treasure of insights into Pauline doctrine. His emphasis on *historia salutis* (history of salvation), which Gaffin picks up, was one of my most fascinating discoveries in seminary. Although he overstates his case at points (e.g., making union with Christ almost always redemptive-historical and hardly ever mystical), Ridderbos is a needed corrective for those of us who were trained to think primarily in terms of *ordo salutis* (the order or method by which Christ's saving work is applied to us), which is a heritage from the Puritans. Do wrestle with this profound work. [*EvQ* 1/78; *ExpTim* 2/78; *JSNT* 71].

★ Schreiner, Thomas R. *Paul, Apostle of God's Glory in Christ*, 2001, 2nd ed. 2020. This evangelical Pauline theology revealed that Carson helped change Schreiner's mind on justification since the publication of *Romans* in BECNT. Well worth buying as an introductory study. Those outside the Baptist and Reformed tradition might not value this exposition of Paul's theology as highly. [*Them* Aut 02; *JETS* 12/02; *Chm* Aut 02; *RelSRev* 4/07; *DenvJ*].

★ Thielman, Frank. *Paul and the Law: A Contextual Approach*, 1994. [*BSac* 4/96; *TJ* Spr 95]. I doubt anyone in evangelicalism knows the topic better than Thielman, with his Duke dissertation, *From Plight to Solution: A Jewish Framework for Understanding Paul's View of the Law in Galatians and Romans* (Brill, 1989) [*NovT* 35.2]. His accessible study of the

NT use of νόμος was published as *The Law and the NT* (1999) [*ExpTim* 6/00]. Other notable evangelical discussions of the topic are Kruse, Schreiner, Westerholm, and especially Carson–O'Brien–Seifrid.

✓ Anderson, Garwood P. *Paul's New Perspective*, 2016. Somewhat comparable to Bird in seeking to blend the NPP with elements of a more traditional Protestant reading of Paul's soteriology. Anderson downplays imputation (in the classic Reformed sense) and teaches a realistic and participationist view (union with Christ). By contrast Calvin emphasized both union with Christ and the imputation of Christ's righteousness (commentary on 2 Cor 5:21). [*JETS* 12/17; *JSNT* 39.5; *Them* 42.3]. See Chester below.

✓ Banks, Robert J. *Paul's Idea of Community*, 3rd ed. 2020. [*Them* 45.2].

☆ Barclay, John M. G. [𝓜], *Paul and the Gift*, 2015. An exceedingly valuable, fresh research (620pp.) of χάρις (often rendered "gift" or "favor") by a leading British academic. Barclay offers "a reconsideration of 'grace' within the anthropology and history of gift, a study of Jewish construals of divine beneficence in the Second Temple period, and, within that context, a new appraisal of Paul's theology of the Christ-event as gift, as it comes to expression in Galatians and Romans" (4). As Garlington also notes, "the book provides a virtual commentary on the bulk of Galatians and Romans" [*BBR* 26.4]. Barclay has changed Pauline studies. [*Bib* 98.1; *Chm* Win 16; *ExpTim* 8/17; *ExpTim* 4/16; *WTJ* Spr 16; *JETS* 6/16; *EvQ* 10/18; *ETL* 94.2; *HBT* 41.2 (discussion); *JSNT* 38.5; *Them* 41.2 (Moo), 41.1 (Schreiner)]. For a précis see *Paul and the Power of Grace* (2020) [*JTS* 4/22; *CBQ* 1/22; *Int* 10/22; *TGA* 3/23; *JSNT* 43.5; *Them* 46.1]. A high-powered discussion within the guild is Edward Adams et al., eds., *The New Perspective on Grace* (2023) [*WTJ* Fall 23].

✓ Barclay, John M. G., and Simon J. Gathercole, eds. [𝓜], *Divine and Human Agency in Paul and His Cultural Environment*, 2008. [*BL* 2009; *ExpTim* 11/09].

✓ Barrett, C. K. ‡ *Essays on Paul*, 1982. [*EvQ* 1/84]. More recent are: *Paul: An Introduction to His Thought* (1994) [*JETS* 12/96; *CTJ* 4/96], and *On Paul: Essays on His Life, Work and Influence in the Early Church* (2003) [*BL* 2005].

Bassler, Jouette. ‡ *Navigating Paul: An Introduction to Key Theological Concepts*, 2007. This book by a well-regarded Pauline scholar could have been better, had she interacted with conservative scholarship on topics such as union with Christ.

✓ Bassler, Jouette, David Hay, and E. Elizabeth Johnson, eds. ‡ *Pauline Theology*, 4 vols., 1991–97. Fortress Press published a vast SBL survey of the topic, moving through the epistles one after another, to understand the contribution of each book.

✓ Becker, Jürgen. ‡ *Paul, Apostle to the Gentiles*, ET 1993. [*ExpTim* 1/94; *Int* 4/95].

✓ Beker, J. Christiaan. ‡ *Paul the Apostle: The Triumph of God in Life and Thought*, 1980. Very influential in its stress on apocalyptic elements in Paul. [*JBL* 101.3]. See also his shorter, more recent books: *Paul's Apocalyptic Gospel* (1982); *The Triumph of God: The Essence of Paul's Thought* (1990); and *Heirs of Paul: Paul's Legacy in the New Testament and in the Church Today* (1991) which mainly deals with the so-called Deutero-Pauline Corpus. For a debate with N. T. Wright, see *Paul: Narrative or Apocalyptic* (2023).

☆ Bird, Michael F. *An Anomalous Jew: Paul among Jews, Greeks, and Romans*, 2016. Valuable overview of Paul studies; Bird critiques the apocalyptic readings. [*Chm* Spr 19; *ExpTim* 12/17; *JTS* 4/18; *JETS* 6/18; *SJT* 71.4; *JSNT* 39.5]. His output is most impressive, for around the same time Bird published a Romans commentary and *Jesus the Eternal Son: Answering Adoptionist Christology* (2017) [*JSNT* 40.5 (Wenham)].

✓ Bird, Michael F. *The Saving Righteousness of God: Studies on Paul, Justification and the New Perspective*, 2006. The author "attempts to reclaim much of Reformed theology in the face of the challenge of the New Perspective" (Foster), viewing those two as compatible to a degree. He seeks a *via media*. [*ExpTim* 1/08; *RelSRev* 9/08; *JETS* 3/09; *EuroJTh* 17.1]. See also his winsome, brief (192-page) *Introducing Paul* (IVP, 2008) [*JETS* 6/10], and his engagement with Dunn, Michael Horton, and others in *Justification: Five Views* (2012) [*SBET* Aut 13].

✓ Bird, Michael F., ed. *Four Views on the Apostle Paul*, 2012. Sharp debate among Schreiner (Baptist), Luke Timothy Johnson (Catholic), Nanos (Jewish), and Douglas Campbell (post-NPP). [*CBQ* 4/14; *JSNT* 35.5; *Chm* Win 13; *Them* 7/13; *RTR* 8/15; *TJ* Spr 14; *JETS* 6/13].

✓ Bird, Michael F., and Preston M. Sprinkle, eds. *The Faith of Jesus Christ: Exegetical, Biblical, and Theological Studies*, 2009. [*Them* 7/10 (Silva); *BBR* 20.4; *JSNT* 33.5; *JETS* 3/11; *BTB* 8/11; *SBET* Aut 11]. Those taking account of the debate should see the comments on Hays under Galatians and also read Benjamin Schliesser, "'Exegetical Amnesia' and ΠΙΣΤΙΣ ΧΡΙΣΤΟΥ: The 'Faith *of* Christ' in Nineteenth-Century Pauline Scholarship," *JTS* 66 (2015): 61–89.

✓ Bird, Michael F., Ruben A. Bühner, Jörg Frey, and Brian Rosner, eds. *Paul within Judaism*, 2023. From an online conference of leading NT scholars.

✓ Blackwell, Ben C. [*M*], *Christosis: Engaging Paul's Soteriology with His Patristic Interpreters*, 2016. Has been generating much discussion. [*Int* 10/18 (Gorman)]. Cf. Gorman below, and M. David Litwa, *We Are Being Transformed: Deification in Paul's Soteriology* (2012).

✓ Blackwell, Ben C., John K. Goodrich, and Jason Maston, eds. *Paul and the Apocalyptic Imagination*, 2016.

✓ Blazowski, Bryan. *The Law's Universal Condemning and Enslaving Power: Reading Paul, the OT, and Second Temple Jewish Literature*, 2019. [*JSNT* 42.5].

✓ Boer, Martinus C. de. ‡ *Paul, Theologian of God's Apocalypse*, 2020. Collected essays from a leader of the apocalyptic school of interpreters (Beker, D. Campbell, Martyn). [*Int* 10/22; *NovT* 63.2; *JSNT* 43.5].

Bornkamm, Günther. ‡ *Paul*, ET 1971. Highly critical biography. [*JBL* 90.4].

✓ Brookins, Timothy A. *Ancient Rhetoric and the Style of Paul's Letters: A Reference Book*, 2022. [*CBQ* 7/23].

✓ Burke, Trevor J. *Adopted into God's Family: Exploring a Pauline Metaphor*, 2006.

✓ Burke, Trevor J., and Brian S. Rosner, eds. *Paul as Missionary*, 2011. [*CBQ* 4/13; *JSNT* 34.5; *Them* 11/11; *BTB* 2/14; *RelSRev* 3/12].

☆ Campbell, Constantine R. *Paul and the Hope of Glory*, 2020. Provides a wise introduction to, and sifting of, theories about Pauline eschatology and apocalyptic thought. The book is especially strong in presenting and analyzing the exegetical evidence. [*WTJ* Spr 21]. Campbell has an introduction: *Reading Paul as Christian Scripture* (2024).

✓ Campbell, Douglas A. ‡ *The Deliverance of God: An Apocalyptic Rereading of Justification in Paul*, 2009. More than any other study, Campbell has set up the apocalyptic and covenant perspectives on Paul in opposition (see Shaw article in *JSNT* 36.2). He pushes a more radical revisionism of Pauline interpretation than the NPP and wants to dispose entirely of a legal framework for understanding justification. This of course requires some gymnastics, and one move—among many in these 1248pp.—is to propose that Rom 1:18–32 is actually the argument of a false teacher which Paul subsequently destroys. [*JSNT* 12/11 (whole issue); *BL* 2010; *JETS* 3/10 (Moo); *Them* 7/10 (Seifrid); *EC* 5/10 (Watson); *EQ* 7/11 (Marshall); *CBQ* 7/11 (de Boer); *Int* 10/10; *Chm* Spr 12; *RTR* 8/12; *ExpTim* 12/10; *BTB* 5/11; *RelSRev* 3/11; *SJT* 65.1]. Another controversial work is *Framing Paul: An Epistolary Biography* (2014) [*ExpTim* 10/15; *BBR* 27.1; *CBQ* 10/16; *JETS* 12/15; *JSNT* 38.5; *Them* 42.2]. For more responses see Tilling, ed., *Beyond Old and New Perspectives* (2014) [*JSNT* 37.5].

✓ Campbell, Douglas A. ‡ *Pauline Dogmatics: The Triumph of God's Love*, 2020. Essentially a huge Barthian exposition of Paul's theology. [*RevExp* 11/21; *CTJ* 4/21; *BBR* 31.1; *CBQ* 7/21; *JTS* 4/22; *Int* 10/22; *JETS* 3/23].

✓ Capes, D. B. *Old Testament Yahweh Texts in Paul's Christology*, 1992. Fine and useful work, summarized in *The Divine Christ* (2018) [*JETS* 9/19; *SJT* 72.4; *JSNT* 41.5].

☆ Capes, David, Rodney Reeves, and E. Randolph Richards. *Rediscovering Paul*, 2007, 2nd ed. 2017. One of the best basic textbooks, engaging, interested in sociology.

✓ Cara, Robert J. *Cracking the Foundation of the New Perspective on Paul*, 2017. [*JETS* 3/18].

✓ Carson, D. A., Peter O'Brien, and Mark Seifrid, eds. *Justification and Variegated Nomism*, 2 vols., 2001–04. Both conservatives and critical scholars cooperate here to produce an incredibly deep and valuable resource for weighing the strengths and weaknesses of E. P. Sanders's interpretation of 1st century Palestinian Judaism as covenantal nomism, as well as other brands of the NPP. I call this the most important response. [*Them* Spr 03, 1/06; *JETS* 3/03; *ExpTim* 6/02; *CBQ* 1/03, 10/05; *TJ* Spr 04 (Dunn), Fall 05; *BBR* 19.1 (Beale); *JETS* 12/05; *TJ* Spr 08 (Beale); *BibInt* 13.1; *DenvJ* 1/02 (Blomberg)].

✓ Carter, T. L. *Paul and the Power of Sin*, 2002.

✓ Casey, Thomas G., and Justin Taylor, eds. ‡ *Paul's Jewish Matrix*, 2011. [*JSNT* 34.5].

✓ Chester, Stephen. *Reading Paul with the Reformers*, 2017. Asserts there is not so large a gap as some suppose between the magisterial Reformers' interpretations of Paul and the NPP. [*JETS* 6/18; *Int* 7/20; *JSNT* 41.5]. Arguing something similar are Anderson (above), and Edwin Chr. Van Driel, *Rethinking Paul: Protestant Theology and Pauline Exegesis* (2021) [*JSNT* 44.5].

✓ Childs, Brevard S. ‡ *The Church's Guide for Reading Paul: The Canonical Shaping of the Pauline Corpus*, 2008. This work furnishes NT scholars with a fresh, outsider's perspective on their Pauline interpretation and with further evidence (as Childs's last book) of the author's extraordinary learning even outside his specialty. [*BTB* 40.1 (negative); *RelSRev* 36.2; *HBT* 31.2 (positive); *Anvil* 26.3–4 (Briggs); *Them* 11/09; *BBR* 21.2].

Conybeare, W. J., and J. S. Howson. *The Life and Epistles of St. Paul*, 1892. A 2-vol. work that has often been reprinted but deserves retirement.

✓ Coulson, John R. *The Righteous Judgment of God: Aspects of Judgment in Paul's Letters*, 2016. A needed reminder of the prominence of the Pauline theme, given that scholarship usually downplays it. [*RTR* 8/17].

✓ Cousar, Charles B. ‡ *The Letters of Paul*, 1996. In the IBT series. Another fine critical introduction, more centered on theology, is Ziesler's *Pauline Christianity* (rev. 1990).

✓ Das, A. Andrew. *Paul, the Law, and the Covenant*, 2001. [*Them* Sum 03; *SwJT* Fall 03; *RTR* 4/04; *TJ* Fall 04 (Hafemann)]; *Paul and the Jews* (2003) [*RTR* 4/05; *Them* Sum 05; *Chm* Sum 06].

✓ Davey, Wesley Thomas. *Suffering as Participation with Christ in the Pauline Corpus*, 2019. A topic that has been deserving closer attention. [*JSNT* 42.5]. See also Siu Fung Wu (ed.), *Suffering in Paul* (2019).

✓ Davies, J. P. [*M*], *Paul among the Apocalypses: An Evaluation of the 'Apocalyptic Paul' in the Context of Jewish and Christian Apocalyptic Literature*, 2016. A St. Andrews diss. in LNTS. [*Presb* Spr 20; *BBR* 27.2; *CBQ* 4/18; *JSNT* 39.5]. More approachable is *The Apocalyptic Paul* (Cascade, 2022) [*JETS* 6/23; *JSNT* 45.5], with its "whistle-stop tour of major figures" (3). A summary is: "The Justice and Deliverance of God: Integrating Forensic and Cosmological in the 'Apocalyptic Paul,'" *CBR* 21 (2022): 338–48. Davies was a pastor and now teaches at Trinity, Bristol.

✓ Davies, W. D. ‡ *Paul and Rabbinic Judaism*, 1948, 1955, 1980. This work did much to spark today's interest in Paul's debt to, and later conflict with, his rabbinic heritage. See also his *Jewish and Pauline Studies* (1984).

✓ Donaldson, Terence. *Paul and the Gentiles: Remapping the Apostle's Convictional World*, 1997. Particularly helpful for tracing the development of the NPP from Stendahl's essay, "The Apostle Paul and the Introspective Conscience of the West," to Dunn and beyond.

✓ Dunn, James D. G. ‡ *The Theology of Paul the Apostle*, 1998. A magnum opus (737pp. + indices), which offers "a fresh, comprehensive treatment of the apostle's theology" (Weima). In its freshness, however, Dunn's *Theology* reinterprets or denies many evangelical doctrines found in Paul: original sin, substitutionary atonement, etc. See my comments under Romans and Galatians. Dunn emphasizes Paul's Jewish background in making sense of his life and theology. Advanced students should consider buying this influential work. [*JETS* 6/01; *SJT* 53.3; *JTS* 4/99; *ThTo* 10/99; *TJ* Spr 99; *CTJ* 11/99; *Int* 1/99; *CBQ* 1/99; *RTR* 4/99; *AsTJ* Fall 99; *RelSRev* 4/99; *ScrB* 1/99; *JSNT* 71; *EvQ* 4/02]. On the specific topic of the NPP, see the convenient collection of Dunn's work (1983–2004) in *The New Perspective on Paul: Collected Essays* (2005, rev. 2008) [*Them* 4/06; *WTJ* Spr 09; *BL* 2006; *RelSRev* 12/08; *JETS* 3/09; *EuroJTh* 15.2]. Despite his revisionism, Dunn still believed "justification by faith alone needs to be reasserted as strongly as ever it was by Paul or by Augustine or by Luther" (87). Among the best brief introductions to the NPP is Yinger, *The New Perspective on Paul* (2011).

✓ Dunn, James D. G., ed. ‡ *The Cambridge Companion to St. Paul*, 2003. For a quick introduction to critical scholarship on Paul, one may turn here [*EvQ* 7/05; *Anvil* 22.1; *DenvJ* 1/04], to Hooker, *Paul: A Short Introduction* (2003) [*Evangel* Sum 04 (Marshall); *Anvil* 20.4], to Thiselton, *The Living Paul* (2009) [*DenvJ* 4/10; *ExpTim* 9/10], or, even better, to Longenecker, ed., *New Cambridge Companion* (2020).

✓ Dunn, James D. G., ed. ‡ *Paul and the Mosaic Law*, 1996, ET 2001. A collection of papers read at the 1994 Durham–Tübingen Research Symposium on Earliest Christianity and Judaism. The contributors are all leading scholars like Hengel, Longenecker, Stanton, Wright, Hays, and Räisänen. [*RelSRev* 1/98, 1/03; *Them* Aut 01].

✓ Eastman, Susan. *Paul and the Person: Reframing Paul's Anthropology*, 2017. Clearly explains that human actors "are both captive and complicit" (111). [*ExpTim* 6/18; *CBQ* 10/18; *JETS* 6/18; *SJT* 72.2; *JSNT* 40.5; *Them* 44.3]. Decades ago, we had Robin Scruggs, *The Last Adam: A Study in Pauline Anthropology* (1966).

✓ Elliott, Neil. ‡ *Liberating Paul: The Justice of God and the Politics of the Apostle*, 1994; *The Arrogance of the Nations: Reading Romans in the Shadow of the Empire* (PCC) 2008. More important political readings of Paul. [*RelSRev* 12/10].

✓ Ellis, E. E. *Paul's Use of the Old Testament*, 1957. A significant signpost. See also his *Pauline Theology: Ministry and Society* (1989) [*WTJ* Fall 91; *CRBR* 1991].

✓ Evans, Craig A., and Aaron W. White, eds. *Who Created Christianity? Fresh Approaches to the Relationship between Paul and Jesus* [D. Wenham FS], 2020. [*ExpTim* 10/21].

☆ Fee, Gordon. *God's Empowering Presence: The Holy Spirit in the Letters of Paul*, 1994. A great book. The prolific Pauline scholar produced a massive study (960pp.) on a neglected topic. There is a definite but moderate Pentecostal slant to this theological work, but in saying that I do not take away from its value. Some of Fee's views (e.g., Spirit-baptism at conversion), if adopted more broadly within his own tradition, could help heal some of the alienation between Pentecostals/charismatics and other evangelicals. The general conclusions of the book are helpful and biblical, because they are drawn through careful exegesis. [*CBQ* 10/95; *RTR* 9/95; *JETS* 9/97; *JBL* Spr 97; *Int* 7/97; *Chm* 111.1].

☆ Fee, Gordon. *Pauline Christology: An Exegetical-Theological Study*, 2007. It is thrilling to see a high Christology developed in a book-by-book study of this quality and thoroughness. That being said, many disagree with his contention that Paul does not use θεός to refer to Christ; cf. Murray Harris's exegesis of Rom 9:5 and Titus 2:13 in *Jesus as God* (1992). On other key points, he rejects a "wisdom Christology" and unfortunately misrepresents complementarian arguments regarding the Son's functional subordination (better "submission," according to Letham). [*RTR* 12/08; *BBR* 19.1; *CBQ* 10/07; *JETS* 6/08; *TJ* Fall 08; *Int* 1/09 (Martin); *WTJ* Spr 09; *ExpTim* 4/08; *RelSRev* 9/08; *BL* 2009; *SBET* Spr 09].

✓ Fitzmyer, Joseph A. ‡ *Paul and His Theology*, 2nd ed. 1989. [*JETS* 6/92; *EvQ* 7/89]. Goes hand in hand with his commentary on Romans and *According to Paul: Studies in the Theology of the Apostle* (1993).

✓ Francis, Fred O., and J. Paul Sampley. ‡ *Pauline Parallels*, 2nd ed. 1984. This synopsis is meant to aid students in recognizing the repetition of phraseology, themes, and images in the Pauline corpus. (No Pastorals here.) See Wilson below.

✓ Fredriksen, Paula. ‡ *Paul: The Pagans' Apostle*, 2017. [*ExpTim* 12/20, 10/21; *BBR* 29.1; *Int* 4/19; *Them* 44.2].

✓ Furnish, Victor Paul. ‡ *Theology and Ethics in Paul*, 1968, (NTL) 2009. A standard work on the issue of Pauline ethics [*JSNT* 33.5], accompanied by *The Moral Teaching of Paul: Selected Issues* (1979, 3rd ed. 2009) [*BL* 2010; *ExpTim* 9/10]. On the same subject, see also *Understanding Paul's Ethics*, ed. Rosner (1995); *Theology and Ethics in Paul and His Interpreters* (Furnish FS), eds. Lovering–Sumney (1996); and Nijay Gupta, "The Theo-Logic of Paul's Ethics in Recent Research," *CBR* 7.3 (2009): 336–61. Recommended for NT ethics more generally are Richard Hays's standard, *The Moral Vision of the NT* (1996), and Richard Burridge on *Imitating Jesus: An Inclusive Approach to NT Ethics* (2007) [*BL* 2009; *SJT* 63.3 (review discussion); *SBET* Spr 09].

☆ Gathercole, Simon. *Defending Substitution: An Essay on Atonement in Paul*, 2015. Precise and concise argument (approx. 120pp.). [*Chm* Win 17; *ExpTim* 7/18; *WTJ* Spr 16; *CTJ* 11/18; *BBR* 26.4; *CBQ* 7/16; *JTS* 4/16; *JETS* 9/16; *JSNT* 38.5; *Them* 40.3]. An earlier, significant essay was D. A. Carson, "Atonement in Romans 3:21–26," in Hill–James, ed., *The Glory of the Atonement* (2004).

✓ Gombis, Timothy G. *Power in Weakness: Paul's Transformed Vision for Ministry*, 2021. Discusses "Paul's biography and theology as a springboard to practical application and as a basis for critique of the church today . . . which often emphasizes, ironically, power and credentials" (Brookins [*CBQ* 7/22]). [*JSNT* 43.5].

☆ Gorman, Michael J. [𝓜], *Apostle of the Crucified Lord*, 2004, 2nd ed. 2017. A full (700pp.), very influential study of Paul, focused mainly on theology. One may term this a conservatively critical content-oriented survey. (He is a Methodist teaching at a Catholic institution.) Without question, Gorman is one of the world's most cited scholars when it comes to Pauline theology. [*Them* Aut 04; *Int* 7/04; *CTJ* 11/04; *RTR* 4/05; *BL* 2005; *SJT* 59.4; *Evangel* Spr 05 (Marshall); *Anvil* 21.3; *DenvJ* 6/04; *CBQ* 10/18; *JTS* 10/19; *JSNT* 40.5]. Also by Gorman are *Cruciformity: Paul's Narrative Spirituality of the Cross* (2001) and *Inhabiting the Cruciform God: Kenosis, Justification, and Theosis in Paul's Narrative Soteriology* (2009) [*BTB* 5/11; *TJ* Fall 12]. By *theosis* he means "transformation into the image of the kenotic, cruciform God" (2009: 161). Further, he argues "that inherent within the very notion of reconciliation/justification are both participation and transformation" (163). More recent are *Becoming the Gospel: Paul, Participation, and Mission* (2015) [*Them* 8/15; *BBR* 26.3; *CBQ* 10/16; *JETS* 12/16; *Int* 10/16; *ETL* 94.2; *JSNT* 39.5] and *Participating in Christ: Explorations in Paul's Theology and Spirituality* (2019) [*CBQ* 7/20; *Int* 10/22; *JTS* 10/21; *JSNT* 42.5; *RevExp* 8/20; *Them* 46.1].

✓ Gray, Patrick. [𝓜], *Paul as a Problem in History and Culture: The Apostle and His Critics through the Centuries*, 2016. The animus in history makes for sobering reading.

✓ Gupta, Nijay. [𝓜], *Paul and the Language of Faith*, 2020. Challenges historic Protestant thinking. "Paul does not intend for πίστις to refer to nonwork, a kind of passive reliance on Christ" (143). [*ExpTim* 10/20; *BBR* 30.3; *JTS* 4/21; *JETS* 12/20; *Int* 10/22; *EvQ* 92.2; *WTJ* Spr 24]. Expect more work to be done, building on Gupta, and especially on Teresa Morgan's research on the whole NT in *Roman Faith and Christian Faith* (2015) [*Int* 1/18; *Them* 40.3] and *The NT and the Theology of Trust* (2022). A classic is Schlatter, *Faith in the NT* (1885, ET 2022) [*JSNT* 45.5; *WTJ* Fall 23].

✓ Gupta, Nijay. [𝓜], *Worship That Makes Sense to Paul: A New Approach to the Theology and Ethics of Paul's Cultic Metaphors*, 2011. Developed from his Durham PhD.

F Gupta, Nijay K., Erin M. Heim, and Scot McKnight, eds. *The State of Pauline Studies*, 2024. I expect it will be required reading for grad students.

✓ Harink, Douglas. [𝓜], *Paul among the Postliberals*, 2003. Much discussed.

✓ Harrill, J. A. ‡ *Paul the Apostle: His Life and Legacy in Their Roman Context*, 2012. [*JTS* 10/15].

✓ Hays, Richard B. ‡ *Echoes of Scripture in the Letters of Paul*, 1989. One of my favorite inter-textual studies on any portion of Scripture. The follow-up book, *The Conversion of the Imagination: Paul as an Interpreter of Israel's Scripture* (2005), is also very stimulating [*RTR* 12/05; *JETS* 3/07; *Them* 4/06; *BL* 2006; *NovT* 49.3; *Evangel* Spr 07].

✓ Heilig, Christoph. ‡ *Hidden Criticism? The Methodology and Plausibility of the Search for a Counter-Imperial Subtext in Paul*, 2015. Yes, as Heilig argues, political readings can be overdone. [*Int* 1/21; *JSNT* 38.5]. His distillation is *The Apostle and the Empire* (2022) [*WTJ* Fall 23]. See also D. Clint Burnett, *Paul & Imperial Divine Honors* (2024).

✓ Hengel, Martin, and Roland Deines. ‡ *The Pre-Christian Paul*, ET 1991. More conservatively critical. Later comes Hengel and Schwemer, *Paul between Damascus and Antioch* (1997).

✓ Hewitt, J. Thomas. *Messiah and Scripture: Paul's 'In Christ' Idiom in its Ancient Jewish Context*, 2020. A scholarly argument that the phrase "is Paul's messianic adaptation of an idiom borrowed from scriptural traditions concerning Abraham's seed (see Gal. 3.14–19), an adaptation which was part of a Jewish interpretive phenomenon which identified Abraham's seed with that of David and so with the messiah" (Williams [*JSNT* 43.5]).

✓ Hill, Wesley. *Paul and the Trinity: Persons, Relations, and the Pauline Letters*, 2015. A much-discussed Durham PhD, challenging how "Paul's God talk" has been conceptualized by leading scholars. Specifically, Hill critiques the "christological model" (with its designations "high" and "low" christology) that has largely replaced the old "trinitarian model," and he means to retrieve in the latter model "the element of the 'relations' that obtain between the trinitarian 'persons'" (1) for the sake of more faithful Pauline exegesis. [*WTJ* Spr 16; *CBQ* 7/16; *JETS* 12/15; *JSNT* 38.5, *Them* 41.1 (Schreiner)].

✓ Hooker, M. D., and S. G. Wilson, eds. ‡ *Paul and Paulinism*, 1982. This FS for C. K. Barrett, though dated, has a wealth of essays.

✓ Horrell, David G. ‡ *Introduction to the Study of Paul*, 3rd ed. 2015. Without question, outstanding as a succinct critical introduction. His treatment of Pauline ethics is *The Making of Christian Morality* (2019) [*JSNT* 42.5].

✓ Horsley, Richard A., ed. ‡ *Paul and Empire: Religion and Power in Roman Imperial Society*, 1997; *Paul and Politics: Ekklesia, Israel, Imperium, Interpretation* (Stendahl FS), 2000. Helpful for understanding the newer political readings of Paul.

✓ Hubbard, Moyer V. *New Creation in Paul's Letters and Thought*, 2002. From CUP.

   Hunter, A. M. [𝓜], *Paul and His Predecessors*, 1961. Also worth noting is Hunter's *The Gospel According to St. Paul*, 1967.

✓ Irons, Charles Lee. *The Righteousness of God: A Lexical Examination of the Covenant-Faithfulness Interpretation*, 2015. [*JETS* 3/16; *JSNT* 38.5].

✓ Jackson, T. Ryan. *New Creation in Paul's Letters*, 2010. [*JSNT* 33.5; *Them* 5/11; *BibInt* 20.4; *RelSRev* 3/11]. Compare Hubbard.

✓ Jervis, L. Ann. [𝓜], *Paul and Time: Life in the Temporality of Christ*, 2023. Fills a real hole in scholarship by considering Paul's statements regarding time, from the vantage point of union with Christ. Only moderately critical.

☆ Jipp, Joshua W. *Christ Is King: Paul's Royal Ideology*, 2015. An important conservative work, actually from Fortress. [*JETS* 6/18; *CBQ* 4/20; *Them* 43.1]. See, too, the well-received *Pauline Theology as a Way of Life* (2023). Compare Hubbard.

✓ Johnson, Luke Timothy. ‡ *The Canonical Paul.* Vol. 1: *Constructing Paul*, 2020; Vol. 2: *Interpreting Paul*, 2021. The two-vol. set, a tour de force, comes from a most stimulating, conservatively critical American Catholic scholar, who accepts all thirteen epistles as authentic. [2020: *ETL* 12/22; *Int* 1/22; *WTJ* Fall 22; *RevExp* 11/21; *BBR* 31.1; *CBQ* 1/21; *JTS* 4/21; *JETS* 3/21; 2021: *BBR* 31.4; *Int* 10/22; *JTS* 4/24].

✓ Käsemann, E. ‡ *Perspectives on Paul*, ET 1971. Brilliant, most provocative. The author built on Schweitzer and launched the "Apocalyptic Perspective" on Paul that Beker, Martyn, de Boer, and Hays (to some degree) develop. As important as any of these essays is "'The Righteousness of God' in Paul," in *NT Questions Today* (ET 1969).

✓ Keck, Leander. ‡ *Christ's First Theologian: The Shape of Paul's Thought*, 2015. [*Int* 1/18; *JSNT* 38.5].

✓ Keener, Craig S. *The Mind of the Spirit: Paul's Approach to Transformed Thinking*, 2016. [*Int* 1/10].

✓ Kim, Seyoon. *The Origin of Paul's Gospel*, 1981, 2nd ed. 2002. To characterize this as a mere restatement of Machen would be unfair. Though pursuing the same questions and coming to similar conclusions, Kim stands in its own right as an immensely learned and valuable work: best book on the subject. [*EvQ* 7/82; *JBL* 103.1]. He critically addresses the Sanders and Dunn theses in *Paul and the New Perspective* (2001) [*JTS* 4/04 (Dunn); *RTR* 12/02; *Them* Sum 03; *CTJ* 4/03; *JETS* 3/03; *JBL* Spr 03; *Int* 4/03; *ExpTim* 8/03; *EvQ* 7/05; *BibInt* 13.1; *DenvJ* 1/02; *Anvil* 20.3].

☆ Kruse, Colin G. *Paul, the Law, and Justification*, 1997. [*JETS* 9/99; *RTR* 8/98].

✓ Laird, Benjamin P. *The Pauline Corpus in Early Christianity: Its Formation, Publication, and Circulation*, 2022. [*JETS* 3/24].

✓ Lau, Te-Li. *Defending Shame: Its Formative Power in Paul's Letters*, 2020. A wise, nuanced treatment of the topic, detailing how shame can be proper and ultimately lead to positive ends in the gospel. [*Presb* Fall 21; *BBR* 31.2; *CBQ* 4/21; *JETS* 6/21; *Int* 1/22; *JSNT* 43.5; *Them* 45.2]. Cf. Jackson Wu, *Reading Romans with Eastern Eyes: Honor and Shame in Paul's Message and Mission* (2019) [*JETS* 6/20].

✓ Litfin, Duane. *Paul's Theology of Preaching*, 1994, rev. 2015. [*JSNT* 38.5].

✓ Longenecker, Bruce W. [𝓜], *Remember the Poor: Paul, Poverty, and the Greco-Roman World*, 2010. [*JTS* 4/12; *Int* 4/12; *JSNT* 34.5; *JETS* 6/12; *RevExp* Sum 12; *BTB* 5/12; *RelSRev* 9/14; *TJ* Spr 12; *BSB* 3/12].

✓ Longenecker, Bruce W., ed. *Narrative Dynamics in Paul: A Critical Assessment*, 2002. An important and high-level discussion, no matter what you think about the value of examining narrative aspects of Paul's thought. Superb! [*ExpTim* 10/04; *Evangel* Spr 05].

✓ Longenecker, Bruce W., ed. ‡ *The New Cambridge Companion to Saint Paul*, 2020. So useful for tracking with current scholarship! See the earlier *Cambridge Companion*, edited by Dunn. [*ELT* 6/22].

✓ Longenecker, Bruce W., and Todd D. Still. [𝓜], *Thinking through Paul: An Introduction to His Life, Letters, and Theology*, 2014. A fine textbook from two prominent Paulinists, which makes concessions to critical scholarship. [*BBR* 25.1; *Chm* Spr 15; *JSNT* 37.5; *Them* 8/15; *JETS* 9/15].

✓ Longenecker, Richard N. *Paul, Apostle of Liberty*, 1964, 2nd ed. 2015. The new edition adds a long essay. [*JSNT* 38.5]. This prolific scholar (†2021) at McMaster had other works on Paul, including his collected *Studies in Paul: Exegetical and Theological* (2004) [*ExpTim* 12/06; *BSac* 1/09]. A fine vol. of essays edited by Longenecker is *The Road from Damascus: The Impact of Paul's Conversion on His Life, Thought and Ministry* (1997) [*DenvJ*]. See his NIGTC on Romans.

✓ Macaskill, Grant. [𝓜], *Union with Christ in the New Testament*, 2013. Outstanding! In this OUP work Macaskill, a prof at Aberdeen, had the benefit of interacting with Con Campbell, but his subject is broader, not just Paul. He emphasizes (overemphasizes?) a covenant basis for union, offering a critique of apocalyptic readings of Paul, as well as Gorman's *theosis* proposal. [*BBR* 24.2; *JTS* 4/15; *ExpTim* 4/15; *Them* 4/14; *SBET* Aut 14; *WTJ* Fall 15; *SJT* 70.1]. The follow-up is *Living in Union with Christ: Paul's Gospel and Christian Moral Identity* (2019) [*CTJ* 11/21; *Int* 7/21; *JSNT* 42.5]. The critique of apocalyptic readings is genially carried further in "History, Providence, and the Apocalyptic Paul," *SJT* 70.4 (2017): 409–26.

Machen, J. Gresham. *The Origin of Paul's Religion*, 1921. Conservative classic.

✓ Malina, Bruce J., and Jerome H. Neyrey. ‡ *Portraits of Paul*, 1996. [*JETS* 6/99].

✓ Malina, Bruce J., and John J. Pilch. ‡ *Social-Science Commentary on the Letters of Paul*, 2006. [*Int* 10/06; *SwJT* Fall 05; *BL* 2007; *BTB* Sum 07; *Them* 5/08].

☆ Marshall, I. Howard, Stephen Travis, and Ian Paul. *Exploring the NT, Vol 2: The Letters and Revelation*, 2002, 2nd ed. 2011. An attractive survey from Britain with a great deal of learning behind it. [*Evangel* Sum 04].

✓ Martin, Ralph P. [𝓜], *Reconciliation: A Study of Paul's Theology*, 1981.

✓ Martyn, J. Louis. ‡ *Theological Issues in the Letters of Paul*, 1997. [*JTS* 4/99; *RelSRev* 4/00; *ThTo* 1/99; *CBQ* 10/98]. See also his work on Galatians.

✓ Matera, Frank J. ‡ *God's Saving Grace: A Pauline Theology*, 2012. [*JETS* 3/14; *BTB* 45.3].

✓ Matlock, R. Barry. *Unveiling the Apocalyptic Paul: Paul's Interpreters and the Rhetoric of Criticism*, 1996. An early critique of Beker, Martyn, and others. [*JTS* 10/97].

✓ McKnight, Scot, and Joseph B. Modica, eds. *The Apostle Paul and the Christian Life: Ethical and Missional Implications of the New Perspective* (2016).

✓ McKnight, Scot, and B. J. Oropeza, eds. *Perspectives on Paul: Five Views*, 2020. More of a focus on soteriology, with contributions by Barclay, Dunn, Das, Pitre, and Zetterholm. [*ExpTim* 2/21; *JETS* 6/22; *CBQ* 1/22].

McRay, John. *Paul: His Life and Teaching*, 2003. A conservative survey. [*Them* Aut 04; *JETS* 9/04; *CTJ* 11/04; *RelSRev* 1/05; *DenvJ* (negative)].

✓ Meeks, W. A. ‡ *The First Urban Christians, The Social World of the Apostle Paul*, 1983. Helped launch the social-scientific approach to Paul. Scholars reflect on the project in *After the First Urban Christians* (2009), eds. Still–Horrell [*JSNT* 33.5; *RelSRev* 12/10].

☆ Morgan, Christopher W., and Robert A. Peterson. *The Glory of God and Paul: Texts, Themes and Theology* (NSBT) 2022. Given the prominence of the theme in Paul (δόξα and δοξάζω appear 21× in Romans alone), I've been waiting for such studies. It is more a survey, however, and whets the appetite for more. [*JETS* 3/23]. See also Berry under Romans.

✓ Moser, Paul K. *Paul's Gospel of Divine Self-Sacrifice: Righteous Reconciliation in Reciprocity*, 2002. The intriguing argument of this CUP issue is that (a) God brings salvation to humanity in a display of divine righteousness, (b) this salvation involves the gift of a righteous self-sacrifice in Jesus, and (c) human beings must respond to divine self-sacrifice with a sacrificial attitude themselves, toward God (Rom 12:1) and in their other relationships. [*ExpTim* 1/23].

✓ Moyise, Steve. [𝓜], *Paul and Scripture: Studying the NT Use of the OT*, 2010. An expert in the burgeoning field gives valuable help to students (160pp.), taking them much further than one might expect from an introduction. I find it helpful to read Moyise and the more conservative Beale alongside each other. See also Porter–Stanley below. [*NovT* 53.4; *EvQ* 1/12; *CBQ* 1/12; *Int* 1/12; *JETS* 6/11; *Them* 11/10; *SBET* Aut 11; *RelSRev* 9/11].

✓ Munck, J. ‡ *Paul and the Salvation of Mankind*, ET 1959.

✓ Murphy-O'Connor, Jerome. ‡ *Paul: A Critical Life*, 1996. [*HBT* 6/98; *RelSRev* 7/97; *JR* 1/98]. His shorter, more engaging, and accessible work is *Paul, His Story* (OUP, 2004). It is rather imaginative too: Saul born about 6 BC to Galilean parents (per the tradition in St. Jerome) who were sold as slaves.

✓ Neyrey, J. H. ‡ *Paul in Other Words*, 1990.

✓ Novenson, Matthew V. [𝓜], *Paul, Then and Now*, 2022. Important essays from the Edinburgh prof.

✓ Novenson, Matthew V., and R. Barry Matlock, eds. ‡ *The Oxford Handbook of Pauline Studies*, 2022. Superb team of essayists assembled! [*Int* 10/22; *JETS* 6/23 (Jipp); *ETL* 9/23].

✓ O'Brien, Peter T. *Gospel and Mission in the Writings of Paul*, 1995.

Pate, C. Marvin. *Apostle of the Last Days: The Life, Letters, and Theology of Paul*, 2013. Argues that an apocalyptic eschatology is the center of his theology. [*Them* 11/14; *ExpTim* 8/15].

✓ Perrin, Nicholas, and Richard B. Hays, eds. *Jesus, Paul, and the People of God: A Theological Dialogue with N. T. Wright*, 2011. From a Wheaton conference. Vanhoozer suggests, echoing F. D. Maurice, that Wright is often right in what he affirms and wrong in what he denies. [*ExpTim* 4/12; *BTB* 5/12]. Two exegetical defenses of penal substitution are I. Howard Marshall's *Aspects of the Atonement* (2008) and Gathercole above.

Pervo, Richard I. ‡ *The Making of Paul: Constructions of the Apostle in Early Christianity*, 2010. A quite critical accounting, about 25 years in the making. [*JTS* 10/11; *RBL* 2011].

Phillips, Thomas E. ‡ *Paul, His Letters, and Acts*, 2009. [*RelSRev* 3/11].

✓ Pitre, Brant, Michael P. Barber, and John A. Kincaid. [𝓜], *Paul, A New Covenant Jew: Rethinking Pauline Theology*, 2019. An important, more conservatively critical, Catholic work, seeking the fuller significance of Paul's background in Judaism. [*JETS* 3/21; *SJT* 74.1; *JSNT* 42.5].

☆ Polhill, J. B. *Paul and His Letters*, 1999. A fine, fairly comprehensive evangelical textbook using a historical approach to reviewing Paul's life, labors, and letters. More up-to-date than Bruce and worth buying. [*DenvJ*].

☆ Porter, Stanley E. *The Apostle Paul: His Life, Thought, and Letters*, 2016. One of the best surveys now available (approx. 450pp.), less concentrated than Bruce on biography. [*Int* 1/10; *JSNT* 39.5; *DenvJ* 1/17].

✓ Porter, Stanley E., ed. *The Pauline Canon*, 2004. From Brill's Pauline Studies series [*EuroJTh* 17.1], which includes more Porter-edited books: *Paul and His Opponents* (2005); *Paul and His Theology* (2006) [*EuroJTh* 18.2; *ExpTim* 7/12]; *Paul's World* (2008) [*BL* 2009; *ExpTim* 6/09; *Them* 5/11]; *Paul: Jew, Greek, and Roman* (2008) [*BTB* 8/10; *BL* 2010; *JTS* 10/11; *RelSRev* 9/10]; *Paul and His Social Relations* (2013) [*JSNT* 36.5; *BTB* 11/14]; and *Paul and Gnosis* (2016) [*Them* 42.1]. Also worth noting is Porter's *Paul in Acts* (1999, 2001) [*RTR* 12/03; *SwJT* Fall 03; *Int* 4/03].

✓ Porter, S. E., and S. A. Adams, eds. *Paul and the Ancient Letter Form*, 2010. Also from Brill's Pauline Studies series. [*Them* 11/10].

✓ Porter, Stanley E., and Bryan R. Dyer, eds. *Paul and Ancient Rhetoric: Theory and Practice in the Hellenistic Context*, 2016. [*JSNT* 39.5].

✓ Porter, S. E., and C. D. Stanley, eds. ‡ *As It Is Written: Studying Paul's Use of Scripture*, 2008. [*NovT* 52.2; *SBET* Spr 10; *BL* 2010; *BBR* 20.3]. Add to this Stanley, ed., *Paul and Scripture: Extending the Conversation* (2012) [*CBQ* 1/15; *JSNT* 36.5]; Porter–Land, eds., *Paul and Scripture* (2019) [*BBR* 30.1; *JTS* 4/21; *JSNT* 42.5]; and Porter–Frewster, eds., *Paul and Pseudepigraphy*, 2013. [*ExpTim* 1/19].

✓ Prothro, James B. *Both Judge and Justifier: Biblical Legal Language and the Act of Justifying*, 2018. A revised Cambridge PhD under Gathercole, skirting much of the NPP controversy to probe a more basic question: What is the act of justifying according to Paul? [*WTJ* Fall 21; *BBR* 31.1; *JETS* 3/19; *JSNT* 41.5; *Them* 44.1].

✓ Räisänen, Heikki. ‡ *Paul and the Law*, ET 1983, Rev. 2010. Contends strongly that Paul is inconsistent. [*JTS* 4/90; *TJ* Spr 84].

Ramsay, W. M. *St. Paul the Traveller and the Roman Citizen*, 1896, 1920.

✓ Richards, E. Randolph. *Paul and First Century Letter Writing*, 2004. Cf. Jerome Murphy-O'Connor, *Paul the Letter-Writer* (1995).

✓ Riesner, Rainer. [*M*], *Paul's Early Period: Chronology, Mission Strategy, Theology*, 1998. A conservatively critical work from a Tübingen scholar (colleague of Hengel and Stuhlmacher), having confidence in the reliability of Acts and the agreement of the Acts narratives with data derived from Paul's letters.

✓ Roetzel, Calvin. ‡ *The Letters of Paul*, 5th ed. 2009. A fine, critically oriented seminary textbook [*JSNT* 33.5]. Added to this is *Paul: The Man and the Myth* (1998) [*JR* 7/01].

✓ Rosner, Brian S. *Paul and the Law: Keeping the Commandments of God*, 2013. An IVP issue with an exegetical and biblical-theological approach to the topic, presenting something of a neo-Lutheran perspective [*Chm* Spr 14; *JETS* 6/14; *Them* 4/14; *SJT* 68.4; *Found* Aut 13].

✓ Rosner, B. S., A. S. Malone, and T. J. Burke, eds. *Paul as Pastor*, 2017. As one reviewer says, "a welcome contribution on an underappreciated aspect of Paul" [*ExpTim* 3/20]. [*JSNT* 41.5; *Them* 44.3]. See also Scot McKnight, *Pastor Paul* (2019) [*ExpTim* 3/20; *Presb* Fall 19].

✓ Sampley, J. Paul, ed. ‡ *Paul in the Greco-Roman World: A Handbook*, 2003, 2nd ed. 2 vols., 2016. "Exceedingly useful," said Proctor of Cambridge, especially for study of the intellectual culture of Paul's day. [*Anvil* 22.4; *BSac* 1/19; *JSNT* 39.5; *Them* 42.3].

✓ Sampley, J. Paul, and Peter Lampe, eds. *Paul and Rhetoric*, 2010. Important for specialists, but see the caution at the end of Darlington's review [*BBR* 23.4]. [*JSNT* 33.5; *ExpTim* 5/11; *RevExp* Sum 12; *RelSRev* 6/11]. Laying out the issues under debate is Michael F. Bird, "Reassessing a Rhetorical Approach to Paul's Letters," *ExpTim* 119 (2008): 374–79.

✓ Sanders, E. P. ‡ *Paul and Palestinian Judaism*, 1977. One of the two or three most important books on Paul in the last fifty years. Most basically, Sanders's contention is that scholarship long mischaracterized 1st century Palestinian Judaism as legalistic, without a theology of grace. By restudying the writings of Judaism, we are corrected to see there twin emphases on election by grace into the covenant and on law-keeping (covenantal nomism) for "staying in" covenant with God and in the covenant community. Sanders then interprets Paul against this backdrop, challenging the traditional understanding of Paul as opposing himself to "salvation by works." This seminal book is critiqued by Gundry [*Bib* 66.1] and others [*WTJ* Spr 82; *TJ* Spr 84; *JBL* 92.2, 104.3; *ThTo* 35.1]. Sanders followed up with *Paul, the Law, and the Jewish People* (1983) and *Paul* (1991), the latter reviewed by Wright [*JTS* 10/92]. Cf. Dunn's "New Perspective," which accepts Sanders's reading of Judaism but (mildly) critiques and revises his reading of Paul. The capstone of Sanders's career is the historically oriented 850-page introduction, *Paul: The Apostle's Life, Letters, and Thought* (Fortress, 2015) [*ExpTim* 9/16; *BBR* 28.3; *JTS* 4/17; *Int* 7/17], which has a dated feel and surprisingly (for a book its size) less interaction with other scholars.

✓ Schellenberg, Ryan S., and Heidi Wendt, eds. ‡ *T&T Clark Handbook to the Historical Paul*, 2022. [*ExpTim* 10/23; *CBQ* 1/24; *JTS* 4/24].

☆ Schnabel, Eckhard J. *Paul the Missionary: Realities, Strategies, and Methods*, 2008. Partially a distillation of his 2-vol. *Early Christian Mission*. How can anyone arrive at a fair, well-balanced understanding of this missionary and his thought without studying his mission work? [*JETS* 9/09; *Them* 7/10]. Cf. Burke and Rosner.

✓ Schnelle, Udo. ‡ *Apostle Paul: His Life and Theology*, 2003, ET 2005. A comprehensive and critically oriented reference work from a famous Halle prof. He doesn't consider Ephesians, Colossians, 2 Thessalonians, or the Pastorals to be Paul's. He delves more into the Hellenistic context of Paul's ministry and teaching. [*JETS* 9/06; *BL* 2007; *RelSRev* 3/08].

☆ Schreiner, Thomas R. *The Law and Its Fulfillment: A Pauline Theology of Law*, 1993. Well-done and comparable to Thielman above. [*TJ* Fall 94]. He also has a textbook: *Interpreting the Pauline Epistles* (2nd ed. 2011).

✓ Schweitzer, Albert. ‡ *The Mysticism of Paul the Apostle*, ET 1931. A riveting, if flawed, exposition of Paul's theology and ethics as deriving from a Jewish-Christian eschatological outlook (including an apocalyptic theology), with an emphasis on a mystical dying and rising with Christ. Justification by faith is a subsidiary aspect of the Apostle's gospel, not the core teaching, and depends upon union with Christ. Schweitzer writes (333), "The problem of the relation between redemption and ethics finds in his teaching a complete solution. Ethic is for him the necessary outward expression of the translation from the earthly world to the super-earthly, which has already taken place in the being-in-Christ." A more extreme idea here is the Christian's loss of "his creatively individual existence and his natural personality" (125).

✓ Scott, James M. ‡ *Adoption as Sons of God: An Exegetical Investigation into the Background of* ΥΙΟΘΕΣΙΑ *in the Pauline Corpus*, 1992. Further, Robert Brian Lewis, *Paul's 'Spirit of Adoption' in Its Roman Imperial Context* (2016) [*ExpTim* 6/17; *BSac* 1/20; *BBR* 27.1; *JTS* 10/17; *JSNT* 39.5] and Erin M. Heim's superb *Adoption in Galatians and Romans: Contemporary Metaphor Theories and the Pauline Huiothesia Metaphors* (2017) [*BibInt* 27.3, 28.3; *JSNT* 40.5; *Them* 42.3]. A theological approach to the once neglected topic is David Garner, *Sons in the Son* (2016) [*Chm* Sum 18].

☆ Seifrid, Mark. *Christ Our Righteousness: Paul's Theology of Justification*, 2000. This IVP issue on a controversial topic is recommended to students, building as it does on his expensive, high-level discussion in *Justification by Faith* (Brill, 1992). [*Chm* Spr 01].

✓ Seifrid, Mark, and Randall Tan. *The Pauline Writings* (IBR Bibliographies), 2002. Still instructive (nearly 250pp.). [*SBET* Spr 03; *RelSRev* 4/03; *BBR* 14.2; *EvQ* 1/05].

✓ Sprinkle, Preston. *Paul and Judaism Revisited*, 2013.

Stewart, J. S. *A Man in Christ: The Vital Elements of St. Paul's Religion*, 1935. Places great emphasis on Paul's phrase "in Christ" and the idea of mystical union with Christ. These emphases—strong in Calvin's interpretation of Paul too—are, in my opinion, the organizing key to Paul's soteriology: we are known, chosen, redeemed, and marked with the Holy Spirit only "in Christ" (Eph 1). This can often be picked up s/h.

✓ Stirewalt, M. Luther. ‡ *Paul: The Letter Writer*, 2003. [*JBL* Fall 04; *Int* 7/04; *CBQ* 4/06; *Evangel* Sum 04 (Marshall)].

✓ Stuhlmacher, Peter. [𝓜], *Revisiting Paul's Doctrine of Justification*, 2001. A vigorous Lutheran protest against the NPP. The author is an outstanding Tübingen scholar. [*JETS* 12/02; *TJ* Spr 03].

✓ Taylor, Walter. ‡ *Paul: Apostle to the Nations*, 2012. Critical introduction (310pp.).

✓ Terrell, Patricia Elyse. ‡ *Paul's Parallels: An Echoes Synopsis*, 2009. Arguably more helpful are Wilson's *Pauline Parallels* (2009), the older Francis–Sampley vol. above, and Ware's *Synopsis*. Note that Terrell is all English and quite lengthy (over 900pp.) because she serially sets down the whole Pauline corpus, Romans to Philemon, to note parallels. The drawbacks are the use of the AV and the tiny typeface.

✓ Thate, Michael J., Kevin J. Vanhoozer, and Constantine Campbell, eds. *"In Christ" in Paul: Explorations in Paul's Theology of Union and Participation*, 2014 (Eerdmans 2018). Includes evangelicals and critical scholars. [*Presb* Spr 19; *BSac* 10/19; *JSNT* 37.5; *Them* 8/15]. More recently, Oxford's Teresa Morgan has a revisionist proposal: *Being 'in Christ' in the Letters of Paul* (2020) [*JTS* 10/22 (Hooker)].

✓ Thiessen, Matthew. ‡ *Paul and the Gentile Problem*, 2016. Contends for a radical NPP: Paul addresses only gentiles. [*Int* 1/20]. The brief follow-up is *A Jewish Paul* (2023) [*WTJ* Spr 24].

☆ Thiselton, Anthony C. [𝓜], *The Living Paul: An Introduction to the Apostle and His Thought*, 2009. A gem. Accomplishes more than I thought possible in 175pp., if one is a student seeking to understand current scholarship and how we arrived here. [*JTS* 10/10; *Int* 1/12; *JSNT* 33.5; *RBL* 2011; *JETS* 6/11; *Them* 7/10; *DenvJ* 13; *SJT* 65.3].

✓ Thompson, James W. ‡ *Apostle of Persuasion: Theology and Rhetoric in the Pauline Letters*,

2020. This conservatively critical study "sketches both the individual rhetoric of various ... letters and the role this rhetoric plays in shaping Paul's theology" [*HBT* 44.2]. [*RevExp* 11/21; *ExpTim* 6/22; *CTJ* 4/21; *JETS* 6/21; *Int* 10/21; *JSNT* 43.5].

✓ Thompson, James W. ‡ *The Church according to Paul: Rediscovering the Community Conformed for Christ*, 2014. Valuable indeed, partly as a corrective for longstanding scholarly prejudices downplaying the ecclesial in Paul. [*WTJ* Fall 15; *Int* 10/16]. More recent and philosophical is Taylor Weaver, *The Scandal of Community* (2021) [*JSNT* 44.5]. Cf. this stress on the communal with Gary W. Burnett, *Paul and the Salvation of the Individual* (2001). See the balancing in Ben C. Dunson, *Individual and Community in Paul's Letter to the Romans* (2012) [*ETL* 91.4].

✓ Tilling, Chris. *Paul's Divine Christology*, 2012. More than a fine technical study, Tilling has had a major impact. This is quite an accomplishment for a PhD, first published in WUNT and now republished by Eerdmans (2015). [*CBQ* 10/14; *TJ* Spr 15; *Them* 11/12; *Int* 7/17; *JSNT* 35.5, 38.5]. See Fee above.

✓ Twelftree, Graham H. *Paul and the Miraculous*, 2013. What does one make of the contrast between a miracle-worker in Acts and Paul's self-presentation in the epistles, rarely raising the issue (e.g., 2 Cor 12:12)? [*BBR* 24.3].

☆ Vos, Geerhardus. *The Pauline Eschatology*, 1952. A classic by old Princeton's great biblical theologian that retains remarkable freshness. Amillennial. I heard it said that the brilliant (secularist) Robert Kraft of the U. of Pennsylvania believed Vos "got" Paul on the issue of imputation and justification better than anyone.

✓ Ware, James P., ed. *Synopsis of the Pauline Letters in Greek and English, Incorporating the Thirteen Pauline Letters and Passages of the Acts of the Apostles Pertaining to Paul*, 2010. Differs from other synopses by including the Greek and by organization. Romans is the base text and Ware places alongside the Romans segments other texts treating the same doctrines/themes (e.g., Prayer, Vice Lists, Wrath of God, New Exodus). See Terrell. Among all the synopses, I find I prefer using Ware and Wilson, each useful in different ways. [*CBQ* 10/12; *ExpTim* 6/11; *Them* 8/11; *RelSRev* 6/11].

✓ Wasserman, Emma. ‡ *Apocalypse as Holy War: Divine Politics and Polemics in the Letters of Paul*, 2018. [*JTS* 10/19 (Davies)].

✓ Watson, Francis. [*M*], *Paul and the Hermeneutics of Faith*, 2nd ed. 2015. A book of profound theology focused on Paul's own hermeneutic. We certainly have not thought enough about Paul as interpreter, as a consummate reader of Scripture. And when Martyn says it is "a stunning book," I take notice. [*CBQ* 7/06; *JTS* 10/05; *JETS* 3/06; *JBL* Fall 06; *Int* 1/07; *JR* 1/07; *Presb* Spr 10; review discussions in *JSNT* 3/06 and *SJT* 59.4].

✓ Watson, Francis. [*M*], *Paul, Judaism, and the Gentiles: Beyond the New Perspective*, rev. ed. 2007. [*BL* 2008; *JTS* 4/10; *Int* 4/09; *Presb* Spr 10; *Anvil* 26.3–4].

☆ Weima, Jeffrey A. D. *Paul the Ancient Letter Writer: An Introduction to Epistolary Analysis*, 2016. Dutch says, "This is a superb study, very readable, with engaging exegetical insights. It deserves to be read by scholars and students alike" [*JSNT* 39.5]. [*CBQ* 1/17; *JETS* 9/17; *RTR* 8/19]. See also Porter–Adams, and Stirewalt above.

✓ Wenham, David. *Paul: Follower of Jesus or Founder of Christianity?* 1995. [*Presb* Fall 95; *TJ* Fall 95; *JBL* Win 96; *HBT* 12/95]. A more recent academic approach to the question is Gerry Schoberg, *Perspectives of Jesus in the Writing of Paul: A Historical Examination of Shared Core Commitments with a View to Determining the Extent of Paul's Dependence on Jesus* (2013) [*JTS* 4/15; *JSNT* 36.5].

✓ Wenham, David. *Paul and Jesus: The True Story*, 2002. Follows Paul's life, journeys, and what he taught the churches. The author long taught at Wycliffe Hall, Oxford.

✓ Westerholm, Stephen. [*M*], *Perspectives Old and New on Paul: The "Lutheran" Paul and His*

*Critics*, 2004. Updates and expands his well-received *Israel's Law and the Church's Faith* (1988)—among the best, most judicious of the early studies of Paul's theology of the Law and the upheaval over the topic. Of course, scholarship has travelled some distance since 1988, and Westerholm has made his contribution more current with *Perspectives*. [*Them* Aut 04; *Int* 10/04; *TJ* Fall 04; *EvQ* 7/05; *RTR* 4/05; *JETS* 3/05; *BL* 2005; *SJT* 60.4; *ExpTim* 1/07; *CurTM* 10/05; *Anvil* 21.4]. For a Westerholm introduction see *Understanding Paul* (2004) [*Evangel* Spr 07 (Oakes)] and the accessible, brief *Justification Reconsidered* (2013) [*WTJ* Fall 14; *JSNT* 36.5; *JETS* 6/14; *CBQ* 7/15; *BSac* 4/18].

✓  Westerholm, Stephen, ed. [𝔐], *The Blackwell Companion to Paul*, 2011. [*CBQ* 4/13; *JTS* 10/12; *JSNT* 34.5; *RelSRev* 9/14].

✓  Westfall, Cynthia Long. *Paul and Gender*, 2016. [*BSac* 10/18].

✓  Wilson, Walter T. *Pauline Parallels: A Comprehensive Guide*, 2009. Treats all 13 epistles in the Pauline corpus, using the NASB. The whole corpus is serially set out, Romans to Philemon, with linguistic/thematic parallels drawn alongside. He also includes a smaller selection of Non-Canonical Parallels (Apocrypha, Philo, Qumran, Plutarch, etc.). See Terrell and Ware. [*BL* 2010; *ExpTim* 3/11].

F  Winter, Bruce W. *The Pauline Corpus against Its Environment*.

✓  Witherington, Ben, III. *Paul's Narrative Thought World*, 1994. Praised by many scholars, but see Spencer's review [*JETS* 12/96]. [*CBQ* 1/96; *HBT* 6/95; *SBET* Spr 97]. Note also his book *The Paul Quest: The Renewed Search for the Jew of Tarsus* (1998) [*ScrB* 7/99; *Chm* Spr 05; *DenvJ*], updated as Witherington–Myers, *Voices and Views on Paul* (2020) [*JSNT* 43.5].

✓  Wolter, Michael. ‡ *Paul: An Outline of His Theology*, ET 2015. Times change. Germans once dominated Pauline studies. That is no longer true, but this vol. is valuable indeed for students interested in current German scholarship. The Bonn prof. Wolter is well-acquainted with Anglophone scholarship too. One should welcome this Baylor U. Press issue. [*ExpTim* 7/16; *CBQ* 1/20; *JETS* 6/17; *Int* 10/16; *ETL* 94.2; *JSNT* 38.5].

✓  Wright, N. T. [𝔐], *The Climax of the Covenant: Christ and the Law in Pauline Theology*, 1991. Essays well worth reading. Exemplifying the exegetical value here is his discussion of Phil 2 on pp.56–98. Wright has been a heavy-hitter among critical evangelical scholars. Many are concerned because here and elsewhere he seems to recast the whole doctrine of justification in ecclesiological terms: it's about who counts as belonging to the people of God. Justification is not about soteriology, how the individual gets saved. Hearing Wright deny penal substitution and imputation, his critics have jumped to defend the Reformation stress on justification as involving imputed righteousness. [*JTS* 10/93; *ThTo* 1/94; *JETS* 12/96]. For an updated exposition of his brand of the NPP, see his "Romans" in NIB and *Paul: Fresh Perspectives*, 2005 [*BL* 2006; *RelSRev* 9/08], titled *Paul: In Fresh Perspective* on the North American side. His answer to his critics—in particular Piper's *The Future of Justification* (2007) [*Chm* Win 09; *EQ* 7/09]—is *Justification: God's Plan and Paul's Vision* (2009) [*EQ* 7/10; *ExpTim* 3/10; *DenvJ* 5/09; *BL* 2010; *Int* 10/10; *BSac* 10/13; *BTB* 5/11; *SJT* 65.3]. See Perrin–Hays above.

✓  Wright, N. T. [𝔐], *Paul and the Faithfulness of God*, 2 vols., 2013. A masterful, grand synthesis of all Wright's work on Paul, encompassing historical research and an exegetically based Pauline theology (about 1600pp.). He seeks "to rethink from the ground up all kinds of previously held views about Paul, his worldview, his theology, and his aims" (61). This set marks a continuation of his Christian Origins series, which began with three vols. on Jesus, then skipped over the Jerusalem beginnings of the church in order to treat Paul. Among reviews I recommend Gathercole's online. [*CBQ* 4/15; *JTS* 4/15 (Dunn); *Int* 7/15; *JSNT* 36.5; *JETS* 3/15; *Them* 4/14; *Anvil* 3/15; *SJT* 68.2 (Barclay); *RTR* 4/14; *SJT* 69.4]. See also *Pauline Perspectives: Essays on Paul 1978–2013* [*JSNT* 36.5; *Chm* Aut 14; *SJT* 69.3]; *Paul and His Recent Interpreters* (2014) [*JETS* 9/16; *Them* 41.1]; and *The Paul Debate* (2016) [*ExpTim* 11/17; *JSNT* 38.5; *Them* 41.1].

☆ Wright, Tom (N. T.). [𝓜], *Paul: A Biography*, 2018. The field of useful, historically well-informed biographies of Paul is not large, and this is one of the best.

✓ Yates, John W. *The Spirit and Creation in Paul*, 2008. "Paul's so-called 'soteriological pneumatology' is perhaps better understood within a wider framework of creation pneumatology." [*JETS* 12/09; *RBL* 6/10; *ExpTim* 4/10; *BL* 2010; *BBR* 21.2; *EQ* 10/10].

☆ Zetterholm, Magnus. ‡ *Approaches to Paul: A Student's Guide to Recent Scholarship*, 2009. [*JETS* 9/10].

NOTES: (1) Bruce Worthington, "Alternate Perspectives beyond the Perspectives," *CBR* 11.3 (2013): 366–87. (2) N. T. Wright, "Paul in Current Anglophone Scholarship," *ExpTim* 123 (2012): 367–81. (3) Michael M. C. Reardon, "Becoming God: Interpreting Pauline Soteriology as Deification," *CBR* 22.1 (2023): 83–107.

# ROMANS

★ Ash, Christopher. *Teaching Romans*, 2 vols., 2009. Marvelously good for preachers (approx. 600pp.). Students will of course pass this by and focus attention on academic heavyweights: Dunn, Fitzmyer, Jewett, Moo, etc.

★ **Cranfield, C. E. B.** [𝓜], (ICC-R) 2 vols., 1975–79. Magisterial! Indispensable for close exegesis. Though you may not agree with some conclusions (e.g., on 5:12ff. and ch. 9), he does lay out carefully all the options. Having read the entire work, I think it is among the best technical exegeses on any NT book. There is an abridgement in pb (1988), but without a treatment of the Greek. It makes Cranfield's conclusions available to a wider readership. Note that he wrote prior to the controversy over E. P. Sanders's thesis and Dunn's development of it. Only later did he respond (urging rejection of Dunn's view); see "'The Works of the Law' in the Epistle to the Romans," *JSNT* 43 (1991): 89–101, reprinted in the collection, *On Romans* (1998). [*RTR* 1/80; *TJ* Spr 80; *JETS* 12/86; *ThTo* 37.1]. If rigorous technical research is not your cup of tea, may I suggest Peterson or Garland?

★ **Kruse, Colin.** (Pillar-R) 2012. The series seeks "above all to make clear the text of Scripture as we have it, . . . [to] interact with the most important informed contemporary debate, but avoid getting mired in undue technical detail," and to blend "rigorous exegesis and exposition, with an eye alert both to biblical theology and to the contemporary relevance of the Bible" (Editor's Preface). Kruse stuck to that task and produced a full, yet manageable commentary for pastors (589pp.). Its strengths are readability, clarity, a to-the-point and level-headed weighing of exegetical options, and satisfying theological reflection (winsome Reformed theology). There is a gentle rather than combative spirit here, with reverence for God's word. If I were to voice a criticism, it would be that the exposition is not so enriched by historical theology (cf. Murray) or *historia salutis* insights (cf. Ridderbos). Kruse's conclusions tend to be traditional: he critiques the NPP in a measured fashion, reads 3:22 as "faith in Jesus Christ," believes ἱλαστήριον includes propitiation, and finds election of individuals, not corporate election, in ch. 9. The corporate "notion of election does not support an explanation of why some Jewish individuals accept the gospel while others do not, which is the reason Paul introduces it" (392). He says "all Israel" refers to the elect of ethnic Israel through time, not a future ingathering as a climactic development (Murray, Cranfield, Dunn, Moo), nor all elect Jews and gentiles composing a "New Israel" (Calvin, Barth, Wright). He replaced Morris. [*WTJ* Spr 13; *CBQ* 7/14; *JSNT* 35.5; *Chm* Win 13; *RTR* 4/13; *Them* 11/13 (Schreiner); *BSac* 10/13; *RelSRev* 9/14; *TJ* Fall 14; *RTR* 4/13; *JETS* 6/13; *Found* Spr 13].

★ **Longenecker, Richard N.** [𝓜], (NIGTC) 2016. Nearly two decades had passed after Moo's and Schreiner's first editions, and we lacked a top-notch, fully up-to-date, technical commentary from an evangelical. Longenecker (†2021) then delivered a 1150-page work, and the three scholars' Romans tomes could be compared. (Each also has a major exegesis of the Greek text of Galatians.) For students especially, Longenecker easily ends up on the recommended list. The foretaste was his 450-page *Introducing Romans* in 2011 [*EvQ* 1/13; *CBQ* 7/13; *JTS* 10/13; *JSNT* 34.5; *Presb* Spr 12; *JETS* 6/12; *ETL* 89.4; *Them* 11/11; *DenvJ* 15; *RTR* 8/15; *BSB* 12/12]. He prefers the subjective genitive understanding of πίστις Ἰησοῦ Χριστοῦ ("faithfulness of Jesus Christ"), accepts in a qualified way the NPP, and sees chs. 5–8 as the focus of the letter. The commentary opens with a 40-page bibliography, and a brief Introduction (39pp.) where he explains the distinctive features of his research. He analyzes what he believes to be the epistle's two models of argumentation: Greco-Roman protreptic discourse and Jewish "remnant" thought/rhetoric. Paul's two main purposes in writing were to communicate the "spiritual gift" of "my gospel" and to seek the Romans' support for the mission to Spain. He explores why Romans has such a high concentration of OT quotations and allusions. At the high point of Romans, ch. 8, he finds a blend of participationist themes ("in Christ," "in the Spirit") and apocalyptic elements. The ethical exhortations of chs. 12ff. are said to be based on the truth of union with Christ. Any weaknesses? Longenecker backs away from a robust doctrine of divine sovereignty and thinks election depends upon foreknowledge of who will receive God's promises by faith; for him human will is ultimately determinative. I fail to see how Paul's argument in ch. 9, under this interpretation, could ever raise the protest, "Is there injustice with God?" Pastors enjoy the sections of Biblical Theology and Contextualization for Today closing each text-unit. Theologians appreciate his attention to the history of interpretation, esp. the church fathers. Note that this NIGTC has less discussion of the Greek than I'd anticipated, and Moo is more up-to-date regarding the scholarship. [*Bib* 99.3; *ExpTim* 10/16; *Presb* Spr 17; *BSac* 10/18; *WTJ* Fall 16; *BBR* 27.1; *JTS* 4/17 (Moo); *JETS* 6/17; *Int* 7/18; *RTR* 12/17; *ETL* 94.2; *JSNT* 39.5; *Them* 43.3].

★ **Moo, Douglas.** (NICNT-R) 1996, 2nd ed. 2018. Replaced Murray and can be regarded as a wise first choice. A large work (1000pp.) that shows shrewd exegetical judgment and understands the theology of the epistle. It was everything I expected when Eerdmans announced that Moo's WEC—noted below—would be reworked for the NICNT series. His conclusions are basically in line with classic Reformed theology (a neo-Lutheran tinge here and there), except his interpretation of ch. 7. He appreciates the importance of union with Christ for interpreting Paul's argument, for example, in ch. 6. I value Moo and Schreiner both for interacting with the Sanders thesis and Dunn's New Perspective. See Moo's NIVAC below, which is also a wise purchase—having both NICNT and NIVAC is not a waste of money or shelf space. In the 2nd edition he changed his mind "on relatively few points of exegesis or theology" (xv), but there is updating throughout. [*Them* 6/00; *JETS* 12/98; *Bib* 78.3; *CBQ* 4/98; *RTR* 9/97; *BSac* 4/98; *JTS* 10/98; *ExpTim* 3/19; *JSNT* 41.5; *WTJ* Fall 20; *CTJ* 4/21]. It is fascinating to compare with Longenecker and Thielman.

★ **Schreiner, Thomas R.** (BECNT) 1998, 2nd ed. 2018. Represents a thorough revision; Schreiner has changed his mind on some key topics. These include righteousness as consistently, exclusively forensic, and the "I" in ch. 7 expressing the Christian's experience. There is interaction with the flood of major studies on Romans over the last two decades. In my opinion this BECNT is an improvement over the 1st edition and definitely deserves to be on pastors' shelves. Many continue, however, to disagree with his "progressive covenantalism" and statements such as this in his *40 Questions about Christians and Biblical Law*: "Paul argues that the entirety of the law has been set aside now that Christ has come. To say that the 'moral' elements of the law continue to be authoritative blunts the truth that the entire Mosaic covenant is no longer in force for believers." See Schreiner's books under Pauline Studies and Galatians. [*Them* 11/99; *Bib* 81.3; *Int* 7/99; *CTJ* 4/01; *DenvJ*; *WTJ* Fall 20; *Int* 10/19].

★ Stott, John. (BST) 1994. Excellent and can be found in both hb and pb. Stott's conclusions are usually in line with conservative Reformed thought (see the cruxes at 5:12ff.; chs. 7, 9, and 11); at the same time, there is a freshness about his exposition which makes it attractive. Thorough and clear at 400pp., with more exegesis than expected in BST. [*Them* 2/98; *JETS* 3/98; *Chm* 109.3]. For more help with exposition, see Boice, Calvin, Hughes, Keller, Lloyd-Jones, Moo (NIVAC), and Philip. From the Arminian side, Osborne is attractive.

★ **Thielman, Frank S.** (ZECNT) 2018. From a veteran Pauline scholar who wrote *Ephesians* for BECNT and has a profound grasp of the theology of the letter. There is plenty of exegetical sagacity, alongside knowledge of the history of interpretation (church fathers to the present) and theological reflection. He also possesses an impressive command of ancient literature and the realia of Roman society. To make proper use of this extensive commentary (745pp.), one needs a working knowledge of Koine Greek. Thielman, who holds the Presbyterian Chair of Theology at Beeson, was assisted here by George Guthrie in developing diagrams of discourse analysis. The introduction is not extensive (23pp.). Regarding specific conclusions, he takes the "I" of ch. 7 to have "a composite character" (Paul and the Roman Christians) and to refer to a previously unbelieving state—"It is unlikely that Paul portrays the struggle of a believer" (369). In 11:26 "all Israel" means "a group of Israelites large enough that they can represent the whole people" (547). [*ExpTim* 3/20; *WTJ* Spr 20; *JETS* 9/20; *JSNT* 41.5].

✓ Abasciano, Brian J. *Paul's Use of the OT in Romans 9:1–9*, 2005. He has follow-up vols. on 9:10–18 (2011) and 9:19–24 (2022), all of which constitute a lengthy and learned Arminian response to Reformed readings. [*JSNT* 45.5].

✓ Achtemeier, Paul. ‡ (I) 1986. A fine, moderately liberal exposition, but this is not Achtemeier at his best. [*JBL* 106.4; *JETS* 3/87].

✓ Adams, Gwenfair Walters, ed. *Romans 1–8* (RCS) 2019. See also Krey below.
  Andria, Solomon. (ABCS) 2012.
  Barnhouse, D. G. 4 vols., 1952–63. From the famous expositor at Tenth Presbyterian, Philadelphia. Slightly dispensational and helpful to preachers. His exegetical judgment is sometimes a bit off-beat. Choose instead Boice (his successor) or Lloyd-Jones.

✓ **Barrett, C. K.** ‡ (BNTC) 1957, 2nd ed. 1991. Not so successful as his commentaries on the Corinthian letters, but still a model of clarity and "remarkably interesting" (Martin). Certain theological inadequacies and errors are pointed out in John Murray's review [*Collected Writings*, Vol. 4: 306ff.]. One of the worst is his statement that "Christ took precisely the same fallen nature that we ourselves have" (156 [1957], 147 [1991])—he here, and in other places too, shows the influence of Barth. Students should be reminded of Barrett's notable survey, *Reading through Romans* (1963).

✓ Barry, David P. *The Exile of Adam in Romans: The Reversal of the Curse against Adam and Israel in the Substructure of Romans 5 and 8*, 2021. A Westminster PhD published by Fortress. [*JETS* 3/23; *JSNT* 45.5].

  Barth, Karl. ‡ 1919, 6th ed. 1929, ET 1933. Truly a turning point in the history of theology! As an exposition of Paul's thought, Barth's *Römerbrief* has definite deficiencies; as a theological treatise in its own right, it changed the theological world. Note also his later *Shorter Commentary on Romans* (ET 1959).
  Bartlett, David L. ‡ (WestBC) 1996. [*Int* 7/97; *CBQ* 4/97].

✓ Bell, Richard H. *No One Seeks for God: An Exegetical and Theological Study of Romans 1.18–3.20*, 1998.

✓ Belleville, Linda L., and A. Andrew Das, eds. *Scripture, Texts, and Tracings in Romans*, 2021. [*JETS* 9/22; *JSNT* 44.5].

✓ Berry, Donald L. *Glory in Romans and the Unified Purpose of God in Redemptive History*, 2016. A PhD study (Amridge?) on a topic needing attention. [*Them* 41.3; *JSNT* 39.5].

☆ **Bird, Michael F.** (SGBC) 2016. Because he has become a major Pauline scholar, the exposition here is noteworthy and worth a close look. Loaded with insights! Bird's "progressive Reformed view" of justification is sympathetic with historic Reformed teaching but also appreciative of, say, Tom Wright's version of the NPP. (Wright is cited more than any other commentator; together they wrote *The NT in Its World* [2019].) Bird thinks "the Lutheran and Reformed interpretation . . . rightly captures Paul's theological texture" but "is deficient at times in grasping the concrete social realities behind Paul's letters" (131). On some key issues, he says 5:12 can be read (with Blocher) as teaching that we are condemned by Adam's sin and by our own (176–80), "the 'I' of 7:7–25 *cannot* be a Christian" (234, emphasis original), and for election in chapter 9 "the focus is corporate, not individual" (323). The 540-page vol. is approachable, pastorally helpful, interesting from start to finish, and the register can be folksy: "Yes, I know that 'gracism' sounds cornier than a cornfield in Cornville, Iowa, but it rings true" (135). The "Live the Story" applications and illustrations make up about 35% of the 540pp. In his concern to communicate in a post-Christian culture, he suggests "we stop using the word 'sin' and find a new term" and "start talking about 'evil' instead" (105).

✓ **Black, Matthew.** ‡ (NCB) 1973, rev. 1989. Has value in the category of brief exegesis, but Bruce is more perceptive and conservative. Black was a learned and mature scholar, but his work had a dated feel even when it appeared. [*RTR* 9/90; *JETS* 9/94].

☆ Boice, James M. 4 vols., 1992–95. Each of the vols. runs about 500pp. This is great preaching from an evangelical leader who long pastored historic Tenth Presbyterian, Philadelphia. [*CTJ* 11/94]. From the British side, one will find model Reformed preaching in Lloyd-Jones, Philip (1987), and Ash (2009).

✓ Bolt, Peter Geoffrey, and James R. Harrison, eds. ‡ *Romans and the Legacy of St. Paul*, 2019. An ecumenical collection of essays. [*ETL* 12/22].

✓ Bray, Gerald, ed. (ACCS) 1998. "A wonderful gateway to the world of patristic thinking relating to this foundational biblical text." This is not a mere culling of materials in the 19th century Schaff set of the church fathers or the Catholic University of America Press's Fathers of the Church series, for Bray presents in English for the first time extensive citations of Origen's commentary. The very best contribution to ACCS? [*Them* 11/99; *NovT* 42.4; *RelSRev* 4/00; *SwJT* Sum 01; *EvQ* 7/02].

Briscoe, D. Stuart. (WCC) 1982. As with the Genesis vol., this is a thoughtful exposition but not especially well-researched.

Brown, John. 1857. A Calvinistic commentary reprinted in 1981 (Baker) and 2003 (Wipf & Stock) which offers a deep theological exposition. Its flavor is reflected in a favorite quote found on pp.38–39: "what to Him who paid the ransom is justice, may be grace, pure grace, to him for whom it is paid." See also Brown on Hebrews and 1 Peter.

☆ Bruce, F. F. (retired TNTC) 1963, rev. 1985. Insightful, handy commentary. See Garland.

✓ Brunner, Frederick Dale. 2021. Eerdmans subtitle is "A Short Commentary." [*Presb* Spr 22; *Int* 10/22; *JSNT* 45.5].

✓ Burns, J. Patout, Jr., with Constantine Newman, eds. *Romans: Interpreted by Early Christian Commentators*, 2012. Compare Bray. [*CBQ* 10/13; *JSNT* 37.5; *ExpTim* 5/13; *BSac* 1/14; *RTR* 8/13].

✓ **Byrne, Brendon.** ‡ (SacP) 1996. "Dense brevity" (Lambrecht). One of the stronger, more widely used American Catholic works. If you're comparing, Fitzmyer is the more careful and skilled exegete, while Byrne is more immediately helpful for proclamation. Byrne uses rhetorical analysis on the letter. [*JBL* Spr 99; *Bib* 78.2; *RelSRev* 1/98].

✓ **Calvin, John.** 1540, ET 1960. See the note at the head of the NT section. Calvin is at his very best here—amazingly, his first commentary. His "patient exegesis is a model of critical and theological thoroughness" (Barrett). "A library without Calvin's Romans and the magnificent English edition of Luther's commentary is sadly impoverished" (Childs).

F   Campbell, Douglas A. ‡ (CCF). See Campbell under Pauline Studies.

✓   Campbell, William S. ‡ *Romans: A Social Identity Commentary*, 2023. A major work (450pp.) from a scholar at U. of Wales, Trinity Saint David, challenging traditional interpretations [*ExpTim* 9/23]. A driving concern is to assert that Jews may find salvation apart from faith in Jesus; cf. the earlier *Paul's Gospel in an Intercultural Context* (1991).

✓ **Crisler, Channing L.** *An Intertextual Commentary on Romans*, 4 vols., 2021–. Regrettably, I've only heard of this. Three vols. are out, and the fourth is to cover chs. 12–16. The author teaches at Anderson University (SC). [*JSNT* 45.5].

✓   Das, A. Andrew. *Solving the Romans Debate*, 2007.

F   Das, A. Andrew. (EEC). The older report was Wayne House and Steve Sullivan.

Denney, James. (Expositor's Greek Testament) 1900. Contains some insights on the Greek text and some probing theology too.

Dodd, C. H. ‡ (Moffatt series) 1932. Represents the old liberal tradition and is famous for its cavalier dismissal of what Paul says about the wrath of God toward sinners.

✓   Donfried, Karl P., ed. ‡ *The Romans Debate*, 1977, rev. 1991. Called "a standard sourcebook" [*JTS* 10/93], this heralded a new approach to Romans more as a situational letter than as a theological treatise. [*CTJ* 4/94; *RTR* 1/96].

☆ Doriani, Daniel M. (REC) 2022. Something of a hybrid: sermonic material is blended with more academic lectures (approx. 550pp.). Doriani contributed *James*, the Matthew set, and *1 Peter* to the series.

✓ **Dunn, James D. G.** [𝓜], (WBC) 2 vols., 1988. A remarkable succession of Durham professors commented on Romans: Barrett, Cranfield, and then Dunn. This huge, brilliant scholarly work rivals Cranfield and is the most important interpretation of Romans along the lines of the NPP. He mastered a tremendous amount of literature to produce this work. However, I am more impressed by Cranfield's mature exegetical judgment and recommend the ICC over the WBC without hesitation (e.g., compare them on 9:5). Dunn was once much more conservative and evangelically minded. Though unable to locate the quote, I recall that he once said Barrett is a better theological guide to Romans than Murray; that tells you something. For more comment on this scholar's views, see Dunn under Pauline Studies and Galatians. The plan had been for Dunn (†2020) to collaborate with Ronald Herms on a revision. [*JTS* 4/91; *CBQ* 7/91; *Int* 1/91; *RTR* 9/90; *Them* 16.2].

F   Eastman, Susan. ‡ (I-R).

✓   Edwards, James R. (NIBC) 1992. A 395-page commentary which is superbly written but, I think, misconstrues Paul somewhat on law and grace. [*EvQ* 4/91; *CTJ* 4/95; *CRBR* 1993].

✓   Esler, Philip F. ‡ *Conflict and Identity in Romans: The Social Setting of Paul's Letter*, 2004. [*ThTo* 7/05; *JR* 7/06; *BibInt* 14.4].

F   Fiddes, Paul. ‡ (BBC).

✓ **Fitzmyer, Joseph.** ‡ (AB) 1993. About 800pp. of first-rate critical commentary. The author was an independent-minded Jesuit priest who also produced the exceptional works on Luke, Acts, 1 Corinthians, and Philemon for the AB series. In this Romans commentary, conservative Protestants were pleasantly surprised to find Fitzmyer agreeing with their interpretation at more than a few points. However, this is not my choice for a theological guide. Strongly recommended for advanced students, but it is not so useful for pastors. [*PSB* 15.3; *Int* 10/95; *CBQ* 7/95; *JBL* Win 95; *NovT* 37.2].

✓ Fowler, Paul B. *The Structure of Romans: The Argument of Paul's Letter*, 2016. From Fortress, probing Romans's preponderance of rhetorical questions.

☆ **Garland, David.** (TNTC-R) 2021. Replaced Bruce and is a model of compactness, yet full enough to accomplish much (over 500pp.). Truly a brilliant and dependable work by a veteran commentator (see Mark, Luke, 1 and 2 Corinthians, Colossians). His leanings are Reformed.

✓ Gathercole, Simon J. *Where Is Boasting? Early Jewish Soteriology and Paul's Response in Romans 1–5*, 2002. An important critique of the NPP, written as a dissertation under Dunn—more than a few were surprised. Gathercole is now a Cambridge professor. [*JBL* Fall 04; *Int* 7/04; *ExpTim* 8/03; *JSNT* 12/03; *JR* 7/04; *EvQ* 1/05; *WTJ* Fall 05; *BibInt* 13.1; *SJT* 62.1; *TJ* Fall 04 (Moo); *DenvJ* 1/02 (Blomberg); *Anvil* 20.4].

✓ **Gaventa, Beverly Roberts.** ‡ (NTL) 2024. Have not seen it, but I fully expect the emerita NT professor at Princeton Seminary has written a leading, perhaps landmark, moderately critical commentary for students and pastors. Do look it up (445pp.).

✓ Gaventa, Beverly Roberts, ed. ‡ *Apocalyptic Paul: Cosmos and Anthropos in Romans 5–8*, 2013. [*JSNT* 36.5; *ExpTim* 6/15; *SJT* 69.2]. She also wrote *When in Romans: An Invitation to Linger with the Gospel according to Paul* (2016). [*WTJ* Fall 17; *Int* 1/18; *SJT* 71.1; *JSNT* 40.5].

✓ Godet, Frederic. 1883. Quite perceptive as an Arminian exposition and worth consulting for the history of exegesis—Godet is frequently cited in Moo's NICNT. This commentary and the huge vol. on John's Gospel are Godet's best known, but see the works on Luke and 1 Corinthians as well. Now free online.

✓ Gorman, Michael J. [𝓜], 2022. Coming from a somewhat conservative Methodist perspective and subtitled "A Theological and Pastoral Commentary." As expected, it is highly readable and engaging, with an emphasis on Paul's mission, a participationist theology (union with Christ in a new life), and how the gospel transforms sinners. See also his works listed under Pauline Studies. [*Int* 10/22; *CBQ* 7/23; *JSNT* 45.5; *JTS* 10/23].

Greathouse, William M., and George Lyons. (New Beacon Bible Commentary) 2 vols., 2008. A 570-page work "in the Wesleyan Tradition."

✓ Haacker, Klaus. ‡ *The Theology of Paul's Letter to the Romans*, 2003. [*ExpTim* 9/04].

✓ Hahn, Scott W. [𝓜], (CCSS) 2017. The author is many things: famously a convert from conservative Presbyterianism, an apologist (author of *Rome Sweet Home*), and an astute Bible scholar with a strong commitment to a biblical-theological approach. Bird accurately describes this book: "One of the best commentaries available on Romans from within the Catholic tradition." [*JSNT* 40.5].

☆ Haldane, Robert. (GS) 1874. Anyone familiar with Haldane's experiences in Geneva will take an interest in this reprint by Banner and by Kregel. An exposition full of heart.

☆ Harrison, Everett F., and Donald A. Hagner. (EBCR) 2008. They have done much to help preachers with what is provided here in 217pp. The theological orientation is broadly and winsomely Reformed (e.g., 9:6–13). Just to note, Hagner does not buy into the NPP and, as one might expect, made great improvements to the EBC by Harrison (1976).

✓ Harrison, James R. ‡ *Reading Romans with Roman Eyes*, 2020. Nine learned essays plus a conclusion, with special focus on the historical background of the letter. An important book! [*ETL* 12/22; *CBQ* 10/21; *JTS* 10/21]. The quick follow-up is Harrison–Welborn, eds., *The First Urban Churches 6: Rome and Ostia* (2021) [*JSNT* 44.5].

☆ **Harvey, John D.** (KEL) 2019. Competent exegetically, of more manageable size (400pp.), warm-hearted, and helpful for those seeking to apply the text to life. Harvey is a conservative Presbyterian and has long taught seminarians at Columbia International University. His vol. has less interaction with NT scholarship. Harvey also published *Romans* (EGGNT) in 2017, which is excellent for Greek students, though at times he does not adequately lay out the interpretive options. [*CTJ* 11/18; *JETS* 6/18; *JSNT* 40.5]. Comparing the two, you should choose KEL if you desire more theological and pastoral reflection.

✓ Hay, David M., and E. Elizabeth Johnson, eds. ‡ *Pauline Theology*, Vol. 3, *Romans*, 1995.

Hendriksen, William. (NTC) 1980–81. Not one of the better vols. in the series, though I'm sure many students and pastors have found it helpful. His last commentary, *Romans*, lacks some of the vigor of earlier works. [*WTJ* Fall 82; *EvQ* 10/90].

Hodge, Charles. (GS) 1864. Was eclipsed by Murray as the best Reformed study. Still, it is valuable as a theological exposition and for understanding the flow and connection of Paul's thought (important for Romans). Church historians recognize Hodge as one of the greats among American systematic theologians during the 19th century. He taught at Princeton Seminary his entire life and wrote solid works on Romans, Corinthians, and Ephesians. Besides the GS reprint (1972), see also the edited CrossC (1994). The full text is free online.

Holland, Tom. *Romans: The Divine Marriage—A Biblical Theological Commentary*, 2011. [*EvQ* 1/13].

☆ Hughes, R. Kent. (PTW) 1991. See under Mark. This Romans exposition is 352pp.

✓ **Hultgren, Arland J.** ‡ 2011. Known for a fine book on the parables, Hultgren delivers here a major, mid-sized work from a moderately critical, Lutheran perspective. After a brief introduction (27pp.), there is a detailed 570-page commentary plus eight appendices. It seems he has read everybody; I can't find any modern scholar of note he has not cited. (Luther and Calvin are missing.) There are some more traditional elements in his interpretation (e.g., an objective genitive at 3:22), but he rejects the "alien righteousness" idea in δικαιοσύνη θεοῦ (3:21–22), rejects a christological statement in 9:5, and writes off any relevance of 1:27–27 to debates about same-sex practices and relationships (such is the difference between ancient practices and homosexuality today). Porter (see Note 3 below) has biting criticism of Hultgren's grammatical comments. [*EvQ* 1/13 (Marshall); *CBQ* 7/13 (Furnish); *JTS* 10/12; *Int* 4/12; *JSNT* 35.5; *RTR* 4/15; *Presb* Fall 12; *JETS* 9/12; *ExpTim* 1/12; *ETL* 89.4; *DenvJ* 15 (Blomberg); *BTB* 8/13; *TJ* Fall 12].

Hunter, A. M. [*M*], (Torch) 1955. An older exposition by a professor at Aberdeen, noted as having one of Scotland's more conservative divinity faculties.

✓ Jervis, L. Ann. [*M*], *The Purpose of Romans: A Comparative Letter Structure Investigation*, 1991.

✓ **Jewett, Robert.** ‡ (Herm) 2007. A formidable tome (1100pp.) by a leading American scholar, independent-minded and long at Garrett-Evangelical, Chicago. Was the fullest exegesis to appear in a couple of decades, containing copious footnotes. Jewett approaches the text with an array of critical tools, with special place given to socio-rhetorical interpretation. His general thesis is cogent enough and focused: "Paul writes to gain support for a mission to the barbarians in Spain, which requires that the gospel of impartial, divine righteousness revealed in Christ be clarified to rid it of prejudicial elements that are currently dividing the congregations in Rome." He interacts a good bit with Dunn's WBC, following his lead at a few points but also criticizing the New Perspective without engaging deeply in the controversy. What he shares with the NPP is a tendency "to let the ecclesiological dimension of Paul's gospel—setting Gentile believers on a par with Jews in the people of God—trump Paul's soteriological aim" (Rainbow). While one cannot help being impressed with the learning here, I agree with Moo [*JETS* 12/07] when he classes this as less distinguished as a theological commentary. Such an assessment makes sense since Jewett does not view the letter as a theological treatise. Cf. Donfried. [*Int* 4/08; *JSNT* 9/08 (a review discussion); *NovT*

50.3; *ExpTim* 10/07; *RelSRev* 9/08; *BSac* 1/09; *BBR* 19.3 (Schreiner); *Anvil* 26.3–4; *EC* 5/10 (Reasoner); *RelSRev* 12/10]. *Romans: A Shorter Commentary* was released in 2013.

✓ **Johnson, Luke Timothy.** ‡ *Reading Romans: A Literary and Theological Commentary* (RNT) 1997. [*RelSRev* 4/03]. Well-done, open to the text, and less traditional from the Roman Catholic side.

✓ **Käsemann, Ernst.** ‡ ET 1980. This vigorous, individualistic commentary builds on a Lutheran base and makes for a strenuous intellectual workout. Not necessarily dependable as a guide through Paul's thought, Käsemann's provocative exposition is, like Barth's, a theological treatise in its own right. This has been one of the five or six most influential commentaries on Romans (in English) from the academic point of view. He detects the influence of apocalyptic, stressing that δικαιοσύνη θεοῦ is God's inbreaking and saving power; he powerfully influenced Martyn, Beker, D. Campbell, and a host of others. [*EvQ* 4/82; *JETS* 9/81; *Them* 7.3].

✓ Kaylor, R. David. ‡ *Paul's Covenant Community: Jew and Gentile in Romans*, 1988.

✓ **Keck, Leander.** ‡ (ANTC) 2005. Highly successful as a learned, to-the-point, critical exegesis by a famous Pauline scholar at Yale. In a disciplined way, the author sticks to explicating Paul's line of thought/argument (e.g., ch. 9). One senses throughout that a lifetime of wrestling with Paul lies behind this work of compressed scholarship (400pp.). His sympathy with the text might lead some to classify Keck as mildly critical. I bought this. Cf. with Matera. [*JETS* 6/06; *BL* 2006; *ExpTim* 2/07; *EuroJTh* 15.2].

Keener, Craig. (NCCS) 2009. The author teaches at Asbury Seminary and is a coeditor for the series. In contrast to Keener's other massive efforts (see John and Acts), this is only 272pp. His commentary is sensitive to rhetoric and informed by deep learning in 1st century literature. [*JETS* 6/10; *CBQ* 4/11; *JSNT* 34.5].

☆ Keller, Tim. *Romans 1–7 for You*, 2014; *Romans 8–16 for You*, 2015. It is good to see what the notable pastor of Redeemer Presbyterian, Manhattan did with this weighty epistle. Clearly Keller found ch. 8 an especially deep mine for preaching transforming grace. An easy read worth considering. See also Judges and Galatians.

Knox, John. ‡ (IB) 1954.

✓ Krey, Philip D. W., and Peter S. D. Krey, eds. *Romans 9–16* (RCS) 2016. See Adams above.

✓ Lampe, Peter. ‡ *From Paul to Valentinus: The Christians in the City of Rome of the First Three Centuries*, 2000.

✓ Lancaster, Sarah Heaner. ‡ (Belief) 2015. [*Int* 1/18].

Leenhardt, F. J. ‡ ET 1961. More of a pastor's commentary, from a German Catholic.

F Letham, Robert. (HGV).

✓ Levy, Ian Christopher, Philip D. W. Krey, and Thomas Ryan, eds. (BMT) 2013. Of special interest for the history of interpretation. [*JSNT* 36.5; *ExpTim* 9/14].

✓ Lightfoot, J. B. 1904. See under 1 & 2 Thessalonians.

☆ Lloyd-Jones, D. Martyn. 14 vols., 1970–2003. These expositions were published by Zondervan and Banner of Truth, covering chs. 1–14, but don't expect any more vols. to complete the epistle. Health problems brought a sudden end both to Lloyd-Jones's exposition at 14:17 and to his pastorate at Westminster Chapel, London. Most Reformed pastors know the virtues and worth of these powerful sermons. The set comes highly recommended by Moo.

☆ Luther, Martin. 1515–16. Several editions and translations are available. I suggest the pb Library of Christian Classics edition (WJK) or the hb in the series Luther's Works (Concordia). There is contagious excitement in these lectures because Luther had recently "discovered" the gospel. It is a wonderful experience to read these pages and grasp the liberty of Christ's gospel along with Luther. It was Luther's preface to this commentary that God used to convert John Wesley.

MacArthur, John. 2 vols., 1991–94. See Matthew for a review of the series.

F   Macaskill, Grant. (ITC).

F   Marshall, I. Howard, and Stephen N. Williams. [𝓜], (THC).

✓   **Matera, Frank J.** ‡ (Paideia) 2010. Appropriately, a fuller vol. (350pp.), and one of the best in the series. Matera is highly regarded and taught at Catholic University. He has written a concise exegesis that selectively acquaints readers with scholarship, keeps an eye constantly on the ancient context, and draws theological conclusions that are in the critical mainstream. [*CBQ* 7/12; *Int* 4/12; *ExpTim* 7/11; *Them* 8/11; *RelSRev* 12/11].

✓   McKnight, Scot. [𝓜], *Reading Romans Backwards*, 2019. Pursues a novel, edgy, back-to-front reading strategy, making sense of chs. 1–8 especially by wrestling with chs. 12–16 and the tension between the "weak" and "strong." The Apostle "turns the judgmental Weak into a stereotyped character he calls the Judge (2:1)" (108). As McKnight interprets the book, 1:18–32 is to be labelled the judgmental speech of the Torah-observant weak person. This seems to me to undercut the full demonstration of human unrighteousness, in contradistinction to divine righteousness declared in the gospel. [*Int* 7/21; *SJT* 73.4; *JSNT* 42.5].

☆   McKnight, Scot, and Joseph B. Modica, eds. *Preaching Romans: Four Perspectives*, 2019. Receiving plaudits. [*JSNT* 42.5; *RevExp* 11/22].

Merida, Tony. *Exalting Jesus in Romans* (CCE) 2021.

☆   **Middendorf, Michael P.** (ConcC) 2 vols., 2013–16. Any wanting a capably done, exegetical commentary from a confessional Lutheran standpoint will find Middendorf very appealing. Along with his treatment of the Greek text, he provides a good measure of theological discussion and preaching helps. Because of the volumes' size and thoroughness (848 + 800pp.), I suppose that few besides the most diligent pastors and conservative scholars will give attention to it. Middendorf published his Concordia Seminary dissertation, *The "I" in the Storm: A Study of Romans 7*, in 1997. [*JSNT* 37.5].

✓   **Moo, Douglas.** *Romans 1–8* (WEC) 1991. A huge entry (almost 600pp.), quite valuable then. Now hard to find. When WEC died, Moo undertook to reformat his work and complete it for NICNT. See Moo above. [*Them* 10/92; *CTJ* 4/92].

☆   Moo, Douglas J. (NIVAC) 2000. Great for pastors, but should not replace Moo's NICNT on your to-buy-list. The same can be said for his college textbook *Encountering the Book of Romans* (2nd ed. 2014) [*Them* Sum 04; *RelSRev* 1/04; *RTR* 8/03; *Anvil* 20.4; *JSNT* 37.5].

✓   **Morris, Leon.** (retired Pillar) 1988. In 1990, say, Morris deserved a place on the pastor's shelf, but now we have Moo, Schreiner, and Kruse (his replacement). A conservative Anglican, Morris held firmly to the moderately Calvinistic Thirty-Nine Articles of Religion. This dependable work for pastors (578pp.) bore similarities to Murray's theological interpretation, but was more up-to-date and cognizant of developments in the NT field. The vol. was less valuable to students, however, because Morris did not deal directly with Sanders and Dunn. That shortcoming made the arrival of Moo's NICNT even more welcome. [*EvQ* 7/90; *JBL* Win 89; *RTR* 1/92; *Evangel* Sum 90].

✓   Moule, H. C. G. (CBSC) 1879. A perceptive exegetical work. There is also a devotional exposition in EB (1894) which would be useful for sermon preparation. Both were republished, and, while reissue does not always indicate value, here it does.

✓   Mounce, Robert H. (NAC) 1995. His NICNT on Revelation indicated his fine scholarship, but this is aimed more at pastors than students. [*Them* 1/97; *JETS* 3/98; *TJ* Spr 97].

☆   **Murray, John.** (retired NICNT) 1959–65. A truly great theological commentary, showing good exegetical judgment. Murray was Professor of Systematics at Westminster Seminary. This is especially helpful to the expositor because it is so focused on Paul's flow of thought and message. (Schreiner is also strong in this area.) Murray did not interact as much with the (old) secondary literature and, therefore, was never valued highly by NT specialists—not valued as highly by those outside the Reformed tradition either. Decades ago, Silva counseled that Murray and Cranfield be your first purchases on Romans; I hazard the guess that today he might say Moo, Cranfield, Longenecker, and Murray. Murray's work was replaced by Moo, but Eerdmans kept Murray in print, though not with the NICNT cover. In 2010 Murray dropped from my recommended purchases, but you should consider it if you are Reformed. (I read every page.) Westminster Seminary Press has reset this classic and bound it (superbly) with a Sinclair Ferguson "Introduction to the 2022 Edition."

✓ Myers, Jason A. *Paul, The Apostle of Obedience: Reading Obedience in Romans*, 2023. Such a study has seemed to me long overdue, given the significant bracketing phrase εἰς ὑπακοὴν πίστεως in 1:5 and 16:26. [*JSNT* 45.5].

Newell, William R. 1938. Very strongly dispensational with a somewhat practical focus. Remains in print.

Newman, B. M., and E. A. Nida. (UBS) 1973.

✓ **Nygren, Anders.** ‡ ET 1952. A highly respected theological commentary from a Lutheran scholar. Thin on the last eight chapters. Still in print.

Olyott, Stuart J. *The Gospel as It Really Is* (Welwyn) 1979.

F Oropeza, B. J. 2 vols.

☆ **Osborne, Grant.** (IVPNT) 2004. This commentary of over 400pp. was contributed by the series editor. It is exactly the right book, if one wants a compact, evangelical Arminian exegesis. I regard Osborne as fairer than Witherington in dealing with the Arminian–Calvinist controversy. It is slightly less helpful than some others in IVPNT for addressing contemporary relevance concerns. [*JETS* 3/05; *Them* 4/06; *RelSRev* 1/07; *Anvil* 22.2]. Do note that Osborne wrote a later "verse-by-verse" commentary for ONTC (2017).

Pate, C. Marvin. (TTC) 2013. From a prof at Ouachita Baptist University. I have not seen it, but one review says he proposes that Romans's structure somehow reflects ancient Hittite suzerainty treaties (330pp.). [*JSNT* 36.5; *TJ* Fall 14].

☆ **Peterson, David G.** (BTCP) 2017; (EBTC) 2020. What an admirable, theological exposition (much exegesis too) and sifting of the most important scholarship on the epistle! Peterson treats the Greek but remains accessible. His theology is conservative Anglican (an emeritus prof at Moore College) and winsomely Reformed. He packs much into the handbook, with a 29-page Introduction and 474pp of verse-by-verse commentary. He suggests "A New Approach" to structural analysis (10–19), using Tobin somewhat. The "Biblical and Theological Themes" section (31–79) accomplishes a lot of good. Calvin described the chief virtue of any commentator as *perspicua brevitas*, and here you have it. [*JETS* 9/18; *JSNT* 44.5].

☆ Philip, James. *The Power of God*, 1987. Prized by Reformed Christians in the UK. Philip was deeply intellectual, and a most thoughtful preacher, devoted to prayer (†2009). Romans was said to be his favorite book. Sinclair Ferguson once said, "Perhaps no other living preacher or pastor in the English-speaking world (in all probability the entire world!) has so frequently exposed his congregation to the faithful, patient and vibrant exposition of Paul's greatest letter." Cf. Ash.

☆ Piper, John. *The Justification of God*, 1983, rev. 1992. The subtitle is "An Exegetical and Theological Study of Romans 9:1–23." This solid, in-depth commentary by a Baptist minister is a good addition to a pastor's library. Piper ably argues that Paul is concerned with the election and reprobation of individuals. Originally the work was a Munich dissertation. [*WTJ* Spr 84; *RTR* 1/84; *EvQ* 1/88; *JETS* 12/83].

✓ **Porter, Stanley E.** 2015. A stand-alone "Linguistic and Literary Commentary" from Sheffield Phoenix (310pp.). The prodigious author applies his Systemic Functional Linguistics to the epistle, explaining how it "reflects the ancient letter form with Paul's two major additions, the thanksgiving and parenesis," and how ch. 5 is "the climax of Paul's argument" (36). The exegesis is incisive and clear, despite the abundance of in-text citations and parenthetical remarks breaking up the flow somewhat. Porter reads ch. 5 as arguing that "on account of [Adam bringing sin and death into the world] or because of that, Paul says, all humans sin, and thus death passes through to all humans" (125). Rom 9:5 is understood as praise to Christ as God (183). [*Them* 41.1 (Schreiner)].

☆ **Porter, Stanley E., and David I. Yoon.** (BHGNT) 2023. Because of Porter's stature as a grammarian—and perhaps his pungency in critiquing others' linguistic lapses—this is intriguing and worthwhile. Students and pastors receive good help (400pp.) in walking through the Greek text.

✓ Reasoner, Mark. *Romans in Full Circle: A History of Interpretation*, 2005. [*ExpTim* 6/09]. This follows a fine CUP monograph on *The Strong and the Weak: Romans 14.1–15.13 in Context* (1999).

✓ **Sanday, W., and A. C. Headlam.** [𝔐], (retired ICC) 1895; 5th ed. 1902. "Should in no way be disregarded" (Martin). One of the very best from the old series. Even if the advanced student has purchased Cranfield, it still would not be unwise to pick up Sanday & Headlam s/h. Porter prizes this work, even with its age, as "still a more important and reliable guide to the Greek text of Romans than many if not most commentaries written since" (see Note 3 below).

✓ Schlatter, Adolf. 1935, 1952, ET 1995. A most thoughtful older German commentary, which emphasizes the righteousness of God as the unifying theme of this epistle. God's "righteousness establishes a relationship in which justice is effective." As David Kuck has noted, Schlatter's emphasis here anticipates Käsemann's reading of Paul in some respects. [*Them* 2/99; *JETS* 3/98; *RTR* 1/97; *SwJT* Sum 96; *HBT* 6/98]. In my personal study of Romans, the righteousness of God works well as an integrating theme. That righteousness is declared in the gospel (1:16–17); contradistinguished by sin or human unrighteousness (1:18–3:20); imputed in justification (3:21–5:21); imparted in sanctification (6:1–8:39); defended as sinners challenge God's purposes in election (9–11); and practiced in all of life (12–16).

✓ **Schnabel, Eckhard J.** *Der Brief des Paulus an die Römer*, 2 vols., 2015–16. An exception is made to the rule of not citing German works. This huge, learned set (approx. 1500pp.) by the Gordon-Conwell prof should not be missed. [*BBR* 27.3; *Them* 44.1].

✓ Schnelle, Udo, ed. ‡ *The Letter to the Romans*, 2009. A huge vol. of 44 papers delivered at the Colloquium Biblicum Lovaniense. [*ExpTim* 8/10].

Shedd, William G. T. 1879. Has been reprinted. Shedd was another of the great 19th century systematic theologians who commented on Romans. This work is interesting and important in the history of exegesis because Shedd took a realistic view of imputation in 5:12ff. (cf. Hodge's and Murray's "representative" or "federal" view).

✓ Sherwood, Aaron. 2020. Subtitled "A Structural, Thematic, and Exegetical Commentary," large-scale (over 900pp.), and published by Lexham outside of any series. The author earned a PhD at Durham and teaches at Regent College. I have not seen this. [*JSNT* 44.5].

✓ Soderlund, Sven, and N. T. Wright, eds. *Romans and the People of God*, 1999. [*EvQ* 4/02].

F Still, Todd. ‡ (NCBC).

Stott, John R. W. *Men Made New*, 1966. A succinct and masterful exposition of Romans 5–8. It used to be reprinted but must now be o/p since the BST vol. is available.

✓ Stowers, S. K. *A Rereading of Romans*, 1994. Influential for arguing that Romans is not theological per se, but a missive aimed at developing a community ethos in the church.

✓ **Stuhlmacher, Peter.** [𝔐], ET 1994. A major but compact work by the brilliant Tübingen scholar, published in pb by WJK. Definitely to be consulted. Stuhlmacher has been one of the most conservative professors of NT in Germany. [*JETS* 12/96; *Int* 10/96; *HBT* 12/95].

✓ Sumney, Jerry L., ed. ‡ *Reading Paul's Letter to the Romans*, 2012. Orienting essays from leading critics, published by SBL. [*Int* 4/14].

✓ **Talbert, Charles.** ‡ (S&H) 2002. The highly respected Baptist theologian and Baylor professor here contributes an attractively presented, accessible exposition of Paul's letter, focusing largely on rhetorical features and following Paul's sustained argument. Talbert is rather uncomfortable with Reformed theology. His 340pp. have less interaction with opposing views. [*JETS* 9/04; *Int* 7/04; *DenvJ* 1/03 (Blomberg, sagacious)].

✓ **Thiselton, Anthony.** [*M*], *Discovering Romans*, 2016. Colin Brown of Fuller commends this: "For those who want to understand what Paul was driving at and why he wrote in the way he did, Thiselton's *Discovering Romans* is without equal." [*Int* 4/18; *JSNT* 39.5].

Thomas, W. H. Griffith. *Romans: A Devotional Commentary*, 3 vols., 1912. Since 1946, this edifying book was repeatedly reprinted by Eerdmans in a one-vol. pb.

✓ Timmins, Will N. *Romans 7 and Christian Identity: A Study of 'I' in Its Literary Context*, 2017. Very fine and clear scholarship on this old, contested issue. The revised Cambridge PhD draws the conclusion that the "I" is "representative" of "a believer in Christ who confesses an ongoing Adamic, anthropological condition of fleshliness" (8). Schreiner has been influenced by my friend Timmins's work here. [*WTJ* Spr 21; *CBQ* 7/19; *JTS* 10/19; *JETS* 12/18; *RB* 125.3; *JSNT* 41.5]. See also Wilder, ed., *Perspectives on Our Struggle with Sin: 3 Views of Romans 7* (2011) [*DenvJ* 4/16].

✓ Tobin, Thomas H. ‡ *Paul's Rhetoric in Its Contexts: The Argument of Romans*, 2004. [*EuroJTh* 15.1 (Bird)].

✓ Toews, John E. (BCBC) 2004.

Waetjen, Herman. ‡ 2011. The subtitle of the commentary, "Salvation as Justice and the Deconstruction of Law," indicates a postmodern work.

F Westerholm, Stephen. [*M*], (Illum). This would follow his "unmatched" (Reasoner) *Romans: Text, Readers, and the History of Interpretation*, 2022. [*ExpTim* 6/23; *CBQ* 1/24].

✓ Wilk, Florian, and J. Ross Wagner, eds. ‡ *Between Gospel and Election: Explorations in the Interpretation of Romans 9–11*, 2010. [*JSNT* 34.5].

☆ **Witherington, Ben, III** (with Darlene Hyatt). (SRC) 2004. Alongside Osborne's IVPNT, the best evangelical Arminian commentary on Romans. There is more theology here than in some of his other works, and necessarily so. For a review of this essentially one-man series, see my comments under 1 Corinthians. Besides exegesis and rhetorical analysis, there is exposition and application, occasionally with almost militant Arminianism—he is displeased at Augustinian/Reformed dominance among Romans commentators. Some are put off by a feminism that strangely bemoans "the lack of genuine dialogue" between camps and then roundly condemns the "blatantly sexist statements" of Southern Baptists and complementarians in general (403). Students learn from Witherington's discussion of the interrelation of the parts of the letter; his outline is oriented toward rhetorical aspects instead of theology. [*Int* 7/04; *DenvJ* 1/04; *RTR* 12/08; *JETS* 6/05; *SwJT* Spr 05; *Them* 4/06; *BL* 2005; *SBET* Spr 05; *RelSRev* 1/06; *BTB* Sum 06; *ExpTim* 1/05; *Anvil* 22.2].

☆ **Wright, N. T.** [*M*], (NIB) 2002. This is not just good, it's a really good read. Certainly one of my favorite commentaries, though I disagree with him at points (see Wright under Pauline Studies above). Wright is extraordinarily influential in debates over Paul's theology and NT theology more generally. Here we have a most engaging exposition (375pp.), which finds the righteousness/justice of God to be the central theme. Comparing the two leading Romans commentaries that propound the NPP, I find Wright more attractive than Dunn. Porter (Note 3 below) offers sharp criticism: "Wright's linguistic abilities are disappointing." [*WTJ* Fall 03]. For "a deep dive" into ch. 8, see Wright's exposition *Into the Heart of Romans* (2023).

☆ Yarbrough, Robert. "Romans" in *Romans–Galatians* (ESVEC) 2020. The whole vol. (640pp.) provides ample help to expositors wanting to get at the message of these epistles, without delving much into the difficult exegetical details. Yarbrough's 200pp. are thoughtful, well-informed, and worthwhile. Even encouraging to the soul! The same can be said for Naselli on 1 Corinthians, Ortlund on 2 Corinthians, and Thielman on Galatians.

F   Yeago, David. (Brazos).

✓   **Ziesler, John.** ‡ (TPI) 1989. Builds on his CUP monograph, *The Meaning of Righteousness in Paul* (1972). Ziesler has been a major work, reflecting the influence of E. P. Sanders. He is extraordinarily well-read. [*CBQ* 4/92; *Them* 1/92; *ExpTim* 3/90].

NOTES: (1) There are other valuable works on Romans, but I have to stop somewhere. (2) James C. Miller, "The Romans Debate: 1991–2001," *CurBS* 9 (2001): 306–49. (3) Stanley E. Porter, "Commentaries on the Book of Romans" (365–404), in *On the Writing of NT Commentaries*, eds. Porter–Schnabel, cited in the Introduction.

# 1 CORINTHIANS

★   Blomberg, Craig L. (NIVAC) 1994. Thoughtful and suggestive, providing trustworthy exegesis and guidance for exposition. Blomberg seems an irenic gentleman, and, as the epistle deals with contentious topics, he wades carefully into the deep water of controversy. Not to be used as a shortcut past one's own exegesis directly to application—and Blomberg would not want you to do such a thing anyway. Well worth the preacher's money. [*JETS* 3/98]. Good expositional helps are fewer for this book, and alongside NIVAC one could add works from among Barnett, Hays, Johnson, Kistemaker, Prior, Um, and Vang.

★   **Ciampa, Roy E., and Brian S. Rosner.** (Pillar) 2010. A strength of this full commentary (870pp.), in line with Ciampa's past work on *The Presence and Function of Scripture in Galatians 1 and 2* (1998), is research into Paul's interpretation of OT texts. Rosner was an editor of the *New Dictionary of Biblical Theology*, and so it is not surprising that a biblical-theological approach is another attractive feature. Ciampa (Aberdeen PhD) is now at Samford, and Rosner (Cambridge PhD) lectures at Moore College, Sydney. I found here linguistic sophistication, good knowledge of the literary and cultural background, insights from the rhetorical angle, and wise moves in the direction of application. They see Paul pressing the point that the Corinthian church needed to mature by hearing a challenge to avoid social/cultural entrapments and live out the gospel. While Fee (2014) may be judged more rigorous and perceptive, more tautly argued too, Pillar would be a fine choice for pastors and students seeking a solid, accessible exegetical tool with much to say theologically. [*CBQ* 1/13 (Garland); *Int* 10/12; *JSNT* 34.5; *Chm* Spr 14; *JETS* 12/11; *ExpTim* 9/11; *Them* 11/11; *DenvJ* 14; *RelSRev* 9/13; *TJ* Spr 13; *ETL* 91.4].

★   Fee, Gordon. [𝔐], (NICNT) 1987, rev. 2014. Has easily been the best mid-level commentary in English—Carson's and Silva's first choice, at least until Garland. It is so thorough and learned that one must have it. However, you may not wish to follow him at every point. His exposition of chs. 12–14 is clearly informed by his Pentecostal convictions, and he has strong feminist leanings (e.g., excising 14:34–35 completely out of the text without any external evidence to back his decision). Yet he can be critical of his Pentecostal heritage, as when he agrees that Paul in 12:13 teaches the Spirit-baptism of every convert. See my comments on Carson below. [*WTJ* Fall 89; *JBL* 108.1; *EvQ* 10/88; *JETS* 9/89; *NovT* 31.2]. Fee revised this (about 960pp.) as part of the ongoing updating of the series. (He admits, however, that he was unable to consult all the new literature since 1987.) He did not change his mind on much at all and continues to insist that mere displacement of 14:34–35 in the Western textual tradition justifies challenging the verses' authenticity—in all fairness, it must be noted that many others make the same move (which strikes some of us as blurring the line between text-critical and literary-critical work). He uses the 2011 NIV. Compare with the slightly shorter Ciampa and Rosner. [*WTJ* Spr 15; *JSNT* 37.5; *ExpTim* 8/15; *BSac* 1/17; *RevExp* 5/22; *DenvJ* 4/16].

★ **Gardner, Paul D.** (ZECNT) 2018. He did his Cambridge PhD on this epistle and, as he told me in Cambridge some years ago, has repeatedly preached through it over the decades. This extensive commentary (over 750pp.) can be warmly commended for its dependable, insightful exegetical remarks and theology. Gardner has taught NT and also served as a pastor, both within the Church of England and, later, the PCA. This ZECNT is of use to students but is especially geared for pastors who have studied Greek. In my opinion, the series editors and Gardner have kept the work somewhat accessible to those without Greek too, since translation is found alongside the Greek. Davids writes, "all can learn from the pastoral tone, the broad reading, and the particular rhetorical viewpoint of this monumental work" [*JETS* 12/18]. It is intriguing to read Jongkind's suggestion that "community markers and community unity" is the main underlying issue Paul addresses, rather than Gardner's "possession of wisdom and knowledge." [*JSNT* 41.5].

★ **Garland, David E.** (BECNT) 2003. The author previously completed a major, mid-level commentary on 2 Corinthians, and this work is stronger for that earlier research into the Corinthian correspondence. Garland is a much-published Baptist evangelical, and his work here is thorough and praiseworthy. Pastors should note that, in line with the series title, this is more a work of exegesis than theological exposition, though there is a good measure of theology and even hints at application. Garland is more accessible as a commentary on the Greek text than Thiselton. Carson's first pick. [*CBQ* 1/05; *JETS* 3/05; *Int* 7/05; *JSNT* 6/05; *RelSRev* 1/05; *ExpTim* 9/05].

★ **Thiselton, Anthony C.** [𝓜], (NIGTC) 2000. This 1400-page exegesis leaves no stones unturned. Thiselton was without doubt a world-class NT scholar, noted especially for expertise in biblical and philosophical hermeneutics. Magnificent! Most pastors will find a tome like this intimidating. (Fee is big enough already.) But those who love to dig deep will find their efforts repaid in full here. Often the reader will appreciate the author's patient, meticulous, circumspect exegesis—in the best British classical tradition. Thiselton was welcomed by students of 1 Corinthians because, outside of foreign language works, we had not seen a major commentary on the Greek text for decades. Then we got NIGTC, BECNT, and AYB. Also to be noted, this is the most intelligent, thorough, and useful application yet of speech-act theory to any biblical text. [*RTR* 12/01; *Them* Spr/Sum 02; *JTS* 4/02; *JBL* Spr 02; *Int* 1/02; *ExpTim* 8/01; *NovT* 44.2; *HBT* 6/02; *AsTJ* Spr 03; *JSNT* 6/04; *SwJT* Fall 01; *RelSRev* 7/02; *EvQ* 1/05; *JR* 7/02 (Furnish); *Evangel* Spr 02].

★ **Thiselton, Anthony C.** [𝓜], *1 Corinthians: A Shorter Exegetical & Pastoral Commentary*, 2006. More than a mere digest of his NIGTC, Thiselton wrote a fresh exposition which reveals that the epistle continued to be on his mind and heart. Preachers who find the earlier comprehensive work too daunting will appreciate this briefer work (300pp.); the bonus is that the author includes sections offering wise pastoral reflection on the text's contemporary application. But students can learn here too! Note his discussion (and acceptance) of Winter's interpretation of 12:3 (193–95). [*RTR* 4/08; *CBQ* 10/07; *JTS* 4/08; *BL* 2008; *ExpTim* 7/07; *Anvil* 25.2; *SJT* 64.2].

✓ Adams, Edward, and David Horrell, eds. ‡ *Christianity at Corinth: The Quest for the Pauline Church*, 2004. [*DenvJ* 3/05].

✓ Bailey, Kenneth E. *Paul through Mediterranean Eyes: Cultural Studies on 1 Corinthians*, 2011. [*Int* 1/13; *JSNT* 34.5; *JETS* 9/12; *ExpTim* 1/13; *Them* 4/12; *BTB* 8/12; *SBET* Spr 14; *TJ* Spr 12].

Baker, William. (CorBC) 2008. This vol. includes Ralph Martin on 2 Corinthians.

☆ Barnett, Paul. (Focus) 2000. Considering his superb NICNT on 2 Corinthians, as well as his long teaching and pastoral experience (retired Bishop of North Sydney), our expectation was that this Focus vol. would be judicious, mature, and ever so useful. That hope wasn't disappointed (310pp.).

☆ **Barrett, C. K.** ‡ (BNTC) 1968. The first choice in most bibliographies prior to Fee's appearance in 1987, and it is easy to see why. As Furnish once said, Barrett is "instructive even when it is not fully persuasive" (*II Corinthians*, p.ix). I recommended this for purchase in the first six editions, but newer, better works are available for both pastors and students. Barrett has been well mined by today's scholarship.

✓ Barth, Karl. [𝓜], *The Resurrection of the Dead*, ET 1933. Mainly a theological exposition of ch. 15. There is some real power here. I have hope that he did indeed believe in a physical resurrection. (T. F. Torrance relates that, when he urged Barth to leave more room for an incarnational theology, Barth gently reminded him that the incarnation was in fact given its due weight in his theology, that he upheld the doctrine of a *leibliche Auferstehung*, or bodily resurrection.)

Bender, Kimlyn J. [𝓜], (Brazos) 2022. A strong entry in the series by an astute Baptist theologian at Truett. [*ExpTim* 10/23].

F   Bonnington, Mark. (THC).

✓ Bowens, Lisa Marie. ‡ *An Apostle in Battle: Paul and Spiritual Warfare in 2 Corinthians 12:1–10*, 2017. Published in WUNT.

✓ Bray, Gerald, ed. *1–2 Corinthians* (ACCS) 1999. [*SwJT* Fall 00; *RelSRev* 4/00; *EvQ* 7/02].

Brookins, Timothy A. (RNT) 2020. A brief "Literary and Theological Commentary" (the subtitle), building on the research for BHGNT. [*CBQ* 10/22; *Int* 10/22].

☆ **Brookins, Timothy A., and Bruce W. Longenecker.** (BHGNT) 2 vols., 2016. A blessing for all Greek students, and easier to use than most in the series. Each vol. is about 250pp., and perhaps the two could better have been bound together. [*CBQ* 7/18; *RevExp* 5/20].

F   Brown, Alexandra R. ‡ (NTL).

☆ **Bruce, F. F.** *1 and 2 Corinthians* (NCB) 1971. Quite brief—256pp. on both epistles—but valuable. He compresses much information into the format and has sound exegetical judgment. The one difference I have with Bruce is over the interpretation of κεφαλή at 11:3. I believe "head" in context clearly means "authority over" and not "source." Also supportive of this understanding is (1) Paul's usage of the word in Eph 1:22 and Col 2:10; (2) the analogy of the husband's headship to Christ's at Eph 5:23; and (3) the articles of Fitzmyer and Grudem regarding the word's extracanonical use—e.g., Grudem's articles in *Recovering Biblical Manhood and Womanhood* (1991) and *JETS* 3/01.

✓ Burke, Trevor J., and J. Keith Elliott, eds. *Paul and the Corinthians: Studies on a Community in Conflict*, 2003. A Thrall FS with a wealth of essays on both epistles. [*NovT* 47.2].

Campbell, Charles L. ‡ (Belief) 2018. [*Int* 4/19].

☆ **Carson, D. A.** *Showing the Spirit: A Theological Exposition of 1 Corinthians 12–14*, 1987. Years ago I used to say that, if I could have only two books on 1 Corinthians, as a pastor I'd choose Fee and this 200-page commentary to counterbalance him on several points. Just the 10pp. on 14:33b–36 are worth the price of the book. The exegesis is detailed and slightly technical where it most needs to be. Because it was difficult to obtain, I no longer recommended its purchase. Carson has been kept in print. See also *The Cross and Christian Ministry: Studies in 1 Corinthians* (1993). [*RTR* 1/90; *Them* 1/90; *EvQ* 4/89; *SBET* Spr 90].

F   Clarke, Andrew. (WBC). Once announced for 2013. Clarke taught at Aberdeen.

✓ **Collins, Raymond F.** ‡ (SacP) 1999. A probing commentary from the Catholic tradition. Students benefit from consulting this full work (almost 700pp.), which is so well-done that it could be regarded as a "Gordon Fee from the critical side." [*CBQ* 7/00; *Bib* 82.1; *SwJT* Fall 00; *ScrB* 1/01; *RB* 4/01; *Them* Spr/Sum 02].

✓ **Conzelmann, Hans.** ‡ (Herm) ET 1975. A highly critical work that had been regarded by many as the standard technical exegesis of this letter. While Conzelmann will always be consulted by specialists, newer works like Thiselton and Fitzmyer have displaced it. [*JBL* 89.1; *Them* 1 (1976): 56].

Dever, Mark. *Twelve Challenges Churches Face*, 2008. A quickly moving and engaging exposition of the letter.

✓ Dunn, James D. G. [𝓜], (NT Guides) 1995. A critical introduction to the main exegetical and theological issues faced by scholarship. Because of the influence of the author in Pauline studies, the guide should be consulted by students.

✓ Ellingworth, Paul, and H. A. Hatton. (UBS) 1985.

✓ **Ellis, E. Earl.** (ICC) 2022. Published by T&T Clark. Much work for the ICC had been done at the time of Ellis's death (†2010), and an editor (Terry Wilder) readied the material (approx. 450pp.), mainly covering chs. 1–13. The content is highly technical, as expected for the intended series, but evangelical in orientation (e.g., see his discussion of ἱλαστήριον as "propitiation" on p.386). [*RelSRev* 9/22]. Holloway will be very different.

Findlay, G. G. (Expositor's Greek Testament) 1901. Can be kept in reserve. For other Findlay works, see Thessalonians and John's Epistles.

✓ **Fitzmyer, Joseph A.** ‡ (AB-R) 2008. This very full work (660pp.) is among a scholar's first choices for a technical commentary reference. The philology, syntactical analysis, and bibliographies are a boon to students. Slightly on the downside, this is a more independent work in that he limits his interaction with other major commentaries like Thiselton and Schrage. He was trying to keep the book of manageable size. See the author's other AB vols. on Luke, Acts, Romans, and Philemon, all of them methodologically consonant with his work, *The Interpretation of Scripture: In Defense of the Historical-Critical Method* (2008). [*RBL* (Thiselton); *ThTo* 7/09; *JETS* 12/09; *Them* 7/09; *ExpTim* 11/09; *Int* 7/09 (Witherington); *EuroJTh* 18.2].

✓ Friesen, Steven J., Daniel N. Showalter, and James C. Walters, eds. *Corinth in Context: Comparative Studies on Religion and Society*, 2010. [*JTS* 10/11; *JSNT* 33.5; *ExpTim* 5/11; *Them* 8/11; *RelSRev* 9/11; *TJ* Spr 11]. See also Showalter and Friesen, eds., *Urban Religion in Roman Corinth* (2005).

✓ Furnish, Victor Paul. ‡ 1999. From the Cambridge NT Theology series.

Godet, Frederic. 1886–87. A mine of exposition to which preachers have turned again and again. Still useful because of its length and insight. Available free online.

Gromacki, R. G. *Called to Be Saints*, 1977. A popularly styled, evangelical exposition.

Grosheide, F. W. (retired NICNT) 1953. Replaced by Fee. Grosheide was never considered the strongest effort, and few view him as still worth consulting. Those wanting a solidly Reformed exposition should look up NTC, Gardner, or Hodge (free online).

F   Hardin, Justin K. (SGBC).

✓ Harrison, James R., and L. L. Welborn, eds. *The First Urban Churches 2: Roman Corinth*, 2016.

Harrisville, Roy A. ‡ (Augsburg NT Commentary) 1987. [*CRBR* 1989].

☆ **Hays, Richard B.** [𝓜], (I) 1997. This commentary is so good and lively, from a less critical angle, that it is a top choice in mainline circles. The evangelical pastor, though probably wanting to tone down the apocalyptic emphasis, could put this to good use, with its sociological and literary analysis, its ethical discussion, and its theology. Hays is always an interesting read. [*TJ* Spr 00; *Int* 1/99; *CBQ* 7/99].

✓ Héring, Jean. ‡ ET 1962. A significant older French work in translation. Advanced students may wish to consult his provocative exegesis, though this work does not have its former prominence.

☆ Hodge, Charles. *I and II Corinthians* (GS) 1857–59. Some may have considered it a quirky choice, but I once included this on the recommended list. The two commentaries were bound together in the GS hb (1974) and published separately in pb by Eerdmans (1993). I came to appreciate their theological worth for pastors (e.g., on 1 Cor 15). And one does need a theological commentary on this letter. But cf. Kistemaker.

Hodge, Charles. (CrossC) 1995. [*SBET* Spr 97]. An edited pb version.

F   Holloway, Paul A. ‡ (ICC-R). See his work on Philippians.

✓ **Horsley, Richard A.** ‡ (ANTC) 1998. A fresh exegesis which runs down a particular track, one (thankfully) not taken by most. Horsley reconstructs the church situation. He thinks that those "primarily addressed in 1 Corinthians . . . focused on their personal relationship with heavenly *Sophia* (Wisdom). . . . As revealed apparently by the wisdom teacher Jesus and his apostle Apollos, *Sophia* provided her devotees with true spiritual knowledge of the divine and immortality of the soul" (37). Because of its individuality (eccentricity) and heterodox conclusions, this won't be used as much as some other ANTC. Not for pastors. [*CBQ* 1/00; *RelSRev* 4/00; *SwJT* Sum 01].

☆ Johnson, Alan F. (IVPNT) 2004. The author is a veteran NT scholar, providing a competent exegesis with brief consideration of contemporary relevance questions. [*JETS* 3/06; *Them* 4/06; *BL* 2005; *RelSRev* 7/06].

✓ **Keener, Craig.** [*M*], *1–2 Corinthians* (NCBC) 2005. At less than 250pp. for both books, Keener seems a bit thin. That being said, Keener is well-informed and interprets the letters from a socio-rhetorical angle. As usual for Keener, he is strong on details but a little less successful at the macro-level. Students will benefit from looking up his Suggested Reading sections: pp.11–19 and 152–55; do note, however, that the suggestions are weighted toward critical works, ignoring some valuable conservative monographs and articles. [*CBQ* 10/06; *JTS* 4/07; *JETS* 9/06; *BL* 2006; *RB* 4/07; *RelSRev* 4/07; *BSac* 1/07; *ExpTim* 8/06; *Anvil* 23.2]. There is now a report that Keener will produce another commentary on this epistle. No series is listed for this, and it may be another huge, stand-alone scholarly work like *Matthew* (Eerdmans), *John* (Hendrickson), *Acts*, and *Galatians* (Baker).

☆ Kistemaker, Simon J. (NTC) 1993. Well worth owning (590pp.) as a sure-footed theological guide, even if it is not the most original, scintillating commentary. Kistemaker's works tend to be fairly even in quality. NTC is especially of value to preachers, and the Reformed theology here is a plus! Kistemaker is much better on the Greek text than Hodge, if you are comparing them. See Carson above. [*CTJ* 11/95; *RTR* 9/96].

✓ Kovacs, Judith L., ed. *1 Corinthians: Interpreted by Early Christian Commentators*, 2005. I find the Bray edited vol. above easier to use and slightly more useful. Kovacs is much fuller in quotation length, however, thus providing a better sense of literary context for the selections. [*Chm* Aut 06; *JTS* 10/07; *BL* 2006; *RB* 4/07; *RelSRev* 3/08; *Pro Ecclesia* Win 09].

✓ Lightfoot, J. B. 1904. See under 1 & 2 Thessalonians.

Lockwood, Gregory J. (ConcC) 2000. I have yet to see this 648-page book.

MacArthur, John. 1984. See Matthew for a review of the series.

✓ Manetsch, Scott, ed. (RCS) 2017.

Mare, W. Harold. (EBC) 1976. See Verbrugge.

✓ Mitchell, Margaret M. ‡ *Paul and the Rhetoric of Reconciliation: An Exegetical Investigation of Language and Composition of 1 Corinthians*, 1991. She has added *Paul, the Corinthians and the Birth of Christian Hermeneutics* (2012).

✓ Moffatt, James. ‡ (Moffatt) 1943. This older standard reference work, long ago superseded, is still cited. Quite critical, with rigorous historical inquiry.

Montague, George T. ‡ (CCSS) 2011. [*CBQ* 10/13; *Int* 1/13; *JSNT* 35.5; *RelSRev* 12/13].

☆ Morris, Leon. (retired TNTC) 1958, rev. 1988. Morris insightfully reads the text and is recommended as a small, handy guide through the book. See Schreiner.

✓ Murphy-O'Connor, Jerome. ‡ *St. Paul's Corinth: Texts and Archaeology*, 3rd ed. 2002. From the trenchant NT prof at the École Biblique in Jerusalem, who had expertise in archaeology, among several research fields. The spirit of criticism in this book and in its companion on Ephesus (see below) is rather negative. His collected articles will be of interest to all students: *Keys to First Corinthians: Revisiting the Major Issues* (OUP, 2009) [*Int* 10/11].

☆ Naselli, Andrew David. "1 Corinthians" in *Romans–Galatians* (ESVEC) 2020. See Yarbrough under Romans.

   Nash, Robert Scott. ‡ (S&H) 2009. I have yet to use this (467pp.), but the respected Matera calls it "a first-rate commentary" [*Int* 10/11].

F  Nasrallah, Laura. ‡ (Herm). See the old Conzelmann above.

   Naylor, Peter. (EPSC) 2004. Conservative Reformed exposition.

F  Nighswander, Dan. (BCBC).

F  Okland, Jorunn. (BBC).

   Oropeza, B. J. (NCCS) 2017. From an able scholar. Follows on the heels of his 2016 commentary on 2 Corinthians in RRA.

   Orr, W. F., and J. A. Walther. ‡ (retired AB) 1976. Of some worth perhaps for its introduction, but the exegesis is too spotty to be dependable. One of the less valuable commentaries in the series, now replaced by Fitzmyer.

   Parry, R. St. John. [𝓜], (Cambridge Greek Testament for Schools and Colleges) 1926, 1937. Remains a useful tool for the student working through the original.

✓ **Perkins, Pheme.** ‡ (Paideia) 2012. As with most of the Paideia vols., Perkins's work is well-informed and concise as a critical exegesis. She is highly regarded as a scholar. [*CBQ* 4/14; *Int* 10/13; *JSNT* 35.5; *RelSRev* 12/13; *TJ* Spr 15].

☆ Prior, David. (BST) 1985. Successfully pursues the aims of the series. This same author has also written on the Minor Prophets for the BST series. [*JETS* 3/87; *Chm* 101.4].

   Proctor, John. ‡ *First and Second Corinthians* (WestBC) 2015. [*ExpTim* 12/15].

   Riddlebarger, Kim. (LCEC) 2013. Lengthy exposition (about 450pp.) by a learned, conservative Reformed pastor in California.

✓ **Robertson, A., and A. Plummer.** [𝓜], (ICC) 2nd ed. 1914. A magnificent piece of work for its time, which is still widely consulted today. (Some seminary professors, e.g., George Knight, used to recommend its purchase as recently as the late 1980s.) This classic pays close attention to technical matters.

   Ruef, J. S. ‡ 1978. Once worth consulting but now outstripped.

✓ Sampley, J. Paul. ‡ (NIB) 2002. This scholar contributed both 1 and 2 Corinthians to NIB (separate vols.). The interpretation of 1 Corinthians (230pp.) seems to emphasize community living and ethical matters. But there can also be a tendency to skirt today's politicized topics like homosexuality (e.g., 6:9–11) where the Apostle takes them up.

☆ **Schreiner, Thomas R.** (TNTC-R) 2018. Replaces Morris's trusty entry. Those desiring a more concise (337pp.), stimulating exegesis from a conservative angle can wisely make this their choice. The newer vols. in Tyndale are more expositional and likely to address application issues, and Schreiner stoutly defends his Baptistic reading of a couple texts (e.g., at 7:14). [*RTR* 12/19].

F  Smith, Jay E. (EGGNT).

☆ Soards, Marion L. [𝓜], (NIBC) 1999. Nearly 400pp. of conservatively critical comment from a prof at Louisville Seminary (Presbyterian). [*RTR* 4/01; *EvQ* 1/02; *Chm* Sum 04].

   Stanley, Arthur P. *The Epistles of Paul to the Corinthians*, 1882. A classic reprinted years ago, but most will be indifferent to it, considering the other resources available.

F  Starling, David. (EBTC)?

☆ Stott, John R. W. *Calling Christian Leaders*, 2002. This 150-page exposition of chs. 1–4 can be recommended to preachers. [*Chm* Aut 02].

✓ Talbert, C. H. ‡ *Reading Corinthians: A Literary and Theological Commentary on 1 &
2 Corinthians* (RNT) 1987, rev. 2002. A quick-paced literary treatment "concerned to
understand large thought units and their relationship to Pauline thoughts as a whole"
(1). Talbert discusses 2 Corinthians in three separate parts. There is little interaction with
fellow scholars (224pp.).

☆ **Taylor, Mark.** (NAC) 2014. Any looking for a workmanlike, mid-level commentary from a
conservative Baptist angle will welcome this publication. Taylor teaches at Southwestern
Baptist Seminary in Fort Worth, Texas, and there are approximately 420pp. of introduction
and commentary. It does not really break new ground, but is a dependable tool for its
intended audience. [*Chm* Spr 15; *JETS* 6/15; *Them* 7/14].

Thrall, Margaret. [*M*], *The First and Second Letters of Paul to the Corinthians* (CBC) 1965.
A capable scholar, Thrall has followed this up with a far more weighty commentary on
2 Corinthians in the ICC.

☆ Um, Stephen. (PTW) 2015. Sermonic material from a well educated (St. Andrews PhD),
dynamic, culturally engaged pastor at Citylife (PCA), Boston. I found the 32 messages
(350pp.) theologically perceptive, with wise, searching application.

Vang, Preben. (TTC) 2014. I have not seen this tool for preachers (253pp.), but I must pass on
to readers that the vol. has received praise. [*BSac* 7/15].

☆ Verbrugge, Verlyn. (EBCR) 2008. For preachers rather than students. This commentary of a
little over 170pp. is clear and simple without being simplistic. His exegetical decisions are
consistently the right ones, in my opinion (e.g., rejecting the ploy of excising 14:34–35/6).
I was saddened at his passing (†2015).

F  Wanamaker, C. (RRA).

F  ~~Wannenwetsch, B.~~ (Brazos).

F  Weima, Jeffrey. (EEC). The old report was H. Wayne House.

✓ Winter, Bruce. *After Paul Left Corinth*, 2001. A much-cited work for research on both epistles,
gathering evidence to understand what may have happened to the church community later.
Highly recommended! Cf. Harrison and Welborn above.

☆ **Witherington, Ben, III.** *Conflict and Community in Corinth: A Socio-Rhetorical Commentary
on 1 & 2 Corinthians*, 1995. Asks different, literary questions and provides a fresh reading.
This isn't just another commentary. Specifically, Witherington pursues the "wholesale
application of classical rhetorical categories" (Bill Salier) to the Corinthian correspondence. His many books complement other, more traditionally styled commentaries. I like
Witherington's insights, but, as has been pointed out in reviews, he seems to be over-
published or publishing too rapidly. This is betrayed in the poor proofreading some books
have received, especially earlier ones. See his other vols. on Mark, John, Acts, Romans,
Galatians, and Philippians. In fact, he has published on the whole NT canon. [*Them* 10/97;
*JETS* 3/98; *TJ* Spr 96; *Bib* 77.3; *Int* 1/97; *CBQ* 1/97].

F  Works, Carla Swafford. (CCF).

Wright, N. T. *Paul for Everyone: 1 Corinthians*, 2003. [*Chm* Win 05].

NOTES: (1) See John Ziesler's article surveying commentaries on 1 Corinthians in *ExpTim*,
6/86. (2) Matthew R. Malcomb reviews "The Structure and Theme of First Corinthians in
Recent Research," *CBR* 14 (2016): 256–69.

# 2 CORINTHIANS

★ **Barnett, Paul.** (NICNT-R) 1997. "Now the evangelical commentary of choice on II Corinthians,"
said E. E. Ellis, prior to the publication of NIGTC. And it still competes for the best mid-level

work available to pastors. Barnett follows Hughes in strongly defending the unity of the letter, unlike Thrall and Martin who find a compilation of three letters, and Barrett, Bruce, and Furnish who find two. There is also a judicious discussion of introductory matters—an important thing for a commentary on 2 Corinthians. Readers find much good theology here from a Sydney Anglican bishop. See BST below. [*RTR* 8/98; *SwJT* Spr 98; *CBQ* 10/98; *Bib* 79.1; *EvQ* 7/99; *JTS* 10/99; *Chm* 113.1; more critical are *Them* 5/99; *WTJ* Spr 01]. See also his study, *The Corinthian Question: Why Did the Church Oppose Paul?* (2011) [*JSNT* 34.5].

★ **Garland, David E.** (NAC) 1999; (CSC) 2nd ed. 2021. This manageable revised work, by a very gifted scholar and writer, reaps a rich harvest from other commentaries. And Garland himself is a veteran interpreter with many major books to his credit. Though I long made NICNT my first pick among commentaries on the English text, this vol. can take Barnett's place as a priority purchase for evangelical pastors, particularly those whose Greek is rusty and who are intimidated by the size or price of NIGTC and BECNT. [*Them* Sum 03; *JETS* 9/01].

★ **Guthrie, George H.** (BECNT) 2015. A very welcome exegesis of the Greek text by a scholar known for his landmark work on Hebrews. He applied himself diligently to the task of exegeting Paul's most difficult and fraught epistle; along the way he offers "a fresh look at certain interpretive issues" (Preface). I suggest that this large-scale work (650pp.) is best used by students and scholar-pastors, not as a sole resource, but alongside other major commentaries. That said, I'm finding I reach for Guthrie first. Its greatest strengths lie in the areas of bibliography; discussion of OT influences; analysis of grammar, literary structure, discourse, and rhetoric; exegetical and theological good sense; clarity of writing; and an engagingly warm tone. This was his first commentary on a Pauline epistle. [*ExpTim* 1/16; *WTJ* Fall 16; *BBR* 28.3; *CBQ* 4/16; *JETS* 3/17; *JSNT* 38.5; *Them* 40.3].

★ Hafemann, Scott J. (NIVAC) 2000. One of the largest and best researched vols. in the series—see his twin monographs: *Suffering and the Spirit on 2 Cor. 2:14–3:3* (1986) and *Paul, Moses, and the History of Israel: The Letter/Spirit Contrast and the Argument from Scripture in 2 Corinthians 3* (1995, 2005) [*EuroJTh* 16.2]. Hafemann did not produce the once-anticipated BECNT, so we are glad for this full work (over 500pp.), which is of value to students as well as pastors. Those looking for more pastoral/devotional expositions might consider Carson, Casto, Belleville, Hughes, Kistemaker, and the old work by Denney.

★ **Harris, Murray J.** (NIGTC) 2005. A publishing event! This is what NT students waited for. Harris is a fitting complement to Thiselton's definitive NIGTC commentary on Paul's First Letter to the Corinthians. He builds on his EBC work (see below), but this technical vol. far outstrips the earlier commentary. It offers a thoroughly satisfying exegesis and more theology than the series often has. There is meticulous discussion of grammatical matters (no verbal aspect theory). The one drawback is the price. Think of this conservative work as an investment which will repay study for years to come. While students may turn to Harris first, they will also be wise to consult Furnish, Thrall, Guthrie, Martin (2nd ed.), and Barrett. [*CBQ* 10/05; *Int* 7/06; *BBR* 16.1, 16.2; *JTS* 4/07; *BSac* 4/06; *JETS* 3/06; *TJ* Spr 06; *BL* 2006; *NovT* 50.2; *ExpTim* 12/06; *Presb* Spr 07].

F   Adewuya, J. Ayodeji. (NCCS).

Arthur, J. Philip. (Welwyn) 2001. Thoughtful expositional work from a Reformed Baptist pastor in the UK (250pp.).

✓ Baker, William R. (College Press NIV Commentary) 1999. Blomberg calls this 470-page work "probably the best vol. in the series thus far." [*Them* Aut 00; *JETS* 9/01].

☆ Barnett, Paul. (BST) 1988. The series is consistently thoughtful and stimulating for the preacher. No doubt, Stott the editor had a lot to do with keeping the standards high. Barnett is a leading example of the Reformed Anglicans associated with Moore College in Sydney. See the NICNT entry above. [*JETS* 12/91].

☆ **Barrett, C. K.** ‡ (BNTC) 1973. Much in the mold of the commentary on the first epistle, though for some reason I value the earlier one more. Carson continued to make this his first pick even in 1993. Preachers will appreciate how the commentary is often theologically charged and eloquent (see 8:9 and his reference to "the absolute naked poverty of crucifixion"). I used to include this among my recommended purchases, and this compact exegesis is still a smart buy, especially if you agree with the ancient Greek saying that "a big book is a big evil." [*JBL* 94.3].

☆ **Belleville, Linda.** (IVPNT) 1996. Careful, succinct exegesis (350pp.) is paired here with some fine theological reflection and pastoral application. Argues well for the unity of the letter. If all the vols. in the series were like this one, Fee on Philippians, and Marshall on 1 Peter, one might buy the whole set. [*Chm* 112.2].

Bernard, J. H. (Expositor's Greek Testament) 1903. Keep in reserve.

✓ Best, Ernest. ‡ (I) 1987. Perhaps the author put less effort into this book than he did into other projects.

✓ **Betz, Hans Dieter.** ‡ *2 Corinthians 8 & 9: A Commentary on Two Administrative Letters of the Apostle Paul* (Herm) ET 1985. Applies rhetorical criticism just to these two chapters. Students should certainly use their discernment here. Betz wrote on Galatians in the same distinguished technical series. [*JBL* 106.4].

✓ Bieringer, R., E. Nathan, and D. Kurek-Chomycz, eds. *2 Corinthians: A Bibliography*, 2008. Nearly 2000 entries. [*NovT* 52.3]. Also edited by Bieringer, Kurek-Chomycz, et al. is *Theologizing in the Corinthian Conflict: Studies in the Exegesis and Theology of 2 Corinthians* (2013) [*CBQ* 7/15; *BBR* 26.1].

✓ Bray, Gerald, ed. *1–2 Corinthians* (ACCS) 1999. See 1 Corinthians.

F  Briones, David E. (EEC).

☆ **Bruce, F. F.** (NCB) 1971. See under 1 Corinthians.

Bultmann, Rudolf. ‡ 1976, ET 1985. As students familiar with the radical critic might predict, he really disassembles the text. From KEK and can be ignored.

✓ Burke, Trevor, and J. K. Elliott, eds. *Paul and the Corinthians: Studies on a Community in Conflict*, 2003. A Festschrift vol. for Dr. Thrall.

☆ Carson, D. A. *From Triumphalism to Maturity*, 1984 = *A Model of Christian Maturity*, 2007. Preaching the last four chapters can be extraordinarily difficult because of the change in Paul's mood from chs. 9 to 10. This exposition can really help the pastor, but one should get the above recommended exegetical works first. This used to be on my "to buy" list in early editions. I am glad that it remains in print. Please note the change in title. [*Evangel* Spr 88; *EvQ* 4/87; *JETS* 9/85; *BSac* 1/08].

Casto, Trent. (REC) 2023. Regrettably, I have had no access to these 28 edited sermons (330 pp.), preached at Covenant Church (PCA) in Naples, Florida. The pastor is said to be thoughtful, earnest, faithful in his ministry, and a great speaker.

✓ **Collins, Raymond F.** ‡ (Paideia) 2013. A veteran Catholic scholar, Collins offers a succinct, more conservatively critical 270-page exegesis. He wrote for SacP on 1 Corinthians and NTL on the Pastorals. [*Int* 4/15; *CBQ* 7/15; *DenvJ* 17; *TJ* Fall 14].

✓ **Danker, Frederick.** [𝓜], 1989. Has lots to offer. Danker takes particular interest in the sociology of benefaction as a key to unlocking the main message of the epistle. Reads the letter as a unity, though chs. 10–13 are said to be written somewhat later. His broad learning is much in evidence. [*JTS* 4/91; *CRBR* 1991].

Denney, James. (EB) 1894. Ralph Martin gave this work a glowing recommendation and calls it "remarkably fresh and apropos on many issues." Denney is probably the best of the old homiletical commentaries.

☆ Diehl, Judith A. (SGBC) 2020. Offers a thoughtful, insightful interpretation (380pp.), with emphasis on application ("Live the Story"). Has good discussion of the theme of suffering, but in an accessible, relational style that is fitting for this extremely personal letter that reveals the "only too human Paul" (77). I missed any reference to Barnett or Guthrie. Diehl was on faculty at Denver Seminary.

Filson, Floyd V. ‡ (IB) 1953.

✓ **Furnish, Victor Paul.** ‡ (AB) 1984. A thorough introduction, full bibliography (dated), and well-reasoned exegesis from the critical angle. This is still among the best scholarly commentaries, though too detailed and academic for most pastors (600pp.). I commend the moderately critical work especially to advanced students who will relish the scholarship—but cf. Harris, Guthrie, Martin, and Thrall. He somewhat tentatively concludes that 6:14–7:1 comes from another hand. Pastors searching for another exegetical work, who think Furnish too full, should consider Belleville. [*WTJ* Fall 87; *ExpTim* 6/85; *JBL* 106.2; *EvQ* 7/87; *JETS* 9/85; *ThTo* 42.4].

F Gooder, Paula. ‡ (BBC). Her earlier study was *Only the Third Heaven? 2 Corinthians 12.1–10 and Heavenly Ascent* (2006) in LNTS.

F Gooder, Paula. (NIGTC-R). This would replace Harris.

F Graebe, Peter. (PentC).

F Hagen Pifer, Jeanette. (ZECNT). Previously she has written on *Faith as Participation* (2019) [*JSNT* 42.5].

☆ Harris, Murray J. (EBCR) 2008. Distills down to 130pp. his hugely detailed NIGTC. Valuable indeed! As with Keener's NCBC on Acts, I could again quote Oliver Wendell Holmes Sr. The old Harris EBC (1976) was an excellent, packed commentary of 100pp., but it sat alongside weaker works in that vol. 10.

✓ Hay, David M., ed. ‡ *Pauline Theology, Vol. 2: 1 and 2 Corinthians*, 1993.

✓ Héring, Jean. ‡ ET 1967. A significant work, previously cited often in the literature on 2 Corinthians. See under 1 Corinthians.

☆ Hodge, Charles. (GS) 1857–59. See under 1 Corinthians. Note the CrossC below.

Hodge, Charles. (CrossC) 1995. [*SBET* Spr 97].

Hubbard, Moyer V. (TTC) 2017. Said to be a clear, well-written, concise work (250pp.) by a Talbot professor with an Oxford DPhil. I have not seen it.

☆ Hughes, Philip Edgcumbe. (retired NICNT) 1962. Dependable, and especially valued for its theological insights into this very personal and emotional letter (see the rich commentary on chs. 3–6). Hughes also stood out for drawing insights from the church fathers. After 2 Corinthians received a lot of scholarly attention, long overdue, in recent decades, Hughes really seemed dated. There is still some value in Hughes (he was once among the top choices), and the vol. should not be discarded by pastors.

☆ Hughes, R. Kent. (PTW) 2006. Great for expositors! [*BSac* 7/06].

✓ Keener, Craig. [𝓜], *1–2 Corinthians* (NCBC) 2005. See under 1 Corinthians.

☆ Kistemaker, Simon J. (NTC) 1997. One of his last works.

☆ Kruse, Colin. (TNTC) 1987, rev. 2015. The original was a good, solid commentary, but with Harris, Furnish, Martin, Bruce, Barnett, and Barrett on my shelf, I found Kruse didn't add to my study. It was excellent for the money, though. I used to call it the best brief commentary by far before Belleville and Scott came along. [*RTR* 5/88; *Evangel* Sum 89]. The revision is a considerable improvement (288pp.).

☆ **Kruse, Colin G.** (EGGNT) 2020. A sure-footed walk through the Greek, and a joy to use. His past work in TNTC demonstrates Kruse has an excellent grasp of the message of the letter, not only of the grammatical-syntactical fine points. EGGNT is for pastors as well as students.

✓ **Lambrecht, Jan.** ‡ (SacP) 1999. Not as full (250pp.) as many others in the series and does not appear to interact as much with scholarship. Appearances can be deceiving. Lambrecht is a brilliant scholar and an expert on this so-difficult section of the Pauline corpus. Though he has not given us his very best work, he provides a valuable exegesis and theological interpretation from the critical angle. By the way, it is a more conservatively critical approach that he takes, upholding the unity and integrity of the epistle. Students should not miss this. [*Int* 1/00; *SwJT* Fall 00; *CBQ* 10/00; *ExpTim* 8/08].

Lightfoot, J. B. *The Epistles of 2 Corinthians and 1 Peter: A Newly Discovered Commentary*, 2016. Somewhat fragmentary remains of his research but worth noting. See Lightfoot under Acts. [*JSNT* 40.5; *BSac* 10/17].

☆ **Long, Fredrick J.** (BHGNT) 2015. A fine guide indeed through the rather complex Greek of this letter (300pp.). Previously Long published the important monograph *Ancient Rhetoric and Paul's Apology: The Compositional Unity of 2 Corinthians* (CUP, 2004).

✓ Manetsch, Scott, ed. (RCS) 2017.

☆ **Martin, Ralph P.** [𝓜], (WBC) 1986, rev. 2014. A leading scholarly work coming out about the same time as Furnish and competing with that AB. One had to be grateful to the energetic "R. P. M." (secret nickname among suffering students at Fuller) for all his painstaking work, as both an author and NT editor for WBC. His commentary was a success and demonstrated complete bibliographical control. To my mind, though, Furnish had a little more to offer in the way of well-considered exegesis. Their critical stances were very similar, as were their conclusions. Martin's theology was more conservative, and, as Hafemann once noted, he provided "the standard reference work for the history of interpretation." Harris's NIGTC and Thrall's ICC superseded both WBC and AB as guides through the exegetical options, and we are enriched, too, by Guthrie's research. [*WTJ* Fall 87; *SJT* 42.3; *RTR* 5/87; *JBL* 107.3]. Martin's revision (700pp.) is again a leading bibliographical help for students. Sadly, he didn't live to see its appearance (†2013). Note that some of the material, marked with gray-shaded paper, is contributed by several former students. Though the vol. is about 150pp. longer than the earlier edition, the commentary itself is only lightly revised. [*JSNT* 37.5; *Them* 4/15].

Martin, Ralph P. [𝓜], (CorBC) 2008. Paired with William Baker on 1 Corinthians and offering a scaled-down version of his WBC above. It has a more conservative feel.

✓ **Matera, Frank J.** ‡ (NTL) 2003. A leading, mid-level, critical commentary that argues for the unity of the letter (325pp.). Students should certainly consult this, especially for its discussion of rhetorical questions. There are some similarities of approach between Matera and Lambrecht, both lauded Catholic scholars. [*CBQ* 10/04; *Int* 7/04; *ExpTim* 4/04; *RelSRev* 4/04; *JETS* 3/05; *RB* 10/05; *CurTM* 8/05].

✓ McCant, Jerry W. ‡ (Read) 1999. [*JETS* 9/01; *Int* 10/02; *RelSRev* 4/01].

F  Meyer, Jason. (EBTC)?

Minor, Mitzi L. ‡ (S&H) 2009. I have yet to use Minor (257pp.). [*Int* 10/11 (Matera)].

F  Mitchell, Margaret. ‡ (Herm). See also Betz.

✓ Murphy-O'Connor, Jerome. ‡ 1991. From the Cambridge NT Theology series.

✓ Murphy-O'Connor, Jerome. ‡ *St. Paul's Corinth: Texts and Archaeology*, 3rd ed. 2002. See under 1 Corinthians.

Naylor, Peter. (EPSC) 2 vols., 2002. Extensive, conservative Reformed exposition from a learned, veteran English pastor. [*Evangel* Spr 05].

✓ Omanson, R. L., and J. Ellington. (UBS) 1994. [*JETS* 9/97].

✓ **Oropeza, B. J.** ‡ *Exploring Second Corinthians* (RRA) 2016. An enormous work, said to be some 850pp., which I have not seen. Oropeza teaches at Azuza Pacific, is prolific, and has a keen interest in intertextuality. [*JSNT* 39.5].

☆ Ortlund, Dane. "2 Corinthians" in *Romans–Galatians* (ESVEC) 2020. See Yarbrough under Romans.

✓ **Plummer, Alfred.** [𝓜], (retired ICC) 1915. More conservative, and a success in its day. Still consulted by students and scholars, but this is not the classic that the ICC was on 1 Corinthians. In any case it has now been replaced by Thrall.

Proctor, John. ‡ *First and Second Corinthians* (WestBC) 2015. [*ExpTim* 12/15].

✓ Roetzel, Calvin. ‡ (ANTC) 2007. The compact exegetical reference by a noted American Pauline scholar strangely does not list Barnett, Harris, or Martin in its bibliography. How did that happen? Roetzel follows the five-letter hypothesis and organizes his commentary in a somewhat confusing way. [*BL* 2009].

✓ Sampley, J. Paul. ‡ (NIB) 2000. [*SewaneeThRev* Easter 01].

✓ Savage, Timothy B. *Power through Weakness: Paul's Understanding of Christian Ministry in 2 Corinthians*, 1996. Originally an excellent Cambridge dissertation submitted in 1986, subsequently revised and updated.

☆ Scott, James M. (NIBC) 1998. A fine piece of work of middling length (267pp.), which competes with Kruse to be the "best bargain" in pb for the student. Scott was current with his NT scholarship, but courageous to buck the critical consensus and argue for the unity of the letter.

☆ **Seifrid, Mark A.** (Pillar) 2014. A diligent pastor's reference that saves space and time by focusing on the text, not citations of other scholars. Seifrid is a capable Pauline scholar and well-read; he just doesn't exhibit all his learning here. (I'm still surprised, though, that he nowhere interacts with Barnett, Barrett, and Matera.) The Introduction of 13pp. is followed by 500pp. of theologically oriented commentary. The work is "somewhat dense and requires very close attention," says Burnett [*JSNT* 37.5]. After 23 years at Southern Seminary (Baptist), he moved back to his Lutheran roots, joining Concordia Seminary in 2015. As Quarles notes [*SBJT* Spr 15], Seifrid cites Luther more than any other writer (28×). Amazingly, Luther citations appear more often than Harris, Furnish, Garland, Martin, and Belleville combined. Readers might have appreciated more dialogue with other scholars, especially in those places where Seifrid takes unusual positions (e.g., rejecting the concessive reading of ὤν at 8:9). [*Chm* Aut 16; *BBR* 27.1; *CBQ* 7/16; *JTS* 10/15; *JETS* 9/15].

☆ Shillington, V. George. (BCBC) 1998. Certainly one of the best in the NT series. The author, who teaches in Canada, did his PhD on Paul under E. P. Sanders at McMaster. He writes with good scholarship in vigorous prose. Deep, yet accessible to laypeople.

Stanley, Arthur P. *The Epistles of Paul to the Corinthians*, 1882. See 1 Corinthians.

Stegman, Thomas D. ‡ (CCSS) 2009. [*RBL* 8/10 (Collins); *CBQ* 4/12; *RelSRev* 12/11].

✓ Talbert, C. H. ‡ *Reading Corinthians: A Literary and Theological Commentary on 1 & 2 Corinthians* (RNT) 1987, rev. 2002. See 1 Corinthians.

Tasker, R. V. G. (retired TNTC) 1958. Replaced by Kruse, but insightful in short compass.

✓ Thiselton, Anthony C. [𝓜], *2 Corinthians: A Short Exegetical and Pastoral Commentary*, 2020. Quite useful for its insight and brevity (approx. 150pp.). [*ExpTim* 4/22].

✓ **Thrall, Margaret E.** [𝓜], (ICC-R) 2 vols., 1994–2000. The result of over three decades' research on 2 Corinthians, building on her popularly styled CBC (1965) and upon Furnish and Martin too. Thrall's set replaces Plummer and could be considered for purchase by advanced students and academically inclined pastors, but the cost is too steep ($190 in pb). She is judicious yet unafraid to challenge consensus and go her separate way. The first vol. of 500pp. includes an introduction and exegesis of chs. 1–7. The second vol. adds another 400pp. of commentary along with helpful excursuses and two concluding essays.

Though not without a few demerits, this set presents a most exacting exegesis of the Greek, carefully laying out the grammatical options. She holds that 2 Corinthians is a compilation of three letters. [*Bib* 77.2; *ExpTim* 1/95; *JTS* 10/96, 4/02; *SwJT* Spr 95; *JBL* Fall 96; *JETS* 9/97; *Them* Spr 03; *ExpTim* 8/01; *NovT* 44.2; *JSNT* 9/01; *JR* 1/03; *EvQ* 10/04; *SJT* 58.3; *Anvil* 18.4 (Barclay)]. Thrall is conservatively critical and has ties to the broader evangelical movement in the UK—e.g., writing reviews for *EvQ*. These vols. can be quite useful to conservative interpreters (mainly specialists), if they are willing to plow through very dense, difficult material. "Even the knowledgeable exegete will find Thrall's work slow going," says Belleville.

F   Tilling, Chris. (NICNT-R). See Tilling under Pauline Studies.
F   Towner, Philip. (THC).
Wan, Sze-kar. ‡ *Power in Weakness* (NT in Context) 2000. [*Int* 10/02].
F   Wan, Sze-kar. ‡ (Illum).
F   ~~Wannenwetsch, Bernd.~~ (Brazos).
✓   Winter, Bruce. *After Paul Left Corinth*, 2001. See under 1 Corinthians.
Wire, Antoinette Clark. ‡ (Wisdom) 2019. [*Int* 10/22; *JSNT* 42.5].
☆   **Witherington, Ben, III.** *Conflict and Community in Corinth: A Socio-Rhetorical Commentary on 1 & 2 Corinthians*, 1995. See under 1 Corinthians above.
Wright, N. T. *Paul for Everyone: 2 Corinthians*, 2003. [*Chm* Win 05].
✓   Young, Frances, and David Ford. *Meaning and Truth in 2 Corinthians*, 1987.

# GALATIANS

★   **deSilva, David.** (NICNT-R) 2018. Replaces Fung. As with his work on Hebrews, a well-written, careful yet stimulating exegesis, with strengths in historical backdrop and socio-rhetorical analysis. There is thorough research behind it (see deSilva below), but not the bulk of footnotes other scholars produce. The lengthy Introduction is superb, insisting on the Southern Galatian theory and proposing that Galatians is an "advisory type" letter, not "an example of forensic or judicial rhetoric" (94) with Paul defending himself against rival teachers. (Over the years Galatians has been treated to an astonishing number of fine rhetorical analyses.) As with Cohick's *Ephesians*, this NICNT has a wealth of excursuses. At 2:16 deSilva takes *pistis Christou* as most probably an objective genitive: "trusting Jesus" (235). I noted his good emphasis on the Spirit empowering the Christian for good works, but balked at some of his ideas about righteousness and final justification on the basis of works. (The language reflected more a version of the NPP than the Reformation's justification by faith alone ["free imputation of Christ's righteousness"], with good works as the necessary evidence of that vital faith which is the only causal ground of justification at the Last Day [see Calvin's *Institutes* 3.3.1; 3.11.13–20; 3.13.1–3.18.10]. Is deSilva adequately steering clear of Trent's assertion that works complete justification? In line with his Methodism, he sees justification as a process leading "to a consummation, at the future judgment, when God's initial gracious verdict on the sinner is—or, it may be, is not—confirmed" [219, Barrett's wording].) One weakness would be a lack of interaction with scholarship on union with Christ. Still, this is certainly a commentary the studious, well-trained pastor would want on the shelf. [*ETL* 3/22; *ExpTim* 6/19 (Tuckett); *JETS* 9/19; *Int* 1/20; *JSNT* 41.5].
★   **George, Timothy.** (NAC) 1994; (CSC) 2nd ed. 2020. Still worth a close look, because George has done a substantial revision, digesting nearly three decades of Galatians scholarship (including Dunn, Martyn, Gorman, Moo, and Schreiner). There is much to appreciate about this theologically astute, traditionally styled commentary. It meets pastors' needs since it is so focused on Paul's message. He is of greater assistance to the expositor than the exegete, for he is more engaged with the history of interpretation and less engaged

with NT scholarship. (George is an extraordinarily learned, veteran Reformation scholar and church historian.) There is solid exegesis here, though. Because commentaries often cover the same ground, it is advantageous to consult a work that has a rather different approach. [*WTJ* Fall 95; *EvQ* 10/96; *Them* 10/97; *JETS* 9/98; *CRBR* 1995].

★ **Longenecker, Richard N.** [*M*], (WBC) 1990. Superb introduction (119pp.), taking the South Galatian view. At points he should have treated the Scriptures with more respect, as when he speaks of the inspired Apostle unfairly caricaturing his opponents' teaching and activity (lxxxix)—are we to sympathize with the opponents? All that aside, this was once the best I knew of in the category of Greek exegesis (323pp.). Now Moo gets the nod. Galatians is probably better served with commentaries on the Greek text than any other NT book. There is an *embarras de richesse* here: Lightfoot, Burton, Bruce, Betz, Longenecker, Martyn, Schreiner, Moo, and Das. One criticism has been that Longenecker "tries too often to combine the older and newer approaches in a synthesis of contradictory interpretations" [*BSB* 12/96]. See also Longenecker's *The Triumph of Abraham's God* (1998) and his *Romans*. Note the forthcoming McCaulley. Many might prefer the handy Oakes to Longenecker. [*WTJ* Spr 93; *JTS* 10/92; *EvQ* 7/93; *JBL* Win 93; *CBQ* 10/92; *Them* 4/92; *JETS* 9/95; *CTJ* 11/92; *AsTJ* Spr 92].

★ **Moo, Douglas J.** (BECNT) 2013. Everything I'd hoped: mature scholarship (interacting with important literature), penetrating exegesis of the Greek, a healthy measure of theological exposition, displaying an enviable mastery of the Pauline corpus (with close comparison work on Romans in probing the NPP), fairly laying out all the exegetical options. If I could have but one commentary handy as I read my Greek NT, this would be my choice; what's more, I expect it may still be my top choice in ten years. The only suggested improvement would be that, although incorporation into Christ is termed "the theological center from which the various lines of Paul's theological reasoning radiate" (33), more could be said about union with Christ. What is said, though, is right on target (55–57, 155, 251–56). Students will most definitely compare Moo with the acclaimed de Boer, Oakes, deSilva, etc. [*BBR* 24.4; *JETS* 12/14; *ExpTim* 5/15; *Them* 4/14; *DenvJ* 18; *Int* 10/15 (Das)]. An excellent essay (35pp.) on the way to the BECNT was "Justification in Galatians," in *Understanding the Times* (Carson FS, 2011).

★ Ryken, Philip. (REC) 2005. Model theological and practical exposition. While students pass this by, pastors enjoy edifying food for the soul. Happy and healthy is the church fed like this. With regard to expositional and devotional helps, we are well-supplied; besides Ryken and Wilson, see Calvin, Gupta, Harmon, Keller, McKnight, Stott, and Thielman.

★ **Schreiner, Thomas R.** (ZECNT) 2010. In Moo and Schreiner, American evangelicalism had two stellar, well-written commentaries on the Greek text of Galatians in a three-year span. This is the more approachable and contains discussion of application, while Moo interacts with more scholarship, is denser, more deliberate, and rigorous. Students and scholarly pastors will want both for their thorough, dependable exegesis and satisfying theological interpretation—both scholars have a Reformed orientation and, while appreciating some of the corrective offered by the New Perspective, follow the more traditional approach. Note that Schreiner pushes his Baptist beliefs harder (e.g., p.257) and to me sounds dogmatic, even off-base, at a few contentious points. E.g., OT scholars I know would be mystified and disappointed at the assertion that the Abrahamic and Mosaic covenants "are fundamentally opposed" (232). He also speaks of "a fundamental incompatibility." Would that he reread Calvin on 3:21. Is Schreiner's way of speaking tied to the problematic idea of some that the Mosaic covenant is a "republication" of a supposed covenant of works with Adam? [*BBR* 22.3; *JSNT* 34.5 (Oakes); *Chm* Sum 14; *Them* 4/12; *DenvJ* 15; *TJ* Spr 13; *JETS* 3/12].

★ Wilson, Todd. (PTW) 2013. The author receives high commendations from the likes of Moo, Gathercole, and Schreiner. Think of this as competition for Ryken; Wilson's background

(Cambridge PhD on Galatians) and 30pp. of exegetical notes (229–58) mean this is the better-studied product. I am happy to recommend both sermonic vols. to pastors. (Full of grace, I can't judge between them.) By the way, Wilson's dissertation was *The Curse of the Law and the Crisis in Galatia* (2007).

Arichea, D. C., and E. A. Nida. (UBS) 1976.

Augustine. *Augustine's Commentary on Galatians*, ET 2003. A fresh OUP translation and pleasingly full introduction by Eric Plumer.

F  Barclay, John M. G. [𝓜], (ITC). Eagerly awaited by many scholars, and will build on his older research in *Obeying the Truth: Paul's Ethics in Galatians* (1988).

Barnes, Peter. (EPSC) 2006. A fine conservative exposition, of good length (350pp.), by a Presbyterian pastor and church historian in Australia. It is clear and accessible enough to be a help to pastors and also educated laity. Barnes makes clear his opposition to the NPP.

✓  Barrett, C. K. ‡ *Freedom and Obligation*, 1985. A rigorous and penetrating study of Paul's argument. [*JBL* 106.4; *ThTo* 44.2].

Bedford, Nancy. ‡ (Belief) 2016. [*Int* 1/19].

✓  **Betz, Hans Dieter.** ‡ (Herm) 1979. This major work stimulated others to utilize classical rhetorical analysis in studying the epistles. In fact, as Hays writes, "the agenda for the interpretation of Galatians during the past twenty years [1980–2000] has been set by . . . Betz's Hermeneia commentary . . . (see, e.g., the commentaries of R. N. Longenecker and B. Witherington, which seek in various ways to correct, refine, and expand upon Betz's analysis of the rhetorical structure)." The vol. is aimed at scholars, and pastors should look to other commentaries for help with the text and message of Galatians. [*WTJ* Fall 83; *TJ* Spr 80; *JBL* 100.2]. For a critique of rhetorical approaches see Kern, *Rhetoric and Galatians* (CUP, 1998).

Bligh, J. ‡ 1969. A huge commentary by an English Roman Catholic, dated and not of much use, in my view. [*JBL* 89.1].

✓  **Boer, Martinus C. de.** ‡ (NTL) 2011. Praised by Oakes, his former colleague, as "now the benchmark for thorough work on the letter." After a 15-page, to-the-point introduction, de Boer offers 400pp. of exegesis that demonstrate why he has the reputation of being a profound, penetrating, clear thinker. He seeks to trace what Paul is meaning to say and "the intended readers' likely reception of his words" (2). He favors the northern Galatian theory, the "faith of Christ" idea in 2:16, and follows lines of interpretation similar to Martyn's (e.g., Paul appropriates Jewish apocalyptic eschatology). The letter contains five summaries of the gospel and the rhetorical climax is taken to be 5:1. Paul, in using vocabulary from the stem *dikai-*, "gives them new, nonforensic meanings" (186). "God rectifies (makes just/righteous) those who believe in Christ by delivering them from enslaving powers" (191). The theology of the letter is constantly kept in view. De Boer taught at Princeton Seminary, Manchester, and the Free University. [*WTJ* Spr 13 (Silva); *BBR* 23.1; *CBQ* 7/13; *Int* 7/12; *JETS* 6/12; *BTB* 8/14; *RelSRev* 6/13; *SJT* 68.1].

Boice, James M. (EBC) 1976. Helpful for pastors in communicating Paul's message, but didn't add to the discussion from an academic point of view. See Rapa.

✓  Bray, Gerald L., ed. *Galatians, Ephesians* (RCS) 2011. What a superb companion to modern-day commentaries! Bray's selectivity is brilliant. He provides a reminder that the magisterial Reformers were astute exegetes as well as theologians.

Bring, Ragnar. ET 1961. An o/p Lutheran work of less use today. At one time it was praised as "extremely perceptive" (Cousar) for theological reflection.

☆  **Bruce, F. F.** (NIGTC) 1982. In the 1980s this was my top pick for a work on the Greek text, showing wise exegetical judgment and providing expert discussion of the historical background. This is still such a good technical commentary that many well-trained pastors will wish to add it to their library at some point—I use Bruce nearly as much as Longenecker. However, there are two drawbacks: Bruce is not much expositional help, and he hardly discusses the then-emerging NPP. [*WTJ* Fall 83; *RTR* 5/83; *JETS* 9/82; *JBL* 104.2].

F   Burer, Michael. (EEC) 2024. By a Dallas Seminary prof (540pp.).

✓   **Burton, E. D.** ‡ (ICC) 1921. One of the best, fullest entries in the old series. For detailed, close exegesis academics still use Burton, but I doubt that pastors will be willing to dig through these pages. A number of his theological conclusions are fundamentally wrong-headed. Students should not miss the valuable appendix (363ff).

☆   Calvin, John. *Sermons on Galatians*, 1557–58, ET 1997. A welcome modern translation of the Reformer's lengthy sermon series (671pp.), published by Banner. [*CTJ* 11/98; *SBET* Aut 99]. Note the 16th century Golding translation reprinted in 1995 by Old Paths [*RelSRev* 27.2].

F   Carson, D. A. (Pillar).

   Cole, R. Alan. (TNTC) 1965, rev. 1989. Useful, handy, but undistinguished.

✓   Cousar, Charles. ‡ (I) 1982. An older theological exposition from a moderately liberal, influential Presbyterian at Columbia Seminary. At the time, higher-critical issues tended not to color the interpretation of Galatians quite as much because there is agreement on the unity of the letter and Paul's authorship. Cousar is a stronger vol. in the series, but feels quite dated (158pp.). [*Int* 7/83].

   Cousar, Charles B. ‡ *Reading Galatians, Philippians, and 1 Thessalonians* (RNT) 2001.

✓   Cummins, Stephen Anthony. *Paul and the Crucified Christ in Antioch: Maccabean Martyrdom and Galatians 1 and 2*, 2001.

☆   **Das, A. Andrew.** (ConcC) 2014. A well-recognized, deeply learned, trenchant Pauline scholar in the U.S., Das has written one of the strongest, most learned NT vols. (over 700pp.) in this large-scale conservative Lutheran series. Concordia is mainly for well-trained pastors, but Das's *Galatians* merits wider use because it is more engaged with current scholarly debates. He is so right: "the time is ripe for a Lutheran commentary on Galatians that takes on the full range of modern scholarship on the letter" (xiv), and he delivered! His work is highly theological. The treatment of 2:17, a difficult text, and a couple of others struck me as odd. [*JSNT* 37.5; *JETS* 12/15; *Int* 1/16]. Making a few waves since is *Paul and the Stories of Israel: Grand Thematic Narratives in Galatians* (2016) [*JETS* 6/17; *JSNT* 39.5; *Them* 45.3].

☆   **deSilva, David A.** (BHGNT) 2014. See deSilva above, and note his *Sri Lankan Commentary* of 2011 [*JSNT* 34.5]. Taking a slightly different approach than other Baylor Handbook guides, deSilva pays close attention to rhetoric as well as the fine points of lexical and grammatical analysis (195pp.). He does more than merely lay out the options; see his argument for the objective genitive at 2:16 (43). A more profitable representative of the well-conceived and executed series.

✓   **Dunn, James D. G.** [𝓜], (BNTC) 1993. From a Pauline scholar of immense stature with a special interest in the Apostle's theology of the law. Dunn pushes hard what he calls "The New Perspective on Paul," *BJRL* 65 (1983). Most conservatives disagree with his interpretation of Paul's argument (i.e., that Paul was opposing himself, not to confidence in human merit and works-righteousness, but to Jewish exclusivism). This full commentary (400pp.)—far more scholarly than might first appear—is definitely to be consulted for papers, but I believe the pastor should look elsewhere for a trusty theological guide through Galatians. Students note its companion, *The Theology of Paul's Letter to the Galatians* (CUP, 1993) [*JBL* Win 95; *SJT* 51.2]; "it would be hard to think of a better introduction to the new perspective on Paul than this book" (Rosner). Two early appraisals of Dunn's theology worth mentioning, alongside the numerous books referenced above under "Pauline Studies," are Silva, "The Law and Christianity: Dunn's New Synthesis," *WTJ* Fall 91; and Hagner's "Paul and Judaism, The Jewish Matrix of Early Christianity: Issues in the Current Debate," *BBR* 3 (1993): 111–130. [*WTJ* Fall 95; *RTR* 9/94; *JETS* 9/98; *SwJT* Fall 97].

✓ Eastman, Susan Grove. ‡ *Recovering Paul's Mother Tongue: Language and Theology in Galatians*, 2007.

✓ Edwards, Mark J., ed. *Galatians, Ephesians, Philippians* (ACCS) 1999. [*RelSRev* 4/00; *EvQ* 7/02].

✓ Elliott, Mark, Scott Hafemann, N. T. Wright, and John Frederick, eds. *Galatians and Christian Theology: Justification, the Gospel, and Ethics in Paul's Letter*, 2014. Not to be missed. [*ExpTim* 1/16; *BBR* 26.3; *JETS* 12/15].

✓ Esler, Philip F. ‡ (New Testament Readings) 1998. [*ScrB* 1/99; *RB* 108.1; *BibInt* 9.1].

☆ Fee, Gordon. (PentC) 2007. A balancing act here as Fee sets out to write a commentary "for others within my tradition," while his "first intent is to understand Paul's letter on its own terms, not in terms of a special agenda" (viii). He adds that a major concern is "to help people read Galatians as if the Reformation had never happened" (1). Hmm. Another fact indicates that Fee was attempting a fresh reading: the bibliography has but eleven entries. But it's Fee, so it's worth perusing. I think he's right on a key point of criticism of the Protestant tradition; in reading Galatians (with Luther and Pope Leo X in the back of our minds, and justification at the front of our minds) we have sometimes given less attention to Paul's orienting concern in 3:3: "having *begun* by the Spirit, are you now trying to *finish* by means of the flesh?" Fee says elsewhere, "This is the question to which the entire argument of the letter is devoted as a response" (*God's Empowering Presence*, 384). The book is the product of four decades of teaching Paul (257pp.). [*JETS* 6/09].

Fesko, J. V. (LCEC) 2012. Conservative exposition by a theology prof at RTS (once at Westminster California). Some highly regard this work, but I have not seen it.

☆ Fung, R. Y. K. (retired NICNT) 1988. A lucid mid-level commentary, building on Bruce (Fung trained under him at Manchester) and of greater help expositionally than NIGTC. It is a laudable effort, but has not aged well. I'm not sure of the reason for so many references to Kittel's *TDNT*. Students need to be made aware of Barr's well-founded criticisms of that famous dictionary, and cautioned against a naïve use of the word study method. Barr's proposition needs to ring in our ears: theological thinking is done mainly in the phrase and the sentence, not in the word. Now see the deSilva NICNT. [*WTJ* Fall 89; *JETS* 6/90; *JTS* 10/90; *EvQ* 7/90].

Garlington, Don. 3rd ed. 2007. A substantial exegesis and exposition, reflecting the NPP and Dunn's influence. (The author did PhD studies at Durham.)

Greene-McCreight, Kathryn. ‡ (Brazos) 2023. The author is a spiritual director at Berkeley Divinity School, Yale. I have not seen this. [*ExpTim* 11/23].

☆ **Gupta, Nijay K.** (SGBC) 2023. An inviting, well-written theological and practical commentary and a fine representative of the series. Like McKnight (see below), the series editor, Gupta is strongly influenced by Dunn and the NPP, as well as by Gorman. At stake in Paul's conflict with the preachers of "a different gospel" (1:6) was "what it means to be a part of God's family." Gupta repeatedly finds an emphasis on the "family theme" (esp. in ch. 4). He terms it a myth that "Galatians is about justification by faith" (13) and views "2:20 as the headline verse for this letter" (14). In line with his *Paul and the Language of Faith* (2020)—see under "Pauline Studies"—he takes *faith* to be "an active mode of engagement and receptivity" (18); it is not "a work in and of itself," nor is it passive. His applications try to avoid politics but tend to be progressive evangelical in tone (e.g., pp. 151–55). My chief criticism is his seeming lack of awareness that justification as "forensic declaration" and as received only in our faith-union with Christ were *both* tenaciously held by the magisterial

Reformers (82–83). Students might note that he edits the New Word Biblical Themes series and has contributed the approximately 150-page inaugural entry on Galatians (2024).

Guthrie, Donald. (NCB) 1969. A model of clarity in the way it expounds Paul's line of thinking. There is not a wasted word, no sidelights. Guthrie shows that he has the gift for distilling things down and explaining the theology here. This also means that he is not so penetrating as others. Quite dated. [*RTR* 5/70].

☆ Hansen, Walter. (IVPNT) 1994. Deserves recognition as a fine work in its class: brief exegesis and exposition (212pp.). Earlier he published "a very valuable monograph" (Silva) on *Abraham in Galatians: Epistolary and Rhetorical Contexts* (1989). As he briefly interacts with the NPP, he "finally sides" (Hagner) with its opponents. See Hansen on Philippians. [*WTJ* Fall 95 (Silva); *JETS* 9/98 (Hagner); *Chm* 109.1 (more critical)].

☆ **Harmon, Matthew S.** (EBTC) 2021. Previously, the Grace Seminary prof (Wheaton PhD) wrote a pastoral commentary on Philippians (Mentor). This one too is very well-researched and rewarding. I value it especially for the Biblical and Theological Themes (373–478), but the treatment of the Greek text is fine. I agree with Harmon that it is a false dichotomy to set the apocalyptic and salvation-historical approaches entirely against each other. He seeks "a more holistic reading" (373). For a great many evangelical pastors, this book will be near the top of the list. [*JSNT* 45.5].

F   Harmon, Matthew S. (EGGNT).

✓ **Hays, Richard B.** [*M*], (NIB) 2000. Takes up some of Martyn's views, which Hays considers so important. Of course Hays is a major force among Paulinists in his own right—see his diss., *The Faith of Jesus Christ* (1983, 2nd ed. 2001 [*Evangel* Aut 03]), and a favorite book of mine, *Echoes of Scripture in the Letters of Paul* (1989). Though brief (166 large pp.), NIB may be considered among the best commentaries on Galatians, especially for those pastors without time for huge vols. like AB. Both exegesis and "Reflection" are superbly done and stimulating, even for one like me who disagrees on a number of issues. By the way, don't be too quick to follow Hays's argument for πίστις Χριστοῦ as a subjective genitive; see Roy A. Harrisville, "Before ΠΙΣΤΙΣ ΧΡΙΣΤΟΥ: The Objective Genitive as Good Greek," *NovT* 48.4 (2006): 353–58; Barry Matlock, "Detheologizing the ΠΙΣΤΙΣ ΧΡΙΣΤΟΥ Debate," *NovT* 42 (2000): 1–24; and Cranfield's cautionary essay (81–97) in the book *On Romans* (1998). For fuller discussions one can look up the Dunn–Hays dialogue in the 2001 edition of the dissertation, and Bird–Sprinkle under "Pauline Studies." Complicating things further is Kevin Grasso, "A Linguistic Analysis of πίστις Χριστοῦ: The Case for a Third View," *JSNT* 43 (2020): 108–44.

F   Heim, Erin M. (BGW).

Hendriksen, William. (NTC) 1969.

Jervis, Ann. [*M*], (NIBC) 1999. Well-informed, concise exegesis (160pp.), by a Wycliffe College, Toronto professor. Jervis favors a NPP interpretation (Sanders and Dunn). [*Int* 7/00; *Chm* Win 00; *RTR* 4/01].

F   Jervis, Ann. ‡? (Illum).

Johnson, Terry L. (Mentor) 2012. A substantial pastoral-devotional work. Christian Focus gave us two Galatians expositions in the series. See McWilliams.

☆ **Keener, Craig S.** 2019. Stamina required! As we have come to expect (after his Acts set), Keener delivers a huge tome (588-page commentary), evidencing his dazzling command of ancient sources and the secondary literature (125-page bibliography). Along with his own translation and exegetical work (with less discussion of the Greek than I had expected), there are 34 excurses. Do distinguish this from the condensed 2018 Cambridge commentary on the NRSV. One reviewer estimates that "70% of the text of the longer work is found in the shorter" (Jones [*Them* 45.2]); the 2019 work has "much more extensive documentation in the notes." As with the deSilva NICNT, readers are treated to a major, learned, socio-rhetorical commentary from a Methodist perspective. The differences are deSilva's more manageable length for busy pastors, openness to the NPP, and greater focus on the text's message. For historical background and literary context, Keener is invaluable. Advanced students and the best-trained pastors will gravitate toward this. [*ExpTim* 10/21; *CBQ* 7/21; *JETS* 12/20; *Int* 10/20 (Das); *BSac* 4/21; *JSNT* 42.5 (Oakes)].

Keller, Tim. *Galatians for You*, 2013. See Romans.

✓ Levy, Ian Christopher, ed. (BMT) 2011. [*Chm* Sum 13; *ETL* 88.4; *CBQ* 10/16].

✓ **Lightfoot, J. B.** 1865. Hard to believe, but a case can be made that this oft-reprinted work is still among the richest exegeses around. Carson sells it short when he writes that Lightfoot has been mined so thoroughly that he hardly adds anything to more modern treatments. It continues to be mined because it is an enduring classic. Students and pastors gain from mining it too; the exercise is a lesson in appreciating the worth of classic commentaries. *Evangel* [Sum 1989] assesses Lightfoot's contributions to scholarship. Note his Philippians and Colossians–Philemon, all free online.

✓ **Lührmann, Dieter.** ‡ (ContC) ET 1992. A more manageable German exegesis (Lutheran), not as full as many of the other scholarly works on this list (168pp.). Lührmann concentrates on theology and does not provide a technical, historical, and linguistic commentary. The Germans no longer dominate Pauline studies as they once did. [*WTJ* Fall 95; *SJT* 49.4].

☆ **Luther, Martin.** 1519 and 1535. I recommend Concordia's edition of the two commentaries in *Luther's Works* (vols. 26 and 27, ET 1963–64). One of the two was available in an 1839 translation reprinted in 1979. I also saw a modern "Today's English" edition (Camacho, 2018). In 1998 the work was edited for CrossC; that pb edition is certainly the cheapest. Because Luther is free online (ccel.org), I removed the purchase recommendation. "It is Luther's Commentary on Galatians which has stimulated generations of readers to sense the power of Paul" (Childs). But perhaps it isn't the power of Paul or the vigor of Luther; it is the emancipating power *of Christ* which comes through in these commentaries. Lightfoot gives this note of praise: "The value of Luther's work stands apart from and in some respects higher than its merits as a commentary" (ix).

Lyons, George. (NBBC) 2010. "A Commentary in the Wesleyan Tradition," it should serve well its intended audience. [*BBR* 23.1; *CBQ* 1/14; *Int* 4/14; *ExpTim* 6/13].

MacArthur, John. 1987. Useful for its pastoral concern and passion for proclamation, but students look elsewhere for help. See further comments under Matthew.

✓ Machen, J. Gresham. *Notes on Galatians*, 1972. Fragmentary but incisive. The student could learn much about exegesis here. Machen takes a "North Galatian" view.

F McCaulley, Esau. (WBC-R). To replace Longenecker. Previously, he wrote *Sharing in the Son's Inheritance: Davidic Messianism and Paul's Worldwide Interpretation of the Abrahamic Land Promise in Galatians* (2019) [*JSNT* 42.5].

☆ McKnight, Scot. (NIVAC) 1995. McKnight's mentors were Dunn and E. P. Sanders. This is a fine homiletical commentary from that perspective. However, some of us think that, according to the NPP, Galatians's argument has a much narrower application than the traditional interpretation and is more or less confined to pastoral problems in the 1st century. In other words, Dunn's thesis makes applying Galatians today difficult. McKnight is the NT editor of the series. [*JETS* 3/98; *ATJ* 29]. Cf. Gupta.

McWilliams, David B. (Mentor) 2009. Edifying, Reformed exposition.

✓ **Martyn, J. Louis.** ‡ (AB) 1997. A favorite of NT specialists. Hays calls it "a work of provocative scholarship, unmatched in its penetrating insight and theological depth by any NT commentary of our generation." That's overdoing it, but this AB gains such high praise because it, somewhat like Barth's work on Romans, is a theological treatise in its own right.

Martyn understands Galatians to be "the reproclamation of the gospel in the form of an evangelistic sermon" (22). He develops Käsemann's "apocalyptic gospel" idea and points to 4:3–5 as "the theological center of the letter" (388). The grace of God is understood as operating more on the grand, cosmological scale (God's invasion in the cross), and less on the level of the individual (the dominant Protestant emphasis since Luther). He downplays forensic elements in the book. Some reviewers, e.g., Carson, believe that Martyn's exegetical judgment can frequently be called into question. He is not for the average pastor, but scholarly types may find Martyn fascinating. [*JR* 4/00; *ExpTim* 5/00; *Int* 10/98; *CBQ* 4/99; *PSB* 21.1; *JSNT* 75; *AsTJ* Spr 02; *JBL* Sum 00; *RBL*; *DenvJ*].

✓ **Matera, Frank J.** ‡ (SacP) 1992. Cousar, also a commentator on this Bible book, gives Matera very high marks. Those wanting a moderately critical reading of Galatians from the Catholic perspective should look this up. Matera essentially follows Dunn's views on the heresy of the Jewish missionaries. I usually read Dunn rather than Matera. [*ExpTim* 3/93; *Int* 4/94; *CBQ* 10/94; *CRBR* 1994; *ExpTim* 8/08].

☆ Morris, Leon. 1996. Accessible, useful, and dependable (191pp.). This is not unlike Morris's *Romans* in style and worth. It will not spark great excitement, but it does the job of providing pastors with solid phrase-by-phrase exposition. Morris has a standard commentary format with good attention paid to details like word study. It is less useful to students. [*Them* 2/00; *SBET* Spr 97].

✓ Nanos, Mark D., ed. ‡ *The Galatians Debate*, 2002. Students gain much from consulting this collection of twenty-three articles. [*RelSRev* 10/03; *JTS* 10/04; *WTJ* Fall 03; *RTR* 4/04; *TJ* Fall 04]. There is also his published dissertation: *The Irony of Galatians* (2001) [*HBT* 12/02; *JETS* 3/03; *JBL* Sum 02; *Int* 7/03; *ExpTim* 2/03; *JR* 10/02; *JTS* 10/05; *JSS* Spr 04; *BibInt* 12.4].

Ngewa, Samuel. (ABCS) 2010. The author was my senior colleague at Nairobi Evangelical Graduate School of Theology. The briefer exposition (195pp.) is thoughtful, accessible, and well-written, with a winsome personal touch (e.g., his witnessing story on p.123). See his work on the Pastorals. [*DenvJ* 14].

☆ **Oakes, Peter.** [𝓜], (Paideia) 2015. Best in the series? A model of compressed, well-informed scholarship (200pp.), Oakes's commentary was eagerly awaited. He is among the leading participants in Pauline studies, is a careful exegete, articulates well the positions of other writers, and brings his impressive learning in the 1st century social-historical context to bear on his interpretation. A strong point here is Oakes's clear reasoning through Paul's argument, and the discussion is on a high level (e.g., pp.80–91). [*ExpTim* 12/15; *BSac* 7/18; *BBR* 26.3; *CBQ* 4/19; *JETS* 6/16; *Int* 7/17; *JSNT* 38.5 (Wenham)]. See also the recent T&T Clark intro *Rethinking Galatians* (2021) by Oakes and colleague Boakye [*JETS* 6/22; *JSNT* 43.5].

Osborne, Grant R. (ONTC) 2017. See under Commentary Series.

Perkins, Pheme. ‡ *Abraham's Divided Children* (NT in Context) 2001.

Platt, David, and Tony Merida. *Exalting Jesus in Galatians* (CCE) 2014.

✓ Plumer, Eric. *Augustine's Commentary on Galatians: Introduction, Text, Translation, and Notes* (OUP) ET 2003. [*EuroJTh* 15.1].

Ramsay, W. M. *A Historical Commentary on St. Paul's Epistle to the Galatians*, 2nd ed. 1900.

Rapa, Robert K. (EBCR) 2008. The author did a dissertation on *The Meaning of "Works of the Law" in Galatians and Romans*. My sense is that the scholar was not given adequate space, and the commentary section (80 of 92pp.) is less useful as a result.

✓ Riches, John. ‡ *Galatians through the Centuries* (BBC) 2008. [*CBQ* 4/09; *BL* 2009; *ExpTim* 7/09; *Int* 7/10; *EuroJTh* 18.1].

Ridderbos, Herman. (retired NICNT) 1953. Replaced by Fung. Though insightful and theologically astute in its day, Ridderbos's work suffered on account of brevity. [*WTJ* Spr 54]. Get his more mature reflections in *Paul: An Outline of His Theology*.

✓ Silva, Moisés. *Interpreting Galatians*, 2001. This fine book is nearly identical to a 1996 issue, *Explorations in Exegetical Method: Galatians as a Test Case* [*JETS* 9/99]. It was preliminary to a BECNT, but see Moo. [*Them* Spr 03; *SwJT* Spr 03; *BBR* 14.2].

✓ **Soards, Marion L., and Darrell J. Pursiful.** [𝓜], (S&H) 2015. Fairly full for the series (nearly 350pp.), intelligent, and engagingly written from a mainline perspective. The coauthors are influenced by the NPP (see pp.111–12) and the apocalyptic interpretation of Martyn.

☆ Stott, John R. W. *Only One Way: The Message of Galatians* (BST) 1968. Long praised by expositors, Stott was a recommended purchase through 2010. His ability to grasp the theology of the text, his practicality, and his ability to communicate make this an ideal tool for sermon work. Many have made use of it as a handbook for Bible studies, and devotional guide. If one doesn't want books of sermons (Ryken, Wilson), buy Stott. The 2020 "revised edition" is a light editing, years after Stott's passing (†2011).

Tenney, Merrill C. 1950.

☆ Thielman, Frank. "Galatians" in *Romans–Galatians* (ESVEC) 2020. See Yarbrough under Romans.

F **Tuckett, Christopher M.** ‡ (ICC-R) 2024. A magnum opus from the series editor?

F Van Voorst, Robert. (~~ECC~~). What happens after the series' demise?

Vanhoye, Albert, and Peter S. Williamson. ‡ (CCSS) 2019. The French Jesuit Vanhoye (†2021) was a Cardinal and rector emeritus at the Pontifical Biblical Institute. His work, originally a textbook in Rome, is translated and adapted here by Williamson and Marsha Daigle-Williamson. [*CBQ* 7/20; *JSNT* 42.5].

Weidmann, Frederick W. ‡ (WestBC) 2012. [*Int* 7/13].

✓ Williams, Jarvis J. (NCCS) 2020. Seems to write in an edgy, unsettling way on an edgy letter (180pp.). Williams is on faculty at Southern Seminary (Baptist) and has previously written on the law in Paul's theology, Galatians, Romans, and racism. Galatians 2 and 3 receive the closest scrutiny here. See his *Christ Redeemed 'Us' from the Curse of the Law* (2019) [*JSNT* 42.5, 44.5].

✓ **Williams, Sam K.** ‡ (ANTC) 1997. Compact. Has received some rather favorable reviews as a lucid, non-technical presentation of the conclusions of important critical scholarship. Williams treats the Apostle's arguments as "matters of opinion—Paul's opinion," and argues that his "polemical charges provide an unreliable basis for characterizing the aims and motives of these Jewish-Christian missionaries" (25). I wish he had more sympathy with Paul and his gospel. [*Int* 7/98; *CBQ* 10/98].

☆ **Witherington, Ben, III.** *Grace in Galatia: A Commentary on Paul's Letter to the Galatians*, 1998. Quite well-done and full (459pp.). Pastors could put this to excellent use. Personally, I regret the way he directs a critique at missionaries—always an "easy mark"—on p.458; and I add that he gets the facts of the story wrong (there was no hint of "cultural imperialism," and it was not Africa). See my comments under 1 Corinthians. [*Int* 7/99; *RelSRev* 4/00; *RB* 108.1; *JSNT* 76].

Witherup, Ronald D. ‡ *Galatians: Life in the New Creation*, 2020. Catholic exposition.

F Wright, N. T. (THC). Will this appear? Hints at Wright's approach are given in "The Letter to Galatians: Exegesis and Theology," in *Between Two Horizons* (2000).

✓ **Wright, N. T.** [𝓜], (CCF) 2021. The first issue of an approachable Eerdmans series focused on the intersection of theology and spiritual formation. As always, Wright excels at putting his own theological interpretation across in a forceful and engaging way. And as with his major Romans commentary, he is a fascinating read from the NPP angle. He repeatedly issues rebuttals of traditional Protestant interpretations—e.g., soteriology, he says, is definitely not the main concern of the epistle. Ecclesiology is the thrust instead: "Paul is advocating a *messianic eschatology* with a *messianic family*" (162). (See the "Pauline Studies" section above.) Call this "a clear distillation of Wright's main project for reinterpreting Paul and Judaism" [*RelSRev* 3/22]. [*WTJ* Spr 22; *ExpTim* 5/22; *CBQ* 7/22; *Int* 10/22 (Matera)].

✓ Yoon, David I. *A Discourse Analysis of Galatians and the New Perspective on Paul*, 2019. [*CBQ* 4/21; *JSNT* 42.5].

# EPHESIANS

★ **Arnold, Clinton E.** (ZECNT) 2010. Builds on an Aberdeen PhD, *Ephesians: Power and Magic* (1989). Arnold is general editor of the series and fittingly published one of the first entries. He acknowledges Guthrie's help in refining the "text diagrams," a defining feature of ZECNT. Because it treats the original, pastors need at least a year of Greek to make best use of this large exegesis (nearly 500pp.). Expositors are happy that Arnold devotes greater attention to texts that are a challenge to preach (e.g., 5:21–33, given 50pp.) and makes suggestions for applying the message. (He is in the complementarian camp.) I found his exegesis and theological exposition dependable. He makes a contribution in discussing the letter's purpose (41–46), though others find "little obvious purpose" (Muddiman). He refines O'Brien's construal: the purpose is "to affirm [the Ephesian churches] in their new identity in Christ as a means of strengthening them in their . . . struggle with the powers of darkness, to promote greater unity between Jews and Gentiles . . . , and to stimulate . . . transformation of their lifestyles . . . [with regard to] purity and holiness" (45). [*BBR* 22.1; *JSNT* 34.5; *Chm* Aut 13; *JETS* 6/12; *ExpTim* 10/11; *DenvJ* 15].

★ **Campbell, Constantine R.** (Pillar-R) 2023. After his excellent *Paul and Union with Christ* (2012), *Paul and the Hope of Glory* (2020), and painstaking BHGNT on the sister letter, Colossians, I can hardly think of a better selection of a scholar to comment on Ephesians. (I say that, despite reservations about the Porter and Campbell thesis that the Greek verbal system is semantically encoded for aspect only and not tense.) He has taught the letter since 2006, has the finest of theological minds, is a conservative Anglican, and seems irenic in nature. This is a fresh reading of the epistle, not a commentary on the commentaries and other secondary literature. His interaction with other commentators is rather limited, though I was happy to see Cohick's NICNT repeatedly referenced. (In a beautiful gesture he dedicates the vol. to O'Brien, his former "teacher, colleague, and mentor" [xiii].) [*BBR* 33.4].

★ Chapell, Bryan. (REC) 2009. Creative, clear, and polished sermonic material on the epistle Dodd once termed "the crown of Paulinism." While the theological exposition is fine, preachers may appreciate Chapell's ideas for illustration and application most of all. An excellent vol. to set alongside Ryken's REC on Galatians. Students show less interest in this, unless it's homiletics class, in which case they'll learn much. (Chapell was my prof.) Other fine expositions for pastors are Boice, Calvin's *Sermons*, Ferguson, Hughes, Lloyd-Jones, Snodgrass, Roberts, Gardner, and Merkle.

★ **Cohick, Lynn H.** (NICNT-R) 2020. Replaces Bruce and will be a favorite evangelical commentary for many years (approx. 440pp.). Cohick has a superb command of ancient Greek literature and lucidly explains the Ephesian religious context. She is committed to a moderate version of the NPP and egalitarianism; with regard to the latter, she has done extensive previous research on the household codes. I can heartily recommend this purchase for students and studious pastors—there is so much to be learned here!—but perhaps not as a first choice. At certain cruxes, such as 1:22b, 2:1–10, and 5:21–33, Thielman is preferable. Waters says, "Cohick's understanding of the grace of salvation as limited to the setting aside of cultural norms mischaracterises grace in Ephesians. By 'works' (2:9), Paul has in mind the sinner's deeds of performance. Since Paul ties the Christian's 'good works' to the

Christian's 'walk' (2:10), we are likewise bound to understand sinners' works in terms of their 'walk' (2:2), that is, in terms of 'trespasses and sins' (2:1)" [*RTR* 4/23]. Her excursus on supersessionism confused me, as she grants that "the Christian message is supersessionary" (192) yet also seems open to a *Sonderweg* ("special path") for Jews in covenant with God but not as Christ-followers (191). Might one or two of her comments—e.g., a husband's love "frees the wife to be her own person" (367)—be read in unhelpful ways within the context of the West's dominant "expressive individualism"? [*WTJ* Fall 22; *ExpTim* 1/21; *BBR* 32.1; *Presb* Spr 22; *CBQ* 1/22; *Int* 10/22; *RevExp* 5/23]. Ten years earlier, she wrote *Ephesians* for NCCS (2010); that is briefer, more popularly written (190pp.) [*ExpTim* 4/14; *RelSRev* 6/12].

★ Stott, John. *God's New Society: The Message of Ephesians* (BST) 1979. Almost 300pp. Has the same qualities as his vol. on Galatians and is even better—don't miss it! Stott is remarkable for drawing from the best of previous works. Through his expositions, he is a pastor to pastors. [*JETS* 6/80].

★ **Thielman, Frank.** (BECNT) 2010. Appreciating the previous work of this Beeson prof. and PCA minister, I anticipated this major exegesis (520pp.) being a top pick. Hoehner can be daunting for busy pastors, and this proves handier for students and expository preachers working through the Greek. Thielman's strengths are deep learning in rhetoric and ancient literature (the classics and church fathers), judicious interaction with the best scholarship, discussion of the circumstances that prompted the letter (building on Trebilco), and theological exposition. (I expected robust and wide-ranging theological discussion after seeing his *Theology of the NT*.) Thielman is quite readable and accessible for a book with in-text citations and so much Greek. Moo writes, "This commentary will join Hoehner and O'Brien as the first references on Ephesians to which I turn." For students and pastors exegeting the original, this would be the smart first purchase. See also Larkin for a handy, thorough, and current guide for coming to grips with syntactical questions in the Greek text. [*BBR* 21.3; *CBQ* 4/12; *JETS* 12/11; *ExpTim* 7/11; *Them* 11/11; *BSac* 1/13; *RelSRev* 6/11].

Abbott, T. K. [𝓜] (retired ICC) 1897. Covers Ephesians and Colossians. Not all that remarkable even decades ago, Abbott can be safely ignored. See Best below.

☆ Allen, Michael. (Brazos) 2021. A briefer but worthy exposition, by a younger systematics prof at RTS (Wheaton PhD) after the passing of the illustrious John Webster (†2016), who originally had the contract. Allen has a good understanding of the history of doctrine and theological interpretation of Ephesians. [*RelSRev* 12/22; *JSNT* 44.5].

Barth, Karl. 1921–22, ET 2017. The first time in English. [*Int* 10/18; *JSNT* 40.5].

✓ **Barth, Markus.** ‡ (AB) 2 vols., 1975. An amazingly full (850pp.) and rigorous treatment, this has a predictable theological *Tendenz*, and follows some lines of thought suggested by his father's work. These vols. were once classed as indispensable to the advanced student and scholarly pastor, and will hold your interest. Argues for Pauline authorship and so is more conservative in some ways than Lincoln. [*WTJ* Fall 75].

☆ **Baugh, S. M.** (EEC) 2016. A large-scale (600pp.), diligently researched, and theologically oriented exegesis from a conservative Presbyterian prof (Westminster California), now emeritus. Baugh is a well-rounded scholar and particularly astute in his handling of ancient history and the fine points of Greek grammar. Also, he writes clearly (though I smiled when I found a 7.5-line sentence) and has his firm opinions. Baugh is excellent but perhaps marginally outside the top tier. Let it be noted finally that he often gives good theological guidance in his Selected Bibliography sections. [*BSac* 7/20].

Beare, Francis W. ‡ (IB) 1952.

✓ **Best, Ernest.** ‡ (ICC-R) 1998. Along with Lincoln, this is an all-important detailed exegesis of the Greek text from the critical camp that denies Pauline authorship. Best comes from Northern Ireland and a Presbyterian background. Students will surely consult this, but few pastors will consider purchasing Best to be money well spent. [*JTS* 10/99; *NovT* 41.2; *Int* 4/99; *CBQ* 10/99; *RTR* 4/99; *SwJT* Spr 00; *RelSRev* 1/01; *EvQ* 10/01; *JETS* 6/01]. As with other recent NT commentaries in ICC, Best was abridged and issued in pb (2004) [*BL* 2005]. For further reading, see his *Essays on Ephesians* (1997) [*JSNT* 72].

✓  Black, Allen, Christine M. Thomas, and Trevor W. Thompson, eds. *Ephesos as a Religious Center under the Principate*, 2022. A FS for Richard Oster. [*BBR* 33.2]. See also both Harrison–Welborn and Koester (below).

☆  **Bock, Darrell L.** (TNTC-R) 2019. An excellent replacement for Foulkes. Remarkably clear and useful as a quick reference. Bock is a veteran commentator and displays consistently sensible judgment in his exegesis. Bock seems to have a deep affection for Ephesians, knows it well, and can crystalize the issues; it is no surprise to read that he has taught this epistle to Dallas exegesis students for twenty years. He terms himself a "mostly Jesus and Gospels person," but he handles this epistle with aplomb. [*JETS* 9/20].

☆  Boice, James M. 1988. I found it to be a very useful book of sermons.

✓  Bratcher, R. G., and E. A. Nida. (UBS) 1982.

✓  Bray, Gerald L., ed. *Galatians, Ephesians* (RCS) 2011. See under Galatians.

✓  **Bruce, F. F.** *The Epistles to the Colossians, to Philemon and to the Ephesians* (retired NICNT) 1984. Replaced Simpson's weak half-vol. entry in the series. Bruce's sensible, well-informed commentary spends about 200pp. on Ephesians. Previously this had been a recommended purchase. Bruce still has value (s/h) but is now replaced in NICNT by Cohick. [*RTR* 5/85; *JETS* 6/86; *Them* 1/86]. Bruce also published an earlier exposition, which was more popular in its appeal (1961).

F  Burke, Trevor. (EBTC)?

Caird, G. B. [*M*], (New Clarendon) 1976. Covers the "Prison Epistles" (Ephesians, Philippians, Colossians and Philemon) with lucid, incisive comments in brief compass. Similar in character to Houlden but much better. The spirit of criticism here is quite mild; he upholds Paul's authorship of both Ephesians and Colossians. No brief work on the Prison Epistles competes with Caird.

☆  Calvin, John. *John Calvin's Sermons on Ephesians*, ET 1973. A separate vol. from the commentary. "For the homilest an excellent purchase" (Childs). Over 700pp. of penetrating exposition. Especially helpful for preaching through the packed theology in chs. 1–3. In early editions I recommended this for purchase.

✓  Caragounis, Chrys C. *The Ephesian Mysterion: Meaning and Content*, 1977.

☆  **deSilva, David A.** (NCBC) 2022. Excels in exploring the fine points of the discourse as it develops, and in presenting the rhetorical and sociocultural background. "Ephesians has the character of a 'liturgical homily' with the minimum epistolary requirements" (4) and "would fall within the broad realm of epideictic rhetoric" (6). The author is ordained in the United Methodist Church, deeply learned, and recognized as an expert on the NT epistles—see Galatians and Hebrews. Though he is critically engaged and can sound [*M*], deSilva has contributed a more conservative vol. in the series and is "inclined to accept the letter's claim to represent Paul's mind and voice" (31). Both thorough (350pp.) and of real value. As expected, the honor-dishonor theme gets close attention in the commentary. [*ExpTim* 4/23].

Donelson, Lewis. ‡ *Colossians, Ephesians, 1 and 2 Timothy, and Titus* (WestBC) 1996. [*RelSRev* 7/97; *Int* 1/98].

Eadie, J. A. 1883. This sturdy old work, which comments on the Greek text, is cited several times by Markus Barth. One of the richest 19th century commentaries.

✓ Edwards, Mark J., ed. *Galatians, Ephesians, Philippians* (ACCS) 1999.

☆ Ferdinando, Keith. *The Message of Spiritual Warfare* (BST) 2016. Very wise and more wide-ranging than a study of Eph 6. He was long in Africa. [*Them* 42.1].

☆ Ferguson, Sinclair B. *Let's Study Ephesians*, 2005. On the popular level I have not found anything better for group Bible studies or devotional reading (205pp.).

Foulkes, F. (retired TNTC) 1963, rev. 1989. Not outstanding but of value. [*JETS* 6/92].

✓ **Fowl, Stephen E.** [𝓜], (NTL) 2012. Fowl teaches at Loyola and is more conservative than most writing for NTL. He hesitates to take a position on the authorship question: "I find the arguments so finely balanced that my decisions about this could vary from day to day." So as to avoid "clumsy formulations," he "will refer to the author . . . as Paul" (28). But such introductory matters are less important to Fowl, and he moves quickly to the text. The exegesis is succinct (215pp.), usually shrewd, and oriented toward theological exposition. See Philippians. [*Int* 1/14; *JSNT* 36.5; *DenvJ* 16; *RevExp* 2/14].

☆ Gardner, Paul. (Focus) 2007. The author, who has been a NT lecturer (Cambridge PhD) and done effective pastoral work as an Anglican and Presbyterian (PCA) minister, writes excellent expositions. This is among them. See also 1 Corinthians and 1–2 Peter.

Garrard, David J. 2023. A brief Wipf & Stock commentary.

✓ Glahn, Sandra L. *Nobody's Mother: Artemis of the Ephesians in Antiquity and the New Testament*, 2023. [*Them* 49.1].

☆ Gombis, Timothy G. *The Drama of Ephesians*, 2010. Eminently worthwhile as a brief, "profoundly spiritual reading" (Turner) of the epistle, building upon the technical scholarship in his PhD. [*BBR* 21.3; *EvQ* 1/13 (Turner); *Them* 11/11; *BSac* 4/13].

Goodwin, Thomas. *An Exposition of Ephesians, Chapter 1 to 2:10*, Repr. 1958. Truly a monumental Puritan exposition (824pp.), by one of the most influential Nonconformists of his time (1600–79). To complete the epistle in a second vol., Sovereign Grace Publishers joined this with the lengthy *Exposition of Ephesians, Chapter 2:11 to 6:18* by Paul Bayne (d. 1617), an earlier Puritan worthy, and also Calvin's brief comments on 6:19–24 (repr. 1959). All free online.

Gurnall, William. *The Christian in Complete Armour*, 1662–65. A Puritan classic on ch. 6 and a rich example of "experimental" (practical) divinity. I once counseled adding it to your library as a devotional work. John Newton paid Gurnall's tome the highest compliment when he said that if he might read only one book beside the Bible, he would choose this. Note that Gurnall has been updated in more modern prose and published in pb by Banner of Truth. I also saw a 2011 Hendrickson reprint (1865 ed.). [*WTJ* Fall 59; *Chm* 107.2; *ExpTim* 10/12]. Save your money: it's free online.

Hamilton, Ian. (LCEC) 2017. Regrettably, I have not seen this exposition by my former pastor in Cambridge. What a fine theological mind he has!

✓ Harrison, James R., and L. L. Welborn, eds. *The First Urban Churches 3: Ephesus*, 2018.

✓ Heil, John Paul. *Ephesians: Empowerment to Walk in Love for the Unity of All in Christ*, 2007. Looks for chiasms everywhere. Carson says, "worth pondering." Heil is a Catholic priest who earned his doctorate at Pontifical Biblical Institute.

F  Heim, Erin M. (WBC-R). To replace Lincoln.

Hendriksen, William. (NTC) 1967. More helpful to the preacher theologically than exegetically.

Hodge, Charles. (GS) 1856 original. Of good value theologically and for understanding the Apostle's train of thought. Banner of Truth issued a hb reprint in 1964, followed by a 1980 Baker Books pb edition. In 1994 it was edited for inclusion in the Crossway Classic series. I believe I prefer Hodge (now free online) to Hendriksen.

☆ **Hoehner, Harold W.** 2002. Rivals Markus Barth as the fullest, most detailed exegesis ever written on Ephesians (900pp.)—and less accessible for that reason. I term this Hoehner's magnum opus; it is the fruit of many years of intense study. He provides a dependable (older style) grammatico-historical exegesis of the Greek, and in smaller measure a reverential theological exposition (somewhat dispensational). For decades to come, it will be a useful tool on the desk of bookish pastors. For a briefer Hoehner commentary, see below. Note that this was selected in previous editions as a recommended purchase, but Thielman displaces it, especially for those preferring a shorter exegesis. Scholarly preachers planning a full expository series will make this purchase. Students ought to read the 60-page defense of Paul's authorship. [*Them* Sum 04; *JETS* 12/03; *JSNT* 9/04; *SBET* Aut 05; *RelSRev* 1/04; *BBR* 16.1; *Int* 1/05; *ExpTim* 3/09; *DenvJ* 1/03; *Anvil* 21.3].

☆ Hoehner, Harold. (CorBC) 2008. In this multiauthor vol. Hoehner covers Ephesians; Philip Comfort treats the Philippian and Thessalonian correspondence; and Peter Davids well covers Colossians and Philemon. See above the huge Hoehner work, of which this provides a profitable distillation.

Houlden, J. Leslie. ‡ (Pelican) 1977. See Caird above.

☆ Hughes, R. Kent. (PTW) 1990. See under Mark.

✓ Immendörfer, Michael. *Ephesians and Artemis: The Cult of the Great Goddess of Ephesus as the Epistle's Context*, 2017. A revised U. of Wales PhD. [*JETS* 9/19; *ETL* 97.2; *JSNT* 40.5]. See also Rogers below.

✓ Jeal, Roy R. ‡ *Integrating Theology and Ethics in Ephesians*, 2000.

Kitchen, M. ‡ (Read) 1994.

☆ **Klein, William W.** (EBCR) 2006. A concise, well-researched exegesis (153pp.) by a seasoned prof at Denver Seminary. He offers a fuller introduction than many entries in EBCR, selective interaction with leading commentaries, and a measure of theological discussion. His theology is more Arminian (corporate view of election), and he takes a gently complementarian approach to the household code (essential equality but a willing submission to the husband). There is still value in Klein's massive *Book of Ephesians: An Annotated Bibliography*, published in 1996 (over 300pp.).

✓ Koester, Helmut, ed. ‡ *Ephesos: Metropolis of Asia: An Interdisciplinary Approach to Its Archaeology, Religion, and Culture*, 1995.

Kreitzer, Larry. ‡ (Epworth) 1979. This is highly praised and a bit like Stott, except it comes from the critical (deutero-Pauline) side.

Kuruvilla, Abraham. 2018. See the Pastorals for another of these useful books of "theological commentary for preachers." I've not seen this.

☆ **Larkin, William.** (BHGNT) 2009. His 196-page handbook guides the student through the problems and nuances of the Greek text (linguistics and syntax). It is done so expertly, and in such a detailed fashion, that even a NT professor could use it as a reference. See Larkin under Acts. [*CBQ* 7/11; *JSNT* 33.5; *BSac* 4/11].

✓ Lightfoot, J. B. 1904. See under 1 & 2 Thessalonians.

☆ **Lincoln, Andrew T.** ‡ (WBC) 1990. His diss. on Ephesians, *Paradise Now and Not Yet* (1981), led us to expect great things. And this is a great commentary (550pp.), but unfortunately Lincoln changed his mind on authorship and became more critical after completing his Cambridge PhD. The work is somewhat vitiated for conservatives by his denial of Pauline authorship. He uses some space distinguishing the theology of Ephesians from that of the genuine Paul. Honestly, the deutero-Pauline arguments he adduces do not strike me as strong. Mainly for advanced students and scholarly pastors, who also enjoy his *Theology of the Later Pauline Letters* (CUP, 1993). The average pastor is not able to appreciate and put to good use the wealth of data and scholarly argument here. Most preachers will hold that Thielman and Campbell, without Lincoln, provide more than enough exegetical guidance. [*WTJ* Fall 92; *CBQ* 1/93; *EvQ* 4/93; *RTR* 9/93; *JBL* 113.2; *Them* 1/92]. N. B.: In a preaching series,

I found that Robinson on the Greek gave me more sound guidance per hour invested. Yes, scholars will not want to be without Lincoln for detailed exegesis, but pastors who give the Scriptures the highest credit rating and are time-pressed might prefer Robinson.

☆ Lloyd-Jones, D. Martyn. 1974–82. Among bookish pastors this 8-vol. exposition needs no commendation. "Eminently worthwhile, but only if you read very quickly" (Carson). [*JETS* 6/82].

F   Long, F. J. (RRA).

MacArthur, John. 1986. See Matthew for my perhaps too-harsh review of this series of sermonic/expositional vols.

✓ **MacDonald, Margaret Y.** ‡ *Colossians and Ephesians* (SacP) 2000. Of note because of her social-scientific approach to these epistles, which she blends with more traditional historical-critical discussion. She takes the standard critical line on introductory matters. [*Int* 10/01; *ExpTim* 3/02; *RelSRev* 10/03; *ExpTim* 8/08; *BSac* 7/10].

Mackay, John A. [*M*], *God's Order*, 1953. Can be picked up s/h. It is one of the most thought-provoking old expositions. Mackay (pronounced "Mc-eye") was President of Princeton Seminary (1936–59). Readers catch his enthusiasm for Ephesians, because "to this book I owe my life" (6) and because of the epistle's ecumenical vision.

☆ MaGee, Gregory S., and Jeffrey D. Arthurs. (Kerux) 2021. A successful effort to blend an exegetical and expositional approach. [*ExpTim* 4/23 (Cohick); *JSNT* 45.5].

✓ Martin, Ralph P. ‡ *Ephesians, Colossians, and Philemon* (I) 1991. Already in the 1970s he had published his verdict that Ephesians is deutero-Pauline, and I wonder if he (NT editor for WBC) influenced Lincoln to adopt the same position. Martin taught at Fuller Seminary and Sheffield. He is best known for editing and writing for the Word series (*2 Corinthians* and *James*), and for his several works on Philippians. Though he was a prominent Pauline scholar, his theological exposition here is too brief (156pp.) to compete with other fine works available. His theology was more conservative than his position on introductory matters. See also Colossians. [*CRBR* 1994; *CBQ* 7/93; *BSac* 1/93].

Merida, Tony. *Exalting Jesus in Ephesians* (CCE) 2014.

☆ **Merkle, Benjamin L.** (EGGNT) 2016. Not as full as some other vols. in the series (230pp.), but, considering Merkle's ability and the challenges of the Greek in Ephesians, this book is a blessing for students. See especially the syntactical/structural layouts and For Further Study (bibliography) segments. See ESVEC below. Blomberg has a critical review. [*BSac* 10/18; *EvQ* 4/18; *JSNT* 40.5; *DenvJ* vol. 20 (Blomberg)].

☆ Merkle, Benjamin L. "Ephesians" in *Ephesians–Philemon* (ESVEC) 2018. One discovers fairly consistent and high quality across the expositions in this vol. As with the rest of the set, the wider coverage makes this an intelligent purchase for the pastor. For the Ephesians portion, Merkle is learned and careful in the exegetical work (see EGGNT above). For Philippians, see Meyer, while Wilson treats Colossians–Philemon. Chapman comments on Thessalonians, and Burk covers the Pastorals.

✓ **Mitton, C. Leslie.** ‡ (NCB) 1981. A packed, moderately critical exegesis denying Pauline authorship. Mitton is useful in the hands of discerning students. Prior to the publication of Lincoln, Best, and Schnackenburg (in ET), Mitton was more important to consult for understanding the standard critical approach. His London dissertation, *The Epistle to the Ephesians: Its Authorship, Origin and Purpose* (Clarendon, 1951), still stands as the classic presentation in English of arguments for the epistle being a post-Pauline production. Those wanting a well-grounded, orthodox response to the critics will find a compact answer in the NT introductions by Guthrie and Carson–Moo, a fuller defense in Hoehner, and a full-length monograph by van Roon (below).

☆ Morris, Leon. *Expository Reflections on the Letter to the Ephesians*, 1994. In the same style as his *Reflections* vols. on John, this 240-page book clarifies the meaning of the text, brings out contemporary application, and includes some illustration. [*JETS* 9/96].

✓ **Muddiman, John.** ‡ (BNTC) 2001. A provocative work of 338pp. by an Oxford scholar challenging the critical position on authorship. Muddiman contends that Ephesians is an authentic letter, but edited and expanded later in the 1st century. The exegesis (with his own translation) is penetrating, and I aver it should be better known in the USA than it is. [*JTS* 10/02; *Int* 4/03; *ExpTim* 8/01; *JR* 7/02; *RelSRev* 7/02; *RTR* 4/07; *RB* 7/05; *Anvil* 19.4].

✓ Murphy-O'Connor, Jerome. ‡ *St. Paul's Ephesus: Texts and Archaeology*, 2008. See the companion vol. under 1 Corinthians. Advanced students will benefit from perusing this. [*JETS* 3/09; *CBQ* 7/09]. See also Koester above.

**O'Brien, Peter T.** (Pillar) 1999. Once regarded as the pastor's first choice, especially if one preferred a forthrightly evangelical commentary upholding Pauline authorship. I did have differences with O'Brien; along with most major interpreters (Calvin, Mitton, Lincoln, Best, Fowl) I take διὰ πίστεως in 2:8 as referring to our faith, not Christ's faith/faithfulness. This book had the same good qualities as his vols. on Colossians–Philemon and Philippians. O'Brien built well on Lincoln. At 500pp. it was fuller than most in Pillar. Sadly, this commentary contains acknowledged "clear-cut, but unintentional, plagiarism," and Eerdmans withdrew it from the market (2016). [*RTR* 12/00; *SwJT* Fall 00; *RelSRev* 7/00; *Them* Spr 01; *JSNT* 6/01; *JETS* 12/01; *Evangel* Aut 02].

Olyott, Stuart J. *Alive in Christ* (Welwyn) 1994.

Osborne, Grant R. (ONTC) 2017. See under Commentary Series.

Patzia, Arthur. [𝓜], *Ephesians, Colossians, Philemon* (NIBC) 1990. The Fuller Seminary professor believes Paul probably wrote Colossians, but not Ephesians. Not a bad value for your money in pb (300pp.).

✓ **Perkins, Pheme.** ‡ (NIB) 2000. Succinct (115pp.), perceptive, and well-written from the critical angle. Perkins also did Mark in this series. See below. [*SewaneeThRev* Easter 01].

✓ **Perkins, Pheme.** ‡ (ANTC) 1997. [*Int* 7/98; *CBQ* 10/98; *RelSRev* 7/98].

☆ Roberts, Mark D. (SGBC) 2016. By a PCUSA faculty member at Fuller Seminary, who specializes in leadership. Roberts is comfortable with Pauline authorship of the Prison Epistles, which is a change from his critical views decades ago as an undergrad and PhD student in NT at Harvard. Roberts has an excellent mind, and his work (260pp.) is valuable to preachers. [*ExpTim* 7/18; *JSNT* 40.5; *DenvJ* 8/18].

✓ **Robinson, J. Armitage.** 2nd ed. 1904. A true classic. "The old standard English commentary of Armitage Robinson has held up quite well, and is actually more useful than Westcott who is always impressive" (Childs). This entry in the old Macmillan series has three parts: an exposition; the Greek text accompanied by extensive exegetical and philological notes; and 80pp. of useful essays and text-critical notes. Reprinted repeatedly: by Kregel (1980), Lutterworth (2002), Wipf & Stock (2003), and Forgotten Books (2012). If you love your Greek NT, want to build a larger, high-quality commentary collection, and find a copy of this, you might buy it. Now free online.

✓ Rogers, Guy MacLean. ‡ *The Mysteries of Artemis*, 2012. See also the literature cited and Rogers's *The Sacred Identity of Ephesos: Foundation Myths of a Roman City* (1991).

✓ Rollock, Robert. ET 2021. From the Latin. The author (1555–99) had a major impact on the Scottish Church by his godliness and learning. [*Presb* Fall 22].

✓ **Roon, A. van.** *The Authenticity of Ephesians*, 1969, ET 1974. A masterful dissertation, favorably reviewed in *WTJ* Fall 77 (by Lincoln, no less!) and *EvQ* 10/77. As an older, in-depth defense of Pauline authorship, it was probably the best. Though somewhat difficult to read in its English dress (the translation isn't the best), it is worthwhile reading for the student. Free at Internet Archive.

✓ **Schnackenburg, Rudolf.** ‡ ET 1991. A most important scholarly commentary from the critical camp—alongside Barth, Best, and Lincoln. It was Childs's first choice before Lincoln came out. Perkins says Schnackenburg provides a "particularly helpful analysis of the logical flow of the letter" (366). This Catholic scholar is best known for studies and commentaries on the Johannine literature. [*ExpTim* 3/93; *JBL* 104.2; *EvQ* 1/96].

Schüssler Fiorenza, Elisabeth. ‡ (Wisdom) 2017. She regularly reads "against the grain," using a radical feminist hermeneutic. [*Int* 4/19; *JSNT* 41.5].

Simpson, E. K. (retired NICNT) 1957. See Bruce above.

✓ Simon, Mark A. *Living to the Praise of God's Glory: A Missional Reading of Ephesians*, 2021. Well-done and takes a fresh approach to the letter. [*JSNT* 44.5].

Simpson, Benjamin I. (BGI) 2020. Regrettably I have not seen it.

Slater, Thomas B. ‡ (S&H) 2012. A compact (189pp.) critical commentary written by a McAfee professor and former Methodist Episcopal pastor. If one has access to the likes of Lincoln, Best, and Schnackenburg, I doubt this adds much. The expense may discourage some from making the purchase. [*CBQ* 4/14 (Lincoln); *Int* 10/13].

☆ Snodgrass, Klyne. (NIVAC) 1996. By a veteran evangelical at North Park Seminary. He knows Ephesians like the back of his hand and is well-qualified to guide expositors through the text to relevant contemporary application. His selection of quotes, both to help along exposition and to help push application, is often superb. The vol. speaks to the pastor's mind and heart. I am very glad for Snodgrass's emphasis upon union with Christ. Still, I judge Stott a better, safer theological guide through Ephesians, especially for discussion of election. Snodgrass understands election in terms of "God valuing us" (59)—he tries to backtrack on p.64 and deny that personal merit or accomplishment pertain to divine election. When he protests so much for human freedom and responsibility and when he asserts a corporate view of election (à la Barth, Torrance), Reformed folk don't want to follow him. Many will feel he is fighting shy of Paul's teaching.

✓ Starling, David I. *Reading Ephesians and Colossians* (RNT) 2020. Subtitled "a Literary and Theological Commentary." Starling was a Baptist pastor and now teaches at Morling College in Sydney; he regards both epistles as authentic. [*RelSRev* 4/22; *BBR* 31.4; *CBQ* 7/22; *Int* 10/22; *Them* 46.2].

F   Sterling, Gregory. ‡ (Herm).

Stoeckhardt, George. ET 1987. A 19th century, conservative Lutheran work by a productive scholar.

✓ **Talbert, Charles H.** ‡ *Ephesians and Colossians* (Paideia) 2007. From a respected NT critic at Baylor who serves as a general editor for the series. Ephesians and Colossians may have been taken together here because of the many thematic similarities (literary dependence questions), and also because many scholars, Talbert among them, view the two as pseudonymous. The exegesis is compact and well-informed. [*ExpTim* 9/08; *RelSRev* 3/09; *DenvJ* 4/08; *JETS* 12/08; *BL* 2009; *BBR* 20.1; *CBQ* 7/09; *Int* 4/09].

✓ Trebilco, Paul. [𝓜], *The Early Christians in Ephesus from Paul to Ignatius*, 2005. A massive historical research (826pp.) that aids the biblical scholar in background studies, though Trebilco discounts the usefulness of the epistle for his own work. This was republished by Eerdmans in 2007 [*CBQ* 7/10].

F   Turner, Max. (NIGTC). Should be quite good, rivaling Lincoln, Hoehner, Best, etc.

F   Turner, Max. (THC).

Uprichard, Harry. (EPSC) 2004. A helpful, wise exposition by a Presbyterian pastor in Northern Ireland who did a doctorate on Paul.

Verhey, Allen, and Joseph S. Harvard. ‡ (Belief) 2011. [*Int* 10/12; *Chm* Aut 13].

✓ **Westcott, B. F.** 1906. Will always be consulted as a careful, dependable work. One of the very best of the older Greek commentaries. Free online. See also Robinson above.

F  Wilder, Terry. (NAC). A mighty long wait for *Ephesians* in this series. Will it still be released as NAC, after CSC has come along to replace the series?

Williamson, Peter S. ‡ (CCSS) 2009. [*RelSRev* 36.2; *CBQ* 1/11; *Int* 1/13].

✓ **Winger, Thomas M.** (ConcC) 2015. An exceedingly full (800pp.), stalwartly conservative Lutheran exegesis of the Greek text and theological exposition—clearly a labor of love. The introduction alone is nearly 170pp. and offers a thorough defense of Pauline authorship. Winger emphasizes Ephesus as the intended destination; this is not a general, circular epistle. Ephesians is mainly a sermon with a "baptismal character" (xvi), and that sacrament "undergirds and permeates the entire letter" (xvii; cf. 144–47); I have doubts such a thesis can be sustained. [*BSac* 7/18].

☆ **Witherington, Ben, III.** *The Letters to Philemon, the Colossians, and the Ephesians* (SRC) 2007. The prodigious Methodist added this 400-page commentary to his socio-rhetorical project. Since there is disagreement over, and much to say about, the rhetorical form and intention in these particular Pauline epistles, his work here is notable. One expert on classical rhetoric, Harrill, says Witherington's thesis that Paul adopted "an Asiatic style" is absurd because no such thing existed; but I have seen references to an Asian school/style in Quintilian (*Inst.* 12.10.16–19). The basic interpretive approach of this vol. is like that of his other works: Romans, Corinthians, Galatians, etc. [*RTR* 12/08; *CBQ* 10/08 (Harrill); *BL* 2009; *BTB* 2/10; *RevExp* Win 09; *Anvil* 26.3–4].

Wood, A. Skevington. (EBC) 1978. See Klein above.

✓ **Yoder Neufeld, Thomas R.** [*M*], (BCBC) 2002. This Mennonite commentary is 400pp. and seeks to hold to a mediating position in the critical debates; he lands more on the pseudonymity side. Yoder wrote his Harvard dissertation on Ephesians and the armor of God image, so perhaps ch. 6 is where he has the most to say. [*JETS* 9/04; *Int* 4/03].

NOTE: Pastors will benefit from reading T. David Gordon's article, "'Equipping' Ministry in Ephesians 4?" in *JETS* 3/94; cf. Sydney H. T. Page, "Whose Ministry? A Re-appraisal of Ephesians 4:12," *NovT* 47.1 (2005): 26–46.

# PHILIPPIANS

★ **Fee, Gordon.** (NICNT-R) 1995. The outstanding Pauline scholar (†2022) produced a stellar replacement for Müller. Like Fee's hefty commentary on 1 Corinthians in this series—of which he was general editor—*Philippians* is very full (528pp.). Even after NICNT arrived, I preferred O'Brien's vol. for both detailed exegesis and theology. However, Fee has more application, is more accessible to beginning students, and somehow seems more attractive in its layout. A pastor's top pick, not to be confused with Fee's briefer IVPNT listed below. [*CBQ* 7/97; *ExpTim* 3/96; *EvQ* 7/99; *JETS* 3/98; *WTJ* Spr 96; *Int* 7/97; *RTR* 9/97; *JTS* 10/98; *RelSRev* 7/97; *Anvil* 17.1; *Chm* Win 10]. For my own study, I now reach first for Guthrie, Fee, Hansen, and Hellerman; they work well together. Students should note that these four, plus Silva, O'Brien, and N. T. Wright—see his article, referenced below—are in essential agreement regarding the *kenosis* passage (2:6), all of them accepting the Harvard research of Roy W. Hoover: "The *Harpagmos* Enigma," *HTR* 64 [1971]: 95–119. Reinforcing Hoover is Michael Martin, "Ἁρπαγμός Revisited: A Philological Reexamination of the NT's 'Most Difficult Word,'" *JBL* 135 [2016]: 175–94.

★ **Guthrie, George H.** (ZECNT) 2023. Over the years, numerous contributors to the series would thank Guthrie in a preface for, say, "invaluable and meticulous help with the grammatical charting" (Gardner, *1 Corinthians*, 12). That ZECNT is so clearly executed and useful owes much to Guthrie as associate editor, with his decades of experience in discourse analysis. I was therefore eager to see this commentary on the Greek, expecting a standout vol. in an already strong series. No disappointment here! The author previously proved himself to be a skillful, insightful, and careful exegete (see Hebrews, 2 Corinthians), and I think he gives us some of his very best work here, especially in tracing the argument or flow of thought (325pp. + indexes). The theological exposition is learned, excellent, and also warm-hearted (just as my friend is, personally). His wide knowledge of the Bible is seen in a 25-page Scripture Index. Students and pastors both should buy Guthrie and then Fee. When one reads the enthusiastic endorsements within the vol., they are no exaggeration. Not a downside really, but the task remains for an evangelical to produce a larger-scale, critically engaged sorting of all the scholarship on Philippians; I think more particularly of works in German (Pilhofer [1995, 2009], Standhartinger [2021], etc.), despite their penchant for wearisome redaction theories.

★ **Hansen, G. Walter.** (Pillar) 2009. A full (355pp.), readable commentary by a noted Paul scholar, displaying remarkably clear and mature scholarship. Hansen argues that the letter's dominant themes are the gospel of Christ and the community in Christ (30); key words are participation, fellowship, and thanks. In his discussion of 2:5–11, he comes to sounder theological conclusions than his old Fuller colleague Ralph Martin. At 3:9, which is important in the NPP debate, he supports the traditional readings of "my righteousness" (gently critiquing Dunn and Wright) and "faith in Christ" (critiquing Hays). As Carson writes in the Editor's Preface, readers benefit from the insights of a seminary professor who previously served as a pastor and missionary. Just to note, Hansen wrote *Galatians* for IVPNT. [*Them* 4/10; *Chm* Aut 10; *BBR* 21.1; *CBQ* 4/11; *JSNT* 33.5; *Presb* Fall 11; *JETS* 12/10; *BSac* 4/11; *DenvJ* 14; *RevExp* Sum 11; *RelSRev* 3/12].

★ **Silva, Moisés.** (BECNT) 1992, 2nd ed. 2005. A superb, compact commentary which, in its 1st edition—either WEC (1988) or the reformatted BECNT—was my first choice before NIGTC and Fee's NICNT came out. Silva shows a sensitivity to language and employs sound hermeneutical principles (his specialty is lexical semantics). Though widely read and interacting with most of the literature, he always keeps Paul's line of thought in view. In other words, he doesn't distract the reader with side issues or a severely academic focus on minutiae. There is a humble tone to this commentary which is appropriate for a work on Philippians, but at the same time it briefly expounds Paul's themes in a grand way. The 2nd ed. is about 230pp. [*JETS* 12/90; *EvQ* 10/91; *ExpTim* 3/90; *Them* 10/90; *TJ* Spr 94; *CRBR* 1991; *BL* 2006; *ExpTim* 5/06].

★ Thielman, Frank. (NIVAC) 1995. Considered one of the very best in the NT section of the series. The brief exegetical portions are judicious, and Thielman's theological exposition (with homiletical direction) is very good. See Motyer, Lloyd-Jones, Carson, Harmon, Cohick, Johnson, Hughes, and Boice for more expositional help.

✓ Ascough, Richard S. ‡ *Paul's Macedonian Association: The Social Context of Philippians and 1 Thessalonians*, 2003.

✓ Barth, Karl. ‡ ET 1962. As one might expect, this is a perceptive theological treatment in brief compass. There was a "40th Anniversary Edition" from WJK.

✓ Beare, F. W. ‡ (retired BNTC) 1959, 3rd ed. 1973. Often consulted, but not so valuable as some think. His construal of the book's editing is unbelievable. And now it has been replaced in the series by the impressive Bockmuehl.

Belleville, Linda L. (NCCS) 2021. A strong entry in a compact series (98pp.).

✓ **Bird, Michael F., and Nijay K. Gupta.** (NCBC) 2020. Well-done in short compass (30-page Introduction, and 165pp. of exegesis). The coauthors are open to the NPP, write lucidly, and are able to crystalize issues. Bird speaks of generally leaning toward an objective genitive rendering of *pistis Christou* but preferring the subjective at Phil 3:9 (139–44). There is solid research behind the commentary, and good direction with regard to bibliography (28–32). [*JSNT* 43.5]. See also Gupta below.

☆ **Bockmuehl, Markus N. A.** [*M*], (BNTC-R) 1998. A major, conservatively critical interpretation for students to consult. Bockmuehl can be compared with the recommended commentaries above in helpfulness to the pastor; if this were the only book you had on Philippians, you would be well-served. The discussion of such matters as partition theories is conducted at a high level. Contains a good measure of theology, and, as noted by Carson, his treatment of the hymn is excellent. This author has done a careful and oft-cited work on *Revelation and Mystery in Ancient Judaism and Pauline Christianity* (1990). See Beare above. [*RelSRev* 10/99].

☆ Boice, James M. 1982. Updated by Baker Books to be based on the NIV text.

F Briones, David E. To be published by Crossway.

Briscoe, Stuart. *Philippians: Happiness beyond Our Happenings*, 1993.

☆ **Brown, Jeannine K.** (TNTC-R) 2022. Replaced Martin. An excellent and lucid exegesis, from a conservative but critically engaged scholar. She takes *pistis Christou* at 3:9 as a subjective genitive ("the faithfulness of Christ"), which disappointed but did not surprise me. [*BBR* 32.4].

Bruce, F. F. (NIBC) Originally 1983. Like Martin's Tyndale work, this is handy. Call it perceptive, to the point, and rather brief (probably too brief to aid pastors much).

Caird, G. B. [*M*], (New Clarendon) 1976. See under Ephesians.

☆ Carson, D. A. *Basics for Believers: An Exposition of Philippians*, 1996. Among the very best, most substantive, sermonic expositions. Preachers, buy this!

Cassidy, Richard J. ‡ *A Roman Commentary on St. Paul's Letter to the Philippians*, 2020. A moderately critical Catholic study (200pp.), focused as a political reading. [*Int* 1/22; *JSNT* 44.5].

☆ Chapman, David. (Focus) 2012. Though a pastorally oriented exposition and not the place students will turn, Chapman's work of about 280pp has good study behind it. He earned his PhD at Cambridge and is Professor of NT and Archaeology at Covenant Seminary. See Chapman under Jesus & Gospels Research.

✓ Chrysostom, John. *Homilies on Paul's Letter to the Philippians*, ET 2013. The eloquent sermons in Greek, plus a fine Pauline Allen translation (SBL). [*ETL* 90.1].

☆ Cohick, Lynn H. (SGBC) 2013. The author combines clear, not-too-detailed exegesis—informed by her enviable knowledge of the ancient Greco-Roman world—with warm exposition, illustrative material, and application. There is much to like about this book for pastors. It competes with Thielman as the best in its category and is Blomberg's favorite. Regrettably there is no bibliography. [*JETS* 9/14].

✓ **Collange, Jean-François.** ‡ ET 1979. Provocative, lots of sparkle, but less dependable in its exegetical judgment. A Martin favorite because of its "Gallic verve and élan." More critical in his view of authorship and composition, Collange, in a manner similar to Beare, tries to read the epistle as a mixed-up composite of three letters.

Comfort, Philip. (CorBC) 2008. See Hoehner under Ephesians.

Cousar, Charles B. ‡ *Reading Galatians, Philippians, and 1 Thessalonians* (RNT) 2001.

Cousar, Charles B. ‡ *Philippians and Philemon* (NTL) 2009. The Columbia Seminary prof (†2014) produced a thin vol., with less than 90pp. on Philippians and about 10 on Philemon.

He mentioned an illness in his foreword; does that help explain why it is half the length we would expect from NTL? This cannot be classed as a reference tool and is scheduled for replacement by Gupta. [*RBL*; *ExpTim* 6/10; *BL* 2010; *Int* 1/11]. See Cousar's earlier commentaries on Galatians (I) and Philippians (above).

Craddock, Fred B. ‡ (I) 1985. Craddock is best known for his work in the area of homiletics; he is less a NT specialist. This work is only 84pp. [*JETS* 6/87].

✓ Edwards, Mark J. *Galatians, Ephesians, Philippians* (ACCS) 1999.

☆ Fee, Gordon. (IVPNT) 1999. Though very well-done, this cannot compare with Fee's NICNT above. I'd prefer to sit under the ministry of a preacher who used the fuller work. [*Chm* Win 00; *Them* Spr 01].

✓ **Flemming, Dean.** (NBBC) 2009. See under Commentary Series. This may be the very best and best-researched entry in New Beacon (270pp.). [*JETS* 9/10; *Int* 1/11; *JSNT* 33.5; *ExpTim* 10/10; *BSac* 10/11; *RevExp* Spr 11]. His recent, popular study guide is *Self-Giving Love* (2021).

☆ **Fowl, Stephen E.** [𝓜], (THC) 2005. A full (254pp.), very readable interpretation, welcomed by students and pastors alike. I found it among the more winsome books on Philippians. There is adequate exegetical scholarship undergirding his theological and ethical reflections (centered on the American context). Yet there are theological questions issuing from the text, especially 2:5–11, that Fowl does not adequately address. He has an evangelical background—studied under Hawthorne—and teaches theology at Loyola. He leans toward a reader-response approach to hermeneutics. [*EvQ* 10/07; *RTR* 4/07; *CBQ* 10/06; *Them* 10/06; *Int* 7/07; *BL* 2007; *RB* 4/07; *RelSRev* 9/08; *Pro Ecclesia* Win 09; *JTS* 10/09; *Anvil* 24.4].

✓ Friesen, Steven J., Michalis Lychounas, and Daniel N. Schowalter, eds. ‡ *Philippi, From* Colonia Augusta *to* Communitas Christiana: *Religion and Society in Transition*, 2022. [*JSNT* 45.5].

☆ Garland, D. E. (EBCR) 2006. One of the most insightful brief (85pp.) commentaries on Philippians I have run across. This is bound in vol. 12: Ephesians–Philemon.

✓ **Gnilka, Joachim.** ‡ ET 1971. From the great 1967 Herders commentary; scholars now use the German 4th edition (1987).

✓ Gupta, Nijay K. *Reading Philippians: A Theological Introduction*, 2020. [*Int* 10/22; *JSNT* 43.5].

F  Gupta, Nijay G. *Philippians and Philemon* (NTL-R). See Cousar above.

Halstead, Elizabeth Steele, et al., eds. *Dwelling with Philippians*, 2010. Breaks the commentary mold with a "blend of devotional literature, study guides, poetry, and gripping artwork" (Mittelstadt [*RelSRev* 12/11]).

Hamm, Dennis. ‡ *Philippians, Colossians, and Philemon* (CCSS) 2013. [*CBQ* 1/18].

☆ **Harmon, Matthew.** (Mentor) 2015. Dipping into it, I found it exegetically well-grounded and judicious, thorough (468pp.), and devotional (e.g., hymns quoted). Pastors can make excellent use of it; students can too, as there is good discussion of the Greek. Silva notes [*WTJ* Spr 16] that Harmon is particularly strong in discussing the OT background of the epistle. The author teaches at Grace College & Seminary, Indiana. I predict many would make this a top pick after using it. [*Them* 8/15; *JETS* 6/16; *JSNT* 38.5].

✓ Harrison, James R., and L. L. Welborn, eds. *The First Urban Churches 4: Roman Philippi*, 2018.

☆ **Hawthorne, Gerald F.** (WBC) 1983, rev. 2004. Before Silva, O'Brien, and Fee came along, Carson wrote that this is "probably the most serviceable commentary." Hawthorne put us in his debt by his painstaking work, and Silva definitely builds on him. However, his independent-minded exegesis at times left me wondering if he was trying too hard to say something new. His theological exposition of the "Hymn" in ch. 2 did not satisfy me. The 1983 vol., like WBC as a whole, was geared for scholars and diligent students. But now we have "what is virtually a new work" (xii) with Ralph Martin's rewrite. The revision is much longer (about 360pp. vs. 262pp.). In comparing the two, one finds extensive newer bibliographies, and Martin occasionally retains Hawthorne's original section of Explanation while adding a section of his own thoughts, where the two differ—see the Application of the hymn (2:5–11) on pp.132–34. [*WTJ* Fall 84; *RTR* 5/84; *JBL* 104.4; *EvQ* 4/85; *JETS* 12/83; *ExpTim* 3/08].

Heil, John Paul. ‡ *Philippians: Let Us Rejoice in Being Conformed to Christ*, 2010. Pursues a "text-centered, literary-rhetorical, and audience-oriented" (9) reading which discovers chiastic structures everywhere. Heil has produced similar studies on Romans, Ephesians, and James, and they are worth looking at. [*JSNT* 33.5; *RelSRev* 9/12].

☆ **Hellerman, Joseph H.** (EGGNT) 2015. A guide to the Greek (285pp.), written by a Talbot (Biola) professor, which is carefully produced and among the strongest entries in the developing series. Pastors will be happy that, in addition to his help with grammar issues, Hellerman offers extensive preaching suggestions. He includes a good measure of discussion of theology and the sociocultural background to the epistle. [*ExpTim* 5/16; *BSac* 4/18; *JETS* 9/16; *RTR* 8/19; *JSNT* 39.5]. Earlier he wrote the superb *Reconstructing Honor in Roman Philippi* (2005), treating the hymn.

Hendriksen, William. *Philippians, Colossians, and Philemon* (NTC) 1962. Not one of his strongest efforts but has been trusty for many pastors.

✓ **Holloway, Paul A.** ‡ (Herm) 2017. A more compact (200pp.) rather than exhaustive technical work, displaying strong interest in ancient rhetorical conventions (here a unified "letter of consolation") and philosophical currents. The Sewanee professor appears to have little interest in theological questions here, and he can be dismissive of scholars even remotely conservative. He traces a believable social setting and set of circumstances to which the letter speaks. Holloway's learned commentary has received a warm welcome in the academy and will be a standard reference tool for decades to come. Questions have been raised, though, about his reading of Paul's message as more philosophical (esp. Stoic) and his neglect of some important scholars. Holloway's Chicago PhD was published as *Consolation in Philippians* (2001). According to his CV, he is under contract to write on 1 Corinthians for ICC. [*ExpTim* 8/18; *JETS* 3/19; *Int* 10/19; *NovT* 61.1].

✓ **Hooker, Morna.** ‡ (NIB) 2000. As with Perkins on Ephesians, this is a succinct (80pp.), insightful, and well-written commentary from the critical angle. [*SewaneeThRev* Easter 01].

☆ Hughes, R. Kent. (PTW) 2007. This work has been combined with his *Colossians and Philemon* in a new one-vol. edition using the ESV (2013).

Hunsinger, George. [*M*], (Brazos) 2020. Profound theological and ecclesial engagement with the biblical text, by a prominent Barth scholar at Princeton Seminary. Though biblical scholars have generally been lukewarm toward this series, many pastors and theologians have been delighted. [*ExpTim* 6/21; *Int* 4/23; *JSNT* 44.5].

✓ Jennings, Mark A. *The Price of Partnership in the Letter of Paul to the Philippians*, 2017. By an adjunct prof at Gordon-Conwell. Argues that Paul's intention in the entire letter is to exhort the Philippian church to continue their support of his ministry. [*Int* 7/19; *JSNT* 41.5].

☆ Johnson, Dennis E. (REC) 2013. From a prof at Westminster Seminary California. The sermonic material here is the product of thorough Bible study, theological reflection, and skillful homiletical practice. Warmly commended to preachers.

Kent, Homer A., Jr. (EBC) 1978. Skip this and go to Garland's EBCR.

☆ **Keown, Mark J.** (EEC) 2 vols., 2017. An exceedingly thorough exegesis and exposition (1100pp.) by a Presbyterian minister and NT lecturer at Laidlaw College in Auckland. (He has also published a 1500-page set entitled *Discovering the NT*, 2018–22 [*JSNT* 41.5].) In the NT section of this conservative series, Keown has produced one of the stronger commentaries. The theological discussion is sound and healthy. The one surprise is his (previously published) view that a clause in 1:14, translated as a somewhat secretive "I am not making known," hints that the Apostle is accepting the help of friends to escape Roman custody (vol. 1: pp.253–54). I regard this as too full for the pastor's study. [*BBR* 29.2; *BSac* 7/21; *JSNT* 41.5].

✓ **Lightfoot, J. B.** 6th ed. 1881. Still one of the most valuable works on Philippians. See Silva's introduction for a fine review of this vol.'s worth. Lightfoot treats the Greek text. His interpretive comments have been heavily edited for a popular audience in the Crossway Classic edition (1994). The full 1881 text is free online.

☆ Lloyd-Jones, D. Martyn. 2 vols., 1989–90. This exposition would be a very wise addition to the pastor's library. Not nearly so long as his other works (e.g., his 8 vols. on Ephesians), which may be a plus. It was reprinted by Baker (1999) in one vol.: *The Life of Joy and Peace: An Exposition of Philippians*. I came close to including the cheaper edition among my recommendations for purchase.

Loh, I.-J., and E. A. Nida. (UBS) 1977.

✓ Marchal, Joseph A., ed. ‡ *The People beside Paul: The Philippian Assembly and History from Below*, 2015. [*ETL* 94.2].

Marshall, I. Howard. (Epworth) 1991. This preacher's commentary would have been very useful, had it been more available in North America.

**Martin, Ralph P.** [𝓜], (retired TNTC) 1959, rev. 1987. Handy for pastors. The earlier edition is not to be disdained or discarded; Martin was more conservative then. Now replaced by Brown. See also Martin's NCB below and his rewrite of the Hawthorne WBC.

✓ **Martin, Ralph P.** [𝓜], (NCB) 1976. Takes a different approach to the letter than TNTC: more academic and technical. Carson notes that his interpretation of 2:1–11 has been influenced for the worse by Käsemann's "Odyssey of Christ" idea. [*EvQ* 10/77]. Later Martin would write that Christ's *kenosis* "entails a suspension of His role as the divine Image by His taking on an image which is Man's" (*A Hymn of Christ*, 196), and I reject this. That monograph on Phil 2 was originally published by Tyndale House, intended for scholars and entitled *Carmen Christi* (1967, rev. 1983) [*EvQ* 10/85]. The later version is *A Hymn of Christ* (IVP, rev. 1997), which examines the hymn at great length. Further research on the topic by various scholars is presented in *Where Christology Began: Essays on Philippians 2*, eds. R. P. Martin and B. J. Dodd (1998). Finally, see Hawthorne above for Martin's last contribution to Philippians studies.

✓ Melick, Richard R., Jr. *Philippians, Colossians and Philemon* (NAC) 1991. Fits well into the series and meets its aims (384pp.). [*EvQ* 1/94; *ThTo* 10/93; *JETS* 3/96].

Merida, Tony, and Francis Chan. *Exalting Jesus in Philippians* (CCE) 2016.

☆ Meyer, Jason C. "Philippians" in *Ephesians–Philemon* (ESVEC) 2018. See Merkle under Ephesians.

Migliore, Daniel L. ‡ *Philippians and Philemon* (Belief) 2014. The Princeton theologian, now emeritus, offers a robust exposition with frequent interaction with Augustine, Calvin, Edwards, and Barth. One of the best in an uneven series. [*Int* 10/16].

F Moo, Douglas. (EBTC)?

Moore, Thomas S. (BGI) 2019. Regrettably, I have not seen it.

Moore, Thomas, and Timothy D. Sprankle. (Kerux) 2019. I have not seen it.

☆ Motyer, J. Alec. (BST) 1984. Builds on his 1966 book, *The Richness of Christ*. Apposite comments with a good deal of practical worth for the preacher. In early editions of this guide, I recommended this for purchase, but I now (slightly) prefer Thielman in this category of exposition. A 2020 revision has "lightly updated language" after the author passed away (†2016). See Motyer's excellent vols. on Exodus and Isaiah. [*JETS* 3/85].

Müller, Jac J. (retired NICNT) 1955. Brief, aged, and wasn't stellar to begin with. This work was once noted because Müller's dissertation examined *The Kenotic Theory in Post-Reformation Theology* (1931). Note: printings prior to 1984 included his NICNT on Philemon. Müller was replaced by Fee.

✓ Nimmo, Paul T., and Keith L. Johnson, eds. *Kenosis: The Self-Emptying of Christ in Scripture and Theology*, 2022. Invaluable, wide-ranging exegetical, theological, and historical-theological essays focusing on Phil 2:7. [*JSNT* 45.5].

☆ Novokovic, Lidija. (BHGNT) 2020. Another fine entry in the ever-useful technical series. The Baylor prof takes readers deep into the grammar and syntax. Quite an education here! [*JSNT* 43.5].

✓ **Oakes, Peter.** [*M*], *Philippians: From People to Letter*, 2001. A most important, fresh investigation of the social setting (esp. in relation to Roman imperial ideology). [*EvQ* 1/05; *BTB* Win 05; *Anvil* 20.2; *RelSRev* 12/10].

**O'Brien, Peter T.** (NIGTC) 1991. Once the best technical commentary and a first choice (close to 600pp.), if your Greek was good and your interests more scholarly. It exceeded the standard set in his WBC on Colossians–Philemon. O'Brien is soundly Reformed theologically, exegetically perceptive, and very thorough. Oakes [*BSB* 9/97] was right to say "the proliferation of detail sometimes makes it hard to see the wood for the trees" in this "magisterial" work, while "Fee keeps the wood very clearly in view." Sadly, there is acknowledged plagiarism in this NIGTC and Eerdmans withdrew it (2016). O'Brien still sits on my shelf, but I now turn to Guthrie instead. See his books on Hebrews and Ephesians. [*WTJ* Fall 92; *CBQ* 1/93; *JBL* Fall 93; *RTR* 9/93; *JETS* 9/95; *Bib* 75.1].

Osborne, Grant R. (ONTC) 2017. See under Commentary Series.

✓ Osiek, Carolyn. ‡ *Philippians, Philemon* (ANTC) 2000.

F Perkins, Pheme. ‡ *Philippians, Colossians, and Philemon* (Illum).

Plummer, Alfred. 1919. You can ignore it at this point.

✓ Reed, Jeffrey. *A Discourse Analysis of Philippians*, 1997.

✓ **Reumann, John.** ‡ (AYB) 2008. Sadly, the prof at Lutheran Seminary, Philadelphia died mere months before his massive (800-page) technical work saw publication. Because of size, it proves to be a work consulted by students/scholars on specific pericopae, but read in full by very few. It is extremely dense. I looked forward to seeing interaction with it in Holloway and a potential Wright ICC. Reumann believes the epistle is an amalgamation of three letters. Bird–Gupta refer to this as "a goldmine of word studies, quick surveys of scholarly views, and brief discussions of interpretive options" (31). [*Int* 10/09; *BBR* 20.3; *JETS* 12/10; *ExpTim* 9/11; *BSac* 7/11].

✓ **Still, Todd D.** *Philippians and Philemon* (S&H) 2011. The author is a proficient evangelical Pauline scholar, teaching at Baylor, and he has produced a readable, succinct (195-page) commentary. I judge this to be one of the more conservative entries in S&H and serviceable for pastors (but the pb is $53). He gives good attention to the flow of thought in the epistles and makes wise exegetical decisions. [*Int* 4/12].

✓ **Sumney, Jerry L.** *Philippians: A Greek Student's Intermediate Reader*, 2007. Poring over this would be like a Greek refresher course for many pastors. The author wrote *Colossians* for the prestigious NTL. [*RelSRev* 9/08; *BL* 2009; *Anvil* 26.3–4; *Them* 5/11].

Tamez, Elsa, Cynthia Kittredge, Claire Colombo, and Alicia Batten. ‡ *Philippians, Colossians, Philemon* (Wisdom) 2017. Tamez is responsible for Philippians, Batten for Philemon, and Kittredge–Colombo for Colossians. [*Int* 1/10; *JSNT* 41.5].

✓ Thompson, James W., and Bruce W. Longenecker. [*M*], *Philippians and Philemon* (Paideia), 2016. [*Int* 7/18; *JSNT* 39.5].

✓ **Thurston, Bonnie B., and Judith Ryan.** ‡ *Philippians and Philemon* (SacP) 2005. I have not had much opportunity to use this 290-page work. Vining says, "No new ground is covered in these commentaries." There is well-informed exegesis from a critical Catholic perspective; theological conclusions are drawn with some tentativeness. [*CBQ* 1/07; *Int* 7/06; *BL* 2006; *RB* 10/05; *RelSRev* 1/06; *ExpTim* 2/06; *BSac* 7/07].

✓ Tomlin, Graham, ed. *Philippians, Colossians* (RCS) 2013.

F  Trier, Daniel J. (ITC).

✓  Verhoef, Eduard. *Philippi: How Christianity Began in Europe: The Epistle to the Philippians and the Excavations at Philippi*, 2013. Attractive and informative.

✓  Vincent, M. R. ‡ (ICC) 1897. Treats Philemon too.

✓  Ware, James P. ‡ *Paul and the Mission of the Church: Philippians in Ancient Jewish Context*, 2005, 2011. [*CBQ* 4/13; *RelSRev* 3/13; *TJ* Spr 13].

F  Watson, D. F. (RRA).

☆  **Witherington, Ben, III.** (SRC) 2011. This fine "Socio-Rhetorical Commentary" is full (about 300pp.) and builds upon his earlier *Friendship and Finances: The Letter of Paul to the Philippians* (1994) in the TPI NT in Context series [*JETS* 12/96; *SBET* Aut 96]. Witherington has had a rethink about the letter and pursues a different methodology in 2011. [*RelSRev* 9/12; *BBR* 23.3; *CBQ* 1/14; *JTS* 4/14; *Int* 1/13; *JSNT* 35.5; *JETS* 9/12; *ExpTim* 12/12; *BTB* 2/15]. See the reviews of his other works under 1 Corinthians.

F  Wright, N. T. [𝔐], (ICC-R). For an exceptionally clear study of the kenosis text, see "ἁρπαγμός and the Meaning of Philippians 2:5–11," *JTS* 37 (1986): 321–52.

F  Zerbe, Gordon. (BCBC).

NOTES: See (1) I. Howard Marshall, "Which Is the Best Commentary? 12. Philippians," *ExpTim* 11/91. (2) Todd D. Still, "An Overview of Recent Scholarly Literature on Philippians," *ExpTim* 119.9 (2008): 422–28. (3) Walter Liefeld's section on Philippians commentaries (241–52) in "The Preaching Relevance of Commentaries," in *On the Writing of New Testament Commentaries*, eds. Porter–Schnabel, cited in the Introduction. (4) Gregory Fewster, "The Philippians 'Christ Hymn': Trends in Critical Scholarship," *CBR* 13.2 (2015): 191–206.

# COLOSSIANS

NOTE: Since it is customary in series to treat Philemon with Colossians in one vol., I marked with [P] those works that follow the pattern. That custom has arisen because Philemon was resident in Colossae, and Onesimus is mentioned in both epistles.

★  **Beale, G. K.** (BECNT) 2019. [P] The accolades from Rosner are deserved: the exegesis of the Greek text (475pp.) is "marked not only by impressive erudition and judicious judgment on complex issues but also by extraordinary theological depth." Especially of value are the meticulous and thorough textual analysis, the discussion of OT allusions, and "how the Jewish exegetical tradition interpreted these" (xi). Let us be reminded, however, that Colossians never directly cites the OT. Perhaps Beale overreaches? The Philemon segment is 70pp. Readers find good interaction with other scholars, but that is not a primary aim (the very short intros are indicative of this). He does not seem to have seen McKnight's *Colossians*. By comparison with McKnight's *Philemon*, Beale sets out contrasts between slavery in the Greco-Roman world and that in antebellum America; this needs to be done. The complication is that slavery in Paul's day could be less abusive and denigrating—so many tutors/teachers and other professionals were slaves—or it could be tortuous, with crucifixion being termed *servile supplicium*, "a slave's punishment." Now my first choice for pastors who can handle Greek, but I like Moo to counterbalance or complement Beale in spots. [*ExpTim* 11/19 (Foster); *Presb* Fall 19; *BBR* 30.2; *CBQ* 4/21; *JETS* 6/20; *EvQ* 92.3; *RevExp* 5/22; *JSNT* 42.5; *DenvJ* 23].

★  Garland, David E. (NIVAC) 1998. [P] The Truett Seminary (Baylor) prof has written a number of impressive commentaries, including *Mark* in NIVAC, *2 Corinthians* in NAC, and 1 Corinthians in BECNT. Not only does Garland frequently provide wise homiletical direction, he also interacts with the best scholarship then available, including Dunn and Barth–Blanke. Among these recommendations, my counsel to pastors is start with Moo, then buy Beale or Garland next, depending on whether one wants more exegetical or expositional help. Other leading pastoral/devotional books would be Hughes, Thompson, Wilson, Lucas, and Woodhouse.

★ **McKnight, Scot.** [𝓜], *The Letter to the Colossians* (NICNT-R) 2018. He seems to have lived in this epistle for long years, is deeply learned, and writes in an engaging, conversational (e.g., "riff off"), sometimes clever style. McKnight attributes more influence to secretaries than most allow: Paul "being mediated by" this or that secretary or coworkers in various letters. "I do not think Paul wrote any of the letters because it is far more likely that Paul was behind all of the letters. We have no pure Pauline letters, no 'undisputed' or 'genuine' Pauline letters, but only letters in which we hear the voice of Paul standing alongside coworkers and (probably) professional scribes" (18). As Gorman says in his review [*Int* 7/20], "it will be hard for many to imagine Romans as anything but undiluted Paul." McKnight cites Sappington's description of the Colossian error—"Strikingly similar to the ascetic-mystical piety of Jewish Apocalypticism" (28)—and especially commends Ian Smith's similar interpretation. But is the epistle presenting an accurate picture? McKnight thinks it possible "that Paul has transposed the problems he's facing at Ephesus . . . onto the canvas at Colossae in his more polemical moments in the letter" (29). (See above McKnight's *Reading Romans Backwards* for another troubling criticism of Pauline Scripture.) This is a full (over 400pp.) reference commentary, providing a repository of others' scholarship with some long quotes. [*ETL* 3/22; *ExpTim* 8/18; *Presb* Spr 19; *BBR* 30.2; *CBQ* 7/19; *JTS* 10/19; *JETS* 3/19; *BSac* 1/21; *JSNT* 41.5]. See McKnight's other vols. in the series: James, Philemon.

★ **Moo, Douglas J.** (Pillar) 2008. 2nd ed. 2024. [P] As expected of the veteran Pauline scholar, a high-quality, leading exegetical commentary with theological sensitivity. Students are glad for the wise sifting of the literature and Moo's clarity. There is no question that this thorough work is the pastor's first pick (471pp.), unless one requires a work directly treating the Greek (see Beale and Pao). The new edition represents a valuable update and expansion (about 50pp.). [*JETS* 9/09; *Them* 4/10; *Presb* Spr 09; *ExpTim* 9/09; *CBQ* 4/10 (Arnold); *BL* 2010; *Int* 4/11 (Sumney); *Chm* Win 12; *RTR* 8/10; *BSac* 10/10; *DenvJ* 14]. Moo's NICNT on Romans is also a first pick.

★ **Pao, David W.** (ZECNT) 2012. [P] The author has a Harvard PhD, heads the NT department at TEDS, and is a well-read Pauline scholar. He contributes a full, astute commentary (415pp.) that fits well in the series. I'd suggest that the work with the Greek text, the structural outlines, and close exegesis are more valuable than the Theology in Application sections, though it's all stimulating and well worth reading. He often brings a fresh perspective to the discussion table. E.g., see his discussion of spirituality and eschatology, putting to death unworthy earthly behaviors, and putting on Christ as a "new uniform" (230–35). My opinion is that, in assessing the beliefs of Paul's opponents, Pao is correct that "[t]he evidence . . . appears to favor a syncretism with Jewish elements providing the controlling framework" (31). [*JETS* 12/13; *Them* 11/13; *BSac* 4/13].

Abbott, T. K. [𝓜], (ICC) 1897. See under Ephesians. Wilson now replaces Abbott.

✓ Anderson, Janice Capel. ‡ *Colossians: Authorship, Rhetoric, and Code*, 2019. From the T&T Clark Study Guides series. [*JSNT* 42.5].

Appéré, Guy. *Mystery of Christ* (Welwyn) 1984.

F Arnold, Clinton E. (WBC-R). Replaces O'Brien. Philemon will be a separate vol.

✓ Arnold, Clinton E. *The Colossian Syncretism*, 1995. Proposes that the heresy opposed was not incipient Gnosticism (1st century gnosis teaching) nor a philosophical tradition, but rather a regional, syncretistic folk religion that had adopted certain elements of Judaism. A work of note for NT students. But there are such diverse views! Besides Arnold's vol. and the standard commentary discussions, students should see W. A. Meeks and F. O. Francis, eds., *Conflict at Colosse* (rev. 1975); Richard DeMaris's *The Colossian Controversy: Wisdom in Dispute at Colosse* (1994); Troy Martin's *By Philosophy and Empty Deceit: Colossians as Response to a Cynic Critique* (1996); Thomas Sappington's *Revelation and Redemption at Colosse* (1991); and Ian K. Smith, *Heavenly Perspective: A Study of the Apostle Paul's Response to a Jewish Mystical Movement at Colossae* (2006).

✓ Barclay, John M. G. ‡ (NT Guides) 1997. [P] A superb entry in the series.

Barclay, William. ‡ *The All-Sufficient Christ*, 1963. Quite a study to get the pastor thinking. Different from the Daily Study Bible.

✓ **Barth, Markus, and Helmut Blanke.** [𝔐], (AB) ET 1994. A major work, following Barth's 2-vol. AB set on Ephesians. Their commentary on Philemon is published in ECC. This vol. on Colossians is essentially a mid-1980s piece of work. Using the maxim, *in dubio pro reo* (when in doubt, for the accused), they urge that Pauline authorship be upheld (125). Students should certainly consult Barth–Blanke, along with the recommended works above, Dunn, Wilson, Foster, Lohse, etc.

☆ Bird, Michael. (NCCS) 2009. [P] The author, now at Ridley College in Melbourne, coedits the series with Craig Keener. Bird is a keen, energetic participant in today's debates about Jesus and Paul. He consistently engages the text theologically and deserves the strong reviews he has received for this 160-page book, written for pastors. Students can learn here too; see the section on The Colossian Philosophy (15–26). [*JETS* 9/10; *CBQ* 10/11; *JSNT* 34.5].

Bratcher, R. G., and E. A. Nida. (UBS) 1977. [P]

✓ **Bruce, F. F.** (retired NICNT) 1957, rev. 1984. [P] See under Ephesians. Up until the 2001 edition of this guide, Bruce's vol. was always recommended for purchase. It remains a smart buy, but not a top pick. Just as good on Colossians as on Ephesians.

✓ Cadwallader, Alan H. ‡ *Colossae, Colossians, Philemon: The Interface*, 2023. Represents some 25 years of research (750pp.) and seeks "to provide as complete a coverage as possible of the material evidence of Colossae as can be recovered to date" (13). Foster rightly terms it a "monumental work" [*ExpTim* 10/23].

✓ Cadwallader, Alan H., and Michael Trainor, eds. *Colossae in Space and Time: Linking to an Ancient City*, 2011. "First-rate," according to Foster [*JSNT* 35.5]. "No serious work on . . . Colossians will be able to ignore this volume."

Caird, G. B. [𝔐], (New Clarendon) 1976. [P] See under Ephesians.

☆ **Campbell, Constantine.** (BHGNT) 2013. [P] A reliable, insightful guide to translation and exegesis of the two epistles (144pp.). The author teaches at Sydney College of Divinity (previously at TEDS and Moore), is a good Paulinist, and contributes to debates about Greek verbal aspect. There is some discourse analysis also. Compare with the fuller Harris, which is stronger on syntactical matters. [*JSNT* 36.5; *Them* 4/14]. See Campbell under Ephesians.

Carson, H. M. (retired TNTC) 1960. [P] Healthy and strong theology (Reformed Anglicanism), but the exegesis did not probe to any depth. See Wright and Thompson.

F   Cassidy, Richard T. (Paideia). [P]

✓ Copenhaver, Adam. *Reconstructing the Historical Background of Paul's Rhetoric in the Letter to the Colossians*, 2018. A significant Aberdeen PhD, published in LNTS. [*JSNT* 41.5].

Copenhaver, Adam, and Jeffrey D. Arthur. (Kerux) 2022. [P] I have not seen it.

Davenant, John. (GS) 2005. A large work (900pp.) by a Puritan professor in Cambridge; he presents the learning of his age (1579–1641). The commentary is profound but not easy to use. [*RTR* 4/06]. Now free online.

☆ Davids, Peter. (CorBC) 2008. [P] See Hoehner under Ephesians.

Deterding, Paul E. (ConcC) 2003. I have hardly used it. At 200pp. it is one of the briefest entries in the series—by comparison the Philemon vol. is nearly twice as long. The author is a solidly conservative Lutheran pastor (ThD), who suggests this epistle has "the most profound Christology in all the NT" (xii). He thinks the Colossian heresy was an "incipient Gnosticism" (12), but his scholarship on the issue is dated.

F   Dodson, Joseph R. (CSC). [P] Would replace Melick's treatment.

Donelson, Lewis. ‡ (WestBC) 1996. See Ephesians.

☆ **Dunn, James D. G.** [*M*], (NIGTC) 1996. [P] A prolific Paulinist, Dunn also published major commentaries on Romans, Galatians, and the Pastorals. This 400-page vol. rivaled O'Brien as a first-rate technical work on these epistles. Students wanted both side by side. Evangelical pastors will prefer Beale, Moo, and Pao. Dunn sits on the fence with regard to authorship; he seems to describe the epistle as deutero-, but not post-Pauline. His assertion regarding the theological problem at Colossae—a forceful Judaism—is "the most striking contribution of the commentary" (Achtemeier). His article on the topic was "The Colossian Philosophy: A Confident Jewish Apologia," *Bib* 76 (1995): 153–81. See the comments under Pauline Studies, Romans, and Galatians. [*Them* 1/97; *JETS* 3/99, 6/99; *JBL* Win 97; *JTS* 4/97; *CTJ* 4/98; *Int* 1/98; *CBQ* 7/97; *Chm* 112.4; *RelSRev* 7/97].

☆ **Foster, Paul.** ‡ (BNTC) 2016. The Edinburgh professor, well known as an editor and regular reviewer at *ExpTim*, did brilliant work here (450pp.). The commentary is thorough, sophisticated yet understated (sober weighing of all evidence), and well-researched. One of the best in the series, but Foster "with hesitation" denies Pauline authorship (80). I cannot think of any mid-level (as opposed to very technical) critical treatment I'd rather have on my shelf. Don't miss his treatment of archaeological data. Key features are Foster's discussion of "prosopography" and downplaying a Jewish aspect to the so-called Colossian Heresy (cf. McKnight). [*ExpTim* 11/17; *ETL* 94.4; *JETS* 12/17 (Arnold); *JSNT* 39.5].

✓ Gorday, Peter, ed. *Colossians, 1–2 Thessalonians, 1–2 Timothy, Titus, Philemon* (ACCS) 2000. [P] [*SwJT* Sum 01].

☆ **Gupta, Nijay K.** [*M*], (S&H) 2013. The author did a Durham PhD and has made his name in Pauline studies. This is not a major, detailed work (205pp.), but it is quite readable, thoughtful, and well-argued. There is creativity too, as Gupta uses key terms in the epistle to reconstruct an imaginary letter from the philosophers Paul opposed (18). He acknowledges Michael Gorman as a mentor: "Much of the ethical perspective of this commentary (particularly the epistemological-moral framework of 'cruciformity') owes an incalculable debt to" Gorman's books and articles (xiv). [*Int* 4/15; *Them* 4/14; *BSac* 10/16].

Hamm, Dennis. ‡ *Philippians, Colossians, and Philemon* (CCSS) 2013. [P]

☆ **Harris, Murray J.** (EGGNT) 1991, 2nd ed. 2010. [P] Not a full-blown commentary, Harris is the first in a proposed 20-vol. series of guides to exegeting the Greek NT. See under Commentary Series. Few books could be better for encouraging pastors to stay in, or get back into, their Greek NT and mine out the riches there. This vol. includes structural outlines, incisive exegetical comments on grammar and rhetoric, and some homiletical suggestions from the original. Harris also has a major commentary on 2 Corinthians. Long a recommended purchase on this list, Harris was displaced by Pao. [*WTJ* Spr 93; *CBQ* 10/92; *ExpTim* 3/93; *JETS* 9/95; *CTJ* 11/92; *Them* 11/10; *BSac* 10/12].

✓ **Harrison, James R., and L. L. Welborn, eds.** *The First Urban Churches 5: Colossae, Hierapolis, and Laodicea*, 2019.

✓ **Hay, David M.** ‡ (ANTC) 2000. More accessible as a critical exegesis (182pp.), compared with the numerous technical, larger-scale commentaries. Overall, a very competent work scholarship-wise, which fulfills the aims of the series, but not stellar. Theology is a problem, as he pushes "the notion of cosmoswide salvation" (63). [*CBQ* 10/03; *Anvil* 18.2].

Hendriksen, William. (NTC) 1965. See under Philippians.

Houlden, J. Leslie. ‡ (Pelican) 1977. See under Ephesians.

☆ Hughes, R. Kent. (PTW) 1989. [P] One of the best expositions available. See under Mark.

F  Jeal, R. R. (RRA).

Johnston, George. ‡ (retired NCB) 1967. [P] Quickly replaced; see Martin.

✓  Kiley, Mark. ‡ *Colossians as Pseudepigraphy*, 1986. Presents in full the arguments for the more critical position. I note in passing that even Kümmel, the old standard critical Introduction in Germany, upheld Pauline authorship of Colossians.

F  Klauck, Hans-Josef. ‡ (Herm). See Lohse below.

✓  **Lightfoot, J. B.** 2nd ed. 1879. [P] Often reprinted, but now free online. Another classic like his works on the Greek text of Galatians and Philippians. This continues to be consulted by scholars; e.g., Dunn's NIGTC cites Lightfoot about as much as any other commentator. For Greekless readers, there is the CrossC edition (1997).

✓  **Lincoln, Andrew T.** ‡ (NIB) 2000. Especially of note (115pp.) because of his influential past work on Ephesians, the sister letter to Colossians. Lincoln tentatively concludes that Colossians, too, is deutero-Pauline (pseudonymous). [*SewaneeThRev* Easter 01].

✓  **Lohse, E.** ‡ (Herm) ET 1971. [P] Still among the leading technical commentaries coming from the critical camp, Lohse has been an exegetical mine for the specialist. As is typical of German scholarship, he denies Pauline authorship of the letter. Deadening and too dense for pastors. Quite dated; see Klauck above. [*JBL* 89.4, 91.4; *ThTo* 30.2].

☆  Lucas, R. C. (BST) 1980. [P] Even if one disagrees with Lucas's ideas about the doctrinal problem Paul faced in Colossae, there is still a lot here to stimulate the preacher to think practically. There are only 7pp. on Philemon; cf. Garland who has 83pp.

MacArthur, John. 1992. [P] See my review of the series under Matthew. [*BSac* 1/95].

✓  **MacDonald, Margaret Y.** ‡ *Colossians and Ephesians* (SacP) 2000. See Ephesians above.

Martin, Ernest D. (BCBC) 1993. [P] Praised by D. A. Carson.

✓  **Martin, Ralph P.** [𝓜], (NCB) 1974, rev. 1981. [P] Quite good for the exegete, though this work has declined in value with the passing of time. [*EvQ* 1/75]. You could also profitably look up his popular-level exposition which is entitled *Colossians: The Church's Lord and the Christian's Liberty* (1972). See also the next, more recent entry.

✓  Martin, Ralph P. [𝓜], *Ephesians, Colossians, and Philemon* (I) 1991. [P] With little hesitation, he denies Pauline authorship of Ephesians. For Colossians, his "persuasion is to stay with Paul's authorial responsibility for the letter, though with some hesitation" (98). See under Ephesians.

F  McCaulley, Esau. (SGBC). [P]

Melick, Richard R., Jr. (NAC) 1991. [P] See under Philippians.

✓  **Moule, C. F. D.** [𝓜], (CGTC) 1957. [P] Has a well-deserved reputation as a fine exegetical tool for working with the Greek and will be consulted for a long time. Moule was one of the greatest NT exegetes of his era. Cf. Harris.

**O'Brien, Peter T.** (WBC) 1982. [P] Was regarded as one of the best in the series and the best on this book. O'Brien's seemed a model commentary on the Greek text, though some quibbled over a lack of text-critical help. Dunn rivaled this work. For a commentary on the Greek text, my preference for O'Brien over Dunn was slight. Sadly, however, this book contains admitted plagiarism, and Zondervan withdrew it (2016). Reports are that Clinton Arnold will replace it. [*WTJ* Fall 84; *RTR* 1/83; *EvQ* 1/85].

Osborne, Grant R. (ONTC) 2016. [P] See under Commentary Series.

Pace, R. Scott, and Daniel L. Akin. *Exalting Jesus in Colossians & Philemon* (CCE) 2021. [P]

Patzia, Arthur. (NIBC) 1990. [P] See under Ephesians.

F  Perkins, Pheme. ‡ *Philippians, Colossians, and Philemon* (Illum).

Phillips, Richard D. (REC) 2024. [P]. Announced, but I have not seen it.

F Pitts, Andrew. *Colossians* (EEC). Another report had Seth Ehorn (who did Philemon).

✓ **Pokorný, Petr.** ‡ ET 1991. Published by Hendrickson. Denies Pauline authorship and has been a significant scholarly exegesis for students to note. [*JBL* Spr 93; *JTS* 10/92; *CBQ* 10/92; *Them* 4/93].

✓ **Schweizer, Eduard.** ‡ ET 1982. From EKK (see the Commentary Series section). "One of the best in the series; and this work combines full knowledge of the relevant literature with some down-to-earth exegesis" (Carson). Fairly useful to studious pastors, though it should be noted that Schweizer rejects Pauline authorship. I bought a pb edition decades ago and found it rich, but it's less important now. [*ExpTim* 3/83].

✓ **Seitz, Christopher.** [*M*], (Brazos) 2014. Seitz is an OT specialist known for his canonical approach and lively theological mind, and theological reflection is the point here. See his discussion of the influence of the OT on Paul (38–45). [*ExpTim* 7/15; *Them* 4/15; *BSac* 1/17; *CBQ* 1/16; *JETS* 9/15; *Int* 10/16 (Sumney)].

✓ Starling, David I. *Reading Ephesians and Colossians* (RNT) 2020. See under Ephesians.

✓ **Sumney, Jerry L.** ‡ (NTL) 2008. The author teaches at Lexington and did a PhD on Paul at Perkins (SMU). His commentary (300pp.) argues for pseudonymity, as expected from this prestigious series. But along the way he seems tentative about his conclusion and dates the epistle remarkably early (AD 62–64). Sumney's approach is more historical-critical, usually thorough, and good on background issues; however his page-and-a-half discussion of the false teaching (10–12) was disappointing. I have had less occasion to use Sumney. [*JETS* 9/09; *CBQ* 10/09; *ExpTim* 1/10; *BL* 2010; *Int* 1/11 (Martin); *BSac* 1/11].

✓ Talbert, Charles H. ‡ *Ephesians and Colossians* (Paideia) 2007. See under Ephesians.

Tamez, Elsa, Cynthia Kittredge, Claire Colombo, and Alicia Batten. ‡ *Philippians, Colossians, Philemon* (Wisdom) 2017. See under Philippians.

☆ Thiselton, Anthony C. 2020. Subtitled "A Short Exegetical and Pastoral Commentary" and a very mature piece of work. See under 1 Corinthians. [*RelSRev* 12/22; *JSNT* 43.5].

☆ **Thompson, Alan J.** (TNTC-R) 2022. [P] Replaces N. T. Wright and offers a solid, insightful exegesis of the two epistles. I found no major surprises in terms of interpretation but came away impressed by his careful, sure-footed work. Thompson did his doctorate at TEDS and teaches in Sydney. This is a pearl among shorter exegetical works. [*BBR* 32.4; *Them* 48.1].

☆ **Thompson, Marianne Meye.** [*M*], (THC) 2005. [P] A thoughtful, well-researched, and well-written theological commentary. Though Thompson is a more critically oriented evangelical, her conclusions on introductory matters are solidly conservative. I regard this as one of the best 21st century works on Colossians. See also her fine work on 2 Corinthians and John. Some might want to move this up to the recommended list. [*CBQ* 7/07; *JETS* 12/06; *BL* 2007; *RB* 4/07; *RelSRev* 1/07; *BTB* Win 08; *JTS* 10/09; *Anvil* 24.3].

Thurston, Bonnie. ‡ *Reading Colossians, Ephesians & 2 Thessalonians: A Literary and Theological Commentary*, 1995. These three letters are grouped together, apparently because of the common critical view that they are pseudonymous.

✓ Tidball, Derek. *The Reality Is Christ: The Message of Colossians for Today*, 1999. One of the best popular-level expositions (250pp.), with excellent research behind it, and written by a Baptist minister who was Principal of London Bible College.

✓ Tomlin, Graham, ed. *Philippians, Colossians* (RCS) 2013.

Vaughn, Curtis. (EBC) 1978. Better than others in the vol.

✓ Wall, Robert. (IVPNT) 1993. [P] The Seattle Pacific prof also authored commentaries on Revelation for NIBC and on James. This little vol. (225pp.) brings out the relevance of these epistles for the church today. The series was expensive in hb for what it has to offer, but is now in pb. Wall, a Dallas Seminary graduate (ThD), is a leading proponent of canonical criticism, coauthoring the Sheffield vol. *The NT As Canon: A Reader in Canonical Criticism.* [*RTR* 5/94; *CRBR* 1994; *Chm* Win 12].

F  White, Joel. (EBTC)? [P]

    Williams, A. Lukyn. (Cambridge Greek Testament for Schools and Colleges) 1907. [P] Use Moule instead.

☆ Wilson, Alistair I. "Colossians, Philemon" in *Ephesians–Philemon* (ESVEC) 2018. See Merkle under Ephesians.

✓ **Wilson, R. McL.** ‡ (ICC-R) 2005. [P] Has the expected ICC wealth of detail, but some regard Wilson as deficient as a thorough, authoritative exegesis. I view it as meeting ICC standards but not being one of the strongest vols. in the series. While it is among the major reference works for students, pastors find mid-level works by Moo and M. Thompson and the technical exegeses of Beale, Dunn, and Harris more approachable and useful. Wilson rejects Pauline authorship in an understated British sort of way. His discussions of Gnosticism and the Colossian Hymn are important. [*CBQ* 7/07; *JETS* 3/07; *Int* 1/08; *NovT* 50.1; *ExpTim* 11/06; *EuroJTh* 16.1; *JSNT* 37.5].

✓ Wilson, Walter T. ‡ *Paul and the Hope of Glory: Education and Exhortation in the Epistle to the Colossians*, 1997.

☆ **Witherington, Ben, III.** *The Letters to Philemon, the Colossians and Ephesians* (SRC) 2007. [P] See Ephesians.

☆ Woodhouse, John. (Focus) 2011. [P] The former Principal of Moore Theological College in Sydney has a remarkable gift for writing theological expositions; see 1–2 Samuel. This NT study is one of the most lucid and thoughtful I have found on these letters. It has maturity and "heart." Tidball is similar.

☆ **Wright, N. T.** (retired TNTC) 1986. [P] Deserved the rave reviews it received when it first appeared. Those familiar with the high caliber of this scholar's work will not be disappointed here. I read this all the way through and recommended its purchase until 2005. Wright has some strong views, and I'd not use it on its own. Wright's work retired H. M. Carson in Tyndale; now see Thompson. Note: compare Wright and Moo on the Colossian heresy; I think the latter is closer to getting it right. No doubt this pb remains a good buy on Colossians. [*Them* 1/88; *RTR* 9/87; *EvQ* 7/88; *Chm* 101.4]. A more popular treatment by Wright is *Paul for Everyone: The Prison Letters* (2002).

NOTE: Nijay Gupta, "New Commentaries on Colossians: Survey of Approaches, Analysis of Trends, and the State of Research," *Them* 35.1 (2010).

# 1–2 THESSALONIANS

★ **Fee, Gordon.** (NICNT-R) 2009. Nearly measures up to his past work (1 Corinthians, Philippians in NICNT) and is, without question, a recommended purchase. Though there is a disappointingly brief introduction—compare the 11pp. here (on two epistles even) with his 55pp. in *Philippians*—Fee makes up for that lack with a disciplined focus on the text and sober, thorough, penetrating exegesis. Both students and pastors appreciate the satisfying measure of theological reflection. Note: there is less scholarly interaction than hoped for. I suspect that less study went into this NICNT than the other two. See Morris below. Fee can be a top pick for a pastor's exegetical reference, especially for those without Greek. [*JETS* 6/10 (Weima); *RBL* 7/10; *BL* 2010; *Them* 7/10; *CBQ* 10/10 (Donfried); *JTS* 4/11; *Int* 7/11; *ExpTim* 7/11; *DenvJ* 14; *BTB* 2/12; *BSB* 6/11]. Those with a strong interest in eschatological debates may be disappointed with his downplaying such issues; such readers may repair to a giant dissertation, on the longer letter at least, by Luckensmeyer, *The Eschatology of First Thessalonians* (2009) [*JSNT* 33.5; *RelSRev* 6/11].

★ **Green, Gene.** (Pillar) 2002. Well-done, thoroughly evangelical, careful in its exegesis, and pitched at pastors rather than specialists. Green has been a good place for pastors to start (less in-depth is Beale). Students value the sure-footed exegesis. On the negative side, as Marshall points out [*Them* Spr 04], there is less exposition and biblical theology than pastors want; also the emphasis on patron-client relations seems overdone. Prior to Fee's appearance, I said Thessalonians lacked an obvious pastor's first choice, sufficiently well-rounded in the areas of both detailed exegesis and theological exposition, but I added that Green is very good as a mid-level work. [*RTR* 8/03; *JETS* 9/03; *ExpTim* 11/03; *RelSRev* 10/03; *Chm* Spr 04; *Int* 1/05; *NovT* 46.4; *DenvJ* 1/03].

★ Holmes, Michael. (NIVAC) 1998. One of the more successful in the series at meeting the stated aims. Preachers are so well served by Stott and Holmes! [*CTJ* 4/99].

★ **Kim, Seyoon, and F. F. Bruce.** (WBC-R) 2nd ed. 2023. At 700pp., about three times the length of Bruce's edition (see below). Kim was his student at Manchester, and he has well honored his mentor with this extensive and mature exegesis. The current Rylands Professor in Manchester, Peter Oakes, calls it "a wonderful commentary, incorporating Bruce's textual notes but essentially a new work." It "faithfully and effectively inherits both Bruce's concern for well contextualized and judicious interpretation and Bruce's skill in producing writing that will be very fruitful in the life of today's churches" (endorsement). A main strength here is the historical research, but Kim is theologically astute as well and has some fresh proposals (e.g., at 2 Thess 2:3–12). He argues for "the essential unity and continuity of Pauline theology between 1 Thessalonians and his later letters" (14). He also explores "the presence of Paul's justification doctrine in 2 Thessalonians as decisive evidence" for authenticity (112). Readers need a working knowledge of Greek to put this masterful exegesis to good use. Because these once-neglected letters have been receiving closer attention in recent decades, Kim's wise sifting of the literature is invaluable. (Students welcome the full bibliographies.) What astonishing wealth to have Malherbe, Weima, and Kim–Bruce! Specialists consult Kim's "companion volume" of essays, *Paul's Gospel for the Thessalonians and Others* (2022) [*Them* 49.1].

★ **Shogren, Gary S.** (ZECNT) 2012. A warm-hearted missionary with academic credentials (Aberdeen PhD), Shogren has taught at a Costa Rican seminary for many years. Not surprisingly, he is sensitive to how Scripture is read in different contexts. He is thorough (335pp.), a dependable guide through the Greek, adept at producing discourse-structure outlines, a capable exegete, and he draws out rich theology on the way toward applying the message. In other words, a fine, well-rounded tool. A student buying this will also find it useful in the pastorate. He is critical of a pretribulational rapture interpretation (37, 251). [*JETS* 9/13 (Weima); *Them* 11/13 (Green)].

★ Stott, John. *The Gospel and the End of Time* (BST) 1991. An excellent complement to technical exegeses. All of Stott's expositions are worth the money, and this one (200pp.) also has an inductive study guide that could be put to good use in a small group. Stott draws from a number of major commentaries (hadn't seen Wanamaker), but one reviewer would have been glad for interaction with more current scholarship (e.g., Malherbe's 1987 book). [*EvQ* 4/95].

★ **Weima, Jeffrey A. D.** (BECNT) 2014. I recommend Weima enthusiastically. The able conservative scholar teaches at Calvin Seminary and has for many years been at the forefront of Thessalonians scholarship. I eagerly awaited his commentary, not only because I expected it to be an "authoritative commentary on 1 and 2 Thessalonians," as Porter calls it, but also because these two epistles had lacked a standout evangelical exegetical treatment on the technical side. Weima's comprehensive (about 670pp.), detailed, and incisive work fills the need; it is my first choice for those who have Greek. Cf. Kim–Bruce, which I now count just as valuable. There is a fine presentation of arguments for the authenticity of the second epistle. [*ExpTim* 9/15; *BBR* 25.2; *CTJ* 4/16; *WTJ* Spr 16; *CBQ* 4/16 (hyper-critical); *JETS* 9/16; *NovT* 58.4; *Them* 41.2]. Advanced students may consult Weima–Porter, *An Annotated Bibliography of 1 and 2 Thessalonians* (1998).

F   Adams, Sean A. *A Linguistic Commentary on 1 and 2 Thessalonians.* At one stage the author had announced this as forthcoming from Brill.

F   Allison, Dale C. ‡ (Illum).

F   Ascough, R. S. (RRA).

☆   **Beale, Gregory.** (IVPNT) 2003. Very well-done, ably mixing exegesis and theological exposition, and pointing ahead to application today. As with his outstanding work on Revelation, Beale gives special attention to the OT background of the NT text. I would have no quarrel with anyone who thinks this deserves a place on the list above (265pp.). If a pastor could buy only one book, this would work well. [*EvQ* 7/05; *JETS* 6/05; *Them* 4/06; *RelSRev* 4/06; *ExpTim* 2/05; *Evangel* Sum 06; *Anvil* 22.2; *Chm* Aut 11].

✓   **Best, Ernest.** ‡ (BNTC) 1972. One of the most valuable in the old series. Advanced students appreciate this penetrating work, though it explains the English text (RSV). Best remains a standard work to consult, but note that the 1977 and 1979 revisions only added to the bibliography. It is not entirely satisfactory on the issue of the authorship of 2 Thessalonians, but Best does assume both letters came from Paul's hand (in conjunction with fellow workers). It is disturbing to see how, since the late 1970s, scholarship has moved toward rejecting the authenticity of the second epistle. Best produced a magnum opus on Ephesians in the ICC. [*JBL* 93.2].

✓   **Boring, M. Eugene.** ‡ (NTL) 2015. A leading critical interpretation (380pp.), following on the heels of his *Mark* in NTL. Boring is a veteran scholar, retired from Brite Divinity School. Those familiar with his large-scale NT Introduction (2012) know that he rejects the Pauline authorship of the second letter. [*BBR* 26.4 (Weima); *CBQ* 4/19; *Int* 1/17].

F   Bowens, Lisa Marie. (NICNT-R). Would replace Fee.

✓   Bridges, Linda McKinnish. ‡ (S&H) 2008. It seems the governing assumption is "that the believers in Thessaloniki were artisans who lived, worked, and worshiped in their workshop" (8) and that these letters address a predominantly male community and betray an androcentric viewpoint. Bridges suggests that "a feminine perspective is absent, either by force or ignorance." Her purpose, then, is to take up "the challenge of creating new worlds of meaning that will be more inclusive and available to all the readers" (12). She treats 2 Thessalonians as pseudonymous. The feel of the work is odd. On the one hand it can be intensely personal and even autobiographical. On the other, it can be inaccessibly academic; e.g., the Introduction begins with a lengthy quote from that famous theorist of dialogism and intertextuality, Mikhail Bakhtin. The vol. is less useful than others in S&H as a theological exposition for pastors; students may find it stimulating. [*CTJ* 4/10; *Int* 1/10 (Weima); *NovT* 53.2].

☆   **Brookins, Timothy A.** (Paideia) 2021. Completes the series and is a strong representative due to its concise exegesis. Brookins defends the authenticity of the second epistle. He draws on the best scholarship and has good judgment exegetically (over 200pp.). Well worth buying, unless one seeks a more thorough and theologically robust expositional work. Somewhat surprising is the multiplicity of citations to eight works of Seneca. [*CBQ* 1/23; *Int* 7/23; *JSNT* 44.5].

✓ **Bruce, F. F.** (retired WBC) 1982. See Kim above. Bruce was long among the most useful commentaries for students and pastors reading the Greek. It was marked by his characteristic thoroughness (though I wished it were longer), carefully weighed comments on the text, and good historical sense (always his forte). Once it was Silva's first choice and a recommended purchase in this guide (1990–2005), though I always wanted a supplemental theological exposition alongside. [*JBL* 104.2; *JETS* 6/83; *RTR* 1/84; *EvQ* 1/85; *Chm* 101.1].

☆ **Byron, John.** (SGBC) 2014. Pleasing as a full theological treatment of the letters (310pp.). The author trained at Durham and teaches at Ashland. According to the series remit, he reads Paul in terms of the whole story of God's revelation in Scripture (he explicitly draws on Hagner and McKnight here). The one main theme "is the ongoing need for the Thessalonians to put their hope in God" (9). He inspires the confidence of his reader in his scholarship, but he writes for the church. He shares lesser-known facts (e.g., on p.20, the canonical order of Paul's Letters simply reflects their length, not chronology or importance—though Thessalonians to Timothy doesn't exactly fit the scheme). Byron writes well.

Calvin, John. (CrossC) 1999. Better to read the full commentary online (Pringle translation of 1851), or consult the 1960 Mackenzie translation (Torrance edition).

Cara, Robert. (EPSC) 2009. By a prof at RTS Charlotte. I regret I've not seen it.

☆ Chapman, David W. "1–2 Thessalonians" in *Ephesians–Philemon* (ESVEC) 2018. See Merkle under Ephesians.

F  Chapman, David W. (EGGNT).

✓ Collins, Raymond F., ed. ‡ *The Thessalonian Correspondence*, 1990. Nearly 40 papers in the BETL series. Earlier influential essays appeared in Collins, ed., *Studies on the First Letter to the Thessalonians* (1984).

Comfort, Philip. (CorBC) 2008. See Hoehner under Ephesians.

Cousar, Charles B. ‡ *Reading Galatians, Philippians, and 1 Thessalonians* (RNT) 2001.

Denney, James. (EB) 1892. Long a mainstay in pastors' libraries and still useful for sermon preparation, if read along with careful exegetical works like Fee, Green, etc.

✓ Donfried, Karl P. ‡ *Paul, Thessalonica, and Early Christianity*, 2002. Brilliant critical essays. [*JTS* 10/03; *ExpTim* 6/04; *RelSRev* 1/05]. See also the Donfried–Beutler edited vol., *The Thessalonians Debate* (2000) [*CTJ* 4/01; *RelSRev* 4/01; *JTS* 10/01].

Duncan, Ligon. *1 & 2 Thessalonians for You*, 2023. Have not seen it.

Eadie, John. 1877. A learned, leading Greek exegesis . . . 150 years ago (370pp.), by a conservative Scottish Presbyterian. Reprinted by Baker (1979), and now free online.

Elias, Jacob W. (BCBC) 1995. Accomplishes well the aims of the series.

✓ Eubank, Nathan. ‡ (CCSS) 2019. By a well-trained, conservatively critical Catholic scholar, this has received plaudits as a clear, more accessible commentary. A stronger entry in the series. [*BBR* 31.1; *CBQ* 10/20; *JSNT* 42.5].

✓ Farrow, Douglas. [𝓜], (Brazos) 2020. "The volume well combines New Testament studies and Christian theology" (Thiselton). The author is a Catholic prof at McGill, has done influential work on the Ascension, and here provides excellent help for those seeking to relate these early epistles and their theology to our time. [*CBQ* 7/22].

✓ Findlay, G. G. (Cambridge Greek Testament for Schools & Colleges) 1904. Was reprinted in 1982 by Baker. Reprints do not always indicate value, but Findlay has held value and is one of my favorite older commentaries. The author earlier did the more accessible CBSC (1894), which is free online.

✓ **Frame, J. E.** (ICC) 1912. Still useful for fuller research. Carson, I believe, may underestimate its worth, given that Fee cites Frame 44×. I was surprised to find it free online.

✓ **Furnish, Victor Paul.** ‡ (ANTC) 2007. The reputation of the author led me to expect a high-quality exegesis, and I was not disappointed. For a compact (204pp.), critical exegetical commentary, you can't do any better; this is especially true of 1 Thessalonians—he is too brief on 2 Thessalonians (40pp.) for my liking. Furnish is a deeply learned, mature Pauline scholar. He says the evidence indicates that 2 Thessalonians is deutero-Pauline, but is open to interpreting the letter as authentic. See his strong *II Corinthians* in AB. [*Int* 7/08; *RelSRev* 9/08; *BL* 2009].

✓ Gatiss, Lee, and Bradley G. Green, eds. *1–2 Thessalonians, 1–2 Timothy, Titus, Philemon* (RCS) 2019.

✓ Gaventa, Beverly Roberts. ‡ (I) 1998. Judged to be a success, but it cannot be a first choice. Though a thin vol., there is much packed into it for the expositor. Disappointingly, she decides 2 Thessalonians is deutero-Pauline. [*NovT* 41.4; *Int* 4/99; *RelSRev* 10/99].

Gillman, Florence, Mary Ann Beavis, and HyeRan Kim-Cragg. ‡ (Wisdom) 2016. [*CBQ* 1/19; *JSNT* 40.5].

✓ Gorday, Peter, ed. *Colossians, 1–2 Thessalonians, 1–2 Timothy, Titus, Philemon* (ACCS) 2000.

☆ Grant, James H. (PTW) 2011. The author pastors Trinity Reformed Church in Rossville, TN, and is clearly a thoughtful, gifted preacher. Grant can be recommended to those preparing expositional messages and Bible studies, and to those desiring devotional reading on these attractive letters.

✓ Gupta, Nijay K. [𝓜], (NCCS) 2016. Part of a remarkable wave of stimulating commentaries on the Thessalonian letters (Weima, Boring, Byron, Johnson, etc.). Combined with the Zondervan work (below), Gupta has done the church and academy a fine service. This exegetical and expositional work is solidly researched, clear, and insightful (approx. 160pp.). [*Chm* Aut 18; *ExpTim* 4/18; *Int* 1/18 (Weima); *JSNT* 39.5, 40.5].

✓ Gupta, Nijay K. [𝓜], (ZCINT) 2019. Not a commentary but a fulsome introduction (approx. 300pp.). The discussion of the authenticity of 2 Thessalonians is quite lengthy (197–220); Gupta cautiously supports Pauline authorship, in part because those who deny it have not constructed "a convincing scenario that would necessitate such a pseudepigraphal letter." [*Presb* Fall 19; *CTJ* 4/20; *BBR* 31.2; *CBQ* 7/20; *JETS* 6/20; *DenvJ* 9/19].

✓ Harrison, James R., and L. L. Welborn, eds. *The First Urban Churches 7: Thessalonica*, 2022.

Hendriksen, William. (NTC) 1955. Now bound with the Pastorals. See my comments there. Long a mainstay for Reformed pastors.

Hiebert, D. Edmond. 1971. A full-length exposition which numbers of pastors have found helpful. Strongly dispensational.

Howell, Mark. *Exalting Jesus in 1 & 2 Thessalonians* (CCE) 2015.

Jackman, David. *The Authentic Church: What Are Our Priorities before Christ Comes Again?* 2001. Valuable for preachers and for devotional study (about 175pp.).

✓ Jewett, Robert. ‡ *The Thessalonian Correspondence: Pauline Rhetoric and Millenarian Piety*, 1986. An important monograph arguing that the Letters were written to counteract an overrealized eschatology.

✓ Johanson, Bruce C. *To All the Brethren: A Text-Linguistic and Rhetorical Approach to 1 Thessalonians*, 1987. An Uppsala dissertation.

✓ **Johnson, Andy.** (THC) 2016. Distinctive and to be appreciated is the missional perspective the author brings to this theological exegesis. Because the Thessalonian correspondence often receives less attention by scholars (and preachers), I value the essays on the letters' theological contribution (224–329). Johnson is a senior professor teaching at Nazarene Seminary in Kansas City. Well-done in many respects. See Cara for a critique of Johnson's theological positions (Arminianism, supporting the NPP and denying imputed righteousness, a subjective genitive reading of πίστις Ἰησοῦ Χριστοῦ, etc.). [*BBR* 27.3; *JETS* 12/17 (Cara); *JSNT* 39.5; *RevExp* 5/19].

✓ **Lightfoot, J. B.** *Notes on the Epistles of Paul*, 1904. Students ought to be aware of this reprint.

Lightfoot and his friends, Westcott and Hort, planned to write commentaries on the Greek text of each NT book. Some were published, but the trio did not live to see the series' completion. Among Lightfoot's commentaries in progress when he died are those included in this 325-page work: 1 and 2 Thessalonians (complete), 1 Corinthians 1–7, Romans 1–7, and Ephesians 1:1–14. The vol. stands alongside his famous exegeses of Galatians, Philippians, and Colossians–Philemon. All are free online.

F   Luijendijk, AnneMarie. ‡ (Herm). A new assignment after the passing of Harvard's Helmut Koester in 2016. Luijendijk teaches at Princeton.

✓   MacDougall, Daniel W. *The Authenticity of 2 Thessalonians*, 2016. An Aberdeen PhD.

☆   **Malherbe, Abraham.** ‡ (AB) 2000. Very important for students, with more dependable exegesis than some other brilliant AB commentaries (e.g., Martyn on Galatians and Elliott on 1 Peter). Prior to this major exegesis, Malherbe had published a good bit on Thessalonians already; see especially his *Paul and the Thessalonians: The Philosophical Tradition of Pastoral Care* (1987). He was Professor Emeritus at Yale (†2012) and heartened evangelicals by his defense of the second letter's authenticity. There is much else to praise here. Malherbe sticks to the task of close exegesis, and the scholarly standards are exceedingly rigorous. His conclusions tend to be conservatively critical. The work is even fuller than its 500pp. might indicate; there is nary a wasted sentence. Specialists interested in Paul's sociocultural context and his "church rhetoric" find this AB invaluable. On the issue of rhetorical analysis, Malherbe concludes that "Paul made extensive use of the conventions of discourse used by philosophers who aimed at the moral and intellectual reformation of their listeners" (96). Scholarly pastors learn much here, even as they wish there were more theology and less citations of other ancient literature. [*CBQ* 4/02; *JETS* 9/02; *JBL* Sum 02; *ExpTim* 1/02; *Bib* 83.1; *NovT* 44.4; *JR* 4/04; *RelSRev* 1/03 (lengthy reviews); *DenvJ*].

Malone, Andrew S. *To Walk and to Please God: A Theology of 1 & 2 Thessalonians*, 2024. I have yet to see it.

☆   **Marshall, I. Howard.** [𝓜], (NCB) 1983. One of his better efforts earlier in his career, though an exegesis in shorter compass (235pp.). He self-consciously builds on the foundation of Best and also discusses Trilling's influential German work (combating Trilling's arguments for pseudonymity). Highly recommended and mildly critical. Reprinted by Regent College in 2002. [*WTJ* Spr 85; *Them* 1/85; *JETS* 12/83].

Marshall, Molly T. ‡ (Belief) 2022. I have yet to see it.

Martin, D. Michael. (NAC) 1995. As a slight surprise to me, considering the Southern Baptist character of the series, Martin cannot find a pretribulational rapture in Thessalonians. Neither can I. The author teaches at Golden Gate Baptist Seminary. Wanamaker calls this 300-page commentary a work of solid scholarship, but it is not first-rate. See Moo below. [*BSac* 1/98; *Them* 1/97; *RelSRev* 10/97].

Mayhue, Richard. (Focus) 1999. The chart on p.13 alerts readers that it is a dispensational exposition—unusual in the series. Mayhue taught at The Master's Seminary.

Menken, Maarten J. J. ‡ *2 Thessalonians* (NT Readings) 1994.

Míguez, Néstor O. ‡ *The Practice of Hope: Ideology and Intention in 1 Thessalonians* (PCC) ET 2012. A political (liberation) reading, using ideological criticism.

✓   **Milligan, George.** ‡ 1908. A great scholar's treatment of the Greek text in the venerable Macmillan series. Milligan has long been consulted. He was more critical in his day but did not reject the authenticity of the second epistle (xcii). Now free online.

Moffatt, James. ‡ (Expositor's Greek Testament) 1910.

F   Moo, Douglas J. (CSC). To replace Martin.

Moore, A. L. ‡ (NCB) 1969. Too brief to do much good; replaced by Marshall.

☆   **Morris, Leon.** (retired NICNT) 1959, rev. 1991. Replaced by Fee. Morris had a shorter, more popularly styled work in Tyndale (listed below), but this was preferred as the more thorough and scholarly. Regrettably, with the NICNT the 1991 revision was not extensive. In 1993 this vol. was George Knight's first choice for the pastor. Because Morris was more balanced between exegesis and exposition than Bruce or NIGTC, I considered it a good first purchase, but Green took Morris's place.

☆ Morris, Leon. (TNTC) 1957, rev. 1984. See NICNT above. [*JETS* 12/85].

✓ Nasrallah, Laura, Charalambos Bakirtzis, and Steven J. Friesen, eds. *From Roman to Early Christian Thessalonike: Studies in Religion and Archaeology*, 2010. [*JSNT* 34.5].

✓ Nicholl, Colin R. *From Hope to Despair in Thessalonica: Situating 1 and 2 Thessalonians*, 2004. [*JETS* 6/05; *Them* Sum 05; *JR* 10/05; *ExpTim* 5/05].

Osborne, Grant R. (ONTC) 2018. See under Commentary Series.

✓ Paddison, Angus. [𝓜], *Theological Hermeneutics and 1 Thessalonians*, 2005. A profound discussion of different traditions of reading the epistle theologically (historical-critical, Aquinas, Calvin). Originally a Glasgow PhD, published by CUP.

Palmer, Earl. (GNC) 1985. Can be ignored.

☆ Phillips, Richard D. (REC) 2015. Thoughtful, *very* thorough, fulsome sermonic material from a prominent PCA pastor. [*Chm* Win 16].

Plummer, Alfred. 1918.

F Porter, Stanley E. (ICC-R). To replace Frame. Donfried (†2022) once had the contract.

✓ **Richard, Earl J.** ‡ (SacP) 1995. A quality, major critical commentary, sensitive to rhetorical matters and focused on philology, and certainly to be consulted by students. The author taught at Loyola and says 2 Thessalonians is deutero-Pauline. When published, Richard was remarkably the "only significant commentary in English over the past century and a half that has tried to make sense of this letter as a forgery" (Fee, 237). [*EvQ* 4/99; *JBL* Win 97 (Weima); *CBQ* 10/97; *SwJT* Spr 99; *RelSRev* 4/97].

Smith, Abraham. ‡ (NIB) 2000. About 100pp. from an African American prof at Andover-Newton who doubts Paul wrote 2 Thessalonians. Smith does not probe deeply enough to help students much, and the critical orientation makes this NIB work less suitable for evangelical pastors. [*SewaneeThRev* Easter 01].

F Still, Todd D. (NIGTC-R). Would replace Wanamaker. Still's PhD was *Conflict at Thessalonica: A Pauline Church and Its Neighbours* (1999).

F Tabb, Brian. (EEC). Previously Robert Thomas was listed.

✓ Thiselton, Anthony. *1 & 2 Thessalonians: Through the Centuries* (BBC) 2011. Fine reception history. [*JTS* 10/13; *JSNT* 34.5; *ExpTim* 10/11].

✓ Thomas, Robert L. (EBCR) 2006. A 125-page improvement on his 1978 EBC, which was dispensational (old-style) and careful, but not so penetrating. I think this may be the best presentation of that tradition among Thessalonians commentaries. Thomas has written a major 2-vol. exegesis of Revelation. See EEC below.

☆ **Wanamaker, Charles A.** [𝓜], (NIGTC) 1990. Carson's first pick from 1993 to 2007, though I am sure he never bought Wanamaker's reversal of the Letters' order. A perceptive commentary on the Greek, notable for its use of social scientific research. It is long on rhetorical analysis but sometimes short on theology. Wanamaker should definitely be consulted by students. The work seemed marginally less valuable to preachers than Bruce's more traditionally styled commentary, yet with Stott and Holmes on hand that was not so serious a problem. For a more recent and accessible socio-rhetorical commentary, see Witherington. Weima displaced Wanamaker on my purchase list. [*JBL* Sum 92; *CBQ* 1/92; *Int* 10/92; *RTR* 5/92; *JETS* 9/95; *CTJ* 4/92; *Bib* 73.3].

Ward, Ronald A. 1973. Helpful exposition with good study behind it. Was more highly valued by pastors back in the 1970s and 80s. See Ward on the Pastorals below.

Weatherly, Jon A. (College Press NIV Commentary) 1996.

Whiteley, D. E. ‡ (New Clarendon) 1969. One of the better works in the series.

F  Wilder, Terry. (EBTC)?

Williams, David J. (NIBC) 1992. Competent, well-researched, and quite handy, too, at about 150pp. It once competed with Morris's TNTC as a best bargain pb for the student. [*CRBR* 1994 (Wanamaker, negative)].

☆ **Witherington, Ben, III.** (SRC) 2006. The prolific scholar's work on Thessalonians is clear, accessible, fairly full (286pp.), and provides a fresh socio-rhetorical interpretation. He is practiced at writing such commentaries. Note that he disagrees with Malherbe for giving prominence to epistolary rather than rhetorical considerations (17). See Witherington's earlier work on Matthew, Mark, John, Acts, Romans, Corinthians, Galatians, etc. This vol. is among the best. [*CBQ* 10/07; *JTS* 4/08; *BL* 2007; *RelSRev* 4/07; *ExpTim* 7/07; *DenvJ* 1/07; *NovT* 51.4 (Burke); *Anvil* 25.1].

NOTES: (1) Sean A. Adams, "Evaluating 1 Thessalonians: An Outline of Holistic Approaches to 1 Thessalonians in the Last 25 Years," *CBR* 8.1 (2009): 51–70. (2) Stanley Porter, "Developments in German and French Thessalonians Research: A Survey and Critique," *CurBS* 7 (1999): 309–34.

# THE PASTORAL EPISTLES

★ Hughes, R. Kent, and Bryan Chapell. (PTW) 2000. A fine piece of work, not only for its sound exposition but also for the guidance it provides the pastor toward appropriate application. Good research stands behind this commentary, though they constantly misspell the name Torrance. They even managed to consult and cite Mounce (also published in 2000). Students and scholars won't spring for this, but preachers will. Those who would prefer an exegetical rather than homiletical commentary should look at Marshall's ICC, Knight, Johnson's AB, and Quinn (Titus).

★ **Marshall, I. Howard.** [*M*], (ICC-R) 1999. Called "splendid" by Barrett. On the project he had Towner's assistance. The exegesis is masterful and will be influential for a generation. Academically inclined pastors want to buy this. Marshall and Towner sympathize with the traditional position on authorship, and "have tried to present the message of the letters as they are ostensibly meant to be understood, as letters from Paul to Timothy and Titus" (xiv). Still, they—Marshall in particular—reject direct Pauline authorship and propose that authentic Pauline materials were posthumously edited. The use of the term pseudonymity, with its attached nuances of deceit/fraud, is avoided (84); Marshall prefers "allonymity" instead. Second Timothy is viewed as having a more patent Pauline character and as providing "the spur for the writing of the subsequent two letters" (86). They read 1 Timothy 2 as prohibiting public teaching of men by women but conclude it is a time-bound text, relevant only to the 1st century situation. Whatever my disagreements with Marshall and Towner on interpretive cruxes, I treasure this 869-page vol. The price is prohibitively high, so I recommend Mounce or Knight for pastors scouting for a commentary on the Greek. Advanced students and the best-trained pastors (with means) can purchase the ICC in pb. [*NovT* 42.3; *ExpTim* 5/00; *EvQ* 10/01; *JTS* 10/01; *JETS* 9/01; *BSac* 4/02; *JSNT* 9/01; *Evangel* Aut 02]. Note his update in Köstenberger–Wilder: "The Pastoral Epistles in Recent Study" (268–324), with its reviews of commentaries published 2000–10, research on the epistles' structure, literary approaches, pseudepigraphy, and theology.

★ **Mounce, William.** (WBC) 2000. A huge vol. (cxxxvi + 600pp.), by a former Gordon-Conwell prof, giving us a detailed, scholarly Greek exegesis. Yet he aims more to benefit the pastor and the church than the academy and is alert to pastoral concerns and questions. He seems to believe, as I do, that the Scriptures belong to the church and theology is best done in the church context. On conservatives' big issues he takes friendly positions, defending both the authenticity of the letters (with Luke as amanuensis) and a traditional reading of Paul's instruction regarding the role of women in the church. He arrives at his positions through disciplined exegesis and weighing all the evidence. The handling of the Greek shows the attention to detail and carefulness one expects from a fine grammarian. Scholarly pastors, especially the frugal ones, will probably want to buy this first for study of the Greek, but they will also want Marshall, Porter, Knight, and Johnson's AB ready at hand for exegesis. [*JETS* 6/02; *BSac* 7/02; *Evangel* Aut 02; *Anvil* 20.2].

★ **Porter, Stanley E.** 2023. An exacting "Commentary on the Greek Text" (860pp., plus the 70-page Bibliography). Published by Baker as a stand-alone work, not the anticipated BECNT. The author describes his effort as "a different kind of commentary," which "paves new ground," is "iconoclastic," and linguistically oriented (Preface). Yarbrough writes, with his usual generous spirit, "If Mount Rushmore honored great and recent English-language commentaries on the Pastorals, alongside the works of I. Howard Marshall, Philip Towner, and Gerald Bray would now appear this offering by Stanley E. Porter" (endorsement). Keener speaks of it as "one of the most, if not *the* most, detailed grammatical commentaries on the Greek text. . . . [It] exhibits Porter's signature approach to Systemic Functional Linguistics and offers a plethora of new insights for scholarly discussion." More academically oriented persons, especially if fascinated by linguistics, will best appreciate Porter's aims and accomplishment; he seems to write as a linguist for fellow linguists. I find Porter most helpful for understanding the text at the clausal level and for following the epistles' lines of thought. He firmly defends Pauline authorship, refuting the language arguments for pseudonymity or a fragmentary hypothesis (e.g., Harrison): "linguistic variation is the product of register/genre variation rather than authorship variation." There is little in the way of theological exposition. Porter stakes out a *"restricting harmful practices* view" in reading 1 Tim 2:12: "I do not commission a woman to teach falsely or to have abusive authority over a man but to be in orderliness." He claims not to have found much help in consulting "conventional" commentaries and "looked to Knight and especially Marshall/Towner as repositories of references to the variety of scholarly opinions."

★ Stott, John R. W. *Guard the Gospel: The Message of 2 Timothy* (BST) 1973; *Guard the Truth: The Message of 1 Timothy and Titus* (BST) 1996. Everything you would expect of Stott. I wish IVP USA would combine the two slim vols., as IVP did in Britain. [*Chm* 112.1].

★ **Towner, Philip H.** (NICNT) 2006. Here we learn that Towner was not in full agreement with Marshall on the authorship issue (see Marshall above). He tentatively upholds the authenticity of the Letters (83–88). His discussion of 1 Timothy 2:8–15 is influenced by Bruce Winter's scholarship on the "new Roman woman" [*JTS* 10/05], and he critiques both the complementarian and feminist arguments (he is egalitarian). He wants to jettison the label "Pastoral Epistles" because it tends to encourage "a corpus mentality" among interpreters and obscure the individuality of each letter. Theological reflection is a strong point of this NICNT, though he does not venture as much into application issues as he did in IVPNT (see below). Towner builds upon his fine dissertation and his IVPNT. He worked so long and carefully on these epistles and produced such a full (886pp.), well-rounded, and insightful commentary, that many will want to make this their first pick. Marshall calls it "arguably the finest and most useful commentary based on the English text of the letters (with adequate discussion of matters Greek in the footnotes)." [*CBQ* 7/07; *BBR* 17.2; *JTS* 4/08; *BL* 2007; *NovT* 49.2; *RB* 10/08 (Murphy-O'Connor, hypercritical); *ExpTim* 6/07; *RelSRev* 7/07 (Malherbe); *JETS* 9/08; *BSac* 7/08].

★ **Yarbrough, Robert W.** *The Letters to Timothy and Titus* (Pillar) 2018. Clearly a leading evangelical commentary for students and pastors! As with WBC and NICNT, many will happily make this a first choice; Yarbrough has the advantage of being able to interact with those sterling works (and the Marshall–Towner ICC). Greekless readers should start here, and those with the language might too. There is so much wisdom and learning, as Yarbrough deals at length with introductory matters, exegetical tangles, and (a strength of the series) the theology in the text. But what especially comes across is the pastor's heart behind Paul's writing—see the section "Paul as Working Pastor." Another distinguishing mark is the exceedingly close attention to word use and patterns (see his 31 tables). Yarbrough has a calm, winsome treatment of 1 Tim 2:11–3:13; his view is complementarian. Note that he also has an outstanding BECNT on the Johannine Letters. [*WTJ* Spr 23; *BBR* 30.1; *JETS* 12/19; *BSac* 4/21].

✓ Aageson, James W. ‡ *Paul, the Pastoral Epistles, and the Early Church*, 2007.
✓ Arichea, Daniel C., and Howard A. Hatton. (UBS) 1995.
☆ Barcley, William B. *1 & 2 Timothy* (EPSC) 2005. By a prof at RTS in Jackson. Directly serves preachers with its focus on the message and application. Easy to read (315pp.).
✓ Barrett, C. K. ‡ (New Clarendon) 1963. Insightful in brief compass.
✓ **Bassler, Jouette M.** ‡ (ANTC) 1996. Better than Houlden or Hanson. Perfect for students who want to consult a probing critical exegesis but don't have time to tackle the new ICC-R, Quinn–Wacker, or another dauntingly full work. Bassler rejects the Pastorals as authentic Pauline epistles. [*RelSRev* 1/98].
F Beale, G. K., and Christopher A. Beetham. (ZECNT).
F Belleville, Linda, Jon C. Laansma, and J. Ramsey Michaels. *1 Timothy, 2 Timothy, Titus, Hebrews* (CorBC) 2009. Bound together, Belleville is responsible for 1 Timothy, Laansma takes 2 Timothy and Titus, and Michaels comments on Hebrews.
✓ Bernard, J. H. 1899. Reprinted in 1980 by Baker in their Thornapple series.
✓ **Bray, Gerald L.** (ITC) 2019. Coming from a distinguished church historian, this work excels in presenting the history of interpretation and reflecting on points of doctrine. That fresh perspective, married to good exegetical and theological judgment, well complements other major works that emphasize detailed interaction with the Greek text plus the ins-and-outs of NT scholarship. Bray has an unflinching confidence in biblical authority (about 550pp.). I smiled at Yarbrough's description: "Bray's interpretation . . . is free of unhealthy preoccupation with what the perceived specialist [NT] authorities allow to be said at present" [*JETS* 12/20]. In short, one of the most stimulating, useful, and expensive commentaries on these letters. [*ExpTim* 12/19; *JSNT* 42.5].
☆ Burk, Denny. "1–2 Timothy, Titus" in *Ephesians–Philemon* (ESVEC) 2018. See Merkle under Ephesians.
   Calvin, John. (CrossC) 1998. Better to read the full commentary online for free.
☆ Calvin, John. *Sermons on Titus*, ET 2015; *Sermons on 1 Timothy*, ET 2018; and *Sermons on 2 Timothy*, ET 2018. [*RTR* 8/21]. Cause for great celebration is the Banner of Truth release of Robert White's fresh translation of Calvin's *Sermons* [*RTR* 8/21]. The three-vol. set lucidly renders the original 1561 French publication and has approx. 1600pp. Previously, some bookish pastors had invested in Banner's "Facsimile Edition" of the 1579 "L. T." (Laurence Tomson) translation. However, as with the Banner facsimile of Calvin's *Sermons on Job*, the Elizabethan English and typeface made it a chore to read. In passing, one can mention the Ray Van Neste and Brian Denker book of *John Calvin's Sermons on 1 Timothy* (2016); it is "revised and updated" from the 1579 translation.

✓ **Collins, Raymond F.** ‡ (NTL) 2002. The first vol. in the series, this is a major mid-level (400-page) commentary from a renowned prof at Catholic University of America. The introduction's conclusions are mainstream critical, denying Pauline authorship (the epistles are said to be a later interpretation of the true Paulines). Collins shows interest in rhetorical features and the links the Pastorals have with Hellenistic literature. He scarcely interacts with other commentaries. (Here is one case where a lack of a modern author index does not handicap the reader.) C. K. Barrett rates this as excellent. The chief difficulty here is the anticipated audience; students will want more interaction with other scholars' views, and preachers will desire more discussion of the theological message, with hints at contemporary relevance. [*JTS* 10/04; *CBQ* 4/03; *JETS* 9/03; *BSac* 4/05; *ExpTim* 9/03; *ThTo* 4/04; *Int* 1/05; *RelSRev* 10/03 (Malherbe); *BBR* 14.1 (Marshall); *CurTM* 8/05].

✓ **Dibelius, Martin, and Hans Conzelmann.** ‡ (Herm) 1966, ET 1972. Long the standard critical commentary for exegetes, Dibelius–Conzelmann has a mine of information for the advanced student, especially on the Greco-Roman literary backdrop. Highly critical and, of course, rejects Pauline authorship. There is little here for the pastor. Its brevity and age, as well as the shift away from exclusively historical-critical research, limit its value today. See Fitzgerald. [*ExpTim* 10/73; *Int* 1/74].

Donelson, Lewis. ‡ (WestBC) 1996. He made his mark in scholarship with *Pseudepigraphy and Ethical Argument in the Pastoral Epistles* (1986). See Ephesians.

☆ Doriani, Daniel M., and Richard D. Phillips. *2 Timothy, Titus* (REC) 2020. See Ryken for another hefty vol. of sermons, especially valued in conservative Reformed circles.

✓ **Dunn, James D. G.** ‡ (NIB) 2000. Has insights (105pp.) but does not intend to compete with full-length technical commentaries. Dunn sits on the fence regarding authorship, but leans toward a position similar to Marshall's. He argues that "pseudonymous writing would be attributed to the originator only if it was deemed to be an appropriate elaboration or extension of the original" (780)—a separate discussion of this issue can be found in Dunn's article on "Pseudepigraphy" in IVP's *Dictionary of the Later NT and Its Developments*. This NIB work includes some wise application. [*SewaneeThRev* Easter 01].

Earle, Ralph. (EBC) 1978. Covers 1–2 Timothy. Not so valuable. See Köstenberger.

Easton, B. S. ‡ 1948. Finds some genuinely Pauline material. Essentially liberal.

Ellicott, C. J. 3rd ed. 1864. An old classic which most have forgotten.

Fairbairn, Patrick. (GS) 1874. A classic reprinted numerous times. Now free online.

☆ **Fee, Gordon.** (NIBC) Originally 1984, 1988. Excellent, accessible, and fuller than many in the series. Very insightful, even if his interpretation of a couple important passages is disappointing. "Fee has worked hard at building a more or less believable 'life setting' that ties the contents of these three little books together" (Carson). In brief compass, it surpassed Kelly (barely) and Guthrie as the best exegesis. However, Fee is less valuable now. (I recommended its purchase until 2009.) Quite a number of evangelical commentaries have appeared since 1990. [*JETS* 12/91].

✓ **Fiore, Benjamin.** ‡ (SacP) 2007. This critical Catholic exegesis is not as full (253pp.) as some other vols. in the series and not so strong on theological reflection. Its strength is in the area of rhetorical/literary research, which makes sense since the author trained in the classics. He rejects Pauline authorship. Malherbe regards this as "a splendid contribution to Sacra Pagina." [*CBQ* 1/09; *Int* 1/09; *ExpTim* 8/08; *RelSRev* 3/09 (Malherbe)].

F Fitzgerald, John T. ‡ (Herm). To replace Dibelius–Conzelmann.

✓ Gatiss, Lee, and Bradley G. Green, eds. *1–2 Thessalonians, 1–2 Timothy, Titus, Philemon* (RCS) 2019.

Gealy, Fred D. ‡ (IB–Exegesis) 1955. Once made a contribution. He regards the letters as pseudonymous. With all the newer works available, you can safely ignore Gealy.

Gloer, W. Hulitt. ‡ (S&H) 2010. After a review of the arguments against Pauline authorship, Gloer says he "will assume authenticity and a date in the mid 60s" (11). There is little interaction with other commentators except Collins. He is Professor of Preaching and Christian Scripture at Baylor. See RNT below.

Gloer, W. Hulitt, and Perry L. Stepp. ‡ *Reading Paul's Letters to Individuals* (RNT) 2008. The vol. of 280pp. treats Philemon, Titus, and 1–2 Timothy (in that order).

✓ Gorday, Peter, ed. *Colossians, 1–2 Thessalonians, 1–2 Timothy, Titus, Philemon* (ACCS) 2000.

☆ **Guthrie, Donald.** (retired TNTC) 1957, rev. 1990. Most valuable for its sturdy defense of Pauline authorship, but one can get that in his massive NT introduction. Generally speaking, Guthrie is still useful, offers an insightful and dependable exegesis, and has been a wise purchase on the part of pastors. See Padilla below.

✓ **Hanson, A. T.** ‡ (NCB) 1982. Previously he also published *Studies in the Pastoral Epistles* (1968) and wrote the vol. for CBC. Quite critical. [*ExpTim* 12/84].

Harding, Mark. ‡ *What Are They Saying about the Pastoral Epistles?* 2001.

Harrison, P. N. ‡ *The Problem of the Pastoral Epistles*, 1921.

Hendriksen, William. (NTC) 1957. Now bound with 1–2 Thessalonians. Has long sat on the bookshelves of Presbyterian and Reformed pastors. Hendriksen still provides some good theological guidance. See NTC in the Commentary Series section.

Hiebert, D. Edmond. (EBC) 1978. Covers Titus and offers some help to pastors, but not students. See Earle.

F Hoklotubbe, T. Christopher. (NIGTC-R). To replace Knight. Meanwhile, see his essay in Gupta–Heim–McKnight, eds., *The State of Pauline Studies* (2024).

Houlden, J. L. ‡ (Penguin) 1976. Was reprinted in Britain by SCM (1989). Has some insights, more than you might expect from such a short work. Argues the critical line.

Huizenga, Annette Bourland. ‡ (Wisdom) 2016. Oakes says the author makes "a well-contextualized case for a reading of the Pastoral Epistles as patriarchal texts to be resistantly engaged with" [*JSNT* 40.5]. [*CBQ* 7/18; *Int* 10/19].

✓ **Hutson, Christopher R.** ‡ (Paideia) 2019. Of use as a quick exegetical reference (280pp. with bibliography). I consider Hutson's one of the best, most interesting liberal treatments of these books—it is arguably one of the best in the series too, if one is thinking about lucidity, exegetical ability, and scholarship. (If one is thinking of "best" in the sense of utility for a Bible-believing pastor's library, then I won't say it. He terms the epistles a "transparent forgery" [2].) Hutson is an Abilene prof who did his Yale PhD (under Malherbe) on the Pastorals; he wears his considerable learning lightly, with good command of the ancient literary milieu. [*Int* 10/21; *JSNT* 42.5].

☆ **Johnson, Luke Timothy.** ‡ *1 & 2 Timothy* (AB) 2001. A conservatively critical Catholic scholar, Johnson upheld Pauline authorship in his esteemed introduction, *The Writings of the NT: An Interpretation* (3rd ed. 2010). This vol. on Timothy is a bracing challenge to the conventional wisdom that the Pastorals should be treated together as a body and are pseudonymous. Need I say that evangelicals were delighted with this shot across the bow of critical scholarship? The liberals, by contrast, were not pleased [*JR* 1/03]. Johnson's exegesis is well-done, so well-done that the scholarly pastor will want to buy this to use alongside the new ICC-R, WBC, NICNT, and NIGTC—all musts for the student. See Quinn below for the companion AB vol. on Titus. [*ExpTim* 8/01; *CBQ* 4/02; *JETS* 6/03; *NovT* 44.2; *HBT* 6/02; *RelSRev* 7/02; *JBL* Spr 02 (Towner); *TJ* Fall 02 (Yarbrough); *BibInt* 10.1 (Marshall); *DenvJ*]. Students should note that this commentary, at least on the correspondence with Timothy, supersedes Johnson's 1996 pb, *Letters to Paul's Delegates: 1 Timothy, 2 Timothy, Titus* ("NT in Context" series) [*Int* 7/98; *SwJT* Spr 98].

Johnson, Luke Timothy. ‡ (Knox Preaching Guides) 1987.

Karris, Robert J. ‡ (NTM) 1979.

☆ **Kelly, J. N. D.** [𝓜], (BNTC) 1963. Definitely one of the best in the series. Was reprinted by Baker in the Thornapple series. Decades ago, Kelly was my first choice and can still be considered for purchase; he had an outstanding grasp of the milieu of the 1st century church, had an excellent theological mind, was a judicious exegete, and a fine writer (in a British essay style—think "Ox-bridge"). He also upheld Pauline authorship with surprising vigor. [*WTJ* Spr 65].

✓ Kidson, Lyn M. ‡ *Persuading Shipwrecked Men: The Rhetorical Strategies of 1 Timothy 1*, 2021. A Macquarie PhD highly regarded by McKnight.

☆ **Knight, George W.** (NIGTC) 1992. Was once my first pick (540pp.). It is careful, well-grounded theologically, contains a good defense of Pauline authorship, and provides a probing, phrase-by-phrase exegesis of the Greek text. Conservative through and through, Knight pays more attention to theology and pastoral concerns than some others in the series (e.g., Ellingworth on Hebrews). However, the method is far more exegetical than expositional. This is the fruit of many years in the Pastorals, going back to his ThD on the Faithful Sayings (published 1968). One is glad for all the interaction with the Ridderbos Dutch commentary. With the passage of time, Knight is a little less useful to students. [*ExpTim* 1/95; *Them* 5/94].

☆ **Köstenberger, Andreas.** (EBCR) 2006. Well-done and a marked improvement over the older series. Many pastors put this to good use as a dependable guide, but now see BTCP (below). Students will look at this as a quick reference if they don't have time to delve into the very lengthy technical exegeses of Marshall, Quinn, Mounce, Towner, etc. Köstenberger also coedited with Terry Wilder the useful vol., *Entrusted with the Gospel: Paul's Theology in the Pastoral Epistles* (2010) [*Them* 7/10; *JETS* 6/11; *RelSRev* 9/11; *TJ* Spr 11].

☆ **Köstenberger, Andreas J.** (BTCP) 2017; (EBTC) 2020. Quite wide-ranging in terms of theological issues, and insightful. The Biblical and Theological Themes section of nearly 200pp. follows a 300-page expositional commentary on the three epistles. This book builds on his earlier contribution to EBCR (above), here "with a special focus on the biblical theological dimension" (xvii). He does well in treating (more briefly) the exegetical questions and is adroit at "big-picture" theological reflection. Certainly among the best evangelical commentaries, despite a need for better editing; note Percival's review [*Chm* Aut 18]. See also Köstenberger's books on John's Gospel. [*JETS* 9/18; *JSNT* 44.5].

✓ Krause, Deborah. ‡ *1 Timothy* (Read) 2004. A feminist interpretation, hostile to Paul (i.e., Paul's interpreter in this pseudonymous letter) and to what she alleges are apostolic attempts to misuse authority to control or silence others. [*JTS* 4/06; *Int* 10/06; *BL* 2005; *RelSRev* 1/06].

☆ Kuruvilla, Abraham. 2021. The author is developing an extensive set of vols. of "theological commentary for preachers" for the OT (Genesis, Judges) and NT (Mark, Ephesians). They are handy, thoughtful, and often point to structures in the text (e.g., chiasms). Kuruvilla teaches at Dallas and has evident gifts as a Bible interpreter and homiletician. [*JSNT* 44.5].

✓ Lea, Thomas, and Hayne Griffin. (NAC) 1992. A full exegesis and exposition (352pp.), reasonably well-done, which argues for the authenticity of the letters.

☆ Liefeld, Walter L. (NIVAC) 1999. Very fine work, but I judge it to be not quite as successful as Stott or Hughes–Chapell. Marshall [*BSB* 3/01] praises it highly, for "Liefeld provides excellent preparatory material for preachers." Egalitarian. [*BSac* 4/02; *Evangel* Aut 02].

☆ Lloyd-Jones, D. Martyn. *I Am Not Ashamed*, 1986. Contains eleven challenging sermons on 2 Timothy 1:21.

✓ **Lock, W.** [𝓜], (retired ICC) 1924. An acclaimed commentary on the Greek text during its time. It is still useful, but eclipsed by newer exegetical works. Lock tentatively upheld Pauline authorship. Has been replaced by Marshall.

✓ Long, Thomas G. ‡ (Belief) 2016. A theological exposition by a retired Emory homiletician. [*CBQ* 10/17; *Int* 1/18].

MacArthur, John. *1 Timothy*, 1995; *2 Timothy*, 1995; *Titus*, 1996. The strength of this series of expositions lies in practical insight and bold application rather than in careful exegesis. Many pastors and Sunday School teachers find it useful. See further comments on the series under Matthew.

✓ **McKnight, Scot.** [*M*], (NCBC) 2023. Succinct, critically engaged exegesis (220pp.), from an egalitarian and progressive evangelical perspective. Quite useful. As in his NICNT on Colossians, McKnight views each of Paul's epistles as collaborative: "the result of conversations with coworkers, with drafts and final drafts, and then—and only then—someone actually putting quill to parchment" (6). "Paul did not write any of his letters" (9). He doubts pseudonymity but agrees with Towner that it's "not possible to prove the authenticity of the letters to Timothy and Titus" (10).

McWilliams, David B. (LCEC) 2015. Regrettably, I have not seen this more homiletically styled work. The veteran pastor used to teach at Westminster Dallas/Redeemer.

Milne, Douglas J. W. (Focus) 1996. An exposition I have not seen.

Montague, George T. [*M*], (CCSS) 2008. An accessible Catholic exposition of about 250pp. The author assumes the letters are from Paul (23). One critical reviewer (Beavis) recommends Fiore instead, because of the "traditionalist bent" of Montague's work. [*JETS* 6/10; *CBQ* 7/10; *RelSRev* 9/09].

Moule, H. C. G. *The Second Epistle of Timothy*, 1905. A devotional commentary concentrating on the message and its application to the heart. Treasured by preachers.

F  Nel, Marius. (SGBC).

✓ Nes, Jermo van. *Pauline Language and the Pastoral Epistles: A Study of Linguistic Variation in the Corpus Paulinum*, 2017. An enormous investigation published by Brill, questioning the critical consensus and the "hidden presumption" that "linguistic variation is best explained by author variation" (1–2). [*WTJ* Spr 19; *BBR* 29.1; *JTS* 10/19; *JETS* 6/19; *JSNT* 41.5].

Ngewa, Samuel M. (ABCS) 2009. The main strength here is warm, clear pastoral exposition (466pp.) focusing on the questions and needs of the African church. The author is NT editor for the series. See also Ngewa's expositions of John's Gospel and Galatians. Recommended for purchase by *DenvJ*. [*JETS* 6/10; *CBQ* 7/10; *JSNT* 33.5; *DenvJ* 13].

✓ Oden, Thomas C. [*M*], (I) 1989. A pleasant surprise (for the series) was his defense of Pauline authorship (192pp.). The famous Drew professor of theology (†2016) was moving in a conservative direction for some time, calling the church to resist modernity and postmodernity and return to the faith of our fathers—the church fathers. He is profitably consulted for theological reflection. [*JETS* 6/92; *Int* 7/91; *CTJ* 4/91; *CRBR* 1991].

☆ Padilla, Osvaldo. (TNTC-R) 2022. Replaces Guthrie and is well-written as a succinct exegetical reference (about 300pp.). The author teaches at Beeson. See his past work on Acts.

✓ **Pao, David.** (BrillEC) 2023. The inaugural vol. in the series. Like the Greek exegesis published by Porter (who edits the new Brill series), Pao's is a huge undertaking, with 70pp. of introduction and bibliography, followed by 660pp. of Greek exegesis. Regrettably I've yet to find a copy, and I'm seeing a price of $300. It would be no surprise if this commentary proves to be among the top three or four evangelical works in usefulness to students. Pao is a veteran scholar (25 years at TEDS), who wrote the ZECNT on Colossians and Philemon.

☆ **Perkins, Larry J.** (BHGNT) 2017. Well-done, and "a sure-footed guide to the major features of these Greek texts" [*ExpTim* 6/19]. [*JSNT* 41.5].

Platt, David, Daniel L. Akin, and Tony Merida. *Exalting Jesus in 1 & 2 Timothy and Titus* (CCE) 2013.

Plummer, Alfred. (EB) 1907.

✓ **Quinn, Jerome D.** ‡ *The Letter to Titus* (AB) 1990. A leading critical commentary by a Catholic scholar, and one of the most exhaustive works on Titus ever (334pp.). The accompanying vol. on Timothy (below) was published outside AB. Quinn's decision to complete first the Titus commentary reflects his conviction that that epistle was issued prior to 1 & 2 Timothy. He suggests that the PE were written as a "third roll" by the author of Luke–Acts, and has closest of connections to the authentic Pauline tradition. Quinn's work is comprehensive, moderately critical, superb for word studies, and of use to students. I do not judge the ECC *Timothy* tome below to be as successful as this AB.

✓ **Quinn, Jerome D., and William C. Wacker.** ‡ *The First and Second Letters to Timothy* (ECC) 2000. Originally intended for AB, but Quinn's untimely death (1988) drastically slowed the production. I was glad, finally, to see the appearance of this 800-page commentary. There are a few odd aspects to the tome, however; chief among them for me is the transliteration of the Greek when this lengthy work will be used by very few besides students and scholars. Marshall praised this vol. while calling it uneven in editing; in a more critical moment he termed it "poorly organized and dull" [*BSB* 3/01]. See Quinn above. Note that the work has been republished in a two-vol. pb. [*ExpTim* 10/00; *SwJT* Fall 00; *JBL* Spr 01; *NovT* 43.1 (2001); *JTS* 4/01; *CBQ* 1/01; *Them* Spr/Sum 02; *JETS* 9/01; *Int* 1/02; *RelSRev* 4/01; *Chm* Sum 01; *EvQ* 7/05; *SJT* 60.1].

☆ Ryken, Philip. *1 Timothy* (REC) 2007. Great for pastors. See his similar works on 1 Kings, Luke, and Galatians.

Saarinen, Risto. ‡ *The Pastoral Epistles with Philemon & Jude* (Brazos) 2008. Has been praised by the likes of I. Howard Marshall for doing "an excellent job of mediating the insights of recent large-scale works in a readable exposition that concentrates on theology, bringing in from time to time the contributions of such expositors as Chrysostom and Calvin." The Pastorals are his main focus, and he regards them as pseudonymous. [*RelSRev* 9/09; *BL* 2010; *CBQ* 10/10].

✓ Simpson, E. K. 1954. This work on the Greek used to be often consulted, owing to the relative paucity of good commentaries on the original text. But since 1990 we have seen a wonderful crop of works published, and Simpson is no longer so valuable.

Spencer, Aída Besançon. (NCCS) 2 vols., 2013–14. The author teaches at Gordon-Conwell (MA) and has published on Paul's literary style and on evangelical feminism.

F  Stanley, Steve. (EEC). A recent report omitted Dennis O. Wretlind as coauthor.

☆ Towner, Philip. (IVPNT) 1994. After his Aberdeen dissertation on the Pastorals under Marshall, *The Goal of Our Instruction* (1989)—it is outstanding, by the way—Towner served as Marshall's research assistant and as a UBS consultant. This learned, insightful commentary for IVPNT succinctly treats the exegetical issues and then the message of these books (208pp.). A very fine representative of the series. NICNT (see above) has superseded IVPNT as a scholarly resource. [*JETS* 12/96; *Chm* Win 12].

✓ Trebilco, Paul, Simon H. Rae, and Deolito Vistar. *1 Timothy* (Asia) 2023. Subtitled "A Pastoral and Contextual Commentary" (approx. 170pp.). Though written on a popular level, the work is of value; Trebilco is a world-class social historian of the Greco-Roman era, with a focus on Asia Minor and social identity. See Trebilco under Ephesians. (WorldCat shows a 2006 ed. too.).

Twomey, Jay. ‡ (BBC) 2009. Reception history. [*JTS* 4/11; *ExpTim* 10/11].

F  Van Neste, Ray. (EGGNT). I appreciated his earlier research on *Cohesion and Structure in the Pastoral Epistles* (2005). See also Perkins above.

☆ **Wall, Robert, and Richard B. Steele.** (THC) 2012. "Essential reading today" (Towner [*ExpTim* 1/14]). Wall is responsible for the Introduction (1–53) and the commentary, using the James Sanders-style canonical approach for which he is known. He claims that rejection of Pauline authorship "has had a de-canonizing effect" on today's readers (1). For him canonical concerns trump historical-critical ones, and the exposition is highly theological. Following the commentaries are Rule of Faith Readings, i.e., lengthy synthesizing theological essays.

Steele contributes the Methodist case studies sections (201–14, 319–29, 390–401). Titus receives relatively less attention (70pp.). Wall and Steele are forcefully egalitarian. [*CBQ* 4/15; *JSNT* 36.5; *RTR* 4/15; *JETS* 12/13; *RelSRev* 3/14; *TJ* Spr 15].

Ward, Ronald A. 1974. This companion to his Thessalonians commentary has 280 full pages of deep, spiritual exposition. The author was well-trained in NT (University of London PhD) and long served as a pastor in the Anglican Church in Canada.

F Wilder, Terry. (Mentor).

☆ **Witherington, Ben, III.** *Letters and Homilies for Hellenized Christians: A Socio-Rhetorical Commentary on Titus, 1–2 Timothy, and 1–3 John*, 2006. This and its companion on Hebrews, James, and Jude (*Letters and Homilies for Jewish Christians*, 2007) are of the same ilk as the author's many other commentaries. They are stimulating, insightful, and useful for exegesis, though I have found them less satisfying for theological reflection. He is in the egalitarian camp. [*Chm* Win 07; *CBQ* 1/08; *ExpTim* 6/08].

Young, Frances. ‡ *The Theology of the Pastoral Epistles*, 1994.

Zehr, Paul. (BCBC) 2010. The author has long served the Mennonite Church in supervised pastoral education. This is not so much for students.

NOTES: (1) For news on Pastorals scholarship, see https://pastoralepistles.com, the Van Neste and Bumgardner site. (2) There is important literature on 1 Timothy 2:9–15, a crux in the interpretation of the Pastorals. I cite an important early journal article by Douglas J. Moo on "1 Timothy 2:11–15: Meaning and Significance," *TJ* 1 (1980): 62–83. Philip Payne's reply to this article, together with Moo's surrejoinder, was published in No. 2 (1981): 169–222. These represent a learned staking-out of the complementarian and egalitarian positions. Taking the debate to a higher level was the *Christianity Today* "1993 Book of the Year," *Recovering Biblical Manhood and Womanhood* (Crossway, 1991). For a full-length hashing out of the issues in a debate format, see *Two Views on Women in Ministry* (Zondervan, 2001, rev. 2005) and *Women in the Church* (IVP, 1995) [*JETS* 9/98; *TJ* Spr 96]. Probably the most influential work from the complementarian side exegeting the 1 Timothy text is *Women in the Church: An Analysis and Application of 1 Timothy 2:9–15* (Baker, 1995, 3rd ed. 2016) [*Chm* Sum 18], supplemented by Wayne Grudem's *Evangelical Feminism and Biblical Truth* (2005). The fullest treatments of the egalitarian position are now Keener's *Paul, Women, and Wives* (1992); *Discovering Biblical Equality* (3rd ed. 2021), ed. by Pierce–Westfall; Payne's *Man and Woman, One in Christ* (2009) [*DenvJ* 2/10 (Blomberg); *CBQ* 1/11; *JSNT* 33.5; *JETS* 3/11 (two)]; J. M. Holmes's 2000 monograph, *Text in a Whirlwind: A Critique of Four Exegetical Devices at 1 Timothy 2.9–15*; and Cynthia Long Westfall, *Paul and Gender* (2016) [*CTJ* 11/18; *BBR* 27.4; *CBQ* 10/17; *Int* 1/18; *RTR* 12/19; *Them* 43.2]. On one disputed point new evidence needs to be considered; see Al Wolters, "An Early Parallel of αὐθεντεῖν in 1 Tim 2:12," *JETS* 54 (2011): 673–84. (3) I. Howard Marshall has several surveys of literature on the Pastorals, including "Some Recent Commentaries on the Pastoral Epistles," *ExpTim* 1/06, and "The Pastoral Epistles in Recent Study" in Köstenberger–Wilder, above. (3) For more high-level discussion of the Pastorals, their authenticity, and their place in the canon, see Hoklotubbe above and the Porter and Wall articles in *BBR* 5 (1995) and 6 (1996). (4) Aldred A. Genade, "The Letter to Titus in Recent Scholarship," *CBR* 9.1 (2010): 48–62.

# PHILEMON

NOTE: See Colossians.

★ **Fitzmyer, J. A.** ‡ *The Letter to Philemon* (AB) 2000. Most will think the Colossians–Philemon vols. recommended above adequate for covering this letter's 25 verses. But any seeking to build a first-class exegetical library can add Fitzmyer. He is ever the patient, thorough exegete and provides excellent treatment of background matters (though I disagree on Onesimus's plight). Like Dunn and a few others, he holds that Onesimus was not a *fugitivus*, "but rather a slave who has been in some domestic trouble with his master Philemon and who has come to seek the intervention of an *amicus domini* (friend of the master) in the hope that he might be restored peacefully to his former status" (18). This Catholic wrote the AB vols. on Luke, Acts, Romans, and 1 Corinthians. [*CBQ* 10/01; *JTS* 10/01; *Int* 7/02; *SwJT* Fall 01; *RelSRev* 10/01; *BBR* 11.2; *DenvJ*; *ExpTim* 3/10].

★ **McKnight, Scot. [𝓜]**, *The Letter to Philemon* (NICNT-R) 2017. A major commentary! At certain points (discussion of possible homosexual abuse of the enslaved Onesimus by Philemon), McKnight engages in distracting speculation and seems to address the academy rather than the church. His conclusion regarding the circumstances is more traditional: Onesimus as runaway slave. His judgment of Paul's ethical framework is not: compared with us, the Apostle "was blind to the immorality of slavery as an institution" (11). He spends so much time and space on an essay about ancient and modern slavery that, though fascinated, I almost forgot I was reading a Bible commentary. (The anti-racist activism message proved distracting for me.) McKnight suggests that the book was quite early (AD 53–55) and composed in Ephesus. [*CTJ* 4/19; *Chm* Sum 18; *ExpTim* 5/18; *Presb* Fall 18; *BSac* 7/20; *Int* 7/20; *ETL* 96.4; *JSNT* 40.5]. Note his other entries in the series: James, Colossians.

F   Arnold, Clinton E., and Daniel K. Darko. (WBC-R). Separate from Arnold's *Colossians*.

✓   Barclay, John M. G. "Paul, Philemon and the Dilemma of Christian Slave-Ownership," *NTS* 37 (1991): 161–86. This article, alongside Nordling's of the same year, presents potent arguments for the traditional runaway-slave interpretation. See also his NT Guides vol. (1997).

✓   **Barth, Markus, and Helmut Blanke.** ‡ (ECC) 2000. An unbelievably big vol. (544pp.) on a brief epistle. See their AB on Colossians, intended as a companion to this commentary. It is a rich resource for researching the social-historical background of the letter, the Greek text, and the history of interpretation. But do take note that the vol. was so long in production that the research was over 10 years old when it appeared. Will this ever be surpassed in comprehensiveness? I fear that such interpretive overkill tends rather to obscure than to clarify things. [*ExpTim* 4/01; *SwJT* Fall 01; *JETS* 12/01; *Evangel* Sum 02; more perceptive: *JBL* Sum 02; *Bib* 83.2; *JTS* 10/01 (Moule)].

✓   Beavis, Mary Ann. ‡ *The First Christian Slave: Onesimus in Context*, 2021. Quite critical, and seeks to "reconstruct a voice for Onesimus." [*CBQ* 4/23; *Int* 10/22; *JSNT* 44.5].

F   Briones, David E. (ITC). The contracted author teaches at Westminster, California.

✓   Burtchaell, James T. ‡ *Philemon's Problem: A Theology of Grace*, 1973, rev. 1998. This is a difficult book to characterize. It treats matters of ancient slavery, the master-slave motif in Scripture, Paul's Epistle to Philemon, and the theological theme of grace (with application to today). Sadly, the Notre Dame academic (†2015) had to resign his post due to allegations he admitted were true. [*EvQ* 4/02].

✓   Byron, John. *Slavery Metaphors in Early Judaism and Pauline Christianity*, 2003; *Recent Research on Paul and Slavery*, 2008. Other influential books on the topic are Jennifer Glancy, *Slavery in Early Christianity* (OUP, 2002) and J. Albert Harrill, *Slaves in the NT* (2006).

✓   **Callahan, A. D.** ‡ *Embassy of Onesimus: The Letter of Paul to Philemon*, 1997. The revisionist thesis that Onesimus was no fugitive slave, but rather the estranged brother of Philemon, doesn't fly (see Fitzmyer's critique, pp.19–20). [*CBQ* 10/98; *RelSRev* 4/98].

   Cousar, Charles B. ‡ *Philippians and Philemon* (NTL) 2009. See under Philippians.

Ehorn, Seth. (EEC) 2011–digital. I have not seen this work.

✓ Felder, Cain Hope. [𝓜], (NIB) 2000. A good, up-to-date commentary by a prof at Howard University. Felder appreciates evangelical scholarship and addresses the slavery issue with poignancy and good sense. For preachers. [*SewaneeThRev* Easter 01].

✓ Gatiss, Lee, and Bradley G. Green, eds. *1–2 Thessalonians, 1–2 Timothy, Titus, Philemon* (RCS) 2019.

✓ Gloer, W. Hulitt, and Perry L. Stepp. ‡ *Reading Paul's Letters to Individuals* (RNT) 2008. This vol. of 280pp. treats Philemon, Titus, and 1–2 Timothy (in that order).

✓ Ip, Alex Hon Ho. *A Socio-Rhetorical Interpretation of the Letter of Philemon in Light of the New Institutional Economics*, 2017. Published in the prestigious WUNT and challenging the runaway slave theory. [*BSac* 7/21; *JSNT* 41.5].

✓ **Jeal, Roy R.** ‡ *Exploring Philemon* (RRA) 2015. Has received a good reception as a socio-rhetorical commentary, published by SBL. [*ExpTim* 11/17; *CBQ* 10/17; *BibInt* 26.4].

✓ Johnson, Matthew V., James A. Noel, and Demetrius K. Williams, eds. ‡ *Onesimus, Our Brother* (PCC) 2012. There is a growing body of scholarship challenging what has been a consensus, that one should see marked differences between the ancient institution of slavery and the American variety (and so be slow to draw comparisons). The essays here contribute to the debate. [*CBQ* 1/14; *JSNT* 35.5; *RelSRev* 6/13]. One of the first to issue the challenge was Orlando Patterson, *Slavery and Social Death* (Harvard, 1985).

✓ Knox, John. ‡ *Philemon among the Letters of Paul*, 1935, 2nd ed. 1959. Proffered a much-debated revisionist thesis about the letter's circumstances and recipient. Archippus, he says, was the slave-owner, not Philemon, and the runaway slave Onesimus should be identified with the later bishop of Ephesus mentioned by Ignatius. Said bishop was a major influence in the formation of the Pauline canon (and the epistle's inclusion).

✓ **Kreitzer, Larry J.** ‡ (Read) 2008. Nearly 200pp., comprised of history of interpretation, a small commentary, and seven more chapters on quite a variety of topics, including some reception history. [*RBL*; *RelSRev* 12/09].

Migliore, Daniel L. ‡ *Philippians and Philemon* (Belief) 2014. See under Philippians.

Müller, J. J. (retired NICNT) 1955. Philemon was originally bound with his Philippians commentary and is o/p. Replaced by Bruce, then by McKnight.

✓ **Nordling, John G.** (ConcC) 2004 This large-scale (379pp.) Lutheran work reveals deeper learning than some other vols. in the series. He is one of the strongest defenders of the traditional interpretation; see his long article in *JSNT* 41 (1991). As with Barth–Blanke, I fear most pastors would be wearied and discouraged using such a large commentary on little Philemon. [*EvQ* 10/07].

✓ **Osiek, Carolyn.** ‡ *Philippians, Philemon* (ANTC) 2000. Only 20pp. on the shorter letter.

✓ Petersen, Norman R. ‡ *Rediscovering Paul: Philemon and the Sociology of Paul's Narrative World*, 1985. A judicious and important monograph, not a commentary, on the social situation.

Rupprecht, Arthur A. (EBC) 1978. Merely 15pp. Now replaced by EBCR.

F Saarinen, Risto. *I–II Timothy, Philemon* (Brazos) 2008. [*BSac* 1/11].

✓ Seesengood, Robert Paul. ‡ *Philemon: An Introduction and Study Guide*, 2017. [*Int* 4/19; *JSNT* 40.5].

✓ **Still, Todd D.** *Philippians and Philemon* (S&H) 2011. See under Philippians.

✓ Stöger, A. ‡ *The Epistle to Philemon* (The NT for Spiritual Reading) ET 1971.

Tamez, Elsa, Cynthia Kittredge, Claire Colombo, and Alicia Batten. ‡ *Philippians, Colossians, Philemon* (Wisdom) 2017. See under Philippians.

☆ Thompson, James W., and **Bruce W. Longenecker.** *Philippians and Philemon* (Paideia) 2016. It is Longenecker who contributes on Philemon: a superb, lucid, 45-page exegetical treatment, judiciously sifting through various theories or readings, and ending with a lengthy bibliography. He wisely agrees with F. F. Bruce: the brief letter "brings us into an atmosphere in which the institution [of slavery] could only wilt and die" (195).

✓ Tolmie, D. Francois, ed. ‡ *Philemon in Perspective: Interpreting a Pauline Letter*, 2010. A large vol. (391pp.) of essays issuing from an international colloquium. The lead contribution is "Tendencies in the Research on the Letter to Philemon since 1980" by Tolmie. Students might even start with this work. [*BBR* 21.4; *JSNT* 33.5; *Them* 41.2].

✓ **Thurston, Bonnie B., and Judith Ryan.** ‡ *Philippians and Philemon* (SacP) 2004. See under Philippians.

✓ **Vincent, M. R.** ‡ (ICC) 1897, 5th ed. 1955. Bound up with the Philippians commentary.

F   White, Michael L. ‡ (Herm).

✓ Young, Stephen E. ‡ *Our Brother Beloved: Purpose and Community in Paul's Letter to Philemon*, 2021. A significant, revisionary sociological interpretation. [*Int* 10/22 (McKnight); *JSNT* 44.5; *WTJ* Fall 23].

NOTES: (1) Jonathan J. Hatter, "Currents in Biblical Research, Slavery and the Enslaved in the Roman World, the Jewish World, and the Synoptic Gospels," *CBR* 20 (2021): 97–127. (2) Peter M. Head, "Onesimus the Letter Carrier and the Initial Reception of Paul's Letter to Philemon," *JTS* 71 (2020): 628–56.

# HEBREWS

★ **Cockerill, Gareth Lee.** (NICNT-R) 2012. Building on his earlier accessible commentary, the author wrote a fuller (750pp.), more academic vol. for NICNT, replacing Bruce. I find him strong on finer points of exegesis, rhetorical, and structural analysis (not that I agree with all his structures), and showing close familiarity with the scholarship, but he seems less helpful in his discussion of theology. There is a confident Arminianism here, and Cockerill at points does not lay out the other options (e.g., at 6:4–8), which surprised me in such a widely used series. (And NICNT used to have a more Reformed flavor too.) Stressing that Hebrews *is* a sermon, not merely has a sermonic character, he consistently terms the author "the pastor," who warns the congregation against "reverting to a spiritual immaturity totally inappropriate for experienced believers" (16). Cockerill seems not "to take the term 'Jewish Christian' in an ethnic sense"; rather it "describes both Jews and Gentiles who give allegiance to Christ while insisting on or feeling the need of various Jewish associations or practices" (20). He also finds "ties with the world of Jewish apocalyptic" (26)—not a routine Hebrews commentary, then. If you are a student wanting a stimulating, relatively recent exegesis, or if Cockerill represents your own theological position, then this belongs on your recommended list. If you do not fit either of those two categories, he might drop off the list. [*CBQ* 4/14; *JTS* 10/14 (Attridge); *Int* 7/14; *JSNT* 35.5; *Chm* Sum 14; *JETS* 3/13; *Bib* 95.1; *CTJ* 4/14; *DenvJ* 16; *BTB* 11/14].

★ **Grindheim, Sigurd.** (Pillar-R) 2023. Quite full, with a 70-page Introduction and 630pp. of theologically charged exegesis. (But considering the extensiveness of the footnotes, the commentary is not as long as one might think.) The author has taught at TEDS (where he earned his PhD under Carson), Ethiopian Graduate School of Theology, Fjellhaug, and Western Norway U. of Applied Sciences. Past publications in biblical theology mark him as a good choice for the series. Grindheim acknowledges a special debt to the technical commentaries by Attridge and Spicq. He classes Hebrews as "an artistically crafted sermon" (32) and "one of the richest" books in the NT, both stylistically and theologically. I find him to be learned (see Index of Names), careful, and a dependable interpreter who communicates clearly. He also has an excellent handle on the history of interpretation (from the church fathers to today). Both pastors and students will find plentiful insights and much to stimulate their own reflection. E.g., "The relational nature of the author's theology also explains the ominous notes that are struck throughout his exposition. Because God has come so near in his Son, it is now possible to act more offensively toward him than ever before" (69). He disagrees with Gäbel, Moffitt, and Jamieson (392–98) and concludes that "the language of a heavenly sanctuary describes Jesus's death on the cross from God's perspective, as an event of heavenly significance" (392). Grindheim is good for the soul. Replaces O'Brien.

★ **Guthrie, George H.** (NIVAC) 1998. Normally I would not urge students to consult NIVAC for exegesis, but this is an exception. Guthrie had long been doing rhetorico-discourse analysis and been concerned to understand *The Structure of Hebrews*, the title of his 1991 dissertation for Southwestern Baptist (Brill, 1994; Baker, 1998). That doctoral work was termed "an invaluable road map through one of the letter's thorniest problems" [*RelSRev* 10/97]; Lane provides in his WBC a fine review of Guthrie's contributions (xc–xcviii). Besides the exegetical help in the NIVAC, there is real theological and homiletical worth in the vol. Also on the list of best expositional helps are Kent Hughes, Phillips, Owen, Raymond Brown, John Brown, and Kistemaker.

★ **Lane, William.** [𝓜], (WBC) 2 vols., 1991. If you desire an exegesis of the Greek that leaves no stone unturned, this has been the best piece of scholarship from the evangelical perspective, arguably the best piece of scholarship from any perspective. (Years ago, George Guthrie termed Lane and Attridge the two best technical commentaries.) In 2016 I added that we would benefit from a rigorous, more current exegesis of the Greek from an evangelical; WBC and NIGTC are now over thirty years old. No wonder Moo's arrival is so welcome! A mountain of work—12 to 15 years' worth—went into the Lane set. Students naturally wish to consult Attridge, Ellingworth, Koester, Cockerill, etc., but Reformed pastors with Calvin, G. Guthrie, Lane, and Moo have all they need. Among few weaknesses is the relative lack of attention given to 6:4–6. Lane's views on the book's message are available to a wider segment of Bible students in his earlier *Hebrews: Call to Commitment* (1985). Lane also wrote a fine commentary on Mark. [*CBQ* 1/93; *ExpTim* 5/93; *RTR* 9/93; *Them* 1/93; *WTJ* Spr 94; *CRBR* 1994]. See deSilva below.

★ **Moo, Douglas J.** (ZECNT) 2024. Before seeing a prepublication draft, I knew this had potential to be among the top choices. There were high expectations because of the author's learning and long experience as a commentator on a half-dozen epistles. But there was another reason: Hebrews lends itself to discourse analysis and a rhetorical approach. As Moo writes, a "distinctive feature of Hebrews is the sophisticated rhetoric the author uses to argue his case. No other New Testament book comes even close to the style of Hebrews, with its frequent *inclusios*, chiasms, and other stylistic mechanisms" (1). The commentary does an outstanding job of tracing the flow of the argument; both students and preachers will therefore find themselves in Moo's debt. The shortish Introduction (17pp.) admirably weighs the evidence for authorship, destination, date, audience and occasion, the worldview of Hebrews, and the literary structure; he models succinct, judicious scholarship. I find the exegesis and exposition to be mature and satisfying; e.g., see the discussion of Heb 9 and "a two-stage understanding of atonement. The death of Jesus on the cross is the essential first step and, in many ways, the decisive moment, since all else flows from that act. But the completion of the atoning act takes place once the exalted Jesus enters the heavenly sanctuary with his blood" (540). Homiletical musings appear in concluding Theology in Application sections. One appendix treats "Some Theological Emphases in Hebrews" (533–42) and has a redemptive-historical orientation. Moo is indeed a top choice for exegesis, theological reflection, and his pastoral points (e.g., pp.204–9).

★ **Peeler, Amy.** (CCF) 2024. The Wheaton prof and Associate Rector at St. Mark's Episcopal, Geneva, IL, has done significant, much-cited research on Hebrews in recent years. (In 2014 she published *You Are My Son* within LNTS.) Though hers is a pastoral commentary (440pp.), students will learn much here. The book can easily be recommended, with its clear and engaging writing, highly theological approach, attention to OT citations and other canonical connections (building on Richard Hays's scholarship), use of the church fathers, fine exegesis, and focus on "Christian formation." Peeler transliterates all Greek words and provides her own translation of the book. On the fraught question of supersessionist theology, she is careful and nuanced but states, "This sermon holds the scandal of exclusive salvation found in Jesus, the Jewish Messiah" (11). She is sympathetic to Moffitt's thesis (7–8) but frames the discussion, to my thinking, in a more acceptable way. Regarding the warning text of ch. 6, she says "repentance from [falling away] is impossible in the sense that Christ cannot go through the process of defeating death and winning salvation again," but there can be a "return to the work Christ has already done" (169). Some of Peeler's work, such as *Women and the Gender of God* (2022), has a critical orientation [𝓜], but that is less in evidence here.

★ **Peterson, David G.** (TNTC-R) 2020. The author returns to the epistle upon which he wrote his impressive Manchester PhD, *Hebrews and Perfection* (CUP, 1982). This revised Tyndale is just outstanding as a briefer exegesis and theological analysis, and I recommend Peterson to students as well as pastors. He probes more deeply than you might assume. All the difficulties with theology in Hebrews are handled with aplomb, yet with a humble spirit before the text.

F   Alexander, Loveday, and Philip Alexander. ‡ (ICC-R). I expect this is a long way off.

☆ **Allen, David L.** (NAC) 2010. Offers a full introduction (70pp.) and a well-researched commentary (535pp.). Allen is Dean and a professor of preaching at Southwestern Baptist Seminary. Along the way he also wrote *Lukan Authorship of Hebrews* (2010) [*JETS* 12/11 (Guthrie); *Them* 5/11; *RelSRev* 3/11]. There are some idiosyncrasies here, but I am not dismissive. He has far more interaction with the scholarship than what is usual in NAC, and pastors may find the vol. less of a handbook and a little more difficult to use. (There are 50pp. on 6:4–8 alone; might Allen better have published a long article and summarized it here? Also he pays somewhat closer attention to the exegetical details than the big picture.) Useful, though the exegesis is not always convincing. [*Them* 8/11; *JETS* 3/12].

✓ **Attridge, Harold W.** ‡ (Herm) 1989. An enormously learned study, handling the text with considerable respect. Together with Lane, Ellingworth, and Koester, easily a top-four exegetical reference. Carson wrote, "no serious student of the text can afford to ignore this" (425pp.). Attridge taught at Notre Dame and Yale, with expertise in the areas of Greco-Roman philosophy and Gnosticism. He pays special attention to the structure of the epistle and the rhetorical skills of the author, whoever he was. Use with some discernment. [*Bib* 72.2; *JTS* 10/90; *JBL* Fall 91; *CBQ* 10/91; *Int* 1/92]. Students benefit from consulting his collected *Essays on John and Hebrews* (2010) [*JSNT* 34.5].

Barclay, William. [𝓜], (DSB) 1957. A fine little vol., perhaps best in the series.

✓ Bateman, Herbert W., IV, ed. *Four Views on the Warning Passages in Hebrews*, 2007. Participating were Cockerill and Osborne from the Arminian side, with Fanning and Gleason representing a more Reformed interpretation. Guthrie offers a wise, winsome Conclusion (430–45).

Bateman, Herbert W., IV, and Steven W. Smith. (Kerux) 2021. I have not seen it.

✓ Bauckham, Richard, et al., eds. *The Epistle to the Hebrews and Christian Theology*, 2009.

St. Andrews sponsors an annual Conference on Scripture and Theology, seeking to bridge the longstanding divide between systematic theologians and biblical scholars. This large work (nearly 500pp.) is a Conference product, containing high-quality exegetical and theological essays. Contributors are generally more conservative critics, from Theology and both the OT and NT guilds, with several famous evangelicals (Marshall and Witherington). [*ExpTim* 5/10; *BL* 2010; *JTS* 4/11; *Chm* Sum 12; *RBL* 2011]. Another collection was Bauckham–Driver–Hart–MacDonald, eds., *A Cloud of Witnesses* (2008).

Beavis, Mary Ann, and HyeRan Kim-Cragg. ‡ (Wisdom) 2015. [*CBQ* 1/18; *JTS* 4/18; *Int* 4/18; *JSNT* 38.5].

☆ **Blackwell, Ben C., John K. Goodrich, and Jason Maston, eds.** *Reading Hebrews in Context: The Sermon and Second Temple Judaism*, 2023. Twenty briefer essays by leading scholars, each treating successive sections of the epistle. The vol. thus serves as a unique collaborative commentary, focusing on the "literary and conceptual world from which Hebrews emerged" (xiii).

✓ Brennan, Nick. *Divine Christology in the Epistle to the Hebrews: The Son as God*, 2021. Called an "excellent dissertation" by Cockerill, reviewing Jamieson's *The Paradox of Sonship* [*JETS* 3/22]. Brennan has some critique of Moffitt. [*CBQ* 9/23].

☆ Brown, John. (GS) 1862, reprint 1961. Mainly a theological exposition, sharing many of the characteristics one finds in the Puritans. Brown was a godly, learned pastor and professor in Scotland. Spiritually edifying. See his works on Romans and 1 Peter.

☆ Brown, Raymond. (BST) 1982. Not to be confused with Raymond E. Brown, the liberal Catholic. Preachers could put this to good use, but it is not so valuable as some others in BST (notably Stott). Brown is less helpful in understanding the connection between the doctrinal and hortatory sections. [*WTJ* Spr 87; *JETS* 9/82].

Bruce, A. B. 1899. Has a strongly theological orientation. Reprinted, but free online.

☆ **Bruce, F. F.** (retired NICNT) 1964, rev. 1990. Bruce's deliberate, well-reasoned exegesis made this valuable, even as one of the top two choices, for many years. Back in the 1980s conservatives were pretty well agreed that Bruce and Hughes were indispensable and a well-matched pair. Unfortunately, as Carson pointed out, the revision undertaken by Bruce was not extensive, and one gained little in replacing the first edition with the revision. (I must add to Carson, however, that the author offered his own fresh translation in 1990.) Still serviceable, Bruce dropped from my recommended list in 2010. For his other commentaries, see Acts, Ephesians, and Thessalonians. [*JBL* 12/65; *NovT* 34.3; *CTJ* 4/91].

Buchanan, G. W. ‡ (retired AB) 1972. An earlier entry in the series. Though Buchanan was a noted scholar, this was not one of the stronger works on Hebrews or better entries in the series. It was replaced by Koester.

Bucher, Debra J., and Estella Boggs Horning. ‡ (BCBC) 2024. I have had little opportunity to use this 240-page Anabaptist commentary. The two authors are more liberal in their theological approach, critical especially of traditional Christian readings of the epistle. They "rely a great deal" on Eisenbaum's notes in *The Jewish Annotated New Testament* (2nd ed., 2017) and "cannot in good conscience read Scripture in ways that minimize the value of other religious traditions" (42).

✓ Calvin, John. 1551. His brilliant grasp of the theological argument in Hebrews is not to be missed. Remember the strong recommendation to purchase his NT commentaries in the Torrance edition.

☆ **Cara, Robert J.** (Mentor) 2024. Excellent from a conservative Reformed perspective, clearly written, and highly theological (nearly 600pp. [large-print] with the bibliography). Readers note his keen interest in creeds and historical theology. Pastors will find him a wise, mature guide for both exegetical questions and exposition. Greek is cited in the text, but always with a gloss; those without the language skills can make full use of this commentary. Some may question whether the covenant of redemption doctrine, with its elaborate superstructure in Reformed scholasticism, rests on an adequate exegetical foundation (see pp.251–52, 266, 553).

Cockerill, Gareth L. *Hebrews: A Bible Commentary in the Wesleyan Tradition*, 1999. "Written with the purpose of enabling the Christian in the pew to understand God's message in the book of Hebrews" (315). See his NICNT above.

✓ Cockerill, Gareth Lee, Craig G. Bartholomew, and Benjamin T. Quinn, eds. *Divine Action in Hebrews and the Ongoing Priesthood of Jesus*, 2023.

✓ Compton, Jared. *Psalm 110 and the Logic of Hebrews*, 2015. [*Them* 42.2 (Guthrie)].

✓ Craddock, Fred B. ‡ (NIB) 1998. From a famous emeritus professor of preaching and NT. See Long below.

✓ Delitzsch, Franz. 2 vols., ET 1868–70. A technical work and part of the exceedingly rich tradition of German commentary on Hebrews over the past 150 years (Bleek, Braun, Michel, Riggenbach, Grässer, Weiss). In between writing those masterful vols. on the OT for KD, he found time for this weighty, incisive commentary. Recommended more for students. Reprinted by Klock & Klock.

☆ **deSilva, David A.** *Perseverance in Gratitude: A Socio-Rhetorical Commentary on the Epistle "to the Hebrews"* (SRC) 2000. Marks a continuation of Witherington's program to provide (Vernon Robbins-esque) socio-rhetorical commentaries on the NT. The 500-page vol. is successful enough that I bought deSilva; he asks and answers some questions not taken up in more traditionally styled commentaries. He convincingly proposes that "the rhetorical situation of Hebrews (as an address . . . urging the maintenance of loyalty and obedience) must govern its application and appropriation" (242). See what he does with 6:4–8 to get the flavor of this work, which serves well as a complement to the exegetical treatments by Lane, Ellingworth, Attridge, etc. At points, though, he may press the material into the mold of his patronage thesis (see Motyer, Attridge reviews). He questions the traditional view of "the Christian addressees as exclusively, or predominantly, Jewish in origin" (2). I counsel more studious pastors to consider buying this as a stimulating, fresh reading. [*ExpTim* 10/00; *CBQ* 10/00; *Int* 4/01; *JTS* 4/01; *EvQ* 1/02; *Them* Aut 02; *Bib* 82.4 (Attridge); *Anvil* 18.2 (Motyer)]. His dissertation is often cited: *Despising Shame* (1995, rev. 2008). See below a forthcoming second major commentary.

F  deSilva, David A. (WBC-R). Replacing Lane's two volumes. As we wait, there is a fine "Cascade Companion" introduction: *The Letter to the Hebrews in Social-Scientific Perspective* (2012) [*Int* 7/13], added alongside his *Perseverance* (above).

✓ Docherty, Susan E. ‡ *The Use of the Old Testament in Hebrews*, 2009.

☆ **Ellingworth, Paul.** [𝓜], (NIGTC) 1993. A massive, erudite work (760pp.) which should be consulted for papers and, like Attridge, will definitely be of interest to the pastor wanting a first-class exegetical library. (Earlier he wrote a 731-page Aberdeen PhD on Hebrews.) Lane is better for pastors, for this NIGTC is more detail-oriented (especially philological) and less theological. The biggest plus is that this patient scholar was able to interact with WBC and Hermeneia. Ellingworth's exegesis here is complemented by a briefer 1991 Epworth Commentary for preachers. His NIGTC is a very smart purchase for the more scholarly. [*ExpTim* 1/95; *RTR* 9/94; *Them* 1/95; *CBQ* 7/94; *CRBR* 1994].

F  Fanning, Buist. (EEC).

☆ **France, Richard T.** (EBCR) 2006. Replaces Morris from the old EBC and is a real improvement, though I could wish for something fuller than these 175pp. France is especially known for his large-scale, quality works on the Synoptics.

✓ Gelardini, G., ed. ‡ *Hebrews: Contemporary Models—New Insights*, 2005.

✓ Gelardini, Gabriella, and Harold Attridge, eds. ‡ *Hebrews in Contexts*, 2016. A sizeable collection of SBL essays. [*JSNT* 39.5; *Them* 42.1]. For Gelardini's own collected essays, see *Deciphering the Worlds of Hebrews* (2021).

Gench, Frances Taylor. ‡ *Hebrews and James* (WestBC) 1996. [*Int* 7/98; *RelSRev* 7/98].

F Gheorghita, Radu. (SGBC).

☆ Gordon, Robert P. (Read) 2000, 2nd ed. 2008. The author, now retired as Regius Prof. of Hebrew in Cambridge, here offers a shorter study of Hebrews. Other *Alttestamentler* (OT specialists) have written insightfully on this epistle in the past (e.g., Delitzsch); Gordon shows again that they have a lot to say. His 2nd edition discusses further the supersessionism controversy and makes the point that both Judaism and Christianity represent "a significant break with the religion of the Hebrew Bible/Old Testament." Gordon's study, not really a commentary per se, is in a class all by itself. See also his work on Samuel. [*JTS* 10/01; *Anvil* 18.3].

Gouge, William. Reprint of 1866 ed. This huge commentary has a reputation to match its size among lovers of the Puritans. Gouge died in 1653. The subtitle is "Being the Substance of Thirty Years' Wednesday's Lectures at Blackfriars, London." Free online.

✓ Gray, Patrick, and Amy Peeler. *Hebrews: An Introduction and Study Guide*, 2020. [*JTS* 4/22; *JSNT* 43.5].

✓ Griffiths, Jonathan, ed. *The Perfect Saviour: Key Themes in Hebrews*, 2012. Evangelical essays from IVP on the theology of the letter. In passing I note Griffiths's worthwhile PhD: *Hebrews and Divine Speech* (2014) [*Them* 8/15; *JETS* 6/16].

Guthrie, Donald. (retired TNTC) 1983. A fine replacement vol. in the series. Now becoming dated itself. [*EvQ* 1/85]. See Peterson.

☆ Hagner, Donald A. (NIBC) 1990. One of the best in the category of non-technical exegesis and exposition (278pp.). Hagner is a fine exegete and writes clearly. Certainly worth more than a skim. Added to this commentary is a college textbook, *Encountering the Epistle to the Hebrews* (2002), given warm reviews [*Them* Spr 04; *Int* 7/03; *RelSRev* 7/03; *JETS* 6/03]; the beginning student would do well to start with it (cf. Gray–Peeler).

F Hall, R. (RRA).

✓ Harrington, Daniel J. ‡ *What Are They Saying about the Letter to the Hebrews?* 2005. [*JETS* 9/06; *BTB* Fall 06].

☆ **Harris, Dana M.** (EGGNT) 2019. Fulfils several of the purposes of a typical commentary, but the series focuses on the fine details of the Greek. EGGNT is consistently strong and quite valuable for its grammatical, syntactical, and structural analyses. Harris teaches at TEDS, knows Hebrews extremely well, and was given good space (450pp.). There are preaching suggestions also. Warmly recommended. [*Presb* Spr 20; *Them* 44.3].

F **Harris, Dana M.** (BGW) 2024?

F Hart, David. (Brazos). Another report has David Nelson.

✓ Healy, Mary. ‡ (CCSS) 2016. Very well-done and engaging from a Catholic and more pastoral angle. Written by a coeditor of the series. [*CBQ* 4/17; *JSNT* 39.5].

✓ Heen, Erik M., and Philip D. W. Krey, eds. (ACCS) 2005. [*JETS* 6/06].

✓ Heil, John Paul. *Hebrews: Chiastic Structures and Audience Response*, 2010. A large (475pp.) work with a fresh approach to the intriguing epistle. Heil says (2), "This new proposal is distinguished by the discovery of multiple levels of macro- and microchiastic patterns that, in a consistent and concerted way, drive the rhetorical rhythm within the persuasive strategy of Hebrews as 'the word of the encouragement' (Heb 13:22)." The overall thesis may not be convincing (I'd say way overblown), but the parallels are fascinating, illuminating, and worth further exploration.

Héring, Jean. ‡ ET 1970. In his survey Martin might again have referred to Gallic verve when reviewing this quite critical work. See under 1 Corinthians.

Hewitt, Thomas. (retired TNTC) 1960. Donald Guthrie replaced it. See Peterson above.

☆ **Hughes, Philip E.** 1977. Highly intelligent, largely theological commentary, complementing Lane beautifully. Hughes used to be my first choice—for pastors, that is. Has been valuable for decades because he was as fine a theologian as he was a biblical scholar, and you need a penetrating theological commentary on Hebrews. Remarkably, Hughes also had expertise in church history, and this vol. is esteemed for his choice citations of the church fathers. He knew the history of interpretation well, and leads us to draw on those rich resources. The work is nearly 600pp., and the theology is in line with the Reformation tradition. The author was an Anglican who taught at Westminster, Philadelphia at the close of his career. This vol. has been published in both hb and pb. Are there weaknesses? Well, Peter Head points to one [*BSB* 9/06]: "Hughes' interest in reading Hebrews in the light of the rest of the NT may actually blunt his appreciation of its distinctive theological witness." If you are more interested in the history of interpretation and Reformed theologically, add this to your list. [*WTJ* Spr 79; *RTR* 5/78; *JBL* 9/79].

☆ Hughes, R. Kent. (PTW) 2 vols., 1993. See under Mark. This would be a good addition to the preacher's shelf. Compare Phillips. The ESV edition is a single vol. (2015).

✓ Hurst, L. D. *The Epistle to the Hebrews: Its Background of Thought*, 1990.

Isaacs, Marie E. ‡ *Reading Hebrews & James* (RNT) 2002.

✓ Jamieson, R. B. *Jesus' Death and Heavenly Offering in Hebrews*, 2019. A revised Cambridge PhD on a highly theological topic. [*JETS* 12/19; *EvQ* 92.2; *JSNT* 42.5; *RevExp* 2/20; *Them* 45.1]. See also his book, *The Paradox of Sonship: Christology in the Epistle to the Hebrews* (2021) [*JETS* 3/22; *Them* 46.3]. What an able younger scholar! However, I do not follow him in denying that Jesus occupied the office of (high) priest during his earthly career (91–92). Jamieson asserts, "the cross is not where and when he offers himself" (178). I reply, there was certainly his "perfection" in the resurrection and ascension (5:9–10), and we may even speak of "consecration" along with an honorific title, but that does not preclude his priestly activity prior. In my view 9:14 speaks of his offering, as priestly representative of God's people, at the time of the cross. [*ExpTim* 1/23]. Note the theological classic by Meeter, *The Heavenly High Priesthood of Christ* (1916).

F Jewett, Robert. ‡ (NCBC).

☆ Jobes, Karen. *Letters to the Church: A Survey of Hebrews and the General Epistles*, 2011. A substantial textbook (478pp.), born out of her Wheaton College lectures. She is an able pedagogue, and many more students are now likely to appreciate her skill. [*CBQ* 7/13; *JSNT* 34.5; *JETS* 12/12; *ExpTim* 10/12; *Them* 11/12; *BTB* 5/14].

☆ Johnson, Dennis E. "Hebrews" in *Hebrews–Revelation* (ESVEC) 2018. All around fine work in the 750-page vol., though many readers may particularly value the longer contributions on Hebrews and Revelation. Accompanying Johnson's solid and sound theological exposition are Plummer on James, Storms on 1 Peter, Harmon on 2 Peter/Jude, Van Neste on John's Letters, and Schreiner on Revelation.

✓ **Johnson, Luke Timothy.** ‡ (NTL) 2006. The veteran scholar with a Catholic background has written some of the best NT commentaries from a mildly to moderately critical viewpoint (see Luke, Acts, Timothy, and James). Among accessible, middle-length interpretations of Hebrews from the critical camp, this is a standard work. He emphasizes the theme of discipleship and traces the influence of Platonism (especially Philo) upon the argument/ theology of the epistle. Evangelical readers may be troubled by Johnson's excursus on the Old and New Covenants, where he joins most critics in rejecting any kind of supersession-ism. What is noteworthy is that he contends that Hebrews itself rejects supersessionism, allowing for the continuance of the old way of worship without reference to Christ, viewing the Old Covenant as remaining valid for those in the old camp (but not for those who would return to it?). Students do not find lengthy interaction with scholarship. [*Chm* Aut 08; *CBQ* 4/07; *JETS* 9/07; *Int* 4/08; *BL* 2008; *ThTo* 4/08; *ExpTim* 12/07; *RelSRev* 3/08; *Bib* 90.3; *HBT* 29.1; *BBR* 20.3 (Guthrie)].

☆ **Kistemaker, Simon J.** (NTC) 1984. Builds on his dissertation, *The Psalm Citations in the Epistle to the Hebrews* (1961). Because of that previous research one might have expected a more scholarly work, but Kistemaker is writing for this specific series. Has value for the preacher especially. [*RTR* 9/85].

☆ **Kleinig, John W.** (ConcC) 2017. The author had a fine preparation by previously writing the Leviticus vol. for Concordia. Class this as one of the fullest commentaries available (740pp.), and as of good value for students and pastors within and outside of his conservative Lutheran tradition. (Many, however, likely will think he goes overboard in his sacramental interpretations; on this point see Peterson's critique [*BBR* 28.1].) Like numerous others, Kleinig takes the epistle to be sermonic in form. [*JSNT* 40.5].

✓ **Koester, Craig R.** ‡ (AB-R) 2001. Replaces Buchanan. This must be placed alongside the large-scale exegeses of Lane, Attridge, and Ellingworth as a first-rate reference tool. While most interpretations amplify the superiority-of-Christ idea as central to Hebrews, Koester thinks the purposes of God for his people is the main theme. He is an unusually gifted exegete and has written what are arguably the two strongest, more recent NT vols. in the AB/AYB series: see Revelation. [*JTS* 4/02; *ExpTim* 3/02; *RelSRev* 1/03; *DenvJ* 1/02 (Blomberg)].

☆ Laansma, Jon C. 2017. Originally intended for TTC, this is subtitled "A Commentary for Preaching, Teaching, and Bible Study." Laansma, who teaches at Wheaton, avoids technical issues and does so well in driving at the main point. His intended reader "wants a specialist to get straight to the bottom line with each passage" (xiii). [*ExpTim* 3/20; *JETS* 9/18; *JSNT* 41.5]. Twenty years prior, he published an important PhD on the rest motif in the NT, with good attention to Hebrews: *'I Will Give You Rest'* (1997).

✓ Laansma, Jon C., George H. Guthrie, and Cynthia Long Westfall, eds. *So Great a Salvation: A Dialogue on the Atonement in Hebrews*, 2019. A collection of evangelical essays on the topic, published in LNTS. [*WTJ* Spr 20; *BBR* 31.1; *JTS* 10/20; *JETS* 12/20].

Lang, G. H. 1951. F. F. Bruce once wrote, "For drawing out and applying to the conscience the practical lessons of the epistle G. H. Lang has few rivals" (NICNT, 1964, xii).

✓ Lindars, Barnabas. ‡ *The Theology of the Letter to the Hebrews*, 1991. From CUP.

Long, D. Stephen. ‡ (Belief) 2011. [*Int* 4/13; *CTJ* 4/14].

Long, Thomas G. ‡ (I) 1997. Well-written. Some might wish he had written more. After a mere 3pp. of introduction, Long provides 146pp. of commentary. Call this a stand-by—such a brief commentary does less to help the preacher unlock the riches of this Bible book. In liberal circles, this book, Craddock, and Johnson are the usually recommended preacher's commentaries. [*ThTo* 1/98; *Int* 7/98; *CBQ* 7/98; *RelSRev* 7/98].

MacArthur, John. 1983. See Matthew for a review of the series, of which this was the first vol.

✓ Mackie, Scott D., ed. ‡ *The Letter to the Hebrews: Critical Readings*, 2018. From T&T Clark (475pp.). Quite an education here, reading a wise selection of the most influential essays over the decades. [*Them* 44.1].

✓ Mason, Eric F., and Kevin B. McCruden, eds. *Reading the Epistle to the Hebrews: A Resource for Students*, 2011. A selection of the best critical essays, published (for convenience?) by SBL. [*CBQ* 1/15; *JSNT* 34.5; *JETS* 3/13; *ExpTim* 2/13; *ETL* 89.4].

McKnight, Edgar, and Christopher Church. ‡ *Hebrews–James* (S&H), 2004. This vol. is something of an odd blend. First, the seasoned NT scholar McKnight provides an understated commentary on Hebrews (320pp.), with much information to help pastors draw their own conclusions. He gives guidance as *you* read and *you* make application. Church (95pp.), on the other hand, forcefully reads James with you and makes many specific applications.

The two commentaries have a different feel, one more academic and reflective, the other more urgent and preachy. [*Int* 7/06].

☆ Michaels, J. Ramsey. (CorBC) 2009. See Belleville under Pastorals.

✓ **Mitchell, Alan C.** ‡ (SacP). 2007. The full (357pp.), accessible, critical commentary completes the Catholic series. Mitchell downplays what others see as the Jewish orientation of the epistle, and treats the material as best falling into the genre of homily. Good attention is paid to rhetorical aspects. Sometimes the exegesis, in my opinion, seems to miss the point; e.g., despite the following stern verse, Mitchell argues that 10:26 "may mean that attempting any other rites of purification is senseless, since that end has been accomplished by Christ's death." [*CBQ* 4/08; *RelSRev* 7/07; *ExpTim* 8/08].

✓ **Moffatt, James.** ‡ (ICC) 1924. "A strong commentary, but more useful to teachers than to preachers" (Childs). Bold, rigorous exegesis. This was the standard reference work for scholars generations ago. Still worth consulting on technical aspects.

✓ Moffitt, David M. [𝓜], *Atonement and the Logic of Resurrection in the Epistle to the Hebrews*, 2011. A very impressive study, discussed by many, including R. B. Jamieson in "When and Where Did Jesus Offer Himself?" *CBR* 15 (2017): 338–68. [*JTS* 10/13]. More recent is Moffitt's *Rethinking the Atonement: New Perspectives on Jesus's Death, Resurrection, and Ascension* (2022) [*JSNT* 45.5; *SJT* 76.4; *ExpTim* 8/23; *WTJ* Fall 23], a collection of essays which Vanhoozer considers "a Copernican Revolution in atonement theology." I have my disagreements exegetically.

✓ Moffitt, David M., and Eric F. Mason, eds. [‡ and 𝓜], *Son, Sacrifice, and Great Shepherd*, 2020. A fine collection of essays from SBL. [*JSNT* 43.5].

Mohler, R. Albert, Jr. *Exalting Jesus in Hebrews* (CCE) 2017.

✓ Montefiore, H. W. ‡ (BNTC) 1964. Martin had impressive things to say about this, but I struggle to understand why. It was a good, serviceable commentary for its day, but hardly a first or second choice. Moderately critical. [*WTJ* Spr 66].

Morris, Leon. (EBC) 1981. All in all, not his best day (150pp.). See France.

F Motyer, Steve. (THC).

✓ Moyise, Steve. ‡ *The Later NT Writers and Scripture*, 2012. See under Acts.

Murray, Andrew. *The Holiest of All*, 1894. A devotional classic which, for all its heart-warming thoughts, isn't so solid in its exegetical base. Not to be discarded, Murray should always be checked against a careful scholarly work. Murray ministered in the South African Dutch Reformed Church and was a main proponent of the Keswick "victorious life" teaching. Several other devotional gems are: F. B. Meyer's *The Way into the Holiest*, H. C. G. Moule's *Studies in Hebrews*, and Griffith Thomas's *Hebrews, A Devotional Commentary* (each shows a Keswick influence).

**O'Brien, Peter T.** (Pillar) 2010. After completing a trio of commentaries on the Prison Epistles, where he demonstrated exceptional ability in exegeting the Greek, rhetorical interpretation, and theological exposition, O'Brien produced *Hebrews*, which I termed my first choice for the pastor's study. I also quoted Ellingworth: "I cannot commend this work too highly." Sadly, it contains admitted plagiarism, and Eerdmans withdrew it from the market (2016). [*DenvJ* 7/10; *Them* 7/10; *BBR* 23.4; *CBQ* 1/14; *JSNT* 33.5; *Chm* Sum 14; *RTR* 4/11; *JETS* 6/11; *RelSRev* 9/11]. I discovered that O'Brien's NSBT vol., *God Has Spoken in His Son* (2016), is also withdrawn.

☆ Osborne, Grant R., with George H. Guthrie. *Hebrews: Verse by Verse*, 2021. Posthumously published and of very good value for pastors and well-read laypeople. Osborne's theology was a classic Arminianism.

☆ Owen, John. 7 vols. 1668–74 (1980 Baker reprint). All the rigor, theological profundity, and verbosity you would expect from the greatest scholar among the Puritans. Can be an extraordinarily difficult chore to work through this, but hard work does pay off. This set was abridged into a one-vol. work and published as *Hebrews: The Epistle of Warning* (Kregel pb). More recent is the Crossway Classic abridgement (1998), which is probably what the average pastor would find most conducive to personal study. Reformed congregations with a tradition of deep Bible teaching could add CrossC to their libraries. [*SBET* Sum 93]. Note, though, that the whole work is free online.

☆ **Pfitzner, Victor C.** ‡ (ANTC) 1997. One of the best in the series. The author, a Lutheran scholar teaching in Australia, gives both a mature and fresh interpretation which demonstrates "that every climactic point in the book is a statement about worship" (Lane). Pfitzner's reflections on a Bible-based theology of worship can spur evangelicals to give that topic more thought than they often do. A very fine, compact exegesis that expertly draws connections between texts. He also uses the older and newer structural studies like Vanhoye and Guthrie. Some conservatives would say Pfitzner is not always the best theological guide. [*AsTJ* Fall 99; *RelSRev* 1/99].

☆ Phillips, Richard D. (REC) 2006. One of the best practical/devotional works available. Readers will find it especially rich and thoughtful on ch. 11; Phillips builds on his earlier book *Faith Victorious: Finding Strength and Hope from Hebrews 11* (2002). The author is pastor of Second Presbyterian (PCA) in Greenville, SC. The vol. is well stocked with helpful material (650pp.) for expositors.

F Pierce, Madison N. (BECNT). Carson was once listed for this. Pierce teaches at Western Theological Seminary (MI) and published a well-respected Durham PhD, *Divine Discourse in the Epistle to the Hebrews* (2020) [*BBR* 31.2; *JETS* 6/21; *JSNT* 44.5; *Them* 46.3].

Pink, Arthur. 1954. A huge vol. of exposition published for many years by Baker. Verbose but suggestive to the expositor who speed reads.

Rayburn, Robert S. *Evangelical Commentary on the Bible* (one-vol.), 1989. Argues the terms "old covenant" and "new covenant" should not be understood as having religio-historical significance, but as describing the religion of legalism and the religion of faith in all ages (BC and AD). This can be said in response: Hebrews has derogatory things to say about the old covenant because after Christ the OT cultus is a closed door. The new age has come in the appearance of a better Prophet and Priest. Adhering oneself to the old economy is *now* the way of unbelief because such an act disregards Messiah's coming and his self-sacrifice. (See Calvin's *Institutes*, 2.9–11).

✓ Rittgers, Ronald K., ed. *Hebrews, James* (RCS) 2017. [*Int* 10/20].

✓ Schenck, Kenneth. ‡ *A New Perspective on Hebrews*, 2019. [*RevExp* 8/21].

☆ **Schreiner, Thomas R.** (BTCP) 2015; (EBTC) 2020. The author does consistently strong work, and many pastors will go buy this theological exposition. Southern Baptist types with an affinity for moderately Reformed theology (especially if distilled down for busy preachers) will possibly view this as a first choice. Schreiner describes his commentary as "relatively brief and nontechnical" (1). If it helps thousands take doctrine more seriously and to discover the riches of biblical theology, as developed in this epistle, I am enthusiastic in welcoming his book. The 2020 version has a 49-page Introduction, 380pp. of commentary, and nine essays on theological themes (65pp.). If Lane and Cockerill would demand too much time, consider this (much easier reading). [*BBR* 32.2; *JETS* 3/16].

Stedman, Ray C. (IVPNT) 1992. Helpful for communicators, less so for students. Stedman published a fair number of expositions on both OT and NT books. This is probably the least scholarly contribution to IVPNT. [*Chm* 107.4].

☆ **Thompson, James W.** ‡ (Paideia) 2008. It is hard to find anything more valuable than this in the category of compact (288pp.), moderately critical exegesis. Thompson's research on Hebrews goes back to a 1974 dissertation. He is recognized as an expert in detailing the philosophical background to the epistle (more the Greco-Roman than the OT and Jewish background). See Moo's review of Thompson's weaknesses as an exegetical reference for one moving text-by-text. [*ExpTim* 12/09; *Int* 4/10; *BBR* 20.2 (Moo); *CBQ* 4/10; *BL* 2010; *Them* 7/10].

✓ Trotter, Andrew H. *Interpreting the Epistle to the Hebrews* (Guides to NT Exegesis), 1997. Not a commentary, but a fine introduction for students [*JSNT* 75]. A little more recent is Harrington.

✓ Vanhoye, Albert. ‡ *Structure and Message of the Epistle to the Hebrews*, 1989. See also *A Different Priest* (2011), which approaches Hebrews as an example of biblical/Semitic rhetoric as opposed to Greco-Roman rhetoric [*DenvJ* 15]. Note that Paulist Press published a Vanhoye commentary in late 2015 (272pp.) [*ExpTim* 7/16; *JETS* 12/17; *JSNT* 38.5]. A selection of his essays can be found in *A Perfect Priest* (2018) [*JSNT* 41.5].

✓ Vos, Geerhardus. *The Teaching of the Epistle to the Hebrews*, 1956. This is a true gem. If you plan to do any work on the theology in Hebrews, you would do well to read this rich biblical-theological study. Reprinted from time to time by P&R.

✓ **Westcott, B. F.** 3rd ed. 1920. Even today regarded as a valuable classic; it "remains impressive and is especially rich in Patristic references" (Childs). Westcott was often reprinted and was a wise purchase. Now free online.

F  Westfall, Cynthia L. (BHGNT). Her published dissertation, *A Discourse Analysis of the Letter to the Hebrews* (2005), is already a highly useful commentary for advanced students [*Bib* 88.2; *ExpTim* 8/07].

F  Westfall, Cynthia Long. (NCCS).

Wilson, R. McL. ‡ (NCB) 1987. A good entry, but in view of the many great works now available you won't pay much attention to it. Wilson is slightly over 250pp.

☆ **Witherington, Ben, III.** *Letters and Homilies for Jewish Christians: A Socio-Rhetorical Commentary on Hebrews, James and Jude*, 2007. Stunningly, this marks the completion of his project to comment on the entire NT (in various series). The vol. is well-done and useful to both students and pastors. [*BL* 2009; *DenvJ* 1/08; *Chm* Sum 12; *ExpTim* 2/12; *RelSRev* 6/11].

NOTES: (1) George Guthrie, "Hebrews' Use of the Old Testament: Recent Trends in Research," *CBR* 1.2 (2003): 271–94. (2) Barry C. Joslin, "Can Hebrews Be Structured? An Assessment of Eight Approaches," *CBR* 61 (2007): 99–129. (3) J. C. McCullough has written four valuable articles in *Irish Biblical Studies* surveying Hebrews scholarship; see *IBS* numbers 2, 3, and 16. (4) Peter Head, formerly with Tyndale House (Cambridge), shows himself to be a shrewd judge of the best commentaries on Hebrews as he reviews a dozen of them in *BSB* 9/06.

# JAMES

★ **Blomberg, Craig L., and Mariam J. Kamell.** (ZECNT) 2008. A promising start to the series (see Commentary Series). Both pastors and students warmly welcomed this handy (288pp.), well-written vol., which leads the reader through grammatical analysis and other matters of exegesis. A strength here is the wise way that the coauthors point out the key questions and problems faced in interpreting James. The coauthors do so well in moving from exegesis to exposition to application that pastors would be more than satisfied with this as a first pick. I will voice a complaint, however, about the number of sections (7) into which the commentary is divided. For the weaknesses of the book, see Davids's review. [*JETS* 9/09; *Them* 7/09; *CBQ* 7/09 (Davids); *ExpTim* 2/10 (Hartin); *BTB* 8/10; *BL* 2010; *BSac* 10/10]. See also Kovalishyn below.

★ Doriani, Daniel. (REC) 2007. A very worthwhile homiletical commentary to use after having carefully done one's exegesis. The author has taught NT at Covenant Seminary and pastored in St. Louis. As I expected, Doriani's exegesis is well-studied and dependable. [*JETS* 6/08]. Other splendid pastoral helps are Manton, Hughes, Motyer, Blanchard (more devotional), and Nystrom (offering more cultural critique).

★ **Johnson, Luke Timothy.** ‡ (AB) 1995. Brilliant! A sizable (347pp. + indices) work from a conservative critic with a Catholic background. Johnson is of great use to those interested in rhetorical criticism; he's proven himself skillful in a broad range of exegetical tasks. Students appreciate his attention to the history of interpretation. While most expositors will bypass this, the scholarly pastor wanting a first-class exegetical library will buy it—my five "musts" are Moo (Pillar), McCartney (BECNT), McKnight (NICNT), Allison (ICC), and Johnson (AB), while keeping Davids handy. In shorter compass (about 50pp.), Johnson does "James" in the NIB. For more from him, see Luke, Acts, Timothy, and Hebrews. [*JETS* 3/99; *Int* 7/97; *RelSRev* 1/97; *JR* 1/98]. Students consult his *Brother of Jesus, Friend of God: Studies in the Letter of James* (2004). [*JTS* 10/05; *SJT* 59.4; *CurTM* 4/05; *ExpTim* 2/05; *HBT* 29.2].

★ **McCartney, Dan G.** (BECNT) 2009. The author taught for decades at Westminster, Philadelphia and Redeemer Seminary (TX). He is a very careful, thorough exegete and has a fine theological mind. As one might expect from a WTS professor, the approach is both rigorously Reformed and fresh; McCartney does not simply recycle older views. I consider it well-rounded: "exegetically rewarding, theologically rooted, and pastorally wise" (Schreiner). While pastors will probably still buy Moo's Pillar or the ZECNT first, students might well make McCartney their choice. For advanced students of the Greek NT, the bibliography is valuable but not as full as I had expected. The reference tool (335pp.) deserves the warmest of welcomes. See McKnight below. [*DenvJ* 6/10 (Blomberg); *JSNT* 33.5; *JETS* 3/11; *ExpTim* 3/12].

★ **McKnight, Scot.** (NICNT-R) 2011. The author is an accomplished, astute evangelical commentator, writing here mainly for students and academically minded pastors. Interacting with the best scholarship, McKnight carefully weighs the exegetical options and draws well-considered conclusions—a time or two he left me hanging. This has to be among the top picks, especially for its being lucid, thorough (over 500pp.), and fairly up-to-date. He shows caution in (finally) favoring the identification of James as the brother of our Lord, upholding Jacobean authorship, and settling on an early date (50s). "McKnight resists any precise analysis of the letter's circumstances. His commentary is attentive to text rather than speculative about context" (Proctor [*BSB* 6/12]). He wisely argues that the teachings of Paul and James are "more complementary than identical or contradictory" (263). One might question whether James is quite so focused on the trial of economic stress as McKnight makes it out to be. Instead of centering on the theme of perfection, he sees the ethic in James as "a Torah observance in a messianic key" (47)—on this point see Ellis's review [*JTS* 4/13]. Some pastors may struggle with the academic language in places; one paragraph includes the words protreptic, paraenesis, reify, and ambit. See Adamson below. [*BBR* 23.3; *CBQ* 1/14; *JSNT* 34.5; *JETS* 12/11 (McCartney); *ExpTim* 3/12; *ETL* 89.4; *Them* 8/11; *BSac* 10/13; *DenvJ* 14; *RevExp* Sum 12; *BTB* 11/14].

★ **Moo, Douglas.** (Pillar) 2000, 2nd ed. 2021. Superseding the 1985 TNTC, the 1st ed. was twice as long and a fresh interpretation. The 2nd is considerably updated and expanded (320pp.), as he had opportunity to interact with the research of Allison, Blomberg–Kamell, McCartney, and McKnight. After a well-written, satisfying introduction of 65pp., readers are treated to over 250pp. of careful exegesis and theological reflection. Moo's thorough knowledge of Romans leads to expert discussion of the differences and similarities between the two letters—an issue pastors often wind up explaining in their teaching ministry. (Johnson also has some learned discussion of the topic.) Moo, however, reads James on its own terms and avoids the trap of interpreting the epistle by reference to Paul. This has been, hands down, the first choice for the evangelical pastor, but it has competition. [*Int* 1/01; *RTR* 8/00; *SwJT* Spr 01; *CBQ* 4/01; *Them* Spr 04; *EvQ* 10/03; *JETS* 9/02; *Chm* Aut 01; *BBR* 12.1 (Davids); *Evangel* Spr 02; *WTJ* Fall 22; *Presb* Spr 22; *CBQ* 10/22].

☆ **Adam, A. K. M.** (BHGNT) 2013. Worthwhile for those wanting a safe pair of hands to guide them through an exegesis of the Greek (146pp.). Cf. Vlachos, which does a bit more for the preacher.

✓ **Adamson, J. B.** (retired NICNT) 1976. A good work, but didn't have the best scholarly reception. Carson summed up the problem when he described it as "disproportionately dependent on Hellenistic parallels at the expense of Jewish sources." One may compare Adamson with Davids on a few passages to see Carson's point. Adamson made his contribution to scholarship less in NICNT and more in his monograph *James, The Man and His Message* (1989). That 500-page work answers his detractors [*CRBR* 1991; *WTJ* Spr 91; *JETS* 6/92; *Evangel* Sum 92; *Chm* 104.2; *TJ* Spr 89 (McKnight)]. See McKnight.

Adewuya, J. Ayodeji. *An African Commentary on the Letter of James*, 2023.

✓ **Allison, Dale C.** ‡ (ICC-R) 2013. Replaced Ropes. Allison, a professor long at Pittsburgh Seminary (PCUSA), contributed what will be classed for decades as a leading technical exegesis. He leaves no stone unturned. After 110pp. of introduction, he provides about 700pp. of densely packed, painstakingly detailed textual criticism, lexical analysis, historical and archaeological study, literary research, exegesis, theological discussion, and reception history. One gets the sense that he truly *has* read everything. His approach is more historical-critical, in line with the series, concluding that James is a pseudepigraphal diaspora letter, with a sermonic and paranetic orientation. He guesses it was written from Rome instead of Palestine and that the author, whoever he was, knew of Paul's epistles. The lack of indices disappoints. [*JETS* 6/14; *ExpTim* 7/15; *Them* 11/14; *Int* 10/17].

Anderson, Kelly, and Daniel Keating. ‡ *James, First, Second, and Third John* (CCSS) 2017.

F   Baker, Bill. (THC).

Baker, William R., and Thomas D. Ellsworth. [𝕸], *Preaching James*, 2004. From Chalice. Baker did an Aberdeen PhD on *Personal Speech-Ethics in the Epistle of James*.

Bateman, Herbert W., IV, and William Varner. (BGI) 2022. I have not seen this guide to the Greek text. [*SBJT* 26.3].

F   Batten, Alicia. ‡ (Illum). See her *What Are They Saying about the Letter of James?* (2009) [*JETS* 12/10], and *Friendship and Benefaction in James* (2017).

✓ Batten, Alicia, and John Kloppenborg, eds. ‡ *James, 1 & 2 Peter, and Early Jesus Traditions*, 2014. [*ExpTim* 9/15].

☆ **Bauckham, Richard.** [𝕸], *James: Wisdom of James, Disciple of Jesus the Sage* (NT Readings) 1999. This fresh reading of James's epistle is well worth consulting, both by students interested in exegesis and the structure of the letter (influenced, he says, by "Jewish wisdom instruction") and by preachers who are eager to apply the message to hearers' hearts and lives. Bauckham is conservatively critical, and his wisdom genre identification has convinced many (but cf. the more cautious approach of McKnight and McCartney). Don't miss this (256pp.). It is less pricey than before and can be heartily recommended for purchase. [*JTS* 4/02].

☆ Blanchard, John. *Truth for Life: A Devotional Commentary on the Epistle of James*, 2nd ed. 1986. Years ago, I wanted to include this among the recommendations. Its 400pp. are eminently practical, good food for the soul, and directly serve preachers in their task of applying Scripture to life. [*EvQ* 10/84].

Boice, James Montgomery. *Sure I Believe—So What!* 1994. Fine sermonic material.

✓ Bray, Gerald, ed. *James, 1–2 Peter, 1–3 John, Jude* (ACCS) 2000. Fascinating reading and instructive for all who study how these epistles were first interpreted by the church. There are fresh insights and remarks to ponder on nearly every page (xxx + 288pp.).

✓ **Brosend, William F.** [𝔐], *James and Jude* (NCBC) 2004. Follows Vernon Robbins's socio-rhetorical approach. It received good reviews. Brosend takes a conservative stance, arguing that the two letters are well treated together, as written by Jesus's half-brothers. [*Int* 1/07; *BL* 2005; *RelSRev* 1/05; *ExpTim* 10/05].

Burdick, Donald W. (EBC) 1981. See Guthrie.

F  Chapman, David. (EBTC)?

✓ Chester, Andrew, and Ralph P. Martin. ‡ *The Theology of the Letters of James, Peter, and Jude*, 1994. From CUP.

✓ Cheung, Luke L. *The Genre, Composition and Hermeneutics of James*, 2003.

✓ Chilton, Bruce, and Craig A. Evans, eds. *James the Just and Christian Origins*, 1999.

✓ Chilton, Bruce, and Jacob Neusner, eds. *The Brother of Jesus*, 2001. Essays from an SBL consultation. See also Bernheim, *James, Brother of Jesus* (1997); Painter's *Just James* (below); Johnson's *Brother of Jesus* (above); and Hartin's *James of Jerusalem* (2004). "Deservedly ignored" (McKnight) is Eisenman, *James the Brother of Jesus*.

Crowe, Brandon D. *The Message of the General Epistles in the History of Redemption*, 2015. Helpful, popular-level study guide for James, and the epistles of Peter, John, and Jude (185pp.). From P&R. It will not be noted under succeeding books.

F  Crowe, Brandon D. (EEC). To replace the Varner vol.

☆ **Davids, Peter.** (NIGTC) 1982. In the 1980s the first choice of Childs, Carson, and Martin. You should note that the author contributed the brief, more popularly styled commentary in NIBC (1989). NIGTC is of much greater value, especially if one is studying the Greek. Davids argues that James the Just received some sort of editorial assistance and that there is a discernable structure to the epistle's argument. Compare with Laws. For students or scholarly pastors, Davids remains an excellent work, worth consulting. [*JETS* 6/83; *WTJ* Fall 84; *JBL* 102.4; *RTR* 9/83].

✓ **Davids, Peter H.** *A Theology of James, Peter, and Jude* (Biblical Theology of the NT) 2014. Because the contribution of these letters to NT theology is usually underappreciated, I was delighted to see Davids's vol., written after publishing three major commentaries on these books. I understand he moved over to Rome in 2014. [*JETS* 3/16].

✓ **Dibelius, M., and H. Greeven.** ‡ (Herm) 1964, ET 1976. Long a standard exegetical tool for specialists and advanced students. By its critical and atomizing approach the commentary does injustice to the tone and message of James, stripping this vibrant book of all theology, and, for me, losing all sense for connection of thought in the epistle. Dibelius–Greeven is of little use to pastors. The German original was the 7th ed. KEK from 1921, and it was revised up to 1964. [*JBL* 85.2].

✓ Dvorak, James D., and Zachary K. Dawson, eds. 2019. A lengthy collection of technical essays in the McMaster Linguistic Exegesis of the NT. [*Int* 10/20; *NovT* 62.2].

✓ Ellis, Nicholas. *The Hermeneutics of Divine Testing: Cosmic Trials and Biblical Interpretation in the Epistle of James and Other Jewish Literature*, 2015. [*Them* 40.3].

Gench, Frances Taylor. ‡ *Hebrews and James* (WestBC) 1996. [*Int* 7/98].

F  George, Timothy. (Brazos).

☆ **Giese, Curtis P.** (ConcC) 2021. Quite valuable, not only as a highly competent, thorough exegesis and Lutheran exposition for learned ministers (450pp.), but also for historical theological reasons. The author "puts to bed" some misconceptions about Luther's theology with regard to the epistle (50–62). Bauckham applauds how Giese "highlights James's emphasis on 'the giving God' who lavishes on us his gifts of salvation." Also, how he "restores the balance by directing attention to Luther's many appreciative exegetical comments on James." I appreciated Giese's structural, rhetorical, and grammatical analyses, all leading to robust discussion of theology and application concerns.

✓ Gowler, David B. ‡ (BBC) 2014. Reception history, guided by a more reader-centered approach. [*ExpTim* 1/15; *Them* 11/14; *RevExp* 11/14; *CBQ* 4/16].

F   Green, Joel B. [𝓜], (NTL).

☆ Guthrie, George. (EBCR) 2006. Quality, concise (75pp.), accessible evangelical exegesis from a scholar who has published important work on Hebrews and 2 Corinthians.

✓ **Hartin, Patrick J.** ‡ (SacP) 2003. Deeper scholarship here (319pp.) than in most Sacra Pagina entries, which tend to wear their learning lightly. Compare this work, by a Catholic priest at Gonzaga, with Johnson above. Hartin holds that James of Jerusalem is the author of the material, which was collected and published in one letter soon after his death. Cargal once said this "commentary represents 'the state of the art' in research on the letter of James." One of his particular interests is *James and the Q Sayings of Jesus* (1991), originally his dissertation. [*Int* 10/04 (Johnson); *ExpTim* 6/04; *JETS* 3/05; *CBQ* 10/04 (Cargal)].

Hiebert, D. Edmond. 1979, rev. 1992. An exposition published by Moody. Quite full.

✓ Hort, F. J. A. [𝓜], 1909. This weighty exegetical treatment of the Greek covers most of the epistle—it was left incomplete, ending at 4:7—and was published by Macmillan (xxxiii + 118pp.). More conservative in its criticism. Now free online.

☆ Hughes, R. Kent. (PTW) 1991. See under Mark. Compare with Doriani.

Isaacs, Marie E. ‡ *Reading Hebrews & James* (RNT) 2002.

☆ Jobes, Karen. *Letters to the Church*, 2011. See under Hebrews.

Johnson, Luke Timothy. ‡ (NIB) 1998. For students this should be passed over in favor of the larger AB (above), which is a major resource for scholarship. Preachers find some of their proclamation concerns addressed in the 50-page NIB contribution.

☆ Johnstone, Robert. (GS) 1871. A thoughtful, reverent exposition which many pastors have used. Now free online.

✓ Jónsson, Sigurvin Lárus. ‡ *James among the Classicists: Reading the Letter of James in Light of Ancient Literary Criticism*, 2021. A revised Aarhus dissertation.

☆ Keddie, Gordon J. *The Practical Christian* (Welwyn) 1989.

Kendall, R. T. *Justification by Works*, 2001; *The Way of Wisdom*, 2002. About 650pp. of bold preaching at Westminster Chapel, London. The reading of 2:14 is odd. Generally, I find him intelligent but less trustworthy as an interpreter.

☆ Kistemaker, Simon J. *James and 1–3 John* (NTC) 1986. [*Them* 4/88].

F   Kloppenborg, John S. ‡ (Herm). To replace Dibelius–Greeven.

F   Kovalishyn, Mariam J. (Kamell). (SGBC). See Blomberg–Kamell above.

✓ Laato, T. "Justification according to James: A Comparison with Paul," *TJ* 18 (1997): 43–84. Counted important reading by several leading scholars (Moo and McCartney).

✓ **Laws, Sophie.** ‡ (BNTC) 1980. Perceptive, packed, and highly praised by scholars. In the 1980s Davids and Laws were probably the two most important reference commentaries. She was more accessible than Davids in that she explains the English text. However, she has obviously done her homework in the original. Laws argues for a late date and Roman provenance, which seems less likely than the setting proposed by Davids, that James addresses Jewish Messianists in the 50s and 60s. Laws's approach also entails a rejection of Jacobean authorship. More critical than Davids. [*ExpTim* 1/81; *JBL* 102.4; *JETS* 9/82; *ThTo* 38.3].

✓ Lockett, Darian R. *Letters from the Pillar Apostles: The Formation of the Catholic Epistles as a Canonical Collection*, 2017. From a respected Talbot scholar. [*Int* 10/20; *JETS* 12/17; *JSNT* 41.5; *Them* 42.3]. On a more popular level, Lockett has also published what serves as exceptionally useful intro: *Letters for the Church: Reading James, 1–2 Peter, 1–3 John, and Jude as Canon* (2021) [*JETS* 6/22; *RevExp* 5/22]. For a collection of nearly thirty oft-cited essays, see Lockett, ed., *The Catholic Epistles: Critical Readings* (2021) [*TGA* 3/23; *JSNT* 43.5]; cf. Mason–Lockett below.

F  Lockett, Darian R. (CSC). To replace Richardson. The author will build on his St. Andrews PhD, *Purity and Worldview in the Epistle of James* (2008).

MacArthur, John. 1998. See Matthew for a review of the series. This is one of the better vols. he has done, which makes sense because the epistle presses home one of MacArthur's main pastoral concerns over the years: the danger of "easy believism" or "cheap grace," which disregards the ethical demands of the gospel (see, e.g., his 1993 *Faith Works*).

Manton, Thomas. (GS) 1651, 1693. For twenty-five years I surprised many by including this Puritan classic on the purchase list. Manton has a rich vein of practical theology a pastor can mine out during an entire lifetime of ministry. I'm guessing that now most preachers would prefer an up-to-date work such as Doriani. Also, Manton is free online. Note: reading literature from another era and culture can provide the interpreter with a different perspective. Manton helps at points where we may have 21st century blinders on. (Look up online C. S. Lewis's essay "On the Reading of Old Books.") More accessible than the GS edition is the CrossC pb version (1995) [*SBET* Spr 97].

☆ **Martin, Ralph P.** [𝓜], (WBC) 1988. Probably used the odd WBC format better than anyone else. In his lengthy introduction (100pp.), Martin well treats the author issue (xxi–lxix) and has an interesting rhetorical analysis. This commentary is a success, even if you don't buy into his idea of a 2-stage compositional history (lxxvii, trying to balance the Greek style and Palestinian flavor). I admit to slight irritation when Martin attributes so much to some "enterprising editor," even questioning that James intended a letter to be sent, and then declares that we cannot tell whether the editor succeeded in his publishing venture, whatever his purposes. Besides such introductory issues, I am more trusting of Davids's exegetical judgment in commenting on pericopae. As always, Martin's bibliography is superb (but now dated). For more scholarly types. [*WTJ* Spr 92; *EvQ* 10/92; *RTR* 9/90; *CBQ* 10/91; *Them* 4/91; *Chm* 105.2].

Mason, Eric F., and Darian R. Lockett, eds. ‡ *Reading the Epistle of James: A Resource for Students*, 2019. Published by SBL. [*ExpTim* 8/20; *Int* 10/20; *JSNT* 42.5].

Maynard-Reid, Pedrito U. ‡ *Poverty and Wealth in James*, 1987. An Orbis issue, "organized according to its exegesis of select passages . . . that just happen to have the sharpest ideological edge and the greatest sociocultural implications" (Brosend, 25).

✓ **Mayor, J. B.** [𝓜], 3rd ed. 1910, 1913. Another mammoth work in the old Macmillan series (600pp.). I once counseled advanced students to obtain a copy of this work, but it is now free online. Mayor did for James and 2 Peter–Jude what Selwyn did for 1 Peter, except with less flair. Mayor is deeply learned, conservatively critical in the old British tradition, and treats the Greek text in detail.

✓ Mitton, C. L. ‡ 1966. A stimulating exposition (o/p), better than his Ephesians commentary, especially for pastors. Mitton posits a Palestinian milieu and points to a date in the 50s.

Moffatt, James. ‡ (Moffatt) 1928. Covers the General Epistles. Moffatt was always liberal, deeply learned, and scintillating at the same time.

☆ Moo, Douglas. (TNTC) 1986, rev. 2015. Superb and succinct (240pp.). The commentary was Moo's earlier effort, which was superseded by his Pillar (above). It contains a great deal of practical and pithy comments, besides astute scholarly judgment. Pastors with this slender pb are well served. Students will take up the much fuller Pillar vol. instead.

Moore-Keish, Martha L. ‡ (Belief) 2019. [*Int* 10/20].

✓ Morgan, Christopher W. *A Theology of James*, 2010. From P&R. [*BSac* 7/12].

☆ Motyer, J. Alec. (BST) 1985. Lives up to the standards of the series. Blanchard, though more diffuse, is just as useful as Motyer to the preacher. In editions of this guide prior to 2001, Motyer was a recommended purchase. Still a smart buy for two main reasons: it is an inexpensive pb, and Motyer's OT expertise gives him special insight into the letter's theological background. [*JETS* 3/87].

✓ Moyise, Steve. ‡ *The Later NT Writers and Scripture*, 2012. See under Acts.

✓ Niebuhr, Karl-Wilhelm, and Robert W. Wall, eds. ‡ *The Catholic Epistles and Apostolic Tradition*, 2009. Arose out of years of work by the SNTS Seminar on the Catholic Epistles. Half the sixteen essays are on James. [*JSNT* 33.5; *RBL* 2011; *ExpTim* 6/11; *BTB* 11/11].

✓ Nienhuis, David R., and Robert W. Wall. *Reading the Epistles of James, Peter, John, and Jude as Scripture: The Shaping and Shape of a Canonical Collection*, 2013. Their argument is that these letters "came into the canon as an intentional collection—implicitly the church's intention—arranged not by chronology or length, but by a 'canonical logic', that is, 'in a sequence that recommends an order of reading for maximal benefit' for forming disciples" (Lockett [*JTS* 10/14]). It is stimulating to read arguments for canonical shaping of NT corpora; cf. scholarship on Psalms and the Twelve Minor Prophets. [*JSNT* 36.5; *JETS* 12/14; *ExpTim* 5/15; *Them* 7/14; *CBQ* 1/16; *Int* 1/16; *RTR* 4/16]. See also Lockett above.

☆ Nystrom, David. (NIVAC) 1997. The author's forte is ancient history and contemporary cultural critique, not NT scholarship. While the literature cited in Contemporary Significance sections is current, Nystrom uses little periodical literature and seems largely dependent on Davids, Laws, and Martin in researching the Original Meaning. He does helpfully draw from the Caird–Hurst *NT Theology* (1994). In short, this vol. provokes pastors to make application but is weak in the exegetical foundation laid beforehand.

Osborne, Grant. (CorBC) 2011. I have not seen this, but know that Osborne wrote on James, 1–2 Peter, and Jude, while M. Robert Mulholland contributed Revelation. The vol. is said to be over 600pp.

☆ Osborne, Grant R. (ONTC) 2019. See under Commentary Series.

✓ Painter, John. ‡ *Just James: The Brother of Jesus in History and Tradition*, 1999, 2nd ed. 2005. Helpful "sourcebook for the study of the letter of James" (Brosend). [*Anvil* 17.3].

✓ **Painter, John, and David deSilva.** ‡ *James and Jude* (Paideia) 2012. Painter is responsible for the James exegesis while deSilva does Jude. I have scarcely used this, but it joins strong scholarship with good accessibility. One of the better vols. in the series. [*CBQ* 4/14; *Int* 7/15; *ExpTim* 12/13; *RevExp* 5/15; *RelSRev* 9/14; *TJ* Fall 14].

✓ **Perkins, Pheme.** ‡ *First and Second Peter, James, and Jude* (I) 1995. Covering all four letters in 200pp. makes this too thin at points to help its intended clergy readership. (By contrast, Tyndale treats them in 700pp.) Another problem noted by reviewers—ironically in the direction of inaccessibility—is the more academic orientation that renders it less serviceable to those without a solid scholarly background. [*JETS* 9/97; *ThTo* 1/97; *Int* 4/97; *CBQ* 10/96; *CRBR* 1996].

Platt, David. *Exalting Jesus in James* (CCE) 2014.

Plummer, Alfred. *General Epistles of St. James and St. Jude* (EB) 1891. Still cited.

☆ Plummer, Robert L. "James" in *Hebrews–Revelation* (ESVEC) 2018. See Johnson under Hebrews.

F Reese, Ruth Anne. (NCCS).

Reicke, Bo. ‡ (retired AB) 1964. Covered Peter and Jude as well; the comment was too cursory to make it very worthwhile. Rejects Jacobean authorship. Replacements are: Johnson on this epistle, Elliott on 1 Peter, and Neyrey on 2 Peter/Jude.

Richardson, Kurt. (NAC) 1997. The author taught at Gordon-Conwell, and his commentary is full enough at 272pp. to accomplish some good. The exegesis tends to be weak, however, and

I predict you will much prefer Moo's Pillar vol. This is not one of the stronger contributions to the series. [*BSac* 10/99].

Rittgers, Ronald K., ed. *Hebrews, James* (RCS) 2017. See under Hebrews.

✓ **Ropes, J. H.** ‡ (retired ICC) 1916. Though students find the best help on technical issues in Mayor, Dibelius–Greeven, Davids, Martin, Johnson, McCartney, and Allison, they could consult Ropes and Hort too. Those older commentaries retain some value and are cited in the more recent works. Ropes is more critical than Hort or Mayor and argued for pseudonymity. Now free online.

Ross, Alexander. (retired NICNT) 1954. Replaced by Adamson. Carson spoke of it as "a book warmly devotional in tone but offering no serious help in the difficult passages."

Runge, Steven E. *James: A Visual and Textual Guide*, 2016. Rather reinvents the genre of biblical commentary by using discourse analysis. Runge has several such guides (Romans, Philippians) that focus attention on *how* the authors say what they do and *how* the arguments of the letters develop. The series has the title High Definition Commentary.

Sidebottom, E. M. ‡ (NCB) 1967. Also covered Jude and 2 Peter, but was too brief to do much good. Would likely have been replaced, if the series had continued.

✓ Sleeper, C. Freeman. ‡ (ANTC) 1998. Some reviewers called this 150-page, compact exegesis a success, but it does not compete with the likes of Davids, Moo. [*Int* 7/01].

**Spencer, Aída Besançon.** (KEL) 2020. Clear and extensive in its treatment of exegetical and interpretive issues (approx. 280pp of commentary). Spencer is one of the longest–serving faculty members at Gordon-Conwell. I have not used this vol. enough to review it properly. [*BBR* 31.1].

☆ Stulac, George. (IVPNT) 1993. A practical exposition of some 190pp. by a PCA pastor. Some give it high marks, not so much for scholarly penetration but for pastoral insight and an earnest, humble spirit that is in line with the epistle's tone. Students need to look elsewhere for exegetical helps. [*Chm* 109.1].

Tasker, R. V. G. (retired TNTC) 1957. A brief, perceptive work replaced by Moo.

✓ Taylor, Mark Edward. *A Text-Linguistic Investigation into the Discourse Structure of James*, 2006. Cf. Cargal's *Restoring the Diaspora* (1993).

**Varner, William.** (EEC) 2014. See Crowe above. Decades ago, the author was a popular speaker and writer in dispensational circles. This vol. treats the Greek text (600pp.), applies discourse analysis (as did a 2011 Kress commentary), and includes Application and Devotional Implications sections. It was withdrawn in 2016 due to admitted plagiarism. After a thorough revision, Varner published again on the Greek text of James in 2017 (Fontes Press).

☆ **Vlachos, Chris A.** (EGGNT) 2013. The author took a PhD at Wheaton and here contributes well to the restarted series. I've used it only briefly, but agree with the warm commendation by Kamell that Vlachos provides "a beautiful distillation of the critical questions" regarding Greek grammar and syntax [*JETS* 9/13]. Another selling point is Vlachos's including homiletical suggestions. [*Them* 7/13].

F  Wachob, W. H. (RRA).

✓ **Wall, Robert W.** *Community of the Wise: The Letter of James*, 1997. Exceedingly full (335pp.) for the series of which it is a part, the TPI NT in Context. (Contrast Sloyan's 76pp. on John's Epistles.) Wall describes his intention: "my work seeks to expose a layer of meaning by mining the text within the context of scripture itself—a canonical *Sitz im Leben*" (1). This is a fine contribution. [*Int* 7/98; *DenvJ*]. Cf. Nienhuis–Wall above.

✓ Webb, Robert L., John S. Kloppenborg, eds. ‡ *Reading James with New Eyes: Methodological Reassessments of the Letter of James*, 2007.

Webber, Randall C. ‡ *Reader Response Analysis of the Epistle of James*, 1996.

☆ **Witherington, Ben, III.** *Letters and Homilies for Jewish Christians: A Socio-Rhetorical Commentary on Hebrews, James and Jude*, 2007. The introduction and commentary on James stretch over 170pp.

NOTES: (1) Ruth B. Edwards, "Which Is the Best Commentary? XV. The Epistle of James," *ExpTim* 6/92. (2) Todd Penner, "The Epistle of James in Current Research," *CurBS* 7 (1999): 257–308. (3) Scot McKnight, "James and His Commentaries" (405–19), in *On the Writing of NT Commentaries*, eds. Porter and Schnabel, cited in the Introduction.

# 1 PETER

★ Clowney, Edmund. (BST) 1989. A favorite of mine. His exegetical decisions are well-considered, and his theological interpretation is very valuable. One of the best-informed entries in the series. He was also a communicator (former President of Westminster Seminary and Professor of Homiletics and Practical Theology). This work is interesting from start to finish; you can read it straight through. Compare with McKnight, who is stronger in NT scholarship. [*Evangel* Win 89; *JETS* 12/92; *RTR* 1/92; *CTJ* 11/90; *Chm* 103.3].

★ **Davids, Peter.** (NICNT) 1990. My first choice among mid-level works. The earlier James commentary led us to expect a lot, and those expectations were not disappointed. This is an ideal commentary: careful exegesis, superb theological reflection, thorough yet pithy. As I was preaching through 1 Peter myself in 1990, Davids was the most lucid and helpful in wrestling with the cruxes: 3:18–22 and 4:1, 6. [*CRBR* 1992; *Them* 1/92; *CBQ* 7/92; *Evangel* Sum 92; *NovT* 35.3]. See also Davids's *Theology* (2014) under James.

★ Doriani, Daniel M. (REC) 2014. Given very high marks by Carson: "exemplary in its careful handling of the text, theological robustness, and fresh writing . . . loaded with the best kind of application." Pastors will rejoice to read such model preaching. Compare with McKnight, Helm, and Marshall as expositional helps. [*WTJ* Fall 15].

★ **Grudem, Wayne.** (TNTC-R) 1988, rev. 2024. The updating is substantial (258pp.), though the author has modified his views in only a few places (xix). In both editions he sought to produce a more independent work and is successful in delivering fresh insights. I still believe the general editors (Morris, then Schnabel) made a very wise choice in Grudem, who gives good attention to theological questions, as well as exegesis. (His Cambridge PhD was in NT.) Compare with other commentaries on "preaching to the spirits in prison" (3:18–20); the minority view adopted here—"Christ went and preached through Noah to those [Noah's generation] who are now spirits in the prison of hell" (214)—is carefully, fully explained (178–214). Grudem is following the venerable tradition of Augustine and Aquinas at this point. Note that the commentary gives less attention to chapters 4 and 5 (220–58). [*WTJ* Fall 89; *JETS* 6/91; *CTJ* 4/90].

★ **Jobes, Karen H.** (BECNT) 2005, 2nd ed. 2022. My first choice. "Thankfully manageable in size (ca. 350 pages . . . ), this is nonetheless a major critical commentary" (Green, re. 1st ed.). Jobes has done much work on the Septuagint (Westminster PhD) and has contributed the Esther vol. to NIVAC. The up-to-date bibliography and interaction with recent technical commentaries make this a superb reference vol. for students. Her special contributions, besides the solid exegesis, are: a proposal that the recipients were converts, possibly from Rome, displaced to Asia Minor; assessment of the LXX/OG background; and a research of the quality of the Greek. Pastors can benefit much from the fine exegesis. [*CBQ* 4/06; *JETS* 3/07; *BL* 2006; *NovT* 49.4; *BSac* 10/07; *ExpTim* 5/06; *BBR* 19.3 (Hafemann); *SBJT* 26.3]. Students will consult Jobes alongside the major heavyweight commentaries of Williams–Horrell, Keener, Achtemeier, Elliott, and Michaels, with more than a nod to Selwyn, Goppelt, Kelly, and Feldmeier. See also Jobes's textbook survey, *Letters to the Church* (2011).

★ **Keener, Craig S.** 2021. As with his host of other major commentaries, Keener here is thorough (over 400pp. + 95-page bibliography) and of great value for his profound knowledge of the historical, socio-rhetorical, and literary background of the NT. But this work has less interaction with the secondary literature (xi–xii). See his fresh translation and twenty-five "A Closer Look" excursuses. Keener argues for Petrine authorship and writes from a conservative Methodist stance. Occasionally I felt overwhelmed by extrabiblical and Greco-Roman literature, as compared with his treatment of biblical (esp. OT) influences/citations. This is an evangelical commentary in the first rank, and well complements others in that genre with its wide exploration of "the cultural encyclopaedia informing the letter" (Sleeman [*JSNT* 44.5]). Only the most diligent and academically inclined will make the purchase. [*ExpTim* 11/21; *JETS* 3/22; *CBQ* 10/22; *Int* 7/23; *TGA* 3/23; *Them* 47.1].

★ **Schreiner, Thomas.** *1, 2 Peter, Jude* (NAC) 2003; (CSC) 2nd ed. 2020. One of the best vols. in the NT series. Though Schreiner gives a very good study of 1 Peter, with plenty of bibliographical help for students, I have valued this vol. even more for 2 Peter and Jude because of the long-standing lack of evangelical exegetical commentaries on that portion (Davids and Green have now supplied that lack). Preachers will appreciate the author's clarity, exegetical good sense, and focus upon theological exposition (more or less Reformed). Blomberg rightly says, "If someone could afford only one commentary on these three letters together, then this is the obvious one to choose, with no close rivals" [*DenvJ* 1/04]. That is even truer now that CSC has appeared; see also 2 Peter below. [*RelSRev* 4/04; *JETS* 12/04; *BSac* 10/05].

☆ **Achtemeier, Paul J.** ‡ (Herm) 1996. Of greater interest to the NT academic than the average pastor. This 400-page work argues for pseudonymity and a date between 80 and 100. I find Achtemeier more theologically sensitive than others in the series. (The theology drawn out is more conservative than the conclusions on introductory matters.) Students are advised to take notice of it in their research; prior to the new ICC, Achtemeier was regarded, alongside Elliott's AB, as *the* leading full-scale critical commentary available. The advanced student or scholarly pastor could put this superb work to good use; I prefer it to Elliott, Michaels, and Goppelt because of Achtemeier's sensible, even masterful, well-rounded exegesis. Will have a long shelf life. [*JETS* 6/99; *JBL* Spr 98; *WTJ* Fall 96; *Int* 1/98; *CBQ* 1/98; *SJT* 51.3; *RelSRev* 7/97].

Adams, Jay E. 1979. A popular commentary, digging into theology and worth skimming.

Bartlett, David L. ‡ (NIB) 1998. The 90-page exposition, from a Yale professor of preaching, dates the book near the close of the 1st century.

✓ Batten, Alicia, and John Kloppenborg, eds. ‡ *James, 1 & 2 Peter, and Early Jesus Traditions*, 2014. [*ExpTim* 9/15].

✓ Beare, F. W. ‡ 1947, 3rd ed. 1970. Beare immediately followed Selwyn and put forward a rather more critical interpretation of the epistle. Scholars remember him for his proposal that we read 1:3–4:11 as a "baptismal discourse" (25–27), but today it is hard to find anyone who believes the letter springs from a homily or liturgy. Discussion of 1 Peter since 1947 has taken as its starting point these two works. Beare denies Petrine authorship in this most valuable of his commentaries.

☆ Bentley, Michael. *Living for Christ* (WCS on 1 & 2 Peter) 1990.

✓ **Best, Ernest.** ‡ (NCB) 1971. Useful for reference, but not as important as his later *Thessalonians* (BNTC) or *Ephesians* (ICC). Best denies the authenticity of this letter.

✓ **Bigg, C. A.** ‡ (retired ICC) 1902. Still useful for technical work. Bigg covers Jude and 1–2 Peter.

He defends Petrine authorship of the first letter but rejects 2 Peter as pseudonymous. See Williams and Horrell.

Blum, Edwin A. (EBC) 1981. Insightful and clear, but too brief. See Charles below.

✓ Bockmuehl, Markus. ‡ *Simon Peter in Scripture and Memory*, 2012. Not a commentary, but an excellent help for understanding the apostolic figure [*EvQ* 4/14; *CBQ* 4/14; *Int* 10/14; *JETS* 9/13; *Them* 7/13; *RevExp* Spr 13; *RelSRev* 3/14; *TJ* Fall 14; *JTS* 4/16], complementing his more scholarly earlier book *The Remembered Peter* (2010) [*Them* 5/11; *RelSRev* 6/11]. Other works on the subject include Larry Helyer, *The Life and Witness of Peter* (2012) [*CBQ* 7/14; *JETS* 12/13; *Them* 7/13; *DenvJ* 16; *RevExp* 2/15], which may be the best entry point; Martin Hengel's more critically oriented *Saint Peter: The Underestimated Apostle* (ET 2010) [*JSNT* 33.5; *Chm* Spr 14; *JETS* 9/11 (Davids); *ExpTim* 6/11; *Them* 11/12; *BTB* 5/12; *RelSRev* 6/12]; and *Peter in Early Christianity* (2015), eds. Bond–Hurtado [*BBR* 26.4; *ETL* 94.1; *JSNT* 38.5; *Them* 42.2]. A popular-level evangelical biography is Barnett, *The Importance of Peter in Earliest Christianity* (2016) [*Them* 42.2].

✓ Boring, M. Eugene. ‡ (ANTC) 1999. Boring argues for pseudonymity and, conservatives would say, is not the safest theological guide to the epistle. As he presses his case for universalism, he takes issue with other writers such as Achtemeier.

✓ Bray, Gerald, ed. *James, 1–2 Peter, 1–3 John, Jude* (ACCS) 2000. See James above.

Briscoe, D. Stuart. *When the Going Gets Tough*, 1982. Engaging sermons on 1 Peter.

F Brown, Jeannine K. (NICNT). To replace Davids's excellent work.

Brown, John. (GS) 2 vols., repr. 1975. Originally 3 vols. entitled *Expository Discourses on First Peter* (1848). A huge Calvinistic work (over 1200pp.) that is rich and suggestive theologically for anyone willing to wade through it. Somewhat in the Puritan vein with regard to style and substance; Brown says "his obligations are peculiarly great" to Leighton (ix). Free online.

✓ Campbell, Barth L. *Honor, Shame, and the Rhetoric of 1 Peter*, 1998. A classical rhetorical approach; compare with Martin's understanding of rhetoric and structure.

☆ Charles, J. Daryl. (EBCR) 2006. This author contributes the commentary on 1–2 Peter and Jude. Earlier he did 2 Peter and Jude in BCBC.

✓ Chester, Andrew, and Ralph P. Martin. ‡ *The Theology of the Letters of James, Peter, and Jude*, 1994. From CUP.

Craddock, Fred. ‡ *First and Second Peter and Jude* (WestBC) 1996. The expositor may learn a lot here, but students will turn to more exegetical works. Craddock is agnostic about authorship but favors the pseudonymity position. [*CBQ* 4/97; *RelSRev* 10/97].

✓ Cranfield, C. E. B. [𝓜], (Torch) 1960. Covers both of Peter's epistles and Jude. It is most insightful and penetrating, as one would expect from Cranfield. There was also an earlier work on 1 Peter (1950), eclipsed by this entry. Fairly mild in its critical stance on 1 Peter.

✓ Dalton, William J. ‡ *Christ's Proclamation to the Spirits: A Study of 1 Peter 3:18–4:6*, 1965, rev. 1989. Certainly one of the most important monographs published on this epistle over the last sixty years. Nearly all commentators (e.g., Davids, Achtemeier, Elliott, Jobes, and Michaels, but with an odd twist) follow his interpretation. See also Pierce.

✓ **Donelson, Lewis R.** ‡ *I & II Peter and Jude* (NTL) 2010. Useful to those seeking a mid-level, compact (285pp.) critical commentary. The author teaches at Austin Presbyterian Seminary and rejects the authenticity of all three epistles. He writes, "Christianity . . . exists as an intersection of readings of the OT, stories and traditions about Jesus, and the demands of living in the Roman world and the still-emerging church. The commentaries that follow will show that each letter gathers those forces in its own way" (2–3). Donelson is dependably liberal in theology. E.g., "this reading seems unlikely because the NT persistently resists the later Christian notion that in death the body . . . dies while the spirit lives on" (109). [*CBQ* 10/11; *JSNT* 34.5; *JETS* 6/11].

☆ **Dubis, Mark.** (BHGNT) 2010. Given that 1 Peter is a major exegetical challenge, this guide to the Greek is most welcome. I have not used it much, but it is said to be expertly done (220pp.). The author wrote his dissertation on 1 Peter at Union Seminary, Virginia, under Achtemeier. [*JSNT* 34.5; *ExpTim* 12/11].

F   Edwards, Dennis R. (WBC-R). To replace Ramsey Michaels's 1988 work.

☆   Edwards, Dennis R. (SGBC) 2017. Accomplishes a lot of good as an accessible, well-informed, mid-length exegesis and theological exposition. Edwards is well-educated (PhD) and has a heart for the church, having spent decades in urban pastorates. However, as noted by one reviewer [*WTJ* Spr 21], his applications in a few places could be disconcerting. For example, as one who rejects patriarchy (134), the North Park Seminary dean quotes, and seems to agree with, a Rachel Held Evans blog equating the complementarian interpretation of the NT household codes (wives' submitting to their husbands) to using those codes to approve of chattel slavery (135). [*JSNT* 40.5].

✓   Egan, Patrick T. *Ecclesiology and the Scriptural Narrative of I Peter*, 2016. A St. Andrews PhD. The author "seeks to account for all uses of scripture in 1 Peter in a comprehensive manner" (x). [*JSNT* 39.5]. For the UK, James Clarke issued it in 2017.

✓   **Elliott, John H.** ‡ (AB) 2000. Huge in size and erudition (900pp.). Few, if any, knew the literature on 1 Peter as well or contributed so much to contemporary Petrine scholarship as Elliott. He argued for pseudonymity and took a heavily sociological approach. His earlier work is *A Home for the Homeless: A Sociological Exegesis of 1 Peter, Its Situation and Strategy* (1981, rev. 1990). I cannot agree with him that the aliens and strangers were literally homeless; this is a case where sociological research should not trump biblical theology. See Achtemeier above. Advanced students once leaned hard on Elliott for bibliographical help. [*CBQ* 10/01; *NovT* 46.3].

✓   **Feldmeier, Reinhard.** ‡ 2005, ET 2008. A welcome 317-page Greek exegesis from Baylor U. Press. Davids is the translator, and when a productive scholar takes time out to do a translation project, we expect there is good reason. German readers should note that the ET is a revision of, and improvement on, the original edition. Horrell says Feldmeier "offers much insight in a short space" (*1 Peter*, p.29), and Hagner calls it "an exceptional commentary that is not only brilliant academically, but one that is also edifying." On authorship Feldmeier tentatively concludes that the weight of evidence is against the Apostle Peter (38). [*CBQ* 1/10; *ExpTim* 7/09 (Horrell); *Int* 1/11].

☆   Forbes, Greg W. (EGGNT) 2014. Very well-done. [*WTJ* Spr 15; *JSNT* 37.5].

☆   Gardner, Paul. *1 and 2 Peter and Jude* (Focus) 2013. A treatment of 1 Peter has been added to his *2 Peter and Jude* (1998). See 2 Peter.

F   Glenny, W. Edward. (EEC).

González, Catherine Gunsalus. ‡ *1 & 2 Peter and Jude* (Belief) 2010. [*Int* 7/12].

☆   **Goppelt, Leonhard.** ‡ 1978, ET 1993. A valuable tool from KEK. In the German it has been of immense help to scholars for its technical and theological discussion. The commentary is probably most notable for its sociological approach. Goppelt, along with nearly all German NT scholars, rejects Petrine authorship. [*JBL* 100.1]. He is well-known for his useful 2-vol. NT Theology (1975–76, ET 1981–82).

☆   **Green, Joel B.** (THC) 2007. The Fuller scholar delivers a fresh exegesis with extended reflection on the epistle's contribution to NT Theology. As with Marshall on this same epistle, the author's Methodist convictions are not so much on display. Along with Fowl on Philippians and Thompson on Colossians, this is one of the best vols. in the THC series. For a probing critique see Gene Green in *JETS*. [*RTR* 12/08; *CBQ* 10/08; *ExpTim* 1/09; *JETS* 12/08; *BL* 2009].

✓   Green, Gene L. *Vox Petri: A Theology of Peter*, 2019. This large, ambitious project (approx. 450pp.) builds on decades of research and accomplishes much good. Note that, though he believes 2 Peter to be authentic (see his fine BECNT), he cautiously leaves that epistle to one side, due to the historical critics' denying it to Peter. Green, then, draws mainly from Mark, Acts, and 1 Peter. The practical effect is that 2 Peter is even more of an outlier. [*Presb* Spr 20, Fall 21; *BBR* 31.4; *JETS* 3/21; *JSNT* 44.5 (Horrell)]. See Bockmuehl above.

F   Hafemann, Scott. (Pillar).

Harink, Douglas. [*M*], *1 & 2 Peter* (Brazos) 2009. Wide-ranging, lively, provocative theological interpretation, directly challenging many traditional views—a book not unlike his *Paul among the Postliberals* (2003). Harink's ear is attuned to apocalyptic notes (Martyn has been a key personal influence), and he assumes "the theological legitimacy" of taking Peter as the author of both letters, "without making a historical-critical judgment" (23). [*ExpTim* 9/10, 7/12; *CBQ* 10/10; *JSNT* 33.5].

☆ Helm, David R. *1 & 2 Peter and Jude* (PTW) 2008. Fine work, which can be compared to Doriani. The bonus with this PTW vol. is that it covers three epistles, not just 1 Peter (360pp.). Helm is easy to recommend to anyone wanting a book of sermons—one that includes solid teaching and preaching (exhortation).

Hiebert, D. Edmond. 1984. A lengthy commentary which seeks to be both exegetical and expositional. Has some attractive features, but is not as penetrating as some other works. Dispensational. [*JETS* 9/85].

☆ **Hillyer, Norman.** *1 & 2 Peter, Jude* (NIBC) 1992. Clear and useful for its size (300pp.)—"both concise and incisive even in its exegesis of difficult verses" (B. Campbell). The approach here is thoroughly evangelical. Call this a bargain. [*RTR* 1/96; *Them* 1/96; *CRBR* 1994 (Davids)].

✓ Holloway, Paul A. ‡ *Coping with Prejudice: 1 Peter in Social-Psychological Perspective*, 2009. [*JTS* 10/11; *JSNT* 33.5].

✓ Hort, F. J. A. 1898. Though fragmentary and covering only 1:1–2:17, this work is worth noting for its exegesis (see Michaels, p.x). Intended for the old Macmillan series.

✓ Hunter, A. M. [*M*], (IB) 1957. I find he always has something profitable to say, but few ministers make use of IB anymore. Takes a more conservatively critical approach.

Johnstone, Robert. 1888. Among exegeses of the Greek text in English, this was the most substantial and erudite work of the 19th century, written by a respected professor at United Presbyterian College, Edinburgh. James Family reprinted the 425-page commentary in 1978. Johnstone's blend of learning with evangelical and Reformed theology led Banner of Truth to include his *James* in their Geneva Series. *The First Epistle of Peter*, by contrast, is less accessible, with its long paragraphs, discussion of scholarly disputes, and occasional Latin quotes (e.g., p.9).

Keating, Daniel. ‡ *First and Second Peter, Jude* (CCSS) 2011. [*JSNT* 35.5].

☆ **Kelly, J. N. D.** [*M*], (BNTC) 1969. Valued by all scholars and by studious pastors, this commentary covers both of the epistles of Peter and Jude. It is a judicious work by a renowned authority on the early church. Unfortunately he follows the critical line on the authorship of 2 Peter. Also reprinted by Baker (Thornapple). [*JBL* 89.4].

☆ Kistemaker, Simon J. *Peter and Jude* (NTC) 1987. Though not profound, it serves the pastor as a sturdy theological guide through these very theological epistles. Strongly supports the stance of believing scholarship regarding the authenticity of both 1 & 2 Peter. His exegetical decisions are well-grounded and clearly explained. Schreiner has done us a similar service more recently. [*WTJ* Fall 89; *CTJ* 11/90].

✓ Knight, Jonathan. ‡ (NT Guides) 1995. For a quick survey of scholarship.

☆ Leighton, Robert. 1693–94. A classic work of full theological exposition, extremely valuable to the pastor willing to work through it—Philip Schaff termed it "immortal." Was reprinted by Kregel in 1972. Leighton (500pp.) was edited down and included in the Crossway Classic series; see below. The full text is free online.

Leighton, Robert, and W. H. Griffith Thomas. *1 & 2 Peter* (CrossC) 1999.

✓ Liebengood, Kelly D. *The Eschatology of 1 Peter: Considering the Influence of Zechariah 9–14*, 2014. Issued by CUP.

✓ Lightfoot, J. B. *The Epistles of 2 Corinthians and 1 Peter*, 2016. Somewhat fragmentary remains of his research, but worth noting. [*JSNT* 40.5].

   Lillie, John. *Lectures on the First and Second Epistles of Peter*, 1869. A large, learned exposition from a native Scotsman and American Presbyterian. Reprinted by Klock & Klock (1978). Its theological discussion is robust and mature, interacting with a host of interpreters: the church fathers, Reformers, Bengel, Alford, leading British and German exegetes of his day, and the poets.

✓ Lockett, Darian R. See the works listed above under "James."

✓ Luther, Martin. 1522–27. His commentaries on the Catholic Epistles are available in both a 19th and 20th century translation. The single vol. published by Concordia (1967) is the one to possess, if you wish to purchase the work, though the earlier one is serviceable. Do not expect to find a commentary on the Epistle of James—the "epistle of straw," as the Saxon Reformer once termed it—in this vol.

   MacArthur, John. 2004. See Matthew for a review of the series.

☆ **Marshall, I Howard.** (IVPNT) 1991. Marshall was general editor, and his work always carried a weight of scholarship. This is a very fine book, satisfying in its exegesis and contemporary application. There is a great deal more substance to this work than one might suppose looking at its slim size—reminds me of Cranfield. Years ago I went so far as to say this would be an excellent first purchase for a pastor. [*CRBR* 1992].

F   Martin, Troy. (NIGTC). Building on a PhD, *Metaphor and Composition in 1 Peter* (1992).

✓ Mason, Eric F., and Troy W. Martin, eds. ‡ *Reading 1–2 Peter and Jude*, 2014. Subtitled "A Resource for Students," the 275-page book contains fourteen SBL essays. [*CBQ* 10/15].

☆ McKnight, Scot. (NIVAC) 1996. The author edited the NT series and here contributes a model commentary for it. See NIVAC under Commentary Series. Almost 300pp.

F   McNutt, Jennifer Powell, ed. *1–2 Peter, 1–3 John, Jude* (RCS).

F   Melick, Richard. *1–2 Peter, Jude* (EBTC)?

☆ **Michaels, J. Ramsey.** [𝓜], (WBC) 1988. A remarkably learned work which advanced the scholarly discussion a good ways. It was Carson's and Silva's first choice in the early 1990s. Though I dislike Michaels's fence-sitting in the Introduction (lxii–lxvii), I was impressed with his erudition and greatly helped in my understanding of 1 Peter. Surprisingly, Michaels wants to argue that the evidence supports both Petrine authorship and a date in the 70s—a view earlier put forward by A. M. Ramsay. Advanced students especially may want to purchase this, but compare with Achtemeier, Selwyn, Elliott, and Jobes (who was able to interact with all the previous scholarship). See Edwards above. [*JTS* 40.2; *WTJ* Fall 89; *JETS* 12/91; *Them* 1/92; *CTJ* 11/90; *Chm* 104.1; *CRBR* 1990 (Elliot, too negative)].

   Miller, Donald G. [𝓜], *On This Rock: A Commentary on First Peter*, 1993. Mainly a theological exposition designed to appeal to a wide audience.

   Miller, Timothy E., and Bryan Murawski. (Kerux) 2023. I have not seen it.

   Moffatt, James. ‡ (Moffatt) 1928. See under James. Moffatt upheld Petrine authorship (the letter being dictated to Silvanus).

   Mounce, Robert H. *A Living Hope*, 1982. Covers both epistles of Peter. This popularly styled commentary is appreciated for its warm-hearted tone, clarity, and thoughtfulness.

✓ Moyise, Steve. ‡ *The Later NT Writers and Scripture*, 2012. See under Acts.

✓ Nienhuis, David R., and Robert W. Wall. *Reading the Epistles of James, Peter, John, and Jude as Scripture*, 2013. See under James.

   Nisbet, Alexander. (GS) 1658. Covers 1 and 2 Peter, and this Puritan surprisingly wasn't verbose. Banner of Truth thankfully reset the classic in modern typeface.

Osborne, Grant. (CorBC) 2011. See James.

Perkins, Pheme. ‡ (I) 1995. See James above.

Perkins, Pheme, Patricia McDonald, and Eloise Rosenblatt. ‡ *1–2 Peter, Jude* (Wisdom) 2022. [*JSNT* 45.5].

✓ Pierce, Chad T. [*M*], *Spirits and the Proclamation of Christ*, 2011. A fresh study of *3:18–22* with an extensive history of research, concluding "it is impossible to specify a single tradition-historical explanation behind this passage in 1 Peter" (236). [*JSNT* 34.5]. Cf. Dalton.

F  Pierce, Madison N. (BGW).

Powers, Daniel. *1 & 2 Peter, Jude: A Commentary in the Wesleyan Tradition*, 2010.

☆ **Reese, Ruth Anne.** [*M*], (NCBC) 2022. Complements her earlier labors on 2 Peter and Jude. At 315pp this is fuller than other entries in the series; Reese includes comparatively more application and "appropriation" (3), with openness to feminist and postcolonial criticisms. She "has a particular interest in the relationship between 1 Peter and various themes in the Hebrew Bible, such as exodus, exile, or glory" (Foster [*ExpTim* 4/23]). [*JSNT* 45.5].

Reicke, Bo. ‡ (AB) 1964. See under James. Argues for Petrine authorship through Silvanus.

✓ Richard, Earl J. ‡ *Reading 1 Peter, Jude, and 2 Peter: A Literary and Theological Commentary* (RNT) 2000. The work of an able Catholic exegete (400pp.).

✓ Sargent, Benjamin. *Written to Serve: The Use of Scripture in 1 Peter*, 2015. Most welcome! [*CBQ* 7/16; *JSNT* 38.5; *NovT* 59.2; *JSNT* 38.5]. An influential earlier discussion of the same was William Schutter, *Hermeneutic and Composition in 1 Peter* (1989).

☆ **Selwyn, E. G.** [*M*], (Macmillan) 1946. A magisterial work in its day, still consulted by all engaged in serious study. Reprinted in Baker's Thornapple series (1981). In spots I find it marginally more useful than WBC for working through the Greek. I used to recommend Michaels's WBC above because it was fairly up-to-date and discussed Dalton, and because Selwyn was o/p and difficult to obtain. Selwyn defends Petrine authorship but through Silvanus. [*WTJ* Fall 47]. See also his valuable, lengthy 1964 essay on "Eschatology in 1 Peter," in *The Background of the New Testament and Its Eschatology* (Dodd FS).

✓ **Senior, Donald,** and Daniel Harrington. ‡ *1 Peter, Jude, 2 Peter* (SacP) 2003. Jude and 2 Peter are treated by Harrington. More critical positions—all three epistles pseudonymous—are assumed regarding authorship issues. (Doesn't this serve to diminish St. Peter's place in the early church?) This is learned and accessible as a commentary reference, but it does not break any new ground. The authors are both in the top rank of American Catholic scholars. [*ExpTim* 5/04; *RelSRev* 1/04; *JETS* 12/04; *Int* 4/05].

Skaggs, Rebecca. *1 Peter, 2 Peter, Jude* (PentC) 2004. [*ExpTim* 4/06].

☆ Storms, Sam. "1 Peter" in *Hebrews–Revelation* (ESVEC) 2018. See Johnson under Hebrews.

✓ Talbert, Charles H., ed. ‡ *Perspectives on First Peter*, 1986.

F  Toit, Sean du. (NCCS).

✓ Vinson, Richard B., Richard F. Wilson, and Watson E. Mills. ‡ *1 & 2 Peter, Jude* (S&H) 2010. Of the three, Vinson's treatment of 1 Peter is the most thorough (255pp.) and well-informed by scholarship. He denies apostolic authorship. Wilson, a theologian rather than a NT scholar, does 2 Peter, reaching generally mainstream critical conclusions and writing well (261–365). I find Mills's work on Jude cursory, with essentially a 2-page introduction and 30pp. of commentary. [*Int* 1/13].

Walls, A. F., and A. M. Stibbs. (retired TNTC) 1962. Walls contributed the introduction and Stibbs did the commentary. This is replaced by Grudem and can be ignored.

Waltner, Erland, and J. Daryl Charles. *1–2 Peter, Jude* (BCBC) 1999. Waltner writes on 1 Peter in this good vol., perhaps the most conservative in the NT series thus far. See Charles above. [*Int* 1/01; *JETS* 9/01].

✓ Watson, Duane F., and Terrance Callan. ‡ *First and Second Peter* (Paideia) 2012. Watson contributes the work on 1 Peter and is somewhat more conservative and theological than his partner. [*CBQ* 4/14; *Int* 7/13; *JSNT* 35.5].

✓ Webb, Robert L., and Betsy Bauman-Martin, eds. ‡ *Reading First Peter with New Eyes: Methodological Reassessments of the Letter of First Peter,* 2007. [*ExpTim* 8/08; *BibInt* 18.1]. See especially Boring's updated essay on "Narrative Dynamics in First Peter."

F   Wilkins, Michael. (ZECNT).

✓ Williams, Martin. *The Doctrine of Salvation in the First Letter of Peter,* 2011. A Presbyterian minister's PhD work, published by CUP. [*JTS* 4/15; *JSNT* 35.5; *JETS* 12/12; *ExpTim* 12/12; *Them* 11/12; *BTB* 11/13; *RelSRev* 12/13].

✓ **Williams, Travis B., and David G. Horrell.** ‡ (ICC-R) 2 vols., 2023. A truly stunning achievement and monument to prodigious scholarship! Elliott was encyclopedic, and this more so. As the collaborators hint in the Preface, the set is destined to be consulted as a technical reference—"A compendium of scholarship" for years to come (xi)—but read through by scarcely anyone. After a 290-page Introduction, concluding that the epistle is pseudonymous (162), the pair provide over 1200pp. of the most painstaking textual, philological, grammatical, and exegetical commentary, and finally a 160-page bibliography. There are no indices. A saving grace is the provision of well-written summaries of the authors' conclusions at the end of each pericope. (E.g., after nearly 110pp. on 3:18–22, there is a two-page summary.) The history of interpretation is covered more thoroughly than expected. Williams previously published monographs on the letter: *Persecution in 1 Peter* (2012) [*JTS* 10/13; *RelSRev* 6/14; *JETS* 7/14, 12/14] and *Good Works in 1 Peter* (2014). Horrell, his doctoral supervisor at Exeter, has written the highly regarded *1 Peter* in T&T Clark's NT Guides series [*ExpTim* 5/09; *BL* 2009; *RelSRev* 9/09; *BTB* 8/10], as well as *Becoming Christian: Essays on 1 Peter and the Making of Christian Identity* (2013) [*JSNT* 36.5; *ExpTim* 5/14]. There was an earlier Horrell commentary, assisting preachers, on *The Epistles of Peter and Jude* (1998) in the Epworth series [*Anvil* 17.3]. With regard to the ICC, Foster says its "impact will only be correctly assessed over multiple decades" [*ExpTim* 7/23].

☆ Witherington, Ben, III. *Letters and Homilies for Hellenized Christians, Vol. II: A Socio-Rhetorical Commentary on 1–2 Peter,* 2008. A much fuller work (400pp.) than some of his recent vols. on the epistles. I have not been able to review this as yet.

NOTE: (1) Mark Dubis, "Research on 1 Peter: A Survey of Scholarly Literature Since 1985," *CBR* 4.2 (2006): 199–239. (2) Travis Williams's survey of scholarship in *CBR* 10.2 (2012).

# 2 PETER

NOTE: Since it is customary in series to treat Jude and 2 Peter in one volume, I have marked with [J] those works that follow the pattern. See also the Jude section below.

★ **Bauckham, Richard J.** [𝓜], *Jude, 2 Peter* (WBC) 1983. [J] The first choice of Carson, Silva, Martin, and Childs. Simply put, this was once regarded as the best exegetical commentary on the Greek text of 2 Peter/Jude in any language. The author told me (2016) that he is revising it with Darian Lockett; it might be best to hold off purchasing the 1983 edition. Readers should be apprised that Bauckham rejects Petrine authorship. (The order of books in his title indicates his conclusion that Jude came first and 2 Peter is literarily dependent.) For a conservative assessment of Bauckham's thesis that 2 Peter is testamentary writing and his arguments for pseudonymity, see Davids and G. Green. This vol. is very useful to students and to scholarly evangelical pastors, who will likely conclude that the author's theology is healthier fare than his historical criticism. (He belongs to the critically oriented wing of British evangelicalism, and so I have marked him as mediating or [*M*].) Compare to Neyrey. [*EvQ* 7/85; *RTR* 9/83; *JETS* 3/84; *TJ* Fall 84; *Them* 9/85; *JBL* 104.3].

★ **Davids, Peter H.** (Pillar) 2006. [J] In the absence of a NICNT, this fills a gap in the preacher's library. Davids has a well-established reputation as a commentator on the General Epistles; his works on James and 1 Peter have both exegetical merit and rich theological exposition. This vol. includes a learned discussion of the relationship between the two epistles, concluding (with Bauckham) that Jude came first and 2 Peter shows signs of literary dependence. At the same time, he says Bauckham's case for pseudonymity is not proven. His exegesis is scholarly and reliable, and the robust theological discussion helps both students and preachers. Students will keep Bauckham and G. Green close at hand, but pastors can wisely make this their first pick (even if evangelicals were surprised to hear he joined the Catholic Church in 2014). [*BBR* 18.1; *Chm* Win 07; *RTR* 12/07; *CBQ* 10/07; *JETS* 9/07; *BL* 2007; *RelSRev* 7/07; *ExpTim* 5/07; *DenvJ* 5/07; *BSac* 10/08; *Anvil* 25.1]. See also Davids's *Theology* (2014) under James and the BHGNT below.

★ **Green, Gene L.** (BECNT) 2008. [J] Can be placed alongside Davids as a dependably conservative work on two epistles for which we earlier had little in the way of evangelical exegesis besides E. M. B. Green. It is especially strong in discussing the historical, cultural, and intellectual background. He helpfully reopens debate of the Bauckham thesis that 2 Peter is testamentary literature, suggesting that a testamentary section (1:12–15) does not make the whole letter such. This 420-page work is a boon for evangelical students, and studious pastors will buy this as a supplement to Davids and Moo. [*DenvJ* 1/09; *JETS* 3/10; *CBQ* 7/09; *ExpTim* 6/10 (Davids)].

★ **Lloyd-Jones, D. Martyn.** *Sermons on 2 Peter*, 1983. There is probably nothing better to get a sense for the power of this epistle when preached by one with full confidence in the authority of the Holy Scriptures. These 25 sermons were originally delivered in London's Westminster Chapel in 1946–47, immediately after the apocalyptic horrors of World War II. Still more homiletical help is available in Helm, Lucas–Green, Harmon, Nisbet, and the two CrossC vols. listed below.

★ **Moo, Douglas J.** (NIVAC) 1996. [J] Moves so well and wisely from exegesis of the ancient text to discerning the contemporary message that lazy pastors might be tempted to let Moo do all their work for them. I used to say this vol. should be the model for the whole NT series. Note that Moo also does Romans for this series.

★ **Schreiner, Thomas.** *1, 2 Peter, Jude* (NAC) 2003; (CSC) 2020. See under 1 Peter. Excellent. Though Schreiner gives a very good study of 1 Peter, with plenty of bibliographical help for students, I used to value this vol. even more for his treatment of 2 Peter and Jude because of the lack of evangelical exegetical commentaries on that portion. For so long we had little more than Michael Green's slim Tyndale vol., and Green did not interact with much scholarship in his exegesis. I spoke of this NAC in 2005 as the average pastor's first choice for a mid-level exegesis and exposition of 2 Peter and Jude. With the appearance of both Davids and Gene Green, Schreiner was not quite the standout work. With the 2020 thorough revision, it remains the clear choice of evangelical pastors desiring a one-vol. exegesis and exposition of the three epistles—a smart purchase for its quality, coverage (three epistles at low cost), and sound theology.

Adams, Thomas. *A Commentary on the Second Epistle General of St. Peter*, ca. 1633. This huge Puritan classic was reprinted by Soli Deo Gloria in 1990. Now free online.

Barnett, A. E. ‡ *The Second Epistle of Peter* (IB) 1957. Can be passed over.

☆ Bentley, Michael. *Living for Christ* (WCS on 1 & 2 Peter) 1993.

✓ **Bigg, C. A.** ‡ (ICC) 1902. [J] See 1 Peter above.

✓ Blum, Edwin A. (EBC) 1981. See 1 Peter above.

✓ Bray, Gerald, ed. *James, 1–2 Peter, 1–3 John, Jude* (ACCS) 2000. See James above.

☆ Brown, John. *Parting Counsels: 2 Peter Chapter 1* (GS) 1856. Has a Puritan flavor to it—Spurgeon called him "a Puritan born out of due time"—and provides much commentary on the theological message. Reprinted by Banner in 1980. Brown has other full expositions of Romans, Hebrews, and 1 Peter.

✓ **Callan, Terrance.** ‡ *Acknowledging the Divine Benefactor: The Second Letter of Peter*, 2015. Following his teacher Vernon Robbins in examining the "textures of texts" (socio-rhetorical interpretation), Callan has produced a substantial (200pp.), stimulating work. [*JSNT* 38.5]. See also his Paideia work with Watson on 1–2 Peter.

☆ **Charles, J. Daryl.** (EBCR) 2006. This author contributes on 1–2 Peter and Jude (a total of 165pp.). See Waltner below for an earlier Charles commentary. I would use this more recent commentary instead of BCBC. Let me add that I believe Charles's EBCR is the best brief exegesis of Jude for conservative pastors (29pp.).

Craddock, Fred. ‡ (WestBC) 1996. [J] See 1 Peter above.

✓ **Cranfield, C. E. B.** ‡ (Torch) 1960. [J] See 1 Peter above.

☆ **Davids, Peter H.** (BHGNT) 2011. [J] An expert walk-through of the Greek text, useful to students and pastors for sharpening their skills. See his Pillar above. [*JSNT* 34.5].

✓ **Donelson, Lewis R.** ‡ *I & II Peter and Jude* (NTL) 2010. See 1 Peter.

✓ **Frey, Jörg.** ‡ 2015, ET 2018. [J] Subtitled "A Theological Commentary" and of interest to advanced students. The extensive and detailed historical-critical work (430pp + 50-page bibliography), by a Zurich professor, develops his thesis that 2 Peter is dependent on the *Apocalypse of Peter*. (Bauckham now criticizes this thesis; see his essay in Frey–den Dulk–van der Watt, eds., *2 Peter and the Apocalypse of Peter: Towards a New Perspective* [2019].) Both epistles are said to be pseudonymous and second century, with 2 Peter literarily dependent on Jude. Already Frey is regarded as an important major commentary. [*ExpTim* 5/19; *JTS* 4/22; *Int* 1/21].

☆ Gardner, Paul. (Focus) 1998. [J] One of the best in the series with excellent exegesis in the background. (Gardner once taught NT at Oak Hill College, London.) Pastors can benefit from the theological exposition, and I cannot think of a better book on these letters to put in the hands of an eager lay Bible student. See 1 Peter.

✓ **Giese, Curtis P.** (ConcC) 2012. [J] I believe Giese was a wise choice to author this because he has undertaken intensive studies in Jewish literature of the Greco-Roman period and in the early church fathers. He follows the series pattern in a disciplined way, offering textual notes (lots of syntax), exegesis of the Greek, and ample theological exposition (in the Lutheran mode). The good-sized vol. (373pp.) sometimes wanders a bit from the explicit teaching of the text in order to reassure readers regarding the doctrines of their church (e.g., consubstantiation and closed communion on p.138). Overall, worth consulting. [*CBQ* 1/14].

✓ Gilmour, Michael J. [𝓜], *The Significance of Parallels between 2 Peter and Other Early Christian Literature*, 2002. He sounds a cautionary note in "Reflections on the Authorship of 2 Peter," *EvQ* 73 (2001): 291–309.

González, Catherine Gunsalus. ‡ *1 & 2 Peter and Jude* (Belief) 2010.

☆ **Green, E. M. B.** (TNTC) 1968, rev. 1987. [J] A sturdy defense of the letter's authenticity, together with a solid exegesis. This is a fine little commentary from a prominent evangelical in the Church of England; for so long in conservative circles it was the standard work on 2 Peter/Jude in pastors' and churches' libraries, in part because there was hardly anything else. In the first six editions, I listed it as recommended for purchase. Reformed folk note his

Arminianism in the interpretation of 2 Peter 3:9. See Green's other well-received works on Matthew's Gospel. [*WTJ* Fall 69].

Harink, Douglas. [𝓜], *1 & 2 Peter* (Brazos), 2009. See under 1 Peter.

☆ Harmon, Matthew S. "2 Peter, Jude" in *Hebrews–Revelation* (ESVEC) 2018. See Johnson under Hebrews.

Harvey, Robert W., and Philip H. Towner. (IVPNT) 2009. [J] The late Harvey was mostly responsible for 2 Peter and he offers mainly a devotional reading. Towner then offers a solid exegesis of Jude, but one that can be challenged, according to a reviewer, when it "repeatedly makes the assertion that the letter is a missional document intended to offer hope to Jude's opponents" [*BL* 2010]. Gauged for pastors. [*JETS* 9/09 (Davids); *Chm* Aut 11].

☆ Helm, David R. *1 & 2 Peter and Jude* (PTW) 2008. See 1 Peter.

☆ Hillyer, Norman. (NIBC) 1992. [J] See 1 Peter above.

F   Hultin, Jeremy. ‡ (Herm). [J]

James, Montague Rhodes. (Cambridge Greek Testament) 1912. [J]

☆ Jobes, Karen. *Letters to the Church*, 2011. See under Hebrews.

F   Joseph, Abson. (SGBC). [J] Previously Rosalee Ewell was listed.

Keating, Daniel. ‡ *First and Second Peter, Jude* (CCSS) 2011. [*CBQ* 10/13].

☆ **Kelly, J. N. D.** [𝓜], (BNTC) 1969. [J] See 1 Peter above. Many would argue this is still among the very best general treatments of 2 Peter. Kelly's writing is a model of clarity, and I have used him extensively over the years.

☆ Kistemaker, Simon J. (NTC) 1987. [J] See 1 Peter above.

✓ **Kraftchick, Stephen.** ‡ (ANTC) 2002. [J] I have not used this 190-page commentary. It is given a good review by Davids [*CBQ* 7/03]. The critical stance will be off-putting for many evangelicals. [*RelSRev* 7/03; *JETS* 9/03].

☆ Leighton, Robert, and W. H. Griffith Thomas. *1 & 2 Peter* (CrossC) 1999. An edifying exposition for the church. For Jude see the Manton vol. in the series.

✓ Lockett, Darian R. See the works listed above under "James."

☆ Lucas, R. C., and Christopher Green. *The Message of 2 Peter and Jude* (BST) 1995. [J] Dick Lucas, a famous British evangelical Anglican, also contributed the BST vol. on Colossians. There are a great many nuggets here for the preacher, and I'll call them gold (235pp.). [*RelSRev* 10/97].

Luther, Martin. *The Catholic Epistles*, 1522–27. [J] See 1 Peter above.

✓ Mason, Eric F., and Troy W. Martin, eds. ‡ *Reading 1–2 Peter and Jude*, 2014. Subtitled "A Resource for Students," the 275-page book contains fourteen SBL essays.

✓ **Mayor, J. B.** [𝓜], *Second Peter and Jude*, 1907. [J] A companion to Mayor's James commentary and Selwyn's encyclopedic First Peter in the Macmillan series, with the same exhaustive approach to grammatico-historical exegesis; few stones are left unturned. Advanced students are encouraged to look this up. Mayor denies Petrine authorship, but he is less dogmatic than many critics on the issue: "there is not that chasm between 1 and 2 Peter which some would try to make out" (civ). The Macmillan work was reprinted but it is now free online. Note too that Mayor has a fine old 70-page commentary on Jude in the *Expositor's Greek Testament* (1897).

Mbuvi, Andrew. (NCCS) 2016. [J] A middle-length exposition by a fine African scholar, teaching at Shaw University, North Carolina. Worth looking up. [*JSNT* 40.5]. Earlier he published a Westminster PhD: *Temple, Exile, and Identity in 1 Peter* (2007).

F   McNutt, Jennifer Powell, ed. *1–2 Peter, 1–3 John, Jude* (RCS).

F   Melick, Richard. *1–2 Peter, Jude* (EBTC)?

Moffatt, James. ‡ (Moffatt) 1928. [J] See James above.

Mounce, Robert. 1982. See 1 Peter above.

✓ Moyise, Steve. ‡ *The Later NT Writers and Scripture*, 2012. See under Acts.

✓ **Neyrey, Jerome H.** ‡ (AB-R) 1993. [J] In its close exegesis of the Greek, this work is said by some to compete with WBC as a first choice for scholars, but does not supersede it. I found Bauckham to be a shrewder, more balanced exegete and a better guide into the theology of these epistles. Some of the conclusions in this AB replacement for Reicke are far-fetched. A Catholic professor, Neyrey follows the critical line—arguing both letters are pseudonymous—and the commentary is close to 300pp., including introduction and indices. Students value it for its application of the methods of social-scientific research, though the arrival of several major commentaries (2003–) makes it less important to students than was the case at the turn of the century. [*Int* 10/95; *JBL* Sum 95].

✓ Nienhuis, David R., and Robert W. Wall. *Reading the Epistles of James, Peter, John, and Jude as Scripture*, 2013. See under James.

Nisbet, Alexander. (GS) 1658. See 1 Peter above.

Osborne, Grant. (CorBC) 2011. [J] See James.

Perkins, Pheme. ‡ (I) 1995. [J] See James above. Gene Green finds much of value here as a theological exposition of 2 Peter/Jude [*BSB* 12/03].

Perkins, Pheme, Patricia McDonald, and Eloise Rosenblatt. ‡ *1–2 Peter, Jude* (Wisdom) 2022.

Powers, Daniel. *1 & 2 Peter, Jude: A Commentary in the Wesleyan Tradition*, 2010.

✓ **Reese, Ruth Anne.** [𝓜], (THC) 2007. [J] The Asbury Seminary prof gives almost as much space to Jude as to 2 Peter. She earlier published *Writing Jude: The Reader, the Text, and the Author* (2000). Reese pursues a canonical reading of these books and avoids taking positions on the higher-critical issues. I find her theological reflection careful and thought-provoking yet deficient, starting as it does from a definition of theology itself (see p.3) that neglects divine revelation and is largely anthropocentric. Her approach seems tied to a more postmodern way of thinking, e.g., the idea that our beliefs in community are the source of our knowledge. Her work represents one of the few attempts to interpret these two epistles using contemporary literary theory. Note that Davids says the commentary on 2 Peter "is significantly weaker than her work on Jude." [*CBQ* 4/09; *RelSRev* 9/08; *JETS* 9/08 (Davids); *BL* 2009; *ExpTim* 7/09 (Davids)].

Reicke, Bo. ‡ (retired AB) 1964. [J] See James above.

✓ Richard, Earl J. ‡ *Reading 1 Peter, Jude, and 2 Peter: A Literary and Theological Commentary* (Reading the NT) 2000. [J] This work of nearly 400pp. is published by Smyth and Helwys but not in their S&H series.

✓ Senior, Donald, and **Daniel J. Harrington.** ‡ *1 Peter, Jude, 2 Peter* (SacP) 2003. [J] Harrington is responsible for the latter two epistles. See 1 Peter above.

Shaddix, James, and Daniel L. Akin. *Exalting Jesus in 2 Peter and Jude* (CCE) 2018. [J]

Sidebottom, E. M. ‡ (NCB) 1967. [J] See James above.

Skaggs, Rebecca. *1 Peter, 2 Peter, Jude* (PentC) 2004. [*ExpTim* 4/06].

F  Smith, Shively T. J. (NIGTC). [J] Previously Hafemann was listed.

F  Stewart, Alexander. (EEC). See Bateman's *Jude*.

Vinson, Richard B., Richard F. Wilson, and Watson E. Mills. *1 & 2 Peter, Jude* (S&H) 2010. See Vinson under 1 Peter.

✓ Waltner, Erland, and **J. Daryl Charles.** *1–2 Peter, Jude* (BCBC) 1999. [J] Charles has previously done much work on both 2 Peter and Jude and makes a decent contribution here. Though not a major commentary, this has been a good reference for students because of the research that lies behind the work. I note in passing Gene Green's disappointment with this commentary [*BSB* 12/03]. See Charles's more recent EBCR above. See also under Jude below. [*Int* 1/01; *JETS* 9/01].

✓ Watson, Duane F. ‡ (NIB) 1998. [J] Not of great account in my opinion, and better on Jude than on 2 Peter. Greek students will probably learn much more from his Duke PhD, *Invention, Arrangement, and Style: Rhetorical Criticism of Jude and 2 Peter* (1988), which began to establish his reputation as a leader in the field of rhetorical studies on the NT.

✓ Watson, Duane F., and **Terrance Callan.** ‡ *First and Second Peter* (Paideia) 2012. Callan contributed 2 Peter, and his work is all the more worth consulting because exegeses are thin on the ground (approx. 90pp.). See 1 Peter.

F   Webb, Robert L. (NICNT). [J] Originally this was to be a joint work with Peter Davids (for Davids see Pillar and BHGNT above). Webb teaches at McMaster University. There is a foretaste of his interpretation of Jude in "The Use of 'Story' in the Letter of Jude," *JSNT* 31.1 (2008): 53–87.

F   Webb, Robert L. (RRA). [J]

✓ Webb, Robert L., and Duane F. Watson, eds. [*M*], *Reading Second Peter with New Eyes: Methodological Reassessments of the Letter of Second Peter,* 2010. [*JSNT* 33.5; *ExpTim* 7/12; *RelSRev* 3/14].

F   Wilder, Terry L. (EGGNT). [J]

☆ **Witherington, Ben, III.** *Letters and Homilies for Hellenized Christians, Vol. II: A Socio-Rhetorical Commentary on 1–2 Peter,* 2008. A much fuller work (400pp.) than some of his recent vols. on the epistles. I have not been able to review this thoroughly.

F   Yarbrough, Robert W. (ZECNT). [J]


# THE EPISTLES OF JOHN

★ Burge, Gary. (NIVAC) 1996. Highly praised by a number of pastor friends. This is a good addition to the other recommendations—all strong on exegesis and theological exposition—because of its fuller discussion of how John's Letters might best be applied today. Burge has some good exegesis, too, but that is not the main value of his commentary here. He is unsure whether the Fourth Gospel and John's Epistles come from the same hand. *DenvJ* [2015] made Jobes, Kruse, Yarbrough, and Burge its top four picks. [*JETS* 6/99]. My favorite pastoral expositions besides Burge and Campbell (and all just as valuable) are: O'Donnell, Allen, and Lloyd-Jones.

★ Campbell, Constantine R. (SGBC) 2017. Does a laudable job of sifting the best exegetical scholarship, while adding his own fine insights (on the Greek, union with Christ). Students certainly benefit. More than some others in SGBC, Campbell's vol. explains the textual basis for his thoughts on application. He is a sound theological guide (230pp.), and his mature pastoral reflections are just as valuable. Happy and blessed is the congregation taught John's Epistles in this manner. [*JSNT* 40.5].

★ Jobes, Karen H. (ZECNT) 2014. See her previous work on Esther, 1 Peter. This 325-page Greek exegesis was born out of a decade of experience lecturing on John's Letters at Wheaton Grad School. Because ZECNT includes a translation in graphical layout and emphasizes the Greek text's flow of thought, besides a fine commentary section, this is helpful in new and distinct ways, alongside Pillar and other series. Pastors find her work all the more useful for their study because she proceeds on the assumption that, "while the letters must be allowed their own voice, they cannot be properly understood without reference to John's Gospel as the interpretive framework for metaphors, images, and theology common to both" (14). Jobes intentionally does not systematically engage interpreters who push a hypothetical Johannine Community theory, and also avoids a polemical reading of 1 John that tries to reconstruct with specificity the false teaching(s) being confronted. I found the Theology in Application sections to be apt and thought-provoking. [*Chm* Win 18; *JETS* 9/16]. See also Jobes's textbook survey, *Letters to the Church* (2011).

★ **Kruse, Colin G.** (Pillar) 2000, 2nd ed. 2020. Prior to Yarbrough and Jobes, the 1st ed. was valuable as probably the best recent evangelical exegesis. (There hadn't been much competition.) The pluses were its confidence in the authority of God's Word, spiritual insight, manageable size (250pp.), and distillation of much current scholarship. On the negative side, the commentary was thinner on 2 & 3 John (32 of 184pp. total). The 2nd ed. is an enlarged revision and update, but not a complete rewrite. Yarbrough says it is "distinguished in its clarity, graciousness, and lightness of touch. . . . Readers may learn less of the scholarly buzz, but they will learn a great deal about the flow and meaning of what these Scriptures say" [*Presb* Spr 20]. Kruse argues for authorship by John the Apostle. Dependable is the right adjective here, even though Collins is correct in pointing out instances where Kruse follows the NIV and could have paid closer attention to the Greek (e.g., abundant use of μένω). Pastors working without the Greek might start with Kruse, but those delving into the original will prefer the guidance provided by Yarbrough and Jobes. [*RTR* 12/00; *Int* 4/01; *SwJT* Spr 01; *EvQ* 7/03; *JETS* 12/01; *Chm* Aut 01; *Presb* Fall 05 (Collins); *Evangel* Spr 02; *Anvil* 19.3].

★ **Stott, John R. W.** (TNTC) 1964, rev. 1988. Probably the best in the series. I used to go so far as to recommend the expositor purchase Stott first, and that remains good advice, though it sticks mainly to the exegetical task (not full exposition). You can use it the rest of your life. Of course, students need a tool which is in-depth and which interacts with current scholarship, and they will likely bypass this on their way to the major scholarly series (AB, BECNT, NTL, WBC, Herm). [*RTR* 5/89].

★ **Yarbrough, Robert.** (BECNT) 2008. Sterling. This replaced Smalley on my list and is my top pick for studious pastors. The author is a PCA minister, trained under Howard Marshall at Aberdeen, who headed the NT Department at TEDS, and coedits this series. He teaches at Covenant Seminary. The exegesis of the Greek is both carefully thorough (464pp.) and aimed at exposition of the theological message. I welcome his attention to the history of interpretation, with special place given to Augustine, Calvin, and Schlatter (one of his favorites). Students appreciate his interaction with well-sifted, modern Johannine scholarship, though more could have been done to engage with critical views at variance with conservative ones; some will see this as a plus perhaps. After the rehashing of the Martyn/Brown thesis in so many commentaries, it may be refreshing to read this one. He plows a different furrow. Foster suggests that Yarbrough and Lieu are well paired, since the former's weak spot (2–3 John) is precisely where Lieu is strongest. Preachers will find help—more than usual in BECNT—as they seek to discern the pastoral implications of the text. [*JETS* 9/09; *DenvJ* 1/09; *RBL*; *CTJ* 11/09; *BSac* 7/10; *ExpTim* 8/09 (Foster); *TJ* Spr 10; *CBQ* 7/10; *BBR* 21.2 (Jobes)].

☆ **Akin, Daniel L.** (NAC) 2001. The 250-page commentary is similar to Kruse in some respects (same intended audience of pastors). It is solid, reveals substantial research on the part of the author, and would be a good purchase for pastors. Akin is President of Southeastern Baptist Theological Seminary. [*Them* Sum 04; *JETS* 9/02; *BSac* 7/03].

Akin, Daniel L. *Exalting Jesus in 1, 2, 3 John* (CCE) 2014. Building upon his NAC above.

☆ Allen, David L. (PTW) 2013. Considerably more attention is paid to 1 John (20 sermons) than 2–3 John (one sermon each). Allen has been a homiletics prof and loves the deeper, riper sermonic material in Augustine, Luther, Calvin, Wesley, Edwards, and Spurgeon. A fine, worthwhile book for preachers (over 300pp.). "He opens up John's epistles with admirable clarity and force" (Yarbrough).

Anderson, Kelly, and Daniel Keating. ‡ *James, First, Second, and Third John* (CCSS) 2017.

Barker, Glenn W. (EBC) 1981. Now honorably retired. See Thatcher.

Bateman, Herbert W., IV, and Aaron C. Peer. (BGI) 2018. I have not seen it. [*JETS* 12/19].

**Bennett, Thomas Andrew.** (THC) 2021. About 200pp. of exegesis, followed by 32 theological essays. Written by a prof at Fuller. Regrettably, I've not used this yet. [*ExpTim* 5/22; *CBQ* 10/22; *Int* 1/23].

✓ Black, C. Clifton. ‡ (NIB) 1998. A little over 100pp. of solid scholarship.

☆ Bowsher, Clive. *Life in the Son*, 2023. See under John's Gospel.

✓ Bray, Gerald, ed. *James, 1–2 Peter, 1–3 John, Jude* (ACCS) 2000. See James above.

✓ Brooke, A. E. ‡ (ICC) 1912. Remains somewhat useful as a reference on technical questions.

☆ **Brown, Raymond E.** ‡ (AB) 1982. *"Commentaire monumental"* (Bonnard)! Brown was a Catholic who long taught at Union Seminary, New York. Only for the advanced student and specialist. See also Brown's commentary on John's Gospel—the epistles were not written by the evangelist, he argues. This is by no means a conservative work and it is too full (800 jam-packed pages) for the average pastor. Still, the commentary is self-recommending as an enormously learned tome and a high point in Johannine scholarship. Quite influential is his argument (building on Meeks's 1972 article, "The Man from Heaven in Johannine Sectarianism") that these Epistles reflect controversy in *The Community of the Beloved Disciple* (his 1979 title) over the proper understanding of the Johannine tradition. Years ago, though I did not buy this argument, in some ways I preferred Brown to the more conservative but less rigorous Smalley. Advanced students and academically inclined pastors might invest in this, if they want more than Yarbrough and Jobes. But cf. Schnackenburg. [*JBL* 103.4].

☆ Bruce, F. F. 1970. A solid brief commentary, very much to the point. Were it not for Stott, it might have been the best popular exegetical work. Has been bound with Bruce's work on John's Gospel.

Bultmann, Rudolf. ‡ (Herm) ET 1973. One of this scholar's last publications (completed 1967). Quite slim (115pp. plus bibliography), radically critical, and not all that influential at this stage, though at one time it was. Don't bother with it, unless you are an advanced student deeply engaging the question of where Johannine scholarship has come from. Bultmann has now been replaced in the series; see Strecker below.

✓ **Burdick, Donald W.** 1985. One of the largest evangelical works (475pp.) on John's Epistles. Has a number of good points and is a good value in pb, but it cannot be among the top choices. Note: this work should be distinguished from his earlier, much briefer work (also) for Moody Press.

Calvin, John, and Matthew Henry. *1, 2, 3 John* (CrossC) 1998. Better to consult the unedited commentaries online for free.

Candlish, Robert. *1 John* (GS) 1866. A full exposition by a 19th century Scottish pastor and professor. It was good to see the work get a new lease on life by being added to the GS series. [*SBET* Fall 95]. Now free online.

F Carson, Donald. (NIGTC). Will this ever appear? It would be cause for celebration.

F Ciampa, Roy E. (TNTC-R). Would replace Stott.

✓ Culpepper, R. Alan, and Paul N. Anderson, eds. ‡ *Communities in Dispute: Current Scholarship on the Johannine Epistles*, 2014. [*NovT* 58.3].

☆ Culy, Martin M. (BHGNT) 2004. One of the first in the series. A brief, worthy guide (155pp.) through the basics of lexical and grammatical analysis. Fledgling Greek students can learn exegesis well with it. [*EvQ* 1/07; *BL* 2006; *ExpTim* 9/06].

Derickson, Gary. (EEC) 2014. The second vol. in the series, after Varner on *James*, Derickson's exegesis of the Greek appears to be thoroughly researched, though not so wisely selective in whom he engages. He is hostile to Calvinism at points and pushes a Zane Hodges-style

"Absolutely Free" grace. Obedience, to Derickson, is not a test of life or evidence of justification (135). I'm puzzled by some statements: "it is possible for a regenerate person not
to know God personally, relationally" (137). I've hardly used this tome (760pp.).

Dodd, C. H. ‡ (Moffatt) 1946. A classic with all of Dodd's brilliance, but from an evangelical
perspective the theology is atrocious. "Wildly out of sympathy with the text," says Carson.
Still cited often; e.g., Campbell does so 14×.

Findlay, G. G. *Fellowship in Life Eternal*, 1909. A justly famous, old devotional study, to which
pastors have turned again and again. The same can be said for Law's book below. Findlay
only treats 1 John.

✓ Grayston, Kenneth. [𝓜], (NCB) 1984. Challenges the usual conclusion of modern scholarship
that the letters are a good bit later than the Fourth Gospel (12). Grayston is cited today
mainly for that original theory. Of interest to students rather than pastors. [*JETS* 9/85;
*ExpTim* 12/84; *Them* 1/86; *EvQ* 1/87].

✓ **Haas, C., M. deJonge, and J. L. Swellengrebel.** (UBS) 1972, rev. 1994. Marshall had high
praise for the first edition: "an extremely valuable book, useful to all students and not
merely to Bible translators." The revised edition is 214pp.

Harris, W. Hall. *1, 2, 3 John: Comfort and Counsel for a Church in Crisis*, 2003. From a Dallas
Seminary prof, this is an exegesis of the Greek text, published by Biblical Studies Press
(292pp.). I have not seen the work, which is praised in Glynn's *Survey*.

F Hill, Wesley. (ITC).

✓ Houlden, J. L. ‡ (BNTC) 1973, 2nd ed. 1994. Retains some value (something of a signpost along
the way), but it is not worth poring over. The tone is quite critical. As the Preface makes
clear, Houlden's revision does not "tinker with the body of the text." The updating is "an
essay of description and assessment" on two decades of scholarly developments (155–60).
[*JBL* 94.4].

☆ Jackman, David. (BST) 1988. An exposition which builds on Stott's TNTC (first edition). More
useful to the expositor than to the student.

☆ Johnson, Thomas. (NIBC) 1993. A fine work of about 180pp. which is more up-to-date than
Stott with regard to NT scholarship and more exegetical, but is not quite as helpful to the
expositor. For a compact exegesis, Rensberger is more rigorous and critical. [*Chm* 108.1;
*CRBR* 1994].

Jones, Peter Rhea. [𝓜], (S&H) 2009. Deciding "at the outset to ground my analysis in my
own exegesis primarily" (xv), Jones has less interaction with the scholarly literature. The
commentary has value and is of good length (294pp.), but at points I found the writing style
awkward (see Pastoral-Polemical, p.105). Jones is a mature pastor and former seminary
prof (McAfee), keenly interested in rhetoric and literary criticism. [*Int* 10/11].

☆ Kistemaker, Simon J. (NTC) 1986. See under James.

☆ Köstenberger, Andreas. *A Theology of John's Gospel and Letters*, 2009. See John's Gospel.

✓ Kysar, Robert. ‡ (Augsburg Commentary) 1986. [*JETS* 6/90].

☆ Law, Robert. *The Tests of Life*, 1909. See Findlay above. Stott mined this work and used Law's
idea that 1 John encourages readers to test themselves whether they have true life in Christ
(tests of love, doctrine, obedience). You will find Law more valuable than Findlay, and he
is free online.

✓ **Lieu, Judith M.** ‡ (NTL) 2008. Reasonably full (336pp.) and standing in the top rank of critical
commentaries. Especially welcome because there had been few excellent exegeses published
by either the critics or evangelicals since the mid-1980s. Lieu builds upon two notable
scholarly monographs: *The Second and Third Epistles of John: History and Background*
(1986) and *The Theology of the Johannine Epistles* (CUP, 1991) [*CRBR* 1993]. She presented
wise caveats regarding the dominant Brown thesis, and emerged as an authority on this

literature. (Lady Margaret's Professor of Divinity in Cambridge (2007–18), Lieu has been President of SNTS.) The book description gives her central thesis: "Each letter shows how an early Christian author responded to threats against authority by recourse to the correct teachings of the faith and a proper understanding of the relationship between Jesus and God. Together, these letters argue for a bond of unity among believers, based on fidelity to the truth of God." In line with the critics' consensus, she believes 1–3 John exhibit no signs of knowing the Fourth Gospel. [*JETS* 9/09; *ExpTim* 8/09; *Int* 7/09 (Kysar); *BL* 2010; *RelSRev* 9/10; *BSB* 6/12].

✓ Lieu, Judith M., and Martinus C. de Boer, eds. ‡ *The Oxford Handbook of Johannine Studies*, 2019. See under John's Gospel.

☆ Lloyd-Jones, D. Martyn. *Fellowship with God* (1993); *Walking with God* (1993); *Children of God* (1993); *The Love of God* (1994); *Life in God* (1994). This sermon series is well worth consideration. I am glad that the publisher, Crossway, put it all in one cheaper, fat (736pp.) vol., *Life in Christ* (2002).

☆ **Marshall, I. Howard.** (NICNT) 1978. A splendid commentary, though some take issue with Marshall's forthright Arminianism. (He was a Methodist minister, long on the faculty at Aberdeen, and regarded as an elder statesman of evangelical NT scholarship in Britain.) He writes with the pastor in mind, and this was the evangelical standard that pastors used alongside Stott's gem. The introduction disappoints some conservatives in that he states his uncertainty about the author's identity. At least he believes that the three came from the same hand. This vol. is still valuable to students for its full survey of introductory issues—Smalley referred his own readers to it (1984, p.xxi). Marshall also wrote magisterial commentaries on Luke and the Pastoral Epistles, and a fine TNTC on Acts. [*WTJ* Fall 79; *JBL* 99.4; *EvQ* 4/79].

F   Martin, Michael. (EBTC)?

F   Mburu, Elizabeth. (WBC-R). To replace Smalley.

     McDermond, J. E. (BCBC) 2011. Thoughtful Anabaptist exposition.

F   McNutt, Jennifer Powell, ed. *1–2 Peter, 1–3 John, Jude* (RCS).

✓ Moloney, Francis J. ‡ *Letters to the Johannine Circle: 1–3 John*, 2020. Concise commentary, commissioned by the Catholic Biblical Association. [*Int* 4/23].

✓ Moyise, Steve. ‡ *The Later NT Writers and Scripture*, 2012. See under Acts.

☆ Ngewa, Samuel. (NCCS) 2019. The author is a veteran, beloved professor in Kenya and has previously published expositions of John's Gospel, Galatians, and the Pastorals.

✓ Nienhuis, David R., and Robert W. Wall. *Reading the Epistles of James, Peter, John, and Jude as Scripture*, 2013. See under James.

☆ O'Donnell, Douglas Sean. *1–3 John* (REC) 2015. Among volumes of (scholarly) sermons on these letters, O'Donnell should be counted especially rewarding. He has a fine theological mind, excellent training, and a knack for applying the Bible's message in a searching way (200pp.). Students will pass this by.

F   Ok, Janette H. (NICNT-R). Would replace Marshall.

✓ **Painter, John.** ‡ (SacP) 2002. Recognized especially for its lengthy introduction—over a quarter of the 410-page vol.—and for his interpretation of the epistles as reflecting a polemical situation within the Johannine community. He dialogues with Brown a good bit in the technical "Notes." More of a literary and historical commentary than a theological one. Preachers will likely find less to assist them here. [*CBQ* 10/03; *Int* 7/03].

✓ **Parsenios, George L.** [𝓜], (Paideia) 2014. A 165-page exegesis from a former prof at Princeton Seminary, now at St. Vladimir's Seminary, that appears to be well-done. He sees the Gospel and Letters as from the same hand(s), with the latter interpreting the former. [*JSNT* 37.5; *BSac* 10/17].

Plummer, Alfred. (Cambridge Greek Testament) 1886. Reprinted from time to time. But if you want one of the older works, pick up Westcott.

Plummer, Robert L., and E. Roderick Elledge. (EGGNT) 2024. I have yet to see it.

Porter, Stanley E., and Andrew K. Gabriel, eds. *Johannine Writings and Apocalyptic: An Annotated Bibliography*, 2013.

✓ Rainbow, Paul A. *Johannine Theology: The Gospel, the Epistles, and the Apocalypse*, 2014. See under John.

✓ **Rensberger, David.** ‡ (ANTC) 1997. Among the leading compact critical exegeses and shows the influence of Brown's thesis. Of special interest to students. More directed toward meeting the expositor's need is the next entry. [*Int* 1/99].

Rensberger, David. ‡ (WestBC) 2001. A slim vol. of only 130pp., this work probably will not be a preference among evangelicals because of its critical theological orientation. Rensberger is sometimes out of sympathy with the text, and his adoption of the Martyn/Brown thesis, I find, makes application of the epistles' message today more difficult. [*Them* Spr/Sum 02; *ExpTim* 8/02; *SwJT* Spr 02; *RelSRev* 4/02].

F Root, Michael. (Brazos).

Ross, Alexander. (retired NICNT) 1954. Replaced by Marshall and long o/p.

✓ **Schnackenburg, Rudolf.** ‡ 1984, ET 1992. Like fellow scholar Brown, Schnackenburg is a critical Catholic who produced in-depth commentaries on the Gospel of John and the Epistles. Both scholars moved left since they first began commenting on the Johannine Literature, the late Brown more so. Schnackenburg was also more conservative than Brown to begin with. This exceptionally fine scholarly work, translated out of the German (Herders series), is 302pp. This is Childs's first choice and is given high marks by Carson and Yarbrough. It will find its way into more students' hands than pastors'. I bought it. [*Int* 1/94; *JETS* 9/96; *BSac* 7/93].

☆ **Schuchard, Bruce G.** (ConcC) 2012. Quite the hefty vol. (about 750pp.). There is extensive research behind it and constant interaction with the likes of Yarbrough, Lieu, Brown, Schnackenburg, etc.—the lengthy quotes and number of footnotes were at times distracting to me. The discussion of grammar in the "Textual Notes" is extremely thorough and granular (e.g., 13pp. and 113 footnotes on 4:1–6). Like Grayston, he dates the letters earlier than the Fourth Gospel. An Amazon review gripes about all the Greek sentence diagraming, but one can put greater stock in Yarbrough's praise for the work's usefulness to both students and preachers. [*CBQ* 1/15; *BSac* 7/16].

✓ Sloyan, G. S. ‡ *Walking in the Truth: Perseverers and Deserters—The First, Second, and Third Letters of John*, 1995. A very slim work in the series NT in Context.

☆ **Smalley, Stephen S.** [*M*], (WBC) 1984, rev. 2007. A solid, respectable vol. by a scholar at home in the Johannine literature. So much was to be learned from the 1984 work, which began to show its age. Though I preferred Brown in some ways, I was always convinced that Smalley was more useful to the pastor, in part because WBC was more manageable at half the length. Students appreciated Smalley for his extensive interaction with the many works available in the early 1980s on these epistles in all the languages. It was happy news to get a thoroughly revised edition (xxxi + 376pp.). At the same time, I regret that he still pushes the Johannine Community interpretation like he does. He "remain[s] convinced that the Johannine corpus . . . enshrines the history of a volatile community, gathering in some sense around John the Apostle, the Beloved Disciple, and that it is possible to trace the story of his church from the Apocalypse, through the Gospel, and thence to the Epistles" (viii). I wish he'd taken opportunity to interact with Strecker, Klauck, and Kruse in the new edition. See Smalley under John's Gospel and Revelation. Was Silva's first choice years ago. Yarbrough replaced this on my list. [*WTJ* Fall 86; *RTR* 9/85; *JBL* 106.1; *EvQ* 4/87; *JETS* 3/86]. See Mburu above.

✓ Smith, D. Moody. ‡ (I) 1991. This author has long been a noted contributor to Johannine scholarship, and some students may wish to consult this shorter work (155pp.)—I wish he had written twice as much. Smith (†2016) had been under contract to write the ICC. See also his commentary on John's Gospel. [*CRBR* 1993].

✓ **Strecker, Georg.** ‡ (Herm) 1989, ET 1996. Replaced Bultmann in both KEK and Hermeneia; Strecker studied under him at Marburg. This is a translation of a rigorous, radical, historical-critical vol., and extends to somewhat over 300 large pages. Compare this technical exegesis with the more accessible and rewarding Schnackenburg. Advanced students will use Strecker, but not pastors. (The latter will think the world is turned upside down when Strecker argues the Presbyter had nonorthodox teaching and "Diotrephes . . . stands closer to the orthodox side" [263].) While praising many features of this demanding commentary (e.g., the wealth of 19 excursuses), Grayston wonders if scholars should hold off producing such works until the whole corpus of Qumran material has been examined (Strecker does little in that area). [*JETS* 6/99; *JTS* 10/97 (Grayston); *Bib* 74.1; *JBL* Win 00].

✓ **Streett, Daniel R.** *They Went Out from Us: The Identity of the Opponents in First John,* 2011. [*BBR* 22.4; *CBQ* 4/13; *JSNT* 34.5; *RTR* 8/12; *JETS* 6/12].

  Thatcher, Tom. (EBCR) 2006. Replaces Barker in the earlier EBC. It fits the bill as a brief exegesis (125pp.), but worryingly has a single bibliographical entry later than 1992.

  Thomas, John Christopher. *1 John, 2 John, 3 John* (PentC) 2004. [*ExpTim* 4/06; *Anvil* 22.4 (Smalley)].

☆ **Thompson, Marianne Meye.** [𝓜], (IVPNT) 1992. A useful 168-page commentary, written with pastors in mind, including both exegesis and application (with preaching-style illustrations). The interpretive work has good research behind it, but the application (often the truly hard work of preaching) is less useful. Perhaps she comes off sounding too much like an academic. A solid representative of the series. [*Them* 5/94; *Chm* Spr 95].

☆ Van Neste, Ray. "1, 2, 3 John" in *Hebrews–Revelation* (ESVEC) 2018. See Johnson under Hebrews.

✓ **Wahlde, Urban C. von.** ‡ *The Gospel and Letters of John* (ECC) 3 vols., 2010. See under John's Gospel. The commentary on the letters is 434pp.

✓ **Watson, Duane F.** ‡ (NCBC) 2024. Shines as a briefer (210-page), less technical, rhetorically oriented exegesis. The focus on rhetoric (how the author of the letters seeks to persuade recipients) provides a different angle in analysis, complementing other commentaries. Watson is influenced by Brown as he construes a conflict within the community addressed. The writer "struggled to convince [recipients] to adhere to the theology and ethics of the Johannine tradition against challenges posed by secessionists from their own ranks. His rhetorical arsenal is rich and varied." Watson makes plentiful use of Bultmann, but no use of Jobes, Kruse, or Yarbrough.

F Watson, Duane F. ‡ (RRA).

✓ **Westcott, B. F.** 1902. "A classic of lasting value" (Childs). He comments on the Greek text. Pastors of several generations relied heavily on Westcott, which was reprinted often—the latest was Wipf & Stock in 2001—but it is now free online.

F Wilder, Terry L. (EGGNT). He is also doing 2 Peter–Jude for the series.

  Williamson, Rick. *1, 2, & 3 John: A Commentary in the Wesleyan Tradition,* 2010.

☆ **Witherington, Ben, III.** *Letters and Homilies for Hellenized Christians: Vol. I: A Socio-Rhetorical Commentary on Titus, 1–2 Timothy, and 1–3 John,* 2006.

F Yieh, John. ‡ (Illum).

NOTES: (1) D. Moody Smith, "The Epistles of John: What's New Since Brooke's ICC in 1912?" *ExpTim* 120.8 (2009): 373–84. (2) There are two review-essays by Klaus Scholtissek in *CurBS* 6 (1998) and 9 (2001), and they pay special attention to German works. (3) Matthew Jensen, "The Structure and Argument of I John: A Survey of Proposals," *CBR* 12.2 (2014): 194–215.

# JUDE
NOTE: See 2 Peter above.

✓ **Bateman, Herbert W., IV.** (EEC) 2015 digital, 2017. An enormous conservative tome, discussing the Greek text (including a fair bit of valuable text-critical discussion), the historical and religious background, theology, and preaching/devotional points. The author earned a PhD at Dallas Seminary, has decades of teaching experience, and wrote Kregel's *Interpreting the General Letters* (2013) [*CBQ* 10/15]. He is convinced that Jude is a condemnation specifically of the Judean Zealots; not all of Bateman's readers are so convinced. Count this as valuable to students and preachers, especially those who are assiduous (approx. 500pp.). [*BBR* 29.1; *JETS* 12/18 (Lockett); *JSNT* 41.5].

✓ Bauckham, Richard J. [𝓜], *Jude and the Relatives of Jesus in the Early Church*, 1990. A follow-up to the masterful WBC on 2 Peter/Jude and his study of James.

Benton, John. *Slandering the Angels: The Message of Jude* (Welwyn) 1999. I have not seen this, but it is said to be about 190pp. in length, which is substantial indeed for this epistle. Pastors might consider Benton.

✓ **Brosend, William.** ‡ *James and Jude* (NCBC) 2004.

✓ Charles, J. Daryl. *Literary Strategy in the Epistle of Jude*, 1993. A significant evangelical study. See Charles (EBCR) and Waltner under 2 Peter.

Jenkyn, William. *Jude*, 1652. Manton self-consciously built on this Puritan work, which he regarded as exceptional. Jenkyn has been reprinted but is free online.

Jones, P. R. *The Epistle of Jude as Expounded by the Fathers*, 2001.

✓ Landon, Charles. *A Text-Critical Study of the Epistle of Jude*, 1996.

✓ Lockett, Darian R. See the works listed above under "James."

✓ Lyle, Kenneth R. *Ethical Admonition in the Epistle of Jude*, 1998.

☆ Manton, Thomas. *Jude* (GS) 1658. Extends to almost 400pp. in typical Puritan fashion. Those who readily profit from Puritan writings are encouraged to look up this beautifully bound vol., reprinted in 1989. Now free online too. "Full of deep application," says *Evangel* [Sum 90]. I consider the scaled-down, modern language version of Manton's *Jude* in the Crossway Classics edition (1999) to be very useful.

F   McNutt, Jennifer Powell, ed. *1–2 Peter, 1–3 John, Jude* (RCS).

✓ **Painter, John, and David deSilva.** ‡ *James and Jude* (Paideia) 2012. See James above. More accurately, deSilva is conservatively critical [𝓜]; see his book, *The Jewish Teachers of Jesus, James, and Jude* (2012).

Plummer, Alfred. *General Epistles of St. James and St. Jude* (EB) 1891. Still cited in the literature and free online.

✓ Reese, Ruth Anne. ‡ *Writing Jude: The Reader, the Text, and the Author*, 2000. This dissertation, with its reader-response criticism, led to the THC commentary on 2 Peter and Jude. I confess I learned less here about Jude, as Reese invited much reflection on "the openness and possibilities of language" (158). There seemed to be more Barthes, Foucault, Freud, and Lacan than NT study. [*BibInt* 12.4].

✓ Robinson, Alexandra. ‡ *Jude on the Attack: A Comparative Analysis of the Epistle of Jude, Jewish Judgment Oracles, and Greco-Roman Invective*, 2018. A solid Macquarie PhD, published in LNTS. [*CBQ* 10/19; *JETS* 3/19; *JSNT* 41.5].

☆ Saarinen, Risto. *The Pastoral Epistles with Philemon & Jude* (Brazos) 2008. See under Pastorals.

✓ Wasserman, Tommy. *The Epistle of Jude: Its Text and Transmission*, 2006. A stunningly thorough study of text-critical issues. [*CBQ* 7/07; *BBR* 18.1; *BL* 2008; *NovT* 50.3; *ExpTim* 5/07; *Them* 5/08]. Earlier we had Charles Landon, *A Text-Critical Study of the Epistle of Jude* (1996).

✓  Watson, Duane F. ‡ *Invention, Arrangement, and Style: Rhetorical Criticism of Jude and 2 Peter*, 1988. See under 2 Peter.

✓  Webb, Robert L., and Peter H. Davids, eds. ‡ *Reading Jude with New Eyes: Methodological Reassessments in the Letter of Jude*, 2008. [*ExpTim* 7/09; *BL* 2010]. *Them* 47.1

✓  Wilson, William Renay, II. *Jude's Apocalyptic Eschatology as Theological Exclusivism*, 2021. [*Them* 47.1].

☆  **Witherington, Ben, III.** *Letters and Homilies for Jewish Christians: A Socio-Rhetorical Commentary on Hebrews, James and Jude*, 2007.

# REVELATION

NOTE: I hesitate to make strong recommendations on Revelation. There is a wide range of interpretations, and one's own eschatological views can influence value-judgments. Some key approaches are (1) preterist: Revelation points to its immediate historical context and is mostly already fulfilled; (2) historicist: Revelation predicts the whole course of Christian history; (3) futurist: Revelation is primarily fulfilled in the final events of history—there are both simpler and wildly extreme interpretive positions here; and (4) idealist: Revelation is a symbolic portrayal of the struggle between God and Satan, not so tied to historical events. Also, there are many scholars today who, in emphasizing the apocalyptic genre, argue that Revelation is more an encouragement and witness to Christian endurance in the face of imperial Roman and cultural pressure/persecution. I believe you can best use this section if you know my position. While taking the prophetic character of the book seriously (1:3), I cannot take a strictly futurist approach. The highly symbolic character of the apocalyptic genre present here—which ironically *conceals* as much as it *reveals*—makes me very cautious about details and inclined to sympathize somewhat with idealist interpretations. (A similar mixed position is taken by Beasley-Murray, A. Johnson, Ladd, Morris, Mounce, and Osborne.) Still, I am compelled by my own exegesis of Rev 20 to take a historic premillennial stance. I try to evaluate the works available without much reference to my own convictions. As it falls out, two of the six full-length recommendations are amil, one is premil, one is progressive dispensational, one is hesitant to decide, another (Schreiner) propounds what seems a novel view, and a final one (Paul) is standoffish about applying a doctrinal system. All have been praised by scholars of every stripe. All are notable for sensitivity to the book's tension between apocalyptic and the prophetic tradition, both of which impacted 1st century Jews and Christians. Those unfamiliar with apocalyptic might digest George Ladd's article in *ISBE, Revised*. (For more in-depth study there is a bibliography above, following Daniel.) It is best to avoid the plethora of fanciful works which view Revelation as a forecast of imminent world events (esp. in the Middle East), seemingly written for 20th and now 21st century Americans, with scant relevance to the early church. Would that more people heeded the ancient advice of Irenaeus: "It is . . . more certain, and less hazardous to await the fulfillment of the prophecy, than to be making surmises, and casting about for names that may present themselves" (*Against All Heresies*, 5.30.3). Here is a challenge for all to take to heart: "If responsible interpreters do not make the effort to set forth the message of Revelation in terms that are faithful both to Scripture and to our own times, this task goes by default to others" (Boring, p.59).

★  **Beale, G. K.** (NIGTC) 1999. His published PhD led us to expect a fine piece of work, and this is a treat, especially for those who love the Greek NT. It can be regarded as the best, most exacting evangelical exegesis. A pleasant surprise is that Beale provides a good bit more theology than we are used to receiving from this series. His approach is "eclecticism, or a redemptive-historical form of modified idealism" (48). The best feature of this work is its treatment of Revelation's OT background; I expected this. (In my opinion, though, Beale fails to do full justice to the influence of Ezekiel.) Compare with Aune's set. [*Them* 2/00; *TJ* Spr 00; *JBL* Spr 00; *WTJ* Spr 00; *Bib* 81.3; *Int* 1/00; *RTR* 12/00; *RelSRev* 7/00; *HBT* 12/02 (Aune)]. Many pastors are scared off by the price and size of this tome (1200pp.). There is a remedy, however. Unless you are an academic, you might consider buying *Revelation: A Shorter Commentary* (2015) in pb, which is still quite full (over 500pp.) but does not treat the Greek directly. In some respects it is the clearer work. [*Chm* Aut 16; *ExpTim* 11/16; *JSNT* 38.5]. Students note another of Beale's titles, *John's Use of the OT in Revelation* (1998).

★ **Fanning, Buist M.** (ZECNT) 2020. Far more than simply the most learned, widely useful dispensational treatment. The interpretive scheme is somewhat eclectic but mainly influenced by progressive dispensationalism (cf. Saucy, Blaising, Bock); see pp.40–49 with its more sophisticated discussion of typology. Fanning interacts constantly with other viewpoints, including important German scholarship (e.g., Lichtenberger, Satake). The Dallas professor emeritus steps away from a *strictly* literal approach (cf. Robert Thomas) and pays good attention to the heavy symbolism, while also highlighting the prophetic (1:3), futurist aspects. He reads the book as unfolding chronologically, not in recapitulation. Fanning has an enviable knowledge of Scripture more broadly, a keen theological mind, an irenic temperament, and an astute grasp of Greek—his Oxford DPhil on verbal aspect, published in 1990, was groundbreaking. The discourse analysis alone may be worth the price of the book. He does not simply "go over the same ground" as earlier commentators and so can be stimulating (where one agrees or disagrees). With regard to introductory matters, he does not think the Apostle John authored the book (28). Building from this, he believes "the theology of Rev is distinctive enough so that treatment of Rev apart from the theology of the Gospel and Epistles is the best option" (568). Students will especially value Fanning, Paul, and Schreiner, not forgetting Koester, for their more current bibliographies; my other recommended works are more than twenty years old. [*DenvJ* 45.3; *Them* 45.3].

★ Johnson, Dennis. *The Triumph of the Lamb*, 2001. This is a suggestive exposition with an amillennial perspective and a sensitivity to biblical-theological themes, anticipated in earlier Scripture and developed in Revelation. (Goldsworthy and Poythress use a similar approach.) I expected Johnson would be good, but it's better than I had hoped. For another very useful commentary of his, see Acts.

★ Keener, Craig S. (NIVAC) 2000. Shows insight and learning—the Author Index extends 10pp., "Other Ancient Sources" to 16pp. (He previously wrote the *IVP Bible Background Commentary*.) This is a book for students and expositors. In the exegesis sections (Original Meaning), there is good interaction with Aune and Beale. Theologically, he likes to cut the difference between premillennialists and amillennialists. Though there is not always the maturity of reflection and synthesis one finds elsewhere in NIVAC, Keener does well in stimulating the preacher to think hard about the rather complex move from interpreting Revelation responsibly to applying the book's message helpfully. He was given a most difficult task and did it well. Though a strong partisan on some theological points, Keener here is very fair to various schools of interpretation. [*RelSRev* 7/03]. More of the best preaching helps are Hamilton, Gardner, Michaels, Poythress, Phillips, and Wilcock. Advanced students, less interested in homiletics, can bypass Johnson and Keener to head straight for Koester, with Aune and Bauckham's books close at hand too.

★ **Mounce, Robert.** (NICNT) 1977, rev. 1998. Once the most scholarly of the evangelical works I suggested for purchase. The first edition was the result of fifteen years' intensive research on the book, and with the revision "a good piece of work has been turned into an even better one" (I. Howard Marshall). This or Beale's "Shorter Commentary" would be a fine first choice for the average pastor. In Beale's 1999 tome we have an excellent detailed commentary on the Greek, but this work by Mounce contains in the notes some close exegesis of the original and some text criticism for those who don't want to take out a bank loan to purchase NIGTC. Mounce takes a historic premillennial position, but is fair and appreciative in dealing with the amillennial point of view. See deSilva. [*CTJ* 13.2; *JBL* 9/79; *EvQ* 7/78, 7/99; *TJ* Spr 00; *RelSRev* 4/01].

★ **Paul, Ian.** (TNTC-R) 2018. A top-notch replacement vol. for the sensible, dependable Morris. Paul is wide-read (though his learning is worn lightly), insightful, adept at sifting through exegetical options, and takes a somewhat more scholarly approach to the text (in the sense of being critically engaged). His is one of the less conservative TNTC. The commentary is fuller than Morris, with Paul's 56-page Introduction and 315pp. of exegesis. The handling of 20:1–10 impressed me; a quick example of his fine work is how he guides modern readers away from misconstruing the ancient use of locks and keys (325). [*NovT* 60.4; *EvQ* 4/19].

★ **Schreiner, Thomas R.** (BECNT-R) 2023. Replaces Osborne, which is surprising given the quality and continued usefulness of the earlier vol. Schreiner (820pp.) is of similar length. Preceding this were Schreiner's exposition in ESVEC below (2018) and *The Joy of Hearing: A Theology of the Book of Revelation* (2021) [*JETS* 12/22]. Both the exegesis and theological exposition are learned, rich, fair-minded, clear, and accessible (especially for a commentary on the Greek). He gives extensive attention to others' interpretations; e.g., I found about 125 citations of Satake's German commentary, and nearly 1000 among Aune, Beale, and Koester. His 65-page intro argues for authorship by the Apostle John (12) and a recapitulatory structure instead of "a linear ongoing narrative" (62). Over the decades Schreiner has "advocated both premillennialism and amillennialism" but found problems with each. He now defends "new-creation millennialism" as a persuasive via media "that retains the best features of amillennialism and the best features of premillennialism" (677; cf. Mealy below). I predict that many will happily term this their first pick. See his major works on Romans, Galatians, Hebrews, 1–2 Peter and Jude.

★ **Weima, Jeffrey A. D.** *The Sermons to the Seven Churches of Revelation: A Commentary and Guide*, 2021. A lengthy and astute commentary (275pp.) by a fine Reformed NT scholar, known as an expert on ancient epistolary conventions and structuring (see "Pauline Studies"). He challenges the "letters" classification. As a bonus there are (intellectually demanding) sample sermons concluding each chapter; "this book models the important move from the study to the pulpit or classroom" (1). Boxall writes [*ExpTim* 3/23], "Weima's reflection on the subtlety of idolatry is especially well done." [*BBR* 32.4; *CTJ* 11/22; *Int* 4/23; *JETS* 3/23; *JSNT* 44.5]. Surely the best historical study on these chapters has been Hemer (below), superseding the old work by W. M. Ramsay. More critical is Worth (below). See Hort (below) and Archbishop Trench (6th ed. 1897) for classics on the Greek. For expositions of the letters, see the notes on Stott below.

Akin, Daniel L. *Exalting Jesus in Revelation* (CCE) 2016.

✓ Alford, Henry. *Alford's Greek Testament*, 1875. A seminal treatment which caused the premillenarian ranks to swell in the 19th century. Alford continues to be quoted by commentators, especially his argument on the two resurrections in vol. IV, p.732. Free online.

✓ Allen, Garrick V. *Manuscripts of the Book of Revelation*, 2020. [*ExpTim* 11/21]. Previously CUP published his PhD: *The Book of Revelation and Early Jewish Textual Culture* (2017), which examined the use of OT texts in Revelation [*JETS* 6/19].

✓ Allen, Garrick V., Ian Paul, and Simon P. Woodman, eds. ‡ *The Book of Revelation: Currents in British Research on the Apocalypse*, 2015. [*JSNT* 39.5].

✓ **Aune, David E.** [𝓜], (WBC) 3 vols., 1997–1998. From his journal articles I anticipated it would be thorough, very scholarly, moderately critical, "linguistically well-informed" (Porter), and have a few idiosyncratic views. I guessed right. Go to Aune and Beale for first-rate exegeses that will long serve the academic world; I believe you will judge Beale to be the better balanced and more judicious. Also, Beale is far more interested in theology. Aune, by contrast, joins those who "bracket theology" (xlviii). Boring considers the commentary's most helpful contribution to be where Aune shares "his vast knowledge of the Hellenistic world and its literature." This 3-vol. work (nearly 1600pp.) is quite a foil to Beale, who emphasizes rather the OT background of the Apocalypse. One could wish for more in the introduction on history of interpretation. Need I say this is more of a scholar's reference set than a tool for the working pastor? Students can make excellent use of his vol. of essays listed previously under Apocalyptic Literature. Aune reportedly plans a revised WBC. [*ExpTim* 11/99; *RelSRev* 10/98, 7/00, 10/00; *Bib* 79.4; *JTS* 10/99; *NovT* 42.2; *Int* 7/00; *Chm* Spr 01; *JETS* 9/00].

✓ Barr, David L. ‡ *Tales of the End: A Narrative Commentary on the Book of Revelation*, 1998. Something of a postmodern take. [*RelSRev* 7/00]. See also the two SBL collections of essays that Barr edited: *Reading the Book of Revelation: A Resource for Students* (2003) [*BL* 2005; *CBQ* 10/04] and *The Reality of Apocalypse* (2006), composed of cutting-edge studies on intertextuality, genre, rhetoric, political readings, and ritual [*ExpTim* 8/08].

Battle, Michael. ‡ *Heaven on Earth: God's Call to Community in the Book of Revelation*, 2017. From WJK, by an Episcopal moral theologian associated with Desmond Tutu.

✓ Bauckham, Richard. [𝓜], *The Theology of the Book of Revelation*, 1993. [*JETS* 9/97; *CBQ* 7/94]. Coming out about the same time was his book of essays, *The Climax of Prophecy: Studies on the Book of Revelation* (1993), which Ian Paul once termed "perhaps the most significant English-language work on Revelation in recent years" [*BSB* 9/06]. These two are still productive goldmines.

☆ **Beasley-Murray, George R.** [𝓜], (NCB) 1974. Brilliant for its time and mildly critical, with more of a stress on apocalyptic than prophecy. This "richly suggestive" (Martin) commentary offered a historic premillennial interpretation of ch. 20. In early editions of this guide I always recommended buying both NCB and NICNT. Unfortunately, this good book has become harder to find. [*EvQ* 7/75].

✓ **Beckwith, I. T.** 1919. One of the best old scholarly commentaries. More conservative than Charles. Still to be consulted for work in the Greek text, and now free online. His discussion of the history of interpretation remains quite useful (318–36).

Beeke, Joel R. (LCEC) 2016. Less a commentary than a lengthy (600-page) book of sermons on the KJV, by the President of Puritan Reformed Seminary. [*CTJ* 11/18].

✓ Blackwell, Ben C., John K. Goodrich, and Jason Maston, eds. *Reading Revelation in Context: John's Apocalypse and Second Temple Judaism*, 2019. Another in a series; see Blackwell under Hebrews. [*JETS* 6/20; *JSNT* 42.5; *Them* 45.2].

✓ **Blount, Brian K.** ‡ (NTL) 2009. The author was previously a pastor, prof at Princeton Seminary, and President of Union Seminary-PSCE, Richmond. He writes as a moderate critic who sees connections between the courageous faith of the early church, with her nonviolent protest against Roman idolatry and injustice, and the experience of African American Christians. Regarding historical setting, Blount dates the book to ca. 95 and contends that persecution under Domitian was at the time a real, but as yet largely unrealized, threat to Christians in the empire. [*Int* 7/10; *ExpTim* 2/10; *BL* 2010; *BTB* 5/11]. An earlier politically engaged reading was *Can I Get a Witness? Reading Revelation through African American Culture* (2005) [*ThTo* 1/06].

Boring, M. Eugene. ‡ (I) 1989. Treats Revelation in 240pp. A careful and well-received exposition which is widely used in more liberal pastoral circles. Professor Boring is fond of the universal salvation idea. [*Int* 4/91; *CRBR* 1991]. See his other major commentaries on Mark and Thessalonians.

✓ **Boxall, Ian.** [𝓜], (BNTC-R) 2006. A solid replacement for Caird's stellar vol. There is a tendency in NT scholarship to downplay any severe Roman persecution as the contextual key to the message of Revelation (e.g., Thompson's ANTC). Boxall gives greater weight to that pressing concern within the faithful community. The author is a mildly critical Oxford scholar and a most gifted exegete. [*JETS* 9/07]. A previous publication was *Revelation Vision and Insight: An Introduction to the Apocalypse* (2002). More recently, we have heard of a forthcoming ICC, replacing Charles.

✓ **Bratcher, R. G., and H. A. Hatton.** (UBS) 1993. A fairly full vol. of 352pp., called "invaluable" by Thompson. [*CRBR* 1995].

✓ **Brighton, Louis.** (ConcC) 1999. The author is Emeritus Professor of NT at Concordia Seminary, St. Louis. This is a full-scale, well-rounded technical commentary (673pp.) from a conservative Lutheran perspective. He later published the Concordia Popular Commentary (2009) [*CBQ* 7/11].

Brooks, Richard. *The Lamb Is All the Glory* (Welwyn) 1986.

✓ Buchanan, George Wesley. ‡ (Mellen Biblical Commentary) 1993. A huge scholarly commentary of nearly 700pp., which pays special attention to Revelation's relationship to other texts. Students may never see this o/p book (originally $140) without recourse to interlibrary loan. [*SwJT* Spr 98].

Bullinger, E. W. 1909. A large work reprinted by Kregel in 1990—why I don't know. It deserves to be buried. Though a scholar of some repute long ago, Bullinger and his "ultra-dispensationalism" were vigorously rejected by dispensationalists: Ironside called it "an absolutely Satanic perversion of the truth."

✓ Burr, David, ed. (BMT) 2019. Focuses more narrowly on Franciscan interpretation in the 12th and 13th centuries. [*ExpTim* 8/20; *CBQ* 1/21].

✓ **Caird, G. B.** ‡ (retired BNTC) 1966, rev. 1984. Similar to NCB in its interpretive approach, but slightly more critical. Caird's commentary has been one of the most highly regarded works on Revelation. He was an incisive exegete indeed. The drawback is that it is now so dated. See Boxall. [*JBL* 86.2].

F   Carson, D. A. (Pillar-R). I expect this is a long way off. See Hughes below.

✓ **Charles, R. H.** ‡ (ICC) 2 vols., 1920. The extraordinarily learned Charles produced an enduring classic with this mine of technical information for students. Though it will be consulted for scholarly work well into the 21st century, the set "has nothing to offer the preacher" [*BSB* 9/06]. Charles was groundbreaking in interpreting Revelation using all his background studies in Daniel, OT Apocrypha, and Pseudepigrapha. See also Swete. Free online. Note the forthcoming Boxall.

Chilton, David. *The Days of Vengeance*, 1987. A large work offering a postmillennial exposition with a Reconstructionist flavor (radical preterist). Chilton is not generous in handling opposing viewpoints, and his dogmatism in dating the Apocalypse prior to Jerusalem's fall (AD 70) flies in the face of too much evidence. Still, there is theological insight in this commentary and it presses the overall point that Christ's ultimate victory ought to mean everything to the Christian today. Chilton substantially moderated his theonomic views before his untimely death.

✓ Clouse, Robert, ed. *The Meaning of the Millennium: Four Views*, 1977. The Hoekema and Ladd interaction is top-notch. Similar books are: Pate, ed., *Four Views on the Book of Revelation* (1998); Bock, ed., *Three Views on the Millennium and Beyond* (1999); and Hultberg, ed., *Three Views on the Rapture* (2nd ed., 2010).

✓ Court, J. M. ‡ *Revelation*, 1994. This is an introduction, not a commentary, useful for reviewing developments in scholarship (especially continental European).

☆ Culy, Martin M. *The Book of Revelation: The Rest of the Story*, 2017. Not a commentary, but an intriguing study of the Seven Letters, their themes, and how the rest of the book might be heard or interpreted by the members of those churches of Asia Minor (265pp.). Culy has been a driving force behind, and editor of, BHGNT. [*JETS* 12/18].

F deSilva, David A. (NICNT-R). Would replace Mounce.

✓ **deSilva, David A.** *Seeing Things John's Way* (SRC) 2009. A mid-scale work (416pp.), focused upon "The Rhetoric of the Book of Revelation" (the subtitle), and aiming to explain the relevance of the Apocalypse to today's church. The strength of the Ashland professor's work is, as some might expect, more in the academic area of classical rhetorical-critical analysis. I find it less helpful for pulpit concerns of theological reflection and application. For more on where he positions himself regarding rhetorical approaches to Revelation, see "What Has Athens to Do with Patmos?" *CBR* 6 (2008): 256–89. [*CBQ* 4/12; *Int* 10/10; *JSNT* 33.5; *JETS* 12/10; *ExpTim* 11/10; *BibInt* 18.4; *DenvJ* 13; *RelSRev* 3/11]. More recent is *Discovering Revelation: Content, Interpretation, Reception* (2021), which does an impressive job covering the main introductory questions in the Discovering Biblical Texts series. [*JETS* 6/22; *CBQ* 7/22; *Int* 1/23]. For his other commentaries, see Hebrews and Galatians.

Durham, James. 1658. A 1000-page exposition, treasured by lovers of the Puritans, reprinted by Old Paths (2000), and now free online. Spurgeon recommended Durham's gospel "savour" more than his lines of interpretation. This author's *Song of Solomon* was also republished, but by Banner. [*CTJ* 11/01].

☆ Duvall, J. Scott. (TTC) 2014. Students familiar with Revelation scholarship will not learn much here, but Duvall is an attractive, clearly written, well-organized, conservative book for pastors (320pp.). He comes across as a born teacher. The approach is open to the text and where it leads, and is insightful on exegetical and theological questions. He frequently makes applications to daily life. I find the Illustrating the Text segments less helpful. In my opinion, unless the illustration is brilliant, it's best to leave it out and use the space for other purposes. (Isn't the best illustrative material usually the speaker's own?) [*BSac* 4/17].

Elliott, E. B. *Horæ Apocalypticæ*, 4 vols., 5th ed. 1862. The labor of the man's life (2500pp.). Odd in some respects, but called "the standard work" of Spurgeon's day.

✓ **Farrer, Austin M.** ‡ *The Rebirth of Images*, 1949; *The Revelation of St. John the Divine*, 1964. The latter is a penetrating, provocative commentary first published at Oxford's Clarendon Press, still useful to consult, though not a reliable guide. Caird says Farrer "first opened my eyes to John's use of the imagination and taught me to see in him both an exegete and a supreme literary artist" (v).

☆ **Fee, Gordon.** (NCCS) 2010. The author taught at Regent College, wrote many commentaries, and edited the NICNT series. As one would expect, Fee is learned and deliberate in taking up exegetical issues, but I argue that less research went into this work. Over the years I have come to have a higher opinion of his book here and his interpretive sagacity. His eschatological positioning seems a bit eclectic. [*CBQ* 7/12; *JTS* 4/14; *Int* 1/12; *JSNT* 34.5; *DenvJ* 14; *RTR* 8/15].

F Fisk, Bruce N. (EGGNT).

Ford, J. Massyngberde. ‡ (retired AB) 1975. One of the most startlingly eccentric commentaries—on a Bible book that has had more than its share. She says Revelation is the product of John the Baptist and his circle and is a decidedly Jewish Apocalypse, pre-Christian in parts. Wild and woolly ideas! Advanced students may wish to consult her work for its references to the DSS (many references incorrect, according to Carson) and church fathers. Yale replaced this with Koester. [*JBL* 9/76].

F   Friesen, Steven J. ‡ (Herm). Earlier he wrote the well-received *Imperial Cults and the Apocalypse of John: Reading Revelation in the Ruins* (OUP, 2001), which one can read alongside Kraybill. See Schüssler Fiorenza for the earlier announcement, which I now doubt.

☆   Gardner, Paul. (Focus) 2008. Simply one of the best (and least expensive) Reformed expositions of the book (310pp.). Written on the popular level, even sermonic, with an amillennial perspective.

Gentry, Kenneth L., Jr. *The Divorce of Israel: A Redemptive-Historical Interpretation*, 2 vols., 2023. The author pastored Presbyterian churches and has been publishing on Revelation for nearly four decades as a leading voice for postmillennialism. This gargantuan 1600-page commentary was, according to Gentry, due for release in September 2023, but I have not seen it. For another preterist commentary, see Leithart below. An earlier Gentry study was *Before Jerusalem Fell* (rev. 1998).

Glasson, T. F. 1965. Published by CUP.

☆   Goldsworthy, Graeme. *The Gospel in Revelation*, 1984. It is hard to think of a better book for Bible study groups than this 160-page theological guide. The author has an excellent background in biblical studies, especially the OT, and here uses the key of biblical theology to unlock the riches of Revelation. He makes the truths of Scripture exciting and practical for the Christian life. See the other books in his Trilogy (subsequently bound together): *Gospel and Wisdom* and *Gospel and Kingdom*.

González, Catherine Gunsalus, and Justo L. González. ‡ (WestBC) 1997. [*RelSRev* 10/98, 7/00].

Gorman, Michael J. [𝓜], *Reading Revelation Responsibly: Uncivil Worship and Witness, Following the Lamb into the New Creation*, 2011. On a popular level.

Gregg, Steve, ed. *Revelation: Four Views—A Parallel Commentary*, 1997.

Guthrie, Donald. *The Relevance of John's Apocalypse*, 1987. This fine book of lectures moves beyond the fine points of exegesis and questions of Revelation's meaning for the future to examine the practical relevance of the book for the church today.

☆   Hamilton, James M. (PTW) 2012. In some circles, full sermon series on Revelation are a rarity, perhaps due to preachers' fears of being unable to answer congregants' questions. (I myself preached only on the Seven Letters.) Hamilton has done a fine job in producing a 400-page vol. of sermons on chs. 1–22, which may stimulate many to commence a book-length exposition. He takes a historic premillennial approach (with an interest in biblical theology), but the book is edifying and useful to any evangelical pastor. Like all the best preaching, it can be engrossing. [*Them* 11/12; *RelSRev* 12/13].

✓   **Harrington, Wilfred.** ‡ (SacP) 1993. Exemplifies some of the best contemporary Catholic scholarship and is worth consulting by the student (270pp.). Compared with some other vols. in the series, this early entry is brief. Harrington believes the Apocalypse was not written during a severe persecution (cf. Thompson). [*SwJT* Spr 95; *CRBR* 1994; *ExpTim* 8/08].

✓   Hays, Richard B., and Stefan Alkier, eds. ‡ *Revelation and the Politics of Apocalyptic Interpretation*, 2012. From a conference at Duke. [*CBQ* 10/14; *JETS* 6/13].

✓   Heil, John Paul. ‡ 2014. A literary-critical commentary by a prof at Catholic University of America; Heil has produced a number of such and claims to find many chiastic structures. [*CBQ* 4/16].

☆   **Hemer, Colin J.** *The Letters to the Seven Churches of Asia in Their Local Setting*, 1986 (2001 reprint in pb). A great piece of historical scholarship which also serves the expositor's needs. Reading this may prompt the preacher to plan a series. See Weima above, Stott and Worth below. [*EvQ* 1/02; *SwJT* Spr 02; *RelSRev* 7/03].

Hendriksen, William. *More Than Conquerors*, 1939. One of his first books and has a different scheme of interpretation: recapitulation. This exposition has long been a favorite in Reformed circles. Idealist.

Henry, Matthew. (CrossC) 1999. The full commentary is free online.

Hoeksema, Herman, and Homer C. Hoeksema. *Behold, He Cometh!* 2nd ed. 2000. Large exposition out of the Protestant Reformed Church.

✓ Hort, F. J. A. [𝓜], *The Apocalypse of St. John I–III*, 1908. Rigorous exegesis; it is a pity he was unable to complete it.

Hoskins, Paul M. 2017. I have not seen it. [*Them* 42.3].

☆ Hughes, Philip E. (Pillar) 1991. About 250pp., this theological exposition is suggestive from the amillennial angle but not up to the standard he set in his Hebrews commentary. I think you will prefer Hughes to Hendriksen. For even better amillennial expositions, see Dennis Johnson and Kistemaker. Eerdmans let this go o/p; see Carson above for the future replacement. [*WTJ* Fall 92; *EvQ* 7/92; *CTJ* 4/91; *CRBR* 1992].

✓ Jauhiainen, Marko. ‡ *The Use of Zechariah in Revelation*, 2005. A Cambridge PhD.

☆ **Johnson, Alan F.** (EBCR) 2006. His EBC (1981) was one of the best in the NT section (200pp.) and offered a historic premillennial interpretation. The length of the new work is similar to the old. This remains one of the most useful shorter evangelical exegeses.

☆ Johnson, Darrell W. *Discipleship on the Edge: An Expository Journey through the Book of Revelation*, 2004. The author teaches pastoral theology at Regent College and here offers 412pp. of sermonic material. Stimulating, without question.

Kelly, Douglas F. (Mentor) 2012. Large vol. of sermons on the KJV. [*Them* 7/13].

✓ Kiddle, Martin. ‡ (Moffatt series) 1940. Continues to be consulted by scholars working on Revelation. An in-depth work, but not as valuable as its length might imply (450pp.).

✓ Kik, J. Marcellus. *Revelation Twenty, An Exposition*, 1955. There are fewer postmillennial commentaries, and this one is in the classic postmillennial mold. See also his *Eschatology of Victory* (1971). Those interested in a postmillennial work from the Christian Reconstruction camp should consult Chilton.

☆ **Kistemaker, Simon J.** (NTC) 2001. This highly theological, amillennial exposition has been used as a seminary textbook (over 600pp.). Years ago, I saluted Professor Kistemaker (†2017) for completing the series, which has proved its usefulness to the church. It was a huge task he undertook. [*Them* Aut 02; *JETS* 3/03; *Int* 1/03].

✓ Knight, Jonathan. ‡ (Read) 1999. [*ExpTim* 1/00; *Them* Spr 01; *WTJ* Spr 02].

✓ **Koester, Craig R.** ‡ (AYB-R) 2014. Replaces Ford, and written by the author of *Hebrews* in the series. This is masterful and most definitely a purchase recommendation for the scholarly pastor. Koester teaches at Luther Seminary and has the best critical introduction in print: *Revelation and the End of All Things* (2001, rev. 2018) [*ExpTim* 9/18; *CBQ* 7/19; *JSNT* 41.5; *RevExp* 2/19]. Scholars must take account of AYB, with its 120-page Introduction, 50-page bibliography, and 650pp. of exegesis in small type. Koester has a strong academic reputation and displays broad and deep learning as he treats the history of interpretation, historical issues (doubts the Apostle John wrote the Gospel, the Epistles, or Revelation, p.66), social setting, literary aspects, rhetoric, and the text. The commentary portion is impressively detailed, with much technical discussion, but also readable. Excellent use of ancient artifacts is made in interpreting the message (e.g., p.694f). His take? "I read Revelation as a forward-moving spiral in which scenes of conflict lead to celebration in heaven over and over again, until 'all is done' in New Jerusalem" (xiv). He offers more of an amillennial interpretation (786–88). After first being priced at $125 in hb, Koester is thankfully now available in pb. [*Them* 4/15; *ExpTim* 11/15; *BBR* 25.3; *CBQ* 1/18; *Int* 1/16].

✓ Koester, Craig R., ed. ‡ *The Oxford Handbook of the Book of Revelation*, 2020. [*ETL* 6/22; *CBQ* 4/23; *JETS* 6/22].

✓ Kraybill, J. N. ‡ *Imperial Cult and Commerce in John's Apocalypse*, 1996. A Mennonite perspective. More recent and accessible is *Apocalypse and Allegiance: Worship, Politics, and*

*Devotion in the Book of Revelation* (2010) [*CBQ* 10/11; *JETS* 6/11; *Them* 11/10]. Yet another treatment of the historical topic is the S. R. F. Price vol., *Rituals and Power: The Roman Imperial Cult in Asia Minor* (CUP, 1984).

Kuyper, Abraham. ET 1935. Full (350pp.) and one of the better old amillennial expositions for the pastor. Heavily theological, which one would expect from the great founder of, and theology prof at, the Free U. of Amsterdam.

☆ **Ladd, George E.** 1972. Relative to NCB and NICNT, Ladd has a greater stress on futurist aspects. But I hasten to add that he is famously a proponent of historic premillennialism, not dispensationalism. Many of his writings deal with eschatology. (Building very much on Ladd's foundation is Blomberg–Chung [eds.], *A Case for Historic Premillennialism* [2009] [*Them* 7/09].) This is a dependable commentary and a premillennial favorite, with a sharp eye for theological themes. Lots of preachers love this one and Wilcock's BST. [*WTJ* Spr 73; *EvQ* 1/75]. Reprinted in ECBC in 2018.

LaHaye, Tim. *Revelation Unveiled*, 1999. Popularizing old-style dispensationalism. With the author's name recognition, this sold like mad. See Michaels below.

✓ **Leithart, Peter J.** (ITC) 2 vols., 2018. Approx. 900pp. of heavily typological commentary, that ranges regularly all over the Bible and is often surprisingly informal, chatty, and pastoral. It's a wild ride, with "occasional, unsystematic, eccentric excursions into theology, history, sociology, economics, or whatever else the text brought to mind" (2:439). The preterist postmillennial scheme dominates. Leithart dates the Apocalypse to the AD 60s, and the bulk of the book prophesies cataclysmic events a few years later. He interprets the prophesied fall of 'Babylon' in ch. 18 as the Roman assault on Jerusalem in AD 70. "The harlot city Babylon, called Egypt and Sodom and compared with Tyre, is *Jerusalem*" (1:31). Replacing it is the new Jerusalem in 21:9–22:5, "the city that Christians now inhabit, the church of the millennial age" (2:439). [*Bib* 100.3; *Them* 43.3].

☆ Longman, Tremper, III. (TOTE) 2022. Given the density of OT allusions in Revelation, this is a welcome publication. The author revisits a favorite theme of his: the divine warrior. The mid-sized commentary (350pp.) is a help to preachers, but, according to one reviewer, "does not aim to give a contribution for an academic audience" (Gallusz [*JSNT* 45.5]). [*JETS* 9/22].

✓ Lupieri, Edmondo F. [𝓜], ET 2006. A fairly extensive exegetical work, translated from the Italian and published by Eerdmans.

MacArthur, John. 2 vols., 1999–2000. Still selling very well as a huge set of dispensational sermons (approx. 640pp.). See Matthew for a review of the series.

✓ Malina, Bruce J., and John J. Pilch. ‡ *A Social-Science Commentary on the Book of Revelation*, 2000. Published by Fortress. The authors take up many issues and interpretive methods scarcely used in more traditional commentaries. I found the appendix helpful for getting a quick view of the structural development of the Bible book and some of its more significant literary features. The line of interpretation (John as an astral prophet) is weird and forced. [*JR* 10/01; *RelSRev* 7/03].

Mangina, Joseph L. (Brazos) 2010. I have yet to use this book. [*BBR* 21.2; *CBQ* 1/12; *ExpTim* 1/11; *Them* 11/10; *BSac* 1/13].

☆ **Mathewson, David L.** (BHGNT) 2016. Supremely qualified to offer meticulous analysis of the difficult Greek here, Mathewson previously published *Verbal Aspect in the Book of Revelation* (2010). [*BSac* 7/18; *JSNT* 39.5]. I believe he has the BGW contract. Most recent is *A Companion to the Book of Revelation* (2020).

Mauro, Philip. *Things Which Soon Must Come to Pass*, 1925. A hefty conservative commentary (amillennial), often reprinted.

McKnight, Scot, with Cody Matchett. *Revelation for the Rest of Us*, 2023. Popular-level, yet a thoughtful presentation of the book's message and "divine politics, a view of government and power that subverts the sinful patterns of 'Babylon' today" (publisher's blurb).

✓ Mealy, J. Webb. [𝓜], *After the Thousand Years: Resurrection and Judgment in Revelation 20*, 1992. A Sheffield PhD with an intriguing new paradigm: "new-creation millennialism," positively explored by Schnabel (*JETS* 64:785–95) and Schreiner (BECNT above).

☆ **Michaels, J. Ramsey.** [𝓜], (IVPNT) 1997. The well-known scholar also published a fine introduction, *Interpreting the Book of Revelation* (Baker, 1992) [*CRBR* 1994]. The popularly styled IVPNT is well-done; I would like to see it get into the hands of many people tempted to get their eschatology from the *Left Behind* series. Here is a taste from *Interpreting*: "The purpose of preaching from Revelation is to evoke first wonder and then faithfulness to the slain Lamb, not to explain the book away or reduce it to a blueprint of the future. The preacher's task is to stand out of the way and let the book's images do their work" (146). Michaels joins those who view apocalyptic as an inadequate genre identification for Revelation. [*RelSRev* 7/00; *Chm* Win 06].

✓ Middleton, Paul. ‡ *The Violence of the Lamb*, 2018. Deeply learned, and does "not approach the Apocalypse as Christian scripture" (x). In his violent triumph, "God is as much a power of domination as any other power" (Pippin, quoted on p.237). The closing sentence: "Those who look to the Apocalypse to find a model of non-violent resistance as a counterpoint to violence in today's world, will find it neither in the slain Lamb nor the slaughtered martyrs" (238). [*JSNT* 41.5].

Minear, Paul. ‡ *I Saw a New Earth*, 1968. Listed mainly for the value of its bibliography. [*JBL* 89.4].

Moffatt, James. ‡ (Expositor's Greek Testament) 1910.

✓ **Moloney, Francis J.** *The Apocalypse of John*, 2020. Offers a different, narratological take on Revelation, "not so much to be understood as a text addressed to the first Christian communities struggling under Roman persecution, but rather as an immersion in the pascal mystery" [*Bib* 103.3]. The main message is less "God's definitive eschatological triumph over evil" and more "the perennial saving effects of Jesus' death and resurrection" (1). Published by Baker Academic and approx. 400pp. [*ExpTim* 9/21; *BBR* 31.3; *JSNT* 43.5]. For other commentaries by this Roman Catholic, see Mark and John.

F  Moo, Jonathan A. (SGBC).

☆ **Morris, Leon.** (retired TNTC) 1969, rev. 1987. A well-informed work in the series and amillennial in interpretation. Fine introduction and 210pp. of insightful, crystal-clear exposition with more stress on the prophetic tradition. In early editions I included Morris on my recommended purchase list. Note his helpful slim vol. on *Apocalyptic* (1972).

✓ Moyise, Steve. ‡ *The OT in the Book of Revelation*, 1995. Other major works on the topic are Beale, *John's Use of the OT* (above), and Fekkes, *Isaiah and Prophetic Traditions in the Book of Revelation* (1994).

✓ Moyise, Steve, ed. ‡ *Studies in the Book of Revelation*, 2001. [*Them* Aut 03; *JTS* 10/03]. See also his book, *The Later NT Writers and Scripture* (2012), under Acts.

Mulholland, M. Robert. (CorBC) 2011. I regret that I have not used it. The vol. in which Revelation is found also contains James, 1–2 Peter, and Jude, all covered by Osborne.

✓ **Murphy, Frederick J.** ‡ *Fallen Is Babylon: The Revelation to John* (NT in Context) 1998. Nearly 500pp. in length, this is definitely a reference book for students. Still, it is accessible to a broader audience interested in literary readings of biblical texts. His book on apocalyptic is recommended. [*RelSRev* 7/00].

Newell, William R. 1935. See under Romans. This was perhaps the favorite exposition among dispensational pastors before Walvoord was published.

✓ Neyrey, Jerome H. ‡ *Hearing Revelation 1–3: Listening with Greek Rhetoric and Culture*, 2019. By a recognized Jesuit NT scholar. [*CBQ* 4/21].

☆ **Osborne, Grant.** (retired BECNT) 2002. Very well-done and more accessible than one might think for a commentary on the Greek. The expositor who feels intimidated by the size and scholarship of Beale might take a step down and buy this instead. Like Mounce, Osborne offers a premillennial interpretation of ch. 20 (expected of a TEDS prof) but is a model of fairness in dealing with other positions. This work directly serves the preacher's interests, and I regard his theological reflections as rich, even though my theology differs from his. [*RTR* 8/04; *Them* Spr 04; *JETS* 12/03; *Int* 4/04; *SBET* Spr 03; *RelSRev* 10/03; *CTJ* 11/04; *ExpTim* 5/06]. See Schreiner above for a surprising replacement. Will Osborne be allowed to go o/p? Even as it is being retired, Osborne will continue to be valued highly for many years to come; it was a recommended purchase in this guide (2005–16). Do be aware that Osborne also has a shorter (375pp.), more popular-level exposition, *Revelation: Verse by Verse*, in ONTC (2016).

☆ Pate, C. Marvin. *Interpreting Revelation and Other Apocalyptic Literature: An Exegetical Handbook*, 2016. Conservative and has the goal to "examine apocalyptic literature as it begins in the OT, develops in Second Temple Judaism, and culminates in the NT, especially in . . . Revelation, all the while demonstrating how to communicate the message of that literature to today's audience" (21). [*ExpTim* 11/17; *JETS* 3/18].

✓ **Patterson, Paige.** (NAC) 2012. A dispensational work noted for its clear, readable exegesis (about 300pp.). Patterson is a giant figure in the Southern Baptist Convention and served as President of Criswell College, Southeastern Baptist Seminary, and Southwestern Baptist. Though not so penetrating with regard to scholarship, this is on the purchase list of thousands of pastors in the premil, pretrib camp. Compare with Walvoord, Thomas—both more traditional dispensationalists—and Fanning (progressive dispensational). [*JETS* 12/13; *Them* 11/14; *BSac* 1/14].

Peterson, Eugene H. *Reversed Thunder: The Revelation of John and the Praying Imagination*, 1988. More of a meditation, and often praised highly: "Unsurpassed," Witherington says, "for dealing with the spiritual substance" of the book. I've not read it.

F Peterson, Rodney L., ed. (RCS).

☆ Phillips, Richard D. (REC) 2017. An enormous vol. of exposition (715pp.) from a Reformed and amillennial perspective, valued by many pastors and laypeople. He takes texts of about 3–5 verses for each sermon. There are few similarly large-scale collections of sermons: Douglas Kelly and John MacArthur. As noted by one reviewer, Phillips had been mentored by James Montgomery Boice, and he "cites Boice's unpublished manuscript throughout the first seven chapters, offering the reader a window into Boice's final sermons before 'his promotion into the very scenes about which he had been preaching'" [*WTJ* Fall 19].

Pieters, Albertus. 1950. A notable commentary in the preterist tradition.

☆ Poythress, Vern. *The Returning King: A Guide to the Book of Revelation*, 2000. This pastoral and theological exposition is especially notable for its clarity in presenting the recapitulation scheme of amillennial interpretation and its gracious spirit in interacting with other positions. It also introduced me to the author's fascinating idea of "counterfeiting." This P&R issue is a good addition to either pastors' or church libraries. I imagine that the book got its start in Poythress's "Notes on Revelation" in *New Geneva Study Bible* (1995), one of the best sections in that Nelson project.

✓ **Prigent, Pierre.** ‡ *Commentary on the Apocalypse of St. John*, ET 2001. A huge (717pp.) and deeply learned work which gives much attention to both the historical background and the Apocalypse's indebtedness to the OT. Often cited in the literature (over 100× by Schreiner) and now in a third French edition (2014).

✓ Rainbow, Paul A. *Johannine Theology: The Gospel, the Epistles, and the Apocalypse*, 2014. See under John.

Ramsey, James B. (GS) 1873. This posthumously published exposition only covers the first 11 chapters.

✓ Ramsay, W. M. *The Letters to the Seven Churches of Asia*, 1905. Another of Ramsay's excellent historical-archaeological studies, now dated. See Hemer and Worth.

☆ **Reddish, Mitchell G.** ‡ (S&H) 2001. A readable, critically informed exposition in the Baptist tradition, this 440-page work is given a very warm review by Aune. The author teaches at Stetson U. in Florida. The retail price may keep it off many pastors' shelves. [*RelSRev* 7/03].

✓ **Resseguie, James L.** [𝓜], *The Revelation of John: A Narrative Commentary*, 2009. While insights abound, his hermeneutical approach has been questioned by some. Said by Fanning to be "really helpful" for following the flow of the text and "highly recommended." Even if one disagrees with a fair number of interpretive decisions, having a rather different hermeneutical approach in a commentary on Revelation stimulates good reflection. He emphasizes the new exodus theme. Compare with Barr's *Tales of the End*, and take note of Resseguie's earlier scholarship in *Revelation Unsealed: A Narrative Critical Approach to John's Apocalypse* (Brill, 1998). [*Them* 11/09; *JETS* 6/10; *ExpTim* 2/10; *BL* 2010; *CBQ* 10/10; *Int* 7/11; *RTR* 8/12; *RevExp* Spr 11; *BTB* 2/11].

✓ Robinson, Andrea L. *Temple of Presence: The Christological Fulfillment of Ezekiel 40–48 in Revelation 21:1–22:5*, 2019. Capably argued New Orleans Baptist PhD. [*JETS* 9/19].

✓ **Roloff, Jürgen.** ‡ (ContC) 1984, ET 1993. Useful, but unfortunately not as thorough as most others in the series (250pp.). There is less interaction with other points of view than one might hope for. This is not a technical work (i.e., a comprehensive historical and linguistic commentary) and is quite accessible, even to well-educated laity. [*PSB* 15.2; *Int* 4/95; *SwJT* Spr 95; *SJT* 49.3].

✓ **Rowland, Christopher C.** ‡ (NIB) 1998. The most significant contribution to NIB vol. XII. Rowland is an Oxford don who writes with flair in an essay style. He is renowned as an expert on the place of apocalyptic in Judaism and early Christianity; see *The Open Heaven* (1982). His introduction includes a fine overview of the history of interpretation (especially some little-known British movements and liberation theology) and the use and misuse of the Apocalypse. Note that biblical scholarship is not the emphasis here, and Rowland scarcely ever interacts with evangelicals. He believes Revelation leads us to resist the idolatries and demands for compromise issuing from the dominant culture, wherever we may be, and to put our hope in a sovereign God. Actually, a better book for preachers may be his 1993 Epworth Commentary.

F Schnabel, Eckhard. (EBTC)?

☆ Schreiner, Thomas. "Revelation" in *Hebrews–Revelation* (ESVEC) 2018. See Johnson under Hebrews. Schreiner has a more recent scholarly work for BECNT (above).

F Schüssler Fiorenza, Elisabeth. ‡ (Herm)? Students note her essays, *The Book of Revelation: Justice and Judgment* (rev. 1998), and her brief 1991 commentary, *Revelation: Vision of a Just World*, both outlining her "perspective from below," interest in rhetoric, and liberationist-feminist interpretation. See Friesen.

Seiss, J. A. 1909. A lengthy dispensational work which was reprinted many times.

Skaggs, Rebecca, and Priscilla C. Benham. (PentC) 2009. Earlier, Skaggs contributed the vol. on Peter & Jude in this series. [*ExpTim* 6/10; *BL* 2010].

☆ **Smalley, Stephen S.** [𝓜], 2005. Subtitled "A Commentary on the Greek Text of the Apocalypse" and published by SPCK (IVP in North America), this full (597pp.) and densely packed vol. contains much interaction with other scholars' writings. Smalley has concentrated for decades on the Johannine literature and knows it well. He interprets Revelation as "a creative and coherent drama" in two acts (1:9–11:19; 12:1–22:17) and as a unity authored by John the Apostle (= the Beloved Disciple) shortly before AD 70. This is a very good book for both students and academically minded ministers. A few reviewers allege that the book has a more traditional feel, paying less attention to cutting-edge social scientific and rhetorical approaches. Like Osborne, it is a more accessible commentary on the Greek than Aune or Beale. The general approach is more or less idealist. [*JETS* 12/06; *BL* 2006; *BTB* Win 07; *BSac* 7/07; *ExpTim* 8/06].

☆ **Stewart, Alexander E.** (EGGNT) 2024. Certainly worthwhile as a careful, thorough guide through Revelation's Greek text and language, with their peculiarities. In comparison with the excellent Mathewson, Stewart has the additional help of 16 sections of "Homiletical Suggestions" throughout (265pp.).

☆ Stott, John R. W. *What Christ Thinks of the Church*, 1958, rev. 1990. A slim vol. on the letters to the churches, recommended in all previous editions of this guide (now see Weima above). Marvelously suggestive for pastors. For more expositions of Revelation 1–3, look up Culy (above) and MacArthur's *Christ's Call to Reform the Church* (2018). Among older books, see Barclay (1957—different from DSB), or, even better, Marcus Loane's *They Overcame* (1971).

F   Stuckenbruck, Loren. ‡ (Illum).

✓ **Sweet, John P.** ‡ (WPC, now TPI) 1979. A highly acclaimed vol. which was lengthier than others in the now defunct Pelican series. Though Sweet is showing its age, I continue calling this one of the best briefer commentaries on Revelation. [*JETS* 6/80].

✓ **Swete, H. B.** 3rd ed. 1911. A classic comparable to Beckwith and the more liberal Charles. Swete is a careful, in-depth study on the Greek text and is still useful. Has been reprinted and is now free online.

☆ Tabb, Brian. *All Things New: Revelation as Canonical Capstone* (NSBT) 2019. Has been praised highly by Culy as "an example of biblical theology at its best" [*JETS* 6/21], building upon Bauckham's masterful *Climax of Prophecy*. [*Them* 45.3].

F   Tabb, Brian. (EEC). An earlier report was Mike Stallard, a dispensationalist.

Tenney, Merrill C. *Interpreting Revelation*, 1957. An introduction to the issues facing the expositor and to the various schemes of interpretation. Premillennial (158).

✓ **Thomas, John Christopher, and Frank Macchia.** (THC) 2016. One of the largest vols. in the series (650pp.), with a long Introduction (much on "History of Effects"), a 330-page theologically oriented exegesis by Thomas, and 220pp. of Macchia's theological essays. Both gentlemen are capable Pentecostal scholars. [*JETS* 6/17; *JSNT* 40.5; *DenvJ* 4/17].

✓ **Thomas, Robert.** (intended for WEC?) 2 vols., 1992–95. Totaling over 1200pp., the set presents a massive exegetical study from an older-style dispensational perspective. Though more moderate than Walvoord (in openness to other views), it still presses hard the literal interpretation—"The proper procedure is to assume a literal interpretation of each symbolic representation provided to John unless a particular factor in the text indicates it should be interpreted figuratively" (36). I believe only those sharing Thomas's doctrinal commitment will give it a high grade. On the plus side, he gives copious citations of others' works and views, sometimes approaching being a catena or chain of extracts. A valuable reference for students. [*WTJ* Spr 93; *BSac* 4/94, 7/96].

✓ **Thompson, Leonard L.** ‡ (ANTC) 1998. From an expert on the historical background. (See *The Book of Revelation: Apocalypse and Empire* [1990] [*JR* 1/92], which sparked a resurgence of interest in the social setting.) This is among the best compact commentaries from the critical camp (190pp.). Some strongly disagree when he gives a positive reassessment of Domitian's reign, arguing that Revelation was written to a community living in peace and that there was no persecution setting. [*RelSRev* 7/00].

☆ **Tonstad, Sigve K.** (Paideia) 2019. Fascinating story here of a physician who then studied theology and did a PhD at St. Andrews on "the cosmic narratives of Revelation" (*Saving God's Reputation*, 2006). He takes the Apostle John to be the author. This fine entry in the series is distinguished by narratological and theological insight on the exegetical level, joined to some excellent contemporary reflection. Note that he dismisses conservative "Armageddon theology" in America (234). A criticism from some is that Tonstad seems to overreact to "interpreters [who] reflexively and uncritically assign the calamities in the book to divine agency" (39). Cf. Middleton perhaps? Tonstad sees ch. 12 as "the hub" (37–38) with its emphasis upon cosmic conflict and the exposure of Satan's agency in the violence of the book. All of history's meaning and God's final justice for "victims" is to be revealed in the Lamb (281–82), the victim who was "killed with violence" (5:6), who is both the revealed and the revealer. [*ExpTim* 1/22; *CBQ* 4/21; *Int* 1/22; *JSNT* 42.5].

☆ Trafton, Joseph L. (RNT) 2005. I like this book. It is subtitled "A Literary and Theological Commentary" and contains good insights from a conservative angle.

✓ Wainwright, Arthur. ‡ *Mysterious Apocalypse*, 1993. Well-done introduction.

Walhout, Edwin. *Revelation Down to Earth: Making Sense of the Apocalypse of John*, 2000. The retired CRC minister says his commentary "explains this difficult book of the Bible from a pastoral point of view" (1). It is a thoughtful personal reading, foregoing much interaction with scholarly literature except when he discusses the structure of the Apocalypse.

☆ **Wall, Robert.** (NIBC) 1991. Fairly full for the series at over 300pp. The reviews are a bit mixed. [*WTJ* Spr 93; *EvQ* 10/97; *Them* 4/96; *CRBR* 1994].

Walvoord, John F. 1966. Illustrates what old-style dispensationalists do with the book. This has been a standard pretribulational commentary. I cannot recommend it as a guide. These days, if I want to read the classic dispensational interpretation of a passage (and have time), I look up Thomas. (More up-to-date and moderate is Fanning.) Walvoord tends to be irritatingly dismissive of other approaches.

✓ Weinrich, William C., ed. (ACCS) 2005. [*BL* 2007; *ExpTim* 1/17].

☆ Wilcock, Michael. (BST) 1975. Different type of interpretation, but most stimulating for anyone preaching or teaching through this book. Decades ago I nearly included this among the recommended purchases. [*EvQ* 4/76].

Williamson, Peter S. ‡ (CCSS) 2015. I have not seen it. [*Int* 7/17].

✓ **Witherington, Ben, III.** (NCBC) 2003. This launched the series, with Witherington himself serving as general editor. As might be expected in light of his past work, he pays attention to both historical backdrop and socio-rhetorical analysis. He writes that "John is what Eusebius was later to call a 'chiliast,' a believer in a thousand-year reign" upon the earth (291). Students will appreciate the bibliographical guidance on pp.51–64. [*ExpTim* 9/04; *RelSRev* 4/04; *JETS* 3/05; *Int* 7/05; *CBQ* 4/09; *BL* 2005; *Anvil* 22.1].

✓ Worth, Roland H. *The Seven Cities of the Apocalypse and Roman Culture*, 1999; *The Seven Cities of the Apocalypse and Greco-Asian Culture*, 1999. See Hemer above.

✓ Yarbro Collins, Adela. ‡ *Crisis and Catharsis: The Power of the Apocalypse*, 1984.

✓ Yarbro Collins, Adela, ed. ‡ *New Perspectives on the Book of Revelation*, 2017. From a Leuven Colloquium. [*NovT* 61.1; *RB* 126.4].

Yeatts, John R. (BCBC) 2003. Comes from the pacifist tradition. [*Int* 4/04].

NOTES: (1) Ian Paul, "Ebbing and Flowing: Scholarly Developments in Study of the Book of Revelation," *ExpTim* 119.11 (2008): 523–31. (2) Michael Naylor has reviewed the recent scholarship on "The Roman Imperial Cult and Revelation," *CBR* 8.2 (2010): 207–39. (3) Lois K. Fuller Dow, "Commentaries on Revelation" (421–48), in *On the Writing of NT Commentaries*, eds. Porter–Schnabel, cited in the Introduction.

# BARGAINS FOR A
# BARE-BONES LIBRARY

THESE CHOICES WILL, I hope, provide the average student or pastor with the best resources, given an extremely limited budget. The following might be termed best bargains, though few would be a first choice if one had plenty of shekels to spend. Or you might think of these as emergency purchases, where, say, you really want a commentary for a new Sunday School class on Exodus but only wish to spend $20. Or you may regard these as arguably some top choices for the studious layperson. I have chosen for the most part one vol. commentaries in paperback with an evangelical perspective. (Believing scholarship should, I think, be given a priority in building a personal library of restricted size.) The choices also tend to be exegetical rather than homiletical in their aim. Several things to consider: (a) don't miss all the free commentaries online, such as Calvin, Keil & Delitzsch, and Matthew Henry—see ccel.org and other sites; (b) buying books s/h often saves 50–60 percent; (c) it could be that with scarce resources you would be best off buying a commentary series or two digitally. Since commentaries are often sold at a discount in entire sets, you also might consider building your library around a series, like the Tyndale OT and NT Commentaries, or the *Expositor's Bible Commentary, Revised.* In this list, names appear in the order of preference—perhaps with cost as a leading consideration—where the connectives "and" or "or" are used.

## OLD TESTAMENT

| | |
|---|---|
| GENESIS | **Steinmann** (TOTC-R) or Hartley (NIBC) or Kidner (TOTC); *For Gen–Exod combined, Ross (CorBC)* |
| EXODUS | **Alexander** (TTC) or Motyer (BST); *For Gen–Exod combined, Oswalt (CorBC)* |
| LEVITICUS | **Sklar** (TOTC-R) or Tidball (BST); *Tidball is more expositional.* |
| NUMBERS | **Wenham** (TOTC); *Might look for the old Ashley s/h (NICOT).* |
| DEUTERONOMY | **Wright** (NIBC) or Woods (TOTC); *Wright is more expositional.* |
| JOSHUA | **Hess** (TOTC) or Firth (BST); *Firth is more expositional.* |
| JUDGES/RUTH | **Evans** (TOTC-R) or, even better, s/h Block (NAC); *For an exposition, Davis (Judges) and Ferguson (Ruth).* |
| SAMUEL | **Long** (TOTC-R) or Baldwin (TOTC); *Possibly better, Vannoy s/h.* |
| KINGS | **Provan** (NIBC) |
| CHRONICLES | **Selman** (TOTC); *Far better Boda s/h.* |
| EZRA–NEHEMIAH | **Petter** (NIVAC) or Lorein (TOTC-R) for well-trained; *Kidner (TOTC) is a classic; Allen (NIBC) is fine and [M].* |
| ESTHER | **Jobes** (NIVAC) or Laniak (NIBC) or Reid (TOTC-R) or Firth (BST, expositional); *Baldwin (TOTC) is a beautiful classic.* |
| JOB | **Wilson** (NIBC) or Andersen (TOTC) |
| PSALMS | **Longman** (TOTC-R); *Kidner (TOTC) still appeals.* |
| PROVERBS | **Wilson** (TOTC-R); *Kidner (TOTC) is a classic.* |
| ECCLESIASTES | **Hubbard** (WCC, one-vol. Eccl–Song) or Kidner (BST) |
| SONG OF SONGS | **Duguid** (TOTC-R); *Or Hubbard's one-vol. Eccl–Song, or Carr (TOTC)* |

| | |
|---|---|
| ISAIAH | **Motyer** (TOTC) or Wegner (TOTC-R) |
| JEREMIAH/LAM. | **Lalleman** (TOTC-R) or Longman (NIBC); *Wright BST more expositional* |
| EZEKIEL | **Hilber** or Wright (BST); *Wright more expositional. Even better Duguid s/h.* |
| DANIEL | **House** (TOTC-R) or Baldwin (TOTC); *Or Davis (BST, more expositional)* |
| MINOR PROPHETS | **McComiskey, ed. in one vol.**; *On one prophet, probably buy TOTC-R (e.g., Routledge on Hosea).* |

# NEW TESTAMENT

| | |
|---|---|
| MATTHEW | **France** (TNTC) or Mounce (NIBC); *Perhaps Carson's old EBC s/h.* |
| SERMON ON MT. | **Stott** (BST) |
| MARK | **Schnabel** (TNTC-R) |
| LUKE | **Perrin** (TNTC-R) or Bock (IVPNT) or Evans (NIBC) |
| JOHN | **Kruse** (TNTC) |
| ACTS | **Marshall** (TNTC) or Stott (BST, expositional); *Possibly s/h Longenecker (EBC)* |
| ROMANS | **Garland** (TNTC-R) or Stott (BST); *Great s/h buys are Moo (NIVAC), Morris, and Murray* |
| 1 CORINTHIANS | **Schreiner** (TNTC-R); *Or Kistemaker s/h* |
| 2 CORINTHIANS | **Kruse** (TNTC); *Or Kistemaker s/h* |
| GALATIANS | **Hansen** (IVPNT) or Cole (TNTC), or Stott (BST, expositional); *Consider s/h George* |
| EPHESIANS | **Bock** (TNTC-R) or Stott (BST); *Consider s/h Bruce (Eph–Col–Phlm)* |
| PHILIPPIANS | **Fee** (IVPNT) or Brown (TNTC-R) or Chapman; *Fee (NICNT) worth the extra money* |
| COLOSSIANS | **Thompson** (TNTC-R) or Wright (TNTC); *Consider s/h Bruce (Eph–Col–Phlm)* |
| THESSALONIANS | **Beale** (IVPNT) or Williams (NIBC) or Morris (TNTC); *Pastors may prefer Stott.* |
| PASTORALS | **Padilla** (TNTC-R) or Towner (IVPNT) or Fee (NIBC) |
| PHILEMON | ***See Colossians commentary incorporating Philemon*** |
| HEBREWS | **Peterson** (TNTC-R); *Bruce or G. Guthrie s/h* |
| JAMES | **Moo** (TNTC-R) or Davids (NIBC) |
| 1 PETER | **Hillyer** (NIBC, on 1–2 Peter, Jude = cheapest) or Grudem (TNTC-R); *Cf. Schreiner (Peter–Jude) is ideal.* |
| 2 PETER/JUDE | **Hillyer** (NIBC, on 1–2 Peter, Jude = cheapest) or Green (TNTC); *Cf. Schreiner* |
| 1–3 JOHN | **Stott** (TNTC) or Johnson (NIBC) |
| REVELATION | **Paul** (TNTC-R) or Michaels (IVPNT s/h); *Perhaps Mounce s/h or Ladd (ECBC)* |

# AN IDEAL BASIC LIBRARY FOR THE PASTOR

THESE CHOICES WILL, I hope, provide the average well-trained student or pastor (MDiv) with the best resources for a basic library, given a typical (?) budget. I sought to pick works that young pastors could grow into, rather than grow out of (because not engaging the text deeply enough). I wish to clarify that this is only a beginning library, restricted to two commentaries per Bible book and balanced between detailed exegesis and theological-practical exposition. In the case of certain Bible books, I have mentioned works that would be complementary or perhaps preferred by the more advanced student or scholarly pastor. Names appear in the order of preference where the connectives "and" or "or" are used. (Believing scholarship should, I think, be given a priority in building a personal library of restricted size.) I have selected a few more technical works (using original Hebrew or Greek) for the NT than OT, since pastors tend to use them more.

## OLD TESTAMENT COMMENTARIES

GENESIS
**Wenham and/or Mathews** (exegesis), **then Ross** or Walton (exposition); *Hamilton is also first-rate, and Goldingay [M] enormously stimulating.*

EXODUS
**Alexander and/or Stuart** (exegesis), **then Wright or Enns** (exposition); *perhaps add Childs, if you are more academic.*

LEVITICUS
**Sklar** (ZECOT) **or Wenham**, then Ross (exposition); *compare Hess. Advanced students see Milgrom (AB) as the standard reference.*

NUMBERS
**Morales or Ashley** (2022), or Wenham (for the frugal), **then Sklar or Duguid** (exposition); *add Milgrom for detail work. Much is learned from Awabdy.*

DEUTERONOMY
**McConville** or Woods (for the frugal), **then Block** (NIVAC, exposition); *Arnold's developing NICOT set is a priority for the best trained.*

JOSHUA
**Firth or Goldingay** [M], or Hess (for the frugal), **then Hubbard** (NIVAC, exposition); *the more scholarly will strongly consider Butler (2nd ed.). Howard is more conservative and probably the most dependable exegesis.*

JUDGES
**Boda–Conway** (if you have Hebrew) **and Block or Webb**; *pastors will add an exposition.*

RUTH
**Block** (ZECOT) **or Lau, then McKeown**; *for more expositional help, consider Duguid. Already own Hubbard? You're in good shape.*

SAMUEL
**Firth or Vannoy, then Arnold** (exposition); *add AB, NICOT, WBC for more detailed exegesis and textual criticism. Preachers should consider Woodhouse and Davis.*

KINGS
**Wray Beal** or House, **and Provan**; *scholarly types will consider AB, Hobbs, and Sweeney. Preachers will look for more expositional help.*

CHRONICLES
**Kaminski and/or Boda** (exegesis), **then Hill or Pratt** (exposition); *the scholarly need more exegesis and will consider Japhet, and the reference works of Klein and Knoppers. Merrill is insightful and solidly conservative.*

EZRA–NEHEMIAH
**Smith** (ZECOT) **and Harrington**; *an academic certainly adds WBC, while the pastor will pick up NIVAC.*

| | |
|---|---|
| ESTHER | **Tomasino** (exegesis), **and Jobes or Firth** (exposition); *some may prefer the simpler exegesis of Baldwin. Take a look at Steinmann. Advanced students find Bush, Berlin, and Fox stimulating.* |
| JOB | **Longman or Hartley** (exegesis), **then Ash or Walton** (exposition); *Hebrew students will certainly make Clines a priority and weigh buying Seow.* |
| PSALMS | **Ross or Bullock** (exegesis), **then Wilson and Tucker–Grant** (exposition); *VanGemeren remains useful. Advanced students consult Goldingay, Kraus, and Hermeneia.* |
| PROVERBS | **Waltke** (NICOT for studious) or **Overland or Longman** (exegesis), **then O'Dowd or Koptak** (exposition); *advanced students may buy Fox and Waltke to start off, with Ansberry a fine complement on discourse.* |
| ECCLESIASTES | **Bartholomew** (exegesis), **and Enns** or Hubbard or Provan (for exposition); *either Fredericks or Longman is a good pick if you agree with him. Seow and Fox are top-notch for scholars.* |
| SONG OF SONGS | **Hess or Longman** (exegesis), **then Duguid** (or an exposition); *the scholarly want more technical works: Fishbane, Murphy, Keel.* |
| ISAIAH | **Smith and Motyer** (1993) **or Oswalt** (NICOT); *an exposition is missing, and preachers can look to add Oswalt (NIVAC) or Webb. Calvin is a big help here, too. The studious appreciate McConville (2023), Wildberger, ICC, and Paul.* |
| JEREMIAH | **Goldingay** [𝓜] **or Mackay** (more conservative, less rigorous), **then Wright or Dearman** (exposition); *see the note at the head of the Jeremiah section. Students start with Lundbom, Holladay, and Allen. Prior to the price-hike, I urged scholarly pastors to buy AB first and quickly add a theological exposition (not Lundbom's area of interest).* |
| LAMENTATIONS | **Goldingay** [𝓜] **or House** (exegesis), **then Wright** or Parry (exposition); *advanced students will seek out OTL.* |
| EZEKIEL | **Block, then Duguid**; *Zimmerli and Greenberg–Cook are invaluable from the critical angle, but best appreciated by academic types. If Block is too heavy or expensive, see Hilber or Joyce* [𝓜]. |
| DANIEL | **Widder** (ZECOT) **or Goldingay** [𝓜], **then Longman** (exposition); *perhaps add more of a conservative counterbalance with Baldwin or Davis's BST. Students pay attention to Collins (Herm). Depending on your theology, consider Steinmann or Tanner.* |
| MINOR PROPHETS | **McComiskey set**; **Hwang or Dearman** (Hosea); **Barker** (Joel); **Carroll R.** (Amos); **Stuart** (Hosea–Jonah); **Block** (Obad); **Youngblood** (Jonah); **Waltke** (Micah, 2007); **Renz** (Nahum–Zeph); **Taylor–Clendenen** (Haggai and Mal) **or Petterson** (Haggai–Mal); **and Boda** (Zech, 2015). *Pastors may add Smith's NIVAC on Hosea–Amos–Micah, Baker on Joel–Obadiah–Malachi, Bruckner on Jonah–Nahum–Habakkuk–Zephaniah, and perhaps Boda on Haggai–Zechariah. Students will want to add a few gems like Paul on Amos (Herm), Sasson on Jonah (AB), Timmer on Nahum (ZECOT), Andersen on Habakkuk (AB), Berlin on Zephaniah (AB), Meyers–Meyers on Haggai–Zechariah (AB), Hill on Malachi (AB), and Tucker on Malachi (ZECOT).* |

# NEW TESTAMENT COMMENTARIES

| | |
|---|---|
| NEW TESTAMENT | **Calvin's Commentaries** (Torrance Ed.) |
| MATTHEW | **Carson or France** (NICNT, fuller), **then Nolland** or Hagner (for detailed Greek exegesis)—one of the pair should be France or Nolland (as newer |

works); *the best recent pastoral exposition is Quarles. NT aficionados, with ambition to do a PhD in that field, need a rich uncle to buy them the sets by Davies–Allison and by Luz. Preachers sensing a need for expositional help may get NIVAC or Doriani.*

| | |
|---|---|
| SERMON ON MT. | **Guelich, then Lloyd-Jones** or Stott (for exposition and application) |
| MARK | **France or Strauss or Stein** (Greek text), **then Garland** (exposition); *what a quandary choosing among the commentaries on the Greek! France is my favorite, but Stein is six years younger and robust in his older-style historical approach (redaction). Strauss is fresh, well-rounded, and more sensitive to applicational concerns. If the pastor thinks the Greek works too demanding, buy Pillar or Bock (2015).* |
| LUKE | **Garland or Bock** (BECNT), **and Edwards** or Green; *none can match Bock's thoroughness; those who think him too fat or expensive have an easy choice for a well-rounded single-vol. on the Greek: buy Garland. Edwards is a superb choice for those not needing a Greek commentary. Preachers will add an exposition to this mix, say a Hughes or Ryken or Bock.* |
| JOHN | **Carson or Michaels, then Klink** (Greek text) **or Burge** (exposition); *advanced students will also look at Keener, Barrett, Brown, and Schnackenburg for detailed exegetical help.* |
| ACTS | **Peterson** (Pillar), **then Schnabel or Bock** (Greek text), **or Stott** (exposition); *for the true scholar the Barrett set will be a first or second purchase, and Keener is stunning. Look at WBC.* |
| ROMANS | **Moo** (NICNT-R), **then Cranfield** (ICC) **or Thielman** (more conservative, Greek text), **or Stott** (exposition); *students note Longenecker, Fitzmyer, and Jewett. Schreiner (2018) is a really smart choice.* |
| 1 CORINTHIANS | **Garland** (builds on Fee) **or Fee** (2014), **then Blomberg** (practical exposition) **or Thiselton** (exhaustive on the Greek text); *it's hard to pass by Fee, even if you disagree. It would be unfair not to mention the Pillar entry, which is pitched just right for pastors, and Gardner's ZECNT.* |
| 2 CORINTHIANS | **Barnett** (NICNT) **or Garland, then Hafemann** (exposition), **or Harris or Guthrie** (Greek text); *frankly I'd not wish to do without either Harris or Guthrie, and the more scholarly might start with that pair.* |
| GALATIANS | **Moo, and Schreiner** (Greek text) **or deSilva** (NICNT), then some exposition; *George or Witherington are good for expositors (if your Greek isn't up to ZECNT). Keener is impressive.* |
| EPHESIANS | **Thielman or Arnold** (Greek text), **and Campbell or Cohick** (NICNT); *pastors will add an exposition. Leading scholarly/technical works include Lincoln, Best, Hoehner, Fowl; check Baugh too.* |
| PHILIPPIANS | **Guthrie** (ZECNT, Greek) **or Fee** (NICNT), then Thielman (exposition); *Hansen is fine.* |
| COLOSSIANS | **Beale** (BECNT, Greek) **and Moo, then McKnight** (English text) **or Garland** (exposition); *add Dunn for scholars.* |
| THESSALONIANS | **Weima or Kim–Bruce** (Greek) **and Fee or Green**, then Stott (for preachers); *Shogren is splendid too and some say deserves to be a priority. Students put Malherbe and Wanamaker to good use.* |
| PASTORALS | **Yarbrough or Towner** (NICNT), **then Porter or Mounce** (Greek text); *pastors will hunt for an exposition such as Stott or Hughes–Chapell. For me Marshall, Knight, and Johnson are indispensable for work with the Greek.* |
| PHILEMON | ***See Colossians commentaries incorporating Philemon*** |

HEBREWS  **Moo or Lane** (WBC, Greek exegesis), **then G. Guthrie** (exposition); *Consider Grindheim's full work (2023). Arminians may prefer to start with Cockerill (NICNT). Scholars prize Hermeneia, NIGTC, and AB.*

JAMES  **Moo** (Pillar-R) **or McKnight, and McCartney** (Greek text); *scholarly types might make Johnson's AB a second or third purchase, and pastors will want an additional expositional help.*

1 PETER  **Jobes** (Greek, 2022) **and Davids,** then an exposition; *the scholarly are tempted to take out bank loans to obtain Achtemeier, Williams–Horrell, and Elliott.*

2 PETER/JUDE  **Davids** (Pillar), **then Green** (BECNT for Greek exegesis) **or Moo** (exposition); *if you're the scholarly type, do acquire Bauckham (brilliant, despite its age!).*

1–3 JOHN  **Yarbrough and Jobes** (Greek text), **or Kruse** (Greekless readers), then an exposition; *for research purposes Schnackenburg, Lieu, and Brown.*

REVELATION  **Schreiner** (BECNT) **and Beale** (NIGTC, Greek text), **or Mounce** (1998, English text), then consider an exposition (Osborne 2016 perhaps, Gardner, Dennis Johnson?); *pastors finding Beale a struggle financially, academically, or time-wise should try "Shorter" Beale (2015). From the dispensational angle, see Fanning. Scholars treasure Aune and Koester.*

## OLD TESTAMENT RESEARCH TOOLS

1. *BHS*, but note that one replacement (among several projects), *Biblia Hebraica Quinta*, is already appearing (2004–). Pastors struggling to stick with their Hebrew should consider *A Reader's Hebrew Bible* (Zondervan, 2008) [*Them* 7/09; *EuroJTh* 18.2], available also within the largest vol. I've ever seen (2250pp.): *A Reader's Hebrew and Greek Bible* (2010) [*BTB* 2/12]. Alternatively, look up Vance–Athas–Avrahami, *BHS, A Reader's Edition* (Deutsche Bibelgesellschaft / Hendrickson, 2014).

2. David Clines's *Concise Dictionary of Classical Hebrew* (2009) [*RBL* 5/11], in preference to Holladay's trusty lexicon.

3. *New International Dictionary of OT Theology and Exegesis* [*JETS* 6/99; *ExpTim* 1/00; *Chm* 112.1].

4. For a holistic grammar, I'll be a realist and tell pastors to use the textbook they got in seminary—hopefully yours moves a bit beyond the basics into the intermediate range. To make better sense of your grammar, you're likely to find Gary Long of good assistance: *Grammatical Concepts 101 for Biblical Hebrew* (rev. ed. 2013) [*EvQ* 4/14]. See below for reference grammars.

5. I've been converted to recommend *Williams' Hebrew Syntax* (Beckman, 3rd ed. 2007) for its broad coverage but also ease of use [*HS* 2008], instead of Waltke–O'Connor. Williams is brilliant for the classroom and for reference.

6. High-powered Bible study software. Gone are the days when I recommended a concordance to the Hebrew OT by Even–Shoshan (all Hebrew) or Kohlenberger–Swanson [*JSOT* 84] (for those with only basic Hebrew).

7. *Old Testament Exegesis* (5th ed. 2022) by Douglas Stuart [2009 ed.: *ExpTim* 5/11; *BTB* 8/11] or Jason DeRouchie's *How to Understand and Apply the OT* (2017) [*JETS* 9/17; *Them* 42.2]. From the critical side, William P. Brown's *Handbook to OT Exegesis* (2017) is an admirable textbook [*Them* 42.3; *HBT* 9/18; *Them* 42.3].

8. Two or three OT Introductions, choosing among Longman–Dillard (2nd ed. 2006) [*JETS* 3/97], Hess (2016) [*BBR* 27.3; *CBQ* 10/18; *JETS* 9/17; *Them* 42.3], Childs (1979, critical), and maybe the old Harrison (with information on the history of scholarship hard to find else-

where). Brilliant and conservatively critical is Hubbard–Dearman (2018), though it is weaker on theological message [*JETS* 12/18; *RevExp* 11/20; *Them* 43.3]. Many will also want to consider the conservative Lutheran work by Lessing and Steinmann: *Prepare the Way of the Lord* (2014).

9. Among OT surveys, consider Arnold–Beyer, *Encountering the Old Testament* (4th ed. 2024) [*ExpTim* 6/16], which is an enjoyable read, or the trusted textbook by Hill–Walton, now in a 4th ed. (2023). Still useful despite its age is LaSor–Hubbard–Bush (1996 ed.) [*JSS* Spr 00].

10. OT Histories by Provan–Long–Longman (2nd ed. 2015) [*RTR* 8/06; *BSac* 7/05; *CJ* 10/05; *JSOT* 42.5] and Merrill (2nd ed. 2008) [*TJ* Spr 09].

11. Consider King–Stager, *Life in Biblical Israel* (2001) [*Them* Sum 03; *WTJ* Spr 03; *Int* 1/03; *JETS* 12/04; *JNES* 7/07; *DenvJ* 1/02 (Hess); *Evangel* Sum 03], if you will in fact read the beautiful book.

12. Among OT Theology books, which I argue are among the most helpful vols. on a preacher's shelf, I can recommend House (1998); Martens's *God's Design* (2nd ed. 1994, 3rd ed. 1998, 4th ed. 2015); Routledge's work for IVP (2008) [*DenvJ* 14]; and Robertson's *The Christ of the Covenants*. Stimulating from the more critical side are Goldingay's set (2003–09) [*Chm* Win 07; *CBQ* 4/05, 11/07; *JTS* 10/05, 4/09; *JETS* 6/05, 6/11; *Them* Win 05; *BSac* 7/06; *Int* 4/06, 4/08; *TynBul* 57.1; *ExpTim* 1/05; *SJT* 63.1 (Chapman, Brueggemann); *Anvil* 22.3 (Moberly); *DenvJ* 4/08 (Hess)]; the liberal, postmodern Brueggemann (1997) [*Them* Aut 99; *Int* 1/99; *CTJ* 4/00; *JETS* 12/99; *TynBul* 57.1; *DenvJ* 13]; and classics by Eichrodt (ET 1961–67) and von Rad (ET 1962–65). Regrettably, I was less impressed with Waltke's huge 2007 effort as an OT Theology—especially when Ruth and Ecclesiastes together get about as many pages as "Prophets" (805–27) and "Prophetic Books" (828–49); on the plus side Waltke gives much attention to what he terms NT intertextuality [*JETS* 3/09; *BSac* 4/09; *VT* 60.1; *Them* 7/09].

## Scholarly Students Will Likely Want to Add:

13. *HALOT* (2 vol. "Study Edition") [*Them* Aut 02]. Advanced students should consult the Sheffield *Dictionary of Classical Hebrew* (1993–2011) in the library [*CBQ* 4/09]; it is now under revision (2018–) [*ExpTim* 5/20]. Those with German can make excellent use of the 18th ed. of Gesenius, *Hebräisches und Aramäisches Handwörterbuch über das Alte Testament* (2013). I can also heartily recommend the HB text and accompanying "Semantic Dictionary of Biblical Hebrew" (based on semantic domains), free online from UBS: https://translation.bible/tools-resources/semantic-dictionary-of-biblical-hebrew/.

14. The Waltke–O'Connor Hebrew Syntax [*JSS* Aut 91; *CRBR* 1992], alongside Williams. I also find useful Arnold–Choi, *A Guide to Biblical Hebrew Syntax* (CUP, 2003, 2nd ed. 2018), but note the critiques [*HS* 2005; *VT* 55.4; *ExpTim* 3/05]. Students take an interest in Noonan, *Advances in the Study of Biblical Hebrew and Aramaic* (2020) [*Them* 46.1].

15. The Joüon–Muraoka (rev. 2006) [*HS* 2007; *ExpTim* 6/10] reference grammar—specialists can't do without it. (I have found the old classic Gesenius (GKC) reference free online.) There is *A Biblical Hebrew Reference Grammar* by van der Merwe–Naudé–Kroeze as well [*JETS* 9/01; *JSS* Aut 01], now in a 2nd ed. [*BBR* 29.1], which I use constantly. Those specializing in Semitics should acquaint themselves with Brill's 4-vol. *Encyclopedia of Hebrew Language and Linguistics* (2013) in their school libraries: astonishing in its breadth and depth and expense [*Them* 11/14; *JJS* 65.2]. For comparative Semitics, another rich resource is *A Companion to Ancient Near Eastern Languages*, ed. Rebecca Hasselbach-Andee (Wiley Blackwell, 2020) [*BBR* 31.2]. Advanced students await the *Oxford Grammar of Biblical Hebrew* (2028?).

16. A copy of the LXX, plus the Lust–Eynikel–Houspie *Greek-English Lexicon of the Septuagint* (3rd ed. 2016); cheaper is a s/h copy of the Liddell & Scott Greek Lexicon: Abridged.

For those doing more extensive work in the LXX, there is only one stop: Muraoka, *A Greek English Lexicon of the Septuagint* (2009)—"an indispensable tool for everyone who studies the Septuagint or works with it in any way" [*WTJ* Fall 10 (Silva)]. [*JAJ* 1.1; *NovT* 52.3; *BBR* 21.4; *CBQ* 10/10; *JTS* 4/12; *Presb* Fall 11; *JJS* 63.2]. A marvelous follow-up was Muraoka, *A Greek-Hebrew/Aramaic Two-Way Index to the Septuagint* (2010) [*NovT* 53.4; *CBQ* 10/11]. Now capping off these efforts, Muraoka has published *A Syntax of Septuagint Greek* (2016) [*JETS* 9/18]. The standard translation is Pietersma–Wright, eds., *A New English Translation of the Septuagint* (OUP, 2007) [*NovT* 52.3; *ExpTim* 3/13]. Making a specific recommendation of a LXX to buy, I believe most seminary graduates would find especially useful the enormous 2-vol. *Septuaginta: A Reader's Edition* (2018) [*WTJ* Fall 19]; those with better Greek can read the old Rahlfs. As a few final notes, specialists await more vols. in the Bons edited *Historical and Theological Lexicon of the Septuagint* (2020–) [*ETL* 97.4]. For comparison work many have used Tov–Polak, *The Revised CATSS Hebrew/Greek Parallel Text* (2004). For an introduction, see Jobes–Silva, *Invitation to the Septuagint* (2nd ed. 2015) [*DenvJ* 10/17], augmented by Aiken's *T&T Clark Companion to the Septuagint* (2015) and *The T&T Clark Handbook of Septuagint Research*, edited by Ross and Glenny (2021).

17. An Aramaic grammar (we are spoiled for choice here): Alger Johns's *Short Grammar of Biblical Aramaic* (1972); Frederick Greenspahn, *An Introduction to Aramaic* (2nd ed. 2003) [*JETS* 9/01; *JSS* Spr 03, Aut 06; *HS* 43; *VT*, 55.1; *ExpTim* 12/04]; A. Steinmann's *Fundamental Biblical Aramaic* (2004) [*JETS* 6/05]; Franz Rosenthal, *A Grammar of Biblical Aramaic* 7th ed. (Harrassowitz, 2006); Elisha Qimron, *Biblical Aramaic* (Bialik Institute, 1993); Miles Van Pelt's *Basics of Biblical Aramaic* (2011, 2nd ed. 2023) [*JESOT* 1.1]; or Andreas Schuele, *An Introduction to Biblical Aramaic* (WJK, 2012) [*BBR* 23.2; *Int* 10/14; *JSS* Spr 16]. For those who want a simpler book to get quickly into the text, I recommend Schuele, and he'll send you to Rosenthal as a reference grammar. Van Pelt works quite well too. Superb and not assuming a knowledge of biblical Hebrew is Erik Reymond, *Complete Aramaic* (2021) [*JJS* Aut 23]. For those with real language ability, Greenspahn is a smart choice. To develop some facility in reading, one might use Muraoka, *A Biblical Aramaic Reader with an Outline Grammar* (2015). Lastly, students should note the magnificent and full reference grammar of Edward Cook: *Biblical Aramaic and Related Dialects: An Introduction* (CUP, 2022) [*Or* 91.3]. For an Aramaic lexicon, see *HALOT*; Ernst Vogt, *A Lexicon of Biblical Aramaic* (ET 2011) [*ETL* 88.1]; and the *Comprehensive Aramaic Lexicon* (CAL) at <https://cal.huc.edu>. (Remember, no Aramaic in *DCH*.)

18. *TDOT*. Note that vol. 16 (ET 2018) is the "Aramaic Dictionary" [*BBR* 30.1].

19. Five useful histories are Bright (3rd or 4th ed.); Shanks, ed., *Ancient Israel: From Abraham to the Roman Destruction of the Temple* (rev. 1999) [*DenvJ*]; the more critical Miller–Hayes, *A History of Ancient Israel and Judah* (2nd ed. 2006) [*BL* 2007]; the sumptuous Hoyland–Williamson, *Oxford Illustrated History of the Holy Land* (2018); and, for advanced students, the moderately critical Frevel, *History of Ancient Israel* (ET 2023). Extremely valuable for other purposes is Arnold–Hess, eds., *Ancient Israel's History: An Introduction to Issues and Sources* (2014) [*VT* 66.3; *BBR* 26.2; *CBQ* 10/15; *RBL* 2017 and *DenvJ* 2/17]. To gain familiarity with the wider ANE context, see Arnold–Strawn, eds., *The World around the OT: The People and Places of the ANE* (2016) [*JSOT* 42.5; *Them* 42.2].; and Greer–Hilber–Walton, eds., *Behind the Scenes of the OT* (2018) [*JSOT* 43.5; *ExpTim* 8/19; *Them* 46.1]—magnificent! Those wanting to complement King–Stager (#11 above) should look up Yamauchi–Wilson, *Dictionary of Daily Life in Biblical Israel and Post-Biblical Antiquity* (one-vol. 2017) [*ETL* 94.2].

20. *The Face of Old Testament Studies*, eds. Baker–Arnold [*Chm* Spr 06]. Update needed.

21. An up-to-date critical introduction, such as John J. Collins's 3rd ed. (Fortress, 2018) [2014: *JSOT* 39.5; 2018: *BBR* 29.4].

22. All the IVP "black dictionaries" on the OT.

23. A reference guide to textual criticism, such as the authoritative Emanuel Tov's fourth ed. *Textual Criticism of the Hebrew Bible* (2022). The second ed. of Brotzman and Tully, *Old Testament Textual Criticism* (Baker, 2016) is an inexpensive alternative that I assign to my undergrad students [*ExpTim* 2/17; *BBR* 27.2]. For a well-conceived bibliography of resources, see DeRouchie, *How to Understand and Apply the OT* (2017), pp.151–56.

24. One last item not to be missed is Greidanus's *Preaching Christ from the Old Testament: A Contemporary Hermeneutical Method* (Eerdmans, 1999), "of interest to biblical theologians as well as preachers" [*JSOT* 89; *Int* 4/00; *Chm* Sum 00; *EvQ* 10/01; *CTJ* 4/01; *Anvil* 19.1].

# NEW TESTAMENT RESEARCH TOOLS

1. Either the UBS *Greek New Testament*, 5th ed. [*JTS* 10/14; *NovT* 57.1] or the Nestle–Aland *Novum Testamentum Graece*, 28th ed. [*JTS* 64.1; *NovT* 56.4; *WTJ* Spr 13; *JETS* 3/13]. Some pastors struggling to stick with their Greek might consider *The UBS Greek New Testament: A Reader's Edition* (2007) [*Them* 4/09; *NovT* 53.4; *RelSRev* 12/11], or *A Reader's Greek New Testament* (Zondervan, 3rd ed. 2015), now available too within *A Reader's Hebrew and Greek Bible* (2010) [*BTB* 2/12], which is 2250pp.

2. Roger L. Omanson, *A Textual Guide to the Greek NT* (UBS, 2006), for keen students practicing textual criticism. Note that the older Bruce Metzger, *A Textual Commentary on the Greek NT*, has information not found in Omanson. Longer and sensible discussions of the major text-critical issues can be found in Philip Comfort's *NT Text and Translation Commentary* (2008) [*CBQ* 1/12].

3. After discussions with friends who are NT specialists, I now recommend Danker, *The Concise Greek-English Lexicon of the NT* (2009) [*NovT* 52.3; 55.4; *CBQ* 10/11; *JTS* 10/10], for pastors and students because of cost, ease of use, and being more up-to-date than BDAG on a few points. However, those specializing in NT must obtain BDAG.

4. *NIDNTTE*, ed. Silva (2014) [*Them* 4/15; *BSac* 7/15; *ExpTim* 11/15; *BBR* 26.1; *CBQ* 7/16], or the "Concise" version of the same (2021), ed. Beetham [*Presb* Spr 22; *TGA* 9/23]. The old edition was *NIDNTT* (1975–78, 1986), also condensed in the one-vol. *NIV Theological Dictionary of NT Words*. I find the one-vol. *TDNT, Abridged* (1985) can't compare with *NIDNTTE*.

5. A solid intermediate-advanced Greek grammar, such as Wallace's *Greek Grammar beyond the Basics*, which is easier to use than the old standard Blass–Debrunner–Funk. Those interested in a terminal degree in NT will find helpful indeed Con Campbell's *Advances in the Study of Greek* (2015), though some issue caveats re. verbal aspect [*Them* 40.3].

6. High-powered Bible study software, instead of a recent concordance to the Greek NT. The expensive print editions one might use in the library are Bachmann–Slaby (De Gruyter) and Moulten–Geden–Marshall (6th ed.) [*NovT* 45.2; *Them* Spr 03; *BBR* 14.2; *JETS* 3/03; *Anvil* 20.1; *CurTM* 4/06]. If one's Greek is rusted out, then see Kohlenberger–Goodrick–Swanson.

7. *NT Exegesis* (4th ed. 2010) by Gordon Fee. Blomberg–Markley, *A Handbook of NT Exegesis* (2010), also works well [*BBR* 21.4; *CTJ* 11/11; *EQ* 7/11; *CBQ* 4/14; *JETS* 9/11; *ExpTim* 8/11; *Them* 8/11; *BSac* 10/12; *RelSRev* 6/13]. Some now say Naselli, *How to Understand and Apply the NT* (2017) [*Them* 42.2], is the best on the topic.

8. NT Introduction by Carson–Moo (2nd ed. 2005) [*Chm* 107.4; *CRBR* 1994; *ExpTim* 1/08; *Anvil* 24.1] for its clarity, and supplemented by the recent works of both deSilva (IVP, 2004, 2nd ed. 2018) [*Them* 1/06; *Chm* Spr 06; *Anvil* 22.3], with his narrative and rhetorical interests,

and Campbell–Pennington (2020) [*Them* 46.1]. Just to note, Guthrie (rev. 1990) has information on the history of scholarship difficult to find elsewhere. The slightly more critical work by Powell (Baker, 2009, 2nd ed. 2018) [*BL* 2010; *Int* 7/11; *JSNT* 32.5; *RBL* 2011; *JETS* 3/11; *ExpTim* 8/11; *BTB* 5/11; *JSNT* 41.5] has interests similar to deSilva. I am impressed with the beautiful presentation in Köstenberger–Kellum–Quarles (B&H, 2009, 2nd ed. 2016) [*SBET* Spr 10 (Marshall); *RBL* 8/10 (Hartin); *JETS* 6/12; *JSNT* 40.5], which Hartin has described as "a masterful piece of work that interacts fairly with modern biblical scholarship." I wouldn't be surprised if it is the favorite of many NT profs. Hagner's mediating work, published by Baker (2012), reflects a lifetime of study and teaching [*BBR* 24.2 (Yarbrough); *CBQ* 10/14; *Int* 4/15; *JETS* 12/13 (Blomberg)]. The Wright–Bird 2019 entry has, to my mind, an unclear purpose, though it is extremely engaging [*BBR* 31.2; *JETS* 3/21; *Int* 1/22; *JSNT* 42.5; *DenvJ* 23]. My favorite moderately critical reference is Holladay (see #14 below).

9.  NT History vol. by Paul Barnett: *Jesus and the Rise of Early Christianity* (1999) [*TJ* Spr 03]. Alternately one can pick up a copy of the F. F. Bruce classic *NT History* (1969). Witherington was not playing to his strength in *NT History: A Narrative Account* (2001) [*Them* Aut 02; *JETS* 3/03]. See also Green–McDonald (#17 below).

10. Some mix of the NT Theologies by Ladd (rev. 1993); Thielman (2005) [*JETS* 9/06; *Them* 4/09]; Beale (2011) [*BBR* 24.1; *Int* 1/13; *JSNT* 35.5; *JETS* 12/12; *Them* 7/12 (Marshall); *JESOT* 3.1 (Boda); *DenvJ* 16; *RelSRev* 9/12]; I. Howard Marshall (IVP, 2004) [*Chm* Spr 07; *CBQ* 7/05; *BBR* 18.1; *JETS* 12/05; *Them* 10/05; *Int* 1/06; *SJT* 62.1; *RelSRev* 1/05; *ExpTim* 1/06]; Blomberg (2018) [*ExpTim* 12/19; *Int* 1/21]; and Schnabel (2023). Compare Schreiner (2008), who uses a thematic approach in an often-inspiring manner [*Them* 4/09; *RelSRev* 3/09; *JETS* 3/09 (Blomberg); *CBQ* 10/09; *JSNT* 32.5 (Oakes)]. Witherington has an enormous 2-vol. work entitled *The Indelible Image* (2009–10), from an evangelical Methodist perspective [*Them* 11/10]. Another highly touted, useful NT Theology is Caird's (1996)

11. Among content surveys, the set by Craig Blomberg (*Jesus and the Gospels*, 1997, 3rd ed. 2022; *From Pentecost to Patmos*, 2006, 2nd ed. 2021) [*Chm* Win 07] and Luke Timothy Johnson's *The Writings of the NT* (3rd ed. 2010) are hard to beat as introductions to the NT literature, as opposed to introductions to NT scholarship. A most enjoyable read is Elwell–Yarbrough, *Encountering the NT* (4th ed. 2022).

## *Scholarly Students Will Likely Want to Add:*

12. *The Greek New Testament*, "Tyndale House Edition" (THE) [*Chm* Aut 18; *ExpTim* 8/18].

13. The BDAG Greek Lexicon (2000) [*JTS* 4/03; *JETS* 12/03; *JBL* Win 01]. Having the domains approach in the Louw–Nida *Greek-English Lexicon* (UBS, 2nd ed. 1989) is quite helpful as well, though the 2-vol. set needs updating. I recommend getting acquainted with John A. L. Lee, *A History of NT Lexicography* (2003), and the massive 3-vol. Giannakis, ed., *Encyclopedia of Ancient Greek Language and Linguistics* (Brill, 2014). I have not heard how far along John A. L. Lee and G. H. R. Horsley are with *A Greek-English Lexicon of the NT with Documentary Parallels*. Advanced students find eminently useful the Liddell–Scott–Jones *Greek-English Lexicon* (LSJ), available free from those responsible for Thesaurus Linguae Graecae (TLG) at https://stephanus.tlg.uci.edu/.

14. Carl Holladay, *Introduction to the NT: Reference Edition* (2017). Other standout critical works are Brown's NT Introduction [*JBL* Spr 99; *CTJ* 11/98] and Eugene Boring, *An Introduction to the NT* (2012) [*CBQ* 10/14; *Int* 4/15; *ExpTim* 12/13; *RelSRev* 6/14].

15. *The State of NT Studies*, eds. McKnight–Gupta (2019) [*ExpTim* 4/20; *BBR* 31.1; *JETS* 6/20 (Blomberg); *Int* 10/22; *JSNT* 42.5 (Wenham)]. Still useful is the older vol. *The Face of NT Studies*, eds. McKnight–Osborne [*Chm* Spr 06].

16. Barrett's *The NT Background* (rev. 1989) or the user-friendly Elwell–Yarbrough, eds., *Readings from the First-Century World* (1998).
17. *The World of the NT: Cultural, Social, and Historical Contexts*, eds. Green and McDonald (Baker Academic, 2013).
18. Since more and more commentaries are making use of discourse analysis, advanced students might like to acquaint themselves with Steven Runge, *Discourse Grammar of the Greek NT* (2010). To grasp the variety of approaches, consult Scacewater, ed., *Discourse Analysis of the NT Writings* (2020).
19. N. T. Wright's *The Resurrection of the Son of God*.
20. Aland's *Synopsis Quattuor Evangeliorum* [*NovT* 29.2]. One of the best English synopses is Dewey–Miller, *The Complete Gospel Parallels* (2012), especially if you want access to the Apocryphal Gospels [*CBQ* 4/14].
21. Metzger's *Text of the NT* (3rd ed. 1992, 4th ed. 2005 [*JTS* 10/06 (panned); *JETS* 12/06; *NovT* 48.2]) or the Alands' *Text of the NT* (2nd ed. 1989).
22. All the IVP "black dictionaries" on the NT.

## RESEARCH TOOLS FOR THE WHOLE BIBLE

1. At least five good translations of the Bible, in addition to the venerable AV/KJV. The most useful to me are specific editions: *NIV Study Bible*, *ESV Study Bible* [*Them* 4/09], *Harper-Collins Study Bible* (NRSV with Apocrypha), *Tanakh* (NJPS, the 1985 Jewish translation, especially in *The Jewish Study Bible*, 2nd ed. of 2014), RSV, and *New Jerusalem Bible* (Catholic translation using "Yahweh"). Hebrew students find fascinating and stimulating Robert Alter's stylized translation, now complete in a 3-vol. set (2019) [*JJS* 71.2]. He writes, "The unacknowledged heresy underlying most modern English versions of the Bible is the use of translation as a vehicle for *explaining* the Bible instead of representing it in another language, and in the most egregious instances this amounts to explaining away the Bible" (xv). I find I refer only occasionally to the New Living Translation (NLT). I consider *The Message* to be too loose a paraphrase. [For reviews of the ESV specifically, see *RTR* 8/03 (critical); *SwJT* Sum 02; *Anvil* 20.4; the large articles on translations in *ExpTim* 4/03, 10/03; and Leland Ryken, *The Word of God in English: Criteria for Excellence in Bible Translation* (Crossway, 2002), reviewed in *VT* 57.1.]
2. An analytical concordance, even an old one (e.g., Young's), still comes in handy.
3. *New Bible Dictionary*, then buy the *International Standard Bible Encyclopedia* (Revised).
4. *New Dictionary of Biblical Theology* [*EvQ* 7/04; *Them* Aut 01; *CTJ* 11/03; *JETS* 12/02].
5. A good atlas: perhaps the Currid–Barrett *Crossway ESV Bible Atlas* (2010) [*Presb* Spr 11; *Them* 5/11]; *The New Moody Atlas of the Bible* (2009) by Beitzel [*Them* 11/09; *VT* 60.3; *Presb* Fall 10; *ExpTim* 4/11; *Them* 5/11]; *The Zondervan Atlas of the Bible* by Rasmussen (rev. 2010) [*JETS* 12/10; *Them* 5/11]; or *The IVP Atlas of Bible History* [*CBQ* 10/07]. Another excellent reference is the *Oxford Bible Atlas* (4th ed. 2007). A slightly different, impressive work is Beitzel, ed., *Biblica, The Bible Atlas: A Social and Historical Journey through the Lands of the Bible* (2007). If you can afford it, you could buy either the Aharoni–Avi-Yonah *Carta Biblical Atlas* (5th ed. 2011) or Rainey–Notley, *The Sacred Bridge* (2006) [*BBR* 17.1], both of which are excellent for intertestamental Jewish history, too. For a cheaper epitome of Rainey–Notley, see *Carta's New Century Handbook and Atlas of the Bible* (2007) [*BBR* 19.3]. Another large expensive work is Pritchard's beautiful *Harper Atlas of the Bible*. University libraries may have several exquisite vols.: *Tübinger Bibelatlas* (2001), Princeton's *Barrington Atlas of the Greek and Roman World* (2000), and Brill's *Historical Atlas of the*

*Ancient World* (2010). My personal favorites are Currid–Barrett (2010), Beitzel (2009), and either of the Rainey–Notley works. If you're broke, try Rasmussen's *Zondervan Essential Atlas* (2013), which used to sell for about $15 in pb [*JETS* 9/14]. A most helpful resource alongside your atlas is J. J. Bimson, ed., *Illustrated Encyclopedia of Bible Places* (1995).

6. Geerhardus Vos's *Biblical Theology* is still a brilliant, seminal read.

7. The more scholarly will certainly save up to buy the *Anchor Bible Dictionary* (1992), which I usually prefer to the *New Interpreter's Dictionary of the Bible* (2006–09).

8. Kevin Vanhoozer, *Is There a Meaning in This Text?* [*JETS* 12/01; *JBL* Fall 01], should be required for any evangelical seriously wrestling with contemporary literary theory and the denial of determinate meaning in texts.

9. Klein–Blomberg–Hubbard, *Introduction to Biblical Interpretation* (3rd ed. 2017) [*ExpTim* 2/18; *BBR* 28.3], and Thiselton's denser *Hermeneutics: An Introduction* (2009) [*CBQ* 4/11; *ExpTim* 5/11; *Them* 11/10; *RevExp* Spr 11; *BTB* 2/12; *SBET* Aut 12; *SJT* 65.4]. More focused on philosophical trends and closely argued is Porter–Robinson, *Hermeneutics: An Introduction to Interpretive Theory* (2011) [*ExpTim* 11/13]. There is much to love about the ambitious textbook by Craig Bartholomew (640pp.): *Introducing Biblical Hermeneutics* (2015) [*JETS* 6/16].

10. *Dictionary for Theological Interpretation of the Bible*, ed. Vanhoozer [*CBQ* 10/06; *TJ* Fall 07; *Int* 1/07; *ExpTim* 11/08; *SJT* 62.2; *DenvJ*; *BL* 2007].

11. Consider either the *Zondervan Dictionary of Biblical Imagery*, ed. John Beck (2011), or the *Dictionary of Biblical Imagery*, eds. Leland Ryken et al. (IVP, 1998).

# The Ultimate
# Reference Library

AN UNFORTUNATE FELLOW ONCE quipped, "If my ship ever comes in, there's sure to be a dock strike." This list gives my choices for a first-class library of English-language exegetical commentaries, were my ship ever to come in. Money is of no concern here; scholarship is. The emphasis is less on expositional helps and more on comprehensive and detailed technical works from a variety of perspectives that will appeal to, or stimulate, the scholarly pastor, advanced student, and specialist. I am concerned to put evangelical treatments up front and will separate the conservative and critical works with a dash. Works are generally listed in order of preference within the divisions of conservative and critical works, but that's not to say I don't prefer the first critical work listed to the second or third evangelical work (e.g., I'd buy Milgrom on Leviticus after getting Sklar). I attempted to keep the number of works to 10–12 per book but at times failed spectacularly (Judges, Psalms, Isaiah, Micah, and Romans). I admit that this dream list has been inspired by Appendix B in Longman's 1995 commentary survey. It's fun to dream.

## OLD TESTAMENT

| | |
|---|---|
| OLD TESTAMENT | Calvin, Keil & Delitzsch (both sets are free online) |
| GENESIS | Wenham, Hamilton, Mathews, Goldingay [*M*], Collins (*Reading Genesis Well*)—Westermann, Sarna, Carr, Brueggemann, Day (*From Creation to Babel*) |
| EXODUS | Alexander (Apollos), Stuart, Hamilton, Wright, Cassuto (trad. Jewish), Enns—Houtman, Davies, Sarna, Fretheim, Childs, Propp, Dozeman, Johnstone |
| LEVITICUS | Sklar (2023), Hartley, Wenham, Kiuchi, Hess, Gane—Milgrom, Levine, Watts, Balentine, Gerstenberger |
| NUMBERS | Morales, Ashley, Awabdy, Morales, Wenham, Cole, Harrison—Milgrom, Levine, Olson, Knierim–Coats |
| DEUTERONOMY | McConville, Arnold, Block, Wright, Christensen (2001), Craigie—Lundbom, Weinfeld, Miller, Tigay, Nelson, Driver |
| JOSHUA | Butler [*M*], Firth, Goldingay [*M*], Howard, Hess, Hawk [*M*], Hubbard, Pitkänen—Dozeman, Nelson, Rösel |
| JUDGES | Boda–Conway, Block, Butler, Webb, Beldman—Smiths (Herm), Sasson, Spronk, Schneider, Nelson, Lindars, O'Connell, Boling, Frolov, Niditch, Moore |
| RUTH | Block (ZECOT), Lau, Hubbard, Bush, McKeown, Hawk [*M*]—Eskenazi-Frymer-Kensky, Schipper, Campbell, Nielsen, Sakenfeld, LaCocque, Sasson |
| SAMUEL | Firth, Steinmann, Tsumura, Youngblood, Vannoy, Long, Gordon—Klein, McCarter, Anderson, Auld, Fokkelman |
| KINGS | Wray Beal, Maier, Provan, House, Wiseman—Cogan–Tadmor, Hobbs [*M*], Sweeney, Walsh [*M*], McKenzie, Long, Mulder, Brueggemann |

| | |
|---|---|
| CHRONICLES | Dillard, Boda, Kaminski, Williamson [*M*], Hahn (Catholic), Merrill, Selman—Japhet [*M*], Knoppers [*M*], Klein, Johnstone, McKenzie, Levin |
| EZRA–NEHEMIAH | Williamson [*M*], Harrington, Smith, Steinmann, Fensham, Kidner—Eskenazi, Fried, Becking, Blenkinsopp, Klein |
| ESTHER | Tomasino, Bush, Jobes, Steinmann(?), Grossman, Laniak, Baldwin, Firth—Berlin, Levenson, Fox, Brown, Macchi, Clines, Berg |
| JOB | Hartley, Longman, Wilson, Andersen—Clines, Seow, Habel, Gordis, Balentine, Janzen, Pope |
| PSALMS | Ross, Goldingay [*M*], NICOT [*M*], Bullock, VanGemeren, Ḥakham (trad. Jewish), Craigie, Tate, Allen, Wilson, Tucker–Grant—Hossfeld–Zenger, Kraus, Mays, Gerstenberger |
| PROVERBS | Waltke, Overland, Ansberry, Steinmann, Van Leeuwen, Longman—Fox, Loader, Schipper, Murphy, Perdue, Clifford |
| ECCLESIASTES | Bartholomew, Goldingay, Longman, Enns, Kidner—Weeks, Seow, Fox, Schoors, Murphy, Crenshaw, Krüger, Whybray, Duncan |
| SONG OF SONGS | Hess, Garrett, Dharamraj, Longman, Duguid, Estes—Murphy, Exum, Fishbane, Assis, Keel, Fox |
| ISAIAH | McConville, Smith, Motyer, Oswalt—Williamson, Wildberger, Goldingay-Payne, Goldingay (*Message*), Roberts, Paul, Beuken, Sweeney, Childs, Baltzer, Seitz, Westermann, Koole |
| JEREMIAH | Goldingay [*M*], Lalleman, Mackay, Thompson, Wright—Lundbom [*M*], Holladay, Fretheim, Allen, Stulman, McKane, Brueggemann |
| LAMENTATIONS | Goldingay [*M*], House, Parry, Provan, Wright, Allen [*M*]—Berlin, Salters, Hillers, Renkema, Dobbs-Allsopp, Assis, Westermann, Berman |
| EZEKIEL | Block, Duguid, Hummel—Zimmerli, Greenberg, Cook, Joyce, Darr, Milgrom-Block, Allen, Hals, Cooke |
| DANIEL | Widder (2023), Steinmann, Tanner, Baldwin, Longman, Sprinkle, Hill—Goldingay (2019), Collins, Newsom, Lucas [*M*], Montgomery |
| THE TWELVE | Sweeney, Nogalski |
| HOSEA | Dearman, Hwang, Moon, Stuart, Goldingay [*M*], McComiskey—Andersen-Freedman, Macintosh, Gruber, Wolff, Ben Zvi |
| JOEL | Barker (2020), Dillard, Hadjiev, Stuart, Goldingay [*M*], Strazicich, Allen—Nogalski (2023), Wolff, Crenshaw, Assis, Seitz, Barton |
| AMOS | Carroll R. (2020), Smith, Hoyt, Hadjiev, Stuart, Goldingay [*M*], Lessing—Paul, Andersen–Freedman [*M*], Eidevall, Wolff, Jeremias |
| OBADIAH | Raabe, Block, Stuart, Phillips, Niehaus, Jenson [*M*], Goldingay [*M*], Allen—Nogalski (2023), Wolff, Renkema, Barton, Watts, Ben Zvi |
| JONAH | Youngblood, Stuart, Phillips, Alexander, Hoyt, Goldingay [*M*], Jenson [*M*], Nixon—Niditch, Nogalski (2023), Erickson, AYB (2023), Sasson, Wolff, Trible |
| MICAH | Waltke (2007), Dempster, Gignilliat, Soenksen, Phillips, Hoyt, Goldingay [*M*], Jenson [*M*], Allen—de Moor, Andersen–Freedman [*M*], Wolff, Hillers, Becking, Smith-Christopher, Ben Zvi, Zapff |
| NAHUM | Renz, Timmer, Longman, Robertson, Patterson, Christensen [*M*]—Roberts, Spronk, Floyd |
| HABAKKUK | Renz, Turner, Thomas, Robertson, Patterson, Booth(?)—Andersen [*M*], Roberts, Floyd, Fuller |
| ZEPHANIAH | Renz, Robertson, Motyer, Patterson—Sweeney, Berlin, Vlaardingerbroek, Roberts, Ben Zvi, Floyd |

| | |
|---|---|
| HAGGAI | Koopmans, Meadowcroft, Motyer, Kessler, Jacobs, Taylor, Petterson, Merrill—Meyers, Wolff, Petersen, Barker, Floyd |
| ZECHARIAH | Boda, Wolters, Petterson, Lessing, McComiskey, Klein—Meyers, Petersen, Conrad, Floyd |
| MALACHI | Tucker, Hill, Snyman, Ross, Clendenen, Stuart, Petterson, Jacobs, Merrill—Petersen, Glazier-McDonald, Floyd, Schart |

# NEW TESTAMENT

| | |
|---|---|
| NEW TESTAMENT | Calvin's Commentaries (Torrance Ed.) |
| MATTHEW | France, Carson, Nolland [*M*], Keener, Hagner, Osborne, Turner—Davies-Allison, Luz, Culpepper, Wilson |
| SERMON ON MT. | Guelich, Pennington, Lloyd-Jones (for theology)—Betz |
| MARK | France, Stein, Evans, Strauss, Guelich [*M*], Edwards, Gundry, Bock, Witherington—Yarbro Collins, Marcus, Boring, Focant, Moloney, Hooker, Cranfield [*M*] |
| LUKE | Bock, Garland, Edwards, Green, Marshall [*M*], Stein, Nolland [*M*]—Fitzmyer, Bovon, Wolter, Spencer, Carroll, Johnson |
| JOHN | Carson, Keener, Michaels, Klink, Thompson [*M*], Ridderbos—Barrett, Brown, Schnackenburg, Lincoln, Beutler, Smith |
| ACTS | Keener, Peterson, Schnabel, Walton (incomplete), Bock, Witherington, Marshall—Barrett, Fitzmyer, Holladay, Pervo, Johnson, Haenchen, Conzelmann |
| ROMANS | Moo (2018), Longenecker [*M*], Thielman, Schreiner (2018), Kruse, Murray, Peterson—Cranfield, Dunn, Jewett, Fitzmyer, Hultgren, Käsemann, Wright, Keck |
| 1 CORINTHIANS | Thiselton [*M*], Garland, Fee (2014), Gardner, Ciampa–Rosner, Witherington—Barrett, Fitzmyer, Hays, Collins, Robertson–Plummer, Conzelmann |
| 2 CORINTHIANS | Harris, Guthrie, Barnett, Seifrid, Witherington—Thrall, Martin (2014), Furnish, Barrett, Matera |
| GALATIANS | Moo, Schreiner, deSilva, Keener, Das, George (2020), Longenecker, Bruce—Tuckett, Martyn, Betz, de Boer, Oakes [*M*], Dunn |
| EPHESIANS | Thielman, Cohick, Campbell, Arnold, Hoehner, Baugh, Robinson—Lincoln, Best, Barth, Schnackenburg, Fowl, Muddiman |
| PHILIPPIANS | Guthrie, Fee (NICNT), Hansen, Silva, Bockmuehl [*M*], Hawthorne (2004), Keown—Holloway, Reumann |
| COLOSSIANS | Beale, Moo, McKnight, Pao, Thompson—Dunn, R. M. Wilson, Foster, Barth–Blanke, Schweizer, Sumney, Lohse |
| THESSALONIANS | Weima, Fee, Shogren, Wanamaker, Green, Beale, Gupta (ZCINT)—Malherbe, Boring, Richard, Best |
| PASTORALS | Mounce, Towner (NICNT), Porter, Pao?, Knight, Bray, Kelly—Marshall-Towner [*M*], Johnson on Timothy (AB), Quinn on Titus, Quinn–Wacker on Timothy, Dibelius–Conzelmann |
| PHILEMON | McKnight, Nordling—Fitzmyer, Barth–Blanke, Kreitzer |
| HEBREWS | Moo, Lane (WBC), Grindheim, Peeler, Peterson, Ellingworth, Cockerill, Hughes, deSilva, Bruce, Guthrie—Attridge, Koester, Johnson |
| JAMES | McCartney, McKnight, Moo (2021), Blomberg–Kamell, Davids (NIGTC)—Allison, Johnson (AB), Martin [*M*], Laws, Hartin, Mayor |

| | |
|---|---|
| 1 PETER | Jobes, Keener, Davids, Michaels, Schreiner (2020), Selwyn, Reese, Grudem—Achtemeier, Williams–Horrell, Elliott, Feldmeier, Donelson, Goppelt |
| 2 PETER/JUDE | Davids, G. Green, Moo, Schreiner (2020), Reese (Jude)—Bauckham, Kelly, Neyrey, Frey, Donelson, Mayor |
| 1–3 JOHN | Yarbrough, Jobes, Kruse (2020), Smalley (2007) [𝓜], Marshall, Stott—Brown, Schnackenburg, Lieu, Strecker |
| REVELATION | Beale, Schreiner, Osborne (2002), Mounce, Smalley, Hemer, Fanning[1]—Koester, Aune, Caird, Boxall, Charles |

## OMNIA IN GLORIAM DEI

---

1. I believe there is a need to include at least one dispensational commentary (especially in light of how millions follow that theological system), and Fanning is the most scholarly.

# INDEX OF NAMES

Decker, Rodney J., 48–49, 344, 348
deClaissé-Walford, Nancy L., 63, 187
Deines, Roland, 288
de Jong, H., 135
de Jong, Matthjs, 223
De La Torre, Miguel A., 73
DelHousaye, John, 322
Delitzsch, Franz, 27, 36, 53, 73, 175,
    187, 192, 200, 206, 208,
    216, 228, 472, 473, 521, 533
Dell, Katharine, 33, 168, 169, 170,
    172, 175, 179, 180, 198,
    200, 208
DeLong, Kindalee Pfremmer, 352,
    355
Demarest, Gary W., 93
de Moor, Johannes C., 295, 534
Dempsey, Carol, 228
Denney, James, 400, 415, 416–17, 456
Denton, Donald L., Jr., 322
de Petris, Paolo, 180
Deppe, Dean, 33
De Pury, A., 110
Derickson, Gary, 49, 500–501
DeRouchie, Jason, 19, 35, 106, 304,
    526, 529
deSilva, David, 32, 60, 420, 421, 423,
    424, 426, 431, 469, 472,
    484, 505, 508, 511, 525,
    529, 530, 535
De Silva, Ivan D. V., 199, 204
Deterding, Paul E., 447
De Troyer, Kristin, 164
Deutsch, R. R., 279, 317
Dever, Mark, 110–11, 112, 411
DeVries, Simon, 141, 143, 151
De Waard, Jan, 129, 243, 284
Dewrell, Heath, 273
Dharamraj, Havilah, 129, 143, 148,
    216, 252, 534
Dhorme, Edouard, 175
Diamond, A. R. P., 238, 239, 242, 243
Dibelius, Martin, 60, 481, 482,
    485, 535
Dicken, Frank, 352
Dickson, David, 187, 245, 331
Dicou, Bert, 285
Diehl, Judith A., 328, 417
Dietrich, Walter, 299, 302, 304
Dijk, Karl, 28
Dijkstra, Meindert, 281
Dilday, Russell H., 144
DiLella, A. A., 260
Dillard, Raymond B., 141, 149, 151,
    153, 154, 157, 158, 265, 269,
    277, 526, 534
Dillow, S. J., 216, 218
Dimant, Devorah, 259
Dinkler, Michal Beth, 352
Di Pede, Elena, 269
Dirksen, Peter B., 151
DiTommaso, Lorenzo, 259, 266, 267
Dobbs-Allsopp, F. W., 168, 169, 216,
    245, 534
Docherty, Susan E., 319, 472
Dockery, David, 34

Dodd, B. J., 442
Dodd, C. H., 33, 362, 370, 400, 429,
    492, 501
Dods, Marcus, 73, 362
Dodson, Joseph R., 23, 447
Doedens, J. J. T., 73
Donahue, John, 60, 344, 345, 347,
    370
Donaldson, Terence, 385
Donelson, Lewis, 431, 447, 460, 488,
    495, 536
Donfried, Karl P., 400, 402, 450,
    453, 456
Doorly, William, 274
Doriani, Daniel, 59, 329, 331, 332,
    340, 343, 356, 400, 460,
    478–79, 482, 483, 486,
    490, 525
Dorsey, David A., 30, 173
Douglas, Mary, 93, 94, 101
Douma, J., 88
Dow, Lois K. Fuller, 519
Dowd, Sharyn, 345
Dowden, Landon, 164, 252
Dozeman, Thomas B., 66–67, 83,
    101, 102, 115, 533
Driesbach, Jason, 115, 130
Drinkard, Joel F., Jr., 239
Driver, Samuel R. (S. R.), 73, 83, 104,
    106, 136, 138, 176, 206,
    252, 259, 269, 278, 281, 307,
    471, 533
Dubis, Mark, 488, 493
Dubovsky, Peter, 144
Duguid, Iain M., 21, 49, 50, 57, 59,
    73, 87, 94, 96, 98, 99, 100,
    102, 123, 128, 130, 161–62,
    167, 182, 214, 215, 216, 217,
    229, 249, 250, 251, 252,
    256, 257, 303, 306, 307,
    308, 312, 316, 521, 522, 523,
    524, 534
Duke, Rodney K., 151, 155
Dungan, David Laird, 322
Dunham, Kyle, 210
Dunn, James D. G., 14, 56, 57, 320,
    322, 328, 345, 375, 379, 384,
    385, 386, 389, 390, 392, 395,
    396, 397, 400, 401, 402, 404,
    407, 411, 420, 423–24, 425,
    426, 427, 438, 445, 446, 447,
    448, 450, 460, 466, 525, 535
Dunnam, Maxie D., 83
Duran, Nicole Wilkinson, 60
Durham, James, 216, 511
Durham, John I., 83
Durusau, Patrick, 37
Duvall, J. Scott, 23, 511
Dvorak, James D., 481
Dyer, Bryan R., 325, 335, 391
Dyer, John, 21, 23

Eadie, J. A., 431
Eadie, John, 453
Earl, Douglas S., 111, 116
Earle, Ralph, 460, 461

Eastman, Susan Grove, 386, 400, 424
Easton, B. S., 460
Eaton, J. H. (John), 187–88, 193, 285,
    299, 302, 304
Eaton, Michael, 208, 209, 211
Eck, Joachim, 227
Eddinger, Terry W., 316
Eddy, Paul Rhodes, 320, 323
Edelman, Diana V., 150, 285
Edenburg, Cynthia, 138
Edlin, Jim, 259
Edwards, Dennis, 489, 491
Edwards, James R., 22, 323, 341, 346,
    350, 379, 400, 525, 535
Edwards, Jonathan, 442, 499
Edwards, Mark J., 362, 424, 432, 440
Edwards, Ruth, 339, 362, 486
Egan, Patrick T., 489
Ehorn, Seth, 83, 449, 467
Ehrlich, Carl, 158
Eichler, Barry, 190
Eichrodt, Walther, 252, 527
Eklund, Rebekah, 340, 350, 352
Elias, Jacob W., 453
Ellicott, C. J., 460
Ellington, John, 139, 146, 153,
    262, 418
Ellingworth, Paul, 62, 411, 462, 469,
    470, 472, 475, 476, 535
Elliott, E. B., 511
Elliott, J. Keith, 410, 416
Elliott, John H., 455, 484, 486, 487,
    488, 491, 493, 526, 536
Elliott, John K., 267
Elliott, M., 218
Elliott, Mark W., 76, 93, 188, 228,
    268, 379, 424
Elliott, M. Timothea, 217
Elliott, Neil, 386
Ellis, E. E., 352, 386, 411
Ellis, Peter F., 362
Ellis, Nicholas, 479, 481
Ellison, H. L., 83, 246, 289, 291
Ellsworth, Thomas D., 144, 480
Ellul, Jacques, 144, 208, 289
Elowsky, Joel C., 362
Emadi, Samuel, 74
Emerton, John A., 52, 169
Emmerson, Grace I., 222, 274
Endres, John C., 155
English, Donald, 345
Enns, Peter, 13, 21, 57, 72, 80, 83, 87,
    168, 169, 170, 205, 206, 319,
    523, 524, 533, 534
Erdman, Charles R., 101
Erdmann, Chr. Fr. David, 138
Erickson, Amy, 134, 167, 214, 220,
    249, 289, 291, 534
Erisman, Angela Roskop, 101
Escott, Timothy R., 158
Eskenazi, Tamara Cohn, 130, 158,
    159, 165, 533, 534
Esler, Philip F., 400, 424
Estelle, Bryan D., 83, 87, 200, 287,
    289
Estes, Daniel J., 169, 170, 176, 188,

# About the Author

**JOHN F. EVANS** is Lecturer in Old Testament & Hebrew at Union School of Theology in Bridgend, Wales.

Born in North Carolina, Dr. Evans grew up in Indiana as the son and grandson of Presbyterian ministers. Previously he pastored two congregations of the Presbyterian Church in America (PCA) and served for twenty years as a missionary, eventually as Head of the Biblical Studies Department at Nairobi Evangelical Graduate School of Theology. (NEGST is now a constituent school of Africa International University.)

He was educated at the Stony Brook School (Stony Brook, NY); Calvin College, BA (Grand Rapids, MI); Covenant Theological Seminary, MDiv and ThM (St. Louis, MO); and Universiteit van Stellenbosch, DTh (Stellenbosch, South Africa). He did postdoctoral work in Cambridge, England. He has authored *You Shall Know that I Am Yahweh: An Inner-Biblical Interpretation of Ezekiel's Recognition Formula* (Eisenbrauns).

Dr. Evans is married to Heidi, and between them they have five children and four grandchildren. He enjoys music, hiking the rugged Welsh coast, and photography.